May 20–22, 2015
Pittsburgh, PA, USA

I0028976

Association for Computing Machinery

Advancing Computing as a Science & Profession

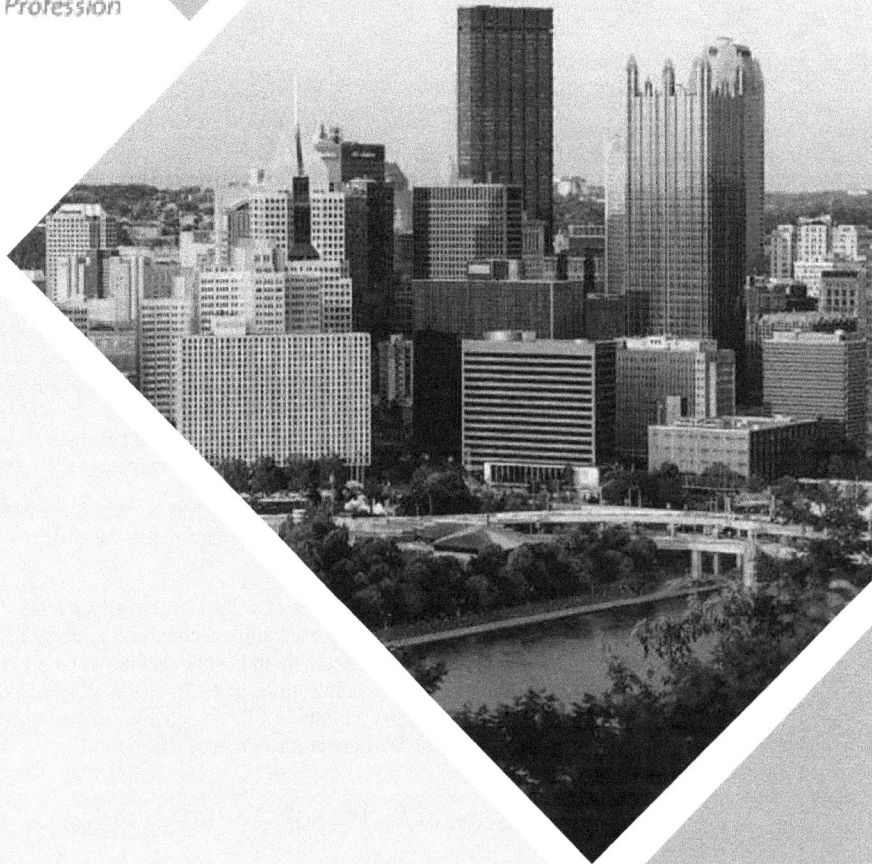

GLSVLSI'15
The 25th edition of the
2015 Great Lakes Symposium on VLSI

Sponsored by:

ACM SIGDA

Incooperation with:

IEEE

**Association for
Computing Machinery**

Advancing Computing as a Science & Profession

The Association for Computing Machinery
2 Penn Plaza, Suite 701
New York, New York 10121-0701

Notice to Past Authors of ACM-Published Articles
ACM intends to create a complete electronic archive of all articles and/or other material previously published by ACM. If you have written a work that has been previously published by ACM in any journal or conference proceedings prior to 1978, or any SIG Newsletter at any time, and you do NOT want this work to appear in the ACM Digital Library, please inform permissions@acm.org, stating the title of the work, the author(s), and where and when published.

ISBN: 978-1-4503-3474-7 (Digital)

ISBN: 978-1-4503-3861-5 (Print)

Additional copies may be ordered prepaid from:

ACM Order Department
PO Box 30777
New York, NY 10087-0777, USA

Phone: 1-800-342-6626 (USA and Canada)
+1-212-626-0500 (Global)
Fax: +1-212-944-1318
E-mail: acmhelp@acm.org
Hours of Operation: 8:30 am – 4:30 pm ET

Printed in the USA

Foreword

Welcome to the 25th edition of the *Great Lakes Symposium on VLSI (GLSVLSI) 2015* held at the Pittsburgh Marriott City Center in Pittsburgh, Pennsylvania, USA. GLSVLSI is a premier venue for the dissemination of manuscripts of the highest quality in all areas related to VLSI, devices, and system-level design. The venue of this year's GLSVLSI is Pittsburgh, which continues GLSVLSI's meetings near noted bodies of water. Pittsburgh is the famous confluence of the Allegheny and Monongahela rivers to form the Ohio River. The Ohio River links with the Mississippi River to reach the Gulf of Mexico, and while not a "great lake", it is a great body of water. Pittsburgh is one of the US oldest cities due to its water passages and also boasts a wonderful geography rich with hiking, water sports, skiing, and many other outdoor activities. You will also find a rich cultural heritage here due to great gifts by philanthropist Andrew Carnegie and cultural treasures like Stephen Foster and Andy Warhol as well as a world class symphony orchestra, museums of art and natural history, and the U.S. National Aviary. We truly believe that Pittsburgh is a *great location* for a symposium on VLSI 2015 and you will enjoy the beautiful city as well as the program over the three days of this year's GLSVLSI activity.

This year, GLSVLSI is co-located with the IEEE Computer Society Microelectronics Systems Education (MSE) conference. This brings another facet to the scope of the GLSVLSI meeting to include pedagogical innovations as well as research innovations in the area of VLSI and microsystems. Your full conference registration will entitle you to attend sessions at either GLSVLSI or MSE as your interests dictate.

Moreover, this year's special theme for GLSVLSI is related to *Biology and the cross overs between VLSI, CAD, and Biology*. To support this theme, we have included several keynote talks from recognized experts in both biology and computing technologies. On Wednesday we will open the symposium with Krishnendu Chakrabarty, William H. Younger Distinguished Professor at Duke University who will speak about Digital Microfluidic Biochips. On Thursday, Lynn H. Matthias Professor Zhenqiang (Jack) Ma will talk about his work in bio-neural graphene sensors for in vivo imaging and optogenetics. Finally, Friday's keynote will host Dr. Andrew Schwartz, Professor of Neurobiology at the University of Pittsburgh, who will discuss recent advances in brain-controlled prosthetics for paralysis. Additionally, we have four terrific special sessions including sessions on BioEDA and Neuromorphic Computing that supplement our special theme. The speakers of each special session are internationally renowned experts and they will discuss the state-of-the-art progress in these emerging domains from multidisciplinary perspectives.

As for the technical meeting, GLSVLSI 2015 was a resounding success: 148 papers were submitted, including authors from 34 different countries, of which 41 papers were accepted as full papers for oral presentation at the symposium (with a 28% acceptance rate). Including poster papers, a total of 60 papers will be included in the symposium and published in the symposium proceedings. Of the authors of these papers in the program, 48% are from North America, 23% from Asia, 23% from Europe, 2.5% from Africa, 2.5% from South America, and 1% from Australia. The final technical program consists of 21 long presentations and 20 short presentations in 11 oral sessions and 19 posters in two poster sessions. Special sessions add another 14 exciting papers to the proceedings of the symposium.

GLSVLSI 2015 starts on Wednesday, May 20th 2015, with an exciting line up of speakers on a broad range of issues including resiliency and robustness, new methods in CAD and circuits, interconnects and network-on-chips, and energy efficient systems. On the second day, in addition to continuing the discussion on resiliency and robustness, CAD, and VLSI design challenges, we have a session focused on emerging technologies and post-CMOS VLSI. On the third day, we have dedicated a session to power and temperature-aware design, accompanying the CAD and circuits tracks. The technical program of GLSVLSI 2015 includes two parallel tracks to allow longer presentations and discussions during the three days of the symposium. Concurrently, MSE will offer a third parallel section. Overall, there are 10 regular sessions, 4 special sessions, and 2 poster sessions in the technical program and a session on the first day of the symposium where the "best paper award" candidates will have the opportunity to present their outstanding work.

The social program of GLSVLSI 2015 includes two special events this year. The first event consists on a reception cocktail on Tuesday evening sponsored by the University of Pittsburgh. Then, on Wednesday, May 20th a joint GLSVLSI/MSE Gala will be held at the Marriott with evening speaker Erik Brunvand, Professor at the University of Utah, speaking about the "art" of VLSI.

Finally, we would like to thank all the members of the Technical Program Committee and the secondary reviewers, who have done a great job in evaluating the submissions and determining the final high quality technical program of GLSVLSI 2015. The Track Chairs have done an outstanding job in ensuring that each submitted paper was consistently reviewed and helping to prepare the final program. In addition, the other members of the Organizing Committees (Laleh Bejhat, Xin Li, Xin Fu, Miroslav Velev, Danella Zhao, and Theocharis Theocharides) should be also commended for providing excellent service with respect to publication, special sessions, publicity, registration, finances, organization of the event and web presence to make this new edition of GLSVLSI a great success.

We trust that you will find GLSVLSI 2015 rewarding in meeting your highest expectation of quality and technical advancement as reflected in these proceedings and the technical presentations.

Alex K. Jones and Hai (Helen) Li
General Co-Chairs

Ayse K. Coskun and Martin Margala
Program Co-Chairs

Table of Contents

Poster Session 1
Session Chair: Tali Moreshet *(Boston University)*

Session: Energy Efficient Systems
Session Chair: Baris Taskin *(Drexel University)*

Special Session: Advances in Neuromorphic Architectures and Future Applications
Session Chair: Cyrille Chavet *(Université de Bretagne-Sud)*

Poster Session 2
Session Chair: Matthias Fuegger *(Max Planck Institute)*

Session: Emerging Technologies
Session Chair: Yiran Chen *(University of Pittsburgh)*

Session: CAD and Circuits I
Session Chair: Fabrizio Lombardi *(Northeastern University)*

Keynote IV
Session Chair: Martin Margala *(University of Massachusetts Lowell)*

Special Session: Bio Design Automation
Session Chair: Yu Wang *(Tsinghua University)*

Special Session: Emerging Computing Paradigm for Error-Tolerant Applications: Approximate Computing and Stochastic Computing
Session Chair: Yiran Chen *(University of Pittsburgh)*

Session: CAD and Circuits II

Session Chair: Miroslav Velev *(Aries Design Automation, USA)*

Session: Power and Temperature-Aware Design

Session Chair: Bei Yu *(University of Texas at Austin)*

Author Index

GLSVLSI Conference Organization

General Chairs: Alex K. Jones *(University of Pittsburgh, USA)*
Hai (Helen) Li *(University of Pittsburgh, USA)*

Program Chairs: Ayse K. Coskun *(Boston University, USA)*
Martin Margala *(University of Massachusetts, Lowell, USA)*

Proceedings Chair: Laleh Behjat *(University of Calgary, Canada)*

Web Chair: Theocharis Theocharides *(University of Cyprus, Cyprus)*

Finance Chair: Danella Zhao *(University of Louisana at Lafayette, USA)*

Publicity Chair: Xin Fu *(University of Houston, Texas, USA)*

Registration Chair: Miroslav Velev *(Aries Design Automation, USA)*

Special Sessions Chair: Xin Li *(Carnegie Mellon University, USA)*

Steering Committee: Joe Cavallaro *(Rice University, USA)*
David Atienza, *(EPFL, Switzerland)*
Jose Ayala *(University Complutense Madrid, Spain)*
Iris Bahar *(Brown University, USA)*
Sanjukta Bhanja *(University of South Florida, USA)*
Erik Brunvand *(University of Utah, USA)*
Yehea Ismail *(American University of Cairo, Egypt)*
John Lach *(University of Virginia, USA)*
Tong Zhang *(Rensselaer Polytechnic Institute)*
Fabrizio Lombardi *(Northeastern University, USA)*
Enrico Macii *(Politecnico di Torino, Italy)*
Gang Qu *(University of Maryland, USA)*
Ken Stevens *(University of Utah, USA)*
Yuan Xie *(Penn State University, USA)*
Zhiyuan Yan *(Lehigh University, USA)*
Hai Zhou *(Northwestern University, USA)*

Program Committee:

Nadine Azemard
Giovanni Beltrame
Alberto Bocca
Youcef Bouchebaba
Francesco Bruschi
Andreas Burg
Andrea Calimera
Koushik Chakraborty
Vikas Chandra
Xi Chen
Minsu Choi
Philippe Coussy
Bishnu Das
Shamik Das
Jason Doege
Rolf Drechsler
Liu Duo
Jennifer Dworak
Fabrizio Ferrandi
Dhruva Ghai
Prasun Ghosal
Ann Gordon-Ross
Domenik Helms
Houman Homayoun
Jiang Hu
Chih-Tsun Huang
Niraj Jha
Antonio Jimenez
Ajay Joshi
Kyung-Ki Kim
Vonkyung Kim
Yong-Bin Kim
Selcuk Kose
Dhireesha Kudithipudi
Akash Kumar
Erik Larsson
Sébastien Lebeux
Karthikeyan Lingasubramanian
Marisa López-Vallejo
Yan Luo
Alberto Macii
Rabi Mahapatra
Michail Maniatakos
Brett Meyer

Saraju Mohanty
Alberto Nannarelli
Gabriela Nicolescu
Nicola Nicolici
Chrysostomos Nicopoulos
Dimin Niu
Marvin Onabajo
Sule Ozev
Preeti Panda
Sudeep Pasricha
Frederic Petrot
Massimo Poncino
Sherief Reda
Garrett Rose
Emre Salman
Ashoka Sathanur
Ioannis Savidis
Anirban Sengupta
Yu Shimeng
Matteo Sonza Reorda
Saket Srivastava
James Stine
Guangyu Sun
Zhenyu Sun
Mehdi Tahoori
Baris Taskin
Himanshu Thapliyal
Aida Todri-Sanial
Nur Touba
Spyros Tragoudas
Jelena Trajkovic
Diego Vázquez
Miroslav Velev
Lei Wang
Li-C Wang
Yanzhi Wang
Xiaoqing Wen
James Wingfield
Tian Xia
Sungjoo Yoo
Joseph Zambreno
Wei Zhang
Jishen Zhao
Geng Zheng

Additional Reviewers:

Zaid Al-Bayati
Arman Allahyari-Abhari
Samira Ataei
Gasser Ayad
Dominique Borrione
Chun-Hsiang Chang
Vivek Chaturvedi
Hari Chauhan
Shuang Chen
Yongsuk Choi
Tiansong Cui
Yexin Deng
Junpeng Feng
Bin Gao
Daniel Grosse
Mohammad Hossein Hajkazemi
Mohammad Shihabul Haque
Chin Hau Hoo
Pablo Ituero
Phillip Jones
Sara Karimi
Mohammad Khavari Tavana
Abhinav Kranti
Ulrich Kuehne
Xue Lin

Maria Malik
Kevin Martin
Sandeep Miryala
Katayoun Neshatpour
Tuan Nguyen
Yuchi Ni
Piotr Olejarz
Madhukar Reddy Pappireddy
Biplab Patra
Nam Khanh Pham
Laurence Pierre
Paul Pop
Roberto Giorgio Rizzo
Alireza Shafaei Bejestan
Mathias Soeken
Dimitrios Stamoulis
Jannis Stoppe
Valerio Tenace
Garima Thakral
Harikrishnan Thelakkat
Kainan Wang
Ke Wang
Li Xu
Seyed Alireza Zahrai
Marina Zlochisti

GLSVLSI 2015 Sponsor & Supporter

Sponsor:

siG da
special interest group on
acm
design automation

In cooperation with: **IEEE**

Digital Microfluidic Biochips: Towards Functional Diversity, More than Moore, and Cyberphysical Integration

[Wednesday Keynote]

Krishnendu Chakrabarty
Electrical and Computer Engineering
Duke University
Box 90291, 130 Hudson Hall
Durham, NC 27708
krish@ee.duke.edu

ABSTRACT

Advances in droplet-based "digital" microfluidics have led to the emergence of biochip devices for automating laboratory procedures in biochemistry and molecular biology. These devices enable the precise control of nanoliter-volume droplets of biochemical samples and reagents. Therefore, integrated circuit (IC) technology can be used to transport and transport "chemical payload" in the form of micro/nanofluidic droplets. As a result, non-traditional biomedical applications and markets (e.g., high-throughout DNA sequencing, portable and point-of-care clinical diagnostics, protein crystallization for drug discovery), and fundamentally new uses are opening up for ICs and systems.

However, continued growth depends on advances in chip integration and design-automation tools. Design automation is needed to ensure that biochips are as versatile as the macro-labs that they are intended to replace, and researchers can thereby envision an automated design flow for biochips, in the same way as design automation revolutionized IC design in the 80s and 90s.

This talk will first provide an overview of market drivers such as immunoassays, DNA sequencing, clinical chemistry, etc., and electrowetting-based digital microfludic biochips. The audience will next learn about design automation, design-for-testability, and reconfiguration aspects of digital microfluidic biochips. Synthesis tools will be described to map assay protocols from the lab bench to a droplet-based microfluidic platform and generate an optimized schedule of bioassay operations, the binding of assay operations to functional units, and the layout and droplet-flow paths for the biochip. The role of the digital microfluidic platform as a "programmable and reconfigurable processor" for biochemical applications will be highlighted. Finally, the speaker will demonstrate dynamic adaptation of bioassays through cyberphysical system integration and sensor-driven on-chip error recovery.

Categories and Subject Descriptors

A.0 [**General Literature**]: GENERAL—*Conference proceedings*

General Terms

Keynote

GLSVLSI'15, May 20–22, 2015, Pittsburgh, PA, USA.
ACM 978-1-4503-3474-7/15/05.
http://dx.doi.org/10.1145/2742060.2745701.

BIOGRAPHY

Krishnendu Chakrabarty received the B. Tech. degree from the Indian Institute of Technology, Kharagpur, in 1990, and the M.S.E. and Ph.D. degrees from the University of Michigan, Ann Arbor, in 1992 and 1995, respectively. He is now the William H. Younger Distinguished Professor of Engineering in the Department of Professor of Electrical and Computer Engineering and Professor of Computer Science at Duke University. In addition, he serves as the Executive Director of Graduate Studies in Electrical and Computer Engineering. Prof. Chakrabarty is a recipient of the National Science Foundation Early Faculty (CAREER) award, the Office of Naval Research Young Investigator award, the Humboldt Research Award from the Alexander von Humboldt Foundation, Germany, and 10 best paper awards at major IEEE conferences. He is also a recipient of the Distinguished Alumnus Award from the Indian Institute of Technology, Kharagpur.

Prof. Chakrabarty's current research projects include: testing and design-for-testability of integrated circuits; resilience in system-on-chip designs; digital microfluidics, biochips, and cyberphysical systems; optimization of enterprise systems. Prof. Chakrabarty is a Fellow of ACM, a Fellow of IEEE, and a Golden Core Member of the IEEE Computer Society. He holds five US patents, with several patents pending. He was a 2009 Invitational Fellow of the Japan Society for the Promotion of Science. He served as a Distinguished Visitor of the IEEE Computer Society during 2005-2007 and 2010-2012, and as a Distinguished Lecturer of the IEEE Circuits and Systems Society during 2006-2007 and 2012-2013. Currently he serves as an ACM Distinguished Speaker.

Prof. Chakrabarty served as the Editor-in-Chief of *IEEE Design & Test of Computers* during 2010-2012. Currently he serves as the Editor-in-Chief of *ACM Journal on Emerging Technologies in Computing Systems* and *IEEE Transactions on VLSI Systems.* He is also an Associate Editor of *IEEE Transactions on Computers, IEEE Transactions on Biomedical Circuits and Systems, IEEE Transactions on Multiscale Computing Systems, ACM Transactions on Design Automation of Electronic Systems.*

Efficient Test Application for Rapid Multi-Temperature Testing

Nima Aghaee, Zebo Peng, and Petru Eles
Embedded Systems Laboratory (ESLAB), Linkoping University, Sweden
{nima.aghaee, zebo.peng, petru.eles}@liu.se

ABSTRACT

Different defects may manifest themselves at different temperatures. Therefore, the tests that target such temperature-dependent defects must be applied at different temperatures appropriate for detecting them. Such multi-temperature testing scheme applies tests at different required temperatures. It is known that a test's power dissipation depends on the previously applied test. Therefore, the same set of tests when organized differently dissipates different amounts of power. The technique proposed in this paper organizes the tests efficiently so that the resulted power levels lead to the required temperatures. Consequently a rapid multi-temperature testing is achieved. Experimental studies demonstrate the efficiency of the proposed technique.

Categories and Subject Descriptors

B.7.3 [**INTEGRATED CIRCUITS**]: Reliability and Testing – *Test generation.*

Keywords

Temperature-dependent defects; multi-temperature testing; temperature simulation; test ordering; test scheduling; 3D stacked IC (3D-SIC)

1. INTRODUCTION

Modern semiconductors manufactured with deep submicron technologies are prone to environment-sensitive defects. Such defects might be sensitive to parameters like supply voltage, clock frequency, and temperature [1–2]. Temperature-dependent defects are an important part of the problem [3–5], and they manifest themselves at different temperatures.

An example for such an environment-sensitive defect is a kind of resistive open that is a major cause of test escapes [1]. It occurs when a metal line has a resistance small enough to be considered as connected at normal temperatures. But at high temperatures the resistance increases to the degree that the line is practically disconnected. This occurs since the electric conductance of the metal has negative temperature coefficient. Therefore, it is expected that a large number of such defects manifest themselves only at high temperature. On the other hand, there are other defects that manifest themselves only at low temperature [1].

Beside the temperature coefficient for conductivity, thermal expansion may also cause temperature-dependent defects [1]. The Dark Via defect, which appears at low temperature, can be caused by voids between interconnect and via [1]. This low-temperature defect can be explained with thermal expansion in metal which fills up the voids and increases the conductivity [3]. Large voids at low temperature shrink at high temperature because of thermal expansion. Consequently, the electric resistance of the via may decrease. Similar defects also exist for other technologies and materials. For example, some defects for a different technology are studied in [6] and interface voids are discussed along with sidewall voids and bulk voids as causes for temperature-dependent defects. Note that modern 3D Stacked IC (3D-SIC) designs that contain a large number of Through Silicon Vias (TSV) are, in particular, susceptible to such defects.

Another type of hard-to-diagnose temperature-dependent defect is silicide open [7]. Silicide is the material used to build local interconnects. Such a local interconnect, in its perfect condition, has a positive temperature coefficient for resistance. But a defective silicide interconnect will have a negative temperature coefficient [7]. Detecting such silicide defects at high temperature is difficult since this interconnect's resistance is not significantly larger than that of a non-defective interconnect. These defects must be tested for at low temperature since a recognizable difference between the defective and non-defective chips exists at low temperature [7].

An experimental study on resistive-open and stuck-open defects is performed in [8]. Both resistive-open and stuck-open defects are relatively common, but resistive-opens are more frequent. The effects of the environmental parameters are studied and some diagnosis schemes are proposed in [8]. It is concluded that the appropriate test temperatures for such temperature-dependent defects could be found based on the location of the defects and the properties of the materials involved in those defects [8]. Consequently, tests that target these defects are generated. These temperatures and test patterns are the inputs to the multi-temperature testing scheme that is the focus of this paper.

This paper focuses on core-based designs that allow parallel test of different cores. Testing different cores in parallel drastically reduces the overall test time. Multi-temperature testing can be performed by using heat chambers. A disadvantage of this approach is that only one temperature at a time can be enforced on the die. Consequently the degree of parallelism is reduced and multi-temperature testing will take a very long time. Other disadvantages of heat chambers include extra cost for the chambers and higher power consumption. In order to avoid such problems, our proposed approach is based on adjusting the cores' power dissipations during testing so that the desired temperatures are rapidly achieved. This approach enables also multiple cores to be tested at different temperatures simultaneously.

A test's power dissipation depends on the previously applied test. Consequently, the power dissipation generated by a series of tests depends on the order in which they are organized [9–12]. This fact is used in this paper in order to adjust the tests' power values so that the desired temperatures for different cores are achieved. If the desired temperatures are higher than what can be achieved by the available tests, specially designed high power stimuli are used in addition to the tests.

GLSVLSI '15, May 20 - 22, 2015, Pittsburgh, PA, USA
Copyright 2015 ACM 978-1-4503-3474-7/15/05…$15.00
http://dx.doi.org/10.1145/2742060.2742064

2. Background and Related Works

2.1 Test Power Dependency on Test Order

A wide range of modern microelectronic devices are core-based designs, including the growing number of 3D stacked ICs. The test techniques for all these ICs are scan based. A test's switching activity depends on the changes of its bits from the previous test to the current one and the state of the scan chain's flip flops. The scan chain's state is also determined by the previous test. This phenomenon is utilized in multiple works in order to modify the tests' power profiles.

A power minimization technique based on test vector ordering is proposed in [9]. The objective is to minimize the tests' average switching activity. It is shown that the test ordering problem is NP-hard [9].

A technique for test time reduction under power constraints is proposed in [10]. Peak powers for tests are taken into account. These peak values depend on the order of the tests. The tests are ordered so that the peak powers for different cores are not overlapped [10].

Reducing power variations in order to reduce the temperature variations during burn-in is discussed in [11]. The variation reduction is achieved by test ordering [11].

Peak power reduction by proper ordering of tests is studied in [12]. The peak power values are captured in a complete directed graph. Then a number of graph based approaches are introduced to minimize the peak power [12].

2.2 Related Test Scheduling Techniques

A multi-temperature testing scheme is introduced in [3]. The proposed method does not utilize a test ordering technique. The required temperatures are achieved by introducing high power stimuli (*heating sequences*) and no stimuli (*cooling*) intervals. If a core is colder than the required temperature, a heating sequence will heat it up. If it is warmer than the required temperature, a cooling interval gives it the opportunity to cool down [3].

Another multi-temperature testing technique is introduced in [4]. The temperature-dependent tests are initially arranged in increasing required temperature. This technique neglects the tests power values and focuses on the required temperatures (temperatures that the temperature-dependent tests should be performed at). Then proper start times for different temperature-dependent tests are found [4].

The negative effects of process variation on multi-temperature testing are addressed in [5]. A stochastic optimization is introduced to reduce the impact of process variation. The optimization objective is to minimize the combined cost of: (1) ICs tested at wrong temperatures; (2) ICs overheated by receiving too much power; and (3) test application time [5]. The advantages of test reordering are ignored in this paper.

In general, the existing multi-temperature testing schemes focus on the temperature-dependent tests, thus, leaving the normal tests to be applied separately. Moreover, these existing techniques do not utilize test reordering. Instead they make use of heating sequences and cooling intervals. On the other hand, the existing test ordering techniques focus on power issues and do not take the temperature into account while ordering the tests. This paper, proposes a test ordering and scheduling technique that efficiently creates the required temperatures. Moreover the normal tests are accommodated in the schedule, while ordering the tests, along with the temperature-dependent tests.

3. Motivational Examples

Consider a 4-bit scan chain as shown in Fig. 1. Assume that 0101, 1111, and 1010 are three tests to be applied. The power dissipated in the circuit under test depends on the test orders. In the current example we focus only on scan chain part of the design. Different orders of these tests will cause different transition counts and consequently different power values. For example, the order 1010-1111-0101, as shown in Fig. 1a, results in a total of 12 transitions during shift-in. Another test order, 1111-1010-0101, as shown in Fig. 1b, results in 22 transitions and therefore higher power dissipation. Assuming that the core is too warm, arranging the tests in their low power order may avoid an additional cooling interval. Alternatively, if the core is too cold the high power arrangement of the same tests may replace an unnecessary heating sequence. This will ensure that TAM is not unnecessarily occupied by dummy heating sequence. Both situations help to shorten the test application time.

Consider an IC with three cores, each having four tests, as shown in Fig. 2. Two of the tests are cold, meaning that they require a low temperature (blue squares with T). The other two are hot, requiring a high temperature (red squares with T). It is assumed that the process starts at cold (room) temperature. Cold tests need one cooling interval (blue square) if they are to follow other tests. Hot tests need heating stimuli application (red square) beforehand. White spaces indicate unavailability of the TAM. The TAM is only available to two cores at a time.

A naïve technique is proposed in [4] that arranges the tests with increasing required temperatures. Consequently, the tests with high required temperature are accumulated at the end as shown in Fig. 2a. The heat transfer phenomenon is one of the arguments for this arrangement. Core 1's heat will warm up core 2 and 3 (and vice versa) and, therefore, it is appropriate to perform their hot tests at the same time (assuming that they will not approach the overheating temperature limit). This arrangement, however, will not utilize the TAM efficiently. In general, hot tests excessively occupy TAM in order to receive heating sequences. On the other hand, cold tests underutilize the TAM because of many required cooling intervals. A balanced TAM access pattern can be achieved by the alternative arrangement given in Fig. 2b. It achieves a faster test by mixing the hot and cold tests. In short, it is beneficial to look into the alternative orders for the temperature-dependent tests, instead of having a fixed order similar to [4].

4. Problem Formulation

Assume that there are M modules in an IC (on one layer in a normal IC or on multiple layers in a 3D-SIC) and their tests could be started and stopped independently (e.g., the modules are cores with core

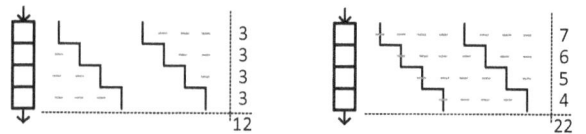

Figure 1. Test orders. (a) A low power order . (b) A high power order.

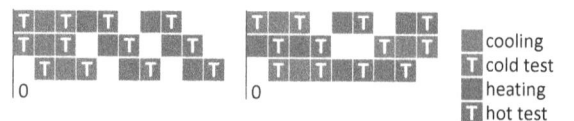

cooling
cold test
heating
hot test

Figure 2. Test temperature orders. (a) Cold tests first. (b) Mixed temperatures.

wrappers in a core-based design). Assume that module m has N_m tests. The set of tests consists of the temperature-dependent tests in addition to the normal tests. Normal tests do not require a specific temperature for their correct application. Temperature-dependent test s for module m is required to be performed when module m's temperature is between a low temperature limit $\theta_{m,s}^L$ and a high temperature limit $\theta_{m,s}^H$. The required temperature, $\hat{\theta}_{m,s}$, is then defined as:

$$\hat{\theta}_{m,s} = (\theta_{m,s}^L + \theta_{m,s}^H)/2.$$

The normal tests are separately specified as don't-cares.

The power dissipated during a test application, as discussed before, also depends on the previous test. Assuming that test $s_{m,s}$ for module m immediately follows test $s_{m,u}$, the dynamic power is denoted by $p_{m,u-s}^d$. The total test's power sequence, denoted by $p_{m,u-s}$, consists of the dynamic power, $p_{m,u-s}^d$, plus the stray power, denoted by $\widehat{p_m}$. The stray power is defined as the power dissipation that cannot be controlled by the test schedule. This includes the static power (including temperature-dependent leakage power) and the power dissipated by the clock network.

All test information can be captured in a graph. Consider an IC that has two modules ($M = 2$). Assume that module m_0 has two tests ($N_0 = 2$) as shown in Fig. 3a. Module m_1 has three tests ($N_1 = 3$) as shown in Fig. 3b. Assume that the two tests for module m_0 should be performed at 40°C and 70°C. Tests for module m_1 should be performed at 40°C, 70°C, and 100°C, respectively. Note that when $\hat{\theta}_{0,1} = 70°C$, test can be performed in the interval $[\theta_{0,1}^L \ \theta_{0,1}^H]$ (e.g., [60° 80°]). Total test powers are shown on the edges in Fig. 3. Although not shown in Fig. 3, usually there is a large number of thermally don't-care (normal) tests.

There are a number of reasons including the TAM structure that limit the tests that can run in parallel. It is assumed that a validity checker exists which updates the set of Valid Tests (VaT) if a new test can be performed simultaneously with the tests that are already selected. This is based on the knowledge of previously applied tests plus the partial set of tests selected to be applied next. For example, assume that in Fig. 3 $s_{0,0}$ and $s_{1,0}$ have been performed previously. Assume that $s_{0,1}$ is already selected to be applied next. In this case VaT is $\{s_{1,1} \ s_{1,2}\}$. Meaning that either of $s_{1,1}$ or $s_{1,2}$ can be applied in parallel with $s_{0,1}$ without violating TAM or power constrains.

In order to convert the power values into temperature values (i.e., temperature simulation) a temperature model similar to HotSpot [13] is used. The thermal behavior of an IC is captured in the following system of ordinary differential equations [14].

$$A \times \frac{d}{dt}\boldsymbol{\Theta} + B \times \boldsymbol{\Theta} = P \tag{1}$$

This thermal model divides the IC into a number of thermal elements. Heat capacities of these elements are captured in matrix A. Thermal conductance values are captured in matrix B. In this equation, $\boldsymbol{\Theta}$ is the temperature vector and P is the power.

Temperature of module m is denoted by θ_m ($\theta_m \in \boldsymbol{\Theta}$) and it should satisfy the condition $\theta_{m,s}^L \leq \theta_m \leq \theta_{m,s}^H$ during the application of test

s. The IC's temperature at the beginning of the testing process is assumed to be equal to the ambient temperature $\theta^{ambient}$. The modules' temperatures should be kept below overheating temperature $\theta^{Overheating}$ (including a safety margin) to avoid wrong test results and damage to the chip. This is true even for thermally don't-care tests.

The goal is to schedule the tests so that all the tests are performed correctly (inside the requested temperature intervals) and the total Test Application Time (TAT) is a minimized. This is mainly achieved by reordering the tests, including the normal tests. In case some cooling is required, it is achieved by halting a test. For additional heating, high power heating nodes are introduced. By adding such features to a test graph, an Enhanced Test Graph (ETG) is achieved. An example for ETG is shown in Fig 5. The power dissipation during a halt for cooling is equal to the stray power, $\widehat{p_m}$. High power heating nodes (red node in Fig. 4) are introduced into the ETG for situations where a fast heating cannot be achieved without them. They are similar to heating sequences used in [3–5]. Note that the green node in Fig. 4 is a normal test.

The next step in generating the ETG is the addition of the average power and the steady state temperatures to the edges. These steady state temperatures are used later to estimate the temperature achieved by a certain edge in infinite time. For this purpose, the average edge's power, denoted by $\overline{p_{m,u-s}}$, is considered. It is assumed that all other modules are receiving their corresponding stray powers ($\widehat{p_k}, k \neq m$). These powers are put together in P^{SS} vector. The steady state temperature, denoted by $\theta_{m,u-s}^{SS}$, is the m-th element in the temperatures vector, $\boldsymbol{\Theta}^{SS}$. It is computed as [15]:

$$\boldsymbol{\Theta}^{SS} = \theta^{ambient} + B^{-1} \times P^{SS} \tag{2}$$

The inputs to the proposed method include the enhanced test graph, ETG, IC's thermal model, constraints on the TAM (used to update the valid tests, VaT), power-related specifications, ambient temperature, $\theta^{ambient}$, and overheating temperature, $\theta^{Overheating}$. The output is a test schedule with a minimal test application time, TAT.

5. Proposed Scheduling Technique

The proposed technique gradually constructs the schedule based on repetition of two successive ordering processes: Ordering of the Temperature-dependent tests (OT) and Ordering of the Mixed nodes (OM). OT is to decide which temperature-dependent tests for which modules are preferred with regard to their required temperatures. Normal tests and heating nodes are neglected for the moment. It produces a list of the temperature-dependent nodes that should be scheduled next. These nodes are taken from the test graph (e.g., Fig. 3). Therefore, such a list shows the temperatures that should be achieved, as well. These temperatures are supposed to be achieved by the ordering of ETG nodes that OM advises. OM combines normal tests, heating nodes, and halts together with the tests listed by OT. OM scheduling is based on temperature simulations. OT and OM are repeated one after the other until all the tests are scheduled.

It may happen that all temperature-dependent tests are performed before all normal tests are completed. In such a scenario, OT takes

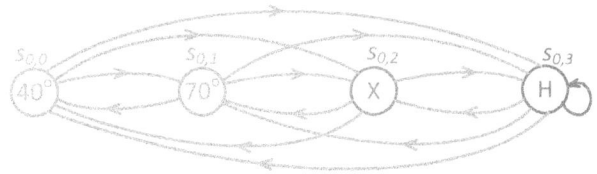

Figure 4. An enhanced test graph, ETG, showing a thermally don't-care (X) node, and a heating node (H).

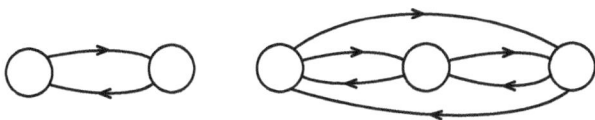

Figure 3. Test graphs for (a) module m_0 (b) module m_1.

the steady state temperatures that correspond to the normal tests as their required temperatures. These remaining normal tests then go through OM, but the only temperature manipulation that may happen, is halting to avoid overheating. This way, the remaining normal tests are scheduled.

5.1 OT: ORDERING OF THE TEMPERATURE-DEPENDENT TESTS

The role of OT is to receive a set of tests that are already selected to be applied together, and return one test that is appropriate to be applied along with them. Let us explain the OT process using an example. Consider an IC with three modules. Assume that only two of the modules can be tested simultaneously due to TAM limitation. The test graphs for modules m_0 is similar to Fig. 3a. m_1 and m_2's test graphs are similar to Fig. 3b. We start with a cold test, for example $s_{0,0}$ and then check the VaT for other tests that can be performed in parallel. Let us assume that apart from $s_{0,1}$ all other nodes are a valid choice. In order to decide which test to run in parallel, we use a fitness function (denoted by F). It returns a fitness value for each one of the alternative tests. The test with largest fitness value is then selected. Assuming that $s_{0,0}$ is already selected and

$$F(s_{1,0}) > F(s_{1,1}), F(s_{1,2}), F(s_{2,0}), F(s_{2,1}), \text{ and } F(s_{2,2}),$$

$s_{1,0}$ is selected to be applied along with $s_{0,0}$. The fitness function, F, contains F_0, F_1, and F_2. F_0 is defined as:

$$F_0(s_{k,u}) = \sum_{m,s} |\hat{\theta}_{m,s} - \hat{\theta}_{k,u}| \tag{3a}$$

While m and s sweep among the tests that are already selected ($s_{m,s}$), k and u represent the candidate test, $s_{k,u}$, that is being evaluated for fitness. Following the previous example, for $F(s_{2,1})$, $m = 0$, $k = 2$, $s = 0$, and $u = 1$. In the general case, the sum covers multiple tests, and therefore multiple values for m and s are visited (always $(m,s) \neq (k,u)$). $|x|$ denotes the absolute value of x. As mentioned in the second part of the motivational example, a balanced TAM access pattern is in trade-off with exploiting the transferred heat. F_0 is the sum of temperature differences among modules for a certain selection of tests. It implies that diverse test temperatures are favorable. This helps to balance the TAM load (similar to Fig. 2b). Besides, it reduces the risk of hot tests running together and needing excessive cooling.

F_1 is defined as:

$$F_1(s_{k,u}) = -\sum_{m,s} |\hat{\theta}_{m,s} - \hat{\theta}_{k,u}| \times b_{m,k} \tag{3b}$$

F_1 is in favor of having similar temperatures to exploit the heat transfer phenomenon. A similar temperature means a smaller value is subtracted from the fitness function. F_1 is the sum of temperature differences multiplied by thermal conductance values between those modules ($b_{m,k} \in \boldsymbol{B}$). A very small heat transfer among modules means that the argument for having similar temperatures is weak. This thought experiment can be verified by assuming very small thermal conductance values ($b_{m,k} \cong 0$). This removes F_1 from the fitness function while the term supporting diverse test temperatures (i.e., F_0) remains. In a 3D-SIC, if module m is located on top of module k and there are many TSVs connecting them, then the thermal conductance between them (i.e., $b_{m,k}$) will be relatively large. Consequently, having similar required temperatures, in this case, will be a great advantage in terms of F_1.

Another aspect to be taken into account is the module/test alternatives that require large temperature changes. For example a module with current temperature of 30°C should change directly to

100°C in order to support an upcoming test. This undesirable effect is captured in the fitness function by the inclusion of F_2:

$$F_2(s_{k,u}) = -|\theta_k - \hat{\theta}_{k,u}| \tag{3c}$$

Let us explain F_2 by considering $F(s_{1,2})$ as an example. The required temperatures for the upcoming test ($\hat{\theta}_{1,2} = 100°C$) is much higher than the current module temperatures, (assume that $\theta_1 = 30°C$ at the moment). Consequently, a large value, $F_2 = -|-70°C|$, will be subtracted from the fitness function, giving a small F. Inclusion of F_2 in F will prevent generating a schedule with frequent changes between cold and hot tests. Such an undesirable scenario will lead to excessively time-consuming heating and cooling actions.

The complete fitness function is defined as:

$$F(s_{k,u}) = (F_0 + \lambda_1 \times F_1 + \lambda_2 \times F_2 + K) \times r_k \tag{4}$$

Where λ_1 and λ_2 are coefficients introduced to balance F_1 and F_2 against F_0. Their values will be optimized in an outer optimization loop. The weighted sum of F_is, ($F_0 + \lambda_1 \times F_1 + \lambda_2 \times F_2$), may add up to a negative number as previously explained in equations 3abc. Therefore, a non-negative value denoted by K, is introduced in order to prevent the fitness values from becoming negative. If ($F_0 + \lambda_1 \times F_1 + \lambda_2 \times F_2$) is non-negative for all alternatives, then $K = 0$, otherwise

$$K = \left| \min_{all\ alternative\ values\ for\ k\ \&\ u} \{F_0 + \lambda_1 \times F_1 + \lambda_2 \times F_2\} \right|.$$

A negative weighted sum is undesirable because then the final multiplication in the fitness function will reduce the fitness values (for Fs with negative values), while it is expected to increase them.

At last the accumulated values are multiplied by the remaining test length for module m_k, denoted by r_k. This multiplication is to favor the selection of modules that have a large remaining set of tests. This way, the interleaving opportunities are maximized. This means that the cases that a module utilizes other modules' cooling intervals for its testing or heating is increased. The opposite case is when the test for many modules finishes rapidly while some modules have a lot of tests to complete. When these few modules release the TAM to cool down, there is no other module to utilize the available TAM. This is another kind of TAM underutilization that must be avoided.

The fitness function is also useful when ordering the thermally don't-care (i.e., normal) tests. This takes place when no temperature-dependent test is left to be visited. In this case, the steady state temperatures, $\theta_{m,u-s}^{ss}$, (u is the latest ETG node visited in module m) are used instead of the required temperatures, $\hat{\theta}_{m,s}$, in equations 3 and 4.

5.2 OM: ORDERING OF THE MIXED NODES

Now that the upcoming temperature-dependent tests are specified by OT, OM should deliver their required temperatures. This is done by scheduling the ETG nodes (e.g., Fig. 4) such that the proper power values leading to such temperatures are obtained. This is similar to the case discussed at the beginning of the motivational example.

The desired schedule could be seen as a path in the enhanced test graph, ETG. Nodes corresponding to the tests should be visited at least once, at correct temperature. When all of them are visited, the test process is completed. Finding such a path with a minimal test application time is the aim of this section. This is an NP-hard problem [9], [11] and therefore a heuristic is introduced to tackle it.

OT has already found the proper list of temperature-dependent tests to be applied next. If the temperatures are right, these nodes are immediately visited. But, if a module needs heating, then some other nodes should be visited first, for heating. This includes heating nodes or high power normal tests. If a module needs cooling, then either it is halted or it visits some low power normal tests.

Let us explain this procedure using the example given in Fig. 5. Consider an ETG with five nodes: two temperature-dependent tests ($\hat{\theta}_{0,0} = 70°C$ and $\hat{\theta}_{0,1} = 40°C$); a low power normal test, $s_{0,2}$, and a high power normal test, $s_{0,3}$; and finally a heating node, $s_{0,4}$. OT indicates that $s_{0,0}$ should be tested first. Assuming that the initial IC's temperature is equal to the ambient temperature, $\theta^{ambient} = 30°C$, heating is required. Therefore, $s_{0,3}$ is visited first. The test is performed and the module is heated (temperature curve obtained by temperature simulation is shown in blue in Fig. 5). Since the temperature is still less than 70°C, the heating node is visited. At last, $s_{0,0}$ can be visited and an OM step is completed. OT is again activated, returning $s_{0,1}$ as the next temperature-dependent test. The module's temperature is too high and therefore, the low power normal test, $s_{0,2}$ is visited. Although the temperature reduces, it is still too warm, therefore, a halt is introduced. This leaves the TAM unoccupied for other modules. Finally the temperature reaches 40°C and $s_{0,1}$ can be visited, ending the test procedure. The resulted ETG path is shown by black arrows in Fig. 5, overlaid on the temperature curve.

When the temperature is lower than required, important decisions are made by OM: whether to visit a normal test or a heating node? The dilemma is that although a normal test heats up the module less efficiently compared with a heating node, it reduces the TAT by visiting a test. To answer this question, we focus on the most powerful test among the remaining normal tests and the most powerful heating node among the heating nodes. Note that the heating node has never less power than a test because in such situations, that test must be copied as a heating node. The decision is made based on a Heating Criterion (HC). HC depends on the steady state temperatures that are previously calculated for ETG as well as the current temperatures:

$$HC = \frac{\theta^{SS}_{m,s-x} - \theta_m}{\theta^{SS}_{m,s-h} - \theta_m} \tag{5a}$$

The above equation is written for module m, assuming that the current node is s. Index h is the heating node and x is the thermally don't-care test. When the normal test is very powerful ($\overline{p_{m,s-x}} \cong \overline{p_{m,s-h}}$), HC will be almost equal to one. This indicates that there is not much difference between the heating times of the two options and therefore the normal test is probably a better choice since it reduces the size of the remaining tests. On the other extreme, when the normal test is very weak ($\theta^{SS}_{m,s-x} \cong \theta_m$), HC will be almost equal to zero. This indicates that the heating node is probably a better choice since the normal test increases the temperature very slowly. We compare HC with a threshold value denoted by ψ to decide:

$$\begin{cases} \text{heating node, if } HC < \psi \\ \text{normal test, otherwise} \end{cases} \tag{5b}$$

The value of ψ will be optimized in an outer optimization loop. For the moment, we assume that it is given. Similarly a Cooling Criterion (CC) is defined to decide between a low power normal test and halting the test for cooling:

$$CC = \frac{\theta_m - \theta^{SS}_{m,s-x}}{\theta_m - \theta^{SS}_{m,stray\_power}} \tag{6a}$$

$$\begin{cases} \text{halt, if } CC < \varphi \\ \text{normal test, otherwise} \end{cases} \tag{6b}$$

When the normal test is very weak ($\overline{p_{m,s-x}} \cong \widehat{p_m}$), CC will be almost equal to one. This indicates that there is not much difference between the cooling times of the two options and therefore normal test is probably a better choice since it reduces the size of the remaining tests. On the other extreme, when the normal test is not that weak ($\theta^{SS}_{m,s-x} \cong \theta_m$), CC will be almost equal to zero. This indicates that halting is probably a better choice since the normal test decreases the temperature very slowly. CC is compared with a threshold denoted by φ to make the decision. The value of φ will be optimized in the outer optimization loop, along with ψ.

The proper ordering of the nodes that is represented as a path in the ETG is discussed above (e.g., an ETG path is shown overlaid on the temperature curve in Fig. 5). There is yet another important aspect: the time-related schedule that incorporates such an ETG path. For example, in Fig. 5, when applying the heating node, $s_{0,4}$, if the 70°C temperature is reached before $s_{0,4}$ finishes, it is a good idea to stop running $s_{0,4}$. Such interrupts, due to higher temperatures than needed or is safe (e.g., overheating temperature) are always possible. If this is a heating node, like this case, the operation continues by immediately visiting the next node in the path. Otherwise, if a running test was halted, that same test continues after the module is sufficiently cooled. The power values are updated in such cases.

The proper moments to stop heating/cooling and start/resume a test are determined, offline, using temperature simulations. Cooling is introduced when $\theta_m \geq \theta^H_m$ or $\theta_m \geq \theta^{overheating}$. Heating is introduced when $\theta_m \leq \theta^L_m$. Heating/cooling continues until the temperature reaches $\hat{\theta}_{m,s} + \mu$ for a low power test or $\hat{\theta}_{m,s} - \gamma$ for a high power test. Therefore, testing starts when:

$$\begin{cases} \theta_m reaches (\hat{\theta}_{m,s} + \mu), if \theta^{SS}_{m,u-s} > \hat{\theta}_{m,s} \\ \theta_m reaches (\hat{\theta}_{m,s} - \gamma), otherwise \end{cases} \tag{7}$$

Assuming that the current test for module m is u, the criterion for test s being high power is that the steady state temperature achievable by s (being performed immediately after u) is larger than the test s's required temperature ($\theta^{SS}_{m,u-s} > \hat{\theta}_{m,s}$). μ and γ values are optimized in the outer optimization loop along with φ, ψ, λ_1, and λ_2. The outer optimization loop is a straightforward implementation of the canonical version of particle swarm optimization introduced in [16]. The objective is to achieve a minimal test application time while all tests are applied at correct temperatures.

6. Experimental Results

Experiments have been performed to demonstrate that the proposed technique can efficiently achieve the required temperatures. For comparison purpose, the approach proposed in [3], which performs multi-temperature test scheduling without reordering of test patterns, is used as the baseline. As mentioned before, multi-temperature testing should be considered for modern 3D stacked ICs

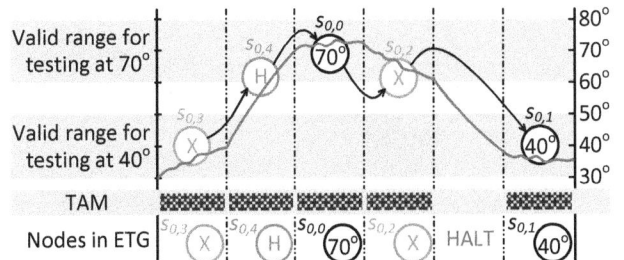

Figure 5. Temperature curves for an ordered ETG with five nodes.

7

as well as normal 2D ICs. Therefore, multi-layer 3D-SICs are also considered for our experiments.

The proposed technique is evaluated on a set of 24 experimental ICs as detailed in Table 1. Column 1 is the IC's number. These ICs have one to four stacked dies (column 2). The ICs with one layer represent a normal 2D IC. The ICs with more than one layer represent a 3D-SIC design. Each die accommodates 2, 12, 20, 30, 42, and 49 modules resulting in 2 to 196 modules per IC as shown in column 3. The proposed approach achieves shorter TAT compared with the baseline approach for all of the experimental ICs. The percentage changes are reported in column 4.

Compared with the baseline approach, the proposed approach is more complicated for one decision-point[1] in the schedule. On the other hand, the proposed approach produces shorter schedules which mean less decision-points. The CPU times that include the time taken by the outer optimization loop (i.e., PSO) are reported in columns 5 and 6. In general, the proposed approach is slightly faster than the baseline approach, as shown in column 7. This means that in average, shorter schedules (smaller TAT) compensate for the more complicated and time-consuming decision-points.

CPU times, in general, grow with the number of modules and layers as shown in Fig. 6. The growth rate is acceptably low and the scheduling process for the largest IC (number 24) takes less than 10 minutes to complete.

7. Conclusions

Multi-temperature testing is used in order to detect the temperature-dependent defects. The existing multi-temperature testing procedures do not utilize opportunities offered by the dependency of test power dissipation on the order of the tests. Besides, combining the normal tests with temperature-dependent tests is not addressed by the existing techniques. In this paper we propose an efficient test application technique to order and combine the normal tests and the temperature-dependent tests in order to achieve a rapid multi-temperature test process.

8. References

[1]   W. Needham, C. Prunty, and E. H. Yeoh, "High volume microprocessor test escapes, an analysis of defects our tests are missing," *ITC 1998.*

[2]   J. Segura, A. Keshavarzi, J. Soden, and C. Hawkins, "Parametric failures in CMOS ICs–a defect-based analysis," *ITC 2002.*

[3]   Z. He, Z. Peng, and P. Eles, "Multi-temperature testing for core-based system-on-chip," *DATE 2010.*

[4]   C. Yao, K. K. Saluja, and P. Ramanathan, "Temperature dependent test scheduling for multi-core system-on-chip," *ATS 2011.*

[5]   N. Aghaee, Z. Peng, and P. Eles, "Process-variation aware multi-temperature test scheduling," *VLSI Design 2014.*

[6]   E. Zschech, E. Langer, H.-J. Engelmann, and K. Dittmar, "Physical failure analysis in semiconductor industry— challenges of the copper interconnect process," *Mater. Sci. Semicond. Process.*, vol. 5, no. 4–5, pp. 457–464, Aug. 2002.

[7]   C.-W. Tseng, E. J. McCluskey, X. Shao, and D. M. Wu, "Cold delay defect screening," *VTS 2000.*

[8]   J. C. Li, C.-W. Tseng, and E. J. McCluskey, "Testing for resistive opens and stuck opens," *ITC 2001.*

[9]   V. Dabholkar, S. Chakravarty, I. Pomeranz, and S. Reddy, "Techniques for minimizing power dissipation in scan and combinational circuits during test application," *IEEE Trans. Comput.-Aided Des. Integr. Circuits Syst.*, vol. 17, no. 12, pp. 1325–1333, Dec. 1998.

[10]   P. M. Rosinger, B. M. Al-Hashimi, and N. Nicolici, "Power profile manipulation: a new approach for reducing test application time under power constraints," *IEEE Trans. Comput.-Aided Des. Integr. Circuits Syst.*, vol. 21, no. 10, pp. 1217–1225, Oct. 2002.

[11]   S. Bahukudumbi and K. Chakrabarty, "Power management using test-pattern ordering for wafer-level test during burn-in," *IEEE Trans. Very Large Scale Integr. VLSI Syst.*, vol. 17, no. 12, pp. 1730–1741, Dec. 2009.

[12]   J. T. Tudu, E. Larsson, V. Singh, and V. D. Agrawal, "On minimization of peak power for scan circuit during test," *ETS 2009.*

[13]   Wei Huang, S. Ghosh, S. Velusamy, K. Sankaranarayanan, K. Skadron, and M. R. Stan, "HotSpot: a compact thermal modeling methodology for early-stage VLSI design," *IEEE Trans. Very Large Scale Integr. VLSI Syst.*, vol. 14, no. 5, pp. 501–513, May 2006.

[14]   N. Aghaee, Z. Peng, and P. Eles, "Process-variation and temperature aware SoC test scheduling technique," *J. Electron. Test.*, vol. 29, no. 4, pp. 499–520, Aug. 2013.

[15]   N. Aghaee, Z. Peng, and P. Eles, "An efficient temperature-gradient based burn-in technique for 3D stacked ICs," *DATE 2014.*

[16]   R. Poli, J. Kennedy, and T. Blackwell, "Particle swarm optimization," *Swarm Intell.*, vol. 1, no. 1, pp. 33–57, Jun. 2007.

[1]A decision-point is a point that a module's state (testing/heating/cooling) or its node in the ETG may change.

TABLE 1.   EXPERIMENTAL RESULTS

IC specifications		Percentage change in TAT	CPU time [sec]		Percentage change in CPU time
Number of layers	*Number of modules*		*Baseline Approach*	*Proposed Approach*	
1	1	2	−46.94	1	1	0
2	1	12	−31.81	1	1	0
3	1	20	−34.18	2	1	−50.00
4	1	30	−13.45	4	3	−25.00
5	1	42	−24.33	4	4	0
6	1	49	−35.30	5	5	0
7	2	4	−28.80	1	1	0
8	2	24	−30.51	3	2	−33.33
9	2	40	−30.02	6	6	0
10	2	60	−25.92	12	9	−25
11	2	84	−27.54	22	17	−22.73
12	2	98	−23.10	31	23	−25.81
13	3	6	−63.64	1	1	0
14	3	36	−48.93	10	10	0
15	3	60	−47.99	24	20	−16.67
16	3	90	−43.84	55	60	9.09
17	3	126	−29.59	99	70	−29.29
18	3	147	−41.77	146	128	−12.33
19	4	8	−35.48	2	2	0
20	4	48	−32.00	29	19	−34.48
21	4	80	−56.06	74	74	0
22	4	120	−47.69	166	196	18.07
23	4	168	−37.60	318	221	−30.50
24	4	196	−36.41	411	457	11.19
	Average		−36.37			−11.12

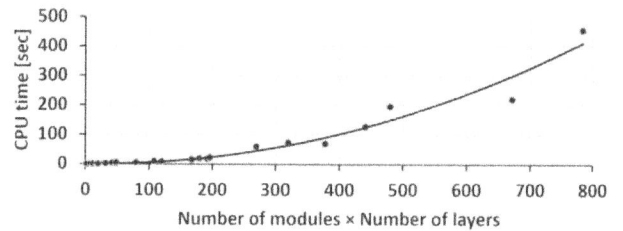

Figure 6.   CPU time growth.

Playing with Fire: Transactional Memory Revisited for Error-Resilient and Energy-Efficient MPSoC Execution

Dimitra Papagiannopoulou
Brown University
dimitra_papagiannopoulou@brown.edu

Andrea Marongiu
ETH Zurich
mandrea@iis.ee.ethz.ch

Tali Moreshet
Boston University
talim@bu.edu

Luca Benini
ETH Zurich
lbenini@iis.ee.ethz.ch

Maurice Herlihy
Brown University
mph@cs.brown.edu

Iris Bahar
Brown University
iris_bahar@brown.edu

ABSTRACT

As silicon integration technology pushes toward atomic dimensions, errors due to static and dynamic variability are an increasing concern. To avoid such errors, designers often turn to "guardband" restrictions on the operating frequency and voltage. If guardbands are too conservative, they limit performance and waste energy, but less conservative guardbands risk moving the system closer to its Critical Operating Point (COP), a frequency-voltage pair that, if surpassed, causes massive instruction failures. In this paper, we propose a novel scheme that allows to dynamically adjust to an evolving COP and operate at highly reduced margins, while guaranteeing forward progress. Specifically, our scheme dynamically monitors the platform and adaptively adjusts to the COP among multiple cores, using lightweight checkpointing and roll-back mechanisms adopted from Hardware Transactional Memory (HTM) for error recovery. Experiments demonstrate that our technique is particularly effective in saving energy while also offering safe execution guarantees. To the best of our knowledge, this work is the first to describe a full-fledged HTM implementation for error-resilient and energy-efficient MPSoC execution.

1. INTRODUCTION

Scaling of physical dimensions in semiconductor devices has opened the way to heterogeneous embedded SoCs integrating host processors and many-core accelerators in the same chip [5], but at a price of ever-increasing static and dynamic hardware variability [2]. Spatial die-to-die and within-die static variations ultimately induce performance and power mismatches between the cores in a many-core array, introducing heterogeneity in a nominally homogeneous system (formally identical processing resources). Dynamic variations depend on the operating conditions of the chip, and include aging, supply voltage drops and temperature fluctuations. The most common consequence of variations is

path delay uncertainty. Circuit designers typically use conservative guardbands on the operating frequency or voltage to ensure safe system operation, with the obvious consequent loss of operational efficiency. When the guardbands are reduced, or when the system is aggressively operated far from a safe point, the delay uncertainty manifests itself either as an intermittent timing error [7] [4] or a critical operating point (COP) [17]. Timing errors may ultimately cause erroneous instructions with wrong outputs being stored or, worse, incorrect control flow. COP defines a voltage and frequency pair at which a core is error-free. If the voltage is decreased below (or the frequency is increased beyond) the COP, the core will face a massive number of errors [17]. The COP effect is highly pronounced in well-optimized designs [11] [15] due to so-called "path walls".

Circuit level error detection and correction (EDAC) techniques [7] [4] can transparently detect and correct timing errors, with the side-effect of an increased execution time and energy. Indeed, techniques such as *multiple-issue instruction replay* [4] to correct an errant instruction incur the cost of flushing the pipeline and executing N+1 replicas of the instruction (N being the number of pipeline stages). In addition, while EDAC techniques are suitable for handling sporadic errors, they are obviously not a good solution for the "all-or-nothing" effect of the COP. In principle the COP can be determined for a particular chip after its production, and the most efficient yet safe voltage/frequency pair for the chip could be configured at that time. However, due to static and dynamic variations, the COP may actually change over space and time. As a result, the "safe" operating point may i) differ from one core to another (imposing to conservatively tune the entire chip to meet the requirements of the most critical core) and ii) suddenly become unsafe due to aging, temperature fluctuations or voltage drops.

In this paper, we propose an integrated HW/SW scheme that addresses both types of variation phenomena, and particularly to dynamically adjust to an evolving COP, thus enabling the system to operate at highly reduced margins without sacrificing performance, while at the same time guaranteeing forward progress at reduced energy levels. More specifically, our approach dynamically monitors the platform and adaptively adjusts to the COP among multiple cores, using lightweight checkpointing and roll-back mechanisms adapted from Hardware Transactional Memory (HTM) for error recovery. In particular, we support two distinct types of recovery mechanisms: non-critical and critical. Non-critical recovery is required whenever an error takes place

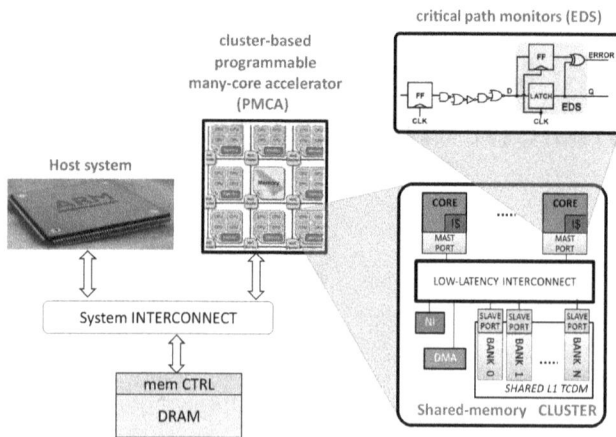

Figure 1: Target platform high level view.

in the datapath (e.g., the multiplier). In this case the consequence of an error is that incorrect data may be stored in memory. Critical recovery is required when an error takes place in the control part of the processor pipeline (e.g., instruction fetch/decode). This type of error breaks the original control flow of the program and prevents any software-based solution from taking control.

We assume the platform is initially configured to operate at a safe, reference operating voltage (i.e., with safe margins to hide all variability effects). Every time a new transaction is started, our technique optimistically lowers the voltage in small steps, individually on each core. If sporadic or non-critical errors take place, the HTM-inspired techniques intervene and ensure correct program behavior and progress. If systematic or critical errors take place, then the system reverts to the previous stable operating point. If over time the COP changes, the technique is re-activated and the system is re-calibrated. Using cycle-accurate simulation models, annotated with power/performance numbers extracted from a silicon implementation of the target platform, we show that the proposed technique can achieve up to 40% energy savings with respect to using conservative voltage margins, over different benchmarks. To the best of our knowledge, this work is the first to i) describe a full-fledged HTM implementation for error-resilient and energy-efficient MPSoC execution; ii) provide realistic energy saving measurements using real-life benchmarks.

The rest of the paper is organized as follows. In Section 2 we provide details of the target platform, and in Section 3 we describe the proposed techniques. The experimental setup and results are discussed in Section 4, and we compare to related work in Section 5. Section 6 concludes the paper.

2. TARGET ARCHITECTURE

Our HW/SW design is driven to a large extent by the target architecture (Fig. 1). We envision a general-purpose *host* processor, coupled with a programmable many-core accelerator (PMCA) composed of several tens of simple cores, where critical computation kernels of an application can be offloaded to improve overall performance/Watt. We assume that the host core is operated with safe margins. Our work focuses on the PMCA, and in particular in a design that leverages a multi-cluster configuration to overcome scalability limitations [5] [10] [18]. Our goal is to improve energy

efficiency by operating the PMCA "dangerously close" to the COP, while exploiting the HTM to avoid failures.

In this multi-cluster configuration, simple processing elements are grouped into clusters sharing high-performance local interconnect and memory. Several clusters are replicated and interconnected through a scalable medium such as a network-on-chip (NoC), while within a cluster a limited number of simple processors (typically 4 to 16) share an L1 tightly-coupled data memory (TCDM). The TCDM is configured as a shared multi-banked scratchpad memory[1] that enables concurrent accesses to different memory banks. Simultaneous accesses to the same bank are serialized in a round-robin fashion. Accesses to memory external to the cluster go through a network interface. The basic synchronization mechanism is provided via standard *test-and-set* registers.

On top of this baseline cluster we design our HTM extensions for error-tolerance. More specifically, we revisit existing checkpointing and rollback mechanisms that have been employed for HTM, to now be used as a lightweight mechanism for fast and efficient error recovery.

The architecture implemented in this work consists of a single computation cluster, featuring 8 cores with private I$ (1 KByte) and 16 TCDM banks (256KB), plus external (main) L2 memory (2MB). The TCDM is implemented using two different technologies: 6-transistor SRAM and Standard Cell Memory (SCM). SCM achieves lower density (~3X) than SRAM, but can reliably operate at the same voltage ranges as the rest of the logic. SRAM requires higher voltages to operate reliably, thus consume (~4X) the energy [13]. We use SCM to implement storage that needs to always be reliable (e.g., to implement function calls, for control-flow data and for instruction cache), while program data is stored in SRAM and our HTM techniques are used to recover from errors.

All the base performance/energy/area numbers used in this work are derived from a silicon implementation of the platform in 28nm STMicroelectronics UTB FD-SOI technology, and integrated in a cycle-accurate SystemC simulator (see Section 4). The cluster is able to operate over a wide range of frequencies (from 20MHz @ 0.5V up to 450MHz @ 1.2V). In this work the target frequency is 200MHz, with a nominal voltage of 0.84. Due to process variation the required V_{dd} for a safe operating condition may actually vary among cores (we observe up to 0.04V increase). Different sources of dynamic variations also increase the minimum voltage level required for safe operation. The baseline platform considers safe margins to compensate for all sources of variability, and is thus conservatively operated at a reference voltage of 1V.

Any errors caused by dynamic variation need to be detected at runtime. We assume each core is equipped with error-detection circuitry such as *error-detection sequential* (EDS) [4]. In particular, since our techniques try to optimistically lower the voltage and adapt to an evolving COP, we need to always be able to recover from two types of errors:

1. **Non-critical errors** are those that originate from timing delays along the datapath (e.g., multiplier) and ultimately lead to writing a bad value on memory.
2. **Critical errors** are those that occur in the control part of the processor pipeline (instruction fetch/decode) and ultimately lead to catastrophic failures.

---

[1]Not a data cache. Coherency is managed via explicit copies.

Our simulation models were augmented to have both types of paths monitored via EDS.

3. IMPLEMENTATION

Our proposed scheme borrows key concepts from Hardware Transactional Memory (HTM) to provide a mechanism for error recovery. Traditionally, HTM requires two key components: i) some form of *bookkeeping* (for keeping track of read/write data conflicts), and ii) *data versioning* (for keeping track of speculative and non-speculative versions of data in case it is necessary to rollback and recover from a data conflict). For our purposes, we only need to implement data versioning and rollback in order to recover from variability-induced errors. Our design uses the TCDM memory to hold both speculative and non-speculative data. Data logs are distributed across the TCDM memory banks, so that each bank is responsible for handling recovery only for its associated data.

3.1 Checkpointing and Rollback

We protect all the parallel parts of the program from errors by enclosing them within transactions (see Sec. 3.4). At the beginning of each transaction (*Transaction Start*) we save the internal state of the core (i.e. program counter, stack pointer, internal registers, stack contents) to be able to roll back in case of errors. *Error resolution* can be eager or lazy, meaning that we can resolve the error by aborting the transaction and rolling back right away or wait until the end of the transactional region to do so. For our design, we consider both variants. For non-critical errors we follow lazy error resolution since we want to avoid the cost of frequent error checking. We fine tune our transactional regions' sizes to be small enough so that if errors start occurring, it won't be long before they get detected and the core's voltage is adjusted to safer levels. In the lazy error recovery scheme, when a transaction completes execution (*Transaction End*) we check whether (non-critical) errors have been encountered by the core executing the transaction. If no errors are detected the transaction *commits*, the checkpointing information is discarded and speculative changes to the data become permanent. If errors are detected the transaction *aborts*, and a *rollback* mechanism restores the internal core state. In addition, data are restored to their original values and speculative copies are discarded. For critical errors an interrupt is generated by path monitors, and error resolution employs an eager scheme (see Sec. 3.3)

3.2 Data Versioning

Data Versioning can also be either eager or lazy. Lazy data versioning keeps the original data in place and buffers the speculative data updates in different locations (allowing for fast error recovery). Eager data versioning makes speculative changes in place and stores back-up copies of the original data in separate places (allowing for fast commits but slow abort handling). We expect that our scheme will incur relatively low error rates; therefore aborts due to errors will be infrequent and we can choose an eager data versioning mechanism.

In this work, we propose a *distributed per-address log* data versioning scheme that is simple, fast, and significantly more space efficient than state-of-the art transactional memory approaches for embedded systems [16]. Figure 2 depicts how the *distributed per-address log* design works. In this

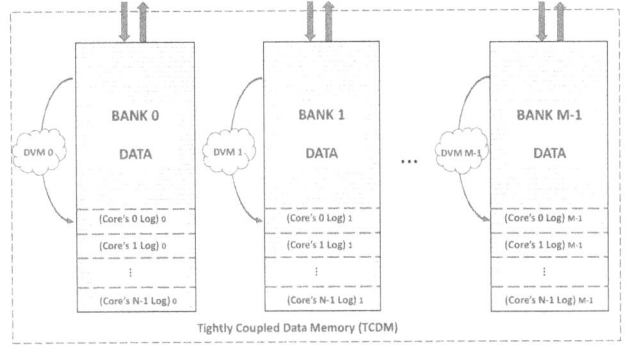

Figure 2: Distributed per-address log scheme for M banks and N cores.

design, distributed per-address logs are used to save backups of the original values of data that are written during transactions, so that they can be recovered in case of errors. Since memory is distributed across multiple memory banks that accept and serve access requests in parallel, having a central control logic to manage the distributed logs would not be efficient. For this reason, we divide the transactional handling and log managing responsibilities across multiple control modules, one for each bank of the TCDM, that we call *Data Versioning Modules (DVM)*. Each bank's DVM is a control block that monitors transactional accesses to the bank and manages the cores' logs that reside in that bank. It is also responsible for restoring the log data of the cores that abort their transactions and cleaning the logs of the cores that commit their transactions. All banks' DVMs work in parallel and independently of each other. At every bank of the TCDM, we keep a fixed-size log space for each core in the system. Each core's log holds the addresses that belong to that bank and are written transactionally by that core. In this way, we keep a log space only for the addresses of the bank that are actually written transactionally. At the same time, with this distributed log design we avoid cross-bank data exchange when saving and restoring the log, since each addresses' log falls within the same bank. Thus the log saving and restoration process is triggered internally by the DVM of each bank and it does not require interaction with the DVMs of other banks.

When a core writes transactionally to an address of a bank, its log is traversed to check whether it already holds an entry for that address. If not, a new log entry is created to store the original data of the address. Note that the data only need to be logged the first time the address is written within a specific transaction. Therefore, the log size depends on the write footprint of each transaction. Since the log of each core is distributed among all the TCDM banks, we expect that the log writes will also be divided among the banks. The size of each core's log space per bank is a parameter in our design, so it can be easily adjusted to the needs of different applications domains. In case of an overflow, our technique resorts to software-managed logging into the main L2 memory. The capability of tuning the transactions' granularity is intuitively key to reducing the number of overflows. Using the technique described in Section 3.4, we found that 1KB total log size per core (64B in each TCDM bank) is adequate for our target applications. Overall, the logs for all the cores occupy roughly 3% of the total TCDM space.

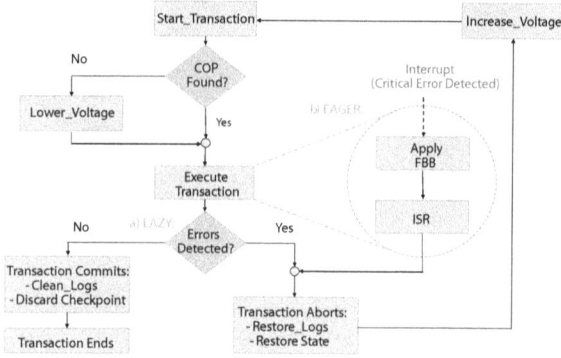

Figure 3: Control Flow of an error-resilient transaction.

If an error is detected and a transaction must abort, each bank's log is traversed to restore the original data back to its proper address. If a transaction commits, the logs associated with that transaction are all discarded and the speculative data now becomes non-speculative.

3.3 Error-Resilient Transactions

The flowchart in Figure 3 describes the semantics of our *error-resilient transactions* (ERT). We start with all platform components set at the safe reference voltage level (1.0V). Each time a core encounters a new transaction it saves its internal state and current stack and checks whether the self-calibration procedure was previously completed and the COP for this core is known. If the COP is still unknown, the executing core optimistically lowers its voltage level by a pre-defined step (0.02V). If the COP has already been reached, then no voltage adjustment is made.

If the transaction end is reached without errors being detected, the transaction *Commits*. A *clean_logs()* process is activated at each bank's DVM to clean up the saved log of the committing core in the respective bank. Note that all these processes are triggered simultaneously by the DVMs of all memory banks. If errors are detected, then the transaction *aborts*. A *restore_logs()* process is activated simultaneously at each bank's DVM to restore all the saved log values of the aborted core. The internal state of the aborted core is restored, its voltage is adjusted back to the previous safe level (*increase_voltage()*) (a +0.02V voltage increase beyond the recently found COP) and the core is ready to retry the transaction. From this point on, the voltage level is no longer reduced when starting a new transaction[2].

3.4 Programming model

Similar to prior approaches [1] [8], we have chosen to integrate transactional memory into OpenMP, a widespread and easy-to-use programming model. An OpenMP program starts on a single thread of execution (the *master*). Once the **parallel** directive is encountered, additional threads are created, and execute the code enclosed within the syntactic boundaries of the construct. The work is parallelized among threads using *worksharing* directives. For illustration purposes we describe here one of the most used among such directives: dynamic loops. Figure 4 shows a code snippet

---

[2] In case a temperature reduction is detected, the voltage can be further decreased, as the COP has "moved" downwards.

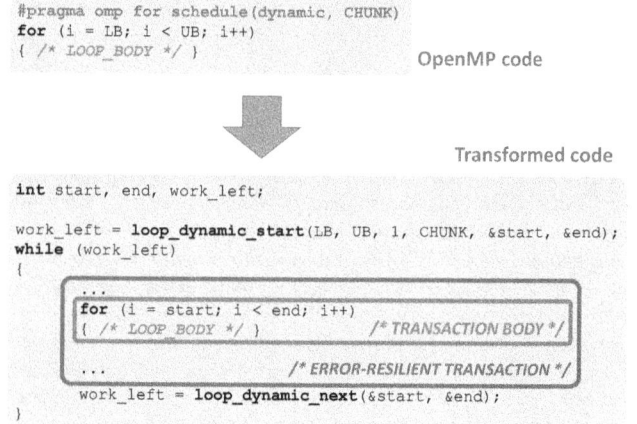

Figure 4: Transformed OpenMP dynamic loop

with a **#pragma omp for** directive, used to distribute loop iterations among threads. The **schedule(dynamic, CHUNK)** clause is used to specify that iterations should be grouped in smaller sets of size CHUNK, and distributed in a dynamic (first come, first served) fashion.

The bottom part of Figure 4 shows how this is achieved once the code is transformed by an OpenMP compiler. Runtime library calls are inserted to interact with an iteration scheduler. First, the scheduler is initialized (**loop_dynamic_start**) passing as parameters the original loop bounds (LB, UB), stride and CHUNK. If there are iterations available the function returns a positive integer (stored in **work_left**) and initializes the input parameters **start** and **end** with lower and upper boundaries for the current chunk of iterations. The original loop body is then executed for these iteration instances and a new call to the runtime library (**loop_dynamic_next**) repeats the process until there are no iterations left.

This mechanism can be easily augmented to wrap each CHUNK of loop iterations within an *error-resilient transaction* (ERT). Thus, transaction granularity at the application level may be adjusted by modifying the CHUNK parameter or with OpenMP loop scheduling clauses. This is important for performance as well as energy efficiency since transaction granularity can impact error-rate in our context.

The same scheme can be easily applied to other OpenMP constructs (**sections**, **task**, etc.). Moreover, to ensure robust execution at every point in program execution, we silently define ERT boundaries wherever an OpenMP construct is encountered. The sequential execution in the master thread is also wrapped in an ERT. Additional ERTs can be manually outlined in the code if necessary.

4. EXPERIMENTAL RESULTS

The proposed architecture has been modeled in Virtual SoC [3], a SystemC-based cycle-accurate virtual platform for heterogeneous System-On-Chip simulation, with back-annotated energy numbers for every system component. The performance, energy, and area numbers are derived from an implementation of the platform in STMicroelectronics 28nm UTB FD-SOI technology. This approach couples the advantages of very accurate power models with the simulation speed of the SystemC models. On average, the virtual platform shows a maximum error in timing accuracy below 6% with respect to a complete RTL simulation of the

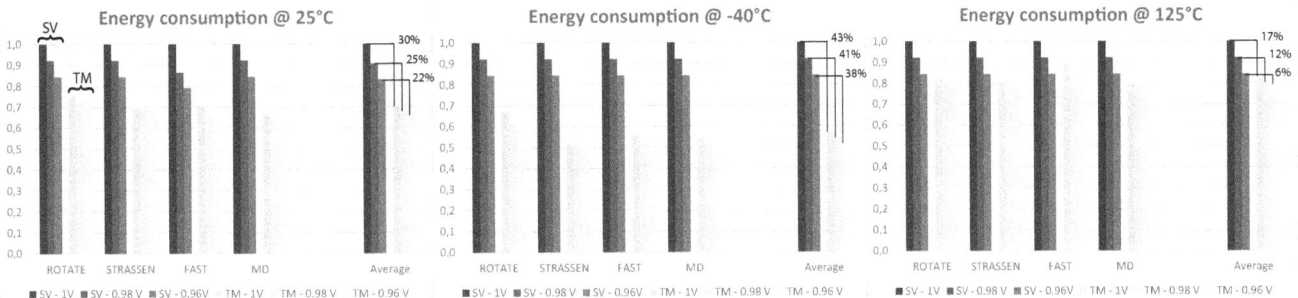

Figure 5: Energy consumption at various operating conditions (voltage, temperature). Steady voltage (SV) versus transactional memory (TM).

same benchmark. We have conducted our evaluations using real-life benchmarks from the computer vision domain: *Rotate* (image rotation), *Strassen* (matrix multiplication), *Fast* (corner detection) and *Mahalanobis-Distance* (cluster analysis and classification).

4.1 Overhead characterization

As a first experiment, we measured the overhead of the proposed HW/SW support for error-resilience in terms of energy and execution delay. The energy overhead for our technique is quite modest: on average, only 1.7% across all benchmarks and never more than 5% of the total system energy. Similarly, execution time overhead is a reasonable 6.6% maximum.

Further detailing the analysis for distributed logs, on average, transactional writes took 0.7 to 1.5 extra cycles to complete and increased total execution time by only 0.5%. The log restoration time clearly depends on the data footprint of the target application: the higher the number of writes within a transaction, the bigger the size of the logs. For each address that needs to be restored, 2 cycles are spent, one for reading the original value from the log space and one for writing it back to its original address. The worst case restoration time per core in isolation is 32 cycles, which may be up to 8 times slower in the unlikely event that all cores were rolling back at the same time. Log restoration time never accounted for more than 3% of the total benchmark execution time. The area overhead of our proposed scheme is quite small. In particular, our distributed per-address logging scheme is space-efficient; the total log space occupies only 3% of the TCDM space. Moreover, based on [4], the area overhead introduced by EDS is nominal.

4.2 Energy characterization

Next, we conducted a set of measurements to assess the energy saving capabilities of our technique. The effect of static within die variations is modeled in our platform by considering different nominal voltages for the target frequency (200MHz) among cores, with a maximum variation of 0.04V (0.84V to 0.88V). To explore how the lowest safe voltage level changes due to temperature variations, we ran our experiments at three different temperature corners ($25°C$, $-40°C$ and $125°C$).

We compare our transactional memory inspired techniques (**TM**) to a conservative *steady-voltage* (**SV**) technique, which uses voltage margins (guardbands) to absorb the effects of static and dynamic variations. From the measurements on silicon we observe that in the worst case, a 0.96V operating voltage would be sufficient to compensate for static and tem-

perature variations. In practice, to also account for other sources of dynamic variations (e.g., aging, voltage drops) even more conservative voltage margins would be necessary. Thus, for each temperature corner we consider three reference voltage levels for the SV configurations (1.0V, 0.98V, 0.96V) that remain unchanged throughout execution.

Figure 5 shows for each temperature corner the total system energy consumption of each configuration, normalized to the baseline SV configuration at reference voltage 1.0V. For each application we show two groups of three bars. The three leftmost bars correspond to the SV technique, for the three reference voltage levels. The three rightmost bars correspond to our TM technique, starting at the three different reference voltages.

Our technique achieves significant energy savings compared to conservative execution at a steady reference voltage, for each temperature corner. Intuitively, we observe that at lower temperatures the energy improvement is significantly better compared to higher temperature corners; at lower temperatures the COP moves toward lower voltage levels, leading to larger energy savings. For example, when using a reference voltage of 1.0V and operating at $-40°C$, on average our technique can save 43% of the energy consumed by the conservative SV technique. Even when our reference voltage is lower, our TM configurations still achieve better energy savings (e.g., at $-40°C$, on average TM-0.98V is 41% more energy efficient than SV-0.98V and TM-0.96V is 38% more efficient than SV-0.96V). At ambient temperatures, energy savings diminish, but are still quite substantial (i.e., 30%, 25%, and 22% on average relative to the 3 different reference voltages). Even at $125°C$ energy savings can still be realized (i.e., 17%, 12%, and 6% relative to the 3 respective reference voltages). Overall, our results show a robust, versatile, and cost-effective technique to saving energy while guaranteeing safe execution.

5. RELATED WORK

Many circuit-level error detection and correction techniques continuously monitor path delay variations [7, 4]. When an error is detected, a recovery technique is enabled that prevents the erroneous instruction from corrupting the architectural state. Examples of recovery techniques include instruction replay at half clock frequency and multiple-issue instruction replay at the same frequency [4]. While ensuring correct system behavior, these techniques impose substantial error recovery costs for many-core chips operating at near-threshold voltage [9] to save power.

Software techniques are often more effective at providing energy-efficient robustness to errors, by exposing variability

13

at lower levels of the software stack. Early approaches focus on course-grained tasks [12] [6], lack generality (as they call for custom programming methodologies) or are only suitable for a specific class of approximate computing programs, in addition to imposing high recovery cycle overhead. A more recent approach based on OpenMP extensions [19] has shown good potential for reducing the recovery cost incurred by HW-based error-correction techniques. Our approach has some key differences. First, it can deal both with sporadic timing errors (like [19]) and with systematic, COP-like error models. To the best of our knowledge our approach is the first to combine SW and HW techniques for dealing with COP. Second, [19] requires error detection and correction (multiple-issue instruction replay) in the HW, as the SW technique alone cannot guarantee complete reliability.

Other works utilized transactional memory for error recovery. The authors of [20] proposed transaction encoding, a software implementation that combines encoded processing for error detection and TM for error recovery. While this design uses TM for checkpointing and rollback as we do, it offers a pure software solution, uses encoded processing for error detection, and does not address energy-efficiency. FaulTM-multi[22], is an HTM-based fault detection and recovery scheme for multi-threaded applications, with relatively low performance overhead and good error coverage. However, it does not target reducing energy consumption, which is central to our implementation. The authors of [21] studied how combining different error detection mechanisms and TM could potentially improve energy efficiency, but they did not provide an actual implementation. To the best of our knowledge, our work is the first to provide a full-fledged HTM implementation for error resilient execution that specifically targets energy savings.

There are various ways to implement eager data versioning. In [14], the authors use per-thread software transaction logs with a stack-based structure, stored in cacheable virtual memory, to hold the original value/address pairs. Since our target architecture has a distributed shared memory space rather than private L1 caches, these logs would result in excessive cross-bank data exchanges, creating big communication delays. Alternatively, the authors of [16] chose to create a mirroring address to hold original data for each address in the memory space. While simple, this design is not space efficient since memory space must be doubled in order to hold the mirrors of all the addresses. Our distributed per-address logging scheme is considerably more space-efficient (only 3% of the TCDM space is reserved for logs).

6. CONCLUSIONS AND FUTURE WORK

In this work, we presented a novel HW/SW scheme adopted from hardware transactional memory that dynamically adjusts the operating voltage to an evolving COP in order to operate at highly reduced margins. Our lightweight scheme is integrated into the OpenMP model, making it easy to program and easy to adjust transaction granularity. Experimental results demonstrate that our technique is particularly effective at saving energy while also offering safe execution guarantees. Based on our findings we draw the conclusion that playing with fire (ie. dangerously close to the COP) instead of using conservative guardbands, pays off, when our lightweight HTM mechanism is used. To the best of our knowledge, this is the first full-fledged implementation of HTM for error resilient execution that targets

reducing energy consumption. Future work will consider a broader range of voltage adjustment strategies due to COP variations.

7. ACKNOWLEDGMENTS

This work was supported in part by NSF grants CNS-1319095, CNS-1319495 and CNS-1301924. The authors would also like to thank Davide Rossi for his help with the error modeling.

8. REFERENCES

[1] W. Baek, et al., The OpenTM transactional application programming interface. *PACT*, p. 376–387, 2007.

[2] S. Borkar, et al., Parameter variations and impact on circuits and microarchitecture. *DAC*, p. 338–342, June 2003.

[3] D. Bortolotti, et al., VirtualSoC: A full-system simulation environment for massively parallel heterogeneous system-on-chip. *IPDPS*, p. 2182–2187, 2013.

[4] K. Bowman, et al., A 45nm resilient microprocessor core for dynamic variation tolerance. *JSSC*, 46(1):194–208, Jan 2011.

[5] D. Melpignano, et al. Platform 2012, a many-core computing accelerator for embedded SoCs: Performance evaluation of visual analytics applications. *DAC*, p. 1137–1142, 2012.

[6] S. Dighe, et al., Within-die variation-aware dynamic-voltage-frequency-scaling with optimal core allocation and thread hopping for the 80-core teraflops processor. *JSSC*, 46(1):184–193, Jan 2011.

[7] D. Ernst, et al., Razor: A low-power pipeline based on circuit-level timing speculation. *MICRO*, p. 7–, 2003.

[8] C. Ferri, et al., SoC-TM: Integrated HW/SW support for transactional memory programming on embedded mpsocs. *CODES*, p. 39–48, Taiwan, Oct 2011.

[9] M. Kakoee, et al., Variation-tolerant architecture for ultra low power shared-l1 processor clusters. *TCAS II*, 59(12):927–931, Dec 2012.

[10] Kalray. MPPA 256 - Programmable Manycore Processor. www.kalray.eu/products/mppa-manycore/mppa-256/.

[11] V. B. Kleeberger, et al., Workload- and instruction-aware timing analysis: The missing link between technology and system-level resilience. *DAC*, p. 49:1–49:6, 2014.

[12] L. Leem, et al., ERSA: Error resilient system architecture for probabilistic applications. *DATE*, p. 1560–1565, 2010.

[13] P. Meinerzhagen, et al., Benchmarking of Standard-Cell Based Memories in the Sub-Domain in 65-nm CMOS Technology. *JETCAS*, 2011.

[14] K. E. Moore, et al., LogTM: Log-based transactional memory. *HPCA*, p. 254–265, 2006.

[15] S. Narayanan, et al., Testing the critical operating point (COP) hypothesis using FPGA emulation of timing errors in over-scaled soft-processors. *SELSE*, 2009.

[16] D. Papagiannopoulou, et al., Speculative synchronization for coherence-free embedded NUMA architectures. *SAMOS*, p. 99–106, July 2014.

[17] J. Patel. CMOS process variations: A critical operation point hypothesis. web.stanford.edu/class/ee380/Abstracts/080402-jhpatel.pdf, 2008.

[18] Plurality Ltd. The hypercore architecture, white paper. Technical Report version 1.7, April 2010.

[19] A. Rahimi, et al., Improving resilience to timing errors by exposing variability effects to software in tightly-coupled processor clusters. *JETCAS*, 4(2):216–229, 2014.

[20] J.-T. Wamhoff, et al., Transactional encoding for tolerating transient hardware errors. *SSS*, volume 8255 of *LNCS*, p. 1–16. Springer Intl. Pub., 2013.

[21] G. Yalcin, et al., Combining error detection and transactional memory for energy-efficient computing below safe operation margins. *PDP 2014*, p. 248–255, Feb 2014.

[22] G. Yalcin, et al., Fault tolerance for multi-threaded applications by leveraging hardware transactional memory. *Computing Frontiers*, p. 4:1–4:9, 2013.

DRAM based Intrinsic Physical Unclonable Functions for System Level Security

Fatemeh Tehranipoor, Nima Karimian, Kan Xiao, and John Chandy
Dept. of Electrical Engineering and Computer Engineering
University of Connecticut
Storrs, CT, USA
{f.tehrani, nima, kanxiao, chandy}@engr.uconn.edu

ABSTRACT

Physical Unclonable Functions (PUF) are the result of random uncontrollable variables in the manufacturing process. A PUF can be used as a source of random but reliable data for applications such as generating chip identification and encryption keys. Among various types of PUFs, an intrinsic PUF is the result of a preexisting manufacturing process, does not require any additional circuitry, and is cost effective. In this paper, we introduce an intrinsic PUF based on dynamic random access memories (DRAM). DRAM PUFs can be used in low cost identification applications and also have several advantages over other PUFs such as large input patterns. The DRAM PUF relies on the fact that the capacitor in the DRAM initializes to random values at startup. We demonstrate real DRAM PUFs and describe an experimental setup to test different operating conditions on three DRAMs to achieve the highest reliable results. Finally, we select the most stable bits to use as chip ID using our enrollment algorithm.

Categories and Subject Descriptors

B.3.1 [**Semiconductor Memories**]: Dynamic Memories;
K.6.5 [**Security and Protection**]: Authentication;
B.7.3 [**Reliability and Testing**]

General Terms

Hardware, Security, Identification

Keywords

Physically Unclonable Function, Dynamic Random Access Memory, System Level Security, Operating Conditions

1. INTRODUCTION

In recent years, due to the trend in globalization, system integrators have had to deal with integrated circuit (IC)/intellectual property (IP) counterfeiting more than ever and this surge in counterfeit hardware has driven the need for more secure chip authentication. Among the sources of counterfeit chips are discarded chips

GLSVLSI'15, May 20–22, 2015, Pittsburgh, PA, USA.
Copyright is held by the owner/author(s). Publication rights licensed to ACM.
ACM 978-1-4503-3474-7/15/05 ...$15.00.
http://http://dx.doi.org/10.1145/2742060.2742069.

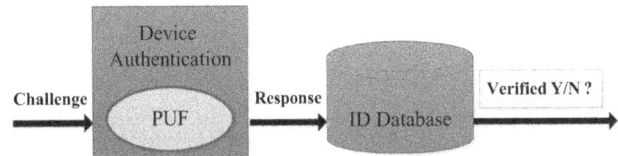

Figure 1: System Level Physical Unclonable Function

reintroduced into the supply chain and fabrication of cheap copies that pass as authentic without significant scrutiny. Random process variability can be used to generate intrinsic identifiers through the use of Physically Unclonable Functions (PUFs). A PUF is a multiple-input multiple-output function that has hard-to-predict dependency between the outputs and the inputs. The PUF inputs and outputs map a set of challenges to a set of responses which are called Challenge-Response Pairs (CRPs). Because the PUF is derived from random process variation, it is very difficult, if not impossible, to predict the responses from a particular challenge or construct a function to do so in hardware or in software. In terms of security, PUFs show better resilience against tampering compared to other solutions. Even though PUFs are manufactured with high precision, any external physical influence will change the PUF behavior and thus, cause the intrinsic ID to be changed. A PUF is a promising solution to many security issues due its ability to generate an IC unique identifier that can resist cloning attempts as well as physical tampering. As an example, in [6] and [12], PUFs were used for device authentication and unique ID generation.

Figure 1 shows the flow for using a PUF for device authentication. A system integrator who wants to authenticate a particular IC will issue a given challenge to the PUF embedded within the device. The PUF's response can then be verified with a trusted database.

1.1 System level Security

Most electronic systems are not designed with security in mind, and as a result, there are always threats from attackers to alter these systems and leak secret information from them. Even if the systems are securely designed, there is no assurance that the delivered system is authentic. System level security mechanisms can use a subsystem on the board to prevent any altering or modification in system functionality and stop or reset the system if any anomalous behavior has been detected. While it is difficult to authenticate the trustworthiness of any particular IC on a system board, a unique identifier, such as a PUF embedded in an IC can be used to give the IC a unique identity. However, with Commercial Off-The-Shelf (COTS) parts, a PUF or chip ID may not be available, so mechanisms for intrinsic PUF identification are needed. In this paper, we present an intrinsic DRAM PUF that can be used to authenticate electronic systems on which DRAMs are present.

1.2 Prior Related Works

The topic of Physical Unclonable Functions has gained considerable attention in the past few years, yielding several proposed approaches for these functions. PUFs designed during the past decade have mostly fallen into two broad categories that can be described as "strong PUFs" and "weak PUFs". Strong PUFs are typically used for authentication, while weak PUFs are used for key storage. The first class of PUFs leveraging manufacturing variability are weak PUFs. These PUFs can be thought of as PUFs that directly digitize some "fingerprint" of the circuit. This direct measurement results in a digital signature that can be used for cryptographic purposes. The second class of PUFs which are strong PUFs differ from weak PUFs in that a strong PUF can support a large number of CRPs. As a result, a strong PUF can be authenticated directly without using any cryptographic hardware. The fundamental difference between weak and strong PUFs is the number of unique challenges that the PUF can process [4]. Furthermore, there are three types of PUF architectures - namely, cover-based PUF, memory-based PUF, and delay-based PUF. Cover-based PUF can be further divided into the categories of optical PUF and electric PUF. DRAM PUF is an example of a memory-based PUF which has the advantage of large input pattern and large input challenges [13]. PUFs have attracted a great deal of attention and as a result various kinds of PUFs has been proposed for key generation/ID, such as SRAM PUF [14, 5], RO-PUF [7], Arbiter PUF, Clock PUF, etc. Many methods have already been proposed for identification and authentication of ICs such as in [12, 10].

1.3 Contributions and Paper Organization

In this paper, we explore the possibility of intrinsic PUFs within COTS DRAM ICs. The motivation to examine these devices is that DRAMs have some unique advantages.

(i) Large input pattern: Because of the large number of available bits in a typical DRAM, one generate a large set of input challenges and correspondingly large output responses. This characteristic of DRAM PUF is very valuable, because the large set of challenge/response pairs makes it cost prohibitive to replicate or clone.

(ii) Cost-effective: Since many computer systems have some form of DRAM on board, DRAMs can be used as an effective system-level PUF. It is also much cheaper than SRAM. Thus DRAM PUFs could be a source of random but reliable data for generating board identifications (chip ID).

However, PUFs intrinsic to DRAM ICs have not been explored extensively. Our primary contribution is the identification of a DRAM PUF based on start up values. We examine the effect of various operating conditions such as temperature variation, voltage variation, and aging which may influence the behavior of the DRAM PUF. Finally, we propose a selection mechanism to isolate highly stable bits within the large set of available bits in a DRAM.

The rest of the paper is organized as follows: Section 2 describes our DRAM PUF approach; Section 3 presents the experimental data and analysis - particularly measured results that demonstrate the effectiveness of DRAM PUF in terms of uniqueness, reliability and randomness compared to the other kinds of PUFs. Finally, concluding remarks and future works are given in Section 6.

2. DRAM PUF APPROACH

DRAM memory cells are comprised of a paired transistor and capacitor. While ideally every DRAM cell should be identical, man-

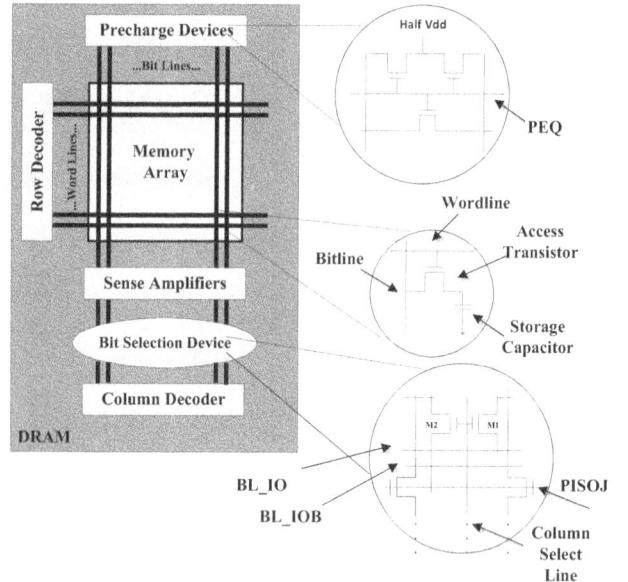

Figure 2: Memory Structure of a One-Transistor DRAM Array

ufacturing imperfections cause slight physical variations in each cell. These physical variation characteristics can be used to develop PUFs. The only previous work on DRAM PUF has been based on altering or disabling the refresh cycle [6]. Modern DRAM chips have a built-in self-refresh module, as they not only require a power supply to retain data, but must also be periodically refreshed to prevent their data contents from fading away from the capacitors in their integrated circuits. The essential approach with refresh-based DRAM PUFs is to initialize all cells to '1' and then after some time, with refresh turned off, some of the cells will leak to '0'. The randomness of which cells leak to '0' provide the opportunity for a PUF. The difficulty with using these refresh or retention based methods for a PUF, is that it may take several minutes to hours for sufficient cells to flip to '0'. Another potential approach is to use the remanence property of DRAMs. Contrary to popular belief, DRAMs can hold their values for surprisingly long intervals without power. DRAM cells retain their contents for a few seconds to minutes at room temperature. In fact, it has been demonstrated that sensitive information can be extracted from volatile memories due to data remanence effects [2, 3]. In this PUF approach, instead of turning refresh off, one could turn the power off to the DRAM, thus reducing the challenge time from hours to minutes.

In our observation of DRAM refresh and remanence properties, however, we noticed that certain DRAMs actually exhibit behavior similar to SRAMs, i.e. they have seemingly random startup values. In other words, the cells do not initialize to '0' as would be expected. Thus, as with SRAMs, these startup values provide a potential for creating a PUF. The reason for this random startup behavior can be explained by the interaction of precharge, row decoder, and column select lines when the device is powered up. Figure 2 shows the structure of a typical DRAM array. Bits are stored either by charging the storage capacitor to V_{DD} or discharging it to ground. In order to reduce the electric field stress on the capacitor, one of the plates of the capacitor is usually biased to $\frac{V_{DD}}{2}$. PEQ is the signal to precharge the bitlines. In normal operation, before reading the cell, the bitline is precharged to $\frac{V_{DD}}{2}$, and when the wordline is activated, the bitline voltage will change slightly depending on the

Figure 3: Test setup with Xilinx Spartan 6 FPGA (left) and off-the-shelf DRAM (right)

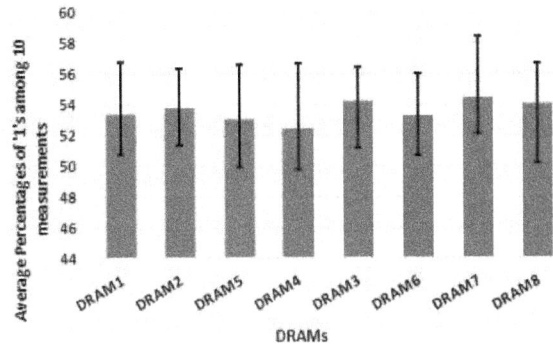

Figure 4: Uniformity of DRAMs across 10 measurements for each of 8 DRAMs (average percentages of 1s values)

capacitance of the storage capacitor. This slight change is detected by the sense amplifier as a '1' or '0'. In other words, the level of the bitlines eventually reaches V_{DD} or ground. At startup, however, the storage capacitor has neither been charged to V_{DD} nor discharged to ground. Thus the startup voltage of each capacitor is equal to the bias voltage, $\frac{V_{DD}}{2}$, which is equal to the bitline precharge voltage. The sense amplifier is then equally likely to read a '1' or '0'. However, because of manufacturing variations, the storage capacitance of each bit will have slight differences, which leads to biasing of each bit to either a '1' or a '0'. This behavior is what allows the startup values of the DRAM to function as a PUF.

3. DRAM PUF CHARACTERIZATION

3.1 Experimental Platform

This section describes the experimental setup used for the data collection. We use eight different 1 MBit Hitachi HM51100AL CMOS DRAMs in a DIP package. The DRAM was mounted on and wired to a prototyping board that includes a high-speed connector to connect with a Xilinx Spartan-6 FPGA on a Digilent Atlys board. The FPGA was programmed to control the test sequence supplied to the DRAM chip and transmit the outputs of the DRAM to a computer using an on-board USB-UART module. The complete experimental set up is shown in Figure 3.

3.2 Uniformity of the Memory

We start with an examination of the uniformity of a DRAM-based PUF. Ideally, 50% of the bits should be '1' and 50% should be '0'. For each of the 8 DRAMs used for startup value experiments, we took 10 measurements of the uniformity - i.e. the percentage of bits that were '1' or '0' at startup. As shown in Figure 4, without any write operation to the DRAM cells, they have start up values and some of the cells values are one. While not perfectly uniform, the uniformity is close enough to ideal that with proper bit selection it can be used as a PUF. This error bar shows the average, minimum and maximum percentage of '1' values of each DRAM (DRAM1 to DRAM8) across different trials. As an example for DRAM1, the average, minimum and maximum percentages of 1's among all 10 measurements are 53.35%, 50.73% and 56.78%, respectively. As can be seen, there is a slight bias to '1' in all the DRAMs. Also, we looked at the distribution of 1's within some of the DRAMs (DRAM1, DRAM2 and DRAM3) to make sure that they are not accumulated in some parts and saw that they are uniformly distributed across all the DRAM cells.

3.3 PUF Stability Evaluation against Environmental and Operating Conditions

In this section, we examine the stability of the DRAM PUF bits under various environmental operating conditions. A stable bit is a bit which does not change in any trial. There are various parameters that can affect PUF stability such as process variation, PUF activity, temperature, supply voltage, etc. Others have proposed PUFs that take into account both process and environmental variations such as crosstalk which magnifies chip-to-chip signature randomness and uniqueness [13]. One of the unique aspects of our work is the stability evaluation against different operating conditions for more than one physical PUF. We did all the experiments for three of the DRAMs which we call them DRAM1, DRAM2 and DRAM3.

We start with baseline measurements (*Nominal Condition (NC)*) with the temperature set to 25 °C and the voltage to 5 V. For each DRAM, we took 10 measurements whereby we read all 1,048,576 (2^{20}) startup bits. The results (Table 1) show that for DRAM1, 37.9% of the startup values were read as '0' across all 10 measurements and likewise 43.5% were read as '1' across all 10 measurements. The remaining 18.6% of bits read as both '0' and '1', and as such are marked as unstable. The results show that the majority of bits are stable, meaning that one can have high confidence that the bits will be the same at reconstruction in normal operating conditions as they were at enrollment. In subsequent sections we will examine the effect of varying operating conditions on stability.

Table 1: DRAMs Stability across all Nominal Conditions

DRAM1		DRAM2		DRAM3	
Bit Value		Bit Value		Bit Value	
0	1	0	1	0	1
37.9 %	43.5 %	27.9 %	37.6 %	26.6 %	37.7 %

3.3.1 Impact of Temperature Variation on Stability

Temperature plays a large role in memory decay by affecting power leakage at the transistor level. There is a clear correlation between temperature and DRAM remanence. Moreover, it has been demonstrated that temperature variations have a much greater impact on bit stability than supply voltage variations for SRAM PUF [14]. In fact, we do not expect similar effects on our startup-value based DRAM PUF. We performed the experiments by sweeping the temperature from 0 °C to 80 °C using a Temptronic TP04100A ThermoStream Thermal Inducting System. The Thermostream system delivers controlled temperature with speed and precision to devices and modules for thermal cycling and testing.

Our measurements show that the temperature can have an impact on bit stability. In Table 2, we show the bit stability under both high temperature (80 °C) and low temperature (0 °C) conditions. NC-HT and NC-LT compare the stability of the DRAMs data under high temperature (HT) and low temperature (LT) condition to the nominal condition (NC) stability, respectively. Twelve measurements at low temperature and high temperature are taken (6 from each voltage) to illustrate the changes of start up values under temperature variations. Note that the number of measurements for nominal condition is 10. From Table 2, for DRAM1, our data indicates that 78.8% (37.2%+41.6%) of cells remain stable and are unaffected by the high temperature. At low temperature for DRAM1, however, only 49.9% (23.8%+26.1%) of cells remain stable, indicating that low temperature has more of an effect on bit stability. We also can see that for DRAM2 and DRAM3 the effect of low temperature on the stability of bits is much more than the high temperature effect.

Table 2: DRAMs Stability under Different Operating Conditions

	DRAM1		DRAM2		DRAM3	
	Bit Value		Bit Value		Bit Value	
	0	1	0	1	0	1
DRAMs Stability under Different Temperature Conditions						
NC-HT	37.2%	41.6%	27.9%	36.5%	21.4%	28.4%
NC-LT	23.8%	26.1%	23.7%	30.7%	17.5%	26.8%
DRAMs Stability under Different Voltage Conditions						
NC-HV	25.2%	30.2%	22.8%	31.5%	10.4%	20.1%
NC-LV	16.7%	26.6%	8.0%	18.7%	5.8%	18.0%
DRAMs Stability under Aging						
NC-AA	33.2%	37.8%	27.4%	37.6%	23.9%	31.2%

3.3.2 Impact of Voltage Variation on Stability

Similarly to the temperature variation, here, we observe the effect of voltage variation on PUF stability. We vary the nominal supply by 10% up and 10% down, and observe the PUF's stability. Twelve measurements of startup values are taken at low voltage (4.5v) and high voltage (5.5v) (6 from each voltage).

In Table 2, we show the bit stability under both high and low voltage conditions for different DRAMs. Again, NC-HV and NC-LV compare the stability of the DRAMs data under high temperature (HV) and low temperature (LV) condition to the nominal condition (NC) stability, respectively. At high voltage, for DRAM1, our data indicates that 55.4% of cells are stable, and at low voltage, 43.3% of cells are stable. We see that voltage variations can have a much greater impact on the bit stability than temperature variation. As with DRAM1, voltage variation has an effect on DRAM2 and DRAM3 also. Table 2 indicates that low voltage has more effect on bit stability than high voltage and this is true for all three DRAMs.

3.3.3 Impact of Aging on PUF Stability

Finally, we explore the potential impact of aging on the stability of the DRAM PUF. VLSI phenomena such as negative bias temperature instability (NBTI), hot carrier injection (HCI) and electromigration and temperature-dependent dielectric breakdown (TDDB) are some of the causes of aging. NBTI is enhanced by high temperature and high supply voltage. High switching rate of a circuit as well as excess supply voltage enhance HCI effect. A high operating voltage as well as higher temperatures can accelerate TDDB. In [9, 8, 1], they evaluated the impact of the aging on different kinds of PUFs such as RO and FPGA-based PUFs.

In this section, we look at the stability of cells as the DRAM1, DRAM2 and DRAM3 age. To accelerate the aging, we performed burn-in of the DRAM using the Thermostream burn-in system.

We did 8 hours of high-temperature aging at 80 °C on DRAM1, DRAM2 and DRAM3 to approximate the effects of 6 months of aging. The impact of this aging on DRAM PUF stability is shown in Table 2. NC-AA compares the stability of the aged DRAMs data to the nominal condition stability. For the three DRAMs we tested we find that between 55-71% of cells remain stable after aging.

3.3.4 Multi-device Evaluation

In this section, we consider the effect of different operating conditions on various devices. We selected the three same DIP DRAMs, DRAM1, DRAM2 and DRAM3, to be tested under different conditions. These tests were applied for the entire 1 MBit memory of each DRAM. For each condition, we did 6-10 tests, collected data and the percentage of the stability among those data (for example for the high temperature condition, we had 6-10 different measurements). A bit is marked stable if it has the same result for all measurements. As shown in Figure 5a, you can see the percentages of ones plus zeros under different operating conditions between DRAM1 (blue), DRAM2 (orange) and DRAM3 (gray).

In the nominal condition, DRAMs have 60% to 80% stable bits. However, at high temperature the stability is actually higher at over 90% for three DRAMs). In other words, somewhat non-intuitively, high temperature actually helps stability of the DRAM bits at startup. For other conditions, low temperature, high voltage, and aging, both DRAMs again exhibit similar stability. However, some conditions manifests different behavior. This is an example of the difference in manufacturing processes that allows chips to be functionally identical but still exhibits differences at the margins.

In Figure 5b, we compare each of the conditions with the nominal condition. In other words, we see how many bits remain the same across multiple measurements at the nominal condition as well as the extreme condition under test. As we can see, between 20% and 80% of the bits remain stable at any condition for DRAM1, DRAM2 and DRAM3. However, the behaviors of all DRAMs under low voltage condition is different from other conditions.

In the context of a PUF, if we were to use all of the nominal condition bits for enrollment, we see that reconstruction of the bits under different conditions could result in half of the bits or more being flipped. This would result in the need for high levels of error correction. Thus, it is important that we enroll bits intelligently, such that we are more likely to select bits that won't flip under different conditions. We discuss our selection algorithm below.

4. ENROLLMENT ALGORITHM FOR GENERATING PUF ID

A key part of using a PUF to generate a unique ID or key is the enrollment process - i.e. the selection of bits to use for the ID. For example, in our 1 MBit DRAMs, one could randomly select 128 bits to use as a key. However, as the data in Figure 5 shows, many of those bits would not be stable under different conditions. Thus, during reconstruction, the bits may be different.

4.1 Bit Selection Procedure Based on Neighbors Stability Status

In this section, we describe an algorithm to select a set of bits for an ID/key that has a high likelihood of being stable. The key insight of the algorithm is that we use spatial information within the DRAMs to infer the stability of a bit cell. The approach is similar to the selection algorithm used by Xiao et al. for SRAM PUF bit selection [14] except that in our approach we take advantage of the fact that we have a better idea of the layout of cells in the DRAMs.

(a)

(b)

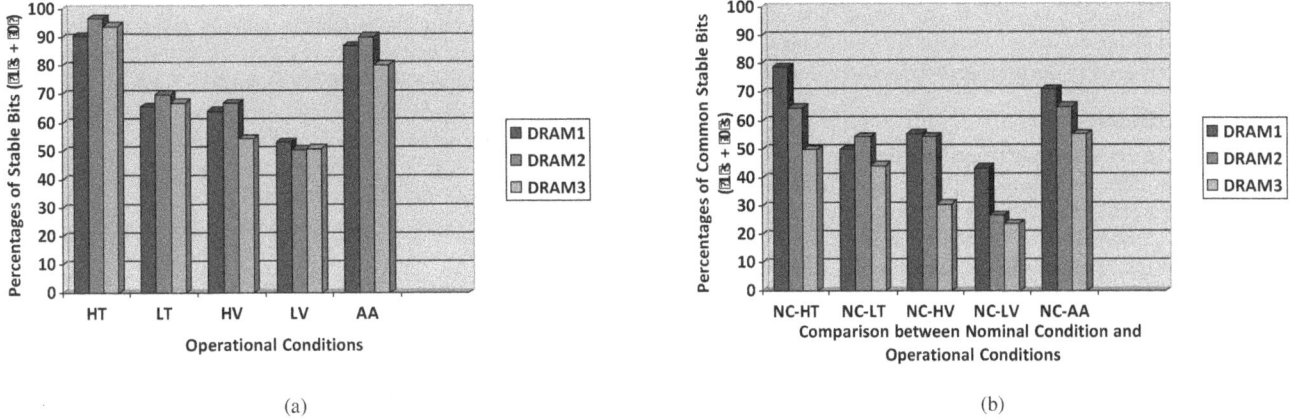

Figure 5: (a) Percentages of stable bits (ones and zeros) for each condition across multiple measurements for DRAM1, DRAM2 and DRAM3. (b) Percentages of the common stable bits (ones and zeros) compared to the Nominal Condition (NC) for DRAM1, DRAM2 and DRAM3.

In other words, we have a grid for memory rows and columns that can give us a very good picture of the cell distribution in the memory array. Thus, spatial correlations (neighborhood stable cells) can be made in both x and y directions.

The basic algorithm is shown in Algorithm 1. The DRAM is organized as an array of cells - in our case for a 1 MBit DRAM the array is 1024 rows by 1024 columns. We count the number of stable bits (ones and zeros) in each row and then select rows that have more stable bits than specific thresholds (T1 and T2). Thresholds have been chosen based on experimentation in order to select 2048 bits (16 128-bits keys). In the ideal case, half will be zeros and half ones, among 1 MBit data in the next level of the algorithm. T1 and T2 are the thresholds for choosing rows that have more stable 1s and 0s, respectively. Among selected rows, those bits that have stable neighbors also identified as potential highly stable bits suitable for enrollment as the PUF ID/key. As mentioned in [14], a stable cell which is surrounded by more stable cells is more likely to remain stable because its neighboring cells have experienced similar operating conditions such as aging effects. As an example, assume that row number i is selected as the one that has a large number of stable bits. If row number $i-1$ and $i+1$ also were selected, row i is one of the best that contains the most stable bits. After that, we can look at the neighbors of each stable bits in that row to choose the ones that have more stable neighbors around it and finally is the best one to be used as ID bits.

As mentioned before, we used this selection algorithm to select 16 128-bit keys from the available bits and compared it to a naive baseline algorithm where 16 keys are selected at random from the 1 MBit set. In both cases, the enrollment is done based on either one or two distinct measurements. In other words, $n = 1$ and $n = 2$ for the algorithm in Algorithm 1. The baseline case only uses 1 or 2 nominal case measurements, whereas our selection algorithm uses 5-10 measurements - 1 or 2 each for NC, LV, HV, LT, and HT. Aging is not used for enrollment because of the time involved and since it also shortens the lifetime of the device.

We evaluate the effectiveness of the selection algorithm by comparing the effect on reconstruction of the 16 keys. Ideally, on reconstruction we should read back the same bits. Table 3 shows the number of bits that flipped across the three different reconstruct attempts and across all conditions including aging for DRAM1, DRAM2 and DRAM3. As can be seen, the use of our selection algorithm reduces the number of bit flips for DRAM1 from nearly 70% in average for the baseline to below 8% in average which is sufficient for using the PUF for chip identification. In fact, our results show that we can also use this PUF for key generation with minimal ECC check bits. Furthermore, using more measurements during enrollment can decrease the number of bit flips.

Table 3: Percentage of Bit Flips after Enrollment Algorithm

	DRAM1		DRAM2		DRAM3	
	n=1	n=2	n=1	n=2	n=1	n=2
Baseline	68.0%	72.8%	75.0%	77.2%	69.5%	71.4%
Our Algorithm	13.2%	2.4%	12.2%	6.3%	9.3%	8.6%

5. EXPERIMENTAL RESULTS VALIDATION

5.1 Reliability

In this section, the reliability of the DRAM cells will be discussed. Generally, reliability of a PUF means that a given PUF can regenerate the same bits consistently. In our work, we chose stable bits based on random selection and also the proposed highly stable bit selection algorithm as discussed in the previous section. Various measurements from different operating conditions (HT, LT, etc) were used for each DRAM to apply the bit selection algorithm on

---

Algorithm 1: Highly Stable Bit selection Algorithm

1: Apply n measurements for each operating conditions
2: Find bits that are stable across all n measurements of all conditions (NC, HT, LT, HV, LV) for the DRAM being enrolled. Note that we do not perform aging during enrollment because it is not practical to age the chip because of the time involved.
3: Count number of stable bits (ones and zeros separately) in each DRAM row
4: Select rows R that have more stable bits than selected thresholds ($T1$ for 1s and $T2$ for 0s) which have been selected based experimentation in order to select 2048 bits.
5: For each row $r \in R$, enroll bits (r, j) that have a neighborhood of stable bits where r is the row number and j is the column number. The neighborhood of stable bits is defined such that row $r-1 \in R$ and $r+1 \in R$ and bits $(r, j-1)$ and $(r, j+1)$ are also stable.

---

them. Then, based on the number of distinct measurements (n=1 or n=2), we can determine which approach produced fewer bit flips during the reconstruction phase. Our results show clearly that there is a relationship between better stability with bit selection and a lower number of distinct measurements (*n*), as shown in Table 3.

5.2 Uniqueness

In this section, we want to evaluate the uniqueness of the DRAM PUF. Therefore we calculated the average Hamming distance between all pairs of IDs that were extracted from the different PUFs (DRAM1, DRAM2 and DRAM3) based on our bit selection algorithm. The results from the selection algorithm (SA) approach compared to the random (R) approach show that our approach produces IDs that have Hamming Distances closer to the ideal 50%.

Table 4: Inter and Intra-die Hamming Distance calculations

	DRAM1		DRAM2		DRAM3	
	R	SA	R	SA	R	SA
DRAM1	24.2%	52.3%	58.4%	48.1%	41.4%	50.7%
DRAM2	58.4%	48.1%	40.6%	51.6%	45.6%	**50.0%**
DRAM3	41.4%	50.7%	45.6%	**50.0%**	22.7%	46.5%

5.3 Randomness

In PUF design, the randomness of the data is very important as it can prevent the prediction of the cell values or the ID bits. In other words, perfectly random data means that the PUF cells are generated independently of each other, and the value of the next cell cannot be predicted, regardless of how many cells have already been produced. The NIST Test Suite (NTS) is a statistical package consisting of different types of tests to test the randomness of binary sequences. Each statistical test is used to calculate a p-value that shows the randomness of the given sequences based on that test. If a p-value for a test is determined to be equal to 1, then the sequence appears to have perfect randomness. A p-value >= 0.01 would means that sequence would be considered to be random with a confidence of 99% [11]. In our work, the randomness of the DRAMs bits was tested using the NIST test suite. The p-values of the selective tests such as Frequency, Block frequency and Cumulative sums are (0.52, 0.61 and 0.7 for DRAM1), (0.41, 0.53 and 0.65 for DRAM2) and (0.66, 0.81 and 0.68 for DRAM3), respectively. Thus, our DRAM PUF data can also considered to be random with 99% confidence.

6. CONCLUSIONS AND FUTURE WORK

In this paper, we proposed a memory based PUF that is based on DRAM startup values. We also describe an algorithm to find the most stable bits for enrollment. There is significant correlation between PUF instabilities that are caused due to voltage, which can be leveraged by PUF designers in designing stable PUFs. In fact, our analysis showed that temperature variation has a major impact on DRAM PUF stability. Despite the many advantages of DRAM PUF, there are still many challenges. As future work, we consider investigating further enhancements to the algorithm to improve the enrollment process. We also intend to observe the suitability of DRAM remanence for use as a PUF.

Acknowledgment

This work was supported in part by a grant from Comcast Corp. and Honeywell Corp. Any opinions, findings and conclusions or recommendations expressed in this material are those of the authors and do not necessarily reflect those of Comcast or Honeywell.

7. REFERENCES

[1] GARG, A., AND KIM, T. Design of sram puf with improved uniformity and reliability utilizing device aging effect. In *Circuits and Systems (ISCAS), 2014 IEEE International Symposium on* (June 2014), pp. 1941–1944.

[2] GRUHN, M., AND MULLER, T. On the practicability of cold boot attacks. In *Availability, Reliability and Security (ARES), 2013 Eighth International Conference on* (Sept 2013), pp. 390–397.

[3] GUTMANN, P. Data remanence in semiconductor devices. In *Proceedings of the 10th Conference on USENIX Security Symposium - Volume 10* (Berkeley, CA, USA, 2001), SSYM'01, USENIX Association.

[4] HERDER, C., YU, M.-D., KOUSHANFAR, F., AND DEVADAS, S. Physical unclonable functions and applications: A tutorial. *Proceedings of the IEEE 102*, 8 (Aug 2014), 1126–1141.

[5] HOLCOMB, D., BURLESON, W., AND FU, K. Power-up sram state as an identifying fingerprint and source of true random numbers. *Computers, IEEE Transactions on 58*, 9 (Sept 2009), 1198–1210.

[6] KELLER, C., GURKAYNAK, F., KAESLIN, H., AND FELBER, N. Dynamic memory-based physically unclonable function for the generation of unique identifiers and true random numbers. In *Circuits and Systems (ISCAS), 2014 IEEE International Symposium on* (June 2014), pp. 2740–2743.

[7] MAITI, A., CASARONA, J., MCHALE, L., AND SCHAUMONT, P. A large scale characterization of ro-puf. In *Hardware-Oriented Security and Trust (HOST), 2010 IEEE International Symposium on* (June 2010), pp. 94–99.

[8] MAITI, A., MCDOUGALL, L., AND SCHAUMONT, P. The impact of aging on an fpga-based physical unclonable function. In *Field Programmable Logic and Applications (FPL), 2011 International Conference on* (Sept 2011), pp. 151–156.

[9] MEGUERDICHIAN, S., AND POTKONJAK, M. Device aging-based physically unclonable functions. In *Design Automation Conference (DAC), 2011 48th ACM/EDAC/IEEE* (June 2011), pp. 288–289.

[10] OZTURK, E., HAMMOURI, G., AND SUNAR, B. Physical unclonable function with tristate buffers. In *Circuits and Systems, 2008. ISCAS 2008. IEEE International Symposium on* (May 2008), pp. 3194–3197.

[11] RUKHIN, A., SOTO, J., NECHVATAL, J., SMID, M., AND BARKER, E. A statistical test suite for random and pseudorandom number generators for cryptographic applications. Tech. rep., DTIC Document, 2001.

[12] SUH, G., AND DEVADAS, S. Physical unclonable functions for device authentication and secret key generation. In *Design Automation Conference, 2007. DAC '07. 44th ACM/IEEE* (June 2007), pp. 9–14.

[13] WANG, X., AND TEHRANIPOOR, M. Novel physical unclonable function with process and environmental variations. In *Design, Automation Test in Europe Conference Exhibition (DATE), 2010* (March 2010), pp. 1065–1070.

[14] XIAO, K., RAHMAN, M., FORTE, D., HUANG, Y., SU, M., AND TEHRANIPOOR, M. Bit selection algorithm suitable for high-volume production of sram-puf. In *Hardware-Oriented Security and Trust (HOST), 2014 IEEE International Symposium on* (May 2014), pp. 101–106.

An Effective TSV Self-Repair Scheme for 3D-Stacked ICs

Songwei Pei [1], Jingdong Zhang [1], Yu Jin [1], Song Jin [2], Jun Liu [3], and Weizhi Xu [4]

[1] College of Information and Technology, Beijing University of Chemical Technology, Beijing 100029, China
[2] Department of Electronic and Communication Engineering,
School of Electrical and Electronic Engineering, North China Electric Power University, Baoding 071003, China
[3] School of Computer and Information, Hefei University of Technology, Hefei 230009, China
[4] Institute of Microelectronics, Tsinghua University, Beijing 100190, China
peisw@mail.buct.edu.cn

ABSTRACT

Various types of defects are prone to be occurred inside the TSV during the manufacturing and bonding steps, thereby severely impacting the yield of 3D-stacked ICs. Moreover, several types of TSV defects are latent and may easily escape detection during the manufacturing test. However, these latent TSVs are prone to degrade during the field operation and may eventually become faulty and then destroy the entire 3D-stacked IC. To tackle the above problems, in this paper, we present an effective TSV self-repair scheme for 3D-stacked ICs. By designing redundant TSVs and a TSV self-repair architecture, the proposed scheme can effectively repair faulty TSVs detected by manufacturing test for improving the yield of 3D-stacked ICs. Moreover, the latent TSVS failed and then detected during the in-field operation can also be self-repaired, thereby elevating the 3D ICs' quality and reliability. Experimental results are presented to validate the proposed method.

Categories and Subject Descriptors

B.7.3 [**Integrated Circuits**]: Reliability and Testing.

General Terms

Performance, Design, Reliability.

Keywords

3D-Stacked IC; TSV Repair; Reliability; Yield;

1. INTRODUCTION

With the rapidly increasing of planar chip complexity, interconnect has emerged as one of the most important performance bottlenecks. The reason is that the delay of long interconnect has become a dominant source in the delay of modern planar chip [1]. Through Silicon Via (TSV) based three-dimensional integrated circuit (3D-stacked IC) technology provides a promising way to overcome this bottleneck, and has attracted great attentions in semiconductor industry [2]. This kind of 3D-stacked IC is implemented by integrating multiple silicon layers through vertical wires called TSV. Hence, the 3D-stacked

IC can provide benefits including low latency, low power, high speed, etc., by replacing the long interconnects with shorter TSVs [1, 3].

It has been reported that a number of companies have developed their TSV-based 3D-stacked IC products to fully exert the advantages of this emerging technology [4, 5]. Although many benefits can be obtained through 3D integration, the TSV-based 3D ICs may suffer from serious manufacturing yield loss. One of the primary reasons is that the yield of TSV is far from satisfactory under the current manufacturing process. In general, various types of defects are prone to occur inside the TSV during the manufacturing and bonding steps, thereby severely impacting the yield of TSV. It is well known that micro-voids may be formed inside the TSVs during the metallization process due to the insufficiently filling of TSVs. After the fabrication of TSVs, the wafer typically needs to be thinned to be less than 100μm [6] to expose the TSV tips for bonding consecutive stacks. This wafer thinning process may lead to the surface roughness, and give rise to the yield loss of later stack bonding. Moreover, the misalignment of bond pad of TSV when bonding consecutive stacks would also decrease the yield of TSV. Actually, in addition to the above mentioned failure cases, TSV may also fail caused by other mechanisms such as process variations, mechanical stress, etc. [7]. It has been reported in [8] that up to twelve different types of TSV defects could be incurred during the 3D integration process, most of which are induced during the manufacturing steps, while the rest is induced during the bonding steps.

Clearly, the failure of a single TSV can cause the entire chip fail even though the other components of the chip are known to be good. Hence, in order to improve the yield and the quality of 3D-stacked ICs, several faulty TSV repair strategies have been proposed and typically use the neighboring TSVs to replace faulty TSVs. In practice, however, the faulty TSVs are typically clustered in a small area during the TSV manufacturing and bonding process. Then if one TSV is faulty, its neighboring TSVs are also probably faulty. Moreover, it is worth noting that several types of the defects occurred in the TSVs are latent and easily escape detection during the manufacturing test [9, 10]. For example, the TSV interfacial cracks are often undetectable during the manufacturing test, but they are prone to degrade during the in-field operation and may eventually become a complete open defect and then destroy the entire chip. Clearly, burn-in for screening latent defects occurred in TSV during manufacturing test could be costly and its effectiveness is also uncertain [10]. Consequently, it is imperative to design an effective TSV repair scheme, by which not only the faulty TSV, including the clustered faulty TSVs, detected during manufacturing test can be repaired for improving the yield of 3D ICs, but also the faulty TSVs failed during the in-field operation can be repaired for elevating the chip's reliability.

1.1 Previous Work

Several related faulty TSV recovery works have been conducted in the literatures to elevate the yield and reliability of 3D-stacked ICs.

Kang et al. [11] presented a TSV recovery scheme for faulty TSVs to elevate the yield of 3D DRAM products. In this scheme, TSVs are bundled into groups, each of which includes 4 signal TSVs and 2 redundant TSVs. The yield of 3D DRAM can be significantly elevated since any 2 faulty TSVs within each group can be tolerated through this scheme. However, up to 50% of additional TSVs need to be designed in this scheme, thus rendering a very high cost.

Hsieh et al. [12] presented a signal shifting scheme for faulty TSV tolerance. The TSV blocks are configured to TSV chains respectively. Each TSV chain includes a redundant TSV. If there is a TSV failed in the TSV chain, it can be repaired using the redundant TSV of the corresponding TSV chain by signal shifting. Cleary, by restricting the redundancy ratio to a limited value, the cost of this faulty TSV recovery scheme could be very low. However, only one faulty TSV can be tolerated in a TSV chain, thus the effectiveness of this scheme will be limited.

Loi et al. [13] presented a faulty TSV tolerance scheme using redundant TSVs for 3-D network-on-chip, in which redundant TSV rows or columns are added to the TSV grids. Suppose that a redundant TSV is added for each column of TSV grid, which means a redundant TSV row is added, then each faulty TSV can be repaired by the redundant TSV of the same column through 2×1 XBARs. In this work, for each unidirectional 3D link, which consists of 32 data signals and 6 flow control signals, if four redundant TSVs are added, the yield can be elevated from 68% to 98%.

Zhao et al. [14] presented a TSV grouping method for faulty TSV recovery. In the method, the grouping ratio, which represents the number of signal TSVs and the redundant TSVs placed in a group, can be calculated based on the probability analysis for successfully repairing faulty TSVs. For each assigned TSV group, it may include multiple redundant TSVs, and hence each TSV in a group can have multiple repair candidates. Therefore, this method can be applied for clustered faulty TSVs repairing.

Jiang et al. [15] proposed a TSV redundancy architecture using dedicated switches to handle clustered TSV faults. Based on this architecture, the corresponding repair algorithm is also presented. In this method, the faulty TSVs can be repaired with redundant ones very flexibly by using the dedicated switches. The faulty TSV can even be repaired by a redundant TSV that placed far apart, thus providing an effective way for faulty TSV recovery, especially for clustered TSV faults. However, all the above methods cannot meet the requirement for repairing the TSVs that failed during the in-field operation.

Recently, the TSV self-repair for TSVs that failed during the in-field operation get noticed in literatures [10, 16]. Nicolaidis et al. [16] proposed a built-in self-repair method that can be used for on-line faulty TSV recovery. In this scheme, the faulty TSVs can be firstly detected by interconnect BIST strategies, and then recorded into the diagnosis vector DV. After that, the TSV-BISR, which consists of repair logic and crossover switch, can repair the faulty TSVs under the control of DV. In order to reduce the area cost, the repair logic is implemented as iterative function in the scheme. However, the area cost of this scheme is still considerable.

Jiang et al. [10] also proposed an in-field TSV repair framework for improving the reliability of 3D-stacked ICs. This scheme is built upon the TSV repair architecture previously proposed in [15], assuming there exists a processor and a non-volatile memory in the 3D-stacked IC. In the proposed scheme, the online testing is conducted periodically or triggered by events firstly. Then the TSV repair algorithm is called upon to find repair paths for the detected faulty TSVs. However, this method cannot be applied to the 3D-stacked ICs without processor or non-volatile memory.

1.2 Contribution and Paper Organization

In this paper, an effective faulty TSV self-repair scheme for 3D-stacked ICs is presented, by which the faulty TSVs can be repaired by redundant TSVs under the control of repair controllers automatically. The expected number of faulty TSVs repairable in a TSV bundle can be achieved by specifying the corresponding number of redundant TSVs. Since the proposed TSV repair scheme can repair faulty TSVs by automatically propagating the functional signals through fault-free TSVs, it can be applied to repair both the TSVs failed during manufacturing test and the TSVs failed during in-field operation.

The remainder of the paper is organized as follows. Section 2 describes the proposed TSV self-repair scheme. Section 3 presents the experimental results. Section 4 concludes the paper.

2. THE PROPOSED TSV SELF-REPAIR SCHEME

In this section, the TSV self-repair scheme is proposed, which can be used to repair faulty TSVs, including clustering faulty TSVs, detected by manufacturing test. Moreover, the TSVs failed and then detected during the in-field operation can also be repaired by the proposed scheme. In the following subsections, the basic architecture of the TSV repair scheme will be presented firstly, and then the operation of the TSV repair scheme will be described. Finally, we will present the calculation for the number of redundant TSVs and repair controllers.

2.1 The Basic Architecture of the TSV Repair Scheme

The basic architecture of the proposed TSV repair scheme is shown in Figure 1, which can be used to repair the faulty TSVs using redundant TSVs by adaptive propagating the functional signals through fault-free TSVs. The adaptive propagating from functional signals to fault-free TSVs is controlled by the repair controllers. For the sake of graphic clarity without loss of generality, only three functional signals and five TSVs (including 3 regular TSVs and 2 redundant TSVs) are presented in Figure 1 to explain the basic principle of the proposed architecture.

As shown in Figure 1, Signal1~3 represent three functional signals to be propagated through TSVs. Test1~5 represent the test results of the five TSVs denoted as TSV1 to TSV5, while the logic high or low values of Test1~5 indicate whether the corresponding TSV is good or faulty. It should be noted that Test1~5 can be obtained by various TSV test methods such as proposed in [17] and in [18], et al. The TSV test method is beyond the scope of this paper. In this paper, we assume that the Test signal can indicate the state of TSV detected during manufacturing test and in-field operation. Since only 2 redundant

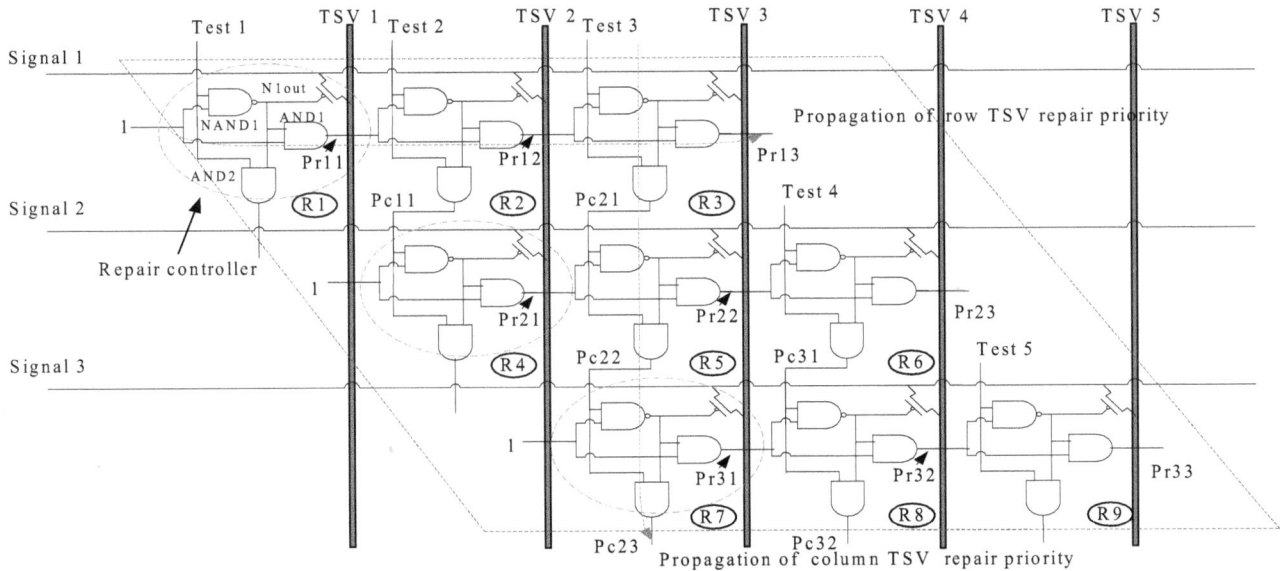

Figure 1. The proposed TSV repair scheme

TSVs are assumed in Figure 1 for the sake of graphic clarity, at most 2 faulty TSVs can be repaired by redundant TSVs. However, it should be noted that the proposed scheme can be easily expanded to include more regular TSVs and redundant TSVs. It can be seen from Figure 1 that the number of repair controllers for each functional signal depends on the number of redundant TSVs. As shown in Figure 1, the number of repair controllers for each functional signal is equal to the number of redundant TSVs plus one. The total number of repair controllers can thus be obtained by calculating the product of the number of functional signals and the repair controllers for each functional signal. For example, assume that 100 regular TSVs and 4 redundant TSVs are grouped together in a TSV bundle, and then the total number of repair controllers is 500.

2.2 The Operation of the TSV Repair Scheme

In the following, we mainly consider the architecture of Figure 1 and two representative cases of TSV failure to analysis the function of the proposed TSV repair scheme. The considered cases include that only 1 TSV is faulty and 2 TSVs are faulty respectively. Suppose that the repair controllers have been remarked as R1 to R9 according to the row and left first.

For the first case, without loss of generality, here we assume that only TSV2 is faulty, which can be the manufacturing defect or the latent defect that failed and then detected during in-field operation. The TSV repair process is analyzed in the following. Clearly, Test1~5 will be set to logic high, low, high, high, and high value in this case. Hence, the N1out in R1 will be set to logic low value. Therefore, Signal1 will be connected to TSV1 by opening the PMOS of R1. Meanwhile, it is worth noting that the Pr11 will also be set to logic low value, which is a control value for NAND and AND gates. Hence, the corresponding N1out in the rest of the repair controllers of the row will be controlled to logic high values, thus rendering disconnecting between this functional signal and the other TSVs.

In fact, the up functional signals have high priority to connect the left fault-free TSVs. If a functional signal is connected to a specific TSV, the Pr11 of the corresponding repair controller will be set to logic low value to prevent the functional signal from connecting the rest of TSVs. Otherwise, the Pr11 of the corresponding repair controller will be controlled to logic high value, which indicates that the priority will be passed to the right repair controllers for finding the possible connection between this signal and other TSVs. For example, if the TSV1 is faulty, then the Pr11 of R1 will be set to logic high value to allow this functional signal to connect to other TSVs. This process is also referred to as the propagation of row TSV repair priority. Clearly, the proposed repair scheme can ensure that a functional signal can only connect to a sole TSV to avoid conflict. It can be concluded that only TSV1 will be connected to the Signal1 in the first case.

Due to the TSV2 is assumed to be faulty, it can also be easily analyzed from Figure 1 that the Pc11 will be set to logic low value. The logic low value of Pc11 will cause the Pr21 to be set to logic high value and renders disconnecting between Sginal2 and TSV2. However, it should be noted that Pc21 and Pr21 would be set to logic high values in this case. Hence, the N1out in R5 will be set to logic low value, resulting in Signal2 connecting to TSV3. Meanwhile, the Pr22 will be set to logic low value to prevent the rest TSVs from connecting to Signal2. Moreover, it should be noted that Pc22 will also be set to logic low value. In fact, the up functional signals have high priority to connect to a specific TSV. If the up functional signal doesn't require connecting to the TSV, the AND2 of the corresponding repair controller will output a logic high value, which indicates that the priority will be passed to the down repair controller for finding the possible connection between the down signals and this TSV. Otherwise, the AND2 of the corresponding repair controller will output a logic low value to prevent the down signals from connecting to this TSV. This mechanism can ensure that the TSV connects to a sole functional signal in the same column to avoid conflict. This process is also referred to as the propagation of column TSV repair priority. Likewise, since both Pc31 and Pr31 will be set to logic high values, Signal3 would connect to TSV4. Based on the above analysis, we can conclude that the Signal1, Signal2, and Signal3 will only connect to TSV1, TSV3, and TSV4 for signal transfer. Consequently, the faulty TSV2 is automatically repaired through the redundant TSV4.

As mentioned above and shown in Figure 1, since 2 redundant TSVs are added to the proposed TSV repair scheme, the TSV repair scheme can then repair up to 2 faulty TSVs. In the following, without loss of generality, we will analyze the TSV repair process targeting that both TSV2 and TSV3 are faulty. In fact, this case can also represent a faulty TSVs cluster. In this case, as analyzed above, Signal1 will connect to the TSV1. Since the TSV2 and TSV3 are all faulty, Pr22 will be set to logic high value according to the propagation of row TSV repair priority. Therefore, Signal2 will connect to TSV4. Similarly, the Pr22 will be set to logic high value according to both the propagation of row and column TSV repair priority. Hence, the N1out of R9 will be set to logic low value. Therefore, Signal3 will connect to TSV5. Based on the above analysis, we can conclude that the proposed repair scheme can self-repair the faulty TSVs cluster, TSV2 and TSV3, by automatically propagating the Signal1, Signal2, and Signal 3 through the fault-free TSVs, TSV1, TSV4, and TSV5, thus the reliability of the 3D-statcked ICs can be improved.

Clearly, if TSV1~3 are all fault-free, the repair process based on the proposed TSV repair scheme is much simpler. The Signal1, Signal2, and Signal 3 will automatically connect to TSV1, TSV2, and TSV3 for signal transferring. Through the above discuss, we can conclude that the proposed TSV repair scheme can self-repair the faulty TSVs with redundant TSVs automatically. The maximum number of the faulty TSVs that can be repaired relies on the number of redundant TSVs.

2.3 The Calculation for the number of redundant TSVs and repair controllers

To calculate the number of redundant TSVs and repair controllers for obtaining a satisfactory reparability, a commonly used probability model for TSV defects is introduced in the following.

For clustering TSV defects, it is a consensus that the close vicinity of a TSV defect center will have a higher defect probability [19, 14]. The defect probability of TSV_i, denoted as P_i, is inversely proportional to the distance between TSV_i and the existing defect center, and can be expressed as

$$P_i \propto (\frac{1}{d_{ij}})^\alpha \qquad (1)$$

where d_{ij} represents the distance between TSV_i and the cluster center and α represents the clustering coefficient.

Suppose a TSV bundle has m TSVs supporting n functional signals with a result of r redundant TSVs ($r=m-n$), then up to r faulty TSVs can be repaired by the proposed scheme. Hence, the reparability can be obtained by calculating the probability that the number of faulty TSVs in a bundle is less than r. Let S represents the faulty TSVs set, in which are $x(x<r)$ different TSVs random selected from the total $n+r$ TSVs. The total number of elements in the S is denoted as C $(n+r, x)$. Then the probability that exact x TSVs are failed in the TSV bundle can be calculated as

$$R_x = \sum_{i=0}^{C(n+r,x)} \left(\prod_{k \in Si} P_k \prod_{j \notin Si} (1-P_j) \right) \qquad (2)$$

where P_k and P_j represent the calculated defective probabilities for TSV k and j from (1). For simplicity, an average defective probability, denoted as p, can be assumed for calculating the R_x. Then (2) can be approximated as [15]

$$R_x = C(n+r,x)\left(p^x(1-p)^{n+r-x}\right) \qquad (3)$$

The reparability of the proposed scheme for a TSV bundle, R_b, can then be calculated by cumulating R_x for $0 \le x \le r$.

$$R_b = \sum_{x=0}^{r} (R_x) \qquad (4)$$

It should be noted that the 3D ICs may contain a large number of TSVs, which are typically grouped into many TSV bundles. Suppose the number of TSV bundles is y. Therefore, the reparability of the total 3D-stacked IC, denoted as R, can be calculated as

$$R = R_b^{y} \qquad (5)$$

Consequently, with a specific number of TSVs in the TSV bundle, the number of required redundant TSVs and repair controllers can be derived through (3) for a 3D-stacked IC with known number of TSVs to achieve an expected reparability.

3. EXPERIMENTAL RESULTS

3.1 Experimental Setup

The proposed TSV repair scheme, which supports to automatically repair the faulty TSVs with redundant TSVs, was implemented using a commercial 90nm CMOS technology in this work. In order to verify the effectiveness of the proposed scheme, two main experiments are conducted, including the functional verification for the proposed TSV repair scheme and the analysis of reparability for the proposed scheme respectively.

In the first experiment, three representative cases of TSV failures, which includes that all TSVs are fault-free, only 1 TSV is faulty, and 2 TSVs are faulty respectively, are considered to verify the function of the proposed scheme. The functional verification for the proposed TSV repair scheme is conducted by using HSPICE. In the second experiment, the average of TSV defective probability is assumed between 5×10^{-5} and 1×10^{-3}, which is a reasonable range as reported in [15].

3.2 Results and Analysis

The signal waveforms for the proposed TSV repair scheme targeting the cases that all TSVs are fault-free, only 1 TSV is faulty, and 2 TSVs are faulty are shown in Figure 2(a) , Figure 2(b), and Figure 2(c) respectively. As shown in Figure 2(a), the Test signals set to logic high values indicate that all TSVs are fault-free. By differentiating the waveforms between the Signals and TSVs in Figure 2(a), it can be easily known that Signal1, Signal2, and Signal 3 are successfully connected to TSV1, TSV2, and TSV3 for signal transferring. Likewise, as shown in Figure 2(b), the Test2 signal set to logic low value indicates that TSV2 is faulty. It can also be easily seen from the simulation results that TSV1, TSV3, and TSV4 are automatically selected for Signal1, Signal2, and Signal 3 to transfer data, which verified that the proposed scheme can self-repair the faulty TSV. As shown in Figure 2(c), both Test2 and Test3 signals are set to logic low values, which indicates clustering TSV defects, TSV2 and TSV3, are occurred. However, it can be noted that the proposed scheme can still tolerate the faulty TSVs and automatically select the TSV1, TSV4, and TSV5 for Signal1, Signal2, and Signal 3 to transfer data. Through the above experimental results, it can be concluded that the proposed TSV repair scheme can self-repair the faulty TSVs with redundant TSVs.

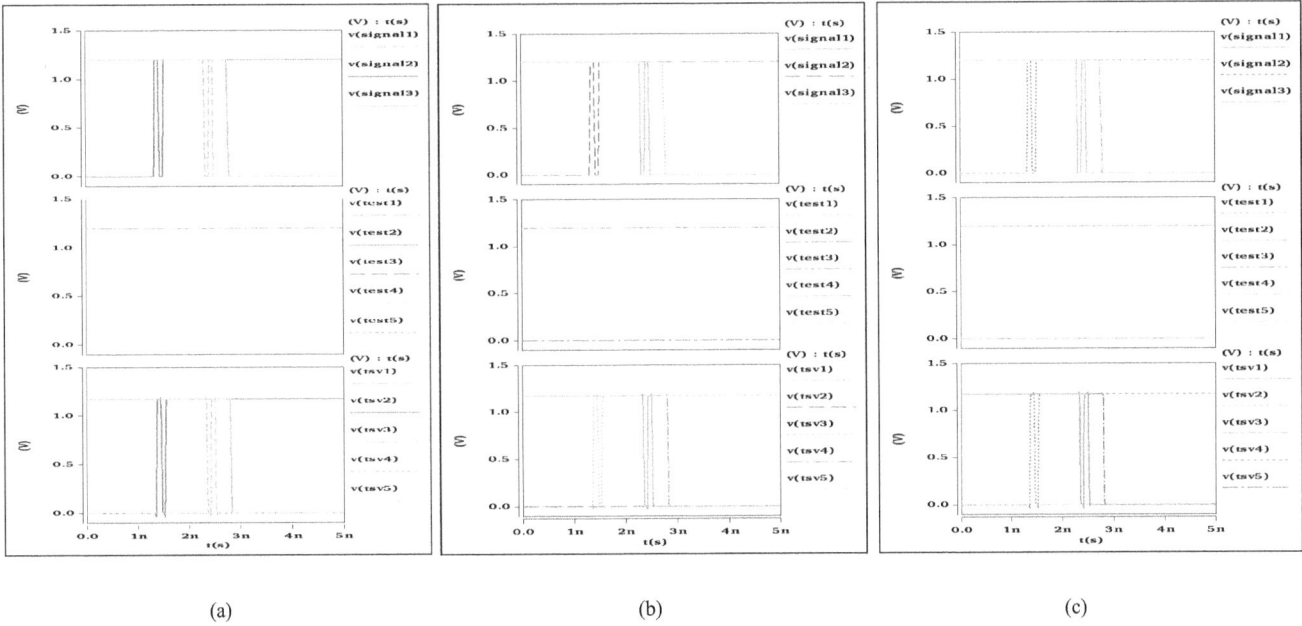

Figure 2. Simulated waveform for TSV repair, (a)all TSVs are fault-free; (b) only TSV2 is fault; (c) both TSV2 and TSV3 are faulty

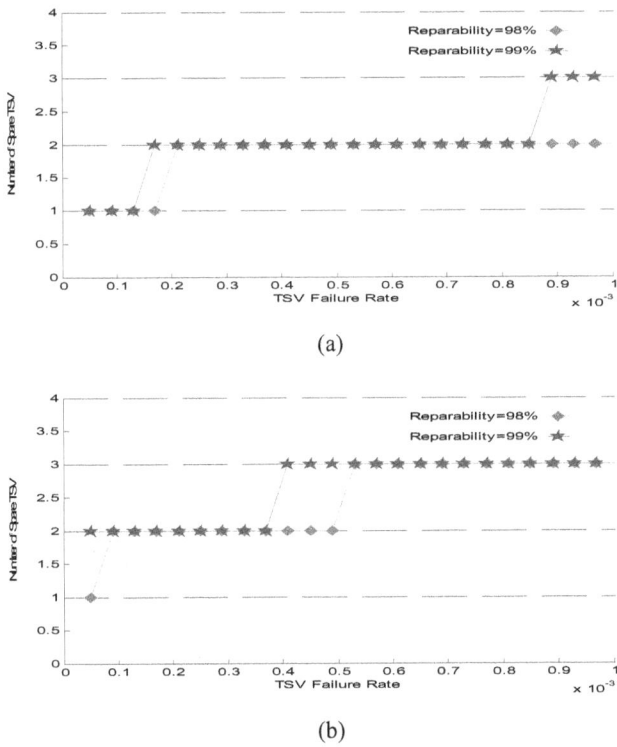

(a)

(b)

Figure 3. The number of required redundant TSVs, (a) 10K TSVs; (b) 100K TSVs

To achieve a satisfactory faulty TSV reparability by using the proposed scheme, the minimum number of redundant TSVs should be reserved for each TSV bundle. In this work, the number of regular TSVs in a bundle is assumed to be 100 [14]. The total numbers of regular TSVs in the 3D-stacked ICs are assumed to be 10K and 100K respectively. Assume the target value of

reparability for the 3D-stacked ICs are 98% and 99% respectively, the minimum number of redundant TSVs required for each TSV bundle can then be derived from (5) considering the average of TSV defective probability assumed earlier. As can be seen from Figure 3, by using the proposed scheme, the number of redundant TSVs for each TSV bundle is limited. Clearly, the number of regular TSVs in a TSV bundle can be decreased, while keeping the same number of redundant TSVs, for coping with more serious TSV failure situations. It should be noted that the number of repair controllers for each regular TSV is equal to the number of redundant TSVs of each TSV bundle plus one. Hence, the total number of repair controllers required for the 3D-stacked IC wouldn't be increased with the decreasing size of a TSV bundle.

3.3 Cost Analysis and Comparison

As calculated for the 3D-stacked ICs described above, it requires at most 3 redundant TSVs for each TSV bundle to achieve a satisfactory reparability by using the proposed scheme. Hence, the cost of the extra logic gates for each regular TSV is at most 4 repair controllers. Table I shows the area cost of the extra logics in the proposed scheme for the 3D-stacked ICs with 10K and 100K TSVs, while the target value of reparability is set to 99% and the TSV failure rate is assumed to be $5*10^{-4}$.

Table 1. Cost Analysis for the case that the target vale of reparability=99% and the TSV failure rate=$5*10^{-4}$

	(Reparability=99%; TSV Failure rate=$5*10^{-4}$)	
#Regular TSVs	10k	100k
#Spare TSVs	200	300
Area of extra logic(μm^2)	235200	3136000

Table II compares the attributes of the area of extra logics, filed of application and repair time for the proposed method with those of [10]. As discussed above, the proposed scheme requires at most 4 repair controllers per regular TSV for faulty TSV recovery, and each repair controller consists of 1 NAND and 2

25

AND gates. As shown in [10, 15], three MX3 gates are required for each regular TSV for faulty TSV recovery. From the commercial 90nm CMOS technology library, it can be obtained that the minimum numbers of transistors for NAND, AND, and MX3 gates are 6, 8 and 24 respectively. Hence, the numbers of transistors for the extra logic per regular TSV are 64 and 72 for the proposed scheme and [10] respectively. Moreover, the method in [10] requires that the target 3d-stacked ICs includes a processor core and non-volatile memory for in-field TSV repair, while the proposed scheme doesn't have this requirement. Furthermore, the repair time for the proposed scheme will be relatively low, since the repair process is conducted by hardware automatically, while the method in [10] is conducted by running the repair algorithm.

Table 2. Comparisons to previous work

Attributes	Proposed method	[10]
Area of extra logic per regular TSV (# Transistors)	64	72
Field of application	Unlimited	Limited
Repair time	Low	Relatively high

4. CONCLUSIONS

In this paper, we have proposed a faulty TSVs self-repair scheme for 3D-stacked ICs, which can be used to repair the faulty TSVs by redundant TSVs effectively. By designing the repair controllers and the interconnect architecture, the mechanism for row and column TSV repair priority propagation is realized, which can assure that a functional signal can only connect to a sole TSV to avoid conflict. Moreover, the proposed TSV repair scheme can automatically repair both the TSVs failed during manufacturing test and TSVs failed during in-field operation. Experimental results obtained by HSPICE simulations verified the function of the proposed scheme. The cost of the proposed scheme is also analyzed and can be acceptable.

5. ACKNOWLEDGMENTS

This work was supported in part by National Natural Science Foundation of China (NSFC) under grant No.(61402031, 61306049, 61204027).

6. REFERENCES

[1] Y. Xie, G. H. Loh, B. Black, and K. Bernstein, "Design Space Exploration for 3D Architectures," ACM Journal on Emerging Technologies in Computing Systems (JETC), vol.2,no.2,pp.65-103, 2006.

[2] H.Yoshikawa, et al., "Chip scale camera module (CSCM) using through-silicon-via (TSV)," Proceedings of IEEE International Solid- State Circuits Conference, 2009, pp.476-477.

[3] W.Davis et al., "Demystifying 3D ICs: The Pros and Cons of going Vertical," IEEE Design & Test, vol.22, no.6, pp.498-510, 2005.

[4] U.Kang,et al., "8Gb 3-D DDR3 DRAM Using Through Silicon-Via Technology," IEEE Journal of Solid-State Circuits (JSSC), vol.45, no.1,pp.111-119,2010.

[5] M.Kawano, et al., "A 3D packaging technology for 4 Gbit stacked DRAM with 3Gbps data transfer," Proceedings of IEEE International Electron Devices Meeting, 2006, pp.1-4.

[6] P.Garrou, C.Bower, and P.Ramm, "Handbook of 3D Integration: Technology and Application of 3D Integrated Circuits," Weinheim: WILEY-VCH Verlag GmbH&Co.KGaA, 2008, Vol.1-2.

[7] S.Ryu,k.Lu,X.Zhang,J.Im, P.Ho, and R.Huang, " Impact of near-surface thermal stresses on interfacial reliability of through-silicon vias for 3-D interconnects", IEEE Transactions on Device and Materials Reliability, vol. 11, no.1, pp.35-43,2011.

[8] C.-N . Peng, et al., "Electrical tests for three-dimensional ICs(3DICs) with TSVs," International Test Conference 3D-test Workshop,2010.

[9] A.Karmarkar, X.Xu, and V.Moroz, "Performance and reliability analysis of 3D-integration structures employing through silicon via (TSV)," Proceedings of IEEE International Reliability Physics Symposium, 2009, pp.682-687.

[10] L.Jiang, F.Ye ,Q.Xu, K.Chakrabarty, and B.Eklow, " On effetive and efficient In-Field TSV Repair for Stacked 3D ICs," Proceedings of ACM/IEEE Design Automation Conference, pp: 1-6, 2013

[11] U.Kang,et al., "8Gb 3-D DDR3 DRAM Using Through Silicon-Via Technology," IEEE Journal of Solid-State Circuits (JSSC), vol.45, no.1,pp.111-119,2010.

[12] A.-C.Hsieh.T.-T.Hwang,M.-T.Chang, M.-H.Tsai,C.-M.Tsent, and H.-C.Li,"TSV redundancy:Architecture and design issures in 3-D IC," Proceedings of IEEE/ACM Design, Automation, and Test in Europe (DATE), pp: 166-171, 2010

[13] I. Loi, S. Mitra, et al., "A Low-Overhead Fault Tolerance Scheme for TSV-Based 3D Network on Chip Links," In Proceedings of IEEE/ACM International Conference on Computer-Aided Design (ICCAD), pp.598-602, 2008.

[14] Y.Zhao, S.Khursheed, and B.M. Al-Hashimi, "Cost-Effective TSV Grouping for Yield Improvement of 3D-ICs," In Proceedings of IEEE Asian Test Symposium (ATS), pp.201-206, 2011.

[15] L.Jiang, Q. Xu, and B.Eklow, "On effective Through-Silicon via Repair for 3D-stacked ICs," IEEE Transactions on Computer-Aided Design of Integrated Circuits and System, Vol.32, No.4, pp.559-571, 2013.

[16] M.Nicolaidis, V. Pasca, and L. Anghel, "Through-silicon-via built-in self-repair for aggressive 3D integration," IEEE International On-Line Testing Symposium (IOLTS), pp.91-96, 2012.

[17] E.J. Marinissen and Y. Zorian, "Testing 3D Chips Containing Through-Silicon Vias," In Proceedings of International Test Conference (ITC), pp.1-11, 2009.

[18] E.J.Marinissen, "Testing TSV-based three-dimensional stacked ICs", Proceedings of IEEE/ACM Design, Automation & Test in Europe Conference & Exhibition (DATE), pp. 1689-1694, 2010.

[19] M.B. Tahoori, "Defects, yield, and design in sublithographic nano-electronics," Proceedings of IEEE International Symposium on Defect and Fault Tolerance in VLSI Systems, 2005, pp.3-11.

Electromigration-aware Clock Tree Synthesis for TSV-based 3D-ICs

Tiantao Lu and Ankur Srivastava

Dept. of Electrical and Computer Engineering, University of Maryland, College Park, MD, U.S.A.

{ttlu, ankurs}@umd.edu

ABSTRACT

In 3D-IC technology, electromigration (EM) degradation has become severe due to the high thermal-mechanical stress induced by the Through-Silicon-Vias (TSVs). However, little has been done on designing an EM-robust clock tree for 3D-ICs. In this paper, we propose a systematic EM-aware clock tree synthesis design flow, to enhance the 3D clock tree's EM reliability, with little interference to clock tree's performance metrics such as total wire length and clock skew. We develop a simple TSV's EM objective function based on multi-physics of the mass transportation equation, and validate it against the finite element method (FEM) simulation. Then we use this objective function to formulate a heuristic, based on integer linear programming (ILP), which places the clock TSVs such that the clock tree's EM reliability is maximized. Results show that the our heuristic is able to increase 3D clock's EM lifetime by more than 3.63x with little wire length overhead, while maintaining zero clock skew.

Categories and Subject Descriptors

B.8.2 [**Performance and Reliability**]: Performance Analysis and Design Aids; J.6 [**Computer-Aided Engineering**]: Computer-aided design (CAD)

Keywords

3D Clock tree; electromigration; hydrostatic stress; MTTF

1. INTRODUCTION

Electromigration (EM) degradation has become one of the most crucial failure causes in modern VLSI circuit. EM refers to the migration of atoms in solid-state conductors, which is caused by multiple factors such as current density, thermal mechanical stress, and temperature distribution. The migration of atoms will form hillocks and voids over time, and eventually leads to severe interconnect failure such as short-circuit and open-circuit, respectively.

Designing an EM-robust 3D-ICs is a very challenging task, for the following three reasons. Firstly, unlike 2D-ICs, where redundant wires and vias are widely used to enable on-line reconfiguration of interconnects [10], 3D-ICs must consider TSV's high manufacturing cost and low yield, which make the redundant design less feasible. Secondly, in 3D-ICs, EM is a strong function of thermal mechanical stress. High thermal mechanical stress is observed around the Through-Silicon-Vias (TSVs) and the neighboring interconnects [8, 12]. This arises from the significant difference between the

coefficients of thermal expansion (CTE) of TSV filling material such as copper ($1.77 \times 10^{-5}K^{-1}$), and silicon substrate ($3.05 \times 10^{-6}K^{-1}$). When TSVs are cooled from a high stress-free annealing temperature to a low working temperature, tensile and compressive stresses are formed inside the TSV and the substrate. Moreover, when multiple TSVs are closely placed, their stress fields influence each other. This high stress field severely deteriorates TSV's EM reliability. Thirdly, due to the poor thermal conductance of inter-layer dielectric (less than $1W \cdot m^{-1} \cdot K^{-1}$, as compared to Si, which is $149W \cdot m^{-1} \cdot K^{-1}$), local temperature hotspot is inclined to appear. This makes TSVs degrade at different rates. Combining these three factors, a holistic EM optimization scheme that takes both stress and thermal profile into account is highly necessary.

Traditional 2D clock tree is largely considered as EM-immune due to clock signal's bi-directional and symmetric AC current. The influence of thermal mechanical stress and temperature on EM for a planer wire is not pronounced either. However, for 3D-IC's clock tree, high thermal mechanical stress as well as localized temperature dramatically accelerates EM. In addition, since clock tree synthesis is usually performed after logic cell's placement, the layout whitespace available for clock TSVs is limited. When multiple TSVs are placed close to each other, their stress fields therefore their EM trends become mutually influenced. The relative positions of one and its neighboring TSVs decide the TSV's EM-lifetime. A straightforward method to eliminate this interrelation and to simplify TSV's placement procedure is to apply Keep-Out-Zone (KOZ) for each TSV, but KOZ could be large so it may become infeasible to place all TSVs within a constrained whitespace area.

There has been some active research on modeling and designing general EM-robust 3D-ICs. For example, Pak et al. investigated a single TSV's EM trend using finite element method (FEM) [12], but it requires lots of memory and simulation time thus is infeasible for chip-level EM optimization. Pathak et al. set up look-up tables that exhaustively investigate the impact of stress, current, or temperature on metal wire's EM trend, and performed a chip-scale EM analysis for metal wires [13]. A follow-up work discussed the influence of TSV's thermal mechanical stress field on neighboring wires and proposed methodology on deciding wire's routing directions [11]. However, both papers [13, 11] only consider the EM in planar metal wires but don't recognize the EM inside TSVs. EM inside TSVs is a much complicated phenomenon as it is affected by neighboring TSVs. We demonstrate that due to the high stress gradient inside TSVs, TSVs are much more prone to EM failure rather than planar interconnects.

Previous works on 3D clock synthesis have primarily focused on minimizing clock power and performance metrics. Kim et al. extended the 2D deferred-merge-embedding (DME) [5] to generate a 3D zero-skew clock tree [9]. A cutting-based approach for abstract clock tree generation was implemented by Zhao et al., and physical routing was carried out to minimize clock slew and total wire length [16]. Shang et al. examined the influence of thermal variation on

3D clock tree, and inserted thermal TSVs for skew reduction [14].

To the best of our knowledge, how to design a 3D EM-robust clock tree has not been investigated. As the optimal TSV allocation for highest EM reliability may contradict with the optimal TSV allocation from clock skew and wire length's perspective, a chip-level optimization needs to be considered to achieve the optimal trade-off between clock network's performance and reliability. Furthermore, as FEM modeling for TSV's EM is too time consuming and not applicable for chip-scale optimization, there is a need to develop an efficient TSV's EM objective function.

The primary contributions of this work are as follows.

1. We propose an EM-aware clock tree synthesis design flow for 3D-ICs (Section 5);

2. We derive and validate an efficient objective function for chip-scale estimation of TSV's EM (Section 4.2), which correlates well with multi-physics based FEM simulations (Section 2.1 and 4);

3. We formulate an ILP problem to place the clock TSVs such that TSV's mean time to failure (MTTF) is maximized while clock skew remains zero, and clock wire length overhead is low (Section 6).

2. BACKGROUND

In this section, we introduce several related works in estimating and optimizing TSV's EM, and also summarize the traditional EM-unaware clock tree design flow for 3D-ICs.

2.1 TSV EM's physical equation

Interconnect's wear-out due to EM was expressed by the empirical Black equation [4]. The Black equation is based on the observation that the life time of a single metal wire is inversely proportional to the current density. However, recent experimental work [7] shows that the current density is not the only driving force for TSV's EM. TSV's wear-out is subject to several interacting forces including current density, thermal mechanical stress gradient, temperature gradient, and atomic concentration gradient. The physics of TSV's EM can be described by the following time-dependent multi-physics mass transportation equations.

$$\frac{\partial c}{\partial t} + \nabla \cdot [-D \nabla c + \frac{Dc \vec{j} e\rho Z}{kT} + \frac{Dc\Omega}{kT} \cdot (\nabla(\sigma)) + \frac{DcQ^\star}{kT} \cdot \frac{\nabla(T)}{T}] = 0 \quad (1)$$

$$D = D_0 \cdot exp\left(\frac{\Omega\sigma - E_a}{kT}\right) \quad (2)$$

$$\sigma = \frac{\sigma_x + \sigma_y + \sigma_z}{3} \quad (3)$$

where c is atomic concentration, t is time, D is diffusivity, j is current density, e is electron charge, Z is effective charge, Ω is atomic volume, σ is hydrostatic stress, $Q^\star$ is heat of transport, ρ is resistivity, k is Boltzmann constant, T is temperature, and E_a is activation energy. The hydrostatic stress, σ, as shown in Eqn.3, is a scalar value, which is the average of principal stress values along x, y, and z axis.

2.2 Thermal Simulation

As Eqn.1 indicates that TSV's EM strongly depends on temperature, we estimate the 3D-IC's thermal profile for a given power consumption using the compact thermal model proposed by Tsai et al.[15], as shown in Eqn.4.

$$T = T_{ambient} + \begin{bmatrix} R_{1,1} & R_{1,2} & \cdots & R_{1,s} \\ R_{2,1} & R_{2,2} & \cdots & R_{2,s} \\ \vdots & \vdots & \ddots & \vdots \\ R_{n,1} & R_{n,2} & \cdots & R_{n,s} \end{bmatrix} \begin{bmatrix} P_1 \\ P_2 \\ \vdots \\ P_s \end{bmatrix} \quad (4)$$

where T is an $n \times 1$ vector, representing TSV's locations, $T_{ambient}$ is the ambient temperature, $R_{n \times m}$ is the transfer thermal resistance matrix, and $P_i(i = 1, \cdots, s)$ are s power sources. The calculation of matrix R is similar to Tsai's work [15] except that we also consider the TSV's thermal resistance in this paper.

2.3 Stress Superposition Principle

The CTE mismatch between TSV and silicon substrate induces significant thermal mechanical stress during TSV's fabrication process. When multiple TSVs are present, we assume the TSV and silicon substrate are linearly elastic structures, then according to the stress superposition principle explained in multiple papers [8, ?, ?], the stress coming from several different bodies is the sum of the stress applied separately. In other words, the stress value at a certain point is the accumulative TSV-induced stress caused by each TSV:

$$\sigma = \sum_{i=1}^{n} \sigma_i. \quad (5)$$

where σ is the total stress at the point of interest and σ_i is the stress value at this point induced by the ith TSV.

2.4 Traditional 3D clock tree design flow

Traditional 3D clock tree synthesis mainly comprises two phases: abstract clock tree generation and wire embedding [9, 16]. The abstract clock tree is a binary single-root tree topology. The leaves of the abstract clock tree represent all clock sinks. The layer index (Z coordinate) of each intermediate clock tree node is determined such that a minimum number of TSVs is used [9], or the usage of TSVs is well controlled [16]. The second phase, wire embedding, using the abstract clock tree as input, aims to minimize various objective functions such as total wire length, clock skew, clock slew, clock power and etc. The most common objective is to minimize total wire length while ensuring zero clock skew. Deferred-merge-embedding (2D-DME) algorithm was proposed by Chao et al. [5] and was extended to the three dimensional space (3D-DME) [9]. Both DME algorithms start with pairs of clock sinks, and iteratively find the solution space, namely, the "merging segments" (MS) for each of the intermediate tree node, with zero clock skew as constraint and minimum wire length as objective. MS is basically the set of points on which the intermediate clock tress node can be located such that there is zero skew in the subtree rooted at that intermediate node. After all the solution spaces have been determined, the exact location of the intermediate tree node is decided such that the Manhattan distance to its parent node is minimized. In 3D-DME, clock TSVs are inserted when two children nodes are not at the same layer. Clock TSVs will be placed at the same locations as their parent node to obtain minimum wire length. To conclude, DME algorithms ensure zero clock skew while producing near-optimal clock wire length results.

3. FEM SIMULATION

Eqn.1 shows all four driving forces of EM: atomic concentration gradient, current density, thermal mechanical stress gradient, and temperature gradient. The atomic concentration c, is difficult to solve analytically thus requires FEM simulation. In this section, we set up detailed FEM based solver in COMSOL [1] to numerically simulate a *single* TSV and adjacent planer wire's EM, induced by current density, this *single* TSV's own stress gradient, and thermal gradient caused by Joule heating. Section 4.3 presents the case where *multiple* TSVs are present and shows that their stress fields and EM trends become mutually influenced.

The structure of the TSV and its material property is the same as the paper authored by Pak et al. [12]. TSV comprises a cylindrical cone and two landing pads. Each landing pad is connected to a metal wire. We assume that the TSV diameter is $4\mu m$, landing pad is $5\mu m \times 5\mu m$, and TSV's height is $31.2\mu m$. The wires connecting to both ends of TSV have a dimension of $0.2\mu m \times 0.2\mu m \times 10\mu m$ (width $\times$ height $\times$ length). Wires and TSVs are imposed with a symmetric clock current signal, with a magnitude of 0.4 mA. In this paper, we assume that the asymmetrical current induced by asymmetrical rise/fall behavior of clock tree buffers is negligible. The current density inside the wires is $1\times10^{10} A \cdot m^{-3}$. TSV's annealing temperature is set to be 573K. Wire's joule heating effect is considered in the model to calculate the temperature distribution. The initial atomic concentration is $1.5\times10^{28}cm^{-3}$. MTTF is defined as the length of time elapses when the atomic concentration has 5% deviation from the initial value [7, 12]. Though MTTF varies depending on different failure criteria, the trend remains similar. Thus in this paper we use a normalized MTTF to represent the TSV's lifetime subject to EM.

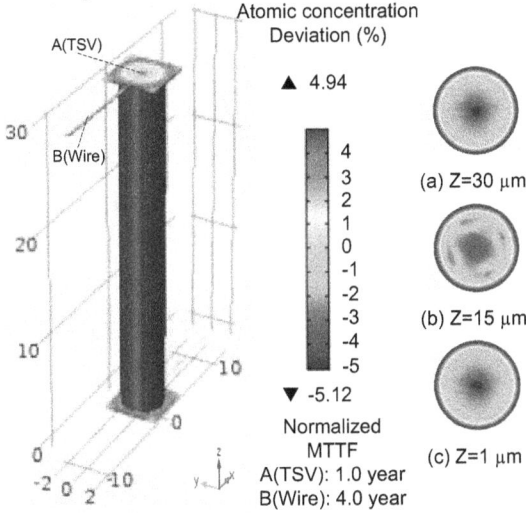

Figure 1: Atomic concentration deviation at $t = MTTF$ in a clock TSV and neighboring planer wire.

Fig.1 shows the simulation result. We have three observations from Fig.1. (1) Metal atoms migrate from TSV's center to its periphery. Our simulation result matches with some experimental TSV's EM testing data [6], where void appears in the central areas of the TSV. The radial movement of atoms can be explained by the mismatch of coefficient of thermal expansions (CTEs) between TSV filling materials (copper, for example) and the silicon substrate. Since $CTE_{Cu} = 1.77 \times 10^{-5} >> CTE_{Si} = 3.05 \times 10^{-6}$, when the TSV structure is cooled from annealing temperature, radical tensile stress is formed inside the TSV, pulling metal atoms from the center to the periphery. (2) Compared to the EM inside XY plane, the vertical migration of atoms is far less significant. This is because the major stress gradient happens at the interface between TSV cone and the substrate, which is inside XY plane. Although clock current flows along Z direction, it is bi-directional thus its impact on the EM is less significant. Previous EM study [12] also supports our observation, where the vertical EM is far less significant than the EM in the XY plane. (3) TSV's MTTF is four times longer than the planar wire's lifetime, making the TSV, rather than the wire, become the most EM-vulnerable device in 3D clock tree.

Besides the EM trends, we also observe that the temperature distribution inside the TSVs is quite uniform. This is because copper is an ideal heat conductor, which spreads wire and TSV's Joule heat evenly. The detailed thermal distribution is omitted for brevity.

4. OBJECTIVE FUNCTION

Solving the differential equation (Eqn.1) using the FEM-based TSV's EM model in Section 2.1 takes about one hour for one TSV. Considering numerous chip-scale thermal and stress profiles and their complicated influences on TSV's EM, FEM model is not capable of handling chip-scale TSV's EM optimization problems. In this paper we derive a simple TSV EM's objective based on the physical mass transportation equation, and then validate it against accurate but time-consuming FEM simulation.

4.1 Simplifying EM multiphysics equation

As we describe in Eqn.1, atomic concentration gradient, current density, thermal mechanical stress gradient, and temperature gradient are four driving forces for EM. However, in 3D clock TSV's structure, current is bi-directional, and temperature is uniformly distributed inside the TSV, and the second term ∇c, the atomic concentration gradient, is a "recovery force" once EM happens. The primary EM driving force for clock TSV is the thermal mechanical stress gradient, thus we can simplify Eqn.1 for clock TSV's EM, as below.

$$\frac{\partial c}{\partial t} + D\nabla \cdot \left[\frac{c\Omega}{kT} \cdot (\nabla(\sigma)) \right] = 0 \qquad (6)$$

Considering EM trend is more significant in the XY plane rather than along the Z direction, Eqn.6 can further be simplified as follows.

$$\frac{\partial c}{\partial t} + \frac{D\Omega}{kT}\left[\frac{\partial c}{\partial x} \cdot \frac{\partial \sigma}{\partial x} + \frac{\partial c}{\partial y} \cdot \frac{\partial \sigma}{\partial y} + c \cdot \left(\frac{\partial^2 \sigma}{\partial x^2} + \frac{\partial^2 \sigma}{\partial y^2} \right) \right] = 0 \quad (7)$$

As we regard 5% derivation as the EM failure criteria, $\frac{\partial c}{\partial x}$, $\frac{\partial c}{\partial y} << c$, and finally we have:

$$\frac{\partial c}{\partial t} + \frac{Dc\Omega}{kT}\left(\frac{\partial^2 \sigma}{\partial x^2} + \frac{\partial^2 \sigma}{\partial y^2} \right) = 0 \qquad (8)$$

For a given TSV distribution and thermal profile, which result in a fixed σ and T, Eqn.8 is a simple ODE, leading to the following MTTF solution (we substitute D by Eqn.2 and notice that $\Omega\sigma << E_a$).

$$MTTF = \frac{kT \cdot exp(\frac{E_a}{kT})}{D_0\Omega \cdot \left(\frac{\partial^2 \sigma}{\partial x^2} + \frac{\partial^2 \sigma}{\partial y^2} \right)} \cdot ln\left(\frac{c_0}{c_t} \right) \qquad (9)$$

where c_0 is the initial atomic concentration, and c_t is the threshold concentration at which TSV fails.

4.2 TSV EM's Objective Function

In Eqn.9, $k, E_a, D_0, \Omega, c_0, c_t$ are all constants, therefore, for a given thermal and stress profile, Eqn.10 represents the intensity of a single TSV's EM. Therefore, in this paper, we use Eqn.10 as an objective function in optimizing TSV's EM. The following section validates our EM objective function to FEM-based simulation results.

$$OBJ\,(Single\,TSV): \frac{1}{T \cdot exp(\frac{E_a}{kT})} \cdot \left(\frac{\partial^2 \sigma}{\partial x^2} + \frac{\partial^2 \sigma}{\partial y^2} \right) \qquad (10)$$

4.3 Model Validation

Now we demonstrate that Eqn.10 is an accurate objective function for TSV's EM. We set up experiments to calculate the correlation coefficient between our objective function, Eqn.10, and FEM based simulation. Six cases of TSV placement configurations are employed in our experiment. All six cases are performed in an EM simulation framework in COMSOL, using the multi-physics mass transportation equation as in Eqn.1. Fig.2(a) indicates the single TSV case, where TSV's EM is caused solely by its own stress gradient. Fig.2(b)-(e) contain multiple TSVs, where the central TSV (yellow) is under influences of neighboring TSV's (blue) thermal mechanical stress field. We change the distance from central and neighboring TSV's center, d, from $5\mu m$ to $9\mu m$. Neighboring TSVs are randomly placed in the last case, as shown in Fig.2(f). The TSV's working temperature is set to 293 K for Fig.2(a) to (e), while random thermal map is applied in Fig.2(f).

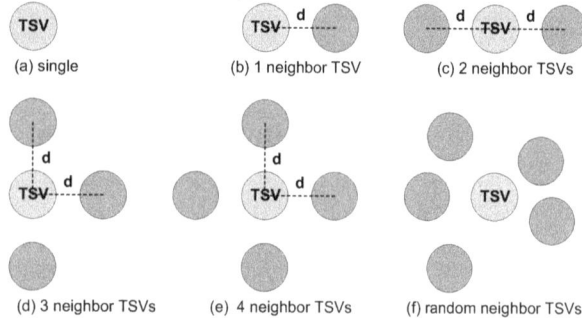

Figure 2: TSV placement configurations.

The FEM based simulation results are summarized in Fig.3. As the distance (d) between central and neighboring TSVs uniformly increases, TSV's MTTF increases. However, when TSV distance (d) is fixed, increasing the number of neighboring TSVs does not always degrade TSV's MTTF. For instance, Fig.3(b) has the fewest neighboring TSVs but the shortest MTTF value in all cases, while Fig.3(e) possesses the most neighboring TSVs but the longest MTTF value. This is because the configuration of neighboring TSVs in Fig.3(e) produces the lowest stress gradients on the central TSV. These observations imply that when multiple TSVs are present, the angle and relative distance between the central TSV and the neighboring TSVs are vital in deciding the central TSV's EM lifetime. In other words, the idea of simply keeping TSVs away from each other by applying KOZ might not guarantee the optimal EM reliability. A quantitative physics-based objective function, such as Eqn.10 is fundamentally better than the KOZ approach to account for TSV's mutual influences on stress as well as EM.

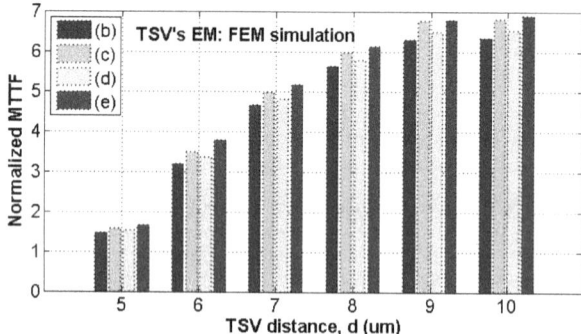

Figure 3: TSV's MTTF using FEM simulation for Fig.2(b)-(e), with various TSV distance.

Fig.4 presents the correlation between the MTTF values calculated from Eqn.9 using our objective function (Eqn.10) and MTTF from FEM simulation.

We use the Pearson's Correlation Coefficient (Pearson's r) to quantify the correlation between our objective function, and the FEM simulation result. Pearson's r is the normalized covariance among two vectors, which is a mathematical way of capturing how good a model is to the real data. As shown in Fig.4, our Pearson's r is 99.0%, meaning that our MTTF estimation function, Eqn.9, is well correlated with FEM simulation, thus accurately predicts the trends of TSV's EM.

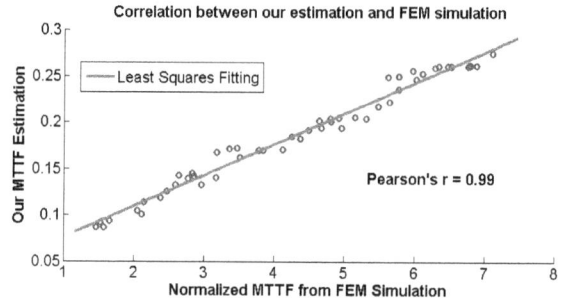

Figure 4: MTTF correlation between our estimation (Eqn.9) and FEM simulation (based on Eqn.1)

5. EM-AWARE DESIGN FLOW

Our EM-aware 3D clock synthesis design flow is summarized in Fig.5. In this paper, we assume the abstract clock tree is given. After performing the 3D-DME algorithm [9], we have an initial TSV placement. This initial TSV placement is determined such that the overall clock wire length is minimized. This is followed by chip-scale thermal simulation. We regard the logic cells (clock sinks) as power sources, and solve the heat transfer equation (Eqn.4) [15]. The next step is to rearrange the location of TSVs such that the clock TSVs' EM lifetime maximized, using an ILP formulation. Then we fix the clock TSV's locations, and layer-by-layer route the clock tree using 2D-DME algorithm [5] to ensure zero clock skew.

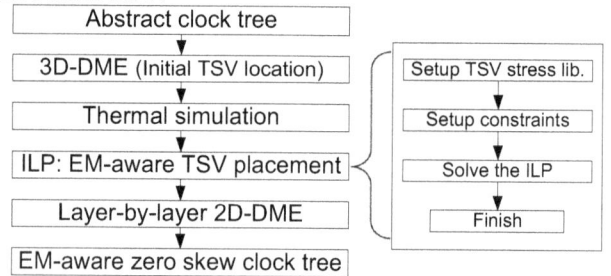

Figure 5: Design flow: EM-aware 3D clock synthesis.

The ILP step consists of three parts. Firstly we build up a clock TSV's temperature-dependent stress library. As explained earlier, the thermal mechanical stress at a certain point, σ, is a function of (1) neighboring TSVs' locations, and (2) the temperature at that point. In order to capture the stress value under various thermal profiles and TSV distributions, we set up a library to record the stress distribution for a single TSV, under various operating temperatures. When a TSV is surrounded by multiple neighboring TSVs, we extract from the library the stress distribution file at the corresponding temperature for each of the neighboring TSVs, and then apply the stress superposition principle (Eqn.5) to calculate the stress value at the central TSV. We use FEM to simulate a single TSV's thermal mechanical behavior under a set of operating temperatures, with fixed annealing temperature. Both the stress data inside the TSV and around the TSV (in silicon) are collected.

Secondly, we impose a placement bounding box (BB) to constrain the placement region for each clock TSV. This constraint mitigates the clock tree's wire length overhead, and can be tuned to adjust the trade-off between TSV's reliability and clock tree's overall wire length. At last the ILP problem is relaxed into an linear programming (LP) problem and is solved by any LP solver. The details of the ILP problem are elaborated in Section 6.

It is worth mentioning that another approach to deal with TSV's EM is simply applying KOZ for each clock TSV. By keeping TSVs far away from each other, KOZs help eliminate the mutual influences of TSVs' stress field thus the EM trend. However, KOZs occupy large layout area thus might be infeasible in case that layout whitespace is limited. Moreover, the discussions in Section.4.3 point out that the KOZ approach might produce sub-optimal results because it lacks the knowledge of how the stress field can affect TSV's EM. Section 7 will show our EM-aware TSV placement algorithm truly outperforms the KOZ approach.

6. TSV PLACMENT: AN ILP PROBLEM

In this section, we formally state the EM-aware clock TSV placement problem, formulate it as an ILP problem and then solve it using LP relaxation.

Problem Statement: Given an initial TSV distribution and a thermal profile, the EM-aware clock TSV placement problem attempts to optimize the location of each TSV, such that the maximum EM among all clock TSVs is minimized.

For illustration purpose, we assume 2-layer 3D-ICs in this section, although our algorithm can be extended to arbitrary number of layers as well, as we present in the result section. We assign each clock TSV a bounding box (BB). The BB is a set of layout whitespace grids that are near to the initial location of the clock TSV. Clock TSV can only move inside the corresponding BB. The BB is used to alleviate the wire length overhead when a clock TSV is moved from its "optimal" location from a pure wire length minimization standpoint (3D-DME). The size of BB is decided by the amount of wire length penalty we are willing to tolerate by the EM-aware TSV reallocation. Clock TSVs and their BBs are numbered from 1 to n, where n is the total number of clock TSVs. Each grid (i, j) inside k^{th} BB is associated with one unknown binary variable $x_{k,i,j}$, as indicated in Eqn.11. This formulation includes the situation where a grid could be associated with multiple variables if multiple BBs overlaps at this grid.

$$x_{k,i,j} = \begin{cases} 1, & if\ k^{th}\ TSV\ is\ located\ at\ grid\ (i,j); \\ 0, & otherwise. \end{cases} \quad (11)$$

We denote the stress value at grid (i, j) as $\sigma_{i,j}$. We also denote a single TSV's stress profile at temperature T as ξ^T. For a given logic placement, we assume its thermal profile is fixed. This is because the BBs only allow local changes in TSV's locations, thus we assume the transfer thermal resistance matrix in Eqn.4 is fixed when TSVs relocate. According to the stress superposition principle 5, when multiple TSVs are present, $\sigma_{i,j}$ can be expressed using the superposition rule by summing up the stress induced by each individual TSV, as follows.

$$\sigma_{i,j} = \sum_{a=1}^{m} \sum_{b=1}^{m} \xi_{a,b,i,j}^{T_{a,b}} \sum_{k=1}^{n} x_{k,a,b}. \quad (12)$$

where m is the horizontal mesh size, n is the total number of TSVs, $\xi_{a,b,i,j}^{T_{a,b}}$ is the stress value at the grid (i, j) induced by a single TSV centered at grid (a,b), and the term $\sum_{k=1}^{n} x_{k,a,b}$ denotes whether a TSV is placed at grid (a, b) or not. Since clock tree synthesis is performed after power planning and logic cell's placement, we only consider the stress field induced by clock TSVs, and other TSVs (power-ground, signal TSVs) have fixed locations thus their stress field is constant.

We assume the 3D-IC's EM lifetime is decided by the minimum MTTF among all TSVs, so we formulate an ILP problem to minimize the maximum TSV's EM. We impose two constraints: (1) the kth TSV is located inside k^{th} BB (constraint 13b), and (2) each grid (i, j) can have no more than

one TSV (constraint 13c).

$$Min \left(Max\ \frac{1}{T_{i,j} \cdot exp(\frac{E_a}{kT_{i,j}})} \cdot \left| \frac{\partial^2 \sigma_{i,j}}{\partial x^2} + \frac{\partial^2 \sigma_{i,j}}{\partial y^2} \right| \right) \quad (13a)$$

$$s.t. \sum_{i=1}^{m} \sum_{j=1}^{n} x_{k,i,j} = 1, \quad \forall k; \quad (13b)$$

$$\sum_{k=1}^{m} x_{k,i,j} \leq 1, \quad \forall (i,j); \quad (13c)$$

$$x_{k,i,j} = 0\ or\ 1, \quad \forall (k,i,j). \quad (13d)$$

where $T_{i,j}$ is the temperature at the grid (i, j), which is a fixed value under the assumption that all the clock sinks have fixed locations. Eqn.13 can be further transformed into the following equivalent form.

$$Min: f$$

$$s.t. \frac{1}{T_{i,j} \cdot exp(\frac{E_a}{kT_{i,j}})} \cdot \left(\frac{\partial^2 \sigma_{i,j}}{\partial x^2} + \frac{\partial^2 \sigma_{i,j}}{\partial y^2} \right) \leq f \quad (14a)$$

$$-\frac{1}{T_{i,j} \cdot exp(\frac{E_a}{kT_{i,j}})} \cdot \left(\frac{\partial^2 \sigma_{i,j}}{\partial x^2} + \frac{\partial^2 \sigma_{i,j}}{\partial y^2} \right) \leq f \quad (14b)$$

$$Constraints \quad (13b) - (13d)$$

where $\sigma_{i,j}$ is estimated by Eqn.12, while the seond-order stress term is linearized using forward difference method, as shown in Eqn.15.

$$\frac{\partial^2 \sigma_{i,j}}{\partial x^2} + \frac{\partial^2 \sigma_{i,j}}{\partial y^2} = \frac{\sigma_{i+1,j} + \sigma_{i-1,j} - 2\sigma_{i,j}}{\triangle^2} + \frac{\sigma_{i,j+1} + \sigma_{i,j-1} - 2\sigma_{i,j}}{\triangle^2}. \quad (15)$$

where $\triangle$ is the mesh size.

Eqn.14 is an ILP problem, in which the binary integer constraint can be relaxed to $0 \leq x_{k,i,j} \leq 1$, and we use efficient LP solvers to solve the resulting LP as a heuristic.

7. RESULTS AND DISCUSSIONS

We implement our algorithms in Matlab and C++, by an Intel Core i5 3.1GHz CPU and 12GB RAM.

7.1 Simulation setup

We evaluate the performance of our EM-aware 3D clock tree synthesis design flow based on the benchmark circuits from ISPD clock network synthesis contest [2]. Since the benchmark circuits are originally designed for 2D chip (with an area of A), we randomly partition all the clock sinks into N layers, with an area of $\frac{A}{N}$ on each layer. Although our algorithm can be applied to arbitrary number of layers, in this paper, we focus on 4-layer 3D-ICs ($N = 4$) for simplicity. For a given TSV bound, we generate the abstract clock tree, starting from a root node, in a top-down manner: (1) if there's only one TSV available, the clock sinks which have the same Z index as the root node form one child of the rood node, while all other sinks form the other child. (2) Otherwise the 3D-IC's layout is partitioned into two sub-layout, in X/Y plane, and the same top-down partition is applied recursively. Our approach is similar to the 3D-MMM algorithm proposed by Zhao et al [16].

Since clock tree synthesis is usually performed after floor-planning and placement, where limited whitespace is available, we randomly generate several layout whitespaces for clock TSVs, where clock TSVs are placed. We also assign random power dissipations for clock sinks. We also assume conventional air cooling is applied at the top of the 3D-IC while all other sides are adiabatic. The ambient temperature $T_{ambient}$ is 293K.

The ILP problem proposed in Section 6 is solved by an academic solver called Mosek [3].

Table 1: WL and MTTF comparison between 3D-DME and our EM-aware 3D clock tree design flow. WL=wire length (μm), MTTF = Mean time to failure (normalized)

ckt	Area constr.	3D-DME		Our design flow		Increase (%)	
		WL	MTTF	WL	MTTF	WL	MTTF
f11	strict	124963	0.93	128077	4.34	2.5	366.7
	medium	124421	1.01	125541	5.32	0.9	426.7
	loose	124159	1.27	124268	6.61	0.1	420.5
f12	strict	74313	1.05	75982	4.33	2.2	312.4
	medium	74177	1.14	76261	5.28	2.8	363.2
	loose	73741	1.42	75257	6.69	2.1	371.1
f21	strict	91813	0.91	92909	4.18	1.2	359.3
	medium	91665	1.11	92889	5.34	1.3	381.1
	loose	91481	1.37	92646	6.59	1.3	381.0
f22	strict	58649	1.11	60647	5.08	3.4	357.7
	medium	58247	1.26	59709	5.17	2.5	310.3
	loose	58064	1.41	59697	6.78	2.8	380.9
f31	strict	219663	0.81	239848	1.52	9.2	87.7
	medium	219434	0.92	225931	5.04	3.0	447.8
	loose	219146	1.13	223972	6.24	2.2	452.2
f32	strict	176892	0.97	187927	4.05	6.2	317.5
	mediu	175488	1.09	185708	5.13	5.8	370.6
	loose	175300	1.21	184187	6.47	5.1	434.7
Avg	-	-	-	-	-	3.0	363.4

Table 2: WL and MTTF comparison between KOZ design and our EM-aware 3D clock tree design flow.

ckt	Area constr.	Keep-out-zone (KOZ) design						EM-aware versus *best* KOZ	
		d =6 um		d =7 um		d = 8 um		Increase(%)	
		WL	MTTF	WL	MTTF	WL	MTTF	WL	MTTF
f11	strict	**125087**	**3.16**	INF	INF	INF	INF	2.4	37.3
	med.	124562	3.23	**124597**	**4.21**	INF	INF	0.8	26.4
	loose	124141	3.62	124274	4.48	**124305**	**6.05**	0.0	9.3
f12	strict	**75102**	**3.18**	INF	INF	INF	INF	1.2	36.2
	med.	74754	3.34	**75487**	**4.34**	INF	INF	1.0	21.7
	loose	74103	3.85	74978	4.98	**75484**	**6.21**	-0.3	7.7
f21	strict	**92468**	**3.12**	INF	INF	INF	INF	0.5	34.0
	med.	92003	3.20	**92688**	**4.39**	INF	INF	0.2	21.6
	loose	91870	3.72	92104	4.85	**92371**	**6.14**	0.3	7.3
f22	strict	59143	3.28	**59736**	**4.15**	INF	INF	1.5	22.4
	med.	58954	3.57	**59427**	**4.41**	INF	INF	0.5	17.2
	loose	58455	3.82	58571	5.04	**60271**	**6.22**	-1.0	9.0
f31	strict	INF	INF	INF	INF	INF	INF	-	-
	med.	224584	2.95	**227749**	**4.01**	INF	INF	-0.8	25.7
	loose	220680	3.31	221478	4.36	**230463**	**5.77**	-2.8	8.1
f32	strict	**182107**	**3.04**	INF	INF	INF	INF	3.2	33.2
	med.	180037	3.19	**182140**	**4.15**	INF	INF	2.0	23.6
	loose	178013	3.35	179877	4.42	**185462**	**6.07**	-0.7	6.6
Avg	-	-	-	-	-	-	-	0.7	23.0

"INF" = Infeasible.

7.2 TSV stress library

We perform single TSV's thermal mechanical stress simulation in COMSOL Multiphysics [1], a finite element solver. TSV's annealing temperature is set to be 573K. 51 TSV stress files are created to store the stress value with a TSV's temperature varying from 293K to 393K.

7.3 3D clock tree's MTTF and wire length

Our simulation results are summarized in Table.1. Three sets of layout whitespace constraint (for clock TSV placement) are imposed on six ISPD benchmarks (strict = $6400\mu m^2$, medium = $10000\mu m^2$, loose = $14400\mu m^2$). Total wire length and MTTF values using traditional 3D-DME based clock tree synthesis approach, are also shown as a comparison. In 3D-DME, d, the minimum distance between two TSVs' center, is set to be 5 μm. Table.1 shows that compared to 3D-DME, our EM-aware design improves the TSV's MTTF in every benchmark, and on average, we enhances the TSV's MTTF by 3.63**x**, with only 3% wire length overhead. Note that our EM-aware design flow still ensures zero clock skew because of the layer-by-layer 2D-DME procedure.

The KOZ based approach, is also implemented, as shown in Table.2. For each area constraint in each benchmark, we enumerate d from $6\mu m$ to $8\mu m$. As d increases, KOZ becomes larger and the mutual stress and EM influences between neighboring TSVs becomes less thus MTTF values increases. However, with limited availability of layout whitespace, TSV placement with a large KOZ might be infeasible (represented as "INF" in the table). Wire length and MTTF results using our EM-aware design flow (shown in Table.1) are compared to the *best* (in terms of MTTF) feasible KOZ-based design, which are highlighted in **bold**, and the increases in both wire length (WL) and MTTF values are listed in the last two columns.

Compared to the *best* KOZ based design, on average our EM-aware design flow is still better, with 23.0% longer MTTF, and only 0.7% wire length overhead.

8. CONCLUSION

This paper proposes an EM-aware clock tree synthesis design flow for 3D-ICs. A simple TSV's EM objective function is derived and validated. We formulate an ILP problem to place clock TSVs such that 3D clock tree's EM reliability is maximized. Results show that our algorithm is able to produce a zero-skew EM-robust 3D clock tree, which possesses 3.63**x** higher MTTF, compared to 3D-DME based

EM-unaware design flow, and 23.0% higher MTTF, compared to the *best* KOZ-based approach, with negligible wire length overhead.

Acknowledgment

The authors acknowledge that this work has been funded by NSF grant 0917057.

9. REFERENCES

[1] COMSOL Multiphysics. http://www.comsol.com/.
[2] Ispd 2009 clock network synthesis contest. http://ispd.cc/contests/09/ispd09cts.html.
[3] Mosek. http://www.mosek.com/.
[4] J. Black. Mass transport of aluminum by momentum exchange with conducting electrons. In *Reliability Physics Symposium*, pages 1 – 6, 2005.
[5] T.-H. Chao, et al. Zero skew clock routing with minimum wirelength. *IEEE Transactions on Circuits and Systems II: Analog and Digital Signal Processing*, 1992.
[6] T. Frank, et al. Reliability of TSV interconnects: Electromigration, thermal cycling, and impact on above metal level dielectric. *Microelectronics Reliability*, pages 17 – 29, 2013.
[7] L. L. JianPing Jing and G. Meng. Electromigration Simulation for Metal Lines. *Journal of Electronic Packaging*, 2010.
[8] M. Jung, et al. TSV stress-aware full-chip mechanical reliability analysis and optimization for 3D IC. In *Design Automation Conference*, pages 188–193, 2011.
[9] T.-Y. Kim and T. Kim. Clock Tree Synthesis for TSV-based 3D IC Designs. *ACM Trans. Des. Autom. Electron. Syst.*, 2011.
[10] K.-Y. Lee, et al. Fast and Optimal Redundant Via Insertion. *IEEE Transactions on Computer-Aided Design of Integrated Circuits and Systems*, pages 2197–2208, Dec 2008.
[11] J. Pak, et al. Electromigration-aware routing for 3D ICs with stress-aware EM modeling. In *IEEE/ACM International Conference on Computer-Aided Design*, pages 325–332, 2012.
[12] J. Pak, et al. Modeling of electromigration in through-silicon-via based 3D IC. In *Electronic Components and Technology Conference (ECTC)*, pages 1420–1427, 2011.
[13] M. Pathak, et al. Electromigration modeling and full-chip reliability analysis for BEOL interconnect in TSV-based 3D ICs. In *IEEE/ACM International Conference on Computer-Aided Design*, pages 555–562, 2011.
[14] Y. Shang, et al. Thermal-reliable 3D clock-tree synthesis considering nonlinear electrical-thermal-coupled TSV model. In *Asia and South Pacific Design Automation Conference*, pages 693–698, 2013.
[15] C.-H. Tsai and S.-M. Kang. Cell-level Placement for Improving Substrate Thermal Distribution. *Trans. Comp.-Aided Des. Integ. Cir. Sys.*, pages 253–266, Nov. 2006.
[16] X. Zhao, et al. Low-Power and Reliable Clock Network Design for Through-Silicon Via (TSV) Based 3D ICs. *IEEE Transactions on Components, Packaging and Manufacturing Technology*, 2011.

Layout Characterization and Power Density Analysis for Shorted-Gate and Independent-Gate 7nm FinFET Standard Cells

Tiansong Cui, Bowen Chen, Yanzhi Wang, Shahin Nazarian and Massoud Pedram
University of Southern California
Los Angeles, CA, USA
{tcui, bowenche, yanzhiwa, shahin, pedram}@usc.edu

ABSTRACT

In this paper, a power density analysis is presented for 7nm FinFET technology node based on both shorted-gate (SG) and independent-gate (IG) standard cells operating in multiple supply voltage regimes. A Liberty-formatted standard cell library is constructed by selecting the appropriate number of fins for the pull-up and pull-down networks of each logic cell. Next, each cell is characterized by doing SPICE simulations to calculate the propagation delays and output transition times as a function of input transition times and load capacitance values. Finally, the power density of 7nm FinFET technology node is analyzed and compared with the 45 nm CMOS technology node for different circuits. Experimental result shows that the power density of each 7nm FinFET circuit is 3-20 times larger than that of 45nm CMOS circuit under the spacer-defined technology. Experimental result also shows that the back-gate signal enables a better control of power consumption for independent-gate FinFETs.

Categories and Subject Descriptors

B.8.2 [**Performance and Reliability**]: Performance Analysis and Design Aids

Keywords

FinFET; Layout; Power Density; Independent Gate Control

1. INTRODUCTION

Thermal effect has gained growing attention to VLSI designers due to the increasing packing density and power consumption of VLSI circuits [1]. The need to reduce the power consumption of digital circuits in order to meet thermal constraints has caused aggressive voltage scaling from the traditional super-threshold regime to the near/sub-threshold regime[2][3]. In addition, with the dramatic downscaling of layout geometries, the traditional bulk CMOS technology is facing significant challenges due to several reasons such as the increasing leakage power and short-channel effects (SCEs) [4]. FinFET devices, a special kind of quasi-planar double gate devices, have attracted a lot of attention as an alternative to the bulk CMOS when technology scales beyond the 32nm technology node, owing to their superior performance [5][6], better scalability

GLSVLSI'15, May 20–22, 2015, Pittsburgh, PA, USA.
Copyright 2015 ACM 978-1-4503-3474-7/15/05 $15.00
http://dx.doi.org/10.1145/2742060.2742093.

[7], lower leakage [8], and stronger immunization to process variations [9].

Due to the promising future of the nanoscale FinFET devices, considerable research efforts have been made to study their models and characteristics. Among all of them, a unique feature of FinFET devices is the independent gate control, i.e., the front gate and the back gate can be controlled by separate signals, which enables more flexible circuit designs [10]. Due to the capacitor coupling of the front gate and the back gate, the threshold voltage of the front-gate-controlled FET varies in response to the back gate biasing, and vice versa [11]. Previous work [12] utilized the independent gate control for FinFETs in the pull-down network of an SRAM cell to keep the $20\,pA/\mu m$ standby power budget, whereas the authors of [13] studied joint gate sizing and negative biasing on the back gate of FinFET devices and demonstrated significant power reduction.

Although the fabrication and application of independent gate control in FinFET devices have been well researched, none of the previous works have focused on the thermal-effect analysis caused by independent gate control, especially for future ultra-scaled FinFETs. Considering that power-density has a strong and direct impact on the thermal characteristics of VLSI circuits, we present a power density analysis for 7nm FinFET technology node operating in super-threshold and near-threshold operation regimes, including both shorted-gate (SG) and independent-gate (IG) devices based on a created Liberty-formatted standard cell library [?]. For each logic cell in this library, we select the appropriate number of fins for the pull-up and pull-down networks, calculate the delay and power parameters, and then use the lambda-based layout design rules to characterize the FinFET cell layout. All cell layouts are designed using the same height to help with floorplanning flexibility, cell interconnection, and eventually area reduction. Finally, the power density of the 7nm FinFET technology node is analyzed and compared with the state-of-the-art 45nm CMOS technology node for different ISCAS benchmarks by calculating the ratio of total power consumption and estimated area. Experimental results confirm that the power density of a circuit in 7nm FinFET node can be at least 3 to 20 times larger than that in 45nm CMOS node under the spacer-defined technology. In addition, we also apply different voltage levels to the back-gate signal of the independent-gate cells. It shows that the back-gate signal enables a better control of power consumption for independent-gate FinFETs.

The rest of this paper is organized as follows. Section 2 introduces the properties of 7nm FinFET devices including the independent gate control. Section 3 explains the library format and characterization flow. The layout characterization details are elaborated in Section 4. We show the synthesis results as well as the power density reports in Section 5 and conclude the paper in Section 6.

2. BACKGROUND

FinFET devices show better suppression of the short channel effect, lower energy consumption, higher supply voltage scaling capability, and higher ON/OFF current ratio compared with the bulk CMOS counterparts [6]. In this paper, we focus on 7nm Fin-FET technology node including both shorted-gate and independent-gate FinFET devices operating in both near-threshold and super-threshold supply voltage regimes. Near-threshold operation regime achieves reduced energy consumption at the cost of degradation of circuit speed. To enable both low power and high performance applications, we perform power density analysis under two supply voltages: 0.3V for near-threshold regime and 0.45V for super-threshold regime.

2.1 7nm FinFET Technology Node

The structure of a 7nm FinFET device is shown in Figure 1. The FinFET device consists of a thin silicon body with thickness of T_{fin}, which is wrapped by gate electrodes. The device is termed quasi-planar as the current flows in parallel with the wafer plane, and the channel is formed perpendicular to the plane. The effective gate length L_G is twice as large as the fin height h_{fin}. The spacer length L_{SP} is an important design parameter that directly relates to the short channel effects [14]. The FinFET structure allows for fabrication of separate front and back gates. In this structure, each fin is essentially the parallel connection of the front-gate-controlled FET and the back-gate-controlled FET, both with a width equal to the fin height h_{fin}.

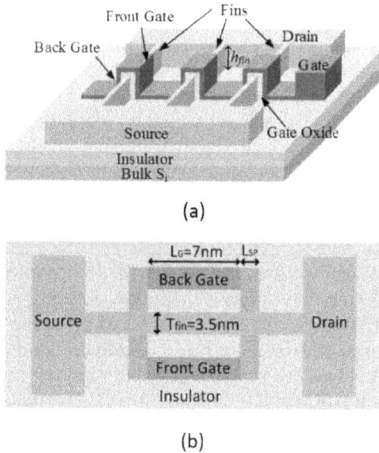

(a)

(b)

Figure 1: (a) Perspective view and (b) top view of the 7nm FinFET device.

2.2 Independent Gate Control for FinFET Devices

A unique feature of FinFET devices is the independent gate control, where the front and back gates can be tied to the same or different control signals, allowing for more flexible circuit designs. Due to capacitor coupling of the front gate and the back gate of a FinFET transistor, the threshold voltage of the front-gate-controlled FET varies in response to the back-gate voltage, and vice versa [15]. Figure 2 shows the relationship between the threshold voltage of the front-gate-controlled FET and the back-gate voltage from the Hspice simulation. Under a relatively small back-gate voltage, a linear relationship between the change of the threshold voltage of front-gate and the back-gate voltage is observed (suppose that we consider N-type FETs).

The unique feature of independent gate control is exploited in previous works [10]-[13], where different implementation modes of FinFET logic gates are proposed and applied. For the N-type or P-type fin, there are two different connection modes: (i) the shorted-gate (SG) mode, where the front gate and the back gate of the fin are tied together to the input signal, and (ii) the independent gate (IG) mode, where one of the gate is driven by the input signal

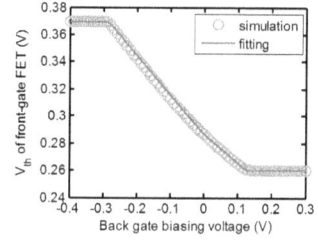

Figure 2: V_{th} of the front-gate-controlled N-type FET vs. back-gate voltage.

and the other is connected to a pre-defined biasing voltage or to the ground. For multiple-input logic cells (e.g., NAND, NOR), there is another IG mode connection where the front gate and back gate are driven by different input signals [16]. These different modes achieve a trade-off between power consumption and rise/fall delay. We illustrate in Figure 3 three examples of implementing a FinFET NAND gate.

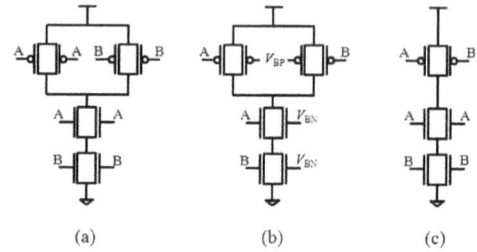

(a)   (b)   (c)

Figure 3: Different FinFET-based NAND gate designs.

In this paper, we perform power density analysis based on both shorted-gate and independent-gate 7nm FinFET standard cells. FinFETs operating designed in shorted-gate mode offer the highest driving strength [17], and we consider shorted-gate FinFETs operating in both near-threshold and super-threshold regimes. On the other hand, independent-gate FinFETs are often used in low power implementations, where a reverse-biasing voltage (i.e., the biasing voltage is low for nFETs and high for pFETs) is used to reduce subthreshold leakage [17]. As a result, we consider independent-gate FinFETs operating in only near-threshold regime, but apply different biasing voltage levels.

3. 7NM FINFET STANDARD CELL LIBRARY CHARACTERIZATION

The main goal of this paper is to perform thermal analysis on a given FinFET circuit, which requires the gate-level implementation of the circuit (in shorted-gate mode or independent-gate mode) and thus the characterization of standard cell library is needed. A standard cell library is a set of high-quality timing and power models that accurately and efficiently capture the behavior of standard cells. The standard cell library is widely used in many design tools for different purposes, such as logic synthesis, static timing analysis, power analysis, high-level design language simulation, and so on, as part of Computer-Aided-Design (CAD). The Liberty library format (.lib), which was first invented by Synopsys a decade ago, has become an industrial standard that is adopted by over 100 semi-conductor vendors and implemented in over 75 production electronic design automation (EDA) tools [?]. Therefore, we build our 7nm FinFET standard cell library in the .lib format. The two major steps of building this library are standard cell sizing and power/timing parameter characterization.

Table 1: Summary of logic cells included in 7nm FinFET standard cell library

Logic Cell	SG Scale	IG Scale
Inverter	1X, 2X, 4X, 8X	1X, 2X
2-input NAND	1X, 2X, 4X, 8X	1X
3-input NAND	1X, 2X, 4X	1X
2-input NOR	1X, 2X, 4X, 8X	1X
3-input NOR	1X, 2X, 4X	1X
AND-OR-INV	1X, 2X, 4X	1X
OR-AND-INV	1X, 2X, 4X	1X
XOR	1X, 2X	1X
XNOR	1X, 2X	1X
MUX	1X, 2X	1X
Latch	1X	1X
D-flip-flop	1X	1X
D-flip-flop w/ S/R	1X	1X

3.1 Standard Cell Sizing

The driving strength of a short-gate or independent-gate Fin-FET device depends on the ratio of fin height and channel length, while both parameters are determined by the fabrication technology. Thus, the FinFET standard cell sizing involves selecting the appropriate number of fins for the pull-up network and pull-down network of each logic cell. The general sizing method is to balance the rise and fall delays of a standard cell. We first investigate the numbers of P-type fins and N-type fins in an inverter that achieve approximately equal rise and fall delays. According to the transregional FinFET model [18], the drain current of a FinFET in the sub- and near-threshold regimes is given by

$$I_{ds} = I_0 e^{\frac{(V_{gs}+\lambda V_{ds}-V_{th})-\alpha(V_{gs}+\lambda V_{ds}-V_{th})^2}{m \cdot v_T}} (1 - e^{\frac{-V_{ds}}{v_T}}) \quad (1)$$

where λ is the drain voltage dependency coefficient (similar to but much smaller than the DIBL coefficient for bulk CMOS devices), v_T is the thermal voltage, and I_0, α, and m are technology-dependent parameters to be derived using Hspice simulation. In order to achieve equal rise and fall delay, the number of P-type fins N_P in an inverter can be determined by

$$N_P = N_N \cdot \frac{I_{ds,N}}{I_{ds,P}} \quad (2)$$

where $I_{ds,N}(I_{ds,P})$ is the drain current of an N-type(P-type) fin when $|V_{gs}| = |V_{ds}| = V_{DD}$, and N_N is the number of N-type fins in the inverter. Based on equation (2) and Hspice simulation, the N_P/N_N ratio can be determined for different size of inverters. We observe that the driving strengths of P-type and N-type fins are balanced for both shorted-gate and independent-gate FinFET inverters using the same size.

We also use the method described in [18] to solve the stack sizing problem and design other combinational and sequential logic cells in near-threshold regime. All the logic cells included in the 7nm FinFET standard cell library are summarized in Table 1. Please note that: (i) For shorted-gate cells, we use the same sizing of FinFET logic cells in the super-threshold regime ($V_{DD} = 0.45V$), since we assume our standard cells support DVFS (dynamic voltage and frequency scaling); (ii) As independent-gate logic cells are designed for low-power use, we include only 1X and 2X scales for inverter and 1X scale for all the other cells.

3.2 Power/Timing Parameter Characterization

When the number of fins of each standard cell is determined, the timing parameters and power parameters need to be calculated and stored in 2D look-up-tables (LUTs) in the input/output pin-level [?]. We obtain the timing and power parameters of each logic cell of interest through Hspice simulations at various input and output conditions based on the Verilog-A based 7nm FinFET device mod-

el. The timing parameters of a logic cell refer to propagation delays and transition times of the output pin when the output makes a transition. For sequential cells such as D flip-flops and latches, the timing parameters also include time check parameters such as the setup time and hold time of the data signal, and the recovery time and removal time of asynchronous control signals. The propagation delays and transition times are represented by using 2D LUTs, which are indexed by input transition times and capacitive load at the output pin. The power parameters in the Liberty library include the leakage power and internal power of a logic cell. The overall power consumption is evaluated by summing up the leakage power, internal power, and switching power (power consumed when charging and discharging the capacitive load). The internal power accounts for the short-circuit power consumption and dynamic power of the diffusion capacitors at the output pin of the logic cell. Also 2D LUTs are used to store internal power values of the output pin related to each input pin. Detailed characterization steps are omitted in this paper because of space limit.

4. 7NM FINFET STANDARD LAYOUT CHARACTERIZATION

The standard cell library characterization enables synthesis and total power estimation of a certain circuit. In order to analyze the power density of 7nm FinFET technology, we also estimate the total area consumption of a given circuit by designing the layout of each cell based on the lambda-based layout design rules for FinFET devices. In this section, we present the layout of each standard cell based on the sizing result of the previous section, including both shorted-gate and independent-gate cells. Our FinFET layout design rules also consider the interconnection between different cells.

4.1 FinFET Layout Design Rules

General understanding of the FinFET layout density is challenged by its dependence on the specific technology adopted to manufacture the "fin" (which is the core of FinFET) [19]. Figure 4 shows the comparison between the layout of a general CMOS device and a shorted-gate FinFET device with four fins. In this FinFET layout structure, a single strip is used for the gate terminal, while source and drain terminals of multiple fins are connected together through a metal wire to make a wider FinFET device. This is different from CMOS devices.

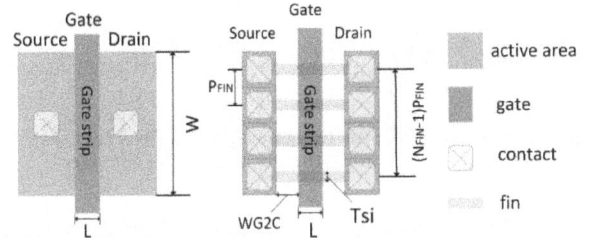

Figure 4: Layout of (a) a general CMOS device and (b) a shorted gate FinFET device with four fins.

In this section, we used the modified lambda-based layout design rules to characterize the layout of each FinFET logic cell. Authors in [20] have reported the major process-related FinFET geometries for 5nm technology and similar values can be derived for 7nm technology, which is shown in Table 2. The detailed process design rules are also included in this table. Notice that generally the layout design rules are similar for CMOS and FinFET technologies because the major difference is on fin fabrication [21]. One critical process-related geometry for FinFET devices shown in Figure 4 is the fin pitch, P_{FIN}, which is defined as the minimum center-to-center distance of two adjacent parallel fins. The value of P_{FIN} is determined by the underlying FinFET technology. More precisely, there are two types of FinFET technologies: (1) lithography-defined technology where lithographic constraints limit the fin pitch spacing, and (2) spacer-defined technology which relaxes the constraints on P_{FIN}, and obtains 2x reduction in the value of P_{FIN} at the cost of a more elaborate and costly lithographic process [22]. In this paper, we focus on the layout characterization of 7nm spacer-defined technology in order to perform a pessimistic estimation on power density in 7nm FinFET technology node.

Table 2: FinFET-specific geometries and design rules

Parameter	Value in 7nm FinFET (nm)	Value in 5nm FinFET (nm)	Comment
L_{FIN}	$2\lambda = 7$	$2\lambda = 7$	Fin length
T_{SI}	3.5	2.725	Fin width
H_{FIN}	14	10.9	Fin height
P_{FIN}	$3\lambda = 10.5$	$3\lambda = 7.5$	Fin pitch using spacer lithography
t_{ox}	1.55	1.09	Oxide thickness
W_C	$3\lambda = 10.5$	$3\lambda = 7.5$	Minimum contact size
W_{M2M}	$3\lambda = 10.5$	$3\lambda = 7.5$	Minimum space between metal wires
W_{G2C}	$2\lambda = 7$	$2\lambda = 5$	Minimum space of gate to contact

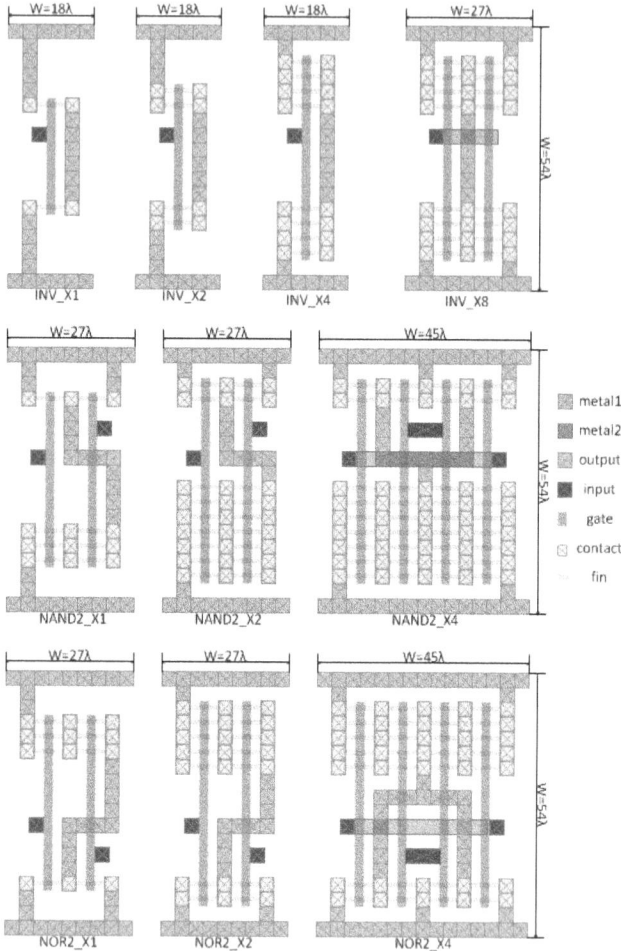

Figure 5: 7nm FinFET shorted-gate layout of inverters, 2-input NAND gates and 2-input NOR gates with different sizes

4.2 7nm FinFET Shorted-Gate Standard Cell Layout

Based on FinFET-specific geometries and design rules, the layouts of shorted-gate standard cells can be determined according to the sizing results of each logic cell, which has been shown in Section 3.1. To achieve higher layout flexibility, the number of fins for certain cells has been slightly adjusted. In addition, considering both area consumption and floorplanning flexibility, all the standard cell layouts are designed with the same height. We set the height of all the cells the same as the standard 2-input 2X NAND (equivalently 2X NOR and 4X inverter) cell in order to achieve the best tradeoff between design flexibility and area waste. These three types of cells occupy over 40% of the total number of cells based on our experimental result for different ISCAS benchmarks, and we have verified that using these three types of cells to determine the standard height will achieve the smallest total area consumption for ISCAS circuits. The shared diffusion and width extension can be

used when we design the layout of larger cells. Figure 5 shows the layout geometry of some basic cells with different sizes. In our standard cell library, all the gates are designed with a fixed height of 54λ. Inverter 1X, 2X and 4X gates achieve an active width of 27λ and the 2-input NAND gates of both 1X and 2X sizes have an active width of 27λ. The 8X inverter and 2-input 4X NAND gate have active widths of 27λ and 45λ respectively by using shared diffusion and width extension. 2-input NOR gate has the same area consumption as 2-input NAND gate of the corresponding size. Notice that the active width has already included the layout interconnect overhead, which is shared by 6λ per cell.

4.3 7nm FinFET Independent-Gate Standard Cell Layout

The introduction of the independent-gate FinFET brings more associated design rules. After the separation of the gate electrodes, each gate segment must be contacted electrically [23]. Therefore, a contact must be placed on the gate poly line between each pair of fins. A major design rule affecting the IG FinFET layout is the "CA over PC to RX" rule [23]. This rule adds a space of W_{M2M} to the distance between two adjacent fins in order to place a contact on every gate segment between every pair of fins, as seen in Figure 6.

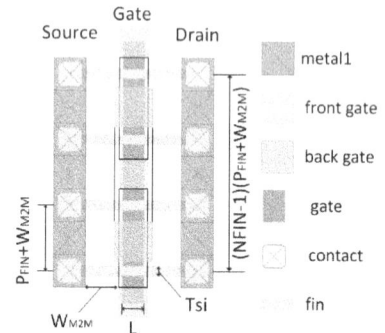

Figure 6: Layout of an independent gate FinFET device with four fins.

The layout of independent-gate standard cells is shown in Figure 7. To maintain the compatibility of FinFET standard cells in different modes, all the IG standard cell layouts are designed with the same height of SG standard cells. In addition, considering that the back-gate control (for Pfet or Nfet) is a kind of global signal, we align the back-gate control signals of different standard cells in order to make it easier for interconnection. The width of IG standard cell turns out to be a little wider than the SG standard cell of the same size.

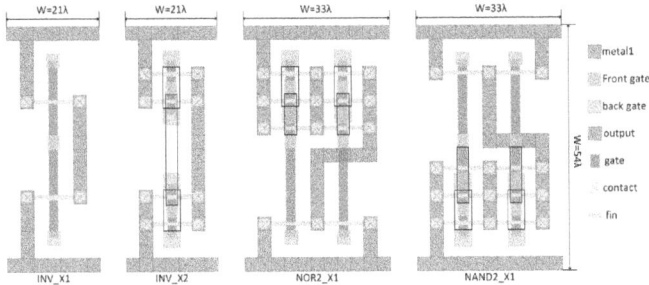

Figure 7: 7nm FinFET independent-gate layout of inverters, 2-input NAND gates and 2-input NOR gates

Table 3: 7nm FinFET Standard Cell Layout Geometries

Cell Type	SG Active Width (λ)	IG Active Width (λ)
Inverter	18, 18, 18, 27	21, 21
2-input NAND	27, 27, 45, 81	33
3-input NAND	36, 63, 117	45
2-input NOR	27, 27, 45, 81	33
3-input NOR	36, 63, 117	45
AND-OR-INV	36, 63, 117	45
OR-AND-INV	36, 63, 117	45
XOR	60, 87	77
XNOR	60, 87	77
MUX	81, 129	105
Latch	90	117
D-flip-flop	156	205
D-flip-flop w/ S/R	192	253

According to the FinFET-specific layout design rules as well as our fixed-height design method, the layout of combinational logic cells and the sequential logic cells can be derived accordingly. The geometries of all the logic cells included in the 7nm FinFET standard cell library are summarized in Table 3.

5. EXPERIMENTAL RESULT AND POWER DENSITY ANALYSIS

To predict the power density values in 7nm FinFET technology, we synthesize various ISCAS benchmark circuits using the developed FinFET standard cell library for both shorted gate mode (in super-threshold regime and near-threshold regime) and independent-gate mode (in near-threshold regime). The power density value is calculated as the ratio of power consumption and the total area of the circuit. We use 45nm CMOS technology for comparison because there are widely-received libraries and thermal analysis results in this technology node. The same circuits are synthesized using the 45nm CMOS library developed by North Carolina State University (NCSU). All benchmark circuits are synthesized by Synopsys Design Compiler.

In order to estimate the power consumption of each circuit in reality, we assume the circuit is operating in a processor with a frequency of f and also we consider an activity factor α, which determines the circuit switching activity. The average power consumption of a circuit can be calculated using:

$$P_{average} = P_{leakage} + \alpha \cdot P_{dynamic} \cdot D \cdot f, \quad (3)$$

where both the leakage power $P_{leakage}$ and the dynamic power $P_{dynamic}$ can be found in the power report from Design Compiler. The value D in this equation represents the circuit delay (which can be found in the timing report) and thus $P_{dynamic} \cdot D$ is the average energy consumption per clock cycle (in other words the average energy consumed inside a circuit when it operates on a new input value). In this paper, the α value is set to be 0.2 and we assume the

circuit is operating under a frequency of 500Mz when estimating the average power consumption. Our estimated power density of 45nm CMOS technology matches the previously reported value, which is around $140mW/mm^2$ [24].

We first analyze the power density comparison between 7nm FinFET shorted-gate circuit and 45nm CMOS circuit for different ISCAS benchmarks, which is summarized in Table 4. One can observe that the power density of 7nm FinFET SG circuits can reach over $1500mW/mm^2$ in near-threshold regime and over $2500mW/mm^2$ in super-threshold regime. These values are much higher than the limit of air cooling (around $1000mW/mm^2$ [25]) and careful thermal management will be needed for FinFET devices operating in shorted-gate mode. Notice that the power density in 7nm FinFET technology can be even higher than these values, because we assume the operating frequency is the same for 45nm CMOS and 7nm FinFET technologies, while in reality, FinFET circuits achieve a much better delay and thus the operating frequency can be higher than that of 45nm CMOS circuits [14].

We also apply different back-gate voltage levels to 7nm IG FinFET circuits, and Table 5 summarizes the power density values of IG FinFET designed ISCAS benchmarks. The reverse biasing voltage level V_{bias} is set to be 0.05V, 0V and -0.05V. We apply V_{bias} to the back-gate voltage of nFETs while the back-gate voltage of pFETs is connected to a voltage level of $(V_{dd} - V_{bias})$. It can be observed that IG FinFET circuits achieve much lower power density values compared with DG FinFET circuits, but even the lowest power density of IG FinFET circuits is still 3 times larger than that of the 45nm CMOS circuit. In addition, the power consumption (as well as the power density) for independent-gate FinFETs can be effectively controlled by the voltage level of V_{bias} because back-gate biasing voltage has an impact on the threshold voltage of the front-gate, which will then affect both dynamic power and leakage power consumption. However, the circuit performance will also be degraded when we reduce the voltage level of V_{bias}. In real FinFET circuit design, we might need to find a suitable V_{bias} level in order to achieve an optimal tradeoff between power density and circuit performance.

Notice that the layouts of shorted-gate and independent-gate FinFET standard cells are designed to be compatible with each other. One might include both SG and IG FinFET standard cells in the library of synthesis, which will result in a circuit with both shorted-gate and independent-gate FinFET devices. The power density of this circuit will be between that of the corresponding pure SG FinFET circuit and pure IG FinFET circuit.

6. CONCLUSION

Nanoscale FinFET devices are emerging as the transistor of choice because they allow for higher voltage scalability and design flexibility. In this paper, we present a power density analysis for 7nm FinFET devices under multiple supply voltage regimes, including shorted-gate and independent-gate standard cells and considering both high performance and low power usage. A Liberty-formatted standard cell library is built and the layout of each cell is characterized based on the lambda-based layout design rules for FinFET devices. Finally, the power density of 7nm FinFET technology node is analyzed and compared with the advanced 45nm CMOS technology node for different circuits. It has been confirmed that under spacer-defined technology, the power density of each 7nm FinFET circuit is about 3 to 20 times larger than that of the same circuit in 45nm CMOS node. We have also shown that the back-gate signal enables a better control of power consumption as well as power density for independent-gate FinFETs.

7. ACKNOWLEDGMENTS

This research is sponsored in part by grants from the PERFECT program of the Defense Advanced Research Projects Agency.

Table 4: Power density analysis for 7nm shorted-gate FinFET and 45nm CMOS circuits

Circuit	FinFET 7nm V_{dd}=0.3V			FinFET 7nm V_{dd}=0.45V			NCSU CMOS 45nm V_{dd}=1.1V		
	Average power (μW)	Total area (μm^2)	Power density (mW/mm^2)	Average power (μW)	Total area (μm^2)	Power density (mW/mm^2)	Average power (μW)	Total area (μm^2)	Power density (mW/mm^2)
c432	9.32	6.76	1380	12.7	5.96	2131	78.9	625	126.3
c499	21.72	17.3	1256	30.8	12.4	2484	78.7	922.8	85.3
c880	11.6	15.3	757	18.9	8.93	2114	74.5	889	83.8
c1355	25.3	20.4	1241	31.3	12.2	2562	117.8	1167	100.9
c1908	26.0	15.3	1702	38.8	16.1	2410	106.9	993.1	107.7
c3540	53.5	35.6	1503	87.7	33.8	2591	396	2768	143

Table 5: Power density analysis for 7nm independent-gate FinFET circuits under V_{dd}=0.3V

Circuit	IG FinFET V_{bias}=0.05V			IG FinFET V_{bias}=0V			IG FinFET V_{bias}=-0.05V		
	Average power (μW)	Total area (μm^2)	Power density (mW/mm^2)	Average power (μW)	Total area (μm^2)	Power density (mW/mm^2)	Average power (μW)	Total area (μm^2)	Power density (mW/mm^2)
c432	4.87	5.06	961	2.88	5.06	569.6	2.28	5.06	450.8
c499	6.95	9.86	705	4.11	9.86	417.3	3.26	9.86	330.2
c880	7.72	13.9	557	4.57	13.9	330.0	3.62	13.9	261.1
c1355	5.85	9.4	623	3.47	9.4	368.7	2.74	9.4	291.8
c1908	8.71	11.4	762	5.16	11.4	451.1	4.08	11.4	356.9
c3540	34.1	29.9	1143	20.2	29.9	677.1	16.0	29.9	535.8

8. REFERENCES

[1] M. Pedram and S. Nazarian, "Thermal modeling, analysis, and management in vlsi circuits: Principles and methods," *Proceedings of the IEEE*, vol. 94, no. 8, pp. 1487–1501, 2006.

[2] R. G. Dreslinski, M. Wieckowski, D. Blaauw, D. Sylvester, and T. Mudge, "Near-threshold computing: Reclaiming moore's law through energy efficient integrated circuits," *Proceedings of the IEEE*, vol. 98, no. 2, pp. 253–266, 2010.

[3] D. Markovic, C. C. Wang, L. P. Alarcon, T.-T. Liu, and J. M. Rabaey, "Ultralow-power design in near-threshold region," *Proceedings of the IEEE*, vol. 98, no. 2, pp. 237–252, 2010.

[4] L. Chang, Y.-k. Choi, D. Ha, P. Ranade, S. Xiong, J. Bokor, C. Hu, and T.-J. King, "Extremely scaled silicon nano-cmos devices," *Proceedings of the IEEE*, vol. 91, no. 11, pp. 1860–1873, 2003.

[5] S. Chaudhuri and N. K. Jha, "Finfet logic circuit optimization with different finfet styles: Lower power possible at higher supply voltage," in *VLSI Design and 2014 13th International Conference on Embedded Systems, 2014 27th International Conference on*. IEEE, 2014, pp. 476–482.

[6] T. Sairam, W. Zhao, and Y. Cao, "Optimizing finfet technology for high-speed and low-power design," in *Proceedings of the 17th ACM Great Lakes symposium on VLSI*. ACM, 2007, pp. 73–77.

[7] C. H. Wann, K. Noda, T. Tanaka, M. Yoshida, and C. Hu, "A comparative study of advanced mosfet concepts," *Electron Devices, IEEE Transactions on*, vol. 43, no. 10, pp. 1742–1753, 1996.

[8] L. Chang, K. J. Yang, Y.-C. Yeo, Y.-K. Choi, T.-J. King, and C. Hu, "Reduction of direct-tunneling gate leakage current in double-gate and ultra-thin body mosfets," in *INTERNATIONAL ELECTRON DEVICES MEETING*. IEEE; 1998, 2001, pp. 99–102.

[9] A. R. Brown, A. Asenov, and J. R. Watling, "Intrinsic fluctuations in sub 10-nm double-gate mosfets introduced by discreteness of charge and matter," *Nanotechnology, IEEE Transactions on*, vol. 1, no. 4, pp. 195–200, 2002.

[10] A. Muttreja, N. Agarwal, and N. K. Jha, "Cmos logic design with independent-gate finfets," in *Computer Design, 2007. ICCD 2007. 25th International Conference on*. IEEE, 2007, pp. 560–567.

[11] F. Crupi, M. Alioto, J. Franco, P. Magnone, M. Togo, N. Horiguchi, and G. Groeseneken, "Understanding the basic advantages of bulk finfets for sub-and near-threshold logic circuits from device measurements," *Circuits and Systems II: Express Briefs, IEEE Transactions on*, vol. 59, no. 7, pp. 439–442, 2012.

[12] T. Cakici, K. Kim, and K. Roy, "Finfet based sram design for low standby power applications," in *Quality Electronic Design, 2007. ISQED '07. 8th International Symposium on*. IEEE, 2007, pp. 127–132.

[13] J. Ouyang and Y. Xie, "Power optimization for finfet-based circuits using genetic algorithms," in *SOC Conference, 2008 IEEE International*. IEEE, 2008, pp. 211–214.

[14] S. K. Gupta, W.-S. Cho, A. A. Goud, K. Yogendra, and K. Roy, "Design space exploration of finfets in sub-10nm technologies for energy-efficient near-threshold circuits," in *Device Research Conference (DRC), 2013 71st Annual*. IEEE, 2013, pp. 117–118.

[15] T. Cui, Y. Wang, X. Lin, S. Nazarian, and M. Pedram, "Semi-analytical current source modeling of finfet devices operating in near/sub-threshold regime with independent gate control and considering process variation." in *ASP-DAC*, 2014, pp. 167–172.

[16] T. Cui, S. Chen, Y. Wang, S. Nazarian, and M. Pedram, "An efficient semi-analytical current source model for finfet devices in near/sub-threshold regime considering multiple input switching and stack effect," in *Quality Electronic Design (ISQED), 2014 15th International Symposium on*. IEEE, 2014, pp. 575–581.

[17] N. K. Jha and D. Chen, *Nanoelectronic Circuit Design*. springer, 2010.

[18] X. Lin, Y. Wang, and M. Pedram, "Joint sizing and adaptive independent gate control for finfet circuits operating in multiple voltage regimes using the logical effort method," in *Proceedings of the International Conference on Computer-Aided Design*. IEEE Press, 2013, pp. 444–449.

[19] M. Alioto, "Analysis of layout density in finfet standard cells and impact of fin technology," in *Circuits and Systems (ISCAS), Proceedings of 2010 IEEE International Symposium on*. IEEE, 2010, pp. 3204–3207.

[20] A. A. Goud, S. K. Gupta, S. H. Choday, and K. Roy, "Atomistic tight-binding based evaluation of impact of gate underlap on source to drain tunneling in 5 nm gate length si finfets," in *Device Research Conference (DRC), 2013 71st Annual*. IEEE, 2013, pp. 51–52.

[21] M. Alioto, "Comparative evaluation of layout density in 3t, 4t, and mt finfet standard cells," *Very Large Scale Integration (VLSI) Systems, IEEE Transactions on*, vol. 19, no. 5, pp. 751–762, 2011.

[22] Y.-K. Choi, T.-J. King, and C. Hu, "Nanoscale cmos spacer finfet for the terabit era," *Electron Device Letters, IEEE*, vol. 23, no. 1, pp. 25–27, 2002.

[23] D. M. Fried, "The design, fabrication and characterization of independent-gate finfets," Ph.D. dissertation, Cornell Unive, 2004.

[24] U. Gogineni, J. A. Del Alamo, and C. Putnam, "Rf power potential of 45 nm cmos technology," in *Silicon Monolithic Integrated Circuits in RF Systems (SiRF), 2010 Topical Meeting on*. IEEE, 2010, pp. 204–207.

[25] G. G. Shahidi, "Evolution of cmos technology at 32 nm and beyond," in *Custom Integrated Circuits Conference, 2007. CICC '07. IEEE*. IEEE, 2007, pp. 413–416.

Exploiting the Expressive Power of Graphene Reconfigurable Gates via Post-Synthesis Optimization

Sandeep Miryala, Valerio Tenace,
Andrea Calimera, Enrico Macii,
Massimo Poncino
Politecnico di Torino
Torino, Italy
andrea.calimera@polito.it

Luca Amarú, Giovanni De Micheli,
Pierre-Emmanuel Gaillardon
École Polytechnique Fédérale de Lausanne
Lausanne, Switzerland
pierre-emmanuel.gaillardon@epfl.ch

ABSTRACT

As an answer to the new electronics market demands, semiconductor industry is looking for different materials, new process technologies and alternative design solutions that can support Silicon replacement in the VLSI domain. The recent introduction of graphene, together with the option of electrostatically controlling its doping profile, has shown a possible way to implement fast and power efficient Reconfigurable Gates (RGs). Also, and this is the most important feature considered in this work, those graphene RGs show higher expressive power, i.e., they implement more complex functions, like Majority, MUX, XOR, with less area w.r.t. CMOS counterparts. Unfortunately, state-of-the-art synthesis tools, which have been customized for standard NAND/NOR CMOS gates, do not exploit the aforementioned feature of graphene RGs.

In this paper, we present a post-synthesis tool that translates the gate level netlist obtained from commercial synthesis tools to a more optimized netlist that can efficiently integrate graphene RGs. Results conducted on a set of open-source benchmarks demonstrate that the proposed strategy improves, on average, both area and performance by 17% and 8.17% respectively.

Categories and Subject Descriptors

B.5.2 [**Design Aids**]: Optimization

Keywords

Graphene, P-N junction, Reconfigurable Gate, Synthesis, Optimization

1. INTRODUCTION

Graphene is a single atomic layer of carbon atoms arranged in a honeycomb lattice structure. It was first isolated by mechanical exfoliation in 2004 by researchers at the University of Manchester [1] after decades of experiments from the scientists across the world.

GLSVLSI'15, May 20–22, 2015, Pittsburgh, PA, USA
Copyright 2015 ACM 978-1-4503-3474-7/15/05 ...$15.00
http://dx.doi.org/10.1145/2742060.2742098

Although the mechanical exfoliation process is effective for research purposes, it is not suitable for industries. Thereafter, significant progress in research has led to other methods, e.g., SiC decomposition [2, 3]. The latest one, being Chemical Vapor Deposition (CVD), has finally reported to be a viable solution for mass-production [4].

High carrier mobility and high saturation velocity are what make graphene a perfect material for electronic devices. However, it also shows some drawbacks; the zero band-gap energy distribution, in particular, as the most critical. The latter results in heavy leakage currents when the material is turned-OFF, and hence, poor I_{on}/I_{off} current ratio. Needless to say this poses severe limitations for digital applications which need a clear separation between 0- and 1-logic. One possible way to open a band-gap is given by lithographic patterning of large graphene sheets into narrow stripes ($\sim$ $10nm$), called Graphene Nano Ribbons (GNRs) [5]. However, the patterning process alter the lattice structure of the material and degrades carrier mobility. An alternative strategy to implement graphene switches is to exploit its intrinsic properties rather than modifying them, that is, one can effectively steer carriers across pristine sheets of graphene by means of external voltage potentials as to build equivalent P-N junctions [6]. The latter, when properly connected, can implement reconfigurable logic gates [7], RGs hereafter, which show exceptional properties w.r.t. CMOS gates.

Just few recent works deal with, or are related to, graphene P-N junctions and RGs. In [8, 9], the authors explore multiple architectures for basic logic gates using graphene RGs and characterize them from power and performance, where as [10, 11] discusses the associated models for delay and power for each of the possible timing arcs for graphene RG logic gates. In [12] the authors propose the interesting comparison among various implementation styles for graphene RG-based circuits. From a CAD standpoint, in [13, 14] the authors proposed a novel data structure on the lines of BDD called Biconditional Binary Decision Diagrams (BBDD) which is suitable for representing RG-based circuits.

Till now, graphene RGs were used for realizing elementary Boolean logic gates, like AND/OR/INV/BUF, but not for complex functions, e.g., Majority (MAJ), multi-inputs XOR and others, like XOR followed by AND (XOR-AND) and XOR followed by another XOR (3-input XOR), all of them very common in many arithmetic circuits. Obviously the right use of such complex gates during synthesis and optimization may result in a drastic reduction of circuit complexity and better figures of merit, as area, performance and power.

Unfortunately, commercial synthesis tools are currently customized for managing Sum-of-Product forms, namely, they have been optimized for AND-OR-INV standard cells mapping; hence do not make, or rarely do, use of those complex functions achievable with RGs, even if included in the reference libraries used at the synthesis stage. This work addresses the above limitation proposing a new post-synthesis tool, currently part of a library package written in C, that parses a logic netlist collected from a standard synthesis flow and automatically recognizes and maps unusual complex functions by means of a structural matching&covering procedure. Such mapping is done as to exploit the maximum expressive power of RGs. With this method, it is possible to reduce not only total number of gates (17% on average) but also improve the average performance (8.17%) of graphene integrated circuits.

2. GRAPHENE RECONFIGURABLE GATE

A graphene reconfigurable logic gate, 3D view given in Figure 1-(a), consists of four layers [15]. The bottom layer has three metal back-gates ($\overline{U}$, S and U) isolated each other by oxide ($\approx 18nm$). A thick oxide layer is growth on top of these three back-gates, while a graphene sheet is deposited on top. Three front metal-to-graphene contacts (A, Z, B) are then connected to the graphene sheet. The central front-contact Z acts as an output pin and the other two front-contacts, namely A and B, will serve as inputs to the reconfigurable logic gate. Notice that the triangular form of the back-gates (bottom view in Figure1-(b)) is fundamental for proper functionality of the RG; interested reader can refer to [15] for more details.

The graphene material adapts its doping profile based on the polarity of the back-gate potentials, hence it requires bipolar voltages: $+V_{dd}/2$ to form n-type; $-V_{dd}/2$ to form p-type regions [16]. This infers logic '1'corresponds to $+V_{dd}/2$ and logic '0'corresponds to $-V_{dd}/2$.

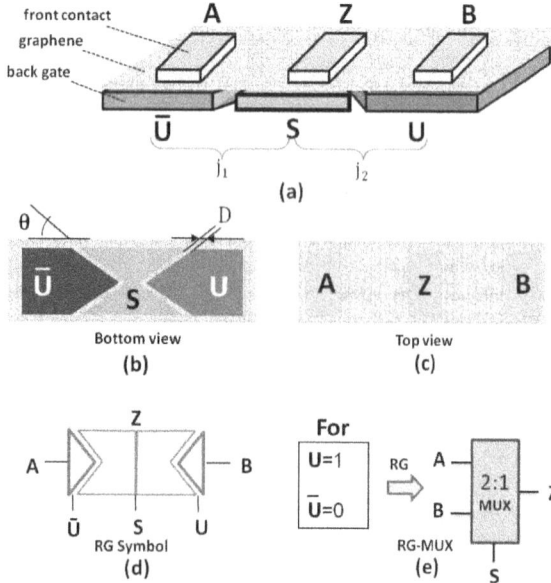

Figure 1: Structure of reconfigurable logic gate

An RG is made of two adjacent junctions (j_1 and j_2 in Fig. 1-(a)), the first between A-Z, the other between B-Z. It operates according to the type of junctions formed (i.e., p-n/n-p

or p-p/n-n); alike potentials fed to two adjacent back-gates induce a p-p/n-n junction, while, opposite polarities form a p-n/n-p junction. The cross resistance of p-p/n-n is $\simeq 300\Omega$ (the ON State) while as for a p-n/n-p junction is $\simeq 3 \cdot 10^5\Omega$ (the OFF state) [7]. Depending on the doping configuration, the inputs carriers injected at the two front-contacts A and B eventually reach the output front-contact Z. The back-gates U and $\overline{U}$ receives complementary potentials as to guarantee that only one of the two junctions can be ON at the same time and thus to avoid short-circuits across inputs A and B.

From a functional viewpoint the behavior of an RG is summarized as follows:

- When S and U receive opposite voltage signals the junction j_1 between A-Z is ON, while j_2 between B-Z is OFF. Hence, the output potential at Z follows that the input at A. This can be written in boolean form as $(S \oplus U) \cdot A$. Where $\oplus$ is represents the XOR operator.

- When S and U receive same voltage signals, the junction j_1 between A-Z is OFF, while the junction j_2 between B-Z is ON. Hence, the output Z follows the input at B. This can be written in boolean form as $(S \odot U)B$. Where $\odot$ is XNOR operator.

- The overall functionality of the Graphene Reconfigurable gate can be written as
$Z = (S \oplus U) \cdot A + (S \odot U) \cdot B$

In order to support electrical simulation, we implemented a Verilog-A macro whose model card is integrated within SPICE simulator. Such a model is borrowed from [7] and [8] to which interested reader can refer for more accurate details.

3. DIGITAL LIBRARY WITH RGS

3.1 Basic Boolean Functions

The RG is used as a primitive to build basic 2-input logic gates [8]. Those used in this work, i.e., INV, OR, AND, XOR, have been summarized in Figure 2. All of them except the XOR, are implemented using a single RG, whereas the XOR needs two RGs. It is worth noticing that terminals U and $\overline{U}$ (not reported in the picture) are fed fixed voltages, i.e., $+V_{dd}/2$ and $-V_{dd}/2$ respectively.

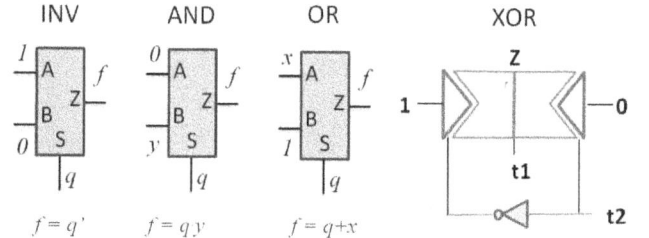

Figure 2: Input configuration for 2-inputs logic gates implementing basic Boolean functions.

Needless to say, any logic function can be implemented with proper connection of basic standard cells. However, a less intuitive, yet more efficient implementation, would better exploit the expressive power of RGs by using the terminals U and $\overline{U}$ as logic inputs; we refer to this implementation as the RG-EXP implementation. In the next subsections we report a quantitative analysis of some complex logic functions typically used in arithmetic circuits, implemented as cascade of standard cells, the STC style, or the RG-EXP style.

3.2 MUltipleXer (MUX)

Implementing the 2:1 MUX using STC, as shown in Fig. 3(b), requires four RGs with total depth of three levels. Note that depth can be used as an estimation of the timing criticality. However, a single RG can naturally implement a 2:1 MUX by just fixing the potential of U to logic '1'; this represents the RG-EXP implementation illustrated in Fig. 3 (a). The area ratio is therefore 4:1, being the RG-EXP 75% more area efficient. The performance comparison between STC

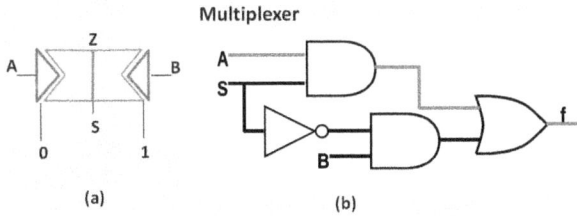

Figure 3: MUX using RG-EXP and STC.

and RG-EXP is reported in Table. 1, where the characterization is done for different input transition time (T_r) with fanout varying from 1 to 5. As can be seen RG-EXP performs substantially better, 55% of delay reduction in the best case (FO=1).

Table 1: Multiplexer function characterization using RG-EXP and STC

Tr (Sec)	2.85E-12		5.65E-12	
FanOut	RG-EXP	STC	RG-EXP	STC
1	9.20E-13	1.87E-12	1.10E-12	2.03E-12
2	1.58E-12	2.47E-12	1.85E-12	2.63E-12
3	2.21E-12	3.06E-12	2.53E-12	3.21E-12
4	2.82E-12	3.64E-12	3.18E-12	3.80E-12
5	3.42E-12	4.22E-12	3.81E-12	4.37E-12

3.3 MAJority Function (MAJ)

Fig. 4 shows the implementation of the majority function, i.e., $f(t1, t2, t3)_{MAJ} = t1 \cdot t2 + t2 \cdot t3 + t3 \cdot t1$, using STCs (a) and RG-EXP (b). Concerning the RG-EXP one, let us explain its functionality by examples. Consider the input configuration of the three inputs $t1$, $t2$ and $t3$ being "101". For such pattern the junction between A-Z is ON (as $t1'=0$ and $t2=0$), while the junction between B-Z is OFF (as $t1=1$ and $t2=0$). Hence the output voltage at Z follows that of the input signal at A, i.e., $t3$, which happens to be '1', which is the right value of the MAJ function when 2 or more inputs are at '1'. Similar reasoning can be done for remaining input patterns. The STC requires four RGs with total depth of tree levels; the area ratio is therefore 4:2, i.e., 50% area savings.

Concerning performance, the Table. 2 shows the delay characterized for different input transition time (T_r) and output load (FanOut). As for the 2:1 MUX gate, the RG-EXP has better performance irrespective of the fanout, 45% of delay reduction in the best case (FO=1), due to lower depth.

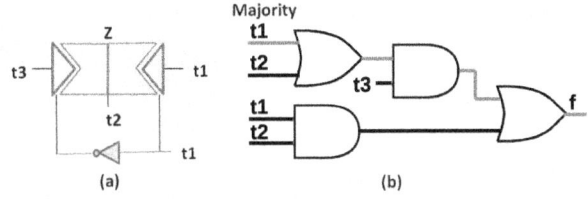

Figure 4: MAJ using RG-EXP and STC.

Table 2: Majority function characterization using RG-EXP and STC

Tr (Sec)	2.85E-012		5.65E-012	
FanOut	RG-EXP	STC	RG-EXP	STC
1	1.29E-012	2.24E-012	1.64E-012	2.63E-012
2	2.08E-012	2.88E-012	2.56E-012	3.31E-012
3	2.78E-012	3.49E-012	3.41E-012	3.96E-012
4	3.43E-012	4.09E-012	4.18E-012	4.60E-012
5	4.05E-012	4.69E-012	4.92E-012	5.22E-012

3.4 XOR-AND

Another complex function that can be efficiently implemented through graphene RG is the XOR-AND (i.e an XOR gate followed by an AND gate), which is a common path in arithmetic circuits. Fig. 5 shows the implementation of XOR-AND with STCs (b) and RG-EXP (a). To explain functionality, consider the combination of the three inputs $t1$, $t2$ and $t3$ to be "101". For such pattern the junction between A-Z is ON (as $t1'=0$, $t2=0$), whereas the junction between B-Z is OFF (as $t1'=1$, $t2=0$). Hence, the signal at Z follows the input on A, i.e., $t3$, which happens to be '1'. Similar reasoning can be done for remaining input patterns.

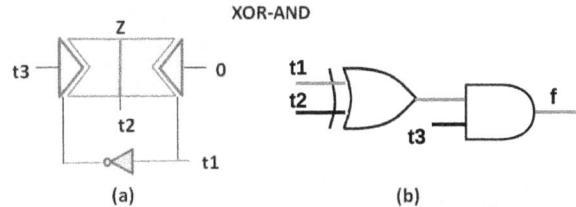

Figure 5: XOR-AND realization using RG-EXP and STC.

The area ratio between STC and RG-EXP is 1:1, i.e., no area savings. Concerning performance, the delay characterized for different input transition time (T_r) and output load (FanOut) is reported in Tab. 3. Again, the RG-EXP shows better performance, 35% in the best case (FO=1).

3.5 XOR-3

It is possible to realize a 3-inputs XOR gate by using a single RG. Fig. 6 shows the implementation of XOR-3 with STCs (b) and RG-EXP (a). Similar to previous cases different inputs patterns turn-ON/OFF one of the two junctions connecting the right input signal to output depending on the input pattern.

The STC implementation requires two XOR gates, each of them requiring two RGs (please refer to Fig.2). The resulting area ratio is 3:4, i.e., 25% area savings. In the best case, the performance savings achieved with RG-EXP is 25% (FO=1), but, due to the presence of an INV at the front contacts, the propagation delay of RG-EXP is worse for FO larger than 3. This suggest that the mapping of 3-inputs

Table 3: XOR-AND function characterization using RG-EXP and STC

Tr (Sec)	2.85E-012		5.65E-012	
FanOut	RG-EXP	STC	RG-EXP	STC
1	1.01E-12	1.50E-12	1.15E-12	1.64E-12
2	1.69E-12	2.10E-12	1.75E-12	2.24E-12
3	2.17E-12	2.68E-12	2.34E-12	2.83E-12
4	2.75E-12	3.27E-12	2.92E-12	3.41E-12
5	3.33E-12	3.85E-12	3.50E-12	3.99E-12

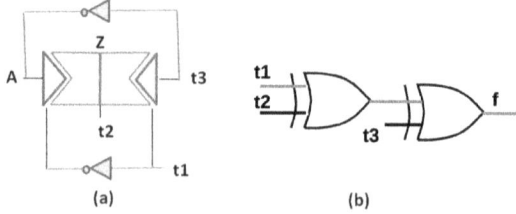

Figure 6: XOR-3 realization using RG-EXP and STC.

XOR with RG-EXP is convenient depending on the current FO.

Table 4: Three input XOR function characterization using RG-EXP and STC

Tr	2.85E-012		5.65E-012	
FanOut	RG-EXP	STC	RG-EXP	STC
1	1.23E-012	1.64E-012	1.49E-012	1.73E-12
2	2.03E-012	2.22E-012	2.46E-012	2.31E-12
3	2.74E-012	2.79E-012	3.33E-012	2.88E-12
4	3.39E-012	3.37E-012	4.12E-012	3.46E-12
5	4.02E-012	3.95E-012	4.86E-012	4.04E-12

4. DESIGN FRAMEWORK FOR RG-BASED CIRCUITS

4.1 Motivational Example

To understand the need of a alternative synthesis strategy and motivate the post-synthesis optimization tool proposed in this work, we briefly report a handcraft analysis for a simple arithmetic benchmark, a 3-bit ripple-carry adder. Fig. 7 reports an abstract view (Acyclic Directed Graph) of its netlist resulted from a standard synthesis flow performed with a commercial tool. Assuming each node has a unit delay, a Static Timing Analysis (STA) returns a critical path delay of 6 units. In reality the delay of each of these nodes differs as it is a function of fanout. However, an attempt to minimize the number of nodes along the critical path increases the probability of reducing the critical path delay. The number in the square box on each edge report the worst-case arrival time of the signals. The worst critical path, highlighted using dotted line, travels from the primary input a0 to the primary output carry.

The sub-tree having as root g10 and leaves a1 and b1 can be covered by the MAJ function (please refer to Fig.4) providing local area and delay savings. The same hold for node g14, while node g20 matches with the structure of the 3-inputs XOR and it might be replaced using the corresponding XOR-3 cell. After these few transformation the new critical path has depth of 4 and the number of standard cells is

reduced from 15 to 10. Simulation results show an improvement in the performance by 20% and an area improvement by 30%.

4.2 Post-Synthesis Mapping

The tool we implemented to perform the post-synthesis optimization is written in C language; it is composed of the following components all of them integrated together:

1. Verilog parser

2. Optimization algorithm

3. Static Timing Analysis (STA) engine

Once the circuit is read by the parser, we archive information in a table-like data structure. Each entry of the table represents a single gate in the benchmark. Connectivity of the gates is conserved by means of original pin names assigned by the commercial synthesis tool.

In order to optimize area/timing features of the input circuits, we implemented optimization algorithm that identifies the RG-EXP functions as discussed in the previous section. After identifying those patterns, we replace them and possibly remove the covered STC gates forming the function in the original netlist with RG-EXP counterparts. When the internal cells covered by the RG-EXP have FO outside the local sub-tree, namely, they drive other external cells in the circuit, they are replaced with a replica as to guarantee the functionality of the circuit. From the Fig. 7, it can be seen that the output of nodes g9 and g6 has fanout of more than 1, i.e., these outputs are input to g16 and g17 respectively. Hence, we have to replicate the nodes g9 and g6 for the functionality of the circuit.

Data: Verilog netlist
Result: Optimized graphene-based netlist
Parse verilog file;
Compute worst-case path with out PST;
Procedure : For identifying majority function
foreach *gate* **do**
  if *gate function is OR* **then**
    if *gate inputs are both AND* **then**
      if *AND input is OR* **then**
        Instantiate a new RG-MUX device;
        Create RG-MUX connections;
        if *gates in pattern has fanout = 1* **then**
          Remove gates;
        end
      end
    end
  end
end
Procedure: For identifying XOR-AND function;
Procedure: For identifying XOR-3 funtion;
Procedure: For identifying Multiplexer;
Compute worst-case path after optimization;

Algorithm 1: Post Synthesis Tool exploiting expressive power of Graphene RG

For each of the four RG-EXPs, we implemented a different match&covering procedure that run iteratively over the circuit. In Alg. 1, we provide the pseudo-code of the entire post-synthesis algorithm, with an unrolled description

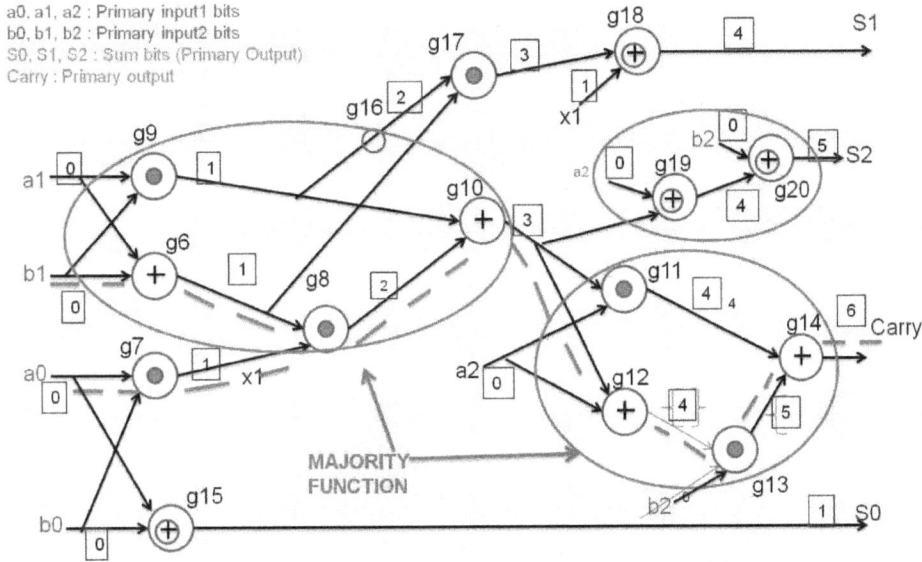

Figure 7: Directed acyclic graph of 3-bit adder.

of the procedure for recognizing MAJ functions. The latter works as follows. First it iterates among the entire set of gates in the circuit. Once an OR gate is recognized it checks whether its two inputs are both connected to AND gates. If that's true, we end up checking whether one of the two AND-gates receive an input from an OR gate. Once the pattern is recognized, it covers the sub-portion of the circuit with the RG-EXP MAJ function. The last step is to check whether it is possible to remove the gates which belong to the recognized pattern. This is possible only if the gates have fanout of 1. In the algorithm we also consider the associative property of the logic gates. In a similar way, there are other procedures to identify the other RG-EXP functions, i.e., XOR-AND, XOR-3, MUX. Finally, a STA is performed once again to identify the worst-case path and measure delay using HSPICE. The STA algorithm is straightforward, as it traverses from primary inputs to primary outputs by considering the worst case arrival-time of each node having delay of logic gates stored in a dedicated look-up table (LUT). Finally traversing the graph in the reverse order, i.e., from PO to PI, paths having maximum delay are marked critical paths.

5. SIMULATION RESULTS

5.1 Implemented Flow

The overall framework used in this work is shown in Fig. 8. The RTL code written in Verilog or VHDL is initially synthesized using conventional synthesis tools. For our work, we have adopted a commercial synthesis tool with technology libraries from STMicroelectronics at 45nm technology node. We used the reduced library set comprising of AND2, OR2, XOR2, NOT, BUF as these cells can be realized using a single Graphene Reconfigurable gate. The synthesized gate level netlist is the main input for the post-synthesis tool which identifies complex logic functions as discussed in the previous section and maps them to graphene RG-EXP. However, the gates that have fanout grater than '1' will be duplicated so that their output signal remains intact. The timing analyzer performs STA on the gate level netlist from

the commercial synthesis tool and our Post Synthesis Tool (PST) to extract the critical path. This critical path is simulated in HSPICE to determine the worst-case performance of the circuit.

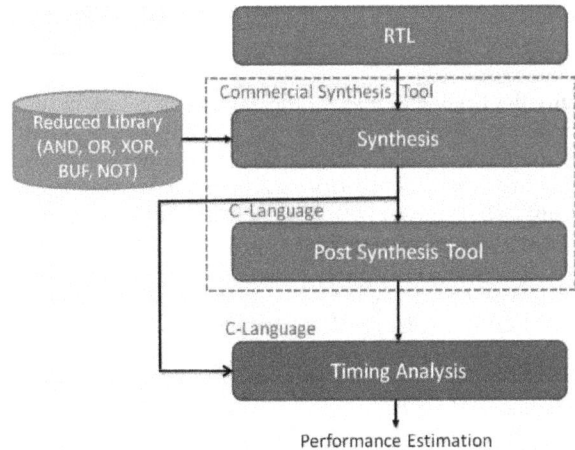

Figure 8: Simulation Framework.

5.2 Collected Results

We compare the results of various benchmarks mapped using conventional synthesis and STCs against those obtained with the proposed tool and RG-EXP.

Tab. 5, reports the number of Primary Inputs (PI) and Primary Outputs (PO) of each benchmark. For the two synthesis strategies (colomns STC and $RG-EXP$), we annotated the depth of the critical path (column $Depth$), the total number of cells (column $\#cells$) and worst-case propagation delay (column $Delay$) from 50% of input signal to 50% of the output signal; notice that delay figures have been obtained through detailed SPICE simulations. We have also annotated the number of RG-EXP functions, i.e., MAJ, MUX, XOR-AND and XOR-3 mapped after the post-synthesis optimization. Finally, column $\%Imp.$ represents the performance improvements resulting from the proposed synthesis strategy.

Table 5: Standard Logic Synthesis Vs. Post-Synthesis Optimization: Area/Performance Analysis

	# PI	# PO	Standard Cell Mapping			Post Synthesis Tool			# MAJ	# XOR-3	# XOR-AND	# MUX	% Imp.
			Depth	# Cells	Delay	Depth	# Cells	Delay					
Add 3bit	6	4	6	15	3.66	4	10	2.92	2	1	0	0	-20.20
Add 8bit	16	9	21	50	10.90	10	40	7.28	7	1	0	0	-33.40
Add 16bit	32	17	45	106	21.80	18	88	13.20	15	1	0	0	-39.40
Mult 4bit	8	8	19	69	10.60	14	60	8.60	3	9	1	0	-18.90
Voter 31	30	1	23	169	13.20	18	97	11.10	20	28	1	0	-16.00
c499	41	32	17	186	10.10	14	150	8.68	2	40	0	0	-14.10
cordic	23	2	17	113	9.47	16	99	8.98	0	0	13	5	-5.17
Maj. 11	11	1	9	42	6.65	7	37	5.33	1	8	4	0	-19.80
Maj. 15	15	1	11	56	6.63	9	49	5.65	1	9	7	0	-14.80
DES	256	245	26	3164	13.30	26	2117	13.30	0	2	86	4	0.00
Comp	11	3	9	40	5.38	9	38	5.38	0	0	6	0	0.00
Sin	34	63	19	1763	9.96	19	1723	9.96	0	0	0	50	0.00
ALU4	14	8	20	1572	10.40	20	1563	10.40	0	0	0	10	0.00
CLA 4bit	9	7	9	29	5.01	8	25	5.20	0	4	10	0	3.77
CLA 8bit	17	9	17	40	8.88	16	32	9.99	32	8	8	0	12.50
c1355	41	32	18	218	10.70	15	182	11.90	2	40	0	0	11.20
Adder_Big	32	16	42	242	21.10	35	230	22.10	4	16	9	1	4.65
Maj. 9	9	1	10	33	6.02	9	29	6.18	0	6	4	0	2.66
Total				7907			6569						8.17

Benchmarks from Add_3bit till majority-15 significantly exploits utilization of complex functions and RG-EXPs. For these circuits, the benefits are not only in terms of area but also in terms of performance, as a reduction of the critical path depth corresponds to shorter propagation delay. These circuits make extensive use of MAJ functions, especially to evaluate the carry, which represents the timing critical path of the circuit.

For circuits from DES to ALU4, the main benefits are in terms of area, while the performance are not affected as no RG-EXP matching are found across the critical path.

For circuits from CLA-4 to Majority-9, due to the presence of many XOR-3 gates, we register substantial area improvements at the cost of some delay penalties. What happens is that it worsens the worst-case performance of the circuit and the reason is well understood from the characterization data of XOR-3 in the previous section.

Overall, on an average, there is 17% improvement in the area of the circuit by adopting PST along with a performance improvement of 8.17%.

6. CONCLUSION AND FUTURE WORK

To exploit the expressive power of graphene RGs a PST is therefore essential or future synthesis tools has to consider these complex functions during optimization. Currently, PST optimizes the netlist to reduce area and for some circuits it reduces the depth of critical path. It may also hamper the performance for some other circuits. However, in our future work we would like to implement the timing driven approach which solely focuses on improving the performance of the circuit. Also, we would like to use the efficiency of BBDD data structure on the portion of the circuit which optimizes performance.

7. REFERENCES

[1] A. K. Geim and K. S. Novoselov, "The rise of graphene," *Nature materials*, vol. 6, no. 3, pp. 183–191, 2007.

[2] G. Deligeorgis, G. Konstantinidis, M. Dragoman, and R. Plana, "Fabrication of graphene devices, issues and prospects," in *CAS Conference*, vol. 01, pp. 21–25, Oct. 2010.

[3] C. Berger *et al.*, "Ultrathin epitaxial graphite: 2D electron gas properties and a route toward graphene-based nanoelectronics," *The Journal of Physical Chemistry B*, vol. 108, no. 52, pp. 19912–19916, 2004.

[4] C. Xu, H. Li, and K. Banerjee, "Modeling, analysis, and design of graphene nano-ribbon interconnects," *IEEE Transaction on Electron Devices*, vol. 56, no. 8, pp. 1567–1578, 2009.

[5] M. Y. Han, B. Özyilmaz, Y. Zhang, and P. Kim, "Energy band-gap engineering of graphene nanoribbons," *Phys. Rev. Lett.*, vol. 98, p. 206805, May 2007.

[6] V. V. Cheianov, V. Fal'ko, and B. L. Altshuler, "The Focusing of Electron Flow and a Veselago Lens in Graphene p-n Junctions," *Science*, vol. 315, no. 5816, pp. 1252–1255, 2007.

[7] S. Tanachutiwat, J. U. Lee, W. Wang, and C. Y. Sung, "Reconfigurable multi-function logic based on graphene p-n junctions," in *DAC*, pp. 883–888, june 2010.

[8] S. Miryala, M. Montazeri, A. Calimera, E. Macii, and M. Poncino, "A Verilog-A model for reconfigurable logic gates based on graphene pn-junctions," in *DATE Conference*, pp. 877–880, March 2013.

[9] V. Tenace, A. Calimera, E. Macii, and M. Poncino, "Pass-XNOR Logic: A new Logic Style for PN-Junction based Graphene Circuits," in *DATE'14: ACM/IEEE Design, Automation and Test in Europe*, pp. 1–4, Mar. 2014.

[10] S. Miryala, A. Calimera, E. Macii, and M. Poncino, "Delay Model for Reconfigurable Logic Gates Based on Graphene PN-junctions," in *GLSVLSI Conference*, pp. 227–232, 2013.

[11] S. Miryala, A. Calimera, E. Macii, and M. Poncino, "Power modeling and characterization of graphene-based logic gates," in *PATMOS International Workshop*, pp. 223–226, Sept 2013.

[12] S. Miryala, A. Calimera, M. Poncino, and E. Macii, "Exploration of different implementation styles for graphene-based reconfigurable gates," in *ICICDT Conference*, pp. 21–24, May 2013.

[13] L. Amaru, P.-E. Gaillardon, and G. De Micheli, "Biconditional BDD: A novel canonical BDD for logic synthesis targeting XOR-rich circuits," in *DATE Conference Exhibition*, pp. 1014–1017, March 2013.

[14] R. I. Bahar, H. Cho, G. D. Hachtel, E. Macii, and F. Somenzi, "Timing analysis of combinational circuits using adds," in *EDAC'94: European Design and Test Conference*, pp. 625–629, 1994.

[15] C.-Y. Sung and J. U. Lee, "Graphene: The ultimate switch," *IEEE Spectrum*, 2012.

[16] K. S. Novoselov *et al.*, "Electric field effect in atomically thin carbon films," *Science*, vol. 306, no. 5696, pp. 666–669, 2004.

A Simulation Framework for Analyzing Transient Effects Due to Thermal Noise in Sub-Threshold Circuits

Marco Donato, R. Iris Bahar, William Patterson and Alexander Zaslavsky
School of Engineering
Brown University
Providence, RI 02912

ABSTRACT

Noise analysis in nonlinear logic circuits requires models that take into account time-varying biasing conditions. When considering thermal noise, which moves the circuit away from its equilibrium point, a correct modeling approach has to go beyond the additive white Gaussian noise (AWGN) used in classical noise analysis. Even when accurate models are available, running standard Monte-Carlo simulations that will expose rare soft errors may still be computationally prohibitive. Probabilistic methods are often preferred for estimating the failure rate. However, these approaches may not provide any insight about the dynamic response to noise events. In this paper, we target both problems in the sub-threshold logic application domain. We first provide a time-domain model for fundamental, technology–independent thermal noise in sub-threshold circuits. Then, we use this model to generate noise input files for SPICE transient analysis. The effectiveness of the approach is demonstrated using 7nm FinFET predictive technology models (PTM) for an inverter and a NAND gate.

Categories and Subject Descriptors

I.6.5 [**Simulation and Modeling**]: Model Development— *Modeling methodologies*

Keywords

thermal noise,noise analysis,time-domain simulation,CMOS logic circuits,sub-threshold circuits

1. INTRODUCTION

The classical approach to modeling thermal noise in electronic circuits assumes that the magnitude of the noise is small enough to consider linear response. The assumption of linearity, however, cannot always be justified in logic circuits, especially when operating in the sub-threshold regime in which the supply voltage V_{DD} is kept below the threshold voltage of the transistors[3][5]. In these operating conditions, the number of electrons in the channel is so small that even small fluctuations can have a pronounced impact on the circuit biasing point.

Therefore, noise analysis for nonlinear logic circuits requires using models that take into account the time dependence of the circuit biasing conditions. The authors of [14] and [13] have shown that taking time-varying biasing conditions when computing the capture and emission rates in random telegraph signal (RTS) noise, can lead to much more accurate models. Their results are useful for obtaining improved spectral noise analysis. The authors of [12] have defined an analytical model for thermal noise. Their approach considers the load capacitor of an inverter as a queue in which the arrival and departure rates are modeled after the forward and reverse drain currents of the transistors. This representation is derived from Sarpeshkar's fundamental work [17] in which the author presented a unified model for thermal noise, viewed as two-sided shot noise process. A queue representation of the output current fluctuations was then used for computing the probability of a soft error in sub-threshold operation. More recently, similar approaches [8][9][10] have been used for modeling the error rate of flip-flops both in sub-threshold and above-threshold operation for end-of-roadmap CMOS technology.

We note that all these works have focused on the analysis of thermal noise in the frequency domain by studying the probability of soft error events. While this has led to some interesting results, we still lack a time-domain framework necessary for capturing the dynamic response to noise in nonlinear circuits. In this paper, we extend the same unified model for thermal and shot noise [8][9][10] to the time domain by modeling the noise fluctuations as a stochastic process.

Our approach requires an understanding of how the statistics of the Poissonian processes describing the charging and discharging rates are affected by the time-varying physical characteristics of the devices. While creating an accurate model for this stochastic process is feasible, the greater challenge is creating one that is computationally-affordable, such that it can be used for simulations over relatively long time frames to capture rare errors that cannot be seen in standard Monte Carlo simulations. This is particularly desirable when doing repeated simulations for design exploration.

For example, if we were to apply this model directly to SPICE circuit simulations, we would need to run a transient analysis in the time range of seconds with time steps on the order of picoseconds, in order to guarantee resolution greater than the fastest response time of the circuit, with the hope of encountering some rare noise pattern that may trigger a soft error in the circuit. Even by employing Monte Carlo methods, this approach would make simulation times too long to be of any practical use.

Instead, our approach is to use a two-step method in which we first look for rare failure-inducing events in the form of stochastic

GLSVLSI'15, May 20–22, 2015, Pittsburgh, PA, USA.
Copyright is held by the owner/author(s). Publication rights licensed to ACM.
ACM 978-1-4503-3474-7/15/05 ...$15.00.
http://dx.doi.org/10.1145/2742060.2742066

current fluctuations using a fast ad-hoc simulator and then extract the desired portion of the time series to simulate the fault in SPICE. As a result, we can potentially compress simulated times of seconds down to the microsecond scale. In addition, our approach allows us to simulate for rare noise events in a matter of a few hours, rather than weeks. We demonstrate the effectiveness of our approach, both in terms of accuracy and simulation time, using 7nm FinFET models.

The remainder of the paper is organized as follows. In Section 2 we briefly review the analytical description of thermal noise in a CMOS transistor as a two-sided Poisson process, as was first shown in [12]. We then extend the analysis in Section 3 by studying the effect of the response time on the noise amplitude. Once we have established the features of the time-domain model, in Section 4 we describe the implementation of the model for a CMOS inverter and a NAND gate using 7nm FinFET predictive technology models (PTM)[18][16]. The results for both gates are validated against the statistical expectations derived from Monte Carlo simulations. In Section 5, we present the our simulation framework and provide some examples showing how this approach preserves the dynamic properties of thermal noise and allows speeding up time-domain SPICE noise simulations.

2. TWO-SIDED POISSON SHOT NOISE

The effect of thermal noise in a logic gate can be explained considering the fluctuations of the charge in the load capacitor C_{out}. If we consider the inverter in Figure 1, the mean flow of electrons in the load capacitance is determined by the equilibrium current flowing in the transistors. In sub-threshold, this current is given by:

$$I_D = I_0 \exp\left(\frac{qV_{gs}}{mkT}\right) \exp\left(\frac{qV_{ds}\lambda_D}{kT}\right) \left[1 - \exp\left(-\frac{qV_{ds}}{kT}\right)\right] \quad (1)$$

where λ_D is the DIBL parameter [20] and m is the ideality factor. Due to thermal agitation of the carriers, the charge stored in C_{out} is not constant. The number of electrons leaving or arriving at the output node is a Poisson distributed random variable and fluctuates in time. We can therefore describe the fluctuations of electrons at the output node as the result of four Poisson processes whose rates are associated with the transistor currents. Each transistor in the inverter has two rates associated with it, one for the forward current and one for the reverse current. For our subthreshold operated gates, the supply voltage $V_{DD} \approx 180mV$. These rates can be conveniently expressed in number of electrons per picosecond [12]:

$$\mu_n = \frac{I_0}{q} \exp\left(\frac{qV_{out}\lambda_D}{kT}\right) \exp\left(\frac{qV_{in}}{mkT}\right) \times 10^{-12} \quad (2)$$

$$\lambda_n = \mu_n \exp\left(\frac{-qV_{out}}{kT}\right) \quad (3)$$

$$\lambda_p = \frac{I_0}{q} \exp\left(\frac{q(V_{DD} - V_{out})\lambda_D}{kT}\right) \exp\left(\frac{q(V_{DD} - V_{in})}{mkT}\right) \times 10^{-12} \quad (4)$$

$$\mu_p = \lambda_p \exp\left(\frac{-q(V_{DD} - V_{out})}{kT}\right) \quad (5)$$

In these formulas we use λ for the rates of the processes charging the capacitor and μ for the rates discharging the capacitor. A property of the Poisson processes allows us to simplify the notation further. If we consider two Poisson processes with rates λ_1 and λ_2, the cumulative number of events associated with the two processes is still a Poisson process with rate $\lambda = \lambda_1 + \lambda_2$. Then, we can assume one Poisson charging process with arrival rate $\lambda = \lambda_n + \lambda_p$ and one Poisson discharging process with departure rate $\mu = \mu_n + \mu_p$.

This final form shows that the thermal noise fluctuations are in fact, the result of two competing Poisson processes. In ideal conditions, the two logic states "1" and "0", correspond to having full charge or zero charge on the output capacitor. Random fluctuations in the electron population for the two equilibrium states change the charge stored in the capacitor and can lead to a switch in the output logic state if the excursion from the equilibrium is large enough. This mechanism was described in [8] using a probabilistic framework based on 2–D Markov chain for analyzing sub–threshold flip–flops and extracting the probability of soft error, *i.e.*, finding the probability of going from the correct stable state to the other as an effect of noise fluctuations. However, it does not help in characterizing the transient behavior of the circuits in the presence of noise. Our goal is to provide an alternative approach that can be used to apply the results from the two-sided shot noise model to time-domain simulations. The value of the rates as extracted directly from the drain current (1) require a good match with the currents from the BSIMCMG model we used in our simulations. The curve fitting obtained by applying the DIBL correction is shown in Figure 2. We used $\lambda_0 = 0.07$ and $m = 1.2$ for the NMOS and $\lambda_0 = 0.08$ and $m = 1.3$ for the PMOS. The mismatch at low values of V_{ds} are due to the fact that we are still considering a relatively simple model for the sub–threshold current, which does not incorporate all the parameters used in the BSIMCMG model. For our simulator, we decided to implement all current and parameter models as a look–up table. This approach helps speeding up the calculations since the parameters have to be computed only once.

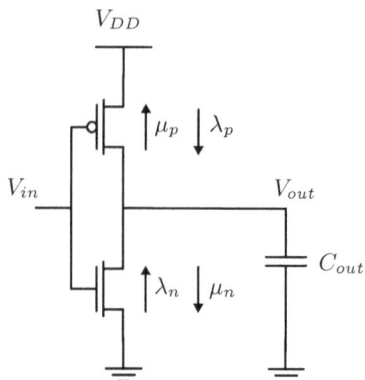

Figure 1: Inverter rates for NMOS and PMOS transistors.

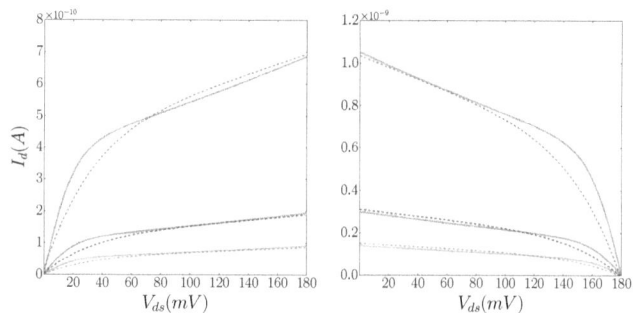

Figure 2: Comparison of the IV curves from the BSIMCMG 7nm FinFET model (solid lines) and the sub–threshold current model from (1) (dashed lines).

46

Should more accuracy be needed, we could still get rid of the mismatch from the curve fitting and implement the look–up tables using parameters extracted directly from SPICE simulations. In our analysis the parameters' calculation were not noticeably affected by the curve fitting approximation. Therefore, we chose to use the simpler current model. The details of the implementation will be discussed in Section 4.

3. ORNSTEIN–UHLENBECK PROCESS – THE EFFECT OF RESPONSE TIME ON NOISE AMPLITUDE

In this section we show how the response time of the circuit affects the final noise amplitude in the time-domain. The Ornstein–Uhlenbeck (OU) process [6][21] was first introduced for the study of Brownian motion. Its current applications span from the study of neural spikes to the representation of stock volatility in financial economics [1][19]. The use of an OU process to describe this circuit essentially extends a single-pole infinite-impulse-response (IIR) model of the circuit rigorously into a statistical description. As we have already established in the previous section, the mean current into the inverter output node is $I_{tot} = I_\lambda - I\mu$. However, the fluctuations in the two Poisson charging and discharging processes are additive and that sum $I_{SHOT} = |I_\lambda| + |I_\mu|$ is proportional to the variance of the shot noise current in the node. To do a time domain simulation of the circuit responding to a process of this type, one selects a small time interval, say Δt, and computes as a random variable a possible estimate the number of electrons entering the node X_t in that interval and from that computes the next output voltage value using the OU process model. This action repeats to produce a time series of output voltages. If Δt is sufficiently large ($\sqrt{\overline{X_t^2}} \geq 50$), then these pulses will resemble a Gaussian process and the calculation can be done very efficiently. However, if Δt is comparable to or larger than the instantaneous time constant of the circuit, then the circuit node voltage will relax back to its original value between pulses and this is not physically accurate. This situation is well described by the Ornstein–Uhlenbeck process [2].

Consider the time series describing the amplitude of the shot current pulses X_t in terms of the number of electrons at each time $t = n\Delta t$, where Δt is the unit time used for counting the number of events from the Poisson distribution. Consider also the instantaneous time constant of the circuit

$$\tau = \frac{1}{g_{dsNMOS} + g_{dsPMOS}} \times C_{out},$$

where C_{out} is the total capacitance at the output node including any input capacitance of the following stages. The resulting thermal voltage noise process V_t is related to X_t by a factor $\Delta V = \frac{q}{C_{out}}$ which is the voltage change due to a single electron on the capacitor. In our simulation $\Delta V = 1.1mV$. The OU process derives from the solution of a stochastic differential equation of the form [1]:

$$dv(t) = -\lambda v(t)dt + dW(t) \tag{6}$$

where $W(t)$ is a Lévy process[7]. Examples of Lévy processes are the Wiener process, used for describing the Brownian motion, and the Poisson process. The discrete time solution of Equation 6 can be expressed as:

$$V_0 = 0, \quad V_t = V_{t-1} \exp\left(-\frac{t}{\tau}\right) + X_t \frac{q}{C_{out}}. \tag{7}$$

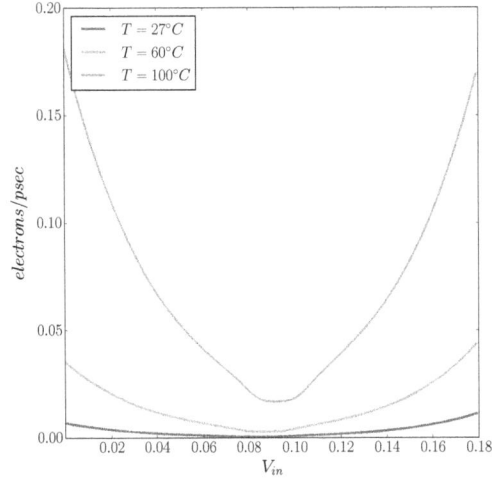

Figure 3: Charging rate λ as a function of the input voltage V_{in} for a CMOS inverter. The rate is expressed in electrons per picosecond.

With this expression for how the time response of the circuit combines with the noise current time series, we can integrate this information with the rates computed above to get the standard deviation of the noise as a function of the biasing point, as explained in the next Section.

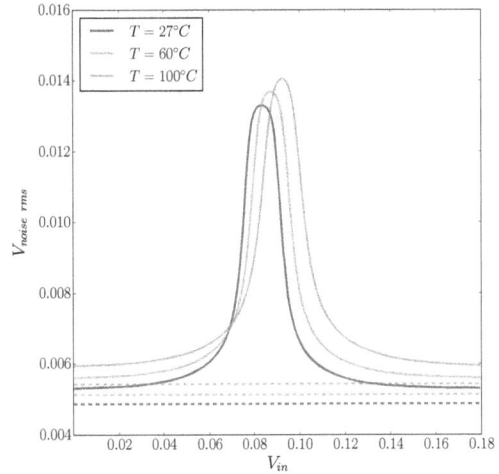

Figure 4: Standard deviation of the output noise voltage as a function of V_{in}. The dashed lines represent the theoretical minimum for thermal noise $(kT/C)^{1/2}$.

4. EXTENDING THE MODEL TO TIME DOMAIN APPLICATIONS

In Section 3, we have presented the basic concepts that allow us to study the statistical behavior of thermal noise in the time-domain. Previous works [12][8][9][10] that have been based on the same two-sided Poisson noise have used inverters or flip-flops. In all these cases, the output noise results from the contribution coming from two transistors. In this Section we first apply the results from Section 3 to a CMOS inverter and then we study how the same model can be extended to more complex gates. We have based our calculations on a 7nm FinFET predictive technology model (PTM). For all the examples show in this work, the capacitive load is equivalent to drain capacitances of the first stage inverter and the gate

47

capacitances of the load inverter. Both inverters were sized using 2 fins for NMOS and PMOS alike. The resulting C_{out} is $149aF$ at $V_{DD} = 180mV$, hence, we assumed a total number of electrons of roughly 168 when $V_{out} = 180mV$.

Figure 3 shows the charging rate for a CMOS inverter at different temperatures. While Figure 3 shows lower rates at $V_{in} = \frac{V_{DD}}{2}$, the noise standard deviation will be the highest at this point. The actual standard deviation of the noise can be obtained combining the Poisson rates with the instantaneous time constant of the circuit as a function of the biasing point. This can be done by counting the average number of electrons in the time constant at a certain input voltage V_{in} and taking the square root of this average. Figure 4 shows the resulting noise rms voltage as a function of the input voltage V_{in}. It is important to notice how the standard deviation curves never go below the theoretical minimum thermal noise $\sqrt{kT/C}$ which would result from the classical noise analysis approach [17][22]. The curves in Figure 4 show the standard deviation of the noise in equilibrium conditions, that is, when the input and output voltage mean values match the voltage transfer curve of the inverter. These curves would depict the noise behavior when the circuit is changing state. A much more interesting situation is shown in Figures 5a and 5b. These two plots represent the case in which the input voltage is at a fixed value and the noise excursion is caused by variations of the output voltage. The asymmetry in the

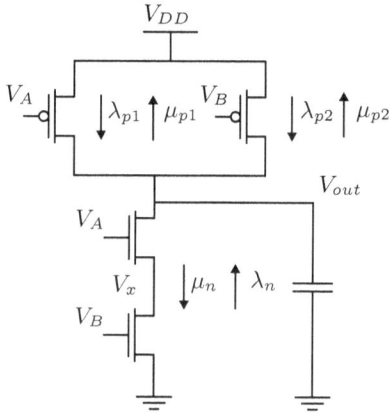

Figure 6: NAND rates. The transistor stack adds a degree of freedom in the calculation of the total noise.

plots from Figure 5a shows how the circuit reacts when it is away from its equilibrium point. For example, the plot on the left shows the case in which $V_{in} = 180mV$. The equilibrium point, where the charging and discharging rates match, is at $V_{out} = 0V$, as expected. For negative values of V_{out}, the charging rate becomes greater than the discharging rate, as the circuit wants to pull the output node back to its stable point. The same behavior appears for positive values of V_{out}, this time with the discharging rate being greater than the charging rate.

The simulation framework used for modeling the inverter can be easily scaled up to more complex multi-input gates. Figure 6 shows the configuration for a NAND gate. In our model, we assume that the total rate for either the charging or the discharging process is made up of three components (i.e., the currents from the two PMOS transistors and the current from the NMOS transistor at the top of the stack). While we do not directly consider the bottom transistor in the pull-down stack for the count of the total rate, its influence in the total noise is given by how the rates of the top

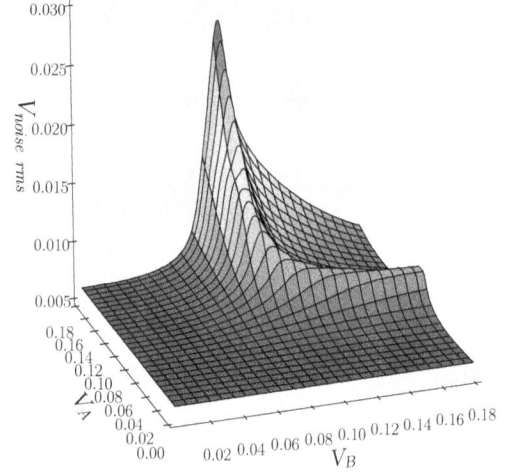

Figure 7: Standard deviation of the output noise voltage as a function of the two inputs V_A and V_B.

transistor are affected by the voltage V_x. This is made more clear by looking at Figure 7. When V_B is high and V_A is varying, the bottom transistor is on and the pull-down network behaves as in the case of the inverter with the rates governed by the V_A. This means that only the forward rate is affected. When V_A is high and V_B is varying, we observe a much higher peak noise. This behavior can be explained by considering that in the latter case, the rates are both controlled by the voltage V_x which varies with V_B.

5. NOISE SIMULATOR

Based on the model description from Section 4, we built our noise simulator. This model was entirely written in C++ with the goal of being able to simulate noise time series in the range of milliseconds to seconds. The algorithm flow can be summarized as in Figure 8. Without loss of generality let us consider the case for an inverter. We start by initializing the parameters at a stable point in the transfer curve of the inverter. For the desired V_{in}, V_{out} pair, we extract the noise parameters λ_t, μ_t and τ_t. At this point we are ready to start the noise samples generation. We generate the Poisson events by counting the inter–arrival times in a period of $50ps$. This value has been chosen so that the integration time is always less than the time constant of the circuit. Since the value of the Poisson rates changes during the simulation, we need to generate the time series from a non–homogeneous Poisson process. A non–homogeneous Poisson process is defined by a time varying rate function $\lambda(t)$. The authors of [11] have shown an efficient way to generate Poisson samples having a time dependent rate function. The algorithm starts by generating Poisson samples in the interval $(0, T]$ with rate $\lambda^* \geq \lambda_t \quad \forall \quad t \in (0, T]$. Then, each sample X_i^* from the series $X_1^*, X_2^*, X_3^*, \ldots X_n^*$ is rejected with probability $1 - \lambda_i/\lambda^*$. The samples that survive this *thinning* procedure, constitute a non–homogeneous Poisson process with with rate function $\lambda(t)$. For our simulator, we generate samples at the highest rate λ_{max} and then add each event to the total count with probability λ_t/λ_{max}[4]. We get the cumulative count at each time–step by subtracting the discharging process count from the charging process count. This value is then translated into an equivalent voltage step ΔV and applied to the time series as shown in Equation 7.

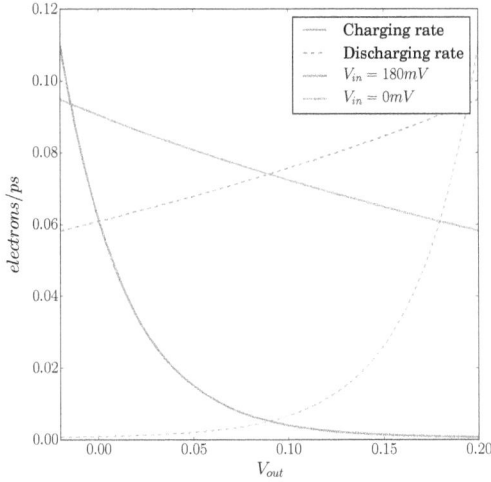

(a) Charging and discharging rates.

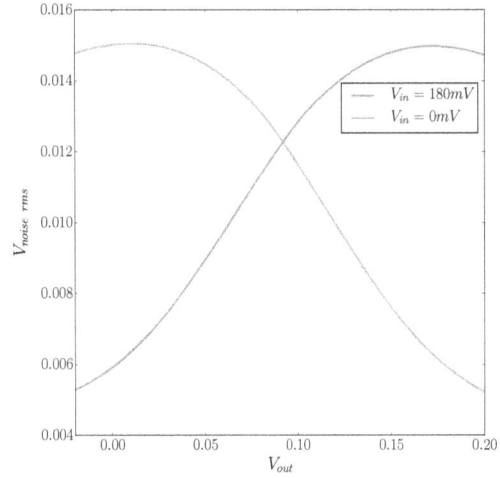

(b) Standard deviation.

Figure 5: Rates and standard deviation of an inverter as a function of the output voltage V_{out}. For the charging and discharging rates, the equilibrium is reached when the values of the two rates are matched.

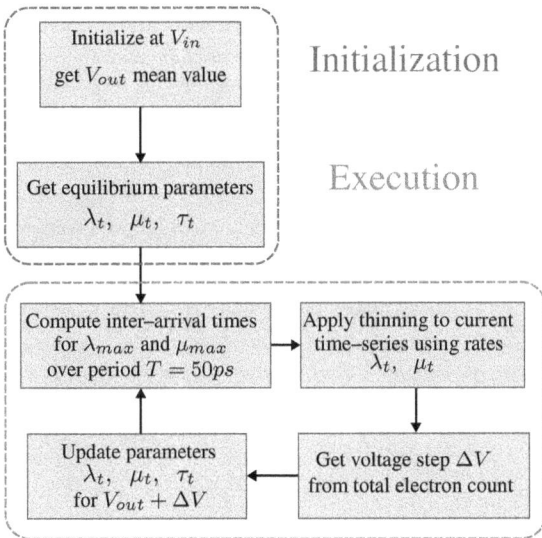

Figure 8: Algorithm flow for the noise simulator.

For each new value of the output voltage, we update the parameters λ_t, μ_t and τ_t, and we proceed to the next iteration of the loop. This last step guarantees that the new noise sample will take into account the deviation from the equilibrium condition. An important requirement of our simulator is to be able to generate long time series without incurring in any periodic pattern. We decided to use the Marsenne-Twister engine [15] which guarantees a period of 2^{19937} (well above our simulation needs). In Figure 9 we compare the accuracy of our approach against SPICE and also evaluate the importance of using the OU process in our approach. In particular, the purple traces in Figure 9 show the the voltage time series results generated from our model (*i.e.* as described in Equation 7). We compare this against the orange traces in Figure 9 which show the response of the SPICE circuit to shot–noise current pulses that were generated from the net electron count derived by our simulator. These current pulses were injected in the output node of the inverter to simulate the actual noise response of the circuit. Finally, the grey traces in Figure 8 show the time series composed of only

the voltage steps $X_t q / C_{out}$ (*i.e.*, ignoring the OU process). From our results in Figure 9 we see that our approach give results in very close agreement to SPICE and the OU process is an important component to achieve accurate results. The performance can be tested on the comparison between the time needed by our noise simulator to generate $100 \mu sec$ of noise samples and the time it takes for SPICE to run a full transient simulation on the same time interval. Our simulator generated the samples in $18.6 sec$ while the SPICE simulation took in total 14.4 minutes, showing that simulation time can be improved by a factor of $47 \times$. Moreover, our simulator takes on average a mere 4 hours to produce a 5σ event. By comparison, SPICE would have to run for almost 10 days to provide the same result. In order to take advantage of this performance improvement, we propose to use our simulator for exploratory analysis of noise transients. By running our simulator for long periods of time, we can extract noise transients from long noise time series, and use SPICE to simulate around rare noise samples in a time range of a few time constants.

6. CONCLUSIONS

In this work, we presented a framework for improving the simulation efficiency of thermal noise in the time domain, starting from the unified shot-thermal noise model. The Ornstein–Uhlenbeck process has been used to capture the correct dynamic response of the circuit while we have guaranteed the correct model behavior to varying biasing conditions using non–homogeneous Poisson processes for modeling the charging and discharging electron flows. Our model can noticeably decrease the simulation time of long thermal noise time–series allowing to capture rare events not only significantly faster than conventional SPICE simulations, but also with comparable physical accuracy. For future work we plan to use our approach as an easier method for evaluating the response of the circuit to rare thermal noise patterns. This will require enabling the simulator to analyze larger and more complex logic circuits. We note that with our current focus on thermal noise, we have not been able to directly compare our results to that of other published works such as [14] and [13] since these works promise non-Monte Carlo methods for modeling nonstationary low–frequency noise phenomena which are fundamentally different from thermal noise. However, we also plan to extend our framework to other noise sources

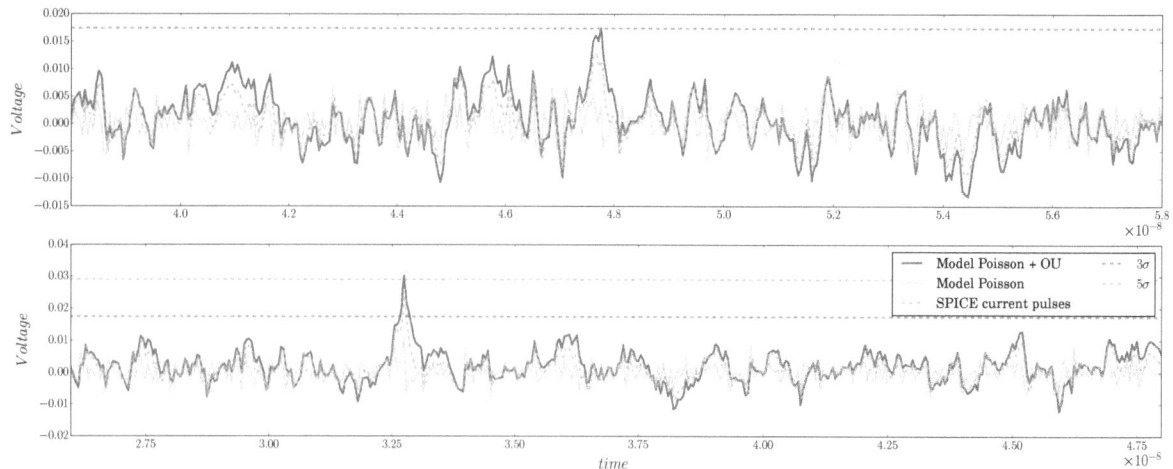

Figure 9: Comparison of the time series generated by our simulator and the SPICE transient response to the shot–noise currents. We used 3σ and 5σ thresholds for the noise events, where $\sigma = (kT/C)^{1/2}$

such as RTS noise, providing better conditions for conducting a comparative study with other models.

7. ACKNOWLEDGEMENTS

This work was supported by the Defense Threat Reduction Agency under Basic Research Award HDTRA1-10-1-0013

8. REFERENCES

[1] O. E. Barndorff-Nielsen and N. Shephard. Non–Gaussian Ornstein–Uhlenbeck-based models and some of their uses in financial economics. *J. R. Stat. Soc. B*, 63(2):167–241, 2001.

[2] E. Bibbona, G. Panfilo, and P. Tavella. The Ornstein–Uhlenbeck process as a model of a low pass filtered white noise. *Metrologia*, 45(6):S117–S126, Dec. 2008.

[3] D. Blaauw, D. Sylvester, Y. Lee, I. Y. Lee, S. Bang, I. Lee, Y. Kim, G. Kim, and H. Ghead. From digital processors to analog building blocks: Enabling new applications through ultra-low voltage design. In *SubVT 2012*.

[4] P. Bratley, B. L. Fox, and L. E. Schrage. *A Guide to Simulation*, volume 2. Springer, 1983.

[5] B. Calhoun, J. Ryan, S. Khanna, M. Putic, and J. Lach. Flexible Circuits and Architectures for Ultralow Power. *Proc. IEEE*, 98(2):267–282, Feb. 2010.

[6] D. T. Gillespie. Exact numerical simulation of the Ornstein-Uhlenbeck process and its integral. *Phys. Rev. E*, 54(2):2084–2091, 1996.

[7] K. Itô. *Stochastic Processes: Lectures Given at Aarhus University*. Springer, 2004.

[8] P. Jannaty, F. Sabou, R. Bahar, J. Mundy, W. Patterson, and A. Zaslavsky. Full two-dimensional markov chain analysis of thermal soft errors in subthreshold nanoscale cmos devices. *IEEE Trans. Device Mater. Rel.*, 11(1):50–59, March 2011.

[9] P. Jannaty, F. C. Sabou, S. T. Le, M. Donato, R. I. Bahar, W. Patterson, J. Mundy, and A. Zaslavsky. Shot-Noise-Induced Failure in Nanoscale Flip-Flops Part I: Numerical Framework. *IEEE Trans. Electron Devices*, 59(3):800–806, Mar. 2012.

[10] P. Jannaty, F. C. Sabou, S. T. Le, M. Donato, R. I. Bahar, W. Patterson, J. Mundy, and A. Zaslavsky. Shot-Noise-Induced Failure in Nanoscale Flip-Flops Part II:

[11] P. A. Lewis and G. S. Shedler. Simulation of nonhomogeneous poisson processes by thinning. *Nav. Res. Logist. Q.*, 26(3):403–413, 1979.

[12] H. Li, J. Mundy, W. Patterson, D. Kazazis, A. Zaslavsky, and R. I. Bahar. Thermally-induced soft errors in nanoscale CMOS circuits. In *NANOARCH*, pages 62–69, Oct. 2007.

[13] A. G. Mahmutoglu and A. Demir. Modeling and Analysis of Nonstationary Low-frequency Noise in Circuit Simulators: Enabling Non Monte Carlo Techniques. In *ICCAD 2014*.

[14] A. G. Mahmutoglu, A. Demir, and J. Roychowdhury. Modeling and analysis of (nonstationary) low frequency noise in nano devices: A synergistic approach based on stochastic chemical kinetics. In *ICCAD 2013*.

[15] M. Matsumoto and T. Nishimura. Mersenne twister: A 623-dimensionally equidistributed uniform pseudo-random number generator. *ACM Trans. Model. Comput. Simul.*, 8(1):3–30, Jan. 1998.

[16] N. Paydavosi, S. Venugopalan, Y. Chauhan, J. Duarte, S. Jandhyala, A. Niknejad, and C. Hu. BSIM–SPICE Models Enable FinFET and UTB IC Designs. *Access, IEEE*, 1:201–215, 2013.

[17] R. Sarpeshkar, T. Delbruck, and C. Mead. White noise in MOS transistors and resistors. *IEEE Circuits Devices Mag.*, 9(6):23–29, 1993.

[18] S. Sinha, G. Yeric, V. Chandra, B. Cline, and Y. Cao. Exploring sub-20nm FinFET design with Predictive Technology Models. In *DAC 2012*, pages 283–288.

[19] P. L. Smith. From Poisson shot noise to the integrated Ornstein–Uhlenbeck process: Neurally principled models of information accumulation in decision-making and response time. *J. Math. Psychol.*, 54(2):266–283, Apr. 2010.

[20] Y. Taur and T. H. Ning. *Fundamentals of Modern VLSI Devices*. Cambridge University Press, Cambridge, UK, 2013.

[21] G. Uhlenbeck and L. Ornstein. On the Theory of the Brownian Motion. *Phys. Rev.*, 36(5):823–841, Sept. 1930.

[22] A. Van der Ziel. *Noise in Solid State Devices and Circuits*. Wiley-Interscience, 1986.

Design of Approximate Unsigned Integer Non-restoring Divider for Inexact Computing

Linbin Chen
ECE Department
Northeastern University
Boston, MA USA
chen.lin@husky.neu.edu

Jie Han
ECE Department
University of Alberta
Edmonton, AB, Canada
jhan8@ualberta.ca

Weiqiang Liu
College of EIE
Nanjing University of Aero.
& Astro., China
liuweiqiang@nuaa.edu.cn

Fabrizio Lombardi
ECE Department.
Northeastern University
Boston, MA USA
lombardi@ece.neu.edu

ABSTRACT

This paper proposes several approximate divider designs; two different levels of approximation (cell and array levels) are investigated for non-restoring division. Three approximate subtractor cells are proposed and designed for the basic subtraction; these cells mitigate accuracy in subtraction with other metrics, such as circuit complexity and power dissipation. At array level, by considering the exact cells, both replacement and truncation schemes are introduced for approximate array divider design. A comprehensive evaluation of approximation at both cell and divider level is pursued. Different circuit metrics including complexity and power dissipation are evaluated by HSPICE simulation. Mean error distance (MED), normalized error distance (NED) and MED-power product (MPP) are provided to substantiate the accuracy and power trade-off of inexact computing. Different applications in image processing are investigated by utilizing the proposed approximate arithmetic circuits.

Categories and Subject Descriptors

B.7.1 [**INTEGRATED CIRCUITS**]: Types and Design Styles – *Algorithms implemented in hardware.*

General Terms

Design, Performance.

Keywords

Inexact computing, Division, Error Distance, Power Dissipation

1. INTRODUCTION

Most computer arithmetic applications are implemented using digital logic circuits, thus operating with a high degree of reliability and accuracy. However, many applications such as multimedia and image processing can tolerate errors and imprecision in computation and still produce meaningful and useful results. The paradigm of inexact computation relies on relaxing fully precise and completely deterministic building modules when for example, designing energy efficient systems. This allows imprecise computation to redirect the existing design process of digital circuits and systems by taking advantage of a decrease in complexity and cost with possibly a potential increase in performance and power efficiency.

Inexact computing is well suited for arithmetic circuits such as adders and multipliers. Recently, five approximate mirror adders (AMAs) have been investigated by logic reduction at transistor level [1]. The three approximate XOR-based adders (AXAs) of [2] show attractive operational profiles for performance, hardware efficiency and power-delay product (PDP), while retaining a good accuracy. Approximate multipliers based on approximate adders have also been proposed, since a multiplier is usually implemented by cascading multiple adders. Some of the less significant bits in the partial products can be truncated [3] while providing error compensation mechanisms; this type of scheme removes some of the adders for a faster execution of this operation. In [4], a simplified 2×2 bit multiplier is used as modular block of a multiplier with larger operand size. An efficient multiplier design using input pre-processing and additional error compensation is proposed for reducing the critical path delay in [5]. To the authors' best knowledge, there have not been any technical literature on an approximate divider (AXD) design. In this paper, the approximate subtractor (AXS) is initially considered as a first level of approximation for a non-restoring AXD (AXDnr). New AXDnr cells (AXDCnr) are proposed and the approximate operation is carried further at divider level by considering different schemes by which exact cells can be replaced by approximate cells or truncated (removed). A comprehensive evaluation of approximation at both cell- and divider-levels is pursued using HSPICE simulation at PTM 32nm technology; various circuit metrics (such as complexity, and power dissipation) are evaluated. MED, NED and MED Power Product are provided to substantiate the accuracy and power trade-off of inexact computing. Different applications in image processing are investigated by utilizing the proposed approximate arithmetic circuits. As for image processing, approximate division often results in a very marginal decrease in quality (as measured by metrics such as PSNR).

2. REVIEW

2.1 Exact Subtractor (EXS)

The functions of an exact subtractor cell (EXSC) and exact full adder cell (EXAC) are quite similar (Table 1). D denotes the difference between X and Y, B_{in} is the borrow bit to the lower position and B_{out} is the borrow bit from the higher position. So, the discussion of EXSC is also applicable to EXAC. An unsigned N-bit ripple EXS can be implemented using N cascading EXSCs.

There are three basic Boolean operations in EXSC and EXAC: XOR/XNOR, AND and OR. Two XOR/XNOR cascaded gates generate the outputs S or D; two AND and one OR gates generate C_{out} or B_{out}. At circuit-level the XOR can be implemented using 3 to 4 transistors (Figure 1(b) or (c)). The XNOR can be implemented using 4 transistors (Figure 1(a)). XOR and XNOR can be used interchangeably to implement the sum output S and the subtraction output D. The AND and OR functions can be implemented using a 2-transistor MUX (Figure 2).

Table 1 EXAC and EXSC Functions

	S or D	C_{out} or B_{out}
EXAC	$S = X \oplus Y \oplus C_{in}$	$C_{out} = \overline{X \oplus Y} \cdot C_{in} + XY$
EXSC	$D = X \oplus Y \oplus B_{in}$	$B_{out} = \overline{X \oplus Y} \cdot B_{in} + \overline{X}Y$

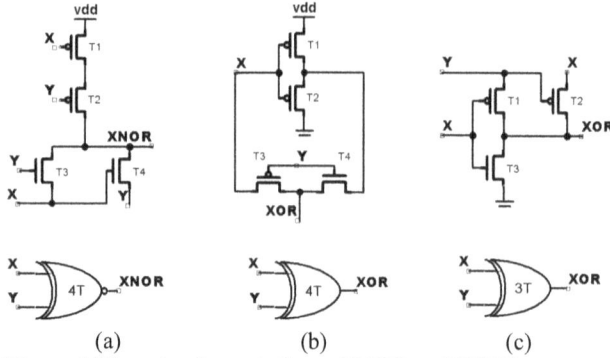

(a) (b) (c)

Figure 1 Three implementations of XOR and XNOR gates and related symbols. (a) 4T XNOR from [6] (b) 4T XOR from [7] and (c) 3T XOR from [8]

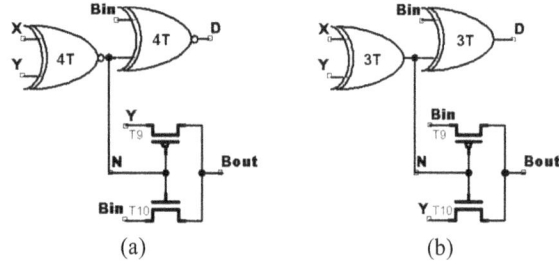

(a) (b)

Figure 2 Implementations of an EXSC (a) based on a 4T XNOR and (b) based on a 3T XOR

Similar to the EXACs in [2], the implementations of the EXSC are shown in Figure 2; when simulating by HSPICE, the signal integrity may be degraded due to the pass transistor logic; thus, a buffer is inserted to preserve an acceptable signal integrity.

2.2 Exact Non-Restoring Divider (EXDnr)

For integer division, the operands are the dividend X and the non-zero divisor Y, and the results of the operation are the quotient Q and the remainder R, i.e.

$$X = YQ + R$$

where the sign of the remainder R is the same as the dividend X and $|R| < |Y|$. A common division algorithm is **non-restoring division** [9].

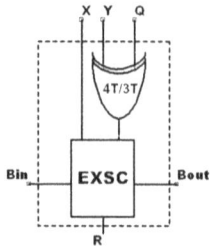

$$R = X \oplus (Y \oplus Q) \oplus B_{in}$$
$$B_{out} = \overline{X \oplus Y \oplus Q} \cdot B_{in} + \overline{X}(Y \oplus Q)$$

Figure 3 EXDCnr and its logic functions using EXSC

Exact Non-Restoring Divider Cell (EXDCnr): An EXDCnr is made of an EXSC and a XOR gate (Figure 3). Q is a control signal such that when Q = 0, EXDCnr is configured as an exact full subtractor (X-Y); when Q = 1, EXDCnr is configured as an

exact full adder (X+Y). This configurable divider cell is the basic building block for an EXDnr.

Exact Non-restoring Divider (EXDnr): A 8-by-4 bits unsigned EXDnr is shown in Figure 4; it computes the unsigned integer division for X[7:0], Y[3:0], Q[3:0] and R[3:0].

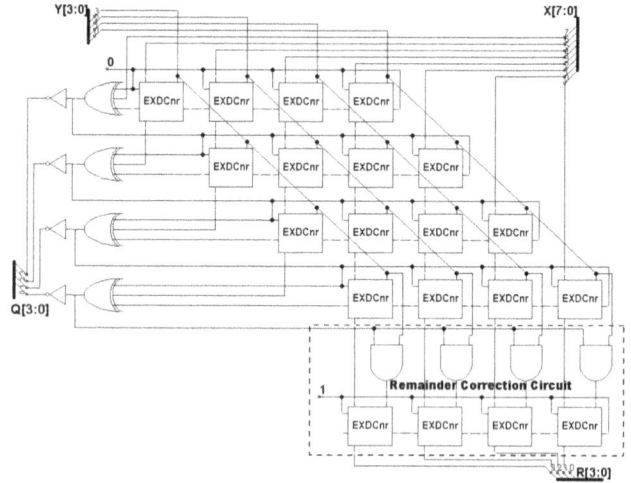

Figure 4 8-to-4 unsigned EXDnr

3. APPROXIMATE SUBTRACTOR (AXS)

3.1 Approximate Subtractor Cell (AXSC)

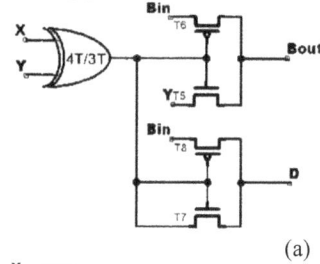

$$D = X \oplus Y + B_{in}$$
$$B_{out} = \overline{X \oplus Y} \cdot B_{in} + \overline{X}Y$$

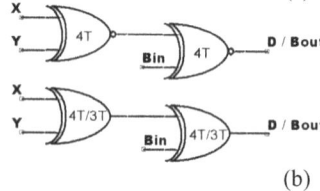

(a)

$$D = X \oplus Y \oplus B_{in}$$
$$B_{out} = D \text{ or } B_{out} = B_{in}$$

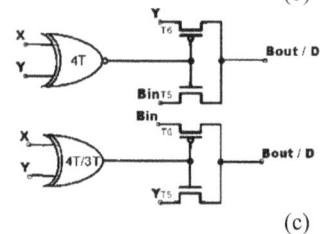

(b)

$$D = B_{out}$$
$$B_{out} = \overline{X \oplus Y} \cdot B_{in} + \overline{X}Y$$

(c)

Figure 5 (a) AXSC1 (b) AXSC2 and (c) AXSC3

Three types of AXSC (AXSC1-AXSC3) are introduced next; their diagrams and functions are shown as Figure 5; two versions (the XOR and XNOR based designs) are proposed for some cells (AXSC2, AXSC3). There are two XOR/XNORs in an EXSC; each of them consists of 4 or 3 transistors. Therefore, the elimination of one of them in an AXS design is an obvious choice for reducing the number of transistors (AXSC1 and AXSC3 abide by this consideration). In the operation of a subtractor, the accuracy of B_{out} is in general more important than D; so, in an AXSC design, B_{out} is unchanged (as in AXSC1 and AXSC3). To reduce the delay, the output signal D and B_{out} can be combined (as occurring in AXSC2 and AXSC3).The truth table for each input combination of these approximate cells is shown in Table 2. The number of transistors and the error distance are shown in Table 3.

Table 2 Truth Table of 3 Proposed AXS Cells

X	Y	B_{in}	EXSC		AXSC1		AXSC2		AXSC3	
			B_{out}	D	B_{out}	D	B_{out}	D	B_{out}	D
0	0	0	0	0	0	0	0	0	0	0
0	0	1	1	1	1	1	1	1	1	1
0	1	0	1	1	1	1	1	1	1	1
0	1	1	1	0	1	**1**	**0**	0	1	**1**
1	0	0	0	1	0	1	**1**	1	0	**0**
1	0	1	0	0	0	**1**	0	0	0	0
1	1	0	0	0	0	0	0	0	0	0
1	1	1	1	1	1	1	1	1	1	1

Table 3 Transistor Count and Error Distance of AXSCs

Subtractor Cell	Transistor Count	Error Distance
EXSC	10	0
AXSC1	8 or 7	2
AXSC2	8, 7 or 6	4
AXSC3	6 or 5	2

3.2 Approximate Subtractor (AXS)

In this section, an N-bit AXS is evaluated. The three types of AXSC are used to replace some of the LSBs of an EXS. The replacement depth d is used to represent the number of the EXSCs replaced by the AXSCs.

3.2.1 MED and NED

In addition to the error distance (ED), the mean error distance (MED) and the normalized error distance (NED) have been proposed [10] by considering the averaging effect of multiple inputs and the normalization of multiple-bit adders. The MED is defined as the mean value of the EDs of all possible outputs for each input. The NED is defined as the MED normalized by the maximum ED that a design incurs. The MED is effective in evaluating multiple-bit approximate arithmetic circuit, while the NED is nearly invariant with the size of an implementation and therefore, is useful in the assessment of a specific type of design.

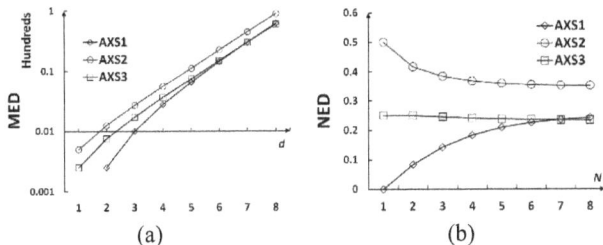

Figure 6 (a) MED of 8-bits AXS with depth d, and (b) NED of N-bit AXS with depth d=N

The MEDs for 8-bit AXS with replacement depth d are shown in Figure 6(a) on a logarithmic scale; AXS1 and AXS3 have the smallest MED, because they nearly preserves the exact computation for subtraction. The NEDs of the proposed AXS with different AXSCs and replacement depth d=N are plotted in Figure 6(b); the value of the NED for different AXS reduces to a constant as the width of the subtractor increases; AXS1 and AXS3 have relative smaller NEDs compared to AXS2.

3.2.2 MED Power Product (MPP)

MPP is used to assess the trade-off between computational accuracy and power consumption for approximate computing circuits. Figure 7(a) shows the dynamic power by exhaustive

simulation using AXSCs in AXS. As the replacement depth d increases, the power consumption decreases. The switching activity of AXS2 is higher (different from AXS1 and AXS3), hence the power of AXS2 is not as good as the other two schemes. MPP is shown in Figure 7 (b). AXS1 has the best MPP when d is low, but it deteriorates at higher values of d. When d increases, AXS3 is the best scheme. On average, the MPP shows that AXS3 is the best choice for an AXS.

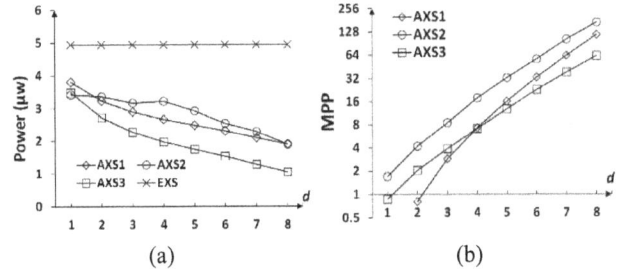

Figure 7 (a) Power and (b) MPP of 8-bit AXS

4. APPROXIMATE NON-RESTORING DIVIDER (AXDnr)

4.1 AXDCnr

The design of an AXDCnr takes advantage of the corresponding AXSC, because subtraction is the basic operation of division. The corresponding AXDCnr1-3 can be derived by substituting the EXSC in Figure 3 with AXSC1-3 presented in previous section.

4.2 AXDnr

4.2.1 Replacement Scheme

A simple divider-level approximation is to use cell replacement, *i.e.* to replace some EXDCnrs in the EXDnr with the AXDCnrs developed in Section 4.1. The approximate cells have a smaller circuit complexity, so making the entire divider less complex and consuming less power. These advantageous features are accomplished at the expenses of introducing errors at the outputs for the quotient Q and/or the remainder R. The errors in Q and R are correlated. So an approximate divider can be designed to have either a more accurate Q with a less accurate R (division), or a more accurate R with a less accurate Q (modulo). Approximation is therefore the process by which exact cell is replaced by an approximate cell; the extent by which this replacement process is performed in a divider is quantified by the depth d, *i.e.* the number of rows (and/or columns) in the divider array with approximate cells. Four types of approximation are used (Figure 8) for the division operation for the accuracies of Q and R.

Vertical Replacement (VR): The least significant (LSB) EXDCnrs in each row of the divider are replaced by AXDCnrs. The depth of the vertical replacement can be increased to further decrease the power while tolerating more errors in the output. Hence, $4 \times d$ EXDCnr cells are replaced with AXDCnr cells in a divider with a vertical approximation of depth d. One example of depth d=2 is shown in Figure 8(a).

Horizontal Replacement (HR): The value of the quotient is mostly related to the borrow signal of each cell in a single row. For example, consider the last row corresponding to the LSB of Q; if the value of R is not of significant concern, then all EXDCnrs in the last row can be replaced with AXDCnrs without losing the accuracy of Q. If some error can be tolerated at Q, then an increase in the depth of the horizontal replacement up to the dth LSB of Q is possible. An example of a horizontal replacement divider of depth d=2 is shown in Figure 8(b).

Square Replacement (SR): By combining the vertical and horizontal replacement; a new configuration is referred to as the square replacement. Hence, in a dth AXDnr, d^2 EXDCnrs are replaced with AXDCnrs. An example of a square replacement AXDnr of depth $d=2$ is shown as Figure 8(c).

Triangle Replacement (TR): Consider the integer pair (i,j) as coordinates of each cell in a divider (Figure 9). An EXDCnr (i,j) ($i<d$ or $j<d$) is replaced by a AXDCnr. So, in a triangle approximation divider with depth d ($d\geq1$), $d(d+1)/2$ EXDCnrs are replaced with AXDCs. An example of a triangle approximation divider with $d=2$ is shown in Figure 8(d).

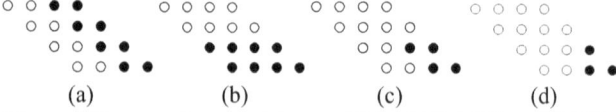

(a)   (b)   (c)   (d)

Figure 8 Four replacement types of 8-to-4 bit AXDnr: (a) VR, (b) HR, (c) SR, and (d) TR. The replaced cells are shaded.

4.2.2 Truncation Scheme

Truncation consists of fully removing at least a cell (so no replacement with AXDCnr(s)); this process is shown by the shaded cells in Figure 8. The input X of the removed cell is left unchanged and moved downwards along the remainder output direction, while the input Y of the removed cell is discarded. Similar to replacement scheme, a truncation scheme has also four configurations: Vertical Truncation (VT), Horizontal Truncation (HT), Square Truncation (ST) and Triangle Truncation (TT).

4.3 Evaluation of AXDnrs

4.3.1 Error Estimation of AXDnrs

Error generation and propagation can be qualitatively analyzed by the location of the replaced or truncated cells in the divider. A so-called *error impact coefficient* (denoted by S) is proposed to simplify the analysis for finding the impact of the inexact or truncated cells in the array divider. An approximate scheme consists of replacing or truncating only a portion of the divider; this leads to different approximate configurations with different accuracy for the output values (Q and R). In a divider, the dividend X and the divisor Y are provided as inputs at the north side, while the quotient Q and the reminder R are generated at the west and the south sides respectively (Figure 9). So, each cell (located at a unique position in the divider) plays a different role in generating an error; intuitively, cell replacement or truncation must not preferably occur at the MSBs of Q and R. Therefore, the coefficients $S_{Q,(ij)}$ and $S_{R,(i,j)}$ are given by

$$\begin{cases} S_{Q,ij} = \dfrac{1}{\sqrt{(i-N)^2+(j-2N+1)^2}} \\ S_{R,ij} = \dfrac{1}{\sqrt{(i+1)^2+(j-N)^2}} \end{cases} (i \in [1,N), j \in [1,2N-1))$$

in which i, j are the coordinates of the cell in the divider ((0,0) is the origin, as shown in (Figure 9). $S_{Q,(ij)}$ is effectively the distance from the MSB cell of Q to a cell position in the divider; $S_{R,(i,j)}$ is the distance from the MSB cell of R to a cell position in the array. Larger $S_{Q,(i,j)}$ or $S_{R,(i,j)}$ is, a greater error is contributed by the (i,j) cell to the final outputs Q_{error} and R_{error}. So, the impacts of errors at the outputs Q and R are given by

$$S_Q = \sum S_{Q,ji} \quad S_R = \sum S_{R,ij}$$

where, $S_{Q,ij}$ and $S_{R,ij}$ are due to cell (i,j) when using an approximate implementation. Figure 10 illustrates the coefficients S_Q and S_R of the replacement or truncation configurations at different depths. The trends for S_Q and S_R are consistent with the

NEDs plotted in Figure 11; so, S_Q and S_R are good qualitative metrics for analyzing different replacement or truncation schemes.

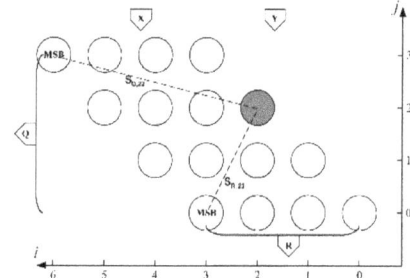

Figure 9 Error impact coefficients S_Q and S_R

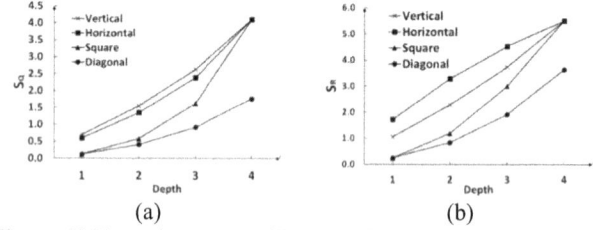

(a)   (b)

Figure 10 Error impact coefficients of different replacement or truncation configurations vs depth: (a) S_Q and (b) S_R

4.3.2 Normalized Error Distance (NED)

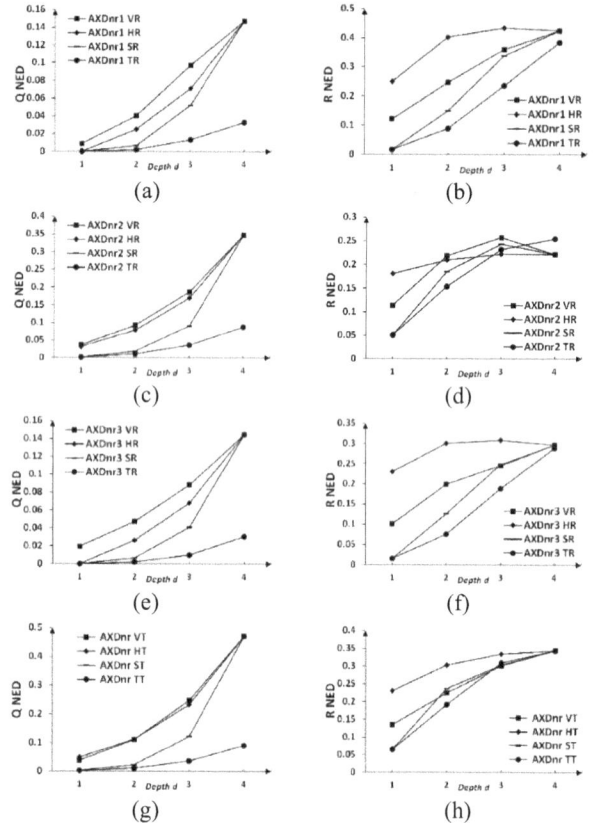

(a)   (b)

(c)   (d)

(e)   (f)

(g)   (h)

Figure 11 NED of AXDnrs for Quotient Q and R (a)(b) AXDnr1, (b)(c) AXDnr2, (d)(e) AXDnr3, (g)(h) Truncation

For a more accurate evaluation of the different approximate designs, the NED has been simulated at different depths (Figure 11). Among the replacement schemes, the error of AXDnr2 is the largest in all cases for Q, but not for R; this is due to the worst (best) accuracy for B_{out} (D) in AXSC2. AXDnr1 and AXDnr3 have on average the smallest NED for both Q and R. Among truncation schemes, the NED of Q is larger than any of its corresponding replacement schemes, because more error is introduced by simply removing a cell compared with replacing it with the proposed AXDC. For both replacement and truncation schemes, the NED of Q for the vertical and horizontal approximations increases rapidly with depth, more than for the square and triangle approximations; the triangle approximation shows the smallest NED for Q compared to the other replacement schemes. The NED of R also increases with replacement depth; moreover, it is larger than the NED of Q. This occurs because the error in R is strongly dependent on the error in Q; however when using a horizontal replacement, the NED of R is less dependent on the replacement depth.

4.3.3 Power consumption

Figure 12 shows the power consumption of AXDnrs versus replacement depth. All AXDnrs consume less power as the replacement depth increases; this is significantly lower than the power consumed by EXDnrs. The power dissipation of the truncation schemes may be slightly larger than the replacement schemes when the depth is small, however the power of a truncation scheme decreases at the highest rate.

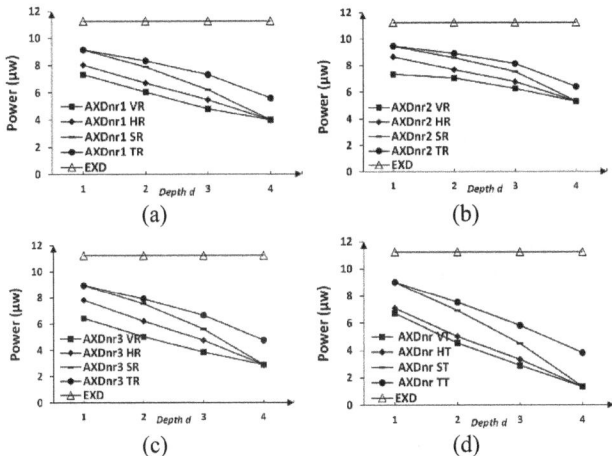

Figure 12 Power consumption of AXDnrs for Quotient Q (a) AXDnr1 (b) AXDnr2 (c) AXDnr3 and (d) Truncation

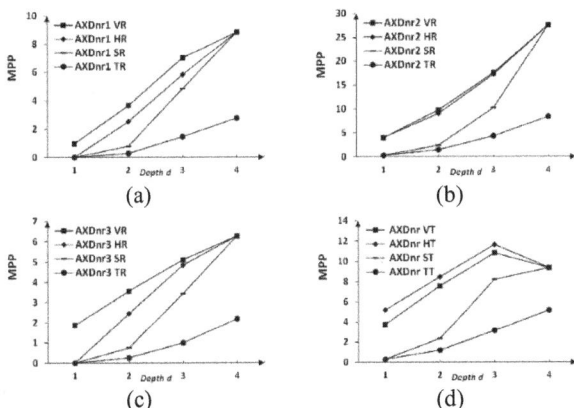

Figure 13 MED Power Product of AXDnrs for Quotient Q (a) AXDnr1 (b) AXDnr2 (c) AXDnr3 and (d) Truncation

4.3.4 MED Power Product (MPP)

To evaluate the tradeoff between computation accuracy and power consumption of the AXDnrs, the MPP of the AXDnrs is calculated and plotted in Figure 13. Although the power saving of a truncation scheme is larger than for a replacement scheme, this

is at the expense of the error; hence, the triangle replacement scheme with AXDnr3 has the smallest MPP. AXDnr3 is very promising for an approximate divider design requiring both high accuracy and low power consumption. AXDnr2 is again shown to be the worst design regardless of the type of replacement. Compared to a replacement scheme, a truncation scheme is not suitable for both high accuracy and low power AXDnr designs.

5. APPLICATIONS

5.1 Pixel Subtraction

Pixel subtraction takes two images as input and produces as output a third image whose values are the subtraction of the second image from the first image on a pixel basis. 8-bit ripple borrow EXS and AXS with replacement depth $d=4$ are used.

Background Removal: In this case, background variations in illumination are subtracted from a scene, such that the foreground objects can be better viewed. For example, the image X in Figure 14 shows some text that has been badly illuminated during capture (*i.e.* there is a strong illumination gradient across the image). If a blank page Y is subtracted from the poorly illuminated image X, the output has a relatively constant illumination. Figure 14 shows the simulation results. The results of AXS1 and AXS3 are better.

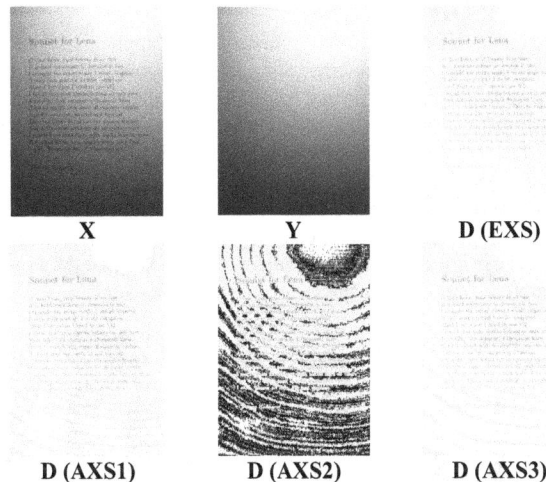

Figure 14 Output images for background removal

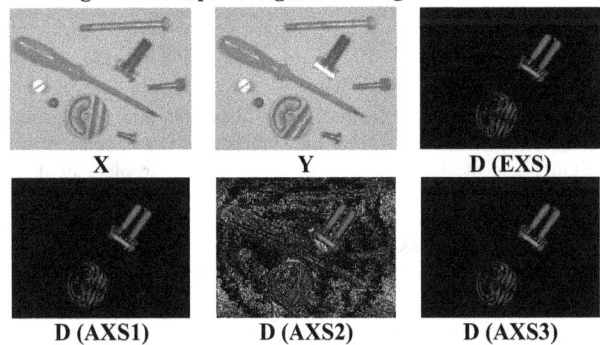

Figure 15 Output images for change detection

Change Detection: The image difference is also used for change detection. If the difference between two frames of a sequence of images is calculated and there is no movement in the scene, then the output image mostly consists of zero value pixels. If there is movement, then the pixels in those regions of the image in which the intensity spatially changes, exhibit significant differences between the two frames. Figure 15 shows the change detection results of a sequence of frames X and Y. AXS1 and AXS3 are capable of detecting the moving part of the image.

The peak signal to noise ratio (PSNR) is commonly used to measure the quality of lossy compression codecs of images. In this case, it is used to assess the quality of the images processed by an inexact arithmetic circuit compared to the ones by an exact arithmetic circuit. For the two image subtraction applications considered in this manuscript, the PSNR results are shown in Figure 16. AXS1 and AXS3 based subtractors have the larger PSNR, so generating the best approximation and the least image errors when replacing EXSCs with AXSCs.

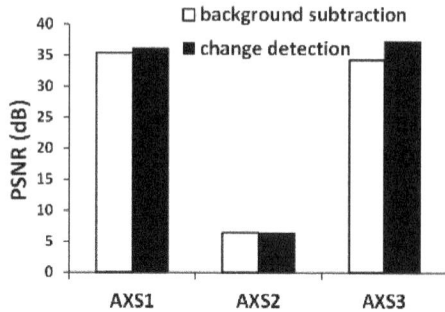

Figure 16 PSNR of AXSs for pixel subtraction

5.2 Pixel Division

The change detection and background removal application can be also realized by division operation. In image analysis, if only integer division is performed, then the results are typically rounded at the output to the next lowest integer. 16-to-8 EXDnr and AXDnr are used to compute the same 8-bit grayscale images as in the previous section; the approximations used in these applications are with depth 3 for VR and HR, depth 2 for VT and HT, depth 5 for SR, depth 4 for ST, depth 7 for TR and depth 5 for TT. These configurations are selected to ensure that the power consumptions are nearly equal.

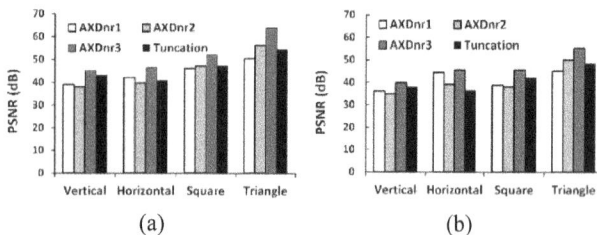

(a)   (b)

Figure 17 Simulated PSNR of pixel division (a) change detection (b) background removal

It can be seen from both change detection and background removal results of Figure 17 that the triangle replacement with AXDnr3 has the best PSNRs while the vertical replacement has overall the worst PSNR.

6. CONCLUSION

This paper has presented a detailed analysis, design and evaluation of dividers that utilize approximate criteria in their operation. As basic operation for division, subtraction has been initially considered. Subsequently, AXDnr have been proposed by introducing approximate computing at cell as well as at divider levels. Division presents unique challenges for approximate computing; it generates two output values (the remainder R and the quotient Q), so changes in cells as well as the dividers may affect one of the outputs more than the other. Hence, different arrangements in the approximate cells have been investigated; these arrangement replaces exact with cells or truncates (eliminates) them according to the direction of computation flow.

The following conclusions can be drawn. (1) The error in Q for different approximation configurations increases with the replacement or truncation depth; the triangle approximation increases at a smaller rate. (2) AXDnr1 and AXDnr3 have on average the smallest NED for Q. However, the error introduced by a truncation scheme is significantly more than a replacement scheme. (3) The error in R due to replacement is significantly larger than the error in Q because R is dependent on Q of previous stage. (4) Power consumption is reduced considerably when the approximation depth increases. Higher the depth, more pronounced is the power reduction. (5) For all depths, AXDnr1 and AXDnr2 consume more power than AXDnr3; the truncation schemes require considerably less power than the replacement schemes. (6) The trade-off between accuracy and power consumption makes an approximate divider design an application specific process. For an application requiring both high accuracy and low power, the MED power product metric shows that AXDnr3 is a good approximate scheme. For Q-oriented applications (image processing), AXDnr3 with a triangle replacement shows the best results.

7. ACKNOWLEDGMENT

This research is supported in part by an NSERC Discovery Grant and by a grant from NSFC (No. 61401197).

8. REFERENCES

[1] Gupta, V., Mohapatra, D., Park, S.P., Raghunathan, A. and Roy, K. 2011. IMPACT: IMPrecise Adders for Low-Power Approximate Computing. In *Proceedings of the International Symposium on Low Power Electronics and Design* (1-3 Aug. 2011), 409-414.

[2] Yang, Z., Jain, A., Liang, J., Han, J. and Lombardi, F. 2013. Approximate XOR/XNOR-based Adders for Inexact Computing. In *Proceedings of the 13th IEEE Conference on Nanotechnology* (5-8 Aug. 2013), 690-693.

[3] Kyaw, K.Y., Goh, W.-L. and Yeo, K.-S. 2010. Low-Power High-Speed Multiplier for Error-Tolerant Application. In *Proceedings of the International Conference of Electron Devices and Solid-State Circuits* (15-17 Dec. 2010), 1-4.

[4] Kulkarni, P., Gupta, P. and Ercegovac, M. 2011. Trading Accuracy for Power with an Underdesigned Multiplier Architecture. In *Proceedings of the 24th International Conference on VLSI Design* (2-7 Jan. 2011), 346-351.

[5] Momeni, A., Han, J., Montuschi, P. and Lombardi, F. 2014. Design and Analysis of Approximate Compressors for Multiplication. *IEEE Trans. Comput.* (Accepted to appear).

[6] Lin, J., Hwang, Y.-T., Sheu, M.-H. and Ho, C.-C. 2007. A Novel High-Speed and Energy Efficient 10-Transistor Full Adder Design. *IEEE Trans. Circuits Syst. I, Reg. Papers 54*, 5, 1050-1059.

[7] Mahmoud, H.A. and Bayoumi, M.A. 1999. A 10-Transistor Low-Power High-Speed Full Adder Cell. In *Proceedings of the IEEE International Symposium on Circuits and Systems* (Jul 1999), 43-46.

[8] Chowdhury, S.R., Banerjee, A., Roy, A. and Saha, H. 2008. A High Speed 8 Transistor Full Adder Design Using Novel 3 Transistor XOR Gates. *International Journal of Electronics, Circuits and Systems 2*, 4, 217-223.

[9] Parhami, B. 2000. *Computer Arithmetic: Algorithms and Hardware Designs*. Oxford University Press.

[10] Liang, J., Han, J. and Lombardi, F. 2013. New Metrics for the Reliability of Approximate and Probabilistic Adders. *IEEE Trans. Comput. 62*, 9, 1760-1771.

Efficient Reliability Analysis of Processor Datapath using Atomistic BTI Variability Models

Dimitrios Stamoulis
Department of ECE
McGill University
Montreal, Canada
dimitrios.stamoulis@mcgill.ca

Dimitrios Rodopoulos
Microlab, School of ECE
NTUA, Athens, Greece
drodo@microlab.ntua.gr

Brett H. Meyer
Department of ECE
McGill University
Montreal, Canada
brett.meyer@mcgill.ca

Dimitrios Soudris
Microlab, School of ECE
NTUA, Athens, Greece
dsoudris@microlab.ntua.gr

Francky Catthoor
imec & KU Leuven
Leuven, Belgium
catthoor@imec.be

Zeljko Zilic
Department of ECE
McGill University
Montreal, Canada
zeljko.zilic@mcgill.ca

ABSTRACT

In this paper, we propose EDA methodologies for efficient, datapath-wide reliability analysis under Bias Temperature Instability (BTI). The proposed EDA flow combines the efficiency of atomistic, pseudo-transient BTI modeling with the accuracy of commercial Static Timing Analysis (STA) tools. In order to reduce the transistor inventory that needs to be tracked by the STA solver, we develop a threshold-pruning methodology to identify the variation-critical part of a design. That way, we accelerate variation-aware STA iterations, with a maximum speedup of 6.82x achieved for representative benchmark circuits. We substantiate the efficiency of the proposed framework for realistic designs. For a CPU datapath, our threshold-pruning technique outperforms built-in pruning commands of the STA solver by 16.87% in terms of runtime improvement. We demonstrate the impact of BTI after three years of operation, with clock frequency degradation up to 24% and functional yield reduction below 90% for higher frequencies.

Categories and Subject Descriptors

B.7.2 [**Integrated Circuits**]: Design Aids—*Simulation, Verification*; B.8.2 [**Hardware**]: Performance and Reliability—*Performance Analysis and Design Aids*

Keywords

Reliability Analysis; Functional Yield Analysis; Bias Temperature Instability (BTI); Static Timing Analysis (STA)

1. INTRODUCTION

Prior art on Bias Temperature Instability (BTI) shows its importance for digital system reliability. Several mod-

eling approaches have been proposed for this phenomenon. The Reaction-Diffusion (RD) model has dominated reliability models and mitigation techniques in prior art [1]. However, the reduction of transistor dimensions has introduced new concerns for the modeling of BTI [2]. Recent defect-based approaches inherently cover transistor aging, accounting for both time-zero/-dependent variability [3,4]. Nonetheless, all previous studies limit their exploration to individual devices, simples gates, SRAM cells and logic blocks.

Literature lacks a comprehensive atomistic BTI modeling flow for datapath-wide reliability analysis of complex CPU modules. In the current paper, we make the following *contributions*: (i) We incorporate a novel, pseudo-transient atomistic BTI methodology [5] with a complete EDA flow, reflecting on the usability of atomistic BTI models for realistic circuits. (ii) We develop a pruning technique to identify the variation-critical part of the transistor inventory that needs to be monitored by an STA tool. We achieve acceleration and reduced memory usage for commercial, transistor-level STA tools with negligible accuracy loss. To the best of our knowledge, this is the *first* study that employs complete reliability analysis for processor-wide reliability metrics, while exploiting the accuracy of atomistic BTI models.

2. RELATED WORK & MOTIVATION

BTI has been studied for more than 30 years as a valid concern for the reliability of Field-Effect Transistors [6]. A modeling approach that has gathered significant momentum throughout the years is the Reaction-Diffusion model [7]. This approach advocates that BTI comes as a result of the breaking of bonds between silicon and hydrogen. This model has been featured in many simulation methods [1], triggering extensive research on BTI countermeasures [8]. Nonetheless, recent literature shows that RD models inherently fail to capture BTI at deca-nanometer technology nodes [9].

Previously, an atomistic approach has evolved, which concentrates on the charge-level activity of gate-stack defects, rather than their actual origin [9]. It attributes the manifestation of BTI to variable numbers of defects, each one with a specific temporal behavior (modeled using time constants) and a certain contribution to overall V_{th} degradation. Minority carriers are trapped and emitted from these sites, leading to V_{th} fluctuations. A variety of related imple-

Table 1: Assessment of SotA: Literature lacks an atomistic BTI flow for subsystem-wide reliability analysis.

Approach	Case Study	Max# FETs	Level of Abstraction
[3,13]	CMOS Logic Gates	6	Gates
[10,14]	6T SRAM cell	6	Gates
[5,11]	subset of SRAM	244	Gates
[15]	Benchmark Circuits	68,000	RTL/ALU
[4]	Array Multiplier	229,376	RTL/ALU
[16]	Logic Subblocks*	N/A **	RTL/ALU
Ours	**CPU module**	1830	Subsystem

* Adders, multipliers, mux-demux and shifter blocks
** Not explicitly reported

mentations exist, modeling BTI either over arbitrary circuit lifetime intervals [10] or in a transient way [11]. However, atomistic BTI modeling comes with increased processing overheads. Recent works have attempted to reconcile the increased accuracy with the computational feasibility of the atomistic BTI model through massive multi-threading [4,12] or novel signal representations [5]. A summary of state-of-the-art (SotA) approaches on atomistic BTI modeling is presented in Table 1.

To fully assess prior art, we sort existing works by the level of abstraction in which BTI modeling has been placed, starting from lower to higher abstraction layers. By inspecting the atomistic BTI-related literature, it is evident that it lacks a comprehensive atomistic BTI modeling flow for subsystem-wide reliability analysis. Previous works have been mostly focusing either on simple CMOS logic gates [3,13] and SRAM cells [5,10,11,14] or on larger netlists of repetitive logic subblocks with reduced functional complexity [4,15,16]. Thus, we observe a limited usability of SotA atomistic BTI models for more complex netlists and realistic CPU modules. This observation constitutes the main motivation behind the current paper. Our goal is to *incorporate an accurate yet efficient BTI modeling methodology with a design flow for credible, subsystem-wide reliability analysis.*

In previous work, a *pseudo-transient* simulation scheme has been devised, enabling fast yet accurate modeling of BTI [5]. We incorporate some of the basic principles of this prior art framework within our proposed EDA flow, aiming to decide on processor-wide reliability metrics, such as yield or maximum clock frequency. However, the atomistic treatment of BTI leads to a statistical and confidence-based perception of those metrics. In other words, given the variable manifestation of BTI it is imperative to employ statistical methods. Thus, another major motivation behind this paper is to accelerate statistical explorations (i.e. Monte-Carlo iterations) used to capture the impact of BTI variability. We develop a pruning algorithm to identify the variation-critical paths to be tracked by a transistor-level STA solver. That way, we alleviate the increased CPU overhead of Monte-Carlo (MC) based reliability analysis, while maintaining the accuracy and the novel features of the atomistic BTI model.

3. PROPOSED EDA METHODOLOGIES

3.1 Transistor-Level V_{th} Modeling

In the context of the current paper, we will introduce two sources of V_{th} variability, (i) a *time-zero* ($\Delta V_{th,\text{TZ}}$) and (ii)

Table 2: BTI model calibration, based on experimental data [17] and the 90 nm Predictive Technology Model [18].

Parameter	Distribution
Operating V_{dd}	$V_{dd} = 0.9$ V $=$ const.
Operating Clock Freq.	$f = 1$ GHz $=$ const.
Temp./Signal Activity	$T = 50°$C $=$ const. / $\alpha = 0.5 =$ const.
Time-Zero pFET	$\Delta V_{th,\text{TZ}} \sim \textbf{Norm}\,(0\text{ V}, 0.0397\text{ V})$
Time-Zero nFET	$\Delta V_{th,\text{TZ}} \sim \textbf{Norm}\,(0\text{ V}, 0.0397\text{ V})$
Defects per pFET	$N_p \sim \textbf{Pois}\,(\lambda = 10^{11} \times \text{Area[cm}^2])$
Defects per nFET	$N_n \sim \textbf{Pois}\,(\lambda = 6.7 \times 10^{10} \times \text{Area[cm}^2])$
Time Const. per Defect (s)	$\log_{10}\left\{\tau_{pV}^*\right\} \sim \textbf{Unif}\,(a = -12, b = 12)$
$\Delta V_{th,\text{TD}}$ per Defect (mV)	$\Delta V_{th,\text{TD}} \sim \textbf{Exp}\,(\eta = 5)$

* p: process, either capture (c) or emission (e)
V: voltage, either high (H) or low (L)

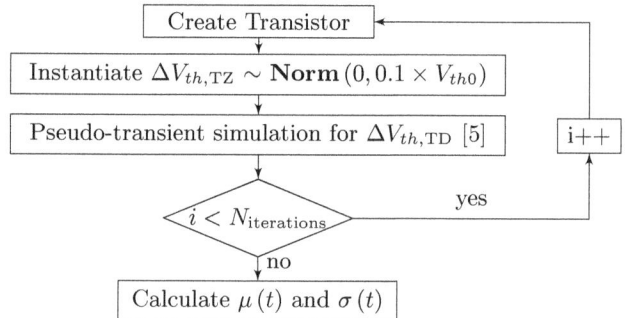

Figure 1: MC iteration scheme to derive distributions for $\Delta V_{th}\,(t)$; we use $N_{\text{iterations}} = 300$ as the halting criterion.

a *time-dependent* ($\Delta V_{th,\text{TD}}\,(t)$) component, as summarized in Equation (1). The former source of variability is typically attributed to fluctuations during the manufacturing process. We will assume that this component is constant throughout the device lifetime and that it follows a Gaussian distribution, namely $\Delta V_{th,\text{TZ}} \sim \textbf{Norm}\,(0, 0.1 \times V_{th0})$, where V_{th0} is the threshold voltage at $V_{bs} = 0$ V, which is typically provided in the transistor modelcard. The latter variability component includes all the time-dependent mechanisms that affect V_{th}, which in our case includes BTI defect activity, simulated according to the atomistic model.

$$\Delta V_{th}\,(t) = \Delta V_{th,\text{TZ}} + \Delta V_{th,\text{TD}}\,(t) \tag{1}$$

In order to enable maximum compatibility with existing STA tools, we choose to express V_{th} variability with a single Gaussian distribution. This design choice also removes the complexity of verbose, circuit-wide, defect databases that were previously utilized [4,5], since we are only interested in the aggregate V_{th} variability at the level of each transistor. As a result, our goal is to create a distribution formulated as $\Delta V_{th}\,(t) \sim \textbf{Norm}\,\{\mu\,(t), \sigma\,(t)\}$. To achieve this goal, we perform a Monte Carlo session per transistor size, where each iteration follows the procedure illustrated in Figure 1, calibrated according to Table 2. Initially, time-zero variabil-

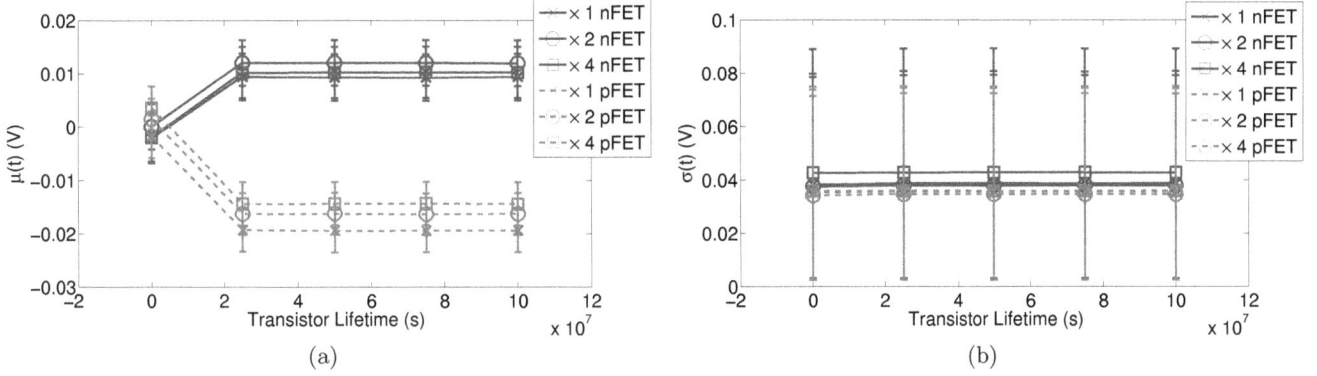

Figure 2: Simulation data for $\Delta V_{th}(t) \sim \mathbf{Norm}\{\mu(t), \sigma(t)\}$, while combining both time-zero and time-dependent variability.

ity is appended. Then, BTI is evaluated over four distinct intervals of transistor lifetime, covering a total of roughly three years (10^8 s). Strides over these intervals are performed according to a "pseudo-transient" simulation setup presented in previous work [5].

After 300 iterations of this process, one can derive estimates for $\mu(t)$ and $\sigma(t)$, by calculating the mean and standard deviation of the available V_{th} data at each point of transistor lifetime. In Figure 2, we present these simulation results, exploring representative FET transistor sizes, assuming the 90 nm Predictive Technology Model [18] and a 95% confidence interval [19]. Given that transistors of the same technology node are typically instantiated at various widths (W), we explore different width values, assuming unit widths of $W = 180$ nm for an nFET and $W = 360$ nm for a pFET. Thus, for the 90 nm technology node the notation "$i \times$ pFET" refers to a pFET with area $A = i \times 360 \times 90$ nm^2 (similarly, for nFETs). This notation is used in the legends of Figure 2.

Based on the results of Figure 2, we can make the following observations: **(i)** The parameter estimation for the distribution of $\Delta V_{th}(t)$ shows a distinct shift after the time-zero instance and remains fairly constant for the rest of the transistor lifetime. This is to be expected given the uniform distribution of defect time constants across the logarithmic time axis. In other words, striking changes in threshold voltage are to be expected if transistor lifetime is inspected logarithmically [3]. This also resembles the power law that is expected by older BTI models, such as the Reaction-Diffusion model [20]. **(ii)** For the considered technology node, transistor area appears to have effectively no impact on BTI impact. This is to be expected, if we consider that the mean V_{th} impact of a single defect is inversely proportional to transistor area, whereas the number of charged traps is positively related to A [21]. In other words, as the transistor area increases (by increasing W) more defects contribute to $\Delta V_{th,TD}$, each of which has a decreased contribution. Thus, increase of W does not affect the aggregate V_{th} variability.

3.2 Efficient Variation-Aware STA

Given the BTI modeling approach presented in the previous Subsection, we now move towards efficiently capturing BTI variability using a transistor-level STA tool. Intuitively, paths with small delay values for all samples do not exhibit significant delay degradation. Hence, we develop a

threshold-pruning technique to identify the variation-critical paths under BTI-induced variations. We create a set of **Python** and **Perl** scripts to implement such functionality. We first develop a parser to port the given gate-level netlist to the transistor level. We also generate all the input-output paths $P_{i,o}$ as candidate search paths. Given the STA compatible netlist, we perform MC iterations to capture the timing impact of BTI variability. Per iteration, we introduce ΔV_{th} variations according to Table 2.

Having delay values across all paths of the circuit per MC iteration and the maximum delay D among all samples, we can apply a simple threshold-pruning condition. In [22], the authors use the following equation:

$$\max_{\Delta\lambda}[d_v^{\text{path}}(\Delta\lambda)] + \varepsilon_{\text{path}}^{\max} < D \qquad (2)$$

where ε is the range that models uncertainty, D is the measured silicon delay and $d(\Delta\lambda)$ is the linear function of the process parameters. This function estimates the worst case delay given a parameter variation vector $\Delta\lambda$. We select this condition as the pruning operator for its simplicity. We properly adjust Equation (2) in the context of our framework by replacing the estimated values with results acquired by the STA solver. The resulting condition is:

$$D_{P_{i,o}} + \varepsilon < D \qquad (3)$$

where $D_{P_{i,o}}$ is the computed delay of the candidate path $P_{i,o}$, D is the maximum delay across all paths and for all MC samples and ε is the range that models uncertainty. It is reasonable to treat the uncertainty range as a deviation from the maximum expected value D, as in [22]. That is,

$$\varepsilon = \alpha \cdot D, \quad \alpha \in [0,1] \qquad (4)$$

Thus, the pruning condition can be written as:

$$D_{P_{i,o}} + \alpha \cdot D < D \Rightarrow$$
$$D_{P_{i,o}} < (1 - \alpha) \cdot D = \kappa D, \quad \kappa \in [0,1] \qquad (5)$$

Instead of initially storing all candidate paths to be later pruned as non-critical, we apply the negation of Equation (5) to directly identify paths as critical. That way, we improve the memory efficiency of our pruning technique, as we store only the critical paths to the initially empty set **P**. The resulting condition of Algorithm 1 is:

$$D_{P_{i,o}} > \kappa \cdot D, \quad \kappa \in [0,1] \qquad (6)$$

In [22], it is shown that the threshold pruning strategy is effective, even for a small introduced range (i.e. $\varepsilon = \pm 1\% \cdot d(\Delta\lambda)$). Therefore, it is quite straightforward to select the κ value accordingly. For the remainder of this paper, we select $\kappa = 99\%$. By applying the pruning operator, we identify the variation-critical paths (set **P**) of the design under test. Given this set, we use scripts that perform Breadth-First search (BFS) to traverse paths **P** and generate the variation-aware STA netlist, which will be referred to as `netlist`+. Inside this file, *only transistors that belong to variation-critical paths are annotated as variational* (i.e. they are assigned parameters or new models), while the rest of them maintain their nominal values. The aforementioned methodology is presented in Algorithm 1.

Algorithm 1 Proposed Pruning Algorithm.

Input: Gate-level HDL design
1: parse HDL / generate STA netlist & $P_{i,o}$ search paths
2: initialize maximum delay $D = 0$ & set $\mathbf{P} \leftarrow \{\emptyset\}$
3: **for all** MC STA samples **do**
4:      introduce BTI variability (Table 2)
5:      find delay per path $P_{i,o}$ and update D
6: **end for**
7: **for all** MC STA samples **do**
8:      **for all** delay values $D_{P_{i,o}}$ **do**
9:          **if** $D_{P_{i,o}} > \kappa \cdot D$ **then**
10:              add $\mathbf{P} \leftarrow P_{i,o}$
11:          **end if**
12:      **end for**
13: **end for**
14: BFS: traverse **P** & generate variation-aware STA netlist
Output: Variation-Aware STA netlist `netlist`+

In order to assess the efficiency of Algorithm 1 we compare against a commercial reference (i.e. Synopsys NanoTime [23]). We apply our method to several ISCAS85 circuits. For 1,000 MC samples, we compare STA iterations of the variation-aware `netlist`+ against default STA sessions where no pruning is applied. The comparison results are shown in Table 3. We observe that our methodology always outperforms traditional STA iterations, while reasonable accuracy is always maintained (i.e. 3.99% maximum error). That is, even for the most pessimistic results, 6.82× speedup and 4.75× memory usage reduction are achieved. This is to be expected, as we reduce the number of variational parameters inside the variation-aware `netlist`+. That way, we reduce the transistor inventory that needs to be monitored for variability by the transistor-level STA tool.

3.3 Proposed EDA Flow

We incorporate the EDA methodologies presented in the previous Subsections with a comprehensive reliability analysis flow, as shown in Figure 3. The variation-aware `netlist`+ is given as an input to the proposed timing analysis flow. Based on the operating conditions (i.e. f_{CLK}, V_{DD}), we generate the proper control script. We introduce BTI-induced variability to the transistor-level `netlist`+, according to Table 2. Hence, we are able to employ accurate yet efficient transistor-level timing analysis using Synopsys NanoTime. Given the MC STA samples, we decide on processor-wide reliability metrics (i.e. functional yield etc).

Table 3: Evaluation of proposed methodology against commercial tool Synopsys NanoTime [23].

Benchmark circuit	Maximum Error	Minimum Speedup	Min Mem Usage Reduction
c499	3.99%	6.82×	4.32×
c880	1.31%	4.01×	3.05×
c1355	2.52%	4.98×	3.86×
c1908	1.36%	3.72×	3.16×
c2670	0.97%	2.67×	2.45×
c3540	2.66%	5.57×	4.75×
c5315	0.84%	5.59×	4.57×
Average	1.95%	4.77×	3.74×

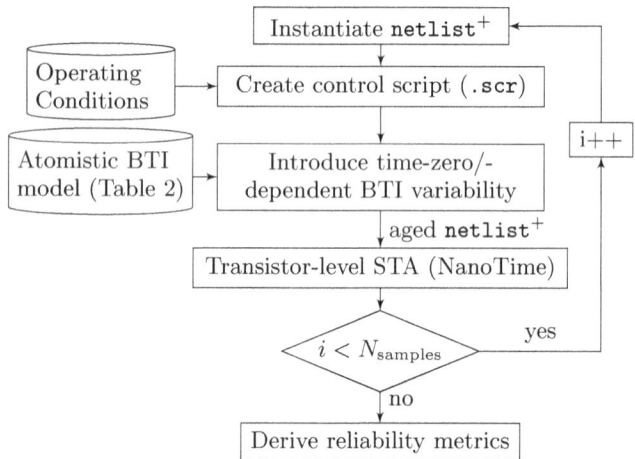

Figure 3: Proposed reliability analysis flow.

4. EXPERIMENTAL RESULTS

4.1 Case Study: OpenRISC Datapath

In order to investigate the usability of the proposed design flow for realistic circuits over their lifetime, we use a modern, open source RISC architecture, namely `OpenRISC` [24]. We focus our exploration on an important CPU module, the datapath. We utilize the 90 nm Predictive Technology Model [18]. We port the exploration to the transistor level, starting from the RTL description. Given the behavioral VHDL code of the datapath module and the target technology, we use Synopsys Design Compiler [25] to generate the optimal gate-level design, in terms of area and speed. The resulting netlist consists of 1830 transistors. We have tested our framework on an AMD®Opteron® server @2.61GHz.

First, we apply Algorithm 1 to the gate-level datapath netlist. We select 150 iterations as an adequate number of MC samples [5]. Compared against pruning-free STA sessions, we achieve 18.69% and 18.29% minimum runtime and memory usage reduction respectively, with 0.84% maximum error. We observe that the performance is highly dependent on the design topology. That is, a significant portion of the datapath corresponds to variation-critical registers, reducing the performance of Algorithm 1 compared to IS-CAS85 benchmarks. Nonetheless, it is worth observing that our approach outperforms the built-in pruning command of the STA solver, achieving up to 16.87% extra runtime improvement. That can be attributed to the phasing of the built-in pruning that is performed after the parsing phase of

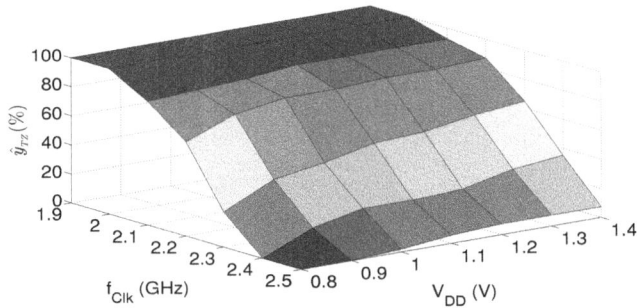

(a) Yield estimation $\hat{y}_{\text{TZ}}$ at time-zero instance

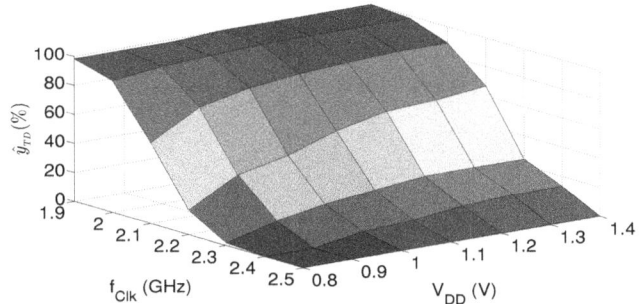

(b) Yield estimation $\hat{y}_{\text{TD}}$ after 3 years of operation

Figure 4: Functional yield analysis : Applying the EDA methodologies proposed in this paper.

all varying parameters [23]. On the contrary, our methodology is decoupled from the STA solver itself. An already "pruned" (in terms of variability) design is generated, reducing the parameters to be captured by the STA solver beforehand.

4.2 Functional Yield Analysis

We now move towards performing a complete reliability analysis, using the flow presented in Figure 3. We estimate the *functional yield* of the module over three years of operation. A sample of this design is defined as *functionally correct* iff the worst path exhibits correct timing behavior (i.e. positive slack), under a particular state of BTI-induced variability. We estimate the functional yield of the target circuit, namely the percentage of samples that exhibit correct functionality at different instances of circuit lifetime. We perform STA MC iterations using Synopsys NanoTime, for a set of different operating points (f, V_{DD}). Based on the "optimal" behavior of our design (i.e. no variability introduced), we select the following 2D exploration space of (f, V_{DD}) pairs:

$$1.9 \text{ GHz} \leq f \leq 2.5 \text{ GHz}, \text{ step} = +0,1 \text{ GHz} \quad (7a)$$
$$0.8 \text{ V} \leq V_{DD} \leq 1.4 \text{ V}, \text{ step} = +0,1 \text{ V} \quad (7b)$$

We introduce time-zero and time-dependent ΔV_{th} variations based on the estimates $\mu(t)$ and $\sigma(t)$ derived in Section 3.1. Again, we select 150 MC samples. As we have already mentioned, the ΔV_{th} distributions remain fairly constant after the time-zero instance. Thus, it is reasonable to select one more instance to capture BTI for the rest of the transistor lifetime. We estimate the functional yield at time-zero instance (Figure 4a) and after three years of operation (Figure 4b). We can observe that BTI significantly affects the proper functionality of our design.

More specifically, we notice the impact immediately after including the time-zero variability. We have non-functional samples starting from 2.1 GHz. That is, compared to the 2.5 GHz optimal frequency of the design without variability, we observe an $f_{\max}$ degradation by 16%. Such degradation is more intense after three years of operation, with the first non-functional samples appearing at 1.9 GHz, resulting in a greater frequency degradation of 24%. Another important observation is that the estimated yield is 0% for frequencies greater than 2.4 GHz in Figure 4b. In other words, the de-

sign loses its functionality completely for higher frequencies during its lifetime due to time-dependent variability. Thus, we stress the importance of properly accounting for BTI-induced variability, in order to achieve functional designs.

4.3 Power-Aware Reliability Analysis

Moreover, we substantiate the usability of our flow as a useful aid for BTI-aware design techniques. A popular power management technique is *voltage scaling*. Figure 4 shows that the number of functional samples decreases as we reduce the supply voltage. As a consequence, decreasing V_{DD} to meet a power constraint could lead to an increased number of non-functional modules. Such observation is of great importance in terms of power-aware design. We define a sample as *functionally correct* for a specific clock frequency f, iff it can meet the timing constraints (i.e. positive slack value), without exceeding a specific power constraint.

To select a representative constraint, we compute the power consumption of the datapath through SPICE simulation for each (f, V_{DD}) pair. We acquire power values varying from 2.07 W up to 9.17 W. We set a power constraint of $P_{\max} = 5$ W. For varying maximum clock frequencies, we estimate the functional yield (Figure 5), assuming a 95% confidence interval [19]. The yield estimations of this Figure provide useful hints regarding power-aware design under BTI variability. For higher frequencies, the functional yield is reduced below 90% under *voltage scaling*, after three years of operation. This observation is fully consistent with a recent, BTI-aware, mitigation technique that suggests progressively increasing supply voltage [5].

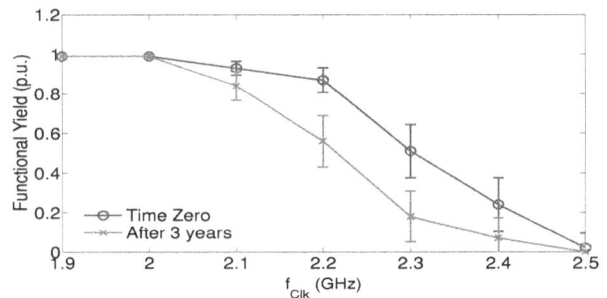

Figure 5: Power-aware reliability analysis: Functional yield of datapath design for varying clock frequencies.

Table 4: Capturing critical path re-ordering while incorporating BTI-induced variability.

	No variability		After 3 years	
	D (ns)	**Path**	**D (ns)**	**Path**
1	0.438	**RdB - X31**	0.514	RstR - X24
...	...	...	...	...
7	0.436	RdB - X25	0.490	RdB - X31
...	...	...	...	...
20	0.431	RdA - X4	0.473	**RdB - X31**

4.4 BTI-Induced Critical Path Re-ordering

Finally, prior art has already provided hints towards capturing the BTI-induced degradation of the critical path [4, 16]. Nonetheless, the experimental results are limited to simple case studies of logic subblocks (i.e. adders, multipliers etc). In the current paper, we fully investigate such observation for an entire CPU module with explicit timing analysis results. In Table 4, we sort paths based on delay values **D** acquired using Synopsys NanoTime for one sample of our reliability analysis. For sake of brevity, we present the first few delay values. By highlighting the critical-path with no variability introduced, it is evident that paths that are not considered critical if BTI is ignored may finally dictate the total circuit delay when time-zero/-dependent activity is incorporated. Thus, we fully substantiate the impact of BTI-induced variability with respect to critical path re-ordering.

5. CONCLUSION

In this paper, we propose a design flow for reliability analysis under BTI-induced variability. We exploit a novel, pseudo-transient BTI approach which alleviates the complexity of atomistic BTI models, while retaining time-zero/-dependent variability. We develop a pruning methodology to efficiently capture transistor variability, using commercial STA tools. We demonstrate the usability of our framework as a useful aid for reliability analysis through realistic testcases. Until now and to the best of our knowledge a time- and workload-dependent yield analysis of an entire CPU module has never been performed with the atomistic BTI model. For a datapath design, we capture the impact of BTI and we present the evolution of processor-wide reliability metrics. After three years of operation, we report a 24% f_{max} degradation and a functional yield reduction below 90% for higher frequencies. We also provide useful hints regarding power-aware design under BTI variability. Finally, we substantiate the impact of BTI-induced variability to critical path re-ordering.

6. ACKNOWLEDGMENTS

The work presented in this paper is partially supported by the Greek State Scholarship Foundation (IKY) and by the FP7-612069-HARPA EU project. The authors would also like to acknowledge CMC Microsystems for the provision of products and services that facilitated this research.

7. REFERENCES

[1] H. Kufluoglu and M. Alam, "A generalized reaction–diffusion model with explicit h–h_2 dynamics for negative-bias temperature-instability (nbti) degradation," *IEEE Trans. on Electron Devices*, 54(5): 1101–1107, 2007.

[2] T. Grasser et al., "Recent advances in understanding the bias temperature instability," in *In IEEE IEDM*, pp. 4.4.1–4.4.4, 2010.

[3] Kaczer, B. et al., "Atomistic approach to variability of bias-temperature instability in circuit simulations," in *IRPS*, 2011, pp. XT.3.1–XT.3.5.

[4] D. Rodopoulos et al., "Understanding timing impact of BTI/RTN with massively threaded atomistic transient simulations," in *IEEE ICICDT*, pp. 1–4, 2014.

[5] D. Rodopoulos et al., "Atomistic pseudo-transient BTI simulation with inherent workload memory," *IEEE TDMR*, 14(2): 704–714, 2014.

[6] K. O. Jeppson et al., "Negative bias stress of mos devices at high electric fields and degradation of mnos devices," *JAP*, vol. 48, no. 5, 1977.

[7] Ogawa, S. et al., "Generalized diffusion-reaction model for the low-field charge-buildup instability at the si-sio$_2$ interface," *Ph. R. B*, 1995.

[8] A. Calimera et al., "Nbti-aware clustered power gating," *ACM Trans. Des. Autom. Electron. Syst.*, vol. 16, no. 1, pp. 3:1–3:25, Nov. 2010.

[9] T. Grasser et al., "The paradigm shift in understanding the bias temperature instability: From reaction–diffusion to switching oxide traps," *IEEE Trans. on Electron Devices*, 58(11): 3652–3666, 2011.

[10] Weckx, P. et al., "Defect-based methodology for workload-dependent circuit lifetime projections – application to sram," in *IEEE IRPS*, 2013.

[11] D. Rodopoulos et al., "Time and workload dependent device variability in circuit simulations," in *IEEE ICICDT*, pp. 1–4, 2011.

[12] G. Lyras et al., "Hypervised transient spice simulations of large netlists amp; workloads on multi-processor systems," in *DATE*, pp. 655–658, 2013.

[13] H. Kukner et al., "Comparison of reaction-diffusion and atomistic trap-based BTI models for logic gates," *IEEE TDMR*, 14(1): 182–193, 2014.

[14] P. Weckx et al., "Non-monte-carlo methodology for high-sigma simulations of circuits under workload-dependent BTI degradation – application to 6t SRAM," in *IRPS*, pp. 5D.2.1–5D.2.6, 2014.

[15] J. Fang and S. Sapatnekar, "Understanding the impact of transistor-level BTI variability," in *IRPS*, pp. CR.2.1–CR.2.6, 2012.

[16] H. Kukner et al., "Degradation analysis of datapath logic subblocks under NBTI aging in FinFET technology," in *ISQED*, pp. 473–479, 2014.

[17] M. Toledano-Luque et al., "Response of a single trap to ac negative bias temperature stress," in *IRPS*, pp. 4A.2.1–4A.2.8, 2011.

[18] Predictive Technology Model, http://ptm.asu.edu/.

[19] T. McConaghy et al., *Variation-Aware Design of Custom Integrated Circuits*. Springer, Oct. 2012.

[20] H. Kufluoglu and M. Alam, "Theory of interface-trap-induced nbti degradation for reduced cross section mosfets," *IEEE Trans. on Electron Devices*, 53(5): 1120–1130, 2006.

[21] M. Toledano-Luque et al., "Degradation of time dependent variability due to interface state generation," in *VLSIT*, pp. T190–T191, 2013.

[22] L. Guerra e Silva et al., "Speedpath analysis under parametric timing models," in *DAC*, 268–273, 2010.

[23] *NanoTime, User Guide*, Synopsys, Inc., 2012.

[24] OpenRISC project, http://opencores.org/or1k/.

[25] *Design Compiler, User Guide*, Synopsys, Inc., 2009.

A Reconfigurable Silicon-Photonic Network with Improved Channel Sharing for Multicore Architectures

Sai Vineel Reddy Chittamuru, Srinivas Desai, Sudeep Pasricha
Department of Electrical and Computer Engineering
Colorado State University, Fort Collins, CO, U.S.A.
{sai.chittamuru, srinivas.desai, sudeep}@@colostate.edu

ABSTRACT

On-chip communication is widely considered to be one of the major performance bottlenecks in contemporary chip multiprocessors (CMPs). With recent advances in silicon nanophotonics, photonic-based networks-on-chip (NoCs) are being considered as a viable option for communication in emerging CMPs as they can enable higher bandwidth and lower power dissipation compared to traditional electrical NoCs. In this paper, we present *UltraNoC*, a novel reconfigurable silicon-photonic NoC architecture that features improved channel sharing and supports dynamic re-prioritization and exchange of bandwidth between clusters of cores running multiple applications, to increase channel utilization and performance. Experimental results show that *UltraNoC* improves throughput by up to 9.8× while reducing latency by up to 55% and energy-delay product by up to 90% over state-of-the-art solutions.

Categories and Subject Descriptors

C.2.1 [Computer-Communication Networks]: Network Architecture and Design—*Network topology*; C.4 [Performance of Systems]: design studies

Keywords

Network-on-chip (NoC), photonic channel sharing, arbitration

1. INTRODUCTION

Advances in technology scaling over the past decade have enabled the integration of billions of transistors on a single die. Such a massive number of transistors has allowed multiple processing cores and more memory to be integrated on a chip, to meet rapidly growing performance demands of modern applications. With hundreds of on-chip cores expected to become a reality in the near future, traditional electrical network-on-chip (NoC) communication fabrics [1], [2] are projected to suffer from cripplingly high power dissipation and severely reduced performance [7]. Crosstalk and electromagnetic interference in metallic interconnects will further worsen the performance and reliability of NoCs with technology scaling.

Recent developments in the area of silicon photonics have enabled their integration with CMOS circuits. On-chip photonic links provide several prolific advantages over their metallic counterparts, including light speed transfers, high bandwidth [3] density by using dense wavelength division multiplexing (DWDM) [3], low power dissipation [4], and low crosstalk [7]. Thus silicon photonics is being considered as an exciting new option for future NoCs. Several photonic devices such as microring resonators, waveguides and photodetectors have already been fabricated and demonstrated at the chip level [5], [6].

GLSVLSI'15, May 20–22, 2015, Pittsburgh, PA, USA.
Copyright © 2015 ACM 978-1-4503-3474-7/15/05...$15.00.
http://dx.doi.org/10.1145/2742060.2742067

These devices have been used as a foundation for several photonic network architectures [8]-[11].

A few prior works emphasize the importance of network resource contention in photonic channels and proposed arbitration techniques to resolve contention [8], [10]. However, a limitation of these approaches is that they do not fully exploit available network bandwidth. Another limitation is that these approaches typically only target single parallel application workloads. In emerging multicore systems where multiple applications execute simultaneously on unique subsets of cores, there is significantly greater variation in temporal and spatial characteristics of network injected traffic. For example, cores running memory intensive tasks can require more network bandwidth than cores running compute intensive tasks [24].

To overcome these shortcomings, we propose a novel photonic NoC architecture called *UltraNoC* that utilizes multiple-write-multiple-read (MWMR) photonic waveguides in a crossbar topology, and supports dynamic performance adaptation to aggressively utilize network bandwidth and meet diverse application demands. We compare *UltraNoC* against architectures with the best-known arbitration mechanisms, for multi-threaded PARSEC [16] workloads on CMP platform sizes ranging from 64-cores to 256-cores. The novel contributions of this paper are:

- A flexible on-chip photonic network architecture (*UltraNoC*) that facilitates selective and reconfigurable prioritization of applications based on their time-varying performance goals;
- A concurrent token stream arbitration that provides multiple simultaneous tokens and increases channel utilization;
- A dynamic bandwidth transfer technique with low overhead, to transfer unused bandwidth among clusters of cores;
- A mechanism to monitor traffic being injected into the network by different co-running applications, to facilitate dynamic arbitration wavelength injection rate modulation.

2. RELATED WORK

A considerable amount of work has focused on the area of photonic NoC design. Several efforts have explored *high-radix low-diameter* photonic crossbar architectures that provide non-blocking connectivity, e.g., [8], [10], [15] and [21]; whereas silicon photonic implementations of *low-radix high-diameter* NoCs have also been investigated in [14], [17], [18], and [20]. Prior work has shown that photonic crossbars are extremely promising architectures to meet future on-chip bandwidths demands, but they can suffer from *(i)* large power dissipation and *(ii)* high contention for resources, especially when using inefficient token-based arbitration schemes. A few techniques to reduce power overhead of photonic NoCs have been proposed in literature. For example, an effective policy for runtime management of the laser source is proposed in [11]. We build on their work to manage power in photonic crossbar NoCs. To reduce contention issues in crossbars, a few improved arbitration techniques have been proposed in [10], [22] that use time division multiplexing (TDM), so that a single data waveguide can be simultaneously used by more than one node in different time slots.

In Flexishare [10], a token stream arbitration scheme is proposed. The scheme requires wavelengths corresponding to each data waveguide to be injected serially into different time slots of an arbitration waveguide. A node writes on the data waveguide only when it gets access to the corresponding arbitration wavelength. Subsequently, the node cannot send data again till its arbitration wavelength is injected into the arbitration waveguide, which takes N cycles for N data waveguides. The scheme leads to channel under-utilization, and performs even worse as the number of nodes and waveguides increase. In [22], the token ring arbitration scheme from Corona [8] was improved with the token channel and token slot arbitration techniques for Multiple-write-single-read (MWSR) crossbars. Token slot arbitration uses TDM and improves upon token channel arbitration by dividing the arbitration waveguide into fixed-size, back-to-back slots, with destination nodes circulating tokens in one-to-one correspondence to slots. A limitation of this approach is that a fixed time gap is required between two arbitration slots to set up data for transmission, which reduces the available time slots to send data. UltraNoC improves upon these prior works by utilizing a more powerful concurrent token stream arbitration strategy, together with reconfigurable cluster prioritization and bandwidth re-allocation to improve MWMR photonic channel utilization.

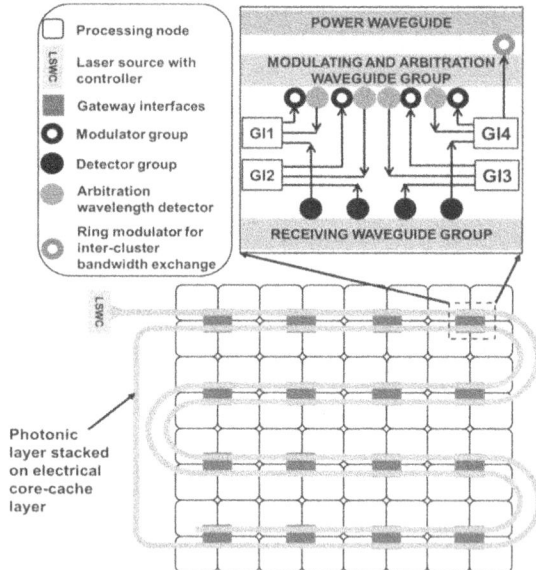

Figure 1: Layout of MWMR crossbar used in UltraNoC along with the arrangement of cores and their respective gateway interfaces.

3. ULTRANOC PHOTONIC NOC OVERVIEW
3.1 Architecture and Terminology

The baseline *UltraNoC* architecture is targeted to a 64-core CMP, as shown in figure 1. We also extend the baseline architecture to a 256-core CMP for the purposes of scalability analysis. Each core has a private L1 and shared L2 cache, with a MOESI protocol to maintain cache coherence. In a 64-core CMP, each group of 8 cores has access to main memory via a dedicated memory controller, whereas in a 256-core CMP, each group of 16 cores has a dedicated memory controller. A node is defined as an entity consisting of one and four cores for the 64-core and 256-core CMP, respectively. Every node in *UltraNoC* is attached to a gateway interface (GI) module that facilitates transfers between the CMOS electrical layer and a photonic layer (with photonic waveguides, modulators, detectors, etc.). The entire chip is divided into four clusters (C_0, C_1, C_2, C_3), where each cluster contains 16 cores in a 64-core CMP and 64 cores in a 256-core CMP.

A detailed layout of the *UltraNoC* architecture is shown in figure 1, where 64 nodes are arranged in an 8×8 mesh. Communication between cores within a node for the 256-core CMP uses an electrical 5×5 NoC router, where four of its input and output port pairs are connected to four cores and the fifth input/output port pair is connected to a GI module. A round-robin arbitration scheme is used within each node for communication between cores and the GI.

Inter-node transfers are facilitated by dual-coiled MWMR waveguide groups, where each group has four MWMR waveguides by default, with each waveguide supporting 64 wavelength DWDM, to facilitate simultaneous transfer of a total of 512 bits of data (cache line) with data modulation at both clock edges. Each MWMR waveguide group in *UltraNoC* passes every node twice in the dual coiled structure to enable a two pass inter-node data communication. A node has the ability to write on the first pass using its ring modulators and read from the waveguide group using its ring detectors in the second pass.

As all nodes are capable of modulating (writing) in an MWMR waveguide group during the first pass, there is a need for arbitration (see Section 3.2 for more details) between sending nodes to ensure that the data of different senders does not destructively overlap on the shared waveguide group. Throughout this paper this first pass portion of the waveguide group is referred to as the *modulating and arbitration waveguide group*. In the second pass of the MWMR waveguide group all nodes receive data through their respective ring detectors; hence this portion of the waveguide group is referred to as the *receiving waveguide group*. Additionally there is a *power waveguide* that runs in parallel with the other waveguides, and carries arbitration wavelengths. This waveguide facilitates our bandwidth transfer and priority adaptation techniques (see Sections 3.3, 3.4).

Figure 1 depicts an expanded view of the collection of GIs for four nodes, which shows the modulating and arbitration, receiving, and power waveguide groups, along with their connection to GIs. There are 64 wavelengths that are utilized for data communication in each MWMR waveguide within each waveguide group, so each ring modulator and detector group has 256 ring modulators and 256 ring detectors, respectively. Each of the 64 wavelengths is assigned to a unique receiving node, such that whenever a receiver detects its corresponding wavelength during a clock cycle, it switches its detectors "on" to receive data in the next clock cycle. All other receivers keep their detectors turned off to save power. We also utilize four arbitration wavelengths, each corresponding to a cluster. For powering the waveguides, we use a broadband off-chip laser source with a laser power controller (LSWC). The LSWC has groups of ring modulators capable of injecting different wavelengths in different clock cycles. As we use 68 DWDM in each MWMR waveguide, there are 68 ring modulators in each ring modulator group in the LSWC. The laser controller also has control logic that can alter the rate of injection of arbitration wavelengths into each waveguide group. More details about LSWC are presented in the next subsections and overhead analysis is presented in Section 4.1.

3.2 MWMR Concurrent Token Stream Arbitration

In *UltraNoC* all of the cores on a chip are partitioned into four clusters ($C_0 - C_3$) and each cluster is assigned a dedicated arbitration wavelength ($\lambda_0 - \lambda_3$). Each MWMR waveguide group is divided into a fixed number of time slots, based on the time taken by light to traverse the waveguide on a die, which is 8 cycles in our architecture. Thus we divide each MWMR waveguide group into 8 time slots. The time slots are classified into three types: *arbitration slot*, *receiver prediction slot*, and *data slot*. For simplicity, figure 2(a) shows an example of the distribution of time slots across 4 MWMR waveguide groups, even though a minimum of 8 MWMR waveguide groups are used in our architecture. In the arbitration slot, the LSWC injects arbitration wavelengths of clusters, selectively using a modulator group to dedicate the arbitration slot to a particular cluster. After a sending node grabs an arbitration wavelength in the arbitration slot, it gets access to the next receiver prediction slot to release the corresponding wavelength of its receiving node. Subsequently, in the next data slot, the sending node modulates data on the 64 wavelengths in each waveguide group assigned for data transfer.

As an example, suppose N_1 in cluster C_0 needs to send data to N_{32} that has a corresponding receiver prediction wavelength w_{32}. N_1 first grabs arbitration wavelength λ_0 which is dedicated to cluster C_0, in the arbitration slot. N_1 then modulates in the next receiver prediction slot, such that only w_{32} (the dedicated wavelength for receiver prediction of N_{32}) is made available by removing all the wavelengths except w_{32} (using its ring modulators) in that receiver prediction slot. On the receiving end at N_{32}, only the detector for wavelength w_{32} is switched on. Once w_{32} is detected, N_{32} prepares to receive data in the next data slot by switching on the remaining detectors in that node. Figure 2(b) shows the position of different slots in the MWMR waveguide group W1 at time cycle 3 for the example in figure 2(a). As our architecture divides each MWMR waveguide group into 8 slots, each slot covers 8 nodes in a particular time instance. The stream of tokens on concurrent slots in waveguide groups allows multiple nodes to inject packets simultaneously, resulting in extremely high channel utilization in the MWMR waveguides. A round-robin arbiter is used within each cluster to resolve contention among the 16 nodes in a cluster, and avoid starvation.

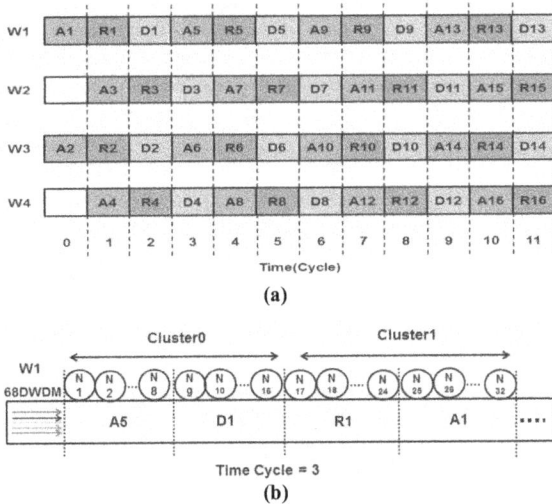

(a)

(b)

Figure 2: (a) Timing diagram of arbitration in UltraNoC, which shows distribution of arbitration (Ai), receiver prediction (Ri)and data slots (Di) across four MWMR waveguide groups (W1–W4); (b) distribution of different slots within MWMR waveguide group W1 at time cycle 3.

3.3 Inter-cluster Bandwidth Exchange

UltraNoC supports inter-cluster bandwidth transfers to further improve channel utilization and overall performance. As an example, if cluster C_0 does not need to transfer data, it transfers its bandwidth to a subsequent cluster C_1. Similarly any cluster can transfer its unused bandwidth to subsequent clusters. Figure 3 presents an overview of the bandwidth transfer technique. The last node in each cluster is provisioned with an extra modulator that is capable of injecting an arbitration wavelength of the next cluster. Whenever a ring detector of the last node of a cluster detects its own arbitration wavelength, and if this node does not have data to transfer, this is a case where the cluster has not used its bandwidth.

To improve channel utilization, the cluster can transfer its unused bandwidth to the next cluster, by having the last node of the cluster inject the arbitration wavelength of the next cluster into the same arbitration slot. To simultaneously remove and inject arbitration wavelengths at the last node of cluster, the arbiter uses information about the current slot of the waveguide and the cluster it belongs to. This information can change across interval windows based on the data received from LSWC (Section 3.4).

Figure 3 illustrates an example of bandwidth transfer. Clusters C_0–C_3 are assigned arbitration wavelengths highlighted with green, yellow, blue, and red respectively. The last node in the first three clusters (node16, node32, and node48) is shown with an extra ring modulator to facilitate the injection of the arbitration wavelength of the next cluster. For this example, nodes in C_0 do not need to transfer any data in the current cycle. Then node16, which is the last node in C_0 removes its cluster's arbitration wavelength (green) from the arbitration slot and injects the arbitration wavelength of C_1 (yellow) so that nodes in C_1 can use this arbitration slot for sending data in the next available data slot. Figure 3 also shows counters at nodes 16, 32, 48, and 64 that are used to count the arbitration wavelength conversions over a time interval. The next subsection presents details about these counters.

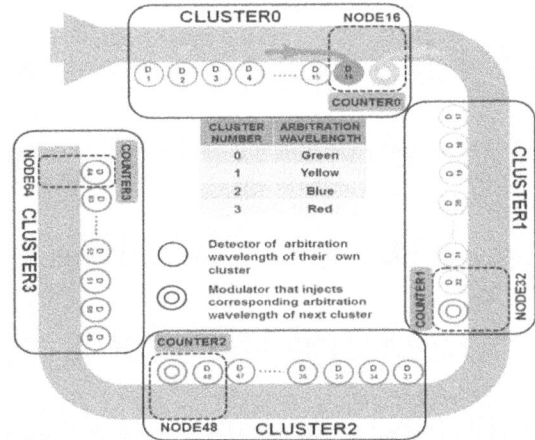

Figure 3: Bandwidth transfer technique: a cluster can transfer its unused bandwidth to the next cluster by absorbing its own arbitration wavelength and releasing arbitration wavelength of next cluster.

3.4 Cluster Priority Adaptation with LSWC Reconfiguration

UltraNoC also supports runtime alteration of allocated bandwidth to each cluster, to closely track changing application bandwidth needs, by altering the number of arbitration slots dedicated to each cluster (i.e., cluster priority). This is essential because while our bandwidth transfer technique can transfer unused arbitration slots from one cluster to another in the direction of concurrent arbitration token stream flow (e.g., C_0 to C_1), it lacks the ability to transfer bandwidth in the opposite direction (e.g., C_1 to C_0). To overcome this limitation, we design a cluster priority adaptation mechanism to more comprehensively manage cluster bandwidth allocations over time. This mechanism also helps to minimize laser power by intelligently reducing the total number of injected arbitration slots for scenarios with low bandwidth requirements. The cluster priority adaptation technique consists of three main steps, as discussed below:

Step 1: Determination of wavelength conversion count: Each cluster C_0 – C_3 has an associated weight w_0 – w_3, which determines the proportion of arbitration slots (and consequently bandwidth or priority) assigned to the cluster. Initially, these weights can be set to be equal, i.e., 0.25 each. At runtime, whenever the last node in a cluster performs a wavelength conversion from its current cluster arbitration wavelength to the next cluster arbitration wavelength, a counter (shown in figure 3) is incremented. This conversion event represents the case where an unused arbitration slot (bandwidth) is transferred from one cluster to another. Over a time interval T, the recorded wavelength conversion counts $WCC_0 - WCC_3$ from each cluster are then used to determine unused bandwidth of each cluster.

Step 2: Calculation of excess arbitration slots: The wavelength conversion count values of different clusters show the aggregated number of excess arbitration slots, which includes excess arbitration slots of the present cluster along with the excess arbitration slots of predecessor clusters. Therefore the excess arbitration slots for the ith cluster (ES_i) are calculated using equation (1) shown below, by subtracting the cluster wavelength conversion count of the predecessor cluster (WCC_{i-1}) from the wavelength conversion count of the cluster under consideration (WCC_i). ES_i values can also be negative, when a cluster consumes a greater number of arbitration slots (made available by predecessor clusters) than its allocated arbitration slots. Such a cluster has a deficit of arbitration slots.

$$ES_i = \begin{cases} WCC_i, & i = 0 \\ WCC_i - WCC_{i-1}, & i > 0 \end{cases} \qquad (1)$$

Step 3: Setting new weight (priority) for each cluster: Based on the estimation of excesses and deficits in arbitration slots assigned across clusters, this final step attempts to adjust weight values of each cluster to eliminate the excesses and deficits. To determine the new weight of the ith cluster $w_i(next)$ for the upcoming time interval, we must subtract the excess weight EW_i of the cluster from its current weight $w_i(current)$. We can calculate EW_i by dividing the excess arbitration slots of the ith cluster (ES_i), calculated in equation (1), by the total number of arbitration slots released in the time interval T, which we denote as K. The equations below show these calculations:

$$EW_i = ES_i / K \qquad (2)$$
$$w_i(next) = w_i(current) - EW_i \qquad (3)$$

Based on the values of the new weights, the LSWC changes the distribution of arbitration wavelengths injected for the next time interval T, such that a cluster with a higher weight will receive more arbitration wavelengths, and has more opportunities to use the waveguides for data transfer. The weight values are also communicated to all clusters, so that arbiters can adjust their local counters to match the new arbitration slot profile in waveguides.

4. EXPERIMENTS
4.1 Experimental Setup

To evaluate our proposed *UltraNoC* architecture, we compared it to an electrical mesh (EMesh) based NoC as well as to two state-of-the-art photonic crossbar NoCs that use smart arbitration techniques: Flexishare with token stream arbitration [10] and Corona with an enhanced token-slot arbitration [22]. We modeled and simulated the architectures at a cycle-accurate granularity with a SystemC-based NoC simulator, for two CMP platform complexities: 64-core and 256-core. We used the PARSEC benchmark suite [16] to create multi-application workloads, with clusters running parallelized versions of different benchmarks.

Table 1 shows the PARSEC benchmarks we considered, classified into three categories according to their memory intensities. *Compute intensive* benchmarks spend most of the time computing and less time communicating with memory; whereas *memory intensive* applications spend a larger portion of their execution time communicating with memory and less time computing within cores. *Hybrid* intensity benchmarks demonstrate both compute and memory intensive phases. We created 12 multi-application workloads from these benchmarks. Each workload

combines 4 benchmarks, and the memory intensity of the workloads varies across the spectrum, from compute intensive to memory intensive. As an example, the SC-BT-BS-VI workload combines parallelized implementations of Streamclusters (SC), Bodytrack (BT), Blackscholes (BS) and Vips (VI), and executes them in clusters C_0, C_1, C_2, and C_3, respectively. Each parallelized benchmark is executed on a group of 16 cores and 64 cores, in the 64-core and 256-core CMP platforms, respectively. Full-system simulation of parallelized PARSEC benchmarks using gem5 [25] was used to generate traces that were fed into our cycle-accurate network simulator. We set a "warm-up" period of 100M instructions and captured traces for 1B instructions.

Table 1: Memory intensity classification of PARSEC benchmarks

Application	Representation	Workload Type
Blackscholes	BS	Compute intensive
Bodytrack	BT	Compute intensive
Vips	VI	Compute intensive
Dedup	DU	Compute intensive
Freqmine	FQ	Hybrid
Ferret	FR	Hybrid
Fluidanimate	FA	Hybrid
X264	X264	Hybrid
Streamclusters	SC	Memory intensive
Canneal	CA	Memory intensive
Facesim	FS	Memory intensive
Swaptions	SW	Memory intensive

We targeted 32nm and 22nm process technologies for the 64-core and 256-core CMPs, respectively. Based on the geometric calculation of the waveguides for a 20mm×20mm chip dimension, we estimated the time needed for light to travel from the first to the last node in a single pass of the MWMR waveguide group in *UltraNoC* as 8 cycles at 5 GHz clock frequency. The same clock and 8 cycle round trip time is also applicable to the waveguides in the Flexishare and Corona photonic crossbar NoCs. Throughout our analysis we use a flit size of 64 bits for EMesh and a total packet size of 512 bits for all photonic NoC architectures. We consider data modulation at both clock edges to enable simultaneous transfer of 512 bits in a single cycle, in the UltraNoC, Flexishare, and Corona architectures.

The static and dynamic energy consumption of electrical routers is based on results obtained from the open-source DSENT tool. Energy consumption of various photonic components for all the photonic NoC architectures are adopted from photonic device characterizations in line with state-of-the-art proposals [19], [23] and shown in Table 2. Here $E_{dynamic}$ is the energy/bit for modulators and photodetectors and $E_{logic-dyn}$ is the energy/bit for the driver circuits of modulators and photodetectors. P_{MWMR} and P_{MWSR} are the static power consumption of an MWMR and an MWSR waveguide group, respectively which includes the power overhead of ring resonator thermal tuning. We consider a ring heating power of 15 μW per ring and detector responsivity of 0.8 A/W [19]. To compute laser power consumption, we calculated photonic loss in components, which sets the photonic laser power budget and correspondingly the electrical laser power.

Finally, based on our gate-level analysis, area overhead due to electrical circuitry (e.g., adders, multipliers) in LSWC is estimated to be 0.011mm^2 at 32nm. We set the reconfiguration delay overhead in *UltraNoC* to be 20 cycles to account for the time to transfer wavelength conversion counter values from each cluster to LSWC, time to determine new priority weights of each cluster, and to update these values in arbiters in each cluster. We set reconfiguration time interval window size in *UltraNoC* to 300 cycles, to balance reconfiguration overhead and performance.

Table 2: Energy and losses for photonic devices [19], [23]

Energy consumption type	Energy
$E_{dynamic}$	0.42 pJ/bit
$E_{logic-dyn}$	0.18 pJ/bit
Static power per waveguide group	**Power**
P_{MWMR} (with 68 DWDM)	3.86 W
P_{MWMR} (with 64 DWDM)	3.73 W
P_{MWSR} (with 64 DWDM)	2.35 W
Photonic loss type	**Loss (in dB)**
Microring through	0.02
Waveguide propagation per cm	1
Waveguide coupler/splitter	0.5
Waveguide bending loss	0.005 per 90^0

4.2 Experimental Results

Our experiments target a 64-core CMP platform and compare network throughput, average packet latency, and energy-delay product (EDP) of *UltraNoC* with the electrical mesh (EMesh), Flexishare with token stream arbitration [10], and Corona with token-slot arbitration [22]. We consider two variants of our architecture: *UltraNoC-8* which uses 8 waveguide groups and *UltraNoC-16* which uses 16 waveguide groups. Figures 4(a)-(c) show the results of this study, with all results normalized with respect to the EMesh results. From the throughput comparison in Figure 4(a), it can be observed that, not surprisingly, all photonic NoCs provide better throughput than EMesh, due to the presence of higher bandwidth photonic links. *UltraNoC* with 8 MWMR waveguide groups (*UltraNoC-8*) has nearly 3× greater throughput compared to Flexishare, with the same number of MWMR waveguides. Even though Flexishare uses MWMR waveguides and time division multiplexing (TDM) as in *UltraNoC*, there are significant differences between the architectures.

In Flexishare, arbitration wavelengths corresponding to MWMR data waveguides are injected serially into the arbitration waveguide and a node that grabs a token in the arbitration waveguide gets exclusive access to the corresponding MWMR data waveguide; whereas in *UltraNoC*, multiple arbitration, reservation and data slots are available concurrently in an MWMR waveguide, such that each MWMR waveguide can be accessed simultaneously by multiple nodes. Moreover, unlike *UltraNoC*, Flexishare does not support priority reconfiguration and bandwidth exchange mechanisms.

UltraNoC-8 also provides higher throughput than Corona. This is because of instances in Corona, where multiple sender nodes attempt to communicate with a single receiver node (e.g., memory controller). Such instances result in the sender nodes attempting to access the single MWSR waveguide connected to the receiver, creating a significant imbalance among MWSR waveguides, with the other waveguides being underutilized while packets get queued waiting for the waveguide connected to the receiver. *UltraNoC* avoids such an imbalance with its use of more efficient MWMR waveguides and improved arbitration.

The *UltraNoC* configuration with 16 waveguide groups (*UltraNoC-16*) with approximately twice the photonic hardware of *UltraNoC-8* provides even better throughput than the other architectures. On average *UltraNoC-8* has 2.8×, 1.6×, and 3.8× higher throughputs compared to Flexishare, Corona and EMesh, respectively. *UltraNoC-16* has 5.3×, 3.2×, and 7.7× higher throughputs compared to Flexishare, Corona and EMesh, respectively. The improvement is somewhat higher for memory intensive workloads than for compute intensive workloads. The large throughput improvement for *UltraNoC* is a direct consequence of avoiding unused bandwidth by transferring it to cores that need it the most, using the bandwidth transfer and priority alteration mechanisms at runtime. These mechanisms also

improve the average packet latency in *UltraNoC*, as shown in Figure 4(b), by reducing the time spent waiting for access to the photonic waveguides. On average *UltraNoC-8* has 17%, 32% and 47% and *UltraNoC-16* has 25%, 40% and 51% lower average packet delay over Flexishare, Corona and EMesh, respectively for the different multi-application workloads.

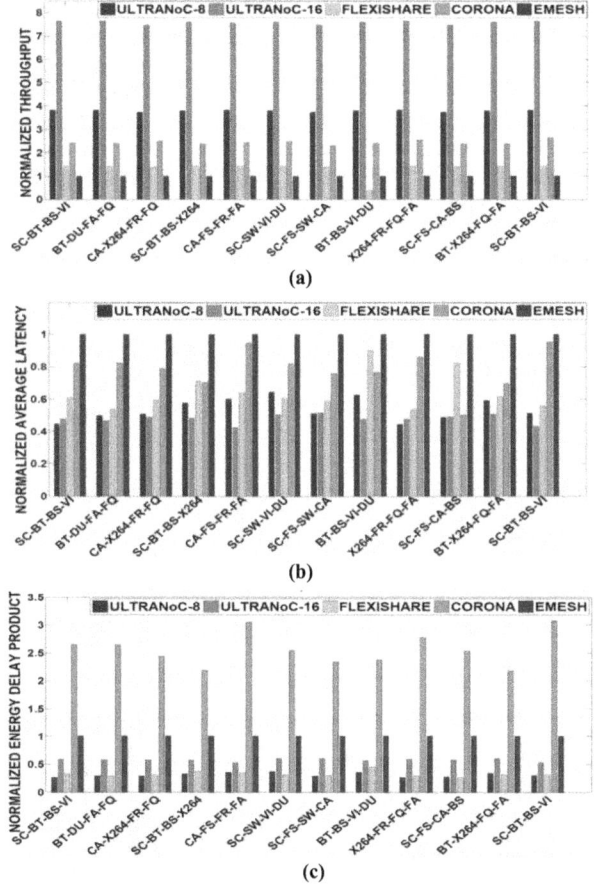

Figure 4: (a) throughput (b) latency (c) EDP comparison of UltraNoC-8 and UltraNoC-16 with other architectures for a 64-core CMP. Results are normalized wrt EMesh.

Figure 4(c) shows the energy-delay product (EDP) comparison between the architectures. It can be observed that on average *UltraNoC-8* has 90%, 70% and 10% lower EDP compared to Corona, EMesh, and Flexishare respectively. Further *UltraNoC-16* has 79% and 45% lower EDP compared to Corona and EMesh. Most of the energy in the photonic architectures was consumed in the form of static energy. A comparison of the photonic hardware between the network architectures (detailed results for modulator and detector ring counts are omitted due to lack of space) shows that *UltraNoC-8* and *UltraNoC-16* have 75% and 50% less photonic hardware compared to Corona but *UltraNoC-16* uses more hardware than Flexishare. This explains why *UltraNoC-16* has a higher EDP than Flexishare, because *UltraNoC-16* uses more photonic hardware (and thus consumes more static energy) than Flexishare, even though the average packet delay for *UltraNoC-16* is lower than Flexishare.

Our final set of experiments explores architecture scalability. We considered a larger 256-core CMP platform by increasing the core concentration in each tile to four to enable higher traffic injection into the network for this scalability study. We evaluated NoC throughput, average packet latency, and EDP for all photonic NoCs. In addition to *UltraNoC-8* and *UltaNoC-16*, we also considered *UltraNoC*-32, a variant of our architecture with 32 waveguide groups. Figures 5(a)-(c) show the results of these experiments. From the throughput results it can also be inferred that on average *UltraNoC*-8 has 3×, 2.8× and 2.6×, *UltraNoC*-16 has 5.7×, 5.3× and 5.7×, and *UltraNoC*-32 has 9.8×, 9× and 9.7× greater throughput compared to EMesh, Corona and Flexishare. The improvements in throughput for *UltraNoC* over Flexishare and Corona are even better for the 256-core CMP, than in the 64-core CMP case. From figure 5(b), it can be seen that on an average *UltraNoC*-8 has 23%, 25% and 48%, *UltraNoC*-16 has 29%, 30% and 53% and *UltraNoC*-32 has 34%, 36% and 55% lower latency compared to Corona, Flexishare and EMesh architectures respectively. Finally, Figure 5(c) shows that on average *UltraNoC*-8 has 88%, 87% and 20% lower EDP compared to EMesh, Corona and Flexishare respectively. Further *UltraNoC*-16 has 77% and 73% and *UltraNoC*-32 has 55% and 51% lower energy delay product compared to EMesh and Corona respectively. The lower EDP of Flexishare compared to *UltraNoC*-16 and *UltraNoC*-32 is due to the lower photonic hardware used in Flexishare, which lowers its power footprint, but also reduces its throughput and increases its latency.

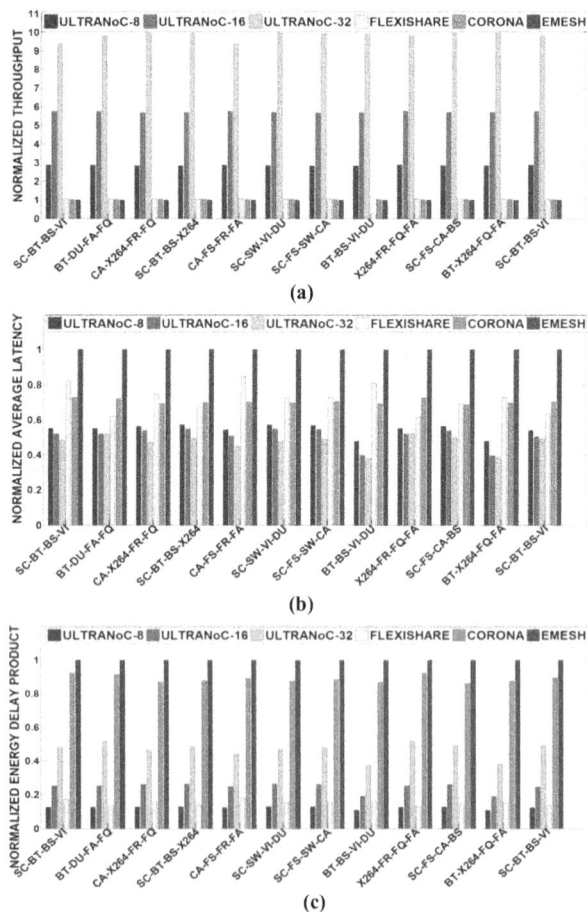

Figure 5: (a) throughput (b) latency (c) EDP comparison of UltraNoC-8, UltraNoC-16 and UltraNoC-32 with other architectures for a 256-core CMP. Results are normalized wrt EMesh.

From the above results, we can summarize that there are variants of *UltraNoC* that can achieve better performance with less hardware compared to existing photonic NoCs, for CMP platforms with low as well as high core counts. The results are a good indicator of the scalability of our proposed *UltraNoC* architecture.

5. CONCLUSIONS

·In this work we presented the *UltraNoC* photonic NoC architecture that features improved channel sharing among cores by using an aggressive concurrent token stream-based arbitration strategy. *UltraNoC* also supports the ability to dynamically transfer bandwidth between clusters of cores and re-prioritize multiple co-running applications to further improve channel utilization and adapt to time-varying application performance goals. *UltraNoC* improves throughput by up to 9.8×, latency by up to 55% and EDP by up to 90% over traditional electrical and state-of-the-art photonic NoC architectures with the best-known arbitration mechanisms. *UltraNoC* also scales well with increasing core counts on a chip.

6. ACKNOWLEDGMENTS

This research is supported by grants from SRC, NSF (CCF-1252500, CCF-1302693), and AFOSR (FA9550-13-1-0110).

REFERENCES

[1] R. Ho, et al., "The future of wires," in *Proc. IEEE*, Apr 2001.
[2] W. J. Dally, B. Towles, "Route packets, not wires," in *DAC*, 2001.
[3] S. Bahirat et al., "OPAL: A Multi-Layer Hybrid Photonic NoC for 3D ICs," in *ASPDAC*, Yokohama, Japan, Jan 2011.
[4] D. A. B. Miller, "Device requirements for optical interconnects to silicon chips," *in IEEE, Special Issue on Silicon Photonics*, 2009.
[5] Q. Xu et al., "12.5gbit/s carrier-injection-based silicon micro-ring silicon modulators," in *Optics Express*, vol. 15,no. 2, Jan. 2007.
[6] S. J. Koester et al., "Ge-on soi-detector/si-cmos-amplifier receivers for high-performance optical communication applications," in *JLT*, vol. 25,no. 1, pp. 46–57, Jan. 2007.
[7] J. D. Owens, et al., "Research challenges for on-chip interconnection networks," in *IEEE Micro*, September-October 2007.
[8] D. Vantrease et al., "Corona: System implications of emerging nanophotonic technology," in *ISCA*, 2008.
[9] Y. Pan et al.,"Firefly: Illuminating future network-on-chip with nanophotonics," in *ISCA*, 2009.
[10] Y. Pan, J. Kim, G. Memik, "Flexishare: Channel sharing for an energy efficient nanophotonic crossbar," in *HPCA*, 2010.
[11] C. Chen, A. Joshi, "Runtime management of laser power in silicon-photonic multibus NoC architecture," in *IEEE JQE*, 2013.
[12] V. Almeida et al., "All-optical switching on a silicon chip" in *Optics Letters*, 29:2867–2869, 2004.
[13] C. A. Barrios, et al., "Low-power-consumption short-length and high-modulation-depth silicon electro-optic modulator" in JLT, 2003.
[14] R. Morris et al., "Power-efficient and high-performance multilevel hybrid nanophotonic interconnect for multicores," in *NOCS* 2010.
[15] J. Psota et al., "ATAC: On-chip optical networks for multicore processors," *Boston Area Archit. Workshop*, pp. 107– 108, Jan. 2007.
[16] C. Bienia et al., "The PARSEC Benchmark Suit: Characterization and Architectural Implications," *in PACT, Oct. 2008.*
[17] M. J. Cianchettiet et al., "Phastlane: a rapid transit optical routing network," in *ISCA*, 2009.
[18] N. Kirman et al., "A power-efficient all-optical on-chip interconnect using wavelength-based oblivious routing," in *ASPLOS* 2010.
[19] X. Zheng et al., "Ultra-efficient 10Gb/s hybrid integrated silicon photonic transmitter and receiver," in *Opt. Express*, Mar 2011.
[20] M. Petracca, et al., "Design exploration of optical interconnection networks for chip multiprocessors," in *HOTI*, Aug. 2008,
[21] A. Joshi et al., "Silicon-Photonic Clos Networks for Global On-Chip Communication", *in NOCS 2009*
[22] D. Vantrease et al., "Light speed arbitration and flow control for nanophotonic interconnects," in *IEEE/ACM MICRO*, Dec. 2009.
[23] P. Grani and S. Bartolini, "Design Options for Optical Ring Interconnect in Future Client Devices," in *ACM JETC, May, 2014.*
[24] T.Pimpalkhute et al., "An application-aware heterogeneous prioritization framework for NoC based chip multiprocessors," in *ISQED 2014.*
[25] N. Binkert et al.,"The gem5 Simulator," in *CA News*, May 2011.

A High-Speed Robust NVM-TCAM Design Using Body Bias Feedback

Bonan Yan[†], Zheng Li[†], Yaojun Zhang[†], Jianlei Yang[†], Weisheng Zhao[*],
Pierre Chor-Fung Chia[‡], Hai Li[†]
[†]University of Pittsburgh, Pittsburgh, Pennsylvania USA
[*]Beihang University, Beijing, China
[‡]Cisco Systems, Inc., San Jose, California
{boy12, zhl85, yaz24, jiy64, hal66}@pitt.edu, weisheng.zhao@u-psud.fr,
chchia@cisco.com

ABSTRACT

As manufacture process scales down rapidly, the design of *ternary content-addressable memory* (TCAM) requiring high storage density, fast access speed and low power consumption becomes very challenging. In recent years, many novel TCAM designs have been inspired by the research on emerging nonvolatile memory technologies, such as *magnetic tunneling junction* (MTJ), *phase change memory* (PCM), and memristor. These designs store a data as the resistive variable of a nonvolatile device, which usually results in limited sensing margin and therefore constrains the searching speed of TCAM architecture severely. To further enhance the performance and robustness of TCAMs, we proposed two novel cell designs that utilize MTJs as data storage units—the symmetrical dual-N structure and the asymmetrical P-N scheme. In both designs, a body bias feedback circuit is integrated to enlarge the sensing margins. Compared with an existing MTJ-based TCAM structure, the tolerance in gate voltage variation of the symmetrical dua-N (asymmetrical P-N) scheme can significantly improve 59.5% (21.2%). The latency and the dynamic energy consumption in one searching operation at the word length of 256 bits are merely $590.35ps$ ($97.89ps$) and $65.05fJ/bit$ ($36.85fJ/bit$), not even mentioning that the use of nonvolatile MTJ devices avoids unnecessary leakage power consumption.

Categories and Subject Descriptors

B.7.1 [**Integrated Circuits**]: Types and Design Styles— *Memory technologies*

General Terms

Design, Performance, Reliability

Keywords

Ternary content-addressable memory (TCAM), nonvolatile memory (NVM), body bias feedback

1. INTRODUCTION

Ternary content-addressable memory (TCAM) compares an input searching data against a table of stored data and returns the address of the matching one(s) [1]. As process technology scales down, the design of conventional SRAM-based TCAMs faces severe difficulties due to the relatively low cell density, large leakage power consumption and deteriorated reliability. Although data is rarely updated in TCAMs, maintaining them in SRAM cells results in huge leakage power consumption which starts dominating the overall energy of TCAM architecture. Moreover, the scaling of SRAM designs has been much slower than that of fabrication processes due to the deteriorating device reliability. Furthermore, the searching speed of SRAM-based TCAMs approaches the design limitation [2].

To increase data storage density, reduce power consumption and improve searching speed, TCAM designs based on emerging *nonvolatile memories* (NVMs) have been extensively studied. The nonvolatile storage of these technologies makes significant reduction in static power consumption [3][4]. The fast access speed and good scalability potentially help improve the TCAM density and enhance the searching speed as well. Among various NVMs, *magnetic tunneling junction* (MTJ) could be one of the best candidates for TCAM design considering its technology readiness and commercialization status [5].

Some examples of the latest MTJ-based TCAM designs include 9-transistors-6-MTJs (9T-6MTJ) [6], 3T-2MTJ [7] and 20T-4MTJ [8] structures. In these designs, a logic bit is represented by the *high or low resistance states* (HRS or LRS) of one or a few MTJ devices and the searching operation is realized through detecting the resistance value. Compared to SRAM-based TCAM with 12 transistors (12T-SRAM) [9], these designs significantly decrease the number of transistors and therefore reduce the cell area [6][7][10]. Particularly, Xu *et al.* proposed a structure which utilizes the voltage-dividing, instead of detecting the exact MTJ resistance value in reading and searching operations [7]. Such a structure effectively reduces the transistor numbers of a single TCAM cell to 3.

However, all these MTJ-based TCAM designs face a severe design challenge—the small difference of MTJ's high and low resistance values (usually only a few KΩ) produces a very limited sensing margin, which significantly degrades the reliability of TCAM design, prolongs the searching latency and induces extra power overhead. The benefits from the

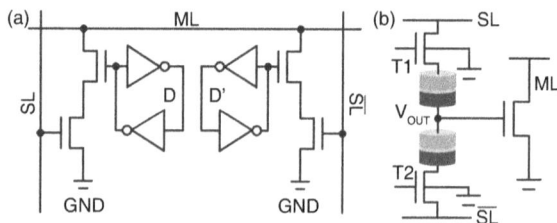

Figure 1: (a) SRAM-based TCAM design; (b) A MTJ-based TCAM cell structure [7].

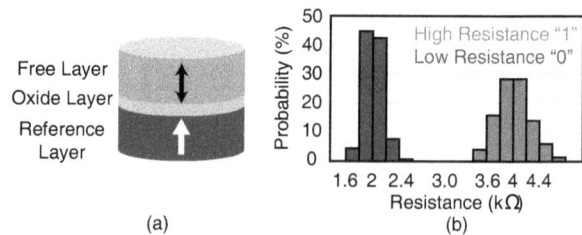

Figure 2: (a) An illustration of MTJ; (b) the MTJ resistance distribution.

nonvolatile device utilization will be also amortized. Very recently, Onizawa *et al.* proposed a 20T-4MTJ TCAM structure with very fast searching performance [8]. However, its cell area and leakage power increase dramatically, even compared with conventional 12T-SRAM version [9].

To conquer the small sensing margin issue and improve the sensing speed and design robustness of MTJ-based TCAMs, we propose two new cell structures, namely, *symmetrical dual-N* and *asymmetrical P-N* designs. Both schemes utilize the voltage dividing scheme [7] for data reading and searching. Besides, a body biasing feedback circuit is embedded. It forms a positive feed mechanism to adaptively adjust the effective resistances of select transistors and therefore improve the sensing margin. We evaluated our designs at $45nm$ CMOS technology [11] and the MTJ model based on the implementation of $40nm$ perpendicular anisotropy structure [12]. The simulations demonstrated significant improvement in sensing speed and energy consumption. For the word length of 256 bits, the symmetrical dual-N scheme can obtain a searching latency of $590.35ps$ and the dynamic energy consumption of $65.05fJ/bit$, under the worst-case scenario. The asymmetrical P-N design has even larger sensing margin, further reducing the searching latency to $97.89ps$ and the dynamic energy consumption to $65.05fJ/bit$.

2. PRELIMINARY

2.1 TCAM

A TCAM cell allows three types of data values: logic 1, logic 0, and X representing a *don't care* value—the state that always output *match* no matter what the searched bit is. In conventional SRAM-based TCAM design, the three different data values are represented by two SRAM cells, as shown in Figure 1(a). The *match line* (ML) is connected to a sense amplifier in reading and searching operations, while a pair of *source lines* (SL and $\overline{SL}$) are used to supply the programming or searching data. Such an SRAM-based TCAM cell requires 12 transistors to achieve a satisfactory reliability and performance, resulting in high leakage power as well as a large cell area.

Figure 1(b) illustrates the fundamental storage principle of an NVM-based TCAM cell [7]. Two *magnetic tunnel junction* (MTJ) devices are used to represent the three possible logic values. The matching function is realized by detecting the voltage at the internal node (V_{OUT}) which is determined by the resistances of the two MTJs as well as transistors T1 and T2. Here, the voltage margin ΔV is defined as

$$\Delta V = |V_{OUT}^{H} - V_{OUT}^{L}|, \qquad (1)$$

where V_{OUT}^{H} and V_{OUT}^{L} respectively denote the lowest bound of *match* condition and the highest possible value in *miss* condition.

The two select transistors (T1 and T2) are necessary to control data access. However, their effective drain-to-source

resistances squeeze the voltage margin ΔV to a limited range, which severely constrains the searching speed and therefore the applications of the design. To address the issue, we propose to utilize body-bias feedback circuit which can enlarge the sensing margin by tuning the effective resistances of the two select transistors properly.

2.2 Basics of MTJ

The structure of a *magnetic tunnel junction* (MTJ) is shown in Figure 2(a). It composes of two ferromagnetic layers (namely the *reference layer* and the *free layer*) and a tunneling oxide layer (e.g., MgO) between the two ferromagnetic layers.

A MTJ can be programmed into two resistance states. When injecting a current from the free layer to the reference layer, the magnetization orientation of the free layer can be switched to be parallel to that of the reference layer. In this case, the MTJ demonstrates a lower resistance value (R_{low}), representing logic "0". Otherwise, the anti-parallel orientation of the two ferromagnetic layers result in a higher resistance (R_{high}), denoting logic "1". The difference between two resistance states is denoted by *tunnel magnetoresistance ratio* (TMR) as $TMR = (R_{high} - R_{low})/R_{low}$.

The logic state stored in a MTJ device can be detected by sensing out the its resistance value R_{MTJ}, which is related to the thickness of the tunneling oxide and the surface area of the device. Thus, process variations can significant affect the MTJ resistance. For example, Figure 2(b) shows the distributions of the high and low resistance values of MTJs in a 64×64 array [13]. The means of the high and low resistance states are $R_{high} = 4K\Omega$ and $R_{low} = 2K\Omega$, respectively. As shown in the figure, the gap between the two resistance states reduces to merely $1K\Omega$ after including the impact of the process variations, making fast read/searching operations very difficult [12].

3. THE BODY BIAS FEEDBACK SCHEME

3.1 Design Principle and Mechanism

To address the small sensing margin and slow searching speed of MTJ-based TCAMs, we propose two new cell structures based on the same basic circuit scheme depicted in Figure 3(a). Same as the 3T-2MTJ TCAM in [7], our designs also use a pair of MTJs (b1 and b2) to represent the three possible logic values. Each MTJ is associated with a select transistor for access control. Instead of directly detecting the exact resistances of MTJs, the proposed design adopts the voltage-dividing property of two serially-connected MTJs as the searching principle.

More importantly, we propose to integrate a body-biasing feedback circuit to enhance the sensing margin. In the work, we denote V_{OUT} as the gate control of the discharging tran-

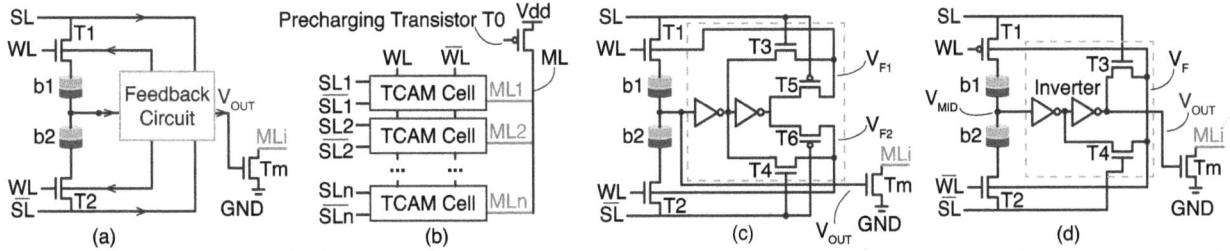

Figure 3: The proposed TCAM designs: (a) The fundamental design, where the arrows indicates signal flow. V_{out} is the gate voltage of Tm. (b) The NVM-based TCAM architecture, in which each word consists of n bits. The match line (ML) is precharged to V_{dd} through T0. (c) The symmetrical Dual-N TCAM cell. V_{F1} and V_{F2} are the feedback signals that respectively control the body bias of T1 and T2. (d) The asymmetrical P-N TCAM cell. A single feedback signal V_F is used to control the body bias of the two select transistors.

sistor Tm. As aforementioned in Section 2.1, the effective drain-to-source resistances of T1 and T2 involve into the voltage dividing function, greatly constraining the ranges of V_{OUT}^H and V_{OUT}^L. Determined by the voltage level of V_{OUT}, the feedback circuit in our designs can adaptively adjust the body controls and hence tune the resistances of T1 and T2, further pulling V_{OUT} toward the expected condition. As such, the voltage margin ΔV increases.

Table 1 summarizes the truth table of the proposed TCAM designs. Two MTJs b1 and b2 together represent the stored data. For example, to save logic "1", b1 and b2 shall be programmed to the high and the low resistance states, respectively, denoting as (b1,b2) = (1,0). And the searching output V_{OUT} is determined by the combination of b1, b2, SL and $\overline{SL}$. To continue the example, if SL and $\overline{SL}$ are respectively set to V_{dd} ("1") and gnd ("0"), V_{OUT} will end at a relatively low voltage level which is not sufficient to turn on the discharging transistor Tm, implying a *match*. On the contrary, a relatively high V_{OUT} can be generated when SL and $\overline{SL}$ are set as "0" and "1", respectively. Tm is turned on to discharge ML, resulting in a *miss*. The *don't care* value in a TCAM cell can be obtained by programming both b1 and b2 to high resistance state. In this case, no matter what combination of SL and $\overline{SL}$, V_{OUT} remains at a relatively low level, corresponding to the *match* condition.

The key of the design is to keep the low level of V_{OUT} below the threshold voltage V_{th} of Tm while making sure that its high level beyond V_{th} [14]. However, V_{OUT} is determined by the voltage dividing of the upper and lower branches so it might not be able to reach the ideal V_{dd} (gnd) as its high (low) level. For convenience and accuracy, we will use "semi-high" and "semi-low" to indicate the level of V_{OUT} from henceforth.

Figure 3(b) illustrates the TCAM architecture of the proposed design. Prior a searching operation, the *match line* (ML) shall be precharged to V_{dd}. During the following searching phase, the *wordlines* (WLs) of the selected cells are raised to high to turn on the select transistors. For any bit i, the searching data and its complementary are supplied to

SL$_i$ and $\overline{SL}_i$, respectively. In the case that the searching bit does not match to the stored bit (*i.e.*, miss), $V_{OUT,i}$ switches to a high level to turn on Tm$_i$ and discharge ML. Even there is only one *miss* condition among the n-bits of a word, ML that is connected to all the n TCAM cells cannot maintain at the high voltage level. In other words, a positive matching signal can be generated only when all the bits produce *match* results and the discharging transistors in all the cells are disabled.

3.2 Symmetrical Dual-N Scheme

We first present the symmetrical dual-N scheme which is shown in Figure 3(c). Here, V_{OUT} is connected to the input of the feedback circuit.

Let's use the case of (b1,b2) = (0,1) to explain how the feedback circuit works in the scheme. If the searching inputs (SL, $\overline{SL}$) = (1,0), V_{OUT} is semi-high. Transistors T3 and T6 are turned on while T4 and T5 remain off. In the situation, V_{F2} as the body bias of T2 becomes much larger than V_{F1}, the body bias of T1. As such, the threshold voltage and hence the resistance of T2 grows faster than those of T1. Th scenario further enlarges the resistance difference of T1 + b1 and T2 + b2, boosting up V_{OUT} to high. The opposite searching inputs, on the contrary, will turn on T4 and T5 and greatly enlarge the resistance of T1 + b1. As a result, V_{OUT} is further pulled down. In summary, a positive feedback loop is formed, which can adaptively tune the resistances of T1 and T2 according to the logic of (b1, b2) and input searching data (SL, $\overline{SL}$). The design aggravates the voltage difference between match and miss conditions, that is, the sensing margin ΔV.

There are totally 11 transistors required in a symmetrical dual-N TCAM cell. Though the feedback circuit can help enhance the sensing margin and improve the robustness of the TCAM design, the access control by NMOS type transistors T1 and T2 always cause threshold voltage drop at the circumstance of passing V_{dd} from either SL or $\overline{SL}$. The corresponding simulation results can be found in Section 4.

3.3 Asymmetrical P-N Scheme

We propose the asymmetrical P-N TCAM design to moderate the voltage drop problem in the symmetrical dual-N

Table 1: Truth Table of NVM-based TCAM Design

Stored Data		SL	$\overline{SL}$	V_{OUT}	Condition
Logic	(b1,b2)				
0	(0,1)	0	1	L	*match*
		1	0	H	*miss*
1	(1,0)	0	1	H	*miss*
		1	0	L	*match*
Don't care	(1,1)	X	$\overline{X}$	L	*match*

Table 2: The Imbalanced V_{OUT} of The Asymmetrical P-N Design

SL	V_{OUT}^H when *miss*	V_{OUT}^L when *match*	ΔV
1.0V	997.85mV	194.88mV	802.97mV
0.0V	998.06mV	370.69mV	627.37mV

71

Table 3: The Comparison of Various TCAM Designs

Design		Dual-N (this work)	P-N (this work)	3T-2MTJ [7]	12T-SRAM [9]
MTJ	TMR	1	1	1	N/A
	R_{low}	$2K\Omega$	$2K\Omega$	$3K\Omega$	N/A
Circuit	Technology Node	$45nm$	$45nm$	$45nm$	$45nm$
	V_{dd}	$1.0V$	$1.0V$	$1.0V$	$1.0V$
	Cell Structure	10T-2MTJ	8T-2MTJ	3T-2MTJ	12T
	Sensing Margin	$189.7mV$	$802.4mV$	$56.45mV$	$792.9mV$
	Sensing Latency†	$590.34ps$	$97.89ps$	$2.3ns$	$132ps$
	Sensing Energy per Search	$65.05fJ/bit$	$36.85fJ/bit$	$80.56fJ/bit$	$90.75fJ/bit$

† The sensing latency was obtained for the word length of 256 bits under the condition that 255 bits match to the input searching data while 1 bit is missed.

scheme. The circuit structure is illustrated in Figure 3(d), where PMOS transistor T1 and NMOS transistor T2 are adopted for access control. Here, V_{OUT} is supplied by the post-amplified signal.

The asymmetrical P-N scheme follows the same fundamental searching principle and the same feedback mechanism as the symmetrical dual-N cell design. Note that the effective resistances of NMOS and PMOS transistors have the opposite dependency on the body bias voltage. More specific, an identical body bias can result in the increase of a NMOS and decrease of a PMOS simultaneously, or vice versa. Thus, we only need two transistors T3 and T4 to supply the body bias in the asymmetrical P-N scheme. The total transistor number reduces to nine.

The most significant difference of the asymmetrical structure from the previous symmetrical version is the use of select transistors. As aforementioned, the threshold voltage drop of NMOS transistor occupies a large portion of the voltage margin, inspiring the symmetrical P-N design. However, the issue cannot be completely solved under all the possible combinations of (b1,b2) and (SL,$\overline{SL}$).

The simulation results in Table 2 show that the asymmetrical P-N scheme helps improve ΔV in most of scenarios except when (b1,b2) = (1,0) and (SL,$\overline{SL}$) = (0,1), which in fact exacerbates swiftly the voltage margin due to the unbalanced gate-source voltage condition. This is a typical design trade-off between the cell area and the sensing margin. Even though, the simulation and analysis in Section 4 still show the asymmetrical P-N design can obtain the best sense margin and therefore the fastest sensing performance.

4. SIMULATIONS AND EVALUATION

We implemented the proposed TCAM designs and evaluated the performance through circuit simulations in Cadence Virtuoso environment. The $45nm$ CMOS technology with the power supply of $V_{dd} = 1V$ was adopted [11]. The MTJ device model was based on the implementation of $40nm$ perpendicular anisotropy structure [15].

We first examine and compare the sensing margins of the proposed schemes with existing MTJ-based TCAM designs [7] as well as conventional 12T-SRAM based on the design in [9]. Table 3 summarizes the simulation results, including the sensing margins, the sensing latency, as well as the energy consumption.

In this section, the major design factors that affects the performance and robustness of MTJ-based TCAMs are discussed and analyzed based on simulation details. Afterwards, the searching speed and power consumptions of the proposed designs are presented and discussed.

4.1 Impact Factors of Sensing Margin

For the proposed TCAM design structures that leverage the voltage dividing for data detection and searching, the sensing performance is greatly affected by the balance of the two access transistors (T1 and T2) as well as the resistance variations of MTJs (b1 and b2). Accordingly, there are three major factors that potentially degrade the sensing margin: the unbalance in gate voltage supplies to T1 and T2, the CMOS process variations, and the MTJ resistance variations. In this subsection, the impacts of these three design factors on the TCAM robustness will be investigated.

4.1.1 The Unbalanced Transistor Gate Voltage

The gate voltage variations of T1 and T2 are firstly investigated. The impacts on V_{OUT} and the sensing margin ΔV are shown in Figure 4. In the simulations, we assume that T1 is turned on with an ideal gate voltage, i.e., $1.0V$ in the symmetric dual-N scheme and $0V$ for an asymmetric P-N cell. The gate voltage of T2 is then swept from $0V$ to $V_{dd} = 1.0V$.

For a design x, $V_{OUT}^H(x)$ and $V_{OUT}^L(x)$ are used to denote the lowest voltage level of V_{OUT} under the miss condition and its highest possible value when the searched and stored bits matches, respectively. The simulation results for three MTJ-based TCAM designs are presented, including the two schemes proposed in this work (Dual-N and P-N) and the 3T-2MTJ design [7] used as the baseline in the work.

Figure 4(a) and (b) demonstrate the exact V_{OUT} and the corresponding sensing margin change of the three designs, which is obtained by

$$\Delta V(x) = |V_{OUT}^H(x) - V_{OUT}^L(x)|. \quad (2)$$

As shown in the figure, V_{OUT} that is dependent on the match and miss conditions changes dramatically with the gate volt-

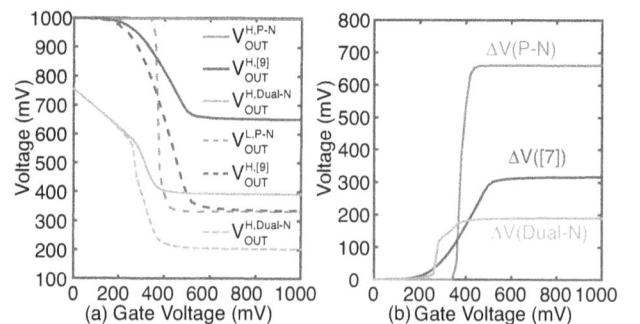

Figure 4: The impact of the gate voltage of access transistors T1 or T2 on (a) V_{OUT} and (b) the voltage margin.

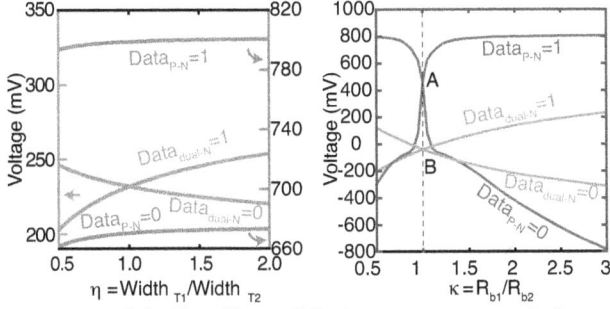

Figure 5: (a) The disequilibrium represented the relation of the sensing margin and the select transistor size ratio η. The $y-axis$ on the left is for the symmetrical dual-N scheme and the right one is for the asymmetrical P-N design. (b) The impact of MTJ resistance variation represented by the change of the voltage margin with the MTJ resistance ratio κ.

age of T2. $\Delta V(x)$ is a key criteria to evaluate the robustness of a given design x. We observe that the asymmetric P-N scheme obtains the highest sensing margin of $627mV$, even when the gate voltage of T2 reduces to about $450mV$. The results demonstrates that the P-N scheme has the strongest resilience on the variations of the access transistor effective resistance .

Comparably, the symmetrical dual-N design has the smallest margins as T2's gate voltage exceeds $600mV$. However, it can steadily maintain the voltage margin in the largest input range – even when the gate voltage of T2 approaches to $300mV$. Thus, under the extremely worst-case scenario when considering all the forms of reliability hazards, the robustness of the symmetrical dual-N design could be the best among these three designs.

4.1.2 The CMOS Process Variations

The process variations can also break the balance of T1 and T2 to cause disequilibrium. So we investigate the impact of variations resulted by CMOS technology.

Figure 5(a) shows the manifestation of disequilibrium represented by the sensing margin versus parameter η which the ratio of transistor dimension, that is, $\eta = \text{Width}_{T1}/\text{Width}_{T2}$. Here, Width_{T1} and Width_{T2} denote the width of transistors T1 and T2, respectively. In the simulation, we keep Width_{T2} unchanged meanwhile changing Width_{T1} to obtain different η. The simulated curves indicate that the variation in η results in distinguished voltage margins.

For the symmetrical dual-N scheme, the largest sensing margin is obtained at $\eta = 1$ when T1 and T2 are identical. Increasing or decreasing η can result in the sensing margin reduction when "0" or "1" is stored in the cell, receptively. Thus the overall system performance degrades. Note that the two curves are not symmetric. This is because we kept Width_{T2} unchanged so that a bigger η corresponds to larger transistors in use. The simulation results also imply that the system performance degradation has a slower rate when increasing the size of T1 and T2, thought it will results in large design area. As for the disequilibrium of P-N design, the voltage margin stays a high level because the V_{OUT} remains amplified after the two-inverter buffer.

4.1.3 The MTJ Resistance Variation

An unavoidable variation factor comes from the NVM storage unit itself. For a MTJ device, the linear variation of

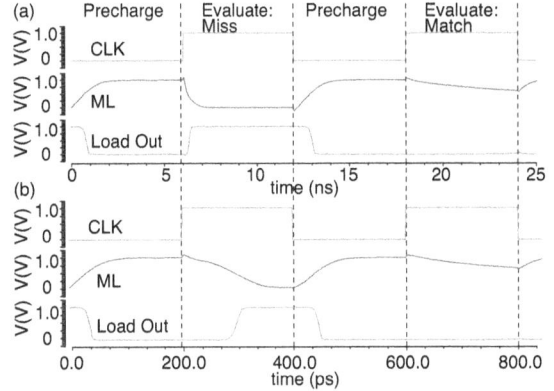

Figure 6: The transient response of key signals: (a) symmetrical dual-N design; (b) asymmetrical P-N design.

the oxide layer thickness can cause the exponential change of the effective MTJ resistance according to the quantum tunnel effect. Thus the impact of MTJ resistance variations should be addressed.

Figure 5(b) shows the change of voltage margins according to the ratio of MTJ resistance $\kappa = R_{b1}/R_{b2}$. Similarly, we fixed R_{b2} in the simulation and changed the value of R_{b1}. Thus, the change of κ indeed reflects the variation of MTJ's TMR ratio, such as

$$\kappa = \begin{cases} (\text{TMR} + 1)^{-1} & \text{if } \kappa \leqslant 1 \\ \text{TMR} + 1 & \text{if } \kappa > 1 \end{cases} \quad (3)$$

As expected, the MTJ variation plays a crucial role in the proposed designs. Naturally, the larger κ induces a bigger gap between the sensing voltages of match and miss conditions. Consequently, the voltage margin is larger.

We also want to point out that at $\kappa = 1$, the cross point of the two curves of the same design refers to the sensing margin induced solely by the feedback circuit. More specific, point A is for the asymmetrical P-N scheme and point B is the one of the symmetric dual-N design. The observation of $\Delta V(A) > \Delta V(B)$ is consistent to the result in Figure 4(b) – the asymmetrical P-N design has a larger voltage margin than that of the symmetrical dual-N design.

4.2 The Searching Speed

The searching speed is the most crucial performance factor of TCAMs, which is directly related to the sensing margin. We compare the sensing speeds of the proposed schemes with the baseline MTJ-based TCAM design [7] and conventional 12T-SRAM [9]. The results are shown in Table 3. Here, the sensing latency was obtain for the word length of 256 bits under the worst-case operation condition: only one bit is different from the input searching bit so that the discharging current at ML is minimal. Compared to the baseline design [7], the searching speed of the asymmetrical dual-N scheme improves $12.7\times$ while the enhancement of the asymmetrical P-N design is more than $76.5\times$.

Figure 6(a,b) presents the transient process during the searching operations for the symmetrical dual-N design and the asymmetrical P-N scheme, respectively. The simulations show a slight degradation on ML voltage level when the evaluation results in a matching. This is because of the electrical charge leakage through the discharging transistors in each TCAM cell, since no keeper is used in the proposed designs. The signal of ML is regulated via an inverter, generating the output signal Load-Out in the figure.

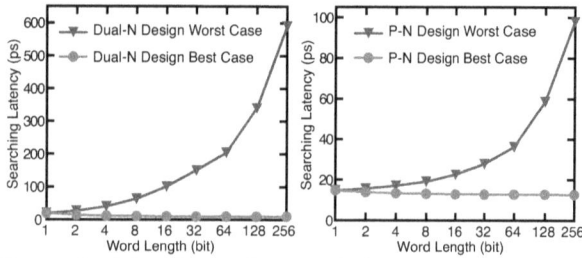

Figure 7: The dependency of the searching latency on the word length. The $y-axis$ on the left is for the asymmetrical P-N design and the right one is for the symmetrical dual-N scheme.

The length of word and the operation condition can also greatly affect the speed of sensing operations as our simulations shown in Figure 7. Same as the above, the worst-case condition occurs when only one bit in the stored data is different from the input searching one. The best-case scenario, in contrast, assume the discrepancy happens at all the bits so that the charge on ML is sunk through the discharging transistors fo all the TCAM cells. The simulation shows that searching speed under the best-case situation doesn't change much as the word length increases. However, the worst-case latency increase quickly as bit number grows and therefore the overall capacitance on ML increases. Comparably, the symmetrical dual-N design with smaller sensing margin is much slower than the asymmetrical P-N design. ical dual-N design are lower than those of the asymmetrical P-N design.

4.3 The Searching Energy Consumption

The energy saving is a key incentive in developing the NVM-based TCAM designs. Compared with conventional SRAM-based TCAMs, the non-volatility of these emerging devices allows zero standby power consumption. Besides, we evaluated the dynamic energy consumption in searching operation and summarized the results in Table 3. Compared with 12T-SRAM design, the proposed symmetrical dual-N and asymmetrical P-N designs can obtain about 35.6% and 63.5% energy savings, respectively.

5. CONCLUSIONS

At advanced technologies, NVM-based TCAM designs possess exceptional potential in density improvement and power saving. However, the emerging nonvolatile storage units encounter insufficient sensing margins that results in low design reliability and poor access speed. We proposed to utilize an adaptive body bias feedback scheme to enhance the sensing margin of MTJ-based TCAMs. Determined by the select transistor types in use, two cell structures were presented: the symmetrical dual-N design and the asymmetrical P-N scheme. We thoroughly analyzed the key design factors that affect the performance and reliability of the proposed TCAMs. Both designs demonstrated distinguished enhancement with the enlarged sense margins, fast searching speed and dynamic energy reduction. These characteristics are remarkably beneficial to commercial applications requiring high-performance TCAMs.

Acknowledgments

This work was supported in part by NSF CNS-1311706, NSF CNS-1342566, and Cisco Systems, Inc. Any opinions, findings and conclusions or recommendations expressed in this material are those of the authors and do not necessarily reflect the views of NSF, Cisco Systems, or their contractors.

6. REFERENCES

[1] K. Pagiamtzis and A. Sheikholeslami, "Content-addressable memory (cam) circuits and architectures: A tutorial and survey," *IEEE Jour. Solid-State Circuits*, vol. 41, no. 3, pp. 712–727, 2006.

[2] Z. Ullah, M. K. Jaiswal, and R. C. Cheung, "E-tcam: An efficient sram-based architecture for tcam," *Circuits, Systems, and Signal Processing*, vol. 33, no. 10, pp. 3123–3144, 2014.

[3] H. Li, X. Wang, Z.-L. Ong, W.-F. Wong, Y. Zhang, P. Wang, and Y. Chen, "Performance, power, and reliability tradeoffs of stt-ram cell subject to architecture-level requirement," *IEEE Trans. Magnetics*, vol. 47, no. 10, pp. 2356–2359, 2011.

[4] Y. Chen, Y. Zhang, and P. Wang, "Probabilistic design in spintronic memory and logic circuit," in *17th Asia and South Pacific Design Automation Conference*, pp. 323–328, IEEE, 2012.

[5] J. Janesky, N. Rizzo, D. Houssameddine, R. Whig, F. Mancoff, M. DeHerrera, J. Sun, M. Schneider, H. Chia, *et al.*, "Device performance in a fully functional 800mhz ddr3 spin torque magnetic random access memory," in *5th IEEE International Memory Workshop*, pp. 17–20, IEEE, 2013.

[6] N. Onizawa, S. Matsunaga, and T. Hanyu, "Design of a soft-error tolerant 9-transistor/6-magnetic-tunnel- junction hybrid cell based nonvolatile tcam," in *IEEE 12th International New Circuits and Systems Conference*, pp. 193–196, IEEE, 2014.

[7] W. Xu, T. Zhang, and Y. Chen, "Design of spin-torque transfer magnetoresistive ram and cam/tcam with high sensing and search speed," *IEEE Trans. Very Large Scale Integration Systems*, vol. 18, no. 1, pp. 66–74, 2010.

[8] N. Onizawa, S. Matsunaga, and T. Hanyu, "A compact soft-error tolerant asynchronous tcam based on a transistor/magnetic-tunnel-junction hybrid dual-rail word structure," in *20th IEEE International Symposium on Asynchronous Circuits and Systems*, pp. 1–8, IEEE, 2014.

[9] Y. Nishi, "Advances in non-volatile memory and storage technology," 2014.

[10] S. Matsunaga, A. Katsumata, M. Natsui, S. Fukami, T. Endoh, H. Ohno, and T. Hanyu, "Fully parallel 6t-2mtj nonvolatile tcam with single-transistor-based self match-line discharge control," in *Symposium on VLSI Circuits*, pp. 298–299, IEEE, 2011.

[11] W. Zhao and Y. Cao, "Predictive technology model for nano-cmos design exploration," *ACM Jour. Emerging Technologies in Computing Systems*, vol. 3, no. 1, p. 1, 2007.

[12] Y. Zhang, X. Wang, and Y. Chen, "Stt-ram cell design optimization for persistent and non-persistent error rate reduction: a statistical design view," in *Proceedings of the International Conference on Computer-Aided Design*, pp. 471–477, IEEE, 2011.

[13] Y. Iba, A. Takahashi, A. Hatada, M. Nakabayashi, C. Yoshida, Y. Yamazaki, *et al.*, "A highly scalable stt-mram fabricated by a novel technique for shrinking a magnetic tunnel junction with reducing processing damage," in *Symposium on VLSI Technology: Digest of Technical Papers*, pp. 1–2, IEEE, 2014.

[14] J. W. Tschanz *et al.*, "Adaptive body bias for reducing impacts of die-to-die and within-die parameter variations on microprocessor frequency and leakage," *IEEE Jour. Solid-State Circuits*, vol. 37, no. 11, p. 1396, 2002.

[15] Y. Zhang, W. Zhao, Y. Lakys, J.-O. Klein, J.-V. Kim, D. Ravelosona, and C. Chappert, "Compact modeling of perpendicular-anisotropy cofeb/mgo magnetic tunnel junctions," *IEEE Trans. Electron Devices*, vol. 59, no. 3, pp. 819–826, 2012.

Characterizing the Activity Factor
in NBTI Aging Models for Embedded Cores

Yukai Chen   Andrea Calimera   Enrico Macii   Massimo Poncino

Department of Control and Computer Engineering
Politecnico di Torino
10129, Torino, Italy

ABSTRACT

In deeply scaled CMOS technologies, device aging causes cores performance parameters to degrade over time. While accurate models to efficiently assess these degradation exist for devices and circuits, no reliable model for processor cores has gained strong acceptance in the literature. In this work, we propose a methodology for deriving an NBTI aging model for embedded cores.

Based on an accurate characterization on the netlist of the core, we were able to (1) prove the independence of the aging on the workload (i.e., executed instructions), and (2) calculate an equivalent average constant aging factor that justifies the use of the baseline model template.

We derived and assessed the proposed model by using a RISC-like processor core implemented in a 45nm process technology as a reference architecture, achieving a maximum error of 2.2% against simulated data on the core netlist.

Categories and Subject Descriptors

J.6 [**Computer-Aided Engineering**]: Computer-aided design (CAD); I.6.4 [**Simulation and Modeling**]: Model Validation and Analysis

General Terms

Design, Experimentation, Performance.

Keywords

Aging, Processors, Reliability, Modeling.

1. INTRODUCTION

In the recent years, a large bulk of research has addressed the issue of NBTI-induced aging. Most of these works have however been focused on logic blocks and SRAM structures; this is because the accurate characterization of NBTI aging requires the availability of the circuit netlist in order to extract the critical paths and the signal probabilities of the relative cells. These information are available for logic circuits during synthesis, and are implicit for SRAM structures whose topology is well-defined. Conversely, this is not the case with processor cores; cores are regarded as black-box, third-party IPs whose netlists are obviously not available.

GLSVLSI'15, May 20–22, 2015, Pittsburgh, PA, USA.
Copyright 2015 ACM 978-1-4503-3474-7/15/05...$15.00.
http://dx.doi.org/10.1145/2742060.2742111.

The state of the art in modeling of the aging of a core relies on simple approximations based on core "usage": an active core will age according to some constant *aging factor*, and it will simply not age when idle ([4]–[8]). The baseline models for the various aging mechanisms can be either analytical (taken from physics, as in [5, 6, 7, 8] or empirical (derived by fitting data as in [4]). The main drawback of these approaches is that the assumption of a constant "aging factor" is neither motivated nor validated; they provide no evidence on (i) how this factor can be computed, (ii) how general (i.e., applicable to other processors) it is. Moreover, the underlying models used in these works refer to the model for a single logic gate; however, extension at the core level of a gate-level model should be proved [8].

In this work, we propose to infer some general properties of an NBTI aging model from the analysis of a core with an available netlist. Our claim is that since most processors share a common architectural concept, the main conclusions will have a reasonably general validity. We target relatively simple embedded processors, for which we can have a better degree of confidence about the generality of the presented results. Our reference "open-netlist" core is a MIPS-based RISC architecture called Plasma [14].

The core netlist is used to obtain detailed aging data using a set of application kernels for characterization; these data are then used to fit the underlying model template. Statistical correctness of the evaluation is guaranteed by using different datasets for the characterization and for the validation. Two are the main conclusions drawn from the validation of the proposed model:

1. **Aging model is roughly independent of the workload.** Quite surprisingly, the impact of different applications and different data sets have negligible impact on the aging of the core.

2. **The aging factor roughly corresponds to the application of a 0.58 static probability at the critical path inputs.** Since the netlist is available, the aging factor can be quantified precisely. This is the fundamental result that motivates the use of a classical NBTI aging gate-level model for application to to an entire logic block.

The proposed model show extremely good accuracy: comparison against simulated values on the netlist yields a maximum error of 2.2%.

2. BACKGROUND AND PREVIOUS WORK

2.1 Background

NBTI occurs when a pMOS transistor is negatively biased (i.e., a logic '0' applied to the gate of the pMOS, called the *stress* state), and manifests itself as an increase of the threshold voltage V_t over time, resulting in turn in a degradation of the delay of a device. Conversely, when a logic

'1' is applied (called *recovery* state), NBTI stress is partially removed, resulting in a decrease of the threshold voltage. A widely used model of NBTI-induced V_t drift is derived from the reaction-diffusion model, and can be summarized as follows [1]:

$$\Delta V_t = \mathcal{A} \cdot f(V_{dd}, V_t, T, \mathbf{R}) \cdot t^n. \qquad (1)$$

The model has three main factors:

1. $\mathcal{A}$ denotes the *aging factor* which reflects the actual stress/recovery pattern;

2. A term including all technological and environmental parameters ($f()$): supply voltage V_{dd}, threshold voltage V_t, temperature T, and all device parameters, lumped here for compactness into set $\mathbf{R}$, comprising oxide geometrical and electrical parameters, activation energy, device size, load, etc. See [1] for the precise mathematical expression of $f()$.

3. The dependence over time. n is $1/4$ or $1/6$ depending on the diffusing species. In this work we use $n = 1/6$.

For a given condition of $\mathbf{R}$, it is the value of $\mathcal{A}$ determines the actual V_t drift. Thanks to some mathematical properties of NBTI aging ([9]), it can be shown that it is possible to use *signal probabilities* instead of actual signal values to determine the effective stress. It is worth remarking that the model of Equation 1 technically applies to an individual transistor and, with minor adaptations, to a logic gate. The translation of the V_t drift on a more macroscopic performance metric such as circuit delay or processor maximum frequency still requires the availability of a netlist to determine the actual critical paths.

2.2 Previous Work

In this section we will review the literature on aging models for processors; for a more in-depth overview of NBTI modeling solutions for generic logic circuits and memories we refer the reader to [10, 2].

The work of [5] presents an NBTI-aware processor (Penelope) in which several aging mitigation strategies are proposed. For evaluation of these strategies, the authors do not use a true aging "model" but rather use an *NBTI efficiency* metric that combines the nominal delay, the TDP (thermal design power) limit, and the NBTI guard-band of the processor. The latter is obtained by choosing the maximum guard-band required by any block, assuming that all paths of the different blocks have been adjusted to fit the cycle time to save power. In some sense this work relies a "static" NBTI model, where aging is not truly evaluated but statically defined in terms of a guard-band for each sub-block.

The authors of [6] adopt a sort of "a priori" model. They assume target processor lifetime of 7 years, and evaluate two different aging rates which increase the delay of the critical paths by 10% and by 25%, respectively, in 7 years. They use an explorative approach for other parameters related to NBTI aging, namely the average fraction of stress time of PMOS transistors, and the the average ratio of PMOS to NMOS transistors in critical paths.

The work of [7] aims at balancing workload in multicores using an aging-related metric. The aging model for a core relies on a traditional gate-level model for a critical path; the authors provide no insight on (i) how the critical path(s) of the processor is detected, and (ii) how the percentage of stress on these critical paths is computed.

Another aging model was proposed in [8]; they adopt the model of Equation 1 as a reference and extend it at the core

level; $\mathcal{A}$ is assumed to be available either by direct characterization on the core or by using specific aging monitors (e.g., [11]). For the first option, they also suggest an approach similar to ours, based on the collection of statistics about delay and core activity at different operating conditions (i.e., V_{DD}, T) running benchmarks with different activity levels A relationship between delay and core activity can be finally established, for example using regression analysis. However, the paper does not specify further details about its implementation nor results.

3. ACTIVITY-SENSITIVE AGING MODEL

The proposed model uses Equation 1 as the baseline template, yet. with two substantial differences:

1. **The aging factor $\mathcal{A}$ is empirically characterized** by a circuit-level analysis of the netlist of the processor;

2. Thanks to empirical evidence resulting from the characterization, it is possible to **use an "equivalent aging factor" for the entire core** (actually, the block containing the critical path). This justifies the assumption of a constant aging factor $\mathcal{A}$ to express the aging of the core, as done also in other works but without a substantiation of this claim.

Although our model is derived using a specific target processor core platform (the Plasma MIPS platform) as a reference, our claim is that since most small embedded cores share a relatively similar architecture, (e.g., RISC-based, relatively shallow pipelines, etc.) the main conclusions drawn here will have a reasonably general validity.

Since Equation 1 expresses a drift in threshold voltage and technically refers to a single gate, our first task in order to model the aging of a processor is to devise a macro-model that (i) tracks a quantity related to the system-level performance of a core, and (ii) uses a "core-level" activity factor (as opposed as a gate-level one).

The first objective can be met by modeling, rather than the drift in threshold voltage, *the maximum operating frequency of the core*. This is done by translating the threshold voltage drift of Equation 1 into a delay degradation using a classical alpha-power law [12], whose inverse determines the maximum operating frequency. Notice that this is possible since our methodology relies on the availability of a core netlist, thus it is possible to accurately extract the critical path by simulation and compute the maximum frequency.

The second requirement implies that we should use an aging factor $\mathcal{A}$ that is some function of the *workload* $\mathbf{W}$. From the core perspective the workload is a mix of applications, whereas at the gate-level this will translate into some signal probability pattern in the circuit. This "core-level" activity factor will therefore represents a sort of mapping of the workload onto signal probability values.

Equation 2 shows the expression of the proposed model.

$$f_{max,aged} = \mathcal{A}(\mathbf{W}) \cdot \mathcal{K}(t, V_{dd}, V_t, T, \mathbf{R}) \cdot f_{max,nom} \qquad (2)$$

where $f_{max,aged}$ is the aged frequency at time t and $f_{max,nom}$ is the nominal frequency of a fresh core. Notice that both $\mathcal{A}$ and $\mathcal{K}$ are scale factors between 0 and 1.

The derivation of the model consists then of two phases. First, the value of the aging factor $\mathcal{A}$ is calculated through the characterization on the core netlist of appropriate workloads. Second, based on the corresponding aging resulting from the applied workloads, the factor $\mathcal{K}$ is empirically determined by fitting the results of the simulation. The details of the methodology are described in the following section.

4. MODEL DERIVATION AND VALIDATION

4.1 Reference Core Platform

The Plasma3 CPU [14] is a synthesizable 32-bit RISC micro-processor implemented in VHDL that executes all MIPS-I user-mode instructions. The main memory contains both instruction and data. The design features an interrupt controller, UART, SRAM or DDR SDRAM controller, and Ethernet controller. Our version is implemented with a three stage pipeline and an additional stage for memory read and writes. The critical path occurs within the execution stage of the core, it includes 110 gates and results into a critical delay of 4.834 ns and a $f_{max,nom}$ of 208.63 MHz.

We chose Plasma as a target platform because it has a relatively general architecture as our platform in order to have a good degree of confidence about the generality of our methodology.

4.2 Simulation Setup and Toolchain

Figure 1 shows the detailed flow of our methodology.

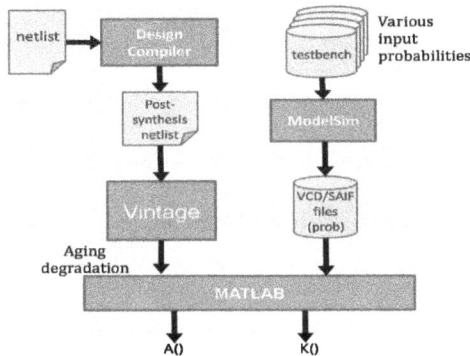

Figure 1: Methodology Implementation.

It uses Synopsys Design Compiler to synthesize the Plasma on the target 45nm cell library, and Mentor Modelsim for the simulation of the Plasma netlist both for characterization (with different signal probabilities on the inputs for $\mathcal{A}$ in $\mathcal{K}$) and for validation. We use Vintage [3], an academic tool that uses aging-characterized libraries to calculate gate-by-gate aging on a critical path, to carry out an NBTI-aware static timing analysis. Finally, Matlab is used for the statistical fitting of $\mathcal{K}$ and $\mathcal{A}$.

4.3 Model Characterization

4.3.1 Characterization of $\mathcal{A}$.

The first step of the methodology is the characterization of $\mathcal{A}$ as a function of the workload. To this purpose, we designed a set of small application kernels that induce different signal probabilities in the core. We chose relatively small kernels because of the limitation of memory size and simulation time. Table 1 lists the set of applications, where **LOC** denotes Lines of Code. In order to further exercise different probability values, strongly data-sensitive applications (sorting ones and CountNumber) have been fed with two input datasets, with different percentages of 0's and 1's. We ran these applications on our platform and extracted the aging with Vintage on the netlist. Figure 2 shows the frequency degradation over time.

The largest difference among applications is 7.14 MHz (about 3.5%); For data-dependent applications, the values represent the average of the two datasets used as inputs. The

Application	LOC	Application	LOC
BubbleSort	396	CountNumber	697
HeapSort	402	CalculatePi	321
QuickSort	456	FFT	781
InsertSort	487	MatrixMult	644
Helloworld	250	ImageConvert	755

Table 1: Application list we tested in our experiment

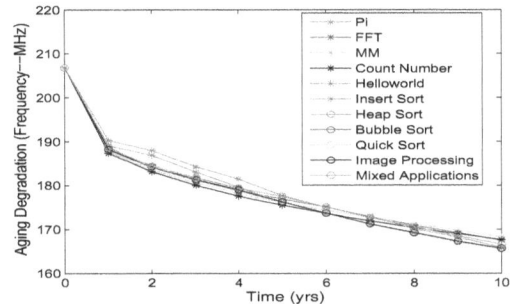

Figure 2: Aging Degradation for Test Applications.

plot seems to suggest that aging degradation is roughly independent of the workload.

To further support this claim, we manually forced all possible static probability values (from all 0's to all 1's in steps of 0.1) at the inputs of the pipeline stage that determines the critical path and have these values propagated into the netlist with Vintage. This experiment guarantees that the workload independence is not a consequence of possible poor choice of application mix, which might possibly exercise only a limited range of signal probabilities. This strategy is similar to approaches typically used to generate power macro-models for RTL power estimation [13].

Even more surprisingly, the simulation of these data confirms the results of Figure 2, as shown in Table 2. The table

Year	Static probability				
	0.0	0.2	0.4	0.6	0.8
0	206.83	206.83	206.83	206.83	206.83
1	191.67	191.64	191.67	191.67	191.64
2	188.52	188.49	188.52	188.52	188.49
3	185.81	185.77	185.81	185.81	185.77
4	182.14	182.09	182.14	182.14	182.09
5	179.05	179.01	179.05	179.05	179.01
6	176.42	176.37	176.42	176.42	176.37
7	173.94	173.89	173.94	173.94	173.89
8	171.82	171.76	171.82	171.82	171.76
9	169.93	169.87	169.93	169.93	169.87
10	167.99	167.92	167.99	167.99	167.92

Table 2: Max Core Frequency [MHz] for Different Input Signal Probabilities.

shows maximum frequency for various input static probability values (columns, in steps of 0.2) vs. time (rows); it is evident from the data that frequency degradation is virtually independent of **input** static probability. The largest difference among all points is only 0.034%.

Such independence of input probabilities allows us to prove the main result of the characterization phase: *since aging is not affected by the input probability values, it is possible to remove the dependency of the workload W from $\mathcal{A}$ in (2).*

However, this property alone does not allow to use a model meant for gate-level aging as Equation 1 at the core level. To this purpose, we need to identify a single, fixed aging factor that can be applied to all the critical gates and that can be characterized once and for all. In order to do this, we artifi-

	Each Aging Year Error[%] (Simulation *VS* Model)									
TB	1	2	3	4	5	6	7	8	9	10
1	1.2	0.2	0.3	0.1	0.0	0.4	0.6	0.4	0.5	0.5
2	1.6	0.7	0.2	0.0	0.2	0.1	0.1	0.1	0.7	0.1
3	0.7	2.0	2.2	1.7	1.7	1.9	2.0	1.5	0.7	0.3

Table 4: Accuracy of our NBTI-aging Model

cially *set different static probability values to* **all signals in the core netlist**. Notice that these values are not logically feasible and can only be forced by writing a corresponding VCD file. The aging factor will be then obtained by finding the best match between the resulting aged frequency values and those of Table 2.

Table 3 reports the frequency values at different times and for different artificially forced probability values on all the internal signals of the cores. As in Table 2, for compactness only values of 0.0, 0.2, 0.4, 0.6, and 0.8 are reported. Aging effects are now sizable, the difference 10-year aging between the worst-case (signals all at 0 probability) and the case with all signals at a 0.8 probability is about 14%.

	Signal probability				
Year	0.0	0.2	0.4	0.6	0.8
0	206.83	206.83	206.83	206.83	206.83
1	184.82	186.02	187.36	189.05	191.24
2	179.55	181.51	183.19	185.27	188.08
3	173.87	176.72	180.07	182.71	185.78
4	169.52	172.55	176.00	180.54	183.98
5	165.87	169.07	172.87	177.55	182.56
6	162.90	166.25	170.09	174.99	181.27
7	160.05	163.64	167.69	172.67	179.70
8	157.62	161.27	165.50	170.70	177.74
9	155.42	159.06	163.40	168.81	176.00
10	153.27	157.10	161.59	167.16	174.60

Table 3: Max Core Frequency [MHz] for Different Static Probability Values for All Signals.

Searching the best match between columns of Table 3 and Table 2 (whose columns are approximately the same) appears to be around a probability value of 0.6. A finer-grain analysis around that point yielded a best match for a probability value of **0.58**. This is equivalent to say that *if we assume a 0.58 static probability value for* **all** *the nodes in the netlist, the core will age approximately as it will under application of typical inputs*. This allows us to use a single, fixed constant aging factor $\mathcal{A}$ to derive our physical term and to also use the gate-level aging model for the whole core without inconsistencies.

Notice that 0.58 is not very far from an intuitive choice of 0.5, in which signal are assumed to change randomly; this suggests that the above result is likely to have a reasonable generality over different platforms. A precise characterization of this value on a given platform would anyway require an analysis similar to the one described here.

4.3.2 Calculation of $\mathcal{K}()$

Now that we have defined an equivalent aging factor, derivation of the physical term $\mathcal{K}()$ becomes straightforward. We take the aging of Table 3 corresponding to $\mathcal{A} = 0.58$ and use Matlab to fit the values to a polynomial curve, after testing different orders of polynomial, we found a fifth-order one has the least error, yielding:

$$\mathcal{K}(t) = -0.014t^5 + 0.015t^4 + 0.025t^3 - 0.048t^2 - 0.048t + 0.86$$

4.4 Model Validation

For the assessment of the model accuracy, we ran three applications not used for the characterization phase: and RGB image conversion (TB1), a matrix manipulation program (TB2) and a mix of the previous two (TB3). Table 4 shows frequency degradation for 1 to 10 years returned by the model and obtained from simulation The comparison shows very good match: the maximum error is 2.2%, while the average over all time points and the three application is only 0.7%.

5. CONCLUSIONS

In this paper we have presented an NBTI aging model for processor cores. The proposed methodology results into two major conclusions: (1) the aging degradation is independent of the workload, (2) it possible to identify an "effective" static probability that can be used as a core-wide stress probability, which allows one to use a gate-level aging model for the entire core. This value has been calculate as a 0.58 stress probability based on a large volume of statistical data. With verification of 45nm silicon data and a RISC processor core architecture(Plasma), our methodology supports statistical aging analysis in standard design flow, improving design predictability and helping avoid pessimistic guard-banding under the increasingly severe NBTI aging effect.

6. REFERENCES

[1] Alam, M. "Reliability-and process-variation aware design of integrated circuits."*Microelectronics Reliability* 48.8 (2008): 1114-1122.

[2] Paul, Bipul C., et al., "Temporal Performance Degradation under NBTI: Estimation and Design for Improved Reliability of Nanoscale Circuits," *DATE-06: Design Automation and Test in Europe*, pp. 1-6, March 2006.

[3] A. Calimera, E. Macii, M. Poncino, "NBTI-Aware Power Gating for Concurrent Leakage and Aging Optimization", *ISLPED'09: ACM International Symposium on Low-Power Design and Electronics*, 2009.

[4] J. Srinivasan, et.al., "Lifetime reliability: towards an architectural solution" IEEE Micro, pp. 70-80, 2005.

[5] Jaume Abella, Xavier Vera, Antonio González, "Penelope: The NBTI-Aware Processor". *40th IEEE/ACM International Symposium on Microarchitecture*, pp. 85-96, 2007.

[6] A. Tiwari, J. Torrellas, "Facelift: Hiding and Slowing Down Aging in Multicores", *41th IEEE/ACM International Symposium on Microarchitecture*, 2008.

[7] J. Sun, et.al., "NBTI Aware Workload Balancing in Multi-core Systems," *ISQED'09: 10th International Symposium on Quality Electronic Design*, March 2009. pp. 833–838.

[8] F. Paterna, A. Acquaviva, L. Benini, "Aging-Aware Energy-Efficient Workload Allocation for Mobile Multimedia Platforms," *IEEE Transactions on Parallel and Distributed Systems, Vol. 24, No. 8, August 2013, pp. 1489–1500*.

[9] Kumar, Sanjay V., Chris H. Kim, and Sachin S. Sapatnekar, "An analytical model for negative bias temperature instability," *ICCAD'06: 2006 IEEE/ACM international conference on Computer-aided design,*pp. 493–496, Nov. 2006.

[10] R. Vattikonda, W. Wang, Y. Cao, "Modeling and minimization of PMOS NBTI effect for robust nanometer design," *DAC-44: ACM Desing Automation Conference*, pp. 1047-1052, 2006.

[11] J. Keane, T.-H. Kim, and C. Kim, "An On-Chip NBTI Sensor for Measuring PMOS Threshold Voltage Degradation," *IEEE Trans. Very Large Scale Integration Systems*, vol. 18, no. 6, pp. 947-956, June 2010.

[12] T. Sakurai, A.R. Newton, "Alpha-Power Law MOSFET Model and its Applications to CMOS Inverter Delay and Other Formulas," *IEEE Journal of Solid-State Circuits*, Vol. 25, No. 2, Apr. 1990, pp. 584–594.

[13] A. Bogliolo, R. Corgnati, E. Macii, M. Poncino, "Parameterized RTL power models for Soft Macros," *IEEE Transactions on VLSI*, Vol. 9, No. 6, pp. 880-887, June 2001.

[14] Plasma Project, http://opencores.org/project,plasma.

Improving Lifetime of Multicore Soft Real-Time Systems through Global Utilization Control

Yue Ma[1], Thidapat Chantem[2], X. Sharon Hu[1], Robert P. Dick[3]
[1]Department of CSE, University of Notre Dame, Notre Dame, IN 46656
[2]Department of ECE, Utah State University, Logan, UT 84322
[3]Department of EECS, University of Michigan, Ann Arbor, MI 48109
Email: {yma1, shu}@nd.edu, tam.chantem@usu.edu, dickrp@umich.edu

ABSTRACT

System lifetime reliability is an important design consideration for many real-time embedded systems. Increasing integrated circuit power density and the subsequent rise in chip temperature negatively impact the lifetime reliability of such systems. Although existing thermal-aware methods are effective in reducing temperature, they may not increase, and may even hamper, the system lifetime reliability. The complicated relationship between temperature and system lifetime requires that reliability be considered explicitly during system design. This paper presents a reliability-aware utilization control framework for homogeneous multicore soft real-time systems. The framework employs a model predictive controller to increase the system lifetime by manipulating the processor utilization. An online heuristic algorithm is introduced to adjust the controller's sampling window in order to reduce the effects of thermal cycling on reliability. Simulation results show that the proposed approach can improve the system mean time to failure by at least 43% and as much as 369% compared to existing techniques.

Categories and Subject Descriptors

B.8.2 [**PERFORMANCE AND RELIABILITY**]: Performance Analysis and Design Aids

Keywords

System-level design; Reliability optimization; Dynamic voltage and frequency scaling

1. INTRODUCTION

Multicore systems provide high performance and power efficiency. However, due to CMOS technology scaling, multicore chips increasingly have higher power density and temperature, which, in turn, reduces system lifetime [5].

There have been a number of research efforts on increasing system lifetime by controlling temperature (e.g., [2, 10, 12]). However, since device lifetime is dependent not only on temperature, but also on temperature variation (thermal cy-

This work was supported in part by NSF under awards CNS-1319904, CNS-1319718, and CNS-1319784 and by Sandia National Laboratory.

cling) [5], temperature reduction strategies alone are suboptimal for maximizing system mean time to failure (MTTF) [6]. Hence, a number of papers have proposed techniques to increase system MTTF directly [1, 3, 4]. Coskun et al. presented a reliability-aware job scheduling and power management approach for multicore systems [1]. However, their work does not consider real-time requirements. Based on wear sensors, Hartman et al. designed a run-time based task mapping algorithm to improve the MTTF of real-time systems [3]. Unfortunately, wear sensors are not yet widely available and can only detect a limited set of integrated circuit (IC) failure mechanisms [11]. Compared to these studies, our approach considers IC-dominant failure mechanisms to improve the lifetime reliability of soft real-time systems.

In this paper, we aim to improve the lifetime reliability of homogeneous multicore systems without sacrificing real-time performance. Since system MTTF depends on both temperature and thermal cycling, we introduce a reliability-aware utilization control framework, called RUC, that jointly optimizes these two factors at the same time. RUC is composed of a global utilization control (GUC) to reduce temperature and a sampling window control (SWC) to reduce thermal cycling. Our main contributions are as follow.

(i) We show that increasing utilization via decreasing execution speed reduces runtime temperature. We exploit this observation to design a model predictive controller (MPC) that keeps the system utilization at a desired value (known as utilization set point) to improve the MTTF without increasing deadline miss rates. The design of MPC considers the real-time constraints as well as MTTF dependency on core temperatures.

(ii) An important parameter in MPC design is the sampling window length (L_{sw}) which impacts system reliability as it affects both core temperatures and thermal cycles. A larger sampling window reduces thermal cycling but increases core temperatures. To achieve the desired trade off between temperature and thermal cycling, we introduce a heuristic to dynamically adjust L_{sw} of the MPC.

We conducted a large set of simulations to assess the effectiveness of our approach. Compared to existing temperature-aware and utilization control mechanisms, our proposed framework achieves, on average, 43% improvement in MTTF, and up to 369% improvement, while allowing more task sets to satisfy real-time constraints.

2. PRELIMINARIES

We consider four main IC-dominant failure mechanisms in this paper: electromigration (EM), stress migration (SM), time dependent dielectric breakdown (TDDB), and thermal cycling (TC) [6]. Figs. 1(a), (b), and (c) depict the MTTF of an example system as a function of amplitude (e.g., the

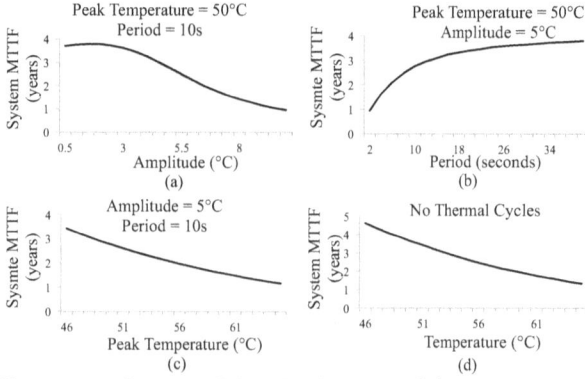

Figure 1: System MTTF due to: (a) amplitude of thermal cycle; (b) period of thermal cycles; (c) peak temperature of thermal cycles; and (d) temperature but no thermal cycles.

difference between the highest (peak) and lowest (valley) temperature), period, and peak temperature, of thermal cycles, respectively, according to a reliability modeling tool [13] with default settings. For comparison purposes, Fig.1 (d) shows the system MTTF due to temperature alone without thermal cycles. As can be seen from Fig.1, the system MTTF is generally higher with lower temperature and smaller thermal cycles, but the precise reliability model is somewhat more complicated.

We focus on homogeneous multicore systems in this paper. Let $M = \{\rho_1, \rho_2, ..., \rho_m\}$ denote the m cores. We assume that these cores have identical thermal and electrical characteristics and initial wear state. The system MTTF of the multicore system is $\min\{MTTF$ of core $\rho_i\}, i = 1, ..., m$, and the MTTF of core ρ_i ($MTTF_i$) can be calculated based on the core's failure rate, or using existing reliability modeling tools, e.g., [13]. For the multicore system under consideration, it has been proven that the system MTTF is maximized if the power is distributed evenly among the cores [11].

Power consumption is the fundamental cause of rising temperature and hence system failure. When a core performs operations, it dissipates dynamic (P_{dyn}) and leakage power (P_{leak}), but when idle only consumes leakage power [10]. Suppose the utilization of a core in a given time interval Δt is $U = \frac{\Delta t_a}{\Delta t}$, where Δt_a is the amount of time that the core executes operations, the average power ($\bar{P}$) can be calculated as

$$\begin{aligned}\bar{P} &= U \times P_{dyn} + P_{leak} \\ &= U \times V^{\alpha_0} \times f \times \alpha_1 + (\alpha_2(f, V) + \alpha_3(f, V) \times T) \times V,\end{aligned} \quad (1)$$

where V and f are the core's voltage and frequency, respectively. $\alpha_0 \geq 1$, $\alpha_1 > 0$, and α_2, α_3 are some voltage/frequency dependent parameters [10].

In term of workloads, we assume that tasks are periodic and already mapped to cores and that no migration is allowed. Workloads may change over time. Tasks on each core are scheduled by a real-time scheduling policy such as earliest deadline first (EDF) or rate monotone (RM) [8]. In a soft real-time system, the late completion of tasks is acceptable but should be avoided. The job of the jth task is denoted by τ_j, which is associated with a tuple $\{e_j, d_j\}$ where e_j is the execution time and d_j is the relative deadline (as well as the period). For a given time duration, thereafter referred to as sampling window k (SW_k), if core ρ_i's frequency is fixed at $f_i(k)$, its utilization can be calculated as

$$U_i(k) = \sum_{\tau_j \in \Gamma(k)} \frac{e_j}{d_j} = \sum_{\tau_j \in \Gamma(k)} \frac{e_j^* + e_j'/f(k)}{d_j}. \quad (2)$$

where e_j' reflects the portion of job execution that is dependent on the core's frequency, and e_j^* is the independent portion. $\Gamma(k)$ is the set of jobs executed in SW_k.

3. PROBLEM FORMULATION

We will use a control theoretic approach to improve the system MTTF by controlling task utilization. Compared to temperature control and MTTF control, utilization control is easier to implement and already widely used in soft real-time systems [9, 12].

Theorem 1. *If in a given time duration, SW_k, core temperatures are constant, then a higher frequency/voltage pair used in SW_k leads to a higher temperature but a lower utilization.*

Theorem 1 indicates that any method to control utilization through manipulations of core's frequency and utilization is also effective in temperature management. Before formulating the utilization control problem, we introduce some notation: $\bar{f}(k)$ is the average frequency over all cores; U^s is the utilization set point; $U^{\max}$ is the upper bound on the utilization to ensure schedulability; $f_{\min}$ and $f_{\max}$ are the lowest and highest core's frequencies allowed, respectively. We aim to solve the following problem:

$$\min \sum_{\rho_i \in M} (U^s - U_i(k))^2. \quad (3)$$

The solution to (3) must satisfy the following constraints:

$$\begin{cases} U_i(k) \leq U^{\max} & \text{for } \rho_i \in M, & (4) \\ -f_{th} \leq f_i(k) - \bar{f}(k) \leq f_{th} & \text{for } \rho_i \in M, \text{ and} & (5) \\ f_{\min} \leq f_i(k) \leq f_{\max} & \text{for } \rho_i \in M. & (6) \end{cases}$$

The first constraint ensures no cores exceed the schedulability bound. According to the system reliability discussion given in Section 2 and [11], the second constraint is introduced to bound the differences in the cores' frequencies, which in turn bound the temperature differences among the cores. The bound on frequency difference, f_{th}, is typically set to 0.1 GHz. The third constraint is used to satisfy the cores' operating requirement.

4. DESIGN OF RUC

4.1 RUC framework

We propose a mechanism to improve system MTTF by solving the optimization problem in Equations (3)-(6) and dynamically adjusting the length of sampling window. We refer to the overall framework as RUC. RUC consists of two main components: global utilization control (GUC) and sampling window control (SWC). GUC reduces temperature by using an MPC, which dynamically adjusts core frequencies to enforce the utilization set point. SWC minimizes thermal cycles by dynamically adjusting L_{sw}.

At the end of SW_k, the utilization of each core is measured. Based on the utilization and MPC settings, MPC solves the optimization problem defined in Equations (3)-(6). The solution consists of the cores' frequencies in the next sampling window and is sent to each core before the start of SW_{k+1}. At the end of SW_k, the measured temperature values are sent to and saved in SWC. Specifically, the temperature measured in the most recent s sampling windows are saved. We refer to the s sampling windows as one profiling window. At the end of each profiling window, a temperature profile is generated. SWC then analyzes this temperature profile and determines whether to increase or reduce the sampling window length in the next profiling window.

4.2 Global utilization control

In this section, we discuss our GUC design to solve the constrained optimization problem in Equations (3)-(6) using an MPC. The basic idea behind any MPC is to optimize a cost function. Hence, we first make a comparison between the constrained optimization problem in Equations (3)-(6) and an MPC cost function optimization problem. After this, we transform the MPC cost function optimization problem to a standard quadratic programming problem to be solved by some existing solvers.

According to control theory, the design of MPC is to minimize a cost function for a given SW_k,

$$J(k) = \sum_{i=N_1}^{N_2} \delta_i [U(k+i) - \rho(k+i)]^2 + \sum_{j=1}^{N_u} \lambda_j [\frac{1}{\Delta f(k+j-1)}]^2, \quad (7)$$

where N_1, N_2, N_u, i, and j are integers, δ_i is the tracking error weight, and λ_i is the control penalty error [12]. The user specified reference trajectory $\rho(k+i)$ defines the ideal trajectory along which the utilization should converge to the set point. The first term in the cost function (7) is a variation of the function in Equation (3). The second term in Equation (7) minimizes the changes in the manipulated variable and does not affect the final result of the optimization problem. Hence, minimizing the cost function (7) under the constraints in Equations (4)-(6) would also lead to the optimal solution to the problem defined in Equations (3)-(6).

We propose using a quadratic programming solver to solve the optimization problem. A standard quadratic programming problem can be written as

$$\min_{\varepsilon} \{\frac{1}{2}\varepsilon^T \Omega \varepsilon + \zeta^T \varepsilon\}, s.t. \begin{cases} A \times \varepsilon \leq b \\ Aeq \times \varepsilon = beq \\ lb \leq \varepsilon \leq ub \end{cases}, \quad (8)$$

where Ω, A, and Aeq are matrices, ζ, b, beq, lb, and ub are vectors, and ε denotes the change in a core's frequency. The key point in MPC design is to transform the problem defined in Equations (4)-(7) to the standard quadratic programming format in Equation (8). Based on ε and the core's frequency inside SW_k, the core's frequency at SW_{k+1} can be directly calculated. We omit the details of the transformation to save space. After the transformation, we can directly solve the quadratic programming problem using a standard solver, e.g., *quadprog* tool in Matlab.

4.3 Sampling window control

The proposed GUC aims to reduce the temperature of the entire multicore chip and to balance the temperature differences among cores, but may introduce thermal cycles. Since a core's frequency and voltage can change from one sampling window to another, sampling window length, L_{sw}, directly impacts thermal cycles. It is difficult to precisely model how the sampling window length affects system reliability, and the complicated reliability model makes finding the best sampling window too time consuming for online use. Hence, to judiciously balance the impact of temperature against that of thermal cycles on system MTTF, we design an efficient online heuristic based on binary search to adjust L_{sw} at runtime.

Since a core's temperature is constant inside each sampling window if a core's frequency is fixed, the aging effect of thermal cycles can be ignored if we only consider a single sampling window. In SWC, we use the concept of profiling window to adjust L_{sw}. A profiling window is composed of s sampling windows with the same length and whose s temperature points, each corresponding to the temperature of the respective sampling window, make up a temperature profile. At the end of each profiling window, we estimate the system MTTF from the temperature profile using a reliability modelling tool [13]. In our experimental evaluations,

---

Algorithm 1: SWC

1:	initialize $Range_s$, $Range_e$, cur, pre, and set $i = 1$
2:	**while** True **then**
3:	**if** at the end of SW_i **then**
4:	measure temperature $T_k(i)$ for each core
5:	$i \leftarrow i + 1$
6:	**if** $i = s$ **then**
7:	$TP(cur) \leftarrow \{T_i(1), \cdots, T_m(i)\}$
8:	calculate $MTTF_{cur}$
9:	**if** cur is the first profiling window **then**
10:	$L_{sw}^c \leftarrow Range_e$
11:	**else**
12:	$L_{sw}^c \leftarrow (Range_s + Range_e)/2$
13:	**if** $MTTF_{cur} \geq MTTF_{pre}$ **then**
14:	$Range_e \leftarrow (Range_s + Range_e)/2$
15:	**else**
16:	$Range_s \leftarrow (Range_s + Range_e)/2$
17:	$i \leftarrow 1$, update cur and pre
18:	**end while**

---

we find that $s = 100$ achieves an precise system MTTF with an acceptable overhead in MTTF calculation. We store and compare the system MTTF in current and previous sampling window, and use the binary search to find the most appropriate sampling windows length.

To find L_{sw}, let $[Range_s, Range_e]$ denote the binary search range. We initially set $Range_s$, which is also the lower bound of L_{sw}, to 1 second to keep the overhead due to RUC under 1% of the sampling window length (based on an Intel Core i5 2.6 GHz and 2 GB memory). To determine an initial value for $Range_e$, we observe that since GUC expects a constant temperature in a given sampling window, so the sampling window length must be smaller than some constant C_{HW}, which depends on runtime environment and hardware platform and is typically on the order of 10 seconds. Moreover, since different hyperperiods (HPs) of a given periodic task set have the same workload, a core's frequency remains the same across different HPs if $L_{sw} = HP$ and utilization set point is fixed. Since a larger L_{sw} leads to higher temperature due to slow frequency scaling, the appropriate value for L_{sw} should be less than or equal to HP. As a result, we initialize $Range_e$ to min$\{HP, C_{HW}\}$. The pseudo code for SWC is given in Alg.1, where L_{sw}^c is L_{sw} in the current sampling window, and cur and pre represent the current and previous profiling window. The search ranger, $[Range_s, Range_e]$, is updated in each iteration until the most appropriate value for L_{sw} is found.

5. EVALUATION

We have conducted a large number of simulation runs to evaluate the effectiveness of RUC. An event-driven simulator was implemented to simulate task execution. Tasks are scheduled using EDF [8] and executed to completion even if they have missed their deadlines. Each benchmark is composed of 50 randomly generated task sets. In each benchmark, the utilization level is kept constant. The utilization levels of the task set considered are 50,60,...,90%. For the task set Γ, the utilization level is defined to be $U_{level} = \sum_{\tau_i \in \Gamma} \frac{e_i}{d_i}$. It is not necessary to evaluate the effectiveness of RUC under low utilization levels since the lowest frequency level would allow all the deadlines to be met while minimizing the core temperatures. To model different task behaviors, we studied two cases: fixed and variable task execution times. For the latter case, actual execution times of jobs are obtained by multiplying the specified execution times by a random value in the range [0.9, 1.1].

The hardware platform consists of 4 homogeneous cores and each of them is an ALPHA 21264 microprocessor, since

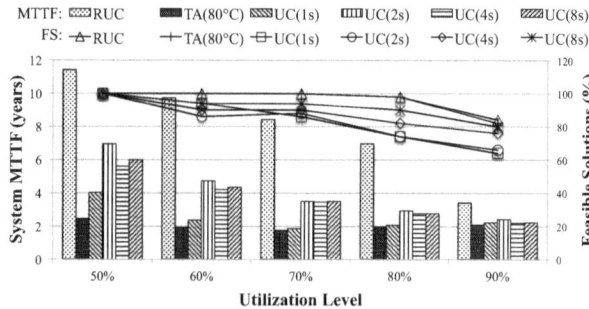

Figure 2: MTTF and FS values obtained by RUC, UC, and TA when tasks' execution times are fixed.

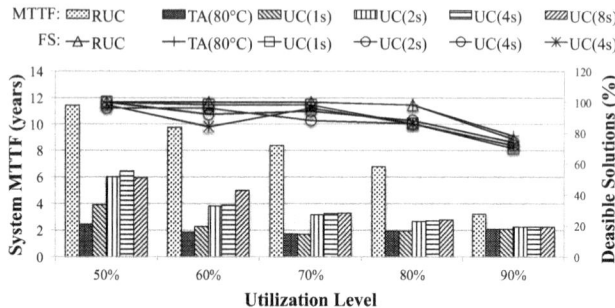

Figure 3: MTTF and FS values obtained by RUC, UC, and TA when tasks' execution times vary dynamically.

it is the only publicly available processor with well established power and thermal models [10]. The processor parameters and constants are listed in Table I. The initial temperature is assumed to be 330°F (56.85°C) and the ambient temperature is 318.15°F (45°C). The runtime temperature is calculated using Hotspot [7].

Table 1: Processor Parameters and Constants [10]

Voltage (V)	Frequency (GHz)	α_1	α_2	α_3
0.7	1.00	1.422	0.1903	15.0
0.8	1.25	2.916	0.2111	15.0
0.9	1.5	5.41	0.234	15.0
1.0	1.75	9.702	0.2592	15.0
1.1	2.00	17.22	0.2867	15.0

We compare the performance of RUC against two representative controller based mechanisms: utilization control (UC) and temperature-aware (TA). Similar to the existing work [9], UC controls a core's frequency to force the utilization to converge to a chosen set point, but it has a fixed L_{sw}. In our simulations, L_{sw} of 1 second (UC(1s)), 2 seconds (UC(2s)), 4 seconds (UC(4s)) and 8 seconds (UC(8s)) are used. As for TA [12], each core's temperature is controlled to converge to its chosen set point. The temperature set point is 80°C, which is below the temperature threshold for hardware throttling [12]. We compare RUC and TA to show that temperature reduction alone is suboptimal in maximizing system MTTF.

We compare RUC, UC and TA in terms of MTTF and real-time performance. Real-time performance is measured by the percentage of feasible solutions (FS), which is the ratio of the number of task sets satisfying their real-time requirements over the total number of task sets. For UC and RUC, the utilization set point is 90% [9]. When tasks execution times are fixed (see Fig.2), the average MTTF values due to RUC for the 5 benchmarks are 11.42, 9.73, 8.43, 6.98, and 3.42 years, respectively. RUC increases MTTF values by up to nearly 364% and at least 52%. In addition, using RUC always results in the highest FS compared to the other

mechanisms in all the benchmarks. These results show that by controlling utilization and adjusting the sampling window length, more real-time task sets can be feasibly scheduled while maximizing system lifetime. RUC exhibits a similar improvement when tasks' execution times vary at runtime (see Fig.3). Its average MTTF values are 11.43, 9.74, 8.40, 6.78, and 3.22 years for the five benchmarks. RUC improves system MTTF by 43%-369% while maintaining FS at a high level. We can conclude that for a variety of different runtime environments, RUC improves system lifetime and increases the schedulability of real-time tasks.

6. CONCLUSIONS

We proposed a reliability-aware utilization control framework to maximize the lifetime of multicore systems under soft real-time constraints. After observing the relationship between reliability and temperature, our mechanism jointly minimizes core temperatures, the temperature differences among cores, and thermal cycling. It uses a model predictive controller to control the core utilization by adjusting a core's frequency/voltage within each sampling window. We also introduced a heuristic to dynamically determine the length of a sampling window. Simulation results reveal that our approach is indeed effective in increasing the lifetime of soft real-time systems. As future work, we plan to extend our mechanism to heterogeneous multicore and hard real-time systems.

References

[1] A. Coskun, et al. Evaluating the impact of job scheduling and power management on processor lifetime for chip multiprocessors. In *Proc. Int. Conf. Measurement and Modeling of Computer System*, pages 169–180, Jun. 2009.

[2] T. Chantem, R. P. Dick, and X. Hu. Temperature-aware scheduling and assignment for hard real-time applications on MPSoCs. *IEEE Trans. VLSI Systems*, 19(10):1884 –1897, Oct. 2011.

[3] A. Hartman and D. Thomas. Lifetime improvement through runtime wear-based task mapping. In *Proc. Int. Conf. Hardware/Software Codesign and System Synthesis*, pages 13–22, Oct. 2012.

[4] A. Hartman, D. Thomas, and B. Meyer. A case for lifetime-aware task mapping in embedded chip multiprocessors. In *Proc. Int. Conf. Hardware/Software Codesign and System Synthesis*, pages 145–154, Oct. 2010.

[5] J. Srinivasan, et al. The impact of technology scaling on lifetime reliability. In *Proc. Int. Conf. Dependable Systems and Networks*, pages 177–186, Jun. 2004.

[6] JEDEC Solid State Technology Association. Failure mechanisms and models for semiconductor devices. *JEDEC Publication*, 2003.

[7] K. Skadron, et al. Temperature-aware microarchitecture: Modeling and implementation. *ACM Trans. Architecture and Code Optimization*, 1(1):94–125, Mar. 2004.

[8] C. Liu and J. Layland. Scheduling algorithm for multiprogramming in a hard-real-time environment. *J. of ACM*, 20(1):46–61, Jan. 1973.

[9] C. Lu, X. Wang, and X. Koutsoukos. Feedback utilization control in distributed real-time systems with end-to-end tasks. *IEEE Trans. Parallel and Distributed Systems*, 16(6):550–561, Jun. 2005.

[10] G. Quan and V. Chaturvedi. Feasibility analysis for temperature-constraint hard real-time periodic tasks. *IEEE Trans. Industrial Informatics*, 6(3):329–339, Aug. 2012.

[11] T. Chantem, et al. Enhancing multicore reliability through wear compensation in online assignment and scheduling. In *Proc. Design, Automation and Test in Europe*, pages 1373–1378, Mar. 2013.

[12] Y. Fu, et al. Feedback thermal control of real-time systems on multicore processors. In *Proc. Int. Conf. Embedded Software*, pages 113–122, Oct. 2012.

[13] Y. Xiang, et al. System-level reliability modeling for MPSoCs. In *Proc. Int. Conf. Hardware/Software Codesign and System Synthesis*, pages 297–306, Oct. 2010.

Directed Self-Assembly Based Cut Mask Optimization for Unidirectional Design

Jiaojiao Ou[†], Bei Yu[†], Jhih-Rong Gao[†], Moshe Preil[‡], Azat Latypov[‡], David Z. Pan[†]

[†]ECE Department, University of Texas at Austin, Austin, TX USA

[‡]GLOBALFOUNDRIES Inc, Santa Clara, CA USA

{jiaojiao, bei, jrgao, dpan}@cerc.utexas.edu, {moshe.preil, azat.latypov}@globalfoundries.com

ABSTRACT

Unidirectional design has attracted lots of attention with the scaling down of technology nodes. However, due to the limitation of traditional lithography, printing the randomly distributed dense cuts becomes a big challenge for highly scaled unidirectional layout. Recently directed self-assembly (DSA) has emerged as a promising lithography technique candidate for cut manufacturing because of its ability to form small cylinders inside the guiding templates and the actual pattern size can be greatly reduced. In this paper, we perform a comprehensive study on the DSA cut mask optimization problem. We first formulate it as integer linear programming (ILP) to assign cuts to different guiding templates, targeting at minimum conflicts and line-end extensions. As ILP may not be scalable for very large size problem, we further propose a speed-up method to decompose the problem into smaller ones and solve them separately. We then merge and legalize the solutions without much loss of result quality. The proposed approaches can be easily extended to handle more DSA guiding patterns with complicated shapes. Experimental results show that our methods can significantly reduce the total number of unresolvable patterns and the line-end extensions for the targeted layouts.

Categories and Subject Descriptors

B.2.7 [**Hardware, Integrated Circuit**]: Design Aids

Keywords

DSA; Cut Mask; Integer Linear Programming

1. INTRODUCTION

As traditional 193i lithography has been pushed to its limit with the scaling down of technology node, industry is looking for the next generation lithography technology, such as multiple patterning lithography, E-beam lithography, extreme ultra violet (EUV), and directed self-assembly (DSA) [1,2]. Recently, DSA has received a lot of attention due to its low cost and high throughput for manufacturing of dense wires and contact layers [3,4].

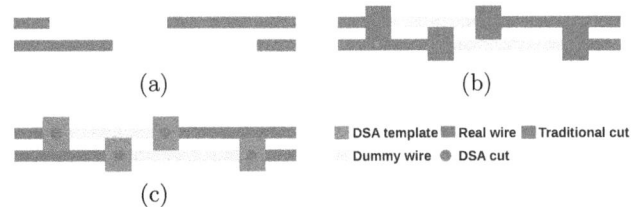

Figure 1: End-cutting of metal wires: (a) target layout, (b) traditional end-cutting, (c) DSA end-cutting.

Several works have been done on the investigation of DSA contact layer fabrication and DSA aware contact layer optimization. Yi et al. [5] demonstrated the fabrication of DSA contacts for unidirectional standard cells. Du et al. [6] proposed a DSA aware contact layer optimization method for 1D standard cell design. Du et al. [7] also proposed a DSA aware routing optimization method which targets at reducing the manufacturing cost and throughput of the via layer.

With the dramatically increased design rules of 2D designs for highly scaled technology nodes, industry is also moving towards the unidirectional design due to its large process window and improved manufacturability [8]. However, manufacturing randomly distributed dense cuts for the metal lines of unidirectional design has become a big challenge for traditional pattern lithography. Firstly, for traditional pattern technique, as shown in Figure 1(b), the cuts may cut across adjacent metal lines. Secondly, for some layouts with tip to tip patterns, traditional lithography might cut extra lines off, thus affecting the connectivity of contacts.

Xiao et al. [9] proposed a DSA cut guiding templates redistribution method for unidirectional standard cell design. The DSA templates are determined for all the cuts by scanning the cuts from the four corners of the pre-constructed conflicted graph. Then these templates are legalized in order to remove overlaps. For overlaps which can not be removed, they are marked as conflicts. However, the proposed process in [9] can not guarantee an optimal result. In *Template Match* step, although it selected the large template to avoid unmarked template, it neglected the relative position of these templates, which introduced a lot of overlap conflicts. Thus, it would take extra efforts and more wire extensions to remove these conflicts.

In this paper, we perform a comprehensive investigation on the DSA based end-cutting problem. We first formulate an ILP to search for optimal solution with minimum wire extensions and conflicts for all test cases. Since for large scale ILP problem the runtime would increase exponentially, we further divide a large layout into several smaller pieces and

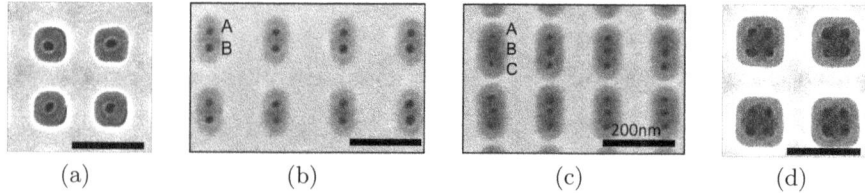

Figure 2: Regular DSA guiding templates SEM images [10]: (a) single-hole template, (b) two-hole template, (c) three-hole template, (d) four-hole template. [Copyright © SPIE, used with permission]

solve them separately without much loss of optimality. For our ILP formulation, it could achieve about 77% less wire extensions on average and zero conflict compared to [9]. For our speed-up method, it could achieve 69% less wire extensions on average, zero conflicts on average and with little sacrifice on runtime.

Our contributions can be summarized as follows:

- We propose an ILP formulation for the DSA cut mask optimization problem, which optimally assigns cuts to different DSA templates with minimum wire extensions and conflicts;

- We propose a speed-up method to solve the problem efficiently;

- Our algorithms can be adaptive to arbitrary types of DSA guiding template shapes, which will be beneficial with the development of DSA manufacturing technique.

The rest of the paper is organized as follows. Section 2 introduces the background of end-cutting process for unidirectional design, DSA guiding template set used in our work, and the definition of DSA cut mask optimization problem. Section 3 proposes the optimal ILP formulation and speed-up method. Section 4 shows the experimental results, and then Section 5 concludes the paper.

2. PRELIMINARIES

2.1 Overview of End-cutting Process

Lines-cut is an effective manufacturing approach [11–13]. For unidirectional layout of metal wires, in order to achieve the circuit connectivity, some parts of the lines should be blocked or cut when printing the unidirectional lines using Self-aligned Double Patterning or other lithography techniques. This cut process can be done by using a trim mask or cut mask. As mentioned in [14, 15], the cut mask can be optimized by the end-cutting approach. That means instead of removing the whole unwanted wires, we just cut up the connectivity of wires by some fixed size cuts, while logical connectivity of the circuit remains the same. By extending the line-end of the wires, some conflicted layout patterns can be resolved for end-cutting approach. For patterns which can not be resolved by wire extension, they will be marked or be printed by alternative lithography technique, such as E-beam [16].

2.2 DSA Guiding Template Type

The shape and size of DSA guiding templates can be adjusted to generate different DSA patterns [17]. However, the variation or overlay of the DSA patterns would increase with the growth of DSA guiding template size and complexity.

For some complex guiding templates, they can even generate some unwanted cylinders inside the template [18]. As reported in [10], some regular DSA guiding templates, shown in Figure 2 could have reasonably good variation controllability and manufacturability. In order to ensure the throughput and manufacturability of the DSA cut for metal lines, we would adopt these regular DSA patterns in our implementation.

2.3 Problem Formulation

We define the DSA cut mask optimization problem as follows:

Problem 1 (DSA Cut Mask Optimization) *Given a unidirectional layout, we are going to cut the metal lines with a predefined DSA guiding template set by assigning cuts to different DSA guiding templates. The target is to minimize the number of unpatternable cuts and total wire extensions by extending the two ends of the wire to fit them into the DSA guiding template.*

3. ALGORITHMS

In this section, we first propose an ILP formulation to find the optimal solution for the problem. Since the ILP formulation is time consuming for very large problem size, we then propose a speed-up method to efficiently solve the problem. Because the guiding patterns are fixed and the metal wires can be extended, it is more difficult than traditional end-cutting problem.

3.1 ILP Formulation

Objective:

Given a unidirectional layout, we are trying to minimize the wire extensions and number of conflicts when applying DSA guiding templates to cut the wires.

$$\text{Minimize} \quad \sum_{i=1}^{n}(x_{2i} - x_{2i-1} - l_i) + W\sum_{i=1}^{2n}\varepsilon_i$$

where W is a constant which denotes the weight of the conflicted cut pattern. If a cut is marked as a conflict, then we should either redesign the layout or adopt other complimentary lithography to remove the conflict, the cost will be quite expensive, thus we define W to be a very big number to reduce the number of conflicts. ε_i is a binary variable indicating the conflicted cut i if it can not be assigned to any DSA templates. x_{2i-1} and x_{2i} are continuous variables indicating the left and right side of wire i, they can also be considered as the horizontal positions for cut $2i - 1$ and $2i$. l_i is a constant which indicates the original length of wire i. n is the number of wires for the layout.

Constraints:

C1: Line-end extension

The line ends of metal wires can only be extended to the left or right of the original design so as not to interrupt the circuit logical connectivity.

$$\begin{cases} x_{2i-1} \leq L_i \\ x_{2i} \geq R_i \\ x_{2i} - x_{2i-1} \leq l_i + \sigma_i \quad i = 1, 2, ..., n \\ x_{2i-1} \geq LL \\ x_{2i} \leq RR \end{cases}$$

σ_i indicates the wire extension limit for each wire. L_i and R_i are constant number indicate the original left and right x-coordinates of wire i. LL and RR are the left and right bound of the layout.

C2: Constraints for templates

For the two line-ends of a wire, we can consider them as two cuts. For each cut, it can be combined with other cuts to be fitted in one DSA guiding template pattern. There might be several templates candidates for each cut, e.g. cut i can be printed by a single-hole template, or it can be combined with cut j and be printed with a two-hole template. Since each cut should be printed by only one template, the constraint is as follows:

$$\sum_{t_j \in T_i} t_j = 1, \forall i \in \{1, 2, \ldots, n\}$$

where T_i is the potential guiding template set for cut i, it includes all the possible DSA guiding templates to print cut i. t_j is a binary variable indicating one of the potential DSA guiding templates. For $t_j \in T_i$, if $t_j = 1$, cut i is printed by t_j. The sum of all potential templates for cut i should be 1. m indicates the total number of potential DSA guiding templates for cut i.

C3: Minimum distance between adjacent templates

Because DSA guiding templates are printed by traditional 193i lithography, adjacent templates should be a minimum distance away from each other. If cut i and cut j are in different templates, without any loss of generality, we use x_i and x_j to indicate the x-coordinate of the two cuts in adjacent templates.

(1) Cuts on the same track

If two cuts are on the same track, we assume that the initial cut i is on the right side of cut j, then x_i is always at least min_s larger than x_j. However, if the two cuts are in the same template t_k or one of the cuts is marked as conflict, then is no such constraint.

$$x_i - x_j + B \times (\varepsilon_i + \varepsilon_j + \sum t_k) \geq min_s, \quad t_k \in (T_i \cap T_j)$$

where B is a very large constant, min_s is the minimum template spacing.

(2) Cuts on adjacent track

If cut i and cut j are on adjacent tracks, since line end can be extended, cut i can be on the left or right side of cut j.

$$\begin{cases} x_i - x_j + B \times (\varepsilon_i + \varepsilon_j + \sum_{t_k \in (T_i \cap T_j)} t_k + d_i^j) \geq min_s \\ x_j - x_i + B \times (\varepsilon_i + \varepsilon_j + \sum_{t_k \in (T_i \cap T_j)} t_k + 1 - d_i^j) \geq min_s \end{cases}$$

where d_i^j is a binary variable denoting the relative position of cut i and cut j. If $d_i^j = 1$, x_i is on the left side of x_j. If $d_i^j = 0$, x_i is on the right side of x_j.

C4: Constraints inside templates

For different DSA guiding patterns, the positions of the inside cuts are different. For two-hole and three-hole vertical templates, the cuts inside them should be aligned vertically; for four-hole template, the horizontal cuts have a certain distance between them, and the vertical aligned cuts have the

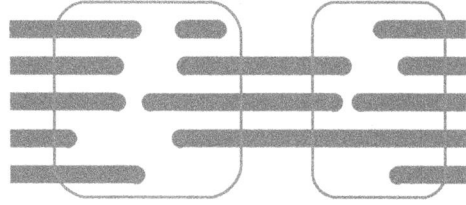

Figure 3: An example of layout division.

same horizontal coordinates. If cut i and cut j are in the same template t_k:

$$\begin{cases} x_i - x_j + B \times (1 - t_k) \geq \theta_k \\ x_i - x_j - B \times (1 - t_k) \leq \theta_k \end{cases}$$

where θ_k indicates the required distance for cut i and j in template t_k.

3.2 Speed-up Method

For large scale size problem, the initial ILP formulation may be quite computational intensive, due to the NP-hardness of ILP problem. For the current biggest benchmark, the number of variables could be more than 90K, and constraints could be more than 70K.

In order to reduce runtime, we can divide the original layouts into several pieces and apply the cut mask optimization algorithm on them separately. After we find the optimal solution for each group, we then merge them together. And there might exist some conflicts on the boundary of each group, therefore we need to remove conflicts after they are merged.

The method consists of three stages: (1) layout division, (2) ILP solution, (3) layout legalization. The ILP formulation is the same as the initial formulation, the *layout division* and *layout legalization* are performed as follows. For layout division, since in the unidirectional layout, some cuts are far away from other adjacent cuts, as shown in Figure 3, there is low possibility that these far away cuts will conflict with each other, thus we can group these adjacent cuts together and find the solution for it. However, if the number of variables in one group is smaller than a certain value, the total initialization time of the ILP solver might exceed the program running time that have been saved, therefore, the number of cuts in each group should be larger than a certain threshold value. Because the number of variables for each group is much less than the original problem, the runtime for each group can be greatly reduced.

After all the optimal solution for each group have been found, there might exist some conflicts or overlaps between DSA guiding templates in different layout groups, we then remove these conflicts by merging adjacent cuts into one or group them into a new DSA templates.

4. EXPERIMENTAL RESULTS

Our algorithms are implemented in C++ and all the experiments are performed on a Linux workstation with Intel Core i7 3.71GHz CPU and 8GB memory. The state-of-the-art ILP solver, Gurobi [19], is used to solve the ILP formulations.

For fair comparison, the six test benchmarks we used in this work are from the authors of [9]. The benchmarks represent the unidirectional metal layers and they are in different sizes. We adopted the DSA guiding template design rule used in [9]. According to the author, the benchmarks are slightly different

Table 1: Comparision with [9]'s method

Case	#Cut	SPIE'13 [9]			ILP			Speed-up		
		#conflict	wire ext.	CPU(s)	#conflict	wire ext.	CPU(s)	#conflict	wire ext.	CPU(s)
1	50	1	201	0.0120	0	28	0.2998	0	28	0.2998
2	100	6	219	0.0234	0	58	2.4799	0	72	0.6698
3	200	12	534	0.0788	0	134	7.8837	0	158	1.4193
4	500	21	1366	0.4159	0	274	354.3260	0	414	2.5163
5	1000	46	2709	1.7431	0	617	86.0026	0	830	4.5137
6	2000	99	5553	7.1713	0	1321	55158.5803	0	1820	9.5318
Avg		30	1764	1.5741	0	405	9268.2621	0	554	3.1585

because the original benchmarks have been overwritten, but the benchmarks are generated by the same method. Since [9] is implemented in MATLAB, the binary is not available to us, we therefore implemented their method to our best effort for comparison.

Table 1 shows the results of comparison in terms of number of conflicts, total wire extensions and runtime for each test benchmark. The second column shows the total number of cuts for each test benchmark. As can be observed from table 1, our ILP formulation and speed-up method have no template conflicts for all the test cases, while on average [9] has 30 remaining conflicts after legalization. Our ILP formulation can achieve about 77% less wire extensions on average, and our speed-up method has about 69% less wire extensions on average than [9]' method. And the speed-up method is about 2934× faster than ILP on average for all the test benchmarks.

5. CONCLUSION

In this paper, we perform a thorough investigation on the DSA based end-cutting problem for unidirectional layout. Two different approaches have been proposed to assign cuts into different DSA guiding templates. The first ILP approach solves the problem and gives a result with 77% less wire extensions and zero conflicts compared to [9]. The speed-up method solves the problem much more efficiently, with 69% less wire extension and zero conflicts. Both of our methods are generic and can be adaptive to different DSA guiding template shapes, which will be beneficial with the development of DSA manufacturing technique.

6. ACKNOWLEDGMENT

This work is supported in part by National Science Foundation (NSF) and Semiconductor Research Corporation (SRC).

7. REFERENCES

[1] D. Z. Pan, B. Yu, and J.-R. Gao, "Design for Manufacturing With Emerging Nanolithography," *IEEE Transactions on CAD*, vol. 32, no. 10, pp. 1453–1472, 2013.

[2] B. Yu, J.-R. Gao, D. Ding, Y. Ban, J.-S. Yang, K. Yuan, M. Cho, and D. Z. Pan, "Dealing with IC Manufacturability in Extreme Scaling," in *Proc. of ICCAD*, 2012, pp. 240–242.

[3] S. Jeong, J. Kim, B. Kim, H. Moon, and S. Kim, "Directed self-assembly of block copolymer for next generation nanolithography," *Materials Today*, vol. 16, no. 12, pp. 468–476, 2013.

[4] Y. Seino, H. Yonemitsu, H. Sato, M. Kanno, H. Kato, K. Kobayashi, A. Kawanishi, T. Azuma, M. Muramatsu, S. Nagahara, T. Kitano, and T. Toshima, "Contact hole shrink process using graphoepitaxial directed self-assembly lithography," *Journal of Microlithography, Microfabrication and Microsystems*, vol. 12, no. 3, 2013.

[5] H. Yi, X.-Y. Bao, J. Zhang, R. Tiberio, J. Conway, L.-W. Chang, S. Mitra, and H.-S. P. Wong, "Contact-hole patterning for random logic circuit using block copolymer directed self-assembly," in *Proc. of SPIE*, vol. 8323, 2012.

[6] Y. Du, D. Guo, M. D. F. Wong, H. Yi, H.-S. P. Wong, H. Zhang, and Q. Ma, "Block copolymer directed self-assembly (DSA) aware contact layer optimization for 10 nm 1D standard cell library," in *Proc. of ICCAD*, 2013, pp. 186–193.

[7] Y. Du, Z. Xiao, M. D. F. Wong, H. Yi, and H.-S. P. Wong, "DSA-Aware Detailed Routing for Via Layer Optimization," in *Proc. of SPIE*, vol. 9049, 2014.

[8] T. Jhaveri, V. Rovner, L. Liebmann, L. Pileggi, A. J. Strojwas, and J. D. Hibbeler, "Co-optimization of circuits, layout and lithography for predictive technology scaling beyond gratings," *IEEE Transactions on CAD*, pp. 509–527, 2010.

[9] Z. Xiao, Y. Du, M. D. F. Wong, and H. Zhang, "DSA Template Mask Determination and Cut Redistribution for Advanced 1D Gridded Design," in *Proc. of SPIE*, vol. 8880, 2013.

[10] H.-S. P. Wong, C. Bencher, H. Yi, X.-Y. Bao, and L.-W. Chang, "Block copolymer directed self-assembly enables sublithographic patterning for device fabrication," in *Proc. of SPIE*, vol. 8323, 2012.

[11] V. Axelrad, K. Mikami, M. Smayling, K. Tsujita, and H. Yaegashi, "Characterization of 1D layout technology at advanced nodes and low k1," in *Proc. of SPIE*, vol. 9052, 2014.

[12] C. Bencher, H. Dai, and Y. Chen, "Gridded design rule scaling: taking the CPU toward the 16nm node," in *Proc. of SPIE*, vol. 7274, 2009.

[13] B. Yu, S. Roy, J.-R. Gao, and D. Z. Pan, "Triple patterning lithography layout decomposition using end-cutting," *Journal of Microlithography, Microfabrication and Microsystems*, vol. 14, no. 1, pp. 011002–011002, 2015.

[14] Y. Ding, C. Chu, and W.-K. Mak, "Throughput optimization for SADP and e-beam based manufacturing of 1D layout," in *Proc. of DAC*, 2014, pp. 1–6.

[15] Y. Du, H. Zhang, M. D. F. Wong, and K.-Y. Chao, "Hybrid lithography optimization with e-beam and immersion processes for 16nm 1D gridded design," in *Proc. of ASPDAC*, 2012, pp. 707–712.

[16] J.-R. Gao, B. Yu, and D. Z. Pan, "Self-aligned double patterning layout decomposition with complementary e-beam lithography," in *Proc. of ASPDAC*, 2014, pp. 143–148.

[17] Y. He, X.-Y. Bao, J. Zhang, C. Bencher, L.-W. Zhang, X. Chen, R. Tiberio, J. Conway, H. Dai, Y. Chen, S. Mitra, and H.-S. P. Wong, "Flexible control of block copolymer directed self-assembly using small, topographical templates: potential lithography solution for integrated circuit contact hole patterning," *Advanced Materials*, vol. 24, no. 23, 2012.

[18] Y. Ma, J. A. Torres, G. Fenger, Y. Granik, J. Ryckaert, G. Vanderberghe, J. Bekaert, and J. Word, "Challenges and opportunities in applying grapho-epitaxy DSA lithography to metal cut and contact/via applications," in *Proc. of SPIE*, vol. 9231, 2014.

[19] "Gurobi." [Online]. Available: http://www.gurobi.com

Skew Bounded Buffer Tree Resynthesis for Clock Power Optimization

Subhendu Roy, Pavlos M. Mattheakis[†], Peter S. Colyer[‡], Laurent Masse-Navette[†],
Pierre-Olivier Ribet[†], David Z. Pan
Department of Electrical and Computer Engineering, University of Texas at Austin, USA
[†]Mentor Graphics, Grenoble, France   [‡]Mentor Graphics, Fremont, USA
subhendu@utexas.edu, {Pavlos_Matthaiakis, Peter_Colyer}@mentor.com,
{Laurent_Masse-Navette, Pierre-Olivier_Ribet}@mentor.com and dpan@ece.utexas.edu

ABSTRACT

With aggressive technology scaling in nanometer regime, a significant fraction of dynamic power is consumed in the clock network due to its high switching activity. Clock networks are typically synthesized and routed to optimize for zero clock skew. However, clock skew optimization is often accompanied with routing overhead which increases the clock net capacitance thereby consuming more power. In this paper, we propose a skew bounded buffer tree resynthesis algorithm to optimize clock net capacitance after the clock network has been synthesized and routed. Our algorithm restricts the skew of the designs within a specified margin from its original skew, and does not introduce any additional Design Rule Check (DRC) violation. Experimental results on industrial designs, with clock networks synthesized and routed by an industrial tool, have demonstrated that our approach can achieve an average reduction of 5.6% and 3.5% in clock net capacitance and clock dynamic power respectively with a marginal overhead in the clock skew.

Categories and Subject Descriptors

B.7.2 [**Hardware, Integrated Circuits**]: Design Aids;

Keywords

Clock tree, dynamic power, post-CTS optimization

1. INTRODUCTION

Clock network synthesis is a fundamental design step in modern ICs. In any synchronous VLSI circuit, the clock network provides the synchronizing signals to the sequential elements (flip-flops). Clock skew is the difference in the clock arrival times between two flip-flops. Although skew has been exploited to cope with the unbalanced data-path delays between the launch and the capture flops [1][2][3][4], skew minimization has long been a prime focus for the CAD engineers [5][6][7][8][9].

GLSVLSI'15, May 22 - 22, 2015, Pittsburgh, PA, USA.
Copyright 2015 ACM 978-1-4503-3474-7/15/05 ...$15.00.
http://dx.doi.org/10.1145/2742060.2742119

Commercial tools synthesize buffered clock trees with specific skew targets in presence of process variations and on-chip-variations [10][11] which along with clock latency (delay from clock root to sink *i.e.*, flip-flops) have been key objectives in ISPD'09 and ISPD'10 contests [12][8]. However, this stringent skew target may not be needed in the late design stage, *i.e.*, after clock tree synthesis (CTS), to achieve the timing closure. Rather, a marginal relaxation in the clock skew might not hurt the timing profile of the design, but could be exploited to optimize the clock net capacitance. Wire sizing and the use of non-default routing with more spacing can potentially improve skew and reduce overall clock tree capacitance [7][13][14], but at the cost of congestion and higher chip area. Several other techniques have been explored in the past to reduce clock dynamic power, such as synthesis-based clock gating [15], data-driven clock gating [16], clock gate cloning [17] and usage of multi-bit-flip-flop (MBFF) [18], but none of them focus primarily on the optimization of the clock net or wire capacitance at the post-CTS stage.

Due to the high switching activity and larger capacitive loads, 30-70% of the dynamic power is dissipated in the clock network [19][20]. The pin capacitance of the clock elements, such as the clock buffers, inverters, clock gates etc., and flip-flops, and the wire capacitance of the clock nets contribute to the clock dynamic power consumption. Recently, the net capacitance has become comparable, and sometimes even higher than the pin capacitance due to several reasons. Firstly, device size is shrinking with technology scaling, and as a result pin capacitance has reduced at much faster rate than the net capacitance. Secondly, with growing design complexity and aggravating variation effect, massive clock gating and skew balancing introduce more and more routing overhead. Consequently, clock net capacitance contributes a significant fraction of the clock dynamic power.

In this paper, we formulate a problem with the target objective of reducing the clock net capacitance of an already synthesized and routed clock tree network, given a specified relaxation margin in the clock skew. A buffer-tree resynthesis algorithm has been proposed which traverses the clock network in a bottom-up fashion, and relocates the clock buffers/inverters guided by mean-centric grid based placement (MCGBP). Since this resynthesis approach has been exercised in the post-CTS stage, semi-global optimizations by moving multiple clock buffers/inverters at a time may not be suitable as it would be disruptive to the timing profile of the design. Instead, we have explored the movement of the clock buffers/inverters one-by-one and ensured that these local transformations do not (i) add any design-rule-check (DRC) violation, such as the maximum load or maximum slew violation etc., and (ii) increase the clock latency apart from meeting a specific skew bound. The key contributions of our paper are summarized as follows:

- To the best of our knowledge, this is the first problem formulation to optimize the clock net capacitance at the post-CTS stage given a specific skew bound.

- A buffer tree resynthesis algorithm has been proposed by mean-centric grid based placement of the clock buffers and inverters in bottom-up fashion without introducing any new DRC violation and increasing the clock latency.

- Our approach has been integrated into an industrial tool, and the execution of this algorithm on 22-65nm industrial designs resulted an average 5.6% reduction in the clock net capacitance with small improvement in the pin capacitance of the clock network.

The rest of the paper is organized as follows. Section 2 describes the problem formulation. Section 3 presents our skew bounded buffer tree resynthesis algorithm. Section 4 presents the experimental results for industrial designs with conclusion in Section 5.

2. PROBLEM FORMULATION

Suppose there are n clock domains in an already synthesized and routed clock tree network. Let WC_{clk} be the total wire capacitance of the clock network. Then the formulation of our problem is as follows:

$$\text{minimize:} \quad WC_{clk}$$
$$\text{subject to:} \quad \forall i \in [1, n] \quad Skew'_i \leq Skew_i + \Delta_{margin} \quad (1)$$

where, $Skew_i$ and $Skew'_i$ are the skew of the ith clock domain before and after the DRC-aware clock network modification respectively and Δ_{margin} is the margin allowed in the skew. By DRC-aware, we mean that the clock network modification is not allowed to introduce any new DRC violation, and in addition not to increase the clock latency. Note that we have used the terms net capacitance and wire capacitance interchangeably throughout the paper.

3. SKEW BOUNDED BUFFER TREE RESYNTHESIS

In this section, we describe our approach. At first, we present the key idea behind the incremental clock tree modification. Then we illustrate why and how the clock network is traversed in the bottom-up fashion. Next, we describe the algorithm for single buffer migration followed by mean-centric grid based placement mechanism to scale this approach.

3.1 Incremental Clock Tree Modification

The key idea of our approach is to size and move the clock buffers or inverters towards its loads. Consider Fig. 1 to illustrate the incremental clock tree modification. For instance, B_2 drives two other clock buffers B_3 and B_4, and B_2 is placed closer to B_3 and B_4 in Fig. 1(b), followed by blockage aware re-routing of the nets n_2, n_3 and n_4. The

new placement of B_2 and the re-routing of the nets (n_2, n_3 and n_4) will impact the clock arrivals in the flip-flops which are at the transitive-fanout (TFO) cone of B_0. Since B_2 is placed closer to its loads, intuitively the wire-load for B_2 would decrease whereas the same for B_0 may increase. However, it ultimately depends on how the re-routing of those nets occurs in the placed design with existing routing. It should be stressed that *global wire-load minimization might not always happen due to the change in routing topology, but also because of routing in different layers.*

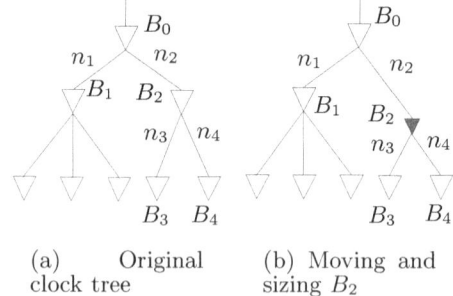

(a) Original clock tree (b) Moving and sizing B_2

Figure 1: Incremental clock tree modification

The benefit of this incremental clock tree modification can be two-fold: (i) it can reduce the total wire-capacitance of the clock nets, and (ii) if the size of B_2 is reduced, it will reduce the pin-capacitance as well. But this can increase the skew of the clock network, and can introduce new DRC violations. So we need to respect these two constraints while physically realizing the transformation.

3.2 Bottom-up Traversal

We adopt a bottom-up traversal of the clock network for performing the incremental modification in the clock tree. This is due to most of the total capacitance of the clock network is associated with the bottom-levels, *i.e.*, closer to the flip-flops. For instance, [9] has shown with one benchmark from ISPD'10 contest [8] that 71% and 12% of the total capacitance are respectively linked with the bottom-most level and second bottom-most level. For each clock domain the incremental modification is performed within the scope of a hyper-net. A hyper-net is a set of logically equivalent or opposite polarity nets which are separated by buffers or inverters in the same physical partition as the root driver of the top net [21]. Note that we do not perform the transformation on any clock-gate or clock-multiplexers, as such an action could worsen the timing pertaining to the enable signals. Fig. 2 shows three hyper-nets, and the traversal order for these hyper-nets can be $HyperNet_1 \rightarrow HyperNet_2 \rightarrow HyperNet_0$. The relative order between $HyperNet_1$ and $HyperNet_2$ is random. But a prioritized ordering can be imposed giving more precedence to the hyper-net with higher switching activity to facilitate more savings in dynamic power.

3.3 Single Buffer Migration (SBM)

Algorithm 1 presents the key steps of Single Buffer Migration (SBM). It works on a buffer or inverter (*cell*) in the clock network. First, the output net of *cell* is obtained, and the bounding box (*bbox*) of the net is calculated (Lines 2-3). At the next stage, we try to find the best position within *bbox* for *cell* for migration, such that the resultant wire-capacitance of the clock network is optimized. However, since this migration occurs after placement in post-

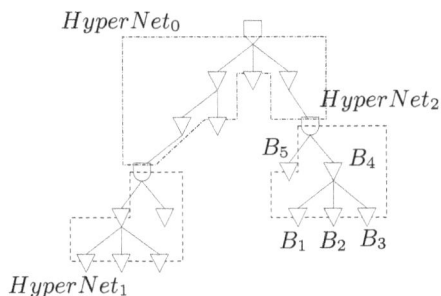

Figure 2: Bottom-up traversal within and across hyper-nets

CTS stage, *cell* can not be moved to any position in order to avoid the placement overlap with the already placed cells. So we find the set of congestion free positions (*positionSet*), and attempt to explore those positions (Lines 4-21). The detailed mechanism for finding these positions will be discussed in Section 3.4.

Algorithm 1 Single Buffer Migration

1: **Procedure** SBM(*cell*);
2: *opnet* ← output net of *cell*;
3: *bbox* ← bounding box of *opnet*;
4: *positionSet* ← congestion free positions within *bbox*;
5: **for all** *pos* ∈ *positionSet* **do**
6:    *cellTypeSet* ← available buffers or inverters in the library;
7:    **for all** *cellType* ∈ *cellTypeSet* **do**
8:       substitute the cell-type of *cell* with *cellType*;
9:       place *cell* in *pos*;
10:      re-route the nets connected to *cell*;
11:      **if** isDRCViolation **then**
12:         continue;
13:      **end if**
14:      **if** $Skew' > Skew + \Delta_{margin}$ **then**
15:         continue;
16:      **end if**
17:      **if** cost(currentSol) < cost(bestSol) **then**
18:         bestSol ← currentSol;
19:      **end if**
20:    **end for**
21: **end for**
22: **return**
23: **end Procedure**

For each available position, we also explore different sizing options for *cell*, followed by re-routing of the clock nets connected to *cell* (Line 10). For instance, if we consider the cell B_2 in Fig. 1, then n_2, n_3 and n_4 will be re-routed. If this migration with sizing and re-routing introduces any new DRC violation, then this move is not accepted (Lines 11-13). We also do not up-size the cells as it could increase the total pin-capacitance of the clock network. In addition, we check if the skew exceeds the pre-specified margin by the move (Lines 14-16). Among all these moves (with sizing), the solution giving the best improvement in wire-capacitance of the clock network is committed by backtracking mechanism (Lines 17-19). It should be stressed that *the algorithm has been integrated to an industrial tool and all these moves are followed by the re-routing of the clock nets along with routing layer assignment by the tool* to get the accurate skew measurement and the improvement in wire-capacitance of the clock network in a fast and incremental way.

However, it is still computationally intensive to explore all congestion free positions and all sizing options. So we propose mean-centric grid-based placement along with pruned sizing options to scale the approach.

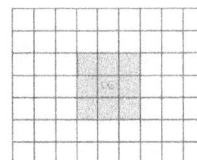

Figure 3: Mean-centric grid exploration with $gridParam = 1$

3.4 Mean-Centric Grid-Based Placement (MCGBM)

In modern designs, a clock net can drive tens of clock buffers or inverters. Although the CAD tools try to place those buffers in geometrical proximity, it may not be always possible, and thus the buffers driven by a net can be placed wide apart. As a result, the area of the bounding box of the clock net can be large, and attempting all congestion free positions in the bounding box can be run-time intensive. On the other hand, the sum of the euclidean distances from a point (x, y) to a set of n points, such as (x_1, y_1), $(x_2, y_2)...(x_n, y_n)$ is given by $\sum_{i=1}^{n} \sqrt{(x - x_i)^2 + (y - y_i)^2}$ and minimized for the mean position, *i.e.*, $x = \frac{\sum_{i=1}^{n} x_i}{n}$, $y = \frac{\sum_{i=1}^{n} y_i}{n}$. So the neighborhood locations of mean position are preferred for capacitance cost optimization.

To move the targeted clock cell accordingly, we divide the bounding box (found in Algorithm 1) into grids of $(2h \times 2w)$, where h and w are the height and width of the cell respectively. Note this grid-granularity is experimentally found to be suitable for solution quality and run-time. To spot the neighborhood of the mean position, we define a parameter called *gridParam*. Suppose the mean position of the net is in a certain grid *gr*. In that case, we will explore all the grids for which the grid distance in x and y co-ordinates from *gr* are both less or equal to *gridParam*. This is explained in Fig 3 representing the grid-based partitioning and the centre of gravity (CG) or mean position of the bounding box. For instance, if *gridParam* = 1, then all shaded grid positions in Fig 3 will be explored for placement.

Additionally, instead of trying with all down-sizing options for the targeted clock buffer or inverter (Line 7 in Algorithm 1), we explore the pre-sorted (according to size) library cells in decreasing order. Once we get a higher cost compared to earlier sizing options, we do not further try to down-size. Experimentally we have observed that this pruning technique does not practically incur any compromise in the solution quality, but saves run-time.

4. EXPERIMENTAL RESULTS

We have implemented the algorithms presented in this work in C++ and run it on a Linux machine with 16-Core 3GHz CPU and 256GB RAM. Table 1 presents the characteristics of 6 industrial designs using cutting-edge technology nodes (22-65nm) along with experimental results run on those designs. The designs are sorted according to the number of cells in the design (Column 3). Columns 2 and 4 represent the technology node and the total number of flip-flops in the designs respectively. Column 5 shows the maximum clock latency (maximum of rise latency and fall latency) in the clock networks of the respective designs. Design 'F' is the biggest design in terms of the total number of cells, whereas design 'D' has biggest clock network with around $136k$ flip-flops. Column 6 presents the ratio of the clock net capacitance (cap_{net}) to the clock pin ca-

Table 1: Design characteristics and clock capacitance/dynamic power reduction

Design	Technology (nm)	# of cells	# of flops	Clock latency (ps)	$\frac{cap_{net}}{cap_{pin}}$	cap_{net} imprv. (%)	cap_{pin} imprv. (%)	P_{dyn} reduction (%)	Run-time (min)
A	65	68,945	11,937	791	0.60:1	4.0	1.0	2.13	25.0
B	65	79,055	11,741	1573	0.66:1	4.7	1.6	2.83	22.4
C	28	128,444	18,967	1034	0.79:1	6.0	0.03	2.66	37.9
D	22	590,392	135,937	1227	2.26:1	3.3	0.4	2.41	245.0
E	28	687,221	34,399	738	2.60:1	9.6	0.84	7.17	56.7
F	28	859,833	37,239	1554	2.25:1	5.7	0.2	4.01	46.3
Average						5.55	0.52	3.54	

pacitance (cap_{pin}). Columns 7 and 8 respectively represent the percentage reduction in cap_{net} and cap_{pin} in the clock network of the designs. Considering the switching activities to be same across all hyper-nets in the clock network, the clock dynamic power (P_{dyn}) improvement is calculated as the weighted sum of the improvements in the net capacitance and the pin capacitance in Column 9. For instance, the improvement in cap_{net} and cap_{pin} for the design 'C' are 6.0% and 0.03% respectively, and the ratio of net to pin capacitance is 0.79:1. So the clock dynamic power improvement would be $6.0 \times \frac{0.79}{1.79} + 0.03 \times \frac{1}{1.79} = 2.66\%$. Column 10 shows the run-time of our approach in each design.

On average, our algorithm achieves respectively 5.55%, 0.52% and 3.54% improvement in cap_{net}, cap_{pin} and P_{dyn}. The pin-capacitance improvement is much smaller as downsizing the buffers to improve cap_{pin} typically (i) introduces maximum slew and maximum load violations and (ii) changes the clock arrivals to a greater extent than just by local move of the buffers, violating the constraints related to the skew and the clock latency. Due to the higher net-to-pin capacitance ratio, the power improvement is higher in the lower technology node, most being for the designs 'E' and 'F' with around 7.2% and 4.0% respectively. It should be stressed that these improvements are *over the baseline clock network synthesized and routed by an industrial tool*. The skew margin is kept at 20ps. gridParam is set to 10 for all these runs. To justify the selection of gridParam, we take the smaller design A and run our algorithm with gridParam = 1, 2, 5, 10, 20 and covering the entire bounding box for each of the nets. Fig. 4 shows the curve for run-time vs. percentage wire-cap reduction. The curve is initially monotonic with gridParam, but starts to flatten beyond gridParam = 10. The maximum run-time is around 4 hours for the design 'D'. This is because although it is not the biggest design, it has the biggest clock network in our benchmark suite.

5. CONCLUSION

To our best knowledge, this is the first work to optimize the clock net capacitance of already synthesized and routed clock networks by a buffer tree resynthesis algorithm. Our approach has been integrated into an industrial tool, and provided an average 5.6% and up to 9.6% improvement in clock net capacitance over the baseline clock networks of industrial designs synthesized and routed by the industrial tool. In terms of clock dynamic power reduction, our algorithm can reduce the clock dynamic power up to 7.2% and 3.5% on average. Since with technology scaling, the percentage contribution of net capacitance is becoming higher and higher in comparison to the pin capacitance, we believe that our approach can potentially reduce more dynamic power in modern designs.

6. REFERENCES

[1] L. F. Chao and H. M. Sha, "Retiming and clock skew for synchronous systems," *ISCAS*, pp. 283–86, 1994.

[2] V. Nawale and T. W. Chen, "Optimal useful clock skew scheduling in the presence of variations using robust ILP formulations," *ICCAD*, pp. 27–32, 2006.

[3] J. P. Fishburn, "Clock skew optimization," *IEEE Trans. on Computers*, vol. 39, no. 7, pp. 945–51, 1990.

[4] X. Liu et al., "Maximizing performance by retiming and clock skew scheduling," *DAC*, pp. 231–36, 1999.

[5] R. Tsay, "Exact zero skew clock routing algorithm," *TCAD*, vol. 12, no. 2, pp. 242–249, 1993.

[6] K. D. Boese and A. B. Kahng, "Zero skew clock-routing trees with minimum wirelength," *ASIC Conference and Exhibit*, pp. 17–21, 1992.

[7] J. L. Tsai et al., "Zero skew clock-tree optimization with buffer insertion/sizing and wire sizing," *TCAD*, vol. 23, no. 4, pp. 565–572, 2004.

[8] C. Sze, "ISPD-2010 high performance clock network synthesis contest," *ISPD*, pp. 143–143, 2010.

[9] R. Ewetz and C. K. Koh, "Local merges for effective redundancy in clock networks," *ISPD*, pp. 162–67, 2013.

[10] X. Shih and Y. Chang, "Fast timing-model independent buffered clock-tree synthesis," *DAC*, pp. 80–85, 2010.

[11] X. Shih et al., "Blockage-avoiding buffered clock tree synthesis for clock latency range and skew minimization," *ASPDAC*, pp. 395–400, 2010.

[12] C. Sze et al., "ISPD-2009 clock network synthesis contest," *ISPD*, pp. 149–50, 2009.

[13] Y. M. Lee et al., "Simultaneous buffer-sizing and wire-sizing for clock trees based on lagrangian relaxation," *VLSI Design*, pp. 587–594, 2002.

[14] A. Kahng, S. Kang, and H. Lee, "Smart non-default routing for clock power reduction," *DAC*, pp. 1–7, 2013.

[15] A. H. Farrahi et al., "Activity-driven clock design," *TCAD*, pp. 705–714, 2001.

[16] S. Wimer and I. Koren, "Design flow for flip-flop grouping in data-driven clock gating," *TVLSI*, pp. 771–78, 2014.

[17] R. Visweshwara et al., "Placement aware clock gate cloning and redistribution methodology," *ISQED*, pp. 432–436, 2012.

[18] S. Lo et al., "Power optimization for clock network with clock gate cloning and flip-flop merging," *ISPD*, pp. 77–84, 2014.

[19] V. G. Oklobdzija et al., *Digital System Clocking: High-Performance and Low-Power Aspects*. Wiley, 2003.

[20] D. Liu and C. Svensson, "Power consumtion estimation in CMOS VLSI chips," *JSSC*, pp. 663–70, 1994.

[21] S. Roy et al., "Clock tree resynthesis for multi-corner multi-mode timing closure," *ISPD*, pp. 69–76, 2014.

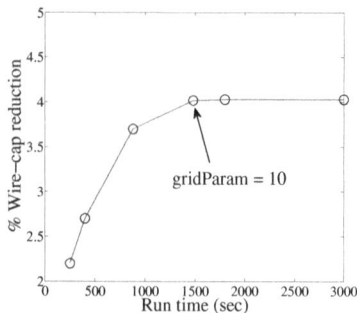

Figure 4: Percentage wire-cap improvement vs. run time trade-off for design A

Novel Designs of Embedded Hybrid Cells for High Performance Memory Circuits

Wei Wei	Kazuteru Namba	Fabrizio Lombardi
ECE Dept, Northeastern University	A.I.S, Chiba University	ECE Dept, Northeastern University
Boston, MA 02115, USA	Chiba, Japan	Boston, MA 02115, USA
+1-617-373-7780	+81-43-290-3255	+1-617-373-4854
wei.w@husky.neu.edu	namba@ieee.org	lombardi@ece.neu.edu

ABSTRACT

Memory design has radically changed in the last few years; the emergence of new technologies has further improved performance and the traditional separation of storage levels between Static Random Access Memory (SRAM) and Dynamic Random Access Memory (DRAM) is not viable as in the past. Recently, the embedded DRAM (eDRAM) has been proposed for cache utilization to improve density while attempting to retain high performance operations; this scheme is often referred as hybrid due to the utilization of different technologies in a memory. In this paper, a hybrid scheme is proposed by adding non-volatile features and related circuits to the SRAM/eDRAM; an Oxide Resistive Random Access Memory (RRAM) is utilized as non-volatile storage in the embedded memory circuit. Different memory cells are proposed in this manuscript; they are evaluated with respect to circuit-level figures of merit as related to operational features (read, write, static noise margin, power delay product) as well as tolerance to event upsets (critical charge) and variations. Extensive simulation results using nanometric PTMs are provided. It is shown that the proposed designs offer substantial improvements over previous hybrid cells as well as a conventional NAND Flash memory cell.

Categories and Subject Descriptors

B.7.1 **[Integrated Circuits]**: Types and Design Styles – *Advanced Technologies, Memory Technologies, VLSI (Very Large Scale Integration).*

General Terms: Design

Keywords

Memory Design, Static and Dynamic random-access-memory, Low power, Hybrid memory, Non-volatile memory

1. INTRODUCTION

Power dissipation of on-chip memory due to leakage is an increasing concern in today's microprocessor design due to the high density and large on-die utilization [1]. While it is well known that on-chip cache is effective in reducing the performance gap between processor and main memory, design of memory

GLSVLSI'15, May 20–22, 2015, Pittsburgh, PA, USA.
Copyright © 2015 ACM 978-1-4503-3474-7/15/05...$15.00.
http://dx.doi.org/10.1145/2742060.2742103

circuits has attracted considerable attention in the technical literature [2, 3, 4]. For example, cache design is significantly impacted by the deterioration of circuit-level performance at lower feature sizes. Moreover as CMOS moves deeper in the nanoscales, circuits must face the challenge to operate at lower supply voltages and account for increased short channel effects.

The Static Random Access Memory (SRAM) and the Dynamic Random Access Memory (DRAM) are been widely used as memory cells; a SRAM is implemented with at least six transistors for fast operational speed. A DRAM requires a smaller number of transistors in a cell, thus attaining a higher density. It is therefore not surprising that the former cell has been extensively used for cache [2, 3], while the latter cell is mostly used for high volume computer storage. Different configurations of cell have been proposed for both SRAM and DRAM to overcome issues as related to stability and retention time. The drawbacks of a SRAM cell are the low signal noise margin (SNM, as measure of stability), circuit complexity, transistor sizing limitations and high leakage during standby. Embedded DRAM (eDRAM) cells achieve lower leakage [5, 6, 17], because the power supply is disabled following data access. An eDRAM incurs in a small circuit complexity, thus further improving chip density.

Non-volatility is a new paradigm for RAM operation [7]; this is made possible by utilizing a Resistive RAM (RRAM) in which resistance switching is implemented. The RRAM represents yet another attractive emerging technology for implementing a RRAM. RRAMs are compatible with a CMOS process flow, while offering further advantages, such as scalability, good operating speeds and ease of fabrication [8, 9]. Moreover, storage of multiple bits on a single memory cell (i.e. on a non binary basis) has also been made possible to increase density [10]. Furthermore, the scaling merit of a RRAM permits to operate at low power, making this non-volatile technology very competitive for large storage. Non-volatile elements are usually added to CMOS-based memory circuits by utilizing stacking for hybrid schemes in which different planes are utilized for the different memory devices [11]. Hybrid schemes utilizing both DRAM and SRAM cells have been proposed in the technical literature.

2. PROPOSED HYBRID MEMORY CELLS

2.1 Improved macrocell

Figure 1 shows the first proposed cell referred as the improved macrocell (MCT); in this cell, the capacitor is replaced by a NMOS transistor within each eDRAM, i.e. data is stored in the gate capacitance.

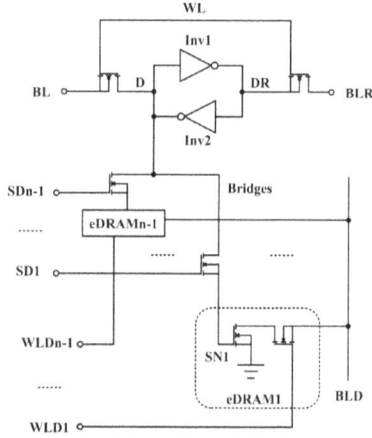

Figure 1. Proposed improved macrocell (MCT)

Similar to MCC [3], the proposed MCT cell has n-1 eDRAM cells; each eDRAM is connected to the SRAM by a NMOS pass transistor (acting as the bridge) and controlled by the corresponding signal from the Selection Decoder (SD). This signal allows the data initially stored in the single SRAM core to be transferred to the Storage Node (SN) of the selected eDRAM. In this scheme, the bridges are bidirectional to allow data transfer between the SRAM and the eDRAM; moreover, no Bitline (BL) is involved in this process, i.e. it is internally controlled.

The "Write" operation is controlled by the Wordline (WL) and stores the data at node D. For the "Read" operation, the corresponding Wordline Read (WLD) is used to transfer the stored data to BL Read (BLD). By utilizing this circuit, the "Read" operation is not destructive for the data stored in an eDRAM. Moreover, each pass transistors act as a bridge between the SRAM core and the eDRAM cell permits a fast transfer of data.

2.2 Non-volatile hybrid memory

Different from the MCT cell, a novel non-volatile hybrid memory is proposed for cache implementation (Figure 2). An embedded RRAM (eRRAM) is added to the eDRAM for non-volatile storage. Although the proposed cell still takes advantage of the bridge, the stored data is controlled, such that the RRAM can be programmed for data transfer from the SRAM core to the eDRAM. To achieve non-volatile storage, the proposed cell requires the execution of the "Reset" operation in the RESET process of the RRAM. Thus, a full operational cycle of the proposed memory cell utilizes the following sequence: "Reset", "Write", "Transfer" and "Read". Each of these operations is given as follows.

Reset: The RRAM is changed back to HRS ahead of the "Write" operation to the SRAM core; this is accomplished by the RESET process described previously. During this step, a "1" is applied to all Word Line RRAMs (WLRs) to turn ON the read transistors and BLD is "0" with no precharging. Hence, irrespective of the data stored in the SRAM, the voltage drop by the RRAM causes a state change to HRS.

Write: the data (appearing on BL and BLR) is written into the 6T SRAM core using WL. During this operation, all SDs, WLDs and WLRs have a "0" value, i.e. data is only stored in the SRAM core.

Transfer: During this state, the data stored in the SRAM cell is transferred to the SN of the selected eDRAM and eRRAM cells

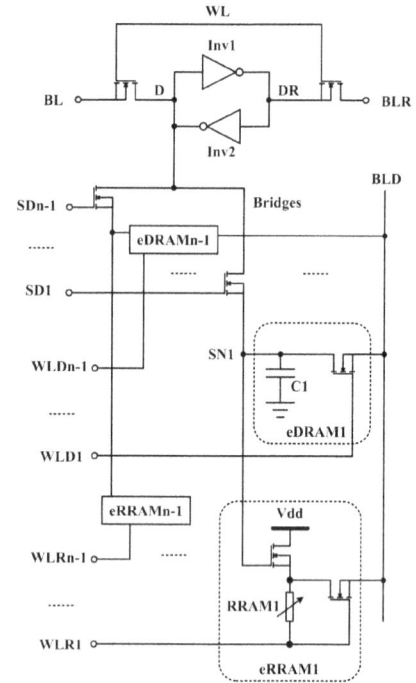

Figure 2. Proposed non-volatile hybrid memory

using the appropriate control signal. For example, if the voltage signal at D is "1", this turns ON the NMOS transistor inside the selected eRRAM and the RRAM is programmed by changing its state from HRS to LRS under a positive voltage drop. If the data is "0", the transistor is kept OFF and the corresponding RRAM is still in HRS. Thus at completion of this step, RRAM1 shows different resistance states as corresponding to the stored information: if SN is "1", it is in LRS; if SN is "0", it is in HRS, respectively. Moreover, the data is also stored in the selected eDRAM.

Read: During the "Read" operation, the selected WLD is changed from "0" to "1", turning ON the read transistor. BLD senses the stored data in the selected eDRAM (note that if the data stored in the eDRAM is lost due to a soft error, the correct data can be read from the RRAM [12]).

The proposed memories are simulated using HSPICE and High Performance (HP) Predictive Technology Models (PTMs) [13]. As per the guidelines of [14], the Cell Ratio (RC) and Pull-up Ratio (RP) for the 6T SRAM core are given by 1.5; in addition, the sizing of the NMOS transistors in an eDRAM and an eRRAM is 1:1.These designs are initially evaluated for power dissipation and performance. The value of n is initially set to 2 to assess the basic features of the memory cells (larger values of n are considered later in this section), i.e. 1 SRAM, 1 eDRAM and 1 eRRAM. Therefore in general, there is only a single SRAM core, while the number of eDRAMs is increased up to n-1; also, the

Table 1. Parameters for memory cell simulation

Parameter	Value
Temperature	25 C
Feature Size	22 nm
Vdd	0.8 V
RRAM Resistances	1 KΩ / 1 MΩ
C1	20 fF

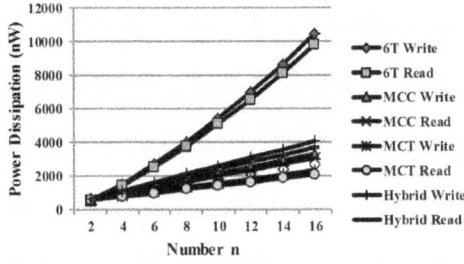

Figure 3. Power dissipation vs n at 22nm

number of eRRAMs in the proposed hybrid cell is assumed to be the same as the number of eDRAMs, i.e. in a hybrid cell for n, there is a single SRAM core and n-1 eDRAMs and n-1 eRRAMs.

The operations of the proposed MCT and the hybrid memory circuits are simulated using the parameters of Table 1; the period of each operation is 10ns to allow sufficient programming time for the RRAM ("Reset" and "Write") [9].

3. CELL EVALUATION

3.1 Power Dissipation

Consider the general case, i.e. n>2. The results are plotted in Figure 3. The power dissipation increases with n, however the rate of increase is dependent on the cell type. The 6T SRAM has the lowest value when n=2; however when n is increased, the MCT cell has the lowest values, while the 6T SRAM has the highest. The proposed hybrid cell incurs in higher power dissipation than both the MCT and MCC cells; however, it still remains substantially less than for a 6T SRAM cell.

3.2 Power Delay Product

The PDP is assessed using the parameters listed in Table 1; the average PDP of these circuits are reported in Table 2 for the two memory operations (i.e. "Write" and "Read") at 22nm feature size. Simulation includes the operations for "Write" and "Read",

Table 2. Power Delay Product of Memory Cells (n=2)

Cell	Operation		PDP (aJ)		
			22 nm	16 nm	10 nm
MCC [3]	Write	SRAM	15.27	11.04	7.42
		SRAM to eDRAM	10.61	7.67	5.15
		eDRAM to SRAM	**10.57**	**7.64**	**5.13**
	Read	SRAM	19.45	13.13	8.82
		eDRAM	30.48	22.02	14.79
MCT	Write	SRAM	14.59	10.85	7.29
		SRAM to eDRAM	**9.25**	**6.69**	**4.49**
		eDRAM to SRAM	10.78	7.79	5.23
	Read	SRAM	18.40	13.29	8.93
		eDRAM	**26.72**	**19.31**	**12.97**
Hybrid	Write	SRAM	15.69	13.65	9.17
		SRAM to eDRAM	11.60	8.38	5.63
		eDRAM to SRAM	10.82	8.06	5.41
	Read	SRAM	19.75	15.53	10.43
		eDRAM	31.47	22.74	15.28
6T	Write	SRAM	**13.18**	**9.53**	**6.40**
	Read	SRAM	**15.26**	**10.30**	**6.92**

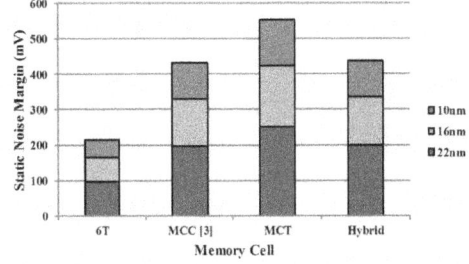

Figure 4. Simulated SNM vs memory cells (n=2)

such as the data stored from the BL and the internal transfer between the SRAM, eDRAM and eRRAM. The proposed MCT cell achieves the best among the three cell types based on the value of PDP due to the improved eDRAM scheme. As expected, the PDP value decreases at lower feature sizes (Table 2), because both the power and delay values are reduced. The proposed MCT cell remains the best among the considered cells (with the hybrid memory having the highest value due to the added RRAM) for the "Write" and "Read" operations.

3.3 Static Noise Margin

The Static Noise Margin (SNM) [14] is assessed for the proposed cells, a 6T SRAM and the MCC cell. Figure 4 shows the SNMs consistently deteriorate at a reduced MOSFET feature size [14]. The three hybrid memory cells (MCT, MCC and hybrid) at 22 nm substantially improve over the SNM value of 97.3mV for a 6T SRAM cell. The MCT cell has the largest value (i.e. 251mV) due to the use of the additional NMOS transistor. The SNM of the proposed non-volatile hybrid memory is mostly determined by the eDRAM with value of 199mV, it is nearly the same as for the MCC cell. A change in SNM is usually caused by the circuitry added to the cell such that the static behavior of the 6T core [14] is also changed. These variations of the SNM fall within the static property of a digital circuit [14] that often depends on the MOSFET threshold voltage. The results show that the cells change this property and improve the SNM. Moreover, the proposed hybrid cell behaves similarly to the MCC cell, because they use the same eDRAM.

3.4 Critical Charge

In a memory circuit, the transient voltage generated by a heavy ion strike, may lead to a Single Event Upset (SEU) as a state change [15]. A SEU is said to occur when the collected energy Q at a particular node is greater than the critical charge, Q_{crit}, i.e. Q_{crit} is the minimum charge that needs to be deposited at the sensitive node of a storage cell to flip (change) the stored bit (data) [16]. Therefore, a node assessment of the cells is pursued to

Table 3. Critical charge and nodes of Memory Cells (n=2)

Node	Memory	Charge (fC)		
		22 nm	16 nm	10 nm
D	6T	1.321	0.832	0.450
	MCC [3]	1.452	0.915	0.495
	MCT	1.486	0.936	0.507
	Hybrid	1.493	0.941	0.509
SN	MCC [3]	8.845	5.573	3.016
	MCT	9.356	5.895	3.190
	Hybrid	10.15	6.396	3.461

Table 4. Ranking of Memory Cells

Metrics	MCC [3]	MCT	Hybrid	6T
Power Dissipation	2	1	3	4
Power Delay Product (PDP)	2	1	3	4
SNM	3	1	2	4
Critical Charge	3	2	1	4

find the critical node and charge. The results are reported in Table 3. From this evaluation, the 6T SRAM presents the least value of charge at the storage node (D). The other three memories show improvements in critical charge, because the additional circuits in these cells increase the capacitance at the storage node. So although the charge for the MCC cell achieves the least improvement, there is no significant difference between them due to the same features in the added eDRAMs. The charges at the SN nodes for the MCC and hybrid cells are larger than for the D nodes due to the large capacitance. Therefore, the critical node is always at D. In addition, the charge values decrease by scaling down with the MOSFET feature size because the internal capacitances are also reduced, thus it also deteriorates the tolerance to an SEU.

4. CONCLUSION

Novel designs of hybrid (SRAM-DRAM) cells have been recently proposed in the technical literature [1, 2, 3]. These designs strive to improve operational performance while saving power dissipation. This manuscript has proposed two additional cell designs referred to as MCT and non-volatile hybrid cell; these designs utilize a Resistive RAM (RRAM) for non-volatile operation. Table 4 shows the ranking of the four memory cells from different perspectives, mostly at circuit level for possible cache implementation. The proposed MCT cell achieves the best performance for most of the other metrics considered in this manuscript. On a relative basis, the proposed non-volatile hybrid memory represents a compromise in design compared with MCC [3]; the hybrid cell is ranked in the middle (i.e. 2nd or 3rd) for most metrics; moreover, the non-volatile storage in the eRRAM is rather pronounced. Furthermore, the simulated results indicate that the non-volatile one has the best tolerance to the soft error with best critical charge, though it presents the penalties on the power dissipations with the added non-volatile storage components. The proposed MCT cell achieves a significant performance improvement and the proposed non-volatile hybrid memory is a good candidate for designing a high performance memory circuit with non-volatile capabilities, excellent tolerance to soft errors. In conclusion, this paper has demonstrated through an extensive analysis and simulation assessment that the proposed two hybrid memory cells offer significant improvements for implementation at nano scaled CMOS.

5. REFERENCES

[1] W. S. Yu, R. Huang, S. Xu et al., "SRAM-DRAM hybrid memory with applications to efficient register files in fine-grained multi-threading," *in Proc. ISCA*, pp. 247-258, 2011.

[2] A. Valero, J. Sahuquillo, S. Petit et al., "An Hybrid eDRAM/SRAM Macrocell to Implement First-Level Data Caches," *Proc. 42nd Ann. IEEE/ACM Int'l Sympo. Microarchitecture*, 2009.

[3] A. Valero, S. Petit, J. Sahuquillo et al., "Design, performance, and energy consumption of eDRAM/SRAM macrocells for L1 data caches," *IEEE Transactions on Computers*, vol. 61, no. 9, 2012.

[4] Y. Z. Chang, F. P. Lai, "Dynamic zero-sensitivity scheme for low-power cache memories," *IEEE Micro*, vol. 25, issue 4, 2005.

[5] W. K. Luk, J. Cai, R. H. Dennard, et al, "A 3-Transistor DRAM Cell with Gated Diode for Enhanced Speed and Retention Time," *2006 Symposium on VLSI Circuits Digest of Technical Papers*, pp. 184-185, 2006.

[6] S. Ganapathy, R. Canal, D. Alexandrescu et al., "A Novel Variation-Tolerant 4T-DRAM Cell with Enhanced Soft-Error Tolerance," *2012 IEEE 30th International Conference on ICCD*, pp. 472-477, 2012.

[7] G. Atwood, S-I Chae and S. S. Y. Shim, "Next Generation Memory," *IEEE Computer Magazine*, no. 8, pp. 21-22, 2013.

[8] H. Akinaga, H. Shima, "Resistive Random Access Memory (ReRAM) Based on Metal Oxides," *Proceedings of the IEEE*, pp. 2237-2251, 2010.

[9] B. Govoreanu, G.S. Kar, Y. Y. Chen, et al., "10x10nm^2 Hf/HfO$_x$ Crossbar Resistive RAM with excellent performance, reliability and low-energy operation," *2011 IEEE International Electron Devices Meeting (IEDM)*, pp. 31.6.1-31.6.4, 2011.

[10] Y. H. Tseng, C. E. Huang, C. H. Kuo et al., "A new high-density and ultrasmall-cell-size contact RRAM (CR-RAM) with fully CMOS-logic-compatible technology and circuits," *IEEE Transactions on Electron Devices*, vol. 58, no. 1, 2011.

[11] W. Wei, K. Namba, J. Han and F. Lombardi, "Design of a Non-Volatile 7T1R SRAM Cell for Instant-on Operation," *IEEE Transactions on Nanotechnology*, vol. 13, issue 15, pp. 905-916, 2014.

[12] W. Wei, K. Namba and F. Lombardi, "Design and Analysis of Non-Volatile Memory Cells for SEU Tolerance," *17th IEEE Symposium on Defect and Fault Tolerance in VLSI and Nanotechnology Systems*, pp. 69-74, 2014.

[13] "Predictive Technology Models (PTM)," *Http://ptm.asu.edu*.

[14] J. M. Rabaey, A. Chandrakasan and B. Nikolic, "Digital Integrated Circuits: A Design Perspective (Second Edition)," *Prentice Hall*, pp. 665, ISBN: 0130909963, 2003.

[15] P. E. Dodd and L. W. Massengill, "Basic Mechanisms and Modeling of Single-Event Upset in Digital Microelectronics," *IEEE Transactions on Nuclear Science*, pp. 583-602, 2003.

[16] C. Detcheverry, C. Dachs, E. Lorfevre et al, "SEU Critical Charge and Sensitive Area in a Submicron CMOS Technology," *IEEE Transactions on Nuclear Science*, vol. 44, pp. 2266-2273, 1997.

[17] W. Wei, K. Namba and F. Lombardi, "Extending Non-Volatile Operation to DRAM Cells," *IEEE Access*, vol. 1, pp. 758-769, 2013.

Dataline Isolated Differential Current Feed/Mode Sense Amplifier for Small I_{cell} SRAM Using FinFET

Bhupendra S. Reniwal[1], Vikas Vijayvargiya[2], Pooran Singh[3], Santosh K. Vishvakarma[4]
Devesh Dwivedi[5]
Nanoscale Devices, VLSI Circuit & System Design Lab, Discipline of Electrical Engineering[1, 2, 3, 4]
Indian Institute of Technology Indore, India[1, 2, 3, 4]
High Speed Serial Links, Analog and Memory IP Development, IBM Bangalore, India[5]
phd11120202@iiti.ac.in[1], skvishvakarma@iiti.ac.in[4]

ABSTRACT

This paper for the first time presents a novel, high-performance and robust current feed sense amplifiers (CF-SA) design for small I_{Cell} SRAM in 20nm Fin-shaped field effect transistor (FinFET) technology. The CFSA incorporates isolated DL current sensing approach which provides the higher Current Ratio Amplification (CRA) factor. The CF-SA significantly outperforms with 66.89% and 31.47% lower sensing delay than CCSA [13] and HSA [8] respectively under similar I_{Cell} and bit-line and data-line capacitance. Our results show that even at the worst corner the CF-SA demonstrates 2.15x and 3.02x higher differential current and 2.23x and 1.7x higher data-line differential voltage with 66.6% and 34.32% higher mean (μ) than those of the best prior arts. Furthermore, failure probability of the proposed design against process parameter variations is rigorously analyzed through Monte Carlo simulations.

Categories and Subject Descriptors

D.3.3 [**VLSI Circuits**]: Current mode sense amplifier (CSA)

Keywords

Static random access memory (SRAM); cell current; Process variation; read yield; delay.

1. INTRODUCTION

Small on-chip Static random access memories (SRAM) are essential to enable low-power platforms that rely on distributed scratchpads. Since SRAMs tend to dominate the area in current multi-core processors, maintaining a small cell size is of critical importance. Therefore SRAM suffers from a decrease in read cell current (I_{CELL}) with an shrinking in device size and V_{DD} but keeping the same threshold voltage. This vulnerability to decreased I_{CELL} is exacerbated in the following situations: 1) small area cell for attempting to achieve smaller area-per-bit; 2) lowering V_{DD} [1]-[2] to reduce power consumption; With continued efforts to reduce the size and bit-line (BL)-pitch, overcoming these issues has become a major challenge in the read operation of SRAMs with a smaller I_{CELL}. Therefore in technologies beyond 45nm, low power current sense amplifier (CSA) design is severely complicated due to decrease in I_{CELL}. Many small memories (Non Volatile Memories and low-voltage SRAMs) employ voltage-mode sense

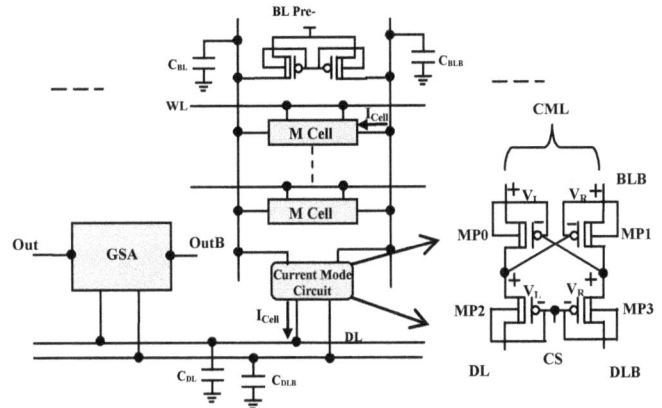

Figure 1: Detailed schematic of conventional current sense amplifier.

amplifier (VSA), [3]-[5] with a long BL developing time to provide tolerance for BL and SA offset; however, this is accomplished at the cost of reduced read speed. Cascode-current-load CSAs (CCL-CSAs) [5], [6]-[7], require long BL settling times and have a small 1st-stage voltage difference when reading a small I_{CELL}. Hybrid SAs [8]-[9] have small differential voltage on the data-lines (DLs) when reading a small I_{CELL}. Current-mirror CSA (CM-CSA) [10]-[12] has fast read speed but cannot sense small I_{CELL}, due to mismatch in the mirror-stage device. Since all of these SA designs utilize the differential output current of the current conveyor, their improvement is only incremental. Reference [13] clearly indicates that the differential current is equal to the current flowing into the cell node where a "0" is stored, i.e., I_{CELL}. In all CSAs and HSAs this differential current develops the differential voltage at DLs. As the input of the global sensing stage, the differential voltage at the DLs should reach up to the offset voltage (V_{os}), to avoid the mismatching issues. Due to this offset and huge DL capacitance, small I_{CELL}, SRAMs suffer from slow read speed and high read fail probability Thus, developing an SA with greater offset tolerance is a prerequisite to achieving high-yield for small I_{CELL}, SRAMs with faster read operation.

Despite this activity in SAs research, there are very few implementations of SAs in FinFET, and multi gate FETs (MugFET), [2], [14]-[17]. In this paper, we propose a new design for SRAM SA by using FinFET technology, besides reducing the sensing delay it improves read yield and decrease effect of data-line capacitance of SRAM. To the best of our knowledge, this is the first work which evaluating read acceleration through boosting differential current in FinFET current mode SA for SRAM. This paper is organized as follows. In Section 2, the conventional CSA and its limitations are reviewed. Section 3 describes the structure and operating principle of the proposed technique. In Section 4,

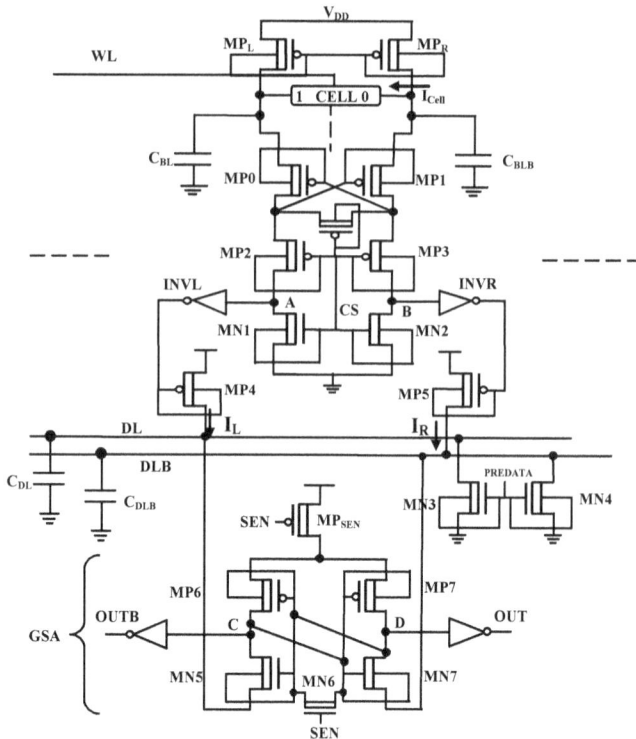

Figure 2: Schematic of current feed sense amplifier with memory column.

the simulation methodology employed for CF-SA with conventional CSA, namely, CCSA [13], the hybrid SA [8], is discussed with commentary on simulation results and comparison followed by an exposition on impact of process variation, device mismatch effects and sensing failure.

2. CONVENTIONAL CURRENT SENSE AMPLIFIER & ITS LIMITATIONS

The conventional current mode SA (CCSA) consists of four equal-sized PMOS transistors as shown in Fig. 1 [13]. Before sensing datalines are precharged to ground. Suppose the cell is accessed (WL=1) and draws I_{CELL}. Now, once column select (CS) signal goes low the CML activates, CML offers a virtual short circuit across the bit-lines. Since the bit-line voltages are equal, the bit-line load currents will also be equal, as well as the bit-line capacitor currents. As the cell draws current I_{CELL}, it follows that the left-hand leg of the SA must pass more current than the right-hand leg. In fact, the difference between these currents is I_{CELL}, the cell current. The drain currents of MP2 and MP3 are passed to current transporting data lines DL and DLB. However, by scaling down of the CMOS technology, the data-line capacitances (C_{DL}, C_{DLB}) may become too large. Therefore, the differential current (I_{CELL}) couldn't produce enough voltage difference to meet offset tolerant requirement of global sensing amplifier (GSA).

3. The PROPOSED CURRENT FEED SA

Fig. 2 shows a simple schematic illustration of the proposed CF-SA with SRAM memory column. The CF-SA uses isolated data-line approach to rapidly generate the 1st-stage voltage difference at small-load internal nodes (A & B), thanks to its DL-decoupled behavior. During the standby mode BL and DL are precharged to V_{DD} and ground via MP_L, MP_R and MN3, MN4 FETs respectively. While CS signal is at logic HIGH, which prechage the node A and B to ground. Therefore the outputs of

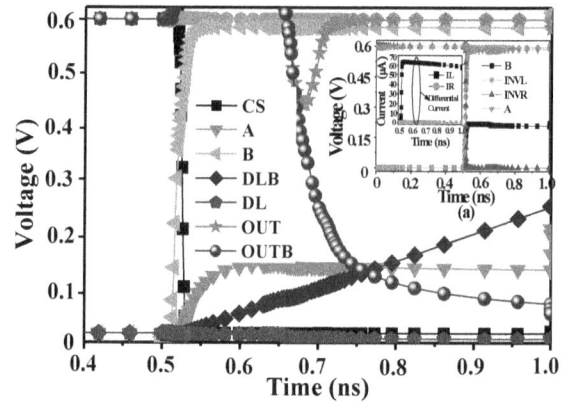

Figure 3: Simulated transient behavior of the CF-SA for V_{DD}=0.6V. Voltage waveforms at various nodes (inset). Differential current in CF-SA (inset).

INVL and INVR become high, which kept MP4 and MP5 in cutoff mode. Subsequently equalization device (MN6) is turned on to clamp the nodes C and D to the equal potential while MP_{SEN} device is turned off to save power. During the read operation both CS and WL signals are triggered to access particular memory cell, creating differential currents and voltage on the BLs. Concurrently MP2 and MP3 are turned on by asserting the CS signal LOW. Owing to the large size BL load FETs (MP_L, MP_R) and the MP0, MP1 of current mode logic, differential currents are quickly transported to the low capacitive nodes A and B, this intern quickly generates the differential potential at these nodes. However the difference in potential of these two nodes is not sufficient to generate the large differential current. Hence, two inverters INVL and INVR are used. INVL and INVR configured with low V_{th} PFET and high V_{th} NFET, which generate the complementary voltage levels. The voltages at nodes A, B and outputs of INVL and INVR are as illustrated in Fig. 3(inset). Finally INL and INR driven the PFETs (MP4 & MP5) and feed larger differential currents Fig. 3 (inset) and develop the large differential voltage at data-lines.

From a topological standpoint, this operation is more robust than that of a CCSA, because large differential is developed at data-lines, which necessitates a higher voltage rise on DLs. Following that, signal sense enable (SEN) asserted LOW which turns ON MP_{SEN} device but turns off MN6 device, thus activating the GSA. This high speed building block subsequently sense and amplifies the voltage difference on the DLs to intermediate outputs at C and D and feeds them to the output inverters to obtain the correct CMOS logic level outputs. Large differential current accelerates the development of the difference (ΔV_{Diff}).

4. Design Methodology & Simulation Results

This section unveils the efficiency of the CF-SA, its design tradeoffs, and a quantitative comparison is made against the CCSA and HSA. The worst-case corner simulations for all designs are performed to verify the results and to compare the performance of the CF-SA with that of the CCSA and HAS. In this comparison, the following values are held for the respective variables: I_{CELL} = 32.02μA, V_{DD}=0.6V, and C_{DL}=100fF with 128 cells per column. A comparison is made against the conventional schemes when all three schemes employ an identical latch as GSA. For the FinFET technology, there are two popular models: UFDG model [18] and PTM [19]. We use the double-gate PTM 20nm technology model and specter as the platform in our FinFET SA simulations. In our

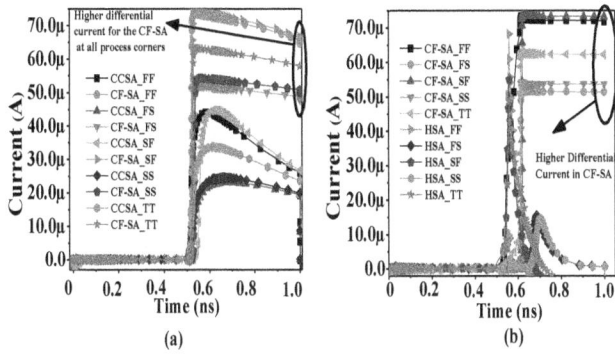

Figure 4: Output differential current across all the process corners for (a) CCSA and CF-SA. (b) CCSA and HAS. The temperature corners considered is 27°C.

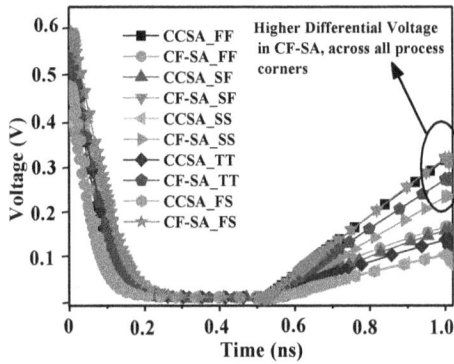

Figure 5: Simulated differential voltage at DLs across all the process corners for CCSA and CF-SA.

simulations, based on the equation $W_{eff} = (2 \times h_{fin} + W_{fin}) \times N_{fin}$, where the fin height h_{fin} and fin width W_{fin} is fixed, we can change the number of fins N_{fin}, to get a reasonable effective channel width W. Fig. 4 shows the relative performance of the SAs at different process corners and verifies the superiority of CF-SA, in terms of differential current at almost every critical corner. In particular, Fig. 4 (a) refers to the case of a CCSA and CF-SA whereas Fig. 4 (b) corresponds to HSA and CF-SA for an equal I_{CELL} (32.02μA). It is worth noticing that CF-SA has two fold of better differential current than CCSA, the differential current is 2.15x and 3.02x higher than the CCSA and HSA, respectively at worst case process corner (SS). Fig. 5 illustrates that CF-SA topology has larger differential, which directly translates into a grater offset tolerance for GSA. Compared to CCSA, the CF-SA provides on average 90% (92 mV against 175 mV) improvement in differential potential at DLs, a larger differential is able to tolerance a larger GSA offset ΔV_{th} and offers the lower cell access time.

To put the comparative analysis in perspective, Fig. 6 plots the simulated differential voltage distribution at datalines, as a result of equal cell current for the CCSA, HSA and CF-SA. The CMC devices size is kept identical for all simulations and variation applied to primary (current) sensing stage only. 1500 point Monte Carlo (MC) analysis, considering V_{th} variation of transistors is performed at worst case process corner. All circuits are simulated at a power supply of 0.6V, $C_{DL}=100fF$ and clock frequency of 1GHz. It is observed from Fig. 6 that the CF-SA gives higher differential voltage, with 59.6% and 18.5% higher mean (μ) than CCSA, and HSA, respectively. We include the results of the sensing delay in simultaneous read scenario. Fig. 7(a) reaffirms

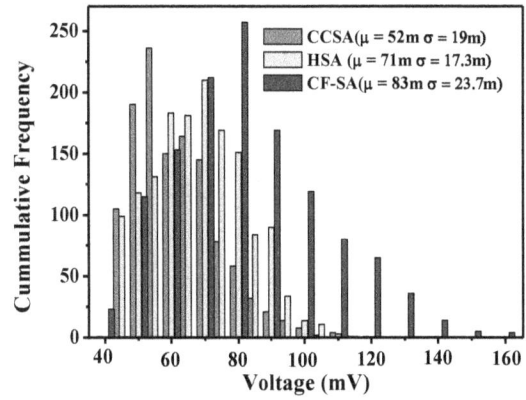

Figure 6: Differential voltage distributions of the designs in comparison using MC simulations at room temperature.

that CF-SA significantly outperforms than other designs with 66.89% and 31.47% lower sensing delay than CCSA and HSA respectively for V_{DD}=0.6V. To gauge the effect of large number of cells over a column in a bigger SRAM macro, we conducted measurements at large number of 6T cells, where values are ranging from 100 to 500 cells/column. In the CF-SA, because of its differential current mode nature no differential discharging of BL capacitance is required, which makes sensing delay less sensitive to BL capacitance as depicted in Fig. 7 (a) (inset). It is apparent that all three designs are insensitive to C_{BL}, as manifested by the almost-horizontal line. This is because all switching nodes are isolated from the highly loaded bit-lines and data-lines In order to gauge the effect of huge DLs capacitance extensive simulations have been carried out by varying the DLs capacitance. Fig. 7 (b) demonstrates, that CF-SA offers enhanced speed robustness against the varying C_{DL} giving a delay sensitivity of only 1.9ps/100fF, which is better than HSA which has 2.78ps/100fF. Although CCSA follows the same trend but failed to sense after 500fF because of lower I_{CELL}.

Circuit characteristics with capturing the local mismatch behavior and V_{th} variation, obtained by MC simulation of 1500 iterations with 6σ parameter variation are shown in Fig. 8 (a). The variations are only performed on the SAs alone. As observed from Fig. 8(a), sensing delay distribution curves for the CCSA and CF-SA cross at 63 ps. Based on the simulation data, our estimation shows that 80.06% of statistical samples in case of CF-SA have sensing delay lower than 63ps, signifying its lower sensing delay compared to CCSA (95.3% of statistical samples in

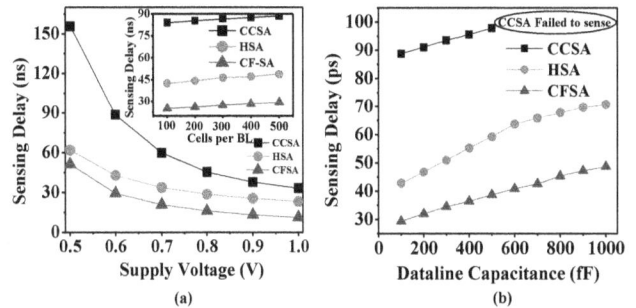

Figure 7: (a) Sensing delay variation with the VDD for CCSA, HSA and CF-SA and Variation of sensing delay with BL capacitance (Inset), (b) Sensing delay variation with data-line capacitance.

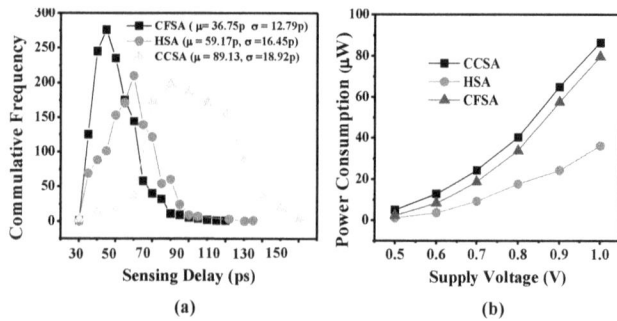

Figure 8: (a) Sensing delay distributions for the designs in comparison, results are from 1500 samples Monte Carlo simulation that vary local parameters (6σ) at room temperature and $C_{BL}=C_{DL}=100fF$, (b) V_{DD} versus read power.

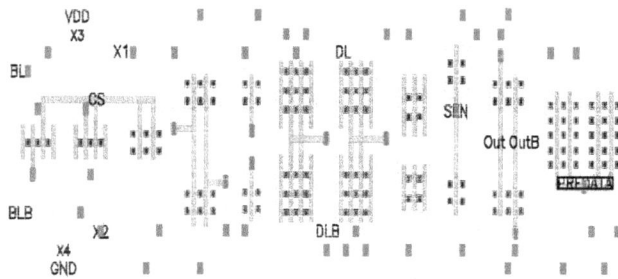

Figure 9: Layout view of current feed sense amplifier.

case of CCSA have sensing delay higher than 63 ps). Similarly 62.06% of statistical samples in case of CF-SA have sensing delay lower than 52ps, signifying its lower sensing delay compared to HSA (27.4% of statistical samples in case of CCSA have sensing delay lower than 52 ps). Fig. 8(b) illustrates the dissipated power for read power dissipation with varying supply voltage. The energy consumption for CF-SA is less than CCSA due to the low power consumption of the amplification stage (GSA) and is also almost independent of the bit-line capacitance as the CMC always maintains the bit-lines close to V_{DD}. Results indicate that CF-SA offers 35.18% savings in energy consumption over CCSA for a 128 cells per column and $C_{DL}=100fF$. On the other hand HSA design exhibits 56.59%, less power than CF-SA due to its better precharging scheme. Table 1 compares all designs based on a different performance metric. Fig. 9 shows how a CF-SA layout can be built using FinFETs [20-21]. The layout design follows the BL pitch for the given technology.

Table 1. Summary of all designs in comparison with CF-SA for $C_{DL}=100fF$ and an operating frequency of 1GHz

	Sensing Delay (ps)	Average Power (μW)	Power Delay Product (fJ)
CCSA	88.73	12.76	1.13
HSA	42.86	3.59	0.15
CFSA	29.37	8.27	0.24

5. CONCLUSION

In this work, for the first time, the FinFET current mode sense amplifier, targeted to small I_{Cell} sensing in SRAM is presented with detailed sensitivity analysis. The SAs were implemented and validated with a 20nm FinFET technology for high read yield and low power applications. The proposed CF-SA, employs data-line isolated current sensing approach, these features enable CF-SA to achieve a read speed 3.02x, 1.45x faster than CCSAs and HSA respectively for sensing 32.02μA on a 100fF data-line. It is shown that, the CF-SA exhibits 2.23x and 1.7x more differential voltage at data-lines than CCSA and HSA. Based on simulation results, we can conclude that CF-SA with isolated data-lines approach has the advantage over the other current mode FinFET SAs in the read operation, such as robust read access against small I_{Cell} and huge data-line capacitance with low sensing delay.

6. REFERENCE

[1] M.-F. Chang et al., "A 0.5 V 4 Mb logic-process compatible embedded resistive RAM (ReRAM) in 65 nm CMOS using low voltage current mode sensing scheme with 45 ns random read time," in *IEEE Int. Solid-State Circuits Conf. (ISSCC) Dig. Tech. Papers*, 2012, pp. 434–435.

[2] C.-Y. Hsieh, M. L Fan, V. Pi-Ho Hu, P. Su and C.-T. Chuang, "Independently-Controlled-Gate FinFET Schmitt Trigger Sub-Threshold SRAMs,"*IEEE Trans. Very Large Scale Integr. (VLSI) Syst.*, vol. 20, no. 7, pp. 1201–1210, July. 2012.

[3] M. E. Sinangil, A. P. Chandrakasan, "Application-Specific SRAM Design Using Output Prediction to Reduce Bit-Line Switching Activity and Statistically Gated Sense Amplifiers for Up to 1.9x Lower Energy/Access," *IEEE J. Solid-State Circuits*, vol. 49, no. 1, pp. 107–117, Jan. 2014.

[4] I. Hayashi et al, "A 250-MHz 18-Mb Full Ternary CAM With Low-Voltage Match line Sensing Scheme in 65-nm CMOS," *IEEE J. Solid-State Circuits*, vol. 48, no. 11, pp. 2671–2680, Jan. 2014.

[5] Yen-Huei Chen et al, "Compact Measurement Schemes for Bit-Line Swing, Sense Amplifier Offset Voltage, and Word-Line Pulse Width to Characterize Sensing Tolerance Margin in a 40 nm Fully Functional Embedded SRAM," *IEEE J. Solid-State Circuits*, vol. 47, no. 4, pp. 2338–2348, April. 2012.

[6] C. J. Chevallier et al., "A 0.13 m 64 Mb multi-layered conductive metal-oxide memory," in *IEEE Int. Solid-State Circuits Conf. (ISSCC) Dig. Tech. Papers*, 2010, pp. 260–261.

[7] F. Bedeschi et al., "A bipolar-selected phase change memory featuring multi-level cell storage," *IEEE J. Solid-State Circuits*, vol. 44, no. 1, pp. 217–227, 2009.

[8] D. Anh-Tuan, K. Zhi-Hui , and Y. Kiat-Seng "Hybrid-Mode SRAM Sense Amplifiers: New Approach on Transistor Sizing," *IEEE Trans. Circuits Syst. II, Exp. Briefs*, vol. 55, no. 10, pp. 986–990, October. 2008.

[9] M. Sharifkhani, E. Rahiminejad, S.M. Jahinuzzaman, and M. Sachdev, "A compact hybrid current/voltage sense amplifier with offset cancellation for high-speed SRAMs," *IEEE Trans. Very Large Scale Integr. (VLSI) Syst.*, vol. 19, no. 5, pp. 883–894, May 2011.

[10] B. Wicht, S. Paul, and D. S-Landsiedel "Analysis and Compensation of the Bitline Multiplexer in SRAM Current Sense Amplifiers," *IEEE J. Solid- State Circuits*, vol. 36, no. 11, pp. 1745–1755, Nov. 2001.

[11] A. Conte, "A high-performance very low-voltage current sense amplifier for nonvolatile memories," *IEEE J. Solid-State Circuits*, vol. 40, no. 2, pp. 507–514, Feb. 2005.

[12] M.-F. Chang et al., "A process variation tolerant embedded split-gate flash memory using pre-stable current sensing scheme," *IEEE J. Solid- State Circuits*, vol. 44, no. 3, pp. 987–994, Mar. 2009.

[13] E. Seevinck, P. J. V. Beers, and H. Ontrop, "Current-mode techniques for high-speed VLSI circuits with application to current SA for CMOS SRAM's," *IEEE J. Solid-State Circuits*, vol. 26, no. 5, pp. 525–536, May 1991.

[14] S. Mukhopadhyay, H. Mahmoodi, and K. Roy, "A Novel High-Performance and Robust Sense Amplifier Using Independent Gate Control in Sub-50-nm Double-Gate MOSFET," *IEEE Trans. Very Large Scale Integr. (VLSI) Syst.*, vol. 14, no. 2, pp. 183–192, FEBRUARY 2006.

[15] M.-L. Fan, V. P.H Hu, Y.-N. Chen, P. Su and C.T. Chuang, "Variability Analysis of Sense Amplifier for FinFET Subthreshold SRAM Applications," *IEEE Trans. Circuits Syst. II, Exp. Briefs*, vol. 59, no. 12, pp. 1031–1035, December. 2008.

[16] M.-Fu Tsai1, J.-H. Tsai, M.-L. Fan, P. Su and C.-T. Chuang, "Variation Tolerant CLSAs for Nanoscale Bulk-CMOS and FinFET SRAM," in IEEE Asia Pacific Conference on Circuits and Systems (APCCAS), 2012. pp. 471–474.

[17] S.S. Rathod, A.K. Saxena, S. Dasgupta, "A low-noise, process-variation-tolerant double-gate FinFET based sense amplifier," Microelectronics Reliability 51 (2011) pp. 773–780.

[18] SOI Group of University of Florida, *UFDG MOSFET Model User Guide (Linux Version)*, 2003. http://www.soi.tec.ufl.edu.

[19] M. Alioto, "Analysis of Layout Density in FinFET Standard Cells and Impact of Fin Technology," in *Proc. IEEE ISCAS*, May. 2010, pp. 3201-3207.

[20] M. Alioto, "Analysis of Layout Density in FinFET Standard Cells and Impact of Fin Technology," in *Proc. IEEE ISCAS*, May. 2010, pp. 3201-3207.

[21] J. Ryckaert et al, , " Design Technology Co optimization for N10," in *Proc. IEEE CICC*, Sep. 2014, pp. 1-8.

Statistically Validating the Impact of Process Variations on Analog and Mixed Signal Designs

Ibtissem Seghaier, Mohamed H. Zaki and Sofiène Tahar
Dept. of Electrical and Computer Engineering,
Concordia University, Montréal, Québec, Canada
{seghaier, mzaki, tahar}@ece.concordia.ca

ABSTRACT

Process variation presents a practical challenge on the performance of analog and mixed signal (AMS) circuits. This paper proposes a Monte Carlo-Jackknife (MC-JK) technique, a variant of Monte Carlo method, to verify process variation affecting the performance and functionality of AMS designs. We use a behavioral model to which we encompass device variation due to $65nm$ technology process. Next, we conduct hypothesis testing based on the MC-JK technique combined with Latin hypercube sampling in a statistical run-time verification environment. Experimental results demonstrate the robustness of our approach in verifying AMS circuits.

Categories and Subject Descriptors

B.7.2 [**Design Aids**]: [Verification, Simulation]

1. INTRODUCTION

Relentless miniaturization of CMOS technology comes with its own compromises. Although it permits an increase in the level of integration, it results on the other hand in more complex designs. This makes AMS design more challenging and dictates a careful verification. Moreover, the diminutive sizing of transistors leads to an ever substantial percentage deviations from the parameters nominal values [4]. Hence, empowering designers with new tools and techniques in order to tape out designs that withstand process variation while meeting strict specification are highly required. To respond to this raising need during early verification, we investigate in this paper a new statistical verification technique that can reduce the Monte Carlo simulation time while ensuring accuracy of the results. The Monte Carlo method is an attractive technique that has a widespread use [8, 3]. Based on repetitive simulations, it permits to evaluate substantive design properties as well as to statistically estimate circuit parameters. To do so, this approach needs a pre-specified underlying distribution, mainly uniform, normal, or log-normal to describe the random variables of process variation effect. Hence, a wrong distribution assumption

leads to a possibility of outright wrong results. This issue has been mooted in a recent research work [7].

This paper addresses the shortcomings of conventional sampling based verification method by (1) providing better parameter space coverage with reduced simulation overhead results from the Latin Hypercube sampling [1] as an alternative to Pseudo Random Monte Carlo sampling; and (2) offering more accurate error margins and hence better verification accuracy is achieved using the Jackknife statistical method to estimate the Monte Carlo distribution parameters.

The rest of this paper is organized as follows: Details of the proposed methodology are given in Section 2. Thereafter, we report experimental results for the verification of a ring oscillator and a Charge Pump PLL in Section 3. Finally, we conclude the paper in Section 4.

2. PROPOSED METHODOLOGY

Figure 1 depicts the overall proposed verification methodology. Given an AMS design description, we derive its behavioral model. Using the process variation libraries created by technology vendors, we then choose a range of parameter deviations for 65nm process. Traditional sampling techniques such as Pseudo Random Sampling (PRS) arranges

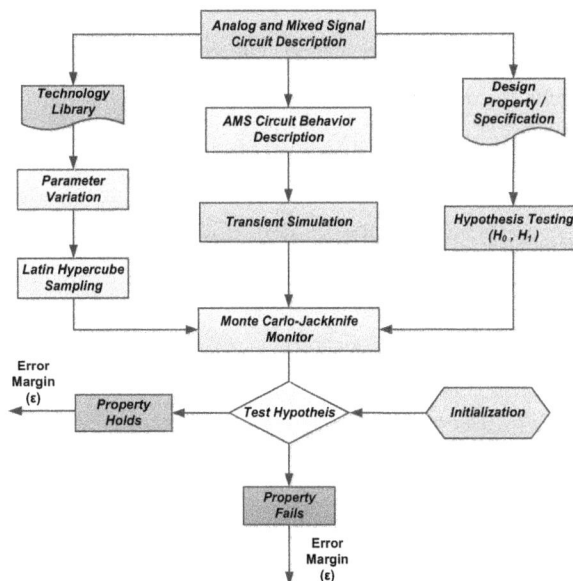

Figure 1: Overview of the proposed methodology

parameter values at some specific corners in the parameter space. When running Monte Carlo simulation, it cannot mimic the system behavior in a global parameter space. However, the Latin Hypercube technique gives samples that could reflect the integral distribution more effectively with a reduced samples variance. In fact, it turns out to be five times more effective than PRS Monte Carlo in yield estimation as shown in [2]. For an efficient sampling procedure from the process variation distribution, the Latin Hypercube Sampling technique is deployed (more details are given in Section 2.1). The AMS circuit is thereafter evaluated for the obtained parameter samples for specific environment constraints, namely the initial values of the voltage and current state variables and simulation parameters (the total simulation time, the simulation step size and so on).

On the other hand, we elucidate a property of interest ($\mathcal{P}$) that the circuit output should comply with. This property is phrased as hypothesis testing problem. It consists of defining a null hypothesis H_0 of $\mathcal{P}$ and an alternative hypothesis H_1 which is naturally the counterexample ($\mathcal{Q}$) opposite to ($\mathcal{P}$). For the chosen parameter variation values and a specified tail test, a critical value based Monte Carlo-Jackknife monitor is carried for a confidence level δ. The property $\mathcal{P}$ is verified if the null hypothesis H_0 is accepted, else the monitor reports a violation. The conclusion of accepting or rejecting H_0 is drawn with an error margin ϵ for a 95% confidence level (see Fig. 1).

2.1 Latin Hypercube Sampling

Latin Hypercube Sampling (LHS) [1] is a an optimized statistical sampling technique to extract parameter values from defined multidimensional distribution. We use LHS to select samples in the process variation space. To construct a Latin hypercube sample of n_p data points from an AMS circuit model with n_d dimensions (state variables) defined from a uniformly distribution $X \sim U(0.1)^{n_d}$, the sampling space is divided in such a way that each of the n_d dimensions are divided into n_b blocks as follows :

$$X_{ij} = \frac{\pi_j(i-1) + U_{ij}}{n_s}, 1 \leq i \leq n_s, 1 \leq j \leq n_d$$

where π_j are uniform random permutations $U_{ij} \sim U[0,1)$ wherein U_{ij} and π_j are independent. LHS has a multiple stratification property:

$$\forall c = 0, ..., n_s - 1, \forall j = 1, ..., n_d$$

$$prob\{1 \leq i \leq n_s | \frac{c}{n_s} \leq X_{ij} < \frac{c+1}{n_s}\} = 1$$

This technique offers variance sampling reduction which results in a better verification coverage.

2.2 Jackknife Technique

The Jackknife technique [6] was originally developed as a nonparametric way to estimate and reduce the bias of an estimator of a population parameter. The bias of an estimator is defined as the difference between the expected value of this estimator and its true value. The Jackknife procedure works as follows: First, remove d data points and calculate the statistic of interest. Second, calculate the pseudo-values according to Equation 1. Then, repeat this process, leaving out d data points at a time to build a distribution of the statistic. Finally, use that distribution to estimate the

---

Algorithm 1 Monte Carlo-Jackknife Verification Algorithm

Require: $V_{out}, T_{obs}, \alpha, test, M, d$
    $N \leftarrow length(V_{out})$
    for $i \leftarrow 1\ to\ N$ **do**
3:      $\theta \leftarrow delete\_d\_Jackknife$
      $T_{JK}(i) \leftarrow Measure\_test\_statistic(\theta)$
    while $test = "upper\ tail\ test"$ **do**
6:      $CV = quantile(T_{JK}, 1 - \alpha)$
      if $CV \geq T_{obs}$ **then**
        Accept H_0
9:      **else**
        Reject H_0
    while $test = "lower\ tail\ test"$ **do**
12:     $CV = quantile(T_{JK}, \alpha)$
      if $CV \leq T_{obs}$ **then**
        Accept H_0
15:     **else**
        Reject H_0
    while $test = "two\ tailed\ test"$ **do**
18:     $CV_L = quantile(T_{JK}, \frac{\alpha}{2})$
      $CV_U = quantile(T_{JK}, \frac{1-\alpha}{2})$
      if $CV_L \geq T_{obs}$ **or** $CV_U \leq T_{obs}$ **then**
21:      *Reject* H_0
      else
        Accept H_0

---

statistic and its uncertainty. For an estimator S, the ith pseudo-value Jackknife of S was calculated as follows:

$$ps_i = NS - (N-1)S_i \quad (1)$$

where S_i is the estimator value for the sample with the ith data point deleted. The Jackknife Confidence Interval (CI) of this estimate for 95% confidence level is then given by:

$$CI_J = \bar{ps} \pm 2\sqrt{\frac{\sigma_J}{N}} \quad (2)$$

where $\quad \sigma_J = \sum \frac{(ps_i - \bar{ps})^2}{N-1}, \quad \bar{ps} = \frac{1}{N}\sum ps_i$

Hence, the Jackknife reduces the bias of the parameter estimates as well as the variance. The detailed procedure for Monte Carlo-Jackknife (MC-JK) based hypothesis testing technique for AMS circuits is illustrated in Algorithm 1, where V_{out} represents the observed circuit output with process variation, M denotes the number of MC-JK samples, d is a parameter for the *deleted_d_jackknife* method, α a chosen significant level and *test* stands for the type of test to be performed. The algorithm starts with drawing M samples from the circuit output V_{out} of size N by leaving out d samples of the output at a time (line 3). The deviation between the output and H_0 is computed using a test statistic estimation T_{JK} for each Jackknife pseudo-sample. Next, the Monte Carlo quantile procedure [8] is employed to measure the critical by type of test: For an upper tail test (line 5)/lower tail test (line 11), the $1 - \alpha/\alpha$ quantiles of the empirical distribution, respectively. In the case of two tailed test, both $1 - \frac{1}{\alpha}$ and $\frac{\alpha}{2}$ quantiles define the lower and upper critical values (lines 18-19). Once the critical value is determined, the monitor decides about the satisfaction or violation of H_0.

3. EXPERIMENTAL RESULTS

In this section, we report the results of the application of our methodology to a ring oscillator and a PLL. All computation and circuit models were performed in a MATLAB environment for $M=1000$ trials and confidence level $\delta = 0.95$. The experiments are run on a 64-bit Windows 7 server with 2.8 GHz processor and 24 GB memory.

3.1 Ring Oscillator

A ring oscillator is a closed-loop chain of an odd number of inverters placed in series with a negative feedback to provide oscillation. Each inverter is composed of a cascaded n-channel and p-channel transistors.

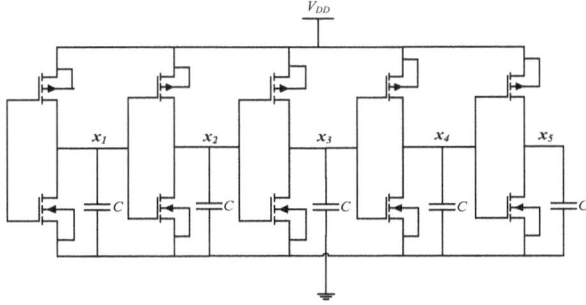

Figure 2: Five-stage CMOS ring oscillator schematic

A five-stage ring oscillator circuit is shown in Fig. 2. To model the influence of the interconnect circuitry, an additional load capacity of C was used. The circuit dynamics are governed by Equation (3):

$$\frac{dx_1}{dt} = -\frac{1}{C}(I_n(x_n, x_1, gnd) + I_p(x_n, x_1, V_{DD})) \quad (3)$$
$$\frac{dx_i}{dt} = -\frac{1}{C}(I_n(x_{i+1}, x_i, gnd) + I_p(x_{i+1}, x_i, V_{DD})), \ \forall i \in [2, n]$$
$$V_{out} = x_n$$

where $\{x_i\}_{i=1}^n$ and gnd stand for the node and ground voltages, respectively. We model the nonlinear current generated by the n-channel and p-channel transistors as functions I_n and I_p, respectively. The node voltages of each of the 5 inverters has been designed to oscillate between the power V_{dd} and the ground gnd at a frequency of 4.5GHz with a tolerance of ± 50MHz. As a result, the null hypothesis H_0 and the alternative hypothesis H_1 can be expressed as:

$$H_0 : \ 4.450 \text{ GHz} \leq f_{osc} \leq 4.550 \text{ GHz}; \quad (4)$$
$$H_1 : \ f_{osc} \geq 4.550 \text{ GHz} \parallel f_{osc} \leq 4.450 \text{ GHz};$$

To study the effect of process variation on the oscillation frequency (f_{osc}), we choose two scenarios:
1) The channel width w_{n_i} of each n-MOS transistor $\{M_{n_i}\}_{i=1}^5$

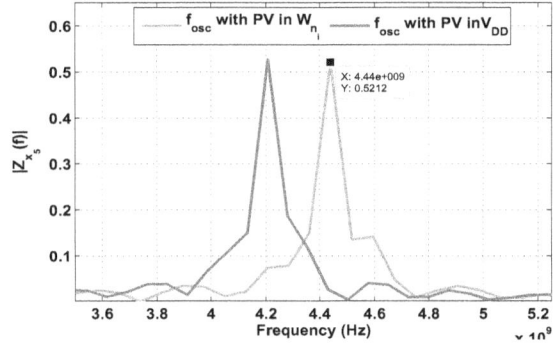

Figure 3: Frequency spectrum of the circuit output

has up to 15%.
2) The power supply voltage V_{DD} is assumed to have 5% variation with Gaussian distribution around the nominal value.

To compute f_{osc}, we employ the Fourier Transform (FT) analysis in MATLAB [5] . A comparison between the Monte Carlo (MC) technique and the proposed approach for the above mentioned scenarios under several process variation factors are summarized in Table 1. Since a two tailed test is chosen, a rejection decision of H_0 is announced if the observed value T_{obs} is within the rejection region ($T_{obs} \in]-\infty, C.V_L] \cup [C.V_L, +\infty[$). It can be noticed from Table 1 that when the percentage of variation increases from 1 to 15% in the case of transistor width deviation (Row 1), both MC and MC-JK techniques report decision changes from acceptance to rejection. However, by sweeping the w_{n_i} up to 10% of variation, an erratic decision between the Monte Carlo and the proposed Jackknife-Monte Carlo is remarked (see Table 1). Moreover, in all cases our approach presents less error margins. This can be explained by the biased estimation of the Monte Carlo technique and the reduced sampling error offered by our approach.

Figure 3 depicts the Single-Sided Amplitude Spectrum of the ring oscillator output x_5 for the two different process variation scenarios. It can be noticed that a great deviation of the tolerated oscillation frequency has been obtained. Therefore, a process variation in the power supply voltage V_{DD} is identified to have a greater effect than a process variation in all 5 n-MOS transistor lengths for 5% trimmed deviation.

3.2 Charge-Pump Phase Locked Loop

We apply the proposed methodology to verify the locking property of a 3rd order dual path Charge Pump PLL (CP-PLL) design shown in Fig. 4. The Phase Frequency Detector (PFD), which is a digital component, operates as follows: The PFD compares the phases of the reference

Table 1: Statistical runtime verification of oscillation frequency of ring oscillator for $\alpha = 0.05$

	$J(ns)$	$C.V_U$		$C.V_L$		T_{obs}		f_{obs} (GHz)		H_0		ϵ (MHz)	
		MC	MC-JK	MC	MC-JK	MC	MC-JK	MC	MC-JK	MC	MC-JK	MC	MC-JK
	1%	-1.487	-1.326	1.487	1.326	1.0389	0.9754	4.51	4.49	Accept	Accept	34.8	16.9
PV	5%	-1.533	-1.378	1.533	1.378	1.0773	0.8559	4.48	4.47	Accept	Accept	25.3	20.3
in W_{n_i}	10%	-1.571	-1.391	1.571	1.391	1.0584	0.8131	4.46	4.47	Accept	**Reject**	32.5	24.9
	15%	-1.652	-1.441	1.652	1.441	2.269	1.938	4.45	4.44	**Reject**	**Reject**	39.0	22.7
PV	1%	-1.845	-1.722	1.845	1.722	0.741	0.825	4.47	4.49	Accept	Accept	17.2	15.6
in	2.5%	-1.883	-1.781	1.883	1.781	-2.179	-1.894	4.46	4.48	Accept	Accept	18.7	16.9
V_{DD}	5%	-1.576	-1.668	1.576	1.668	1.848	1.857	4.25	4.18	**Reject**	**Reject**	25.3	21.7

Table 2: Statistical runtime verification of PLL locking time for $\alpha = 0.05$

case	$J(ns)$	c.v		T_{obs}		N_{obs}		H_0		ϵ	
		MC	MC-JK	MC	MC-JK	MC	MC-JK	MC	MC-JK	MC	MC-JK
	0.5%	1.454	1.361	-2.389	-2.771	971	1098	Accept	Accept	154	138
P.V in VCO	1%	1.527	1.431	0.768	0.592	1229	1274	Accept	Accept	174	146
and LPF	2%	1.676	1.569	13.443	10.782	1479	1583	**Reject**	**Reject**	182	165
	5%	1.541	1.497	162.19	137.08	1847	1643	**Reject**	**Reject**	223	177

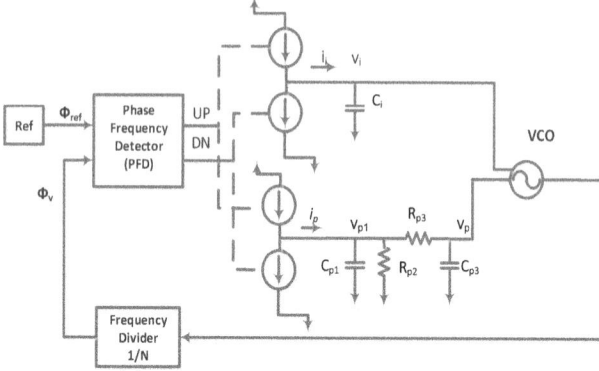

Figure 4: 3rd **order CP-PLL macro model**

signal ϕ_{ref} and the feedback signal ϕ_v during their rising edges. If the phase difference is within the tolerated margins, no current is injected in the Charge Pumps (CP). However, if the reference oscillator leads/lags the feedback signal (ϕ_{ref}/ϕ_v reaches 2π first), then the CP injects current to charge/discharge the Low Pass Filter (LPF) capacitors which increases the control voltage.

The dynamics of the analog PLL components is described by the following equations:

$$\frac{dv_i}{dt} = \frac{1}{C_i}i_i$$
$$\frac{dv_{p1}}{dt} = \frac{1}{C_{p1}}[(\frac{1}{R_{p2}} + \frac{1}{R_{p3}})v_{p1} + \frac{1}{R_{p3}}v_p + i_p]$$
$$\frac{dv_p}{dt} = \frac{1}{C_{p3}R_{p3}}(v_{p1} - v_p) \qquad (5)$$
$$\frac{d\phi_i}{dt} = \frac{1}{N}(K_i v_i + K_p v_p + 2\pi f_0)$$
$$\frac{d\phi_{ref}}{dt} = 2\pi f_0$$

The locking property we attempt to verify can be expressed as: *The required number of cycles for the PLL to lock is less than a certain value ($|\phi_v - \phi_{ref}| \leq 0.2°$)*. This property can be formulated as follows:

$$H_0 \;:\; T_{lock} \leq 1500 \; cycles; \qquad (6)$$
$$H_1 \;:\; T_{lock} > 1500 \; cycles;$$

Table 2 shows the results of verifying the locking time of the CP-PLL circuit using an upper tail test for a significance level $\alpha = 0.05$. We compared the discrepancy between the results obtained using MC and our MC-JK approach. The obtained results demonstrate a good agreement between the two techniques in verifying the PLL locking (H_0 column in

Table 2). Besides, a better verification accuracy is remarked using our approach with an error margins ϵ less than those given by the MC technique. For instance, for 2% process variation in the VCO and LPF the error margin computed using our approach $\epsilon = 165$ cycles while an error estimate of $\epsilon = 182$ cycles has been given by traditional MC.

4. CONCLUSION

In this paper, a Monte Carlo-Jackknife statistical approach is proposed to handle the verification of analog and mixed signal designs under $65nm$ process variation. The proposed technique constructs statistically a sound hypothesis testing approach and hence can be used in lieu of traditional Monte Carlo simulation. For instance, it provides better accuracy with reduced error margin than Monte Carlo. However, MC-JK is more computationally intensive than MC based statistical runtime verification. To alleviate this, we deployed the Latin Hypercube method for a more effective sampling with less trials.

As future work, we plan to extend the proposed approach to online runtime verification fashion for the same accuracy. Moreover, we intend to study more uncertainties in AMS designs such as noise, and initial condition variation.

5. REFERENCES

[1] J. C. Helton et al. Survey of sampling-based methods for uncertainty and sensitivity analysis. *Reliability Engineering & System Safety*, 91(10):1175–1209, 2006.

[2] C. Kuo et al. Efficient trimmed-sample monte carlo methodology and yield-aware design flow for analog circuits. In *Design Automation Conference*, pages 1113–1118, 2012.

[3] L. Lin and W. Burleson. Analysis and mitigation of process variation impacts on power-attack tolerance. In *Design Automation Conference*, pages 238–243, 2009.

[4] J. K. Lorenz et al. Hierarchical simulation of process variations and their impact on circuits and systems: Methodology. *IEEE Transactions on Electron Devices*, 58(8):2218–2226, 2011.

[5] MATLAB. Fast Fourier Transform. `http://www.mathworks.com/help/matlab/ref/fft.html`, 2015.

[6] F. Mecatti, P. L. Conti, and M. G. Ranalli. *Contributions to Sampling Statistics*. Springer, 2013.

[7] R. Narayanan, I. Seghaier, M. H. Zaki, and S. Tahar. Statistical run-time verification of analog circuits in presence of noise and process variation. *IEEE Transaction on VLSI*, 21(10):1811–1822, 2013.

[8] Z. Wang, M. H. Zaki, and S. Tahar. Statistical runtime verification of analog and mixed signal designs. In *Signals, Circuits and Systems*, pages 1–6, 2009.

The Bit-Nibble-Byte MicroEngine (*BnB*) for Efficient Computing on Short Data

Dilip Vasudevan
Department of Computer Science
University of Chicago
Chicago, IL, USA
dilipv@cs.uchicago.edu

Andrew A. Chien
Department of Computer Science
University of Chicago
Chicago, IL, USA
achien@cs.uchicago.edu

ABSTRACT

Energy is a critical challenge in computing performance. Due to "word size creep" from modern CPUs are inefficient for short-data element processing. We propose and evaluate a new microarchitecture called "Bit-Nibble-Byte" (BnB). We describe our design which includes both long fixed point vectors and as well as novel variable length instructions. Together, these features provide energy and performance benefits on a wide range of applications. We evaluate BnB with a detailed design of 5 vector sizes (128,256,512,1024,2048) mapped into 32nm and 7nm transistor technologies, and in combination with a variety of memory systems (DDR3 and HMC). The evaluation is based on both handwritten and compiled code with a custom compiler built for BnB. Our results include significant performance (19x-252x) and energy benefits (5.6x-140.7x) for short bit-field operations typically assumed to require hardwired accelerators and large-scale applications with compiled code.

Categories and Subject Descriptors

C.1.2 [**Processor Architectures**]: Multiple Data Stream Architectures (Multiprocessors); C.1.3 [**Processor Architectures**]: Other Architecture Styles—*Heterogeneous (hybrid) systems, Parallel Processors*

Keywords

Heterogeneous Computing, SIMD, DDR3, Hybrid Memory Cube, Microengines

1. INTRODUCTION

With the current scaling of technology nodes, energy dissipation has become the prime factor compared to the performance. To address this challenge, several different architectures are proposed exploiting the data-level and instruction level parallelism. Multicore system design with

GLSVLSI'15, May 20–22, 2015, Pittsburgh, PA, USA.
Copyright 2015 ACM 978-1-4503-3474-7/15/05 ...$15.00
http://dx.doi.org/10.1145/2742060.2742106.

homogeneous architecture was proposed to address this challenge. But due to the general purpose nature of these cores, several applications still incur higher overhead in terms of performance and energy attributed by the instruction issue cost than the actual workload computation. Heterogeneous computing architecture addresses this challenge by designing architectures with multiple heterogeneous cores tailored to specific application.10x10 paradigm [1] is a systematic approach to heterogeneity in computer architecture design. As a first step towards this goal, this paper introduces one of the microengine named Bit-Nibble-Byte Microengine which constitutes one of the microengine of the 10x10 core.

Motivation: Many applications require short fixed point or bit-level manipulations, but such operations (like shifting, rotation, shuffling and logical operations) are often not well supported on modern architectures.For traditional RISC ISA's, even extended by multimedia extensions, these operations incur high instruction count, runtime, and energy overheads. This challenge motivates us to implement efficient bit level operations supporting several data sizes and better instructions and intrinsics to carry out these operations. Thus we propose efficient an ISA with larger vector size and improved instructions to implement the algorithms efficiently.3D Stacked memory architectures are becoming very popular recently [3],[4]. Given that the proposed micro-engine will require higher bandwidth of data, performance and energy analysis of the BnB MicroEngine with a three-dimensional (3D) stacked memory system is also experimented.

Contributions: The contributions of this paper are as outlined below: 1) Design of BnB, a SIMD instruction set extension and micro-architecture with a scalar and vector (sizes ranging 128,256,512,1024 and 2048) data path that incorporate novel instructions for short data calculations with high efficiency, 2) A detailed empirical study on the impact of the several vector sizes of the BnB micro-engine over Performance and Energy for 6 applications namely GF Multiplication, AES Encryption, AES Decryption, RLE (Run-Length Encoding), 2D convolution and DWT (Discrete Wavelet Transform) is shown, 3) Detailed RTL and Gate Level Implementation of BnB, and evaluation of the performance and energy efficiency on a set of benchmark kernels, using a 32nm and 7nm CMOS process, 4) Integration of BnB microarchitecture implemented at Gate level (Hardware model) with two different memory systems namely DDR and Stacked Memory (software model) which provides knowledge on impact of the change in the memory system model over the performance and energy of the whole system, 5) Demon-

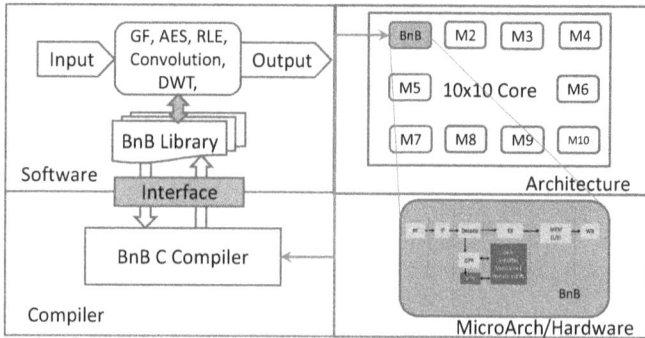

Figure 1: 10x10 Architecture

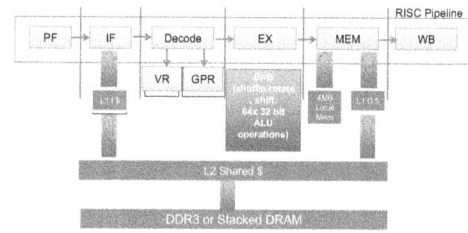

Figure 2: BnB's 6-stage pipelined microarchitecture with Memory Hierarchy (DDR3 or Stacked 3D)

strated the flexibility, programmability of BnB instrinsics and actual C code compiled for the BnB using a BnB compiler over 6 application, 6) Empirical results of running full system models namely BnB-32nm-DDR, BnB-7nm-DDR, BnB-32nm-HMC, BnB-7nm-HMC over 5 different vector sizes (128,256,512,1024,2048) compared with scalar showing clearly how BnB MicroEngine achieves performance and power efficiency by improving 3 aspects of system design namely micro-architectural/ISA enhancement, Memory system upgrade and technology scaling.

The rest of the paper is organized as follows. In section 2, BNB microarchitecture is introduced. In Section 3, the ISA and intrinsics of BnB are proposed. In Section 4, the performance and Energy results of the BNB Micro-engine are presented and compared with the results from scalar version for DDR3 and HMC memory hierarchy. Future work and summary is provided in section 5.

2. BNB ARCHITECTURE

A 10x10 architecture (Figure 1) exploits deep workload analysis to drive co-design of a federated heterogeneous architecture that exploits customization for energy efficiency, but federates a set of customized engines to achieve general-purpose coverage. The BnB micro-engine is one of the 10x10 micro-engines proposed to accelerate short data type based applications.

2.1 BnB Features

BnB's ISA includes sixteen 32-bit general purpose registers, sixteen 2048-bit vector registers. The vector registers are 16x wider than the mainstream 128-bit wide SSE. For table lookup operation, with 128-bit vectors, 16 elements of size 8 bit can be indexed. BnB's 2048 bit vector allows 256 elements of size 8 bits, a 16x table lookup at each instruction. Further, while SSE limits element size to 8, 16,32 bits for most of the instructions, BnB supports 4, 8, 16, 32, 64, 128 bits. Benefits obtained by the proposed BnB architecture over SSE is that there is a 10x improvement obtained by the increase in the vector register size. And novel custom instructions for bit operations provide another 3.75 improvement for a total of 37.5x instruction count improvement.The size of 2048 bits is especially chosen for the reason that this size is sufficient for the applications targeted. For example this size matches the size of the SBOX(256 bytes) in AES algorithm.

2.2 BNB ISA

The BnB microengine is a 6-stage pipelined architecture, comprising Prefetch (PF), Instruction Fetch (IF), Decode (DE), Execute (EX) , Memory (MEM) and Writeback (WB). All the new BnB instructions execute in the execute stage as shown in 2. Figure 2 shows the block diagram for BnB with memory hierarchy. It uses 2 level cache and 2GB memory. The memory hierarchy was modeled as either DDR or HMC.Each BnB instruction and accompanying intrinsic (for direct software access) is shown in the Table. 1. The columns are: intrinsic definition, machine instruction, and description of the functionality.

3. METHODOLOGY AND EXPERIMENT

Design Configurations: BNB micro-architecture was implemented using the Synopsys CAD flow. For cache and memory simulation, DRAMSim2 [6],Cacti [2]and MARSSim[5] are used. We integrate the Synopsys tool flow with the memory hierarchy simulation tool to do full system online simulation. First the C++ model of the micro-engine was generated for functional simulation and then the RTL of the designed microarchitecture was synthesized to gate level using this CAD flow. Two models are evaluated namely Baseline and BnB. All these models are synthesized to gate-level designs using 32nm and 7nm technology and totally 4 models are evaluated namely BnB-DDR-32nm, BnB-DDR-7nm,BnB-HMC-32nm,BnB-HMC-7nm for performance, and energy metrics. Table 2 shows the configuration of the system implemented. Benchmarks were written in ANSI C + intrinsics, and compiled using a custom compiler generated for the BnB MicroEngine based on the BnB architecture description. Thus any benchmark written in ANSI C language is supported.**Benchmarks (short data, and long vectors):** Benchmarks used for the experiments are GF Multiplication, RLE, AES, 2D Convolution and DWT. For GF multiplication, RLE and AES the input size is 128KB. For 2D convolution and DWT the inpuBt size is 640x480 Byte size pixels. For BnB designs, vectorized code of these benchmarks were implemented using BnB intrinsics and large vector data types are compiled using the BnB compiler and run on the BnB microengines.

4. EXPERIMENTAL RESULTS

4.1 Performance

Performance metrics is detailed in this section by evaluating the instruction count, cycle count and execution time of the BnB designs against scalar version.

Table 1: BnB ISA

Intrinsic	Instruction	Description
shuffle_v2k(dst,src,size)	SHUFFLE2K	Do shuffle between two 2048 bit vectors (size = element size to shuffle)
rotate_v2k(dst,size,count)	VROTATE2	Rotate each element of size "size" in "dst" for "count" times
vxor(dst,src)	VXOR	Do bitwise XOR between dst, src and store result in dst
vand(dst,src)	VAND	Do bitwise AND between dst, src and store result in dst
vor(dst,src)	VOR	Do bitwise VOR between dst, src and store result in dst
vmul(dst,src)	VMUL	Do 64 integer multiplication of src and dst and store result in dst
vadd(dst,src)	VADD	Do 64 integer addition of src and dst and store result in dst
vsub(dst,src)	VSUB	Do 64 integer substraction of src and dst and store result in dst
shift_v2k(dst,size,count)	VSHIFT	Shift right each element of size "size" in "dst" "count" times
vcntlz(dst,src)	VCNTLZ	Count number of leading zeros in src and store the count in dst
svxor (dst,src,size)	SVXOR	Do XOR of "src" over each element of "dst" vector of size 32
rvsmov(dst,src,index)	RVSMOV	Store value in "src" register indexed by "index" in "dst" vector.
vrsmov(dst,src,index)	VRSMOV	Store 32 bit indexed by "index" in "src" vector to "dst" register.
lm_2_vec(dst,src), vec_2_lm(dst,src)	LM2VR, VR2LM	Move data to and from local memory

Table 2: Experimental System - Configuration

Parameter	Value
Core type	In-order, 6-stage pipeline
ISA	MIPS-like ISA
Vector register file	2048b x 16 registers
Cache hierarchy	L1-I: 32KB, 2-cyc latency, L1-D: 24KB, 2-cyc latency, Shared L2: 512KB, 10-cyc latency
Main memory DDR3 (Model I)	2GB/4-rank/16-device DDR3
Main memory HMC (Model II)	4GB/4-rank/8-device
Scratch Pad/Local Memory	4 MB

Instruction Count: Figure 3.a shows the comparison of relative instruction count for the six applications mentioned earlier. For GF, with input size of 128KB, scalar required as much as 45 million instructions and BnB required only 512K - 565K instructions. For GF, 79.5X -87.75X reduction in instruction count was noticed. It should be noted that the instruction count for GF multiplication for all vector sizes are in the range around 550K. The reason for the minor change in the count is that the data movement to the vector accounted for more instructions compared to the actual multiplication operations. Alternatively, for the convolution, the effect of vector size is evident from the fact that the instruction count reduction increases from 25x to 237x, when we move from vector size of 128 to 2048 bits. For all the 6 applications instruction count reduction was between 9- 237x.

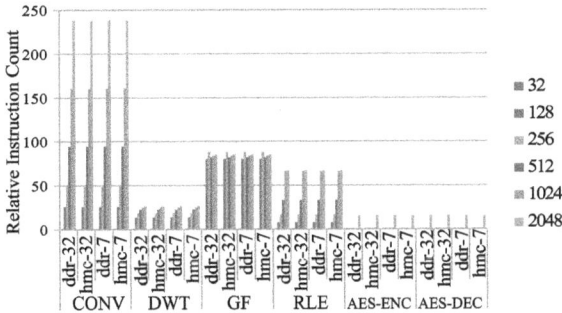

Figure 3: Relative Instruction Count Reduction

Cycle Count/Execution Time: Since we are using multi cycle instructions, the execution time varies compared to instruction count. The performance results for the 6 applications are shown in Figure.4 in *ms*. For the 2D-Convolution and DWT, the bars pass above the graph scale and the actual values are printed next to the bars in "ms". With the technology scaling, the execution time is improved as 32*nm* systems run at 1GHz and 7*nm* systems are running at 4GHz. Most of the benefit on cycle count reduction for convolution and DWT comes by operating on the image

pixels stored in local memory. From Figure. 4 , for 2d convolution, scalar version in 32*nm* technology took around 830 ms and the fastest BnB design was "BnB-2048" executing 2d convolution on a 640x480 pixel image in 3.3 ms. For AES-ENC and AES-DEC, it should be noted that the execution time for scalar, BnB-128,BnB-256,BnB-512 and BnB 1024 are same as they run scalar code.

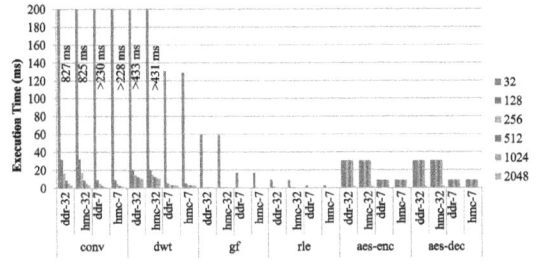

Figure 4: Performance in "ms"

Speedup: The relative performance speedup is shown in Figure. 5 ranges from 19 -248x for BnB designs with DDR3 memory and 20 - 252 x for the BnB designs with HMC memory hierarchy. Convolution achieved the highest speed up of 248x for DDR3 based design and 252x for HMC based designs. For GF application, BnB with 256 bit vector size had highest speedup of 115x for DDR3 based system and 130x for the HMC based system. For AES encoding and decoding BnB-2048 bit system achieved highest benefit of 19x and 21x for DDR3 and HMC based systems respectively. Cycle count reduction due to the computation on data from local memory and the large vector size had high impact on the speedup of AES algorithms. For DWT and RLE the speed up was scaling with vector size with 21x-41x and 7x-61x respectively.

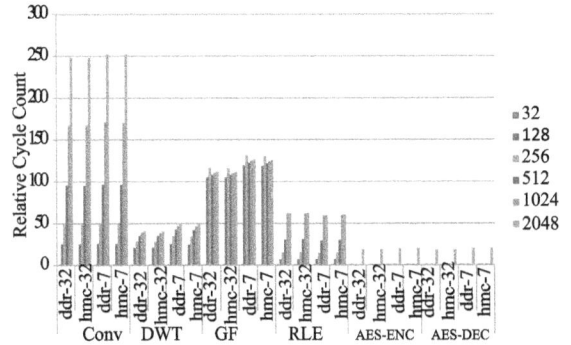

Figure 5: Relative Performance/cycle count

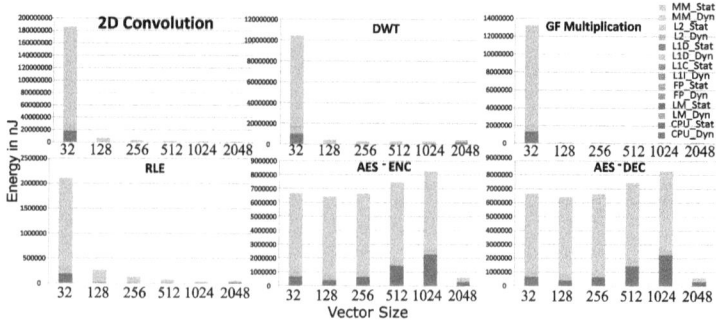

Figure 6: Energy Distribution for $32nm$

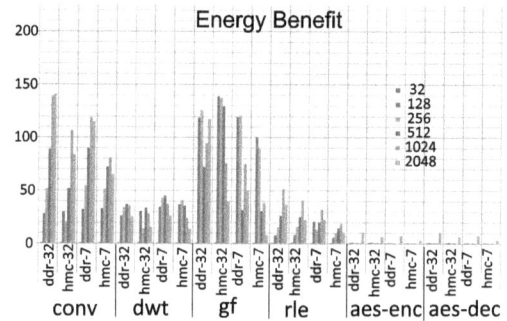

Figure 7: Relative Energy

4.2 Energy

System Energy: The component level energy distribution of the scalar and BnB of different vector sizes is shown in Figure 6.

Operating on the data from the local memory and wider vector datapath influenced the reduction in DRAM energy.For the convolution application, the energy is scaling linearly with the increase in vector size.

However,for the DWT application, the energy was scaling up to the vector size 1024 and for BnB 2048, the energy increased. This is due to the fact that, the balance between larger instruction count reduction with wider vector datapath (dissipating higher power) reaches the equilibrium. Further improvement with BnB-2048 design can be achieved if this data movement is carried out efficiently. Similar trend is seen for the RLE and GF. Nevertheless, there are applications for which most of the computation are vectorized and the energy benefit scales with vector size. An example for this case is the AES application. For AES, the size of S-Box used in the AES algorithm is suitable to the vector size BnB 2048, which is 256 Bytes. As shown in last two graphs of Figure. 6, the energy benefit is higher for BnB-2048 compared to other sizes. The reason for this benefit is of two folds. First, BnB-2048 runs vectorized code and second is that lower vector size designs run the scalar version of the AES.

Energy Benefit: The relative energy benefit of BnB with different vector sizes over scalar version is shown in Figure. 7. It ranges from 7.7x-140.7 x for BnB designs with DDR3 memory and 5.6x - 138.7 x for the BnB designs with HMC memory hierarchy. Convolution achieved the highest benefit of 140.69 x for DDR3 based design and 129x for HMC based designs. For GF application, BnB with 257 bit vector size had highest speedup of 126x for DDR3 based system and BnB with 128 bit vector achieved 138.7x for the HMC based system. For AES encoding and decoding BnB-2048 bit system achieved highest benefit of 10.8x and 7.6x for DDR3 and HMC based systems respectively. For DWT, BnB with 1024 vector size achieved higher benefit of 51x for DDR based system and 40.66x for HMC based system.

4.3 Compute Core and Overall Chip Area

BnB design was implemented in $32nm$ and $5nm$ for 5 different vector sizes (totally 10 different designs were synthesized). For $32nm$, the area of BnB core was ranging from $0.177~mm^2$ to $3.72~mm^2$ (3x - 67x bigger than the scalar version which is $0.055~mm^2$). For $7nm$ design, the area was ranging from $0.003465~mm^2$ to $0.232721~mm^2$. For the whole system of BnB with 2048 vector including the memory hierarchy implemented in $32nm$ and $7nm$, the 4MB local memory consumed 60% of the chip area followed by the L2 cache which consumes 24%. BnB's core constitutes 14% of the total chip area.

5. SUMMARY AND FUTURE WORK

A new microarchitecture for accelerating the lower bit-level operations was proposed in this paper. With the Gate level BnB model integrated with DDR and HMC memory hierarchy, BnB achieved performance benefit ranging from 19x-248x for designs with DDR3 and 20-252 x for the BnB designs with HMC compared to the baseline RISC core with similar memory hierarchies. Energy benefit achieved was from 7.7x-140.7 x for BnB designs with DDR3 memory and 5.6x-138.7 x for the BnB designs with HMC memory hierarchy. Next step is to do physical design of the BnB microarchitecture at $32nm$ and obtained the energy and performance results at layout level.

6. ACKNOWLEDGMENTS

This work is being supported in part by the Defense Advanced Research Projects Agency under award HR0011- 13-2-0014 and the generous Synopsys Academic program.

7. REFERENCES

[1] A.A.Chien, A. Snavely, and M. Gahagan. 10x10: A general-purpose architectural approach to heterogeneity and energy efficiency. In *Proc of the Intl Conf on Computational Science, ICCS , Singapore, 1-3 June, 2011*, pages 1987–1996, 2011.

[2] K. Chen et al. Cacti-3dd: Architecture-level modeling for 3d die-stacked dram main memory. In *DATE*, March 2012.

[3] J. Jeddeloh and B. Keeth. Hybrid memory cube new dram architecture increases density and performance. In *VLSI Technology (VLSIT), 2012 Symp on*, 2012.

[4] Kim et al. 3d-maps: 3d massively parallel processor with stacked memory. In *Solid-State Circuits Conference Digest of Technical Papers (ISSCC), 2012 IEEE International*, pages 188–190, Feb 2012.

[5] A. Patel et al. Marss: A full system simulator for multicore x86 cpus. In *DAC*, 2011.

[6] P. Rosenfeld et al. Dramsim2: A cycle accurate memory system simulator. *Computer Architecture Letters*, 10(1), Jan 2011.

Reduced-latency LLR-based SC List Decoder for Polar Codes

Bo Yuan
University of Minnesota, Twin Cities
200 Union Street SE, Minneapolis, MN 55455
yuan0103@umn.edu

Keshab K. Parhi
University of Minnesota, Twin Cities
200 Union Street SE,Minneapolis, MN 55455
parhi@umn.edu

ABSTRACT

Polar codes, as the new generation of channel codes, have potential applications in communication and storage systems. Successive-cancellation list (SCL) algorithm is the main decoding approach for improving the error-correcting performance of polar codes. Recently low-complexity SCL decoders in the log-likelihood-ratio (LLR) form were proposed to replace the original ones in the likelihood form. However, these LLR-based SCL decoders can only decode 1 bit in one cycle, which leads to very long latency. This paper, for the first time, presents a reduced-latency LLR-based SCL decoder. With the new decoding scheme that determines 2 bits simultaneously, the proposed (n, k) decoder reduces the entire decoding latency from $3n-2$ to $2n-2$ clock cycles with the same critical path delay as the prior LLR-based SCL decoders. As a result, the decoding throughput and hardware efficiency are increased by a factor of 1.5. In addition, compared to a prior reduced-latency non-LLR-based SCL decoder, the proposed work reduces the area by two times as well.

Categories and Subject Descriptors

B.5 [**Hardware**]: Register-Transfer-Level implementation;

B.5.1 [**Design**]: Style (e.g., parallel, pipeline, special-purpose)

Keywords

Polar codes, LLR, Decoder, SC, List, Reduced-latency, VLSI

1. INTRODUCTION

Due to their interesting capacity-achieving property, the research on polar codes [1] has been one of the most active topics among the channel codes. In particular, many investigations [1-7] were conducted to design high-performance decoder. Among those works, successive-cancellation list (SCL) decoding algorithm [1] is viewed as the best decoding approach since it can improve the error-correcting performance of polar codes significantly. However, from the aspect of VLSI design, the original likelihood-based SCL decoders were challenged with the long latency and high complexity. To address these problems, [5] proposed a low-latency likelihood-based 2b-SCL algorithm to reduce the decoding latency. Besides, [6-7] proposed to represent the SCL algorithm with the form of log-likelihood-ratio (LLR) instead of likelihood to save area. However, the above works only focused on reducing either latency or complexity but not both.

GLSVLSI '15, May 20-22, 2015, Pittsburgh, PA, USA
Copyright 2015 ACM 978-1-4503-3474-7/15/05...$15.00
http://dx.doi.org/10.1145/2742060.2742108

This paper, for the first time, presents a reduced-latency LLR-based SCL decoder, which can achieve both low complexity and short latency. Compared to the likelihood-based SCL decoder, the LLR representation in the proposed decoder leads to great reduction in complexity. More importantly, compared to the original LLR-based SCL decoder that only determines 1 bit in one cycle, the proposed decoder, namely *LLR-based 2b-SCL*, enables the decoding of 2 bits simultaneously. As a result, the entire decoding latency is reduced from $3n-2$ to $2n-2$ cycles for (n, k) polar codes. Hardware analysis shows that the proposed LLR-based 2b-SCL decoder achieves 1.5 times increase in decoding throughput and hardware efficiency than the original LLR-based SCL decoder. In addition, compared to non-LLR-based 2b-SCL decoder, this work reduces the entire gate count by a factor of 2.

The rest of this paper is organized as below. Section 2 reviews the polar codes. The proposed LLR-based 2b-SCL decoding algorithm is derived in Section 3. Section 4 presents the hardware architecture. Hardware performance is discussed in Section 5. Section 6 draws the conclusions.

2. REVIEW OF POLAR CODES

2.1 Polar Codes

Different from other block codes, the encoding process of polar codes utilizes the pre-selected frozen positions. For (n, k) polar encoding, the first step is to expand the original k-bit message to an n-bit message $u=(u_1, u_2,...u_n)$. The padded $(n-k)$ bits, which are forced to be "0", are referred to frozen bits that are located at frozen positions. Then, the intermediate message u is multiplied with n-by-n generator matrix G to generate transmitted codeword $x=(x_1, x_2,...x_n)=uG$. Fig. 1 shows an encoder for n=4 polar codes. For details of polar encoding process, the reader is referred to [1].

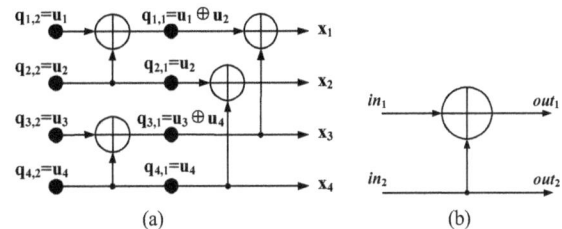

Fig. 1. (a) n=4 polar encoder. (b) Basic unit of encoder, cited from [5].

2.2 Likelihood-based SC Decoder

At the receiver end, the received codeword $y=(y_1, y_2,...y_n)$ is usually different from x due to the corruption of noise. Therefore, a polar SC decoder is used to recover u from y. Fig. 2 shows an example SC decoding procedure for n=4 polar codes. Here the decoder consists of two types of unit, namely as **f** and **g**. Each unit is labelled with a number that indicates the time index when the unit is activated. Notice that at the final stage (stage-2 in this example), a hard-decision unit h is used to output the decoded bit.

As indicated in [5], the functions of **f** and **g** units can be simply derived from encoding procedure. For any polar encoder, the basic computation block is shown in Fig. 1(b). It is seen that this basic block performs left-to-right transformations as $out_1 = in_1 \oplus in_2$ and $out_2 = in_2$, where $\oplus$ is the exclusive-or operation. Correspondingly, the basic block of SC decoder performs the right-to-left estimations from the likelihoods of out_1 and out_2 to the likelihoods of in_1 and in_2 (see Fig.2 (b). Therefore, the expected relationships between the estimated in_1, in_2, out_1 and out_2 are: $\widehat{in}_1 = \widehat{out}_1 \oplus \widehat{out}_2$ and

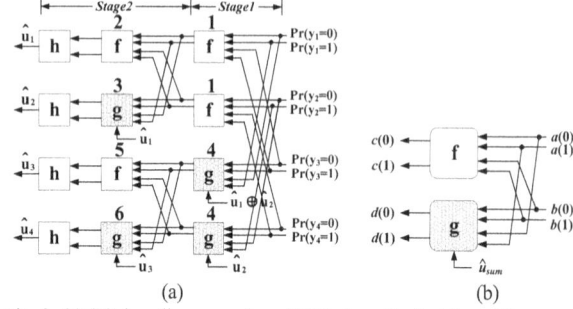

$$\widehat{in}_2 = \widehat{out}_2 \qquad (1).$$

Fig. 2. (a) SC decoding procedure. (b) Basic unit, cited from [5].

With (1), the functions of **f** and **g** can now be developed. Assume the previous decoded bits $\hat{u}_1$, $\hat{u}_2$,... $\hat{u}_{i-1}$ are determined as z_1, z_2,...z_{i-1} and this event is denoted as $\hat{u}_1^{i-1} = z_1^{i-1}$, then we have:

$$c(0) = \Pr(\widehat{in}_1 = 1, \hat{u}_1^{i-1} = z_1^{i-1}) = a(0)b(1) + a(1)b(0) \qquad (2)$$

$$c(1) = \Pr(\widehat{in}_1 = 1, \hat{u}_1^{i-1} = z_1^{i-1}) = a(0)b(1) + a(1)b(0) \qquad (3)$$

$$d(0) = \Pr(\widehat{in}_2 = 0, \widehat{in}_1 = \hat{u}_{sum}, \hat{u}_1^{i-1} = z_1^{i-1}) = a(\hat{u}_{sum})b(0) \qquad (4)$$

$$d(1) = \Pr(\widehat{in}_2 = 1, \widehat{in}_1 = \hat{u}_{sum}, \hat{u}_1^{i-1} = z_1^{i-1}) = a(1 - \hat{u}_{sum})b(1) \qquad (5)$$

Notice that here the likelihood inputs of **f** and **g** units are denoted as $a(0) = \Pr(\widehat{out}_1 = 0, \hat{u}_1^{i-1} = z_1^{i-1})$, $a(1) = \Pr(\widehat{out}_1 = 1, \hat{u}_1^{i-1} = z_1^{i-1})$, $b(0) = \Pr(\widehat{out}_2 = 0, \hat{u}_1^{i-1} = z_1^{i-1})$ and $b(1) = \Pr(\widehat{out}_2 = 1, \hat{u}_1^{i-1} = z_1^{i-1})$.

2.3 Likelihood-Based 2B-SCL Decoder

For practical use of polar codes, SCL algorithm that consists of multiple SC component decoders is usually adopted to improve the performance of polar codes. However, the original SCL algorithm is challenged with its inherent long latency. Because the SCL algorithm can only decode one bit in one cycle, its overall decoding latency is $3n-2$ cycles. To solve this problem, a reduced-latency likelihood-based 2^Kb-SCL decoder was proposed in [5]. Fig. 5 illustrates the difference in metric computation between SCL and 2^Kb-SCL decoder with example $K=1$. It can be seen that for 2b-SCL case the original last stage of SC component decoder is replaced with the metric computation unit (MCU) and zero forcing unit (ZFU) that can calculate the metrics of length-($2i$) each time (see Fig. 3(b)). As a result, 2 bits can be decoded at the same time. As analyzed in [5], the overall decoding latency of 2b-SCL decoder is reduced from $3n-2$ to $2n-2$ cycles. For detail of likelihood-based 2b-SCL algorithm, the reader is referred to [5].

3. LLR-BASED 2B-SCL DECODER

As discussed in Section 2.3, 2^K bits decision were proposed to reduce the latency of SCL decoders. Besides, use of LLR instead of

likelihood in SCL algorithm was proposed in [6-7] to save area. However, these two methods only focused on achieving either low complexity or short latency but not both. In addition, the integration of these two approaches is non-trivial due to their different derivations. As a result, in this subsection we present the LLR-based 2^Kb-SCL algorithm. Notice that here we only show the reformulating procedure for 2b-SCL ($K=1$) case. The derivation for other K will be investigated in the future work.

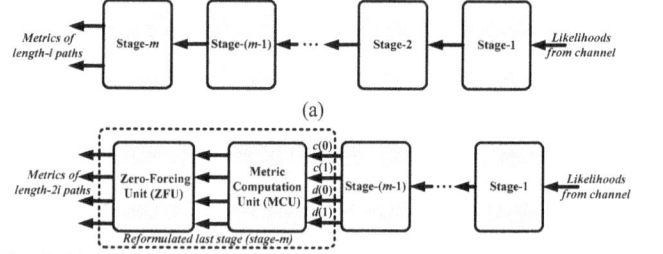

(a)

Fig. 3. (a) Original SC component decoder. (b) Reformulated likelihood-based 2b-SCL component decoder, cited from [5]. Here $m=\log_2 n$.

First, as presented in [4], (2)-(5) that compute propagating messages can be converted into LLR form as below:

$$c = 2\tanh^{-1}(\tanh(\frac{a}{2})\tanh(\frac{b}{2})) \approx sign(a)sign(b)\min(|a|,|b|) \qquad (6)$$

$$d = a(-1)^{\hat{u}_{sum}} + b \qquad (7)$$

where $c=\ln(c(0)/c(1))$, $d=\ln(d(0)/d(1))$, $a=\ln(a(0)/a(1))$ and $b=\ln(b(0)/b(1))$ are the LLR-based messages.

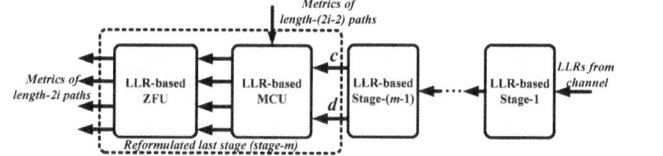

Fig. 4. LLR-based reformulated SC component decoder.

Next, we show how to calculate the metric of length-($2i$) path from the metric of length-($2i-2$) path in the LLR form. Similar to [5], the general idea is to replace the last stage of original decoder with a new LLR-based MCU and ZFU (see Fig. 4). Assume that the current decoded 2 bits are determined as α and β, respectively. Then according to the definition of path metric, the metric of length-($2i$) path is $\Pr(\hat{u}_{2i-1} = \alpha, \hat{u}_{2i} = \beta, \hat{u}_1^{2i-2} = z_1^{2i-2})$. With the use of logarithmic domain representation, we have:

$$M_{\alpha,\beta,2i} = \ln(\Pr(\hat{u}_{2i-1} = \alpha, \hat{u}_{2i} = \beta, \hat{u}_1^{2i-2} = z_1^{2i-2}))), \qquad (8)$$

where $M_{\alpha,\beta,2i}$ represents the metric of length-($2i$) path when $\hat{u}_{2i-1} = \alpha, \hat{u}_{2i} = \beta, \hat{u}_1^{2i-2} = z_1^{2i-2}$.

Notice that (8) can be re-written as below:

$$M_{\alpha,\beta,2i} = \ln(\Pr(\hat{u}_{2i-1} = \alpha, \hat{u}_{2i} = \beta \mid \hat{u}_1^{2i-2} = z_1^{2i-2})))$$

$$=\ln(\Pr(\hat{u}_{2i-1} = \alpha, \hat{u}_{2i} = \beta \mid \hat{u}_1^{2i-2} = z_1^{2i-2})\Pr(\hat{u}_1^{2i-2} = z_1^{2i-2}))$$

$$=\ln(\Pr(\hat{u}_{2i-1} = \alpha, \hat{u}_{2i} = \beta \mid \hat{u}_1^{2i-2} = z_1^{2i-2}))+\ln(\Pr(\hat{u}_1^{2i-2} = z_1^{2i-2})). \qquad (9)$$

Recall that $\Pr(\hat{u}_1^{2i-2} = z_1^{2i-2})$ is the metric of length-($2i-2$) path. Hence (9) can be further reformulated as:

$$M_{\alpha,\beta,2i} = \ln(\Pr(\hat{u}_{2i-1} = \alpha, \hat{u}_{2i} = \beta \mid \hat{u}_1^{2i-2} = z_1^{2i-2})) + M_{2i-2} \quad (10)$$

where $M_{2i-2} = \ln(\Pr(\hat{u}_1^{2i-2} = z_1^{2i-2}))$ is the logarithmic domain metric for length-($2i$-2) path.

In addition, because $\hat{u}_{2i-1}$ and $\hat{u}_{2i}$ are now determined independently, the first item of (10) can be re-written as:

$$\ln(\Pr(\hat{u}_{2i-1} = \alpha, \hat{u}_{2i} = \beta \mid \hat{u}_1^{2i-2} = z_1^{2i-2}))$$

$$= \ln(\Pr(\hat{u}_{2i-1} = \alpha \mid \hat{u}_1^{2i-2} = z_1^{2i-2}) \Pr(\hat{u}_{2i} = \beta \mid \hat{u}_1^{2i-2} = z_1^{2i-2}))$$

$$= \ln(\Pr(\hat{u}_{2i-1} = \alpha \mid \hat{u}_1^{2i-2} = z_1^{2i-2})) + \ln(\Pr(\hat{u}_{2i} = \beta \mid \hat{u}_1^{2i-2} = z_1^{2i-2})) \quad (11)$$

Recall that for the last stage $\widehat{out}_1 = \hat{u}_{2i-1} = \alpha$ and $\widehat{out}_2 = \hat{u}_{2i} = \beta$. Then according to (1), the expected relationship between the inputs and outputs of the basic unit of last stage is $\widehat{in}_1 = \alpha \oplus \beta$ and $\widehat{in}_2 = \beta$. Therefore, we have:

$$\ln(\Pr(\hat{u}_{2i-1} = \alpha \mid \hat{u}_1^{2i-2} = z_1^{2i-2})) = \ln(\Pr(\widehat{in}_1 = \alpha \oplus \beta \mid \hat{u}_1^{2i-2} = z_1^{2i-2})),$$

$$\ln(\Pr(\hat{u}_{2i} = \beta \mid \hat{u}_1^{2i-2} = z_1^{2i-2})) = \ln(\Pr(\widehat{in}_2 = \beta \mid \hat{u}_1^{2i-2} = z_1^{2i-2})). \quad (12)$$

Besides, as shown in Fig. 4, c and d are the LLR-based inputs to the reformulated last stage. Notice c and d can be interpreted as:

$$c = \ln\left(\frac{\Pr(\widehat{in}_1 = 0, \hat{u}_1^{2i-2} = z_1^{2i-2})}{\Pr(\widehat{in}_1 = 1, \hat{u}_1^{2i-2} = z_1^{2i-2})}\right) = \ln\left(\frac{\Pr(\widehat{in}_1 = 0 \mid \hat{u}_1^{2i-2} = z_1^{2i-2})}{\Pr(\widehat{in}_1 = 1 \mid \hat{u}_1^{2i-2} = z_1^{2i-2})}\right),$$

$$d = \ln\left(\frac{\Pr(\widehat{in}_2 = 0, \hat{u}_1^{2i-2} = z_1^{2i-2})}{\Pr(\widehat{in}_2 = 1, \hat{u}_1^{2i-2} = z_1^{2i-2})}\right) = \ln\left(\frac{\Pr(\widehat{in}_2 = 0 \mid \hat{u}_1^{2i-2} = z_1^{2i-2})}{\Pr(\widehat{in}_2 = 1 \mid \hat{u}_1^{2i-2} = z_1^{2i-2})}\right) \quad (13)$$

Since the sum of numerator and denominator in (13) is 1, we have:

$$\Pr(\widehat{in}_1 = \alpha \mid \hat{u}_1^{2i-2} = z_1^{2i-2}) = (e^c)^{1-\alpha} / (e^c + 1)$$

$$\Pr(\widehat{in}_2 = \beta \mid \hat{u}_1^{2i-2} = z_1^{2i-2}) = (e^d)^{1-\beta} / (e^d + 1) \quad (14)$$

Finally, by summarizing (10)(11)(12)(14), we have:

$$M_{\alpha,\beta,2i} = M_{2i-2} + (1-\alpha \oplus \beta)c - \ln(e^c+1) + (1-\beta)d - \ln(e^d+1) \quad (15)$$

(15) describes the LLR-based principle that calculates the metric of length-($2i$) path from the metric of length-($2i$-2) path. However, these equations contain $\ln(\cdot)$ operation that is infeasible for hardware implementation. Therefore, (15) needs to be simplified.

Consider $\ln(1+e^x) \approx x$ for large x; otherwise 0, we can have the approximated equation as (16).

In general, after receiving the LLR-based messages c and d from stage-(m-1), MCU utilizes (16) to replace the current metrics of length-($2i$-2) paths as M_{2i-2} with the new metrics of length-($2i$) survival paths as $M_{\alpha,\beta,2i}$. Then similar to [5], a ZFU unit is used to force some path metrics to zero based on the pre-determined frozen positions. Notice that because the computation is in the LLR form, hence the original forced zero changes to forced negative infinite, namely $-inf$. As a result, the proposed LLR-based 2b-SCL algorithm is summarized as scheme A.

$$M_{\alpha,\beta,2i} \approx \begin{cases} M_{2i-2} - (\alpha \oplus \beta)c - \beta d & c \geq 0 \text{ and } d \geq 0 \\ M_{2i-2} - (\alpha \oplus \beta)c + (1-\beta)d & c \geq 0 \text{ and } d < 0 \\ M_{2i-2} + (1-\alpha \oplus \beta)c - \beta d & c < 0 \text{ and } d \geq 0 \\ M_{2i-2} + (1-\alpha \oplus \beta)c + (1-\beta)d & c < 0 \text{ and } d < 0 \end{cases} \quad (16)$$

Scheme A: LLR-based (n, k) 2b-SC list decoding (LLR-2b-SCL) with list size L

1: **Input:** *Log - Likihood ratios of each bit in the received codeword*
2: **Initialization:** *Path metric $M_0 = 0$ for each survival path*
3: **For** $i = 1$ to $n/2$
4:     For each length-($2i-2$) survival path $(\hat{u}_1, ... \hat{u}_{2i-2}) \triangleq z_1^{2i-2}$ with metric M_{2i-2}
5:     **SC decoding:**
6:         *Activate stage -1 to stage -(m-1) of LLR-based SC component decoder*
7:         *stage -(m-1) output LLR-based message c and d*
8:     **Path Expansion:**
9:         *Expand survival path z_1^{2i-2} to 4 candidate paths $(z_1^{2i-2}, \hat{u}_{2i-1}, \hat{u}_{2i})$:*
10:         *1 length -($2i-2$) path $\Rightarrow$ 4 length -($2i$) paths*
11:     **Metric Computation:**
12:         *Calculate path metrics for 4 length -($2i$) paths $M_{i,0}$ by (16)*
13:         $M_{0,0,2i}$ for path $(z_1^{2i-2}, 0, 0)$, $M_{0,1,2i}$ for path $(z_1^{2i-2}, 0, 1)$
14:         $M_{1,0,2i}$ for path $(z_1^{2i-2}, 0, 0)$, $M_{1,1,2i}$ for path $(z_1^{2i-2}, 0, 1)$.
15:     **Forcing Zero:**
16:         $M_{\alpha,\beta,2i}$ for path $(z_1^{2i-2}, \alpha, \beta)$ with $\alpha, \beta \in \{0,1\}$
17:         **if** $\hat{u}_{2i-1}$ is frozen, **then** $M_{1,0,2i} = -\inf$ and $M_{1,1,2i} = -\inf$.
18:         **if** $\hat{u}_{2i}$ is frozen, **then** $M_{0,1,2i} = -\inf$ and $M_{1,1,2i} = -\inf$.
19:   **End for**
20:     **Compare and Prune:**
21:     *Compare the metrics $M_{\alpha,\beta,2i}$ of all the $4L$ length -($2i$) candidate paths*
22:     *Select L paths with the L largest metrics as the new survival paths*
23: **End for**
24: **Output:** *Choose the length -n survival path with the largest metric*

4. HARDWARE ARCHITECTURE

4.1 Overall Architecture

Based on Scheme-A in Section 3, the overall architecture of LLR-based 2b-SCL decoder is shown in Fig. 5. In general, the L-size 2b-SCL decoder consists of L SC component decoders. Here the SC component decoder is very similar to the one that was discussed in [4]. The only difference is that the last stage is reformulated to an LLR-based MCU and ZFU (see Fig. 4). In addition, the entire LLR-based 2b-SCL decoder contains three types of memory banks, which store the LLR messages, survival paths and the corresponding path metrics, respectively. Besides, as indicated in the line 20~22 in Scheme-A, a sorting block is used to sort the path metric and select the L larger ones.

Because the design of LLR-based PE, memory banks and sorting block has been discussed in [4-5], in this section we focus on the key components of LLR-based 2b-SCL decoder as MCU and ZFU.

4.2 LLR-based MCU&ZFU

Fig. 6 shows the inner architecture of MCU&ZFU block, which implements the function that is described in lines 11~18 in scheme-A. Here the *signal(c)* and *signal(d)* are the control signals that indicate whether the input LLR-based messages c and d are larger than 0 or not. In addition, *ctrl1* and *ctrl2* are the control signals that indicate whether the $\hat{u}_{2i-1}$ and $\hat{u}_{2i}$ are the frozen bits or not. Here the input and output metrics and LLR messages are quantized with q bits. C2S and S2C blocks perform the conversion between sign-magnitude-based and 2's complement-based representations.

5. PERFORMANCE ANALYSIS

Table 1 analyzes the hardware performance of the q-bit quantized LLR-based 2b-SCL decoder with the example (1024, 512) polar code. Here the list size L is 2 and the overall architecture of the decoder is set as line-based architecture. As analyzed in [5], the critical path of the SC list decoder is located in the sorting block. With the use of data path balancing technique in [5], the critical path delays of the proposed LLR-based 2b-SCL decoder and the referred SCL decoders are only $3T_{c\&s}$, where $T_{c\&s}$ represents the critical path of the "compare and swap" operation in the sorting block. Because the proposed LLR-based 2b-SCL can determine 2 bits simultaneously, its overall decoding latency is the same as the likelihood-based 2b-SCL decoder as $2n-2$ clock cycles. As a result, compared to the LLR-based SCL decoder in [7] that has the latency of $3n-2$ cycles, the proposed decoder achieves 33% reduction in decoding latency. In addition, compared to the non-LLR-based 2b-SCL decoder in [5], the proposed decoder saves the total gate count by 50% due to the use of LLR representation.

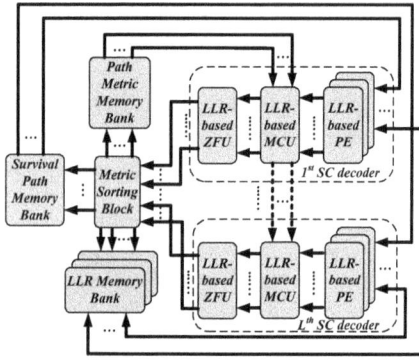

Fig. 5. Overall architecture of LLR-based 2b-SCL decoder.

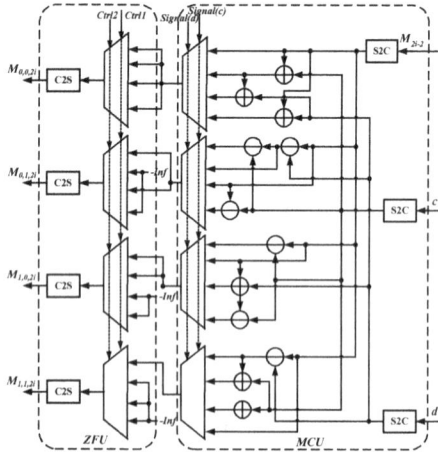

Fig. 6. The architecture of LLR-based MCU and ZFU.

Because the coded decoding throughput of polar decoder is calculated as $n/$(critical path delay*latency), the proposed LLR-based 2b-SCL decoder has 1.5 times speedup in throughput than the LLR-SCL decoder. As seen in Table 1, because the width of quantization bits should be around $q=6$ for negligible decoding performance loss, the area overhead of the proposed LLR-based 2b-SCL decoder is very small (less than 1%). As a result, the hardware efficiency of the proposed decoder, as defined as throughput/gate count, can achieve 1.5 times speedup than the LLR-SCL decoder. In addition, compared to the non-LLR-based 2b-SCL decoder, the proposed LLR-2b-SCL decoder increases the hardware efficiency by 2 times as well.

Table 1. Hardware Analysis of LLR-based 2b-SCL Decoder

Design		LLR-2b-SCL	LLR-SCL [7]	Non-LLR-2b-SCL[5]
PE	**# of PE**	Ln/2=1024		
	Gate count	~17q		~34q
MCU	**# of MCU**	L=2		L=2
	Gate count	~123q/2	~21q/2	~16q
ZFU	**# of ZFU**	L=2	N/A	L=2
	Gate count	~14q		~12q
Sorting	**# of sorting**	1	1	1
	Gate count	~76q	~20q	~64q
Bits of Memory Bank		4096q+2048		8120q +2048
Total Gate Count		~(21731q +2048)	~(21545q +2048)	~(43056q +2048)
Critical Path delay		$3T_{c\&s}$		
Latency (clock cycles)		2046	3070	2046
Throughput (normalized)		~1.5	1	~1.5
Hardware Efficiency (normalized)		~1.5	1	~0.75

6. CONCLUSION

This paper presents LLR-based 2b-SCL decoder that decodes 2 bits simultaneously. Compared to prior SCL decoders, the proposed decoder achieves both low complexity and short latency.

7. REFERENCES

[1] E. Arıkan, "Channel polarization: A method for constructing capacity-achieving codes for symmetric binary-input memoryless channels," *IEEE Trans. Inf. Theory*, 2009.

[2] A. Alamdar-Yazdi and F. R. Kschischang, "A simplified successive-cancellation decoder for polar codes," *IEEE Commun. Lett.*, 2011.

[3] I. Tal and A. Vardy, "List decoding of polar codes," arXiv:1206.0050, 2012.

[4] B. Yuan and K.K. Parhi, "Low-latency successive-cancellation polar decoder architectures using 2-bit decoding," *IEEE Trans. CAS-I*, 2014.

[5] B. Yuan and K.K. Parhi, "Low-Latency Successive-Cancellation List Decoders for Polar Codes with Multi-bit Decision," *IEEE Trans. on VLSI Systems, 2015*

[6] A. Balatsoukas-Stimming, M. Bastani Parizi and A. Burg, "LLR-based Successive Cancellation List Decoding of Polar Codes", in *Proc. of IEEE ICASSP*, 2014.

[7] B. Yuan and K.K. Parhi, "Successive Cancellation List Polar Decoder using Log-likelihood Ratios," in *Proc. of 2014 Asilomar Conf. on Signal, Systems and Computers*, 2014.

Delay, Power and Energy Tradeoffs in Deep Voltage-scaled FPGAs

Monther Abusultan and Sunil P Khatri

ECE Department, Texas A&M University, College Station, TX 77843

ABSTRACT

In this paper, we present a circuit-level analysis of deep voltage-scaled FPGAs, which operate from full supply to sub-threshold voltages. The logic as well as the interconnect of the FPGA are modeled at the circuit level, and their relative contribution to the delay, power and energy of the FPGA are studied by means of circuit simulations. Three representative designs are studied to explore these design trade-offs. We conclude that the energy and delay-minimal FPGA design is one in which both the interconnect and logic are curtailed from scaling below a fixed voltage (about 550mV in our experiments). If power is a more important design factor (at the cost of delay), it is beneficial to operate both the logic and interconnect between 300mV and 800mV.

Categories and Subject Descriptors: B.7.1 [Types and Design Styles]: VLSI (very large scale integration)

Keywords: Low Power FPGA Interconnect; Sub-threshold FPGA; PVT Variation Cancellation; Adaptive Body Bias Control Circuit.

1. INTRODUCTION

The popularity of field programmable gate arrays (FPGAs) [1, 2] as a means to implement digital designs has been growing rapidly. The main reason for this is the effectiveness of the FPGA based design approach for low and mid volume designs. Compared to ASIC and custom designs, FPGAs exhibit a faster design turnaround time and lower non-recurring engineering (NRE) cost. It is conjectured that the recent reduction in the number of ASIC designs [3] (due to the increasing cost of generating IC fabrication masks), has added to the growing popularity of FPGAs.

FPGAs consist of a number of logic islands. Each island implements a small part of the entire logic programmed on the FPGA. Logic islands are made up of one or more look-up tables (LUTs). Each LUT can implement any logic function of up to n inputs (where n varies from 4 to 6 depending on the FPGA device).

Sub-threshold operation holds great promise in the design of extreme low power circuits, with a penalty in delay compared to full supply voltage circuits [4], [5]. These circuits can deliver up to $\sim 200 \times$ lower power, with a ~ 20-$40 \times$ nominal delay penalty. These characteristics make sub-threshold circuits practical for hand-held, sensor network or wearable electronics. However the delay of sub-threshold circuits have an exponential dependence on PVT variations. To address these variations [6, 7, 8, 9] used body biasing. The approaches of [6, 7, 9] use an on-the-fly, dynamic body biasing approach. With such approach, the delay variation was reduced from 2-3 orders of magnitude to about $1.2 \times$.

In this work, we present results on an FPGA design which is able to consume extremely low power when the computational needs are low, and operate at high speed when the computational demands

GLSVLSI'15, May 20–22, 2015, Pittsburgh, PA, USA.
Copyright © 2015 ACM 978-1-4503-3474-7/15/05 ...$15.00.
http://dx.doi.org/10.1145/2742060.2742120.

are high. Past work on this area has focused on the logic (LUT) or interconnect aspects of the design. Our work models *both* the logic and the interconnect, to study the power, delay and energy trade-offs of a sub-threshold FPGA.

The key contributions of our paper are listed below:

- We evaluate an FPGA which can operate over a wide range of supply voltages and operating frequencies.
- Our design is based on the LUT design of [9] which operates from sub-threshold through full supply voltages. The interconnect of our FPGA largely resembles that of a Xilinx Virtex 7 XC7VX550T device.
- We study the trade-off of delay, power and energy by using three benchmark designs.
- Our experiments show for these designs, it is best not to scale the voltage below 550mV, to minimize energy and delay.

The remainder of this paper is organized as follows. Section 2 discusses previous work in the area of sub-threshold FPGAs. Section 3 describes the details of the FPGA design which utilizes dynamic body biasing. Section 4 presents the results of experiments we performed to validate our approach. We conclude with Section 5.

2. PREVIOUS WORK

In [10], the authors evaluated the design of LUT structures that operate at full supply voltage. The authors of [11] study the use of CMOS transmission gates results in FPGA LUTs. In [12], the authors focus on reducing both active and stand-by leakage for a LUT-based FPGA. The authors propose circuit modifications to the output buffers and write blocks of the LUT to reduce leakage. The work of [10], [11] and [12] does not attempt to address sub-threshold LUT operation, or the design of LUTs which have a wide range of operating frequency (and power).

Achieving reliable sub-threshold operation requires compensation of PVT variations, since they have a significant impact on I_{ds} (and hence the worst-case delay of the circuit). Therefore, for reliable operation, a sub-threshold circuit has to include a dynamic mechanism that cancels PVT variations. The sub-threshold FPGA LUT design approach in [9] implements dynamic body bias control for both the NMOS and PMOS devices, to enable the LUT to operate over a wide range of supply voltages as well as operating frequencies. This enables the possibility of trading off the power consumed versus the delay over a wide range of supply voltages. The work of [9] is conceptually similar to those of [6, 13, 7], where the authors proposed the use of a phase-detector and a charge pump to dynamically self-adjust for PVT variations in a sub-threshold design approach for ASICs. In [6, 13, 7] the Nbulk voltage was limited to 0.4 V to avoid forward biasing of the PN junctions.

In [14], the authors present power management and memory architecture enhancements in the Stratix-III and Stratix-IV FPGA architectures. The authors use two levels of body biasing (Vbb_HS for high speed and Vbb_LP for low power) to control static leakage power. In contrast to [9], the work in [14], is not sub-threshold operation capable and the body biasing used is not dynamic.

A review paper on sub-threshold design was presented in [15], in which the authors suggested an ultra dynamic voltage scaling technique, which dynamically scales the power supply voltage to sub-threshold operation. In contrast, traditional dynamic voltage scaling techniques restrict the minimum supply voltage to super-threshold operation [16, 17], providing less aggressive power scaling, while ensuring that PVT variations do not become an issue. Body-biasing based compensation for these variations was mentioned briefly in [15]. The work of [15] is substantially introductory in nature, devoting a good deal of attention to the basics of sub-threshold operation, problems, and challenges. A short section discusses sub-threshold FPGAs, with a focus on interconnect in sub-threshold operation.

Among the previous work, one set of paper focuses on LUT design ([10, 11, 12]) or sub-threshold body biased LUT design ([9, 14]). Another set focuses on interconnect for sub-threshold FPGA ([15]). In contrast, we focus on computing the total delay, power and energy of our sub-threshold FPGA (logic *as well as* interconnect). We use three different benchmark circuits to study the power, delay and energy trade-offs. The FPGA design that we use in our simulations is based on the electrical characteristics of the Xilinx Virtex 7 XC7VX550T FPGA device.

3. APPROACH

3.1 Overview

Previous papers have focused on either sub-threshold FPGA interconnect, or sub-threshold FPGA LUT design. In this paper we study a complete sub-threshold FPGA design (interconnect and logic). The focus is on studying the delay, power and energy trade-offs for an FPGA that can operate over a wide range of supply voltages. The interconnect structure in our FPGA follows that of a Xilinx Virtex 7 XC7VX550T FPGA device. Our sub-threshold FPGA design is implemented using 22 nm PTM [18] technology, while the Xilinx Virtex 7 is implemented using a 28 nm technology node. Our LUT structure is based on the LUT design proposed in [9].

3.2 Building Blocks

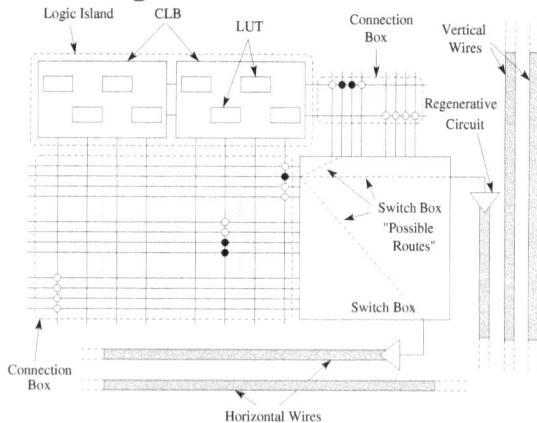

Figure 1: Sub-threshold FPGA Building Blocks

To characterize the behavior of the sub-threshold capable FPGA, we divide the FPGA's architecture into smaller blocks as shown in Figure 1. The building blocks studied in this paper are the Lookup Table (LUT), Connection Box (CB), Switch Box (SB) and Wires of various lengths. The LUTs in our FPGA are clustered in groups of 4 LUTs per configurable logic block (CLB), with two CLBs per *logic island*. This mimics the logic structure of the Xilinx Virtex 7 (XC7VX550T) FPGA device. The wire lengths used in our study are single (L1), double (L2), quad (L4), Long 12 (L12) and Long 18 (L18). These wire lengths substantially follow the wire lengths available in the Xilinx Virtex 7 (XC7VX550T) FPGA with the exception of hex (L6) wires which we omitted for simplicity. The lengths of these wires are multiples of L1, which is the shortest wire available. An L1 wire connects CLBs in adjacent logic islands. Hence, the length of an L1 wire is equal to the distance between two adjacent logic islands.

The delay, power and energy of our FPGA will be split into logic and interconnect. The delay, power and energy of each building block will be accounted for in the computation of the logic or interconnect delay, power and energy depending on whether the building block is a logic or interconnect block. The LUT and CB are considered logic blocks. On the other hand, the SB and wires are considered interconnect blocks.

3.2.1 LUT

The LUT design in our work is similar to the LUT design of [9].

In FPGAs, multiple LUTs are placed in CLBs. These LUTs can be used separately to implement logic functions or can be combined to implement larger logic functions. In our sub-threshold FPGA design, each CLB consists of 4 LUTs following the architecture of the Xilinx Virtex 7 XC7VX550T FPGA device. CLBs are placed such that two CLBs are available in each logic island. Each logic island is dynamically body-bias controlled, in the manner described in [9].

3.2.2 Connection Box

The CB is a group of switches that route signals into and out of the logic island. The CB is implemented as a full matrix of switches that allows each wire leaving (entering) the CLB to connect to a group of wires going into (coming from) an adjacent switch box (SB). Figure 1 shows two connection boxes, one that routes signals into the CLB and the other that routes signals coming out from the CLB. In Figure 1, each switch in the CB is represented by a circle. A solid circle represents an ON switch and an empty circle represents an OFF switch. In our design, switches in the CB are implemented as passgates. The transistors in each CB are dynamically body biased.

3.2.3 Switch Box

The SB is also a group of switches that route signals. SBs can route a signal coming from any source (a wire or a CB) into any destination (which can be either a wire or an adjacent CB, to eventually go into the corresponding CLB). There are several popular SB design topologies, as described in [19, 20, 21]. Although these different SB topologies differ in their routing scheme, they all follow one general rule. This rule is that each signal entering the SB can be only routed to any of three destinations. This means that the difference between these SB topologies only impacts the place and route tools, which need to know the possible routes for each signal. However, from a circuit point of view, each signal entering the SB sees three switches which can either be ON or OFF based on where the signal is routed. This means that our circuit model of the SB is generic, and can support any SB topology. Figure 1 shows a representative SB. The three dashed lines inside the SB depict three potential connections originating from the same input. Similar to the CB, the switches in the SB are also implemented as passgates. These passgates are also dynamically body biased.

In our model, we account for the difference in delay, power and energy of the SB in both the cases when the SB is a) passing a signal between a CB and a wire and b) when it is passing a signal between two wires. It is important to distinguish these two cases because a different input drive strength or load is seen at the output in each of these cases. Our tools infer which of the two models should be used for each SB input after the design is synthesized, placed and routed.

3.2.4 Wires

As mentioned earlier, we have five different wire lengths in our proposed sub-threshold through full supply capable FPGA implementation. These wire lengths are L1, L2, L4, L12 and L18 following that of the Xilinx Virtex 7 XC7VX550T FPGA device. L1 is the shortest wire, used to connect between any two adjacent SBs. The Length of L1 in our FPGA implementation was found to be 18.6 μm, based on the area of each logic island. Consequently, the lengths of the remaining wires, L2, L4, L12 and L18 are 37.2 μm, 74.4 μm, 223.2 μm and 334.8 μm respectively.

We use a regenerative circuit to regenerate the signals before they propagate through a wire segment of length L1. Figure 1 shows both wires and regenerative circuits. These regenerative circuits consist of a low switch-point inverter and a pullup keeper device similar to that used in the LUT design. The size of the NMOS and PMOS devices in the low switch-point inverter are L = 22 nm and W = 88 nm for the NMOS device, and L = 22 nm and W = 44 nm for the PMOS device. The size of the pullup keeper (PMOS) is L = 110 nm and W = 44 nm.

4. EXPERIMENTS

In this section, we discuss the tools that were used to simulate our design. Next, we present and analyze the results of implementing the benchmark circuits on our FPGA (which supports sub-threshold to full supply operation).

4.1 Tools Used in our Simulations

In order to compute the delay, power and energy of a design implemented on our FPGA, we developed two design flows, a physical design flow and a synthesis design flow.

The physical design flow starts by modeling the RC parasitics of the five different wires supported by our FPGA design (L1, L2, L4, L12, L18). A 3-dimensional structure of a metal stack containing the wires was modeled in Raphael [22] to extract the RC parasitics of each wire. The 3-dimensional structure was constructed based on DRC rules obtained from ITRS 2012 specifications [23]. The resultant resistance and capacitance of the modeled wires are converted into a π RC network. This allows us to model the wires as a distributed RC model, in order to produce accurate simulation results when modeling long wires. These π models are then simulated in HSPICE with the rest of the building blocks (LUT, CB and SB) to produce delay, power and energy models which will be used to produce the final delay, power and energy of the benchmark circuits.

The synthesis flow begins by synthesizing the benchmark circuit HDL and generating the routed design in Xilinx Native Circuit Description (NCD) format for the FPGA device chosen (Xilinx Virtex 7 XC7VX550T FPGA in our work). Since we are using an FPGA architecture that matches that of XC7VX550T, the routed design obtained from the Xilinx tools will match our FPGA as well. The next step in the synthesis flow is to convert the NCD netlist into a parseable Xilinx Design Language (XDL) netlist. XDL is a library provided by Xilinx to allow third-party developers to view and edit a design in the NCD format. The XDL netlist provides all the information we need about the LUTs, CBs, SBs and wires used to route the design on the XC7VX550T FPGA device. In order to map the design into our FPGA (which supports sub-threshold to full supply operation), we wrote scripts to perform a mapping of the Xilinx netlist to our FPGA (the only exception is mapping L6 wires in the XC7VX550T to L4 wires in our FPGA model). Once this mapping is completed, we compute the delay, power and energy of the final circuit which are reported later in this paper.

4.2 Benchmark Circuits

We used three benchmark circuits to test our FPGA implementation. The three benchmark circuits that we used are:

- Ethernet IP [24]: IP supported by Xilinx IP generator.
- CopyBlaze [25]: A microprocessor similar to PicoBlaze.
- AVR HP [25]: A hyper-pipelined AVR microcontroller.

4.3 Results and Analysis

In this section, we will discuss the delay, power and energy of the Ethernet IP benchmark Using the results for this benchmark, we propose an optimal approach of operating the FPGA in low power/energy mode. The results of the remaining benchmarks (CopyBlaze and AVR HP) quantitatively match the conclusion drawn from the results of the Ethernet IP benchmark, hence, omitted for brevity.

Figures 2(a), 2(b) and 2(c) show the delay of the Ethernet IP benchmark. The x-axis shows the supply voltage at three different body biasing points (0V to the left, 225mV in the middle and 450mV to the right) and the y-axis shows the delay. The body bias numbers shown in the figure reflect the body bias applied to the NMOS devices. The body bias applied to PMOS devices is numerically equal to VDD minus the body bias reported on the plot. The maximum body bias we allow in our FPGA is 450mV, in order to prevent any diodes from turning on which would cause a current/thermal spike. In Figures 2(a), 2(b) and 2(c) we show the delay of logic and interconnect as the supply is swept from 300mV to 800mV. As expected, the delay of the logic and the interconnect increases as the supply is decreased. The rate at which the delay increases is exponential in the sub-threshold region (following the sub-threshold leakage current equation presented in Section 3). Also, when we compare the curves of the plot at each biasing point, we clearly see that the delay is decreased as the applied body bias is increased. Comparing logic delay and interconnect delay, we see that interconnect delay is consistently larger than logic delay at all points ($\sim 4\times$ larger).

Figure 2(b) and Figure 2(c) show the same plots as in Figure 2(a) except that in Figure 2(b) we limit the supply voltage of the interconnect network between 550mV and 800mV. Note that the logic still operates between 300mV and 800mV. The reason why this particular range was chosen will be discussed later in this section, when we discuss the energy plot. As seen in Figure 2(b), since the supply voltage of the interconnect network is limited to a minimum of 550mV, the delay of interconnect becomes much smaller than that of logic (about $2.9\times$ smaller) at the lowest supply voltage of the FPGA. Figure 2(c) shows the delay of logic and interconnect when we limit the supply voltage of both logic and interconnect between 550mV and 800mV. The delays in Figure 2(c) track those of Figure 2(a) except that the delays are fixed below 550mV indicating that the supply voltage does not drop below that point. In effect 550mV is the lowest supply that the FPGA is operated at.

Figures 2(d), 2(e) and 2(f) show the power consumption of running the Ethernet IP on our FPGA (which supports sub-threshold to full supply operation). Similar to the delay plots, the x-axis shows the supply voltage at three body biasing points. The y-axis shows the power consumed (μW). Figure 2(d) shows that when no body biasing is applied, the logic and interconnect power consumption is similar at lower supply voltages. At higher supply voltages, logic power consumption becomes slightly larger. As we apply more body biasing, the gap between logic power consumption and interconnect power consumption becomes wider. We see the same trend when we limit the supply voltages to a minimum of 550mV. These plots show that the power consumption of the logic components of the Ethernet IP implemented on our FPGA is higher than the power consumed by the interconnect components of the same benchmark.

Figure 2(g), Figure 2(h) and Figure 2(i) show the energy utilization of running the Ethernet IP on our FPGA. The x-axis shows the supply voltage at three body biasing points and the y-axis shows the energy utilized (pJ). Figure 2(g) shows that the energy as the supply voltage is increased from 0.3V to 0.8V at three body biasing points. The interconnect energy curve has a U-shape, clearly indicating an optimal operating point, where the energy has a minimum value at 550mV. Decreasing the supply voltage below this point causes the energy utilization to increase, hence it is practical to limit the supply voltage to voltages higher than 550mV. When the supply voltage drops below 550mV, the drastic increase in delay (for both interconnect and logic) outweighs the savings in power, causing the energy to increase. On the other hand, although the energy used increases as the supply voltage is increased above 550mV, these operating points are useful due to the need to achieve faster operation (the delay decreases as we increase the supply voltage). Therefore, we propose

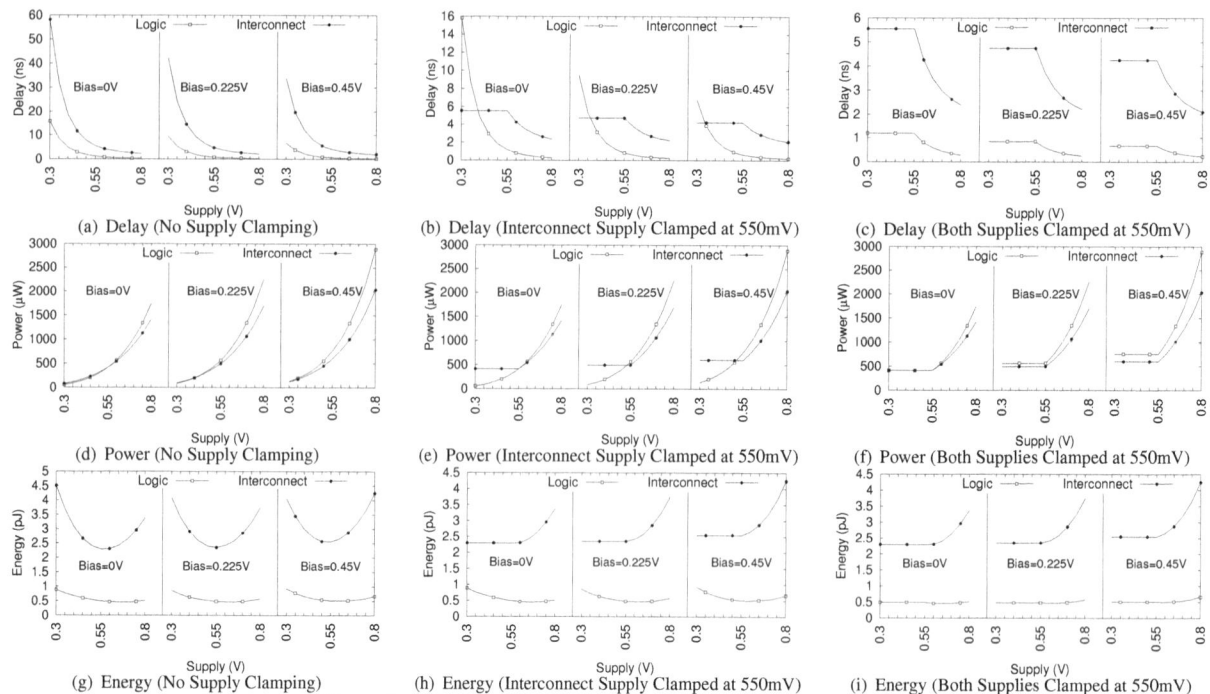

(a) Delay (No Supply Clamping) (b) Delay (Interconnect Supply Clamped at 550mV) (c) Delay (Both Supplies Clamped at 550mV)

(d) Power (No Supply Clamping) (e) Power (Interconnect Supply Clamped at 550mV) (f) Power (Both Supplies Clamped at 550mV)

(g) Energy (No Supply Clamping) (h) Energy (Interconnect Supply Clamped at 550mV) (i) Energy (Both Supplies Clamped at 550mV)

Figure 2: Ethernet IP Benchmark Delay, Power and Energy

limiting the supply voltage of the FPGA interconnect network to the range from 550mV to 800mV as shown Figure 2(h). The logic energy curves are much more flat than the interconnect energy curves, but they still follow the same trend. We see that the energy used by the logic components of the FPGA start increasing as we drop the supply voltage below 550mV. Although the increase in energy is much smaller than its interconnect counterpart, it is also beneficial to limit the logic supply voltage between 550mV and 800mV since decreasing the logic supply voltage below 550mV will increase the delay without saving energy. Consequently, we suggest limiting the supply voltage of the entire sub-threshold FPGA to the range from 550mV to 800mV (configuration (c)). Note that if delay is not an important factor, and power is more important, it would be beneficial to operate both the interconnect and the logic between 300mV and 800mV (configuration (a)). An alternate approach would allow full voltage scaling for logic, but scale the interconnect between 550mV and 800mV (configuration (b)), to obtain improved delay, but higher power than configuration (a).

The trends for the CopyBlaze and AVR HP benchmarks for configurations (a), (b) and (c) are similar to those shown in Figures 2 and are omitted for brevity.

5. CONCLUSIONS

FPGAs are inherently inefficient in terms of power and energy. Since low power/energy designs are very important in contemporary practice, we focus our attention on deep voltage-scaled operation of the FPGA. Our experiments assume the logic and interconnect of a commercial FPGA, and we demonstrate the delay, power and energy trade-offs using three benchmark designs. We conclude that it is most efficient (from a delay and energy standpoint) to operate the FPGA above 550mV. If power is a more important design factor (at the cost of delay), it is beneficial to operate both logic and interconnect between 300mV and 800mV.

6. REFERENCES

[1] S. Trimberger, ed., *Field-Programmable Gate Array Technology.* Netherlands: Kluwer Academic Publishers Group, 1994. ISBN: 9780792394198.

[2] S. D. Brown, R. J. Francis, J. Rose, and Z. G. Vranesic, *Field-programmable gate arrays.* Norwell, MA, USA: Kluwer Academic Publishers, 1992.

[3] A. Sangiovanni-Vincentelli, "The tides of EDA." Keynote Talk, Design Automation Conference, June 2003.

[4] J. Rabaey, *Digital Integrated Circuits: A Design Perspective.* Prentice Hall Electronics and VLSI Series, Prentice Hall, 1996.

[5] N. Weste and K. Eshraghian, *Principles of CMOS VLSI design - a systems perspective.* Addison-Wesley, 1988.

[6] N. Jayakumar and S. P. Khatri, "A variation-tolerant sub-threshold design approach," *Proceedings, Design Automation Conference*, June 2005.

[7] S. Paul, R. Garg, S. P. Khatri, and V. S., "Design and Implementation of a Sub-threshold BFSK Transmitter," *Int'l Symposium on Quality Electronic Design (ISQED)*, Mar. 2009.

[8] J. Zhou, M. Ashouei, D. Kinniment, J. Huisken, and G. Russell, "Extending Synchronization from Super-Threshold to Sub-threshold Region," *IEEE Asynchronous Circuits and Systems (ASYNC)*, 2010.

[9] M. Abusultan and S. P. Khatri, "Look-up table design for deep sub-threshold through full-supply operation," in *Proc. of Int'l Symposium on Field-Programmable Custom Computing Machines*, May 2014.

[10] P. Chow, S. O. Seo, J. Rose, K. Chung, G. Paez-Monzon, and I. Rahardja, "The design of a SRAM-based field-programmable gate array-Part II: Circuit design and layout," *IEEE Trans. on Very Large Scale Integration Systems*, Sept. 1999.

[11] C. Chiasson and V. Betz, "Should FPGAs abandon the pass-gate?," in *Field Programmable Logic and Applications (FPL), 2013 23rd Int'l Conf. on*, 2013.

[12] A. Lodi, L. Ciccarelli, D. Loparco, R. Canegalloa, and R. Guerrieri, "Low leakage design of LUT-based FPGAs," in *Proceedings of the 31st European Solid-State Circuits Conference (ESSCIRC)*, Sept 2005.

[13] N. Jayakumar, R. Garg, B. Gamache, and S. P. Khatri, "A PLA based asynchronous micropipelining approach for subthreshold circuit design," *ACM/IEEE 43rd Design Automation Conference*, Sept. 2006.

[14] D. Lewis, E. Ahmed, D. Cashman, T. Vanderhoek, C. Lane, A. Lee, and P. Pan, "Architectural enhancements in Stratix-III™ and Stratix-IV™," in *Proc. of Int'l Symposium on Field Programmable Gate Arrays*, FPGA '09, 2009.

[15] B. Calhoun, J. Ryan, S. Khanna, M. Putic, and J. Lach, "Flexible Circuits and Architectures for Ultralow Power," *Proc. of the IEEE*, Feb. 2010.

[16] T. Burd, T. Pering, A. Stratakos, and R. Brodersen, "A dynamic voltage scaled microprocessor system," *IEEE Journal of Solid-State Circuits*, Nov. 2010.

[17] S. Lee and T. Sakurai, "Run-time voltage hopping for low-power real-time systems," *Design Automation Conference Proceedings*, 2000.

[18] "PTM website." http://ptm.asu.edu/.

[19] G. G. Lemieux and S. D. Brown, "A detailed routing algorithm for allocating wire segments in field-programmable gate arrays," in *Proc. Physical Design Workshop, Lake Arrowhead, CA*, 1993.

[20] Y.-W. Chang, D. F. Wong, and C. K. Wong, "Universal switch modules for fpga design," *ACM Trans. Des. Autom. Electron. Syst.*, Jan. 1996.

[21] S. J. E. Wilton, *Architectures and Algorithms for Field-programmable Gate Arrays with Embedded Memory.* PhD thesis, 1997.

[22] "Synopsys website." http://www.synopsys.com/.

[23] "ITRS website." http://www.itrs.net/.

[24] "Xilinx website." http://www.xilinx.com/.

[25] "OpenCores website." http://www.opencores.org/.

Phase-based Cache Locking for Embedded Systems

Tosiron Adegbija and Ann Gordon-Ross*

Department of Electrical and Computer Engineering, University of Florida (UF), Gainesville, FL 32611, USA

tosironkbd@ufl.edu & ann@ece.ufl.edu

*Also affiliated with the NSF Center for High-Performance Reconfigurable Computing (CHREC) at UF

ABSTRACT

Since caches are commonly used in embedded systems, which typically have stringent design constraints imposed by physical size, battery capacity, real-time deadlines, etc., much research focuses on cache optimizations, such as improved performance and/or reduced energy consumption. Cache locking is a popular cache optimization that loads and retains/locks selected memory contents from an executing application into the cache to increase the cache's predictability. Previous work has shown that cache locking also has the potential to improve cache performance and energy consumption. In this paper, we introduce *phase-based cache locking*, which leverages an application's varying runtime characteristics to dynamically select the locked memory contents to optimize cache performance and energy consumption. Experimental results show that our phase-based cache locking methodology can improve the data cache's miss rates and energy consumption by an average of 24% and 20%, respectively.

Categories and Subject Descriptors

B.3.2 [**Hardware**]: Memory Structures: Design Styles – *cache memories.*

General Terms

Design.

Keywords

Cache locking, phase-based tuning, energy savings, configurable caches, dynamic optimization.

1. INTRODUCTION AND MOTIVATION

Caches are commonly used in embedded systems to bridge the processor-memory performance gap by exploiting the spatial and temporal locality of memory accesses. However, caches can contribute significantly to overall system energy consumption (e.g., the ARM920T's caches consume up to 44% of the microprocessor's overall energy consumption [15]). Therefore, much research focuses on cache optimizations, such as improved performance and/or reduced energy consumption, while satisfying an embedded system's intrinsic design constraints imposed by physical size, battery capacity, real-time deadlines, consumer market competition, etc.

Cache locking is a popular cache optimization that loads and retains/locks selected contents/memory blocks (regions of

GLSVLSI'15, May 20–22, 2015, Pittsburgh, PA, USA.
Copyright © 2015 ACM 978-1-4503-3474-7/15/05…$15.00.
http://dx.doi.org/10.1145/2742060.2742076

instruction and/or data addresses) from an executing application into the cache. Cache locking can be done either at system startup (static cache locking) or dynamically during runtime (dynamic cache locking), and is available in modern embedded processors, such as the ARM Cortex processors [3]. These cores support special lock subroutines that lock the selected contents into the cache such that locked contents cannot be evicted by the cache's replacement policy. Since accesses to locked contents will always produce a cache hit, these addresses' access times are predictable.

Cache locking traditionally benefits execution time predictability when using caches, especially in real time systems where the worst-case execution time (WCET) must be estimated. In these systems, the cache contents are typically known statically and cache locking ensures that the memory access times and cache related preemption delays are predictable for the locked contents, allowing tighter WCET estimation. Previous work [9] showed that cache locking benefits also include improved cache performance in general purpose embedded systems by eliminating conflict misses and guaranteeing a hit for the locked contents. Additionally, cache locking can result in reduced dynamic energy since cache locking can reduce cache misses, and thus reduce the energy consumed when accessing lower memory levels and associated stalls.

However, cache locking also reduces the cache's overall utilization. Since portions of the cache are exclusively used for the locked contents, the effective cache capacity is reduced and conflict misses may increase for the memory blocks that are not locked. For cache locking to be effective, the locked contents must represent application regions that significantly affect overall cache performance and energy consumption. If the contents are poorly selected, cache locking can significantly degrade performance [21] and/or energy, especially for static cache locking where the locked contents are retained throughout the system's lifetime.

Prior cache locking methods (e.g., [14]) used static cache locking to improve instruction cache predictability in real time systems where the applications and cache contents are known at design time. However, assuming this a priori knowledge limits these methods' applicability to general purpose embedded systems (e.g., smartphones, tablets, etc.), which typically execute a large variety of applications that are unknown at design time. Furthermore, those studies focused on improving predictability without necessarily improving cache performance and/or energy. Alternatively, dynamic cache locking [4][7][21] adjusts the locked contents at runtime to further improve cache predictability and reduce dependence on a priori application and cache content knowledge..

Anand et al. [2], Liang et al. [9], and Liu et al. [10] used cache locking to optimize instruction cache performance in general purpose embedded systems, but none of these works evaluated cache locking's energy benefits. Additionally, since an application typically processes much more data than the number of instructions executed, most prior cache locking methods, if applied directly to the data cache, would require a large data cache and/or potentially result in runtime overhead in terms of performance and/or energy, since complex runtime analysis would be required due to the inherent runtime variability of data caching [21].

Therefore, we propose a new methodology for leveraging cache locking for data cache performance and energy consumption optimizations in general purpose embedded systems. The locked data cache contents are dynamically selected, loaded, and retained at runtime based on the application's intrinsic runtime variable characteristics (e.g., cache miss rates, branch mispredicts, etc.). Unlike instructions, which typically remain fixed during execution, applications process different data streams during runtime, thus our cache locking method dynamically changes the locked contents based on the application's changing data. Prior work showed that *phase classification* can partition an application's execution into execution intervals and group intervals with similar and stable characteristics as *phases*, which typically exhibit data reuse [16]. Our work leverages this data reuse and is based on the premise that cache performance and energy consumption can be optimized if memory blocks with high reuse are locked in the cache, guaranteeing that all accesses to that data are cache hits. Our analyses showed that a few *persistent phases* repeat several times throughout an application's execution, thus we propose to lock those persistent phases' data in the cache, thereby eliminating the conflict misses for those phases.

In this paper, we propose *phase-based cache locking* to dynamically select locked data cache contents for cache performance and energy consumption optimization. We empirically show that cache locking can significantly reduce the data cache's energy consumption when the locked contents are selected to minimize an application's conflict misses.

2. BACKGROUND AND RELATED WORK

Much previous work studied cache locking's execution time predictability benefits and phase classification for exploiting an application's runtime variability in isolation. However, little prior work exploits cache locking for optimizing the cache's performance and/or energy consumption while considering runtime variability. In this section, we present general related work and background on cache locking and phase classification, which we leverage for dynamically selecting the locked contents.

2.1 Cache Locking

Cache locking is primarily used in hard real time systems to improve the cache's predictability and facilitate tighter WCET estimations as compared to a system without cache locking—a non-locking cache. Puaut et al. [14] proposed greedy algorithms for selecting the locked contents in hard real time systems. Vera et al. [21] combined compile-time cache analysis with data cache locking to enable tight WCET estimation in real time systems. Since these works targeted real time embedded systems where the executing applications are typically known a priori, these works have limited applicability to general purpose embedded systems. Furthermore, even though these works improved cache predictability, these works did not explicitly focus on improving the cache performance and the proposed cache locking methods could potentially increase the conflict misses for the memory blocks that are not locked [21].

To improve the cache performance in general purpose embedded systems, Liang et al. [9] presented an instruction cache locking heuristic to select the locked contents in order to realize cache locking's performance benefits by reducing the conflict misses. The proposed heuristic reduced the cache miss rates by up to 24%. Anand et al. [2] used detailed, iterative cache simulations to evaluate the performance benefits for locking different memory blocks. However, due to the detailed cache simulations and number of iterations involved, this method would incur significant runtime

overhead if used for dynamic cache locking. Additionally, since the authors used static cache locking, this method is not applicable to systems where the executing applications are unknown a priori. Liu et al. [10] proposed an algorithm that dynamically determined the instruction cache's locked contents to improve the average-case execution time (ACET). However, these works did not evaluate the energy benefits of cache locking, and since these works focused on the instruction cache, the inherent runtime variability of data caches were not considered.

Using simulations, Asaduzzaman et al. [5] showed that cache locking could potentially improve cache performance and reduce power consumption. Yang et al. [21] used a dynamic programming algorithm to determine the locked contents in order to improve the data cache's power consumption and performance. However, the authors used a compiler-assisted technique that constrained the proposed method to systems where the executing applications were known a priori.

Our work differs from previous cache locking methods by using dynamic cache locking in the data cache to optimize the cache's performance and energy consumption. We propose a phase-based methodology that dynamically selects the locked contents, incurs minimal runtime overhead, and makes our work applicable to general purpose embedded systems where the executing applications may be unknown a priori.

2.2 Phase Classification

Since dynamically leveraging phase characteristics can significantly increase optimization potential by specializing the optimizations to different phases of execution [1][8][17], much prior work explored different phase classification techniques. Sherwood et al. [17] showed that phase classification using basic block distribution was highly correlated with application characteristics, such as cache miss rates, instructions per cycle (IPC), branch mispredictions, etc. Hamerly et al. [8] created SimPoint, which used machine-learning techniques to identify an application's phases by analyzing basic block vectors that were annotated with the block's execution frequency. Shen et al. [16] showed a strong correlation between data locality and an application's phase characteristics, and showed that data reuse patterns could be used to classify phases. Since phase characteristics are strongly correlated with the phases' data reuse patterns, our work leverages phase classification and the phases' data reuse to select an application's locked contents to optimize the data cache's performance and energy consumption.

3. PHASE-BASED CACHE LOCKING

Our phase-based cache locking methodology selects the locked contents such that the cache's performance and energy consumption are improved compared to a default non-locking cache. Additionally, our methodology determines if an application will benefit from cache locking based on the phases' persistence, such that our methodology never degrades the performance and/or energy consumption as compared to a non-locking cache. In this section, we describe our phase-based cache locking architecture, our methodology for selecting the locked contents, and present our phase-based cache locking algorithm.

3.1 Architecture and Implementation

Our work assumes line locking [7], which is supported in the ARM processor family [3]. Line locking enables individual lines to be locked for different cache sets, as opposed to way locking, where all the lines in a particular cache way are locked. Figure 1 depicts our phase-based cache locking architecture for a sample dual-core system, where each core has private level one (L1) instruction and data caches. The phase-based cache locking module (referred to as the locking module for brevity herein) connects directly to each

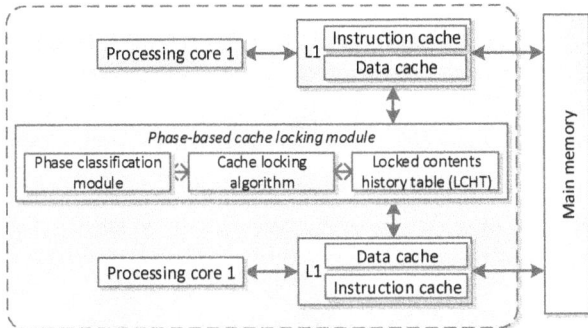

Figure 1. Phase-based cache locking architecture

core's L1 data cache, thus this architecture is extendable to any *n*-core system by connecting the locking module to each core's L1 data cache. Since the locking module contains simple logical operations, the locking module can be implemented using small custom hardware or a lightweight co-processor process to facilitate easy integration into current embedded system microprocessors.

The locking module contains a *phase classification module* to classify the applications' phases and determine the phases' persistence, a *cache locking algorithm*, and a *locked contents history table (LCHT)*. The LCHT is a small hardware or software data structure with per-application entries that retain information (memory addresses and working set sizes) of an application's locked phases' data for subsequent executions of that application. The LCHT's size can be dynamic or fixed depending on the memory constraints of the system, and a replacement policy, such as least recently used (LRU), can be used when the table is full. When a new application is executed, an entry is added to the LCHT.

Figure 2 depicts the LCHT entry's basic structure, which includes: application A_i's identification ID; the memory addresses of A_i's locked contents *lockedContents(Ai)* as selected by the cache locking algorithm; *noLockedContents* and *profile* flags, which default to '0' and indicate if A_i benefits from cache locking and if A_i has been profiled, respectively; and two fields to store A_i's cache miss rate and energy while executing with a non-locking cache for determining if A_i benefits from cache locking (Section 3.3). We estimate the LCHT's overhead in Section 3.4.

Traditional static cache locking restricts the cache's replacement policy from considering locked contents for replacement throughout the system's lifetime. Alternatively, dynamic cache locking inserts special lock and unlock instructions that call the microprocessor's cache locking subroutines. These subroutines disable or enable the cache's replacement policy at the beginning and end of locked contents, respectively. However, since the application code is modified, which alters the application's memory map, data may be

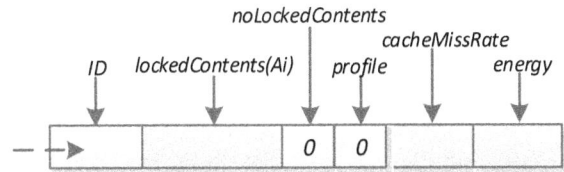

Figure 2. Locked contents history table (LCHT) entry basic structure

written to, and/or read from, the wrong cache sets. Our cache locking methodology avoids application code modification by using the debug registers, which store program counter values that represent the beginning and ending instructions of the locked content's phase. The locking module sets the debug registers such that the exception handler loads and locks the contents in the cache. Using this method does not modify the application's memory map, and can be directly used with any legacy binary. Previous work [4] using a similar method showed that this method accrued negligible runtime overhead.

3.2 Selecting the Locked Contents

To select the locked contents, our phase-based cache locking methodology leverages application execution locality, wherein the majority of an application's execution, measured by the number of dynamic instructions executed, typically occurs within a few persistent phases that access the same data. To ascertain the extent of application execution locality, we analyzed several applications and the applications' phases to evaluate the benefits of locking these phases' data in the cache. Our analysis revealed that for cache locking to provide any cache locking benefits, phase P_i's execution must comprise at least 10% of application A's total execution. Based on this observation, we define a phase P_i as persistent if:

$$P_i \in A : I_{Pi} \geq 0.1 * I_{total} \tag{1}$$

where A represents all of the phases in application A, I_{Pi} is P_i's number of instructions, and I_{total} is A's total number of instructions. We quantify P_i's persistence ρ using the percentage of A's total execution that belongs to P_i, where ρ is given as:

$$\rho = \frac{I_{Pi}}{I_{total}} \tag{2}$$

and ρ is a percentage between 0 and 100%. We note that persistence is a necessary, but not sufficient condition for P_i to provide cache locking benefits.

Figure 3 analyzes phase persistence for an arbitrary subset of applications from SPEC CPU2006 [19]. The x-axis depicts the applications' distinct phases (the number of phases per application varies) and the y-axis depicts the percentage of each application's execution that belongs to each phase (total phase execution percentage for each application totals 100%). We evaluated SPEC benchmarks because these benchmarks show a greater variation during execution than typical embedded system benchmark suites, which typically model specific kernels, rather than complete embedded system applications that would be comprised of several of these kernels (e.g., a digital camera's application would contain specific kernels, such as JPEG compression and decompression, MPEG compression and decompression, etc.).

Figure 3 shows that the majority of applications have a few phases that are significantly more persistent than the other phases, suggesting that these application's phases are amenable to cache locking. For example, 56% of *calculix*'s execution is spent in two phases while the remaining 44% of the execution is spent in the remaining six phases—7% on average for each remaining phase with a 0.03 standard deviation. 51% of *gromacs*'s execution is spent

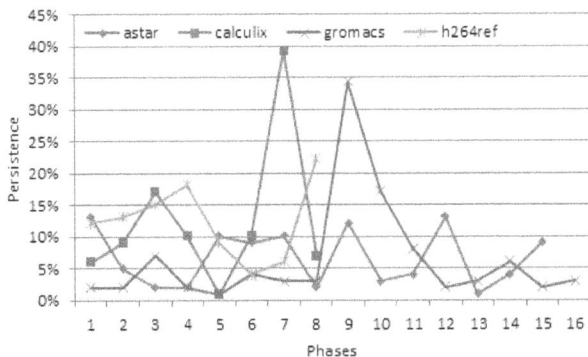

Figure 3. Phase persistence for SPEC2006 benchmarks.

```
1    Inputs: Aᵢ;
2    Outputs: @lockedContents(Ai);
3    if(!(lockedContents(Ai) in LCHT)) {
4        #profile Ai to determine phases and persistence
5            execute(Ai);
6            @phases_Ai, p(phases_Ai) <- profile(Ai);
7            #sort phases' persistence in descending order
8            @pers_phases_Ai = sort {p{$b} <=> p{$a}
9                } @phases_Ai;
10           foreach phase(@pers_phases_Ai) {
11               if(sizeOf(lockedContents(Ai)) <=
12                   sizeOf(maxLockedCache)) {
13                       push(@lockedContents(Ai), phase);
14               }
15               else {
16                   break;
17               }
18           }
19           storeLockedContentsLCHT(Ai);
20           profile = 1;
21   }
22   if(lockedContents(Ai) in LCHT &&
23       profile = 1) {
24           #Ai previously executed once
25           loadAndLock(@lockedContents(Ai));
26           execute(Ai);
27           if(missRates(locking) > missRates(non-locking)
28               || energy(locking) > energy(non-locking))
29           {
30                   noLockedContents = 1;
31           }
32           profile = 0;
33   }
34   elsif(lockedContents(Ai) in LCHT &&
35       profile = 0) {
36           #locked contents have been determined
37           loadAndLock(@lockedContents(Ai));
38   }
39   if(noLockedContents = 1) {
40       #Ai has no locked contents
41       break;
42   }
```

Algorithm 1. Phase-based cache locking algorithm

in two phases while the remaining 49% of the execution time is spent in the remaining fourteen phases—3% on average for each remaining phase with a 0.02 standard deviation. Since only two phases represent nearly half of *calculix* and *gromacs*'s execution, these applications would benefit the most from cache locking if these two most persistent phases were locked in the cache. Alternatively, since *h264ref*'s execution is relatively evenly spread across all of the application's eight phases, *h264ref* has less potential to benefit from phase-based cache locking since no phase has a prominent persistence. Our phase-based cache locking methodology identifies these applications, and executes these applications with a non-locking cache to prevent performance and/or energy degradation. Results in Section 4 verify these persistence-based cache locking benefit hypotheses.

Since phase classification has been extensively studied, and data reuse is highly correlated with phase characteristics, the phase classification module profiles the application with a non-locking cache during the application's first execution. The phase classification module uses a phase classification technique similar to [17] to partition the application's execution into phases and uses Equations (1) and (2) to determine the phases' persistence at runtime. Low-overhead, custom hardware profiles the application and groups the application's intervals into phases. The phases are formed at runtime by tracking the program counter (PC) from committed branch instructions and the number of instructions between the current and previous branch to create a basic block

vector for each execution interval. Each interval's vector is compared with previous vectors, and similar intervals are grouped into phases. We refer the reader to [17] for additional details.

Without loss of generality and considering general purpose embedded systems, our methodology assumes a system without preemption. However, our methodology could easily incorporate preemption by saving the LCHT's profiling state on application preemption, and restoring the profiling state on resumption. Our future work will evaluate the impact of preemption and context switches on our methodology's effectiveness.

3.3 Phase-based Cache Locking Algorithm

Algorithm 1 depicts our phase-based cache locking algorithm, which takes as input application A_i and outputs an array of A_i's locked contents' memory addresses *lockedContents(Ai)* (lines 1-2). For each application A_i, if the LCHT contains no entry for A_i, our cache locking algorithm profiles and selects A_i's locked contents during A_i's first execution using the non-locking cache (lines 3-21). After A_i completes execution, the algorithm selects A_i's locked contents by sorting A_i's persistent phases by persistence in descending order (lines 7-9), and selects phases for locking in descending order until the total data locked by the selected phases exceeds *maxLockedCache* (lines 10-18). The total data is the working set size of the locked contents, where the working set size is calculated by the number of unique 64-byte blocks accessed by the selected phases. *maxLockedCache* is the maximum percentage of the cache that can be locked, and defaults to 50%. We empirically determined that at least 50% of the cache must remain unlocked to minimize conflict misses for the memory blocks that are not locked for an application to benefit from cache locking.

After selecting the locked contents, a new entry for A_i containing A_i's locked contents' memory addresses are added to the LCHT and the *profile* flag is set (lines 19-20). For subsequent executions of A_i, if the LCHT contains an entry for A_i's locked contents and *profile* is set, this is A_i's second execution and the cache locking algorithm locks the selected contents, and determines if A_i will benefit from cache locking after A_i's second complete execution. The cache locking algorithm determines if A_i benefits from cache locking by comparing A_i's cache miss rate and energy consumption while executing with and without locked contents. If cache locking increases the cache miss rate or energy consumption with respect to the non-locking cache, the cache locking algorithm sets the *noLockedContents* flag to '1', implying that A_i does not benefit from cache locking. The cache locking algorithm then sets the *profile* flag to '0' to indicate that cache locking's benefit has been determined for A_i (lines 22-33).

If A_i's locked contents' memory addresses are in the LCHT and the *profile* flag is '0' (i.e., A_i has been previously profiled), *loadAndLock()* triggers the processor's cache locking subroutines (Section 3.1), which load and lock A_i's locked contents in the cache for the duration of A_i's execution (lines 34-38). Alternatively, if *noLockedContents* is set, A_i is executed with the non-locking cache (lines 39-42).

3.4 Computational Complexity and LCHT Hardware Area and Power Overhead

Our phase-based cache locking algorithm sorts the persistent phases N with worst-case time complexity $O(N \log N)$ and selects the locked contents with worst-case time complexity $O(N)$. Given that these operations dominate the algorithm, the algorithm results in minimal computational overhead and has good scalability.

```
totalEnergy = dynamicEnergy + staticEnergy +
          fillEnergy + writebackEnergy + cpuStallEnergy;
dynamicEnergy = totalAccesses * accessEnergy
staticEnergy = (((totalMisses * penalty) +
          (totalHits * hitCycles)) * staticEnergyPerCycle);
staticEnergyPerCycle = dynamicEnergy * 0.25;
fillEnergy = (totalMisses * (linesize/wordsize) *
          readEnergyPerWord);
writebackEnergy = (totalWritebacks * (linesize/wordsize) *
          writeEnergyPerWord);
cpuStallEnergy = (((totalMisses * penalty) + (totalWritebacks *
          writebackPenalty)) * cpuIdleEnergy);
```

Figure 4. Energy model.

To show that our phase-based cache locking methodology constitutes minimal hardware area and power overhead, we estimate the LCHT's hardware/memory requirements. For a 32-entry LCHT, 5 bits store the ID, 32 bits store *lockedContents(Ai)*, 1 bit each stores the *noLockedContents* and *profile* flags, and 16 bits each store the cache miss rate and energy. Using these assumptions, we estimate from a synthesizable VHDL implementation and synthesis using Synopsys Design Compiler [20] that the 32-entry LCHT constitutes an area of 2.48 μm^2 and power consumption of 56.72 μW. Relative to a MIPS32 M14K [12] 90 nm processor, which has an area of 0.21 mm^2 and consumes 12 mW of power at 200 MHz, the 32-entry LCHT constitutes only 1.3% and 0.5% area and power overheads, respectively.

4. EXPERIMENTAL RESULTS
4.1 Experimental Setup
We quantified our phase-based cache locking methodology's performance improvement and energy savings using fifteen benchmarks from the SPEC CPU2006 benchmark suite, compiled to Alpha/OSF binaries and executed using the reference input sets. We used SPEC benchmarks because SPEC applications exhibit greater execution variation (i.e., more distinct phases) than most embedded system benchmarks, and thus more rigorously test our methodology. Since embedded system benchmarks are typically kernels performing a specific task (i.e., few distinct phases), our results are pessimistic. We have verified the suitability of SPEC2006 benchmarks through conversations with personnel in the embedded systems microprocessor manufacturing industry. However, our cache locking methodology presented in this paper and the results are applicable to both embedded system applications and desktop applications. To represent embedded system applications, which are typically much smaller than general purpose applications, we used the first 10 billion instructions [11] from each SPEC benchmark and used SimPoint [8] to classify the benchmarks' phases and determine the phases' persistence.

We simulated cache locking using Simplescalar-AlphaLinux's sim-outorder [18] and drove our simulations using Perl scripts. We modeled an embedded system microprocessor with cache configurations similar to the ARM Cortex A15 [3] microprocessor with 32 KB, 4-way set associative private L1 instruction and data caches with 64 byte line sizes. We used sim-profile to collect information about the phases' memory accesses and data reuse.

Figure 4 depicts the energy model used to calculate the L1 data cache's energy consumption. The model calculates the data cache's dynamic and static energy, the energy required to fill the cache on a miss, the energy consumed during a cache write back, and the energy consumed when the processor is stalled during cache fills and write backs. We assumed instruction and data cache access latencies of 1 cycle and a main memory access latency of 80 cycles, similar to previous work [11]. We used Simplescalar to gather cache statistics, such as *totalMisses, totalAccesses, totalWritebacks,*

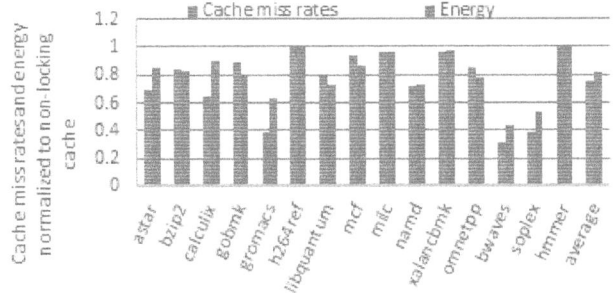

Figure 5. Cache miss rates and energy consumption of phase-based cache locking normalized to a non-locking cache (baseline of one).

etc. We assumed the static energy per cycle to be 25% of the cache's dynamic energy and the CPU idle energy to be 25% of the MIPS M14K processor's active energy [12]. We used CACTI [13] to determine the cache's dynamic energy for 90nm technology.

4.2 Miss Rate and Energy Consumption Analysis Compared to a Non-locking Cache
Figure 5 depicts the data cache's miss rates and energy consumptions for our phase-based cache locking methodology normalized to a non-locking cache (baseline of one). These results depict the system after the cache locking algorithm has selected the locked contents and evaluated the applications' cache locking benefits (i.e., after the first two executions have completed). On average over all of the applications, our cache locking methodology improved the data cache miss rate by 24% compared to the non-locking cache, with improvements as high as 69% for *bwaves* and 61% for both *gromacs* and *soplex*. These applications' cache miss rate improvements were high because a few phases comprised the majority of the applications' execution, and thus substantiates our hypothesis about locking the highly persistent phases. For example, four of *bwaves*'s nineteen phases comprised 47% of *bwaves*' execution. However, locking all four phases would have reduced the effective cache size for the remaining phases and increased those phases' memory blocks' conflict misses. Thus, our cache locking algorithm only locked the two most persistent phases to achieve a 69% miss rate improvement. We observed similar trends for *gromacs* and *soplex*.

However, *h264ref*'s and *hmmer*'s cache miss rates did not improve over the non-locking cache because both applications' phases' persistence were relatively consistent throughout execution, and no one phase was more persistent than any other. For example, since five of *h264ref*'s seven phases comprised 80% of the execution, our cache locking algorithm determined that both applications would not benefit from cache locking, and were executed with the non-locking cache. These results solidify our hypothesis for locking only persistent phases, and if an application's phases do not exhibit persistence, the system should default to a non-locking cache.

With respect to energy consumption, our cache locking methodology improved the data cache's average energy consumption by 20% compared to the non-locking cache, with savings as high as 56% for *bwaves*. Since *h264ref* and *hmmer* did not have any locked contents, phase-based cache locking resulted in the same energy consumption as the non-locking cache. Since our phase-based cache tuning methodology successfully evaluates the benefits of cache locking, and defaults to a non-locking cache when cache locking is not beneficial, there is no cache miss rate and/or energy degradation.

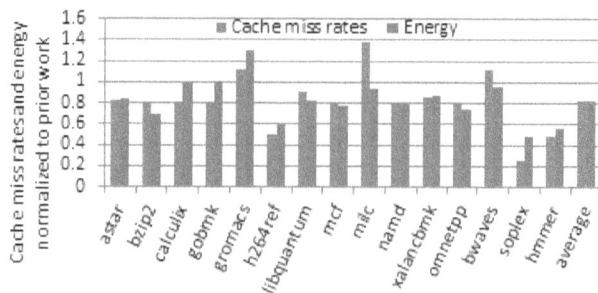

Figure 6. Cache miss rates and energy consumption for phase-based cache locking normalized to prior work (baseline of one).

4.3 Comparison to Prior Work

We compared our phase-based cache locking methodology to prior work that used the cache miss rate to select the locked contents and locked memory blocks with the highest cache miss rates, as determined through extensive runtime analysis [6]. We simulated this method using Simplescalar to provide a close comparison to the state of the art.

Figure 6 depicts the data cache's miss rates and energy consumption when using our phase-based cache locking methodology normalized to prior work (baseline of one). On average over all the applications, phase-based cache locking improved prior work's cache miss rates by 18%, with improvements as high as 74% for *soplex*. Our methodology outperformed prior work for all applications, except *gromacs*, *milc*, and *bwaves* because the memory blocks with the highest miss rates in these applications were included in some, but not all, of the most persistent phases. For example, for *gromacs*, our methodology locked two phases *x* and *y* that comprised of 34% and 17% of the application's execution, respectively. *x* had memory blocks with high miss rates, and these memory blocks were locked by prior work, however, *y*'s memory blocks had very low miss rates, thus, prior work locked different memory blocks that had higher miss rates than *y*'s memory blocks. We can improve our methodology by carrying out runtime analysis to determine the memory blocks' miss rates to lock phases that are persistent and have high miss rates, and we intend to explore this improvement in future work.

Figure 6 also shows that our phase-based cache locking methodology improved the energy consumption as compared to prior work by 17% on average over all of the applications, with improvements as high as 52% for *soplex*. Unlike the cache miss rate comparisons, prior work only outperformed our work for *gromacs* for energy consumption improvement. Prior work locked memory blocks that contributed significantly to *gromacs's* energy consumption due to those blocks' high miss rates. In general, our methodology also improved over the non-locking cache and outperformed prior work on average. These results show that our phase-based cache locking methodology successfully optimizes the data cache's miss rates and energy consumption without extensive runtime analysis.

5. CONCLUSIONS

In this paper, we proposed phase-based cache locking for improving the data cache's performance and energy consumption in general purpose embedded systems where the executing applications may be unknown a priori. Phase-based cache locking leverages fundamentals of phase classification to dynamically select the data cache's locked contents based on the data's associated phase's persistence, with minimal runtime overhead. Compared to a non-locking cache, our phase-based cache locking methodology improved the data cache's miss rates and energy consumptions by an average of 24% and 20%, respectively. In future work, we will extend our phase-based cache locking methodology to tradeoff the phases' persistence with the phases' memory blocks' miss rates to further improve the cache miss rates and energy consumptions. We will also extend our phase-based cache locking methodology to the instruction cache to optimize the instruction cache's miss rates and energy consumption.

6. ACKNOWLEDGEMENTS

This work was supported by the National Science Foundation (CNS-0953447). Any opinions, findings, and conclusions or recommendations expressed in this material are those of the authors and do not necessarily reflect the views of the National Science Foundation.

7. REFERENCES

[1] T. Adegbija, A. Gordon-Ross, and A. Munir, "Phase distance mapping: a phase-based cache tuning methodology for embedded systems," Springer Design Automation for Embedded Systems (DAEM), January 2014.

[2] K. Anand and R. Barua, "Instruction cache locking inside a binary writer," International Conference on Compilers, Architectures and Synthesis for Embedded Systems (CASES), October 2009.

[3] ARM: http://www.arm.com

[4] A. Arnaud and I. Puaut, "Dynamic instruction cache locking in hard real-time systems," International Conference on Real-Time and Network Systems (RTNS), October 2006.

[5] A. Asaduzzaman, I. Mahgoub, and F. Sibai, "Impact of L1 entire locking and L2 way locking on the performance, power consumption, and predictability of multicore real-time systems," International Conference on Computer Systems and Applications, May 2009.

[6] A. Asaduzzaman, F. Sibai, and M. Rani, "Improving cache locking performance of modern embedded systems via the addition of a miss table at the L2 cache level," Journal of System Architecture, April 2010, pp 151-162.

[7] H. Ding, Y. Liang, and T. Mitra, "WCET-Centric Dynamic Instruction Cache Locking," Design, Automation, and Test in Europe (DATE), March 2014.

[8] G. Hamerly, E. Perelman, J. Lau, and B. Calder, "SimPoint 3.0: faster and more flexible program analysis," Journal of Instruction-Level Parallelism, 2005, pp 1-28.

[9] Y. Liang and T. Mitra, "Instruction cache locking using temporal reuse profile," Design Automation Conference (DAC), June 2010.

[10] T. Liu, M. Li, and C. Xue, "Instruction cache locking for embedded systems using probability profile," Journal of Signal Processing Systems, November 2012.

[11] A. Lukefahr, et al., "Composite cores: pushing heterogeneity into a core," International Symposium on Microarchitecture, Dec. 2012.

[12] MIPS32 M14K. http://files.tomek.cedro.info/electronics/doc/mips/MD00688-2B-M14K-APP-01.00.pdf. Accessed 30 July 2014.

[13] N. Muralimanohar and N. P. Jouppi, "Cacti6.0: A tool to model large caches," COMPAQ Western Research Lab, 2009.

[14] I. Puaut and D. Decotigny, "Low-complexity algorithms for static cache locking in multitasking hard real-time systems," Real-Time Systems Symposium (RTSS), 2002.

[15] S. Segars, "Low-power design techniques for microprocessor," International Solid-State Circuits Conference Tutorial, Feb. 2001.

[16] X. Shen, Y. Zhong, and C. Ding, "Locality phase prediction," International Conference on Architectural Support for Programming Languages and Operating Systems (ASPLOS), December 2004.

[17] T. Sherwood, S. Sair, and B. Calder, "Phase tracking and prediction," International Symposium on Computer Architecture, December 2003.

[18] Simplescalar ported to Alpha/Linux with Linux System Calls. http://hhnajafabadi.s3-website-us-east-1.amazonaws.com/mase-alphalinux.htm

[19] SPEC CPU2006. http://www.spec.org/cpu2006

[20] Synopsys Design Compiler, Synopsys Inc. www.synopsys.com

[21] X. Vera, B. Lisper, and J. Xue, "Data cache locking for higher program predictability," ACM SIGMETRICS International Conference on Measurement and Modeling of Computer Systems, June 2003.

A Multilayered Design Approach for Efficient Hybrid 3D Photonics Network-on-chip

Dharanidhar Dang, Biplab Patra, Rabi Mahapatra
Department of Computer Sceince & Engineering
Texas A&M University
{d.dharanidhar,biplab7777,rabi}@tamu.edu

ABSTRACT

In Chip Multiprocessors, traditional metallic interconnects will soon reach their bandwidth and energy dissipation limits. Photonic NoC (PNoC) is a promising alternative to renew higher performance in the advent of rising number of cores on chip. Efficient PNoC architectures are needed to reduce laser related energy consumption and maintain high performance. In this work we propose a novel sandwich layered approach to design a 3D PNoC architecture that is able to reduce no of hops, cross over points, and no of laser sources using multiplexing techniques. The 3D hybrid PNoC uses high performance 5X5 photonic routers incorporating mode division multiplexing (MDM) along with wavelength division multiplexing (WDM) and time division multiplexing (TDM). Experimental results demonstrates an increase in aggregated bandwidth up to 4x while reducing average energy consumption per router by 83% as compared to the recently reported results.

Categories and Subject Descriptors

C.1 [**Processor Architectures**]: Multiple Data Stream Architectures; B.2.2 [**Performance Analysis and Design Aids**]: Simulation—*Algorithms*

General Terms

Theory

Keywords

Photonic Network-On-Chip, Mode Division Multiplexing

1. INTRODUCTION

With rise in number of cores on a chip, there is a demand of new communication paradigm to accomodate large data traffic efficiently. In recent years photonic interconnections have emerged as the most relevant and attractive alternative to traditional electrical interconects[1]. With high speed switching through Micro Ring Resonators[MRR] and low power optical waveguides as transmission medium we can achieve higher bandwidth by exploiting wavelength and mode[2]. PNoC is by far the most promising paradigm to meet the needs of the next generation on-chip communication.

In this paper we propose a sandwich layered approach to design a 3D PNoC architecture by reducing the no. of laser components resulting in reduction in energy consumption and enhancement of aggregate bandwidth. We have incorporated MDM[3] along with WDM to increase the bandwidth of communication by manifolds. As shown in Fig.1 there are three layers as the basic design which can be repeatedly used to build multilayered 3D PNoC. The bottom and the top network layers include two 4X4 mesh of routers connecting processing cores along with multiplexers to carry out laser multiplexing. The sandwiched middle layer known as the laser layer includes mode-locked lasers and circular waveguides to route messages to the appropriate router.

A high performance, low power, scalable and low cost photonic router is the heart of any high performance PNoC. In recent years several photonic router architectures have been proposed in the literature[4][5][6]. In this paper we use a high performance 5 port photonic router based on Cygnus router layout[2] incorporating MDM along with WDM and TDM to design a high performance and low power 3D PNoC.

GLSVLSI '15, May 20 - 22, 2015, Pittsburgh, PA, USA
Copyright 2015 ACM 978-1-4503-3474-7/15/05 ...$15.00.
http://dx.doi.org/10.1145/2742060.2742083.

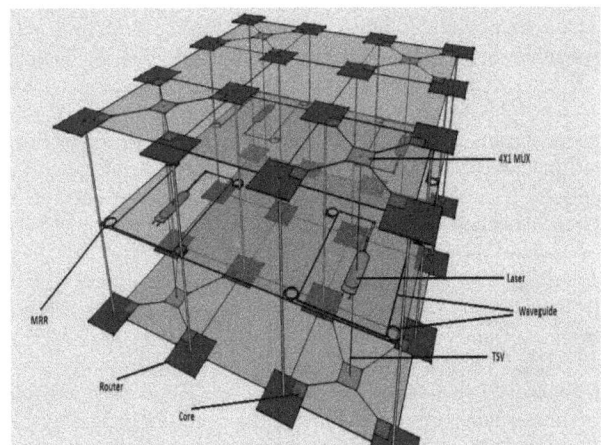

Figure 1: **Three layered Photonic mesh network**

This paper has the following contributions:- (i) It has introduced a novel sandwiched laser-layered architecture as the basic building block for low power 3D PNoC architecture. This approach is the first of its kind to the best of our knowledge. (ii) It incorporates MDM along with WDM and TDM in routers to achieve higher bandwidth and lower power as compared to earlier works. (iii) The results from experiments indicate that :- The bandwidth of communication is about 40 Gbps which is about 4X higher than the recently reported results in[6]. The average energy consumption per router is about 83% lesser than the best reported result in[5]. The insertion loss is reported to be -2dB for the longest optical path which is about 75% less than the recently reported result in[7].

The paper is organized as follows. Section 2 describes the background information on PNoC, 3D stacking and the various building blocks for the proposed PNoC. The architecture of the proposed Sandwich Layered PNoC is described in Section 3. The experiments and results along with the comparative analysis with other photonic routers in literature are presented in Section 4. We conclude the paper in Section 5 with some directions for the future work.

2. BUILDING BLOCKS OF THE ARCHITECTURE

Several 2D Photonic NoC architectures based on mesh[2], torus[1], crossbar[8] and clos[9] topologies have been proposed in recent years. To decrease cross sectional area and crossover points several 3D topologies have also been proposed[5][7]. But there is little attempt to reduce the number of laser components in designing a PNoC which is the primary source of power consumption. The topology we adopted for our design is a 4X4 2D mesh in the network layers. The important building blocks here are routers using MRR based Switches, Through-Silicon Vias(TSVs), and multiplexers for laser multiplexing.

2.1 ROUTER ARCHITECTURE: SWITCHING AND LAYOUT

The photonic router used in the proposed architecture is a 5X5 non-blocking with 5 I/O ports[14]. The communication techniques used in PNoCs are typically of two types. 1- Deterministic switching and 2- Dynamic Switching. In deterministic switching technique, a fixed routing pattern is defined during the network design and optical path between source-destination pair is established by dynamically selecting a specific wavelength[9]. This technique is typically used in wavelength selective passive networks. On the other hand, in dynamic switching technology, routing pattern is dynamically selected by an electronic controller[1][2]. This technique is similar to circuit switching.

Though the former technique exhibits a lower latency than the later[8] but circuit switching networks provide higher aggregate bandwidth by adopting MDM along with WDM and TDM. They are also compact and scalable[4]. The basic switching element MRR is a circularly coiled waveguide which has the property of rotating the optical signal in clockwise direction. The switching time of the MRR is around 10ps. Fig.2a and Fig.2c shows MRRs in OFF condition that allow optical signals to flow from input port to the output labelled as straight port without deflection. However when MRRs are ON (Fig.2b and Fig.2d) they couple the optical

signals from Waveguide A to Waveguide B positioned in the rectangular direction.

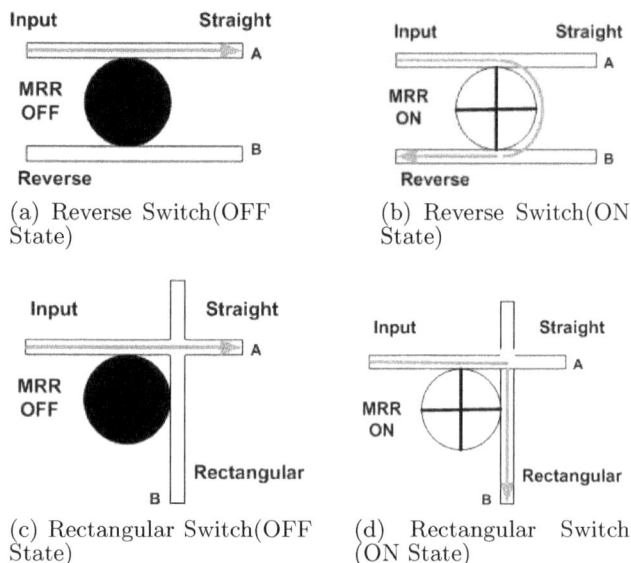

(a) Reverse Switch(OFF State)

(b) Reverse Switch(ON State)

(c) Rectangular Switch(OFF State)

(d) Rectangular Switch (ON State)

Figure 2: MRR Switching

There are two types of switching arrangements namely 1- Reverse switching and 2- Rectangular Switching. Reverse switching deflects the optical signal by 180 degrees with a parallel arrangement of waveguides as shown in Fig.2a and Fig.2b. To switch the optical signal in a 90 degree angle we have an orthogonal arrangement of waveguides known as Rectangular Switching. It may be noted that the parallel reverse switching can also be done by combining two rectangular switches but that would result in two crossover points leading to cross talk and also use of an extra MRR. In the Reverse Switching arrangement as shown in the Fig.2a and Fig.2b the 180 degree deflection takes place without any crossover points and one MRR only. It results in reduction in insertion loss which is about 0.12dB per waveguide crossing and also power as MRR needs a DC current to switch ON and consumes less than 20uW[10].The switching time of MRR is very small and it is 10ps in our case. The photonic router layout as shown in Fig.3 adapted from Cygnus router[2] is composed of a photonic switching fabric made by combining 16 reverse and rectangular switches as mentioned above along with multimode waveguides and a network interface(NI). The router has five bidirectional ports viz. East, West, North, South and the NI port. Each photonic router has a controller within NI for selecting wavelength and mode for optical signal transmission. The router can operate simultaneously on multiple wavelengths using WDM with wavelength spacing equal to the free spectrum range of the MRR. The proposed layout consists of only 14 waveguide crossings, 16 MRRs in the switching fabric and 2 MRRs within NI to set up MDM leading to an optimized design. The NI (Fig.4) is the main control center in the router which comprises of a WDM + MDM + TDM based electrical to optical(E/O) converter, an optical to electrical(O/E) converter and an electrical controller. The E/O converter includes the mode locked laser along with MRR and waveguide arrangements facilitating MDM[3]. This has been shown in

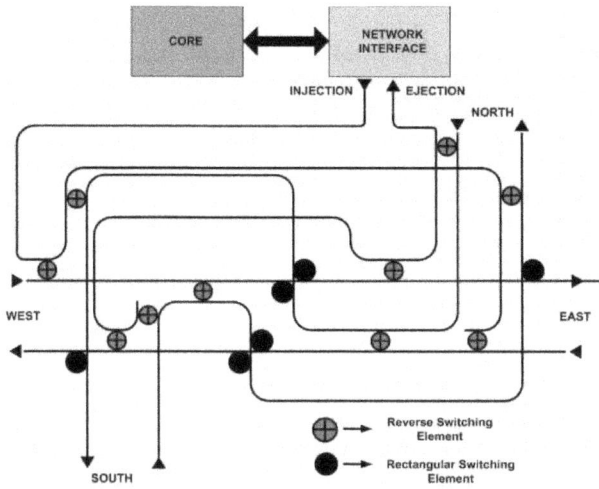

Figure 3: Logical layout of 5×5 photonic router

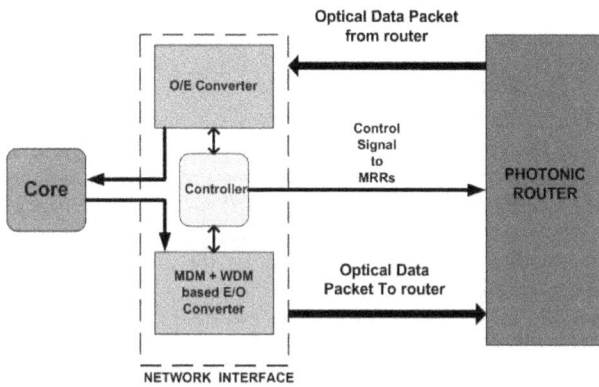

Figure 4: MDM Integrated Network Interface

Fig.5. This results in higher aggregate bandwidth compared to all the previously proposed PNoC architectures.

2.2 MULTILAYER STACKING

Multiple electrical layers for building a 3D architecture are connected with each other by through-silicon-vias(TSVs). The proposed multilayer sandwiched architecture uses TSVs for communication between the laser layer and the network layers. TSVs have very small cross-sectional diameter(4um-10um) and extremely small delay(20 ps for a 20 layer -3D stack)[5]

3. BASIC SANDWICHED LASER-LAYERED PNOC ARCHITECTURE

In the proposed 3 layer sandwiched PNoC architecture, both the top and the bottom layers are network layers and the middle sandwiched layer is the laser layer.
Each of the network layers consist of a 2D mesh network of 16 cores interconnected by 16, 5X5 non-blocking photonic routers as described in Section II. Apart from that there are multimodal waveguides with two channels incorporating WDM and four 4X1 MUXs each dedicated to each of the 4 routers as shown in Fig.1.
In the proposed design the laser layer consists of several waveguides which act as channels to relay the information from a source router to a destination router through the

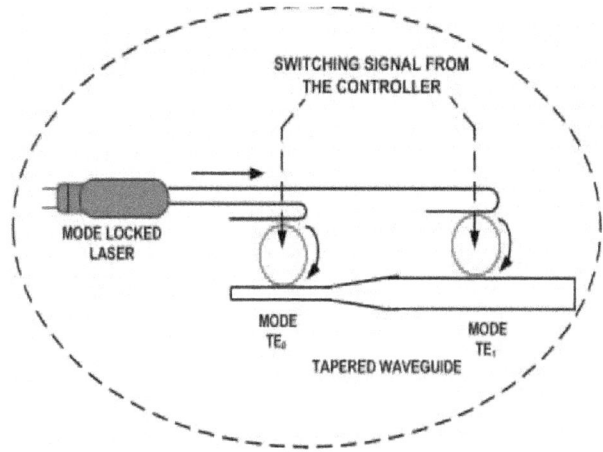

Figure 5: Mode Locked Laser employing MDM

Mode Locked Laser(MLL) in the same layer, selected by the corresponding 4X1 MUX in the network layer. Each laser serves four routers contrary to one laser per router as in almost all PNoC architectures recently proposed.

3.1 MECHANISM AND CONTROL

If a source core 's' wants to send message to a destination core 'd', it first sends a READY signal to the corresponding 4X1 multiplexer (MUX) to check its availability. As it follows the circuit switching mechanism so the route to be followed from source to destination is figured out as soon as the READY signal reaches the MUX. After receiving the acknowledgement from MUX, the core sends the message to the mode locked laser through MUX via TSV. The mode locked laser is controlled by the electronic controller present in the router. It adaptively selects the wavelength and the mode on which the message is to be relayed until the destination core. The controller uses the algorithm as depicted in Algorithm 1.

To relay messages from the top to the bottom layer and vice versa there is one MRR in the laser layer corresponding to each router which helps in tapping the message as it is relayed in the common waveguide channel from the corresponding mode locked laser.
From the above arrangement we can see that with only four lasers we are able to serve 32 cores simultaneously. The various experiments carried out, results and a thorough comparative analysis are presented in the next section.

4. EXPERIMENTS AND RESULTS

IPKISS[11] platform has been used for design and simulation of the 3 layer sandwiched PNoC. This tool allows photonic layout design, virtual fabrication of components in different technologies, physical simulation of components, and optical circuit design and simulation. We custom designed photonic components like MRR, waveguide, mode-locked laser, tapered waveguide, and photodiode required for the proposed architecture. Virtual Fabrication was done in order to validate the components.

Procedure *Core1(s) wants to send Data to Core2(d)*

Data: N= no. of signals transmitting fully or partially along the path

if *N=0* **then**

  Switch ON MRR_0 with λ_0;

  Send Signal from Mode-Locked Laser;

end

if *(N=1) and (mode=TE_0)* **then**

  Switch ON MRR_1 with λ_0;

  Send Signal from Mode-Locked Laser with a (τ + pulse-width) delay;

end

if *(N=2)* **then**

  Switch ON MRR_0 with λ_1;

  Send Signal from Mode-Locked Laser with a $2(\tau$ + pulse-width) delay;

end

if *(N=2) and (mode=TE_0)* **then**

  Switch ON MRR_1 with λ_1;

  Send Signal from Mode-Locked Laser with a $3(\tau$ + pulse-width) delay;

end

Algorithm 1: Controller Algorithm for adaptive mode division multiplexing

4.1 ARCHITECTURE SIMULATION IN IP-KISS

The design parameters adopted to carry out various experiments are depicted in Table 1. MRR of diameter $10\mu m$ was adopted to keep the area of the PNoC foot-print as small as possible without letting the waveguides interfere much. The multimode waveguide in our design supports four optical modes TE_0, TE_1, TE_2 and TE_3 with a refractive index of 2.46. The waveguide also supports multiple wavelengths. The mode-locked laser used has a frequency of 10-GHz. It produces optical signal with a pulse width of 10ps. Each of the pulses contains multiple wavelengths ranging from 1595nm to 1605nm. The laser also produces hundreds of modes. But we are considering modes TE_0, TE_1, TE_2 and TE_3 as the proposed MDM scheme supports 4 modes. Using all these fundamental components, we built the 3 layer sandwiched PNoC in IPKISS and performed the physical simulation.

MRRs and waveguides were integrated to virtually fab-

Table 1: Design Parameters for Experimental Setup

Design Parameters	Value
MRR diameter	$10\mu m$
Waveguide(MRR) width	450nm
Waveguide(Signal Transmission) height	250nm
Waveguide(Signal Transmission) width	450nm
Refractive index Of waveguides	2.46
Pulse-width of Optical Signal	10ps
Frequency(mode-locked laser)	10GHz
Wavelength	1547.5nm& 1550nm

ricate the router. Routers, lasers, TSVs, and waveguides were connected and virtually fabricated. After virtual fabri-

cation to cater design issues, we carried out simulation using CAMFR. CAMFR provides the refractive index profile and optical transmission profile of the fabricated design. Uniform refractive index across the PNoC is necessary for ripple free photonic transmission. After testing the uniformity of refractive index across the router, we simulated the 2-layer PNoC in CAPHE. CAPHE is an optical circuit simulator for time-domain and frequency-domain analysis. It is also used to evaluate the insertion loss in an optical circuit. The insertion loss in the MRR is found to be 0.12dB. Each MRR can be tuned to multiple wavelengths.

4.2 Comparative analysis

In this section the proposed PNoC architecture(PRO) design has been analytically compared with other 3D architectures like R-3PO[5],Corona[7], and Firefly[6]. Various parameters such as optical insertion loss, required no of MRRs and energy consumption for these architectures were analysed.

4.2.1 Number Of MRRs

The no of MRRs used in a PNoC depicts its cross sectional footprint and cost. The number of MRRs used to design each of the 3-D PNoC architectures were compared. In the proposed 3 layer sandwiched PNoC Architecture, 19 MRRs per core are used. 16 MRRs for the router layout, 2 for facilitating WDM+MDM and 1 for tapping the message from the waveguide originating from the mode locked laser. So for 32 cores in the proposed design one needs 608 MRRs. The no of MRRs per core or router(each core associated with one router) for various 3D architectures were compared Fig.6. It is evident from the graph that the proposed architecture outperforms all others. The number of MRRs/Router for the proposed router architecture is about 32.1%, 24% and 17.3% less than R-3PO, Corona & Firefly respectively. Such reduction in the numberof MRRs directly reduces cross-sectional area and cross-over points on chip.

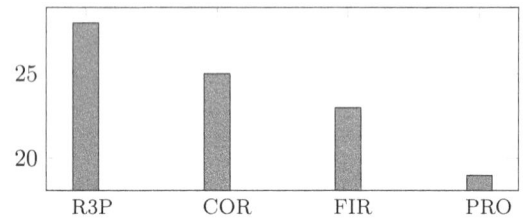

Figure 6: Comparing number of MRRs/Router for different PNoC architectures; R3P:R-3PO, COR:Corona, FIR:Firefly, PRO:proposed sandwiched-3 layer PNoC

4.2.2 Energy Consumption

The total energy consumption in PNoC architectures can be divided into two categories :- optical energy and electrical energy. Electrical energy is consumed by the electrical controller and the optical energy consumption is the sum of laser energy and energy dissipated in the photonic switching fabric.

The laser energy can be determined by the following equation

$$P_{Laser} = P_{Det} + P_{Channel} + M_{Sys} \qquad (1)$$

Here P_{Det} is the photo-detector sensitivity. $P_{channel}$ is the photonic channel loss and M_{sys} is the system margin. The optical insertion loss is the loss in signal power whenever there is a waveguide crossing or bending. The total optical insertion loss is determined by

$$L_{Insertion} = \sum L_{Bending} + \sum L_{Crossing} + \sum L_{MRR} \qquad (2)$$

As per the Equation 2, insertion loss in an optical path accounts for the total no of bendings and crossings of waveguides and MRRs in the message path. To maintain the uniformity and have a fair comparison with other architectures we use the same optical device parameters and loss values as listed in Table 2. The primary function of the electrical

Table 2: Electrical and optical losses

Component	Value	Unit
Laser efficiency	5	dB
Splitter	0.2	dB/cm
Ring Drop	1	dB
Photodetector Sensitivity	-26	dBm

controller is to turn the MRRs ON and OFF. The number of MRRs encountered while the message is relayed from source to destination is determined by the routing algorithm and also the amount of traffic. We analytically determined the electrical energy consumption of the proposed design by dimension order routing scheme. We evaluated the average energy consumption per optical path in the network (P_{path}) and also the average energy consumption per router (P_{router}). We calculated P_{path} using Equation 3. Here P_j represents the energy consumed on j-th path when the bandwidth is 'B'. 'P^*' represents the total number of photonic paths in the NoC. P_{router} is calculated using Equation 4 where 'R' is the average number of photonic routers in all the optical paths.

$$P_{path} = \frac{\sum_{j=1}^{P^*} P_j}{P^* \times B} \qquad (3)$$

$$P_{router} = \frac{P_{path}}{R} \qquad (4)$$

Network-level analysis in Fig.8 shows that the proposed 3D PNoC consumes the average energy per optical path of about 4.8fJ/bit. It is about 20% less than Firefly and almost equal to the Corona architecture. Though as compared to R3PO the average energy per optical path is more but it gets balanced as R3PO has a higher insertion loss. In the proposed router based network, average router energy consumption is 0.32fJ/bit, which is also 83% less than the Corona architecture as shown in Fig.7. The MRRs in the routers of the proposed archirecture are placed in such a manner that it does not need to switch on any MRR for a packet to travel along the row or column. This makes the proposed 3D PNoC highly scalable without worrying about the energy consumption in additional routers on a longer path. From Fig.9 we can see the variation in average energy/path in fJ/bit for different NoC sizes. The graph corresponding to

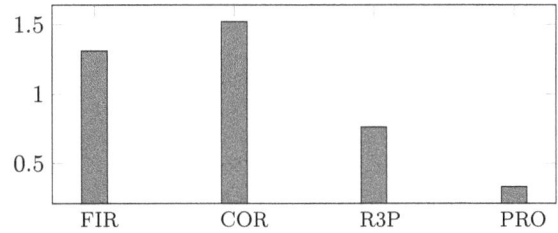

Figure 7: Comparison of energy consumption per router in fJ/bit

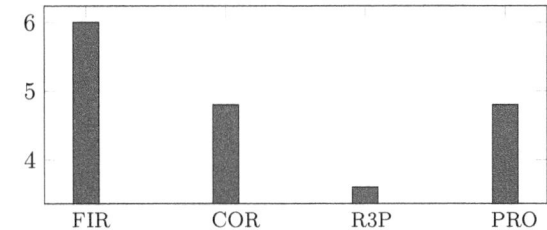

Figure 8: Comparison of average energy consumption per optical path, in fJ/bit

the proposed router and the Corona architecture are almost overlapping with negligible difference.

4.2.3 Optical Insertion Loss

Insertion loss is the loss of signal power whenever a crossing or bending is encountered in a waveguide along the transmission path which includes transferring the optical signal into the MRR. Insertion loss in a NoC determines its feasibility and also the power required by the NI of the router in this case to transmit and receive optical signals. The optical signal must be transmitted with sufficient power so that they can be received in a proper form at the destination. Insertion Loss for an MRR and waveguide crossings are 0.5dB and 0.12 dB respectively.

Insertion Loss varies across input-output pairs in a network. Hence we evaluated the best-case, average-case, and the worst-case insertion losses in all the architectures. It is clear from the result shown in Fig. 10 that the proposed architecture has the lowest insertion loss among all the cases. Compared to R-3PO the proposed router has 65% less best case loss, 45% less average-case loss and 30% less worst-case loss.

4.3 Bandwidth Comparison

Photonic-links deployed in the proposed PNoC has a data rate of 10-Gbps. Deploying MDM and WDM, the proposed architecture offers an overall bandwidth of 40-Gbps. The architecture enhances the photonic-link data rate by 4× compared to 1× enhancement in the most recently reported architecture[5].

4.4 Number of Laser-sources

The laser-multiplexing technique deployed in the proposed architecture allows each laser-source to serve eight cores. This technique reduces the number of on-chip lasers by 87.25% compared to architectures deploying one laser-source per core[6].

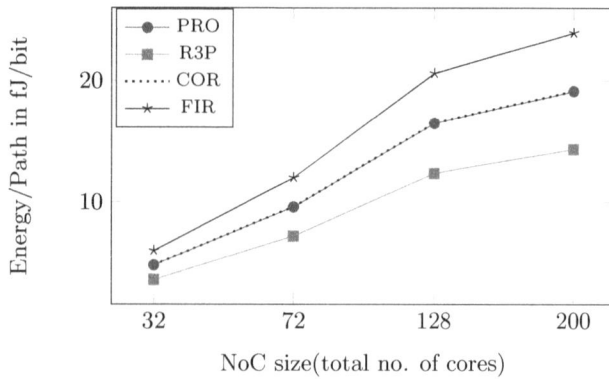

Figure 9: Average energy per Path for different NoC sizes

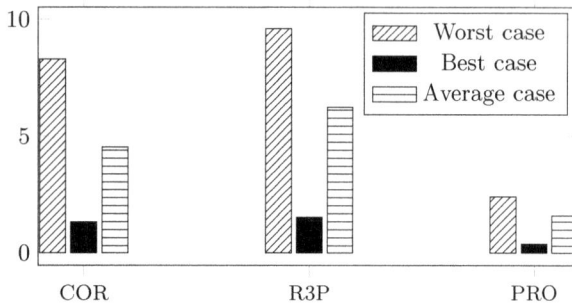

Figure 10: Insertion loss in 4×4 PNoC in dB

5. CONCLUSION

This article introduced a sandwiched 3 layer PNoC architecture and a high performance photonic router microarchitecture by integrating WDM, MDM and TDM techniques. A virtual prototype implementation demonstrates significant improvements in the performance and energy consumption as compared to some other PNoC architectures. This approach can be extended to realize efficient multilayer 3D PNoC designs in the future. A network simulator will be designed to demonstrate the behaviour and eficiency of the proposed architecture in different types of traffic scenarios. MRR properties vary with temperature which affects the overall performance of PNoC. Research will be carried out to design an efficient thermal model of PNoC.

6. ACKNOWLEDGMENTS

The authors acknowledge the support of Luceda Photonics, Belgium for providing IPKISS and CAPHE tools to validate photonic components and cicuits used in the experiment.

7. REFERENCES

[1] A. Shacham, K. Bergman, and L.P. Carloni, *Photonic networks-on-chip for future generations of chip multiprocessors,*, IEEE Trans. Comput.57(9), 1246-1260 (2008).

[2] H.X. Gu, K.H. Mo, J. Xu, and W. Zhang, *A low-power low-cost optical router for optical networks-on-chip in multiprocessor systems-on-chip,* 2009 IEEE Computer Society Annual Symposium on VlSI, 19-24 (2009).

[3] L. Luo, N. Ophir, C. Chen, L. Gabrielli, C. Poitras, K. Bergmen and M. Lipson, *WDM-compatible mode-division multiplexing on a silicon chip,* Nature Communications5,Article number:3069,15 January 2014

[4] L. Yang, R. Ji, L. Zhang, Y. Tian, J. Ding, H. Chen, Y. Lu, P. Zhou and W. jhu *Five-port optical router for photonic networks-on-chip,*Optics Express, Vol. 19, Issue 21, pp. 20258-20268 (2011)

[5] R. Morris, A.K. Kodi, and A. Louri, *Dynamic Reconfiguration of 3D Photonic Networks-on-Chip for Maximizing Performance and Improving Fault Tolerance,* ,MICRO, 2012, pp.282-293.

[6] Y. Pan, P. Kumar, J. Kim, G. Memik, Y. Zhang, A. Choudhary, *Firefly: Illuminating future network-on-chip with nanophotonics,* Int'l Symposium on Computer Architecture (ISCA), 2009.

[7] D. Vantrease et al. *Corona: System Implications of Emerging Nanophotonic Technology,*35th International Symposium on Computer Architecture, 2008. ISCA '08.

[8] C. Batten et al. *Building manycore processor to DRAM networks with monolithic silicon photonics,* High-Performance Interconnects, Symposium on, pp. 21-30, 16th IEEE Symposium on High Performance Interconnects, (2008).

[9] A. Joshi, C. Batten, Y.J. Kwon, S. Beamer, I. Shamim, K. Asanovic, and V. Stojanovic, *Silicon-photonic clos networks for global on-chip communication,* 2009 3rd ACM/IEEE International Symposium on Networks-on-Chip, 124-133 (2009).

[10] A. W. Poon, F. Xu, X. Luo, *Cascaded active silicon microresonator array cross-connect circuits for WDM networks-on-chip,*Proc. SPIE Int.Soc. Opt. Eng. 6898, 689812, 2008.

[11] IPKISS - a generic and modular software framework for parametric design www.ipkiss.org

[12] A. Bianco et al. *Scalability of optical interconnects based on microring resonators* IEEE Photon. Technol. Lett.22(15), 1081-1083 (2010)

[13] Y. Xie et al.*Crosstalk noise and bit error rate analysis for optical network-on-chip,* 47th ACM/EDAC/IEEE Design Automation Conference, 657-660 (2010)

[14] Dang, D.; Patra, B.; Mahapatra, R.; Fiers, M., *Mode-Division-Multiplexed Photonic Router for High Performance Network-on-Chip,* VLSI Design (VLSID), 2015 28th International Conference on , vol., no., pp.111,116, 3-7 Jan. 2015

Analyzing the Dark Silicon Phenomenon in a Many-Core Chip Multi-Processor under Deeply-Scaled Process Technologies

Alireza Shafaei   Yanzhi Wang   Srikanth Ramadurgam

Yuankun Xue   Paul Bogdan   Massoud Pedram

Department of Electrical Engineering
University of Southern California
Los Angeles, CA 90089
{shafaeib, yanzhiwa, ramadurg, yuankunx, pbogdan, pedram}@usc.edu

ABSTRACT

The impact of dark silicon phenomenon on multicore processors under deeply-scaled FinFET technologies is investigated in this paper. To do this accurately, a cross-layer framework, spanning device, circuit, and architecture levels is initially introduced. Using this framework, leakage and dynamic power consumptions as well as frequency levels of in-order and out-of-order (OoO) processor cores, and on-chip cache memories and routers in a network-on-chip-based chip multiprocessor system synthesized in 7nm FinFET technology and operating in both super- and near-threshold voltage regimes are presented. Subsequently, total power consumptions of multicore chips manufactured with (i) OoO and (ii) in-order processor cores are reported and compared. According to our results, for a 64-core chip and 15W thermal design power budget, 64% and 39% dark silicon are observed in OoO and in-order multicores, respectively, under super-threshold regime. These percentages drop to 19% and 0% for OoO and in-order multicores operating in the near-threshold regime, respectively. Furthermore, the highest energy efficiencies are achieved by operating in the near-threshold regime, which points to the effectiveness of near-threshold computing in mitigating the effect of dark silicon phenomenon under deeply-scaled technologies.

Categories and Subject Descriptors

B [**Hardware**]: General

Keywords

FinFET devices, dark silicon, near-threshold computing

1. INTRODUCTION

Transistor dimensions have been shrinking in each technology generation, resulting in more transistors with faster switching speeds in successive technology nodes. On the other hand, in order to maintain the power density at a constant level, the supply voltage, V_{dd}, must also be scaled down by a similar factor as the feature size, which subsequently necessitates a reduced threshold voltage value, V_{th}. Decreasing the V_{th} induces an exponential increase in the OFF (leakage) current of the underlying devices, an effect which is not desired especially under nanometer technology nodes where the leakage power is leading the chip power consumption. As a result, V_{th}, and accordingly V_{dd}, are not scaling proportionally with the feature size. This phenomenon has in turn resulted in increased chip power density. However, our ability to remove heat from VLSI chips (using advanced packaging and cooling technologies) is rather limited. Hence, conventional processor performance scaling (which was mainly achieved by boosting the clock frequency of compute cores from one generation to next) has come to an end. Instead, system designers try to achieve higher computational capacity for their processors by integrating more cores onto the same chip, each core operating at the same peak frequency level as a previous-generation core. Clearly, achieving higher performance with respect to single-threaded applications has come to halt, although the performance on multi-threaded applications and ability to execute multiple concurrent applications on the same chip has been increasing.

Unfortunately, a new limitation (typically referred to as *dark silicon* phenomenon [11, 19, 17]) has arisen. This phenomenon refers to the fact that although we have the silicon real state on a die to integrate many cores onto the same chip, many of the integrated cores cannot be powered up at the same time, because the resulting power consumption will create power densities that will exceed the acceptable limits imposed on any die. The aforesaid limits are typically captured as a *thermal design power* (TDP)[1] for the chip. In other words, even though by scaling-down to new technology nodes and shrinking the transistor sizes, more cores can

---

[1]TDP is the maximum amount of power that chip can safely dissipate through the cooling system.

be packed on a same-area chip, only a subset of cores can be active at any time for a given TDP.

On the other hand, the chip industry is undergoing a technology shift from conventional planar CMOS transistors towards quasi-planar FinFET devices [2, 6, 1]. This is because of the improved (three-dimensional) gate control over the channel which diminishes source and drain controls, thereby reducing short channel effects [18]. Furthermore, a FinFET device offers higher immunity to random variations which mainly result from the undoped channel of FinFET devices [14, 20]. Additionally, the minimum energy point and the minimum energy-delay point of FinFET circuits occur at supply voltage levels lower than that of planar CMOS counterparts [13], enabling more aggressive voltage scalability in FinFET-based circuit designs. Because of these advantages, FinFET devices are currently recognized as a promising choice of device for deeply-scaled technologies, i.e., technology nodes beyond the 10nm regime [15].

It is predicted in [11] that regardless of the chip organization and topology, multicore scaling is power limited and a significant portion of the fixed-size chip needs to be powered-off, e.g., 50% in 8nm. This projection for future technology nodes is in fact based on 2010 release of the ITRS, which does not adequately consider the effect of the transition from bulk CMOS to FinFET process technologies. To mitigate this shortcoming, we present a device-circuit-architecture cross-layer framework to project multicore scaling and demonstrate the dark silicon phenomenon in deeply-scaled FinFET technologies. More precisely, at the device-level, we design and optimize FinFET devices with gate length of 7nm using advanced device simulators from Synopsys TCAD tool suite [5]. We then extract compact Verilog-A models in order to perform fast gate- and circuit-level simulations, and characterize a library of standard cells. Using this library of standard cells, we synthesize processor cores and *network-on-chip* (NoC) routers by using Synopsys Design Compiler, and report their frequency level and power consumption. Furthermore, characteristics of cache memories are derived from a modified version of CACTI with FinFET support [16].

In this paper, in order to study the effect of dark silicon in future technologies, we consider the following multicore platforms: (i) an out-of-order (OoO) multicore processor, where each core is a Nehalem-based OoO processor, and (ii) an in-order multicore processor, where each core is a LEON3 [3] microprocessor. According to our results, for a 64-core chip and 15W TDP budget, 64% (19%) and 39% (0%) dark silicon are observed in OoO and in-order processors, respectively, under super-threshold (near-threshold) regime. For a TDP of 20W, there is no dark silicon in both processors operating in the near-threshold regime, and the amount of dark silicon for super-threshold operation is reduced to 55% and 22% for the OoO and in-order processors, respectively.

The rest of this paper is organized as follows. The cross-layer design framework is introduced in Section 2, followed by the dark silicon prediction methodology for deeply-scaled technologies in Section 3. Prediction results are presented in Section 4, and finally, Section 5 concludes the paper.

2. CROSS-LAYER DESIGN FRAMEWORK

Our objective is to estimate the power consumption of major components of a multicore platform (i.e., processor cores, on-chip cache memories, and NoC routers) in future

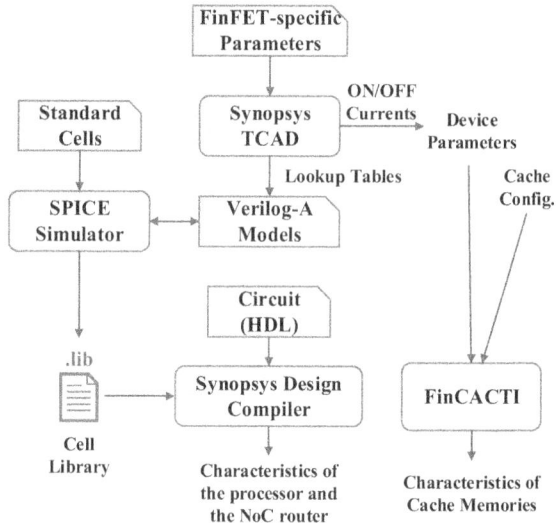

Figure 1: The cross-layer design framework for synthesizing/characterizing processor cores, NoC routers, and cache memories using FinFET devices.

FinFET devices. Subsequently, we will use this information to predict the amount of dark silicon in processors manufactured with such deeply-scaled devices. To do this accurately, we adopt a cross-layer design framework, spanning device, circuit, and architecture levels, which is shown in Figure 1. Details of this framework are described next.

2.1 Device-Level Design

FinFET devices [18] are currently viewed as the technology-of-choice beyond the 22nm regime [2, 6, 1], due to the improved gate control over the channel, and the reduced leakage current, sensitivity to process variations, and short-channel effects. As no industrial data is available, we build and simulate 7nm FinFET devices using Synopsys Sentaurus Device, the advanced multidimensional device simulator from the TCAD tool suite [5]. The gate length of our FinFET devices is 7nm, with 1.5nm gate underlap on each side, resulting in a channel length of 10nm. Furthermore, the nominal operating voltage is 0.45V, the threshold voltage is between 0.2V to 0.25V, and the subthreshold slope is $\sim$80mV/dec, for both NFET and PFET devices.

In this paper, we consider the following two supply voltage operating modes: (i) super-threshold (ST) regime for high performance operation, and (ii) near-threshold (NT) regime for cases where the energy efficiency is the main concern. Characteristics of 7nm FinFETs [10], and for comparison purposes, 16nm PTM planar CMOS transistors [23] are reported in Table 1 for both ST and NT operations. In both regimes, the OFF current of 7nm FinFET devices is lower than that of 16nm PTM counterpart, which is approximately 12$\times$ smaller in the ST regime, but only 2$\times$ smaller in the NT operation mode. Basically, because of the negligible *drain induced barrier lowering* (DIBL) effect in FinFET devices, OFF currents of FinFET devices in ST and NT regimes are almost identical. However, for 16nm planar CMOS devices, the OFF current in the NT regime is $\sim$5$\times$ lower than that of the ST regime.

Table 1: Characteristics of 7nm FinFET and 16nm planar CMOS (PTM) devices for super-threshold (ST) and near-threshold (NT) regimes.

Device Library	Operating Mode	V_{dd} (V)	ON Current (A/μm) NFET	ON Current (A/μm) PFET	OFF Current (A/μm) NFET	OFF Current (A/μm) PFET	ON/OFF Current Ratio NFET	ON/OFF Current Ratio PFET	Reference
7nm FinFET	ST	0.45	8.818e-04	5.504e-04	3.811e-08	5.782e-08	23,140	9,518	[10]
7nm FinFET	NT	0.3	1.494e-04	1.366e-04	3.497e-08	5.675e-08	4,272	2,408	[10]
16nm PTM	ST	0.7	1.397e-03	9.839e-04	4.884e-07	6.084e-07	2,860	1,617	[23]
16nm PTM	NT	0.5	5.415e-04	3.621e-04	1.009e-07	9.081e-08	5,367	3,987	[23]

2.2 Circuit-Level Design

Based on device simulations, we also extract compact Verilog-A models which serve as the interface between the SPICE engine and the device simulator. These SPICE-compatible Verilog-A models allow us to perform fast gate- and circuit-level simulations, compared with the extremely slow device-level simulations. An important application of the Verilog-A models is to characterize a library of standard cells which includes timing and power models as well as layout information for a set of combinational (e.g., INV, NAND, NOR, XOR) and sequential (e.g., latch and D-flip-flop) logic gates [22]. This information is then stored in the Liberty library format (.lib), and are later used in order to synthesize logic circuits, such as processor cores and NoC routers.

We also develop standard 6T and the more robust 8T SRAM cells made of the 7nm FinFET devices, which will be used as the main building blocks of cache memories. For both 6T and 8T SRAM cells, we (i) derive the cell area from the layout information in order to obtain the memory density, (ii) measure the *static noise margin* (SNM) in order to ensure the robust operation of the SRAM cell under deeply-scaled technology nodes, and (iii) calculate the leakage power of the SRAM cell. SNM and leakage power of SRAM cells are measured by SPICE simulations using the Verilog-A models.

2.3 Architecture-Level Evaluation

We synthesize the LEON3 [3] seven-stage processor (with cache memories excluded) and the Open Source NoC Router RTL [7] (with 128-bit link width, and two virtual channels per input port) based on the developed 7nm FinFET standard cell library. The LEON3 is a fully synthesisable VHDL model of a 32-bit processor based on the SPARC-V8 RISC architecture, and is selected as the in-order processor core in this paper. However, for an advanced OoO core, we adopt a Nehalem-based processor, and since we cannot find an RTL description for such processor, the frequency and power consumption are calculated using the McPAT tool [12]. Characteristics of the Nehalem-based processor core are derived under 45nm technology node, but are then scaled down to 7nm FinFET technology. In order to derive the appropriate technology scaling factors, we use Synopsys Design Compiler to synthesize several ISCAS bechmark circuits and processors using 45nm NanGate and 7nm FinFET standard cell libraries (under both ST and NT regimes).

In order to characterize FinFET-based cache memories, we use a modified version of CACTI tool [16], which also supports 7nm FinFET devices as well as the standard 8T SRAM cell. This modified CACTI tool also provides XML files for introducing new technologies and/or devices. By us-

ing these XML interfaces, we are able to characterize cache memories made of 7nm FinFET and 16nm planar CMOS devices. Testing results on a 16KB L1 cache demonstrates that 4.6× per-access energy reduction and 13× leakage power consumption reduction can be achieved when comparing 7nm FinFET and 16nm planar CMOS devices.

3. DARK SILICON PREDICTION METHODOLOGY

The methodology that we use in order to predict the percentage of dark silicon in future multicore processors made of deeply-scaled FinFET devices is described in this section.

3.1 Prediction Methodology for OoO Processors

We project OoO multicore scaling into 7nm gate-length FinFET technology using the following procedure. We adopt the Sniper [9] multicore simulator to execute various applications from the PARSEC [8] and SPLASH2 [21] benchmarks. We adopt a 64-core as the OoO multicore platform built in 45nm bulk CMOS technology, with Nehalem-based cores, individual L1 data and instruction caches with the following configurations: 32KB, 4-way, 3-cycle latency, 1-bank, LRU replacement policy, and individual L2 cache with the following configurations: 256KB, 4-way, 6-cycle latency, 2-bank, LRU replacement policy. The measured operating frequency of the OoO multicore platform is 2.6GHz.

When projecting into 7nm gate-length FinFET technology, we make the assumption that the projected multicore processor with 7nm FinFET technology uses the same core structure and L1/L2 cache configurations with the original processor with 45nm bulk CMOS technology. More specifically, the L1 instruction/data caches and L2 cache still take 3 cycles and 6 cycles, respectively. Since the propagation delay of logic circuits has better scalability with technology nodes than cache memories, the clock frequency of the 7nm FinFET processor will be dominated by cache latency. As a result, the clock frequency of the 7nm FinFET 64-core processor is determined from our modified CACTI tool and is ~5GHz. For the data path using 7nm FinFET technology, we derive the dynamic energy consumption and leakage power consumption from the circuit synthesis results and power traces of the 64-core platform executing benchmarks. Please note that the processing core with 7nm FinFET technology may have larger portion of slack time in each clock cycle because the clock cycle is determined by the cache scaling, and thus, the leakage energy consumption may be more significant in this case.

Table 3: Frequency levels of the adopted processor cores, and the NoC router under 7nm FinFET technology, for super-threshold (ST) and near-threshold (NT) regimes. Frequencies are reported in GHz.

Component	OoO		In-Order	
	ST	NT	ST	NT
Processor	5	3.03	2.86	1.52
Router	4	3.03	2.86	1.52

3.2 Prediction Methodology for In-Order Processors

The in-order multicore platform is a 64-core processor, made of LEON3 cores, with individual L1 data and instruction cache memories with the following configurations: 16KB, direct-mapped, 1-cycle latency, 1-bank, LRU replacement policy, and individual L2 cache with the same configuration as that of the OoO multicore platform. In order to have a single-cycle L1 cache, the operating frequency of the in-order multicore platform is determined by the clock cycle of the L1 cache memory, which is 2.86GHz (measured by FinCACTI tool [16]). On the other hand, since the VHDL description of the LEON3 is available, we can synthesize it using our 7nm FinFET standard cell library. However, because LEON3 is a simple microprocessor, a scaling factor to translate the power consumption of the LEON3 to an actual processor is needed, which is described next.

We adopt a simple OoO processor, called mor1kx (Cappuccino implementation) [4], which is written in Verilog HDL, and synthesize it using Synopsys Design Compiler under our 7nm FinFET standard cell library. We then divide the leakage and dynamic power consumptions of the Nehalem-based core (obtained from McPAT) by the corresponding power component of the mor1kx core (obtained from Design Compiler) in order to derive the factor that scales the power consumption of a simple processor to an actual implementation. By multiplying this scaling factor by the LEON3 results, we can obtain the power consumption of a complex in-order processor. The reason that we are interested in in-order multicore processors is because such processors may be the future trend in many-core platforms.

4. RESULTS AND DISCUSSION

We assume that the multicore processor contains 64 tiles, where each tile is comprised of a processor core (OoO or in-order, depending on the type of the multicore processor), private L1 and L2 cache memories, and an NoC router. Routers are arranged in a two-dimensional 8×8 mesh topology. In this section, we adopt the following multicore platforms: (i) OoO - ST, (ii) OoO - NT, (iii) in-order - ST, and (iv) in-order - NT, where the first term denotes the type of core, and the second term indicates the operating mode of the multicore processor.

Table 2 reports the power consumptions of different components of the adopted multicore platforms for the 7nm FinFET technology. Frequency levels of the core and router for each platform are also shown in Table 3. The OoO processor consumes 1.9× (2.1×) more power compared with its in-order counterpart under the ST (NT) regime. On the other hand, the total power consumption of the OoO (in-order) tile has been reduced from 595mW (315mW) in the ST regime

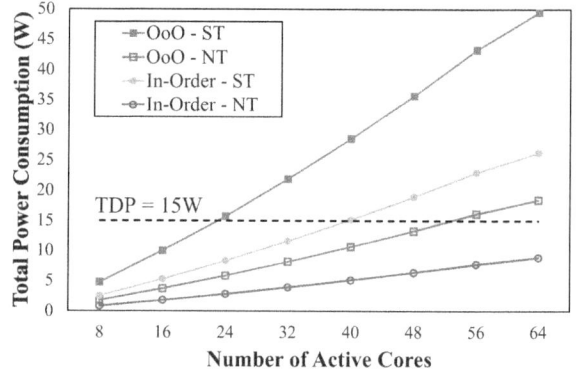

Figure 3: Total power consumption of different multicore platforms under 7nm FinFET technology vs. the number of active (turned-on) cores at the same time. TDP limits the number of cores that can be turned on at the same time, resulting in the dark silicon phenomenon.

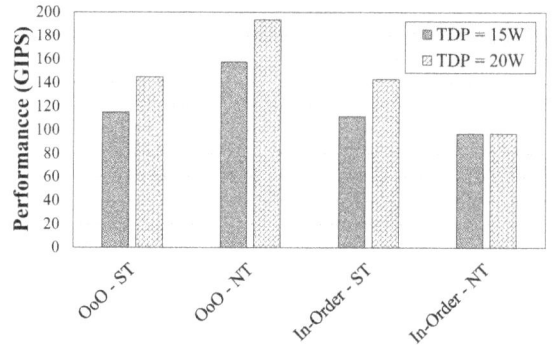

Figure 4: Performance of different multicore platforms under 7nm FinFET technology for TDP=15W and TDP=20W. Performance of a processor is defined as billion instructions per second (GIPS).

to 222mW (107mW) in the NT regime, resulting in 2.7× (3×) power reduction. In fact, using in-order cores and especially operating at the NT regime significantly reduces the power consumption, but this power reduction comes at the cost of performance degradation.

Using the results of Table 2, power breakdowns of the OoO and in-order tiles under ST and NT regimes are calculated and shown in Figure 2. Because of the architectural complexity of the OoO core, the processor is the main component of the power consumption of the OoO tile. However, by moving to a simpler in-order core, L2 cache (because of the high leakage power consumption) becomes the main component of the power consumption of the in-order tile. More precisely, the cache memory system (including L1 and L2 caches) dominates the total power consumption of the in-order processor.

We measure the total power consumption of the adopted multicore platforms, assuming that a subset of cores, varying from 8 to 64, are powered on (active) at the same time. For this purpose, a parallelism penalty of 0.625% is added to the total power consumption per core, which basically is

Table 2: Power consumptions of the OoO and in-order cores, L1 and L2 caches, as well as the NoC router under 7nm FinFET technology, for super-threshold (ST) and near-threshold (NT) regimes. P_{dyn}, P_{leak}, and P_{tot} denote the average dynamic, leakage, and total power consumptions, respectively. No parallelism penalty is assumed for the reported power consumption of the 64-core platform in this table. All powers are reported in mW.

Component	OoO - ST			OoO - NT			In-Order - ST			In-Order - NT		
	P_{dyn}	P_{leak}	P_{tot}	P_{dyn}	P_{leak}	P_{tot}	P_{dyn}	P_{leak}	P_{tot}	P_{dyn}	P_{leak}	P_{tot}
Processor	151	124	275	22	70	93	19	15	34	2	7	9
L1	73	37	110	7	21	29	82	19	102	8	11	19
L2	10	93	104	1	55	56	10	93	104	1	55	56
Router	39	67	106	6	38	44	28	48	76	3	19	22
Tile	273	321	595	36	185	222	140	176	315	15	92	107
64-Core			38,052			14,178			20,188			6,816

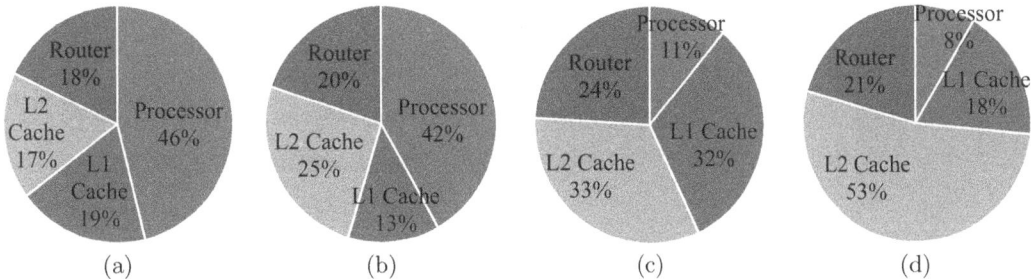

Figure 2: Power breakdowns of the OoO multicore processor in (a) super-threshold (ST) and (b) near-threshold (NT) regimes, and the in-order multicore processor in (c) ST and (d) NT regimes under 7nm FinFET technology.

due to the power overheads imposed by the cache coherency protocol and network congestions in cases where more cores are powered on. Results are illustrated in Figure 3. As can be seen, the in-order multicore platform operating in the NT regime results in the lowest power consumption, and does not experience any dark silicon effect even with TDP = 10W. In other multicore platforms, however, a portion of the core should be powered off, pointing to the existence of the dark silicon on chip.

In order to measure the effect of dark silicon in the adopted multicore platforms, we use TDP = 15W and TDP = 20W. Based on these TDP levels, the maximum number of cores that can be active at the same time, the total power consumption, and the percentage of cores that should be left dark in each multicore processor are reported in Table 4. Based on this table, we make the following observations. For TDP = 15W, 64% (19%) and 39% (0%) dark silicon are observed in OoO and in-order multicores, respectively, under the ST (NT) regime. However, increasing the TDP budget to 20W reduces the amount of dark silicon to 55% and 22% in OoO and in-order multicores operating in the ST regime, respectively, but leaves no dark silicon under the NT regime.

Finally, in order to make a conclusion, the performance as well as the energy efficiency of the multicore platforms are evaluated. For this purpose, performance of the processor is defined as billion instructions per second, and is denoted by $GIPS = N_{max} \times f_{clk}$, where N_{max} and f_{clk} represent the maximum number of active cores at any time and the clock frequency of the processor, respectively. On the other hand, the energy efficiency of the processor is defined as billion instructions per second per watt (or billion instructions per

joule), and is denoted by $GIPS/W = GIPS / P_{total}$, where P_{total} is the total power consumption of the multicore processor when N_{max} cores are active at f_{clk}. Performance and energy efficiency values of the adopted multicore platforms are shown in Figure 4 and Figure 5, respectively. We can observe that for TDP=15W, the OoO processor operating in the near-threshold regime achieves the highest performance as well as the highest energy efficiency among all adopted multicore platforms. The highest energy efficiency under TDP=20W is obtained by using the in-order processor operating in the near-threshold regime, which is because of the extremely low power operation of this platform.

These results point to the effectiveness of the near-threshold operation in mitigating the effect of the dark silicon phenomenon under deeply-scaled FinFET technologies. In fact, the near-threshold operation enhances the performance by allowing more cores to be active at any time, and hence enabling more aggressive parallelism, and also increases the energy efficiency, because of operating in the minimum energy operation point of the system.

5. CONCLUSION

We studied the effect of dark silicon in future FinFET technologies for OoO and in-order multicore processors under ST and NT operating modes. For this purpose, a device-circuit-architecture cross-layer design and analysis framework has been introduced, which is adopted in order to derive the leakage and dynamic power consumptions as well frequency levels of OoO and in-order processor cores, on-chip L1 and L2 cache memories, and NoC routers. According to our results, for a 64-core chip and 15W thermal design power budget, 64% (19%) and 39% (0%) dark silicon are ob-

Table 4: Prediction of dark silicon in different multicore platforms in 7nm FinFET technology under 15W and 20W TDP values.

Multicore Platform	TDP = 15W			TDP = 20W		
	Max # of Active Cores	Total Power (W)	Dark Silicon	Max # of Active Cores	Total Power (W)	Dark Silicon
OoO - ST	23	14.957	64%	29	19.505	55%
OoO - NT	52	14.688	19%	64	19.140	0%
In-Order - ST	39	14.686	39%	50	19.912	22%
In-Order - NT	64	9.202	0%	64	9.202	0%

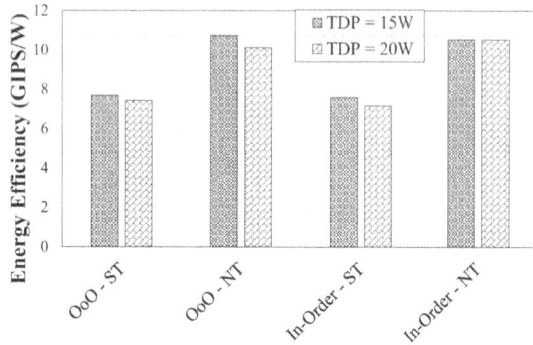

Figure 5: Energy efficiency of different multicore platforms under 7nm FinFET technology for TDP=15W and TDP=20W. Energy efficiency of a processor is defined as billion instructions per second per watt (GIPS/W).

served in OoO and in-order multicores, respectively, under the ST (NT) regime. Furthermore, performance and energy efficiency results of the multicore platforms point to the effectiveness of near-threshold computing in mitigating the effect of dark silicon phenomenon in deeply-scaled FinFET technologies.

6. ACKNOWLEDGMENTS

This research is supported by grants from the PERFECT program of the Defense Advanced Research Projects Agency and the Software and Hardware Foundations of the National Science Foundation.

7. REFERENCES

[1] GLOBALFOUNDRIES 14nm technology. [Online]. Available: http://www.globalfoundries.com/technology-solutions/leading-edge-technology/14-lpe-lpp

[2] Intel®22nm technology. [Online]. Available: http://www.intel.com/content/www/us/en/silicon-innovations/intel-22nm-technology.html

[3] LEON3 processor. [Online]. Available: http://www.gaisler.com/index.php/products/processors/leon3

[4] mor1kx - an OpenRISC Processor IP Core. [Online]. Available: https://github.com/openrisc/mor1kx

[5] Synopsys Technology Computer-Aided Design (TCAD). [Online]. Available: http://www.synopsys.com/tools/tcad

[6] TSMC 16nm technology. [Online]. Available: http://www.tsmc.com/english/dedicatedFoundry/technology/16nm.htm

[7] D. U. Becker. *Efficient Microarchitecture for Network-on-Chip Routers*. PhD thesis, Stanford University, August 2012.

[8] C. Bienia. *Benchmarking Modern Multiprocessors*. PhD thesis, Princeton University, January 2011.

[9] T. Carlson, W. Heirman, and L. Eeckhout. Sniper: Exploring the level of abstraction for scalable and accurate parallel multi-core simulation. In *International Conference for High Performance Computing, Networking, Storage and Analysis (SC)*, pages 1–12, Nov 2011.

[10] S. Chen, Y. Wang, X. Lin, Q. Xie, and M. Pedram. Performance prediction for multiple-threshold 7nm-FinFET-based circuits operating in multiple voltage regimes using a cross-layer simulation framework. In *IEEE SOI-3D-Subthreshold Microelectronics Technology Unified Conference (S3S)*, Oct. 2014.

[11] H. Esmaeilzadeh, E. Blem, R. St. Amant, K. Sankaralingam, and D. Burger. Dark Silicon and the End of Multicore Scaling. In *38th International Symposium on Computer Architecture (ISCA)*, pages 365–376, 2011.

[12] S. Li, J.-H. Ahn, R. Strong, J. Brockman, D. Tullsen, and N. Jouppi. McPAT: An Integrated Power, Area, and Timing Modeling Framework for Multicore and Manycore Architectures. In *42nd International Symposium on Microarchitecture (MICRO-42)*, pages 469–480, Dec 2009.

[13] X. Lin, Y. Wang, and M. Pedram. Joint sizing and adaptive independent gate control for FinFET circuits operating in multiple voltage regimes using the logical effort method. In *IEEE/ACM International Conference on Computer-Aided Design (ICCAD)*, pages 444–449, Nov 2013.

[14] T. Matsukawa, S. O'uchi, K. Endo, Y. Ishikawa, H. Yamauchi, Y. X. Liu, J. Tsukada, K. Sakamoto, and M. Masahara. Comprehensive Analysis of Variability Sources of FinFET Characteristics. In *Symposium on VLSI Technology*, 2009.

[15] E. Nowak, I. Aller, T. Ludwig, K. Kim, R. Joshi, C.-T. Chuang, K. Bernstein, and R. Puri. Turning Silicon on its Edge [Double Gate CMOS/FinFET Technology]. *IEEE Circuits and Devices Magazine*, 20(1):20–31, 2004.

[16] A. Shafaei, Y. Wang, X. Lin, and M. Pedram. FinCACTI: Architectural Analysis and Modeling of Caches with Deeply-Scaled FinFET Devices. In *IEEE Computer Society Annual Symposium on VLSI (ISVLSI)*, July 2014.

[17] M. Shafique, S. Garg, J. Henkel, and D. Marculescu. The EDA Challenges in the Dark Silicon Era: Temperature, Reliability, and Variability Perspectives. In *51st Design Automation Conference (DAC)*, pages 185:1–185:6, 2014.

[18] S. Tang, L. Chang, N. Lindert, Y.-K. Choi, W.-C. Lee, X. Huang, V. Subramanian, J. Bokor, T.-J. King, and C. Hu. Finfet - a quasi-planar double-gate mosfet. In *IEEE International Solid-State Circuits Conference (ISSCC)*, 2001.

[19] M. B. Taylor. Is Dark Silicon Useful?: Harnessing the Four Horsemen of the Coming Dark Silicon Apocalypse. In *49th Design Automation Conference (DAC)*, 2012.

[20] X. Wang, A. Brown, B. Cheng, and A. Asenov. Statistical Variability and Reliability in Nanoscale FinFETs. In *IEEE International Electron Devices Meeting (IEDM)*, pages 5.4.1–5.4.4, Dec 2011.

[21] S. C. Woo, M. Ohara, E. Torrie, J. P. Singh, and A. Gupta. The splash-2 programs: Characterization and methodological considerations. In *Proceedings of the 22Nd Annual International Symposium on Computer Architecture (ISCA)*, ISCA '95, pages 24–36, 1995.

[22] Q. Xie, X. Lin, Y. Wang, M. Dousti, A. Shafaei, M. Ghasemi-Gol, and M. Pedram. 5nm FinFET Standard Cell Library Optimization and Circuit Synthesis in Near-and Super-Threshold Voltage Regimes. In *IEEE Computer Society Annual Symposium on VLSI (ISVLSI)*, July 2014.

[23] W. Zhao and Y. Cao. New Generation of Predictive Technology Model for Sub-45nm Early Design Exploration. *IEEE Transactions on Electron Devices*, 53(11):2816–2823, 2006.

Small-World Network Enabled Energy Efficient and Robust 3D NoC Architectures

Sourav Das, Dongjin Lee, Dae Hyun Kim, Partha Pratim Pande
School of Electrical Engineering and Computer Science
Washington State University, Pullman, USA
{sdas, dlee2, daehyun, pande}@eecs.wsu.edu

ABSTRACT

Three dimensional (3D) Network-on-Chip (NoC) architectures enable design of low power and high performance communication fabrics for multicore chips. In spite of achievable performance benefits, 3D NoCs are still bottlenecked by the planar interconnects. To exploit the benefits introduced by the vertical dimension, it is imperative to explore novel 3D NoC architectures. In this paper, we propose design of a small-world (SW) network based 3D NoCs. We demonstrate that the proposed 3D SW NoC outperforms its conventional 3D mesh-based counterparts. On average, it provides ~25% reduction in the energy delay product (EDP) compared to 3D MESH without introducing any additional link overhead in presence of conventional SPLASH-2 and PARSEC benchmarks. The proposed 3D SW NoC is more robust in presence of TSV failures and performs better than fault-free 3D MESH even in the presence of 25% TSVs failure.

Categories and Subject Descriptors

C.2.1 [**Computer-Communication Networks**]: Network Architecture and Design

General Terms

Algorithms, Performance, Design

Keywords

3D NoC; small-world; latency; energy dissipation; TSV

1. INTRODUCTION

Three dimensional (3D) Network-on-Chip (NoC) is an emerging paradigm that takes advantages of amalgamation of two emerging technologies, NoC and 3D IC. It allows for the creation of new structures that enable significant performance enhancements over more traditional solutions. With freedom in the third dimension, architectures that were impossible or prohibitive due to wiring constraints in planar ICs are now possible, and many 3D implementations can outperform their 2D counterparts. Existing 3D NoC architectures predominantly follow straightforward extension of regular 2D NoCs. However, this does not exploit the advantages provided by the 3D integration technology appropriately. The additional degree of freedom provided by the vertical connections enables design of more efficient irregular architectures. In this context, design of small-world network-based NoC architectures [1] is a notable example. It is already shown that either by inserting long-range shortcuts in a regular mesh architecture to induce small-world effects or by adopting power-law based small-world

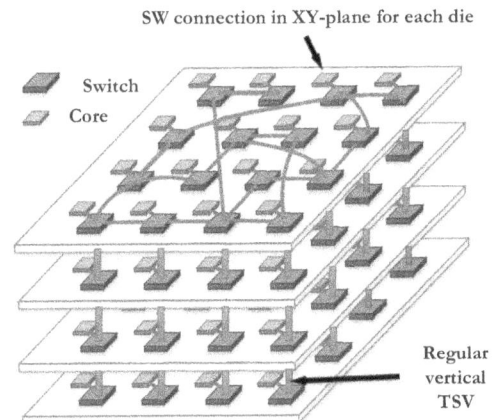

Figure 1: Conceptual view of 3D SW NoC with TSVs. For simplicity, only one logical XY-plane SW connection is shown here.

connectivity it is possible to achieve significant performance gain and lower energy dissipation compared to traditional multi-hop mesh networks [1][2]. In this work, we advocate that this concept of small-worldness should be adopted in 3D NoCs too. More specifically, the vertical links in 3D NoCs should enable design of long-range shortcuts necessary for a small-world network. These vertical connections give rise to close proximity among communicating nodes that would have been far apart in a solely planar system.

In this work, we propose design of 3D small-world (SW) NoC architectures. Considering the perfectly aligned vertical link placement constraints of Through Silicon Vias (TSVs), we first determine the suitable design parameters of 3D SW NoCs. Next, by exploiting the vertical dimension in a 3D IC, the tasks are mapped among the cores in such a way that physically long distant and highly communicating cores are placed along the vertical dimension, and hence overall system performance can be significantly improved. Through rigorous experiments we demonstrate that the proposed architecture is capable of achieving better performance and lower energy dissipation compared to conventional 3D MESH architectures. As the TSVs are costly in terms of fabrication, area overhead, energy dissipation; we investigate the performance degradation of different NoCs due to TSV failure. We demonstrate that for up to 25% of TSV failure, the proposed 3D SW NoC is capable of achieving better performance than a fault-free 3D MESH architecture.

2. RELATED WORK

3D NoC has emerged as one of the compelling solutions to design high performance and low power communication infrastructure for multicore chips. The natural extension of 2D planar architecture was the simple and regular 3D mesh-based NoC, which has been investigated in many existing works [3][4][5]. NoC-bus hybrid architecture was proposed in [6] that used central bus arbiter and

Dynamic Time Division Multiple Access (dTDMA) technique for bus access in the vertical dimension to reduce the network latency. To take advantage of vertical short distance inherent in 3D integration, 3D Dimensionally Decomposed (DimDe) NoC router architecture [7] was developed that reduces the total energy consumption, but latency was not minimized. Reducing the number of input ports, an improved version of 3D NoC router architecture was developed in [8]. As all of these architectures have buses in the Z-dimension, with increase in the network size, they are subject to traffic congestion and high latency under high traffic injection loads. Integration of 3D IC and on-chip photonics was exploited in the design of hybrid NoC architectures [9][10]. These architectures are capable of providing very high bandwidth and low power dissipation. However, the challenges of integrating two emerging paradigms, 3D IC and silicon Nano-photonics have not been overcome yet.

In this work we propose a robust 3D NoC architecture that combines the benefits of reduced vertical distance of 3D ICs and the low hop-count and robustness of small-world architecture. We present detailed design methodologies for developing the 3D SW NoC, evaluate its performance with respect to conventional 3D MESH and other irregular architectures by incorporating suitable network routing algorithms.

3. PROPOSED 3D NOC

Modern complex network theory provides a powerful method to analyze network topologies. Between a regular, locally interconnected mesh network and a completely random Erdös-Rényi topology, there are other classes of graphs, such as small-world and scale-free graphs. Small-world graphs have a very short average path length, defined as the number of hops between any pair of nodes. The average shortest path length of small-world graphs is bounded by a polynomial in log (N), where N is the number of nodes, making them particularly interesting for efficient communication with minimal resources [11]. NoCs incorporating small-world connectivity can perform significantly better than locally interconnected mesh-like networks [1], yet they require far fewer resources than a fully connected system.

3.1 Topology of Network

Our goal is to use the small-world (SW) approach to build a highly efficient 3D-NoC with planar links and TSVs in the vertical dimension. We consider 4 layers in this 3D NoC topology and the dimension of each layer is 10 mm x 10 mm.

3.1.1 Communication path length (μ)

In the proposed 3D NoC topology (Figure 1), each core is connected to a switch; the switches are interconnected using planar and TSV links. The topology of the NoC is a small-world network where the links between switches are established following a power law distribution. More precisely, the probability $P(i,j)$ of establishing a link between two switches i and j, separated by an Euclidean distance ℓ_{ij}, is proportional to the distance raised to a finite power as in [11]:

$$P(i,j) = \frac{\ell_{ij}^{-\alpha} f_{ij}}{\sum_{\forall i} \sum_{\forall j} \ell_{ij}^{-\alpha} f_{ij}} \quad (1)$$

The frequency of traffic interaction between cores, f_{ij}, is also factored in, so that the more frequently communicating cores have a higher probability of having a direct link between them. This frequency is expressed as the percentage of traffic generated from core i that is sent to core j. This approach implicitly optimizes the network architecture for a non-uniform traffic scenario. Getting now into details, the parameter α governs the nature of

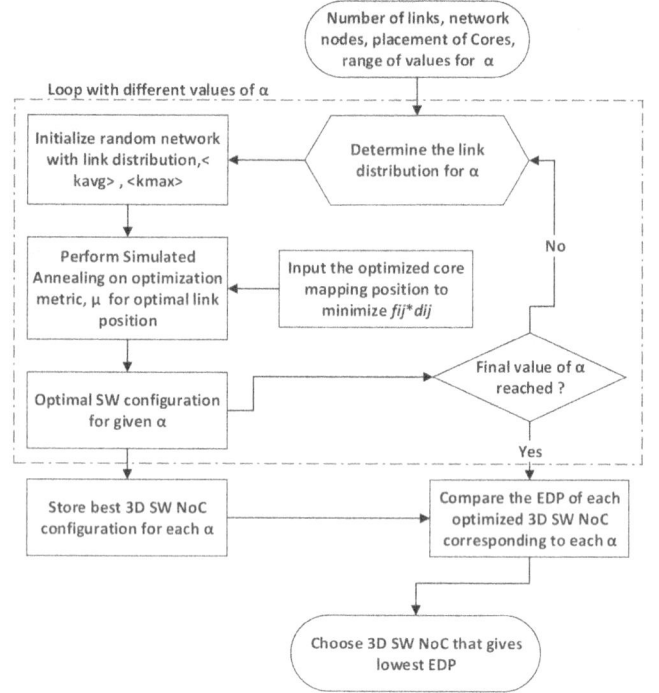

Figure 2: Our network creation algorithm for 3D SW NoC.

connectivity; in particular, a larger α would mean a locally connected network with a few, or even no long-range links. By the same token, a zero value of α would generate an ideal small-world network following the Watts-Strogatz model [11] – one with long-range shortcuts that are virtually independent of the distance between the cores. It has been shown that α being less than $D + 1$, D being the dimension of the network, ensures the small-worldness [12]. Overall, the parameter α, affects the NoC performance significantly. Thus, for our proposed architecture, we first focus on determining the parameter 'α' considering the constraints of the 3D network structure. To be specific, as we consider TSVs for vertical connection, these links need to be perfectly aligned along the z-dimension and we can apply irregularities following power law-based interconnection in the planar dies only.

In order to determine α, we focus on optimizing the parameter, μ, which is the average path length for any message. Optimizing the average path length ensures less utilization of network resources and improvement in the network performance both in terms of latency and energy dissipation. We define μ as the product of hop count, frequency of communication and link length between any pair of source and destination-

$$\mu = \sum_{\forall i} \sum_{\forall i} (m * h_{ij} + d_{ij}) * f_{ij} \quad (2)$$

Where h_{ij} is hop count between switches i and j; m is number of stages inside a NoC switch; f_{ij} is frequency of communication and d_{ij} is physical distance corresponding to each hop calculated along the path. So any network that possesses low μ will achieve low message latency and energy dissipation and hence low energy-delay-product (EDP).

3.1.2 3D SW NoC design steps

As mentioned above, the parameter α governs the nature of the connectivity. Hence, we first determine the value of this parameter that will help us in designing the 3D SW NoC architecture with least EDP. To build 3D SW NoCs with optimum value of α, we develop the design flow shown in Figure 2. The inputs to the flow are the total number of links, the total number of nodes, the locations of the cores, and α. The design flow is as follows:

1. For a given α, we calculate the link length distribution following (1). In this work, we constrain the number of total links equal to that of 3D MESH and the system size is 4x4x4.

2. We follow the constraint of perfectly aligned regular vertical link placement along the z-dimension. This is because along the z-dimension, we use TSVs and they need to be perfectly aligned.

3. The small-world network has an irregular connectivity. Hence, the number of links connected to each switch is not a constant. For fair comparison between our small-world network and 3D MESH, we assume that both of them use the same average number of connections, $<k_{avg}>$ per switch. This also ensures that the 3D SW NoC does not introduce additional links compared to 3D MESH. For a 64-core system, $<k_{avg}>$ is 4.5 considering all the switches including the peripheral ones. In addition, the maximum connectivity per node, $<k_{max}>$, is set to be 7 for the SW network as found in [13] [14].

4. To develop our SW network, we consider the communication frequency f_{ij} between any pair of source and destination nodes and try to optimize μ for network performance. We map the tasks among the cores in such a way that the overall μ decreases. To do this, we place highly communicating and long distant nodes along the vertical dimensions. Placing the physically long links in the vertical dimension provides two benefits. The wireline energy consumption reduces due to the reduction of the link length and the number of repeaters needed in a long planar wire. Moreover, the reduced network latency minimizing the probability of traffic congestion eventually reduces the overall power consumption.

5. After task remapping, we first build a random network with the link distribution determined at step 1. Then simulated annealing (SA) is performed to reduce μ. A solution perturbation method we use in the simulated annealing is to randomly choose an existing link, remove the link, and create a new link of the same length between two other nodes. The convergence criteria are the total number of perturbations, the lowest temperature, and the lowest bound (0.1% in our experiments) on the amount of performance improvement compared to the previous network configuration after a pre-determined number of perturbations. In this way, we develop the optimum 3D SW NoC configuration for a given α.

6. We build the optimum 3D NoC using the above steps for a given α. Consequently, we vary α within a certain range (determined experimentally in section 4) and determine the optimum 3D NoC for each α using our design flow. Finally to choose the optimum value of α for 3D SW NoC, we consider the particular network configuration that minimizes the EDP of the NoC. The simulation results will be shown in Section 4.

Following the above-mentioned steps and considering the constraints of network resources, we can develop optimized 3D SW NoC for any given set of applications.

3.1.3 3D SW- Bus NoC

In addition, we also consider 3D SW-BUS NoC architecture where we replace the network connections (Point-to-Point (P2P)) between the planar layers with TSV bus. As the distance between the individual 2D layers in 3D IC is small, bus is also a possibility for communicating in the Z-dimension [6]. For consistency with [15], our analysis considers the use of a dynamic time-division multiple-access (dTDMA) bus, although any other type of bus may be used as well.

3.2 Other 3D NoCs under Consideration

To benchmark the performance of our proposed 3D SW NoC architecture with respect to other irregular 3D NoCs, we consider the Mesh-Random-Random-Mesh (*mrrm*) and Random-random-random-random (*rrrr*) architecture as suggested in [15]. Like the 3D SW architecture, in this case also we keep the total number of links to be equal to that of a 3D MESH.

The characteristics of these two architectures are:

mrrm: Point to point (P2P) TSV based 3D NoC that consists of two planar layers of mesh-based interconnection architecture and the rest two layers have random interconnection patterns.

rrrr: P2P TSV based 3D NoC that consists of four layers of random interconnection networks.

To construct the *random* architectures for *mrrm* and *rrrr* configurations, 1000 random connection matrices were generated and we obtained the average of the average hop count over these 1000 matrices. Then the particular connection matrix, which has the closest average hop-count to the average of average hop-count, was selected for the *random* architecture

3.3 Routing Algorithm
3.3.1 ALASH

For regular 3D MESH architecture, XYZ or adaptive-Z are the preferred routing algorithms for their simplicity. For irregular architectures such as the small-world network, the topology agnostic Adaptive Layered Shortest Path Routing (ALASH) algorithm is proved to be suitable [16]. ALASH is built upon the layered shortest path (LASH) algorithm, but has better flexibility by allowing each message to adaptively switch paths, letting the message choose its own route at every intermediate switch. We incorporate the ALASH routing for our 3D SW architecture.

3.3.2 Elevator-First (EF)

Recently Elevator-first (EF) algorithm was proposed for 3D NoCs with limited vertical links [17]. To achieve deadlock-free routing in this algorithm, a message is restricted to revisit any xy-layer after it has already left that layer. To ensure this condition for an irregularly-connected xy-layer, we need to make sure that there should be at least one path between every source and destination pair in that layer. This puts additional constraints on irregular networks and SW NoC. Our proposed 3D-SW NoC has an irregular topology in the xy-plane, so we put this additional restriction on the proposed architecture keeping all other design parameters same. The performance of 3D SW NoC with EF algorithm is marked as 3D EF in this paper. We then compare the 3D EF's performance with respect to the ALASH-based design.

4. EXPERIMENTAL RESULTS AND ANALYSIS
4.1 Simulation Setup

To evaluate the performance of the proposed 3D SW NoC, we use a cycle accurate NoC simulator that can simulate any regular or irregular 3D architecture. Our system consists of 64 cores and 64 switches equally partitioned in four layers. Four SPLASH-2 benchmarks, FFT, RADIX, LU, and WATER [18], and five PARSEC benchmarks, DEDUP, VIPS, FLUIDANIMATE, CANNEAL, and BODYTRACK [19] are used. The width of each link is the same as the flit width, which is 32 bits. Each packet consists of 64 flits. The NoC simulator uses switches synthesized from an RTL level design using TSMC 65-nm CMOS process in Synopsys™ Design Vision. All switch ports have a buffer depth of two flits and each switch port has four virtual channels in case of

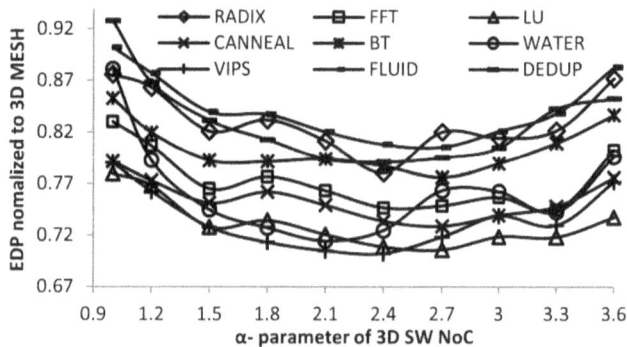

Figure 3: Variation of EDP w.r.t the connectivity parameter α.

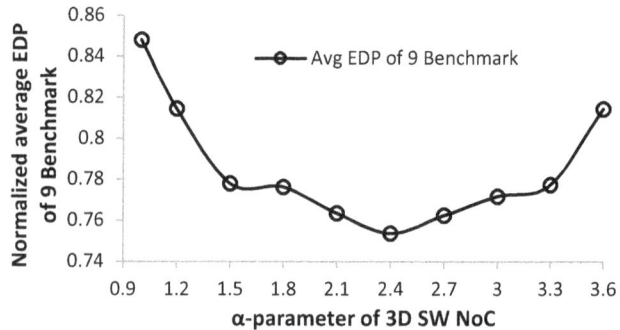

Figure 4: Average normalized EDP of the 9 benchmarks of 3D SW NoC with variation in α (normalized to 3D MESH).

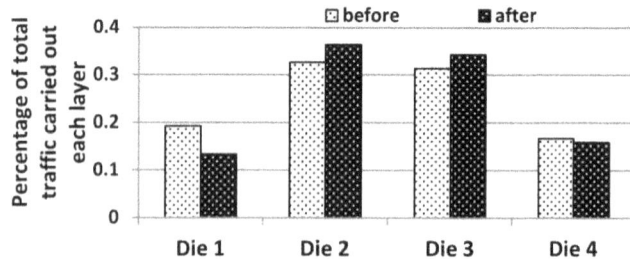

Figure 5: Percentage of total traffic carried out by each layer before and after task remapping.

irregular NoC. Hence, four layers are created in ALASH routing. Energy dissipation of the network switches, inclusive of the routing strategies, were obtained from the synthesized netlist by running Synopsys™ Prime Power, while the energy dissipated by wireline links was obtained through HSPICE simulations, taking into consideration the length of the wireline links.

4.2 Effects of Connectivity Parameter –α and Task remapping

In this section, we first determine the connectivity parameter- α for our proposed 3D SW NoC. We vary the connectivity parameter α from 1.0 to 3.6 and find the best α that gives us the lowest energy-delay product (EDP). Figure 3 shows the EDP values of our 3D SW NoC architecture for each α. The EDP values are normalized to those of 3D MESH NoC for all the benchmarks. As seen from the figure, as α increases from 1.0 to 2.4, the EDP decreases almost steadily. When α is small, large number of long-range links are likely to be placed at the cost of reduced local, short-range links. Although this configuration improves long-distance data exchange, it compromises the local communications, which have larger impact on the EDP than the long-distance communications. Thus, the EDP is high when α is small. As α increases from 2.4 to 3.6, most of the links become local, short-range links and the network approaches the regular multi-hop pattern that also results in high EDP. Therefore, we need to choose a value of α that achieves a compromise between these two extreme cases. If we increase α beyond 3.6, the long-range links become almost non-existent and the NoC architecture becomes very close to 3D MESH. Hence, we do not consider α beyond this.

To visualize the effect of α more clearly, Figure 4 plots the average EDP of the nine benchmarks. As shown in the figure, α=2.4 gives us the lowest EDP on average, so we choose α= 2.4 for our 3D SW NoC design.

Remapping tasks among the cores helps to improve NoC performance. However, task remapping may affect the traffic congestion. Figure 5 shows the percentage of total traffic carried by each die before and after remapping the tasks. We observe from this figure that the task remapping slightly increases the traffic carried by the second and the third dies, but it reduces the traffic in the first and the fourth dies. Therefore, it is clear that our task remapping does not lead to noticeable traffic congestion in any particular layer.

4.3 Comparison with Other Existing NoCs

In this section, we compare the performance of the proposed 3D SW NoC with other 2D and 3D NoC architectures. Especially, we consider the following existing architectures: 2D MESH, 2D small-world (2D SW), and 3D MESH, 3D mesh-bus hybrid architecture (3D MESH-BUS), 3D small-world (3D SW), and 3D SW-bus hybrid architecture (3D SW-BUS). For regular connection of 2D and 3D MESH, we use the XY and XYZ- dimension order routing whereas for all the SW architectures, we use ALASH-based routing. We also implemented the Elevator-first routing algorithm for 3D-SW and 3D SW-BUS NoCs to demonstrate the benefits of ALASH routing algorithm for irregular architectures. The 3D SW and 3D SW-BUS with the Elevator-first algorithm are marked as 3D EF and 3D EF-BUS, respectively. Since we are interested in both network latency and energy consumption, we use the unified EDP for the NoC performance metric. Figure 6 shows energy-delay-product (EDP) values of all the NoC architectures. All the EDP values are normalized to those of the conventional 2D MESH.

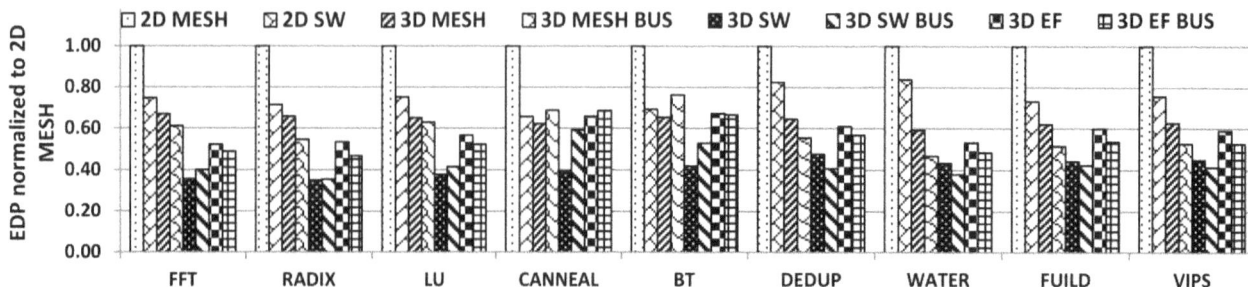

Figure 6: Energy-Delay product (EDP) normalized to 2D MESH for different NoCs.

The EDP for all the 3D NoCs is less than that of the 2D architectures. The value of the communication path length μ as shown in Table 1 helps us to analyze the reduction of EDP for 3D NoCs. Any network with lower value of μ, offers reduced weighted average hop count. On average, messages consume less network resources both from latency and energy perspective for that network. All the 3D NoCs have lower value of μ compared to 2D MESH and 2D SW and hence all of them perform better than 2D NoCs. 3D SW NoC possesses lowest value of μ among all NoCs. For 3D SW NoC, the remapping of the tasks for highly communicating and distant cores along the Z-dimension helps reducing the value of μ from 25.8 to 20.7. As a result, after remapping, the EDP value for 3D SW NoC reduces significantly. On an average, 3D SW shows ~25% reduction in EDP value compared to 3D MESH. Among the different 3D NoCs, 3D SW-BUS shows comparable EDP with 3D SW for relatively lower injection benchmarks i.e. LU, FFT, and VIPS. The bus is shared medium and performs efficiently whenever there are no access contentions among the connected nodes. For low traffic injection scenario, bus works as long range shot cuts between distant nodes without giving rise to contentions. However, for the comparatively higher traffic injection rates e.g. CANNEAL and BODYTRACK, bus access becomes a bottleneck and it results in traffic congestion. So network latency increases for 3D SW BUS and the performance degrades compared to 3D SW.

Next, we compare the performance of ALASH and Elevator-first routing algorithms implemented for the 3D SW and 3D SW-BUS architectures. ALASH routing algorithm ensures shortest path between a source-destination pair. Moreover, ALASH algorithm chooses paths based on traffic density and avoids traffic congestion on switches [14]. As a result it helps minimizing the latency and consequently energy consumption for any NoCs and performs better than other routing algorithms. On the other hand, Elevator-first routing algorithm is suited for 3D NoC with limited number of vertical links; it does not take into account traffic density of the X-Y planes. As a result, on average it encounters more traffic congestion and ultimately reroutes through longer paths compared to ALASH. Hence, by incorporating ALASH-based routing the latencies of 3D SW and 3D SW-BUS are less than 3D EF and 3D EF-BUS NoCs.

4.4 Comparison of 3D SW with Die Level Irregular NoCs

In this section, we compare the performance of the 3D SW NoCs with two recently proposed 3D irregular architectures, mesh-random-random-mesh (*mrrm*) and random-random-random-random (*rrrr*) as described in Section 3.2. Figure 7 shows the EDP for these architectures normalized with respect to the EDP of the 3D MESH. As the figure shows, the 3D SW architecture outperforms the *mrrm* and *rrrr* architectures. The *mrrm* and *rrrr* architectures have random distribution of interconnects instead of the power-law-based distribution. For *rrrr*, the link distribution contains large number of medium- and long-range links with the expense of short range links. As a result, the nearby communication

Table 1: Path length (μ) for different NoCs

NoC type	Communication path length (μ)
2D MESH	37.98
2D SW	34.38
3D MESH	27.72
3D EF	27.2
3D *mrrm*	26.96
3D *rrrr*	27.76
3D SW (w/o task remapping)	25.84
3D SW (w/ task remapping)	20.71

suffers from long latency and power dissipation. In *mrrm*, the link distribution is very close to 3D SW NoC in two layers only whereas the rest of the two layers consist of multi-hop mesh links. The power-law-based 3D SW NoC architecture balances both nearby and long distant communication and hence its performance is superior to both- *rrrr* and *mrrm*. In addition, long-range links are generally traffic attractors, so they lead to higher traffic congestion for some nodes if they are not optimized properly. Finally, as shown in table 1, the average communication path length μ of 3D SW NoC is lowest and hence it performs better than all these irregular architectures.

4.5 Robustness of 3D SW Architecture

The 3D NoC architectures considered here use TSVs for vertical communication. TSVs are subject to failures due to voids, cracks, and misalignment [20]. Thus, we analyze the performance of 3D NoCs for a broad range of TSV failure scenario-5%, 10%, and 25% of the total vertical links. When some of the TSVs fail, we remove them, so the resultant NoC becomes partially vertically connected as suggested in [17]. To evaluate the robustness of our 3D SW NoC architecture and the ALASH routing algorithm separately, we perform two-step experiments. First, we demonstrate the robustness of the 3D SW NoC architecture. We consider the *mrrm* architecture for comparison as it was found to be the best among all the other 3D architectures considered in this work. Then we focus on analyzing the role of the ALASH and EF routing algorithms in presence of TSV failure. The 3D SW NoCs incorporating ALASH and EF algorithms are marked as 3D SW and 3D EF respectively.

Figure 8 shows the EDP of 3D SW NoC, *mrrm* and 3D EF incorporating different TSV failures. The EDP is normalized to a fault-free 3D MESH NoC. The TSV failure scenario has been chosen randomly from one thousand trials. It is seen that, for all range of TSV failures, the EDP of 3D SW NoC is always better than that of *mrrm*. Presence of different irregular connectivity and power-law based link distribution on each die for 3D SW NoC helps increase its robustness in case of TSV failure. In addition, we observe that, 3D SW NoC with 25% of the total vertical links failure has a lower EDP than completely fault free 3D MESH. Moreover, both *mrrm* and 3D EF perform worse than 3D MESH in presence of the same amount of vertical link failure.

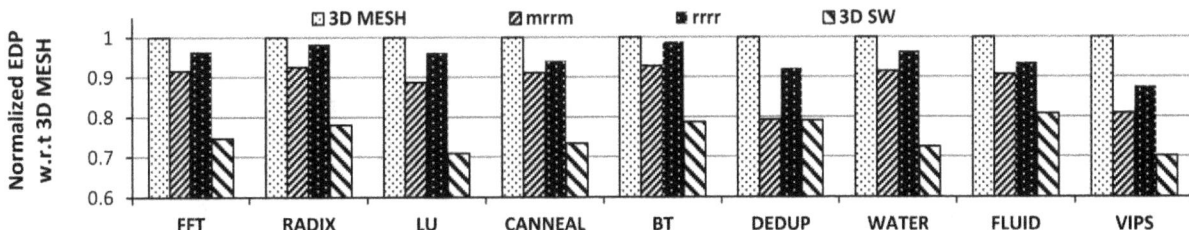

Figure 7: EDP value normalized to 3D MESH for different 3D NoCs.

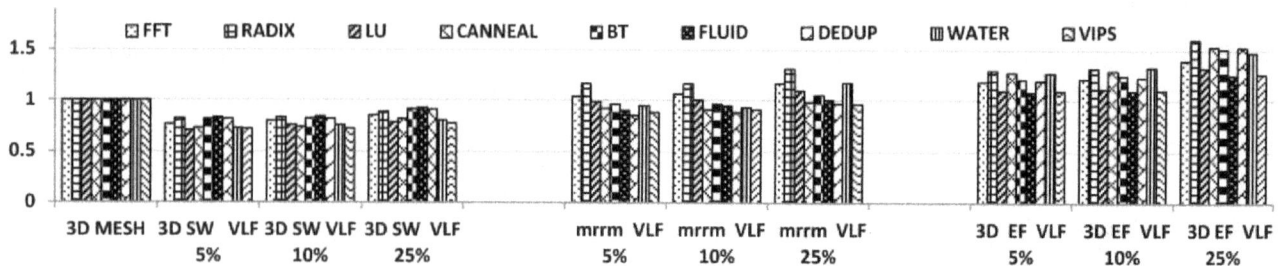

Figure 8: Normalized EDP in presence of random vertical link failure (VLF).

The Elevator-first algorithm mainly focuses on optimizing performance of partially vertically connected 3D NoCs [17]. Here we compare the performance of the NoC with vertical link failures by incorporating the ALASH and EF routing algorithms. ALASH ensures alternative shortest-path in case of link failure by adopting multi-path routing whereas EF always focuses on minimization of vertical distance without ensuring overall minimum path length. Consequently, removing higher number of TSVs from 3D SW NoC increases the traffic congestion probability for some of the vertical links in case of EF algorithm. As a result, the EDP of 3D EF with vertical link failure scenario is always higher than that of 3D SW implemented with ALASH.

5. CONCLUSION

This paper advocates design of small-world network-based 3D NoC architecture that predominantly uses the vertical links as the long-range shortcuts. In this way we are able to bring physically far and highly interacting nodes to logical proximity so that they are easily accessible to each other. This 3D NoC architecture not only outperforms existing regular mesh-based counterparts; it also offers better performance with respect to other recently proposed irregular architectures. The power-law based connectivity of this 3D SW NoC also makes it very robust against TSV failures. Even with 25% vertical link failure, it achieves better performance than fault-free 3D MESH-based NoC.

6. ACKONWLEDGEMENT

This work was supported in part by the US National Science Foundation (NSF) grants CCF-0845504, CNS-1059289, and CCF-1162202, and Army Research Office grant W911NF-12-1-0373.

7. REFERENCES

[1] U. Y. Ogras, R. Marculescu, ""It's a Small World After All": NoC Performance Optimization via Long-Range Link Insertion", IEEE Trans. on VLSI Systems, Vol. 14, pp 693-706, 2006.

[2] C. Teuscher, "Nature-inspired interconnects for self-assembled large-scale network-on-chip designs", e-print arXiv: arXiv: 0704.2852.

[3] V.F. Pavlidis, E. G. FriedMan, "3-D Topologies for Networks on-Chip," IEEE Trans on VLSI Systems, Vol 15, pp. 1081-1090, 2007.

[4] B. S. Feero, P.P. Pande "Networks-on-Chip in a Three-Dimensional Environment: A Performance Evaluation", IEEE Trans. on Computers, Vol 53, pp. 32-45, Aug. 2008.

[5] A.W. Topol, et al. "Three-Dimensional Integrated Circuits," IBM Journal of Research and Development, Vol. 50, nos. 4/5, July 2006.

[6] F. Li, C. Nicopoulos, T. Richardson, Y. Xie, V. Narayanan, M. Kandemir "High-Performance and Fault-Tolerant 3D NoC-Bus Hybrid Architecture Using ARB-NET Based Adaptive Monitoring Platform" IEEE Trans on Computers, Vol. 63, pp. 32-45, Aug. 2008.

[7] J. Kim et al., "A novel dimensionally-decomposed router for on-chip communication in 3D architectures," in Proc. of Annual Intl. Symp. On Computer Architecture, June 2007, pp. 138–149.

[8] A. M. Rahmani et al., "High-Performance and Fault-Tolerant 3D NoC-Bus Hybrid Architecture Using ARB-NET Based Adaptive Monitoring Platform", IEEE Trans. on Computers, vol 63, pp. 734-747, Mar 2014.

[9] D. Vantrease et al., "Corona: System Implications of Emerging Nanophotonic Technology," In Proc. of 35th Int'l Symposium Computer Architecture, pp. 153-164, June 2008.

[10] R. W. Morris, A. K. Kodi, A. Louri, R. D. Whaley"Three-Dimensional Stacked Nanophotonic Network-on-Chip Architecture with Minimal Reconfiguration", IEEE Transaction on Computers, Vol. 63, pp. 243-255, Jan. 2014.

[11] T. Petermann, P. D. L. Rios, "Spatial small-world networks: a wiring-cost perspective", e-print arXiv:cond-mat/0501420.

[12] T. Petermann, P. D. L. Rios, "Physical realizability of small-world networks", Phys. Rev. E 73, Feb 2006.

[13] R. Kim, G. Liu, P. Wettin, R. Marculescu, D. Marculescu, P. P. Pande, "Energy-Efficient VFI-Partitioned Multicore Design Using Wireless NoC Architectures", In Proc. of Intl Conf on, CASES 2014.

[14] P. Wettin et al., "Performance evaluation of wireless NoCs in presence of irregular network routing strategies," in Proc. of DATE, pp.1-6, 2014.

[15] H. Matsutani et al., "Low-Latency Wireless 3D NoCs via Randomized Shortcut Chips", in Proc. of DATE, 2014.

[16] O. Lysne, T. Skeie, S. A. Reinemo, I. Theiss, "Layered Routing in Irregular Networks", IEEE Transaction on Parallel and Distributed System, vol. 17, 2006, pp. 51- 65.

[17] F. Dubois, A. Sheibanyrad, F. Petrot, M. Bahmani, "Elevator-First: A Deadlock-Free Distributed Routing Algorithm for Vertically Partially Connected 3D-NoCs", IEEE Trans. on Computers, vol. 62, 2013, pp. 609-615.

[18] S. C. Woo, M. Ohara, E. Torrie, J. P. Singh, A. Gupta,"The SPLASH-2 programs: characterization and methodological considerations," In Proc. of International Symposium on Computer Architecture, 1995, pp. 24-36.

[19] C. Bienia, "Benchmarking modern multiprocessors", Ph.D. Dissertation, Princeton Univ., Princeton NJ, Jan. 2011.

[20] I. Loi, F. Angiolini, S. Mitra, L. Benini, "Characterization and Implementation of Fault-Tolerant Vertical Links for 3-D Networks-on-Chip", IEEE Trans. Computer Aided Design of Integrated Circuit and System, vol. 30, 2011, pp. 124-134.

A Dynamically Reconfigurable RF NoC for Many-Core

Alexandre Brière[1], Eren Unlu[2], Julien Denoulet[1], Andrea Pinna[1],
Bertrand Granado[1], Francois Pêcheux[1], Yves Louët[2], Christophe Moy[2]

[1]Sorbonne Universités, UPMC Univ Paris 06, UMR 7606, LIP6, F-75005 Paris, France
<firsname.lastname>@lip6.fr

[2]Supélec - IETR, F-35576 Cesson-Sevigne Cedex, France
<firsname.lastname>@supelec.fr

ABSTRACT

With the growing number of cores on chips, conventional electrical interconnects reach scalability limits, leading the way for alternatives like *Radio Frequency* (RF), optical and 3D. Due to the variability of applications, communication needs change over time and across regions of the chip. To address these issues, a dynamically reconfigurable *Network on Chip* (NoC) is proposed. It uses RF and *Orthogonal Frequency Division Multiple Access* (OFDMA) to create communication channels whose allocation allows dynamic reconfiguration. We describe the NoC architecture and the distributed mechanism of dynamic allocation. We study the feasibility of the NoC based on state of the art components and analyze its performances. Static analysis shows that, for point to point communications, its latency is comparable with a 256-node electrical mesh and becomes lower for wider networks. A major feature of this architecture is its broadcast capacity. The RF NoC becomes faster with 32 nodes, achieving a ×3 speedup with 1024. Under realistic traffic models, its dynamic reconfigurability provides up to ×6 lower latency while ensuring fairness.

Categories and Subject Descriptors

C.1.2 [**Processor Architectures**]: Multiple Data Stream Architectures (Multiprocessors)—*Interconnection architectures*

Keywords

Many-Core; NoC; RF; Dynamic; Reconfigurable;

1. INTRODUCTION

With the emergence of *Chip Multi Processor* (CMP), *Network on Chip* (NoC) have been introduced to make the different processing elements soundly communicate together. First generation NoCs based on electrical interconnects have been studied in the past decade. Their bandwidth can be considered as infinite, but they show limitations in terms of

GLSVLSI'15, May 20–22, 2015, Pittsburgh, PA, USA.
Copyright © 2015 ACM 978-1-4503-3474-7/15/05 ...$15.00.
http://dx.doi.org/10.1145/2742060.2742082.

latency, when the number of cores increases. To overcome these limitations, alternatives such as 3D, optical and *Radio Frequency* (RF) are now explored. In this paper, we present a RF NoC with dynamic allocation of communication resources. It takes advantage of RF properties to optimize bandwidth utilization and reduce latency. Section 2 presents an overview of related work. Section 3 describes the RF NoC architecture. Section 4 details the dynamic allocation algorithm. Section 5 presents experimental setups and results, and section 6 concludes the paper.

2. RELATED WORK

2.1 Technology trends

Following recommendations of the ITRS [8], new technologies are explored to overcome limitations of electrical connections. As chips integrate more and more components, distances, and therefore latency, increase. Pioneering contributions try to reduce distances with 3D [12, 15] or reduce traveling time with optic [13, 19] and RF [3, 2].

2.1.1 3D NoC

3D chips are based on stacked layers. In addition to planar connections, each layer has vertical connections with other layers. Some approaches mix 3D with optic [23] or RF [11] by using dedicated layers. 3D offers many advantages, but also adds significant thermal constraints.

2.1.2 Optical NoC

Optical is used to provide shortcuts for long distance communications. The use of optic, like other new technologies, not only allows a gain in bandwidth and latency, but also other architectural innovations such as new cache management policies [10]. A major drawback of optical NoC is the need of an external light source.

2.1.3 RF NoC

Similar to the optic solution, RF waves travels at a speed close to the speed of light. But, unlike optical solutions, RF directly benefits from full compatibility with CMOS technology. RF waves can be transmitted through a waveguide [2] or an antenna [4]. Solutions using antennas have greater flexibility, but they also increase consumption compared to waveguides, and suffer from lesser immunity to interference.

2.2 Communication Resources Allocation

As on-chip traffic is highly heterogeneous in the spatial and temporal domain, available bandwidth is generally un-

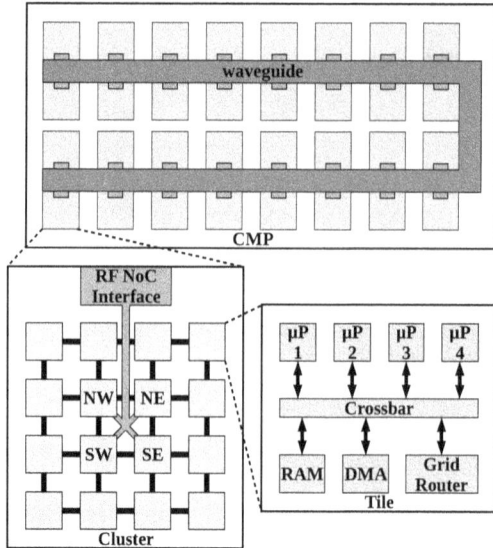

Figure 1: CMP hierarchical RF NoC architecture

derused and the design over-dimensioned in static interconnects. In optical or RF solutions, bandwidth is divided into dedicated channels that allow simultaneous transmissions. In a *Single Write Multiple Read* (SWMR) scheme, each communication channel is allocated to a specific node N so every other node can receive data sent by N [10]. In contrast, *Multiple Write Single Read* (MWSR) allocates each communication channels to a specific node N so it can receive information from other nodes [19]. MWSR has one drawback: it requires an arbitration mechanism in the receiving devices to avoid collision, as multiple nodes may simultaneously transmit data to the same destination node. SWMR supports broadcasting, while MWSR has to copy the broadcast message to each dedicated channel nodes. In terms of energy, all nodes in a SWMR scheme listen to all communication channels in the system (i.e. whole bandwidth). In that case, a node only requires small specific hardware for its pre-dedicated bandwidth. It is the opposite for MWSR: a node only has to listen to its pre-dedicated channel and just needs dedicated hardware to emit over the whole bandwidth. In *Multiple Write Multiple Read* (MWMR), each node can be assigned multiple channels to emit a message, and respectively each node can simultaneously receive data from different channels and nodes [21]. MWMR is the most energy consuming, as it requires arbitration for both emission and reception. It is also by far the most flexible solution and allows more advanced reconfiguration mechanisms.

3. PROPOSED CMP ARCHITECTURE

This section presents the architecture of the hierarchical RF NoC based CMP. As 3D adds significant thermal constraints and optical needs an external light source, RF has been chosen. MWMR is chosen for its flexibility and broadcast capacity. The propagation time in silicon is very short at the scale of a chip (about 0.5 ns for 100 mm), and can be considered almost constant for any source-destination combination. Moreover, the time needed to emit and receive a RF message is also constant. So, the RF NoC allows to transmit data in constant time, unlike router-based NoC, for which transmission duration varies linearly with the distance between source and destination. However, this dura-

tion is still higher than a router-based NoC for short distance communications. So RF must be used only when a certain distance threshold is reached, involving the use of a hierarchical architecture where the RF NoC is the top level communication medium.

3.1 CMP architecture

Figure 1 shows the global architecture of the CMP, with three levels of hierarchy: tiles, clusters and CMP. Each hierarchical level is associated with a specific interconnect: respectively wired crossbar, wired grid and RF global interconnect. The tile is the lowest hierarchical level. It contains a local RAM, a DMA and processors, all connected to the crossbar. The local crossbar is connected to a grid router to access the second level (the wired grid) . A tile is connected by its router to the four nearest tiles, forming a cluster of $M \times M$ tiles. As the increase of the latency limits the size of a cluster, RF NoC is used as a third level interconnect when its latency becomes lower than the grid latency.

3.2 RF NoC architecture

To allow inter cluster communications, each cluster includes a RF NoC interface connected on one side to the four central tiles as illustrated in Figure 1, and on the other side to the waveguide. The RF NoC Interface, pictured in Figure 2, makes use of *Orthogonal Frequency Division Multiplexing* (OFDM). In OFDM, the bandwidth is split into several orthogonal narrow band channels, providing high spectral efficiency, manageable equalization process and robustness. The RF NoC use specifically a medium access scheme based on OFDM called *Orthogonal Frequency Division Multiple Access* (OFDMA). It adds the possibility for multiple senders to simultaneously use the same bandwidth while using only one transceiver per sender.

Data coming from routers of the four central tiles are stored into corresponding FIFOs [1]. The arbiter [2] selects a packet from one of the FIFOs [1], converts it into specific RF NoC *flow units* (flits) and writes it in the FIFO [3] which possesses all the monitoring mechanisms to evaluate the transmit requirements of the cluster. The flit is then serialized [4] into groups of bits according to the chosen modulation (BPSK, QPSK or 16-QAM), and finally creates the appropriate constellation symbol. The demux [5] parallelizes the modulator output to feed the IFFT inputs [6], according to the channels/subcarriers allocated to the cluster. OFDM symbols generated by the IFFT [6] feeds the RF Tx and its DAC [7] and are sent to the waveguide. To transform *OFDM* in *OFDMA*, each cluster is allocated a certain number of subcarriers at every OFDM symbol to transmit its data and perform zero-padding to the rest of subcarriers. This way, the transmitter allows other nodes to send their data on the same OFDM symbol without interference. The choice of subcarriers is indicated by the RF Controller [7] to the demux [5] by the control signal Ⓒ. The other way to tune communication resources is to change the modulation. The choice of the modulation is also performed by the RF Controller according to its allocation algorithm presented in the next section and provided to the modulator by the control signal Ⓑ. Data reception follows the opposite path in all clusters. As each cluster decodes the entire OFDM symbol, data circulating on the RF NoC are visible by all clusters in the CMP. Thus, broadcast is an intrinsic feature of OFDMA. To perform the dynamic bandwidth allocation,

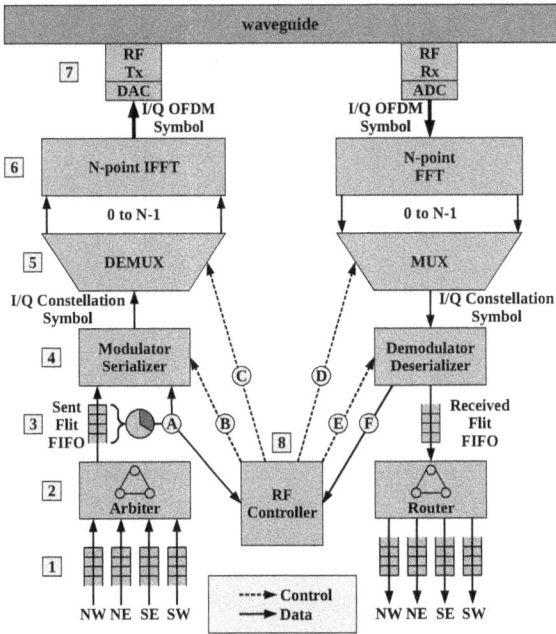

Figure 2: RF NoC Interface

the RF controller 7 evaluates the bandwidth requirements of its own cluster Ⓐ and the needs of other clusters Ⓕ.

4. DYNAMIC BANDWIDTH ALGORITHM

To reach maximum bandwidth occupation, the OFDMA reconfigurability potential must be fully exploited. To do so, efficient algorithms based on instantaneous traffic demands are required to allocate subcarriers among clusters. The most significant metrics for these algorithms are latency and fairness. This issue is clearly linked to *network theory* and efficient solutions rely on state-of-the-art OFDMA schedulers, which optimize these metrics. Little's Law states that to minimize average latency, a scheduler has to maximize the use of bandwidth. Among schedulers for conventional OFDMA networks, we choose *Queue Proportional Scheduler* (QPS) as the best guideline to design our allocation algorithm. QPS is a throughput optimal scheduler and is proven to provide fairness and small instantaneous latency [16]. The scheduler arbitrates N subcarriers to K nodes, proportionally to their instantaneous queue lengths and allows to allocate more subcarriers to nodes that communicate the most.

A distributed bandwidth allocation scheme is used. In the block 3 of Figure 2, clusters compute their *Queue State Information* (QSI) and transmit them simultaneously with payload data to other clusters, thanks to OFDMA intrinsic broadcast feature. When each cluster has collected all other cluster's QSI (Ⓕ in Figure 2), all RF Controller simultaneously execute the bandwidth allocation algorithm. As each RF Controller processes identical data with the same algorithm, they all compute locally the same allocation solution, thus avoiding bandwidth conflict. Transmitting QSI simultaneously with payload and using a distributed algorithm allow to avoid latency and extra communication overhead.

QSI is computed and transmitted every τ symbol, τ being a trade-off parameter. On the one hand, a small value of τ allows optimal allocation but the algorithm is executed more often and QSI transmission more frequent, consuming more bandwidth. On the other hand, larger values of τ result in

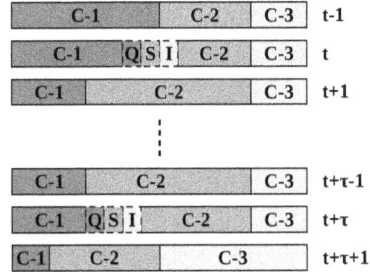

Figure 3: EQPS algorithm with rotating QSI channels on frequency and time

more available bandwidth, but outdated QSIs decrease the algorithm performance.

Expected Queue Proportional Scheduler (EQPS) algorithm is an extension of the original QPS algorithm. It provide the expected future QSI values of clusters. At first each cluster calculates its *Deterministic Queue State Information* (DQSI) which represents the minimum service demand. DQSI is the difference between the last received QSI and the bandwidth allocated during the last τ symbols. It is calculated using equation (1). With Q_i^t, the QSI of cluster i received on symbol t and S_i^t, the number of allocated subcarriers from symbol t to symbol $t+\tau$. Once DQSI is obtained, it is possible to take into account the incoming data to a cluster's transmission queue during the next period of τ symbols. For this purpose, we use *Exponentially Weighted Average Filter* (EWMA). It estimates the next sample by weighting recent observation and previously computed average using equation (2). With A_i^t, the amount of bits arrived during the last τ symbols, and α, a scalar that weighs the effect of historical data compared to instantaneous sample, which is generally between 0.9 and 0.99 [22].

$$\dot{Q}_i^{t+\tau} = \min(0, Q_i^t - S_i^t) \ (1) \quad \hat{A}_i^{t+\tau} = (1-\alpha)A_i^t + \alpha\hat{A}_i^t \ (2)$$

Merging the average arrival, the last QSI value and the current bandwidth allocation, the RF Controllers use equation (3) to calculate $\hat{Q}_i^t$, the estimated QSI for cluster i. Then, using equation (4), they compute S_i^{t+1}, the allocated number of subcarriers to cluster i on symbol $t + \tau$. With N, the number of subcarriers, and K the number of clusters. The result is rounded to the nearest larger integer to guarantee that every non-empty queue gets at least one subcarrier resource, which ensures fairness. Note that, at the end of computation, the total number of allocated subcarriers may exceed N. So extra subcarriers are removed from the nodes with the higher values of S_i^{t+1}.

$$\hat{Q}_i^t = \dot{Q}_i^t + \hat{A}_i^t \ (3) \qquad S_i^{t+1} = \left\lceil N \frac{\hat{Q}_i^t}{\sum_{j=1}^K \hat{Q}_j^t} \right\rceil \ (4)$$

To avoid using the same subcarriers for QSI transmission every τ symbols, as it would constantly induce allocation penalties in some clusters, a *rotating QSI channel* is used during every allocation frame. It maps the QSI channels to different adjacent blocks of subcarriers, by moving the interval one by one. This procedure is illustrated in Figure 3.

5. EXPERIMENTAL SETUP AND RESULT

In this section, we assume a realistic bandwidth of 20 GHz for RF and a CMP with 32 clusters and 4 cores per tile.

CONFIGURATION				
# cores	512	1 024	2 048	4 096
# tiles	128	256	512	1 024
# clusters	32	32	32	32
AREA				
IFFT/FFT [18]	20,27	20,27	20,27	20,27
Tx/Rx [9]	1,23	1,23	1,23	1,23
DAC/ADC [5]	7,36	7,36	7,36	7,36
Wageguide [7]	4,35	6,16	8,71	12,31
RF NoC	**33,21**	**35,02**	**37,57**	**41,18**
Cores	105,32	210,64	421,27	842,55
RAM [6]	4,50	8,99	17,99	35,98
CMP	**143,03**	**254,65**	**476,83**	**919,70**
RF NoC part	**23,22%**	**13,75%**	**7,88%**	**4,48%**
POWER				
IFFT/FFT [18]	4 320	4 320	4 320	4 320
Tx/Rx [9]	400	400	400	400
DAC/ADC [5]	5 184	5 184	5 184	5 184
RF NoC	**9 904**	**9 904**	**9 904**	**9 904**
Cores	19 896	39 793	79 586	159 172
RAM [6]	1 446	2 891	5 782	11 564
CMP	**31 246**	**52 588**	**95 272**	**180 640**
RF NoC part	**31.70%**	**18,83%**	**10,40%**	**5,48%**

Table 1: Chip area (mm^2) and power (mW)

5.1 Surface and power estimation

In order to evaluate the feasibility of a CMP using our RF NoC, we perform a basic estimation of surface and power. We compare these characteristics with those of an existing CMP, the Intel Core i7-5960X.

5.1.1 Experimental setup

Surface and power are calculated on the basis of state of the art components, assuming a 22 nm target technology as used for the i7-5960X. For digital components, equation (5) is used to get S_N, the normalized surface in the target technology N, depending on the surface S_Q in the original technology Q. According to ITRS [8], when the size of transistors decreases by a 0.7 factor, the power consumption decreases by a 0.65 factor. Equation (6) gives W_N, the normalized power consumption in technology N, based on the power consumption W_Q in the original technology Q. The scaling of analog components is not as simple, since it is necessary to take into account other factors. So we directly used the surface and power of state of the art components.

$$S_N = S_Q \times (N/Q)^2 \quad (5) \quad W_N = W_Q \times 0.65^{\log_{0.7}(N/Q)} \quad (6)$$

5.1.2 Result

Table 1 presents surface and power of the components, showing that the RF NoC area is mainly due to FFT/IFFT, ADC/DAC and the waveguide. The rest of the surface is mainly occupied by cores and their caches (ARM Cortex-A5). Compared to the i7-5960X, whose surface is 355 mm^2, the first three cases have a realistic area. The last one seems less realistic with current technology but should be achievable in the future. Power consumption and surface do not vary in the same way. This is due to the increasing length of the waveguide. The surface calculation uses the true length of the waveguide whereas the power calculation uses the average length of the different cases. Table 1 shows that the power consumption of the RF NoC is mainly due to FFT/IFFT and ADC/DAC. Compared to the i7-5960X, whose power consumption is 140 W, all cases are realistic, demonstrating the feasibility of the RF NoC from this point of view. The part of the RF NoC in the global surface and

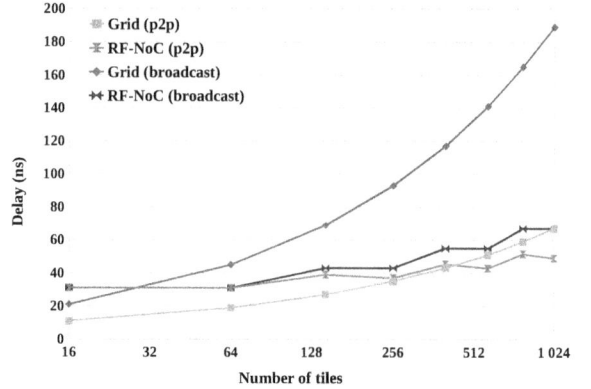

Figure 4: Average latency for P2P flit transfer

power decreases as the number of cores increase, making the RF NoC more and more interesting.

5.2 Intrinsic characteristic evaluation

5.2.1 Experimental setup

The RF NoC is compared with a router based electrical NoC using analytical models. Performance are evaluated in the case of a random traffic without contention. We assume cores running at 1 GHz and a bandwidth divided into 512 subcarriers. A grid router has a latency l_{RG} of 3 cycles, one for reading data, one for selecting the output port and one for writing data to the chosen port. Equation (7) gives D_{CMP}, the average number of crossed routers to go from one tile to another, including the original tile router. We considered a CMP with a grid of $N \times N$ tiles. We get L_{grid} the average latency of a grid with equation (8).

$$D_{CMP} = \frac{2}{3}N + 1 \quad (7) \qquad L_{grid} = D_{CMP} \times l_{RG} \quad (8)$$

The latency of the RF NoC l_{RF} is 25 cycles, which corresponds to the OFDM symbol duration. We also take into account the average number of cycles to go from source to the transmitting RF NoC Interface and from the receiving RF NoC Interface to destination. For a CMP containing clusters of $M \times M$ tiles, the average distance $D_{cluster}$ between tiles and RF router is given by equation (9) if M is even, and equation (10) if M is odd. Equation (11) gives L_{NoC_RF} the average latency of the RF NoC.

$$D_{cluster} = \frac{M}{2} \quad (9) \quad D_{cluster} = \frac{M^2 + 2M - 1}{2M} \quad (10)$$

$$L_{NoC\_RF} = l_{RG} \times D_{cluster} + l_{RF} \quad (11)$$

We can compare the average duration of a flit reception with the RF NoC and with a grid connecting all the tiles of the CMP. We set the number of clusters to 32 and we modify the size of CMP by varying the number of tiles per cluster.

5.2.2 Result

Access to the RF NoC is shared by the four central tiles in the first case, whereas it is in the single central tile in the second case. This different location of the RF router explains the staircase shape of the RF NoC latency curves shown in Figure 4. For point-to-point (P2P) communications, the RF NoC becomes faster for CMPs of at least 512 tiles.

To perform a broadcast, data must cross a maximum of $2N - 1$ routers for a grid and a maximum of $2M$ routers plus the waveguide for the RF NoC, where N is the CMP

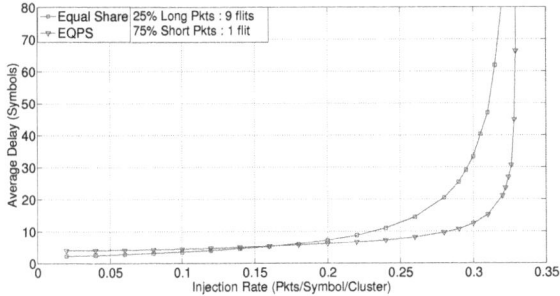

Figure 5: Average latency under Poisson traffic

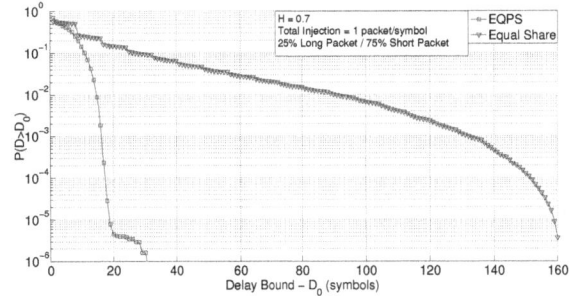

Figure 6: ICDF under realistic traffic model

width while M is the cluster width. Figure 4 shows that the RF NoC is faster for CMPs of at least 32 tiles.

5.3 Evaluation of dynamic allocation

5.3.1 Experimental setup

Note that in this experiment, QPSK is the only used modulation order. Based on experiments, we decide to compute QSI every 8 symbols. It provides the necessary amount of computation time for the RF Controller to perform subcarriers allocation while only 3.125% of bandwidth is used for QSI transmission. Assuming that the shortest packet is one flit, incoming packets are split into 64 bits flits. We divide the 1024 subcarriers into 256 groups of 4 subcarriers modulated with QPSK during 8 symbols, thus providing 64 bits of service during every allocation frame and ensuring that each non-idle node gets a chance to transmit at least one flit. QSI values are 8-bit long, representing a queue of 0 to 255 of awaiting flits. That way, we only need 4 subcarriers to modulate a cluster's QSI on one symbol. So, we use 128 subcarriers during one symbol to transmit all the QSIs.

Messages are either small packets (*read requests, acknowledgements*, etc.), or long packets (*write requests, read responses* followed by *cache lines*). According to [14], we set the proportion of short packets (1 flit - 64 bits) and long packets (9 flits - 576 bits) to 75% and 25%. It is assumed that cache lines are 64 bytes, thus cache coherence packets contain 8 payload flits and 1 overhead flit, featuring all necessary informations (destination, ID, etc.). When a packet is generated, a Bernoulli process determines its length.

We use OMNET++ to test the bandwidth allocation protocol. We focus on inter-cluster communications as we aim to show the benefits of the dynamic allocation algorithm. Thus, we discard intra-cluster communications. We also assume infinite capacity transmit queues. With state-of-the-art on-chip simulators, generating memory traffic by using benchmark applications is not efficient for more than 1000 cores [10]. So we use synthetic models to mimic memory traffic as a first approach.

5.3.2 Results - Uniform On-Chip Traffic

One of the most widely used traffic models for on-chip networks is the *uniform model*, where each node may generate a packet every cycle with a probability p. However, as we have 64 cores per cluster and multiple cycles in an OFDM symbol (with 1 GHz processors, one symbol corresponds to 50 cycles), there may be multiple packets generated in a symbol. As aggregation of multiple independent Bernouilli processes is a Poisson process, we model the number of packets generated in a cluster on each symbol as a Poisson distribution. We compare the dynamic allocation (EQPS) with the case

where subcarriers are statically and equally allocated (Equal Share). Figure 5 shows the packets average latency under Poisson traffic with increasing *injection rate*. Note that, for injection rates smaller than 0.15 packets/symbol/cluster, *Equal Share* performs better than EQPS. Indeed, EQPS re-arbitrates subcarriers every 8 symbols, based on the instantaneous QSI and a moving average, which does not provide high efficiency when queue length values are small. As traffic load increases and instantaneous queue lengths get bigger and bigger, the need to reallocate bandwidth arises and EQPS becomes more efficient, pushing back the saturation threshold of the network.

5.3.3 Results - Realistic On-Chip Traffic

Uniform and Markovian traffic do not accurately capture the features of on-chip traffic. So, new synthetic models have been developed. The fractal and self-similar behavior of CMP memory traffic both in time and space have been observed [1]. One characteristic of memory traffic of shared memory CMP is the *long-range dependence* (LRD) [17]. LRD reflects the temporal similarity of the traffic generation process in different scales of time intervals. It can be modeled by a power-law decaying covariance function : $\gamma(k) = ck^{-\alpha}$, where c is an arbitrary scalar and α is an exponent reflecting the degree of long-range dependence. One method to characterize and generate stochastic long-range dependent traffic is to use *Hurst Parameter*, H, where $H = (2 - \alpha)/2$ [20]. A synthetic traffic model for cache-coherent CMPs, which attains an 95% accuracy compared to real application traces has been proposed [17]. We choose this model to test the RF NoC and EQPS algorithm under realistic on-chip traffic conditions, with $H = 0.7$ (an approximate mean for all kind of applications). To generate traffic with Hurst parameter in OMNET++, we use the method explained in [20], where the number of generated packets by a node at any instance is determined by the aggregation of many *Pareto distributed ON-OFF* processes (we set this number to 500, which is fairly sufficient for each cluster). Similarly, clusters injection rates are assumed to be Gaussian distribution.

We tested our algorithm under non-uniform traffic and plotted the *Inverse Cumulative Probability Density Function* (ICDF), the probability that the latency of a packet is larger than a delay bound, $P(D > D\_0)$. Figure 6 shows ICDF for EQPS and Equal Share, with an injection rate of 1 flit/symbol/cluster. It shows a ×6 improvement, showing the benefits of the EQPS algorithm.

6. CONCLUSION

Current RF and optical NoC create multiple channels requiring several transceivers per cluster, which limit variety and granularity of reconfiguration schemes. We propose in this paper a dynamically reconfigurable RF NoC based on OFDMA. We describe the hierarchical architecture of the CMP using the RF NoC and propose a dynamic bandwidth allocation algorithm. Static analysis shows that RF NoC average latency is comparable with mesh average latency for P2P communications but up to ×3 lower for broadcast. Under realistic traffic models, the dynamic bandwidth allocation algorithm provides up to ×6 lower latency than static schemes. To comfort those promising results, a SystemC model of the architecture is under development so future work can evaluate more precisely performances with benchmarks. Moreover, one can imagine new cache coherency protocols taking advantage of the low cost broadcast of the proposed RF NoC.

7. ACKNOWLEDGMENTS

This work has been supported by the French National Research Agency under grant ANR-12-INSE-0004.

8. REFERENCES

[1] P. Bogdan and R. Marculescu. Statistical physics approaches for network-on-chip traffic characterization. In *IEEE/ACM International Conf on Hardware/Software Codesign*, pages 461–470, 2009.

[2] M. Chang, J. Cong, A. Kaplan, M. Naik, G. Reinman, E. Socher, and S. Tam. Cmp network-on-chip overlaid with multi-band rf-interconnect. In *High Performance Computer Architecture (HPCA), IEEE International Symposium on*, pages 191–202, 2008.

[3] M. Chang, V. P. Roychowdhury, L. Zhang, H. Shin, and Y. Qian. Rf/wireless interconnect for inter-and intra-chip communications. *Proceedings of the IEEE*, 89(4):456–466, 2001.

[4] S. Deb, K. Chang, M. Cosic, A. Ganguly, P. Pande, D. Heo, and B. Belzer. Cmos compatible many-core noc architectures with multi-channel millimeter-wave wireless links. In *Great Lakes Symposium on VLSI (GLSVLSI)*, pages 165–170. ACM, 2012.

[5] Y. Duan and E. Alon. A 12.8 gs/s time-interleaved adc with 25 ghz effective resolution bandwidth and 4.6 enob. *Solid-State Circuits, IEEE Journal of*, 49(8):1725–1738, 2014.

[6] C.-S. Gong, C.-T. Hong, K.-W. Yao, and M.-T. Shiue. A low-power area-efficient sram with enhanced read stability in 0.18-μm cmos. In *Circuits and Systems, APCCAS 2008, IEEE Asia Pacific Conference on*, pages 729–732, 2008.

[7] J. Hu, J. Xu, M. Huang, and H. Wu. A 25-gbps 8-ps/mm transmission line based interconnect for on-chip communications in multi-core chips. In *IEEE MTT-S International Microwave Symposium Digest (IMS)*, pages 1–4, 2013.

[8] ITRS. International technology roadmap for semiconductors report, 2013 version.

[9] K. Jongsun, B. Gyungsu, and M. Chang. A low-overhead and low-power rf transceiver for short-distance on-and off-chip interconnects. *IEICE Transactions on Electronics*, 94(5):854–857, 2011.

[10] G. Kurian, J. Miller, J. Psota, J. Eastep, J. Liu, J. Michel, L. Kimerling, and A. Agarwal. Atac: A 1000-core cache-coherent processor with on-chip optical network. In *International Conference on Parallel Architectures and Compilation Techniques*, pages 477–488. ACM, 2010.

[11] J. Lee, M. Zhu, K. Choi, J. H. Ahn, and R. Sharma. 3d network-on-chip with wireless links through inductive coupling. In *International SoC Design Conference (ISOCC)*, pages 353–356. IEEE, 2011.

[12] F. Li, C. Nicopoulos, T. Richardson, Y. Xie, V. Narayanan, and M. Kandemir. Design and management of 3d chip multiprocessors using network-in-memory. *ACM SIGARCH Computer Architecture News*, 34(2):130–141, 2006.

[13] I. O'Connor. Optical solutions for system-level interconnect. In *International Workshop on System level Interconnect Prediction*, pages 79–88. ACM, 2004.

[14] Y. Pan, J. Kim, and G. Memik. Tuning nanophotonic on-chip network designs for improving memory trafics. In *PICA@ MICRO2009*.

[15] V. Pavlidis and E. Friedman. 3-d topologies for networks-on-chip. *Very Large Scale Integration (VLSI) Systems, IEEE Trans. on*, 15(10):1081–1090, 2007.

[16] K. Seong, R. Narasimhan, and J. M. Cioffi. Queue proportional scheduling in gaussian broadcast channels. In *IEEE International Conference on Communications (ICC)*, pages 1647–1652, 2006.

[17] V. Soteriou, H. Wang, and L.-S. Peh. A statistical traffic model for on-chip interconnection networks. In *IEEE International Symposium on Modeling, Analysis, and Simulation of Computer and Telecommunication Systems (MASCOTS)*, pages 104–116, 2006.

[18] S.-N. Tang, J.-W. Tsai, and T.-Y. Chang. A 2.4-gs/s fft processor for ofdm-based wpan applications. *Circuits and Systems II: Express Briefs, IEEE Transactions on*, 57(6):451–455, 2010.

[19] D. Vantrease, R. Schreiber, M. Monchiero, M. McLaren, N. P. Jouppi, M. Fiorentino, A. Davis, N. Binkert, R. G. Beausoleil, and J. H. Ahn. Corona: System implications of emerging nanophotonic technology. *ACM SIGARCH Computer Architecture News*, 36(3):153–164, 2008.

[20] W. Willinger, M. S. Taqqu, R. Sherman, and D. V. Wilson. Self-similarity through high-variability: statistical analysis of ethernet lan traffic at the source level. *Networking, IEEE/ACM Transactions on*, 5(1):71–86, 1997.

[21] C. Xiao, F. Chang, J. Cong, M. Gill, Z. Huang, C. Liu, G. Reinman, and H. Wu. Stream arbitration: Towards efficient bandwidth utilization for emerging on-chip interconnects. *ACM Transactions on Architecture and Code Optimization (TACO)*, 9(4):60, 2013.

[22] Q. Xu, D.-n. Cheng, and Y.-d. Fu. Traffic feature distribution analysis based on exponentially weighted moving average. In *Computer Science and Automation Engineering (CSAE), IEEE International Conference on*, volume 1, pages 535–539, 2012.

[23] Y. Ye, L. Duan, J. Xu, J. Ouyang, M. Hung, and Y. Xie. 3d optical networks-on-chip (noc) for multiprocessor systems-on-chip (mpsoc). In *3D System Integration (3DIC), IEEE International Conference on*, pages 1–6, 2009.

Computational Thinking Meets Design Thinking: Technology and Arts Collaborations

[Gala Speaker]

Erik Brunvand
Electrical and Computer Engineering
University of Utah
50 S. Central Campus Dr., Rm MEB 3190
Salt Lake City, Utah 84112
elb@cs.utah.edu

ABSTRACT

Are fine arts and technology compatible partners? Do these disciplines support each other or flinch when they are combined like oil and water? Do collaborative efforts provide interesting insights and opportunities for students? For practitioners? There seems to be an explosion of interest in exploring arts and technology connections: new media, digital media, kinetic art, new frontiers, emergent media, interdisciplinary, multidisciplinary, and transdisciplinary are only some of the terms used to describe this fusion of disciplines.

A visit to the SIGGRAPH art gallery or the SIGCHI Interactivity sessions, for example, will showcase a wide variety of uses of computing, embedded control, sensors, and actuators in the service of art. Kinetic art using embedded control is a marriage of art and technology. Artistic sensibility and creativity are required for concept and planning, and computer science and engineering skills are required to realize the artistic vision. However, these different skills are often taught in extremely different parts of a university campus.

In this talk I will start with some thoughts on the nature of combining arts and technology, and show some historical and contemporary examples specifically relating to kinetic art. I will then describe an ongoing collaborative course that involves Computer Science and Art students working together to design and create computer-controlled kinetic art. Students in the course explore interfacing of embedded computer systems with sensors and actuators of all sorts. They also explore physical and conceptual aspects of machine-making as a fine-art sculpture process. Our goal is to enhance the educational experience of both groups of students. We believe that both student groups gain significant and unusual benefits that they can apply in a variety of ways in their respective disciplines.

Categories and Subject Descriptors

A.0 [**General Literature**]: GENERAL—*Conference proceedings*

General Terms

Dinner Speaker

BIOGRAPHY

Erik Brunvand is an Associate Professor in the School of Computing at the University of Utah in Salt Lake City, Utah. His research and teaching interests include the design of application-specific computers, graphics processors, ray tracing hardware and software, asynchronous and self-timed systems, and VLSI. He and his students are currently designing a many-core computer architecture targeted at real-time graphics rendering using ray tracing.

In 2009 he co-developed and taught an arts/tech collaborative course with a colleague in the Department of Art and Art History at the University of Utah entitled Embedded Systems and Kinetic Art that is now in its sixth offering this spring. This course puts computer science and art students into teams to design and build collaborative computer-controlled kinetic artworks. He has also spent time as a visiting scholar in the Digital and Experimental Media Arts (DXARTS) program at the University of Washington (2012).

This interest in arts/tech collaborations has led him to explore a variety of kinetic mixed media art pieces, many involving electronic control. His work has shown in venues such as the SIGGRAPH Art Gallery, the Kimball Art Center, the National Screenprint Biennial, and the Utah Museum of Contemporary Art. He is also a printmaker, and co-founder of Saltgrass Printmakers, a non-profit printmaking studio and gallery in Salt Lake City since 2004.

GLSVLSI'15, May 20–22, 2015, Pittsburgh, PA, USA.
ACM 978-1-4503-3474-7/15/05.
http://dx.doi.org/10.1145/2742060.2742123.

Graphene Neural Sensors for Next Generation In Vivo Imaging and Optogenetics

[Thursday Keynote]

Zhenqiang (Jack) Ma
Lynn H. Matthias Professor in Engineering
Vilas Distinguished Achievement Professor
Electrical and Computer Engineering
University of Wisconsin-Madison
1415 Engineering Drive
Madison, WI 53706
mazq@engr.wisc.edu

ABSTRACT

Graphene has been studied extensively for their properties in the electrical, mechanical, and optical domains. Graphene's flexible, transparent, and bio-compatible characteristics expand its boundaries from electrical applications to biological applications. Here, we present graphene neural sensors that allow for next generation in vivo imaging and optogenetics for its transparency over a broad wavelength spectrum and ultra-mechanical flexibility. The neural sensors implanted on the brain surface in rodents verify their unique abilities, including see-through in vivo imaging via fluorescence microscopy and 3D optical coherence tomography, and performance in advanced optogenetic experiments. The study is expected to deliver key information regarding the use of graphene in biological environments, specifically the brain. Subsequently, the study will have a strong impact on a wide spectrum of research areas spanning electrical engineering, neural science, and neural engineering.

Categories and Subject Descriptors

A.0 [**General Literature**]: GENERAL—*Conference proceedings*

General Terms

Keynote

BIOGRAPHY

Zhenqiang (Jack) Ma received his Ph.D. degree in electrical engineering from the University of Michigan in 2001. Before he joined the faculty at the University of Wisconsin-Madison in 2002, he worked for Conexant Systems and Jazz Semiconductor. He is recognized as a Lynn H. Matthias Professor in Engineering and Vilas Distinguished Achievement Professor in the Department of Electrical and Computer Engineering, with affiliated appointments in Nuclear Engineering, Engineering Physics, Materials Science Program, and UW Energy Institute. His research interests cover semiconductor materials and heterogeneous integration, device physics and technologies, and their applications to electronics, optoelectronics, nanophotonics, energy conversion, bioelectronics, biomimetics, power electronics, and sensors for nuclear materials. He has published over 330 peer-reviewed technical papers related to his research. He received the PECASE, DARPA Young Faculty Award in 2008 and several awards from the University of Wisconsin. He holds 25 US patents.

Acknowledgments

The work discussed in this keynote presentation was completed in collaboration with Professor Justin Williams and Ph.D. student Dong-Wook Park at the University of Wisconsin-Madison.

GLSVLSI'15, May 20–22, 2015, Pittsburgh, PA, USA.
ACM 978-1-4503-3474-7/15/05.
http://dx.doi.org/10.1145/2742060.2745702.

Online and Operand-Aware Detection of Failures Utilizing False Alarm Vectors

Amir Yazdanbakhsh, David Palframan, Azadeh Davoodi, Nam Sung Kim and Mikko Lipasti

Department of Electrical and Computer Engineering

University of Wisconsin at Madison, USA

{yazdanbakhsh, palframan, adavoodi, nskim3}@wisc.edu, mikko@engr.wisc.edu

ABSTRACT

This work presents a framework which detects *online* and at *operand level* of granularity *all* the vectors which excite a set of diagnosed failures in combinational modules. The failures may be of various types and may change over time. We propose to utilize this ability to detect failures at operand level of granularity to improve yield, by not discarding those chips containing failing and redundant computational units as long as they are not failing at the same time. The main challenge in realization of such a framework is the ability for on-chip storage of *all* the (test) vectors which excite the set of diagnosed failures. A major contribution of this work is to significantly *minimize* the number of stored test cubes by inserting only a few but carefully-selected "false alarm" vectors. As a result, a computational unit may be *mis-diagnosed* as failing for a given operand however we show such cases are rare and the chip may continue to be used.

Categories & Subject Descriptors B.7.2. [Integrated Circuits]: Design Aids

General Terms Reliability; Algorithms; Design

Keywords Manufacturing Yield

1. INTRODUCTION

Technology scaling beyond 32nm significantly degrades the manufacturing yield. One way to improve yield is by creating a layout with manufacturing-friendly patterns, for example imposing restrictive design rules or just using regular fabrics [8]. A particular challenge in this approach is to avoid significant degradation in power, area, or performance compared to non-regular and flexible design [12].

Alternatively, redundancy at various levels can be used to improve yield. Many prior proposals suggest exploiting redundancy that *already* exists in high performance processors including [16]. For instance, faulty execution units can be disabled. To avoid the performance penalty due to disabling logic, additional redundancy can be introduced in the form of spare execution units. However this type of redundancy is somewhat coarse-grained and may not be area efficient.

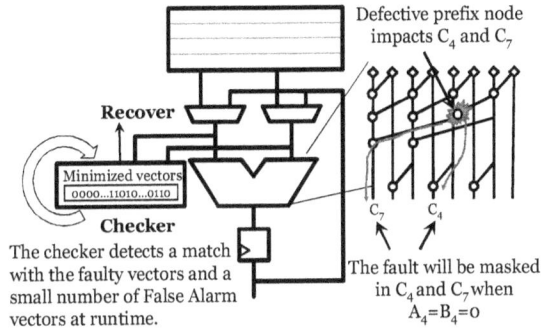

Figure 1: Overview of our framework

For this reason, other proposals suggest the use of fine-grained redundancy at granularity of a bit slice [5, 13], resulting in potentially more area-efficiency, but imposing a significant performance penalty, since many multiplexors are required to route around a potentially bad slice of logic. Other techniques suggest exploiting existing circuit redundancy. For instance, in [14], a small amount of extra logic is added to take advantage of redundancy in the carry logic of Kogge-Stone adders. Though area efficient, the extra logic is on the critical path and may reduce performance.

The degree of redundancy which can be exploited in a chip should be constrained because of the induced area overhead, and the increasing variety of modules in modern processors (e.g., arithmetic logic, multiplier, floating point, bypass logic, etc.) each of which requires its own dedicated redundant module(s). At the same time, the increasing degradation in manufacturing yield requires a higher degree of redundancy. These factors decrease the effectiveness of a scheme solely based on redundancy to improve the yield in challenging technology nodes.

In this work we introduce a *flexible* framework which detects *online* and at *operand level* of granularity *all* the vectors which may excite a set of diagnosed failures in failing combinational modules. Our framework is flexible in the sense that all it needs are the vectors which make a computational unit to fail, and it does not care about the source of the failure. Indeed, as new vectors are identified over time, they can be incorporated with the previous ones and detected by the checker unit. Moreover, unlike some previous works, our implementation does not result in adding extra logic on the critical design paths.

Our framework is based on an on-chip "checker" unit implemented as a TCAM which detects online if a vector feeding a defective combinational module causes an observable failure. Figure 1 shows an example in which the failing module is a Han-Carlson adder [7]. A defect in an internal node only impacts bit positions C_4 and C_7 and will not yield to an observable failure when the input arguments $A_4 = B_4 = 0$. Therefore the adder may continue to be used when there is no match with a failing vector in the checker.

Upon online detection of the failure, the checker sets a recovery flag which in a microprocessor signals re-issue of the operation. In the case of a defect, we propose this re-issue to be by scheduling the operation on a redundant computational unit as long as the redundant unit is not failing for the same vector (but may be failing for other vectors). If it is a failing timing path, the recovery could be re-execution on the same unit after scaling down to a lower frequency.

The main challenge in realization of such a framework is the ability for on-chip storage of *all* the (test) vectors which excite an identified failure. The number of vectors that excite a failure can be numerous even after applying various minimization techniques, thereby making it impossible for on-chip storage and online detection. A major contribution of this work is to significantly minimize the number of stored test cubes by inserting only a few "false alarm" vectors. As a result, a computational unit may be misdiagnosed as failing for a given operand however we show by carefully selecting the false alarms, the number of misdiagnosed cases can be minimized, while the chip can safely be continued to be used and all true failures are guaranteed to be detected. We note, the notion of false alarms in this work is similar to the false triggers in post-silicon debugging in [9].

Our procedure to insert false alarms extends the ESPRESSO tool for two-level logic minimization. It suits a TCAM-based implementation for online checking against test cubes which we also argue is also an area-efficient alternative.

The contributions of this work can be summarized below.

- Introducing a TCAM-based checker unit as a flexible option for online and operand-level fault detection.

- Proposing the use of false alarm vectors which we show helps significantly reduce the TCAM area, with only a slight increase in the number of misdiagnosis, as verified by realistic workloads on microprocessors of different issue widths.

2. DESIGN OF THE CHECKER UNIT

Consider the example of a 2-issue processor shown in Figure 2 (a). The figure shows implementation of the checker unit as a TCAM. The circuitry added for protection is shown in red. For a set of test cubes stored in the TCAM, the operands of the two ALUs are checked online. In case there is a match, a recovery flag is activated indicating the ALU which is going to fail for that operand. The recovery activates the process which ensures the incorrectly-processed instruction will not be committed and instead will be re-issued in the pipeline to the other ALU. The checker can work effectively if the recovery flag is not activated too frequently. Regardless, it allows continuing the use of a failing system, even when potentially two ALUs are failing as long as they don't fail for the same operand. It is also configurable and the set of stored test cubes can be updated if more failures are found over time.

2.1 Area Overhead

Implementing the checker in the above example requires MUXes to send the operands of both ALUs to the checker.

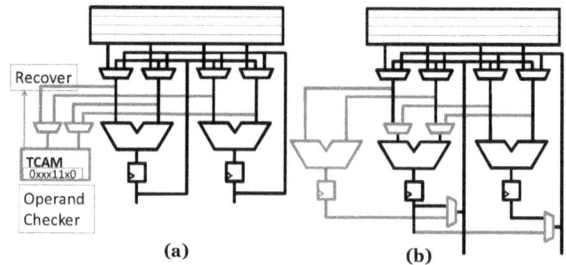

Figure 2: Protect a 2-issue faulty processor using (a) a checker unit; (b) a redundant module

For the 2-wide processor in this example, we need two 2-1 MUXes, each for example of 32 bits. For a 4-wide processor, we need two 4-to-1 (32-bit) MUXes. To understand this area overhead, we compare against a redundancy-based scheme which can be considered as a more conventional way for protection against failures.

In Figure 2(b), we show how a redundant ALU can be added to the 2-issue processor. We need MUXes that can forward (i) the input vector from any potentially-faulty ALU to the third ALU and (ii) the output vector from the redundant ALU to the faulty ALU. The additional MUXes ensure that in case *any* of the three ALUs is failing, the other two can be used. This MUX network can lead to a significant area overhead. For example for the 2-issue processor in Figure 2(b) we show how the third ALU is connected. There are four 2-to-1 (32-bit) MUXes in this case.

The area overhead of (a) and (b) are shown in red. The use of (a) is desirable if it has a lower area than (b). This is apart from other desirable features of (a) including online operand-aware detection of failures and providing a mechanism to work with two failing ALUs as long as they are not failing for the same operand. Moreover, unlike the redundant ALU case, the MUXes in (a) *are not on the critical path*. Thus, these MUXes can be sized much smaller than the MUXes used for the redundancy technique in Figure 2(b).

Two factors may be considered in allotting the area of the checker. First, the checker's area can be decided based on the number and types of modules which need protection, and by comparing with the overhead associated with using other alternatives (e.g., redundancy-based). The second factor limiting the checker's area is the recovery overhead (e.g., total runtime spent on re-execution of instructions).

2.2 Implementation Options

Here we compare two options to implement the checker unit: (i) a Ternary Content Addressable Memory (TCAM), and (ii) a Field-Programmable Gate Array (FPGA). We discuss them further in our simulation results.

1) TCAM: Since all the test cubes after the minimization include many don't care bits, our first and most logical implementation choice is using a TCAM that can match a content line with don't-care bits; note that a traditional CAM cannot be used for the checker unit. A conventional TCAM needs to support a random access to a specific entry to update the key value at runtime. This requires a log2(N)-to-N decoder for a TCAM with N entries. Thus, the decoder takes a notable fraction of the area in a conventional TCAM. However, we do not need such a decoder in our use of TCAM, because each entry must be updated only once, every time the chip is turned on. Therefore, supporting a sequential access to write the test cubes to the TCAM is sufficient, which we implement with a simple counter.

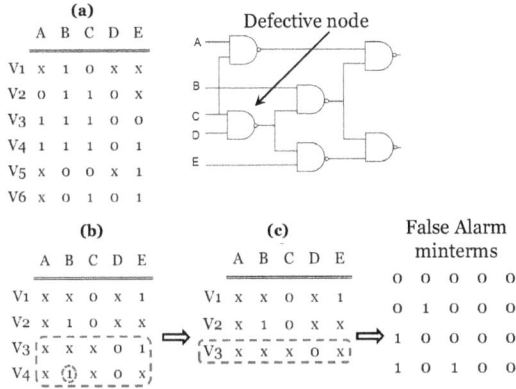

Figure 3: Example of failing C17 circuit; (a) faulty cubes before minimization; (b) faulty cubes after minimization; (c) cubes after adding false alarms

2) FPGA: Our second choice is using an embedded FPGA fabric, which can be implemented with a typical logic device technology. Since our minimized test cubes contain many don't-cares within each cube, synthesizing it to a Boolean function may lead to a very compact circuit that needs only a fraction of FPGA resource.

2.3 Programming the Checker at Startup

In our scheme, we must store test cubes on-chip and ensure they are loaded in the checker unit every time the chip is turned on. The first choice is to store them in the on-chip one-time-programming (OTP) memory (a.k.a. fuses). However, the size of each fuse cell is larger than the SRAM cell used for the checker unit and in practice can double the area overhead. Recently, mounting a flash memory package on a processor package using package-on-package technology began to receive a notable attention [6]. This can provide a large amount of non-volatile storage at a cost far cheaper than on-chip OTP memory integrated with logic device technology. Hence, we assume that the programming values of a detector is stored in the flash memory at no extra cost.

3. TEST CUBE MINIMIZATION

Given a failing path or slow/defective gate, the on-chip checker needs to store all the test cubes exciting the failure. Storing the total number of test cubes is not possible in practice. So in the first step, we aim to minimize the number of test cubes as much as possible. Here we propose to use a 2-level logic minimization tool. This is because it is most suitable for a TCAM-based implementation of the checker which allows storing/parallel-checking against the individual test cubes, containing don't-care bits.

However, even after minimization, the number of test cubes can be prohibitively large. Therefore, we propose false alarm insertion which allows significant reduction/minimization in the number of stored test cubes. Consider an "alarm" function representing a Boolean recovery signal generated by the checker. The on-set of this function is represented by the minimized test cubes. *By adding false alarms we essentially map a few terms from the off-set back into the on-set in order to further minimize the number of test cubes (corresponding to the TCAM entries) as many as possible.* Specifically, using false alarm insertion, we aim to reduce the number of test cubes beneath a target threshold corresponding to the maximum number of entries in the TCAM which we set to *only* 32 test cubes in our simulation setup.

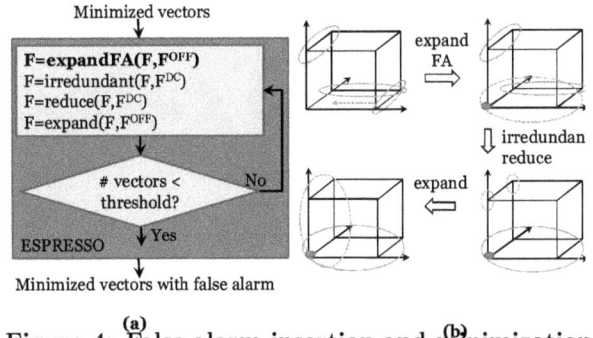

Figure 4: False alarm insertion and minimization

Example: Figure 3 shows these steps for the C17 benchmark circuit from the ISCAS85 suite containing one defective gate. The number of all the test cubes which yield to an observable fault in the outputs are 6 and 4, corresponding to before and after minimization, respectively. In Figure 3(b) v4 is expanded in literal 'B' and as a result it can be merged with v3 (or v3 can be eliminated). Expanding v4 introduces 8 additional minterms. However four of these minterms are already included in v3. So only the remaining four minterms will be false alarms which are listed in the figure. Compared to Figure 3(a), the number of test cubes is dropped by half with the insertion of four false alarms.

3.1 Procedure

Figure 4(a) shows the overview of our procedure. The input is a set of already minimized faulty test cubes. Our goal is to reduce the size of this set beneath a given threshold while minimizing the total number of added false alarms.

Our procedure is comprised of the following two core steps which are tightly integrated and repeated at each iteration. The first step expands a subset of the test cubes by identifying for each cube, a single literal which should be dropped in it. Since the input of the algorithm is an already minimized set, further expansion of a cube may likely make it overlap with the off-set of the function, introducing false alarms at this step. However, the expansion in turn may also help reduce the size of the resulting test cubes, as we showed in the example in Figure 3. Therefore, in the second step, we apply logic minimization to reduce the size of the cubes. Specifically, in our implementation, we integrated step one within the main loop of the ESPRESSO logic minimization algorithm [3] by modifying the corresponding source code from [1].

The details are shown in Figure 4(a). To insert false alarms at step one, we add the expandFA function. Step two is then an ordered sequence of standard logic minimization techniques, namely irredundant (for removing a cube fully contained in another cube), reduce (for breaking a cube into more number of cubes), and expand (for expanding a cube in the on-set of the function). After step 2, if the number of test cubes falls beneath the threshold, false alarm insertion is stopped, otherwise the process is repeated. Note, in the next iteration, a cube which is considered in expandFA may already have false alarms so its further expansion by dropping a literal adds more false alarms.

Figure 4(b) shows an example when applying the above sequence for a function of 3 variables. The on-set of the function are the points in the cube which are included in the circles. Each circle represents a test cube. First, the expandFA procedure expands a cube and as a result one unit of false alarm is added. The on-set of the function is updated to include the false alarm. The expanded cube now

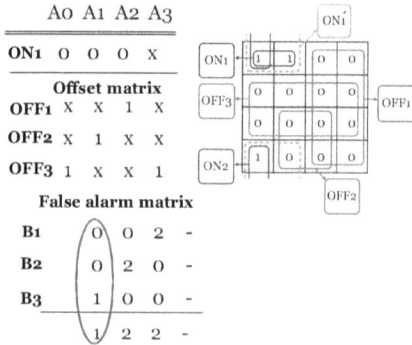

Figure 5: False alarm insertion for one cube

fully contains one of the test cubes which gets identified and removed by the `irredundant` procedure. As a result, the number of test cubes is reduced by one. Next, the `reduce` procedure breaks one test cube into two new cubes which allows its expansion in the on-set of the function (without adding false alarm). The end result is reducing the number of cubes as well as the number of literals.

3.2 False Alarm Insertion for One Cube

At each call of the `expandFA` function, each cube is visited once and considered for expansion to include some of the points in the off-set. Specifically, at iteration i of the algorithm, only the cubes that have up to i number of don't-cares are expanded. This ordering ensures that the cubes with fewer don't-cares are expanded first. Such a cube introduces fewer false alarms if one of its literals is dropped.

Furthermore, if a cube satisfies the expansion requirement, its don't-care count will be increased by one after dropping one literal. Therefore, in the future iterations, it will continue to be expanded, each time by one literal, until the number of test cubes falls beneath the threshold.

For a given cube, the choice of the literal to be dropped is made such that first, overlap with the off-set is minimized (to ensure inserting fewest number of false alarms), and as a secondary objective, the overlap with on-set is maximized (to increase the opportunities for logic minimization in the subsequent step). We explain our procedure for dropping a literal for a single cube to achieve these objectives using the example in Figure 5. Consider the cube ON1 with value 000x in a four-variable function. The off-set is stored in a minimized way using three cubes as shown in the K-map and represented by a matrix. Each row represents one of the cubes in the off-set and a column gives the literal index. Next, a false alarm matrix is formed where each row corresponds to a row in the off-set matrix. The number of columns is equal to the number of literals. An entry in row i and column j designates the number of introduced false alarms between the off-set cube i and (the expanded) cube when literal j is dropped. For example, in Figure 5, dropping literal A0 in ON1, results in its expansion in a new cube denoted by ON1' in the K-map which is shown to overlap with OFF2 in one location, thus for the 1 entry in row 3 and column 1. We then use the summation of each column, giving an upper bound on the total number of false alarms if the corresponding literal is dropped, and select the column with minimum summation to identify the dropped literal.

The upper bound will be tighter if each unit of introduced false alarm is shared among fewer off-set cubes. In our example, the false alarm is only included in OFF2 so the upper bound is equal to the number of false alarms.

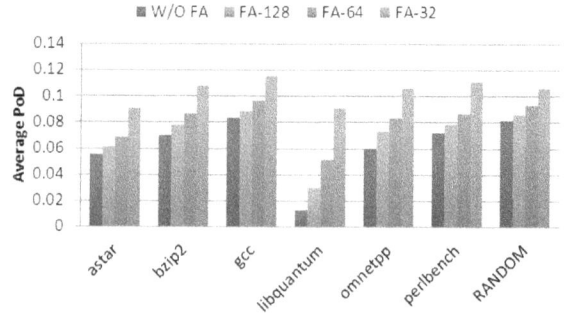

Figure 6: Probability of Detection for a single fault

In case there is a tie when more than one column has the same minimum summation, the one which overlaps with a higher number of on-set cubes is selected which provides opportunity for logic minimization in the subsequent step.

4. SIMULATION RESULTS

We divide our validation into two parts, 1) studying the impact of adding false alarms, and 2) studying the area overhead. In part (1), we study a 32-bit Brent-Kung adder [4] by injecting faults at different locations and study the rate of false alarm insertion. In part (2), we assume the adder is part of a 2-issue and 4-issue microprocessor and analyze the area overhead.

4.1 Impact of False Alarm Insertion

4.1.1 Failure due to A Single Fault

Here we considered single-failure scenarios in various nodes of the adder. For each non-primary input and non-primary output node, we considered two failing cases modeled by a stuck-at-0 and stuck-at-1. For each case, we then generated all the faulty test cubes (which yield to an observable fault in the adder's outputs) using the open-source ATPG tool Atalanta [11]. (Atalanta was able to generate test cubes for about 50% of the nodes in the adder which are the ones considered in our experiments.) The faulty cubes for each case were minimized using the `ESPRESSO` tool [3] using a flow as shown in the example of Figure 3. Minimization reduced the average number of test cubes over the cases from 10,425 to 915 test cubes. Our false alarm procedure was then used for various number of target test cubes (128, 64, and 32 test cubes).

Here we study the impact of false alarm on the frequency of activating the recovery signal. We use simulation for each fault to determine the percentage of the times that the checker activates the recovery signal which we denote by Probability of Detection (PoD). The simulations were done using realistic workloads as well as random input vectors. For the workload-dependent case we considered the benchmarks in the SPEC2006 suite [15]. Specifically, the arguments of the adder were recorded by running each benchmark on an X86 simulator. For the random case, 100K test patterns with uniform probability were generated.

Figure 6 shows the PoD for the following cases: without false alarm insertion (denoted by W/O FA), and with false alarm insertion for target number of test cubes of 128, 64, and 32 bits (denoted by FA-128, FA-64, and FA-32, respectively). For each bar, the reported PoD is averaged over all the corresponding cases.

We make the following observations.

Table 1: Ratio and overhead of false alarms

# cubes	32		64		128	
	FA	FA-Ag	FA	FA-Ag	FA	FA-Ag
astar	0.23	23%	0.11	54%	0.06	75%
bzip2	0.26	6%	0.19	18%	0.13	32%
gcc	0.20	-3%	0.12	18%	0.07	44%
libquantum	0.38	-20%	0.34	-21%	0.29	-23%
omnetpp	0.28	11%	0.20	22%	0.14	41%
perlbench	0.24	12%	0.14	38%	0.09	54%
RANDOM	0.17	39%	0.10	56%	0.05	76%
Average	0.25	10%	0.17	26%	0.12	43%

- Average and variance of PoD degrades with decrease in the number of test cubes (going from 128 to 32). This behavior is expected due to insertion of false alarms.

- Average and variance PoD after inserting false alarms does not degrade significantly in FA-128 or FA-64 or FA-32 compared to W/O FA. (Note the limit on the Y-Axis is only 0.15 probability.)

- The above behavior is true for both workload-dependent and random cases, with the random case typically having a higher PoD especially in the W/O FA case.

We conclude that our false alarm insertion procedure does not degrade the PoD significantly, despite the significant decrease in the number of test cubes (from on average 915 test cubes after logic minimization to 128, 64, and 32 test cubes).

We further implemented a variation of our false alarm insertion algorithm in which at each iteration, all the cubes are expanded using the expandFA procedure. Recall, in our (default) procedure, the cubes with a lower number of don't-cares are expanded in the earlier iterations, thus for a less aggressive strategy. (See Section 3 for the description of the default procedure.) We denote the aggressive and default procedures by FA-Ag and FA, respectively.

The FA-Ag procedure results in adding more false alarms per iteration. However, the number of iterations may be smaller because more minimization is possible due to a higher number of expanded cubes per iteration. Therefore, the total number of false alarms induced by FA-Ag may not necessarily be higher than FA if it finishes in a smaller number of iterations. In this experiment, we compare the number of false alarms in two variations of our procedure.

Specifically, we report the fraction of false alarms from the total number of detections. This can be represented by the quantity $\frac{FA}{FA+TP}$ with FA denoting the number of false alarm minterms and TP the number of true positives when a fault is truly happening.

Table 1 shows this fraction for FA-32, FA-64, and FA-128 in columns 2, 4, 6, respectively. We observe that the fraction of false detections deteriorates from FA-128 to FA-32 which is expected due to insertion of more false alarms. The average ratio of false detections for FA-32, FA-64 and FA-128 are 0.25, 0.17, and 0.12, respectively.

The results for FA-Ag are shown in columns 3, 5, 7, as a percentage of additional false alarms, compared to FA for number of cubes equal to 32, 64, and 128, respectively. The average overheads in false alarms of FA-Ag compared to FA are 10%, 26% and 43%, for 32, 64, and 128, respectively. So on-average FA-Ag results in more overhead with increase in the number of test cubes compared to FA. However, in one case (the libquantum benchmark), FA-Ag resulted in fewer false alarms than the FA case. So the aggressive expansion strategy worked out better in this benchmark for this metric.

4.2 Comparison of Area and Power

In this experiment, we evaluate the areas of TCAM and FPGA-based implementations of the checker within a 2-wide and 4-wide microprocessor. For the area of the checker unit we consider TCAM and FPGA-based implementation, as explained in Section 2 for various number of test cubes (32, 48, 64, 128). So we have four variations: 2+T, 2+F, 4+T, 4+F.

We estimate the area of a TCAM-based checker based on the TCAM cell area in 0.18um technology presented in [2] after applying a scaling factor from [17] for 32nm technology.

To evaluate the area of a FPGA-based checker unit, we first derive the truth table from a test cubes set for a failure. Second, we feed Synopsys Design Compiler (SDC) with the derived truth table and a commercial 32nm standard cell library to synthesize the circuit. Based on a prior work comparing area, timing, and power consumption between ASIC and FPGA implementations through an extensive study [10], we use a scaling factor of 35 to compute the FPGA area from the ASIC; an ASIC implementation is 35 times smaller than FPGA implementation for most combinational logic [10].

In our experiments we compared the areas of the following base cases using redundancy:

- 2+1: This case contains two adders (in a 2-issue microprocessor) with one redundant adder. The diagram of this case, including all necessary MUXes is shown in Figure 2(b). The area is taken after synthesis using Synopsys Design Compiler (SDC) using a 32nm Technology library. The area of this base is 4460 μm^2.

- 4+1: This case contains four adders (in a 4-issue microprocessor) with one redundant adder. The area is computed as reported by SDC after synthesis. Our implementation accounted for all the necessary MUXes, similar to the previous case. The area of this base case is 10837 μm^2.

The above base cases are compared against the following four variations of the checker-based alternative:

- 2+T: This case contains the two adders and instead of one redundant adder, a TCAM is used. The area in this case is computed after synthesizing the two adders and the MUXes for TCAM connection, as shown in Figure 2(a). This post-synthesis area is taken from SDC and is 4682.8 μm^2 which excludes the TCAM area. Next, the TCAM area is also estimated for number of test cubes equal to 128, 64, 48, and 32. The TCAM area for a given size is divided into a memory portion and a shift register (counter) for initial startup, as explained in Section 2. For the memory portion, the area is calculated by scaling the TCAM estimate given in [2] for 0.18um technology using the scaling factor from [17] for 32nm technology. The shift register is synthesized using SDC and 32nm library for different number of test cubes. Table 2 shows the areas of the shift register and the overall area of the TCAM portion in columns 2 and 3 for different number of test cubes. The overall area of 2+T is shown in column 5.

- 4+T: The area of TCAM portion is computed just like the previous case as reported in Table 2 column 3. The remaining part is composed of 4 adders with proper MUX connections to the TCAM. The area of this portion is 11375 μm^2 after synthesis using SDC.

Table 2: Area (in μm^2) of various implementations

#cubes	SR	TCAM	FPGA	2+T	4+T	2+F	4+F
32	259	1126	3618	5587	12280	8079	14455
48	389	1552	4973	6013	12706	9434	15810
64	519	1977	6323	6438	13131	10784	17160
128	1038	3732	15563	8193	14886	20023	26400

Table 3: Overhead of various implementations

#cubes	baseline: 2+1		baseline: 4+1	
	2+F	2+T	4+F	4+T
32	26.6%	-12.5%	7.3%	-8.8%
48	47.8%	-5.8%	17.4%	-5.7%
64	69.0%	0.9%	27.4%	-2.5%
128	213.7%	28.4%	96.0%	10.5%

Overall area of 4+T is shown in column 6 for different number of input vectors.

- 2+F: This case contains two adders and one FPGA for the checker unit. The area of the two adders with proper MUXes is 4460 μm^2 after synthesis using SDC. The area of the FPGA portion for different number of test cubes is listed in column 4. It is obtained by synthesizing the corresponding truth tables of test cubes in ASIC and scaling with a factor of 35, based on an extensive recent study [10] estimating the area of combinational logic to be 35X smaller in ASIC. (For different failures, an FPGA was estimated and the worst-case was over all the failure cases was scaled.) The area of 2+F is given in column 7.

- 4+F: The area of the FPGA portion is the same as previous case (given in column 4). The remaining area of the four adders with proper MUX connections is 10873 μm^2 after synthesis using SDC. The overall area of 4+F is listed in column 8.

All adders and MUXes are 32-bit in the above cases.

Table 3 lists the percentage area overhead of our four variations compared to the areas of the corresponding baselines. The area overheads are listed for the number of test cubes from 32 to 128.

We observe that 2+T and 4+T have 12.5% and 8.8% less area than 2+1 and 4+1 cases, respectively, for 32 number of test cubes. The FPGA-based checker consumes considerably more area than the 2+1 and 4+1 cases. Although the FPGA-based checker for many failures does not require significant area, some failures required a large FPGA, far exceeding the area overhead of integrating a redundant adder. The FPGA-based area can become competitive by not protecting such cases, thus reducing the failure coverage.

Overall, the TCAM-based checker provides similar or lower area for the number of test cubes of 32, 48, and 64.

We also discuss the power overhead of the TCAM-based checker. (We do not consider the FPGA case because in our experiments it always had a high area overhead.) For the TCAM case, we observe that most key values are 0s to program don't-cares in TCAM while the columns filled with don't-cares do not discharge the matching lines. For example, for 32, 48, 64 and 128 test cubes stored in TCAM, over all the failure cases, the number of used (non-don't care) bits are 46, 46, 48, and 50, respectively. Therefore, power consumption of the TCAM-based implementation is not significant.

Based on the TCAM model in [2], we estimate that the TCAM-based checker consumes approximately 347fJ, 472fJ, 602fJ, and 1106fJ per cycle (234mW, 318mW, 406mW, and 746mW for 1.2ns cycle time) for 32, 48, 64, and 128 test cubes, respectively; our checker for 48 test cubes consumes 24% and 48% less power than the 2+1 and 4+1 cases.

5. CONCLUSIONS

We presented a new framework for online detection of failures at operand level of granularity.The core of our framework is a checker unit which gets programmed after identifying one or more failures within combinational modules; it can also be updated upon observing new failures. For a given failure, if an operand yields to an observable fault, it will be detected by our checker and a recovery flag will be activated at runtime. We presented detailed analysis showing that a TCAM-based implementation of our checker has a smaller area than an alternative using a redundant module. This is with the aid of a proposed algorithm to insert a relatively small number of false alarm test cubes, enabling significant degree of minimization in the number of test cubes to be stored in the checker.

6. REFERENCES

[1] ESPRESSO. http://embedded.eecs.berkeley.edu/pubs/downloads/espresso/.
[2] B. Agrawal and T. Sherwood. Modeling TCAM power for next generation network devices. In *ISPASS*, pages 120–129, 2006.
[3] R. K. Brayton, G. D. Hachtel, C. McMullen, and A. L. Sangiovanni-Vincentelli. Logic minimization algorithms for VLSI synthesis. *Kluwer Academic Publishers, Boston, MA*, 1984.
[4] R.P. Brent and H.T. Kung. A regular layout for parallel adders. *IEEE Trans. on Computers*, C-31(3):260 –264, 1982.
[5] Zhan Chen and Israel Koren. Techniques for yield enhancement of vlsi adders. In *ASAP*, pages 222–229, 1995.
[6] A.N. Doboli and E.H. Currie. Introduction to mixed-signal, embedded design. *Springer Science+Business Media, LLC*, 2011.
[7] Tack-Don Han and David A. Carlson. Fast area-efficient VLSI adders. In *IEEE Symp. on Computer Arithmetic*, pages 49–56, 1987.
[8] T. Jhaveri, L. Pileggi, V. Rovner, and A. Strojwas. Maximization of layout printability/manufacturability by extreme layout regularity. In *SPIE*, 2006.
[9] H. F. Ko and N. Nicolici. Mapping trigger conditions onto trigger units during post-silicon validation and debugging. *IEEE Trans. Computers*, 61(11):1563–1575, 2012.
[10] I. Kuon and J. Rose. Measuring the gap between FPGAs and ASICs. *IEEE TCAD*, 26(2):203–215, 2007.
[11] H.K. Lee and D.S. Ha. Atalanta: an efficient ATPG for combinational circuits. *Technical Report; Department of Electrical Engineering, Virginia Polytechnic Institute and State University*, pages 93–12, 1993.
[12] Y-W. Lin, M. Marek-Sadowska, and W. Maly. On cell layout-performance relationships in VeSFET-based, high-density regular circuits. *IEEE TCAD*, 30(2):229–241, 2011.
[13] Kazuteru Namba and Hideo Ito. Design of defect tolerant wallace multiplier. In *PRDC*, pages 300–304, 2005.
[14] P. Ndai, Shih-Lien Lu, Dinesh Somesekhar, and K. Roy. Fine-grained redundancy in adders. In *ISQED*, pages 317–321.
[15] A. Phansalkar, A. Joshi, and L.K. John. Analysis of redundancy and application balance in the SPEC CPU2006 benchmark suite. In *ISCA*, pages 412–423, 2007.
[16] Premkishore Shivakumar, Stephen W. Keckler, Charles R. Moore, and Doug Burger. Exploiting microarchitectural redundancy for defect tolerance. In *ICCD*, pages 35–42, 2012.
[17] J. Srinivasan, S.V. Adve, P. Bose, and J.A. Rivers. The impact of technology scaling on lifetime reliability. In *DSN*, pages 177 – 186, 2004.

Speed Binning Using Machine Learning and On-chip Slack Sensors

Mehdi Sadi [1], Xiaoxiao Wang [2], Leroy Winemberg [3] and Mark M. Tehranipoor [1]

[1]Dept. of Electrical & Computer Engineering, University of Connecticut, Storrs, USA
[2]Beihang University, China;   [3]Freescale Semiconductor, Austin, TX, USA
mehdi.sadi@engr.uconn.edu, wangxiaoxiao@buaa.edu.cn, leroyw@freescale.com,
tehrani@engr.uconn.edu

Abstract

Speed binning of integrated circuits using Fmax test of a SoC requires application of complex functional and structural test patterns. Today's test-pattern-based speed binning techniques incur high test cost in terms of long test time and requires significant effort to generate effective patterns. In this paper we propose a novel speed binning flow that uses path timing slacks, extracted with robust digital embedded sensor IPs, of selected critical/near-critical paths. We apply machine learning techniques to model a predictor considering the extracted slacks and the Fmax values from a set of randomly tested die during wafer sort. The proposed flow has been demonstrated in a SoC circuit at 28/32nm technology. The worst-case miss-binning of the predictor is within 6% of the nominal Fmax.

Categories and Subject Descriptors

B.8.1 [Hardware]: Reliability, Testing, and Fault-Tolerance

Keywords

Speed Binning; Fmax testing; Slack Sensor; Timing Reliability

1. INTRODUCTION

With aggressive technology scaling the transistor density per unit chip area has increased significantly over the past decade. This paved the way for many-core processors and highly integrated System-on-Chips (SoCs). The increased variability in transistor parameters and workload-dependent fluctuations in operating conditions have made harnessing the full benefits of scaling a challenging task [1][2]. Variations can be categorized into three major classes - 1) One-time static process variations due to manufacturing imperfections that cause transistor and interconnect parameters to drift from their designed values. 2) Run-time dynamic variations - power supply noise and temperature fluctuations - resulting shifts in operating conditions. 3) Aging variations, induced by stress from prolonged operations, that cause parametric degradation over time [2]. In terms of spatial locations, the variation can be segmented into die-to-die and within-die components. Variations impact transistor length, width, threshold voltage, oxide thickness etc., all of which directly contribute to path delay fluctuations. As a result, a certain path may show significant discrepancy in the delay between pre- and post-fabrication stages [3][4] and the actual speed limiting paths

might be masked in the simulation phase [5]. Further, the workload-dependent aging variations can cause an initially non-critical path to be critical anytime in the lifetime of the chip [6].

As a result of path delay variations, the maximum operating frequency of a chip (e.g. microprocessors, DSPs, micro-controllers and ASICs) or the Fmax varies from chip-to-chip and wafer-to-wafer. At the production test phase chips are binned according to the operating frequency. Chips in the higher bin are faster and sold at a higher profit. To accurately identify the Fmax it is necessary to excite all the possible critical paths at increasingly higher clock frequencies until any of the capture flip-flops fail. To test the potential critical paths, two types of test patterns - functional and structural - are applied. Functional tests apply patterns that are derived from actual workloads, whereas structural - generally Transition Delay Fault (TDF) and Path Delay Fault (PDF) patterns - are dependent on the circuit topology and are intended to excite certain paths. As far as speed binning accuracy is concerned, functional test patterns are usually superior to structural patterns [7]. After adjusting this maximum passing frequency to account for the required guard-band, the chip Fmax is obtained. The test patterns are generally a combination of functional test patterns, and transition delay fault and path delay fault test patterns. There are two challenges to this approach. Firstly, application of functional test patterns is expensive in terms of required effort to generate patterns and test time [8]. Secondly, frequency sweeping to identify the failing frequency may require many unnecessary intermediate steps [9][10]. Finally, in order to apply delay fault test patterns, the path under test must be testable. To make all the paths testable by structural/functional test patterns, extra test points may be required to be inserted which incur area overhead [11].

Since structural patterns are less expensive to generate compared to functional patterns, there have been significant amount of research to utilize structural test results in estimating actual chip Fmax [7][12]-[14]. In [12], the authors studied the correlation between the structural and functional Fmax using sample chips fabricated with 150nm technology, where a linear relation was established. The authors in [13] demonstrated that structural Fmax based on complex path delay fault patterns exhibited correlation to the actual functional Fmax. In [15] data learning techniques were used to build a Fmax predictor from structural test results. In [9], the authors presented experimental data on test time for server processors where they reported that a major portion of total test time is associated with speed binning.

One of the primary objectives of this work is to reduce the test time and cost associated with speed binning. With the aim of test cost and time reduction, we evaluate the application of machine learning based predictive methodology in speed binning using extracted path slack. In our proposed flow, instead of testing testable paths with patterns which also require clock sweeping, we take a completely different approach - we measure the timing slack of selected number of critical/near-critical paths with embedded sensors to estimate what Fmax is. The use of sensors may slightly increase the design effort, but significantly reduces the Fmax test cost and time as explained in later sections. The design effort is not significant as we insert our slack sensors on selected number of critical/near-critical paths at gate-level netlist. The use of sensors also allow measuring Fmax in the field during functional mode and in-field BIST mode in addition to the manufacturing test mode. In-field Fmax measurement capabilities offer a unique opportunity to understand how circuit aging with time affects Fmax.

In addition to capturing slacks from actual critical/near-critical paths, the multiple number of embedded slack sensors also act as process monitors. In the experimental work of [13] that analyzed data from large number of test chips, it was reported that the use of process monitor sensors, such as ring oscillators, substantially improved the Fmax prediction accuracy.

In light of the above, our objectives and contributions in this work are:

- Development of a novel Fmax prediction framework that eliminates the long test time and cost associated with functional/structural Fmax testing.

- Extracting path slack data from critical/near-critical paths with embedded sensors and using those as features in training machine learning engines.

- In order to ensure that the features of the machine learning tool - the path slacks - capture spatial variation profile, a layout-aware and netlist-level sensor insertion flow is proposed to insert sensor IPs in the synthesized netlist and physically place those at strategic locations across the layout.

The rest of the paper is organized as follows. In Section 2 describes our proposed Fmax framework. The architecture of slack extraction sensor is presented in Section 3. Sensor insertion algorithm is provided in Section 4. Experimental results are presented in Section 5 followed by conclusions in Section 6.

2. PROPOSED SPEED BINNING FLOW

The chip Fmax is limited by the path delay of the most critical path. Because of process variations, noise and aging, the exact critical path cannot be identified at the pre-fabrication stage [16]. As a result any of the critical or near-critical paths - identified from the Static Timing Analysis (STA) or Statistical STA (SSTA) - can be the speed-limiting path for a certain chip depending on the chip-to-chip process variations. Without loss of generality, path slack and Fmax distributions are correlated. As a result, if the impact of process variations on path slack distribution is known, using the slack's correlation with Fmax, one would be able to predict the distribution of Fmax with process variations at time 0, i.e., production test. In order for this approach to be practical, we would require a simpler method to extract path slack in-situ from fabricated chips. Towards this goal, we have designed an all digital sensor IP which is connected to a capture flip-flop, and records the worst-case slack of all the paths that terminate at that capture flip-flop. The use of slack sensors eliminates the frequency sweep stage. Using sensors, this can be accomplished by running a single frequency (i.e. nominal frequency) and capturing the slack data. From the available slack margin at this frequency, a frequency close to the correct Fmax can be inferred.

Our proposed Fmax prediction methodology is depicted in Fig. 1. The essence of this approach is to train a machine learning tool with sufficient training data obtained from Chips under Test and Training (CTT) (Fig. 1(a)) and later use this trained predictor to estimate Fmax for new Chips Under Test (CUT) (Fig. 1(b)). For a sample of chips, the slacks from critical/near-critical paths are measured using embedded slack sensors. Fmax of the same sample chips are measured using clock sweeping of test patterns. The required number of CTTs (marked as black dots on the wafer in Fig. 1(a)) n depend on the characteristics of the data and generally $n \ll k$, where k is the number of remaining CUTs (marked as red dots on the wafer in Fig. 1(b)). Let's assume $\{S_{i1}...S_{im}\}$ represents the slacks from m sensors of the ith chip. The matrix X contains the slack data of each sensor from different samples. In X, there are n samples of

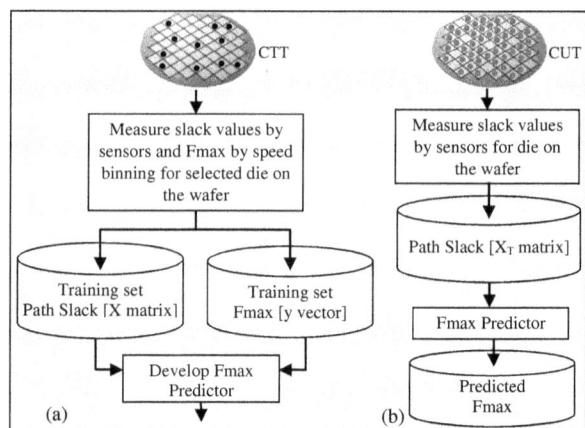

Figure 1: (a) Fmax predictor development from CTTs; (b) Fmax prediction of CUTs using the developed predictor.

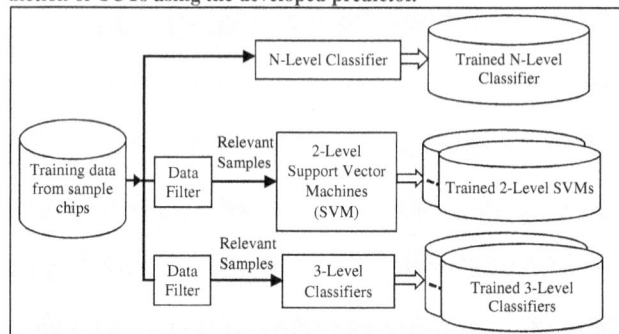

Figure 2: Development of trained classifiers from data of CTTs.

chip and m sensors in each sample. The column vector y contains the Fmax of each of the n chips.

$$X = \begin{bmatrix} S_{11} & \cdots & S_{1m} \\ \vdots & \ddots & \vdots \\ S_{n1} & \cdots & S_{nm} \end{bmatrix} \qquad y = \begin{bmatrix} F_1 \\ \vdots \\ F_n \end{bmatrix}$$

Fig. 2 shows the training process. If there are N discrete levels in the Fmax data, first an N-level classifier is trained with the training data. Then for each of the different N Fmax levels, two binary Support Vector Machines (SVMs) are trained that compares between pairs $(N, N-1)$ and $(N, N+1)$. Finally 3-level classifiers are trained to identify the correct state between levels $N-1$, N and $N+1$.

After the machine learning tools are trained with sufficient number of CTTs, for CUTs, the expensive procedure of functional or structural Fmax testing is omitted and only slacks are measured using the embedded sensors. The Fmax prediction flow using the trained classifiers is demonstrated in Fig. 3. First, the test samples are passed through the N-level classifier which outputs the frequency F. Based on the value of F, the test data are passed to two SVMs that predicts between adjacent levels. If the results of these two SVMs - $F1$ and $F2$ - match with F, the Fmax is taken to be the matched result F. Otherwise, the data are further classified among these three frequencies with the aid of a trained 3-level classifier and the output of this stage $F3$ is finalized as Fmax.

3. THE PATH SLACK SENSOR

An important component of the flow presented in Fig. 1 is a low-cost embedded sensor to accurately measure slack of the selected number of critical/near-critical paths. The circuit diagram of the used slack sensor IP is depicted in Fig. 4. When activated, the sensor monitors and records the worst-case timing slack at the capture flip-flop for all the paths terminating at that particular flip-flop. The sensor probes path ending capture flip-flop's D and Q ports through minimum size buffers. The small size of the buffers ensures

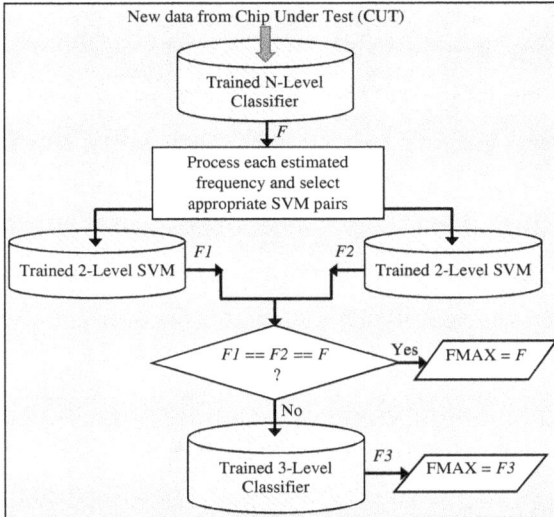

Figure 3: Speed binning flow for CUTs using trained classifiers.

that minimum amount of load capacitance is added to the main circuit path, thus impacting the path delay minimally. A path may experience slightly different rising edge and falling edge transition delays at the D input of the monitored capture flip-flop. Our goal is to deploy multiple instances of the sensor in the layout, hence to limit the area-overhead, we have designed our sensor IP for either rising or falling transition instead of both types of transitions. Based on the flip-flop of interest and path activation patterns, the suitable sensor type would be selected for that particular flip-flop. The different modules of the sensor and their functions are briefly described below.

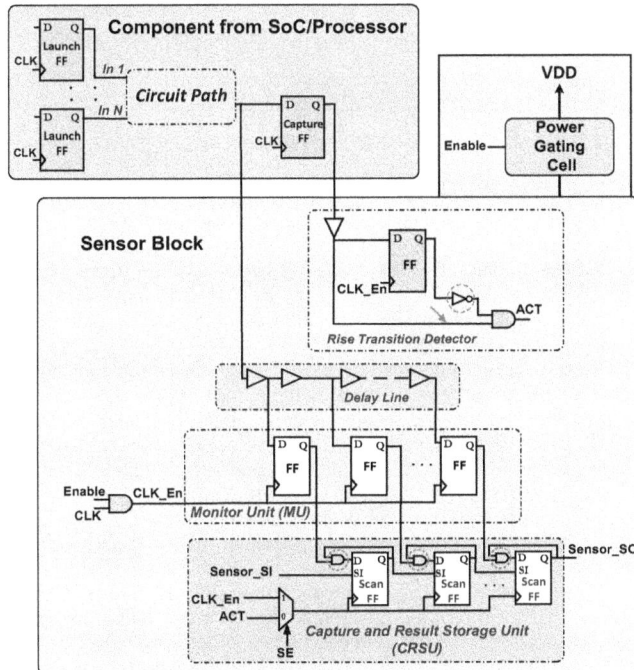

Figure 4: The slack sensor architecture for rising transition.

3.1 Transition Detector

The flip-flop inside the transition detector stores the data sampled by the capture flip-flop in the previous clock (CLK) cycle. This stored value is compared to the data sampled at the capture flip-flop by the current CLK edge. In Fig. 4 the circuitry for a rise transition detector is shown where a pulse is generated at the ACT output

in the event that the current data is logic one and previous a logic zero, indicating a rising transition in the incoming data. The latency between the active edge of the CLK and the pulse at the ACT is the sum of the propagation delays of a buffer and an AND gate. This small latency is irrelevant since the purpose of the ACT pulse is to latch the states from the Monitor Unit (MU) flip-flops to the Capture and Result Storage Unit's (CRSU) scan flip-flop chain. A fall transition detector can be implemented by simply moving the NOT gate (marked with red circle in Fig. 4) to the other input (marked with red arrow) of the AND gate.

3.2 Delay Line and Monitor Unit

The delay line consists of a chain of buffers. The number of required buffer stages depend on the desired slack detection range and unit buffer delay in the selected standard cell library. A flip-flop is attached at the end of each buffer to capture the states at the active CLK edge. The combination of delay line and the flip-flops in the Monitor Unit (MU) convert the timing slack into a corresponding digital data.

3.3 Capture and Result Storage Unit

In Fig. 4 each flip-flop in the scan chain of CRSU samples the corresponding MU flip-flop's output. The flip-flops in this module are clocked by the ACT pulse instead of the system CLK for achieving glitch immunity. For the case of a rising transition monitoring slack sensor, as shown in Fig. 4, the AND gate in front of each scan flip-flop make it sticky, in the sense that if it ever records a zero, it will hold on to the zero until reset or it is scan loaded with logic one. For rising transition, at the initialization stage all the scan flip-flops are set to logic one. To design a falling transition based slack sensor, the AND gates (marked with red circle in Fig. 4) in CRSU module are simply replaced by OR gates and at initialization all the flip-flops of CRSU are reset to logic zero. The OR gates, in this case, will ensure that if the flip-flop ever records a logic one, it will hold on to the one until reset. During the slack evaluation phase SE is set to zero and the flip-flops inside CRSU record the worst-case slack observed at the monitored capture flip-flop. The sensor data extraction process is initiated by setting SE pin to logic high which connects the flip-flops in a scan chain clocked by the main clock and finally the stored slack data is extracted through the Senor_SO pin. For multiple number of sensors, their CRSU are connected by a scan chain for data extraction [17]. The meta-stability issue may occur in at most one of the flip-flops of the MU block if the output from the buffer of the delay line arrive late in the flip-flop's setup time window. Any such meta-stability is automatically resolved in our architecture as we are using two flip-flops in series - forming a synchronizer circuit [18] - with the output of each buffer in the delay line. Even if there occurs a meta-stability in the MU block, the flip-flops of the CRSU will almost always be meta-stability resolved because of the high Mean Time Between Failure (MTBF) of a synchronizer circuit [18] and the designed sticky feature of the CRSU flip-flops.

4. SENSOR INSERTION FLOW

In this Section we develop a layout-aware path selection algorithm for sensor placement. The sensors act as features in our machine learning tool. The candidate capture flip-flops for sensor placement should be selected based on two main criteria - i)the sensors target the critical/near-critical paths and ii)the sensors or features of the machine learning tool should be a good representative of the trend of the data or the chip-to-chip PVT variations. Our proposed sensor insertion flow along with the path selection algorithm, shown in Fig. 5, addresses these criteria. For the first case, it is not practical to place sensors at the end of each of the critical/near-critical paths as the number of these paths are extensive in modern SoCs. Hence, the number of sensors to place are decided by the area-overhead budget. For the second criterion, the proposed algorithm ensures that the sensors cover a wide range of paths and those paths are spatially distributed across the layout. Spatial distribution of the sensors allow monitoring PVT variation effects on the timing critical paths. The flow begins with the synthesis of hardware from RTL

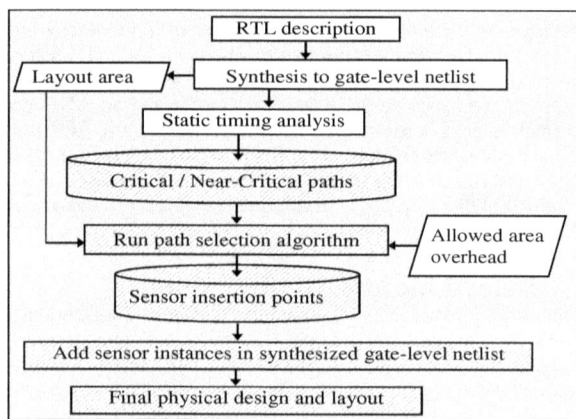

Figure 5: Sensor insertion flow.

to the gate-level netlist. At this stage, based on the the standard cell library used in synthesis and the gate-level netlist, an estimate of the layout area is obtained from the synthesis CAD tool. After that, static timing analysis is performed on the synthesized netlist and critical/near-critical paths (considering both single and multi-cycle paths) are sorted in order of their respective path slacks. Next the Path Selection algorithm is executed. The algorithm takes as input the sorted critical/near critical path list, an estimated area-overhead - which can be 2% to 5% of the main design depending on area-overhead budget - and outputs the sensor insertion points located inside the synthesized netlist of the SoC. In Algorithm 1, Lines 1 to 4 calculate the total number of sensors allowed for the given area-overhead. Lines 5 to 6 identify logical module-aware unique capture flip-flop sets. Since one or more paths can terminate on the same capture flip-flop, only the unique capture flip-flops are identified. In Lines 7 to 10, the total sensors are distributed among the logical modules in the ratio of the modules' share of the total critical/near-critical paths. Lastly, in Lines 11 to 13, the algorithm reports capture flip-flop nodes in the netlist where the sensors will be inserted. Finally, the sensor instances are added inside the synthesized netlist of the SoC at those identified insertion points and the physical design is completed.

Algorithm 1 Path Selection Algorithm

1: Specify area of the sensor module, $Area_{Sensor}$
2: Specify estimated total area of the chip, $Area_{Chip}$
3: Specify allowed area-overhead, $Area_{Overhead}$
4: Total sensors, $Total_{Sensor} = (Area_{Chip} * Area_{Overhead}) / Area_{Sensor}$
5: Read static timing analysis report and create a set of unique capture flip-flops where one or more paths terminate
6: Create a path group for each of the logical modules in the netlist and assign the respective capture flip-flops into that path group
7: **for** (each path group j) **do**
8:     Identify the number of critical/near-critical paths, N_j
9:     Identify contribution to the total number of critical or near-critical paths, $P_j = N_j / \sum N_j$;
10:     Allotted sensor for each path group, $S_j = P_j * Total_{Sensor}$
11:     Select top S_j critical or near-critical paths.
12:     Report the list of capture flip-flops for the selected S_j paths
13: **end for**
    Report the list of sensor insertion points in netlist for each path group j

---

5. EXPERIMENTAL RESULTS

The first step in extracting the path slacks for speed binning using embedded sensors, is to design the sensor IP with appropriate slack detection range. The slack detection range is determined by the number of buffer stages in the delay line. The detection resolution is limited by the delay of a unit buffer. The nominal resolution at typical-typical corner for our selected 28/32nm standard cell library is 20ps [20]. The expected resolution at 14nm and 22nm nodes are 10ps and 6ps, respectively, considering minimum size buffers at nominal conditions [21]. The resolution also sets the maximum round-off error limit of slack measurement. The slack detection

range is set to 15% of the nominal clock period of the SoC in which the sensors would be embedded into. With a nominal clock period of 740ps for our benchmark circuit at the selected standard cell library and sensor resolution of 20ps, 6 buffers are required to cover a 15% slack margin - which is about 111ps.

After deciding the number of required buffers in the delay line, the slack sensor IP was written in Verilog and synthesized with Design Compiler using Synopsys 28/32nm standard cell library [20]. Each sensor occupied a layout area of $136\mu m^2$. A post layout SPICE netlist was extracted and simulated with HSPICE [20]. The sensor calibration results for 28/32nm standard cell library are given in Table 1, where Column 1 reports the slack obtained by subtracting the flip-flop setup time from the delay between the data arrival time and the active clock edge. Column 2 shows the effects of temperature variations on the sensor response at nominal VDD. Since only 6 buffers were used in the delay line, it was observed - for the selected 28/32nm technology library - that the sensor response was invariant of any shift in temperature within 25°C to 75°C, the typical operating temperature range of chips. As mentioned in Section 3, for a rising transition detector, the sensors are initialized with a sensor reading of 111111, before the path slack measurements commence. At the upper detection limit the sensor code is 111110 and as the slack decreases, the sensor code changes from 111110 to 111100, then to 111000 and eventually to the lower detection limit at 000000, where each zero represents slack reduction by an amount equal to the delay of a buffer. Hence, the sensor reading of 111111 and all other states not mentioned in the calibration data of Table 1, indicate that the monitored slack was either negative or beyond the detection range.

Table 1: SENSOR CALIBRATION RESULTS FOR 28/32nm STANDARD CELL LIBRARY

Slack (ps)	Nominal VDD 1.05 V	95% VDD 0.9975 V	90% VDD 0.9450 V
	25°C to 75°C	25°C to 75°C	25°C to 75°C
120	1 1 1 1 1 0	1 1 1 1 1 0	1 1 1 1 0 0
100	1 1 1 1 0 0	1 1 1 1 0 0	1 1 1 0 0 0
80	1 1 1 0 0 0	1 1 1 0 0 0	1 1 0 0 0 0
60	1 1 0 0 0 0	1 1 0 0 0 0	1 1 0 0 0 0
40	1 0 0 0 0 0	1 0 0 0 0 0	1 0 0 0 0 0
20	0 0 0 0 0 0	0 0 0 0 0 0	0 0 0 0 0 0

Since the speed of the buffers, used in the delay line, is sensitive to power supply noise and voltage droop, we analyzed the power supply variation sensitivity of the sensor IP and tabulated the results in Table 1. The effect of voltage droop - slowing down of the sensor as shown for the 90% VDD case in Column 3 - can be easily decoupled from slack data with the aid of power supply noise sensors such as in [19].

As the sensor modules are power gated, the impact of aging degradation are minimal. To assess the impact of process variations on the sensitivity of the sensor we conducted a 150 sample Monte Carlo simulation on the sensor IP. The selected parameters to vary from nominal were transistor length (L), width (W) and threshold voltage (Vth) each by 15% and oxide thickness (Tox) by 4%. All simulations were done within the statistical range of 3 standard deviations (3σ) [17]. It was observed that in all the cases about 95% of the responses matched the expected calibration results as in Table 1, in rest of the cases the sensor response was either slower or faster by an unit buffer delay. These results imply that worst-case observation error is limited to one buffer delay [17].

For implementing our sensor insertion flow to extract path slacks for speed binning, we selected the Floating Point and Graphics Unit (FGU) circuit from the OpenSPARCT2 SoC's SPARC core [22]. The circuits were synthesized to gate level netlist with 28/32nm standard cell library using Design Compiler [20]. For the FGU circuit, from an initial post synthesis timing analysis with Prime-Time [20], the list of all the timing paths sorted in the descending order of nominal delay were obtained. Since one or more paths terminated on each capture flip-flop, the paths were grouped according to the unique capture flip-flops where they terminated and the circuit modules which contained the flip-flops. The layout area of FGU was estimated from the synthesis tool Design Compiler [20]. Since the register file macro module of FGU would be supplied as a hard macro block, in calculating the allowed area-overhead we only considered the area pertaining to the standard cells. The statistics from the sensor insertion flow are shown in Table 2. To assess the effect of number of sensors or features of machine learning tool on prediction accuracy, we varied the area-overhead budgets from 2% to 4%. The corresponding number of capture flip-flops to be monitored by sensors were 30, 45 and 60, respectively, as shown in Columns 5 to 7 in Table 2. As described in Section 4, to ensure that the sensors were distributed spatially across the layout, they were placed proportionally across the different logical modules of the netlist. Column 1 in Table 3 reports the different logical modules of the FGU circuit and Column 2 reports the number of unique capture flip-flops in each logical module. In Column 3 of Table 3 the worst-case slack cut-off range was set as 15% of the nominal clock period. In Columns 5 to 7 of Table 3, the number of allotted sensors for the unique capture flip-flops of the different logical modules are shown for the three different area-overhead budgets.

Table 2: LAYOUT STATISTICS

No. of Cells	No. of Flip-flops	Estimated Layout Area (Non macro)	Each Sensor Area	Allotted Sensors By Area Overhead		
				2%	3%	4%
58802	7514	204304 μm^2	136 μm^2	30	45	60

After finalizing the candidate flip-flops for sensor insertion, the sensor netlist was added to those points inside the synthesized gate level netlist of the FGU. The netlist-level sensor insertion flow was automated with Perl scripts. Finally, the full physical designs of the FGU, with embedded sensor network, was completed with IC Compiler [20]. Fig. 6(a) shows layout of FGU with 60 embedded sensors. From Fig. 6(b), it can be observed that the sensor blocks are distributed across the layout as those were placed inside the different logical modules of the main netlist according to our proposed flow. Fig. 6(b) also indicates that critical/near-critical paths in certain blocks are situated close by, which is dictated by the RTL and circuit design of FGU.

Table 3: SENSOR DISTRIBUTION IN FGU OF OPENSPARCT2

Logical Module Name	No. of Unique Capture Flip-flops	Flip-flops with Worst Slack Below Cut-off		No. of Allotted Slack Sensors (by Area Overhead)		
		Number	Percent of Total	2%	3%	4%
FAC	495	5	0.83	0	1	1
FAD	693	6	1	1	1	1
FDC	76	6	1	1	1	1
FDD	1040	261	43.4	13	19	25
FEC	84	5	0.83	0	0	1
FGD	1102	46	7.7	2	3	4
FIC	65	5	0.83	0	0	1
FPC	699	15	2.5	1	1	2
FPE	97	7	1	1	1	1
FPF	731	56	9.3	2	4	5
FPY	1931	189	31.4	9	14	18

The detailed transistor level circuit netlist of the 60 sensor along with their corresponding monitored paths were extracted from the layout using Synopsys tools [20]. Also the transistor level netlist of the top 20% critical/near-critical paths - identified from post layout timing analysis - were extracted for FMAX identification. While identifying the possible critical paths, both single cycle and multi-cycle paths were considered. For multi-cycle paths, the slacks were normalized according to the cycle count. Because of post-fabrication process variations, it is expected that the delays of these identified critical paths will vary from chip-to-chip. As a result we cannot exactly pinpoint the speed limiting critical path in the pre-fabrication phase. To simulate the effect of post-fabrication process variations,

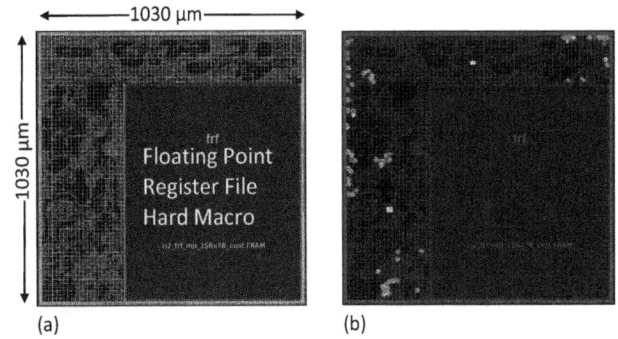

Figure 6: (a) The layout of FGU with embedded sensor network. (b) Cells of sensor modules are highlighted.

we performed 150 point Monte Carlo simulation on the extracted critical paths as well as the sensor-path pairs using HSPICE [20]. The selected parameters to vary from nominal were transistor length (L), width (W) and threshold voltage (Vth) each by 15% and oxide thickness (Tox) by 4%. The simulation time was approximately 25 hours on a system with Intel Xeon processor with 8 cores and 96GB RAM. The path slacks were extracted from the simulations of the sensor-path pairs by exciting them with appropriate stimulus functions generated by Synopsys tools [20]. From detail SPICE simulations of all of the critical/near-critical paths of the circuit, the longest path delay was identified. After adding 10% margin with this delay as guard-band against aging and noise, the minimum CLK period and the Fmax was estimated for each sample. In order to quantize the continuous Fmax values we need to assign a grid size or bin width. To analyze the effect of bin width on prediction mismatch for a nominal operating frequency of 1.35 GHz, we selected two different bin resolutions - 25 MHz and 50 MHz.

The 150 data samples obtained from Monte Carlo simulations were partitioned into a training set consisting of 100 samples and a validation set containing 50 samples. Each of the slacks act as a feature in our machine learning based speed binning flow. The machine learning capabilities of the MATLAB [23] statistical tool box were used to select and train the multi-level classifiers and 2-level SVMs as introduced in Section 3. For multi-level classifiers the TreeBagger algorithm from MATLAB [23] were used. TreeBagger is an adaptive classification algorithm that analyzes the properties of the data features and based on that models and trains a classifier. This trained classifier was later verified with the validation data set. TreeBagger classifiers were used in the first and last stages of our speed binning flow as shown in Fig. 3. The SVM binary classifiers, used in the second stage of the flow, were also designed and trained with MATLAB [23] by taking the relevant data from training data set. After the required classifiers were all trained with the 100 sample training data set, the 50 sample validation data were applied to the trained classifiers and the corresponding predicted Fmax were obtained. These predicted Fmax were later compared with actual Fmax to identify the miss-binning rate.

The results for the 60 sensors/features case are shown in Fig. 7(a) to (f). In Fig. 7(a) the relative importance of each sensor (feature) in modeling the multi-level classifier is depicted. Fig. 7(b) shows the actual Fmax for the 50 sample validation data set. The predicted Fmax and prediction mismatch for bin width of 50 MHz are depicted in Fig. 7(c) and (d), respectively. Prediction results for bin size of 25 MHz is shown in Fig. 7(e) and 7(f). In Table 4 and Table 5 the mismatch at different stages of the classification are reported for the three different numbers of sensors used at 50 MHz and 25 MHz bin width, respectively. It is observed that the SVM classifiers improved the results obtained from the first stage multi-level classifiers for all the cases of sensor counts and bin sizes. Increasing the number of sensors from 30 to 60 improved the prediction accuracy significantly as shown in Columns 5 to 7 in Tables 4 and 5. With 60 sensors, for bin width of 50 MHz, the worst-case mismatch is 2 bin or 100 MHz and occurs only for 4% of the samples as seen in Row 5 of Column 7 in Table 4. For bin width of 25 MHz, the worst-case mismatch is 75 MHz which occurs for only 6% of the samples as reported

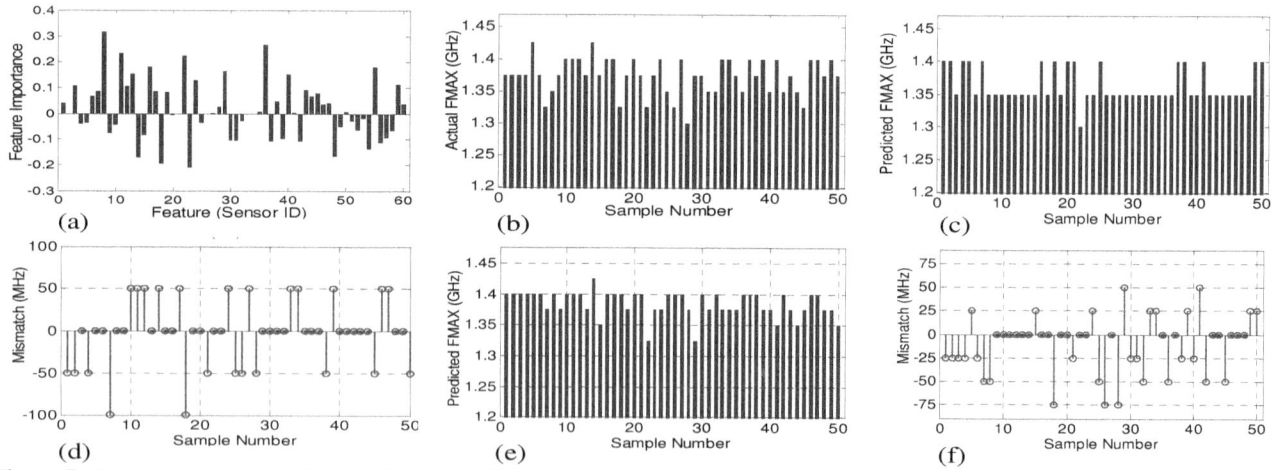

Figure 7: (a) Importance of each feature (Sensor); (b) Actual Fmax of the validation data set; (c) Predicted Fmax for the validation data set with 50 MHz bin size; (d) Prediction mismatch for 50 MHz bin size; (e) Predicted Fmax for the validation data set with 25 MHz bin size; (f) Prediction mismatch for 25 MHz bin size.

in Row 5 of Column 7 in Table 5. Reduction of the bin width decreases the worst-case frequency mismatch. For a nominal CLK frequency around 1.35 GHz and bin width 25 MHz, the worst-case mismatch of 75 MHz translates to only 5.6% frequency or path delay mismatch. The guard-band that is typically added to the nominal path delay in estimating Fmax can mask this mismatch effect and make the predicted Fmax practically acceptable. In regards to the results in Table 4 and 5, it should be noted that in our SPICE Monte Carlo simulation the process variation parameters were randomly selected from a Gaussian distribution without any spatial or global correlation, but in reality for fabricated chips, there are always some correlation between the process parameter variation distribution as experimentally verified in [13]. This correlation is expected to further improve our speed binning accuracy with silicon data.

Table 4: FOR 50MHz BIN SIZE

Mismatch Between Predicted and Actual Fmax	After First Level of Classification			After Final Stage of Classification		
	Number of Sensors			Number of Sensors		
	30	45	60	30	45	60
None (0 MHz)	21	23	24	23	23	25
1 Bin (50 MHz)	27	23	24	25	24	23
2 Bin (100 MHz)	1	4	2	2	3	2
3 Bin (150 MHz)	1	0	0	0	0	0

Table 5: FOR 25 MHz BIN SIZE

Mismatch Between Predicted and Actual Fmax	After First Level of Classification			After Final Stage of Classification		
	Number of Sensors			Number of Sensors		
	30	45	60	30	45	60
None (0 MHz)	15	18	19	17	19	20
1 Bin (25 MHz)	21	17	19	20	16	18
2 Bin (50 MHz)	8	8	8	8	7	9
3 Bin (75 MHz)	5	7	4	4	7	3
4 Bin (100 MHz)	1	0	0	1	0	0

6. CONCLUSIONS

We have proposed a novel speed-binning flow that utilizes the path slacks extracted with on-chip sensors. The path slacks are used as features in modeling and training machine learning tools. The worst-case mismatch between predicted and actual Fmax is within 6%. The proposed framework has the potential to eliminate the high cost associated with conventional pattern-based speed-binning flows.

7. ACKNOWLEDGMENTS

This work was supported by the National Science Foundation under grant CCF-1255898 and by Semiconductor Research Corporation under task 2422.

8. REFERENCES

[1] S. Ghosh and K. Roy, "Parameter variation tolerance and error resiliency: New design paradigm for the nanoscale era," Proc IEEE, vol. 98, pp. 1718-1751, 2010.

[2] S.S. Sapatnekar, "Overcoming variations in nanometer-scale technologies," Emerging and Selected Topics in Circuits and Systems, IEEE Journal on, vol. 1, pp. 5-18, 2011.

[3] P. Das and S.K. Gupta, "Extending pre-silicon delay models for post-silicon tasks: Validation, diagnosis, delay testing, and speed binning," in VLSI Test Symposium (VTS), IEEE 31st, pp. 1-6, 2013.

[4] J. Zeng, R. Guo, W. Cheng, M. Mateja and J. Wang, "Scan-based Speed-path Debug for a Microprocessor," IEEE Design & Test of Computers, 2011.

[5] E.J. Jang, A. Gattiker, S. Nassif and J.A. Abraham, "Efficient and product-representative timing model validation," in VLSI Test Symposium (VTS), IEEE 29th, pp. 90-95, 2011.

[6] M. Ebrahimi et al. "Aging-aware logic synthesis," in Proceedings of the International Conference on Computer-Aided Design, pp. 61-68, 2013.

[7] J. Chen, Jing Zeng, L. Wang, J. Rearick and M. Mateja, "Selecting the most relevant structural Fmax for system Fmax correlation," in VLSI Test Symposium (VTS), 28th, pp. 99-104, 2010.

[8] U. Guin et al., "Functional Fmax test-time reduction using novel DFTs for circuit initialization," in Computer Design (ICCD), IEEE 31st International Conference on, pp. 1-6, 2013.

[9] E. Dimaandal and M. Padilla, "Test-time reduction methodology: Innovative ways to reduce test time for server products," in Electronics Packaging Technology Conference (EPTC 2013), IEEE 15th, pp. 718-722, 2013.

[10] C.K.H. Suresh, E. Yilmaz, S. Ozev and O. Sinanoglu, "Adaptive reduction of the frequency search space for multivdd digital circuits," in Design, Automation & Test in Europe Conference & Exhibition (DATE), pp. 292-295, 2013.

[11] J. Rearick, "Too much delay fault coverage is a bad thing," in Test Conference, Proceedings. International, pp. 624-633, 2001.

[12] B.D. Cory, R. Kapur and B. Underwood, "Speed binning with path delay test in 150nm technology," Design & Test of Computers, IEEE, vol. 20, pp. 41-45, 2003.

[13] K.A. Brand, S. Mitra, E. Volkerink and E.J. McCluskey, "Speed clustering of integrated circuits," in Test Conference, Proceedings. ITC. International, pp. 1128-1137, 2004.

[14] R. Wilson et al., "27.1 A 460MHz at 397mV, 2.6GHz at 1.3V, 32b VLIW DSP, embedding FMAX tracking," in Solid-State Circuits Conference Digest of Technical Papers (ISSCC), IEEE International, pp. 452-453, 2014.

[15] J. Chen, L. Wang, Po-Hsien Chang, Jing Zeng, S. Yu and M. Mateja, "Data learning techniques and methodology for Fmax prediction," in Test Conference, ITC. International, pp. 1-10, 2009.

[16] J. Zeng, J. Wang, C. Chen, M. Mateja and L. Wang, "On evaluating speed path detection of structural tests," in Quality Electronic Design (ISQED), 11th International Symposium on, pp. 570-576, 2010.

[17] M. Sadi, L. Winemberg and M.M. Tehranipoor, "A Robust Digital Sensor IP and Sensor Insertion Flow for In-Situ Path Timing Slack Monitoring in SoCs," in VLSI Test Symposium (VTS), 2015 IEEE 33rd, 2015.

[18] R. Ginosar, "Metastability and Synchronizers: A Tutorial," Design & Test of Computers, IEEE, vol. 28, pp. 23-35, 2011.

[19] M. Sadi, Z. Conroy, B. Eklow, M. Kamm, N. Bidokhti and M.M. Tehranipoor, "An All Digital Distributed Sensor Network Based Framework for Continuous Noise Monitoring and Timing Failure Analysis in SoCs," in Test Symposium (ATS), 2014 IEEE 23rd Asian, pp. 269-274, 2014.

[20] http://www.synopsys.com/COMMUNITY/UNIVERSITYPROGRAM/

[21] http://ptm.asu.edu/

[22] http://www.oracle.com/technetwork/systems/opensparc/index.html

[23] http://www.mathworks.com/products/matlab/

Reconfigurable - Self Adaptive Fault Tolerant Cache Memory for DVS enabled Systems

Michail Mavropoulos, Georgios Keramidas, Grigorios Adamopoulos, Dimitris Nikolos
Department of Computer Engineering & Informatics, University of Patras, Greece
{mavropoulo, gkeramidas, adamopoul, nikolosd}@ceid.upatras.gr

ABSTRACT

Processor caches play a critical role in the performance of today's computer systems. As technology scales, due to manufacturing defects and process variations a large number of cells in a cache is expected to be faulty. The number of faulty cells varies from die to die and in the field of the application depends on the operating conditions (e.g., supply voltage, frequency). Several techniques have been proposed to tolerate faults in caches. A drawback of the redundancy based techniques is that the amount of redundancy is decided at the design time targeting a maximum number of faults, so in cases of a small number of faults (e.g., in the nominal supply voltage in a system with DVS) only a part of the redundant resources is used. In this paper we propose a new reconfigurable-self adaptive fault tolerant cache scheme. The unique characteristic of our scheme is that it uses its resources for both the reduction of the misses caused by the faulty blocks as well as for the reduction of conflict misses, depending on the number of faults, their distribution in the cache, and the running application. Our experimental results for a wide range of scientific applications and a plethora of fault maps with different SRAM failure probabilities reveal that our proposal can achieve significant benefits.

Categories and Subject Descriptors

B.1.3 [**Control Structures and Microprogramming**]: Control Structure Reliability, Testing, and Fault-Tolerance – *Redundant design.*

Keywords

Fault tolerance, processor cache memories, reconfigurable caches.

1. INTRODUCTION

As feature size of ICs continues to shrink, a large number of cells in a memory is expected to be faulty due to manufacturing defects and process variations [5]. Thus, it is becoming increasingly difficult to meet 100% correctness with an acceptable production yield. On the other hand, power consumption has become a key challenge in the design of high performance systems and almost all contemporary processors are equipped with the necessary support to operate in multiple power modes. Reducing

the supply voltage is an effective method to reduce power consumption; hence Dynamic Voltage Scaling (DVS) is widely used to reduce the power consumption of microprocessors. Unfortunately, voltage scaling exponentially increases the impact of process variations on memory cell reliability resulting in an exponential increase in the number of the faulty cells [5]. Failures in memory cells due to voltage scaling typically determine the minimum supply voltage, known as Vccmin, at which the memory can reliably operate. The Vccmin of the processor as a whole is determined by the Vccmin of its on-chip cache memories [25].

To improve cache yield and enable low voltage operation, many techniques have been proposed. A class of these techniques targets to increase the robustness of cache memories to the variations of the device parameters whereas various other techniques try to tolerate the faults stemming from manufacturing defects, variations of the device parameters and aging phenomena.

At circuit level, variations on the traditional 6T (6 transistors) SRAM cell design or designs including 8T [8], 10T [7] cells as well as a Schmidt trigger based 10T SRAM cell [12] have been proposed. However, the above techniques incur significant area overheads. To improve the yield of memories in general and caches in particular, multiple word/bit line redundancy has extensively been used [6, 21]. Although the multiple word/bit lines redundancy improves the yield of memories, it is not suitable to cope with faults appearing due to DVS in the field of the application. At the system level, the usage of Error Correcting Codes (ECC) has been proposed. However, due to the large number of faults, multiple bit error correcting codes should be used. Such codes require high storage overheads, large decoding times, and complex decoders [14]. ECC are suitable for handling soft errors.

The disabling of the faulty cache parts (ways, sets, or blocks) has been extensively studied by many researchers [16, 17, 23]. The drawback of those techniques is the increased number of additional misses as the number of the faulty cache parts increases (graceful degradation). In [15], it was shown that the savings in dynamic energy/power consumption increase when we reduce the supply voltage but only up to a certain point. Further lowering the supply voltage, the increase of the energy/power being consumed for accessing the next cache level due to the increased number of misses, surpasses the savings due to lower supply voltage.

Aiming at the minimization of the number of misses caused by the disabled faulty cache parts, several techniques have been investigated at the cache organization level. A class of techniques is based on restructuring the cache in order to combine partially faulty blocks to get a smaller number of non-faulty lines [5, 11, 18, 19, 20, 22, 25]. These techniques increase the critical path delay of the cache and its complexity. In another class of techniques the reduction of the misses caused by the disabled faulty parts of the cache is achieved by using redundant word-lines in the cache [3], an external spare cache connected to the main cache via an interconnection network [4], a small fully associative spare cache [24], the use of the victim cache [13] or an extra cache [2].

A common drawback of the redundancy based techniques proposed in [3], [4], and [24] is that when the number of the faults in the cache is relatively small (for example in the nominal supply voltage) the extra memory resources are underutilized or not utilized at all. On the other hand, the use of a victim cache [13] exploits well the redundant resources only when the number of faults is very small, reducing the misses caused by conflicts (conflict misses) as well as by faulty blocks. As the number of faults increases its efficiency is rapidly reduced. The extra cache proposed in [2], called RVC cache, targets in providing safe and tight worst-case execution times for hard real-time applications. Recently a fault-tolerant aware (re)placement policy based on a spatial footprint prediction mechanism was proposed [10]. This technique was presented for only 2-way associative faulty caches and is not straightforwardly extensible to higher associative caches.

In this work we propose a reconfigurable, self-adaptive fault tolerant cache memory which is based on the use of a small fully associative extra cache. The extra cache has two modes of operation. In one mode it concurrently plays the role of a victim cache [9], with respect to the conflict misses, and a spare cache [24] with respect to the misses caused by the disabled faulty cache parts; we called that mode VS mode. This mode of operation is used when the number of faults in the cache is smaller than a predefined threshold. In the other mode of operation, the extra cache functions as a spare cache [24]. In the first mode of operation since the number of the faulty blocks is relatively small, the block disabling technique is used. In this mode of operation the percentage of the blocks of the extra cache which is used as redundancy for the faulty blocks of the main cache with respect to that which is used for conflict misses depends on the number of the faults, their distribution in the cache area as well as on the running application. In the second mode of operation the block/n disabling technique is used, where n = 2, 4, ... Although, in the context of this work, we provide a design of the extra cache for n=2, the design can easily be extended for n=4 or 8.

Intuitively, the RVC cache [2] operates as a victim-spare cache too. However, our proposal differs in various aspects:

i) Our proposal aims at improving the average performance for DVS enabled systems, while RVC cache focuses on providing timing guarantees for hard real time applications.

ii) Our proposal is suitable for a wide range of fault probabilities. On the contrary the number of non-faulty blocks in RVC should be at least equal to the number of the faulty blocks of the main cache, rendering it unsuitable for situations with large number of faults.

iii) The proposed mechanism is reconfigurable with two modes of operation. In one mode (small number of faults), the disabling of the faulty parts take place at block level, while in the other mode (large number of faults) at subblock level. RVC has one mode of operation with block level disabling.

Structure of paper. Section 2 outlines the necessary background information. Section 3 presents the motivation of the proposed solution. Section 4 provides the detailed design of the proposed extra cache and describes its synergy with the main cache. Section 5 offers our evaluation results and Section 6 concludes this work.

2. BACKGROUND AND FAULT MODEL

Block disabling was proposed in [23] to enhance the yield of VLSI processors. In block disabling, only one extra bit (called fault flag) per block is required in order to indicate whether a block contains faulty bits in the tag or data area. For subblock disabling

we need one bit (fault flag) per subblock. In the case of a fault in the tag of a block, the fault flags of both subblocks are set. We consider that the fault flags are implemented with robust SRAM cells (e.g., using 10T cells [12]). The detection of the defective cells can be done by BIST based periodic testing in the field for each operating point (i.e., Vcc level). A detailed description of the BIST operation is beyond the scope of this paper.

When the block disabling technique is used in an m-way set associative cache, some sets, those with faulty blocks, have lower effective associativity. LRU does not take into account the faulty blocks of a set. This can reduce performance significantly if the lower associative sets happen to be accessed frequently with access patterns captured with the nominal cache associativity. In cases of large number of faults, applying the block disabling technique, a large volume of blocks is disabled leaving operational only a small part of the cache. In such cases the subblocks disabling technique leaves operational a significantly larger part of the cache.

In an m-way set associative cache equipped with the subblock disabling technique, when the tags of both subblocks are faulty, the block is disabled and the associativity of the set is reduced, as in the case of the block disabling technique. When the required data does not exist in the cache due to a faulty subblock (i.e., the tag lookup operation indicated a cache hit, but the most significant bit of the address offset points to the faulty subblock), then the cache block is evicted and if dirty the valid subblock is written back to the lower cache level. In this case, the request is treated as a normal miss serviced by the cache placement/eviction logic. The operation just described is similar to the operation described in [1].

The performance of an m-way set associative faulty data cache equipped with the block disabling ability and enhanced with a victim cache [9] (a small extra fully associative cache) was investigated in [13]. A set with faulty blocks have lower associativity and the LRU does not take into account the faulty blocks of the set [13]. An evicted block is stored in the victim cache. After a hit in the victim cache the requested block is interchanged with the block of the main cache being in the set defined by the index of the requested block and the frame indicated by the replacement algorithm (LRU in our case) of the main cache.

The spare cache (a small extra fully associative cache) was proposed in [24] for mitigating the misses caused by faults in direct mapped caches. The idea of spare cache can be applied also to m-way set associative caches. In a miss, when the frame indicated by the cache LRU replacement algorithm is faulty, the fetched block is stored in the frame of the spare cache indicated by its (local) LRU. The LRU counters of the main and the spare cache are updated.

A spare cache can be used along with the subblock disabling technique too. In this case the spare cache is again a fully associative cache but its entries are subblocks and its LRU refers to subblocks. On a miss the following three operations may occur. When the LRU block of the main cache is fault free, the miss is treated as a normal miss. When one of the subblocks of the frame indicated by the LRU of the main cache is faulty, the fetched block is stored in part (one subblock) in the correct part of the frame of the main cache and the other subblock in the LRU subblock of the spare cache. When both subblocks of the frame indicated by the LRU of the main cache are faulty, the fetched block should be stored in two subblocks of the spare cache in two steps (depending on the fetch policy this may introduce additional delay).

Fault Model. In order to take into account faults stemming from manufacturing defects, variations of the device parameters, and aging, we consider a wide range of fault probabilities from 5×10^{-5} to 5×10^{-3}. With respect to the location of the faults we consider that the faults are random and uniformly distributed in the tag and the

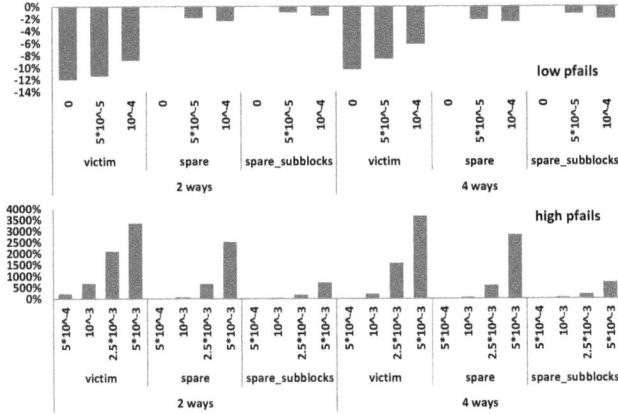

Fig 1: Faulty misses normalized to the misses of a fault-free cache without additional redundant resources.

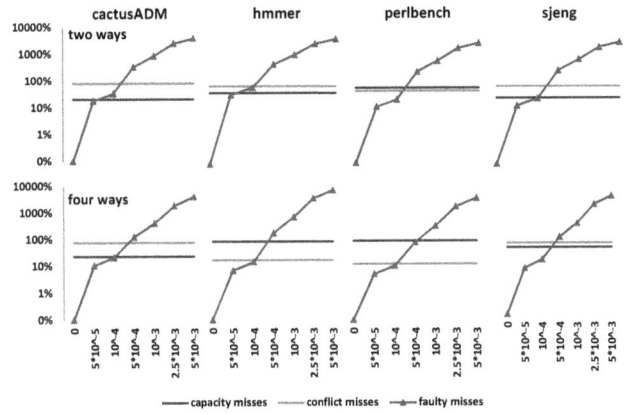

Fig.2: The percentage of faulty (red lines), conflict (green lines) and capacity (blue lines) misses with respect to the total number of misses in a fault free cache.

data bits of the target cache. In addition, we assume that the victim or spare caches are also faulty. In our experiments we used the random function of GNU/Linux to produce 50 random fault maps. Finally, we consider that the fault flags and the LRU counters are implemented with robust SRAM cells.

3. MOTIVATION

Fig. 1 depicts the misses of a faulty first-level 2- and 4-way 16KB data cache (DL1) equipped with the block or subblock (block/2) disabling technique and enhanced with either a victim or a spare cache of 16 blocks. As noted, faults are considered in the DL1 as well as in the victim and spare caches. The illustrated misses are normalized to the misses reported by a fault-free cache without additional redundant resources (victim or spare cache).

From Fig. 1, it is clear that for small fault probabilities (pfails) the usage of the victim cache results in smaller number of misses. However, as the pfail increases, the misses increases very fast toward prohibitively high levels. On the other hand, the extra cache working as a spare cache at block level, and even better at subblock level, restricts significantly the increase of misses. However, in the case of small fault probabilities (for example during nominal supply voltage) using the extra cache as a spare, we do not take a full advantage of the additional redundant resources.

To justify the above behavior of the victim and the spare cache we analyze the sources of misses in fault free and faulty caches. Our aim is to reveal the ratio between the misses caused by disabling faulty cache parts (faulty misses) with respect to the conflict and capacity misses in the corresponding fault free cache. Fig. 2 shows the collected statistics for four SPEC2006 benchmarks. The top and the bottom part of Fig. 2 refer to a 2-way and a 4-way 16KB DL1 respectively. In all graphs, the vertical-axis (percentage of faulty misses with respect to a fault-free cache) is in logarithmic scale, whereas the horizontal axis depicts various pfails. In addition, the leftmost point in the horizontal axis (tagged as "0") corresponds to the non-faulty case.

There are three lines in each graph. The green and the blue lines depict the percentage of conflict and capacity misses with respect to the total number of misses in a fault free cache. The red line shows the percentage of the faulty misses caused by the block disabling technique: [(misses_faulty_cache – misses_fault_free _cache) / misses_fault_free_cache] × 100. We excluded from the graphs the cold misses, since they correspond to less than 1% of the total misses in all studied applications.

Several conclusions can be drawn from Fig. 2. First, the number of conflict misses varies significantly among the

applications. Moreover, for fault probabilities less than or equal to 10^{-4} (low faults volume situation) the number of conflict misses surpasses the number of faulty misses in all cases. Going to higher pfails, the number of reported conflict misses is smaller than the faulty misses. As explained in the previous section, the victim cache, due to faulty block disabling, confronts the misses caused by faults in the main cache as conflict misses. Therefore, the victim cache copes with conflict as well as faulty misses while the spare cache mainly copes with faulty misses. It is known also that the victim cache works poorly with a sizable amount of conflict misses. Due to these reasons, the victim cache gives better results only for small pfails for which the number of faulty misses is limited. In Fig. 1 we can see that the spare cache for pfails equal to 5×10^{-5} and 10^{-4} reduces the misses with respect to the fault free cache. The reason is that for each faulty (sub)block the spare cache may use more than one spare (sub)blocks, increasing this way the apparent associativity of the sets with the faulty (sub)blocks.

Fig. 3 depicts the increase of the misses (percentage of misses in the faulty cache over the misses of a non-faulty cache) caused by four fault distributions for two benchmarks and six fault probabilities from 5×10^{-5} to 5×10^{-3}. It is obvious that the volume of faulty misses depends on the distribution of the faults in the cache memory array as well as on the executing application. For example, in the 10^{-4} pfail case, the faulty misses vary from 34.4% up to 579.1% (bzip2) depending to the fault distribution and for the same fault distribution up to 499% between gobmk and bzip2. The fluctuations of faulty misses are the result of the unique memory behavior of each application in relation to the distribution of the faults in the cache. Thereby, it becomes clear that an ideal fault tolerance cache scheme must be able to adapt its functionality (as we propose in this work) not only to different fault volumes, but also to the manifestation of the impact of the defective cells at the microarchitectural level (i.e., the introduced faulty misses).

From the above analysis, the following remarks can be drawn:

i) For small number of faults, the conflict misses are more than the faulty misses.

ii) For small number of faults, the faulty misses depend heavily on the distribution of faults in the cache structure.

iii) The victim cache confronts better the conflict misses, while the spare cache copes better with the faulty misses.

iv) For a fault free cache, the spare is a waste system resource.

v) For the same fault map, the subblock disabling technique deactivates a smaller part of the cache.

163

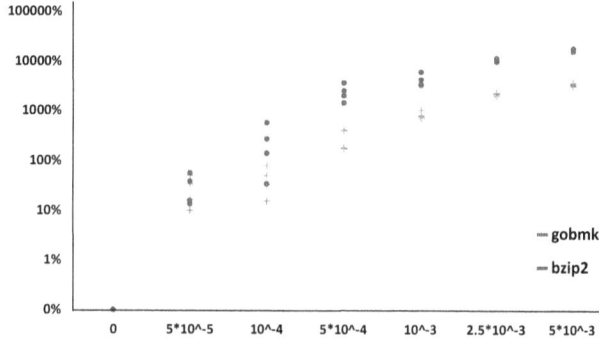

Fig.3: Variations of faulty misses among different fault maps and applications.

The above analysis justifies the proposed reconfigurable, self-adaptive fault tolerant cache with the two modes of operation.

4. PROPOSED MECHANISM

The proposed fully associative extra cache should be able to operate as a VS – cache, with the ability of disabling faulty blocks in both the main and the extra cache, when a control input VS is equal to 1 (VS=1) and as spare cache with the ability of disabling faulty subblocks in both the main cache and the extra cache, when VS=0. To this end, both the main cache and the extra contain separate faulty bits f_i (with i=0, 1) for each subblock to indicate if the specific subblock is fault free (f_i =1) or faulty (f_i=0).

The extra cache consists of two fully associative arrays (Fig. 4). If VS=1, the tag-0 array is deactivated in order to reduce the static power consumption and the operation of the extra cache is based on tag-1. Also in this case (VS=1) when a block is moved in the extra cache the associated tag extended by the value 0 is stored in tag-1 (tag/E) array. The LRU is implemented in two levels. At the higher level, an LRUA shows the least recently used memory array. At the lower level, the LRUL (left) and LRUR (right) show the least recently used subblock in the left/right array respectively.

Fig. 5 sketches the basic operations of our proposal in VS mode (VS=1). For illustration purposes, we assume a 2-way associative cache consisting of eight sets and a 2-entry extra cache. The left part of Fig. 5 illustrates the extra cache functionality in case of a hit in the main cache (Case A in Fig. 5) or a miss in the main cache and a hit in the extra cache (Case B). These two cases may occur when the system core generates a new request. At this point, two policies could be implemented: either the main and the extra cache are checked simultaneously or the extra cache is accessed only in main cache misses. In the latter case, a penalty of one cycle will be introduced; however this policy is considered as more power efficient, since the extra cache is triggered only during

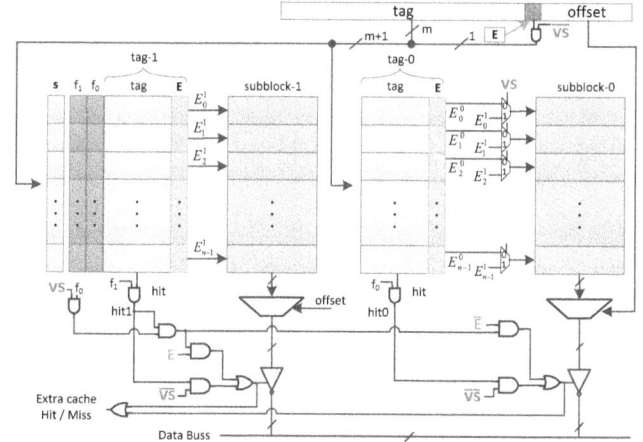

Fig.4: Design of the extra cache. For VS=1 operates as a VS cache with block disabling ability; for VS=0 operates as a spare cache with subblock disabling ability.

cache misses. In any case, both policies achieve significant savings in performance and power than resorting to the lower cache levels.

In Case A, the requested data are forwarded to the core. No more actions are required. In Case B, the upcoming actions are dictated by the "swap bit" (Fig. 5). The swap bit acts as an indicator to distinguish the memory blocks residing in the extra cache. As noted two types of blocks are forwarded to the extra cache. Either blocks that are originally mapped in faulty blocks in the main cache (swap bit is set to "0") or blocks that are mapped in fault free main cache blocks and end up in the extra cache upon their eviction from the main cache (swap bit is set to "1"). In the former case, the extra cache block substitutes a faulty block in the main cache, so the hit process ends when the requested address is forwarded from the extra cache to the core. In the latter case, the requested address is again forwarded to the core, but also the addressed block in the extra cache is swapped with the LRU block of the corresponding set of the main cache (see "swap operation" in left part of Fig. 5). Note that if a faulty block is indicated by the LRU, swap operation cannot be performed.

The right part of Fig. 5 describes the functionality of the proposed mechanism when both the main and the extra cache do not hold the requested data. In this case, a miss request is issued to the next cache level. Upon the requested data arrive, we must identify (by checking the fault flag of the LRU block in the target cache set) if their destination is faulty (Case C) or fault free (Case D). Obviously, in both cases the data are forwarded to core. However, in Case C, the missed data is simply stored in the extra cache and both the LRU of the main cache and the extra cache are

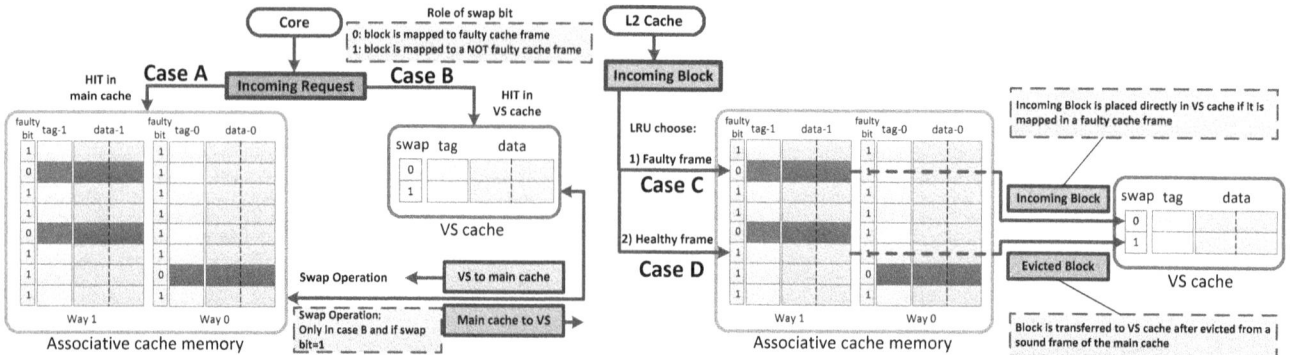

Fig.5: Basic functionality of the extra cache for VS=1 (hit case in the left part and miss case in the right).

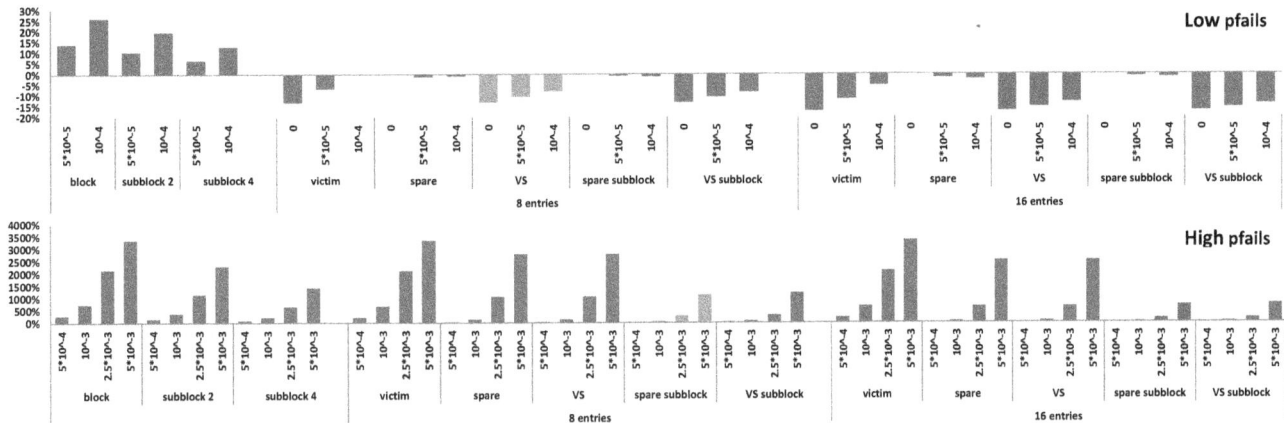

Fig.6: Normalized misses of the studied fault-tolerance mechanisms. The red and green bars show the proposed configuration modes of an 8-entries and 16-entries extra cache respectively.

updated. Conversely, if the target block (according to LRU) in the main cache is fault free, the arriving data fills the block indicated by LRU while the current data are moved to the extra cache. In this case the replaced entry in the extra cache is discarded and, if dirty, written back to the next cache level. Both the LRU of the main and the extra cache are updated. Finally, in all cases, the swap bit is appropriately modified.

5. EVALUATION RESULTS

We performed cycle accurate simulations assuming a dynamic 2-issue core with a 20-entry instruction window. In this work we assume that faults are injected only in first level data caches. We use a 16KB DL1 configured as a 2-way associative cache. Overall, the simulated memory system includes a 16KB/4-way IL1, a 256KB/8-way L2 cache, and a 4GB main memory. The block size is equal to 64 bytes in all cache levels. In addition, we use 18 scientific applications from SPEC2006 suite and we simulate the largest-weight 200-million instruction Simpoint sample per benchmark. For clarity reasons, we opt to show the average numbers of misses reported by each studied technique across all benchmarks normalized to the misses of a fault-free cache.

To showcase the reconfiguration aspects of our proposal with respect to the volume of faults, we present our gathered statistics in two different sets of graphs. In particular, the top graph in Fig. 6 depicts the simulation results assuming SRAM pfails up to 10^{-4} (low-pfail case), whilst the graph in the bottom shows the corresponding results for pfails ranging from 5×10^{-4} to 5×10^{-3} (high-pfail case). In all graphs, the studied pfails are juxtaposed to the horizontal axis. The bars in the top graph of Fig. 6 tagged as "0" illustrate the reporting statistics of a fault-free cache. The green (8-entries extra cache) and the red (16-entries extra cache) bars show how the redundant memory resources as well as the disabling policy (block vs. subblock disabling) should be configured in relation to the volume of faults in the main and the extra cache.

Both graphs of Fig. 6 show the normalized misses of eight fault tolerant mechanisms. In particular, the groups of bars in the left part of the graph, tagged as "block," "subblock2," and "subblock4," depict the impact of faults when the block, subblock, and sub-subblock disabling schemes are employed in the underlying faulty cache (i.e., when one, two, or four faulty flags are assigned to each physical cache frame).

Traversing the x-axis from left to right, the two subsequent groups of bars correspond to 8 and 16 entries extra caches respectively. In each group there are measurements for the "victim" mechanism (configured as in [13]) with block disabling, the

"spare" mechanism (configured as in [24]) with block disabling, the proposed in this paper scheme in "VS" mode with block disabling and the proposed in this paper schemes in spare mode, "spare subblock", and in VS mode, "VS subblock" with subblock disabling. Note that the same block/subblock disabling technique is used in both the main and the extra cache. As mentioned, the y-axis in both graphs of Fig. 6 shows the normalized misses with respect to a fault-free cache (lower values correspond to a better fault tolerance capacity). Note that values below "0" (in y-axis) indicate that the reported number of misses is lower than a fault-free cache.

If we concentrate at the top graph of Fig. 6 (low-pfails), our target is to reveal the fact that our scheme is able to reduce the number of misses compared to a fault free cache even in the presence of faults. This represents a unique characteristic of our mechanism. While typical error recovery mechanisms do manage to reduce the fault-induced misses, those mechanisms fail to increase cache performance when the number of faults is very small or zero (i.e., the additional memory resources are underutilized in low pfails and faulty free situations). On the contrary, our extra cache in VS mode (16-entries VS/red bars) is able to report an average decrease in the number of misses from 13.2% (pfail=10^{-4}) up to 17.3% (no fault case). The reason is that VS cache acts also as temporal memory placeholder of the cache misses that are (with probability) conflict misses.

Comparing our extra cache in VS mode with the victim cache for low pfails (Fig. 6) we can see that as pfail increases the difference in misses increases in favor of our proposal. For example, in the 10^{-4}/16-entries case, the victim cache results in 5.2% reduction of misses compared to a fault-free cache, while our extra cache in VS mode achieves a 13.2% reduction. Obviously, our extra cache reaps the benefits of the victim and the spare cache.

Finally, there is a critical design choice that must be taken at this point: if the disabling mechanism must be applied at the block or subblock level. Obviously, operating at subblock level would result in a higher fault-free memory space in both the main and the extra cache, but the block level disabling technique (due to its simplicity) would offer the potential of a more power efficient solution. As a result, our proposition in low pfails is to rely on the block disabling approach irrespectively of the number of entries in the extra cache (green and red bars in the top graph of Fig. 6).

On the contrary, moving to higher probabilities of faults (bottom graph), it is clear that operating at subblock level exhibits remarkable benefits compared to block level disabling. This can be seen in both VS mode and spare mode. For example in the 5×10^{-3} pfail (the highest probability studied in this work), the absolute difference between block and subblock disabling techniques starts from the 15.8x (8-entries VS mode) up to 18.1x (16-entries spare cache). A second important observation is that in high pfails, the distance between VS mode and spare mode (either at block or subblock level) has been significantly reduced or even nullified. This is an expected result since the misses produced by the defective cache parts dominate over the conflict misses in high pfails. Our extra cache in spare mode usually leads to a slightly better cache performance (more than 10% in some cases) compared to the VS mode. This is apparent in all studied categories (block or subblock disabling and 8-entries or 16-entries extra cache).

Furthermore, this is not the only advantage of spare mode over VS mode in high probabilities of faults. In particular, the spare mode has the extra benefit of lower power consumption (in VS mode after a hit at the extra cache a block is exchanged between the main cache and the extra one). Consequently and as it is further highlighted by the green and red bars in the bottom graph of Fig. 6, our proposition in high pfails is to apply the subblock disabling technique and to function the extra cache as spare cache.

6. CONCLUSION

We propose a reconfigurable fault tolerant cache with two modes of operation which is based on the use of an extra small fully associative cache. In low-failure situations, the extra cache operates as a self-adaptive victim-spare (VS) cache with the ability of disabling faulty blocks in both the main and the extra cache. In high failure situations the extra cache operates as a spare cache with the ability of disabling subblocks in both the main and the extra cache. In VS mode of operation, the proposed scheme offers redundant (spare) memory elements for the faulty blocks of the main cache while concurrently plays the role of the victim cache at block level lowering the conflict misses. The percentage of the blocks of the small extra cache which used as redundant storage for the faulty blocks of the main cache depends on the number of faulty blocks and the executing application, and is self-adaptive.

Acknowledgements

This research has been co-financed by the European Union (European Social Fund – ESF) and Greek national funds through the Operational Program "Education and Lifelong Learning" of the National Strategic Reference Framework (NSRF) - Research Funding Program: Thales "HOLISTIC". Investing in knowledge society through the European Social Fund.

7. REFERENCES

[1] J. Abella et al. "Low Vccmin Fault-Tolerant Cache with Highly Predictable Performance," Proc. of Intl. Symposium on Microarchitecture, 2009.

[2] J. Abella et al. "RVC: A mechanism for time-analyzable real-time processors with faulty Caches," Proc. of High Performance and Embedded Architectures and Compilers, 2011.

[3] A. Ansari et al. "Enabling ultra low voltage system operation by tolerating on-chip cache failures," Proc. of Intl. Symposium on Low power electronics and design, 2009.

[4] A. Ansari et al. "Zerehcache: Armoring cache architectures in high defect density technologies," Proc. of Annual Intl. Symposium on Microarchitecture, 2009.

[5] A. Agarwal et al. "Process Variation in Embedded Memories: Failure Analysis and Variation Aware Architecture," Trans. on Solid State Circuits, 2005.

[6] D. K. Bhavsar and J. H. Edmondson. "Alpha 21164 Testability Strategy," Design & Test of Computers, 1997.

[7] B. Calhoun et al. "A 256kb sub-threshold SRAM in 65nm CMOS," Proc. of Solid-State Circuits Conference, 2006.

[8] G. Chen et al. "Yield-driven near-threshold SRAM design," Trans. on Very Large Scale Integration Systems, 2007.

[9] N. P. Jouppi. "Improving Direct-Mapped Cache Performance by the Addition of a Small Fully-Associative Cache and Prefetch Buffers," Proc. of Intl. Symposium on Computer Architecture, 1990.

[10] G. Keramidas et al. "Spatial pattern prediction based management of faulty data caches," Proc. of Intl. Conference Design, Automation, and Test in Europe. 2014.

[11] C. K. Koh et al. "Tolerating process variations in large, set associative caches: The buddy cache," Trans. on Architecture and Code Optimization , 2009.

[12] J. P. Kulkarni, K. Keejong, and K. Roy. "A 160 mV, fully differential, robust schmitt trigger based sub-threshold SRAM," Proc. of Intl. Symposium of Low Power Electronics and Design, 2007.

[13] N. Ladas, Y. Sazeides, and V. Desmet. "Performance-Effective Operation below Vcc-min," in Proc. of Intl. Symposium on Performance Analysis of systems & Software, 2010.

[14] S. Lin and D. J. Costello. "Error Control Coding (2nd Edition)," Prentice Hall, 2004.

[15] M. A. Makhzan et al. "Limits on Voltage Scaling for Caches Utilizing Fault Tolerant Techniques," Proc. of Intl. Conference on Computer Design, 2007.

[16] S. Ozdemir et al. "Yield-Aware Cache Architectures," Proc. of Intl. Symposium on Microarchitecture, 2006.

[17] F. Pour and M. D. Hill. "Performance implications of tolerating cache faults," Trans. on Computers, 1993.

[18] D. Roberts, N. S. Kim, and T. Mudge. "On-chip cache device scaling limits and effective fault repair techniques in future nanoscale technology," Proc. of Digital System Design Architectures, Methods and Tools, 2007.

[19] A. Sasan et al. "A fault tolerant cache architecture for sub 500mV operation: resizable data composer cache (RDC-cache)," Proc. of Intl. Conference on Compilers, Architecture, and Synthesis for Embedded Systems, 2009.

[20] A. Sasan et al. "Inquisitive Defect Cache: A Means of Combating Manufacturing Induced Process Variation," Trans. on Very Large Scale Integration (VLSI) Systems, 2010.

[21] S. E. Schuster. "Multiple word/bit line redundancy for semiconductor memories," Trans. on Solid State Circuits, 1978.

[22] P. Shirvani and E. McCluskey. "PADded cache: a new fault tolerance technique for cache memories," Proc. of VLSI Test Symposium, 1999.

[23] G. Sohi. "Cache Memory Organization to Enhance the Yield of High-Performance VLSI Processors," Trans. on Computers, 1989.

[24] H.T. Vergos and D. Nikolos. "Performance Recovery in Direct-Mapped Faulty Caches via the Use of a Very Small Fully Associative Spare Cache," Proc. of Intl. Computer Performance and Dependability Symposium, 1995.

[25] C. Wilkerson et.al. "Trading off Cache Capacity for Reliability to Enable Low Voltage Operation," Proc. of Intl. Symposium on Computer Architecture, 2008.

Untrusted Third Party Digital IP cores: Power-Delay Trade-off Driven Exploration of Hardware Trojan Secured Datapath during High Level Synthesis

Anirban Sengupta
Computer Science & Engineering
Indian Institute of Technology
Indore 452020, India
asengupt@iiti.ac.in

Saumya Bhadauria
Computer Science & Engineering
Indian Institute of Technology
Indore 452020, India
phd1301101005@iiti.ac.in

ABSTRACT

An evolutionary algorithm (EA) driven novel design space exploration (DSE) of an optimized hardware Trojan secured datapath based on user power-delay constraint during high level synthesis (HLS) is presented. The focus on hardware Trojan secured datapath generation during HLS has been very little with absolutely zero effort so far in design space exploration of a user multi-objective (MO) constraint optimized hardware Trojan secured datapath. This problem mandates attention as producing a Trojan secured datapath is not inconsequential. Merely the detection process of Trojan is not as straightforward as concurrent error detection (CED) of transient faults as it involves the concept of multiple third party intellectual property (3PIP) vendors to facilitate detection, let aside the exploration process of a user optimized Trojan secured datapath based on MO constraints. The proposed DSE for hardware Trojan detection includes novel problem encoding technique that enables exploration of efficient distinct vendor allocation as well as enables exploration of an optimized Trojan secured datapath structure. The exploration backbone for the proposed approach is bacterial foraging optimization algorithm (BFOA) which is known for its adaptive feature (tumbling/swimming) and simplified model. Results of comparison with recent approach indicated an average improvement in quality of results (QoR) of >14.1%

ACM Classification Keywords

Hardware, Computing Methodologies

Author Keywords

DSE, 3PIP, power, delay, hardware Trojan, BFOA, HLS.

1. INTRODUCTION

Today's hardware systems designed are susceptible to hardware Trojans which are malevolent alterations to the circuit either during design or fabrication. This problem has become pervasive due to globalization of system on chip (SoC) design process increasing major concerns of security and credibility of embedded 3PIPs [2, 7]. During the design stage of a 3PIP, an adversary

GLSVLSI '15, May 20 - 22, 2015, Pittsburgh, PA, USA
Copyright 2015 ACM 978-1-4503-3474-7/15/05...$15.00
http://dx.doi.org/10.1145/2742060.2742061

(possibly an untrustworthy vendor) can deliberately infuse a Trojan logic resulting in malfunctioning of the digital circuit. This matter gets further intricate as hardware Trojans can be of multiple types [3, 5]. In case of high level synthesis, the hardware Trojan mostly considered is the one which is capable of maliciously altering the digital output of a 3PIP. The detection procedure as suggested by [7] is accomplished by having IP cores of same functionality from different vendors. This is because different vendors will have different implementations and it is less likely that both are Trojan infected. Even if they are, the chances of different vendor IPs generating same output behavior is considered extremely uncommon. However, detection process of the Trojan during design of hardware Trojan secured datapath in HLS inevitably requires multiple redundant hardware instances from different vendors, which if not accounted for its power and delay during fitness evaluation, may result in a secured circuit violating user constraint. Therefore, the design process of hardware Trojan secured datapath should govern the usage of adaptive intelligent DSE based on user power-delay constraint as well as effective vendor allocation procedure during scheduling.

1.1 Motivation/Background of BFOA

This paper presents an approach for multi-objective exploration of hardware Trojan secured DMR datapath that satisfy conflicting user constraints as well as yield lower design cost (better fitness). According to the research reported so far, a regular exploration process of scheduling and allocation involving area and delay as design objective is considered intractable [1]. Inclusion of 3PIP hardware Trojan detection ability as additional design objective in such an exploration process would intricate the mechanism and therefore shall require advanced mechanism that offers a simplified model yet without compromising in its ability to find high quality design solution. Methodologies such as BFOA [4] would be considered suitable for such notorious problems because other evolutionary algorithms such as genetic algorithm (GA), hybrid GA and particle swarm optimization (PSO) do not provide flexible options through a simplified model for adaptive searching such as change in directions when a certain search path is being found unproductive. Further, PSO is known to be a highly sensitive algorithm; therefore failing to clinically pre-tune the parameters often may result in premature convergence [8]. On the contrary, BFOA not being highly sensitive, is simple yet adaptive in nature and involves multiple loops such as chemotaxis and dispersal as well as options of tumble/swim [6]. The above framework provides the flexibility to be configured in a proficient way for eliciting efficient search behavior for this problem.

2. RELATED WORK

The focus on hardware Trojan detection during HLS has been very little with absolutely zero effort so far in design space exploration of a user multi-objective constraint optimized hardware Trojan secured datapath. This problem mandates attention as producing a Trojan secured datapath is not inconsequential. Merely the detection process of Trojan is not as straightforward as concurrent error detection (CED) of transient faults as it involves the concept of multiple 3PIP vendors to facilitate detection, let aside the exploration process of a user optimized Trojan secured datapath based on MO constraints. Efficient vendor allocation procedure needs to be devised for Trojan detection during HLS, besides robust and adaptive exploration scheme for hardware Trojan secured datapath. *Note: Trojans that disable specific units but producing no change in the output functionality computationally do not fall within the scope of this paper.*

Authors in [7, 8] adopted a CED technique to detect the malicious output during HLS. A diverse set of 3PIP vendors is used to detect the Trojan's. However, the authors in [7, 8] do not incorporate design space exploration of Trojan secured datapath based on user constraints. Further, it also does not have detailed probing into the allocation procedure of distinct vendor IP to similar operations (which is affects final delay and power of the schedule as established in the proposed work). Lack of consideration of above leads to results in an inferior quality final solution (higher cost). However, [8] provides recovery from Trojan errors besides detection. In [1], the approach is based on side channel analysis and is capable of detecting malicious hardware modifications in the presence of large process variation induced noise. However, for HLS further no optimization is performed in [1] based on power-delay tradeoff. Additionally, authors in [4] introduced an approach which relies on characteristics like path delay and power consumption of the manufactured chips where, the manufactured chips are measured and compared with the expected values to identify Trojan's. This behavior of the approach for Trojan identification and detection is not effective.

3. PROBLEM FORMULATION

Determine an optimal resource configuration, $R_x = \{N(R_1), N(R_2),....N(R_D), V\}$, by exploring the design space of a given data flow graph (DFG), and satisfying conflicting user constraints and minimizing overall cost. Find: Optimal (R_x), with minimum hybrid $Cost(P_T^{DMR}, L_T^{DMR})$, subjected to: $P_T^{DMR} \leq P_{cons}$ and $L_T^{DMR} \leq L_{cons}$ and hardware Trojan fault secured, where D is total available resource types, $N(R_d)$ is the number of instance of a resource type 'd', P_T^{DMR} & L_T^{DMR} are power and delay of a double modular redundant (DMR) design evaluated on user power and delay constraints (P_{cons}, L_{cons}) and V' is the vendor allocation procedure type (where V = '1' or '0').

4. DIFFERENCE IN HARDWARE TROJAN AND TRANSIENT FAULT DETECTION: MOTIVATION OF PROPOSED WORK

The nature of transient faults (TF) is different than hardware Trojan induced faults (HT) in 3PIP's. HT is permanent in nature which remain hidden (and do not vanish) while transient faults are temporary in nature (active for some pico-secs). In context of DSE while dealing with transient faults, exploration can exploit

time redundancy where same hardware unit can be re-used in duplicate unit after the k_c cycle (k_c is the strength of the transient fault). Further, same single vendor providing distinct hardware is sufficient. On the contrary, for hardware Trojan faults it requires minimum two vendors for its successful detection (cases where Trojans leads to disabling hardware units are ignored in this paper, as it falls outside the scope of the proposed work). However so far in the literature, during detection of hardware Trojans, design space exploration to optimize the Trojan secured datapath based on user constraint is not performed. Ignoring DSE process during design of Trojan secured datapath is not pragmatic as this often results in violation of user constraint. Further, past approaches have only attempted to keep distinct hardware (from different vendor) assignment to similar operations in original and duplicate units of a DMR system, but have not probed into a detailed allocation procedure of hardware units inside a DMR schedule (as there can be more than one ways to implement distinct hardware assignment condition, where each ways results in different power and delay (thereby cost) of final DMR. This is due to the fact that same resource type/IP provided from different vendors has slightly different power and delay i.e. both vendors can never produce IPs which are exact replica in parametric values). These aforesaid uncovered aspects of previous approach are addressed through the proposed work.

5. PROPOSED METHODOLOGY

The proposed DSE methodology for generation of optimal hardware Trojan secured datapath (resource configuration as well as optimal vendor allocation procedure) based on user power-delay constraint during HLS is shown in Figure 1. Module library, behavioral description of CDFG and predefined user parametric constraints for power and time execution (or delay) are provided as inputs to the exploration process. A set of control parameters such as 'N_c' (maximum number of chemotaxis steps allowed which is the stopping criterion that indicates the maximum limit of the iterations that the proposed approach is allowed to execute) and 'p' (population size) are used for regulating the BFOA driven exploration process where 'p' indicates the number of individuals/bacterium (initial design solutions) participating in the evolutionary process of exploration. The BFOA driven exploration process has following terminating criteria:

- Terminates when reached designer specified 'N_c'.
- When no improvement is seen in global best among bacteria population over last 10 iterations (chemotactic steps). Significant improvement in global best usually occurs after couple of iterations.

Note: Interested readers may refer to [6] for more details. The proposed methodology presents a novel encoding scheme for bacterium which comprises of a resource array (resource configuration) and vendor allocation procedure type 'V'. Therefore, a bacterium position (candidate design solution) is labeled as R_x:

$$R_x = (\overrightarrow{R_n}, V) \qquad (1)$$

Where, $\overrightarrow{R_n}$ indicates the resource array (resource configuration e.g. number of adders, multipliers etc). The reason behind incorporating the last dimension with vendor allocation procedure type 'V' is discussed in later sections.

5.1 Chemotaxis Algorithm

Movement of a bacterium in BFOA from one position to the other is characterized as a chemotactic movement (chemotaxis). The exploration process comprises of chemotactic algorithm [6]. The chemotaxis function is:

$$\overrightarrow{R_n}(New) = \overrightarrow{R_n}(Last) + C(i)\frac{\Delta(i)}{\sqrt{\Delta^T(i)\Delta(i)}} \qquad \text{where, } \overrightarrow{R_n}(New)$$

and $\overrightarrow{R_n}(Last)$ are the new and old resource configurations of a bacterium solution, $C(i)$ is the step size and $\Delta(i)$ is the tumble vector. The bacterium positions are used to generate a DMR schedule ($SDFG^{DMR}$) with distinct vendor assignment rule to detect the presence of hardware Trojan. Since distinct vendor assignment can be implemented in various ways, therefore, the optimal allocation procedure of hardware units from distinct vendor for similar operations (in original and duplicate) is explored through our proposed scheme, to find an optimized scheduling (this is motivated in our next section). The schedule generated indicates a hardware Trojan secured system. The obtained Trojan secured DMR schedule is evaluated on metrics of power and delay to determine the cost of the Trojan-secured datapath solution. The cost of the Trojan secured datapath solution explored includes power component due to functional resources, interconnect units (mux and demux), comparator as well as overhead incurred from internal buffering (temporary storage of operation output). This internal buffering contributes to the total power since in a DMR similar operation is being done on the two copies (original and duplicate) at different times. The system needs to keep the outputs from both units stored in some internal buffer to compare only when both outputs are ready. This process of evaluating design solutions (bacterium positions) evolves through the proposed DSE using chemotaxis mechanism to generate an optimal hardware Trojan fault secured DMR system that satisfies P_{cons}, L_{cons}, as well as minimizes hybrid cost.

5.2 Motivation of using vendor allocation procedure '*V*' in problem encoding during exploration

In order to detect hardware Trojans a minimum of two vendors are always needed to provide distinctness (*Note*: cases where Trojans lead to disabling hardware units are ignored in this paper, as it falls outside the scope of the proposed work). However, technique of usage of the two vendors during allocation inside the DMR scheduling (i.e. assignment process) of each vendor IPs inside the system during allocation) dictates the final latency and power of entire system. This is because same resource type/IP from two different vendors has different area, power and delay. *Note*: It is assumed that multiplier and adder provided by vendor V1 has area = '2468au' & '2034au', latency = '10000ns' & '265ns', and energy = '10.0pJ' & '0.80pJ' (where energy values have been extracted from [9]) while multiplier and adder provided by vendor V2 has area = '2464au' & '2032au', latency = '11000ns' & '270ns' and energy = '9.8pJ' & '0.739' respectively. Hence, merely using distinctive vendor assignment for detection without probing into the procedure of allocation (assignment) of vendor type in DMR system may lead to skipping of an alternate better solution in context of DSE of an optimal Trojan secured datapath (*this is established in upcoming paragraphs*). Therefore, exploration of an additional dimension, '*V*' (indicating allocation procedure of IP's from different vendor type) which can either be '0' or '1' is incorporated in the bacterium encoding along with resource array. The value of '*V*' as '0' or '1' is interpreted as follows:

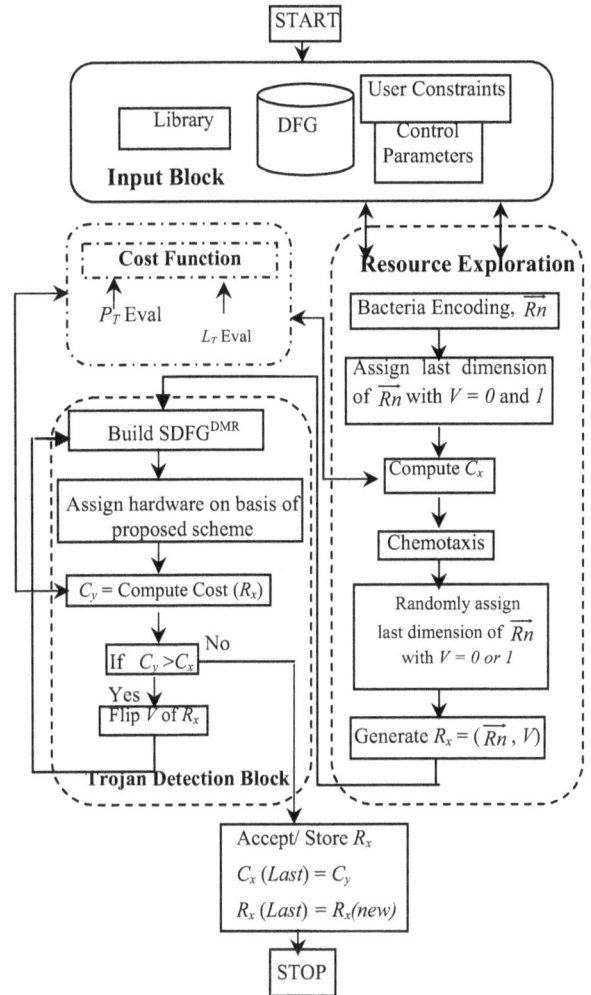

Figure 1. Proposed Methodology

5.2.1 *Vendor allocation procedure (Type 1):* V = 1

- All operations of a specific unit being strictly assigned to resources of **same** vendor type (say: all operations of original unit strictly assigned to **same** vendor '*V1*' and all operations of duplication to **same** vendor '*V2*').

- Similar operations of both original unit U^{OG} and duplicate unit U^{DP} being assigned to different vendors.

5.2.2 *Vendor allocation procedure (Type 2):* V = 0

- **Alternate** vendor assignment to operations in control step of a unit. (example, in Figure 2, operation 3 & 6 assigned alternatively to '*V1*' and '*V2*'. Next multiplication if any would have been assigned to '*V1*' alternately).

- Similar operations of both U^{OG} and U^{DP} being assigned to different vendors.

In both above cases, whenever there is a conflict of operation during scheduling between operation of U^{OG} and U^{DP}, preference is given to the operation of U^{OG} during scheduling. For a resource set $\overrightarrow{R_n}$ = 2(+), 5(*), there are two possible DMR schedules generated for IIR filter benchmark on the basis of $V = 0$ and 1, as seen in Figure 2 and 3. More specifically, for $R_x = (2(+), 5(*), 0)$, the latency is: 23,080ns and power is: 0.58mW; while, for $R_x = (2(+), 5(*), 1)$, the latency is: 22,080ns and power is: 0.88mW.

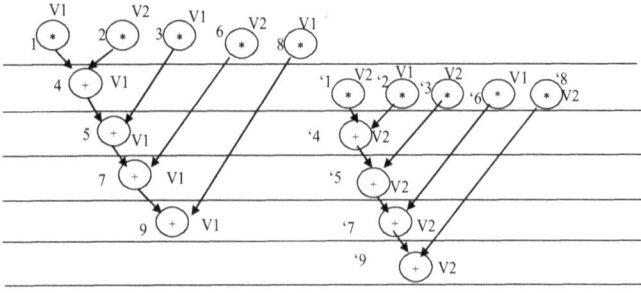

Figure 2. IIR filter for $V = 0$; $\overrightarrow{R_n}$ = 2(+), 5(*) indicating alternate assignment procedure of two vendor types

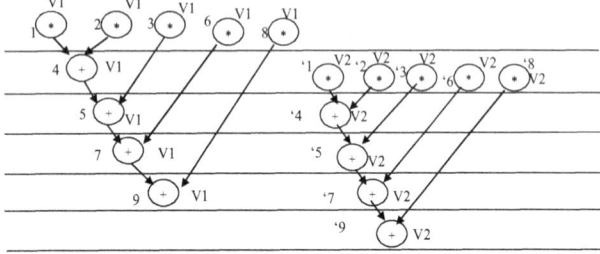

Figure 3. IIR filter for $V = 1$; $\overrightarrow{R_n}$ = 2(+), 5(*) indicating each entire unit strictly assigned to same vendor type (U^{OG} to '$V1$' and U^{DP} to '$V2$')

Clearly, a difference is observed in the delay and power of the two generated scheduling solutions both abiding by distinct vendor type assignment to similar operations for detect ability. The schedules generated in Figure 2 and 3 are both hardware Trojan fault secured (with two vendor needed), however, one is better than the other in different parameter. Only using distinct vendor assignment without probing into the procedure of allocation of vendor type in DMR system may lead to missing of better alternative (or optimal) solution in context of DSE. Therefore, in context of DSE, it is worth to explore the additional dimension 'V' incorporated in the proposed bacterial encoding.

5.3 Evaluation models

In the proposed work, each bacterium position represents a resource array of datapath present in the design space as well as vendor allocation procedure.

5.3.1 Proposed power model

Total power consumption (P_T^{DMR}) by a resource set is represented in terms of Static Power (P_S^{DMR}) and Dynamic Power (P_D^{DMR}). 'P_T^{DMR}' is represented:

$$P_T^{DMR} = P_S^{DMR} + P_D^{DMR} \tag{2}$$

Static power (P_S^{DMR}) considered here is leakage power (due to leakage current) which is a function of resource area and leakage power per transistor. *Note: power due to short circuit current is not considered in this paper.*

$$P_S^{DMR} = (\sum_{j=1}^{2} \sum_{i=1}^{n} (A(R_i^{V_j}) * R_i^{V_j})) * p_c \tag{3}$$

where, $R_i^{V_j}$ is the number of instances utilized from vendor V_j for a resource type R_i, and 'n' is the maximum number of resource type for vendor V_j while $A(R_i^{V_j})$ is the area of a resource type (R_i) corresponding to vendor (V_j); 'p_C' is the power dissipated per transistor. On the other hand, the average dynamic power consumed by a resource configuration is a function of dynamic activity of the resources and can be given as:

$$P_D^{DMR} = \frac{E_{FU}}{L_T^{DMR}} \tag{4}$$

Where, E_{FU} is the total energy consumed by the resources. *Note: The power component includes power due to functional resources, interconnect units (mux and demux), comparator (for error detection) as well as overhead incurred from internal buffering (during temporary storage of operation output in DMR scheduling).The model in eqn. (3) & (4) does not capture the effect of buffering and comparator, however, its impact was considered internally from scheduling during implementation.*

5.3.2 Proposed Delay (Latency) model

For given 'D' functional resources the delay is:

$$L_T^{DMR} = \sum_{c.s=1}^{c.s(\max)} \sum_{j=1}^{2} Max(D(op_i^{Vj}),....D(op_n^{Vj}), D(op_{'i}^{Vj}),......D(op_{'n}^{Vj})) \tag{5}$$

Where, $1 \leq i \leq n$ and '$1 \leq$ '$i \leq$ 'n. (Here, operations in original and duplicate is labeled as i and 'i respectively; n and 'n = maximum number of operations in original and duplicate unit). Here, $D(op_i^{Vj})$ is the delay of operation i, assigned to vendor V_j, $c.s$ represents control steps, while $c.s(max)$ is the maximum number of control steps in a schedule.

5.3.3 Proposed cost model

The proposed fitness function (considering total delay and power consumption of a solution) is defined as:

$$C_f(R_x) = W_1 \frac{P_T^{DMR} - P_{cons}}{P_{\max}^{DMR}} + W_2 \frac{L_T^{DMR} - L_{cons}}{L_{\max}^{DMR}} \tag{6}$$

Where, $C_f(R_x)$ is the cost of bacterium with resource set R_x, P_{max}^{DMR} and L_{max}^{DMR} are the maximum power and delay of the DMR system and W_1 and W_2 are the user defined weights both kept at ½ during exploration to provide equal preference; P_{cons} and L_{cons} are the user constraints for power and latency (delay).

5.4 Demonstration of proposed methodology

This section demonstrates the proposed methodology illustrated in Figure 1 for IIR benchmark.

Step 1: Initialize bacterium: say (2A, 2M) with last dimension.
Step 2: Screen the best bacterium from set (2A, 2M, 0) and (2A, 2M, 1). Evaluation yields Cost (2A, 2M, 0) = 0.003, while Cost (2A, 2M, 1) = 0.07. Selecting R_x (last) = (2A, 2M, 0) and cost as: $C_x = 0.003$.
Step 3: Project the bacterium (2A, 2M) for chemotactic movement.
Step 4: Tumble: [0.0, +1.0]
Step 5: Do chemotaxis on: (2A, 2M) => R_x (new) = (2A, 4M)
Step 6: Randomly, assign last dimension to '0' to (2A, 4M)
Step 7: Generate $R_x(new)$ = (2A, 4M, 0) by keeping last vendor allocation procedure dimension same as R_x (in step 2).
Step 8: Build DMR for $R_x(new)$ = (2A, 4M, 0)
Step 9: Assign hardware on basis of proposed interpretation.

Step 10: Compute cost C_y= Cost (2A, 4M, 0) => C_y= -0.108
Step 11: $C_y < C_x$
Step 18: C_x = -0.108 (assign new value of cost)
Step 19: $R_x(last)$ = (2A, 4M, 0) (assign new value of configuration).

6. RESULTS

The proposed approach as well as [7] both have been implemented in java and run on Intel Core-i5-3210M CPU with 3MB L3 cache memory, 4GB DDR3 primary memory and processor frequency of 2.5 GHz. An average of 10 runs was reported for proposed BFOA DSE with equal weightage to both user objectives of power and delay ($W_1 = W_2 = $ ½). As found during the experiments conducted that the proposed approach is scalable and is able to handle problems of any size (for example, many CDFG benchmarks greater than 100 nodes have been tested and yields final optimal solution with acceptable exploration runtime of ~ 41 secs. For the sake of brevity, the details of all benchmarks have not been reported).

6.1 Results of proposed approach

During experimentation, following optimal settings were made for proposed approach: p= 3, 5 and 7, N_c = 120 based on pre-tunning experiments. Table 1 shows the effect of bacterium size 'p' on the exploration time of proposed DSE method. As evident, it indicates that for all benchmarks with the increase in bacterium size, the exploration time of the proposed approach to find the final solution increases (with the cost of the final solution remaining the same for all bacterium size). The exploration time increase is because of increase in computational complexity per iteration (i.e. the total number of positions evaluated in a run increases with the increase in 'p'). Figure 4 shows a graphical representation of the variation of exploration time with respect to increase in the bacterium size 'p'. Further, as shown Table 2, the proposed approach comprehensively meets the user constraints of delay and power (and minimizes the hybrid cost in eqn. (6) for all benchmarks. For example, in case of IIR benchmark, the proposed approach generates the final optimal solution with power (P_T^{DMR}) = 0.58mW and L_T^{DMR} = 23080ns, which is with the specified user constraints of power and delay (P_{cons} = 0.55mW and L_{cons} = 38945

Table 1. Comparison of exploration time with respect to bacterium size 'p' for proposed approach

Benchmark	Bacterium Size	Exploration time (ms)	Cost of final solution
IIR	3	640	-0.125
	5	703	-0.125
	7	1250	-0.125
MPEG MV	3	7043	-0.251
	5	7657	-0.251
	7	11422	-0.251
ARF	3	1907	-0.192
	5	2156	-0.192
	7	3786	-0.192
IDCT	3	7156	-0.154
	5	7998	-0.154
	7	8328	-0.154
DCT	3	3516	-0.106
	5	3891	-0.106
	7	5977	-0.106
FIR	3	6500	-0.245
	5	7282	-0.245
	7	12532	-0.245

ns). Also, the proposed approach is able to achieve the real optimal solution for all benchmarks as verified with the golden solution found through brute force.

In the proposed work, possibility of false negative outcome (i.e. existing Trojan going undetected) does not exist, as the allocation step satisfies the necessary/sufficient condition of detection by assigning every similar operation of original and duplicate unit to hardware from distinct vendors (this has been established in [7] that for Trojan detection only two vendors are required for creating distinctness). Further we have assumed that the designed DMR system is only vulnerable to those hardware Trojans which are capable of affecting the computational output (thereby the DMR system is assumed free of any other faults affecting final output such as single event transient). Hence the possibility of false positive outcome also does not arise in proposed approach.

6.2 Comparison of proposed approach

QoR indicates the quality of final solution explored yielded by both approaches (proposed and [7]) is an important tool for comparison. The QoR for both the approaches (proposed and [7]) is evaluated by the following function from [6]:

$$QoR = \frac{1}{2}\left(\frac{P_T^{DMR}}{P_{max}^{DMR}} + \frac{L_T^{DMR}}{L_{max}^{DMR}}\right) \quad (7)$$

The area of the single comparator/error detection block responsible to runtime Trojan detection at the final output is also considered in the above QoR function when evaluating its magnitude for both [7] and proposed approach. However, since only a single comparator/error detection block is used in both approaches, hence it has no impact on the QoR of both approaches. However, during QoR comparison, power overhead due to internal buffering (temporary storage of operation output), has been considered for both proposed approach and [7].

Table 3, illustrates the comparative results of the proposed approach and [7] when evaluated on the standard benchmarks. As seen from the results in Table 3, with the introduction of exploration for vendor allocation procedure type 'V' and user constraint driven exploration, the proposed approach generates

Table 2. Results of proposed approach

Benchmark	L_{cons} (ns)	L_T^{DMR} (ns)	P_{cons} (mW)	P_T^{DMR} (mW)	Cost
IIR	38945	23080	0.58	0.58	-0.125
IDCT	119160	77080	1.02	0.93	-0.154
ARF	130810	89890	0.63	0.48	-0.192
MPEG MV	88307	36240	1.48	1.03	-0.251
DCT	175442	153540	0.77	0.59	-0.106
FIR	76387	34890	1.22	0.85	-0.245

Note: mW = miliwatt, ns = nanoseconds

Table 3. Comparison of proposed approach with [7]

Benchmark	Final solution for Trojan Secured datapath (proposed)	Final solution for Trojan Secured datapath [7]	Cost of final solution (proposed)	Cost of final solution [7]	QoR in cost units (proposed)	QoR in cost units [7]	% improvement in QoR
IIR	2(+), 5(*), 0	2(+), 3(*),1	-0.125	-0.016	0.53	0.64	17.1
IDCT	6(+), 4(*), 0	5(+), 3(*),1	-0.154	-0.027	0.50	0.63	20.6
ARF	2(+), 4(*),0	3(+), 3(*),1	-0.192	-0.056	0.49	0.63	22.2
MPEG MV	2(+), 10(*), 0	3(+), 8(*),1	-0.251	-0.226	0.30	0.33	9.0
DCT	4(+), 4(*), 0	5(+), 3(*),1	-0.106	-0.064	0.50	0.54	7.4
FIR	6(+), 6(*), 0	5(+), 5(*),1	-0.245	-0.209	0.33	0.36	8.3

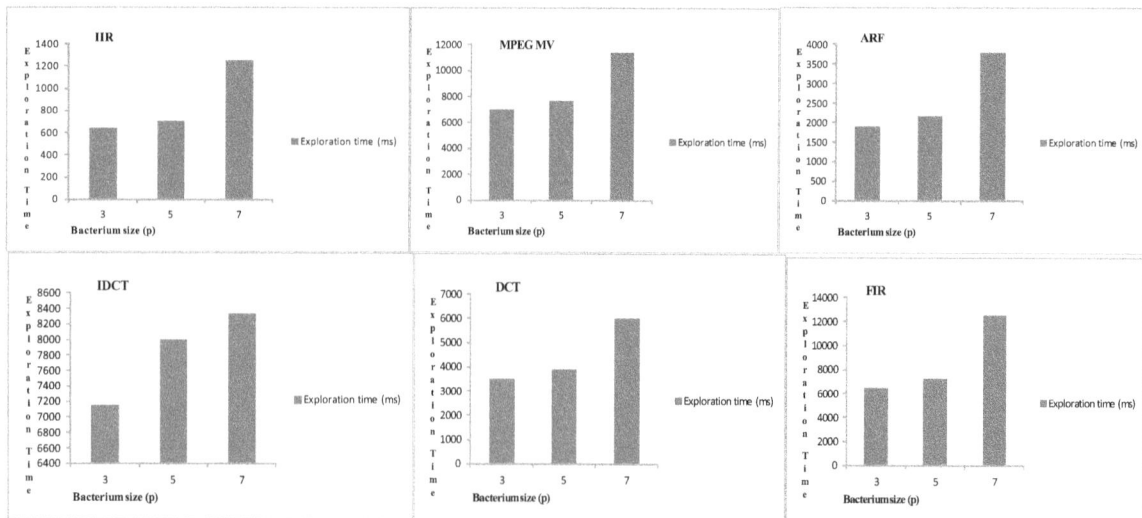

Figure 4. Graphical representation of variation of exploration time (in ms) with respect to change in Bacterium size (p)

better results in comparison to [7]. For example, in ARF benchmark, the proposed approach generates 2(+), 4(*), 0 as the solution (cost of -0.192) which is lesser than the cost of [7] (cost = -0.056). This is because, in previous approach there is no provision of exploring an optimal 'vendor allocation procedure' during scheduling in DMR as well as no optimization scheme based on user power- delay constraint for finding a better alternative solution. Figure 5 shows the comparison of the QoR (in cost units) of the proposed approach with [7]. *Note: Collusion constraints have not been imposed for both approaches during implementation since preventing collusion that leads to disabling of hardware units falls outside the scope of this paper. This paper focuses on only hardware Trojan detection during DSE.*

7. CONCLUSION

A novel DSE approach for hardware Trojan secured datapath based on power-delay tradeoff during HLS is presented. The results when compared with previous approach indicated improved QoR of > 14.1% for the proposed approach.

8. REFERENCES

[1] Narasimhan, S., Du, D., Chakraborty, R., Paul, S., Wolff, F., Papachristou, C., Roy, K., and Bhunia, S. 2010. Multiple-parameter side-channel analysis: A non invasive hardware Trojan detection approach. In *Proceedings 3rd Intl. Symp. Hardware Oriented Security and Trust*, 2010, pp. 13-18. DOI= http://ieeexplore.ieee.org/10.1109/HST.2010.5513122.

[2] Karri, R., Rajendran, J., Rosenfeld, K., and Tehranipoor, M. 2010. Trustworthy Hardware: Identifying and Classifying Hardware Trojans. In *Proc. of the IEEE Computer*, vol. 43, no. 10, 2010, pp. 39-46. DOI = http://ieeexplore.ieee.org/10.1109/MC.2010.299.

[3] Bhunia, S., Abramovici, M., Agrawal, D., Bradley, P., Hsiao, M., Plusquellic, J., and Tehranipoor, M. 2013. Protection against hardware Trojan attacks: Towards a comprehensive solution *Proc of IEEE Design & Test*, vol. 99, 2013, pp. 1–1. DOI=http://ieeexplore.ieee.org/10.1109/MDT.2012.2196252

[4] Jin, Y., and Makris, Y. Hardware Trojan Detection using Path Delay Fingerprint, *Proc of IEEE Intl Workshop on Hardware-Oriented Security and Trust*, 2008, pp. 51-57.

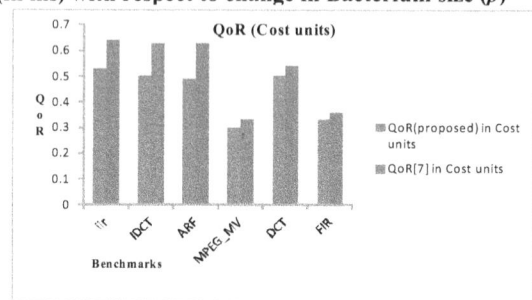

Figure 5. Comparison of QoR with [7]

DOI= http://ieeexplore.ieee.org/10.1109/HST.2008.4559049.

[5] Zhang, X., and Tehranipoor, M. 2011. Case study: Detecting hardware Trojans in third-party digital IP cores. In *Proc. of IEEE International Symposium on Hardware-Oriented Security and Trust*, 2011, pp. 67–70. DOI=http://ieeexplore.ieee.org/10.1109/HST.2011.5954998

[6] Sengupta A., Bhadauria S. 2014. Exploration of Multi-Objective Tradeoff During High Level Synthesis Using Bacterial Chemotaxis and Dispersal, *Elsevier Journal on Procedia Computer Science*, 2014, Volume. 35, pp. 63- 72

[7] Rajendran, J., Huan, Z., Sinanoglu, O., and Karri, R. 2013. High-level synthesis for security and trust. *Proc. of 19th IEEE Intl On-Line Testing Symposium*, 2013, pp.232-233. DOI=http://ieeexplore.ieee.org/10.1109/IOLTS.2013.6604087.

[8] Xiaotong C., Kun M., Liang S., Kaijie W. 2014. High-level synthesis for run-time hardware Trojan detection and recovery, *Proc of 51st ACM/EDAC/IEEE Design Automation Conference (DAC)*, California, 2014, pp. 1 – 6.

[9] Reynders N., Dehaene, W. 2011. A 190mV supply, 10MHz, 90nm CMOS, pipelined sub-threshold adder using variation-resilient circuit techniques. *In Proceedings of the IEEE Asian Solid State Circuits Conference (A-SSCC)* pp. 113-116. DOI=http://ieeexplore.ieee.org/10.1109/ASSCC.2011.6123617.

Multi Replica Bitline Delay Technique for Variation Tolerant Timing of SRAM Sense Amplifiers

Samira Ataei and James E. Stine
Oklahoma State University
Department of Electrical and Computer Engineering
VLSI Computer Architecture Research Group
202 Engineering South
Stillwater, OK 74078, USA
{ataei, james.stine}@okstate.edu

ABSTRACT

Timing variation of sense amplifier enable (SAE) attributable to the random variation of transistor threshold Voltage is reduced by a novel Multi Replica Bitline Delay technique to provide the best tracking with process variations for SRAM applications. Multi replica bitline with a sufficient count of replica cells are utilized in parallel and delay of RBLs is added together to generate timing for sense amplifier (SA). Simulation results in IBM 65nm CMOS technology show that 50% timing variation is reduced at 1.0V supply Voltage.

Categories and Subject Descriptors

B.3 [**MEMORY STRUCTURES**]: Semiconductor Memories—*Static memory (SRAM)*

General Terms

Design

Keywords

SRAM, Variation, Sense amplifier timing

1. INTRODUCTION

As SRAM continues to occupy most of the area in Very Large Scale Integration (VLSI) systems, the speed and power consumption significantly impacts the system performance [1]. In recent years, power dissipation has become an important consideration due to increasing integration and operating speed of devices, as well as the growth of battery operated appliances. Consequently, the demand for fast memories with lower power consumption continues to be an important consideration for future architectures. However, as process technology scales below 100-nm feature sizes for functional and high yields in silicon the traditional design approach

needs to be modified to survive increasing amoutns of variation [1, 4].

To decrease the energy consumption for portable applications, circuit designers have been continually decreasing supply Voltages and SRAMs are no exception to this trend. Unfortunately, however, the threshold Voltage (V_{TH}) has not scaled down as fast as the supply Voltages. Moreover, fluctuations in the V_{TH} cause delay variability of low power circuits across process corners [11, 7]. In case of the SRAMs, the large delay across process corners will demand larger margins in the design of the bitline path and also will result in larger power dissipation and loss of speed.

In general, the read operation in SRAM is the most time consuming access procedure. Generally, the SA amplifies the small Voltage difference on the bitlines at the proper sense timing to realize high-speed operations. Therefore, the SAE signal is extremely important for high speed and low power SRAMs. Unfortunately, with the increased variation effects, such as random dopant fluctuation, accurate generation of timing signals in SRAM are not excessively tolerant. This is because the optimum timing for the SAE is sensitive to Process, Voltage, and Temperature (PVT) variations. Fortunately, the timing generation circuit for SAE in SRAM also undergoes similar variation and may be modeled by a normal distribution. Therefore, the optimum timing for SAE must be determined in relation to the PVT variations [5, 12, 13].

If the SAE arrives early before the bitline difference reaches the SA offset, a read failure may occur and a late-arrived SAE would consume more unnecessary time, thereby wasting the power. Figure 1 depicts the distribution of the T_{BL} (time that bitline Voltage is sufficient for sensing) and the T_{SAE} (time that sense amp activates) considering process variation. Figure 1(a) shows the correct sensing when $T_{BL} < T_{SAE}$ and Figure 1(b) shows the wrong sensing when $T_{BL} > T_{SAE}$. As the technology scales down, these distributions become wider and the probability of wrong sensing could potentially change. Therefore, it is necessary to consider a timing margin in SRAM design as shown in Figure 1(c) and by increasing the timing margin it is possible to guarantee safe sensing operation. The problem is how to determine the adequate timing margin. Furtermore, to complicate the process this solution will result in larger power dissipation and a loss of speed.

The conventional way of generating SAE is to use a replica bitline (RBL) that consists of an additional column of dummy

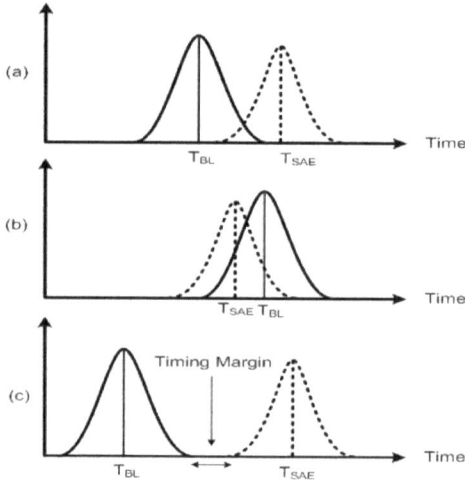

Figure 1: Distribution of timings for sense amps (a) $T_{BL} < T_{SAE}$ (b) $T_{BL} > T_{SAE}$ (c) Time margin.

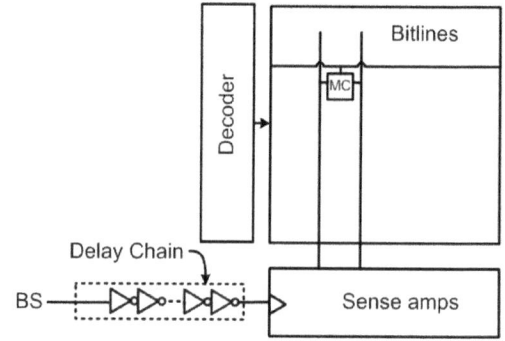

Figure 2: Common sense clock generation architecture.

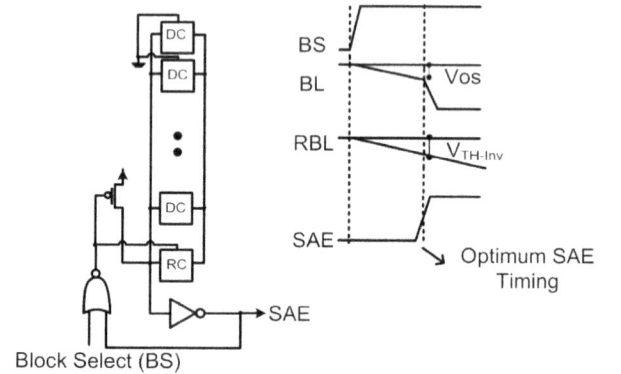

Figure 3: Operational waveforms of conventional replica architecture. (RC=Replica Cell, DC=Dummy Cell)

cells (DC) and replica cells (RC) that track the random process variation in SRAM array [2]. However, the increased variations in scaled technologies, causes the replica column characteristics to vary significantly. Consequently, the random V_{TH} variation cannot be tracked well by the RBL and the RCs, which causes read failures and the cycle time deterioration, especially for small feature sizes. To suppress variation of the RBL delay, several technique has been proposed [3, 6, 8, 9, 14]. However, there are limitations for all these techniques and they cannot track variations well.

This paper presents an architecture to suppress variation of RBL. Using our approach, the proposed archicture utilizes a Multi Replica Bitline Delay (MRBD) technique for the SA read control timing. This technique is more efficient in area compare to other schemes that use multi replica bitline, such as [6] and [14], because this technique uses less number of replica bitline to suppress the variation. The simulation results using IBM 65nm cmos10lpe CMOS technology show that MRBD reduces the timing variation approximately 50% using a 1.0 V supply Voltage compared to a conventional RBL.

The rest of this paper is organized as follows. In Section 2 the timing control technique of the conventional RBL is presented. This is followed by the description of proposed Multi Replica Bitline Delay technique in section 3. Section 4 then presents simulation results evaluating the effectiveness of the proposed techniques. Section 5 concludes the paper.

2. REPLICA BITLINE TECHNIQUE

The prevalent technique to generate the timing signals within the SRAM array uses a scaled inverter chain (Figure 2). The main problem in delay chain method is that the inverter delay does not track the delay of the memory cell over all process corners and environment conditions. For low power SRAMs at low Voltages due to greater impact of threshold and supply Voltage fluctuations on delays, tracking issue is more severe.

These effects discourage the use of delay chain technique, demanding the use of techniques that more closely follow the behavior of the circuit. Different structures have been proposed for this purpose. In [2], the authors presented a

replica bitline technique to match the delay of the activation of the SA and the delay of the propagation of the required Voltage swing at the bitlines. In RBL technique, memory cells drive delay of control path. The delay driven memory cells in control path are same as that of read path; so is the delay shift according to the PVT variation. Therefore, the RBL technique attains self-timed tracking with optimal SAE timing. Using replica circuits, the variation on the delay of the SA activation and bitline swing is minimized. This RBL technique uses a normal memory cell driving a short bitline signal. The short bitline capacitance is set to be a fraction of the main bitline capacitance. This fraction is determined by the required bitline swing for proper sensing.

Figure 3 shows operational waveforms of the conventional timing RBL. The timing for SAE is generated as follows. At first, the RBL and the normal bitlines are precharged to VDD. Next, block select is asserted and selected word line is activated. Then, the RCs discharge the RBL and normal bitlines are also discharged through the accessed cell. The proper timing for SAE is determined when the difference between bitlines Voltages becomes larger than offset Voltage at input transistors of sense amplifier (V_{OS}).

Increased variations in scaled technologies, causes the replica column characteristics to vary considerably. As technology scales down, the device channel area decreases, which lead to an increase in V_{TH} variability ($\sigma_{V_{TH}}$) [5]. The value $\sigma_{V_{TH}}$ is influenced by variation due to process variability. Random dopant fluctuation is the most significant source of process variability in deep submicron CMOS processes. Due to the limited number of dopant atoms in the small channel area, there exists a major variability in the threshold Voltage. Any lack or addition of only a few dopant atoms will lead to a variation in channel dopant concentration, and thus variation in VTH. This variation is described by the following equation [10].

$$\sigma_{V_{TH}} \approx \frac{A_{\Delta V_{TH}}}{\sqrt{W \cdot L}} \quad (1)$$

$\sigma_{V_{TH}}$ is the standard deviation of the difference in the threshold voltage between the two transistors, $A_{\Delta V_{TH}}$ is the Pelgrom constant, W is the width of the transistor, and L is its length. As the random V_{TH} variation becomes larger, the RBL and normal bitline cannot track each other. The delay mismatch of read path to discharge the bitline, and control path to generate SAE induces a fail of read operation or degradation of performance. A technique called Configurable Replica Bitline (CRBL) has been developed to suppresses RBL delay variation by choosing the RCs with small variation to drive a RBL [3]. These cells are selected from many cells based on an added post-silicon test results. The CRBL technique suppresses delay variation to 7% but increases test cost and in new SRAMs with hundreds of modules, the costs of these additional tests can be excessive. Another technique utilizes multiple replica cells (K) in parallel for reducing the threshold variation [9]. In this case, the standard deviation of the timing for the SAE is divided by $K \cdot \sqrt{K}$ [9]. However, the effect of reducing the random V_{TH} variation is limited in the low V_{DD}, because there is an upper limit for the RC count, which decreases as V_{DD} is lowered.

In Multi Stage Replica Bitline technique, the RBL is divided into several stages with the inverter placed between them [6]. The goal of this technique is to increase the number of stages in hopes of suppresing SAE timing variation. However, the delay of additionally inserted inverters increases as number of stages increases and this makes a large difference between the delay of RBL and normal bitlines of array. This drawback forces the replica bitline delay to be decreased in order to keep the total delay constant. Therefore, there is a trade-off between the effect of suppressing SAE timing variation and the inverter delay overhead for this technique.

Still, yet, another technique called the digitized Replica Bitline Delay (DRBD) technique [8] increases the number of replica cells (K), which, subsequently, reduces the variation of the RBL delay. Then, the final timing for SAE is obtained by using a timing multiplier circuit (TMC). The number of gates in the TMC is proportional to K. While increasing K in the RBL suppresses timing variation, it increases variation because of the quantization noise of the TMC. Therefore, the number K is limited in this technique. Another hybrid approach combines the multi stage and multi replica cell techniques to reduce the effect of variations [14]. It also proposes a Timing Addition Circuit (TAC) to add the delay of each stage and generate the correct timing of SAE. Unfortunately, this technique has area penalty due to using multiple stage and abundant gates in TAC and also quantization noise of TAC. There are limitations for all this techniques and they cannot track variation well. Therefore, to suppress variation of RBL, new designs must be developed.

3. MULTI REPLICA BITLINE TECHNIQUE

3.1 Proposed Multi Replica Bitline delay

For suppressing the timing variation of the SAE attributable to the random V_{TH} variation, Multi Replica Bitline Delay ($MRBD$) technique is proposed in this paper. Figure 4 shows the proposed $MRBD$ technique. In proposed $MRBD$, a replica column is divided to M segment. In each segment which we call it a RBL both bitline (BL) and its complementary (BLB) are tied together. Thus, compared with the conventional design when we have the same count of RCs, each bitline capacitance load and RC discharged current are $(2 \cdot C_{BL})/M$ and $2 \cdot I_{read}$, respectively. The delay of each divided replica bitline is therefore $1/M$ of that of the conventional bitline delay and the sum of the delays of all M replica bitline is the same as that of the conventional bitline delay. The proposed scheme also utilizes the multi replica cells (k) in each divided replica column. The activated number of the replica cell in each divided replica bitline is K time of conventional replica bitline. Thus, the current of the RCs of each divided RBL is the K times of the conventional bitline ($K \cdot I_{read}$). Because the random variation of the delay of each RBL is independent event, the total σ is a square root of sum of squares of each replica bitline σ.

As a result, σ of the SAE timing is divided by $\sqrt{M}$ due to M replica bitline and $K \cdot \sqrt{K}$ due to K replica cell in each bitline and $\sqrt{2}$ because of the using both BL and BLB in discharging the RBL. Therefore, σ of the timing for SAE is divided by $K \cdot \sqrt{(2 \cdot M \cdot K)}$. Thus, the variation of the RC current is considerably reduced compared to that in the conventional scheme. Inserted inverters between each RBL increase variation and also shift the mean value of sense amp timing to right. Because of using multiple $RC(K)$ in each RBL, mean value is shifted to left, so, the delay caused by inserted inverters helps to bring mean value of SAE to its proper value. Figure 5 shows the distribution of the SAE timing with the conventional RBL technique and the proposed $MRBD$ technique. As shown in figure 5, compared with the conventional technique, the proposed scheme is able to achieve lower variation of the SAE timing by adjusting the values of M and K.

Figure 6 shows the schematic of the 6T conventional RC and 6T replica cell that is used in this design. In conventional RC two discharged paths are realized. Using two discharge paths suppress the SAE timing variation as mentioned above.

Figure 7 shows the standard deviation with different numbers of RBL and RCs (M, K). As M increases, the capacitance of RBL is reduced. As a result, the standard deviation σ is reduced. However, as shown in table.1, the reduction of the standard deviation σ is no longer effective if M is over 3 because of added inverters. The optimum count of replica cells may exist because both supply Voltage and inserted inverter between RBLs limit reduction of variations. According to the simulation results, the optimum value of M and K are 2 and 4, considering the area overhead of using $MRBD$.

3.2 Final SRAM Architecture

A single column of the designed SRAM is shown in Figure 8. This SRAM has 256 rows and 32 columns. Each column consists of a SA and a write driver. The write driver is sized

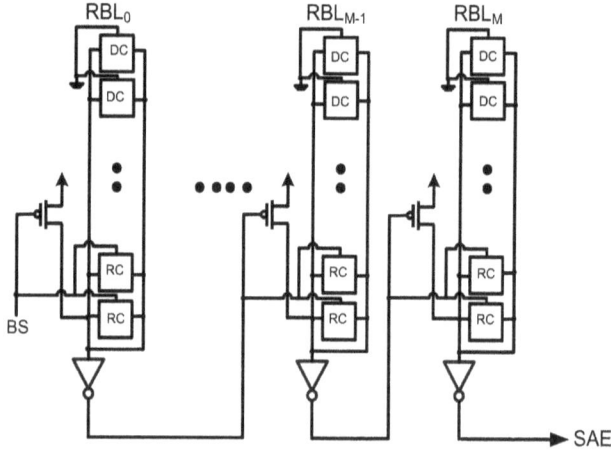

Figure 4: Proposed MRBD technique.

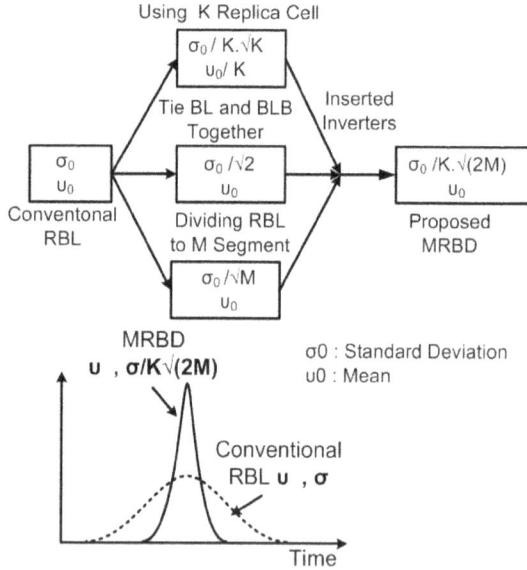

Figure 5: Conventional RBL and proposed MRBD timing variation.

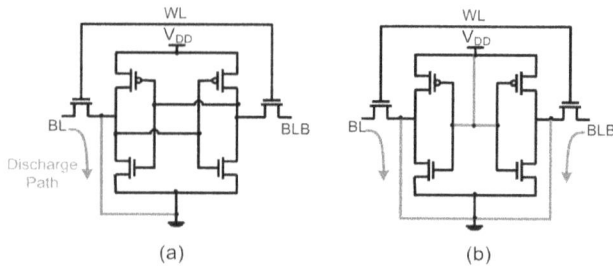

Figure 6: (a) Conventional RC and (b) Proposed RC.

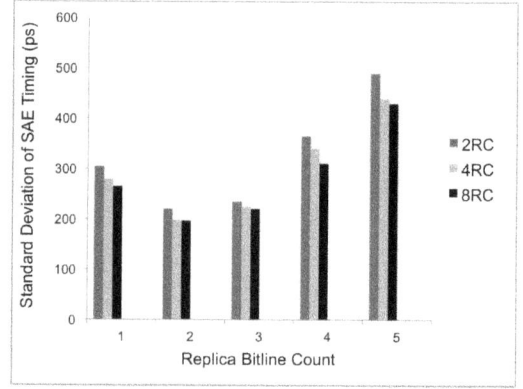

Figure 7: Statistical results for different values of (M,K) (Optimal value = (2,4)).

to reduce the delay of driving the bitline with the data input and consequently to increase the speed of write operation. During Read operation, the Voltage swing of the bitlines is limited to a smaller value whereas a write operation requires full Voltage swing on the bitlines. SA resolves a small input Voltage difference applied to its input terminals to a full swing Voltage level output.

A major part of the access time is the time allotted to develop a signal on the bitlines. This is the time from the rise of the wordline to the time SA is allowed to switch. The latch type SA is chosen in order to apply $MRBD$ technique on it. Using $MRBD$ technique, SAE signal will arrive when the Voltage difference between bitlines is minimum readable value.

By setting the SA to the minimum value required to reliably read any memory cell, the wordline pulse width can be minimized and energy consumption associated with charging and discharging of high capacitive bitlines will be reduced. Also the accessed cell has to develop less swing thus decreasing the memory access time. The minimal bitline swing that can be resolved reliably is limited by the offset of the sense amplifier. The input offsets of sense amplifier (V_{offset}) sets the higher levels for the required BL discharge, thereby increasing the energy consumption. The minimal target value of the required BL discharge ΔV_{min} depends on the technology, sense amplifier design and sizing. If V_{offset} follows a Gaussian distribution with 0 mean and a standard deviation σ_{offset}, then the required minimum BL discharge is expressed in the number of standard deviations (n):

$$\Delta V_{min} \quad > \quad n \cdot \sigma_{offset} = n \cdot \frac{A_{\Delta V_{TH}}}{\sqrt{W \cdot L}} \qquad (2)$$

where σ_{offset} is the standard deviation of the difference in the threshold Voltage between the two input transistors, $A_{\Delta V_{TH}}$ is the Pelgrom constant, W and L are width and length of the sense amplifier input transistor.

Increased random V_{TH} variations also increases the mismatch offset Voltage and necessitates the use of relatively upsized sense amplifiers to ensure correct functionality. In traditional SA design this offset is reduced by increasing the size of the critical transistors [10], which directly represents into increased dynamic energy consumption.

The increase in threshold Voltage aggravates variability for the SRAM cell design. This results in degradation of

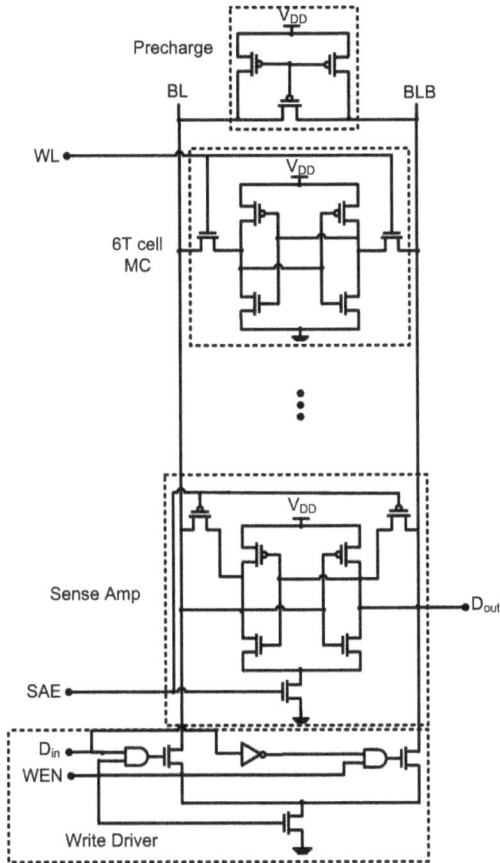

Figure 8: One column of SRAM array.

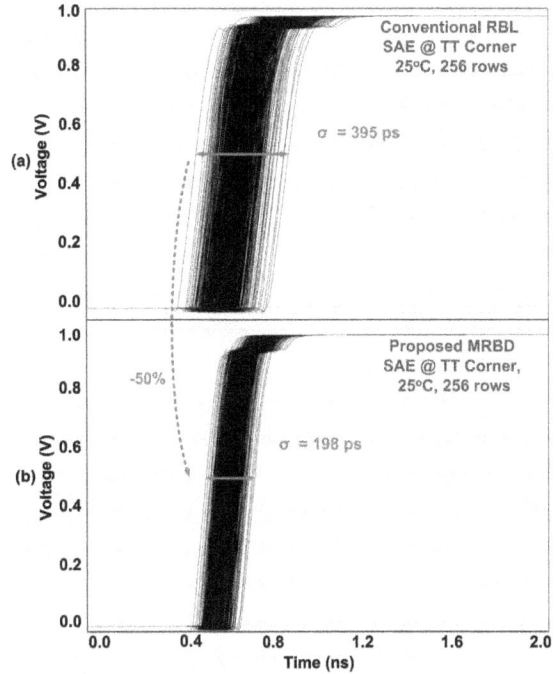

Figure 9: Monte Carlo simulation results of (a) conv. single RBL and (b) proposed MRBD with 256 rows with TT corner.

read static noise margin (SNM) and writeability of SRAM cell. The design optimizations for improving one parameter often end up in worsening the other. Read SNM is of greatest concern; therefore in this paper $6T$ cell design is highly constrained by area, stability, power and performance.

4. SIMULATION RESULTS

Figure 9 shows the 1000 points Monte Carlo simulation results of the proposed MRBD and the conventional single RBL scheme at the supply Voltage of 1.0V. Simulation inclues both inter-die and intra-die variation which provides the most complete representation of statistical variations during chip manufacturing. The number of replica bitlines and replica cells are 2 and 4 for the total 256 rows memory cells. As shown in Figure 9, the standard deviation of the SAE timing with the proposed scheme is 198ps, which is much smaller than 395ps with the conventional scheme. The standard deviation of the SAE timing is decreased by 50%. This scheme is robust to the global variation of the VTH.

Table 1 summarize the simulated performance of the design and compare it with conventional replica bitline technique. Figure 10 shows the Monte Carlo simulation results in FF and SS corners. The $MRBD$ technique may bring additional power consumption and area, by adding more transistors due to applying replica bitline in circuit design. However, this power and area cost is acceptable due to the significant reduction of SAE timing variation. Moreover, the con-

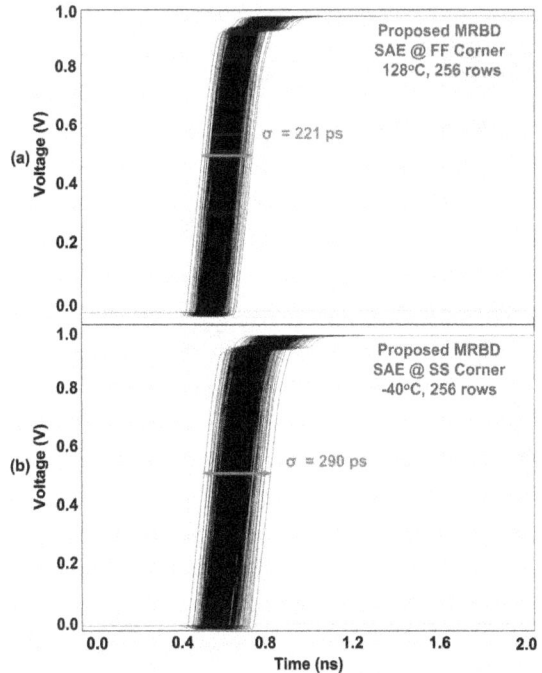

Figure 10: Monte Carlo simulation results of proposed MRBD technique in (a) FF and (b) SS corners.

177

Table 1: Circuit Simulation Results for IBM cmos10lpe 65nm.

Design	Conv. RBL	MRBD
Technology node [nm]	65	65
Organization	256 rows 32 bits	256 rows 32 bits
Power Dissipation	1.26 mW	1.43 mW
Supply Voltage	1.0 V	1.0 V
Standard Deviation	395 ps	198 ps
Transistors	53,874	54,504

ventional scheme requires higher supply Voltage to achieve the same SAE timing variation as the proposed one. Since the power consumption is proportional to square of the supply Voltage, higher supply Voltage can lead to more power. Thus, for achieving same yield, the proposed $MRBD$ can save overall power consumption of SRAM. This technique can be applied to the various row configurations and there is no influence for the column configurations. Therefore, the proposed scheme can be applied to the SRAM compilers. As the capacity of memory becomes larger, the proportion of the $MRBD$ area will be decreased.

5. CONCLUSIONS

A novel Multi replica bitline delay technique is proposed for improving the process variation tolerance of SA read control timing of SRAM. This design is implemented in IBM 65nm CMOS technology. Compared with the conventional RBL design, there is a 50% timing variation reduction at 1.0V supply Voltage while there is a negligible increase in power consumption.

6. ACKNOWLEDGMENTS

This material is based upon work supported by the National Science Foundation under Grant No. CNS-1205685.

7. REFERENCES

[1] International technology roadmap for semiconductors. Technical report. http://public.itrs.net/.

[2] B. Amrutur and M. Horowitz. A replica technique for wordline and sense control in low-power SRAM's. *IEEE Journal of Solid-State Circuits*, 33(8):1208–1219, Aug 1998.

[3] U. Arslan, M. McCartney, M. Bhargava, X. Li, K. Mai, and L. Pileggi. Variation-tolerant SRAM sense-amplifier timing using configurable replica bitlines. In *2008 IEEE Custom Integrated Circuits Conference (CICC)*, pages 415–418, Sept 2008.

[4] A. Chandrakasan, S. Sheng, and R. Brodersen. Low-power CMOS digital design. *IEEE Journal of Solid-State Circuits*, 27(4):473–484, Apr 1992.

[5] R. Houle. Simple statistical analysis techniques to determine optimum sense amp set times. *IEEE Journal of Solid-State Circuits*, 43(8):1816–1825, Aug 2008.

[6] S. Komatsu, M. Yamaoka, M. Morimoto, N. Maeda, Y. Shimazaki, and K. Osada. A 40-nm low-power SRAM with multi-stage replica-bitline technique for reducing timing variation. In *2009 IEEE Custom Integrated Circuits Conference (CICC)*, pages 701–704, Sept 2009.

[7] T. Mizuno, J. Okumtura, and A. Toriumi. Experimental study of threshold Voltage fluctuation due to statistical variation of channel dopant number in MOSFET's. *IEEE Transactions on Electron Devices*, 41(11):2216–2221, Nov 1994.

[8] Y. Niki, A. Kawasumi, A. Suzuki, Y. Takeyama, O. Hirabayashi, K. Kushida, F. Tachibana, Y. Fujimura, and T. Yabe. A digitized replica bitline delay technique for random-variation-tolerant timing generation of SRAM sense amplifiers. *IEEE Journal of Solid-State Circuits*, 46(11):2545–2551, Nov 2011.

[9] K. Osada, J.-U. Shin, M. Khan, Y.-D. Liou, K. Wang, K. Shoji, K. Kuroda, S. Ikeda, and K. Ishibashi. Universal-vdd 0.65-2.0v 32 kb cache using Voltage-adapted timing-generation scheme and a lithographical-symmetric cell. In *2001 IEEE International Solid-State Circuits Conference (ISSCC)*, pages 168–169, Feb 2001.

[10] M. Pelgrom, A. C. J. Duinmaijer, and A. Welbers. Matching properties of MOS transistors. *IEEE Journal of Solid-State Circuits*, 24(5):1433–1439, Oct 1989.

[11] D. Sekar and J. Meindl. The impact of multi-core architectures on design of chip-level interconnect networks. In *IEEE 2007 International Interconnect Technology Conference*, pages 123–125, June 2007.

[12] V. Sharma, S. Cosemans, M. Ashouei, J. Huisken, F. Catthoor, and W. Dehaene. A 4.4 pJ/access 80 mhz, 128 kbit variability resilient SRAM with multi-sized sense amplifier redundancy. *IEEE Journal of Solid-State Circuits*, 46(10):2416–2430, Oct 2011.

[13] N. Verma and A. Chandrakasan. A 65nm 8T sub-V_t SRAM employing sense-amplifier redundancy. In *IEEE International Solid-State Circuits Conference (ISSCC), 2007*, pages 328–606, Feb 2007.

[14] J. Wu, J. Zhu, Y. Xia, and N. Bai. A multiple-stage parallel replica-bitline delay addition technique for reducing timing variation of SRAM sense amplifiers. *IEEE Transactions on Circuits and Systems II: Express Briefs*, 61(4):264–268, April 2014.

MSCS: Multi-hop Segmented Circuit Switching

Donald Kline, Jr.
Computer Engineering
University of Pittsburgh
dek61@pitt.edu

Kai Wang
Computer Science
University of Pittsburgh
kaw139@pitt.edu

Rami Melhem
Computer Science
University of Pittsburgh
melhem@cs.pitt.edu

Alex K. Jones
Electrical and Computer Eng.
University of Pittsburgh
akjones@pitt.edu

ABSTRACT

NoCs (networks-on-chip) are commonly proposed as scalable on-chip interconnects for current and future CMPs (chip multi-processors) and many-core systems. While scalable, the lack of global control can create routing inefficiencies detrimental to the overall network latency. Recently, NoCs have been proposed that allow flits to traverse multiple network switches in a single cycle. This requires a more global view of control to allow routers along the path of a packet to configure their switches collectively. In this paper, we propose a reservation based circuit-switching design, MSCS, which provides simplified global control and multi-hop traversal while reducing latency. MSCS performs network control once per network dimension for the lifetime of a packet, while the leading methods require multiple arbitration steps depending on contention in the network. Furthermore, MSCS can perform control for a packet prior to the availability of resources through reservations, while previous schemes only perform control on-demand. Overall, MSCS can reduce the buffer size by 50% over the leading multi-hop scheme while maintaining a nominal latency improvement (1.4%). With the same buffer resources per port, MSCS achieves a 12.7% latency improvement.

Categories and Subject Descriptors

C.2.1 [**Network Architecture and Design**]: Packet-Switching Networks; Circuit-Switching Networks

General Terms

Network-on-chip; Multi-hop Traversal; Multiprocessing Systems

1. INTRODUCTION

The single threaded computing model driven by improvements in clock frequency that has long dominated the computing industry does not scale using leading edge CMOS technology nodes. As the practical clock rate of a processor is bounded by dynamic power dissipation, this limits the potential performance improvements of single threaded execution. Moreover, performance improvements through architectural techniques, such as instruction level parallelism, that can be efficiently exploited through out-of-order execution have limited scalability. To address this, a large segment of the the computing industry has embraced chip multi-processors (CMPs) while moving away from the single threaded model. Currently, general purpose graphics processing units (GPGPUs) and many-core CMPs are two important examples of highly parallel multi-core computing on a chip. While commodity processors have reached a handful of cores per chip, specialty multi-core processors that scale into the dozens of cores, such as Tilera's Gx [1] series and Intel's Xeon Phi [2], are already commercially available.

For these many-core systems, bus interconnection networks are no longer scalable to support data access and communication demands for these massively parallel CMPs. To address this concern, researchers have typically employed a regular network-on-chip (NoC) interconnection strategy, such as a mesh due to scalability and efficiency advantages over traditional techniques such as a shared bus [3]. Fundamentally, a scalable NoC requires a straightforward capability to add additional nodes on the periphery of the design with minimal change to the fundamental structure of the network, for which the mesh is a good example.

However, the other important aspect of scalability is the distributed control methodology of a NoC such as packet or wormhole switching. In this case, each router in the NoC independently arbitrates and routes locally for traversal to adjacent nodes. Recent research proposes to utilize a clockless repeater link to perform more global control and multi-hop traversal [4] to provide dramatic improvements in message latency and network power consumption. However, this previous work still utilizes basic assumptions of on-demand message routing suitable for distributed control even though messages require coalescing of multiple nodes' arbitration and routing. This limits latency and throughput savings possible in the context of a multi-hop NoC that requires a more global view of control. For example, using on-demand routing [4], packets can continue to spend multiple cycles in local and global arbitration every time the packet stops short of its destination due to contention.

In this work we propose a Multi-hop Segmented Circuit Switching (MSCS) NoC organization that leverages the multi-hop traversal concept [4]. MSCS avoids on-demand circuit establishment by utilizing a more global reservation concept to establish paths through the network, similar to a circuit switch. However, MSCS is scalable as it does not require higher radix switches while still providing full connectivity between nodes. MSCS makes the following contributions:

- Eliminating redundant on-demand arbitration of packets through reservations.

- Prescheduling of resources for reservations to hide arbitration latency in the network.

- Reducing the number of virtual queues at each ingress port to reduce static power in the network while providing a reduced latency over previous approaches.

With a single virtual channel buffer per port, MSCS is still extremely effective at reducing latency. MSCS provides a 12.7% improvement in network latency compared to the leading multihop NoC approach [4] with one buffer per port. Furthermore, MSCS with one buffer per port still demonstrates a small 1.4% latency improvement over on-demand arbitration with two virtual queues per port. Thus, MSCS can dramatically reduce storage buffer overhead in the NoC while maintaining or improving NoC performance.

We describe the related and motivating work for MSCS in Section 2. In Section 3, we explain the proposed MSCS design in detail and describe its implementation. The architectural parameters and experimental methodology used to evaluate the MSCS approach with the results of these experiments for both synthetic and benchmark workloads are related in Section 4. Finally, Section 5 presents conclusions of the impact of the MSCS approach.

2. BACKGROUND AND RELATED WORK

The control latency of NoC routers has been studied as a method to improve message latency through the interconnect. This has been accomplished through the development of speculative routers [5], usage of elastic buffers to reduce the router pipeline stages to as few as two stages [6], and adjusting the router pipeline in an attempt to stabilize network latency [7]. However, those designs still require decentralized and localized network control.

The developments of static and on-demand express virtual channels (EVCs) [8] provide a platform for considering more global thinking about path establishment in NoCs. EVCs provide a "fast" arbitration path for established "circuits" in the context of packet switching networks. Using this concept, circuits can be established based on the requirements of coherence traffic [9], on the history of communication partners [10], or on compiler analysis [11]. Further, using intelligent circuit establishment during a data request (e.g., a shared cache read request in a CMP), the circuit establishment latency for on-demand circuit establishment can be hidden [12]. The commonality of these approaches is that they all gather some form of global information and use this to improve circuit establishment techniques beyond on-demand requests.

The development of circuit establishment using SMART [4], or Single-cycle Multi-hop Asynchronous Repeated Traversal, exacerbates the problem of latencies from arbitration and control in the router. This is due to the dramatic reduction in transmission latency of the multi-hop approach, which amplifies the impact of network pipeline and arbitration delays, such as those introduced during route setup and network contention. MSCS leverages the SMART multi-hop traversal capability and is inspired by the déjà vu routing proposal [13] to create a unique and novel routing approach for multi-hop NoCs. Déjà vu routing uses a separate "control" plane in the network to send out single flit circuit establishment messages to initialize a circuit in the "data" plane. Déjà vu depends on the advance tag match of a cache to initialize the circuit setup prior to the data being available and ultimately sent. This gives the setup packet a head start in the traditional packet-switched control plane to pre-establish the circuit in the data plane. In the following sections we describe both SMART and déjà vu, respectively, in more detail.

2.1 SMART and Multi-hop Traversal

In a standard packet-switching mesh NoC design, when a router sends a flit to a destination N hops away, the flit must be stopped at each router. Each router performs control, typically at the rate of several[1] cycles-per-hop to match the depth of the router pipeline. A more efficient approach would be to collectively configure the N routers involved in the communication of that packet, and then send the flits through those N routers without the impediment of network control at each router. Thus, the *spatial scope* of network control typically influences the performance of the network, while the global element of network control mainly affects the scalability of the network. Therefore, theoretically, the best approach is to combine global control with decentralized hardware. In the case of the packet that traverses N routers, a global-decentralized control scheme would reduce flit latency by $N - 1$ times the individual router latency.

The previously proposed SMART NoC design [4] leverages global-decentralized control and asynchronous repeated traversal and achieves a dramatic flit latency reduction over traditional packet-switching NoCs. SMART allows a group of routers to collectively perform crossbar configuration in one cycle. The group size is dictated by how many repeaters the packet can traverse in a cycle as determined by the cycle length and the underlying implementation technology[2]. After configuration, asynchronous repeated traversal allows a flit to traverse the globally configured path for multiple hops in one cycle without buffering the flit at each intermediate router.

SMART has three pipeline stages: local arbitration (SA-L), global arbitration (SA-G) and flit traversal (FT). SA-L arbitrates local contentions; for instance, if both the central input port (connected to the local node) and the west input port have a flit to be sent to the east port in the same cycle, the router must arbitrate and select a winner input port to use the east output port. SA-G performs the global control and configuration, and determines control of the SMART links which perform multi-hop traversal. Each router could potentially produce a winner flit during the SA-L stage for each direction in every cycle, and thus multiple flits from different routers could enter SA-G stages at the same time. For each router involved in contention, global arbitration is used to select a winning flit, and the router will configure its crossbar accordingly in the FT stage.

To illustrate SMART NoC traversal, an example of four concurrent messages with one-flit packets is shown in Figure 1. This example assumes all four packets enter the FT stage at time 1. Since the path of two messages (red and blue) overlap heading east at router 9, they must be buffered at the input ports to 9. To illustrate which operations can occur in parallel, in the Figure, it is assumed that the bandwidth of each non-SMART link is at least two flits, so both packets perform local (baseline mesh) flit traversal to router 10 at cycle 4[3]. After two more cycles of SA-L and SA-G, the two flits no longer overlap, and can traverse the remainder of this path at cycle 7 using SMART links. The other two messages did not have conflicts on their route, and therefore could be directly delivered to their destination core using SMART links in a single cycle.

2.2 Déjà Vu and Amortized Reservations

Déjà vu routing [13] is a proposed design that exploits the temporal network communication pattern for better performance relative to energy efficiency. A déjà vu network has two network planes; a packet-switched control plane that handles control messages (in-

---

[1]NoC router pipelines are commonly three to five cycles.

[2]In the SMART study, the number of routers that could be traversed in a cycle was determined to be as many as eight [4].

[3]If the bandwidth was a single flit, either the red or blue message would be delayed by an additional cycle in the router 9 pipeline.

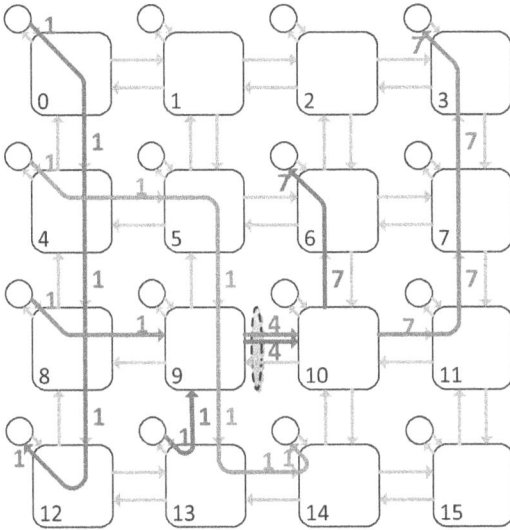

Figure 1: SMART traversal times for four concurrent, independent messages [4].

cluding coherence messages) with an EVC-based circuit-switched data plane. The goal of déjà vu was to save power. Thus, the control plane is a relatively low-bandwidth but fast (higher clock rate) network designed to handle only the relatively smaller width of control messages. In contrast, the data network has a much higher bandwidth but a reduced clock rate.

Déjà vu routing uses the distributed control provided by the control plane to perform more global network control for the data plane. The routing information in the head flit of a data packet is sent as a reservation packet on the control plane. The crux of the déjà vu scheme is that reservations are handled in order of reservation arrival rather than with a specific timestamp estimate as in traditional reservations. While routing the reservation flits for data packets, the control plane resolves the potential contention among packets and reserves resources based on reservation arrival order on the data plane for simple, single cycle data plane control. The reservation based network control essentially expands the *temporal scope* of network control; the network control is performed prior to resource usage. The results of network control (resource allocation and arbitration) are stored for future use.

Déjà vu works in the context of power savings because reservations get a head start on the control plane (the time between cache tag match and data retrieval) and the data plane speed has been reduced. Even though the control plane requires 3-cycle/hop arbitration and the data plane requires a single cycle/hop, the combination of the head start and the faster clock speed typically allows the control packet to arrive at the destination prior to the data catching up, allowing the data plane to operate with a lower clock speed while achieving a similar latency to a packet switch design.

In the next section we describe MSCS which utilizes both the spatial scope notion of SMART and the temporal scope notion of déjà vu to improve the resource utilization of a multi-hop NoC.

3. DESIGN AND IMPLEMENTATION

In this section, we describe the Multi-hop Segmented Circuit Switching router design. MSCS is based on the notion of resource pre-scheduling combined with global control and multi-hop traversal. In MSCS, resources are pre-scheduled for a packet by scheduling the arrival order irrespective of the actual arrival time and as such expands the temporal scope of network control. As a result,

network control is performed at most once or twice for a packet during its lifetime, and temporal redundancy and network latency are reduced. In the next subsections first we describe the MSCS design and then we explore some of the implementation details.

3.1 Design

Multi-hop NoC routing brings the interconnect one step closer to true circuit switching. In traditional circuit switching, the source router must send a circuit setup message to the destination router in advance of a message to setup a circuit. The intermediate routers set and maintain their crossbar configuration according to the setup message. The control overhead is paid once during circuit setup time; when a circuit is established, data packets can traverse the circuit without the impediment of local network control, and no buffer is required for data packets because there is no possible contention. [14]

However, there is a significant drawback with circuit switching: the circuit setup overhead. The source router sends a circuit setup message to the destination router, and has to wait for an acknowledgment from the destination router before sending the data packet. The acknowledgment wait time from the destination router varies depending on the type of network used and the contention experienced by the setup message. The requisitioned resources along the path of a circuit cannot be used by any other circuit during a setup request, creating potential for idle resources, latency degradation, and throughput loss.

MSCS enhances circuit switching with a circuit reservation mechanism. As resources of a router (i.e. crossbar connections and data links) are exclusively allocated in circuit switching to a single circuit request, an allocated resource cannot be reassigned to other circuits until circuit teardown. Thus, circuit switching handles contention through single assignment of a resource. In contrast, MSCS reserves that resource for future use instead of acquiring the resource directly. When the reservation becomes available, which could happen immediately in low contention scenarios, the message is sent. Therefore circuit reservation is analogous to a circuit setup request in traditional circuit switching.

To realize these reservations in MSCS, each router contains a FIFO reservation queue for each network direction. A reservation is popped from the queue when the circuit associated with that reservation is finished sending data, which is similar to circuit teardown in baseline circuit switching. By doing this, resources are granted to circuits in FIFO order, and circuits are also established and torn down in the same order.

MSCS also requires a multi-hop (broadcast) network as the circuit request network. This is needed for two reasons: First, the data network is capable of multi-hop traversal, and thus the circuit request network must match the speed of data network. Second, circuit reservation orders must be globally consistent. Broadcasting ensures that a reservation's en-queue time (and order) is the same for all routers along the route. If two reservations are broadcasted at the same time, then a global priority scheme, or arbitration, is utilized by the routers to determine reservation queuing order.

To increase throughput, MSCS adds a buffer to every input port of the data network to allow messages to traverse available circuit *segments* and buffer data downstream along the message route where earlier reservations are still being satisfied. In contrast to circuit switching, this data buffer adds resource overhead and necessitates buffer flow control but does not require a fully established circuit to send a data packet. This removes the acknowledgment requirement of the complete circuit setup and decreases the circuit control delay compared to circuit switching, even under zero network load. In the next several sections we describe in detail the

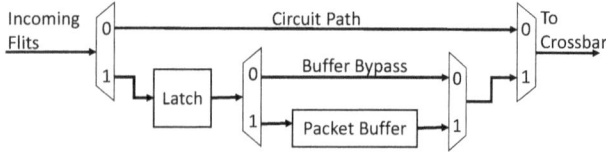

Figure 2: The MSCS input port.

implementation of data path, flow control, and circuit reservation network to realize MSCS.

3.2 Flow Control

The one data buffer per input port in MSCS necessitates buffer flow control. Fortunately, the flow control mechanism of MSCS does not delay the data path, and, consequently, it does not incur performance degradation. We employ a similar multi-hop traversal technique proposed by SMART [4], since the data path of MSCS and SMART are similar.

Multi-hop traversal replaces the traditional clocked wire repeaters with asynchronous repeaters which boost flits and allow fast multi-mm propagation[4]. At the conclusion of a multi-hop traversal, a flit must be latched at the ending router's input port (see Figure 2). Both flit traversal and latching are done in a single cycle. In the cycle following a circuit segment traversal the flit is written into the data buffer if the next circuit segment is not available or if the flit has reached its destination router. If the next segment is available the flit can be reinjected from the latch directly. Note, a flit may not continue along the route if either the current router output port is serving another reservation or if the next buffer downstream does not have sufficient input buffer space to hold the flit.

The latter case is required to ensure that if the available circuit segment ends with the next router it can be appropriately buffered. To accomplish this, MSCS uses on/off flow control. There is one buffer on/off line from each of the neighboring routers. If the line is on, enough buffer space is available and the crossbar connection and input buffering is determined solely by circuit reservation. Otherwise, if the line is off, the input port must buffer the incoming flit and not make any crossbar connection for that direction. To avoid flow control delays, the buffer availability of the subsequent cycle can be determined in the current cycle. For example, the router can report the reservation will be consumed and allow the next reservation to send in the following cycle if it is handling the tail flit of the currently reserved connection.

3.3 Circuit Reservation Request Network

To reduce complexity, we restrict the routing algorithm to X-Y routing (dimension-order routing) with the standard 2D mesh. Thus, the path of a packet has at most one turn. The reservation request procedure is naturally divided into two broadcasts, a request broadcast for the X dimension and another for the Y dimension. For each row or column of the 2D mesh network, the circuit request network is the same as 1D mesh.

Circuit reservations in one dimension: A circuit request network consists of three buses—an arbitration bus, a request bus, and a flow-control bus. The size for these buses per row/column are N bits, $\log(N)$ bits, and N bits, respectively, where N is the size of a row in an $N \times N$ mesh. The source router of a packet uses the request bus to broadcast its circuit request, while the arbitration bus handles potential conflicts among multiple source routers. During the arbitration stage, source routers assert their own bit lines of the arbitration bus, and all the routers use round robin arbitration to chose among the relevant candidate source routers. To broadcast a

---

[4]SMART links are reported to traverse 8 mm in a 2GHz cycle [4].

circuit request, the winner puts the row/column number of the destination node on the request bus. All nodes have the winner source node's row/column number after arbitration, and those nodes also have the destination node's row/column number after the broadcast.

To deal with potential reservation buffer overflow, a router asserts its bit line on the flow-control bus if its reservation buffer is full. A source node will not make a circuit reservation if the circuit has a full router on its path, since the reservation will fail.

Circuit reservations in multiple dimensions: When introducing additional dimensions, for X-Y routing, a packet traverses the entire X dimension first followed by the Y. Each dimension can utilize the circuit reservation from the single dimension case. We assume the packet must re-arbitrate when changing dimension. This could potentially hinder traffic in the first dimension along that route, significantly reducing throughput. We solve this problem by removing the waiting packet for the new dimension to a data buffer separated from the original dimension. We call this a relay buffer as it relays a packet from one dimension to the next.

3.4 Data Path

To build a MSCS 2D mesh crossbar, it is necessary to change the crossbar design of the regular mesh. Figure 4 shows the modified crossbar design. The router has two small crossbars (3x4 and 4x3) instead of a single large 5x5 crossbar. In terms of energy efficiency and area, the two smaller crossbars actually use less power and area than a 5x5 crossbar.

In X-Y routing, a packet turning from the X to Y dimension is buffered at the relay buffer and no longer blocks the X dimension. At this point, the packet makes a circuit reservation for the Y dimension from the relay buffer. The relay buffer serves as a single point of entry of the Y dimension for incoming packets from either the east or west direction. Arbitration is needed to resolve potential contention between central-in (messages that only require the Y dimension) and the relay buffer. The arbitration latency can be amortized by using natural parallelism that exists in the circuit request pipeline, so it does not require an additional pipeline stage.

Further, a control register is required between the data path (crossbar and input port) and the circuit control unit. The control register is a latch that holds the setup signal from the control unit to the crossbar and the input port. The control register is set by the control unit one cycle ahead.

There are only two pipeline stages for MSCS: reservation and traversal. When the reservation entry is generated, it is given to the circuit setup logic to set the control logic in parallel to writing the reservation queue. At the beginning of the next cycle, the control register is already set, and the data path can begin immediately if the resources are available. Furthermore, we add a second read port for the reservation queue to read the top two reservations in order to calculate the next circuit's configuration prior to the current circuit's teardown and establish it immediately in the next cycle. An auxiliary control register is required to store this calculated configuration.

The circuit request latency overhead with no contention is at most two cycles for a packet and only one cycle for requesting a circuit that travels in only one dimension. For a data packet with multiple flits, the overhead is amortized. For circuits that cannot be established for more than one cycle due to contention, the circuit establishment overhead is entirely hidden as the packet must already wait for the contention to clear to use the resource.

To illustrate MSCS NoC traversal, an example of four concurrent messages with one-flit packets is shown in Figure 3. This example assumes all four packets enter the traversal stage at time 1. The green flow's reservation had precedence over the red flow, so the

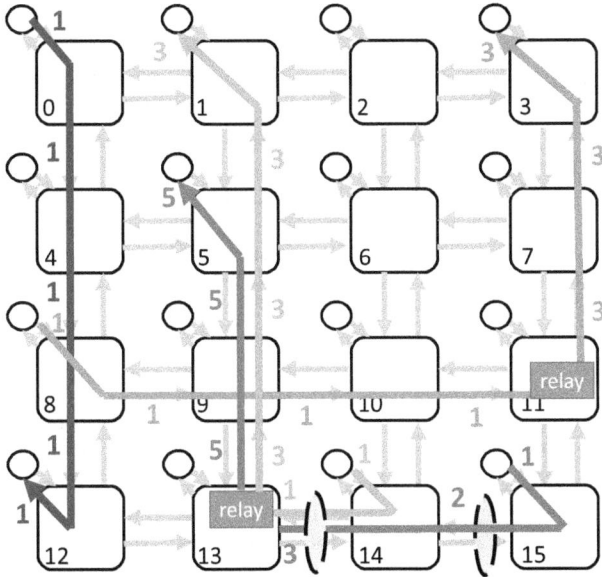

Figure 3: MSCS traversal times for four concurrent, independent messages, with one relay queue. With two relay queues, the red flow could enter a relay queue in router 13 at cycle 2.

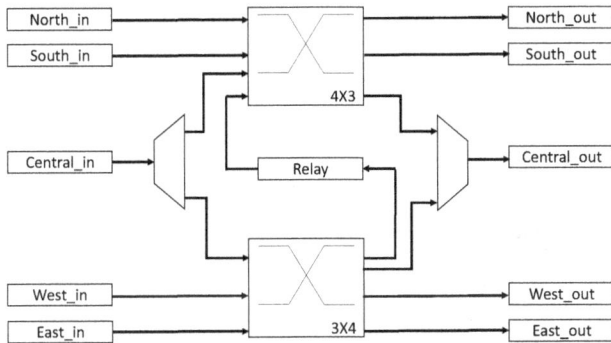

Figure 4: The relay crossbar adjustments for MSCS.

red flow must buffer at the east ingress of router 14. In cycle 2, the red flow can traverse to the east ingress of router 13, as the green flow is now holding the relay buffer. Simultaneously, relay arbitration occurs for the green flow. In the cycle that the green flow leaves the relay queue (cycle 3), the red flow performs switch traversal and buffer write into the relay queue. Following this, the red flow performs arbitration (cycle 4), and finally, in cycle 5 it can complete switch and link traversal to its destination.

3.5 Comparing MSCS with SMART

Both SMART and MSCS use global control and multi-hop traversal, but MSCS uses circuit switching and reservations, while SMART uses on-demand network control. SMART performs arbitrations each cycle on a per packet basis, which incurs latency due to the repeated per packet controls. MSCS's FIFO reservation queues handle and maintain the global and local arbitration, so that circuits can be established when the resources become available without performing latency inducing arbitration at each step.

To illustrate this situation, in both SMART and MSCS, a packet can traverse a circuit segment and be stopped prematurely and short of its intended destination due to downstream buffer occupancy. When the downstream buffer becomes available, the packet can resume its traversal. For MSCS, resuming traversal happens during the same cycle that buffer space becomes available and requires no

control delay due to the circuit reservation. For SMART, there is a minimum additional two cycle startup latency for resuming packet traversal, since SMART needs to perform local and global arbitration each time before sending a packet.

4. RESULTS AND DISCUSSION

To evaluate the impact of MSCS, we constructed a cycle accurate router implementation of MSCS using the gem5 [15] simulator. To assess the relative performance of MSCS, we also implemented SMART faithfully based on the published manuscript [4] and use this state-of-the-art design as our reference for comparison in our evaluation.

We performed both synthetic traffic network only simulations and full system simulations on benchmark workloads. For synthetic traffic simulation, we use an 8×8 as the underlying topology. An 8×8 mesh is appropriate as it is used for existing commercial products such as the Tilera 64 [1], and it is a common topology for performance evaluation in proposed NoC research proposals. Each virtual channel buffer and relay buffer can hold eight flits. For full system simulations, we used a set of selected benchmarks from parsec 2.1 [16] and splash-2 [17] suites. The underlying system uses 64-core CMP with a standard shared last-level cache system with the MESI coherence modeled by Ruby. Each core is a 3-issue out-of-order X86 processing unit. The O3 CPU module in gem5 is used to model the core.

4.1 Synthetic Traffic Analysis

Our synthetic traffic analysis used uniform random traffic. MSCS with a single buffer per port and two and four relay buffers per network node was compared to SMART with two and four virtual channel buffers per input port per node. This compares schemes with a 25% and 50% reduction in virtual queues per node, respectively. The results of average network latency for synthetic traffic with 5-flit packets can be observed in Figure 5. Over the scope of the synthetic results until the start of saturation, the MSCS scheme with two relay buffers per node results in a 50.5% latency reduction over SMART with two virtual queues per input port, and continues to have lower latency with heavy traffic. MSCS with four relay buffers per node produces a 16.7% reduction in network latency through the period depicted in the graph (until the onset of saturation) over SMART with four virtual channel buffers. However, past the onset of saturation, SMART with four virtual channel buffers outperforms MSCS with four relay buffers (and half the virtual queues).

The average packet latency results of uniform random synthetic traffic with packets of just one flit can be observed in Figure 6. Sim-

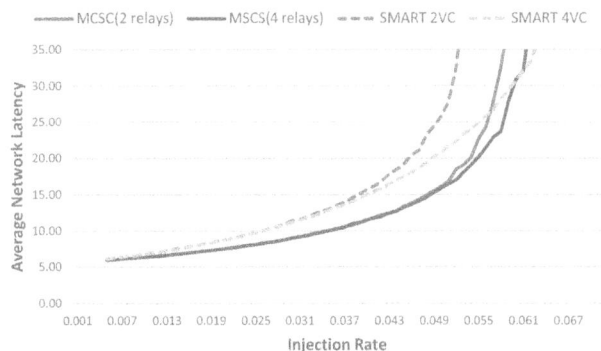

Figure 5: Network latency for synthetic traffic, 5-flit packets.

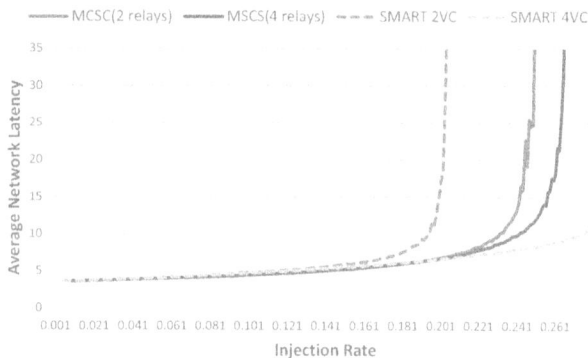

Figure 6: Network latency for synthetic traffic, 1-flit packets.

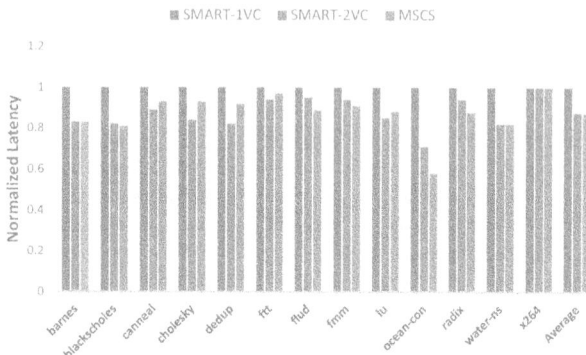

Figure 7: Average network latency normalized to SMART with 1 virtual channel per input port.

ilar to the results for packets with five flits, MSCS with two relay buffers consistently outperforms SMART with two virtual channels per input port over all synthetic input traffic, with an average improvement of 36.6% before saturation. However, SMART with four virtual channels per input port outperforms MSCS with four relay buffers (half the number of virtual channels).

4.2 Full System Evaluations

Average packet latency is shown for full system simulations under various workloads in Figure 7. For this simulation, five flit packets were used, and SMART with one and two virtual channels per port were compared against MSCS with one input buffer per port and one relay buffer per node. On average, MSCS results in a 12.7% reduction from SMART with one virtual channel per port, and a reduction of 1.4% from SMART with two virtual channels per port, despite having 37.5% less buffer requirements per node.

5. CONCLUSION

With the increasing number of cores on a chip, NoCs using traditional routing with local arbitration and traversal have been relied upon due to their scalability. While this approach is scalable, the distributed local control can severely limit minimum network latency. Multi-hop links significantly improve NoC average message latency by allowing flits to traverse multiple hops in a single cycle but require global distributed control. Additional logic surrounding these links provides the global control necessary to reduce latency and increase network utilization.

By adding reservations to multi-hop links and removing all but one virtual queue per port from the data path, we can reduce the static energy from those queues while decreasing average in-network latency over the leading multi-hop proposal, SMART. For benchmark traffic, MSCS results in a 12.7% reduction from SMART with one virtual channel per port, and a reduction of 1.4% from SMART

with two virtual channels per port. This latter savings is achieved despite the reduced buffer capacity because the reservations allow a packet to only perform arbitration once for each dimension.

References

[1] "Tilera. TILE-Gx Processor Family. ONLINE." http://www.tilera.com/products/processors/TILE-Gx_Family, 2014. [Accessed: December 1, 2014.].

[2] "Intel Xeon Phi™ Coprocessors. ONLINE." http://www.intel.com/content/www/us/en/processors/xeon/xeon-phi-coprocessor-overview.html, 2014. [Accessed: December 1, 2014.].

[3] H. G. Lee, N. Chang, U. Y. Ogras, and R. Marculescu, "On-chip Communication Architecture Exploration: A Quantitative Evaluation of Point-to-point, Bus, and Network-on-chip Approaches," *ACM Trans. Des. Autom. Electron. Syst.*, Vol. 12, No. 3, pp. 23:1–23:20, May 2008.

[4] C.-H. O. Chen, S. Park, T. Krishna, S. Subramanian, A. P. Chandrakasan, and L.-S. Peh, "SMART: A single-cycle reconfigurable NoC for SoC applications," *Proc. of DATE, 2013*, pp. 338–343, March 2013.

[5] R. Mullins, A. West, and S. Moore, "The design and implementation of a low-latency on-chip network," *Proc. of ASP-DAC*, p. 6 pp., Jan 2006.

[6] G. Michelogiannakis and W. Dally, "Router designs for elastic buffer on-chip networks," *High Performance Computing Networking, Storage and Analysis, Proceedings of the Conference on*, pp. 1–10, Nov 2009.

[7] P. Zhou, J. Yin, A. Zhai, and S. Sapatnekar, "NoC frequency scaling with flexible-pipeline routers," *Low Power Electronics and Design (ISLPED) 2011 International Symposium on*, pp. 403–408, Aug 2011.

[8] A. Kumar, L.-S. Peh, P. Kundu, and N. K. Jha, "Express Virtual Channels: Towards the Ideal Interconnection Fabric," *Proc. of ISCA*, pp. 150–161, 2007.

[9] N. Jerger, M. Lipasti, and L.-S. Peh, "Circuit-Switched Coherence," *Computer Architecture Letters*, Vol. 6, No. 1, pp. 5–8, January 2007.

[10] A. Abousamra, R. Melhem, and A. Jones, "Winning with Pinning in NoC," *Proc. of HOTI*, pp. 13–21, Aug 2009.

[11] Y. Li, A. Abousamra, R. Melhem, and A. Jones, "Compiler-Assisted Data Distribution and Network Configuration for Chip Multiprocessors," *IEEE Trans. on Parallel and Distributed Systems*, Vol. 23, No. 11, pp. 2058–2066, Nov 2012.

[12] A. Abousamra, A. K. Jones, and R. Melhem, "Proactive Circuit Allocation in Multiplane NoCs," *Proc. of DAC*, pp. 35:1–35:10, 2013.

[13] A. Abousamra, R. Melhem, and A. Jones, "Déjà Vu Switching for Multiplane NoCs," *Proc. of NoCS*, pp. 11–18, May 2012.

[14] K.-C. Chang, J.-S. Shen, and T.-F. Chen, "Evaluation and Design Trade-offs Between Circuit-switched and Packet-switched NOCs for Application-specific SOCs," *Proceedings of the 43rd Annual Design Automation Conference*, DAC '06, (New York, NY, USA), pp. 143–148, ACM, 2006.

[15] N. Binkert, B. Beckmann, G. Black, S. K. Reinhardt, A. Saidi, A. Basu, J. Hestness, D. R. Hower, T. Krishna, S. Sardashti, R. Sen, K. Sewell, M. Shoaib, N. Vaish, M. D. Hill, and D. A. Wood, "The Gem5 Simulator," *SIGARCH Comput. Archit. News*, Vol. 39, No. 2, pp. 1–7, Aug. 2011.

[16] C. Bienia, S. Kumar, J. P. Singh, and K. Li, "The PARSEC benchmark suite: characterization and architectural implications," *Proc. of PACT*, pp. 72–81, 2008.

[17] S. Woo, M. Ohara, E. Torrie, J. Singh, and A. Gupta, "The SPLASH-2 programs: characterization and methodological considerations," *Proc. of ISCA*, pp. 24–36, June 1995.

EDA Challenges for Memristor-Crossbar based Neuromorphic Computing

Beiye Liu, Wei Wen, and Yiran Chen
ECE Department
University of Pittsburgh
Phone: (412) 624-5836
{bel34, wew57, yic52}@pitt.edu

Xin Li
ECE Department
Carnegie Mellon University
Phone: (412) 268-6507
xinli@cmu.edu

Chi-Ruo Wu and Tsung-Yi Ho
CSIE Department
National Cheng Kung University
Phone: +886-6-275-7575
{gtrw, tyho}@csie.ncku.edu.tw

ABSTRACT

The increasing gap between the high data processing capability of modern computing systems and the limited memory bandwidth motivated the recent significant research on *neuromorphic computing systems* (NCS), which are inspired from the working mechanism of human brains. Discovery of memristor further accelerates engineering realization of NCS by leveraging the similarity between synaptic connections in neural networks and programming weight of the memristor. However, to achieve a stable large-scale NCS for practical applications, many essential EDA design challenges still need to be overcome especially the state-of-the-art memristor crossbar structure is adopted. In this paper, we summarize some of our recent published works about enhancing the design robustness and efficiency of memristor crossbar based NCS. The experiments show that the impacts of noises generated by process variations and the IR-drop over the crossbar can be effectively suppressed by our noise-eliminating training method and IR-drop compensation technique. Moreover, our network clustering techniques can alleviate the challenges of limited crossbar scale and routing congestion in NCS implementations.

Categories and Subject Descriptors

B.7.1 [**Integrated Circuits**]: Types and Design Styles–*VLSI (very large scale integration)*.

Keywords

Memristor Crossbar; Neuromorphic Computing; Neural Networks;

1. INTRODUCTION

As Moore's Law is approaching its end [14], technology scaling of conventional CMOS devices slows down and many studies on emerging circuits and devices are being performed. Two promising emerging nano-devices, i.e., spintronic [15] and resistive devices (a.k.a. memristor) [16], draw considerable attentions from the researchers. Besides, the gap between CPU computing capacity and memory accessing bandwidth greatly limits the up-scaling of von Neumann computer architecture, known as "memory wall" problem [17].

Emerging memristor devices has been well received as a promising candidate for next-generation memory [16]. Crossbar structure of memristors can be manufactured with a high integration density at a level of 10^{10} synapses per square inch; the achieved power consumption is also as low as one trillion operations per second (TOPS) per Watt [8][5]. Moreover, the non-volatility and programmability of memristor resistance can efficiently mimic the variable synaptic strengths of biological synapses, using memristor to implement artificial neural network has become a hot research topic [7].

The VLSI realization of brain-inspired computing systems is referred to as neuromorphic computing systems (NCS). Although memristor has demonstrated many attractive characteristics in NCS implementation, there are still many fundamental challenges in designing a robust and efficient NCS. For instance, the computing and training reliability of a memristor crossbar is often deteriorated by process variations and signal noises [5]. As another example, voltage distributed over a crossbar degrades due to wire resistance (a.k.a. IR-drop), which could become severer as the crossbar size increases and therefore, constrain the scalability of the crossbar structure. Finally, a practical neural network is usually so large that one single crossbar may not offer sufficient connections. Utilizing multiple crossbars will raise the routing congestion problem; on the contrary, using memristor to implement a sparse neural network may cause a low crossbar utilization rate.

In this paper, we summarize some of our recent published works about enhancing the design robustness and efficiency of memristor crossbar based NCS.

2. PRELIMINARY

2.1 Memristor Based NCS

Figure 1 illustrates the structure of a feed-forward neural network where input (x_i) neurons are connected with output neurons (y_i) through synapses (w_{ij}). The output message at every output neuron is activated after collecting and weighting messages from all the inputs. In a memristor-based NCS, every synapse is implemented by a memristor and the synaptic weight is represented by the resistance (memristance) of the memristor device. Mathematically, the computation can be formulated as:

GLSVLSI '15, May 20 22, 2015, Pittsburgh, PA, USA.
Copyright 2015 ACM 978-1-4503-3474-7/15/05...$15.00.
http://dx.doi.org/10.1145/2742060.2743754

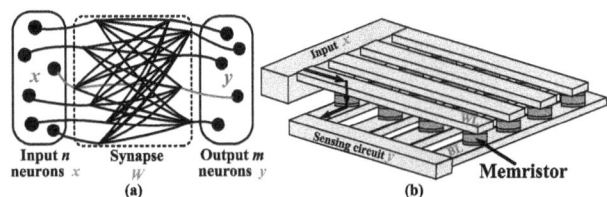

Figure 1. (a) Conceptual overview of a neural network [8]. (b) Circuit architecture of a memristor crossbar [7].

$$y_n = W_{n \times m} \times x_m, \quad (1)$$

where x_m and y_n are the activity patterns of m input neurons and n output neurons, respectively, and $W_{n \times m}$ is the weight matrix denoting synaptic strengths between inputs and outputs. Matrix-vector multiplication in Eq. (1) is the core operation of one of the commonest computation (namely, "recall" process) in NCS. Both network of discrete memristors and memristor crossbar can realize this operation but crossbar is considered as a more efficient way because of its structural similarity [6]. As Figure 1(b) shows, in a recall process, x is mimicked by the input voltage vector applied on the word-lines (WLs), and the bit-lines (BLs) are grounded. Each memristor is programmed to a resistance state representing the weight of the correspondent synapse. The current along each BL is collected and converted to the output voltage vector y by the "neurons" at the output of the crossbar [5].

2.2 Training of Memristor Crossbar

"Training" is another basic computation of NCS. The training of a NCS can be categorized as either close-loop on-device (OLD) training or open-loop off-device (OLD) training. In OLD training, amplitudes and durations of the programming signals are first computed based on different algorithms and applications. Then the memristors in the crossbar are programmed accordingly. On the other hand, CLD is an iterative scheme to update weights (resistances) of memristors according to the feedback from outputs [10].

When programming a memristor crossbar, programming pulses with different amplitudes and durations are applied to the crossbar for a desired resistance matrix R: the voltage of the WL and BL connecting the target memristor (Rij) are set to $+V_{bias}$ and GND, respectively, while all other WLs and BLs are connected to $+V_{bias}/2$. Hence, only Rij is applied with a full V_{bias} above the threshold that can change the device's resistance state, leaving the rest of memristors remain unchanged because they are only "half-selected" with a voltage of $V_{bias}/2$ [11].

3. Design Challenges Overview

In this section, we discuss some challenges in the design and design automation of memristor-based NCS.

3.1 IR-drop

The resistance along the metal wires connected to the memristors in the crossbar causes the IR-drop issue in NCS: the voltage reaching the device could be considerably lower than that supplied by the write driver. In general, the influence of IR-drop on a memristor is determined by its position in the crossbar as well as the resistance states of all memristors. As proved in [11], when all memristors are at their low-resistance state (LRS), both recall and training processes of the memristor crossbar will encounter severe reliability problem, especially when the size of the crossbar is beyond 64×64.

Figure 2 virtualizes the IR-drop issue on a crossbar with a size of 128×128. Figure 2(a) depicts the programming voltage distribution (V') in the training process. The programming voltage from the driver is $2.9V$. V'_{ij} is the voltage reaching the memristor between WL_i and BL_j. The largest IR-drop happens at the far end location as $V'_{(128,128)}$. The worst case and the best case of IR-drop occur when all the memristors are at their HRS (high-resistance state) and LRS, respectively, as shown in Figure 2(b). IR-drop greatly harms the programmability of the memristor crossbar and degrades the computation accuracy of the NCS. Similar trend can be also found during recall process of the NCS.

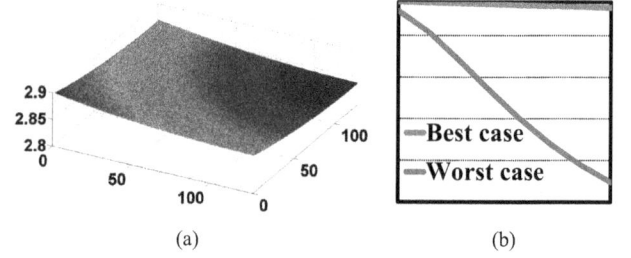

(a)   (b)

Figure 2. (a) Programming voltage distribution on a 128×128 all-HRS-memristor crossbar (the best case). (b) Programming voltage degradation vs. crossbar size [5].

IR-drop significantly affects reliability of the recall and training processes of NCS. During the recall process, input patterns (voltages) are applied on the WLs and outputs are read from the BLs. Because of IR-drop, the BLs that are far from the input driver are subject to the distortion of the voltage applied on the memristors on the BLs and therefore, the distortion of the outputs. During the training process, resistance matrix R of all memristors should be programmed to the value representing the targeted weight matrix. For a memristor initially at HRS state, its final resistance R_{ij} is a function of the voltage (V_{ij}) and the accumulative duration (T_{ij}) of the programming pulse such as:

$$R_{ij} = f(T_{ij}, V_{ij}, R_{HRS}). \quad (2)$$

Due to IR-drop, the actual voltage applied on the memristor is V'_{ij} that is different from the targeted V_{ij} and thus, leading to an inaccurate training result (weight matrix).

3.2 Routing Challenges of NCS Design

In contrast to the limited scale of memristor crossbars that can be manufactured presently, neural networks used in real applications are often very large. For example, DNN (deep neural network) used in [1] is composed of more than 4000 input neurons. The network designed for LDPC coding in IEEE 802.11 also has a similar scale [2]. To implement such large-scale neural networks, three memristor-based schemes can be utilized: (1) pure *discrete synapse (memristor) design* (DSD), (2) pure *multiple crossbar design* (MCD) and (3) a hybrid design trading off between (1) and (2). The DSD is flexible to realize synaptic connections but its area cost increases exponentially with the neuron number because of routing congestion. Inter-crossbar routing congestion is also a major problem in MCD. Moreover, if the neural network is sparse, implementing the network with MCD may cause a low utilization of (the synaptic connections of) the memristor crossbar. We note that the routing congestion and low crossbar utilization problems are very common in some applications with large and sparse neural networks. For example, in LDPC coding based on back propagation algorithm, less than 1% possible connections in the network are actually connected [2]. Considering the pros and cons of DSD and MCD, A hybrid scheme (DSD+MCD) can be promising to overcome these challenges. Given a large and sparse neural network, we proposed a clustering technology to concentrate randomly distributed connections into multiple small clusters. As a result, within-cluster connections are dense and between-cluster

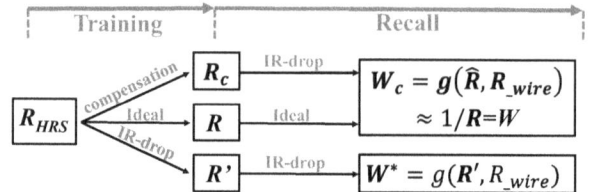

Figure 3. Compensation for both training and recall processes [5].

186

ones are sparse. MCD and DSD respectively realize within- and between-cluster connections, resulting in both high crossbar utilization and low routing congestion. More details will be given in the next section.

4. Solutions for NCS Design Challenges

We proposed some techniques to solve the design challenges of NCS illustrated in Section 3.

4.1 IR-drop Compensation

To alleviate IR-drop issue, compensation techniques can be utilized in recall and training processes of memristor crossbar. Figure 3 gives an overview of IR-drop compensation scheme in [5].

Taking into account the impact of IR-drop during the recall, we define W^* as the actual but distorted weight matrix. W^* is determined by the targeted memristor resistance state R and the wire resistance $R_{\_wire}$ as:

$$W^* = g(R, R_{\_wire}). \quad (3)$$

As shown in Figure 3, the IR-drop compensation scheme optimizes a compensating resistance state R_c that generates a weight matrix W_c close to the ideal target W as:

$$\min_{R_c}\|W - W_c\|^2 = \sum_{i=1}^{n}\sum_{j=1}^{m}(W_{(i,j)} - W_{c(i,j)})^2. \quad (4)$$

Gradient descent algorithm can optimize this target as:

$$R_{c\_k+1} = R_{c\_k} - \gamma\sum_{i=1}^{n}\sum_{j=1}^{m}(2\left(W_{(i,j)} - W_{c(i,j)}\right)\frac{\partial W_{c(i,j)}}{\partial R_{c\_k}}) \quad (5)$$

Here $W_c = g(R_c, R_{\_wire})$ and can be explicitly measured [5].

Different from the recall process, the optimization target of IR-drop compensation in the training process is minimizing the difference between the trained R' and the targeted R that represents desired weight matrix W. As aforementioned, all memristors can be set towards HRS to minimize the IR-drop impact during the training process. As Eq. (2) formulated, the final resistance of a memristor is the function of the programming pulse voltage and duration. Then the IR-drop can be compensated by prolonging the programming duration.

4.2 Memristor Crossbar Reduction

Another method to alleviate the impact of IR-drop is to reduce the scale of the involved computation and thus, the required size of the memristor crossbar [5]. The proposed crossbar reduction scheme is to approximate the weight matrix W ($n \times m$) in Eq. (1) by leveraging singular value decomposition (SVD) as [4]:

$$W = U\sum V \approx W_{appx} = \sum_{i=1}^{r}\delta_i \cdot u_i \cdot v_i. \quad (6)$$

Here U and V are unitary matrices, Σ is an rectangular diagonal matrix with singular values of W. δ_i ($i=1,...r$) are the first r (i.e., the rank of W_{appx}) singular values of W. u_i and v_i are the approximated left and right singular vectors of W, respectively. The dif-

ference between W and W_{appx}, that is $\Delta W = \|W - W_{appx}\|$, is decided by the coverage of $\sum_{i=1}^{r}\delta_i$ on the overall summed $\sum_{i=1}^{m}\delta_i$. The difference, hence, ΔW can be controlled by the value of r. [5] gives the strategy to select r.

Based on the approximation result, we are able to transform the weight connection function in Eq. (1) to:

$$W \cdot x \approx (\sum_{i=1}^{r}\delta_i \cdot u_i \cdot v_i) \cdot x$$
$$= W_{left} \cdot W_{right} \cdot x \quad (7)$$

where

$$W_{left} = [\delta_1 \cdot u_1 ... \delta_r \cdot u_r], W_{right} = \begin{bmatrix} v_1 \\ \vdots \\ v_r \end{bmatrix} \quad (8)$$

Here W was originally represented on an $n \times m$ crossbar and $m \times 1$ vector x is represented by the input voltage vector. Eq. (7) and (8) show that the connection function can be transformed to a new two-stage system that consists of a $n \times r$ weight matrix W_{left} and a $r \times m$ weight matrix W_{right}. Note that $r << n$ or m. This method is named as one-dimensional (1-D) reduction.

Figure 4 illustrates the programming voltage distribution on a 128×128 memristor crossbar when IR-drop is considered. Here all memristors are at LRS to demonstrate the worst-case impact of IR-drop. We highlighted (colored) the memristor locations with a voltage drop higher than V_{bias} /2 under "half-selected" programming scheme introduced in Section 2.2. We name the boundary of the highlighted area as the "hard-limit". Any memristor outside the "hard-limit" will not be effectively programmed because they are practically "half-selected". Increasing the programming voltage to raise the voltage applied on the memristors outside the "hard-limit", however, will affect the memristors that should be "half-selected". Hence, the scale of the "hard-limit" serves as a good measurement of programming robustness of the memristor crossbar. As shown in Figure 4(a), the size of the largest "hard-limit" is 48×48, or say, the maximum dimension of the data that can be processed is only 48. Our "2-D reduction method" proposed in [5] can reduce the required memristor crossbar size at both dimensions. However, by reducing the size of one dimension down to a smaller value, say, $r = 22$, the size of another dimension can be extended to 128, as depicted in Figure 4(b). Such a crossbar is sufficient to process the data with a size of 128 leveraging our proposed 1-D reduction method, as long as the rank of W_{appx} is not higher than 22.

4.3 Neural Network Partitioning

Spectral graph partitioning (also spectral clustering) is a candidate to partition the graph which representing a neural network into multiple groups. The optimization target is to minimize the between-group similarity and maximize the within-group similarities [3]. As the message propagation direction on the neural network has no impact on the optimization function, the neural network can be abstracted as an undirected graph to perform spectral partitioning. In NCS design, by specifying the "similarity" as "the number of connections", the goal of our spectral graph partition-

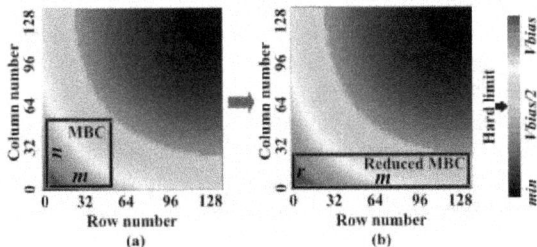

Figure 4: Reduction improves reliability [5].

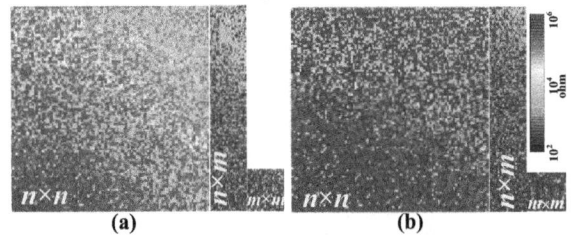

Figure 5. Trained memristor resistance discrepancy (a) without IR-drop compensation. (b) with IR-drop compensation [6].

ing becomes minimizing the (between-group) connections that need to be mapped to DSD and maximizing the (within-groups) connections that fit into the crossbars (MCD), thus, decreasing the routing congestion and increasing the crossbar utilization.

5. Experiments

5.1 Evaluations of IR-drop Compensation and Crossbar Reduction

Figure 5 shows our experiment results about the resistance discrepancy between the targeted crossbar and the actual trained one impacted by IR-drop and process variations. In our experiment, the programmed memristor resistance is assumed to follow the log-normal distribution as $r = r_0 \cdot \exp(\theta)$ [12], where, $\theta \sim N(0, \sigma)$ is Gaussian distribution and r_0 is the mean value.

We use Hopfield network as an example to illustrate the effectiveness of IR-drop compensation and crossbar reduction schemes. A crossbar with a scale of 128×128 (original $n \times n$) can be reduced to 128×19 ($n \times r$) by applying 1-D reduction and to 19×19 ($r \times r$) by 2-D reduction scheme [5]. Here r is set to 15% of n, or the maximum pattern numbers that can be stored in a 128×128 Hopfield network in theory [13]. As Figure 5(a) shows, reduction schemes significantly reduce the resistance discrepancy as the crossbar size decreases, resulting in a higher quality of training. Moreover, as shown in Figure 5(b), the IR-Drop compensation scheme effectively minimizes the crossbar resistance discrepancy. More experiments also showed that the training quality enhancement could substantially improve recall successful rate of the NCS [5].

5.2 Evaluations of clustering

Figure 6(a) and (b) demonstrates the adjacency matrix of a Hopfield network with 200 neurons before and after spectral partitioning, respectively. In the figure, the i-th neuron is indexed on the i-th row (also on the i-th column). A black element at location (i, j) shows the connection between the i-th and the j-th neurons, and an empty (white) space shows no connections. The connection topologies in (a) and (b) are the same and the only difference is the order of the neurons. Reordering neurons through spectral partitioning, clusters are formed in the red squares. Experiment shows that the connections are efficiently concentrated into several dense clusters, which can be efficiently implemented by MCD.

In a hybrid design (DSD+MCD), however, there are still some fundamental challenges need to be solved: Firstly, the size of a formed cluster should not exceed the maximum size of the available crossbars. Conventional spectral partitioning [3], however, does not consider this limitation; Secondly, it is usually difficult to cluster majority of the connections into clusters by simply performing spectral partitioning algorithm because random neural networks may not have a good clustering property. For instance, 52% of total connections in Figure 6(b) are still outside clusters.

6. Conclusion

In this paper, we summarized some EDA challenges in neuromorphic computing system design, such as the IR-drop issue and

the routing congestion and low crossbar utilization of large-scale sparse neural network implementation. We also introduced some techniques, i.e., IR-drop compensation, crossbar reduction and neural network clustering to overcome these challenges.

7. Acknowledgement

This work is partially supported by AFRL FA8750-14-1-0241, NSF CNS-1116171, and HP Lab Innovation Research Program.

8. REFERENCES

[1] D. Ciresan, U. Meier, and J. Schmidhuber, "Multi-column deep neural networks for image classification," *CVPR*, pp. 3642-3649, 2012.

[2] "IEEE Standard for Information technology--Telecommunications and information exchange between systems Local and metropolitan area networks--Specific requirements Part 11: Wireless LAN Medium Access Control (MAC) and Physical Layer (PHY) Specifications," *IEEE Std 802.11*-2012, pp. 1-2793 , 2012.

[3] U. Von Luxburg, "A tutorial on spectral clustering," *Statistics and computing*, vol. 17, pp. 395-416, 2007.

[4] Golub, G. H. and Reinsch, C., "Singular value decomposition and least squares solutions," *Numerische Mathematik*, 1970.

[5] B. Liu, *et al.*, "Reduction and IR-drop compensations techniques for reliable neuromorphic computing systems," *ICCAD*, pp. 63-70, 2014.

[6] B. Liu, *et al.*, "Digital-assisted noise-eliminating training for memristor crossbar-based analog neuromorphic computing engine," *DAC*, pp. 1-6, 2013.

[7] M. Sharad, D. Fan, and K. Roy, "Ultra low power associative computing with spin neurons and resistive crossbar memory," DAC, pp. 1-6, 2013.

[8] M. Hu, *et al*, "Hardware realization of BSB recall function using memristor crossbar arrays," DAC, pp. 498-503, 2012.

[9] P. F. López, *et al*, "A Computational Study of the Diffuse Neighbourhoods in Biological and Artificial Neural Networks," *IJCCI*, pp. 490-495, 2009.

[10] Miao Hu, *et al*, "BSB training scheme implementation on memristor-based circuit," *CISDA*, 2013.

[11] J. Liang and H. S. Wong, "Cross-point memory array without cell selectors—device characteristics and data storage pattern dependencies," , *IEEE Transactions on Electron Devices,* vol. 57, pp. 2531-2538, 2010.

[12] S. R. Lee, *et al.*, "Multi-level switching of triple-layered TaOx RRAM with excellent reliability for storage class memory," *VLSIT*, pp. 71-72, 2012.

[13] J. J. Hopfield, "Neural networks and physical systems with emergent collective computational abilities", *Proceedings of the National Academy of Sciences of the USA*, 1982.

[14] A. Asenov, S. Kaya, and A. R. Brown, "Intrinsic parameter fluctuations in decananometer MOSFETs introduced by gate line edge roughness," *Electron Devices, IEEE Transactions on,* vol. 50, pp. 1254-1260, 2003.

[15] X. Dong, *et al*, , "Circuit and microarchitecture evaluation of 3D stacking magnetic RAM (MRAM) as a universal memory replacement," *DAC* , pp. 554-559, 2008.

[16] D. Niu, Y. Chen, C. Xu, and Y. Xie, "Impact of process variations on emerging memristor," DAC, pp. 877-882, 2010.

[17] S. A. McKee, "Reflections on the memory wall," *the 1st conference on Computing frontiers*, p. 162, 2004.

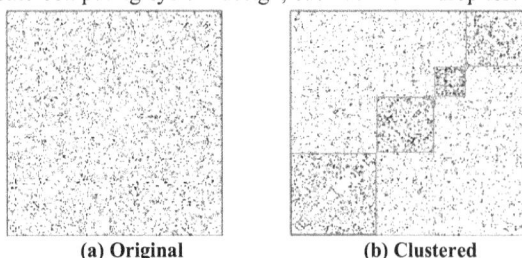

(a) Original   (b) Clustered

Figure 6. Connection matrices before and after partitioning.

Energy Efficient RRAM Spiking Neural Network for Real Time Classification

Yu Wang[1], Tianqi Tang[1], Lixue Xia[1], Boxun Li[1], Peng Gu[1], Hai Li[2], Yuan Xie[3], Huazhong Yang[1]
[1] Dept. of E.E., Tsinghua National Laboratory for Information Science and Technology (TNList),
Centre for Brain Inspired Computing Research (CBICR), Tsinghua University, Beijing, China
[2]Dept. of E.C.E., University of Pittsburgh, Pittsburgh, USA
[3]Dept. of E.C.E., University of California at Santa Barbara, California, USA
e-mail: yu-wang@mail.tsinghua.edu.cn

ABSTRACT

Inspired by the human brain's function and efficiency, neuromorphic computing offers a promising solution for a wide set of tasks, ranging from brain machine interfaces to real-time classification. The spiking neural network (SNN), which encodes and processes information with bionic spikes, is an emerging neuromorphic model with great potential to drastically promote the performance and efficiency of computing systems. However, an energy efficient hardware implementation and the difficulty of training the model significantly limit the application of the spiking neural network. In this work, we address these issues by building an SNN-based energy efficient system for real time classification with metal-oxide resistive switching random-access memory (R-RAM) devices. We implement different training algorithms of SNN, including Spiking Time Dependent Plasticity (STD-P) and Neural Sampling method. Our RRAM SNN systems for these two training algorithms show good power efficiency and recognition performance on realtime classification tasks, such as the MNIST digit recognition. Finally, we propose a possible direction to further improve the classification accuracy by boosting multiple SNNs.

1. INTRODUCTION

The era of Big Data brings new chances and new challenges in many fields especially for the applications needing real-time data processing such as the EEG classification, tracking, etc[1, 2]. These applications demonstrate huge demands for more powerful platforms with higher processing speed, lower energy consumption, and more intelligent mining algorithms. However, the classic "scaling down" method is approaching the limit, making it more and more difficult for CMOS-based computing systems to achieve considerable improvements from the device scaling [3]. Moreover, the memory bandwidth required by high-performance CPUs has also increased beyond what conventional memory architectures can efficiently provide, leading to an ever-increasing "memory wall" challenge to the efficiency of von Neumann

architecture. Therefore, innovation in both device technology and computing architecture is required to overcome these challenges.

The spiking neural network (SNN) is an emerging model which encodes and processes information with sparse time-encoded neural signals in parallel [4]. As a bio-inspired architecture abstracted from actual neural system, SNN not only provides a promising solution to deal with cognitive tasks, such as the object detection and speech recognition, but also inspires new computational paradigms beyond the von Neumann architecture and boolean logics, which can drastically promote the performance and efficiency of computing systems [5, 6].

However, an energy efficient hardware implementation and the difficulty of training the model remain as two important impediments that limit the application of the spiking neural network.

On the one hand, we need an applicable computing platform to utilize the potential ability of SNN. IBM proposes a neurosynaptic core named TrueNorth [7]. To mimic the ultra-low-power processing of brain, TrueNorth uses several approaches to reduce the power consumption. Specifically, TrueNorth uses digital messages between neurons to reduce the communication overhead and event-driven strategy to further save the energy computation [6]. However, the C-MOS based implementation still has some limitations that are hard to avoid, while some RRAM's inherent advantages can overcome these difficulties. First, on-chip SRAM, where the synapse information is stored, is a kind of volatile memory with considerable leakage power, while RRAM is non-volatile with very low leakage power [8]. Another limitation is that TrueNorth may still needs adders to provide the addition operation of neuron function, but RRAM crossbar can do the addition, or the matrix-vector multiplication, with ultra-high energy efficiency by naturally combing the computation and memory together [9, 10, 11]. Consequently, RRAM shows potential on implementing low-power spiking neural network.

On the other hand, from the perspective of algorithm, the efficient training of SNN and mapping a trained SNN onto neuromorphic hardware presents unique challenges. Recent work of SNN mainly focuses on increasing the scalability and level of realism in neural simulation by modeling and simulating thousands to billions of neurons in biological real time [12, 13]. These techniques provide promising tools to study the brain but few of them support practical cognitive applications, such as the handwritten digit recognition. Even TrueNorth [10] uses seven kinds of applications to verify its performance, but the training and mapping methods for spike-oriented network are not discussed in detail. In other words, the mapping problem and efficient training method for SNN, especially for the real-world applications, to achieve an acceptable cognitive performance is severely demanded.

These two problems are always coupled together and only by overcoming these two challenges can we actually utilize the full power of SNN for realtime data processing applications. In this paper, we discuss these two problems with the RRAM based system architecture and two different offline training algorithms of SNN. We use the MNIST digit recognition task[14] as an application example for the realtime classification. The goal of this paper is to design a RRAM-based SNN system with higher classification accuracy and to analyze its strengths and weaknesses compared with other possible implementations.

The main contribution of this paper includes:

1. We compare different training algorithms of spiking neural networks for practical cognitive tasks, including the unsupervised Spike Timing Dependent Plasticity (STDP), and the supervised method, i.e, the Neural Sampling learning method. For STDP, we can NOT provide an acceptable cognitive performance, while the performance of Neural Sampling method is comparable to ANN systems for the MNIST digit recognition task.

2. We propose an RRAM-based implementation of different architectures of spiking neural networks. The R-RAM implementation mainly includes an RRAM crossbar array working as network synapses, an analog design of the spiking neuron, an input encoding scheme, and an mapping algorithm to configure the RRAM-based spiking neural network.

3. We compare the power efficiency and recognition performance of SNN and the RRAM-based artificial neural network (ANN). The experiment results show that ANN can outperform SNN on the recognition accuracy, while SNN usually requires less power consumption. Based on these results, we discuss the possibility of using boosting methods, which combine some weak SNN learners together, to further enhance the recognition accuracy for real-world application.

The rest of this paper is organized as follows: Section II introduces the background for SNN and RRAM-based hardware architecture. We propose two kinds of RRAM-based SNN architectures with two different training algorithms and discuss the potential possibility to boost the recognition accuracy by combining multiple SNNs together in Section III. Finally, Section IV concludes the paper and proposes some future directions for RRAM-based SNN systems.

2. BACKGROUND

The spiking neural network consists of layers of spiking neurons connected by weighted synapses as shown in Fig. 1 [10]. The input data, such as images, will be encoded into the spike trains and then sent into the network. The output of the network can be treated as another representation of the input data, e.g., the corresponding classification results of the input images. According to Fig. 1 , the two most important operations in SNN are (1) the nonlinear function made by spiking neurons; (2) the matrix-vector multiplication based on the synapse weights.

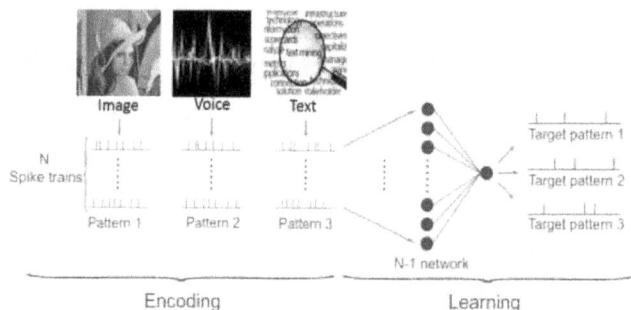

Figure 1: Spiking Neural Network System Flow. [10]

The spiking neural network, especially the two most important operations can be realized by either digital or analog circuits. Different from the digital implementation like TrueNorth, an analog implementation based on CMOS analog neuron and RRAM crossbar is introduced in our design. For the nonlinear function, specific circuits for functions like sigmoid and Leaky Integrate-and-Fire (LIF) have been proposed [15] and used in our design. Thanks to the RRAM crossbar structure, it is possible to get several orders of energy efficiency gain for the matrix-vector multiplication operation for weighted synapse computation [9]. We briefly show how to implement (1) spiking neuron unit; (2) weight matrix crossbar in the following two subsections.

2.1 Analog Spiking Neuron Unit

LIF neuron unit has an energy efficient implementation in the analog mode and the details can be found in [15]. Here we just give the diagram in Fig. 2: The capacitor C_{mem} works as an integrator to accumulate the crossbar output current I_{oj}, which passes through a mirror current source (T_1, T_2). The resistor R_{mem} functions as the leaky path. T_3 works as a digital switch which controls the reset path: Once the voltage on V_{mem} exceeds the threshold V_{th}, the output of the comparator would be set to high voltage level, the flip-flop would send a pulse to the next crossbar and at the same time, the reset path is conducted, which means the voltage on C_{mem} is reset to V_{reset}. Such design[15] is quite power efficiency with the average power consumption of $\sim$300nW. However, it may still bring considerable overhead in very large SNN system design since there are 14 transistors in one complete neuron unit.

2.2 RRAM based Crossbar for synapse weight computation

The RRAM device is a passive two-port element with variable resistance states (an example of 2D filament model of

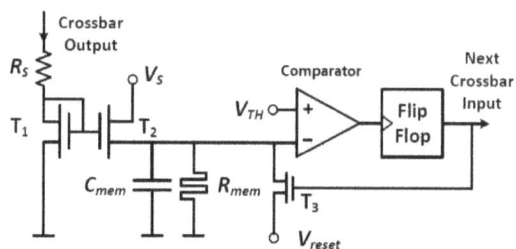

Figure 2: The Circuit Diagram of Analog Spiking Neuron.

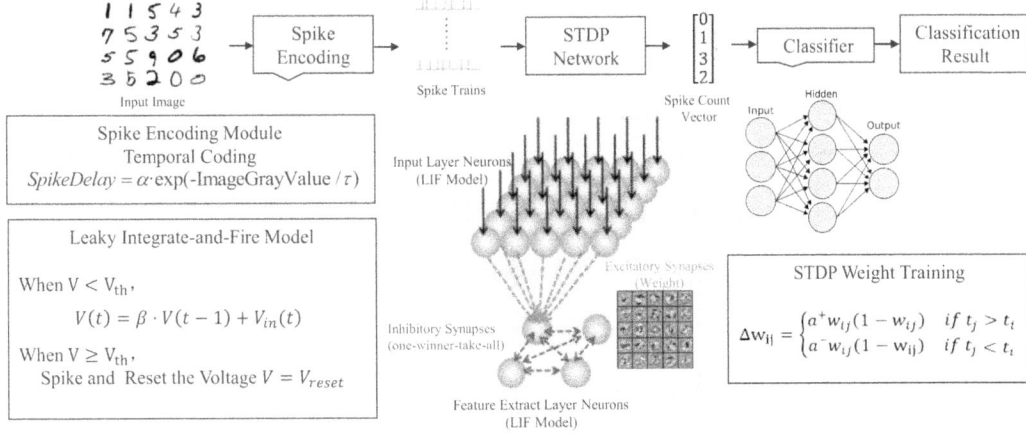

Figure 4: System Structure of Unsupervised Feature Extraction + Supervised Classifier: 2-layer STDP based SNN + 3-layer ANN. [10]

the HfO$_x$ based RRAM is shown in Fig. 3(a)). The most attractive feature of RRAM devices is that they can be used to build resistive cross-point structure, which is also known as the RRAM crossbar array (Fig. 3(b)). Compared with other non-volatile memories like flash, the RRAM crossbar array can naturally transfer the weighted combination of input signals to output voltages and realize the matrix-vector multiplication efficiently by reducing the computation complexity from O(n^2) to O(1).

As shown in Fig. 3(b), the relationship between the input voltage vector ($\vec{V_i}$) and output voltage vector ($\vec{V_o}$) can be expressed as follows [16]:

$$V_{o,j} = \sum_k c_{k,j} \cdot V_{i,k} \tag{1}$$

where k ($k = 1,2,..,N$) and j ($j = 1,2,..,M$) are the index numbers of input and output ports, and the matrix parameter $c_{k,j}$ can be represented by the conductivity of the RRAM device ($g_{k,j}$) and the load resistors (g_s) as:

$$c_{k,j} = \frac{g_{k,j}}{g_s + \sum_{l=1}^{N} g_{k,l}} \tag{2}$$

The continuous variable resistance states of RRAM devices enable a wide range of weight matrices that can be represented by the crossbar. The precision of RRAM crossbar based computation may be limited by Non-Ideal factors,

such as process variations, IR drop[17], drifting of RRAM resistance[18], etc. However, SNN only requires low precision of single synaptic value, meanwhile the binary input and LIF operation also alleviate the precision requirement of matrix vector multiplication. Therefore, the RRAM crossbar array is a promising solution to realize matrix-vector multiplication for synapse weight computation in neural networks.

3. RRAM-BASED SPIKING LEARNING SYSTEM

For a SNN system used for realtime classification applications, an offline training scheme is needed to decide the weights of the neural networks. i.e. coefficients in the crossbar matrix. To our best knowledge, there are two kinds of SNN training methods to build up classification systems: (1) Unsupervised SNN training method, for example, Spike Timing Dependent Plasticity (STDP), is first introduced for extracting features; then the supervised classifier is introduced to finish the classification task. (2) First train an equivalent ANN using the gradient-based method, then transfer ANN to SNN and map SNN to the RRAM-based system for real-world applications. Both offline SNN systems are implemented with RRAM crossbar arrays [10, 11], and the details are shown in the following subsections.

3.1 Unsupervised Feature Extraction + Supervised Classifier

As an unsupervised method, STDP is mainly used for feature extraction. We can not build a complete classification system only based on STDP. A classifier is usually required for practical recognition tasks. Therefore, when mapping the system onto hardware, just as shown in Fig. 4, a five-layer neural network system is introduced: a two-layer spiking based neural network and a three-layer artificial neural network.

The first two layer SNN is trained using an unsupervised learning rule: Spike Timing Dependent Plasticity (STDP) [19], which updates the synaptic weights according to relative spiking time of pre- and post-synaptic neurons. The learning rate is decided by the time interval: the closer the distance between pre- and post-synaptic spikes, the larger the learning rate. The weight updating direction is decided by which neuron spikes first: for the excitatory neuron, if

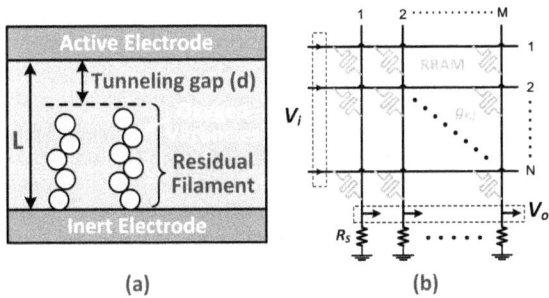

Figure 3: (a). Physical model of the HfO$_x$ based RRAM. (b). Structure of the RRAM Crossbar Array. [11]

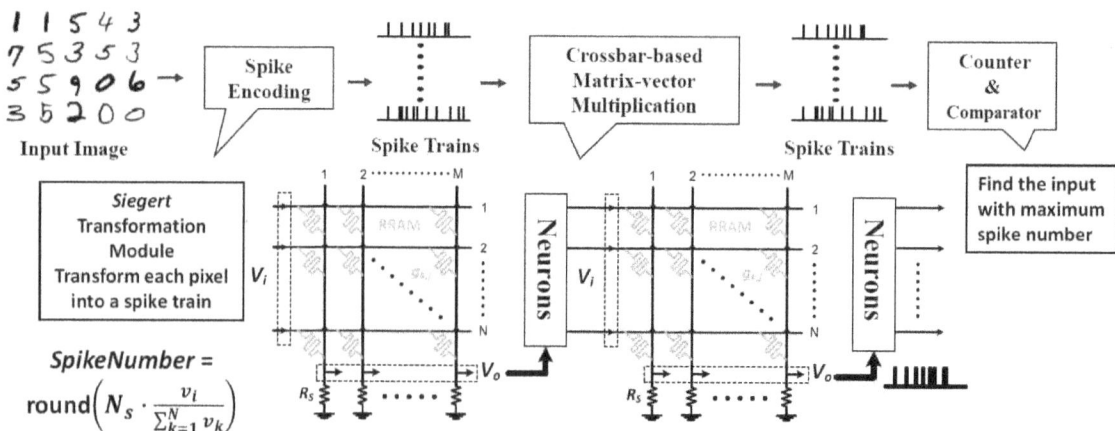

Figure 5: System Structure: Transferring ANN to SNN – Neural Sampling Method. [11]

the post-synaptic neuron spikes later, the synapse will be strengthened; otherwise, it will be weakened. When every synaptic weight no longer changes or is set to 0/1, the learning process is finished.

There is a converting module between the two layer SNN and 3-layer ANN to convert the spike trains into the spiking count vectors. Then the spike count vectors are sent into the following layers of the network (the 3-layer ANN). We use a 3-layer ANN as a classifier to process the features extracted from the input data by the previous 2-layer SNN. We use the CMOS analog neuron in Section II for the LIF neuron; and the RRAM crossbar for synaptic computation in both 2-layer SNN (vector addition) and 3-layer ANN (matrix vector multiplication).

An experiment is made on MNIST digit recognition task to evaluate the RRAM-based SNN system performance. The training algorithm is implemented on the CPU platform where LIF neurons are used in the first two layers and the sigmoid neurons are used in the last three layers. For the testing process (forward propagation of neural networks), we use circuit level simulation where the weight matrix is mapped to RRAM-based crossbar. Since the input images are 28×28 sized 256-level gray images. The five-layer spiking neural network system has five layers of neurons in all and the experiment result with the network size of "784×100SNN + 100×50×10ANN" shows the recognition accuracy of 91.5% on CPU platform and 90% on RRAM-based crossbar model (circuit simulation result). The performance is a little worse than that of the three-layer ANN sized "784×100×10" with the recognition accuracy of 94.3% on CPU platform and 92% on RRAM-based crossbar model (circuit simulation result). Moreover, when we change the supervised classifier into a two-layer SVM and make the system of "784×50 STDP + 50×10 SVM", the recognition accuracy on CPU platform only reaches 90% while the traditional "784×50 PCA + 50×10 SVM" gets the accuracy of 94%. As PCA is usually the baseline for evaluating the performance of feature extraction, STDP does **NOT** demonstrate itself as an exciting method for MNIST digit recognition tasks.

We observe that ANN consumes more power than SNN when ANN use similar or even smaller number of neurons, when both ANN and SNN use RRAM crossbar to implement matrix vector multiplication. Here we only consider the crossbar and the neuron power consumption. For example, the proposed "784×100 SNN + 100×50×10 ANN" consumes 327.36mW on RRAM while the power consumption

increases to 2273.60mW when we directly use "784×100×10 ANN". The power (energy) saving of SNN comparing to ANN mainly comes from the different coding scheme. The input voltage of SNN can be binary since it transforms the numeric information into the temporal domain, so there is no need for SNN to hold a large voltage range to represent multiple input states as implemented in ANN. ANN needs input voltages of 0.9V, but SNN can work with much lower voltage supply (0.1V). Furthermore, binary coding in SNN can avoid the usage of large number of AD/DA on the input and output interfaces. The AD/DA power consumption, which is not considered here, consumes a considerable large portion of total power consumption in the RRAM based NN systems[20].

3.2 Transferring ANN to SNN – Neural Sampling Method

The Neural Sampling method provides a way to transfer ANN to SNN, thus offering a useful training scheme on classification tasks. An equivalent transformation is made between the nonlinear function (named Sigert function, which is similar to sigmoid function) of ANN and the Leaky Integrate-and-Fire (LIF) neuron of SNN. Therefore, it is possible to first train the ANN made up of the stacked Restricted Boltzmann Machine (RBM) structure using Contrastive Divergence (CD) method. In this way, a satisfying recognition accuracy of ANN can be first achieved. And then, the spike-based stacked RBM network with the same synaptic weight matrices can also be implemented for the classification tasks. The system structure is shown in Fig. 5 [11].

Since spike trains propagate in the spiking neural network, original input $x = [x_1, \cdots, x_N]$ should be mapped to spike trains $X(t) = [X_1(t), \cdots, X_N(t)]$ before running the test samples where $X_i(t)$ is a binary train with only two states 0/1. For the ith input channel, the spike train is made of N_t spike pulses with each pulse width T_0, which implies that the spike train lasts for the length of time $N_t \cdot T_0$. Suppose the spike number of all input channels during the given time $N_t \cdot T_0$ is N_s, then the spike count N_i of the ith channel is allocated as:

$$N_i = \sum_{k=0}^{N_t-1} X_i(kT_0) = \text{round}(N_s \cdot \frac{v_i}{\sum_{k=1}^{N} v_k}) \qquad (3)$$

192

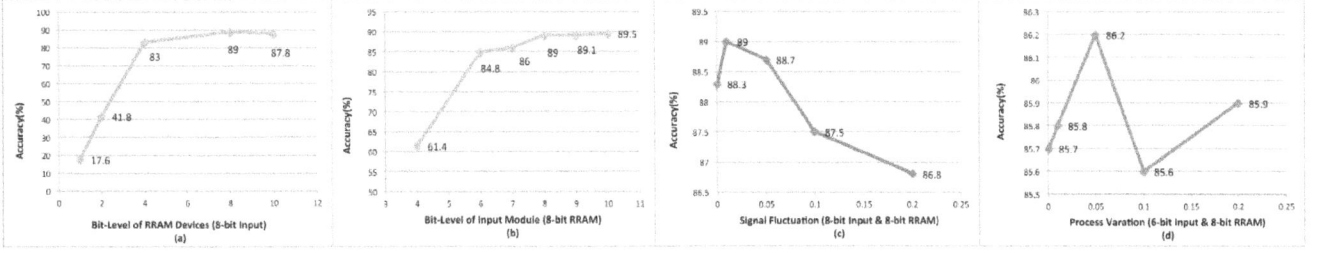

Figure 6: Recognition accuracy under (a). different bit-level of RRAM devices (b). different bit-level of input module, and (c) different degrees of input signal fluctuation (d) different degrees of process variation of RRAM devices. [11]

which implies

$$\frac{N_i}{N_s} = \frac{v_i}{\sum_{i=1}^{N} v_i} \qquad (4)$$

Then the N_i spikes of the ith channel is randomly set on the N_t time intervals. For an ideal mapping, we would like to have $N_i << N_t$ to keep the spike sparsity on the time dimension. However, for the speed efficiency, we would like the running time $N_t \cdot T_0$ to be short. Here, T_0 is defined by the physical clock, i.e. the clock of the pulse generator. which implies that we can only optimize N_t directly. Here, we define the bit level of the input as

$$\log\left(\frac{N_t}{\text{mean}(N_i)}\right) \qquad (5)$$

which evaluates the tradeoff between time efficiency and the accuracy performance.

We train the SNN with the size of $784 \times 500 \times 500 \times 10$. And the parameters are shown in Table 1. The experiment results show that the recognition accuracy of MNIST dataset is 95.4% on the CPU platform and 91.2% on the ideal RRAM-based hardware implementation. The recognition performance decreases about 4% because it is impossible to satisfy with $N_t << N_s$ on the RRAM platform.

We show the results for recognition under different bit level quantization of input signal and RRAM devices, together with RRAM process variation and input signal fluctuation. The simulation results in Fig. 6 (a) show that a 8-bit RRAM device is able to realize a recognition accuracy of nearly 90%. The simulation results in Fig 6 (b) shows that the input signal above 6-bit level achieves satisfying recognition accuracy (>85%). Based on the 8-bit RRAM result, different levels of signal fluctuation are added on the 8-bit input signal. The result shown in Fig 6 (c) demonstrates that the performance of accuracy just decreases ~3% given 20% variation. Fig. 6 (d) shows that when RRAM device is configured to 8-bit level with the 6-bit level input, the performance does not decrease under 20% process variation. The sparsity of the spike train leads to the system robustness, making it insensitive to the input fluctuation and process variation.

Table 1: Important Parameters of the SNN System

Network Size	$784 \times 500 \times 500 \times 10$
Number of Input Spike (N_s)	2000
Number of Pulse Interval (N_t)	128
Input pulse Voltage (V)	1V
The Pulse Width (T_0)	1ns

The power consumption of the system is mainly contributed by three parts: the crossbar, the comparator and the $R_{mem}C_{mem}$ leaky path. The simulation results show that the power consumption is about 3.5 mW on average. However, it takes $N_t = 128$ cycles with the physical clock $T_0 = 1ns$. Though input conversion from numeral values to spike trains leads to about 100X clock rate decrease, the system is able to **complete the recognition task in real time** (~1μs/sample) thanks to the short latency of RRAM device.

3.3 Discussion on How to Boost the Accuracy of SNN

The experiment results in the above subsections show that the recognition accuracy will decay after transferring an ANN to a SNN. However, due to the ultra-high integration density of the RRAM devices and the 0/1 based interfaces of SNN, SNN tends to consume much less circuit area and power compared with ANN. This result inspires us that we may integrate multiple SNN with the same or even less circuit area and power consumption of ANN, and combine these SNNs together to boost the accuracy and robustness of the SNN system.

Previously, we have proposed an ensemble method to boost the accuracy of RRAM-based ANN systems [20], named SAAB (Serial Array Adaptive Boosting), which is inspired by the AdaBoost method [21]. The basic idea of AdaBoost, which is also its major advantage, is to train a series of learners, such as ANNs or SNNs, sequentially, and every time we train a new learner, we try to "force" the new learner to pay more attention to the "hard" samples incorrectly classified by previous trained learners in the training set. The proposed technique can improve the accuracy of ANN by up to 13.05% on average and ensure the system performance under noisy conditions in approximate computation applications.

SAAB boost the computation accuracy at the cost of consuming more power and circuit area. As SNN usually consumes much less area and power compared with the ANN, there is a chance to integrate multiple SNNs under the same circuit resource limitation of ANN. And these SNNs can be boosted together by the similar idea of SAAB. However, the inherent attributions of SNN systems should be considered when designing the boosting algorithm. According to our observation, there are two types of errors in the SNN-based classification tasks: (i). a "traditional" type: more than one neuron in the output layer spikes and the neuron spiking the most is not the target neuron; and (ii). a "special" type of SNN: no neuron in the output layer spikes; It is interesting to observe that most of the wrong trials are the "special" type and it can be reduced slightly when increasing the input spike counts. We regard such samples as "the difficult classifying cases". When seeking for the possibility to make up the performance loss after transferring ANN to SNN with a boosting-based method, this problem should be considered.

4. CONCLUSIONS AND FUTURE WORK

In this paper, we analyzed the possibility of designing R-RAM based SNN system for the realtime classification. Two different SNN systems based on different training algorithms are shown, including the training methods and hardware architecture. We also compare the energy efficiency and accuracy for MNIST application of both systems. Finally, we discuss the possibility of how to boost the accuracy of SNN.

For future work, besides the boosting algorithm for multiple SNNs, we propose the following research directions: (1) Design the basic core structure for large SNN "processor" based on RRAM crossbars. For the two proposed SNN systems in this paper, we design it following the design style of fixed accelerators without considering the scalability or reconfigurability for bigger or different problems. (2) Design on-line learning RRAM based SNN system. To achieve intelligent systems, we need the system to learn by itself. How to use the inherent learning feature of RRAM to build up on-line learning computing system for real world application remains an interesting problem.

Acknowledgment

This work was supported by 973 project 2013CB329000, National Natural Science Foundation of China (No. 61373026), the Importation and Development of High-Caliber Talents Project of Beijing Municipal Institutions, and Tsinghua University Initiative Scientific Research Program.

5. REFERENCES

[1] C. Guger, H. Ramoser, and G. Pfurtscheller, "Real-time eeg analysis with subject-specific spatial patterns for a brain-computer interface (bci)," *Rehabilitation Engineering, IEEE Transactions on*, vol. 8, no. 4, pp. 447–456, 2000.

[2] G. A. Carpenter, S. Grossberg, and J. H. Reynolds, "Artmap: Supervised real-time learning and classification of nonstationary data by a self-organizing neural network," *Neural networks*, vol. 4, no. 5, pp. 565–588, 1991.

[3] H. Esmaeilzadeh, E. Blem, R. St Amant, K. Sankaralingam, and D. Burger, "Dark silicon and the end of multicore scaling," in *ISCA*, 2011, pp. 365–376.

[4] E. Neftci, S. Das, B. Pedroni, K. Kreutz-Delgado, and G. Cauwenberghs, "Event-driven contrastive divergence for spiking neuromorphic systems," *Frontiers in neuroscience*, vol. 7, 2013.

[5] T. Masquelier and S. J. Thorpe, "Unsupervised learning of visual features through spike timing dependent plasticity," *PLoS computational biology*, vol. 3, no. 2, p. e31, 2007.

[6] S. K. Esser, A. Andreopoulos, R. Appuswamy, P. Datta, D. Barch, A. Amir, J. Arthur, A. Cassidy, M. Flickner, P. Merolla *et al.*, "Cognitive computing systems: Algorithms and applications for networks of neurosynaptic cores," in *Neural Networks (IJCNN), The 2013 International Joint Conference on*. IEEE, 2013, pp. 1–10.

[7] P. A. Merolla, J. V. Arthur, R. Alvarez-Icaza, A. S. Cassidy, J. Sawada, F. Akopyan, B. L. Jackson, N. Imam, C. Guo, Y. Nakamura *et al.*, "A million spiking-neuron integrated circuit with a scalable communication network and interface," *Science*, vol. 345, no. 6197, pp. 668–673, 2014.

[8] B. Govoreanu, G. Kar, Y. Chen, V. Paraschiv, S. Kubicek, A. Fantini, I. Radu, L. Goux, S. Clima, R. Degraeve *et al.*, "10× 10nm 2 hf/hfo x crossbar resistive ram with excellent performance, reliability and low-energy operation," in *Electron Devices Meeting (IEDM), 2011 IEEE International*. IEEE, 2011, pp. 31–6.

[9] B. Li, Y. Shan, M. Hu, Y. Wang, Y. Chen, and H. Yang, "Memristor-based approximated computation," in *ISLPED*, 2013, pp. 242–247.

[10] T. Tang, R. Luo, B. Li, H. Li, Y. Wang, and H. Yang, "Energy efficient spiking neural network design with rram devices," in *Integrated Circuits (ISIC), 2014 14th International Symposium on*. IEEE, 2014, pp. 268–271.

[11] T. Tang, L. Xia, B. Li, R. Luo, Y. Wang, Y. Chen, and H. Yang, "Spiking neural network with rram : Can we use it for real-world application?" in *DATE*, 2015.

[12] E. Painkras, L. A. Plana, J. Garside, S. Temple, F. Galluppi, C. Patterson, D. R. Lester, A. D. Brown, and S. B. Furber, "Spinnaker: A 1-w 18-core system-on-chip for massively-parallel neural network simulation," *Solid-State Circuits, IEEE Journal of*, vol. 48, no. 8, pp. 1943–1953, 2013.

[13] R. Wang, T. J. Hamilton, J. Tapson, and A. van Schaik, "An fpga design framework for large-scale spiking neural networks," in *ISCAS*, 2014, pp. 457–460.

[14] Y. LeCun and C. Cortes, "The mnist database of handwritten digits," 1998.

[15] G. Indiveri, "A low-power adaptive integrate-and-fire neuron circuit," in *ISCAS (4)*, 2003, pp. 820–823.

[16] M. Hu, H. Li, Q. Wu, and G. S. Rose, "Hardware realization of bsb recall function using memristor crossbar arrays," in *DAC*, 2012, pp. 498–503.

[17] P. Gu, B. Li, T. Tang, S. Yu, Y. Wang, and H. Yang, "Technological exploration of rram crossbar array for matrix-vector multiplication," in *ASP-DAC*, 2015.

[18] B. Li, Y. Wang, Y. Chen, H. H. Li, and H. Yang, "Ice: inline calibration for memristor crossbar-based computing engine," in *DATE*, 2014.

[19] S. Song, K. D. Miller, and L. F. Abbott, "Competitive hebbian learning through spike-timing-dependent synaptic plasticity," *Nature neuroscience*, vol. 3, no. 9, pp. 919–926, 2000.

[20] B. Li, L. Xia, P. Gu, Y. Wang, and H. Yang, "Merging the interface: Power, area and accuracy co-optimization for rram crossbar-based mixed-signal computing system," in *DAC*, 2015.

[21] Z.-H. Zhou, *Ensemble methods: foundations and algorithms*. CRC Press, 2012.

On-chip Sparse Learning with Resistive Cross-point Array Architecture

Shimeng Yu
School of ECEE, Arizona State University
Tempe, AZ 85287
480-965-1581
shimeng.yu@asu.edu

Yu Cao
School of ECEE, Arizona State University
Tempe, AZ 85287
480-965-1472
ycao@asu.edu

ABSTRACT

Unsupervised learning with sparse coding is widely adopted in applications of feature extraction, pattern classification, and compressive sensing. However, even with the state-of-the-art hardware platform of CPUs/GPUs, solving a sparse coding problem is still expensive in computation. In this paper, the resistive cross-point array architecture (CPA) is proposed to achieve on-chip acceleration of sparse coding, especially the matrix/vector operations that are intensively used in the algorithm. Learning and recognition experiments are conducted with the MNIST handwriting dataset. By co-optimizing the algorithm, architecture, circuit, and resistive synaptic devices, SPICE simulation at 65nm demonstrates that the CPA is able to accelerate sparse coding computation by more than 3800X, compared to software running on an 8-core CPU. Furthermore, this work investigates the technological limitations of a realistic resistive CPA, including reduced ON/OFF range of synaptic devices, nonlinearity in programming, spatial and temporal variations, and interconnect parasitics. The results illustrate both enormous opportunities and practical barriers of resistive CPA in real-time learning on a chip.

1. INTRODUCTION

The biophysical neural system has been a rich source of inspiration for computing beyond the conventional von Neumann architecture. As a bio-plausible model of the visual cortex, sparse coding was successfully developed to reconstruct data vectors using sparse linear combinations of basis vectors [1]-[3]. Such a representation has been adopted in numerous domains, such as image recognition, text mining, and audio processing.

Sparse coding aims to minimize the objective function, $\sum_i \| D \cdot Z_i - x_i \|^2 + \lambda |Z_i|_1$, where x_i is an input vector, λ is the regularization parameter, D is called the dictionary, and Z_i is the feature vector which is assumed to be sparse. Different from traditional feature extraction methods, the D matrix is non-orthogonal and over-complete and thus, far less restrictive in representing input. To quickly reach a stable sparse representation for x_i, state-of-the-art algorithms apply iterative, parallel, or stochastic methods for the two most computationally intensive

tasks: updating the feature vector Z and updating the dictionary D. In this paper, we focus on the Iterative Shrinking-Thresholding Algorithm (ISTA [2]) to update Z due to its inherent parallelism, and the Stochastic Gradient Descent (SGD [3]) to update D exploiting stochasticity for greater efficiency:

Update Z via ISTA: $\sum_i \| D \cdot Z_i - x_i \|^2 + \lambda |Z_i|_1$, where $h_{\lambda/L}$ is the soft thresholding function, and $r_t \triangleq D_t \cdot Z_t - X_t$ is the residual error of data presentation (r).

Update D via SGD: $D_{t+1} \leftarrow D_t - \eta_t \cdot \Delta D_t$, where η_t is the learning rate and $\Delta D_t = r_t \cdot Z_t^T$.

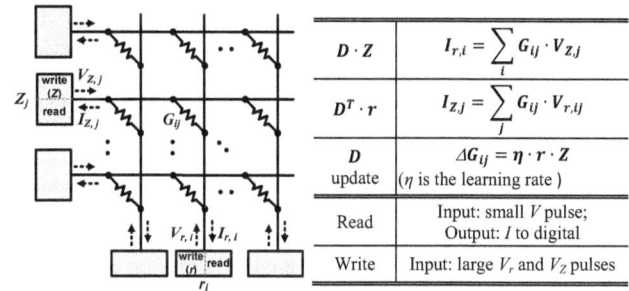

$D \cdot Z$		$I_{r,i} = \sum_i G_{ij} \cdot V_{z,j}$
$D^T \cdot r$		$I_{z,j} = \sum_j G_{ij} \cdot V_{r,ij}$
D update		$\Delta G_{ij} = \eta \cdot r \cdot Z$ (η is the learning rate)
Read		Input: small V pulse; Output: I to digital
Write		Input: large V_r and V_Z pulses

Figure 1. The structure and operations of the resistive CPA.

These learning algorithms are typically implemented in software, and run on a general-purpose CPU/GPU. Limited by the sequential architecture of today's microprocessors, they suffer from a long computing time, especially in dealing with a large D matrix. Thus, it is desirable to have a special hardware that accelerates the learning process beyond such limitations.

2. ACCELERATION WITH CPA

The resistive crosspoint array structure (CPA), shown in Fig. 1, was recently proposed as a promising solution for learning in hardware neural networks [4]. The iterative solution to the sparse coding problem can be realized by mapping the matrix D onto the resistive synaptic device (RSD) [5], and learning takes place through the update step. The quantity X (or r) is associated with one side of the array and Z with the other side. At each cross point, the conductance (G) of a synaptic device, which is non-volatile and compatible with CMOS [5], represents the weight. G of a RSD is increased (or decreased) by a positive (or negative) voltage pulse. The amount of change depends on the voltage value and the pulse width. The basic functions of the CPA include:

Read for Matrix Product: When a voltage is input from $Z(V_{z,j})$, the output current at x_i is $I_{X,i} = \sum G_{ij} \cdot V_{z,j}$. If G encodes D, then a Read corresponds to sensing the current which encodes $D \cdot Z$, which takes in parallel.

Write to Update D: The conductance of the entire array is updated in parallel, rather than sequential operations.

To demonstrate the acceleration, the hardware platform of the resistive CPA is implemented with 65nm standard cells for the digital periphery. For software, ISTA and SGD algorithms are run on a 3.4 GHz CPU with 8 cores. The date set is the handwritten digits, MNIST [6], containing 60,000 training images and 10,000 testing images. The dimension of X is 100 for each 10x10 image patch, and the dimension of Z is 400. The computing is fixed-point, with 6 bits (64 levels in RSD) to represent D and 4 bits (16 levels in the digital periphery) to represent x or z. The non-truncated software results in 97% recognition accuracy and the truncated CPA results in comparable accuracy of 95%.

Table 1. Computation time in software and CPA schemes.

	CPU	CPA
$D \cdot Z$	4.65 ms	2 μs
$D^T \cdot r$	12.6 ms	2 μs
Update D	26.4 μs	336 ns
Total	17.3 ms	4.56 μs
Acceleration		3800X

Table 1 evaluates the computation time with the 65nm resistive CPA, for one image patch. In the hardware scheme, updating z takes 40ns, which consists of 8 special read operations, and updating D consumes 336ns due to a single write operation. Note that per image patch, updating z iterates 100 times for ISTA, and updating D occurs only once. Through dedicated hardware circuits and parallelization, the resistive CPA accelerates the computing by 3800X, compared to the software implementation.

3. TECHNOLOGICAL LIMITATIONS

With an ideal resistive synaptic device (i.e., a linear update of the weight with input voltage pulse), Section 2 demonstrate tremendous speed-up with the CPA architecture. However, in reality, this assumption may not hold. Figure 2(a) shows the microscopic top-view and the device structure of the fabricated $TaOx/TiO_2$ based synaptic device [7]. By applying positive pulses and negative pulses on the RSD device, long-term potentiation (LTP) and long-term depression (LTD) can increase and decrease the conductance, respectively, as shown in Fig. 2(b). It is observed that a non-linear behavior of LTP and LTD commonly exists in today's synaptic devices, possibly due to the inherent drift and diffusion dynamics of the ions/vacancies in these materials. Such significant non-linearity is common among other types of RSDs.

Besides the non-linearity in weight update, another realistic characteristic deviated from an ideal device is the limited ON/OFF weight ratio. The off-state conductance is not perfectly zero, as shown in Fig. 2(b), while the ideal synaptic device

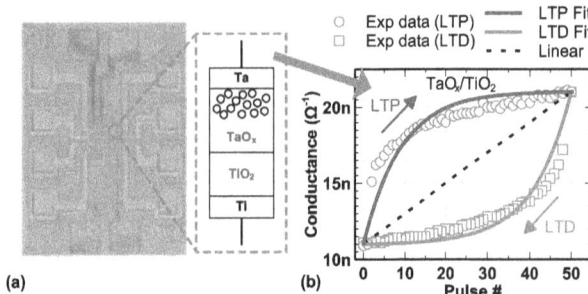

Figure 2. Non-linearity, limited ON/OFF and variations in a realistic synaptic device (RSD) [7].

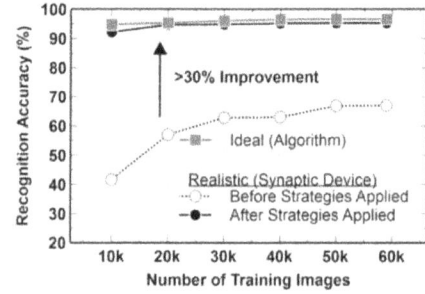

Figure 3. Mitigation of the impact of non-ideal RSD factors on learning accuracy. The solutions include algorithm adaptation for the non-linearity and hardware redundancy for variations.

assumes that the minimum weight is zero. In addition, the device variation is always a concern for the emerging devices. The RSD variation has two aspects, one is the spatial variation from device to device, and the other is the temporal variation from pulse to pulse. All of these realistic device characteristics may degrade the learning performance of the systems. Figure 3 shows the poor recognition accuracy (65%) of the MNIST handwriting digits with the realistic synaptic device behavior, compared to the accuracy with the software approach (97%). Increasing the number of training data sets has limited compensation on the loss of accuracy. To mitigate their impact, a suite of solutions are proposed, ranging from the tuning of the sparse coding algorithm to incorporate the non-linearity, the addition of a dummy column in the CPA to cancel the off state current, and redundant RSD cells to reduce variations. With the proposed strategies applied, the recognition accuracy can increase back to 95%.

As the RSD cells are integrated into an array, further attention should be paid to the increasing parasitics of metal wires. Fortunately, their impact can be well controlled by appropriately sizing up the wire dimension, at an affordable expense of area, energy and latency [8].

4. SUMMARY

The rapid advances in machine learning and data analysis demand much higher computation power that is not possible through conventional technology scaling. The only solution is to perform the computation directly in hardware, with disruptive device and design technologies. The resistive cross-point array presents such a promise. More research is in urgent need to overcome practical limitations by the device properties, in order to deliver a large-scale, real-time learning capability on a chip.

5. REFERENCES

[1] B. A. Olshausen, D. J. Field, "Emergence of simple-cell receptive field properties by learning a sparse code for natural images," *Nature*, vol. 381, no. 6583, pp. 607-609, 1996.

[2] I. Daubechies, M. Defrise, and C. De Mol, "An iterative thresholding algorithm for linear inverse problems with a sparsity constraint," *Communications on pure and applied mathematics*, vol. 57, no. 11, pp. 1413-1457, 2004.

[3] L. Bottou, O. Bousquet, "The tradeoffs of large-scale learning," *Optimization for Machine Learning*, pp. 351, 2011.

[4] J. Seo, B. Lin, M. Kim, P.-Y. Chen, D. Kadetotad, Z. Xu, A. Mohanty, S. Vrudhula, S. Yu, J. Ye, Y. Cao, "On-chip sparse learning acceleration with CMOS and resistive synaptic devices," submitted to *IEEE Trans. Nanotechnology.*

[5] D. Kuzum, S. Yu, and H.-S. P. Wong, "Synaptic electronics: materials, devices and applications," *Nanotechnology*, vol. 24, 382001, 2013.

[6] Y. LeCun, C. Cortes, *The MNIST database of handwritten digits*, 1998.

[7] I.-T. Wang, Y.-C. Lin, Y.-F. Wang, C.-W Hsu, and T.-H. Hou, "3D synaptic architecture with ultralow sub-10 fJ energy per spike for neuromorphic computation," *International Electron Device Meeting*, 2014.

[8] P.-Y. Chen, D. Kadetotad, Z. Xu, A. Mohanty, B. Lin, J. Ye, S. Vrudhula, J. Seo, Y. Cao, S. Yu, "Technology-design co-optimization of resistive cross-point array for accelerating learning algorithms on chip," *Design, Automation & Test in Europe*, 2015.

Origami: A Convolutional Network Accelerator

Lukas Cavigelli, David Gschwend, Christoph Mayer, Samuel Willi, Beat Muheim, Luca Benini
Integrated Systems Laboratory, ETH Zurich
Gloriastr. 53, 8092 Zurich, Switzerland
{cavigelli, benini}@iis.ee.ethz.ch, {davidgs, chmayer, willis, muheim}@ee.ethz.ch

ABSTRACT

Today advanced computer vision (CV) systems of ever increasing complexity are being deployed in a growing number of application scenarios with strong real-time and power constraints. Current trends in CV clearly show a rise of neural network-based algorithms, which have recently broken many object detection and localization records. These approaches are very flexible and can be used to tackle many different challenges by only changing their parameters. In this paper, we present the first convolutional network accelerator which is scalable to network sizes that are currently only handled by workstation GPUs, but remains within the power envelope of embedded systems. The architecture has been implemented on 3.09 mm^2 core area in UMC 65 nm technology, capable of a throughput of 274 GOp/s at 369 GOp/s/W with an external memory bandwidth of just 525 MB/s full-duplex – a decrease of more than 90% from previous work.

Categories and Subject Descriptors

B.7.1 [**Integrated Circuits**]: Types and Design Styles – *Algorithms implemented in hardware, VLSI;* I.2.6 [**Artificial Intelligence**]: Learning – *Connectionism and neural nets.*

Keywords

Machine learning; pattern recognition; classification; computer vision; signal processing; accelerator; VLSI design.

1. INTRODUCTION

Today computer vision technologies are used with great success in many application areas, solving real-world problems in entertainment systems, robotics and surveillance [1]. More and more researchers and engineers are tackling action and object recognition problems with the help of brain-inspired algorithms, featuring *many stages* of feature detectors and classifiers, with lots of parameters that are optimized using the wealth of data that has recently become available. These "deep learning" techniques are achieving record-breaking results on very challenging problems and datasets, outperforming more mature concepts trying to model the specific problem at hand [2]–[4] or joining forces with them [5]. Convolutional Networks (ConvNets) are a prime example of this powerful, yet conceptually simple paradigm. They can be applied to various data sources and perform best when the information is spatially or temporally well-localized, but still has to be seen in a more global context such as in images.

As a testimony of the success of deep learning approaches, several

research programs have been launched, even by major global industrial players (e.g. Facebook, Google, Baidu, Microsoft, IBM), pushing towards deploying services based on brain-inspired machine learning to their customers within a production environment [3], [5], [6]. These companies are mainly interested in running such algorithms on powerful compute clusters in large data centers.

With the increasing number of imaging devices the importance of digital signal processing in imaging continues to grow. The amount of on- and near-sensor computation is rising to thousands of operations per pixel, requiring powerful energy-efficient digital signal processing solutions, often co-integrated with the imaging circuitry itself to reduce overall system cost and size. Such embedded vision systems that extract meaning from imaging data are enabled by more and more energy-efficient, low-cost integrated parallel processing engines (multi-core DSPs, GPUs, platform FPGAs). This permits a new generation of distributed computer vision systems, which can bring huge value to a vast range of applications by reducing the costly data transmission, forwarding only the desired information [1], [7].

Many opportunities for challenging research and innovative applications will pan out from the evolution of advanced embedded video processing and future situational awareness systems. As opposed to conventional visual monitoring systems (CCTVs, IP cameras) that send the video data to a data center to be stored and processed, embedded *smart* cameras process the image data directly on board. This can significantly reduce the amount of data to be transmitted and the required human intervention – the sources of the two most expensive aspects of video surveillance [8]. Embedding convolutional network classifiers in distributed computer vision systems, seems a natural direction of evolution, However, deep neural networks are commonly known for their demand of computing power, making it challenging to bring this computational load within the power envelope of embedded systems – in fact, most state-of-the-art neural networks are currently not only trained, but also evaluated on workstations with powerful GPUs to achieve reasonable performance.

In this paper we present Origami, a convolution network accelerator ASIC, featuring a new architecture which is scalable to TOp/s performance while remaining area- and energy-efficient and keeping I/O throughput within the limits of economical packages and low power budgets.

Organization of the Paper: Section 2 shortly introduces convolutional networks and highlights the need for acceleration. Previous work is investigated in Section 3, discussing available software, FPGA and ASIC implementations and explaining the selection of our design objectives. In Section 4 we present our architecture and its properties. We discuss our results in Section 5 and subsequently conclude the paper with Section 6.

2. CONVOLUTIONAL NETWORKS

Convolutional Networks are always built from the same few basic building blocks: Convolution layers, activation layers and pooling layers. One sequence of convolution, activation and pooling is considered a *stage*, and modern, deep networks often consist of multiple stages. The convolutional network itself is used as a feature extractor, transforming raw data into a higher-dimensional, more meaningful representation. ConvNets particularly preserve locality through their limited filter size, which makes them very suitable for visual data (e.g., in a street scene the pixels in the top left corner contain little information on what is going on in the bottom right corner of an image, but if there are pixels showing the sky all around some segment of the image, this segment is certainly not a car). The feature extraction is then followed by a classifier, such as a normal neural network or a support vector machine.

A stage of a ConvNet can be captured mathematically as

$$\mathbf{y}^{(\ell)} = \text{conv}\big(\mathbf{x}^{(\ell)}, \mathbf{k}^{(\ell)}\big) + \mathbf{b}^{(\ell)}, \qquad \mathbf{x}^{(\ell+1)} = \text{pool}\big(\text{act}\big(\mathbf{y}^{(\ell)}\big)\big),$$

$$y(o,j,i) = b(o) + \sum_{c \in \mathcal{C}_{in}} \sum_{(\Delta j, \Delta i) \in \mathcal{S}_k} k(o,c,\Delta j, \Delta i) x(c, j - \Delta j, i - \Delta i),$$

where ℓ indexes the stages, o indexes the output channels $\mathcal{C}_{out}$ and c indexes the input channels $\mathcal{C}_{in}$. The pixel is identified by the tuple (j,i) and $\mathcal{S}_k$ denotes the support of the filters. In recently published networks, the pooling operation determines the maximum in a small neighborhood for each channel, often on 2×2 areas and with a stride of 2×2. The activation function is applied point-wise for every pixel and every channel. A currently popular choice is the rectified linear unit (ReLU), which designates the function $x \mapsto \max(0, x)$. The activation function introduces non-linearity into neural networks, giving them the potential to be more powerful than linear methods. Typical filter sizes range from 5×5 to 9×9, sometimes even 11×11 [2], [4], [9].

In order to compare the complexity of various networks and the throughput of different implementations, we need a common measure. Evaluating convolutions requires performing many multiply-add operations. We count each multiply-add as two operations to remain compatible with the rest of the literature. For the convolution layer we thus have the number of operations

$$2 n_{out} n_{in} (h_{in} - h_k + 1)(w_{in} - w_k + 1) h_k w_k,$$

where n_{out} is the number of output channels $|\mathcal{C}_{out}|$, n_{in} is the number of $|\mathcal{C}_{in}|$, $h_{in} \times w_{in}$ is the size of the image and $h_k \times w_k$ is the size of the filter in spatial domain. This measure is the most common in neural network literature.

Software and hardware implementations alike often come with a throughput dependent on the actual size of the convolutional layer. While we keep our implementation runtime-configurable to a large extent, we use the ConvNet presented in [10] as a reference for performance evaluation. It has three stages and we

Table 1: Parameters of the three stages of our ref. ConvNet.

	Stage 1	Stage 2	Stage 3
Input size	240×320	117×157	55×75
Input channels	3	16	64
Output channels	16	64	256
# Operations	346 MOp	1682 MOp	5428 MOp
# Filter values	2352	50176	802816

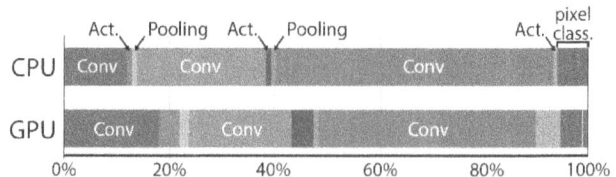

Figure 1: Computation time spent in different stages of our reference scene labeling ConvNet from [10].

assume input images of size 240×320. The resulting sizes and complexities of the individual layers are summarized in Table 1 and use a filter of size 7×7 for all of them. The total number of operations required is 7.57 GOp/frame.

2.1 Computational Effort

The evaluation of most convolutional networks for real applications is computationally very demanding. With the aforementioned scene labeling ConvNet, real-time use at 30 frame/s amounts to 227 GOp/s, which is not possible with any available implementation even on the most recent commercially procurable mobile processors.

When considering hardware acceleration of algorithms in a rapidly changing field such as deep learning, the long-term usability has to be considered as well. While the structure of the networks changes from application to application and over time, better activation functions and pooling operations are found every year. So an overall accelerator is soon outdated, but we can accelerate the commonality among all networks: the convolution operation. Fortunately, this is also the most time consuming part for well-optimized software implementations at 89% of the total computation time for CPU and 79% for GPU implementations, as shown in Figure 1.

3. PREVIOUS WORK
3.1 Software Implementations
Acceleration of convolutional neural networks has been discussed in many papers. There are very fast and user-friendly frameworks publicly available such as Torch [11], Caffe [12] and cuDNN [13], in particular also due to the need to train the networks efficiently. These and other optimized implementations can be used to obtain a performance baseline on desktop workstations and CUDA-compatible embedded processors, such as the Tegra K1. On a GTX780 desktop GPU, the performance can reach up to 3059 GOp/s for some special problems and about 1800 GOp/s on meaningful ConvNets. On the Tegra K1 up to 96 GOp/s can be achieved, with 76 GOp/s being achieved with an actual ConvNet. On both platforms an energy-efficiency of about 7 GOp/s/W considering the power of the entire platform and 14.4 GOp/s/W with differential power measurements can be obtained [10].

3.2 FPGA Implementations
The issues of embeddability and power-efficiency have been addressed by many researchers using FPGA implementations. A popular architecture is the one which started as CNP [14] and was further improved and renamed to NeuFlow [15], [16] and later on nn-X [17].

The CNP was published in 2009 and achieved 12 GOp/s at 15W on a Spartan 3A DSP 3400 FPGA using 18 bit fixed-point arithmetic for the multiplications. It is worth mentioning that it is self-contained, being able to perform all operations necessary in ConvNets and coming with a soft CPU. It also features a

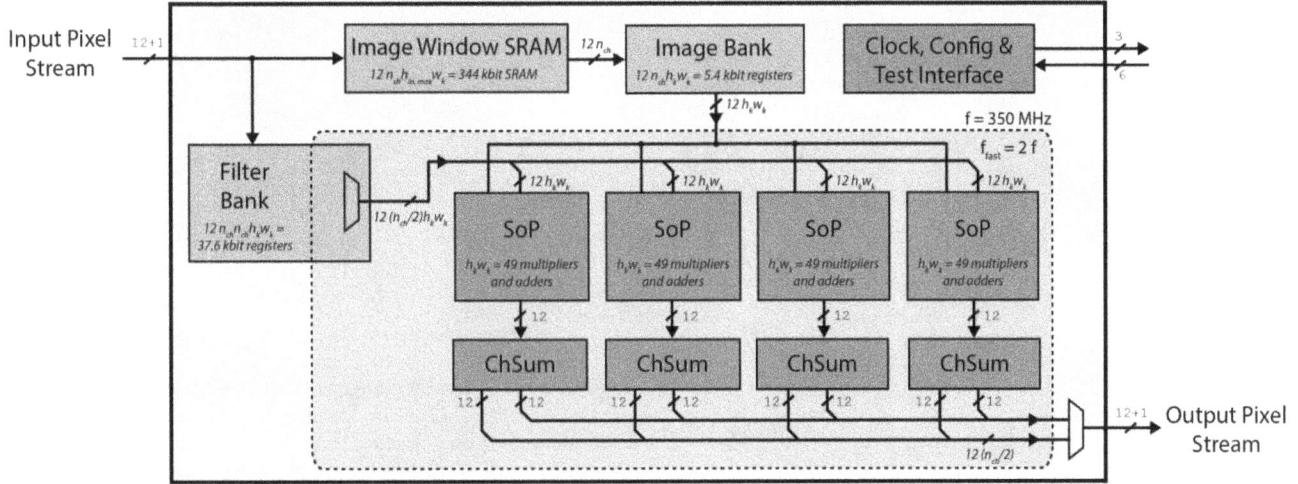

Figure 2: Top-level block diagram of the proposed architecture for the chosen implementation parameters.

compiler, converting network implementations with Torch directly to CNP instructions.

NeuFlow scaled up CNP to multiple convolution engines following the dataflow paradigm and allowing for runtime reconnection of the various processing blocks. The work published in 2011 features a Virtex 6 VLX240T to achieve 147 GOp/s at 11W using 16 bit fixed-point arithmetic.

In 2014, neuFlow was ported to a Zynq XC7Z045 as nn-X, making use of the hard-wired ARM cores. It achieves a throughput of about 200 GOp/s at 4W (FPGA, memory and host) and uses 4×950 MB/s full-duplex memory interfaces.

3.3 ASIC Implementations
In 2012 an ASIC implementation of NeuFlow was published [16]. It was implemented in IBM 45nm SOI technology, using a chip area of 12.5 mm². It achieves a performance of about 300 GOp/s at 0.6W operating at 400 MHz with an external memory bandwidth of 4×1.6 GB/s full-duplex.

To push the limits of what is possible in terms of energy efficiency, simulation (pre-silicon) results in ST 28nm FDSOI have recently been published [18]. The processing core was evaluated for single convolutions of various sizes suitable for ConvNets, achieving 37 GOp/s with 206 GOp/s/W at 0.8V and 1.39 GOp/s with 1375 GOp/s/W at 0.4V with the same implementation.

3.4 Discussion
These existing implementations show that hardware accelerators for ConvNets are feasible with high energy efficiency, giving significant improvements over software implementations.

However, none of the architectures are suitable for high-performance applications due to memory interface limits. The ASIC implementation of neuFlow comes with 299 I/O pins to achieve 300 GOp/s. Applying the aforementioned scene labeling ConvNet to larger images such as full-HD frames requires 5190 GOp/s to get 20 frame/s and there is also a trend towards even more complex ConvNets. Simply scaling this architecture up would require more than 5000 I/O pins or about 110GB/s full-duplex memory bandwidth when based on the nn-X architecture. This problem is not specific to the neuFlow/nn-X implementation, but common to all architectures we are aware of.

In this work we specifically address this issue, reducing the memory bandwidth required to achieve a high computational throughput.

4. ARCHITECTURE & IMPLEMENTATION
A top-level diagram of the ASIC architecture is shown in Figure 2. It is composed of data provider entities for the filter weights and an image window, and four processing channels computing the sum of products and accumulating the results. The data providing circuitry largely runs at a slower frequency f compatible with the I/O drivers, while the data processing units run with a faster clock $f_{fast} = 2f$.

In previous work, convolutions have been performed by loading one filter, loading one input image, and performing a single convolution to produce one output image. With our architecture we want to minimize I/O bandwidth by exploiting the fact that we can load n_{ch}^2 filters, load n_{ch} images, and perform n_{ch}^2 convolutions, to produce n_{ch} output images after summing up the results – effectively reducing the I/O to computation ratio by a factor of almost $1/n_{ch}$.

4.1 Concept of Operation
As we still want to keep the throughput per area high, we need to ensure the required amount of SRAM and register field memory is kept as small as possible without significant impact on performance. We thus store only a moving, w_k pixel wide and maximum $h_{in,max}$ pixel high spatial window of all n input images in SRAM, as shown in Figure 4. The resulting memory has $n_{ch}h_{in,max}$ words of length $12 \cdot w_k$ bit. The present working area of $n_{ch} \times h_k \times w_k$ pixel is always kept in registers and is moved down by one pixel row for one input image after the other, loading w_k new pixels from SRAM every cycle. Once it reaches the bottom of the image, it jumps back to the top and one pixel to the right, stalling the processing units for $n_{ch}(h_k - 1)$ cycles.

The actual computations take place in $n_{ch}/2$ processing chains running at $f_{fast} = 2f$. Each processing chain comes with a sum-of-products (SoP) unit and a channel summer (ChSum). A SoP unit has $h_k w_k$ 12-bit multipliers with 23 bit outputs and an adder tree summing up all the results, finally truncating the results to 12 bit. The channel summer then accumulates the data for two output channels, switching between those channels every cycle of the fast

201

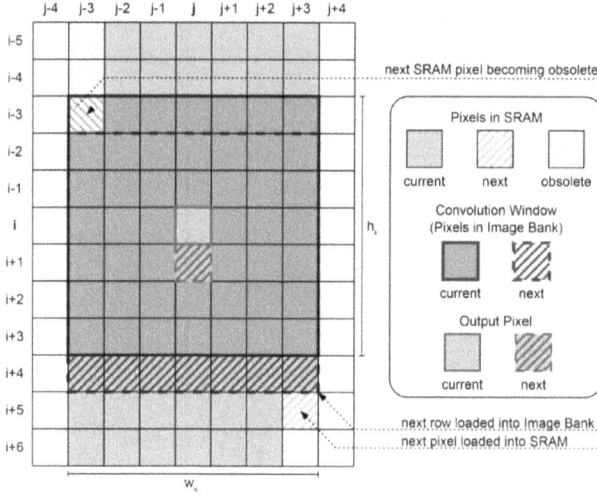

Figure 4: Data stored in the filter and image bank register fields and the image window SRAM.

clock, such that the input image patch has to be changed at the slower frequency only. Each channel summer updates its output every $2n_{ch}$ cycles of the fast clock. The results are then transferred off-chip, fully utilizing the 12 bit bus.

For the implementation, we fixed the filter size $h_k = w_k = 7$ and chose $n_{ch} = 8$. Smaller filters have to be zero-padded and larger filters have to be decomposed into multiple 7×7 filters and added up. To keep the cycles lost during column changes low also for larger image, we chose $h_{in,max} = 512$. For the SRAM, the technology libraries we used did not provide a fast enough module to accommodate $8 \cdot 512$ words of $7 \cdot 12$ bit at 350 MHz. Therefore the SRAM was split into 4 modules of 1024 words each.

4.2 Fixed-Point Analysis

Previous work is not conclusive on the required precision for ConvNets, 16 and 18 bit are the most common values [14], [15], [17], [18]. To determine the optimal data width for our design, we performed a fixed-point analysis based on our reference ConvNet. We replaced all the convolution operations in our software model with fixed-point versions thereof and evaluated the resulting precision depending on the input, output and weight data width. The quality was analyzed based on the per-pixel classification accuracy of 150 test images omitted during training. We used the other 565 images of the Stanford backgrounds dataset [19] to train the network.

Our results have shown that an output length of 12 bit is sufficient to keep the implementation loss below a drop of 0.5% in accuracy. Since the convolution layers are applied repeatedly with little processing between them, we chose the same signal width for the input, although we could have reduced them further. For the filter weights a signal width of 12 bit was selected as well.

4.3 Throughput

The peak throughput of this architecture is given by

$$2n_{SoP}h_k w_k f_{fast} = 274 \text{ GOp/s},$$

with $n_{SoP} = n_{ch}/2 = 4$. At the borders of an image no valid convolution results can be calculated, so the core has to wait for the necessary data to be transferred to the device. These waiting periods occur at the beginning for $w_k - 1$ columns and at the

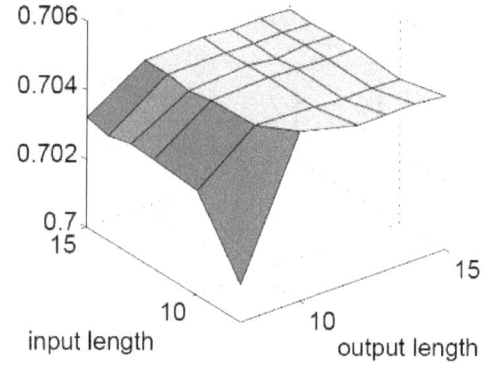

Figure 3: Classification accuracy with filter coefficients stored with 12 bit precision. The single precision implementation achieves an accuracy of 70.3%. Choosing an input length of 12 bit results in an accuracy loss of less than 0.5%.

beginning of each new row for $h_k - 1$ cycles. The effective throughput thus depends on the size of the image:

$$\eta_{border} = \frac{(h_{in} - h_k + 1)(w_{in} - w_k + 1)}{h_{in}w_{in}}.$$

For our reference network and the chosen implementation parameters, this factor is 0.96, 0.91 and 0.82 for stages 1...3, respectively in case of a 240×320 pixel input image. For larger images this is significantly improved, e.g. for a 480×640 image the Stage 3 will get an efficiency factor of 0.91. However, the height of the input image is limited to 512 pixel due to the memory size of the image bank. If larger images are to be processed, they have to be split into horizontal stripes with an overlap of $h_k - 1$ rows.

Before the image transmission can start, the filters have to be loaded through the same bus used to transmit the image data. This causes a loss of a few more cycles. The total number of filter coefficients is $n_{out}n_{in}h_k w_k$, which amounts to 2.4k, 50.2k and 802.8k for the three stages. This results in an additional efficiency factor of

$$\eta_{filterLoad} = \frac{n_{in}h_{in}w_{in}}{n_{out}n_{in}h_k w_k + n_{in}h_{in}w_{in}},$$

which evaluates to 0.98, 0.97 and 0.91 for the three stages.

The number of output and input channels usually does not correspond to the number of output and input channels processed

Table 2: Throughput and efficiency for the individual stages of our reference ConvNet.

	Stage 1	Stage 2	Stage 3
η_{border}	0.96	0.91	0.82
$\eta_{filterLoad}$	0.98	0.97	0.91
η_{blocks}	0.38	1.00	1.00
η	0.36	0.88	0.75
act. throughput	99 GOp/s	241 GOp/s	206 GOp/s
#Operations	173 MOp	841 MOp	2714 MOp
time	1.75 ms	3.49 ms	13.2 ms
average actual throughput: 203 GOp/s			

Table 3: Post-Layout Key Figures as Taped-Out.

Physical Characteristics	
Technology	UMC 65 nm, 8 Metal Layers
Core/Pad Voltage	1.2 V / 2.5 V
Package	QFN-56
# Pads	55 (i: 14, o: 13, clk/test: 8, pwr: 20)
Core Area	3.09 mm^2
Circuit Complexity (w/ SRAM)	912 kGE (1.31 mm^2)
Logic (std. cells)	697 kGE (1.00 mm^2)
On-chip SRAM	344 kbit
Max. Clock Frequency	core: 700 MHz, i/o: 350 MHz
Power[1] @700 MHz, 1.2V	744 mW (core) + 500 mW (pads)
Performance / Throughput	
Max. Throughput	274 GOp/s
Effective Throughput	203 GOp/s
Core Power-Efficiency	369 GOp/s/W

in parallel by this core. This can be overcome by partitioning the output and input channels into blocks of $n_{ch} \times n_{ch}$ and filling in all-zero filters for the unused cases. The outputs of these blocks then have to be summed up pixel-wise off-chip.

This processing in blocks can have a strong additional impact on the efficiency when not fully utilizing the core. While stages 2 and 3 of our reference ConvNet can be perfectly split into 8×8 blocks and thus no performance is lost, Stage 1 has only 3 input channels and can load the core only with $\eta_{blocks} = 3/8$. However, stages with a small number of input or output channels also perform much less operations and efficiency in these cases is thus not that important.

The total throughput with the reference ConvNet running on our implementation is summarized in Table 2, alongside details on the efficiency of the individual stages.

4.4 Implementation Summary

The ASIC has been named ORIGAMI and has been sent for tape-out in UMC 65nm CMOS technology. The design includes several design for test measures, including scan chains and built-in self-tests for the SRAM. The fast clock was generated by XOR-ing two phase-shifted 350 MHz clock signals. The key values of the ASIC have been compiled in Table 3.

After all these design choices, the resulting final area breakdown is shown in Figure 5.

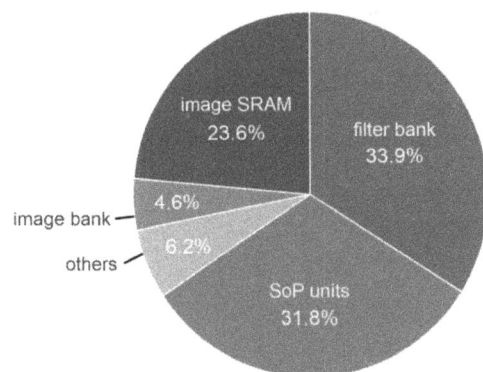

Figure 5: Final core area breakdown.

5. RESULTS & DISCUSSION

We have focused on multiple design aspects in our architecture: I/O bandwidth, throughput per area and power efficiency.

We have achieved a peak throughput of 274 GOp/s and an actual throughput of 203 GOp/s on only 3.09 mm^2 core area in 65 nm technology with a routing density of 69%. Our implementation thus achieves 66 GOp/s/mm^2, compared to 24 GOp/s/mm^2 of the neuFlow chip. This is very important, considering that such an accelerator has to be co-integrated with a processor and potentially many more devices within a SoC.

This ASIC comes with only one input and one output bus of 12 bit each and 3 control pins operating at 350 MHz. This architecture's data I/O bandwidth of 525 MB/s full-duplex for 203 GOp/s, 2.58 MB/GOp, is far better than the results shown in previous work, such as 24.7 MB/GOp for the neuFlow ASIC [16] or 20 MB/GOp for nn-X [17].

The power efficiency of our chip is 369 GOp/s/W without the pads and 220 GOp/s/W if we include the pads. Better results have been reported in literature, e.g. 490 GOp/s/W for the NeuFlow ASIC, and 207 GOp/s/W or even 1375 GOp/s/W in [18]. There are three main aspects influencing energy efficiency: First, we have a higher switching activity in the core, since we change the filter weights at the multiplier inputs with $f_{fast} = 700$ MHz and change also the image input at $f = 350$ MHz. Second, we use small shift registers and SRAM instead of large shift registers to store a stripe of the image. This saves some area and increases energy efficiency. Last but most important, technology scaling also has a significant positive impact, particularly with such a high utilization.

Besides that, it is important to stress the fact that the power to access external memory is not considered in the above estimate. Given the significant I/O bandwidth, this is the dominating factor for the overall system power and energy efficiency. If we consider only the energy used for the data interface of these architectures and assume LPDDR3 memory and a 28 nm implementation, an energy usage of 21 pJ/bit for memory module and PHY with a reasonable output load is realistic with a very high page hit rate and a perfectly-dimensioned memory (based on [20] and the Micron System Power Calculator[2] with values for LPDDR3).

If we scale to 28 nm, our core power would decrease to about 142 mW and the LPDDR3 memory including the PHY would add 180 mW to make a total of 322 mW or 630 GOp/s/W. The neuFlow implementation would use approximately 239 mW, and memory and PHY would require 2.14 W, totaling 2.38 W or 126 GOp/s/W. The implementation of [18] suffers from the same issues, their superior energy efficiency in the processing core is gained with FDSOI technology which could also be applied to our architecture. However, the UMC 65 nm process is currently a more reasonable and accessible choice for a low-cost implementation and has a fast turn-around time.

---

[1] The power usage was simulated running with real data.

[2] www.micron.com/products/support/power-calc

6. CONCLUSION & FUTURE WORK

We have presented the first ConvNet accelerator scalable to multi-TOp/s performance by significantly improving on the external memory bottleneck of previous architectures. Further, it is more area efficient than previously reported results and comes with the lowest-ever reported power consumption when including I/O power and external memory.

Further work with newer technologies, programmable logic and further configurability to build an entire high-performance low-power system are planned alongside investigations into the ConvNet learning-phase to adapt networks for very-low precision accelerators during training.

ACKNOWLEDGMENTS

This work was funded by armasuisse Science & Technology and the ERC MultiTherman project (ERC-AdG-291125).

Figure 6: Post-layout chip graphic

REFERENCES

[1]   F. Porikli, F. Bremond, S. L. Dockstader, J. Ferryman, A. Hoogs, B. C. Lovell, S. Pankanti, B. Rinner, P. Tu, and P. L. Venetianer, "Video surveillance: past, present, and now the future [DSP Forum]," *IEEE Signal Process. Mag.*, vol. 30, pp. 190–198, 2013.

[2]   A. Krizhevsky, I. Sutskever, and G. E. Hinton, "Imagenet classification with deep convolutional neural networks," in *Proc. NIPS'12*, 2012.

[3]   C. Szegedy, W. Liu, Y. Jia, P. Sermanet, S. Reed, D. Anguelov, D. Erhan, V. Vanhoucke, and A. Rabinovich, "Going Deeper with Convolutions," in *arXiv:1409.4842*, 2014.

[4]   P. Sermanet, D. Eigen, X. Zhang, M. Mathieu, R. Fergus, and Y. LeCun, "OverFeat: Integrated Recognition, Localization and Detection using Convolutional Networks," in *arXiv:1312.6229*, 2013.

[5]   Y. Taigman and M. Yang, "Deepface: Closing the gap to human-level performance in face verification," in *Proc. IEEE CVPR'13*, 2013.

[6]   T.-Y. Lin, M. Maire, S. Belongie, J. Hays, P. Perona, D. Ramanan, P. Dollár, and C. L. Zitnick, "Microsoft COCO: Common Objects in Context," in *arXiv:1405.0312*, 2014.

[7]   C. Labovitz, S. Iekel-Johnson, D. McPherson, J. Oberheide, and F. Jahanian, "Internet inter-domain traffic," *ACM SIGCOMM Computer Communication Review*, vol. 40. p. 75, 2010.

[8]   C. Bobda and S. Velipasalar, Eds., *Distributed Embedded Smart Cameras*. Springer, 2014.

[9]   C. Farabet, C. Couprie, L. Najman, and Y. LeCun, "Learning hierarchical features for scene labeling," *IEEE Trans. PAMI*, 2013.

[10]   L. Cavigelli, M. Magno, and L. Benini, "Accelerating Real-Time Embedded Scene Labeling with Convolutional Networks," in *Proc. DAC'15*, 2015.

[11]   R. Collobert, "Torch7: A matlab-like environment for machine learning," *Proc. NIPSW'11*, 2011.

[12]   Y. Jia, "Caffe: An Open Source Convolutional Architecture for Fast Feature Embedding." 2013.

[13]   S. Chetlur, C. Woolley, P. Vandermersch, J. Cohen, J. Tran, B. Catanzaro, and E. Shelhamer, "cuDNN: Efficient Primitives for Deep Learning," in *arXiv:1410.0759*, 2014.

[14]   C. Farabet, C. Poulet, J. Y. Han, and Y. LeCun, "CNP: An FPGA-based processor for Convolutional Networks," in *Proc. IEEE FPL'09*, 2009, vol. 1, no. 1, pp. 32–37.

[15]   C. Farabet, B. Martini, B. Corda, P. Akselrod, E. Culurciello, and Y. LeCun, "NeuFlow: A runtime reconfigurable dataflow processor for vision," in *Proc. IEEE CVPRW'11*, 2011, pp. 109–116.

[16]   P. H. Pham, D. Jelaca, C. Farabet, B. Martini, Y. LeCun, and E. Culurciello, "NeuFlow: Dataflow vision processing system-on-a-chip," in *Midwest Symposium on Circuits and Systems*, 2012, pp. 1044–1047.

[17]   V. Gokhale, J. Jin, A. Dundar, B. Martini, and E. Culurciello, "A 240 G-ops/s Mobile Coprocessor for Deep Neural Networks," in *Proc. IEEE CVPR'14*, 2014, pp. 682–687.

[18]   F. Conti and L. Benini, "A Ultra-Low-Energy Convolution Engine for Fast Brain-Inspired Vision in Multicore Clusters," in *Proc. DATE'15*, 2015.

[19]   S. Gould, R. Fulton, and D. Koller, "Decomposing a scene into geometric and semantically consistent regions," in *Proc. IEEE ICCV'09*, 2009.

[20]   M. Schaffner, F. K. Gürkaynak, A. Smolic, and L. Benini, "DRAM or no-DRAM? Exploring Linear Solver Architectures for Image Domain Warping in 28 nm CMOS," in *Proc. IEEE DATE'15*, 2015.

Restricted Clustered Neural Network for Storing Real Data

Robin Danilo
Université de Bretagne Sud,
Lab-STICC
Lorient, France
robin.danilo@univ-ubs.fr

Vincent Gripon
Electronics Department,
Télécom Bretagne
Brest, France
vincent.gripon@telecom-
bretagne.eu

Philippe Coussy
Université de Bretagne Sud,
Lab-STICC
Lorient, France
philippe.coussy@univ-
ubs.fr

Laura Conde-Canencia
Université de Bretagne Sud,
Lab-STICC
Lorient, France
laura.conde-
canencia@univ-ubs.fr

Warren J. Gross
Department of Electrical and
Computer Engineering, McGill
University
Montreal, Québec, Canada
warren.gross@mcgill.ca

ABSTRACT

Associative memories are an alternative to classical indexed memories that are capable of retrieving a message previously stored when an incomplete version of this message is presented. Recently a new model of associative memory based on binary neurons and binary links has been proposed. This model named Clustered Neural Network (CNN) offers large storage diversity (number of messages stored) and fast message retrieval when implemented in hardware. The performance of this model drops when the stored message distribution is non-uniform. In this paper, we enhance the CNN model to support non-uniform message distribution by adding features of Restricted Boltzmann Machines. In addition, we present a fully parallel hardware design of the model. The proposed implementation multiplies the performance (diversity) of Clustered Neural Networks by a factor of 3 with an increase of complexity of 40%.

1. INTRODUCTION

In conventional computer architectures, data storage is performed by using indexed memories which require explicit addresses to access contents. On the other hand, associative memories allow retrieval of content from partial or noisy version of input data. They are thus suitable for tasks such as nearest neighbor search, mapping and set implementations, and data intrusion systems.

Recently a new model of associative network (parallel implementation of associative memory) known as Clustered Neural Networks (CNNs) has been proposed [4, 5]. This network is composed of a fully interconnected neuron layer. When the distribution of messages is uniform, this model offers a large storing diversity (number of messages stored)

with a good message retrieval ability (probability to retrieve a message). Based on binary units, binary connections and a simple decoding algorithm, this associative network model allows efficient fully-parallel hardware implementations [7, 8, 3]. However, like other models of associative networks [9], diversity strongly depends on the distribution of stored messages. Recent work [2] proposed specific strategies to handle non-uniform distributions. However, these strategies imply to add material that increases the hardware complexity of the architecture.

In this paper, we propose a new approach and its fully-parallel hardware implementation to handle non-uniform distributions in CNN. Our method is similar to Restricted Boltzmann Machines [11, 6]: a hidden layer is added to the network and only the connections between the hidden layer and the input layer are permitted. The resulting network is named Restricted Clustered Neural Network (R-CNN).

The paper is organized as follow: In section II, CNN and non-uniform distributions are briefly discussed. In section III, the proposed model and its fully hardware implementation are presented. In section IV, R-CNN is simulated and compared with CNN. Section V concludes the paper.

2. CLUSTERED NEURAL NETWORK

To store messages composed of c symbols over an alphabet of size ℓ, CNN consists of using a binary neural network composed of c parts (named clusters), each containing ℓ neurons. They are capable of retrieving any of them when some of the symbols are missing.

We denote by $\mathcal{M}$ the set of messages to store. Each message m is composed of c symbols $m_0, \ldots, m_{c-1}$. A partially erased version of m is denoted with $\tilde{m}$. Thus $\tilde{m}$ is such that either $\tilde{m}_i = m_i$ or $\tilde{m}_i$ is unknown.

2.1 Principles

In the rest of this paper, n_{ij} designates the neuron of the cluster i associated with the j-th symbol of the alphabet and v_{ij} its value, $v_{ij} = 1$ means that n_{ij} is active while $v_{ij} = 0$ means that n_{ij} is inactive. Each neuron can be connected by a binary link to any other neuron in another cluster. These binary links are stored in the adjacency matrix $W_A(\mathcal{M})$. By

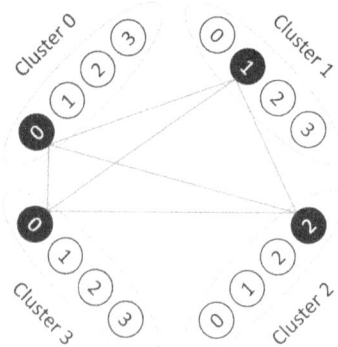

Figure 1: Graphical representation of CNN during the storing process of the message $m = (0, 1, 3, 0)$

convention $w_{(ij)(i'j')} = 1$ means that it exists a binary link between n_{ij} and $n_{i'j'}$.

During the storing process, each message m leads to the activation of one neuron in each cluster in the following manner:

$$v_{ij} = \begin{cases} 1 & \text{if } m_i = j \\ 0 & \text{otherwise} \end{cases} . \quad (1)$$

The connections between the active neurons are then stored in $W_A(\mathcal{M})$. Fig. 1 depicts the graphical representation of a CNN during the storage process of the message $m = (0, 1, 3, 0)$ (here $c = 4$ and $\ell = 4$). The neurons n_{00}, n_{11}, n_{23} and n_{30} are activated and the stored connections are represented by green lines. Storing distinct messages can result in addressing multiple times the same connections, in such case, the corresponding connection is not incremented[1].

During the retrieving process, an incomplete message $\tilde{m}$ is presented to the network leading to the activation of neurons following Eq. 1. As part of the symbols of $\tilde{m}$ are erased, some clusters of the network do not have any active neuron. We call them neutral clusters. The neutral state of each cluster is stored in a vector d, if $d_i = 1$, then, the cluster i is neutral. After this initialization phase, an iterative process is performed in order to retrieve the entire message. This process exploits two important properties of the network:

1. a unique neuron should be active in each cluster of the network,

2. for one stored message, each neuron is connected with all the other neurons of the message.

From these properties, the following activation rule is deduced: a neuron is activated if it is connected with one active neuron from each non-neutral cluster. As shown in [3], this activation rule can be performed by the following boolean function:

$$v_{ij}^{t+1} = (v_{ij}^t \vee d_i^t) \wedge \bigwedge_{i' \neq i} \left(\bigvee_{j'} \left(w_{(ij)(i'j')} \wedge v_{i'j'}^t \right) \vee d_{(i')}^t \right) , \quad (2)$$

where $d_i^t = \overline{\bigwedge_j v_{ij}^t}$.

Note that after an iteration, several neurons may be activated in one cluster. For this reason, the process iterates

[1]Note that the connections in the network are binary.

until eventually only one neuron remains active in each cluster.

Due to the structure of the network, the memory cost of storing $W_A(\mathcal{M})$ is given by:

$$cost_{CNN} = \frac{c(c-1)\ell^2}{2}. \quad (3)$$

The performance of CNNs are evaluated in terms of diversity and message retrieval ability. The diversity is the number of messages that are learned in the network. The message retrieval ability is the probability to retrieve m from $\tilde{m}$.

2.2 Non-Uniform Distribution

CNNs offer their maximal diversity when messages to store are uniformly distributed. Real-world data lead to a significantly lower diversity. Indeed, a non-uniform distribution results in a more frequent occurrence of some symbols and thus an overuse of some neurons in a cluster.

In a CNN, symbols are directly connected together, amplifying the adverse effects of the distribution of these messages. Indeed, an overused neuron will be connected with another overused neuron and so on. This phenomenon has been well studied in [2] and some solutions have been proposed to deal with non-uniform distributions.

To illustrate the problem of non-uniform distribution we have compared the message retrieval ability of a CNN on two data sets. The first one named "Yeast data set" [10] is composed of biological data and contains 1484 instances of 8 real attributes including two constants. We take only the 6 non-constant attributes and quantify them in 64 intervals. Each instance can be seen like a message of 6 symbols over an alphabet of size 64. The second named "Uniform data set" is composed of 1484 random messages of 6 values between 0 and 63 uniformly distributed. For the two data sets, the resulting network is composed of 6 clusters of 64 neurons.

For the two data sets, every message (or instance) is first stored in the network. Then, one message is randomly chosen, two symbols are erased before being provided to the network that must retrieve the erased symbols. This test is repeated 10000 times and the error rate is computed. For the uniform data set, the error rate is equal to 0.3669, while for the Yeast data set the error rate is equal to 0.905.

2.3 Strategies

In [2], three strategies have been proposed. The first (Str1) consists of adding random symbols to extend the messages. These random symbols are associated with hidden clusters (which are not part of the message) to support the input clusters (which are part of the message). The network is thus composed of hidden and input clusters fully interconnected. The second strategy (Str2) is based on increasing the size of clusters instead. Thus a symbol is not associated with a unique neuron in a cluster but with a group of neurons. During the storing process, each time the symbol occurs, one of the corresponding neurons is chosen at random to be its representation. During the retrieving process, the occurrence of one symbol leads to the activation of several neurons in a cluster. The last strategy (Str3) consists of using Huffman lossless compression. The authors thus associate the most frequent symbols with a lot of corresponding neurons whereas least frequent ones are associated with few neurons.

In [2], the three strategies have been simulated for a Gaussian distribution. Str1 gives poor performance compared with the two others. For Str2 it is necessary to multiply by 4 the number of neurons in each cluster to reach the performance of the uniform distribution. As a consequence, the total amount of memory needed to store $W_A(\mathcal{M})$ is multiplied by 16. Str3 offers the best results for the same amount of memory. However, the drawback of Str3 is that it is necessary to preprocess the data before the use of CNN.

3. RESTRICTED CLUSTERED NEURAL NETWORK

In this section we propose a new approach deal with non-uniform distribution. The strategy consists in associating a hidden message randomly generated to the input message. Like the random symbol strategy, we add hidden clusters to the network for the hidden message but instead of using a fully connected CNN we only have connections between the input clusters and the hidden clusters. Thus, when a partially erased message is presented to the network, the hidden message is first retrieved and is then used to retrieve the input message. This procedure is similar to restricted Boltzmann machines and the resulting network is named Restricted CNN (R-CNN). Fig. 2 depicts a graphical representation of a R-CNN.

3.1 Principles

The number of hidden clusters c^h and the number of neurons per hidden cluster ℓ^h must be chosen by the designer depending on the application specification (intended diversity). Neurons of the input and hidden layers are noted by n_{ij}^{in} and n_{ij}^h respectively. In a R-CNN, a neuron of one layer can only be connected to neurons of the other layer. The connections are stored in the adjacency matrix $W_R(\mathcal{M})$, by convention, $w_{(ij)in(i'j')^h} = 1$ means that a binary link exists between n_{ij}^{in} and $n_{i'j'}^h$.

During the storing process, each new input message m^{in} is associated with a *randomly generated* hidden message m^h. m^{in} leads to the activation of one neuron in each input cluster while m^h leads to the activation of one neuron per hidden cluster. The connections between the active neurons of the input layer and the active neurons of the hidden layer are then stored in $W_R(\mathcal{M})$. Fig. 2 depicts the graphical representation of a R-CNN during the storing process of the input message $m^{in} = (0, 1, 3, 0)$, the hidden message $m^h = (0, 2, 0, 3)$ is associated to the input message. The neurons n_{00}^{in}, n_{11}^{in}, n_{23}^{in}, n_{30}^{in}, n_{00}^h, n_{12}^h, n_{21}^h, n_{33}^h are activated and the stored connections are represented by green lines.

During the retrieving process, an incomplete input message $\tilde{m}^{in}$ activates neurons in the input layer. A part of the clusters of the input layer are neutral due to the erased symbols of $\tilde{m}^{in}$. Then an iterative process is performed in order to retrieve the entire message. This process is divided in two steps:

1. activation of the neurons of the hidden layer from the input layer

2. activation of the neurons of the input layer from the hidden layer

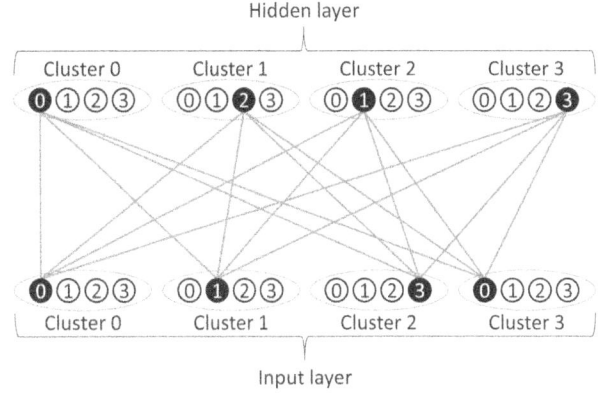

Figure 2: **Graphical representation of R-CNN during the storing process of the message** $m = (0, 1, 3, 0)$

The neurons are activated by the following boolean functions:

$$v_{ij}^{h\ t+1} = \bigwedge_{i'} \left(\bigvee_{j'} \left(w_{(i'j')in(ij)^h} \wedge v_{i'j'}^{in\ t} \right) \vee d_{i'}^{in\ t} \right), \quad (4)$$

where $d_{i'}^{in\ t} = \overline{\bigwedge_{j'} v_{i'j'}^{in\ t}}$.

$$v_{ij}^{in\ t+1} = \bigwedge_{i'} \left(\bigvee_{j'} \left(w_{(ij)in(i'j')^h} \wedge v_{i'j'}^{h\ t} \right) \right), \quad (5)$$

Note that after the first step, each hidden cluster has at least one neuron activated and cannot be neutral.

Due to the structure of the network, the memory cost of storing $W_R(\mathcal{M})$ is given by:

$$cost_{R-CNN} = c.\ell.c^h.\ell^h. \quad (6)$$

3.2 Proposed Architecture

A fully parallel hardware implementation of R-CNN is proposed in this section. First, the generation of random messages for the hidden layer is explained. Then, the storing and activation modules are presented.

3.2.1 Random Message Generation

The messages generated for the hidden layer must be uniformly distributed. For that, the low-complexity simple algorithm proposed in [1] is used. With this algorithm, instead of dividing the set of neurons of the hidden layer into equal clusters, the size of each cluster is chosen to be relatively prime with each other. Relatively prime means that the greatest common divisor is equal to one. The size of the cluster i is ℓ_i^h and the value assigned to this cluster is m_i^h. During initialization, the value 0 is assigned to each cluster, thus the first message generated for the hidden layer is a zeros vector. Then, a new message is generated by assigning to each cluster the value computed from:

$$m_i^{h\ t+1} = (m_i^{h\ t} + 1) \pmod{\ell_i^h}. \quad (7)$$

Tab. 1 shows an example in which the hidden layer is divided in 3 clusters of sizes $\ell_0^h = 3$, $\ell_1^h = 4$, $\ell_2^h = 5$. Each symbol is represented in a cell under its integer form on the first line and under its equivalent one-hot encoded form on the second line. The interests of such algorithm are:

ℓ_i^h	3	4	5
	m_0^h	m_1^h	m_2^h
$m^h\,0$	0	0	0
	0 0 1	0 0 0 1	0 0 0 0 1
$m^h\,1$	1	1	1
	0 1 0	0 0 1 0	0 0 0 1 0
$m^h\,2$	2	2	2
	1 0 0	0 1 0 0	0 0 1 0 0
$m^h\,3$	0	3	3
	0 0 1	1 0 0 0	0 1 0 0 0
$m^h\,4$	1	0	4
	0 1 0	0 0 0 1	1 0 0 0 0
$m^h\,5$	2	1	0
	1 0 0	0 0 1 0	0 0 0 0 1
$m^h\,6$	0	2	1
	0 0 1	0 1 0 0	0 0 0 1 0
$m^h\,7$	1	3	2
	0 0 1	1 0 0 0	0 0 1 0 0
$m^h\,8$	2	0	3
	0 1 0	0 0 0 1	0 1 0 0 0
$m^h\,9$	0	1	4
	1 0 0	0 0 1 0	1 0 0 0 0
$m^h\,10$	1	2	0
	0 0 1	0 1 0 0	0 0 0 0 1
$m^h\,11$	2	3	1
	0 1 0	1 0 0 0	0 0 0 1 0

Table 1: Exemple of messages generated for the hidden layer

1. it automatically produces uniformly distributed messages,

2. it maximizes the Hamming distance between the messages produced,

3. it is easy to implement by using shift registers.

The design of the hidden layer is done as follow: first the number of hidden neurons N^h and the number of hidden clusters c^h are chosen, then, the size ℓ_i^h of each hidden cluster is determined. To determine the size of hidden clusters the mean size is first computed $\ell_{mean}^h = \frac{N^h}{c^h}$ and $c^h - 1$ prime numbers are chosen around ℓ_{mean}^h to be the sizes of the first $c^h - 1$ hidden clusters. The last size is equal to N^h minus the sum of the first $c^h - 1$ sizes. For example, for $N^h = 1536$ and $c^h = 6$, $\ell_{mean}^h = 256$, the $c^h - 1$ first sizes could be $\ell_0^h = 241$, $\ell_1^h = 251$, $\ell_2^h = 257$, $\ell_3^h = 263$, $\ell_4^h = 269$ and the last size should be $\ell_5^h = 1536 - 241 - 251 - 257 - 263 - 269 = 255$. This procedure guarantees that each size is relatively prime with each other.

3.2.2 System Level Architecture

Fig. 3 depicts the system level architecture of a fully parallel hardware implementation of the R-CNN. The system is composed of two neuron layers (input, hidden) each one divided in c and c^h clusters respectively. If the input clusters are of equal sizes, each hidden cluster i has a specific size ℓ_i^h in order to generate random messages uniformly distributed. During both storing and retrieving process, messages of length $\kappa.c$ ($\kappa = log_2(\ell)$) are cut into c symbols of length κ and provided to the Local Maping Modules (LMMs). LMMs realize a one hot encoding of symbols into vectors of ℓ bits where only one bit is set to one. These c vectors of ℓ bits are then stored in the neurons state registers of the input layer.

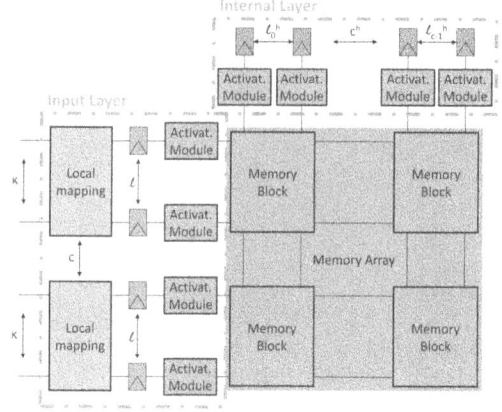

Figure 3: Simplified scheme of the system level architecture

During the storing process, a set of messages is stored in the network by storing the connections between the input layer and the hidden layer in a memory array. This memory array is divided in $c.c^h$ memory blocks composed of massively parallel on-chip registers (flip-flops) for simultaneous access. One block is used to store the connections between an input cluster and a hidden cluster. This operation is done by using the storing module. During the retrieving process, incomplete messages are provided to the system and the stored connections are used to retrieve the erased symbols by alternating between the computation of the values of the hidden state registers and the input state registers. This operation is done by using several activation modules (one per neuron).

3.2.3 Storing Module

During the storing process, each input message is associated with a hidden message generated with the algorithm proposed in [1]. To generate these hidden messages, each hidden cluster i is provided with a shift register whose size corresponds to the size ℓ_i^h of the cluster. For the first hidden message, each shift register has one register set to one and the others to zero. After the storage of each new input message, the bit set to one is shifted.

Fig. 4 depicts the storing module for one memory block between an input cluster and the ith hidden cluster. The input cluster is composed of a set of ℓ neurons state registers while the hidden cluster is composed of a shift register of size ℓ_i^h. Between them, a memory block of size $\ell \times \ell_i^h$, where each row stores the connections of one neuron of the input cluster with all neurons of the hidden cluster. During the storing of an input message, the row of the active neuron of the input cluster is selected with the MUX, and an OR array is used to accumulate the value of the shift register with the previous connections.

3.2.4 Activation Module

During the retrieving process, the activation modules are used to compute the values of every state registers of the input and the hidden layers. Fig. 5 depicts an activation module for the hidden layer (left side) and for the input layer (right side). This activation module implement Eq. 4 and 5.

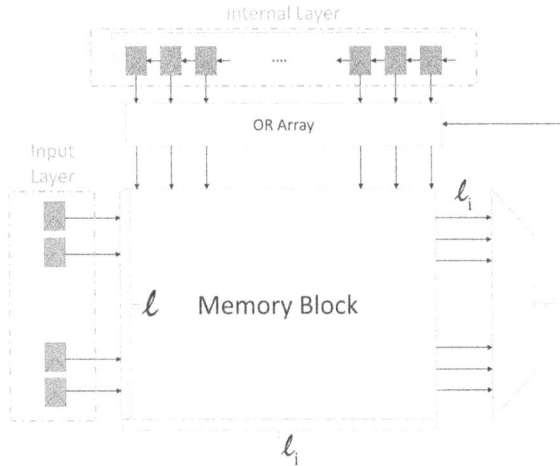

Figure 4: Block diagram of the storing module between a cluster of the input layer and a cluster of size ℓ_i^h of the internal layer

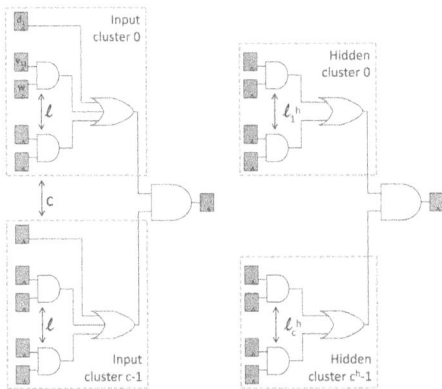

Figure 5: Logic diagram of the activation rule, for the internal layer on the left and the input layer on the right

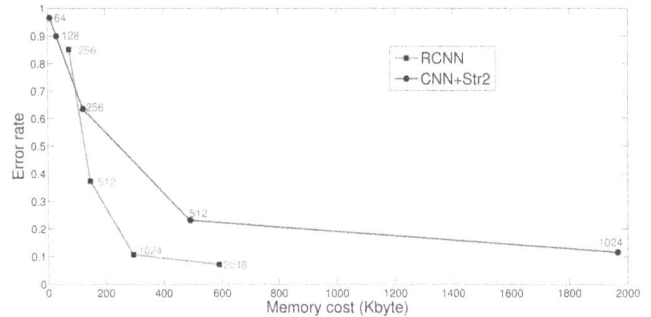

Figure 6: Error rate as a function of memory cost for R-CNN and CNN+Str2

4. RESULTS

In this section we evaluate the memory cost and the retrieval ability of R-CNN for a given diversity. A comparison is done with CNN+Str2 from [2] that is the strategy which offers the best performance without data preprocessing. Then, the proposed architecture is compared with the fully hardware implementation of CNN proposed in [8] and based on Eq. 2.

4.1 Message Retrieving

The "Yeast data set" is used to test the two strategies, R-CNN and CNN+Str2. The 6 non-constants attributes are taken and quantified on 64 intervals. Each instance is thus a message of 6 symbols over an alphabet of size 64. The entire data set is first learned in the network, then one message (or instance) m is chosen at random, two symbols are erased to produce $\tilde{m}$ which is sent to the network in order to retrieve m. This operation is repeated 10000 times and the message retrieval ability is evaluated by computing the error rate (number of successful message retrieval over the total number of trial).

There are several ways to increase the message retrieval ability of R-CNN: increase the size of the hidden clusters, increase the number of hidden clusters, use Str2 on the input layer. From our experiments, the greatest diversity is obtained when the size of hidden clusters is increased and we only show results for this solution.

Fig. 6 shows the error rate as a function of the memory cost for several configurations of CNN+Str2 and R-CNN. The memory cost is computed for CNN+Str2 and R-CNN with Eq.s 3 and 6 respectively. For R-CNN, the number of hidden clusters c^h are fixed to 6 and the network is simulated for different numbers of neurons in the hidden layer. The mean size ℓ_{mean}^h of the hidden clusters is reported on the figure. For CNN+Str2, different sizes of clusters are simulated, these sizes are reported on the figure. We can see in Fig. 6 that R-CNN offers better message retrieval ability than CNN+Str2 for a lower memory cost.

4.2 Complexity Analysis

We know compare the area complexity of the proposed architecture with the CNN implementation proposed in [8]. This comparison is done in NAND gate eq. (based on STMicroelectronics 90nm cell library). Two equivalent configurations of networks are chosen: a CNN with $c = 6$, $\ell = 64$ and a R-CNN with $c = c^h = 6$ and $\ell = \ell_{mean}^h = 64$. Both networks need 4 cycles to retrieve a message.

Tab. 2 presents the area cost for the two implementations. The total cost divided in three parts: the cost of registers used for memory array and neurons, the cost of storing module and the cost of retrieving module. For the CNN implementation, the major part of the area (46%) is used for registers, then the storing module (33%) and finally the retrieving module (21%). The high register cost is due to the fact that the implementation [3] uses two times more memory elements for the memory array than needed (from Eq. 3). The R-CNN implementation uses globally a greater area than the CNN implementation (+43% for the total area). The largest increase comes from the retrieving module (+127%). This is due to the number of neurons two times higher in a R-CNN than in a CNN.

If both networks give the same performance for uniform distribution, the area overhead paid for R-CNN is compensated by better performance for non-uniform distribution. With the CNN configuration studied here, only 25 instances of the "Yeast data set" can be stored with an error rate under 0.01, whereas the number of instances which can be stored in

	CNN [3]	R-CNN
Registers	1.36×10^6	1.63×10^6 $(+20\%)$
Storing	0.97×10^6	1.17×10^6 $(+20\%)$
Retrieving	0.62×10^6	1.41×10^6 $(+127\%)$
Total	2.95×10^6	4.01×10^6 $(+43\%)$

Table 2: Area of CNN ($c = 6$ and $\ell = 64$) and R-CNN ($c = c^h = 6$ and $\ell = \ell^h_{mean} = 64$) in NAND gate eq.

the R-CNN for the same error rate is equal to 76 (multiplied by a factor of 3).

5. CONCLUSION

In this paper, a new model of associative memory named the Restricted Clustered Neural Network (R-CNN) has been introduced. This model is based on the Clustered Neural Network (CNN) and uses Restricted Boltzmann Machine principles in order to increase the diversity of CNN on non-uniform distributions of input messages. A comparison was done between the proposed model and the CNN in terms of memory usage and error rate for a message retrieval task on real data (non-uniform distribution). It has been shown that the R-CNN outperforms CNN for this task with a lower memory usage.

A fully parallel implementation of R-CNN has also been proposed. This implementation has been compared with an equivalent implementation of a basic CNN. Although the area cost is more important for R-CNN, the additional cost ($+43\%$) is largely compensated by better performance (diversity is multiplied by a factor of 3).

The storing algorithm proposed here is simple and easy to implement in hardware. It consists of associating a hidden message uniformly distributed with the input message (non-uniformly distributed). In future work, we will study smarter storing algorithms which choose the hidden message function of input messages.

Acknowledgment

This work has received a French state support granted to the CominLabs excellence laboratory and managed by the National Research Agency in the "Investing for the Fuure" program under reference Nb. ANR-10-LABX-07-01.

6. REFERENCES

[1] E. B. Baum, J. Moody, and F. Wilczek. Internal representations for associative memory. *Biological Cybernetics*, 59(4-5):217–228, 1988.

[2] B. Boguslawski, V. Gripon, F. Seguin, and F. Heitzmann. Huffman coding for storing non-uniformly distributed messages in networks of neural cliques. In *AAAI 2014: the 28th Conference on Artificial Intelligence*, volume 1, pages 262–268, 2014.

[3] R. Danilo, H. Jarollahi, V. Gripon, L. Conde-Canencia, P. Coussy, and W. J. Gross. Algorithm and implementation of an associative memory for oriented edge detection using improved clustered neural networks. In *Circuits and Systems (ISCAS), 2015 IEEE International Symposium on*. IEEE, 2015. to appear.

[4] V. Gripon and C. Berrou. A simple and efficient way to store many messages using neural cliques. In *Proceedings of IEEE Symposium on Computational Intelligence, Cognitive Algorithms, Mind, and Brain*, pages 54–58, Paris, France, April 2011.

[5] V. Gripon and C. Berrou. Sparse neural networks with large learning diversity. *IEEE Transactions on Neural Networks*, 22(7):1087–1096, July 2011.

[6] G. Hinton. Training products of experts by minimizing contrastive divergence. *Neural computation*, 14(8):1771–1800, 2002.

[7] H. Jarollahi, N. Onizawa, V. Gripon, and W. J. Gross. Architecture and implementation of an associative memory using sparse clustered networks. In *Circuits and Systems (ISCAS), 2012 IEEE International Symposium on*, pages 2901–2904. IEEE, 2012.

[8] H. Jarollahi, N. Onizawa, V. Gripon, and W. J. Gross. Reduced-complexity binary-weight-coded associative memories. In *Acoustics, Speech and Signal Processing (ICASSP), 2013 IEEE International Conference on*, pages 2523–2527. IEEE, 2013.

[9] A. Knoblauch, G. Palm, and F. T. Sommer. Memory capacities for synaptic and structural plasticity. *Neural Computation*, 22(2):289–341, 2010.

[10] M. Lichman. UCI machine learning repository. 2013.

[11] P. Smolensky. Information processing in dynamical systems: Foundations of harmony theory. 1986.

NeuroDSP Accelerator for Face Detection Application

Michel Paindavoine
LEAD UMR CNRS - Univ.
Bourgogne
Esplanade Erasme
21065 Dijon, France.
michel.paindavoine@u-
bourgogne.fr

Olivier Boisard
LEAD UMR CNRS - Univ.
Bourgogne
Esplanade Erasme
21065 Dijon, France.
olivier.boisard@u-
bourgogne.fr

Alexandre Carbon
CEA LIST
Paris-Saclay Campus -
Nano-Innov
91191 Gif-sur-Yvette Cedex,
France.
alexandre.carbon@cea.fr

Jean-Marc Philippe
CEA LIST
Paris-Saclay Campus -
Nano-Innov
91191 Gif-sur-Yvette Cedex,
France.
jean-
marc.philippe@cea.fr

Olivier Brousse
GlobalSensing Technologies
14 rue Pierre de Coubertin
21000 Dijon, France.
olivier.brousse@globalsensing.eu

ABSTRACT

Neuro-Inspired Vision approach, based on models from biology, allows to reduce the computational complexity. One of these models - The Hmax model - shows that the recognition of an object in the visual cortex mobilizes V1, V2 and V4 areas. From the computational point of view, V1 corresponds to the area of the directional filters (for example Gabor filters or wavelet filters). This information is then processed in the area V2 in order to obtain local maxima. This new information is then sent to an artificial neural network. This neural processing module corresponds to area V4 of the visual cortex and is intended to categorize objects present in the scene. In order to realize autonomous vision systems (low-power consumption) with such treatments inside, we studied a new architeure of a Neural Processor named NeuroDSP. We describe in this paper an optimized Hmax model implementation on this Neural Processor for a face detection application.

Keywords

Neuro-Inspired Vision, Face Detection, Hmax algorithm, Neural Processor

1. INTRODUCTION

Visual recognition of a familiar object - such as the image of the Eiffel Tower in its natural environment - is obtained easily by a human subject. The execution of the same task on a "classical" computer requires complex and costly algorithms in terms of computing power. Thus, "Neuro-Inspired" approach, based on models from biology, allows to reduce the computational complexity. During the last 20 years many vision models have been proposed such as those from M.Riesenhuber and T.Poggio [1] , Y.Lecun [2] and S.Thorpe [3]. The Hmax model proposed by T.Serre et al [4] , which builds on the work of Poggio, shows that the recognition of an object in the visual cortex mobilizes V1, V2 and V4 areas. From the computational point of view, V1 corresponds to the area of the directional filters (for example Gabor filters or wavelet filters). This information is then processed in the area V2 in order to obtain local maxima. This new information is then sent to an artificial neural network. This neural processing module corresponds to area V4 of the visual cortex and is intended to categorize objects present in the scene.

In order to realize autonomous vision systems (low-power consumption) with such treatments inside, we studied a new architecture of a Neural Processor named NeuroDSP. We describe in this paper an optimized Hmax model implementation on this Neural Processor for a face detection application. In the second section, we introduce the orignal Hmax model and then we show in the third second section how to decrease the amount of calculations in the context a face detection application. In the last section of this article, we describe the implementation of the optimized Hmax model using the new NeuroDSP accelarator.

2. THE HMAX MODEL

HMAX consists in an alternate succession of simple cells and complex cells layers, named S1, C1, S2 and C2. The simple cells layers (S1 and S2) aim to extract features from the input image, while the complex cells layers (C1 and C2) provide invariance to locations and scales of those features. Let's summarize the operations performed by each layer (for details see T.Serre et al [4]):

Table 1: Parameters of Gabor filters used in HMAX S1 layer.

Scale band	C1 spatial pooling grid	Overlap	S1 filter size
Band 1	8×8	4	7×7 9×9
Band 2	10×10	5	11×11 13×13
Band 3	12×12	6	15×15 17×17
Band 4	14×14	7	19×19 21×21
Band 5	16×16	8	23×23 25×25
Band 6	18×18	9	27×27 29×29
Band 7	20×20	10	31×31 33×33
Band 8	22×22	11	35×35 37×37

S1 layer.

This layer consists in a Gabor filters bank, each sensitives to a given orientation and scale. The original framework uses 4 different orientations $(0, \frac{\pi}{4}, \frac{\pi}{2}$ and $\frac{3\pi}{4})$ and 16 scales, resulting in a total of 64 filters.

The parameters of these filters are the same as in [4] ; those parameters are recalled in Table 1.

C1 layer.

In order to provide a first level of invariance to locations and scales, each C1 unit pools over a neighborhood of S1 units across two images of successive scales and same orientation and keeps the maximum.

S2 layer.

This particular layer needs to be trained before it can be used. During the training stage, several patches of various sizes are cropped from images in C1 representation, at random positions and scales. Each patch is cropped at the same position and scale accross the four orientations, and all the selected C1 units values are serialized in order to form a vector. Thus, cropping an $s \times s$ patch results in a vector of $4s^2$ components. During feed-forward, patches are cropped from C1 units at all locations and scales, and feed all S2 units of corresponding sizes. The output of the i-th S2 unit, the vector of which is called X_i, fed with the vector X is given by :

$$S2_i(X) = \exp\left(-\beta \|X - X_i\|\right)$$

where β is a normalization parameter.

C2.

Finally, the maximum output of each S2 units is kept, and the other values are discarded. This provides a complete invariance to scales and locations of the features.

Once HMAX descriptors have been extracted, we use a RBF or a SVM classifier with linear kernel functions to determine the category they belong to.

Figure 4 shows the original Hmax framework with S1, C1, S2 and C2 layers.

3. PROPOSED OPTIMIZATIONS

3.1 Complexity analysis

HMAX was designed to be able to recognize any kind of object, thus it extracts a large variety of features. However, if we are looking for a particular type of object some features may not be as relevant as others.

Let's compute the number of operation in S1, noted as C_{S1}. If we note s_I the side of the input image, s_{f_n} the side of a filter of the nth scale, N_λ the number of scales and N_θ the number of orientations, we have $C_{S1} = N_\theta \sum_{k=1}^{N_\lambda} s_I^2 s_{f_k}^2$. For C1, if we call s_{m_k} the step in pixels between two pooling windows at the kth scale, we have $C_{C1} = N_\theta \sum_{k=1}^{N_\lambda} \left(\frac{s_I}{s_{m_k}}\right)^2 + s_I^2 \frac{N_\lambda}{2}$. Finally, if we call N_n the number of neurons in the RBF net and s_n the size of its neurons, the number C_{Cl} of operations needed by the RBF net to classify a vector is given by $C_{Cl} = 2N_n(s_n + 1)$. Therefore the total number of operations $C_{\text{tt}} = C_{S1} + C_{C1} + C_{Cl}$ needed to recognize an image is given by $C_{\text{tt}} = N_\theta s_I^2 \left[\sum_{k=1}^{N_\lambda} \left(s_{f_k}^2 + \frac{1}{s_{m_k}^2}\right) + \frac{N_\lambda}{2}\right] + 2N_n(s_n + 1)$. This expression shows that reducing the number of orientations N_θ and the size of the vectors sent to the classifier, which itself depends on N_θ and $s_{m_k}^2$, would dramatically reduce the complexity. C_{tt} also depends on s_I^2; however, we found that using smaller input images reduces the system's performance significantly. Therefore, we chose to keep it to 128. The same goes for N_λ.

The previous paragraph showed what one can do to reduce the complexity. Let's see first how to reduce the number of orientations N_θ: Figure ?? shows that features obtained with $\theta = \theta_1 = 0$ seem more relevant than the others, as it brings out the eyes and the mouth. It is however hard to recognize a face on the images obtained for other values of θ. This led us to keep only $\theta = \theta_1$, and thus we have $N_\theta = 1$. Then, by taking a closer look to the Figure ??, we can also see that pixels in a neighborhood have very similar values. This duplication of information may not be necessary. We propose to reduce it by multiplying the size and overlap of the pooling window in the C1 layer by 2 in each dimensions, thus multiplying all the s_{m_n}'s by 2. Furthermore, for a given orientation, there is also a duplication of information accross scales. Figure 3 shows the patches obtained with $\theta = 0$: in all scales the brightest pixels tend to be located around the eyes and the mouth, while other locations tend to have darker pixel. However, instead of simply removing the duplicate information as we did before, we propose to keep it by summing the images as shown in Figure 2.

The rational is that, even if there are duplicated data, the different patches are not similar enough to allow us to simply discard some of them.

Finally, we can optimize out the neural net we use for the final classification. The function used in RBF neural nets is, usually, a Gaussian function, so that the closer a vector is to a learnt example, the higher the neuron's output. We propose to use just either the norm 2 or norm 1 instead of a radial basis function. It will not reduce the complexity much, but norms are somewhat easier to implement on hardware than Gaussian functions, particularly in the case of the norm 1.

Figure 1: Original Hmax framework

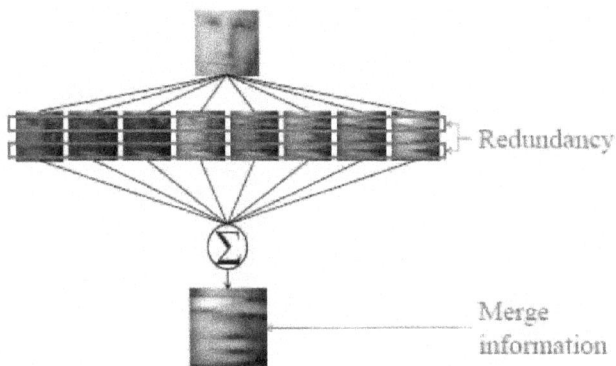

Figure 2: Merging C1 output by summing the images.

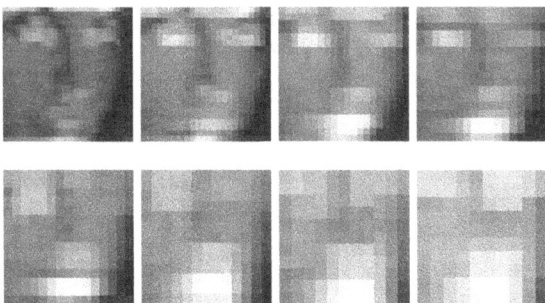

Figure 3: C1 patch pyramid for $\theta = 0$ and all scales.

3.2 Experiments

We applied the optimizations presented in the previous section to a face detection application as shown in figure 4.

Images of faces are provided by the LFWCrop dataset [5], and we used images from the popular Caltech101 dataset [6], without the face pictures, as counter-example of faces. We ran three independent experiments. First, we evaluated the recognition performance of the original algorithm, without any of the proposed optimizations. We then ran a second experiment, this time with all the optimizations we proposed and with the norm 2 instead of the radial basis function. Finally, the third experiment is the same as the second one, but this time with the norm 1.

Those three experiments all consisted in two stages: the learning stage and the testing stage. The learning stage, which aims to train the classifier, consisted in choosing 500 examples of faces from LFWCrop and 250 counter-examples from Caltech101 at random, and applying the following process to all the images: they are first convert to grayscale images, then resized to 128×128. Their histograms are equalized, and they feed HMAX's S1 and C1 layer - the versions of the S1 and C1 algorithms depending of course on the tested optimizations. Once all the images were processed, they were used as examples to train the classifier. Finally all the remaining images are used as the test base: we apply the same aforementionned process, and the RBF net classifies them as "face" or "not-face" - again, the implementation of the RBF functions depends on the tested optimizations.

The classification performances are shown in Figure 5. It appears that the performances are somewhat degraded when using the norm 2-optimized version, and even a more degraded when using the norm 1-optimized version. However, Figure 6 shows that the optimized versions are dramatically less complexe than the original one during classifications. As for the RBF net, the loss in performance between the versions with the norm 1 and the norm 2 is somewhat significant as shown in Figure 5, so the norm 2 version of the optimized algorithm should be prefered.

4. FACE DETECTION IMPLEMENTATION ON NEURODSP PROCESSOR

As introduced in this article, processing chains including neural networks are currently at the heart of researches involving processing and analysis of natural signals.

In this context, GlobalSensing Technologies and CEA LIST, created in 2012 a joint laboratory in order to design a new neuro-inspired processor called NeuroDSP. The architecture of this processor integrates signal and image pre-processing operators (convolution, linear and non-linear image trans-

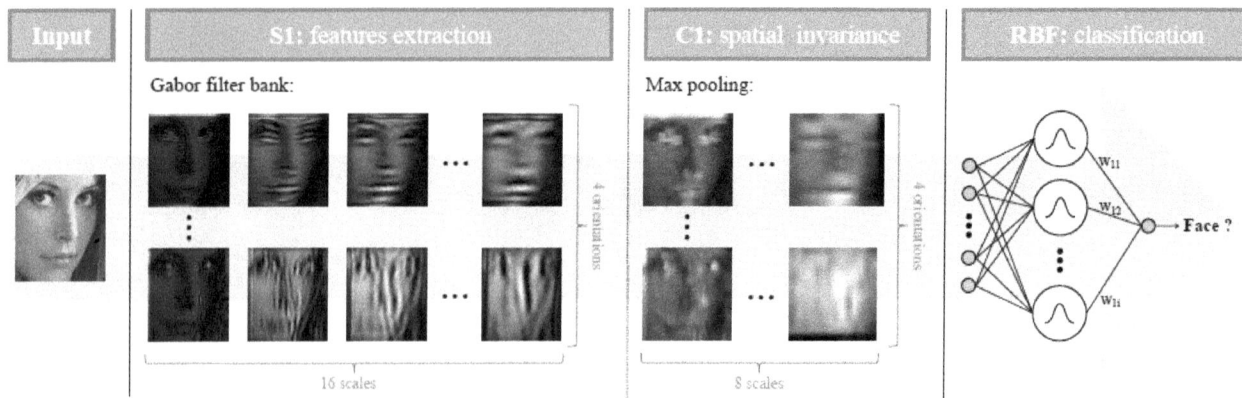

Figure 4: Optimized Hmax framework for Face Detection.

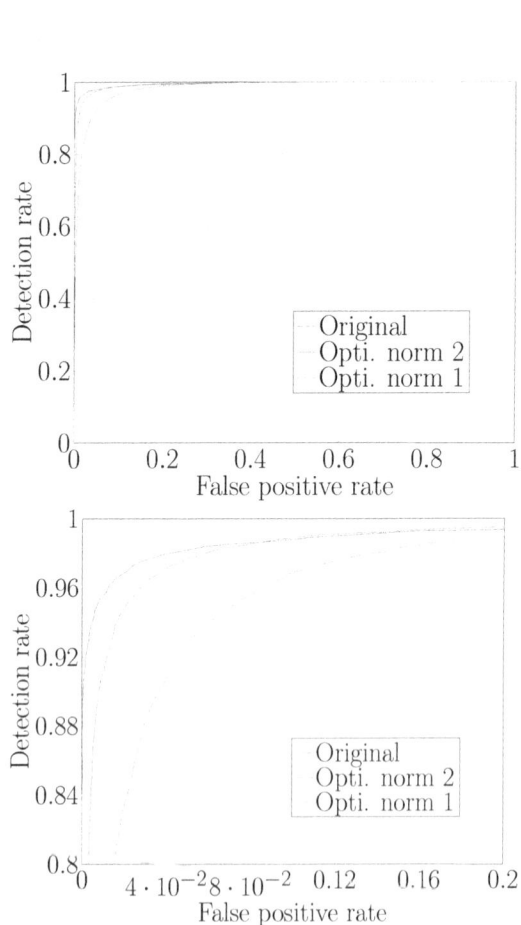

Figure 5: Recognition rates as a function of false positive rates. The "Original" curve shows the performance obtained with the original algorithm, "Opti. norm 2" shows the performance got when using all the optimizations and the norm 2 distance, and "Opti. norm 1" shows the results when using all the optimizations and the norm 1 distance. The Figure on the right hand side is a zoom-in of the Figure on the left hand side.

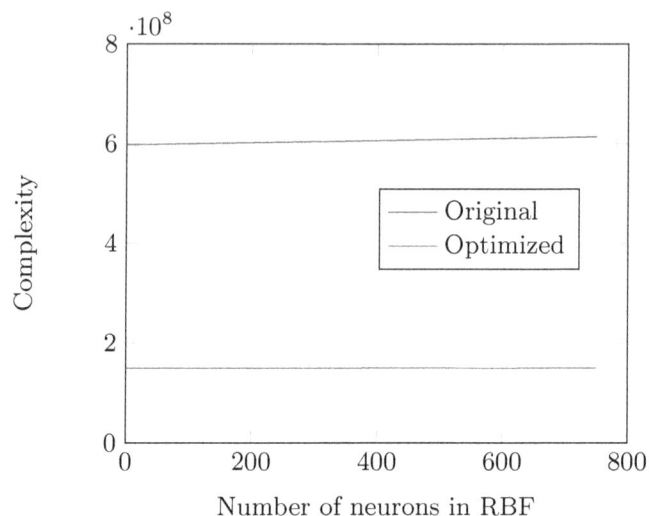

Figure 6: Classification's complexity for one image as a function of the number of neurons in the classifier.

forms) in combination with artificial neural network functions (RBF, KNN, MLP). Thanks to this architecture, NeuroDSP can realize different neuro-inspired chains like Convolutional Neural Network or Hmax.

In this section we present first the main specifications of the NeuroDSP processor and then we show that we can implement the face detection algorithm studied in the previous section.

4.1 NeuroDSP processor description

The full NeuroDSP architecture, illustrated in Figure 7 is based on clusters of 32 elementary processors working in parallel.

The specifications of each cluster are summarized as follows:

- 32 programmable PEs, each can perform image-signal processing and neural functions;

- Optimized for MAC operations:

  - Signal processing: convolution filters, etc.

214

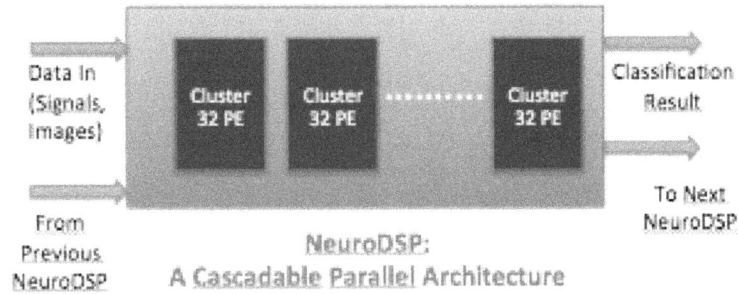

Figure 7: NeuroDSP architecture.

– Neural functions: weighted inputs sum

- Can perform non-linear operations;

- 1 PE represents 1 neuron, PEs can be time multiplexed for implementing bigger networks;

- Optimized memory accesses for data locality and reuse

With this architecture, we can consider a variable number of clusters to accommodate different application domains and related performances.

First implementation have been considered with FPGA and ASIC TSMC 45 nm technology. With this last one, we obtained a preliminary profile result which shows that one PE working at 800MHz can achieve 800 Moperations per second with 1.5mW of power consumption. Thus with a cluster of 32 programmable PEs, more than 25GOPS (1 GOPS=1 Giga operations per second) can be reached with a 48mW power consumption.

4.2 Face detection implementation

In relation to the previous section, we have shown that an optimized Hmax algorithm for face detection needs 16 Gabor Filters (S1 layer) and a C1 spatial pooling layer followed by a RBF neural network.

Considering a 128×128 pixels original face image, we need the following amount of calculations:

- S1 layer:16 filters with kernel from 7×7 to 37×37 (see Table 1) need 9104 MAC per pixel thus 4.5 GMac per second for a 128×128 pixels image working at 30fps (frames per second)

- C1 layer: 9 MOPS (1 OPS= 1 operation per second) for a 128×128 pixels image working at 30fps

- RBF layer: 48 MOPS for a 128×128 pixels image working at 30fps

So, in this application the main amount of calculations corresponds to the S1 layer (Gabor filters). In relation to the NeuroDSP specifications we can see that the face detection algorithm proposed in this article can be easily executed in real time (30 fps) using only one cluster and this with a very low-power consumption (less than 48mW).

5. CONCLUSION

The work presented in this paper is partly done within the NeuroDSP project.[1]

Neuro-inspired algorithms like HMAX studied in this article, extract a large variety of different features from images, so it may be used to recognize any kind of objects. However, when considering a specific object recognition task, some of those feature may not be needed. We considered here a face detection application; discarding the features that do not seem relevant and merging duplicate features allowed us to dramatically reduce the algorithm complexity, while the performance in terms of recognition rate is not much degraded. Thanks to this result, we have shown that the implementation of the optimized Hmax algorithm for face detection is realizable using the NeuroDSP accelarator with a very low-power consumption.

Further work will consist in finding a more general framework allowing to find optimizations depending on the considered application.

6. REFERENCES

[1] Riesenhuber,M. and Poggio, T. *Hierarchical models of object recognition in cortex.* Nature, 1999

[2] LeCun,Y. and Kavukcuoglu,K. and Farabet,C. *Convolutional Networks and Applications in Vision.* IEEE ISCAS 2010

[3] Thorpe,S., Brilhault,A. and Perez-Carrasco, J.A. *Suggestions for a Biologically Inspired Spiking Retina using Order-based Coding.* IEEE ISCAS 2010

[4] Serre,T., Wolf,L., Bileschi,S., Riesenhuber,M. and Poggio, T. *Robust Object Recognition with Cortex-like Mechanisms.* IEEE PAMI vol. 29, num 3, march 2007

[5] G. B. Huang, M. Ramesh, T. Berg, and E. Learned-Miller. *Labeled faces in the wild: A database for studying face recognition in unconstrained environments,* University of Massachusetts, Amherst, Tech. Rep. 07-49, Oct. 2007.

[6] L. Fei-Fei, R. Fergus, and P. Perona, *Learning generative visual models from few training examples: An incremental bayesian approach tested on 101 object categories,* in Conference on Computer Vision and Pattern Recognition Workshop, 2004. CVPRW âĂŹ04, Jun. 2004, pp. 178âĂŞ178

[1] Part of this work was funded by French FUI under the NeuroDSP project with the participation of BPI France, Region Bourgogne, Conseil General de Savoie, Grand Dijon, Arve Indusries and Vitagora..

Space Oblivious Compression: Power Reduction for Non-Volatile Main Memories

Yong Li, Haifeng Xu
Department of ECE, University
of Pittsburgh
Pittsburgh, PA, 15261
{yol26,hax6}@pitt.edu

Rami Melhem
Department of CS, University
of Pittsburgh
Pittsburgh, PA, 15261
melhem@cs.pitt.edu

Alex K. Jones
Department of ECE, University
of Pittsburgh
Pittsburgh, PA, 15261
akjones@pitt.edu

ABSTRACT

Power consumption of main memory has become a critical concern and has led to proposals to employ emerging non-volatile memories (NVMs) to replace or augment DRAM. This paper proposes *Space Oblivious COmpression* (SOCO), an in-place lightweight compression mechanism particularly designed for reducing NVM-based main-memory energy rather than saving space. SOCO can significantly reduce the number of bits written to save considerable energy for NVM-based main memories. By relaxing the goal of a conventional compression, the proposed approach practically eliminates memory addressing and management overheads incurred by compression techniques designed to save space. Our experiments show that SOCO provides more than 50% reduction in bits written, resulting in 23% and 34% energy savings for Spin-transfer Torque (STT)-MRAM and Phase Change Memory (PCM), respectively.

Categories and Subject Descriptors

B.3 [**Hardware**]: Memory Structures—*General*

General Terms

Design, Experimentation, Performance

Keywords

Energy Saving; STT-RAM; PCM; Compression

1. INTRODUCTION

Reducing power consumption of main memory under performance constraints has become the most critical metric in delivering high-performance and low-power computing platforms. A recent study of server class systems shows that main memory consumes 40% of server power [6] exacerbating both the direct energy consumption and the indirect energy contribution required to mitigate the power density/thermal effects (e.g., HVAC) of these systems. This percentage of energy contribution is even higher when the system is in standby mode, a common case for mobile systems, typically to save energy. This has led to several proposals to utilize emerging non-volatile memory (NVMs) such as

phase change memory (PCM) [15] and spin-transfer torque magnetic RAM (STT-MRAM) [9] at the main memory level. These NVMs provide advantages of dramatically reduced static energy consumption by eliminating the need for refresh while also boasting potential advantages in technology scalability and density. Unfortunately, PCM and STT-MRAM have a much higher dynamic write energy than DRAM that can limit their energy advantage.

In this paper we design a simple and efficient mechanism to reduce the impact of dynamic write power in NVM-based main memories called *space oblivious compression* (SOCO). It has been widely observed that data stored in main memory is highly redundant [1, 8, 13]. The key observation of SOCO is that storing compressed data to main memory can be much less expensive than writing the original uncompressed value if the mechanism to eliminate data redundancy (1) is lightweight and (2) avoids addressing complexity. Unfortunately, direct adoption of existing space saving compression schemes, while lightweight, can incur considerable runtime overheads in addressing, access indirection and memory management due to re-organization of data values, variable sized blocks, dynamically changing compression ratios, difficulties in calculating address offsets, etc.

In contrast, SOCO's "compression" is dedicated to reducing power consumption in NVMs rather than the traditional goal of saving memory space. In particular, SOCO leverages a cache-block-level delta-based compression scheme similar to the one used in prior work [14] but utilizes an essentially unmodified page management mechanism to enhance compression effectiveness and reduce overheads compared with the leading capacity oriented scheme [13]. The contributions of this work are enumerated as follows:

- We propose SOCO, a page organization that leverages existing lightweight compression techniques to save NVM-based main memory energy instead of space.

- We demonstrate that SOCO can provide significant energy savings in systems employing PCM and STT-MRAM.

- We demonstrate that SOCO is orthogonal and can be applied effectively with existing NVM-based main memory power optimizing schemes.

Our experiments demonstrate that SOCO reduces bits written by more than 50% with less than 1% performance overhead. For NVM systems employing differential-write, SOCO still provides a significant reduction of 30% of dynamic writes.

2. SPACE OBLIVIOUS COMPRESSION

SOCO is a lightweight compression mechanism that is appropriate to be used as an on-the-fly mechanism and leverages BDI [14] compression. It is different than LCP [13] in that it keeps the compressed data in place. This avoids heavy data alignment, packing,

GLSVLSI'15, May 20–22, 2015, Pittsburgh, PA, USA.
Copyright © 2015 ACM 978-1-4503-3474-7/15/05 ...$15.00.
http://dx.doi.org/10.1145/2742060.2742107.

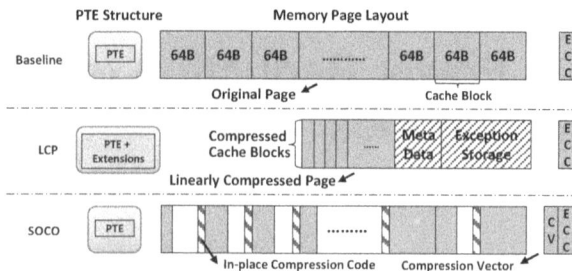

Figure 1: Compression schemes.

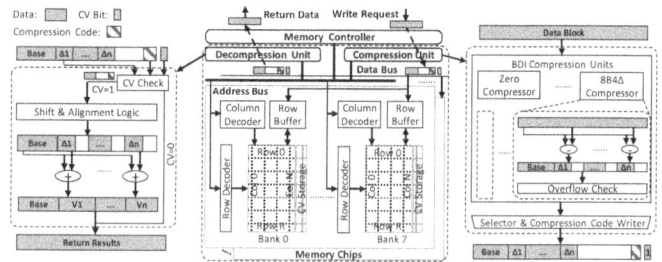

Figure 2: SOCO main memory design

offset computation and addressing overheads typically associated with a space-saving compression mechanisms including LCP. For example, LCP must utilize a single compression pattern for all of the blocks in the page to simplify addressing. In contrast, SOCO can utilize the most efficient pattern for each block as the addressing is identical to the original uncompressed scheme. In the next section we describe the BDI and LCP approach in some detail.

2.1 BDI and LCP Compression

The BDI method [14] leverages redundant patterns (e.g., zero blocks, narrow values and low dynamic range patterns) exhibited by adjacent data bytes/values within a cache block. In particular, BDI divides a cache block into several sub-blocks and represents the entire block as two *base* sub-blocks (a zero sub-block and the first non-zero sub-block) plus the difference information (Δ). Depending on the memory content a block can be compressed into different formats (i.e., 8-Byte Base + 4-Byte Δ, 8-Byte Base + 2-Byte Δ, 8-Byte Base + 1-Byte Δ, 4-Byte Base + 2-Byte Δ, 4-Byte Base + 1-Byte Δ, 2-Byte Base + 1-Byte Δ and zero compression), which are stored as a *compression code* attached to each block and examined for decompression purposes. The compressibility of all the formats are examined by a hardware unit in parallel and the result with the best compression ratio is selected.

In a uncompressed memory space, a page can be decomposed into blocks corresponding to the cache line size as shown in Figure 1 (Baseline). For example, in a system with 4K pages and 64-byte cache lines, each page is divided into 64 64-byte blocks. LCP [13] [Figure 1 (LCP)] compresses all compressible blocks of a memory page into the same format (i.e., all blocks in a page have the same compression code) using a particular compression scheme such as BDI. The common compression code for the page is stored in an extended Page Table Entry (PTE) structure for the page. However, not all blocks can be compressed. Thus, in LCP, each page contains an *exception* region to store uncompressed blocks and a *metadata* area to assist the addressing of compressed/uncompressed blocks, as illustrated in Figure 1 (LCP).

Another overhead of LCP is incurred when an updated data block cannot be accommodated in the compressed region and needs to be copied to the exception area. As LCP manages physical pages with different sizes (i.e., 512-, 1024-, 2048- and 4096- Bytes) for accommodating compressed data, memory writes could result in expensive page resizing faults that take thousands of cycles [18].

2.2 SOCO Compression

Similar to LCP, SOCO operates on cache-line sized memory blocks. We also leverage the lightweight compression scheme of BDI that allows data to be compressed using base+Δ form, zero-compression, or uncompressed as described in Section 2-2.1. Since our primary goal is to reduce bits written and active data bits, rather than saving memory space, we propose an organization of the compressed page different than the LCP scheme to simplify addressing.

In SOCO, each block is marked as either compressed or uncompressed, indicated by a corresponding bit in a *compression vector* (CV) associated with the page (see the SOCO page layout in Figure 1). The CV structure is stored in a non-addressable area similar to the bits required for a scheme such as Flip-N-Write [5]. The additional storage overhead for the CV is small (e.g., 8B compared to 4KB or $< 0.2\%$ overhead in a system with 4KB pages and 64B cache lines). This avoids the need for a metadata or exception region, modification to the PTEs or the Translation Lookaside Buffer (TLB), or memory controllers, as all blocks are stored in place.

In SOCO, compressed blocks require storage of far fewer bits, but the entire space is available should the block require storage in uncompressed fashion. The compression code for compressed blocks is also stored in a fixed location (e.g., the last few bits of the block). For BDI three bits are needed to distinguish eight different compression formats. Writes to the block result in replacing the stored data with new data directly. Storage of compressed values store only the required bits and compression code, avoiding unnecessary writes. This is shown in Figure 1 (SOCO), where the white space indicates unutilized space due to compressed data. Further, changes in the compression status of the block during a write do not incur modifications to the page structures, nor do they trigger page faults as in LCP.

2.3 Integration in Main Memory

SOCO can be implemented by integrating the compression and decompression logic into the serial data-bus interface at the DIMM level. As illustrated in Figure 2, multiple memory chips are laid out in a way similar to the conventional DRAM, except that each memory bank is extended with the CV bits indicating whether the corresponding data rows are compressed.

Upon a write request, the compression unit (the right part of Figure 2) compresses the data block before it is written into the row buffer through the data bus and finally into the storage array (organized as rows and columns). Similar to BDI [14], the compression unit comprises multiple compressors operated in parallel. Each compressor divides the to-be-compressed data block into several sub-blocks (SBs) of a certain length and calculates the difference (i.e., delta) between each sub-block and the *Base* block (the first sub-block) using a subtracter. If the differences for all sub-blocks are within a specific range (e.g., 4 bytes) dictated by the overflow check logic, the compressor reports a compressibility status to the compression selector, which selects the compressor with highest compression ratio based on the reports of all the compressors. Then the compression code writer returns the compressed data with the corresponding compression code indicating how it is compressed. Note that in our design each block is compressed individually, regardless how other blocks in the page are compressed. This greatly simplifies compression unit design. In contrast, LPC requires that all the compressed blocks in one page must be compressed by the same compression method, which requires a global decision for selecting an appropriate compressor and complicates the design.

Upon a read request, the decompression unit is employed to decompress the requested data block read from the row buffer. As shown in the left part of Figure 2, the decompression unit first checks the CV bit after reading the block from memory arrays through the data bus. If the CV bit for the block is 0, the data read out is directly returned as a response to the read request. If, however, the CV bit is 1, shifting logic is used to align delta blocks to the beginning of the corresponding data sub-blocks based on the compression code. Once aligned, the delta information and the base block are fed into a series of adders to compute the original values.

3. EXPERIMENTS AND RESULTS

For performance and power evaluation we use a PIN [16] based in-house simulator to model a 4-issue width, 4GHz CPU with three levels of caches (4-way 16KB, 8-way 1MB, 16-way 4MB) and 4GB main memory. The access time for the three levels of caches are 1, 3, and 20 cycles, respectively and the page fault penalty (4KB) is 3000 cycles. We implement SOCO and LCP techniques in the modeled main memory. To demonstrate that the proposed compression technique is independent of NVM technology, we model both STT-MRAM and PCM and show that our approach achieves consistent performance gains. We use applications from the Rodinia [4] and PARSEC [3] benchmark suites.

Table 1: Memory parameters.

Memory	STT-MRAM	PCM
Read Latency (cycles)	84 (21ns)	192 (48ns)
Write Latency (cycles)	123 (21ns+10ns(*MTJ switch time*))	600 (150ns)
Read Energy (pJ/bit)	1.24 [11]	2.47 [12]
Write Energy (pJ/bit)	3.51 [11]	16.82 [12]
Precharge Power (mW)	7.25 [11]	18.6 ($\approx$ DRAM)
Refresh Power (mW)	0 (no refresh)	0 (no refresh)
Active Power (mW)	91.4 ($\approx$ DRAM)	91.4 ($\approx$ DRAM)

Similar to prior work, we assume STT-MRAM read latency is competitive to DRAM [11]. The STT-MRAM write energy we used in our simulation is 3.51 pJ/bit, or 2.8 times of the read energy. The precharge power is 7.25mW in our STT-MRAM modeling. We adopt the PCM latency and power model used in prior work [12]. Similar to STT-MRAM, reads in PCM are non-destructive and thus, the required precharge power is lower than that of DRAM.

We implement LCP [13] based on the BDI [14] compression scheme, which is also similar to the one used in prior work for PCM [7]. To accelerate meta data accesses for compression and decompression, we use a meta cache of 512 entries with 2-cycle hit latency. In all the compared compression mechanisms we adopt a bitwise LEAP adder design [2] with a power consumption of 9.96 fJ/bit per addition operation with two cycle latency.

3.1 Write Savings

Figures 3a reports the percentage of memory bits written/stored in a baseline uncompressed system that can be eliminated by adopting various compression mechanisms. On the baseline system (Figure 3a), LCP achieves a write reduction from 2% for *srad* to 75% for *particlefilter*. On average, LCP reduces bits written/stored by 41%. Applying SOCO over the baseline system results in a reduction from 13% for *nn* to nearly 80% for *particlefilter*. Noticeably, for some applications such as *srad*, SOCO drastically reduces written/stored bits compared to LCP (from 2% to 75%). This advantage comes from the flexibility of applying a different compression mechanism for each block in the page. On average, using SOCO

reduces 51% of written/stored bits. As such SOCO provides a 17% improvement compared to LCP.

To evaluate the impact of applying LCP and SOCO on a system that employs a NVM-based main memory we consider the impact of using compression schemes combined with the leading method to reduce dynamic write power in NVMs, differential write (DW) [7]. DW compares values to be written with the original values stored and only writes the bits that differ. DW can be viewed as an optimized version of partial writes [11, 12] where dirty status for every bit is tracked so that a bit is flipped only when necessary, thus significantly reducing the number of bits that need to be changed during a write. The results for applying LCP and SOCO to a system that employs DW is shown in Figure 3c. Applying LCP on top of DW provides almost no additional benefit ($<$1%) in terms of written bits. In contrast, combining SOCO with DW achieves a reduction of up to 80% over a DW baseline (*hotspot*) with an average savings over DW of more than 30%.

3.2 System Performance Analysis

Figure 3b shows the execution time of the compared compression mechanisms normalized to the baseline system. Unfortunately, LCP exceptions (e.g., page resizing faults, see Section 2-2.1) can add significant page fault penalties. On average, LCP slows down systems with STT-MRAM and PCM by 39% and 23%, respectively. Since, in Figure 3b, the average performance degradation is dominated by a small number of benchmarks, we recompute an average degradation excluding the two worst performing benchmarks (*srad* and *backprop*). The recomputed average slowdown of LCP becomes 5.1% and 4.6% on STT-MRAM and PCM, respectively. In contrast, SOCO retains the compressed blocks and compression code in place and avoids exception and memory access overheads. As Figure 3b shows, the performance impact from SOCO is negligible. SOCO's minor degradations are mainly caused by compression/decompression latencies and add a nominal 0.18% and 0.1% for STT-MRAM and PCM, respectively.

3.3 Memory Energy Reduction

Figure 3d reports memory energy consumption of the different schemes. For each memory technology, the energy consumption of various mechanisms are normalized to the baseline system with the same memory technology. SOCO has a higher compression ratio than LCP and thus, consumes the lowest read/write dynamic power. Based on our modeling the compression power is negligible. For STT-MRAM, LCP reduces energy consumption by 8.5% while SOCO reduces it by 22.6%. On PCM, the dynamic power constitutes an even larger portion of the overall power consumption compared with STT-MRAM. Thus, reducing bits to write impacts energy more significantly. As such, SOCO reduces the average total energy consumption by 34%, compared to 21.2% by LCP.

4. RELATED WORK

Some prior attempts utilize memory technology independent encoding schemes to reduce the number of bits to program during write operations. In particular, Jacobvitz *et al.* [10] introduce a redundant encoding mechanism in which each possible data word is mapped to a code set named *coset* where multiple encoded words can be selected. Cho *et al.* [5] propose *Flip-N-Write*, a mechanism to reduce bit programming effort by replacing the write operation with a read-modify-write operation. Delta compression [7] is proposed for a hybrid PCM-DRAM main memory. Frequently modified data are updated based on the delta value (achieved by an XOR operation). As a result, fewer writes occur in the main memory. MemZip [17] also uses lightweight compression with the goal

(a) Percentage of written bits saved by SOCO

(b) Performance in execution time (normalized to uncompressed (baseline))

(c) Percentage of written bits saved by SOCO with DW

(d) Energy impact (normalized to total energy consumed by baseline)

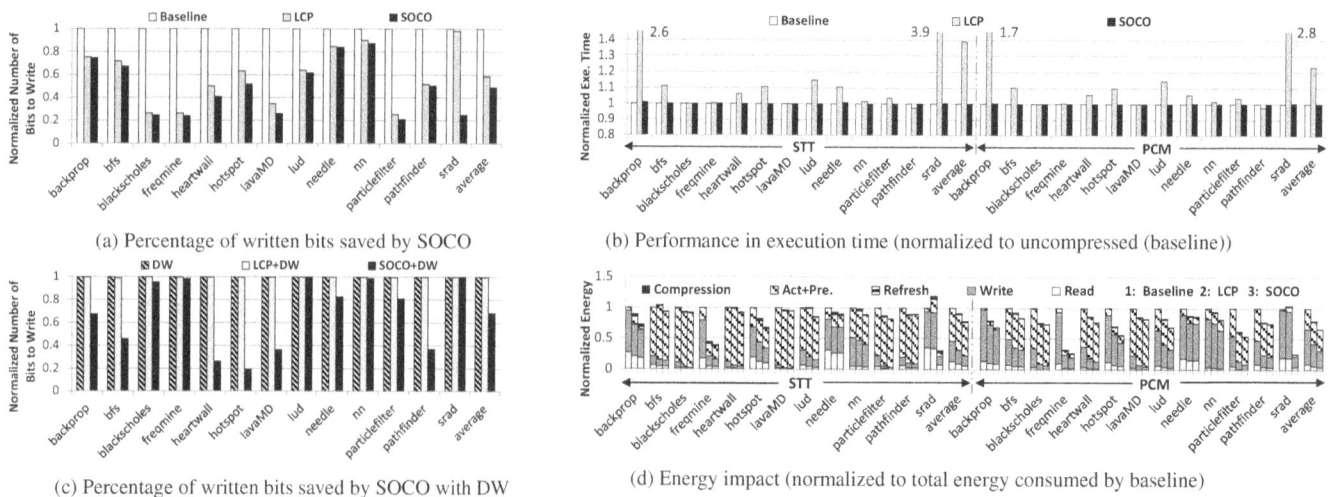

Figure 3: Performance and Energy Results.

to reduce power in the memory system and unlike LCP does not change the memory organization. MemZip's approach is to compress data at the memory controller and reduce power by reducing the amount of data communicated to and from the memory system.

5. CONCLUSION

This paper studies the use of compression techniques to reduce the number of written bits, which translates to energy savings in PCM and STT-MRAM memory technologies. We propose a highly efficient, low overhead, and effective page compression mechanism, SOCO, to compress data for energy optimization rather than improving effective capacity. The outcome of our evaluation for PCM and STT-MRAM memories shows that SOCO introduces practically no latency increase to the memory access path while dramatically reducing the number of bits accessed.

6. ACKNOWLEDGMENTS

This worked is supported by NSF award CCF-1064976, EFRI-1038139, and SAMSUNG SGMI award.

7. REFERENCES

[1] B. Abali, H. Franke, D. E. Poff, R. Saccone, C. O. Schulz, L. M. Herger, and T. B. Smith. Memory expansion technology (mxt): software support and performance. *IBM Journal of Research and Development*, 45(2):287–301, 2001.

[2] M. Alioto and G. Palumbo. Analysis and comparison on full adder block in submicron technology. *IEEE Trans. on (VLSI) Systems*, 10(6):806–823, 2002.

[3] C. Bienia, S. Kumar, J. P. Singh, and K. Li. The parsec benchmark suite: Characterization and architectural implications. Technical Report TR-811-08, Princeton University, January 2008.

[4] S. Che, J. Sheaffer, M. Boyer, L. Szafaryn, L. Wang, and K. Skadron. A characterization of the rodinia benchmark suite with comparison to contemporary cmp workloads. In *Proc. of IISWC*, pages 1–11, 2010.

[5] S. Cho and H. Lee. Flip-n-write: A simple deterministic technique to improve pram write performance, energy and endurance. In *Proc. of MICRO*, pages 347–357, 2009.

[6] Q. Deng, D. Meisner, L. Ramos, T. F. Wenisch, and R. Bianchini. Memscale: Active low-power modes for main memory. *SIGPLAN Not.*, 47(4):225–238, Mar. 2011.

[7] Y. Du, M. Zhou, B. Childers, R. Melhem, and D. Mossé. Delta-compressed caching for overcoming the write bandwidth limitation of hybrid main memory. *ACM Trans. Archit. Code Optim.*, 9(4):55:1–55:20, Jan. 2013.

[8] M. Ekman and P. Stenstrom. A robust main-memory compression scheme. In *Proc. of ISCA*, pages 74–85, Washington, DC, USA, 2005. IEEE Computer Society.

[9] M. Hosomi, H. Yamagishi, T. Yamamoto, and K. B. et al. A novel nonvolatile memory with spin torque transfer magnetization switching: Spin-ram. *IEDM Technical Digest*, 2(25):459–462, 2005.

[10] A. N. Jacobvitz, R. Calderbank, and D. J. Sorin. Coset coding to extend the lifetime of memory. In *Proc. of HPCA*, pages 222–233, 2013.

[11] E. Kültürsay, M. Kandemir, A. Sivasubramaniam, and O. Mutlu. Evaluating stt-ram as an energy-efficient main memory alternative.

[12] B. C. Lee, E. Ipek, O. Mutlu, and D. Burger. Architecting phase change memory as a scalable dram alternative. *SIGARCH Comput. Archit. News*, 37:2–13, June 2009.

[13] G. Pekhimenko, V. Seshadri, Y. Kim, H. Xin, O. Mutlu, M. A. Kozuch, P. B. Gibbons, and T. C. Mowry. Linearly compressed pages: A low-complexity, low-latency main memory compression framework. In *Proc. of MICRO*, 2013.

[14] G. Pekhimenko, V. Seshadri, O. Mutlu, P. B. Gibbons, M. A. Kozuch, and T. C. Mowry. Base-delta-immediate compression: practical data compression for on-chip caches. In *Proc. of PACT*, pages 377–388, 2012.

[15] M. Qureshi, M. Franceschini, and L. Lastras-Montano. Improving read performance of phase change memories via write cancellation and write pausing. In *High Performance Computer Architecture (HPCA), 2010 IEEE 16th International Symposium on*, pages 1–11, jan. 2010.

[16] V. J. Reddi, A. Settle, D. A. Connors, and R. S. Cohn. Pin: a binary instrumentation tool for computer architecture research and education. In *Proc. of WCAE*, 2004.

[17] A. Shafiee, M. Taassori, R. Balasubramonian, and A. Davis. Memzip: Exploring unconventional benefits from memory compression. In *Proc. of HPCA*, pages 638–649, Feb 2014.

[18] X. Wang, J. Zang, Z. Wang, Y. Luo, and X. Li. Selective hardware/software memory virtualization. *SIGPLAN Not.*, 46(7):217–226, Mar. 2011.

Flip-Mirror-Rotate: An Architecture for Bit-write Reduction and Wear Leveling in Non-volatile Memories

Poovaiah M. Palangappa
Electrical and Computer Engineering
University of Pittsburgh, Pittsburgh, PA
pmp30@pitt.edu

Kartik Mohanram
Electrical and Computer Engineering
University of Pittsburgh, Pittsburgh, PA
kartik.mohanram@gmail.com

ABSTRACT

This paper proposes Flip-Mirror-Rotate (FMR), an architecture for bit-write reduction and endurance enhancement in emerging non-volatile memories (NVMs). FMR comprises three components: adaptive Flip-N-Write (aFNW), Mirror-N-Write (MNW), and Rotate-N-Write (RNW). aFNW and MNW focus on word-level bit-write reduction, which reduces NVM dynamic energy while also improving endurance. RNW is an intra-word wear leveling scheme that operates at cache line granularity. The proposed FMR architecture is integrated with frequent pattern compression (FPC) to simultaneously reduce bit-writes and wear in NVMs. Trace-based simulations of the SPEC CPU2006 benchmarks show that for the same memory overhead and $< 1\%$ loss in memory bandwidth, FMR reduces bit-writes (dynamic energy) by 48% (29%) in comparison to classical read-modify-write (DCW), 39% (13%) in comparison to Flip-N-Write (FNW), and 21% (14%) in comparison to FPC. Simultaneously, FMR also reduces the peak bit-writes per cell by 47% in comparison to DCW, 34% in comparison to FNW, and 47% in comparison to FPC, improving NVM endurance.

Categories and Subject Descriptors

B.3.0 [**MEMORY STRUCTURES**]: General

Keywords

Non-volatile Memory; Endurance; Energy; Wear Leveling

1. Introduction

The ITRS projects that non-volatile memory (NVM) technologies such as phase-change memory (PCM) [1], resistive RAM (R-RAM) [2], and spin-transfer torque RAM (STT-RAM) [3] are suitable replacement candidates for DRAM due to their better scalability and lower leakage [4]. However, NVMs present new challenges in comparison to DRAM: asymmetric read/write access latencies, higher power/energy requirements, and limited endurance, which impede their large-scale adoption in computing systems [1–3]. To overcome these problems, a broad set of solutions that rely on data-encoding [5], write scheduling [6–9], data-migration using address translation [10–12], and architectural improvements [13, 14] have been proposed. However, these techniques address either NVM latency, power/energy, or endurance explicitly; this potentially limits their effectiveness in practice. In contrast, solutions that focus on reducing bit-writes, i.e., cell updates in NVMs have the universal

This work was supported by NSF Award CCF-1217738.

technology-independent appeal of simultaneously reducing write latency, lowering dynamic energy, and enhancing endurance.

Flip-N-Write (FNW) [15] and frequent pattern compression (F-PC) [16] are two state-of-the-art techniques that have successfully reduced the number of bit-writes within a data word. FNW compares the existing data in memory with the new data to be written and conditionally performs bit-wise invert or 'flip' on the individual data partitions of a word. Whereas FNW guarantees $\leq n/2$ bit-writes for an n-bit data word and reduces peak-bit writes by 50%, the average bit-write reduction of FNW is $\approx 15\%$. FNW also incurs 1 bit of overhead per partition (byte/half-word/full-word); increasing the number of partitions (and thus overhead) reduces the bit-writes marginally (≈ 3-4%). In addition, FNW cannot reduce bit-writes if the data already yields $\leq n/2$ bit-writes. Further, FNW does not exploit statistical characteristics such as the frequency of occurrence of patterns in the data. Recently, in [16], it has been shown that FPC can be used to compress data to reduce the number of bit-writes in the NVM. It is reported that when 32-bit FPC is integrated with opportunistic wear leveling, it is possible to reduce bit-writes by 2-3× in comparison to FNW. However, although FPC reduces the average number of bit-writes per word, it increases the entropy of a few bit locations within the word. In practice, this may lead to premature failures of these high-entropy cells, lowering NVM endurance.

This paper proposes Flip-Mirror-Rotate (FMR), an architecture for bit-write reduction and endurance enhancement in NVMs. First, since classical FNW cannot be integrated with FPC, we propose adaptive-FNW (aFNW) that extends classical FNW by dynamically adapting partition size to uncompressed/compressed data. aFNW effectively integrates FNW with FPC, resulting in bit-write reductions over both FNW and FPC. Second, we propose Mirror-N-Write (MNW), which conditionally bit-reverses (i.e., mirrors) the data depending on the potential number of bit-writes. Unlike FNW, which is ineffective if an n-bit word already yields $\leq n/2$ bit-writes, MNW reduces the number of bit-writes over and above FNW. Third, we propose Rotate-N-Write (RNW), an intra-word, cache line granularity wear leveling technique that is orthogonal to aFNW, MNW, and FPC. For an overhead of 3 tag bits per 512-bit cache line, RNW 'rotates' writes in offsets of 8 across each 64-bit word to spread the wear across the data word and effectively reduce the peak bit-writes per cell. Finally, we evaluate FMR using memory traces from the SPEC CPU2006 benchmarks.

2. Background and Motivation

Non-volatile memory (NVM) technologies, as an alternative to existing mainstream memory technologies such as DRAM and SRAM, have their advantages in high density, low leakage power, and non-volatility. However, most NVM technologies suffer from high write energy [17], limited endurance [1], and asymmetric read/write latencies [18–21]. Modern NVM modules include energy consumption limits on their operation to prevent the modules from overloading the power supply, and to prevent overheating. How-

Prefix	Pattern encoded	Example	Compressed example	Encoded size	Value space	Compression contribution
000	Zero run	0x0000000000000000	0x0	3 bits	1 value	29.7%
001	8-bit sign-extended	0x000000000000007F	0x17F	11 bits	255 values	1%
010	16-bit sign-extended	0xFFFFFFFFFFFFB6B6	0x2B6B6	19 bits	65280 values	1%
011	Half-word sign-extended	0x0000000076543210	0x376543210	35 bits	$\approx 2^{32}$ values	2.1%
100	Half-word, padded with a zero half-word	0x7654321000000000	0x476543210	35 bits	$\approx 2^{32}$ values	16.4%
101	Two half-words, each a byte sign-extended	0xFFFFBEEF00003CAB	0x5BEEF3CAB	35 bits	$\approx 2^{32}$ values	8.3%
110	Word consisting of four repeated double bytes	0xCAFECAFECAFECAFE	0x6CAFE	19 bits	65534 values	1.1%

Table 1: **64-bit FPC values (inclusive of 3-bit prefix, indicated in red)**

ever, write operations in NVM technologies require more energy per bit in comparison to DRAM due to their high write-current [1]. Hence, NVM modules are restricted to writing a limited amount of data at once, which in turn increases the write latency and impacts performance [14]. Furthermore, since a single write access usually involves both set and reset, the latency of the write operation is determined by the longest latency cell write, creating a bottleneck for individual write operations [21]. Finally, during NVM operation, frequently changed cells are subjected to higher physical stresses, which results in poor data retention and eventual cell failure. This limits the lifetime of these memory cells to around 10^{8-10} writes [1, 17, 22].

2.1 FNW and FPC: Background

Existing solutions based on data-encoding [5], write scheduling [6–9], data-migration using address translation [10–12], and architectural improvements [13, 14] focus exclusively on improving either NVM latency, power/energy, or endurance. However, bit-write reduction techniques can address these limitations simultaneously. The rest of this section focuses on two state-of-the-art bit-write reduction methods—FNW [15] and FPC [23]—and motivates their limitations with examples.

Flip-N-Write (FNW): For n-bit words, FNW computes the Hamming distance, d, between the new data and the existing data. If $d < n/2$, the new data is stored as-is; if $d > n/2$, the bit-wise complement of the data is stored, which guarantees $< n/2$ bit-writes. When $d = n/2$, the data is written in complemented/uncomplemented form consistent with the existing data to avoid redundant flips in the tag bit, which guarantees $n/2$ bit-writes. Note that FNW uses a tag bit for every 16 bits to indicate whether the stored data is complemented/uncomplemented.

Frequent pattern compression (FPC): FPC was originally proposed in [23] for data compression in L2 caches to increase their memory capacity. More recently, in [16], FPC was extended for compression of data written into the NVMs in order to reduce bit-writes. FPC maintains a table of the 8 most frequent patterns. During a write access, if incoming data matches one of the patterns, the data is compressed and stored along with a 3-bit prefix that encodes the pattern match. FPC uses 1 tag bit to indicate whether the stored data is compressed or uncompressed. This paper extends the frequent patterns used by 32-bit FPC [23] to 64-bit word lengths, which is summarized in Table 1 with an example for each frequent pattern. During a read access, the compression tag bit and the 3-bit prefix are used to expand the data to a full word.

2.2 FNW and FPC: Limitations

Although FNW and FPC are successful state-of-the-art techniques to realize bit-write reductions in NVMs, this sub-section illustrates their limitations using examples.

FNW: Consider a 16-bit example in Fig. 1, where the existing data and the new data differ by only 5 bits. Since $5 < 16/2$, the data is written as-is to memory, incurring 5 bit-writes. In other words, FNW is ineffective when writes require $\leq n/2$ cell updates.

Second, consider a 16-bit word example (as shown in Fig. 2), where we apply FNW on two 8-bit data partitions. The incoming

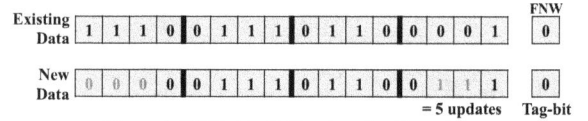

Figure 1: **FNW: Limitation for $\leq n/2$ updates**

16-bit word is compressed to 7-bit data using FPC. Due to compression, the 2nd half-word does not require any bit-writes. Hence, FNW is rendered inactive for this partition and the 2nd tag bit is underutilized. In other words, FNW is not fully effective when it is preceded by compression.

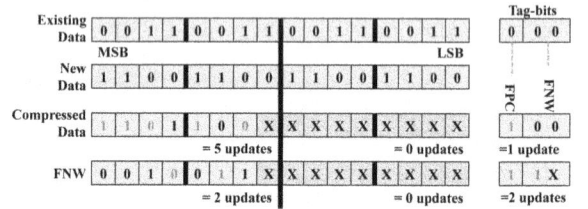

Figure 2: **FNW: Limitation when used with FPC [23]**

FPC: Consider the two examples shown in Fig. 3, where 16-bit words are compressed using 16-bit FPC. In both cases, we see that the higher order bits undergo more bit-writes (i.e., an increase in entropy) in comparison to the lower order bits. Our simulations (discussed in detail in Section 6) show that when FPC is used, bits 63, 62, and 61 used to store the FPC prefix experience a higher number of bit-writes in comparison to uncompressed data. In practice, this may lead to premature failure of these cells. In other words, although FPC is successful in reducing cumulative bit-writes, it may do so at the cost of NVM endurance by increasing the peak bit-writes per cell.

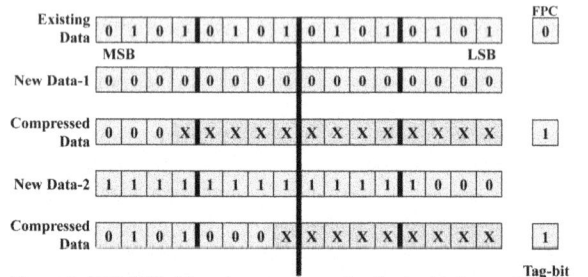

Figure 3: **FPC [23]: Bit-write concentration in the higher order bits**

3. Adaptive Flip-N-Write (aFNW)

Originally, FNW was proposed for bit-write reduction in fixed-width data [15]. However, as illustrated in Fig. 2, FNW is not optimal when it is integrated with FPC. Hence, we propose aFNW, which extends FNW by dynamically adapting data width (partition size) to work with compression techniques such as FPC.

Example: aFNW is illustrated using a 16-bit example (Fig. 4). The existing data in the memory location is chosen arbitrarily for this example. Note that aFNW always follows FPC in the FMR architecture, which is shown in the second and third lines of Fig. 4. Following compression, the 16-bit data is encoded into 8-bit data, where classical FNW results in 5 bit-writes, as shown in the fourth line of Fig. 4. However, aFNW adapts its partition size to 4 bits since the data is compressed, which results in 0 bit-writes in the data field and 2 bit-writes in the tag bits.

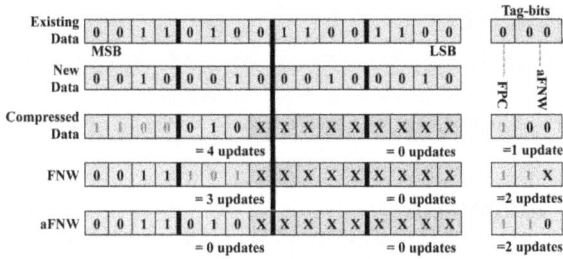

Figure 4: **Illustration of aFNW integrated with FPC**

4. Mirror-N-Write (MNW)

Whenever the Hamming distance between new and existing data is $> n/2$, FNW can reduce it to $< n/2$. However, when the Hamming distance is $\leq n/2$, FNW cannot reduce bit-writes. To address this limitation, we propose mirroring of the data word before it is written into the memory array. For n-bit data, mirroring is defined as taking data in the order of significance $[(n\text{-}1):0]$ and writing it in the form $[0:(n\text{-}1)]$. Note that one tag bit is required to record the status of the data as mirrored/un-mirrored. For uniform data traffic, the average Hamming distance between the existing and incoming data is the same for mirrored/un-mirrored data. However, FPC and FNW operate only on un-mirrored data; this motivates MNW to take advantage of the possibility to reduce bit-writes using data mirroring, regardless of the success of FNW/FPC.

Example: MNW is illustrated using a 16-bit word with 2 aFNW partitions. As shown in Fig. 5, in the absence of MNW, the incoming data results in 3 bit-writes in the first partition and 2 bit-writes in the second partition. FNW cannot further reduce the number of bit-writes since the bit-flips in both the partitions are ≤ 4. However, when MNW is used to mirror the word ($[15:0] \rightarrow [0:15]$) in this example, the 'mirrored' data that results in only 3 bit-writes is written to memory and the tag bit is updated to mirrored.

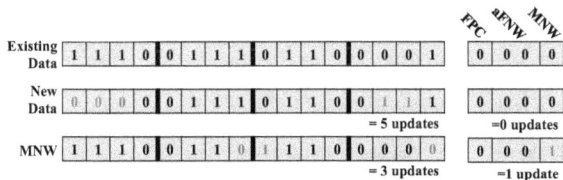

Figure 5: **Illustration of MNW**

5. Wear leveling: Rotate-N-Write

Word-level compression schemes like FPC reduce bit-writes by leveraging program data statistics to eliminate redundant bit-flips. However, in doing so, the bit-writes for a few of these cells are increased in comparison to other cells within the same word. For example, although FPC reduces the total writes across most bit indices in comparison to data-comparison write (DCW, i.e., classical read-modify-write for NVMs [24] used as the baseline in this work), it increases the number of writes for FPC prefix bits (bit indices 63, 62, and 61, shown in Fig. 6(a)). Also, due to the statistical nature of FPC, the higher order bits of a memory word experience more bit-writes in comparison to the lower order bits. Since the endurance of the word is limited by the endurance of its weakest cell, FPC potentially reduces overall NVM endurance. This limitation in FPC motivates RNW, which is a cache line granularity intra-word wear leveling scheme to uniformly spread bit-writes across a word.

RNW operates at cache line granularity since most data transactions between the last level cache and the main memory are in

units of cache lines, either due to 'write-through' or cache evictions. Hence, all the words in a cache line are subjected to the same access patterns. This implies that for any intra-word wear leveling scheme, it is sufficient to maintain a common set of tag bits for all words in the cache line. RNW maintains one global 16-bit counter (GC) for the entire NVM module and one global 3-bit offset register. GC increments every time a write access is received by the NVM module; whenever GC saturates, it resets and increments the offset register. During a write access, the data is offset by $8\times$ the offset register. Along with the data, the global offset register is also recorded using 3 tag bits for each cache line, which is then used to re-align the data during a read access. For an overhead of 3 tag bits per 544-bit cache line (512 data bits and 32 tag bits, at 4 tag bits per 64-bit word for FMR), RNW 'rotates' data in offsets of 8 across each word to spread the wear across the 64-bit data-word and to effectively reduce the peak bit-writes per cell. Note that RNW also 'rotates' tag bits for wear-leveling.

6. Evaluation and Results

The FMR architecture was evaluated using an in-house simulator of memory traces from the SPEC CPU2006 [25] benchmark suite collected using the Intel Pin binary instrumentation tool [26].

Summary: We summarize the results and provide detailed comparison between different schemes in Table 2. We compare bit-writes, energy, and overhead for DCW (classical read-modify-write for NVMs [24] used as the baseline in this work), FNW, and FPC. Our implementation of FPC, aFNW, and MNW requires 1, 2, and 1 bits of overhead, respectively, for a 64-bit data word. This 6.25% overhead is equivalent to the overhead of classical FNW (4 tag bits per 64-bit data-word in 4 16-bit partitions). In addition, RNW requires 3 bits for a 512-bit cache line, which brings FMR overhead to 6.8%. The estimated logic overhead of the FMR controller is $\approx$ 10k gates ($< 0.1\%$ area per NVM module). The FMR architecture was pipelined for bandwidth improvements with the read-path/write-path adding 2/3 clock cycles of latency, which translates to $< 1\%$ reduction in memory bandwidth.

Architecture	Bit-writes	Energy	Overhead
DCW [24]	100%	100%	0%
FNW [15]	84.6%	83%	6.25%
[16] extended to 64-bit FPC	65.8%	82%	1.6%
FMR	51.9%	71%	6.8%

Table 2: **Comparison of bit-writes, energy, and overhead for the 4 schemes considered in this paper, normalized to DCW.**

Bit-writes: The cumulative bit-writes for FNW, FPC, and FMR, normalized to uncompressed data with DCW, is shown in Fig. 7(a). The last entries in Fig. 7(a) are the geometric mean of the bit-write reduction across all benchmarks, which is equivalent to simulating all the benchmarks for the same time. FNW reduces cumulative bit-writes to 84.6% in comparison to DCW, in close agreement with the theoretical estimate of 85% (derivation omitted for brevity). FPC (64-bit data-word with 1 tag bit) reduces the cumulative bit-writes to 65.8% in comparison to DCW, an improvement over FNW. FMR outperforms FNW and FPC, reducing cumulative bit-writes to 51.9%, 61.4%, and 78.9% in comparison to DCW, FNW, FPC, respectively.

Dynamic energy: We also evaluate the impact of FMR on dynamic energy for PCM using the energy/bit numbers of 13.5pJ (19.2pJ) for set (reset) [1]. As shown in Fig. 7(b), FMR reduces the energy by 39%, 13%, and 14% in comparison to DCW, FNW, and FPC, respectively.

Bandwidth: We measure the impact of FMR on memory bandwidth using DRAMSim2 [27], a cycle accurate main memory simulator. The fundamental modifications in DRAMSim2 for NVM

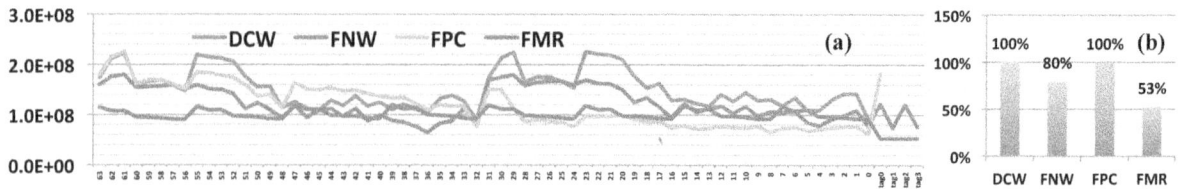

Figure 6: (a) Bit-writes versus bit index in a 64-bit data-word. Note that the tag bits (tag0, tag1, tag2, and tag3) are shown on the far right on the x-axis; (b) Peak bit-writes across all bit indices, normalized to DCW.

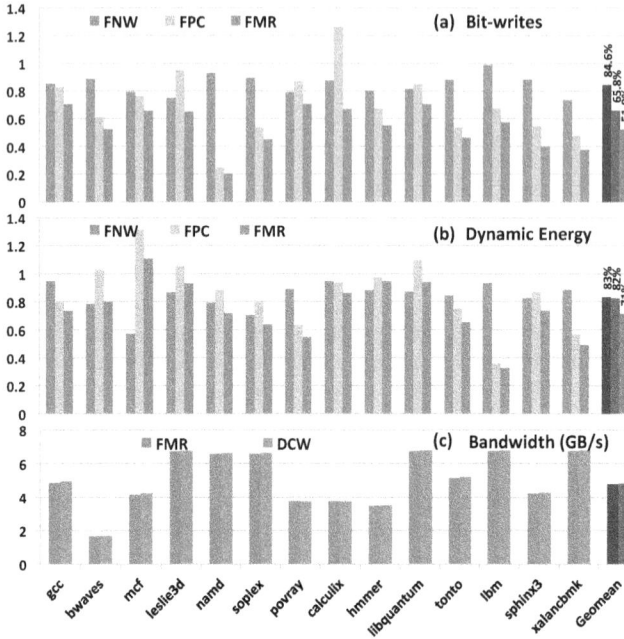

Figure 7: (a) Cumulative bit-writes normalized to DCW; (b) Dynamic energy normalized to DCW; (c) Memory bandwitdh of FMR and DCW.

(PCM in this case) simulation are [28]: row read delay is 27ns, row write delay is 250ns, the reset latency is 40ns, and the set latency is 250ns. We added 2/3 cycles of latency to the read/write path to account for the latency of the synthesized FMR controller. The simulation results in Fig. 7(c) show that the geometric mean of FMR memory bandwidth normalized to DCW is 99.14%, which indicates that the overall loss in memory bandwidth for FMR is negligible ($\approx 0.86\%$) in comparison to DCW.

Wear leveling: To measure wear, the simulator reports the number of bit-writes that occur at each bit index across all words in a run. Sequential scheduling of randomly chosen benchmarks is used to simulate a real workload. In Fig. 6(a), we show the distribution of bit-writes across the bit-indices of a word and the 4 FMR tag bits on the far right. Whereas FPC reduces the cumulative bit-writes over uncompressed data with DCW (area under the curve), FPC concentrates peak bit-writes at bit indices 63, 62, and 61, which negatively affects NVM endurance. On the other hand, FNW reduces the bit-writes across all bit indices in comparison to FPC, i.e., FNW is better for NVM endurance in comparison to both FPC and DCW. Finally, FMR spreads wear uniformly across the entire word, outperforming DCW, FNW, and FPC. Figure 6(b) shows the peak bit-writes encountered across all 64 bit indices for DCW, FNW, FPC, and FMR. We see that RNW within FMR reduces the peak-bit writes by 47%, 34%, and 47% in comparison to DCW, FNW, and FPC, respectively. In summary, RNW improves NVM endurance by 2× in comparison to DCW and FPC and by 1.6× in comparison to FNW.

7. References

[1] B. Lee et al., "Architecting phase change memory as a scalable DRAM alternative," in Proc. Intl. Symp. Computer Architecture, 2009.

[2] I. Baek et al., "Highly scalable nonvolatile resistive memory using simple binary oxide driven by asymmetric unipolar voltage pulses," in Proc. Intl. Electron Devices Meeting, 2004.

[3] E. Kultursay et al., "Evaluating STT-RAM as an energy-efficient main memory alternative," in Proc. Intl. Symp. Perf. Analysis Systems and Software, 2013.

[4] "International technology roadmap for semiconductors," 2011.

[5] J. Li and K. Mohanram, "Write-once-memory-code phase change memory," in Proc. Design, Automation and Test in Europe Conference, 2014.

[6] M. K. Qureshi et al., "Improving read performance of phase change memories via write cancellation and write pausing," in Proc. Intl. Symp. High Performance Computer Architecture, 2010.

[7] M. K. Qureshi et al., "PreSET: Improving performance of phase change memories by exploiting asymmetry in write time," in Proc. Intl. Symp. Computer Architecture, 2012.

[8] Y. Kim, S. Yoo, and S. Lee, "Write performance improvement by hiding R drift latency in phase change RAM," in Proc. Design Automation Conference, 2012.

[9] S. Kwon et al., "Optimizing video application design for phase-change RAM-based main memory," IEEE Trans. VLSI Systems, 2012.

[10] M. Qureshi et al., "Enhancing lifetime and security of PCM-based main memory with start-gap wear leveling," in Proc. Intl. Symp. Microarchitecture, 2009.

[11] G. Wu et al., "CAR: Securing PCM main memory system with cache address remapping," in Proc. Intl. Conference Parallel and Distributed Systems, 2012.

[12] N. Seong et al., "Security refresh: Protecting phase-change memory against malicious wear out," IEEE Micro, 2011.

[13] L. Jiang et al., "Improving write operations in MLC phase change memory," in Proc. Intl. Symp. High Performance Computer Architecture, 2012.

[14] J. Yue and Y. Zhu, "Making write less blocking for read accesses in phase change memory," in Proc. Intl. Symp. Modeling, Analysis Simulation of Computer and Telecommunication Systems, 2012.

[15] S. Cho and H. Lee, "Flip-N-Write: A simple deterministic technique to improve PRAM write performance, energy and endurance," in Proc. Intl. Symp. Microarchitecture, 2009.

[16] D. Dgien et al., "Compression architecture for bit-write reduction in non-volatile memory technologies," in Proc. Intl. Symp. Nanoscale Architectures, 2014.

[17] J. Yue and Y. Zhu, "Accelerating write by exploiting PCM asymmetries," in Proc. Intl. Symp. High Performance Computer Architecture, 2013.

[18] S. Kang et al., "A 0.1-μm 1.8-V 256-Mb phase-change random access memory (PRAM) with 66-mhz sysnchronous burst-read operation," IEEE Journal of Solid-state Circuits, 2007.

[19] I. Song et al., "A 20nm 1.8V 8GB PRAM with 40MB/s program bandwidth," in Proc. Intl. Solid-state Circuits Conference, 2012.

[20] A. Jog et al., "Cache revive: Architecting volatile STT-RAM caches for enhanced performance in CMPs," in Proc. Design Automation Conference, 2012.

[21] C. Xu et al., "Understanding the trade-offs in multi-level cell ReRAM memory design," in Proc. Design Automation Conference, 2013.

[22] Wong et al., "Metal Oxide RRAM," Proceedings of the IEEE, 2012.

[23] A. Alameldeen and D. Wood, "Frequent pattern compression: A significance-based compression scheme for L2 caches," tech. rep., Univerity of Wisconsin-Madison, 2004.

[24] B.-D. Yang et al., "A low power phase-change random access memory using a data-comparison write scheme," in Proc. Intl. Symp. Circuits and Systems, 2007.

[25] "SPEC CPU2006," 2006.

[26] C.-K. Luk et al., "Pin: Building customized program analysis tools with dynamic instrumentation," in Proc. Programming Language Design and Implementation Conference, 2005.

[27] P. Rosenfeld et al., "DRAMSim2: A cycle accurate memory system simulator," Computer Architecture Letters, 2011.

[28] R. A. Bheda et al., "Energy efficient phase change memory based main memory for future high performance systems," in Proc. Intl. Green Computing Conference and Workshops, 2011.

Fine-Grained Voltage Boosting for Improving Yield in Near-Threshold Many-Core Processors

Joonho Kong
School of EE
Kyungpook National University
joonho.kong@knu.ac.kr

Arslan Munir
Dept. of CSE
University of Nevada, Reno
arslan@unr.edu

Farinaz Koushanfar
Dept. of ECE
Rice University
farinaz@rice.edu

ABSTRACT

Process variation is a major impediment in optimizing yield, energy, and performance in near-threshold many-core processors. In this paper, we present a comprehensive analysis on yield losses in near-threshold many-core processors. Based on our analysis, we propose energy-efficient yield improvement techniques for near-threshold many-core processors: SRAM cell arrays and Wordline driver voltage Boosting (SWBoost) and Cache voltage Boosting (CBoost). Results reveal that SWBoost and CBoost improve a chip yield by up to 66% and 83%, respectively. Furthermore, runtime energy overheads of SWBoost and CBoost are only 0.46% and 0.54%, respectively, which are much lower than conventional voltage boosting techniques.

Categories and Subject Descriptors

C.1.2 [**Computer Systems Organization**]: Multiple Data Stream Architectures (Multiprocessors)— *Multiple-instruction-stream, multiple-data-stream processors (MIMD)*

Keywords

Near-threshold computing; process variations; yield; voltage boosting

1. INTRODUCTION

An effective approach to sustain Moore's law and alleviate the dark silicon problem [5] in advanced process technologies is to lower the processor's supply voltage to near the transistor's threshold voltage (V_{th}): a computing paradigm known as near-threshold computing (NTC). Decreasing supply voltage from the nominal operating point (nominal V_{dd} operation is also known as super-threshold computing (STC)) decreases operating frequency and hence performance linearly, leakage power exponentially, and active energy per operation quadratically.

Although NTC enables sustaining Moore's law; process variations, which are caused by manufacturing imperfections and are also an issue in STC, exacerbate in the NTC regime. Each submicron technology generation becomes increasingly susceptible to process variations that manifest across the chip as fluctuations in transistor parameters (mainly, threshold voltage V_{th} and effective gate length L_{eff}) around the nominal values. The parametric variation at NTV causes substantial delay and power variation in circuits of identical processor cores, which limits the maximum operating frequency of the entire many-core

Table 1: Failures classification in many-core processors.

Metric	Element	Category
Timing	Logic	Core logic timing failure
	SRAM & logic	L1-I timing failure
	SRAM & logic	L1-D timing failure
	SRAM & logic	L2 timing failure
Stability	SRAM	L1-I stability failure
	SRAM	L1-D stability failure
	SRAM	L2 stability failure
Power	Chip	Excessive leakage failure

processor [6]. Furthermore, this variation in chips' delay and power consumption beyond design margins severely hurts processors' yield. Improving processors' yield is imperative as it can significantly impact the revenue of a semiconductor industry.

In this paper, we conduct a comprehensive yield analysis in the near-threshold regime and propose efficient yield improvement techniques that selectively boost V_{dd} in a fine-grained manner for many-core processors. Compared to conventional coarse-grained voltage boosting techniques [12][13][15][16], our fine-grained voltage boosting techniques considerably improve processors' yield. Moreover, energy efficiency of our proposed techniques reduces leakage-induced yield losses. Our main contributions are summarized as follows:

- We conduct the first comprehensive component-level analysis of yield losses in a near-threshold tiled many-core processor;
- We identify that SRAM-based structures are most vulnerable to yield losses at NTV and justify the necessity of fine-grained voltage boosting mechanisms;
- We propose fine-grained and selective voltage boosting techniques for tiled many-core processors: SRAM cell arrays and Wordline driver voltage Boosting (SWBoost) and Cache voltage Boosting (CBoost);
- We consider leakage-induced yield losses and reveal ineffectiveness of the previous course-grained voltage boosting techniques. We also quantify yield improvement by our proposed fine-grained voltage boosting techniques over the existing techniques.

2. YIELD ANALYSIS FOR NTC

Operation in near-threshold regime significantly impacts yield of manufactured chips due to enhanced effects of process variation. This section classifies and analyzes yield losses for different process variation severities. We classify failures that cause yield losses into eight different categories as summarized in Table 1.

2.1 Reference NTV many-core architecture

Our reference architecture is a tiled many-core processor consisting of 64 tiles similar to Tilera's TILEPro64 processor [14]. The processor features an 8×8 grid of 64 tiles (processor cores) implemented in 11nm process technology. The nominal V_{dd} and V_{th} are $0.55V$ and $0.33V$ [7], respectively. The architectural parameters for cache memories follow Tilera's TILEPro64 specifications as close as possible [14]. Our NTV many-core processor's cache memories are composed of 8T SRAM cells which are more robust to process variation than 6T SRAM cells [6].

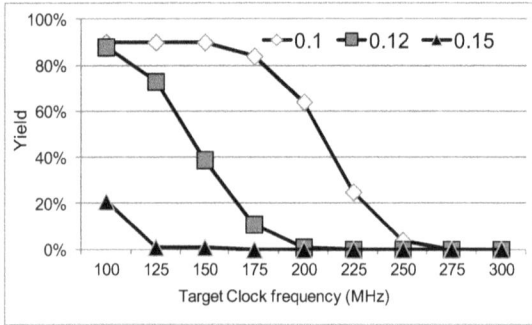

Figure 1: Yield versus target clock frequency for different process variation severities.

2.2 Analysis of Yield Losses

Effect of Target Clock Frequency & Process Variation: Chip yield depends on target clock frequency and process variation severity. Process variation severity is expressed as σ/μ where σ denotes standard deviation of process variation around mean μ. Fig. 1 depicts yield results for various target clock frequencies and three V_{th} process variation severities: $(\sigma/\mu)_{V_{th}} = 0.1$, 0.12, and 0.15 [7]. The L_{eff} variations are exactly half of V_{th} variations for each variation severity and are not denoted for conciseness. We set the leakage yield cutoff to be 10% of the baseline leakage-induced yield loss (approximately matched to the cutoff presented in [8]). We assume the nominal clock frequency (i.e., without process variation) of our target processor to be 1GHz [7].

Results reveal that as the target clock frequencies become higher, yield is significantly reduced. For instance, yield is 0% irrespective of process variation severity when the target clock frequency is higher than 250 MHz. Similarly, obtaining a target clock frequency of 225 MHz when $(\sigma/\mu)_{V_{th}} = 0.1$ is challenging because of diminishing yield. For example, yield is 25% for the target clock frequency of 225 MHz as compared to the yield of 64% for the target clock frequency of 200 MHz. Results indicate that yield decreases as process variation severity increases. For example, yield is only 21% for the target clock frequency of 100 MHz when $(\sigma/\mu)_{V_{th}} = 0.15$. These results verify that yield significantly limits the manufactured chips' performance.

Percentage of Faulty Tiles: Fig. 2 depicts the number of tiles containing faulty microarchitectural components (among L1D\$, L1I\$, L2\$, and core logic) when $(\sigma/\mu)_{V_{th}} = 0.15$. We count the number of tiles containing timing or stability failure in microarchitectural components for a sample of 100 chips where the maximum number of failure occurrences is 64 tiles × 100 chips = 6400. Results reveal that there are more tiles containing one failing component as compared to the tiles with multiple failing components. For example, the number of tiles with one failing component is 34.9% when the target clock frequency is 300 MHz. These results indicate that component-level fine-grained voltage boosting techniques would be more beneficial in terms of yield and energy optimization as compared to tile-level coarse-grained voltage boosting techniques. Consequently, the finer-grained techniques would also be beneficial for a leakage-induced yield loss reduction due to their lower leakage power consumption.

Composition of Yield Losses: Our yield loss analysis in this subsection focuses on component-level failures (i.e., among L1-I, L1-D, L2, and processor core) as classified in Table 1 excluding leakage power failure. We count the number of tiles containing timing or stability failures in microarchitectural components for a sample of 100 chips where the maximum number of failure occurrences is 64 tiles × 100 chips = 6400. Fig. 3 depicts composition of yield losses for $(\sigma/\mu)_{V_{th}} = 0.15$.

Results reveal that the timing failures in 8T SRAM-based components (i.e., caches) are dominating factors in yield

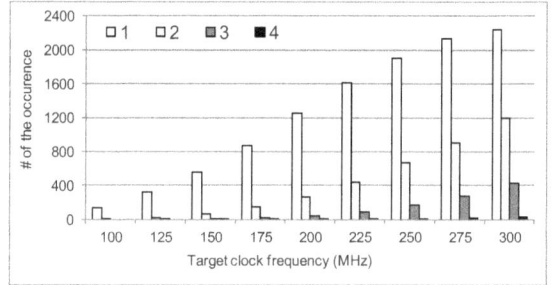

Figure 2: Number of tiles with faulty components out of 100 chips when $(\sigma/\mu)_{V_{th}} = 0.15$.

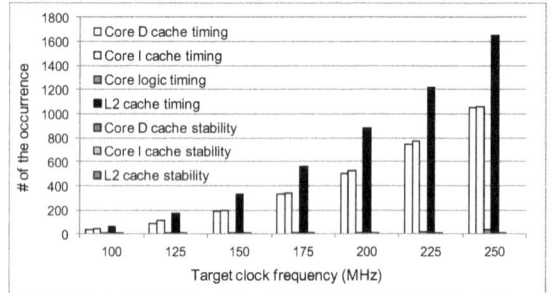

Figure 3: Composition of yield losses.

losses. The core logic timing failures are negligible and only appear when the target frequency $\geq$ 225 MHz. The stability failures are also negligible in our many-core processor operating at 0.55V. Results further indicate that L2 caches are most susceptible to failures due to process variation as compared to other 8T SRAM-based components. The large size of L2 caches as compared to L1 caches result in greater timing failure rate in L2 caches since large cache size implies large number of 8T SRAM cells and a large number of parallel independent delay paths.

3. VOLTAGE BOOSTING TECHNIQUES FOR NTV MANY-CORE PROCESSOR

In this section, we propose fine-grained microarchitectural component-level voltage boosting techniques: SWBoost and CBoost. Our proposed techniques are based on our comprehensive yield analysis, which reveals that SRAM-based components (L1-I, L1-D, and L2 caches) are more susceptible to the effects of process variations than the processor core logic (Section 2.2) in the NTC regime. This section also discusses coarse-grained voltage-boosting techniques proposed in prior work [12][13][16]: tile-level boost (TBoost) and voltage margining (VM). We also provide implementation guidelines of our proposed techniques in this section.

3.1 Proposed Voltage Boosting Techniques

SWBoost: SWBoost supplies the boosted V_{dd} only to the wordline drivers and SRAM cell arrays. The range of boosted V_{dd} is 0.57V–0.65V. SWBoost can provide yield improvements as most failures in cache memories occur due to timing and stability failure in 8T SRAM cells. SWBoost can provide energy savings as compared to boosting the whole tile or whole cache memories. Fig. 4 depicts our proposed boosting techniques. In the case of SWBoost, we only boost wordline and SRAM cell supply voltage. SWBoost is based on dual-voltage rail (DVR); however, SWBoost operates in a finer-grained manner as compared to the conventional DVR [12][13][15][17]. SWBoost selectively applies the boosted V_{dd} to faulty cache components to improve yield and energy efficiency. Two power gating P-type metal-oxide-semiconductor (PMOS) transistors are required for a component, which are employed to select either nominal V_{dd} or boosted V_{dd} for each component. Since there are three cache memory components (L1-I, L1-D, and

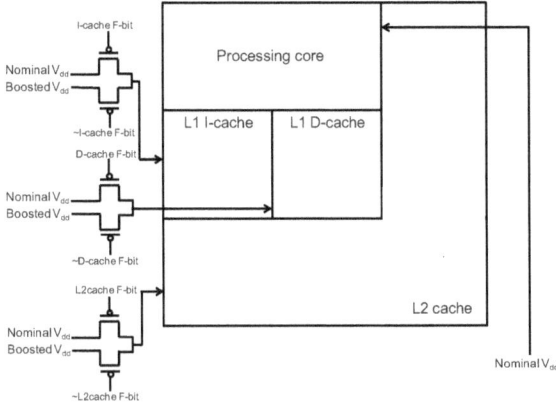

Figure 4: Our proposed voltage boosting technique.

L2) in each tile, a total of six PMOS transistors are needed for each tile. To support SWBoost for all of the 64 tiles in the processor, 384 power gating PMOS transistors are required.

To determine whether to supply nominal or boosted V_{dd} to a cache component, SWBoost uses three fault indicator (F) bits (stored in a non-volatile memory) for each tile: *D-cache F-bit*, *I-cache F-bit*, and *L2cache F-bit*. *D-cache F-bit*, *I-cache F-bit*, and *L2cache F-bit* determine if a timing- or stability-related failure exists in L1-D, L1-I, and L2 cache, respectively. A total of 192 bit non-volatile storage is required for storing these F-bits for our many-core processor ($3 \times 64 = 192$). The contents of these F-bits are determined during the chip testing phase. Since current processors already possess structures for testability, our proposed techniques do not need additional components for testing.

*CBoost:*CBoost has the same V_{dd} boosting range and granularity as that of SWBoost, however, the boosted V_{dd} is supplied to the entire cache memories including cache peripheral circuits (e.g., address decoders and multiplexers). CBoost can provide higher yield than SWBoost as it can alleviate more timing-related failures in cache memories (cache peripheral circuits with the boosted V_{dd} will also be faster than non-boosted V_{dd}), however, CBoost consumes more energy than SWBoost. As in the case of SWBoost, CBoost also needs 384 power gating PMOS transistors and 192 F-bits.

3.2 Existing Voltage Boosting Techniques

*TBoost:*TBoost is a coarse-grained voltage boosting technique that supplies boosted voltage at the tile-level in case of failure in any of the tile's component (processor core, L1-I, L1-D, and L2 cache). In our TBoost implementation, we use the same boosting granularity as presented in [12][13], although prior work does not boost L2 caches.

*Voltage Margining (VM):*VM [16] is a coarse-grained voltage boosting technique that increases the chip-wide V_{dd} to save the faulty chips (or tiles) and improve performance. VM consumes more energy than SWBoost, CBoost, and TBoost because of being coarser-grained than other techniques.

3.3 Implementation Issues

Our proposed fine-grained voltage boosting designs (SWBoost and CBoost) require power gating PMOS transistors and non-volatile F-bits, and hence requires some area overhead. A single power gating PMOS transistor requires huge area compared to regular transistors ($\sim$ 6K transistors) [12], however, the overall area overhead is negligible compared to the total processor area as the state-of-the-art processors integrate more than a billion transistors. A conservative estimate of area overhead of all the power gating PMOS transistors in our many-core

processor is 0.23%. The area overhead of non-volatile storage for 192 F-bits is negligible.

Although our designs use two different voltage levels (nominal and boosted), our designs do not need voltage level converters because of small difference between these voltage levels [11]. In our designs, devices with non-zero threshold voltages can be used in place of voltage level converters.

4. EVALUATION

This section presents evaluation results focusing on yield improvement and energy overhead of our proposed fine-grained voltage boosting techniques (SWBoost and CBoost) and coarse-grained voltage boosting techniques proposed in prior work: TBoost and VM. We also present yield results for the spare tiles (ST) technique for yield improvement: ST_x represents the case when 'x' number of spare tiles are employed for mitigating the effects of process variation. We compare our voltage boosting techniques with a *baseline* case that denotes no voltage boosting or no process variation-aware technique. We investigate the yield results for three different process variation severities: $(\sigma/\mu)_{V_{th}} = 0.1$, 0.12, and 0.15.

4.1 Evaluation setup

For yield estimation, we use VARIUS-NTV [6] process variation model, which is specialized for NTC. We specify V_{th} and L_{eff} variation severities whereas other parameters are set to their default values in VARIUS-NTV. For workload-dependent energy consumption of our many-core processor, we use Snipersim [1] to extract the access counts of each functional unit, which are then given as an input to McPAT [10] scaled for 11nm technology node. We use 15 multi-threaded benchmarks from SPLASH-2 (barnes, cholesky, lu, ocean, radiosity, radix, and raytrace) and PARSEC (blackscholes, bodytrack, dedup, fluidanimate, freqmine, raytrace, streamcluster, and swaptions) for our evaluations.

4.2 Yield

Table 2 summarizes yield results for various boosting techniques with boosted V_{dd} of 0.57V, 0.61V, and 0.65V and spare tiles for various target clock frequencies (TCF) and process variation severities. Results indicate that ST techniques impart best yield when $(\sigma/\mu)_{V_{th}} = 0.1$ and target clock frequency is 200 MHz. Our CBoost technique delivers best yield for relatively high target clock frequencies.

For instance, CBoost enables 54% yield, which is highest across other considered techniques, when target clock frequency is 300 MHz and boosted V_{dd} is 0.65V. CBoost enables 15% yield improvement over TBoost when target clock frequency is 300 MHz and boosted V_{dd} is 0.65V. Better yield of CBoost than TBoost is due to the coarser-grained boosting (tile-wide) of TBoost that results in more power/energy consumption. This additional energy consumption in TBoost causes additional leakage-induced yield losses, which limits the yield attainable from TBoost. SWBoost can obtain comparable yield to CBoost and TBoost when the target frequency is low ($\leq$ 200 MHz), however, the yield attainable from SWBoost decreases sharply as the target frequency increases. VM proffers the worst yield among all the considered techniques due to low leakage power efficiency that results in high leakage-induced yield losses.

Results indicate that attainable yield from all voltage boosting techniques deteriorates for $(\sigma/\mu)_{V_{th}} = 0.12$ and $(\sigma/\mu)_{V_{th}} = 0.15$ due to increased process variations. However, overall trend of yield results across various techniques is similar to the case of $(\sigma/\mu)_{V_{th}} = 0.1$.

4.3 Energy

Fig. 5 shows the geometric mean of normalized energy results for various multi-threaded workloads for $(\sigma/\mu)_{V_{th}} = 0.15$. The 'TBoost_exL2' in Fig. 5 denotes the TBoost technique in which the L2 cache is excluded from the tile-level V_{dd} boosting similar to the technique introduced in

Table 2: Yield results of boosting techniques and spare tiles (TCF denotes target clock frequency and PV process variation).

PV	Boosted V_{dd}	N/A	0.57V				0.61V				0.65V				N/A		
$(\frac{\sigma}{\mu})_{V_{th}}$	TCF	Base	SWBoost	CBoost	TBoost	VM	SWBoost	CBoost	TBoost	VM	SWBoost	CBoost	TBoost	VM	ST$_1$	ST$_2$	ST$_3$
	200MHz	64%	77%	79%	79%	49%	86%	89%	89%	0%	89%	89%	89%	0%	79%	93%	98%
	250MHz	4%	18%	19%	19%	10%	45%	68%	67%	0%	70%	87%	86%	0%	20%	38%	52%
0.1	300MHz	0%	0%	0%	0%	0%	4%	11%	9%	0%	12%	54%	47%	0%	0%	0%	2%
	200MHz	1%	5%	7%	7%	5%	23%	38%	34%	0%	43%	72%	64%	0%	3%	14%	34%
	250MHz	0%	0%	0%	0%	0%	1%	1%	1%	0%	2%	20%	11%	0%	0%	0%	0%
0.12	300MHz	0%	0%	0%	0%	0%	0%	0%	0%	0%	0%	1%	0%	0%	0%	0%	0%
	100MHz	21%	49%	45%	44%	27%	64%	76%	76%	9%	74%	86%	86%	0%	53%	76%	85%
	150MHz	1%	1%	1%	1%	0%	6%	14%	13%	2%	19%	52%	45%	0%	1%	5%	12%
0.15	200MHz	0%	0%	0%	0%	0%	1%	1%	1%	0%	0%	2%	1%	0%	0%	0%	0%

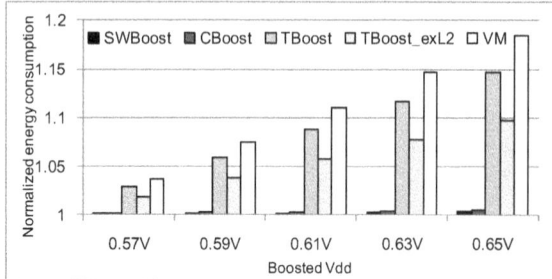

Figure 5: Geometric mean of energy results normalized to the baseline for $(\sigma/\mu)_{V_{th}} = 0.15$.

[12]. Results indicate that SWBoost is most energy-efficient because of fine-grained boosting of only the SRAM arrays and wordline drivers of faulty cache memory components. SWBoost and CBoost show a runtime energy overhead of 0.46% and 0.54% on average, respectively, as compared to the baseline.

5. RELATED WORK

Process variation is a major issue for optimizing yield, performance, and energy in the NTV regime. Several earlier studies investigated cache and multi-core designs for NTC. Chen et al. [2] compared conventional 6T SRAM, single-ended 6T SRAM, and 8T SRAM designs for NTC. Dreslinski et al. [4] proposed an energy-efficient L1 cache architecture for NTC. Dreslinski et al. [3] proposed a multi-voltage, clustered multi-core design that supports different supply voltages and threshold voltages in the caches for each cluster (a group of processor cores was termed as cluster). Our work differs from this work as our proposed designs supply higher V_{dd} to only faulty cache memories for yield improvement. Moreover, our designs do not need V_{th} tuning nor require voltage-level converters, which makes our designs much simpler than that presented in [3].

Miller et al. [13] proposed dual-voltage rails and half speed units for mitigating process variation in the NTV regime. The authors proposed core-level voltage boosting by supplying dual V_{dd}, however, this coarse-grained voltage boosting results in energy and yield inefficiency. Our proposed designs only boost faulty cache memories that present a major bottleneck in yield improvement in NTC. Seo et al. [16] proposed various techniques to mitigate the effects of process variation in near-threshold single instruction multiple data (SIMD) architectures including VM, spare components (cores/tiles), and frequency margining. Results reveal that our proposed fine-grained voltage boosting techniques depict better yield as compared to VM and spare tiles. In [9], a variation-aware SIMD architecture was proposed, however, the proposed design focused only on the processing unit and not on memory components. Karpuzcu et al. [7] proposed a process variation-aware thread scheduling and frequency assignment technique that exploits a heterogeneity of clusters in an NTV many-core processor. Some prior work demonstrated silicon implementations for NTV processors [15] which use different voltages for SRAM arrays for better stability; however, our designs selectively supply the boosted V_{dd} only to the faulty cache memories.

6. CONCLUSIONS

In this paper, we present a comprehensive analysis of yield losses in tile-based many-core processors. Results indicate that SRAM-based components are vulnerable to yield losses in the near-threshold regime. We observe that fine-grained selective voltage boosting techniques not only reduce both timing- and leakage-induced yield losses but also improve runtime energy efficiency. Based on our yield analysis, we propose architectural component-level V_{dd} boosting techniques: SWBoost and CBoost. Results reveal that SWBoost and CBoost improve a chip yield by up to 66% and 83%, respectively. Results also verify that energy overhead of our proposed techniques is significantly less than the conventional techniques. SWBoost is most energy-efficient among all the evaluated techniques with a maximum energy overhead of only 0.46% as compared to the baseline. In our future work, we plan to incorporate a process variation model for interconnect and optimize our design to take into account both interconnects and tiles under process variations in the NTV regime.

7. REFERENCES

[1] T. Carlson, W. Heirman, and L. Eeckhout. Sniper: Exploring the level of abstraction for scalable and accurate parallel multi-core simulation. In the 2011 International Conference for High Performance Computing, Networking, Storage and Analysis (SC), pages 1–12, 2011.

[2] G. K. Chen, D. Blaauw, T. Mudge, D. Sylvester, and N. S. Kim. Yield-driven near-threshold SRAM design. In Proceedings of the 2007 IEEE/ACM international conference on Computer-aided design, pages 660–666, 2007.

[3] R. G. Dreslinkski, B. Zhai, T. Mudge, D. Blaauw, and D. Sylvester. An energy efficient parallel architecture using near threshold operation. In Proceedings of the 16th International Conference on Parallel Architecture and Compilation Techniques, pages 175–188, 2007.

[4] R. G. Dreslinski, G. K. Chen, T. Mudge, D. Blaauw, D. Sylvester, and K. Flautner. Reconfigurable energy efficient near threshold cache architectures. In Proceedings of 41st IEEE/ACM International Symposium on Microarchitecture, pages 459–470, 2008.

[5] H. Esmaeilzadeh, E. Blem, R. S. Amant, K. Sankaralingam, and D. Burger. Dark silicon and the end of multicore scaling. In Computer Architecture (ISCA), 2011 38th Annual International Symposium on, pages 365–376, 2011.

[6] U. R. Karpuzcu, K. B. Kolluru, N. S. Kim, and J. Torrellas. VARIUS-NTV: A microarchitectural model to capture the increased sensitivity of manycores to process variations at near-threshold voltages. In Proceedings of the 2012 42nd Annual IEEE/IFIP International Conference on Dependable Systems and Networks (DSN), pages 1–11, 2012.

[7] U. R. Karpuzcu, A. Sinkar, N. S. Kim, and J. Torrellas. EnergySmart: Toward energy-efficient manycores for near-threshold computing. In Proceedings of the 2013 IEEE 19th International Symposium on High Performance Computer Architecture (HPCA), pages 542–553, 2013.

[8] J. Kong, X. Pan, S. Ozdemir, A. Mohan, G. Memik, and S. W. Chung. Fine-Grain Voltage Tuned Cache Architecture for Yield Management under Process Variations. IEEE Transactions on VLSI Systems, 20(8):1532–1536, 2012.

[9] E. Krimer, R. Pawlowski, M. Erez, and P. Chiang. Synctium: A near-threshold stream processor for energy-constrained parallel applications. IEEE Computer Architecture Letter, 9(1):21–24, 2010.

[10] S. Li, J.-H. Ahn, R. Strong, J. Brockman, D. Tullsen, and N. Jouppi. McPAT: An integrated power, area, and timing modeling framework for multicore and manycore architectures. In the 42nd Annual IEEE/ACM International Symposium on Microarchitecture, pages 469–480, 2009.

[11] X. Liang, G.-Y. Wei, and D. Brooks. ReVIVaL: A variation-tolerant architecture using voltage interpolation and variable latency. In Proceedings of the 35th Annual International Symposium on Computer Architecture, pages 191–202, 2008.

[12] T. N. Miller, X. Pan, R. Thomas, N. Sedaghati, and R. Teodorescu. Booster: Reactive core acceleration for mitigating the effects of process variation and application imbalance in low-voltage chips. In Proceedings of the 2012 IEEE 18th International Symposium on High Performance Computer Architecture (HPCA), pages 27–38, 2012.

[13] T. N. Miller, R. Thomas, and R. Teodorescu. Mitigating the effects of process variation in ultra-low voltage chip multiprocessors using dual supply voltages and half-speed units. Computer Architecture Letters, 11(2):45–48, 2012.

[14] A. Munir, F. Koushanfar, A. Gordon-Ross, and S. Ranka. High-performance optimizations on tiled many-core embedded systems: A matrix multiplication case study. The Journal of Supercomputing, 66(1):431–487, 2013.

[15] G. Ruhl, S. Dighe, S. Jain, S. Khare, and S. Vangal. IA-32 processor with a wide-voltage-operating range in 32-nm CMOS. IEEE Micro, 33(2):28–36, 2013.

[16] S. Seo, R. G. Dreslinski, M. Woh, Y. Park, C. Charkrabari, S. Mahlke, D. Blaauw, and T. Mudge. Process variation in near-threshold wide SIMD architectures. In Proceedings of the 49th Annual Design Automation Conference, pages 980–987, 2012.

[17] B. Stolt, Y. Mittlefehldt, S. Dubey, G. Mittal, M. Lee, J. Friedrich, and E. Fluhr. Design and implementation of the POWER6 microprocessor. IEEE Journal of Solid-State Circuits, 43(1):21–28, 2008.

Approximate Multiplier Architectures Through Partial Product Perforation: Power-Area Tradeoffs Analysis

Georgios Zervakis   Kostas Tsoumanis   Sotirios Xydis

Nicholas Axelos   Kiamal Pekmestzi

School of Electrical and Computer Engineering
National Technical University of Athens
Athens, Greece 15270
{zervakis, kostastsoumanis, sxydis, njaxel, pekmes}@microlab.ntua.gr

ABSTRACT

Approximate computing has received significant attention as a promising strategy to decrease power consumption of inherently error-tolerant applications. Hardware approximation mainly targets arithmetic units, e.g. adders and multipliers. In this paper, we design new approximate hardware multipliers and propose the Partial Product Perforation technique, which omits a number of consecutive partial products by perforating their generation. Through extensive experimental evaluation, we apply the partial product perforation method on different multiplier architectures and expose the optimal configurations for different error values. We show that the partial product perforation delivers reductions of up to 50% in power consumption, 45% in area and 35% in critical delay. Also, the product perforation method is compared with state-of-the-art works on approximate computing that consider the Voltage Over-Scaling (VOS) and logic approximation (i.e. design of approximate compressors) techniques, outperforming them in terms of power dissipation by up to 17% and 20% on average respectively. Finally, with respect to the aforementioned gains, the error value delivered by the proposed product perforation method is smaller by 70% and 99% than the VOS and logic approximation methods respectively.

Categories and Subject Descriptors

B.2 [**Arithmetic and logic structures**]: miscellaneous

Keywords

Approximate computing, Low power, VLSI multiplier

1. INTRODUCTION

In recent years, massive research has been performed in the field of approximate computing at both software and hardware levels. At software level, Sidiroglou et al. [1] proposed the loop perforation technique which skips a number of loop iterations and results in executing a subset of the initial computations, thus saving time and power but producing approximate outputs. Hardware approximation mainly targets arithmetic units. The most commonly used techniques are the truncation, the Voltage Over-Scaling (VOS) and the simplification of a unit's logic complexity (i.e. alteration of the truth table) [2–5]. However, the truncation technique has reportedly proved to provide unsatisfactory results compared to the other methods [3–5]. Extensive research has been conducted on approximate adders [2, 5, 6] providing significant gains in terms of area and power along with exposing small error. Research on more complex components, e.g. multipliers, is essential yet limited due to their complexity. A multiplier comprises three main parts, the Partial Product generation unit, a tree to accumulate the partial products and a final adder [7]. [3] proposed a simplified imprecise 2x2 multiplier and used it to compose larger multiplication circuits. [4] altered the truth table of the 4:2 compressor producing two approximate 4:2 compressors, which they then used in a Dadda tree with 4:2 reduction and proposed two multipliers that outperform [3].

In this paper, we introduce the Partial Product Perforation method for creating approximate hardware multipliers. Inspired from [1], we apply the partial product perforation method on 16 different multiplier architectures. Through extensive experimental evaluation, we present the optimal approximate multiplier configurations, for various error values. More specifically, we use industrial strength tools in order to expose the multiplier architectures that achieve the lowest values of power consumption, area and critical delay for different numbers and ranks of omitted partial products and various error values. We show that the partial product perforation technique delivers reductions of up to 50% in power consumption, 45% in area and 35% in critical delay for 0.1% normalized mean error distance [8]. Compared with state-of-the-art approximate computing works VOS [2] and [4], perforation outperforms them by up to 17% and 20% on average in terms of power dissipation and with the imposed error improving by 70% and 99% respectively.

2. PARTIAL PRODUCT PERFORATION FOR APPROXIMATE MULTIPLIERS

In this section, the partial product perforation method for the design of approximate hardware multipliers is de-

GLSVLSI'15, May 20–22, 2015, Pittsburgh, PA, USA.
Copyright © 2015 ACM 978-1-4503-3474-7/15/05 ...$15.00.
http://dx.doi.org/10.1145/2742060.2742109.

scribed. Consider two n-bit numbers A and B. The result of their multiplication $A \times B$ is obtained after summing all the partial products Ab_i, where b_i is the ith bit of B. Thus,

$$A \times B = \sum_{i=0}^{n-1} Ab_i 2^i. \quad (1)$$

The partial product perforation technique omits the generation of k successive partial products starting from the jth one. A perforated partial product is not inserted in the accumulation tree and hence, n full adders can be removed from it. Applying product perforation with j and k configuration values produces the approximate result

$$A \times B|_{j,k} = \sum_{i=0, i \notin [j, j+k)}^{n-1} Ab_i 2^i, b_i \in [0, 1]. \quad (2)$$

Note that $j \in [0, n-1]$ and $k \in [1, \min(n-j, n-1)]$.

Fig. 1 depicts an example of applying the partial product perforation method on an 8-bit multiplier with $j=2$ and $k=3$ configuration values. Through the proposed approximation technique, the power, area and delay of the multiplication circuit are decreased, making though the computation imprecise. The higher the rank of a perforated partial product, the greater the error imposed at the final result. Also, since the addition is an associative and commutative operation, when more than one partial products are perforated, the total error results from the addition of the errors produced from the perforation of each partial product separately. For example, the error of perforating the partial products of the 2nd and 5th rank is equal to the sum of the error of perforating the 2nd partial product and the error of perforating the 5th one. Therefore, for the rest of the paper, when perforating on more than one partial products, targeting to minimize the imposed error, we perforate on successive ones.

We use the notation $D[j,k,c]$ to label the different approximate multiplier architectural configurations. The parameter "D" refers to the tree architecture, j is the first partial product to be perforated and k the number of the perforated partial products. If no j and k are specified, the respective notation refers to the exact design. Finally, c takes the values "s" for Simple Partial Products (SPP) and "m" for Modified Booth Encoding (MBE). For example Fig. 1a depicts the array[s] configuration, while Fig. 1b the array[2,3,s].

3. EXPLORING THE EFFICIENCY OF PARTIAL PRODUCT PERFORATION

In this section, the partial product perforation method is applied on various multiplier architectures in order to explore how their power consumption, area, delay and accuracy behave considering all possible values for the configuration variables j and k. This analysis can be used to expose the optimal architecture-configuration for determined error

values regarding both power dissipation and area complexity. The latter is critical since different configurations may not have the same impact on a multiplier architecture regarding its power, area and delay. For example, when power consumption is examined, an architecture may be the optimal one when accurate calculations are performed, but a suboptimal when partial product perforation is applied.

Both SPP and MBE techniques are considered in our analysis. Regarding the accumulation tree, the most common architectures are used: 1) Array, 2) Balanced delay, 3) Compressor 4:2, 4) Counter 7:3, 5) Dadda, 6) Dadda with 4:2 compressors, 7) Redundant binary and 8) Wallace [7]. A carry look-ahead adder is used as the final adder.

A critical issue for the approximate computing is the error imposed during computations. In [8] the authors proposed the Error Distance (ED), Mean Error Distance (MED) and Normalized MED ($NMED$) as effective metrics for quantifying the accuracy of approximate arithmetic circuits. ED is defined as the absolute distance of the fully accurate product P and the approximate one P', $ED = |P - P'|$. The MED is the average of EDs for all inputs and $NMED = MED/P_{max}$, where $P_{max} = (2^n - 1)^2$ in the case of an n-bit multiplier [9]. The Relative Error Distance (RED) is defined as $RED = ED/P$ and the Mean RED ($MRED$) is similarly obtained [9]. These metrics are used to evaluate the accuracy of the approximate multipliers.

The flow used for our evaluation is summarized in Fig. 2. For our analysis 16-bit multiplier architectures are considered. They are synthesized using Synopsys Design Compiler and the TSMC 65nm standard cell library. We simulate the designs using Modelsim and calculate their power consumption with Synopsys PrimeTime triggering the average mode of calculation. All the possible combinations of j and k are explored and 1376 architectural configurations are examined in total. The metrics measured for each design are the $NMED$, $MRED$, minimum delay and, at the relaxed clock period of 2ns, its power consumption and area complexity.

In Fig. 3a-3c we depict the power, area and delay measurements for all the examined multiplier architectures, when the partial product perforation method is applied. The configurations of Fig. 3a-3c feature $j=0$ and k varying from 1 to 7 for the SPP-based designs and from 1 to 4 for the MBE-based ones. Note that $NMED < 10^{-3}$ for all designs. It is shown that the more partial products are perforated (i.e. increase of k), the more the evaluated metrics decrease. However, we observe that the power and area scale more gracefully than the delay, mainly due to the existence of the final adder. Among all the accurate designs, the counter7:3[m] has the minimum power, while the Dadda[0,7,m] design is the one consuming the least power among all the approximate designs with 50% power reduction compared to the respective accurate one. The accurate design with the small-

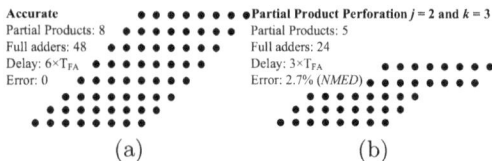

Figure 1: The partial product accumulation tree (a) of an accurate 8-bit multiplier and (b) after applying the partial product perforation with $j = 2$ and $k = 3$. For the delay calculation, we use the delay model of an array tree while T_{FA} is the delay of a full adder.

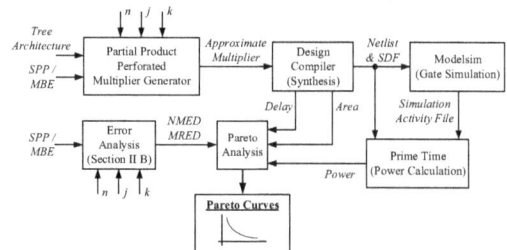

Figure 2: The flow used to evaluate the Partial Product Perforation method on different multiplier architectures.

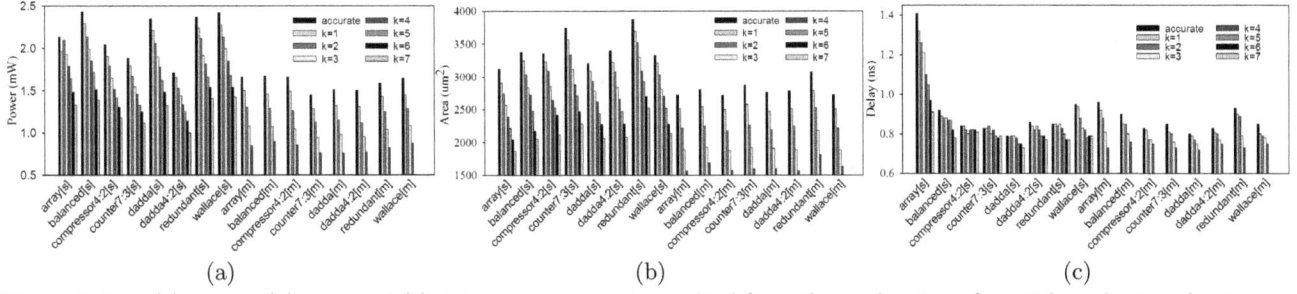

Figure 3: The (a) power, (b) area and (c) delay measurements resulted from the application of partial product perforation on different multiplier architectures. We consider $j = 0$ and $k = 1..7$ for the SPP-based architectures and $k = 1..4$ for MBE-based ones. The power and area values are obtained for clock period 2ns.

est area is the array[m] and the respective approximate one is the array[0,7,m]. The counter7:3[0,7,m] design delivers the greatest area reduction (45%) compared to the accurate counter7:3[m] and is close to the minimum one. The Dadda[s] achieves the minimum delay among all the exact designs and the Dadda[0,7,m] the lowest delay among all, while the array[0,7,s] delivers the greatest delay improvement (35%) compared to the respective accurate design. Finally, it is observed that the MBE-based designs exhibit greater savings compared to the respective ones using the SPP generation technique.

Since power, area and delay metrics scale differently for each multiplier architecture when various error values are considered, we illustrate in Fig. 4 the power-area Pareto curves for different $NMED$ values in order to distinguish the optimal designs. We consider the $NMED$ values of $10^{-4}, 5 \times 10^{-4}$ and 10^{-3} which enclose a large set of different partial product perforation configurations while keeping the error small. The optimal accurate design is the Dadda[m]. Moreover, the Dadda4:2[m] architecture appears in all curves but with different product perforation configuration (different j and k values) depending on the $NMED$ bound. The Dadda[0,2,m], Dadda4:2[0,3,m] and Dadda4:2[0,4,m] designs offer the best power-area tradeoff when $NMED$ takes the values $10^{-4}, 5 \times 10^{-4}$ and 10^{-3} respectively.

The partial product perforation method offers significant power, area and delay savings depending on the error bound and the multiplier architecture. It can achieve up to 50% power, 45% area and 35% delay reductions for only 0.1% error ($NMED < 10^{-3}$). For example, when concerning the Dadda4:2[m] architecture, the configurations appearing in the Pareto curves (Fig. 4) have 20% area and 26% power savings for $NMED < 10^{-4}$, 32% and 37% for $NMED < 5 \times 10^{-4}$ and 44% and 49% for $NMED < 10^{-3}$.

Targeting to elucidate the impact of partial product per-

foration on each multiplier architecture, we examine their power variation (range of power values) for a bounded error. Fig. 5 presents for all the architectures the box plot diagram regarding to power, considering all the product perforation configurations that result to $NMED < 5 \times 10^{-4}$. The MBE-based architectures exhibit smaller variation and lower median than the respective SPP-based ones. The smallest median and variation values are observed for the counter7:3[m] architecture. Thus, its power consumption for various partial product perforation configurations is concentrated in a smaller range making its power behavior more predictable. Such a point is also confirmed in Fig. 4 where the counter7:3[m] for $NMED$ values 5×10^{-4} and 10^{-3} is the Pareto optimal point with the lowest power.

4. EXPERIMENTAL EVALUATION

In this section, we extensively evaluate the efficiency of partial product perforation method in terms of power consumption, area and error, and we compare it with state-of-the-art approximate computing works which either apply logic approximation [4] or the VOS technique [2]. Using the two inexact 4:2 compressors[1] of [4], two approximate 16-bit multipliers ACM1 and ACM2 are implemented and synthesized at 2ns using Synopsys Design Complier and Prime-Time. In order to compare the partial product perforation with the VOS technique, we use the Synopsys Composite Current Source model (CCS) [10]. CCS models are proven to deliver signoff-level accuracy to within 2% of HSPICE simulation, are designed to be scalable for voltage, temperature and process and offer better accuracy than the Non-Linear Delay and Power Models [10]. For the exact multiplier architectures of Section III, we scale the supply voltage from 1V

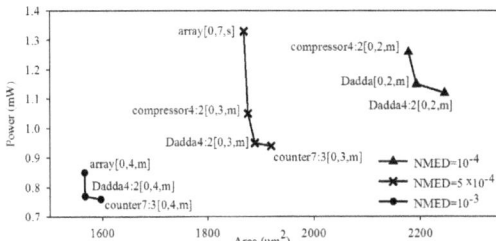

Figure 4: TheThe Power-Area Pareto curves for different $NMED$ values. Each point of a Pareto curve corresponds to a specific architecture-configuration noted next to it.

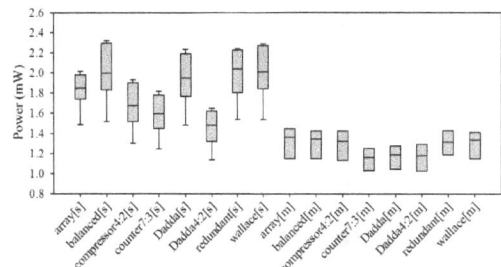

Figure 5: Power box plots of the considered multiplier architectures for all the partial product perforation configurations that result to $NMED < 5 \times 10^{-4}$.

---

[1]We consider logic approximation at the 16 LSB columns.

(nominal) to 0.80V and measure their power consumption and error metrics using 10^5 random generated inputs. All the architectures had similar behavior under VOS and thus, only the results of applying VOS on a Dadda 4:2 multiplier are presented here.

Fig. 6 presents in a comparative manner the power, area, *NMED* and *MRED* measurements of applying 1) four different product perforation configurations, 2) the approximate compressors [4] and 3) VOS on a 16-bit Dadda 4:2 multiplier using SPP (Fig. 6a) and MBE (Fig. 6b). The proposed Partial Product Perforation for the SPP designs included in Fig. 6a, delivers power savings up to 42% and area reduction up to 39% compared to the exact design, while the *NMED* value is at most 4.8×10^{-4} and the *MRED* one is up to 7.8×10^{-3}. The respective values for MBE configurations (Fig. 6b) are 49% power savings, 44% area reduction, 6.3% correct outputs, *NMED* 9.7×10^{-4} and *MRED* 1.4×10^{-2}. The partial product perforation technique shows significant gains compared to the accurate design, the VOS technique and the logic approximation [4] in terms of power and area. Moreover, it has lower relative error (*MRED*) than both the VOS technique and [4]. On average, compared with VOS, the depicted partial product perforation configurations attain 11% lower power consumption and 92% lower *NMED* when SPP is used and 17% and 70% respectively when MBE is used. Compared with [4], when SPP is preferred, the power consumption and the *MRED* are 18% and 29% lower, while when MBE is used, the respective values are 20% and 99%.

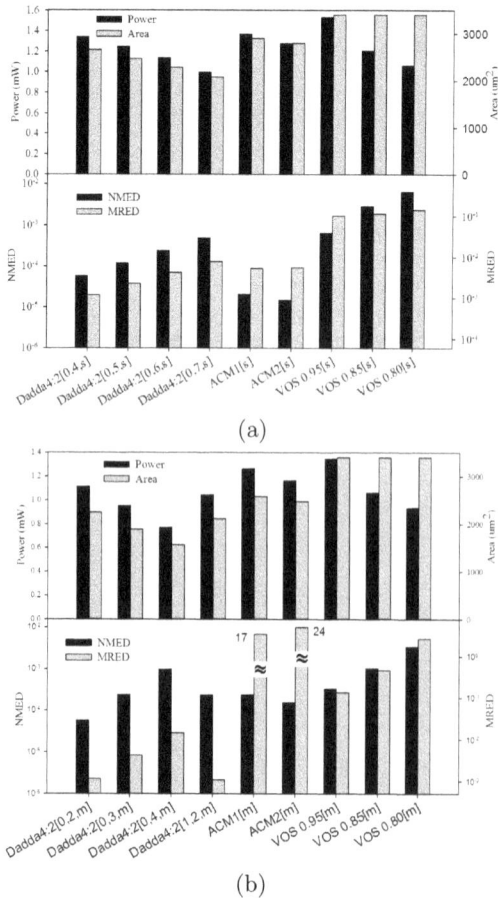

(a)

(b)

Figure 6: Comparison of product perforation with ACM1, ACM2 [4] and VOS for (a) SPP and (b) MBE.

From Fig. 6 it is shown that the product perforation exhibit lower values of *MRED* than ACM2, while having higher *NMED*. The large *NMED* value of partial product perforation means that it may produce large *ED*. However, the small value of *MRED* shows that such large *ED* is insignificant compared to the accurate result. On the other hand, [4] produces smaller *ED* but its errors are of greater significance compared to the exact results.

5. CONCLUSION

In this paper we propose the partial product perforation technique to produce approximate hardware multipliers. The proposed technique omits a number of partial products achieving high area and power savings, while retaining high accuracy. It is applied on the most common multiplier architectures and through a tradeoff analysis of power, area, delay and error, optimal configurations relative to specific error values are proposed. Finally, compared to state-of-art works that use logic approximation and VOS, we achieve significant gains in all metrics examined.

Acknowledgements

This research has been co-financed by the European Union (European Social Fund - ESF) and Greek national funds through the Operational Program "Education and Lifelong Learning" of the National Strategic Reference Framework (NSRF) - Research Funding Program: Thales -UOA- HOLISTIC. Investing in knowledge society through the European Social Fund.

6. REFERENCES

[1] S. Sidiroglou *et al.*, "Managing performance vs. accuracy trade-offs with loop perforation," in *Foundations of software engineering (ESEC/FSE)*, pp. 124–134, Sept. 2011.

[2] Y. Liu *et al.*, "Computation error analysis in digital signal processing systems with overscaled supply voltage," vol. 18, pp. 517–526, Apr. 2010.

[3] P. Kulkarni *et al.*, "Trading accuracy for power with an underdesigned multiplier architecture," in *24th Int. Conf. on VLSI Design*, pp. 346–351, Jan. 2011.

[4] A. Momeni *et al.*, "Design and analysis of approximate compressors for multiplication," vol. PP, Feb. 2014.

[5] V. Gupta *et al.*, "Impact: Imprecise adders for low-power approximate computing," in *Int. Symp. on Low Power Electronics and Design*, pp. 409–414, Aug. 2011.

[6] R. Ye *et al.*, "On reconfiguration-oriented approximate adder design and its application," in *Int. Conf. on Computer-Aided Design*, pp. 48–54, Nov. 2013.

[7] B. Parhami, *Computer Arithmetic: Algorithms and Hardware Designs.* NY: Oxford University Press, 2000.

[8] J. Liang *et al.*, "New metrics for the reliability of approximate and probabilistic adders," vol. 62, pp. 1760–1771, June 2012.

[9] C. Liu *et al.*, "A low-power, high-performance approximate multiplier with configurable partial error recovery," in *Design, Automation and Test in Europe*, Mar. 2014.

[10] G. Mekhtarian, *Composite Current Source (CCS) Modeling Technology Backgrounder.* Synopsys, Inc., Nov. 2005.

A SystemC Platform for Signal Transduction Modelling and Simulation in Systems Biology

Rosario Distefano[1]   Franco Fummi[1]   Carlo Laudanna[2]   Nicola Bombieri[1]

Rosalba Giugno[3]

[1]Dept. Computer Science, University of Verona, Italy
[2]Dept. Patology and Diagnostics, University of Verona, Italy
[3]Dept. Clinical and Molecular Biomedicine, University of Catania, Italy
name.surname@univr.it, giugno@dmi.unict.it

ABSTRACT

Signal transduction is a class of cell's biological processes, which are commonly represented as highly concurrent reactive systems. In the Systems Biology community, modelling and simulation of signal transduction require overcoming issues like discrete event-based execution of complex systems, description from building blocks through composition and encapsulation, description at different levels of granularity, methods for abstraction and refinement. This paper presents a signal transduction modelling and simulation platform based on SystemC, and shows how the platform allows handling the system complexity by modelling it at different abstraction levels. The paper reports the results obtained by applying the platform to model the intracellular signalling network controlling integrin activation mediating leukocyte recruitment from the blood into the tissues.

Categories and Subject Descriptors

Applied computing [**Life and medical sciences**]: [Systems biology]; Applied computing [**Life and medical sciences**]: [Biological networks]; Computing methodologies [**Modeling and simulation**]: [Model development and analysis]

Keywords

Signal transduction, Modeling and simulation, SystemC.

1. INTRODUCTION

Modeling and simulation signal transduction systems is a key requirement for integrating in-vitro and in-vivo experimental data. In-silico simulation allows testing different experimental conditions, thus helping in the discovery of the dynamics that regulate the system. These dynamics include simulating errors in the cellular information processing that are responsible for diseases such as cancer, autoimmunity,

and diabetes [9].

In System Biology, different Software are available for simulation and analysis of biochemical processes or pathways [12, 10, 5, 3]. They can be classified into two categories: those that rely on mathematical models such as ordinary differential equations [4], and those that rely on computational models, like Boolean networks [14], Petri nets [6], interactive state machines [13], and π-calculus [11]. Tools based on mathematical models have the highest potential to accurately describe and simulate the system but they are difficult to apply in case of large systems. Tools based on computational models best apply if precise quantitative relationships of the system are unknown, if the system involves many different variables, or if it changes over time [8].

Despite the adopted tool and model, a common way to explain such complex dynamical systems is to view them as highly concurrent reactive systems, whose design requires (i) techniques for composition and encapsulation starting from building blocks, (ii) methods for modeling at different abstraction levels, and (iii) efficient validation methodologies [7, 5]. All these issues related to concurrent reactive systems have been largely addressed in the past years in the electronic design automation (EDA) field and many methodologies and tools have been proposed to design and verify system-on-chips as well as embedded systems.

This paper presents a platform for modeling and simulation of signal transduction networks. The platform relies on SystemC (*www.systemc.org*), a standard language for modelling and simulation of Hardware/Software systems at different abstraction levels. The paper shows how a generic protein network representing signal transduction can be modelled at different abstraction levels, where each level distinguishes for the accuracy degree of the protein and co-factor models. The platform has been applied for modeling and simulation of the signaling network controlling LFA-1 beta2 integrin activation mediating leukocyte recruitment from the blood into the tissues. Simulation has been conducted to understand how the concerted action of the signaling proteins generate a concurrent modular mechanism of regulation of integrin activation, which is characterized both by topological and dynamic properties such as oscillations and hysteresis. The paper underlines the benefit of modeling the system at different abstraction levels, by showing how the model simulation provides information on the system properties with an accuracy degree proportional to the simulation time.

2. THE SYSTEMC PLATFORM

In System Biology, a signal transduction network consists of a set of biological elements, such as, *proteins* or *co-factors*. Such elements behave as concurrent objects and interact each other through activation or inhibition actions to form signal transduction chains. An element can be activated (or inhibited) by an *upstream element*, and it can activate (or inhibit) a *downstream element*. In the proposed platform, each element behaviour is formally modelled through finite state machines (FSMs) and implemented as a SystemC module through processes. The element modules are finally connected and simulated at system level.

2.1 Modeling of biological elements

The elements of a signal transduction network share a common behavior, which, through a FSM model, is represented by three states: *Inactive*, *Activated* and *Behaving* (see upper side of Figure 1). In the *Inactive* state, the element does not perform any biological function neither interact with other elements. The element becomes *Activated* as soon as an upstream element starts a reaction, which may consist of an activation (e.g., steric activation, phosphorilation, co-factor synthesis, etc.) or inhibition. Once activated, the element is ready to execute its biological function, that is, to react with a downstream element of the chain. Nevertheless, this can happen only after a *delay time*, which represents the time spent by the element to reach the target. Thus, after the delay time, the element state moves to *Behaving*, in which the element executes its biological function. The delay time depends on several factors, such as, the molecular concentrations of the element and of the target. Any element returns to the inactive state either if it receives an inhibition signal by an upstream protein or if the element *lifetime* expires. t represents the time elapsed, which is constantly updated during simulation, while *lifetime* represents the maximum lifetime from the activation instant in which the protein carries out its biological function. In the proposed FSM model, the transition guards (i.e., the conditions controlling the state transitions) are expressed in terms of variables (e.g., delay_time, lifetime) as well as activation or inhibition events raised by upstream elements. To model such a behavior, we define three classes of input/output signals:

- *Unknown inputs (Input_Ui)*: They are inputs whose values depends on the environment characteristics and status, which are unknown at modelling time. Some examples are the *delay time* (i.e., time spent by the protein to reach a protein target), the molecular concentrations, and the element lifetime. For each unknown input, the platform generates different values with the aim of observing, via simulation, how such values affect the biological system dynamics.

- *Topological inputs (Input_Ti)*: They are inputs whose values depend on the topological interactions of the modelled element with upstream elements, such as activation via phosphorylation, steric, co-factor, or inhibition. During simulation, topological inputs may be dynamically set to a value representing an activation or an inhibition action.

- *Topological outputs (Output_Ti)*: They are outputs whose values are set at simulation time and depend on the role of the modelled element towards downstream elements.

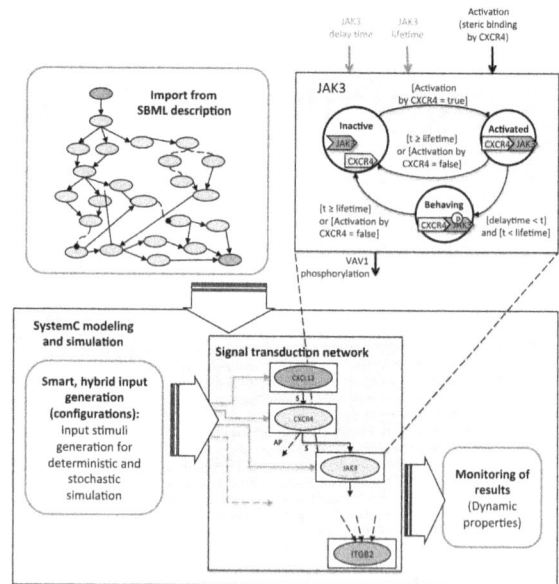

Figure 1: The SystemC platform.

2.2 System-level Simulation Platform

Figure 1 shows the SystemC-based platform, in which the FSM model of the JAK3 protein is reported as example among the elements of the system. All the element modules are connected through SystemC signals, to form the networks. The system of proteins and co-factors is connected to a stimuli generator, which automatically generates patterns of values for each unknown variable. We refer to a pattern of values as *configuration* of the system. A configuration consists of values for each unknown input of the network elements. The platform generates a new configuration and runs (i.e., execute) a dynamic simulation of the system for a given simulation time. During such a run, the platform monitors the system properties (Monitoring of results) by observing the behavior of one ore more network elements (e.g., it monitors the state and the molecular concentration of a given protein). After the simulation time, the platform generates a new configuration and starts a new run. The whole simulation ends when all the possible configurations have been run. The simulation aims at identifying those configurations that lead the system to specific behaviors.

The platform generates the configurations by combining deterministic and probabilistic approaches. The main goal of the input generation is to explore and, at the same time, to handle the solution space through an hybrid approach (i.e., deterministic and probabilistic), by exploiting the the simulation results to drive the generation of a new configuration. The proposed FSM model, which is shared by each network element, allows the corresponding SystemC implementation to be automatically generated from a Systems Biology Markup Language (SBML) description [2]. SBML is a representation format, based on XML, for communicating and storing computational models of biological processes. It is a free and open standard with widespread software support and a community of users and developers. SBML can represent many different classes of biological phenomena, including metabolic networks, cell signaling pathways, regulatory networks, infectious diseases, and many others. It is the de facto standard for representing computational models in systems biology today.

3. ABSTRACTION LEVELS AND SIMULATION ACCURACY

At system-level, concurrency and interaction of signal transduction elements can be modelled and simulated at different levels of accuracy. Consider, for example, the element interaction represented in Figure 2. Protein *P1* may bind with (and, thus, activate) three different target elements (i.e., proteins), *P2*, *P3* and *P4*. In turn, *P2* or *P3* may bind with *P5*, while *P4* may inhibit *P6*. As a result, *P1* may be involved into three different pathways, two of them forming protein complexes (*P1-P2-P5*, *P1-P3-P5*), while the third one to inhibit *P6* (*P1-P4-P6*). Such a dynamic interaction can be viewed at different abstraction levels, as described in the following sections.

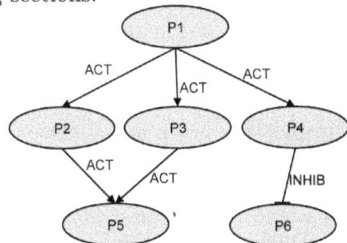

Figure 2: An example of protein network

3.1 High Level Model of Elements

At this level, each network element can establish only one interaction at a time (e.g., *P1* may activate either *P2*, *P3*, or *P4*) and each element may be part of one complex at a time (e.g., P5 may be part of either *P1-P2-P5* or *P1-P3-P5*). Each element behavior is modeled through a single FSM and concurrency is viewed at protein/co-factor level. The element behavior is implemented by a single SystemC process, which is sensible to the input signals coming from upstream elements and writes on output ports to activate/inhibit one of the downstream elements at a time. The element interaction is modeled through boolean signals (i.e., activation/inhibition true or false). The downstream target is chosen by following a probability distribution, which takes into account the molecular concentrations of the target elements. The higher the molecular concentration of a target, the higher the interaction probability.

3.2 Intermediate Level Model of Elements

At this level, each element of the network can establish more than one interactions at a time. (e.g., a subset of molecules of *P1* may activate molecules of *P2*, and a different subset of molecules of P1 may activate *P3*, or *P4*). Each element may be part of one or more complexes at a time (e.g., some molecules of P5 may be part of *P1-P2-P5* and some others may be part of *P1-P3-P5*). Each element behavior is modeled through one or more FSMs and the description granularity allows viewing concurrency among molecular sets of protein/co-factors.

The element behavior is implemented by more SystemC processes, and the number of implemented FSMs is handled dynamically at run time. As soon as a set of molecules of the upstream element reaches the modeled element, a new FSM is created to implement the behavior of the subset of the element molecules interacting with them. The downstream

targets are chosen by following a probability distribution, which takes into account the molecular concentrations of the target elements. Differently from the HLM model, a set of molecules can be split over different targets.

This level allows signal transduction networks to be modeled more accurately than HLM and, thus, it allows analysing their dynamic properties more in detail. On the other hand, it requires implementing many FSMs (which number depends on the system topology) and handling a larger solution space, with a direct impact on the simulation time.

3.3 Low Level Model of Elements

At this level, concurrency is viewed and implemented at molecular level. Each element behavior is modeled through a FSM per molecule. The element behavior is implemented by more SystemC processes, and the number of implemented FSMs corresponds to the molecular number of the system. The downstream target of each element molecule is chosen by following a probability distribution that, still, takes into account the molecular concentrations of the target elements. This level allows signal transduction networks to be modeled with the maximum accuracy. Nevertheless, such a modeling style may lead to the a prohibitive number of FSMs and to an intractable solution space to explore in case of complex systems. Thus, it fits to model subsets of signal transduction networks or to model networks with a reduced molecular number of each element.

4. EXPERIMENTAL RESULTS

The SystemC platform has been applied to model and simulate the leukocyte recruitment system at different abstraction levels, as proposed in Section 3. The model simulations have been conducted to identify the system properties (i.e., the system *configurations*) that lead to oscillating behaviors, and to compare the results obtained at each abstraction level in terms of accuracy and simulation time. The main goal was identifying the configurations that lead to oscillations of ITGB2 with a period of 30-40 ms, which represents the average stopping time of a cell when it interacts with the blood vessel epithelium.

Table 1 reports the characteristics of the system, which have been provided as input (i.e., input assumptions deduced by in-vitro experimental data) to restrict the solution space. Each protein and cofactor (reported in the table with (P) and (C), respectively) have been simulated with different molecular concentrations, within the range reported in column *MConcentration*. The delay time of each protein has been generated within the range reported in column *delay time* and biased as function of the molecular concentration of the target element. The lifetime value in each configuration has been sampled in the range reported in column *lifetime*. For each configuration, the system dynamics have been simulated and monitored for a total time of 250 ms.

For each implementation of the system (i.e., HLM, ILM, LLM), we run 4,194,304 configurations. Table 2 reports the results in terms of simulation time, amount of configurations that lead to oscillations of ITGB2 (in percent over the total amount of configurations), and amount of *useful* rather than *redundant* configurations. We refer as useful those configurations that lead to oscillations and differ each other by at least one input value. A configuration is redundant (and thus it does not represent any new property) when it is a duplicate of any useful configuration, and occurs when a

Table 1: The protein network characteristics

	Unknown inputs		
	MConcentration (# molecules)	delay time (ms)	lifetime (ms)
CXCL12 (P)	1,400	-	250,250
CXCR4 (P)	1,325	2,3	250,250
JAK3 (P)	1,300	2,5	250,250
JAK2 (P)	1,175	2,5	42,42
ABG (P)	1,200	2,5	31,37
VAV1 (P)	1,168	2,2	45,51
RAC1 (P)	1,235	2,6	34,40
RHOA (P)	1,146	2,6	29,35
CDC42 (P)	1,256	2,2	35,41
PLC (P)	1,210	2,4	33,33
IP3 (C)	1,115	2,5	51,57
CA (C)	1,140	2,5	44,50
DAG (C)	1,123	2,5	56,62
RASGRP1 (P)	1,127	2,4	32,38
PLD1 (P)	1,67	2,4	28,28
PIP5K1C (P)	1,234	2,4	27,33
PA (C)	1,322	2,2	63,69
RAP1A (P)	1,364	2,2	34,40
PIP2 (C)	1,243	2,3	55,61
RIAM (P)	1,435	2,4	39,39
RASSF5 (P)	1,134	2,5	32,38
FERMT3 (P)	1,123	2,5	31,31
TLN1 (P)	1,364	2,5	36,36
ITGB2 (P)	1,125	-	43,49

Table 2: Experimental results obtained at each abstraction level. $^*MConcentration \in [1, \lceil max/100 \rceil]$

Level	Config. (#)	Sim.time (min)	Oscill. (%)	Useful config(%)	Redound. config(%)
HLM	4,194,304	10	1.1	0.3	0.7
ILM	4,194,304	150	5.2	2.9	2.1
LLM*	4,194,304	850	1.0	0.96	0.04

Table 3: HLM implementation

# ITGB2 osc.	Periodic osc.		Aperiodic osc.	
	# config.	%	# config.	%
2	85,863	56.99	10,908,147	48.26
3	40,970	27.19	7,390,337	32.7
4	19,017	12.62	3,208,551	14.2
5	4,428	2.94	894,701	3.96
6	368	0.24	173,108	0.77
7	23	0.02	23,851	0.11
8	6	0.00	2,232	0.01

the complexity of such a biological system to be handled by modelling it at different abstraction levels. Experimental results obtained by applying the platform to model the intracellular signalling network controlling integrin activation mediating leukocyte recruitment from the blood into the tissues have been presented and analysed.

6. REFERENCES

[1] The Systems Biology Markup Language. http://www.sbml.org.

[2] N. Bombieri, R. Distefano, G. Scardoni, F. Fummi, C. Laudanna, and R. Giugno. Dynamic modeling and simulation of leukocyte integrin activation through an electronic design automation framework. In *Proc. of the Int. Conf. on Computational Methods in Systems Biology (CMSB) - Springer*, pages 143–154, 2014.

[3] J. C. Butcher. *Numerical Methods for Ordinary Differential Equations*. Wiley, Chichester, UK, 2003.

[4] L. Calzone, F. Fages, and S. Soliman. Biocham: An environment for modeling biological systems and formalizing experimental knowledge. *Bioinformatics*, 22(14):1805–1807, 2006.

[5] C. Chaouiya. Petri net modelling of biological networks. *Brief. in Bioinformatics*, 8(4):210–9, 2007.

[6] J. Fisher, D. Harel, and T. A. Henzinger. Biology as reactivity. *Commun. ACM*, 54(10):72–82, Oct. 2011.

[7] J. Fisher and T. A. Henzinger. Executable cell biology. *Nature Biotechnology*, 25:1239 – 1249, 2007.

[8] E. Gonçalves, J. Bucher, A. Ryll, J. Niklas, K. Mauch, S. Klamt, M. Rocha, and J. Saez-Rodriguez. Bridging the layers: Towards integration of signal transduction, regulation and metabolism into mathematical models. *Molecular BioSystems*, 9(7):1576–1583, 2013.

[9] N. Le Novère and T. Shimizu. Stochsim: modelling of stochastic biomolecular processes. *Bioinformatics*, 17(6):575–576, 2001.

[10] C. Priami. Stochastic pi-calculus. *The Computer Journal*, 38(7):578–589, 1995.

[11] D. Resasco, F. Gao, F. Morgan, I. Novak, J. Schaff, and B. Slepchenko. Virtual cell: computational tools for modeling in cell biology. *Wiley Interdiscip Rev Syst Biol Med*, 4(2):120–140, 2012.

[12] A. Sadot, J. Fisher, D. Barak, Y. Admanit, M. J. Stern, E. J. Hubbard, and D. Harel. Toward verified biological models. *IEEE Trans. on Computational Biology and Bioinformatics*, 5(2):223–34, 2008.

[13] S. Srihari, V. Raman, H. W. Leong, and M. A. Ragan. Evolution and controllability of cancer networks: A boolean perspective. *IEEE/ACM Transactions on Computational Biology and Bioinformatics*, 11(1):83–94, 2013.

configuration value is randomly chosen twice, due to the hybrid deterministic/stochastic approach adopted for the input generation (see Section 2.2). To avoid the state explosion in the LLM model, we implemented the system as explained in Section 3.3, but we reduced its complexity by limiting the maximum molecular concentration of each protein. Table 2 shows that the HLM simulation provides results in less time, even though the quality of such results is lower (i.e., the number of observed oscillations is low and the majority of them are given by redundant configurations). The table shows that the quality of results and the simulation time increase by refining the model. In the LLM simulation, the amount of oscillations is low w.r.t. the higher level implementations since the simulated model is reduced (MConcentration). The table shows that, at this level, the accuracy of the obtained results is the highest. In general, the obtained results confirm the benefit of modeling the system at different abstraction levels, that is, at each level, the model simulation provides information on the system property with an accuracy degree proportional to the simulation time. Finally, Table 3 reports a more detailed analysis of the obtained results (which, for the lack of space, are reported for the HLM simulation only). In particular, Table 3 reports the amount of configurations that lead to the ITGB2 oscillation (# config.), periodic and aperiodic, by grouping them into sets depending on the number of oscillations (# ITGB2 osc.) over the simulated period of 250 ms (i.e., from 2 to 8).

5. CONCLUSIONS

The paper presented a signal transduction modeling and simulation platform based on SystemC. The platform allows

Yield-aware Performance-Cost Characterization for Multi-Core SIMT

Seyyed Hasan Mozafari†, Kevin Skadron‡, and Brett H. Meyer†

†Dept. of Electrical and Computer Engineering
McGill University
Montréal, QC, Canada

‡Computer Science Department
University of Virginia
Charlottesville, VA, USA

seyyed.mozafari@mail.mcgill.ca, skadron@cs.virginia.edu, brett.meyer@mcgill.ca

ABSTRACT

Redundancy is now routinely allocated in circuits, microarchitectural structures, or at the system level, to mitigate mounting manufacturing yield losses. In this paper, we propose *spare lane sharing*, which reduces the cost of multi-core SIMT systems by allowing one of two neighboring cores to make use of a redundant lane if necessary. We have evaluated the performance-cost trade-offs of core-, lane-, and shared-lane-sparing under a variety of benchmarks, and found that for nearly all applications shared-lane-sparing outperforms lane-sparing, reducing cost by up to 20%.

Categories and Subject Descriptors

B.8.1 [**Hardware**]: Performance and Reliability—*Reliability, testing, and fault-tolerance*; C.1.2 [**Processor Architectures**]: Multiple Data Stream Architectures (Multiprocessors)—*Single-instruction-stream, multiple-data-stream processors (SIMD)*

Keywords

Manufacturability; system-level design; redundancy

1. INTRODUCTION

To control costs in the face of mounting yield losses, silicon systems must now be over-provisioned at the circuit level (*e.g.*, guard-bands and noise margins in design rules), microarchitectural level (*e.g.*, using redundant execution units), or system level (*e.g.*, using redundant cores) to ensure that systems with some defects can satisfy specifications and can, therefore, be sold. In this paper, we investigate the application of redundancy to improve the yield of multi-core single-instruction, multiple-thread (SIMT) architectures [1]. Multi-core SIMT architectures present a unique opportunity for yield improvement, as there are multiple levels of design abstraction at which components are already replicated for application *performance* improvement: (a) the system, which consists of multiple thread-parallel cores; and, (b) the

cores, each of which consist of a single front-end unit and multiple, data-parallel processing elements (*lanes*). Because different applications exhibit differences in parallelism, different configurations (e.g., data cache size, number of cores, number of lanes per core) are expected to strike the best performance-cost trade-offs. As the relative mix of components (cores vs. lanes) changes, the most cost-effective strategy for improving yield is also expected to change (redundant cores vs. redundant lanes). However, there are systems that cannot absorb the cost of a spare core and each core by itself cannot amortize the cost of an extra lane.

In this context, we propose the allocation of a *shared spare lane* (SSL) which can be used by either of two neighboring cores to replace a defective lane. We investigate the opportunity to reduce manufacturing costs in the presence of random defects by allocating spare cores, lanes, and shared lanes, in SIMT architecture. We observe, when considering the space of performance-cost trade-offs, that while some design points call for no redundancy (low-cost designs, in particular), and others for core- or lane-sparing, many benefit the most from shared spare lanes. Our experiments reveal that an SSL can be integrated with negligible area overhead, and only 1.3% timing overhead, while reducing costs significantly, especially for applications that call for systems that mix thread- and data-parallel execution.

2. RELATED WORK

Application-specific and reconfigurable single-instruction, multiple data (SIMD) processors are emerging as a low-cost alternative to general-purpose multi-core systems [2][3]. In this paper, we investigate strategies for improving the yield of application-specific SIMT processors [1].

Redundancy is a well-studied technique for improving yield and has been previously employed at a variety of levels of design abstraction, e.g.: at the circuit level, by taking advantage of repetitive structures [4][5], or designing multipurpose functional units [6]; and, at the microarchitecture and system level, by allocating spare cores and functional units [7][8]. Gao et al., [9] considered the effect of shared spare resources on yield for multi-core CPUs; while they investigated the effect of a single redundancy regime (shared modules), we investigate the resulting trade-offs when multiple redundancy schemes are available.

As a consequence of the growing interest in system-level redundancy, a variety of authors have proposed modeling or analysis frameworks for evaluating redundancy strategies in the multi-core era. Several studies have come to the conclusion that as cores proliferate, core-level redundancy is the most cost-effective [7][8]: lower-level techniques incur too great an overhead to cover too few possible defects. Our work develops yield models specifically for multi-core SIMT

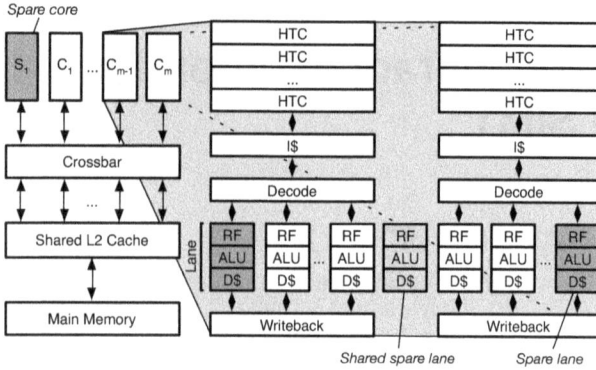

Figure 1: A multi-core SIMT system with spare core, spare lane per core, and shared spare lane.

processors, considering their unique opportunity for yield improvement; we consequently observe that systems that take advantage of data-level parallelism require alternatives to core sparing to achieve cost-effective yield improvement.

3. MULTI-GRANULARITY REDUNDANCY

A multi-core SIMT processor is illustrated in Figure 1 [1]. The architecture consists of a number of cores which communicate, through a crossbar, with a shared L2 cache. Each SIMT core is a multi-processor in its own right, but its redundant functional units (decoder, and write-back) have been removed to improve power and area efficiency for applications that exhibit data-level parallelism. Each core consists of a unified front-end unit, including L1 instruction cache (I\$), hardware thread contexts (HTC), and instruction decoder, processing elements (lanes), and a back-end write-back unit. Each lane consists of a register file (RF), arithmetic and logic unit (ALU), and L1 data cache (D\$).

Multi-core SIMT simultaneously takes advantage of thread-and data-level parallelism (TLP and DLP respectively): cores can execute different threads of the same application, or even different applications, and each core can execute the same instructions on multiple data elements at the same time. Different parallel applications have different working set sizes and mixes of TLP and DLP; therefore, different configurations result in optimal performance [1]. This variability in the design space for multi-core SIMT systems has an important consequence for yield enhancement: systems optimized for different applications may call for different redundancy.

3.1 System Yield

Yield is defined, at the time of manufacturing, as the ratio of working ICs to the total number fabricated [5]. Redundancy improves yield by substituting an operational component for a defective component at manufacturing time, increasing the salable chip count. However, if no defects are present, we assume that the redundant component is unused. Die cost, therefore, is only reduced if the increase in salable dice overwhelms the increase is system area.

The system yield y_{sys} of our SIMT architecture is the product of the yield of different groups of components, namely the cores, y_{cores}, the L2 cache, y_{L2}, and the crossbar, $y_{crossbar}$:

$$y_{sys} = y_{cores} \times y_{L2} \times y_{crossbar}. \qquad (1)$$

Row and column redundancy is standard in SRAM arrays; we assume that the yield of L1 and L2 caches is 1. Furthermore, crossbar yield approaches 1 with the addition of redundant wires [10]. In this case, the yield of the system is equivalent to the yield of the set of cores.

3.2 Core and Lane Sparing

One straightforward way to improve system yield in homogeneous SIMT multiprocessors is to (a) add spare cores or (b) add spare lanes to each core. When a core (lane) is defective, a redundant core (lane) can be substituted for it, as illustrated in Figure 1. As the number of cores (lanes per core) in the system increases, the relative overhead of a single redundant core (lane per core) goes down.

Given a system that requires m operational cores and integrates n spares, where each core has yield y_{core}, the yield of the set of cores y_{cores} is calculated with the binomial distribution:

$$y_{cores} = \sum_{i=m}^{m+n} \binom{m+n}{i} (1 - y_{core})^{m+n-i} (y_{core})^i. \qquad (2)$$

For the sake of simplicity, hereafter the binomial distribution will be denoted $Binom(y, b, s)$ for a system with b components and s spares, where components have yield y.

The yield of a core is dependent on the yield of its components. In this paper, we divide a core into (a) its lanes, (b) its L1 cache ($y_{L1} = 1$), and (c) everything else (skeleton):

$$y_{core} = y_{lanes} \times y_{L1} \times y_{skeleton}. \qquad (3)$$

Given a system where each core requires k operational lanes and integrates l spares, and the yield of each lane is y_{lane}, the yield of the lanes can, like the yield of cores, be calculated with the binomial distribution: $y_{lanes} = Binom(y_{lane}, k, l)$.

We observe from the die photo of AMD Opteron Sledgehammer (130nm SOI) processor that the elements of a single lane occupy more than 72% of the core's area. Our assumption is that the remaining area is not easily protected at low overhead: while some units, such as the hardware thread contexts, are repetitive, the structures are relatively small. Redundancy therefore offers little coverage relative to the total area of a core [7], especially as the number of lanes increases. Consequently, we do not protect them by redundancy within a given core; instead, failure within these elements can be addressed with core sparing.

3.3 Spare Lane Sharing

The homogeneity of lanes, and the significant role they play in SIMT architecture, presents an additional, unique opportunity for low-cost yield enhancement: sharing a spare lane between two cores, illustrated in Figure 1. When the two cores share a spare lane (orange), if either core has a defective lane not covered by spare lanes (gray), or when spare lanes are not available, the shared spare can be employed. The shared spare lane improves yield and reduces costs when spare lanes may otherwise be too costly; from a redundancy perspective, an SSL covers twice the lanes (at half the overhead) compared with a dedicated spare lane.

Integrating a shared spare lane only requires the addition of multiplexors in the decode and write-back units to direct signals to and from the spare lane. To quantify the area and performance overhead of an SSL, we added one between two independent tiles of the FlexGrip GPGPU streaming processor [11]. FlexGrip is very similar in structure to our SIMT architecture. We synthesized the processor using the 65nm TSMC standard library and measured the change in area and clock frequency. We observe that the area overhead (not including the spare lane itself) is less than 0.1% of a single lane; clock frequency falls just 1.3%.

The inclusion of an SSL makes the yield of one core in the pair dependent upon the yield of the other: if one core needs the shared spare lane, it is only available if the other core does not. Consequently, there is no straightforward formula to calculate a single core's yield when both SSL and spare cores are present. Furthermore, the combinatorial space is prohibitively large; simply counting systems that yield or do not is computationally intractable as systems grow. We therefore estimate yield as follows. There are two cases in which both cores that share a spare lane are functional. Neither core needs the shared spare lane when sufficient spare lanes are present or no lanes are defective:

$$y_{lanes\_ssl_1} = Binom(y_{lane}, k, l) \times Binom(y_{lane}, k, l). \quad (4)$$

If one core of a pair has $l + 1$ defective lanes, the pair still yields if the shared spare is not defective:

$$y_{lanes\_ssl_2} = y_{lane} \times \binom{k+l}{l+1} (1 - y_{lane})^{l+1} (y_{lane})^{k-1}$$
$$\times Binom(y_{lane}, k, l). \quad (5)$$

Symmetry in the system means there are two ways to have a core that requires the shared spare lane: $y_{lanes\_ssl_p} = y_{lanes\_ssl_1} + 2 \cdot y_{lanes\_ssl_2}$, and the yield of a single core's lanes can be estimated as $y_{lanes\_ssl} = \sqrt{y_{lanes\_ssl_p}}$.

When spare cores are not present, this model is exact. However, error is introduced when spare cores are available. In this case, the system may yield despite the failure of one of a pair of a cores sharing a spare lane. We approximate the yield with an even number of spare cores as $y_{cores} = Binom(y_{core_{ssl}}, m, n)$, where $y_{core_{ssl}}$ is the yield of a core with a shared spare lane. If an odd number of spare cores are allocated and each but the last has a shared spare lane,

$$y_{cores} = Binom(y_{core_{ssl}}, m, n)(1 - y_{core}) +$$
$$\sum_{i=m}^{m+n+1} \binom{m+n}{i-1} (1 - y_{core_{ssl}})^{m+n-(i-1)} (y_{core_{ssl}})^{(i-1)} (y_{core}). \quad (6)$$

The effect of the introduced error is, in the end, negligible: we observe that, for the defect densities considered, systems that employ more than one type of redundancy (e.g., spare cores and shared spare lanes) are too expensive to fall on the performance-cost Pareto-optimal front. We hypothesize that this may change under higher defect densities; such an investigation is the subject of future work.

4. EXPERIMENTAL SETUP

We used MV5 [12] to simulate the performance of SIMT configurations, consistent with parameters in the literature [1]. We varied the number of cores N, $N \in \{1, 2, 4, 6, \ldots, 20\}$, the number of lanes per core (SIMT width) W and hardware threads per core (SIMT depth) D, $W \& D \in \{1, 2, 4, 8, \ldots, 64\}$ and L1 data cache size S, $S \in \{8, 16, 32, 64\}$ KB. From the parameter space defined above, we selected all configurations with die area within $[50, 250]$ mm^2. We selected benchmarks from Minebench [13], SPLASH-2 [14], and Rodinia [15]: FFT, Filter, HotSpot, LU, MergeSort, Shortest-Path, KMeans, SVM.

We estimated the cost of a configuration as follows. The cost of a die C_{die} is a function of the cost of a wafer C_{wafer}, the number of dice per wafer, and die yield, y_{sys} [16]:

$$C_{die} = \frac{C_{wafer}/(Dice/Wafer)}{y_{sys}}. \quad (7)$$

We assume a wafer radius of $150mm$, a wafer yield of 1, and that wafers cost \$3000 each. y_{sys} is calculated as in

Section 3. The yield of individual components, such as lanes, is calculated with the negative binomial yield model [17, 18]:

$$y_b = \left(1 + \frac{\lambda_b \times A_b}{\alpha}\right)^{-\alpha}. \quad (8)$$

where (α), (λ_b), and (A_b) are the clustering parameter, defect density, and component area, respectively. We assume $\alpha = 4$ and $\lambda_b = 0.025/cm^2$ in $65nm$ [16].

To estimate the chip area we measured the area of functional units based on die photo of an AMD Opteron processor. As this processor is fabricated in $130nm$, we used a scaling factor of 0.7 per generation to scale the processor to $65nm$. While the Opteron and SIMT processors are not architecturally the same, the relative size of the functional units is not expected to vary significantly. Moreover, since the core's area is dominated by the integer ALU and multiplier, the relative size of other components is less important.

5. RESULTS

We conducted a variety of experiments to validate our models and evaluate the different redundancy techniques. To validate our yield models (Section 3), we compared our analytical results with statistical simulation using Monte Carlo Simulation (MCS). We considered 140 large configurations (each with more than 50 cores, and at least 16 lanes per each core), divided into seven equal subsets. Each of the first three subsets are allocated a single type of redundancy, a spare core (SC), spare lane (SL), or shared spare lane (SSL). Each of the second three are allocated a pair of redundancy types (SC+SL, SC+SSL, or SL+SSL). The last subset is allocated all three types. As appropriate, we consider n SC, k SL, and zero or one SSL, where $n \in SC = \{0, 1, \ldots, m\}$, $l \in SL = \{0, 1, \ldots, k\}$ for a system with m cores and k lanes per core. The number of HTC in a configuration is $k + l + s$, where $s = 1$ if an SSL has been integrated. We simulated an unrealistically high defect density $(0.3/cm^2)$ to exaggerate any potential error in the models. We performed 100K trials for each configuration; on average over all subsets, the relative difference in yield between MCS and our models is 0.61% yield, with a 95% confidence interval of 0.76% yield.

Next, we performed exhaustive performance simulation using MV5, simulating 813 configurations (Section 4) with no redundancy for each benchmark. We then added redundancy to each configuration, to the point that its manufacturing cost is greater than the cost of the baseline system, based on a realistic defect density $(0.025/cm^2)$.

From the set of baseline and corresponding defect-tolerant designs, we selected the performance-cost Pareto-optimal front (POF). Designs utilizing SSL pay a 1.3% execution latency penalty. We observe that systems allocated a combination of redundancy types, for the normal defect density, do not appear on the POF; neither do systems with more than a single redundant unit of a given type.

The results of our experiments are summarized in Tables 1. Table 1 lists, by benchmark (App.), the range of configurations that benefit most, in terms of *average relative cost reduction* (ARCR), from each redundancy allocation under consideration: a spare core (SC), spare lane (SL), shared spare lane (SSL), and no redundancy (None). ARCR is defined as the change in cost relative to the baseline design with no redundancy. The best ARCR for each configuration group is indicated in bold; when no redundancy type decreases cost, no ARCR is bolded.

We made the bins in Table 1 as large as possible without complicating their definition (e.g., by combining two disjoint or partially overlapping sets). Consequently, some POF de-

Table 1: ARCR for Performance-cost POF Configurations

App.	Configurations				ARCR (%)		
	Cores	D$ Size	HTC	Lanes	SC	SL	SSL
Filter	[2, 8]	[8, 32]	[16, 64]	[2, 4]	**11.2**	7.9	9.6
	[4, 16]	[16, 32]	[8, 16]	[16, 32]	7.5	**8.3**	7.2
	[1, 2]	[8, 32]	[2, 8]	[1, 4]	-0.9	-1.3	-0.7
KM*	[6, 8]	[8, 32]	[8, 16]	[1, 2]	**7.3**	4.3	5.8
	[4, 16]	[8, 16]	[2, 4]	[4, 16]	5.3	7.1	**8.3**
	[1, 2]	[16, 32]	[1, 4]	[1, 4]	-1.7	-1.8	-0.9
FFT	[8, 16]	[8, 64]	[8, 16]	[1, 4]	**4.5**	3.1	4.0
	[1, 4]	[8, 16]	[1, 8]	[1, 2]	-0.9	-1.6	-1.2
MS+	[16, 20]	[32, 64]	[8, 16]	[1, 4]	**5.6**	4.3	4.7
	[4, 8]	[8, 32]	[4, 8]	[4, 8]	3.6	3.9	**4.5**
	[1, 2]	[8, 16]	[4, 16]	[1, 4]	-0.6	-1.2	-0.8
SP†	[16]	[16, 64]	[8, 32]	[2, 4]	**7.6**	6.1	6.8
	[8]	[16]	[4, 8]	[4, 8]	7.2	7.1	**8.7**
	[1, 2]	[8, 16]	[1, 4]	[1, 4]	-1.1	-1.4	-0.7
HS‡	[16, 20]	[32, 64]	[8, 16]	[1, 4]	**5.5**	4.2	4.8
	[4, 16]	[8, 32]	[4, 16]	[4, 8]	4.7	5.3	**6.0**
	[1, 2]	[16, 32]	[1, 32]	[1, 2]	-1.3	-1.1	-0.5
LU	[16, 20]	[16, 64]	[16, 32]	[1, 4]	**6.2**	4.7	5.6
	[2, 4]	[16, 32]	[4, 8]	[4, 8]	3.5	4.1	**4.5**
	[1, 2]	[8, 16]	[4, 16]	[1, 2]	-0.7	-1.7	-0.9
SVM	[8]	[8]	[8]	[2]	**1.3**	-0.8	-0.5
	[1, 2]	[8, 64]	[1, 32]	[1, 2]	-1.1	-1.0	-0.7

*: KMeans, +: MergeSort, †: ShortestPath, ‡: HotSpot

signs do not fit well into the bins. Each application has, on average, more than 25 POF designs. Three are omitted from Filter, ShortestPath, and MergeSort; seven and five from LU and HotSpot, respectively; and, two and one from FFT and SVM, respectively. In the worst case (LU), incorporation of the outliers results in 0.2% variation in ARCR.

In general, we observe that systems with few cores (1-2 or 4) benefit the most from no redundancy. The cores in these systems often tend to be narrow (1-2 or 4 lanes); consequently, spare cores, lanes, or shared lanes, represent too great an overhead to be absorbed by increases in yield. For configurations with more cores, few lanes, and many HTCs (generally more than eight), SC is the best redundancy regime. Only a spare core covers defects in the HTCs; these systems do not use enough lanes to benefit from lane-level redundancy. Aside from Filter, applications do not generally benefit from a spare lane. Instead, SSL is used for systems with more lanes (generally more than four) and fewer HTC (usually less than eight).

Overall, we observe that when performance-cost Pareto-optimal designs are considered, a shared spare lane is a suitable substitute for a spare lane for most applications. For HotSpot and KMeans, SSL is not only the dominant redundancy technique, representing a greater share of the POF than SC, it also reduces costs about 0.4% more than SC, on average. Moreover, SSL reduces cost more than 0.5% more than SL on average across all benchmarks.

6. CONCLUSIONS

In this paper, we investigated the application of redundancy allocated at different design granularities in the context of multi-core SIMT systems. In addition to evaluating the traditional approaches of core- and lane-sparing, we proposed spare lane sharing. Under spare lane sharing, the cost of the spare lane is amortized across two cores, making it affordable for a wider range of system configurations. Shared spare lanes can be integrated with negligible area and marginal performance overhead.

We observe that when systems consist of a few small cores, no type of redundancy reduces cost: the overhead is too great to be absorbed by increases in yield. Spare cores increase yield best for applications that require many large, narrow cores: in these systems, cores are not dominated by lanes, but by other resources not explicitly protected by redundancy. Only spare cores can cover their failure.

In general, however, most benchmarks perform best on systems with wider cores. In this case, shared spare lanes offer the best reduction in cost. Notably, only a single benchmark, Filter, which requires very wide cores, has designs with spare lanes on its performance-cost Pareto-optimal front. In all other cases, shared spare lanes outperform spare lanes, making them a suitable substitute for spare lanes in the context of yield improvement in multi-core SIMT systems.

Acknowledgements

This research was made possible with funding from Fonds de recherche Nature et technologies du Québec (FRQNT), the US NSF grant MCDA-0903471 and C-FAR, one of the six SRC STARnet Centers, sponsored by MARCO and DARPA, and CAD tools from CMC Microsystems.

7. REFERENCES

[1] J. Meng, et al., "Robust SIMD: Dynamically adapted SIMD width and multi-threading depth," in IPDPS'12.

[2] Y. Lin, et al., "Soda: A low-power architecture for software radio," in ISCA, 2006.

[3] C. Lyuh, et al., "A novel reconfigurable processor using dynamically partitioned simd for multimedia applications," ETRI, vol. 31, no. 6, 2009.

[4] F. Hatori, et al, "Introducing redundancy in field programmable gate arrays," in CICC, 1993.

[5] I. Koren and Z. Koren, "Defect tolerance in VLSI circuits: Techniques and yield analysis," Proceedings of the IEEE, vol. 86, no. 9, 1998.

[6] V. V. Kumar and J. Lach, "Heterogeneous redundancy for fault and defect tolerance with complexity independent area overhead," in DFT, 2003.

[7] S. Premkishore, et al., "Exploiting microarchitectural redundancy for defect tolerance," in ICCD, 2003.

[8] E. Schuchman and T. N. Vijaykumar, "Rescue: a microarchitecture for testability and defect tolerance," in ISCA, 2005.

[9] Y. Gao, et al., "Trading off area, yield and performance via hybrid redundancy in multi-core architectures," in VTS, 2013.

[10] S. Shamshiri and K.-T. Cheng, "Modeling yield, cost, and quality of a spare-enhanced multicore chip," IEEE Tran. Comp., vol. 60, no. 9, 2011.

[11] K. Andryc, et al., "Flexgrip: A soft gpgpu for fpgas," in FPT'13, 2013, pp. 230–237.

[12] J. Meng and K. Skadron, "Avoiding cache thrashing due to private data placement in last-level cache for manycore scaling," in ICCD, 2007.

[13] R. Narayanan, et al., "Minebench: A benchmark suite for data mining workloads," in IISWC, 2006.

[14] S. C. Woo, et al., "The SPLASH-2 programs: Characterization and methodological considerations," in ISCA, 1995.

[15] S. Che, et al., "A performance study of general purpose applications on graphics processors using CUDA," JPDC, Elsevier, vol. 68, no. 10, 2008.

[16] J. L. Hennessy and D. A. Patterson, Computer Architecture: A Quantitative Approach, 5th ed. Morgan Kaufmann Publishers Inc., 2012.

[17] J. Cunningham, "The use and evaluation of yield models in integrated circuit manufacturing," TSM, vol. 3, no. 2, 1990.

[18] J. De Sousa and V. Agrawal, "Reducing the complexity of defect level modelling using the clustering effect," in DATE, 2000.

An Efficient Approach to Sample On-Chip Power Supplies

Luke Murray and Sunil P Khatri
Department of ECEN, Texas A&M University
College Station, Texas, USA
tromboneman@tamu.edu, sunilkhatri@tamu.edu

ABSTRACT

In recent years, post-silicon debugging has become a significantly difficult exercise due to the increase in the size of the electrical state of the IC being debugged, coupled with the limited fraction of this state that is visible to the debug engineer. As the number of transistors increases, the number of possible electrical states increases exponentially, while the amount of information that can be accessed grows at a much slower rate. This difficulty is compounded by the outsourcing of IP blocks, which creates more black boxes that the debug engineer must work around. As a result, when an IC fails tracking down the cause of the failure becomes a monumental task, and debugging becomes more art than science. One source of errors in a test circuit is the fluctuation of the power supplies during a single clock cycle. These supply variations can increase or decrease the speed of a circuit and lead to errors such as hold time violations and setup time violations. This paper presents a circuit that samples precisely the power supply multiple times in a clock cycle, allowing the debug engineer to quantify the variations in the supply over a clock cycle. With this information, a better understanding of the electrical state of the test chip is made possible. The circuit presented in this paper can sample the supply voltage with a quantization of 0.291mV, and the output is linear with an R^2 value of 0.9987.

1. Introduction

Post-silicon debug is complicated due to the presence of billions of on-chip nets and devices, resulting in a very large electrical state to reason about and a limited number of pins to access them. Several electrical effects such as cross-talk, processing variation, temperature, and power supply variations make the task of post-silicon debug even more difficult. Although techniques such as test pattern generation and boundary scans allow for the examination of the digital state of a chip, many of the failure modes of this IC are analog in nature, such as power supply integrity. Knowing the fluctuations of the on-chip power supply over any clock cycle is important to understanding how the power supply is effecting the timing of circuits, and if these changes in timing are responsible for the error, such as hold time and setup time violations, being debugged. This paper presents a method to reconstruct the power supply waveform over a clock cycle.

In our scheme, an IC would have several Supply Testing Units (STUs), each connected to a set of test points on the chip, as shown in Figure 1. In this figure three STUs (STU1, STU2 and STU3) are connected to seven test points (n1 through n7). The test points would be located at points in the power grid that are likely to have problems with droops or spikes; design-time CAD simulations and analysis could be used to identify these potentially problematic locations. Note that these test points may be located at sites that are not easily accessed during the post-silicon debug, such as the power pins of critical logic that are on lower metal layers. Each of the STUs is able to measure the supply voltage at one of the test points, outputing a sequence of binary numbers representing the measured voltage, and reconstruct the power supply waveform for that point. By repeatedly measuring the voltage over a single clock cycle, the supply voltage waveform could be reconstructed for a given time interval of interest for debug purposes. This could then be used by the debug engineers to understand the effects that power supply variations were having on the timing of circuits, and if it led to the error being debugged.

In particular we sample the power supply fifteen times a clock period (assumed to be 1ns) and output a 10-bit number representing the voltage of each sample

The key contributions of this paper are:

- The STU samples the power supply fifteen times a cycle, providing a high-accuracy measurement of the supply voltage at any test point.

- A complete reconstruction of the supply voltage waveform can be performed, enabling accurate debugging.

- Our scheme directly sample the power supply of any location on the die, including locations that are hard to probe using traditional techniques.

- Our scheme is integrated on-die, eliminating the need for expensive instrumentation, depackaging, or depassivation.

The rest of the paper is organized as follows. Section 2 goes over the previous works. In Section 3 the details of the circuit are explained. Then in Section 4 the results of simulations are reported.

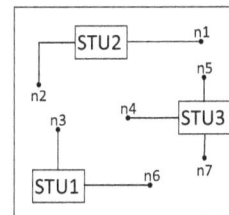

Figure 1: STU Based Architecture to Test Several Candidate Test Points

2. Previous Works

Previous methods of sampling power supply voltages have usually only attempted to sample the power supply once per clock cycle and have relied on indirect methods to measure variations in the power supply. Past approaches often required special off-chip equipment, or were destructive in nature.

One method used in the past to detect spikes or droops in the power supply has been to look at the *effects* the noise would have on a circuit. This can be achieved by looking at the propagation delay of an inverter [1] or on a NAND gate [2]. Similarly, the voltage threshold curve of an inverter can be used to estimate the power supply noise [3]. These methods are indirect and averages, unlike our method.

Other methods have generated *statistics* about the power supply, such as when it crosses a threshold [4], the lowest or highest voltage [5], or the Power Spectral Density (PSD) [6]. These methods can not reconstruct the power supply waveform.

Previous methods have converted the analog supply to a digital output using different types of ADC [7, 8]. However the power supply voltage is not sampled before conversion, resulting in an *average* measurement of the supply over a single clock cycle, losing the changes in the supply that occur *during* a clock cycle.

Methods that use a specialized oscilloscope have also been proposed [9], but are destructive, requiring depackaging and depassivating a part.

Unlike previous works, our scheme is non-destructive, and samples the power supply voltage multiple times a clock cycle.

3. Approach

Our approach works in two phases. First, during the *sampling phase*, the power supply is sampled at a sampling rate F_s (15GHz in our experiments) for S samples. Assuming a clock rate F (1GHz in our experiment) for the test circuit, this produces $S = \frac{F_s}{F}$ samples per clock. For our experiment, S is fifteen samples per clock, which results in fifteen Sample to Pulse Converter (SPC) blocks, one for each sample. Then, in the *conversion phase*, each of the samples collected in the first phase is converted from the stored analog value to a digital count. The resulting sequence of C counts is the output of the STU and can be used to reconstruct the original supply waveform. Note that the number of samples per clock (fifteen in our design) is limited by the conversion speed of the STU. Because the

In practice the conversion rate (F_c) is much slower than the sampling rate (F_s). In particular, our design yields an F_c of 15 MHz. Hence the conversion time for $S = 15$ samples is $\frac{S}{F_c} = 1\mu s$. Therefore, to reconstruct the power supply for K clock cycles, the corresponding experiment should be repeated for $min(K, \frac{F_s}{F_c})$ runs, each run using the same input vectors. This is because every $\frac{F_s}{F_c}$ clock cycle can be sampled then converted during the next $\frac{F_s}{F_c} - 1$ clock cycles before another clock cycle is sampled. During the first run, the 1st, $\frac{F_s}{F_c} + 1$, $2 \times \frac{F_s}{F_c} + 1$, and so forth clock cycles are sampled. Then during the second run, the 2nd, $\frac{F_s}{F_c} + 2$, $2 \times \frac{F_s}{F_c} + 2$, and so forth clock cycles are sampled. After this, the complete waveform could be reconstructed by interleaving the results from each of the runs. If $K < \frac{F_s}{F_c}$, then K experiments are run and the results are concatenated.

The loading effect of our STU on the power net is minimal, since the load capacitance the STU presents is that of two minimum sized transistor diffusions. The capacitance of a power supply node is significantly larger than the loading capacitance of our circuit.

3.1 Block Diagram

A brief overview of our approach is presented next, followed by a discussion of each component of our design.

The datapath of each STU is made up of fifteen Sample to Pulse Converters (SPC) that are connected through a MUX to a counter unit, as shown in Figure 2. At the start of the sampling phase, the control unit produces a 66.67ps pulse on each of the $Ctrl_{read}$ pins of the SPCs The falling edge of the pulse to SPC_1 coincides with the rising edge of SPC_2, whose falling edge coincides with the rising edge of SPC_3, and so on. When the $Ctrl_{read}$ line goes high for any SPC, it reads the voltage from V_{test} (the voltage of the power supply test point being analyzed) into a MIM capacitor inside the SPC.

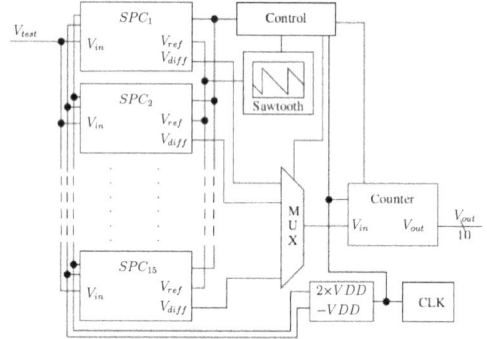

Figure 2: Block Diagram of each Supply Testing Unit (STU)

During the conversion phase, the voltage stored in the MIM capacitors of the SPC is compared (using a Difference Amplifier) to a sawtooth waveform, V_{ref}. This produces a pulse train, where each pulse is high when V_{ref} is greater than the voltage stored in the MIM capacitor C_{SPC} in the SPC. The MUX selects the input to the counter, driving the counter input with a pulse from SPC_1, followed by SPC_2, and so on, up to SPC_{15}. The counter measures the width of each of the pulses and outputs it as V_{out} (a 10-bit number) in Figure 2. The combination of the differential amplifier (in the SPC), the sawtooth waveform generator and the counter function as an ADC. Finally, at the end of the conversion phase, fifteen V_{out} samples have been computed.

Along with a control circuit to synchronize the datapath, there is a ring oscillator clock circuit that produces a 15GHz clock. Additionally, there are two charge pumps to produce -VDD and 2×VDD, which are used by the SPCs

3.2 Sample to Pulse Converter

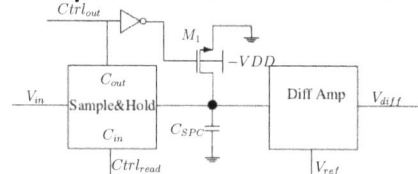

Figure 3: Sample to Pulse Converter (SPC)

The two main parts of the Sample to Pulse Converter are the Sample & Hold (SH) circuit and the Difference Amplifier, which will be covered in Section 3.3 & Section 3.4, respectively. The voltage samples (V_{SH}) stored in the SH circuits (in C_{SH} in Figure 4) can range between $VDD + V_R$ and $VDD - V_R$, where V_R is the maximum on-chip ripple (assumed to be 100mV). The rest of the SPC converts the voltage stored in the SH circuit (in C_{SH}), to a lower voltage that is less than VDD. This is done by charge sharing between the capacitor inside the SH circuit, C_{SH}, and the capacitor between the Sample & Hold and the Difference Amplifier, C_{SPC}, shown in Figure 4 & Figure 3, respectively. When the STU is in the sampling phase, $Ctrl_{out}$ is low, which means that M_1 in Figure 3 is conductive and C_{SPC} is grounded. Then when $Ctrl_{out}$ goes high, C_{SH} and C_{SPC} are effectively shorted, making the voltage of the output of the SH block equal to $\frac{C_{SH}}{C_{SPC}+C_{SH}} \times V_{SH}$, where V_{SH} was the sampled voltage of the SH block.

3.3 Sample & Hold

The Sample & Hold circuit is used to quickly sample the voltage of the power supply at the given test point and store it as a voltage (V_{SH}) in the capacitor C_{SH}. This is done using two complimentary passgates and a capacitor, C_{SH}, as shown in Figure 4. For SPC_i, the $Ctrl_{read}$ pin is connected to the output $Ctrl_i$ from the Sample & Hold part of the control circuit. This signal will go high for a 66.67ns pulse during the sampling phase, allowing C_{SH} to sample the voltage on V_{in}. The C_{out} signal will stay low during the sampling phase, then go high during the conversion phase when the voltage in C_{SH} is shared with the voltage in C_{SPC}, as described above.

There are two specifications that the Sample & Hold circuits must meet. First, the voltage on V_{in} should be faithfully stored into C_{SH} during the sampling phase. Second, the voltage in C_{SH} should be preserved during the conversion phase. To meet the first requirement the sizing of the first passgate (on the left of Figure 4) and the capacitor (C_{SH}) must be such that their RC value is small enough to allow charging during a $\frac{1}{15\text{GHz}}$ period. The second requirement can be met by limiting the leakage during the conversion phase. Part of how this is meet is by heavily reverse biasing all of the MOSFETs in the passgates (set Figure 4) to increase the magnitude of their threshold voltages, hence reducing their leakage. The MOSFET M_1 in the SPC (Figure 3) is reverse biased for the same reasons. The leakage is also controlled by reducing the size of the passgates.

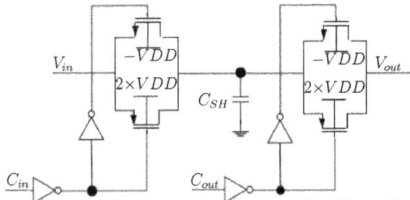

Figure 4: Sample & Hold Circuit

3.4 Difference Amplifier

The Difference Amplifier takes as inputs the sawtooth V_{ref} signal and the voltage stored in C_{SPC}. When $V_{ref} > V_{SPC}$, the output V_{diff} is pulled high and when $V_{ref} < V_{SPC}$ it is pulled low. This creates a train of pulses on the output (V_{diff}) of the Difference Amplifier that have a frequency equal to the frequency of V_{ref} (15MHz). Note that this choice frequency results in fifteen sample being converted in $\frac{15}{15\text{MHz}} = 1\mu s$ The width of each pulse in the pulse train changes with the voltage stored in C_{SPC}. Lower voltages create wider pulses and higher voltages shorter ones. This train of pulses will continue until a new sample is read into C_{SPC}

3.5 Sawtooth Waveform Generator

The sawtooth circuit was designed for a V_{test} range of 0.7V to 0.9V. The output, V_{ref}, is shown in Figure 5. For chips with multiple power domains, the range can be adjusted for each power domain by resizing the gate capacitors in the sawtooth circuit.

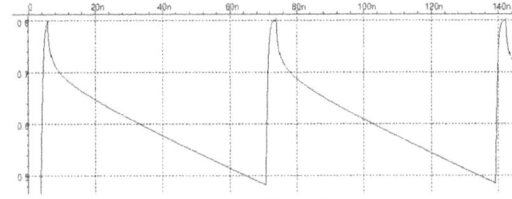

Figure 5: Sawtooth Circuit output at V_{ref}

3.6 Counter

A standard T-Flip Flop counter circuit, see Figure 2, measures the width of the pulse on V_{in}, and outputs a 10-bit number, V_{out}. The value on V_{out} is proportional to the width of the pulse on V_{in} The 15GHz clock is gated with V_{in} and is connected to the counter, so that the counter counts the number of clock pulses while V_{in} is high. When the STU control switches the MUX, to select the V_{diff} from an new SPC, a reset signal is also sent to the counter circuit. Since the counter circuit is standard, a figure for this circuit is omitted.

3.7 Control Circuit

The control circuit is composed of a circuit controlling the $Ctrl_{read}$ pins of the SPC during the sampling phase, and a separate circuit controlling the STU during the conversion phase. The single input to the control circuit is a 2ns wide active high reset pulse, V_{reset}, which dictates when the sampling will start. From V_{reset}, fifteen $Ctrl_{read}$ signals are created using an edge detection circuit and a shift register. The control to the MUX is created using a clock divider to create a 15MHz counter, which is also used to create V_{start}.

3.8 Resonant Clock

The sampling performed by the STU is at a 15GHz frequency, and hence the 15GHz clock must be generated by the STU. This is done using a resonant clock, as described in [10]. This clock works by creating a sinusoidal standing wave oscillation in a Mobius shaped transmission line.

4. Experiment

All of the circuits described in this paper were modeled in HSPICE [11] using a 22nm PTM technology [12]. The nominal VDD for this process is 0.8V. The length of the wire in the Mobius band for the resonant clock was 1026 μm with a width of 20 μm, and a spacing of 20 μm. This achieved a square wave clock signal at 15GHz.

The main experiment was to apply a test voltage to V_{test} and measure the change in V_{out} (see Figure 2) as V_{test} was varied. After the circuit had booted up, V_{test} was changed to the test voltage for that run, and the STU received a 2ns pulse on V_{reset} that would cause the STU to start sampling V_{test}. During this test, V_{test} was swept from 0.7V to 0.9V in 10mV increments. Figure 6 shows the outputted counts on V_{out} for the given voltages on V_{test}. This plot shows that the output count varies linearly, with an R^2 (Coefficient of Determination) value of 0.9987, showing that it is possible to reconstruct the original waveform from the output count. Using the output count seen on V_{out}, and the corresponding voltage on V_{test}, we performed a linear curve fit to obtain the equation $count = 3431.6 \times V_{test} + 2165.5$. From this equation we find that the voltage resolution of our design is $\frac{\Delta V}{count} = 0.291mV$. During this test the 2×VDD and -VDD circuits were not simulated since the HSPICE runtimes were prohibitive. However they were both simulated with fifteen SPCs connected as loads. The measured outputs from the charge pumps from this simulation were used in the overall test of the circuit.

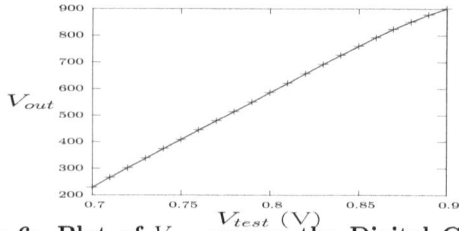

Figure 6: Plot of V_{test} versus the Digital Count on V_{out}

One potential concern with our approach is that after all fifteen SPCs sample the supply value, only one SPC converts its stored value at a time. This leaves open the possibility that even if they all sample the same voltage, they could produce different results, since the stored value of SPC_i could droop (due to leakage currents) before it is converted. To test what happened to the voltage stored in C_{SH} and C_{SPC} over time a voltage of 780mV was sampled by an SPC and the width of V_{diff} (the train of pulses produced by the difference amplifier) was measured over a one microsecond (the conversion period for our setup) timeframe. The result was that there was a decrease of 0.2ns for each pulse, which would decrease the output count by three for each conversion. This means that if, for example, all the SPCs sampled the same V_{test} and SPC_1 outputted 467, then SPC_2 would output 464, and SPC_3 would output 461, and so on. However, this change in the output versus the order of conversion is linear, with R^2 equal to 0.998. Hence, this effect can easily be compensated for by adding $3 \times (i - 1)$ to the results of SPC_i.

The linearity of the sawtooth circuit was also tested, because of the effect of this circuit on the overall circuit's linearity. The result was that over the range of [0.7V, 0.9V] for V_{test}, the sawtooth had an R^2 equal to 0.9977. The sawtooth spend 87.75% of the clock cycle in the [0.7V, 0,9] operating range, which is the percentage of the number of 10 bit outputs that are used.

To test the effects of **processes variation** on the design, several corner cases were run on the Sample & Hold Circuit, since the effect of variations on other blocks can be canceled during calibration. The fast and slow corners were created by a 5% change in transistor width and length and a increase and decrease in temperature of 25 degrees Celsius, respectively. The change in the digital count is at most $\pm$ 3.12% and $\pm$ 2.55%, for the two corners. The R^2 for the fast and slow corners are 0.9918 and 0.9976, respectively. Since the transistors for all the SPC blocks will vary in width, length and temperature together, the near unity R^2 value shows most of the error will be eliminated by calibration. Calibration can be performed by running the STU while the clock to the circuit under test is turned off, so that no switching occurs, and the power supply is constant.

Tolerance to temperature fluctuations after calibration was also tested, with the result that a 1% fluctuation in temperature gave a 0.04% fluctuation in V_{out} and a 5% fluctuation in temperature gave a 2% fluctuation in V_{out}. This shows that a small change in temperature will have an even smaller effect on the results.

Assuming that the wire from any test point to the capacitor (in the Sample & Hold block) is $500\mu m$ in Metal7, the RC time constant was calculated to be 23.8ps. This is below the 33.3ps required by the Nyquist Sampling theorem for 15GHz sampling, ensuring the high frequency component of the power supply will be captured.

The overall area of the STU is 10.77 μm^2. Of the total area, the largest part comes from the control circuit (3.88 μm^2). The resonant clock (3.17 μm^2) and the sawtooth (1.58 μm^2) are the second and third largest sub-circuits of the STU. The control circuit has twenty-nine flip-flops which adds to its size. The resonant clock requires a pair of large inverters to operate and the sawtooth circuit has two large gate capacitors. In addition to the active area, the circuit also requires 27fF worth of MIM (metal-insulator-metal) capacitors that are used for C_{SH}, C_{SPC} and the capacitors in the charge pumps.

5. Conclusion

This paper presents a circuit that can sample the power supply voltage at a fast (15GHz) rate, taking several (15 in our experiments) samples per clock period. These samples are then each converted to a 10 bit output. The circuit is substantial linear with a resolution of $\Delta V = 0.291$mV and an R^2 of 0.9987. This output along with calibration data can be used to completely reconstruct the supply voltage waveform over any interval of time. Furthermore, by sampling the power supply at a rate faster than the test circuits clock, the debug engineer will be able to see how the supply varies over a clock period. This information can then be used to understand the effect that the power supply is having on the timing of circuits. This information can prove to be a crucial aid in the post-silicon debugging of the test chip.

6. References

[1] J. Vázquez and J. de Gyvez, "Power supply noise monitor for signal integrity faults," in *Design, Automation and Test in Europe Conference and Exhibition, 2004. Proceedings*, vol. 2, pp. 1406–1407, IEEE, 2004.

[2] C. Metra, L. Schiano, M. Favalli, and B. Ricco, "Self-checking scheme for the on-line testing of power supply noise," in *Design, Automation and Test in Europe Conference and Exhibition, 2002. Proceedings*, pp. 832–836, IEEE, 2002.

[3] A. Vijayakumar, R. Kumar, and S. Kundu, "On design of low cost power supply noise detection sensor for microprocessors," in *VLSI (ISVLSI), 2012 IEEE Computer Society Annual Symposium on*, pp. 120–125, IEEE, 2012.

[4] A. Muhtaroglu, G. Taylor, and T. Rahal-Arabi, "On-die droop detector for analog sensing of power supply noise," *Solid-State Circuits, IEEE Journal of*, vol. 39, no. 4, pp. 651–660, 2004.

[5] Y. Tamaki, T. Nakura, M. Ikeda, and K. Asada, "A toggle-type peak hold circuit for local power supply noise detection," in *Quality Electronic Design (ASQED), 2010 2nd Asia Symposium on*, pp. 29–32, IEEE, 2010.

[6] E. Alon, V. Stojanovic, and M. Horowitz, "Circuits and techniques for high-resolution measurement of on-chip power supply noise," *Solid-State Circuits, IEEE Journal of*, vol. 40, no. 4, pp. 820–828, 2005.

[7] M. Nagata, J. Nagai, T. Morie, and A. Iwata, "Measurements and analyses of substrate noise waveform in mixed-signal IC environment," *Computer-Aided Design of Integrated Circuits and Systems, IEEE Transactions on*, vol. 19, no. 6, pp. 671–678, 2000.

[8] R. Petersen, P. Pant, P. Lopez, A. Barton, J. Ignowski, and D. Josephson, "Voltage transient detection and induction for debug and test," Test Conference, 2009. ITC 2009. International, 2009.

[9] T. Okumoto, M. Nagata, and K. Taki, "A built-in technique for probing power-supply noise distribution within large-scale digital integrated circuits," in *VLSI Circuits, 2004. Digest of Technical Papers. 2004 Symposium on*, pp. 98–101, IEEE, 2004.

[10] V. Cordero and S. Khatri, "Clock distribution scheme using coplanar transmission lines," in *Design Automation, and Test in Europe (DATE) Conference*, pp. 985–990, IEEE, 2008.

[11] "Synopsys HSPICE." http://www.synopsys.com/tools/Verification/AMSVerification/CircuitSimulation/HSPICE/Pages/default.aspx.

[12] "ASU PTM website." http://www.ptm.asu.edu.

Dynamic Bitstream Length Scaling Energy Effective Stochastic LDPC Decoding

Thomas Marconi and Sorin Cotofana
Computer Engineering Lab, TU Delft, The Netherlands
{T.Marconi, S.D.Cotofana}@tudelft.nl

ABSTRACT

Stochastic Computing (SC) is an attractive solution for implementing Low Density Parity Codes (LDPC) decoders due to its fault tolerance capability and low hardware requirements. However, in practical implementations, SC efficiency is limited by the Stochastic Bitstream (SB) length and by the computation inaccuracies due to non-unique SB representations. In this paper, rather than statically fixing the SB length at run-time, we propose a Dynamic Bitstream Length Scaling (DBLS) technique, which adjusts on-the-fly the SB length such that Quality of Service requirements for energy efficient LDPC decoding are fulfilled. In this way, depending on the communication channel condition, different SB lengths are adaptively utilized such that the best decoding performance vs energy consumption tradeoff is achieved. To evaluate the DBLS practical implications we selected an (1296,648) LDPC with $d_v = 3$ and $d_c = 6$ and implemented our approach and the best state-of-the-art stochastic LDPC decoder with 64-bit edge memory on a Virtex-7 FPGA. Experimental results indicate that our proposal requires 9% more FFs and 3% more LUTs while diminishing the energy consumption by 31-80% and providing 1.5-5.1x higher throughput.

1. INTRODUCTION

Low Density Parity Codes (LDPC) codes, introduced by Gallager in 1962 [6], have a decoding performance which is very close to the Shannon limit [7]. Due to their high error correction capability LDPC codes have been adopted by many communication standards, e.g., WiFi [2], WiMAX [3], DVB-S2 [1], 10GBase-T [4]. Although LDPC decoding is very powerful in terms of error correction it has high computation demands, which have a negative impact on the energy consumption. Given that in communication hand-held devices, a typical LDPC utilization case, to prolong the battery life, low energy LDPC decoding has received substantial attention in the recent past. One of the effective ways to construct LDPC decoders is by using Stochastic Computing

(SC). Due to the SC efficient hardware implementation, SC based LDPC decoders power consumption is substantially smaller than the one relaying on the traditional computation paradigm. However, given the fact that operands are represented as long Stochastic Bitstreams (SB) SC-based implementations inherently exhibit large latency. Consequently, the low power gain could be potentially nullified by the long computation time precluding the SC utilization for low energy LDPC decoder implementations.

In all existing SC-based machines, e.g., LDPC decoders, the SB length is fixed during decoding regardless of the communication channel Signal to Noise Ratio (SNR). To reduce energy consumption while fulfilling Quality of Service (QoS) requirements, in this paper, we propose a Dynamic Bitstream Length Scaling (DBLS), which adapts on-the-fly the SB length according to the channel conditions. Note that in existing SC-based LDPC decoders, the SB length is fixed and decided at design time. In particular, we utilize the communication channel conditions quantified by the current Signal-to-Noise Ratio (SNR) to dynamically adjust the SB length on-the-fly to the minimum value for which the QoS requirements are still satisfied. Although our focus in this work is on applying DBLS to synchronous designs, in principle, our approach is also suitable for asynchronous engines. To evaluate the practical implications of our proposal, we choose a fully parallel implementation of a 64-bit Edge Memory (EM) [12] stochastic (1296,648) LDPC decoder with $d_v = 3$ and $d_c = 6$ as an evaluation vehicle. Our extensive experiments on a Virtex-7 FPGA indicate that at the expense of an area overhead of 9% more FFs and 3% more LUTs, the DBLS technique improves the energy efficiency and throughput by 31-80% and 1.5-5.1x, respectively, while fulfilling the QoS requirements.

The rest of the paper is organized as follows. In Section 2, we discuss the proposed technique while its effectiveness is presented in Section 3. Finally, we close the discussion with some conclusions in Section 4.

2. PROPOSED TECHNIQUE

The Stochastic Computing paradigm proposed by Gaines [5], Ribeiro [11], and Poppelbaum et al. [10] in 1967, represents a number x as a Stochastic Bitstream (SB) $X = X_1 X_2 X_3 ... X_{L_s}$ such that $P(X_i = 1) = x$ where $0 \le x \le 1$ and L_s is the SB length. Thus an SB of L_s bits with N_1 comprising bits being equal to 1, encodes a number $x = \frac{N_1}{L_s}$. This number representation has two main advantages: (i) arithmetic computations can be done with low complexity hardware and (ii) has intrinsic high fault tolerant capabil-

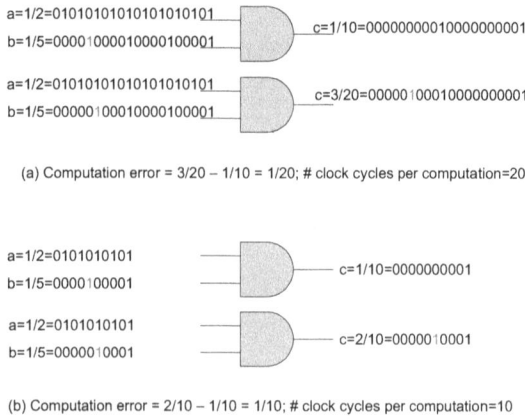

(a) Computation error = 3/20 − 1/10 = 1/20; # clock cycles per computation=20

(b) Computation error = 2/10 − 1/10 = 1/10; # clock cycles per computation=10

Figure 1: Tradeoff of Computation Error and Latency in Stochastic Computing (SC)

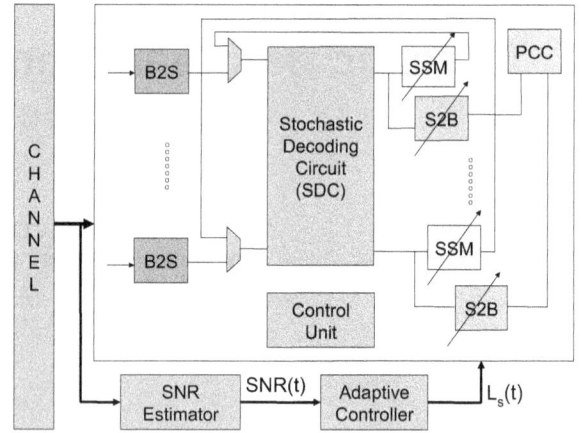

Figure 2: LDPC Decoding with DBLS Technique

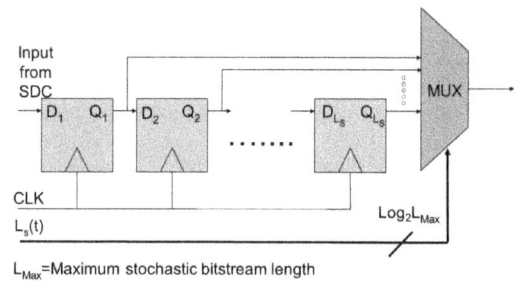

L_{Max}=Maximum stochastic bitstream length

Figure 3: SSM for supporting DBLS technique

ity. This representation allows for the evaluation of complex arithmetic operations by using simple logic gates. For instance, we can use an AND gate to implement a multiplication as illustrated in Figure 1. Moreover, by relying on an identically-weight representation, SC has a high fault tolerant capability, e.g., flipping one bit at position n of an SB with length L_s causes only an $\frac{1}{L_s}$ difference irrespective of the n value while the same bit flip in traditional binary representation creates a 2^{n-1} difference. The main SC drawbacks are: (i) long computation latency due to the required long SB representations and (ii) inaccurate computation results caused by the non-unique number representation. For example, illustrated in Figure 1, a number $a = \frac{1}{2}$ can be represented as a 20-bit SB A=01010101010101010101 or a 10-bit SB A=0101010101 or any other SB that has an equal number of bit 1 and 0. This non-unique representation creates the premises for producing incorrect results. In Figure 1(a), when we change $B_5 B_6$ from 10 to 01, the 2nd AND gate produces an incorrect result; $\frac{1}{2}$ times $\frac{1}{5}$ should be equal to $\frac{1}{10}$ as produced by the 1st AND gate, however, the 2nd AND gate's result is $\frac{3}{20}$. It can be easily observed that the computation error of Fig 1(a) is $\frac{3}{10} - \frac{1}{10} = \frac{1}{20}$ and the computation latency is 20 clock cycles. If we shorten the SB length L_s from 20 to 10 to shorten the computation time from 20 to 10 clock cycles as shown in Fig 1(b), the computation error will increase to $\frac{2}{10} - \frac{1}{10} = \frac{1}{10}$. This simple motivational example clearly demonstrates that various computation error vs latency trade-offs are possible in the SC context. Using longer (shorter) SBs produce more (less) accurate results with longer (shorter) latencies. Since the energy consumption proportionally depends on latency, trading accuracy for energy is also possible.

Trading accuracy at the right time is the key idea behind our proposed technique to diminish energy consumption while fulfilling Quality of Service (QoS) requirements. Trading accuracy in the moment accuracy is needed to fulfill QoS requirements is not a good option. To guaranty QoS while diminishing energy consumption, we need to trade accuracy only in the time moments when QoS can be provided without requiring high computation accuracy. To be able to properly adjust at run time the SB length to the channel status we perform at design time a decoder pre-

characterization, i.e., we measure decoder's Frame Error Rate (FER), Bit Error Rate (BER), energy/bit and throughput under SB length scaling on a variety of noisy channels.

The way we apply the DBLS technique during the LDPC decoding process is presented in Figure 2. We utilize the SNR Estimator present in any standard communication systems, to provide SNR information to the Adaptive Controller. This information is essentially needed to assist the Adaptive Controller in adjusting the SB length $L_s(t)$ based on the instantaneous channel condition represented by SNR(t). Based on SNR(t) and the pre-characterization results, the Adaptive Controller tunes $L_s(t)$ to the minimum value for which the QoS requirements (e.g., BER, FER) are fulfilled. We propose 3 strategies in pre-determining the SB length at design time. Choosing $L_s(t)$ at SNR(t) is done by selecting SB length from pre-characterization results that minimizes (i) BER denoted as Best BER (BB), (ii) FER called as Best FER (BF), or (iii) energy/bit named as Lowest Energy (LE) strategy.

In the following we describe the modus operandi of the proposed adaptive stochastic LDPC decoder. For each received message we first determine the BS length value $L_s(t)$ according to the actual SNR value. This adaptation is done on-the-fly, no decoding stop nor restart is required. Subsequently, in the first $L_s(t)$ clock cycles, soft messages (i.e., probabilities) are converted by the Binary to Stochastic Converter (B2S) blocks to SBs with length $L_s(t)$, bit by bit in each clock cycle. In this first iteration, the multiplexers direct the SBs to the Stochastic Decoder Circuit (SDC), i.e.,

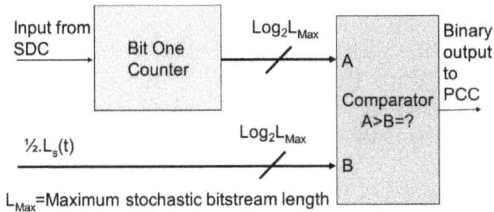

Figure 4: S2B for supporting DBLS technique

Variables Nodes (VNs) and Check Nodes (CNs), for processing. The $L_s(t)$-bit SB produced at each SDC output is stored in the Stochastic Stream Memory (SSM). This SSM should have adjustable size to accommodate our DBLS technique. The architecture of this adjustable SSM is presented in Figure 3. Different from fixed-length SSM, this tunable SSM makes use of a multiplexor to select $Q_{L_s(t)}$ for output. In this way an SB length of up to L_{Max} can be accommodated. In the subsequent $L_s(t)$ clock cycles, the multiplexer inside SSM in collaboration with the multiplexer in Figure 2 feeds back $L_s(t)$-bit stored in SSM as inputs to the SDC for subsequent iterations. At the end of each iteration, the Parity Check Circuit (PCC) verifies the parity constraints for early termination purpose. To do this verification, the PCC makes use of the hard bit values provided by the Stochastic to Binary Converter (S2B). Since DBLS technique needs to support adjustable SB length, the S2B needs to facilitate adjustable SB length hard decisions as presented in Figure 4. By letting the comparator making hard decisions controllable by the Control Unit as indicated in the figure, the variable SB length is supported by S2B. The SB iterative processing stops either when all check nodes are satisfied or when the maximum number of iterations is surpassed.

3. EVALUATION

Although our technique is in principle applicable to any SC machines for which the SB length vs performance relation can be pre-characterized, in this paper, we evaluate its effectiveness by applying it to a fully parallel implementation of the 64-bit EM [12] stochastic LDPC decoder reported as the best SC-based decoder in terms of decoding performance in, e.g., [9]. More precisely, a circuit decoding regular (1296, 648) LDPC code with VN degree of 3 ($d_v = 3$), and PN degree of 6 ($d_c = 6$) is utilized. Input messages in form of probabilities are 4-bit quantized. Each probability is represented by a 16-bit SB. The maximum number of iterations is set at 100. Each iteration takes 16 decoding cycles and for each decoding cycle one clock cycle is needed. The EM decoders with DBLS technique using proposed strategies, denoted as BB, BF, and LE, are evaluated against their original version, named as EM, in terms of: (i) decoding performance, specifically FER and BER, (ii) area - the number of occupied FPGA hardware resources (i.e., FFs and LUTs), (iii) throughput (Mb/s), and (iv) energy/bit (pJ/bit). An Additive White Gaussian Noise (AWGN) channel with Binary Phase Shift Keying (BPSK) modulation (with mapping $0 \rightarrow 1$ and $1 \rightarrow -1$) is generated to mimic a realistic telecommunication channel in our experiments. We apply the Noise-Dependent Scaling (NDS) technique [12] with $\alpha = 3$ and Y=6 to the AWGN channel

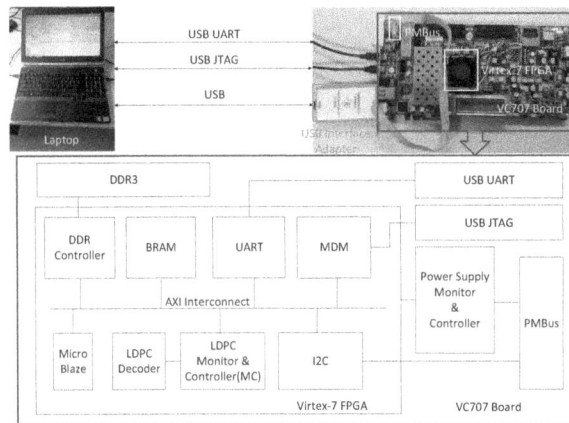

Figure 5: Experimental Hardware Platform

Table 1: Area and Power Consumption

Decoders	Area		Power
	# FFs	# LUTs	(W)
EM	189896	146300	1.85
EM with DBLS	206730	150189	1.855

prior to decoding. Similar to [8], all evaluation figures are obtained from direct FPGA measurements.

To facilitate a real hardware evaluation, we develop an experimental hardware platform that consists of a laptop and a Xilinx VC707 board as depicted in Figure 5. The laptop is dedicated to: (i) designing the hardware platform targeting Xilinx Virtex-7 FPGA: XC7VX485TFFG1761-2 inside the Xilinx board and generating the bitstream files, (ii) downloading the bitstream files for FPGA hardware and the software files for the MicroBlaze through the USB JTAG interface, (iii) monitoring/capturing the number of iterations and decoding outcomes, FER, and BER through the USB UART, and (iv) measuring Energy/bit using the Fusion Digital Power Designer from Texas Instrument through Texas Instrument USB Interface adapter by reading PM-Bus, and accessing Power Supply Monitor and Controller inside the board. To build the evaluation hardware support (e.g., AWGN channel emulator, BPSK modulator, and other functionality for evaluation purpose) and the decoders, the Xilinx board is utilized. The MicroBlaze processor, resident on the FPGA, in collaboration with the LDPC Monitoring and Controller (MC) mainly acts as the evaluation hardware support by accessing software and data stored in BRAM and DDR3. The MC monitors the decoding outcome and conveys 4-bit quantized probabilities from the MicroBlaze to the evaluated decoder. The two possible outcomes of the decoding process are: (i) "success" and (ii) "give up". If all check nodes are satisfied, the outcome is "success". In the case that all check nodes cannot be satisfied after the maximum number of iterations, the system reports "give up". The MicroBlaze processor utilizes these outcomes for computing the statistical results of the experiments (i.e. BER, FER). The laptop displays the experimental results received from FPGA board through USB UART.

The experimental results in terms of FER, BER, energy efficiency, and throughput are presented in Figures 6 and

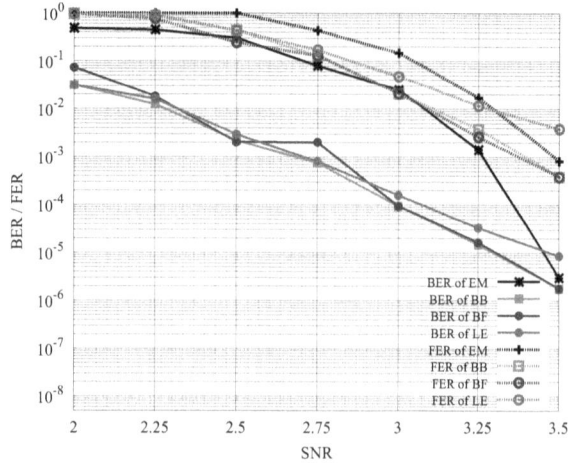

Figure 6: BER and FER

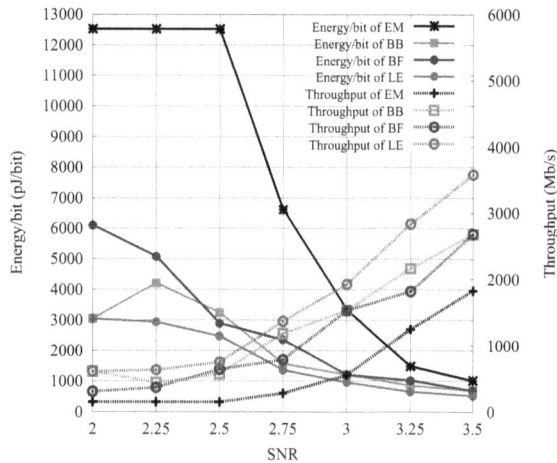

Figure 7: Energy/bit and Throughput

7, respectively. Tables 1 summarizes the amount of FPGA hardware resources required by the decoders and the corresponding power consumption. From these experimental results, one can observes that: (i) The area overhead associated with the DBLS technique in terms of the number of occupied FFs and LUTs is 9% and 3%, respectively. This area overhead is mainly attributed to the additional hardware to support adjustable SB length. The overhead does not affect the maximum clock frequency, which is 182.449 MHz, but it slightly increases power consumption by 0.3%. (ii) Since the computation latency is lowered by shortening SB length, the throughput is increased. Because the energy consumption is proportional to the computation latency, despite the power consumption increase due to (i), the energy/bit is minimized as depicted in Figure 7. (iii) Although the BB strategy is mainly designed to minimize BER, it also reduces the energy/bit by 32-76% when compared to EM due to the higher throughput (1.7-4.2x) achieved by SB length reduction. (iv) The BF strategy is minimizing FER while lowering the energy by 31-77% and increasing the throughput by 1.5-4.3x thanks to its SB length adaptability to SNR. (v) The LE strategy provides the largest energy reduction (49-80%) and

boosts throughput (2.3-5.1x) for a slightly higher FER and BER at SNR=3.5dB. The BER is 8.54×10^{-6}, which is higher than EM's BER, 3.0×10^{-6}. However, if the BER target is higher than 8.54×10^{-6}, the LE scheme still can fulfill the targeted QoS.

4. CONCLUSIONS

In this paper, we proposed a Dynamic Bitstream Length Scaling (DBLS) technique to automatically adjust Stochastic Bitstream length to achieve energy efficient stochastic LDPC decoding. Subject to specified decoding performance constraints and adaptive to communication channel conditions, the technique leverages available performance-energy tradeoffs to deliver satisfying performance while minimizing the energy. When implemented on a Virtex-7 FPGA, despite its area overhead of 9% more FFs and 3% more LUTs, the technique outperforms the best equivalent state of the art counterpart in terms of energy efficiency by 31-80% and throughput by 1.5-5.1x while fulfilling the QoS requirements.

Acknowledgment

This work was supported by the Seventh Framework Programme of the European Union, under the Grant Agreement number 309129 (i-RISC project).

5. REFERENCES

[1] The digital video broadcasting standard.

[2] The ieee 802.11n working group std.

[3] The ieee 802.16 working group std.

[4] Ieee p802.3an (10gbase-t) task force.

[5] B. R. Gaines. Stochastic computing. In *Proceedings of the April 18-20, 1967, Spring Joint Computer Conference*, AFIPS '67 (Spring), pages 149–156, New York, NY, USA, 1967. ACM.

[6] R. Gallager. Low-density parity-check codes. *Information Theory, IRE Transactions on*, 8(1):21–28, January 1962.

[7] D. J. MacKay and R. M. Neal. Near shannon limit performance of low density parity check codes. *Electronics letters*, 32(18):1645–1646, 1996.

[8] T. Marconi, C. Spagnol, E. Popovici, and S. Cotofana. Towards energy effective ldpc decoding by exploiting channel noise variability. In *Very Large Scale Integration (VLSI-SoC), 2014 22nd International Conference on*, pages 1–6, Oct 2014.

[9] A. Naderi, S. Mannor, M. Sawan, and W. Gross. Delayed stochastic decoding of ldpc codes. *Signal Processing, IEEE Transactions on*, 59(11):5617–5626, Nov 2011.

[10] W. J. Poppelbaum, C. Afuso, and J. W. Esch. Stochastic computing elements and systems. In *Proceedings of the November 14-16, 1967, Fall Joint Computer Conference*, AFIPS '67 (Fall), pages 635–644, New York, NY, USA, 1967. ACM.

[11] S. T. Ribeiro. Random-pulse machines. *Electronic Computers, IEEE Transactions on*, EC-16(3):261–276, June 1967.

[12] S. Tehrani, S. Mannor, and W. Gross. Fully parallel stochastic ldpc decoders. *Signal Processing, IEEE Transactions on*, 56(11):5692–5703, Nov 2008.

Dynamic Power Reduction Techniques in On-Chip Photonic Interconnects

Brian Neel
School of EECS
Ohio University
Athens, OH, 45701
bn179706@ohio.edu

Matthew Kennedy
School of EECS
Ohio University
Athens, OH, 45701
mk140409@ohio.edu

Avinash Kodi
School of EECS
Ohio University
Athens, OH, 45701
kodi@ohio.edu

ABSTRACT

Photonic interconnects is a disruptive technology solution that can overcome the power and bandwidth limitations of traditional electrical Network-on-Chips (NoCs). However, the static power dissipated in the external laser may limit the performance of future optical NoCs by dominating the stringent network power budget. From the analysis of real benchmarks for multi-cores, it is observed that high static power is consumed due to the external laser even for low channel utilization. In this paper, we propose runtime power management techniques to reduce the magnitude of laser power consumption by tuning the network in response to actual application characteristics. We scale the number of channels available for communication based on link and buffer utilization. The performance on synthetic and real traffic (PARSEC, Splash-2) for 64-cores indicate that our proposed power scaling technique can reduce optical power by about 70% with less than 1% throughput penalty for real traffic.

Categories and Subject Descriptors

C.1.2 [**Computer Systems Organization**]: Multiprocessors—*Interconnection architectures*

Keywords

Interconnection Architecture, Nanophotonics, Power Reduction

1. INTRODUCTION

There have been several nanophotonic architectures and circuit optimizations related to reducing the external laser power. In [1], multi-bus NoC architecture between private L1 caches and distributed L2 caches which use weighted time division multiplexing to distribute the laser power across multiple buses. The proposed multi-bus NoC switches off laser sources at runtime during low bandwidth requirements to minimize the laser power consumption. In PROBE [2], multiple channels between source and destination are switched

off using table-based prediction method. With a lightweight prediction technique, PROBE scales the bandwidth adaptively to the changing traffic demands while maintaining reasonable performance. This work differs from prior work as we evaluate the tree-based splitter to reduce the amount of optical intensity required by evaluating the network load. This provides a mechanism to increase or decrease the amount of optical intensity by enabling or disabling optical light into different levels of the tree splitter.

The focus of this paper is to design a power efficient reconfigurable optical power tree architecture that can consume energy in proportion to the application load. The proposed design allows the number of optical carrier signals to be reconfigured and time multiplexed across the entire optical network. Since off-chip communication to the laser is slow, the laser is designed to have a number of states corresponding to the number of optical carrier signals that it needs to provide. Then based on buffer and link utilization, a control unit will signal the laser to change states. During laser state changes, the network can still be used at the lower of the two states (current state and destination state) until the laser has stabilized, preventing significant performance degradation. This results in a system where the available bandwidth is tuned to match the network load providing a degree of energy proportionality to the optical network.

2. ARCHITECTURE

2.1 Reconfigurable Optical Power Tree

By strategically tuning the tree ring resonators we can activate and deactivate links. We can then tune the laser source according to the amount of power required by only the active links. For example, by tuning only the ring resonator denoted R_0^0, we can direct all of the laser power to the left half of the power tree, i.e. only the row links. However, as the individual link optical power requirements remain constant, we can simultaneously conserve energy by tuning the laser to source approximately only half of the optical power. The power can be further reduced when only one or two active links are necessary by tuning second and third levels of ring resonators. Figure 2 presents example configurations where only a partial number of links are activated and the optical power is reduced to only half and a quarter of the original optical power respectively. The number of activated links required can be determined at runtime based on fluctuating bandwidth requirements. Since the tree is controlled by MRRs, the active channels can be quickly

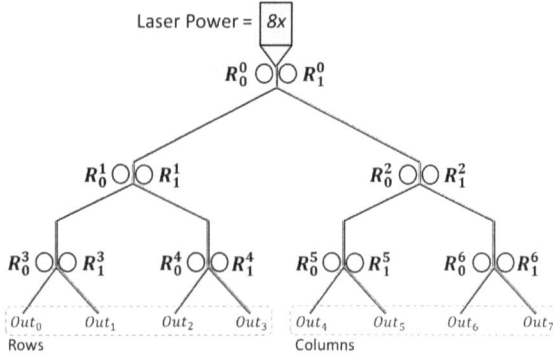

Figure 1: The proposed optical power tree with ring notation. Without any rings activated, the optical laser power is halved at each branch of the tree. This requires approximately 8 times the power required to activate a single link. The left half of the tree corresponds to the row-based links while the right half corresponds to column-based links.

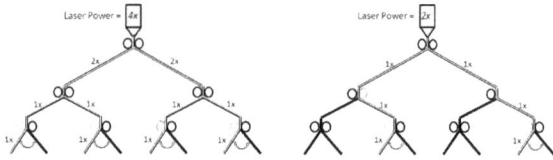

Figure 2: Example cases showing only 4 of the 8 channels (left) and 2 of the 8 channels (right) in the tree active.

reconfigured to any of the physical channels connected to the tree.

2.2 Reconfiguration Algorithm

There are a number of ways to determine when and how to change the laser states. A simple and effective approach is to set thresholds below the saturation point in each state. While the saturation point will vary across application traffic patterns, we chose fixed network load thresholds according to the worst-case traffic pattern, i.e. the pattern with the lowest saturation load. This was done to ensure adequate power is provided in each trial to avoid saturating the network. Methods could be employed to determine appropriate thresholds at runtime, however we save this for future work as it extends beyond the scope of this paper.

We define the laser power states as S_i, where $0 \leq i < log_2(N)$ and N is the number of carrier signals. The number of threshold points required is one less then the number of laser states, where threshold count, TC, is $TC = log_2(N)$. We simulated eight synthetic traffic patterns (explained in Performance Evaluation section) and determined the thresholds used in our evaluation. After determining the thresholds, we estimated the network load based on aggregated buffer and link utilization measurements over a rolling reconfiguration window. We used the aggregated link utilization measurements to determine the total network load. We then compared the estimated network load to the thresholds at the end of the laser reconfiguration window, RW_L, to determine if a state change is necessary. If a state change is necessary, then the laser is signalled to change states and

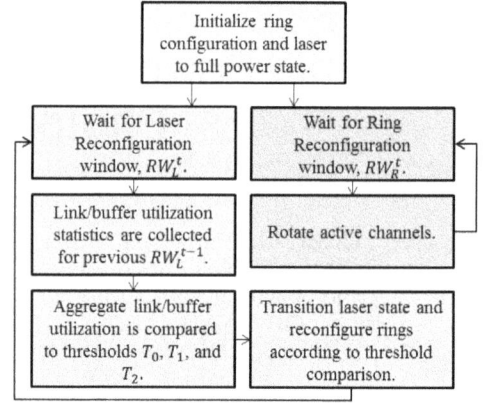

Figure 3: Laser (red) and ring (blue) reconfiguration flow.

wait for a response that the laser is stable at the new state. While waiting for a response back from the laser, the network can continue operating at the lower of the two states. For example, if the laser state is currently S_2 and we are going to transition to S_3, then we can continue operating in S_2. While moving to S_3, the laser will still be providing more light than what is necessary for S_2. However, as we transition down a state then we can immediately operate in the new state as the optical intensity will be less than what is needed for the current state, but always higher than what is needed for the new, lower state. Therefore, even during laser state transitions, the network is still active. Figure 3 depicts the laser and ring reconfiguration flow.

2.3 Active Channel Reconfiguration

By using MRRs to control light within the power tree it is possible to reconfigure the channels available in state S_i to any of the output channels at the leaves of the tree. The ring reconfiguration window, RW_R, can be very small compared to the laser state reconfiguration window, RW_L, as tuning the resonators can be done at 10 Ghz or higher speeds.

In our simulations we set the RW_R to 4, enough cycles to send a packet across each of the active channels, but only if the packet was ready to be sent in the first cycle of the new window. Otherwise, the packet must wait for the next time the channel is available. While round robin provides acceptable performance, it may be possible to further improve performance by skipping channels that do not have packets ready to send on the channel and allow another channel the use of the otherwise wasted bandwidth.

3. CASE STUDY

While an optical flattened butterfly has been chosen as a test case, other photonic architectures with multiple channels may also be compatible with our proposed reconfiguration mechanism. In our flattened butterfly, we combine optical transceivers and electronic switches to design a power-efficient high-performance network as shown in Figure 4. The proposed off-chip broadband light source will generate W_N wavelengths, $\Lambda = \lambda_0, \lambda_1, \lambda_2, \lambda_3, ...\lambda_{W_N-1}$. By transmitting the continuous off-chip carrier signal in both x- and y-directions simultaneously, we modulate the signals at the optical transmitters. Figure 4 shows 4 cores and a shared L2 cache combined together to form a *tile*. This grouping

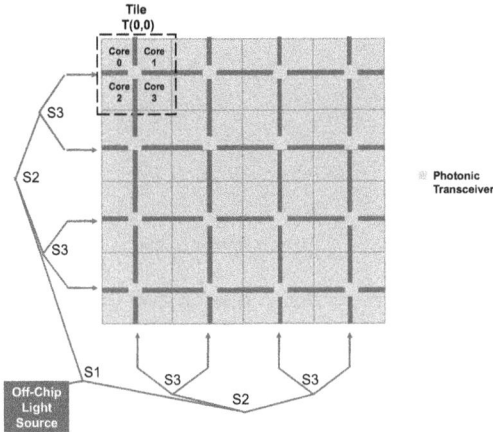

Figure 4: Proposed layout of flattened butterfly architecture for 64 tile architecture. Four tiles are combined into a super-tile. Each waveguide is considered a single optical channel connected to the optical power tree

reduces the cost of the interconnect as every core does not require lasers attached and more importantly, facilitates local communication through cheaper electronic switching [3]. Each tile consists of dual-set (x and y) photonic transceivers and an electronic switch. Optical interconnects are used in two dimensions along the grid similar to an electronic 2D mesh or torus. It takes a maximum of 2 hops to traverse between any two tiles, one hop in the x-dimension and one hop in the y-dimension.

4. PERFORMANCE EVALUATION

4.1 Simulation Methodology

In this section we discuss our simulation methodology and assumptions leading to the results presented in the next section. The proposed optical power tree was simulated using a 64-core implementation of an optical flattened butterfly as the base network architecture. We also assume packets are composed of four 128-bit flits, requiring 4 network cycles to transmit a complete packet between two routers. With this in mind we chose a ring splitter reconfiguration period of 4 network cycles to allow the transmission of a complete network packet before deactivating the channel and reactivating a new channel. This optimizes network performance by preventing congestion of partial packets from building up in the network routers. We assume a 512 network clock cycle window for laser state reconfiguration based on Complement traffic analysis; further analysis is left for future work.

The SPLASH-2 [4], PARSEC [5], and SPEC CPU2006 [6] workloads were used to evaluate the performance of 64-core networks. The results acquired from these two implementations are included in the following section of this paper along with a comparison highlighting the energy savings achieved using the proposed reconfigurable laser architecture.

4.2 Results

Figure 5 shows the latency curves for each individual state for two select traffic patterns. For these simulations, the laser state is fixed and the network load is increased until

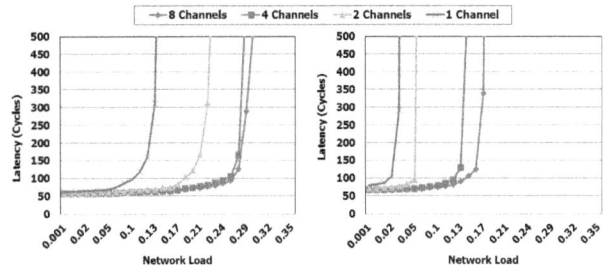

Figure 5: Shows the saturation throughput for each state for a tree with N=3 for synthetic traffic patterns Uniform Random (left) and Complement (right).

the latency spikes at the saturation point. The saturation point is the point where further network demand no longer increases throughput as the network is already working at maximum capacity. Latency is plotted on the y-axis and network load (as a function of network capacity) is on the x-axis. A round robin ring reconfiguration method is used to distribute the active signal across the available channels.

Figure 5 (right) shows the latency curves for Complement traffic pattern which has the lowest saturation point for each state out of all the traffic patterns tested. Complement is used to determine the thresholds used throughout the rest of our testing as we are accounting for the worst case latency in each state. The thresholds are set at $T_0 = 0.01$, $T_1 = 0.05$, and $T_3 = 0.12$. The laser state is determined by estimating network load from buffer and link utilization and comparing it to the thresholds. Therefore, this plot is an important factor in determining the performance of the network.

Figure 6 presents the laser state transitions and network injection rate against elapsed time in network cycles for the Uniform Random synthetic traffic pattern. The network injection rate is stepped up nearly to the network saturation point for the corresponding traffic pattern, and then stepped back down to a near idle network load. The blue network load curve in the figure represents the simulation injection rate as a function of the total network capacity. As this is simply a controlled simulation parameter, this information would not normally be available to the reconfiguration controller without previous knowledge of the application traffic. Reconfiguration decisions must be made according to the estimated network load calculated using buffer and link utilization statistics collected by the laser reconfiguration controller. This calculated network load is included in the plot as the red color coded line. Only when the calculated network load crosses a threshold, denoted by the horizontal dotted lines, will the laser transition to a new power state. We can observe from the figures the laser reconfiguration reacts very rapidly to increasing network load, however, the laser tends to lower it's state at a lagging pace relative to the network injection rate. This is because the reconfiguration algorithm also accounts for buffer utilization which requires several network cycles to drain packets from the router buffers.

While the synthetic traffic simulations help to demonstrate the operation of the proposed design, real traffic simulations were also performed to exhibit the optical power savings achieved by the architecture. Figure 7 presents the laser state transitions for a real traffic trace acquired using

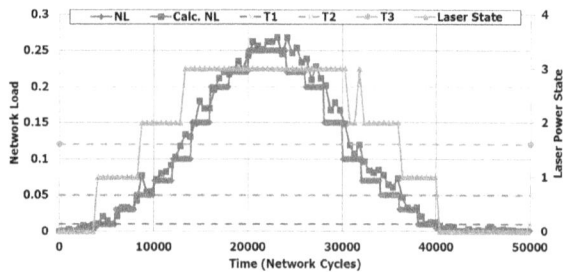

Figure 6: Laser state transitions, network load (NL), and calculated network load (Calc. NL) versus elapsed simulation cycles using Uniform Random synthetic traffic.

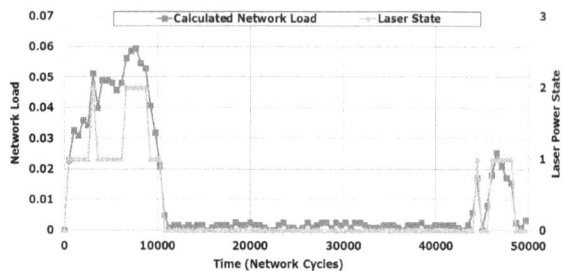

Figure 7: Laser state transitions and calculated network load versus elapsed simulation cycles using PARSEC-Ferret traces.

GEM5 [7]. We simulated the laser reconfigurable architecture using several real traffic traces. On average, optical power consumption was reduced by more than 70% as shown in Figure 8 with virtually no penalty to network throughput compared to the standard optical flattened butterfly architecture as shown in Figure 9.

5. CONCLUSIONS

This work has shown that by using the light source in lower intensity states and time multiplexing the available carrier signals, it is possible to trim the power and provide energy proportionality to the laser. An important aspect of this design is controlling the optical power tree with micro-ring resonators that can provide quick reconfiguration within a single power state. This paper just touches the surface of many aspects of the design such as light source design and reconfiguration algorithms leaving many ideas (laser control, electrical drivers) for future work. However, even with simple reconfiguration algorithms, the simulation results show significant reduction in power for real traffic benchmark traces. More than 70% reduction in power is demonstrated, while providing nearly no throughput penalty at less than 1%.

6. ACKNOWLEDGEMENT

This research was supported by the US National Science Foundation (NSF) awards CCF-1054339 (CAREER), ECCS-1129010, CCF-1318981, ECCS-1342657, and CCF-1420718.

7. REFERENCES

[1] C. Chen and A. Joshi, "Runtime management of laser power in silicon-photonic multibus noc architecture,"

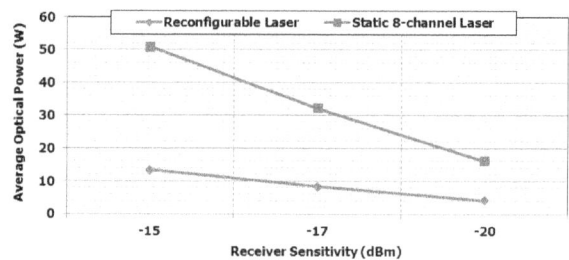

Figure 8: Average laser power consumption using real traffic traces for reconfigurable and static 8-channel laser implementations vs. several receiver sensitivities. Power consumption was simulated for networks with optical receiver sensitivities of -15dBm (conservative), -17dBm, and -20dBm (aggressive).

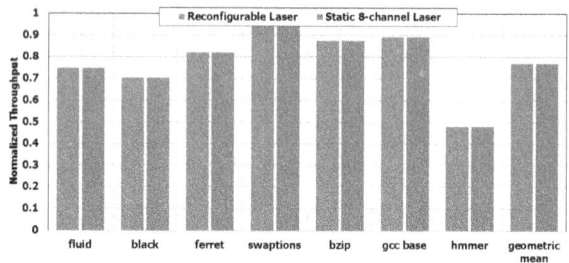

Figure 9: Comparison of normalized network throughput using various real traffic traces for the reconfigurable laser implementation vs. static 8-channel laser implementation.

Journal of Selected Topics in Quantum Electronics, vol. 2, March/April 2013.

[2] L. Zhou and A. K. Kodi, "Probe: Prediction-based optical bandwidth scaling for energy-efficient nocs," in *IEEE/ACM 7th International Symposium on Networks-on-Chip (NoCs)*, 2012.

[3] J. Balfour and W. J. Dally, "Design tradeoffs for tiled cmp on-chip networks," in *Proceedings of the 20th ACM International Conference on Supercomputing (ICS)*, Cairns, Australia, June 28-30 2006, pp. 187–198.

[4] S. Woo, M. Ohara, E. Torrie, J. Singh, and A. Gupta, "The splash-2 program: Characterization and methodological considerations," 1995, pp. 24–36.

[5] C. Bienia, S. Kumar, J. P. Singh, and K. Li, "The parsec benchmark suite: Characterization and architectural implications," in *Proceedings of the 17th International Conference on Parallel Architectures and Compilation Techniques*, October 2008.

[6] J. L. Henning, "Spec cpu suite growth: an historical perspective," *SIGARCH Comput. Archit. News*, vol. 35, pp. 65–68, March 2007.

[7] M. Martin, D. Sorin, B. Beckmann, M. Marty, M. Xu, A. Alameldeen, K. Moore, M. Hill, and D. Wood, "Multifacet's genreal execution-driven multiprocessor simulator (gems) toolset," *ACM SIGARCH Computer Architecture News*, no. 4, pp. 92–99, November 2005.

Design and Characterization of Analog-to-Digital Converters using Graphene P-N Junctions

Roberto Giorgio Rizzo, Sandeep Miryala,
Andrea Calimera, Enrico Macii, Massimo Poncino

Politecnico di Torino, 10129, Torino, ITALY

ABSTRACT

Electrostatically controlled graphene p-n junctions are devices built on single-layer graphene sheets whose in-to-out resistance can be dynamically tuned through external voltage potentials.

While several recent works mainly focused on the possibility of using those devices as a new logic primitive for digital circuits, in this paper we address a complementary problem, that is, how to efficiently implement Analog-to-Digital Converters (ADCs) that can be integrated in future all-graphene flexible ICs.

The contribution of this work is threefold: *(i)* introduce a new ADC architecture that perfectly matches with the main characteristics of graphene p-n junctions; *(ii)* give a first, yet detailed parametric characterization of the proposed ADC architecture as to validate its functionality and quantify its figures of merit; *(iii)* provide a fully automated design flow that, given as input the design specs, i.e., input voltage range, voltage resolution and sampling rate, returns an optimally sized ADC circuitry.

Few case studies also demonstrate p-n junction based graphene ADCs have characteristics in line with those offered by todays' CMOS ones.

Categories and Subject Descriptors

B.7.1 [**Types and Design Styles**]: Advanced technologies

Keywords

Graphene, P-N junction, ADC, design, characterization

1. INTRODUCTION

Since their introduction, Silicon Field-Effect-Transistors (Si-FETs) have been the main technological vehicle for the IC industry, both in the analog and digital domains; even if this technology is approaching its physical limit, it will certainly hold at least for the next decade. Nevertheless, the research community has been engaged in a gold race for discovering

GLSVLSI'15, May 20–22, 2015, Pittsburgh, PA, USA.
Copyright © 2015 ACM 978-1-4503-3474-7/15/05 ...$15.00.
http://dx.doi.org/10.1145/2742060.2742099.

new materials that can sustain the electronic market in the beyond-silicon era.

Graphene [14], a two-dimensional allotrope of Carbon with atoms packed in a honeycomb lattice, has been indicated as the first, real and effective candidate to bring the mission off. Graphene has superior electro-mechanical properties [3, 5] w.r.t. other materials; high conductivity, high carrier mobility, high thermal stability, along with robustness, flexibility and transparency are just few of them. All these characteristics perfectly meet new demands raising from ubiquitous computing and flexible/wearable computing. Needless to say, for such applications the availability of dedicated graphene-based circuits that can support physical signal sensing, sampling, conversion and processing is a true need. Unfortunately, most of the existing works only focus on the latter aspect, that is, data processing [10, 11, 17, 18], while very few, if not nothing at all, has been done for mixed-signal Analog/Digital conversion, the target of this work.

Designing all-graphene Analog-to-Digital Converters (ADCs) is not trivial. The first limitation is the technological wall imposed by graphene. The existing architectures designed for CMOS technologies [2, 19] require active transistors for implementing operational amplifiers. Unfortunately, graphene FETs does not seem a viable solution as those proposed in [7, 21], rely on a patterning process where wide graphene sheets are cut into narrow ribbons (below 10nm). As a side effect, the patterning injects physical defects that alter the level of disorder in the material and degrades most of the electrical properties to the point that it might vanish the benefits of using graphene [6]. As an alternative to patterning, other recent works have proven the possibility to adopt the *Electrostatic doping* [1]. This method allows a fine-tuning of the Fermi Energy (E_F) that can be shifted down in the valence band (to obtain equivalent p-type graphene) or up in the conduction band (to obtain equivalent n-type graphene) using external electrical field applied through split metal gates. Face to face regions with opposite doping profiles form an equivalent p-n junction [4], which can serve as a current switch [16].

From an electrical point of view, however, a graphene p-n junction is a voltage-controlled passive resistor rather than an ideal switch. This makes the scenario more complicated and raise a few questions this work wants to answer: is it possible to implement graphene ADCs by means of pure passive components like graphene p-n junctions? If yes, what are the resulting characteristics of such graphene ADCs?

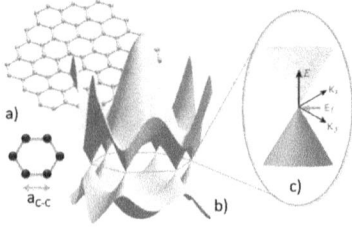

Figure 1: The graphene honeycomb lattice (a), its energy band structure (b) and the linear energy dispersion around the Fermi Energy E_F (c)

Moreover, can they compete with CMOS ADCs, at least for a specific class of physical data, e.g., biometric signals?

In order to get those answers we firstly propose a new ADC architecture which is reminiscent of all-digital CMOS ADCs [20] [8]. It makes use of a voltage-to-time converter, implemented as a chain of p-n junctions, that generates a timing window proportional to the amplitude of the input signal to be converted; the width of the timing window is measured by means of a digital counter, also realized with graphene p-n junctions, that provides the digital representation of the sampled signal. Secondly, we present parametric SPICE simulations that characterize the proposed ADC architecture. Thirdly, we introduce a fully automated design flow with input as the design specs, i.e., input voltage range, voltage resolution and sampling rate, returns a properly sized ADC circuit. Such a design tool is used to generate a few test-cases.

2. BACKGROUND

2.1 Graphene Physics

Graphene was isolated for the first time in 2004 [13, 14]. It consists of a two-dimensional (2D) structure in which carbon atoms are packed in an honeycomb lattice with a bond length a_{C-C} of 1.42Å, Figure 1 (a). The resulting energy band structure is plotted in Figure 1 (b) [15]. From the plot one can notice that conduction and valence curves touch each other at zero energy, where the Fermi energy E_F passes, Figure 1 (c).

The lack of an energy band gap makes graphene semi-metallic, thereby avoiding the material to be completely turned-OFF. This prevents the possibility of using pristine sheets of graphene to implement FETs. Nevertheless, recent works have jointly exploited (i) the massless propagation of carriers in graphene, and (ii) the existence of a tunneling property called *Klein's tunneling*, to devise an electrostatically controlled p-n junction [4] that allows a fine steering of carriers injected into the material.

2.2 Graphene p-n Junction

Figure 2 gives an abstracted view of a graphene p-n junction. Two split metal gates (referred as back gates U and S) are isolated from the graphene sheet by a thick layer of oxide, while two metal-to-graphene contacts (referred as front metal contacts A and Z) are placed on top of the structure and serve as source/drain for the injected carriers. Voltage potentials applied on the two back-gates implement the electrostatic doping [4]: a negate voltage (-V) shifts down the Fermi Energy E_F in the valence band leading to p-type graphene doping; a positive voltage (+V) shifts E_F up in the conduction band leading to n-type graphene doping.

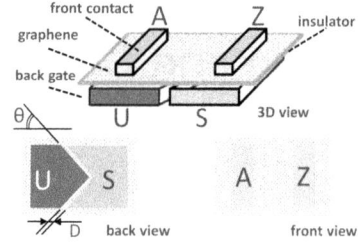

Figure 2: Structure of graphene p-n junction.

Different back gate voltage configurations alters the equivalent resistance R_{AZ} between the front metal contacts A and Z. Opposite voltages form p-n (or n-p) junction. Under this configuration, carriers injected into the p-doped region through the left front contact A cross the potential barrier at the junction edge with a transmission probability $T(\theta)$ that depends on (i) the angle θ between the electron's wave vector $\bar{k}$ and the normal of the junction, and (ii) the width D of the transition region. Equation 1 gives the analytical expression of $T(\theta)$:

$$T(\theta) = cos^2(\theta)e^{-\pi k D sin^2(\theta)} \tag{1}$$

$T(\theta)$ is 1 for those carriers that travel orthogonally toward the junction (i.e., $\theta = 0$), regardless of D, and exponentially decreases for higher values of θ ($T(\theta) = 0$ for $\theta = \pi/2$). A common practice is to force the angle θ to be 45°C by construction; this can be obtained by giving the back-gates a triangular shape as shown Figure 2.

Similar voltages applied at the two back-gates form a n-n (or p-p) junction. Under this configuration, $T(\theta) = 1$, i.e., 100% of carrier transmitted.

From an electrical point of view, this graphene device can be seen as a voltage controlled resistor whose value (R_{AZ}) is in a non-linear relationship with the back-gate voltages [12] [18]; R_{AZ} ranges from a high value R_{OFF}, under p-n configuration, to a low-value R_{ON}, under p-p (n-n) configuration. Figure 3, obtained with a dedicated Verilog-A model,plots R_{AZ} vs. the voltage at gate S when U is fed with a '0'-logic, i.e., $-V_{dd}$ (redline), or '1'-logic, i.e., $+V_{dd}$ (green line). As one can observe, the larger the voltage difference between U and S, the larger the R_{AZ} (due to lower transmission probability). This behavior is exploited in the proposed ADC architecture to obtain a variable-latency delay chain as described in the next section.

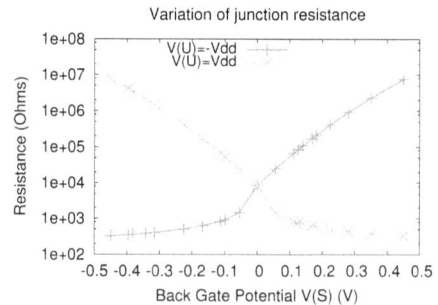

Figure 3: R_{AZ} vs. voltage at the back-gate S

2.3 RG-MUX

The pioneering work [17] proposed the use of graphene p-n junctions as basic primitive to implement a Reconfigurable Graphene Multiplexer (RG-MUX). Figure 4 shows the 3D structure of the RG-MUX; it consists of two back-faced p-n junctions which share a common back-gate (S): $j1$ formed by $\overline{U}$ and S; $j2$ formed by U and S. The right and left sided front contacts A and B serve as inputs, whereas the central one Z as output.

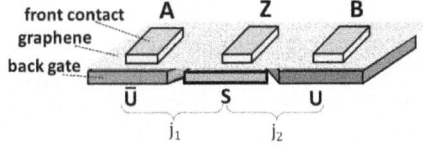

Figure 4: RG-MUX design views.

Pins $\overline{U}$ and U are the *configuration pins* and are always controlled by a complemented logic voltage; the pin S works as selective pin of the MUX. When U='1' ($\overline{U}$='0'), the graphene region above the U gate results as n-doped, while that above the $\overline{U}$ gate as p-doped. Notice that the '1'-logic value is $+V_{dd}/2$ and the '0'-logic value is $-V_{dd}/2$. Under such configuration, if S='0', the central graphene becomes p-type, forming a p-p junction on the left and a p-n junction on the right; the p-p junction shows a low resistance ($R_{AZ}=R_{ON} \approx 300\Omega$), whereas the p-n junction a high resistance ($R_{AZ}=R_{OFF} \approx 10^7\Omega$). Therefore, the output Z follows the input signal associated with the smallest resistive path, i.e., A. On the contrary, if S='1', the central graphene becomes n-type forming a low resistive n-n junction on the right; this forces the output Z to follow B. A dual behavior is observed when U='0' ($\overline{U}$='1'). This conceptually implements a reconfigurable 2-to-1 multiplexer with programmable polarity [9].

3. GRAPHENE ADC ARCHITECTURE

Figure 5 shows the ADC architecture adopted for graphene p-n junctions, the *G-ADC*, inspired by all-digital ADCs for CMOS [20][8].

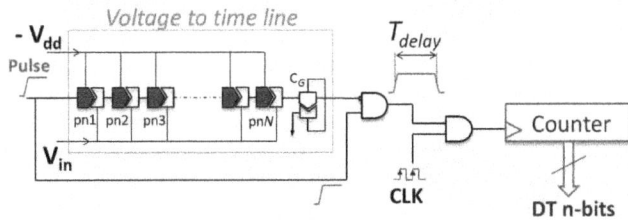

Figure 5: Graphene-ADC architecture.

It consists of two main stages: *(i)* a Voltage-to-Time (VTT) line converter and *(ii)* a digital counter. The VTT line is a chain of p-n junctions connected as follows: one back-gate (the dark one in the picture) fed with a fixed reference voltage, i.e., $-V_{dd}$; the other back-gate (the white one in the picture) connected to the sampled input signal, i.e., V_{in}; the front contacts are tied so as to form a series connection, with the first p-n junction (the leftmost in the picture) receiving a trigger signal, i.e., V_{pulse}. Notice that the length of the chain is a design parameter that changes with ADC specifications. The VTT line ends with a fixed capacitive load, i.e., C_G, implemented by a p-n junction with short circuited front-contacts. Since the resistance of each p-n junction is function of the voltage difference applied at its back-gates (please refer to Section 2), which, in this specific case, is the difference between the reference voltage and the input signal voltage V_{in}, i.e., $|V_{in} - Vdd|$, the in-to-out propagation T_{delay} for V_{pulse} proportionally increases with the amplitude of the input signal V_{in} itself. The first AND gate

receives inputs from the complemented output of the VTT line and V_{pulse}, generates a square signal of width T_{delay} that serves as clock-enable for the digital counter. The counting stored at the end of the conversion is therefore proportional to T_{delay}, namely, a quantized representation of the input signal V_{in}. The next paragraph briefly describes the internal structure of the digital components used in the G-ADC architecture, namely, basic logic gates and digital counter.

RG-MUX based combinational logic gates.
Appropriate input configuration patterns can be fed to the RG-MUX in order to build any Boolean logic function. Those used in the G-ADC, i.e., BUF, INV, AND, MUX, have been summarized in Figure 6. It is worth noticing that terminals U and $\overline{U}$ (not reported in the picture) are fed with fixed voltages, i.e., $+Vdd$ and $-Vdd$ respectively.

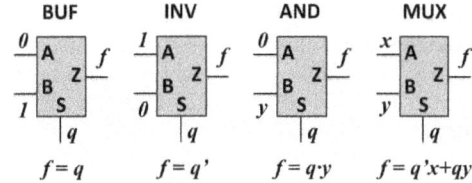

Figure 6: Logic gates using RG-MUXes.

N-bit digital counter.
We implemented the digital counter as a standard flip-flop based frequency divider. As an example, Fig. 7 shows a 4-bit counter realized using D-FlipFlops with outputs taken at {D0, D1, D2, D3}. The flip-flops are designed using a standard master/slave combination of latches; the implementation of a latch using a RG-MUX as primitive is straightforward as it just needs to feedback the output to the input and use the clock as selector.

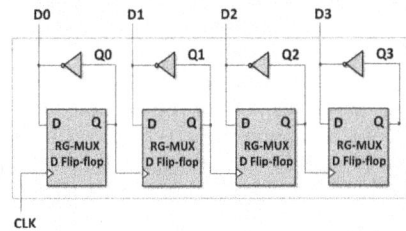

Figure 7: 4-bits digital counter.

4. DESIGN SPECS. & CHARACTERIZATION

In order to make the G-ADC compliant with design specs, the VTT line must be properly sized, both in terms of p-n junction geometries (i.e., width W, junction distance D) and number of stages (i.e., N), and the counter width properly fixed (i.e., N_{bit}). Reported below the main design specs/constraints we take into consideration while designing the G-ADC:

- *Minimum Voltage*: when the G-ADC is fed with the minimum input voltage V_{in-min}, the timing window must be larger than the clock-period so as to allow the LSB of the counter to be incremented [$T_{delay}(V_{in-min}) \geq T_{clk}$]

- *Resolution*: The delay variation between two minimum spaced input samples must be larger than the clock-period as to guarantee at least the increment of one bit through the counter [$\Delta T_{delay}(\Delta V_{Resolution}) \geq T_{clk}$]

- *Dynamic Range*: When the G-ADC is fed with the maximum input voltage V_{in-MAX}, the counting of the timing window width should not generate overflow $[T_{delay}(V_{in-MAX}) < 2^{N_{bit}} \cdot T_{clock}]$; in this work we considered a large dynamic range, i.e., from $0V$ to $V_{dd} = 1.1V$.

The set of parametric characterizations, described in the following paragraphs, helped us to identify the parameters that mostly affect the figures of merit of the G-ADC, the T_{delay} vs. V_{in} dependence in particular. Some of the collected data have been integrated (in the form of Look-Up-Tables) within the optimal sizing procedure, others allowed us to drop from the design space weak variables as to reduce the complexity of the design space. In other words, the goal is to find good knobs that can speed up the optimization/sizing phase.

p-n Junction: Resistance VS. Junction Distance (D).

The transmission probability $T(\theta)$, and hence the equivalent resistance R_{AZ}, of a graphene p-n junction is strongly influenced from the junction distance D. Figure 8 (left) plots R_{AZ} as function of the applied signal V_{in} for three possible values of D. Collected results highlight that the larger the D, the larger the resistance. The most important aspect concerns the sensitivity of R_{AZ} from V_{in} ($\partial R_{AZ}/\partial V_{in}[\Omega/Volt]$) rather than its absolute value. As D gets larger, $\partial R_{AZ}/\partial V_{in}$ substantially increases; this translates into a better ADC response, namely, small voltage changes may cause large resistance and, hence delay, variation. This suggests having D as design knob is a good option.

p-n Junction: Resistance VS. Width (W).

Another physical parameter to be sized which affects R_{AZ} is the junction width W. Figure 8 (center) plots R_{AZ} as function of the applied signal V_{in} for different values of W. Collected results highlight that the larger the W, the larger the resistance. However, differently from D, the sensitivity $\partial R_{AZ}/\partial V_{in}$ is not strongly affected by W. This suggests us to drop the variable W from the optimization space and just fix it at the minimum value (i.e., $W=100nm$) for area optimization.

VTT line: T_{delay} VS. Number of stages (N).

We finally analyzed the main dependence of T_{delay} from number of VTT stages N. Figure 8 (right) reports, as an example, T_{delay} across the VTT line as function of N, when $V_{in} = 100mV$, $W = 100nm$ and $D = 18nm$. As expected T_{delay} gets larger with N by following an Elmore delay model. Knowing the advantage of having a linear relationship from N, we let N be a free design parameter the tool can play with. However, as shown later in the text, N is marginal parameter if compared to D, but can be exploited to extend the input dynamic range of the ADC.

5. AUTOMATED DESIGN FLOW

We implemented a CAD tool which automatically generates an optimum sized SPICE netlist of the G-ADC. The overall flow is shown in Fig. 9. Input parameters are the G-ADC design specs, namely, *Voltage Resolution* (minimum sensed voltage), *Voltage Range* (V_{in-min} and V_{in-MAX}) and *Input Signal Band Frequency*. Look-Up-Tables (LUTs) storing the characterization data are also made available. Notice that in this first version, the operating clock-frequency is

fixed by the designer, at-priory and can't be modified by the tool. The sizing algorithm, described in the next subsection, generates a set of possible G-ADC implementations. More specifically, the algorithm is run for all the possible combination of design parameters, namely, for different values of D ($[18, 36, 54]$ nm) and for all possible number of stages possible (from 1 to 20). Those implementations that matches the design specs, namely, the one representing *pareto* points in the design space, are marked as *good* and are available as output to designers who can decide the best option.

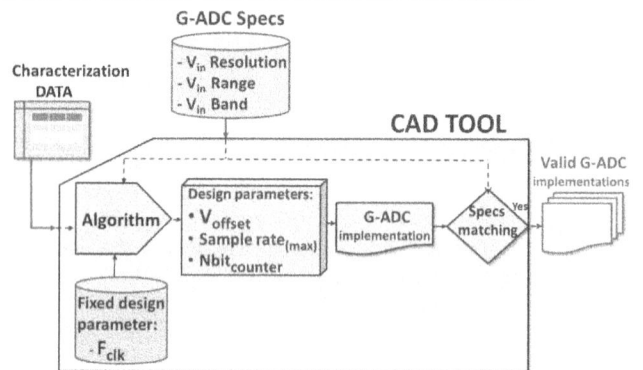

Figure 9: CAD tool for G-ADCs.

5.1 Sizing Algorithm

The sizing algorithm has been implemented as a Matlab script. The execution flow, graphically depicted in Figure 10, consists of three main steps:

1. Receiving as input the value of D and the length of the VTT line N, the algorithm checks whether a voltage offset V_{offset} has to be added to the input signal V_{in}. Such an offset is required to guarantee the matching of both the *Minimum Voltage* and the *Resolution* constraints. A too small V_{in-min}, in fact, might not guarantee a T_{delay} larger than the clock period T_{clk} (needed to increment the counter LSB) at minimum voltage. Then, it has to be ensured that the delay variation between two minimum spaced input samples must be caught (or captured) by the counter, that is, $[\Delta T_{delay}(\Delta V_{Resolution}) \geq T_{clk}]$. To avoid any loss of information, the voltage off-set shifts right V_{in-min} on the $T_{delay} - V_{in}$ curve (as shown in Figure 10) to reasonable values, that is, V'_{in-min}.

2. The second constraint to be met concerns the *Dynamic Range*; the algorithm guarantees that in the worst-case, namely, at maximum input voltage V_{in-MAX}, the counter does not produce overflow. To do so, the delay at full-scale $T_{delay}(FS)=T_{delay}(V_{in-MAX} + V_{offset})$ is extracted from the $T_{delay} - V_{in}$ curve and made available internally for the next step.

3. Having the $T_{delay}(FS)$, the algorithm calculates the maximum *Sampling Rate* the G-ADC can operate and the minimum sufficient number of bits for the counter N_{bit}. Notice that the sampling rate is limited by the $T_{delay}(FS)$, as any new sample can't be processed till the full timing window of the current sample is measured and discharged.

At this point, all the design parameters are fixed and the control is sent back to the main execution flow which checks

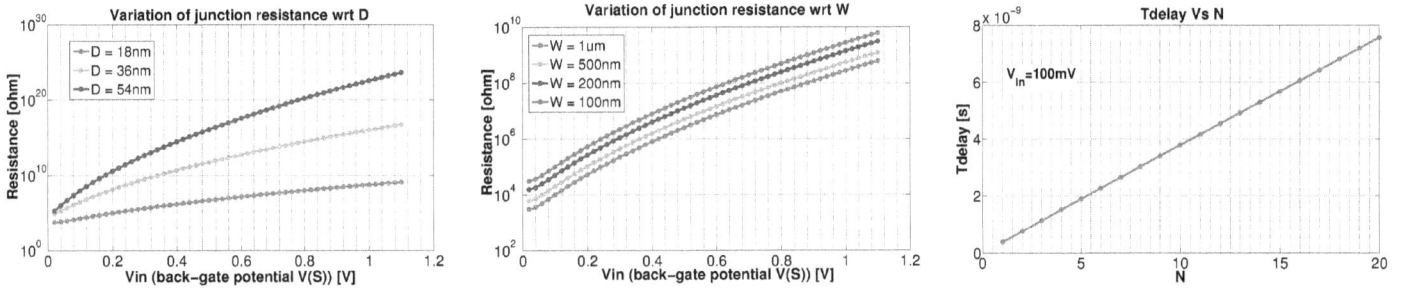

Figure 8: p-n junction: R_{AZ} VS. Distance D (Left) and Width W (Center); VTT line: T_{delay} VS Number of stages.

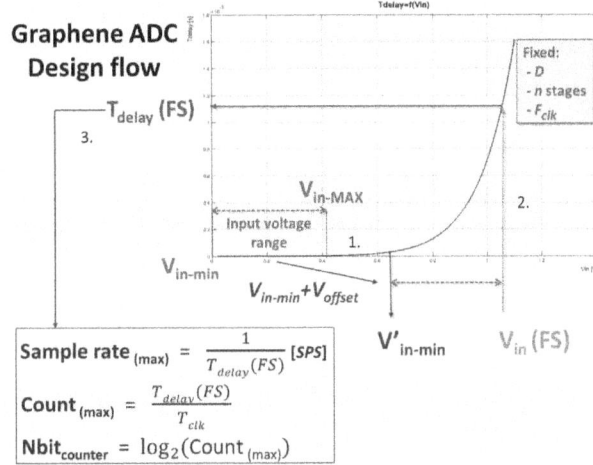

Figure 10: G-ADC design flow algorithm.

the compliance with design specs; if positive, the current implementation is marked as feasible and the algorithm is run again for another combination of design parameters (D and N). In order to have a *good* implementation of the G-ADC, the maximum *Sampling Rate* provided by the CAD tool is required to be at least twice the analog input bandwidth B_{in} (design specs) to satisfy the Nyquist theorem.

6. CASE STUDIES

In this section we describe a few use cases for the proposed CAD tool. The goal is to show some figures of merit of the proposed G-ADC architecture and better explain the existing dependence among design parameters.

Case 1.

Table 1 summarizes the characteristic of the G-ADC implementation returned by the CAD tool for two different set of [*Resolution; Input range*] specs: $200mV$ and $100\mu V$; $800mV$ and $3mV$. We are also considering a specific case in which the designer forces $D = 18nm$ and $N = 1$ (a single pn-junction in the VTT line); the maximum Input-signal Band B_{in} is 50KHz. As per the discussion given in Section 4, $W = 100nm$. The clock frequency is $10GHz$.

We can highlight three main aspects. First. The larger the dynamic input range the larger the $T_{delay}(FS)$; this leads to an higher minimum number of the counter width N_{bit} and a higher conversion time which translates into lower maximum sampling rate. Second. The lower the resolution, the smaller V_{offset} to be added to V_{in-min} (refer to section 5.1, constraint 1). Third. Intuitively, area increases linearly

User-constrained parameters		
$\mathbf{W} = 100nm$, $\mathbf{F}_{clk} = 10GHz$		
$\mathbf{N} = 1$, $\mathbf{D} = 18nm$		
Specs		
$\mathbf{B}_{in} = 50KHz$		
Input range	$200\ mV$	$800\ mV$
Resolution	$100\ \mu V$	$3\ mV$
Output		
Sampling Rate$_{(MAX)}$	$1.45\ MSPS$	$105\ KSPS$
Counter Nbit$_{(MIN)}$	13	17
Voffset	$0.53\ V$	$0.23\ V$
Area	$5.287\mu m^2$	$6.859\mu m^2$

Table 1: Case-1: G-ADC design.

with the number of p-n junction stages N and the number of the counter bits N_{bit}. Notice that the tool evaluates the *active* area of the G-ADC, that is the area occupied by the graphene p-n junction devices only [17].

Case 2.

We consider a single set of [*Resolution; Input range*] specs: $200mV$ and $100\mu V$. Differently from *Case*1, here the number of stages is not constrained, while is the tool that fully explores available options for N; for the sake of space, Table 2 only reports output results for $N = 1$ and $N = 20$. As one can see, there is no large difference between the performance of the two implementations, but the CAD tool provides the designer the possibility to make the optimal choice. The voltage off-set could be a discriminant factor. It is clear that the smaller the V_{offset}, the larger the input range over which the G-ADC can operate when considering a fixed upper-bound of $1.1V$ (please refer to Figure 10); one can therefore decide for the solution with $N=20$, which al-

257

lows smaller V_{offset} and hence potentially larger operating input range at the cost of more area and lower sampling rate. Similar results have been annotated also for other test cases which allowed us to derive the following rule of thumb: *Solutions with smaller N are preferable if sampling-rate and/or area represent the main cost function; solution with larger N are indicated when design specs call for large input range.*

User-constrained parameters		
$\mathbf{W} = 100nm$, $\mathbf{F}_{clk} = 10GHz$		
$\mathbf{D} = 18nm$		
Specs		
$\mathbf{B}_{in} = 50KHz$		
Input range $= 200\ mV$		
Resolution $= 100\ \mu V$		
Output		
N	1	20
Sampling Rate$_{(MAX)}$	$1.45\ MSPS$	$1.1\ MSPS$
Counter Nbit$_{(MIN)}$	13	14
Voffset	$0.53\ V$	$0.26\ V$
Area	$5.287\mu m^2$	$5.878\mu m^2$

Table 2: Case-2: G-ADC design.

Case 3.

As a further example, Table 3 reports the returned G-ADC implementations when also D is left as optimization parameter. Also in this case a single set of $[Resolution;\ Input\ range]$ specs is considered: $100mV$ and $100\mu V$.

User-constrained parameters			
$\mathbf{W} = 100nm$, $\mathbf{F}_{clk} = 10GHz$			
Specs			
$\mathbf{B}_{in} = 50KHz$			
Input range $= 100\ mV$			
Resolution $= 100\ \mu V$			
Output			
D	$18\ nm$	$36\ nm$	$54\ nm$
N	1	1	1
SR$_{(MAX)}$	$3.5\ MSPS$	$1.1\ MSPS$	$105\ KSPS$
Nbit$_{(MIN)}$	12	14	17
Voffset	$0.53\ V$	$0.12\ V$	$0.06\ V$
Area	$4.895\mu m^2$	$5.686\mu m^2$	$6.870\mu m^2$

Table 3: Case-3: G-ADC design.

For $D=36nm$ and $D=54nm$ only G-ADC implementations with $N=1$ match the constraints, hence feasible. Differently, for $D=18nm$, the tool returns feasible implementation for all possible values of N (from 1 to 20); we just reported the case for $N=1$ as to provide a fair comparison among the three implementation. The reason why for increasing values of D only single stage VTT lines are feasible is that for larger N, also $T_{delay}(FS)$ increases substantially making the conversion slower and reducing the maximum sampling rate (which might fall below the threshold $2 \times B_{in}$). It is also worth noticing that the case with $D=18nm$ outperforms the other twos in terms of sampling-rate and area; $D=54nm$ is the case with minimum offset (refer to case 2 to understand the benefits of a smaller offset).

7. CONCLUSIONS

This paper presents an ADC architecture realized using graphene p-n junctions along with its characterization. It introduces, for the first time, the possibility to interface analog and digital domains using all-Graphene devices. We also implemented a CAD tool that allow designers to perform a *what-if* analysis. Characterization results along with few test-cases validate the functionality of the proposed ADC design and quantify some of the main figures of merit.

One of the major limitation for the proposed G-ADC is its non linear conversion behavior. This due to non-linear dependence of the p-n junction resistance from voltage. Some form of linearity correction could be introduced, as an example, using a D/A feedback loop, as exploited in CMOS SAR-ADC. Another viable solution is by using Look Up Tables with stored correction factors for different operating regions.

8. REFERENCES

[1] C. H. Ahn and et al. Electrostatic modification of novel materials. *Rev. Mod. Phys.*, 78(4):1185–1212, Nov. 2006.

[2] B. Black. Analog-to-digital converter architectures and choices for system design. *Analog Dialogue*, 33(8):35–38, 1999.

[3] A. H. Castro Neto, F. Guinea, N. M. R. Peres, K. S. Novoselov, and A. K. Geim. The electronic properties of graphene. *Reviews of Modern Physics*, 81(1):109–162, Jan. 2009.

[4] V. V. Cheianov, V. Fal'ko, and B. L. Altshuler. The focusing of electron flow and a veselago lens in graphene p-n junctions. *Science*, 315(5816):1252–1255, Mar. 2007.

[5] A. K. Geim and K. S. Novoselov. The rise of graphene. *Nature Materials*, 6(6):183–191, Mar. 2007.

[6] X. Jia, J. Campos-Delgado, M. Terrones, V. Meunier, and M. S. Dresselhaus. Graphene edges: a review of their fabrication and characterization. *Nanoscale*, 3(1):86–95, 2011.

[7] Y.-M. Lin, C. Dimitrakopoulos, K. A. Jenkins, D. B. Farmer, H.-Y. Chiu, A. Grill, and P. Avouris. 100-ghz transistors from wafer-scale epitaxial graphene. *Science*, 327(5966):662, 2010.

[8] S. Masuda, T. Watanabe, S. Yamauchi, and T. Terasawa. All-digital quadrature detection with tad for radio-controlled clocks/watches. *IEEE Transaction on Circuits and Systems*, 56(2):285–293, Feb. 2009.

[9] S. Miryala, A. Calimera, E. Macii, and M. Poncino. Delay model for reconfigurable logic gates based on graphene pn-junctions. In *GLSVLSI'13: ACM International Conference on Great Lakes Symposium on VLSI*, pages 227–232, 2013.

[10] S. Miryala, A. Calimera, E. Macii, and M. Poncino. Exploration of different implementation styles for graphene-based reconfigurable gates. In *ICICDT-13: IEEE International Conference on IC Design & Technology*, pages 21–24, May 2013.

[11] S. Miryala, A. Calimera, E. Macii, and M. Poncino. Ultra low-power computation via graphene-based adiabatic logic gates. In *DSD-14: IEEE Euromicro Conference on Digital System Design*, pages 365–371, Aug. 2014.

[12] S. Miryala, M. Montazeri, A. Calimera, E. Macii, and M. Poncino. A verilog-a model for reconfigurable logic gates based on graphene pn-junctions. In *DATE'13: ACM/IEEE Design, Automation and Test in Europe*, pages 1–4, mar 2013.

[13] K. S. Novoselov and et al. Electric field effect in atomically thin carbon films. *Science*, 306(5696):666–669, Oct. 2004.

[14] K. S. Novoselov, D. Jiang, F. Schedin, T. Booth, V. Khotkevich, S. Morozov, and A. K. Geim. Two-dimensional atomic crystals. In *Proceedings of the National Academy of Sciences of The United States of America*, volume 102, pages 10451–10453, Jul. 2005.

[15] H.-S. Philip Wong and D. Akinwande. *Carbon nanotubes and graphene device physics*. Cambridge University Press, 2010.

[16] C.-Y. Sung and J. U. Lee. Graphene:the ultimate switch. *IEEE Spectrum*, Jan. 2012.

[17] S. Tanachutiwat, J. U. Lee, W. Wang, and C. Y. Sung. Reconfigurable multi-function logic based on graphene p-n junctions. In *DAC'10: ACM/IEEE Design Automation Conference*, pages 883–888, Jun. 2010.

[18] V. Tenace, A. Calimera, E. Macii, and M. Poncino. Pass-xnor logic: A new logic style for pn-junction based graphene circuits. In *DATE'14: ACM/IEEE Design, Automation and Test in Europe*, pages 1–4, Mar. 2014.

[19] R. Walden. Analog-to-digital converter survey and analysis. *IEEE Journal on Selected Areas in Communications*, 17(4):539–550, Apr. 1999.

[20] T. Watanabe, T. Mizuno, and Y. Makino. An all-digital analog-to-digital converter with 12-μv/lsb using moving-average filtering. *IEEE Journal of Solid-State Circuits*, 38(1):120–125, Jan. 2003.

[21] H. Yang and et al. Graphene barristor, a triode device with a gate-controlled schottky barrier. *Science*, 336(6085):1140–1143, May 2012.

A Ternary Content Addressable Cell Using a Single Phase Change Memory (PCM)

Pilin Junsangsri, Fabrizio Lombardi

Department of Electrical and Computer Engineering
Northeastern University
Boston, MA 02115, USA
(1) 617-373-4854

Junsangsri.p@husky.neu.edu, lombardi@ece.neu.edu

Jie Han

Department of Electrical and Computer Engineering
University of Alberta
Edmonton, Alberta T6G 2V4, Canada
(1) 780-492-1361

jhan8@ualberta.ca

ABSTRACT

This paper presents the novel design of a Ternary Content Addressable Memory (TCAM); different from existing designs found in the technical literature, this cell utilizes a single Phase Change Memory (PCM) as storage element and ambipolarity for comparison. A memory core consisting of a CMOS transistor and a PCM is employed (1T1P); for the search operation, the data in the 1T1P memory core is read and its value is established using two differential sense amplifiers. Compared with other non-volatile memory cells using emerging technologies (such as PCM-based, and memristor-based), simulation results show that the proposed non-volatile TCAM cell offer significant advantages in terms of power dissipation, PDP for the search operation, write time and reduced circuit complexity (in terms of lower counts in transistors and storage elements).

Categories and Subject Descriptors

B.7.1 [**Integrated Circuits**]: Types and Design Styles – *Advanced Technologies, Memory Technologies, VLSI (Very Large Scale Integration).*

General Terms

Design

Keywords

Ternary Content Addressable Memory (TCAM), Phase Change Memory (PCM), Ambipolar Transistor, Emerging Technology

1. INTRODUCTION

A Ternary Content Addressable Memory (TCAM) is a fully associative memory that implements a lookup-table function using a dedicated comparison circuitry within usually a single clock cycle. It compares the input search data against a table of stored data; the address of the matching data (if any) is then returned [1]. The memory cell in a TCAM stores three states (i.e. '1', '0', '2'). The additional state '2' is also referred to as the "mask" or "don't care" state; it is used for matching to either a '0' or '1' in the input search data process. TCAM is used for applications that allow both exact and partial matches [2], it is mostly used for specific application tasks, such as the longest prefix matching in network

search engines. However, the utilization of a TCAM comes at the cost of increased area and power consumption; these are two of the design parameters that chip designers usually strive to reduce in the nanometric scales. Moreover with an ever increasing number of applications, TCAMs of increasing larger size are often required, thus further exacerbating power consumption [1].

This paper introduces a TCAM cell that is different from the designs found in the technical literature, it employs only a single phase change memory (PCM) as non-volatile storage element and a CMOS transistor as control element in the memory core, i.e. 1T1P. For the search operation, the data in the 1T1P memory core is read and its value is established using differential sense amplifiers. Ambipolar transistors are employed in the circuit for comparing the stored with the search data. The advantage of ambipolarity is that the state of a transistor (ON/OFF) is controlled by the voltage at the polarity gate and can be implemented by a single device (such as a CNTFET) [3]. The proposed ambipolar-based comparator circuit requires two ambipolar transistors for TCAM operation. Simulation results show that the proposed TCAM cell offer significant advantages in terms of write time, search time, power dissipation and reduced transistor count compared to other non-volatile memories when compared with other non-volatile TCAM cells (such as PCM- and memristor-based).

2. REVIEW AND PRELIMINARIES

2.1 Phase Change Memory (PCM)

The phase change memory (PCM) is regarded as one of the most promising alternatives among emerging technologies for non-volatile memory design. PCM has a high density, good speed, low operating voltage, excellent scaling capabilities and compatibility with a complementary metal oxide semiconductor (CMOS) process [4]. Data storage in a PCM is related to the phase transformation of the chalcogenide alloy (e.g. $Ge_2Sb_2Te_5$, GST) that exhibits amorphous and crystalline phases. In the amorphous phase, the resistance of the PCM is high and is commonly referred to as the *reset state*; in the crystalline phase, its resistance is low and is commonly referred to as the *set state* [4]. To program data into a PCM, a pulse with high amplitude is used to melt and quench the PCM to an amorphous phase (*Reset State*), while a longer pulse with low amplitude is used to crystallize the PCM to a crystalline phase (*Set State*) [4].

2.2 Ambipolar Transistor

Different from a traditional (unipolar silicon CMOS) device whose behavior (either p-type or n-type) is determined at fabrication, ambipolar devices can be operated in a switched mode (from p-type to n-type, or vice versa) by changing the gate bias [4] [5]. Ambipolar conduction is characterized by the superposition of electron and hole currents; this behavior has been experimentally reported in different emerging technologies such as carbon nanotubes [3], silicon nanowires [4], graphene [6], and organic semiconductor heterostructures [7]. An ambipolar transistor can be used to control the direction of the current based on the voltage at the so-called *polarity gate*. The second gate (referred to as the Polarity Gate, PG) controls its polarity, i.e. when PG is set to logic '0', the ambipolar transistor behaves like a NMOS; when PG is set to logic '1', it behaves like a PMOS [8]. In the technical literature and to the best knowledge of the authors, there is no HSPICE compatible model to simulate the behavior of an ambipolar transistor; therefore, in this paper, the model of Figure 1a is utilized at macroscopic level for simulating the characteristics of an ambipolar transistor by using four transmission gates and two MOSFETs.

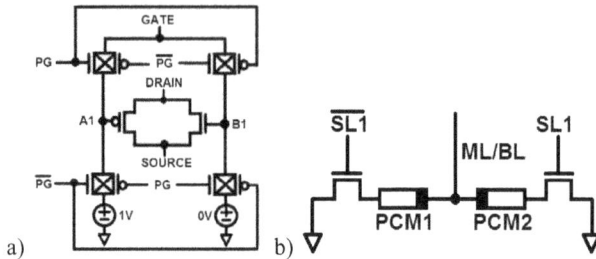

Figure 1. a) Model of an ambipolar transistor b) TCAM [9]

2.3 Existing TCAM Designs

TCAM designs using emerging technologies (such as the memristor and PCM) and CMOS have been extensively analyzed in the technical literature [2] [9] [10]. A CMOS-based TCAM cell employs two SRAMs as storage core [9] and requires 16 transistors. A TCAM with a larger number of transistors [8] incurs in a high power dissipation [10]; moreover, the relatively high leakage current encountered at nanoscale CMOS feature sizes [10] and the volatile nature of operation, are of concern. A memristor-based TCAM cell has been proposed in [2]. Six transistors are employed as control elements, while two memristors are used as storage elements. Since no additional supply voltage is required [2], its power dissipation is less than a CMOS TCAM cell. The TCAM cell of [2] requires a smaller number of transistors; however its write and read times [2] are slower than for a CMOS TCAM cell and a refresh operation is also needed when the cell is consecutively read many times. PCM is another emerging technology that can be employed as storage element in a TCAM cell. The resistance of a PCM remains unchanged if the voltage drop across it is less than the threshold voltage, i.e. no refresh operation is required. In [9], a TCAM cell is proposed by using 2 PCMs and 2 CMOS transistors (Figure 1b). By storing data in the form of PCM resistances, the search operation of a TCAM [9] starts by setting the match voltage (V_{ML}) to 0.4V, while the voltage at the search lines (SL and $\overline{SL}$) is based on the search data. The output of the search operation is presented in the form of a match line current (I_{ML}). The size of the transistors (M1 and M2) of this TCAM [9] must be adjusted until the resistances during the set and reset states are close to the PCM resistances of state '1' and '0' respectively; therefore, the design of this TCAM cell [9] is complicated and difficult to attain in the presence of variations as encountered in the nano scales. Moreover, the output of the search operation [9] is given as a match line current (I_{ML}), a *current sense amplifier* is required. Moreover, the match line current of the TCAM cell [9] during a search operation is very small, i.e. a high-performance current sense amplifier is needed.

3. PROPOSED CELL

This section presents the basic principles of the proposed cell. The basic memory core consists of a phase change memory (PCM) as storage element and a CMOS transistor as control element, i.e. this is a 1T1P memory core. The write and read operations of this 1T1P memory core are established by controlling the voltages at the bitline (BL) and the word lines (WL) as shown in Figure 2a.

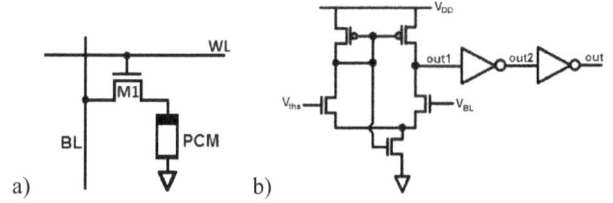

Figure 2. a) The proposed 1T1P core b) Differential sense amplifier [11]

3.1 Write Operation

To write data into the memory core, the write voltage is obtained as input from BL, while WL is used as selection line. When the word line voltage (V_{WL}) is at V_{DD}, M1 is ON, the voltage of BL (V_{BL}) passes through M1 and drops across the PCM. The 1T1P core can be written based on the value of V_{BL}. State '0' corresponds to the amorphous phase of the PCM (high resistance value) while state '1' corresponds to the crystalline phase (low resistance value). State '2' or *don't care* state is given by an intermediate resistance of the PCM (intermediate phase i.e. between the amorphous and the crystalline phases).

3.2 Read Operation

Initially, the bitline is precharged to the Vread value; as the word line is at V_{DD}, M1 is ON. So V_{BL} flows through M1 and drops across the PCM; the data stored in the core is found by checking the value of V_{BL}. If a '1' (low PCM resistance) is stored in the 1T1P core, V_{BL} is easily passed to GND, because for a '1' the value of PCM resistance is very low. However if a '0' is stored, the value of VBL is higher than for state '1'. Therefore, the data stored in the memory core is correctly read.

The value of the read voltage (V_{read}) of the core is limited to V_h because holding voltage is the minimum threshold voltage of PCM. The change from the OFF to ON states (or vice versa) during read operation does not occur in this memory core.

4. CIRCUIT DESIGN

The proposed cell consists of few circuits (in addition to the core) that are analyzed and discussed next.

4.1 Differential Sense Amplifier

The match or mismatch outcome of the proposed TCAM cell is generated by using two differential sense amplifiers for estimating stored data and by employing ambipolar transistors to compare the stored and the search data. A differential sense amplifier [11] (Figure 2b) finds the difference between V_{BL} and the threshold voltage of the differential sense amplifier (V_{ths}), then inverters are employed to drive the voltage difference to the output (V_{out}). If V_{BL} is higher than V_{ths}, then the voltage at node out is at GND, otherwise the voltage at node out is given by V_{DD}.

The values of the threshold voltages of the differential sense amplifiers (V_{ths1}, V_{ths2}) are given between the '0' and '2' and the '2' and '1' states respectively, while the output voltages are given at nodes O1 and O2 (Figure 3a). If a '0' ('1') is stored in the 1T1P core, V_{BL} is high (low). The voltages at O1 and O2 are at GND (V_{DD}) and GND (V_{DD}). However if a '2' is stored in the memory core, V_{BL} takes the intermediate value, i.e. the voltages of nodes O1 and O2 are given by GND and V_{DD} respectively.

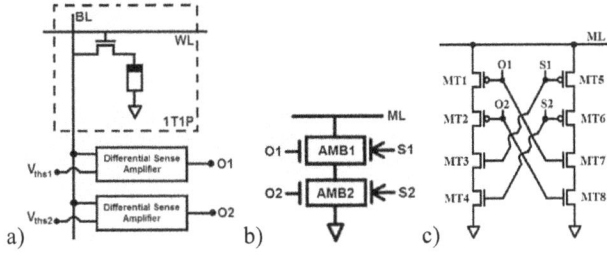

Figure 3. a) 1T1P core and differential sense amplifiers b) Ambipolar-based TCAM comparator circuit c) CMOS-based TCAM comparator circuit

4.2 Comparator Circuit

After the data stored in the 1T1P memory core is adjusted by the differential sense amplifiers and observed as voltages at nodes O1 and O2, a comparison circuit is used to compare the stored with the search voltages.

The *match* or *mismatch* outcome of the proposed TCAM cell is generated using the match line voltage (V_{ML}) for the output of the comparator circuit. An ambipolar-based comparator circuit for TCAM operation (Figure 3b) employs 2 ambipolar transistors. The match or mismatch outcome of the proposed TCAM cell is based on precharging the match line voltage (V_{ML}) to V_{DD}, while the search (stored) data is provided as voltage at lines S1 (O1) and S2 (O2) to the polarity gates of the ambipolar transistors.

Table 1. Voltages at nodes O1, O2, S1, S2, and match line voltage of proposed TCAM comparator circuit

Search	V_{S1}	V_{S2}	Stored	V_{O1}	V_{O2}	V_{ML}	Outcome
	0	0	0	0	0	V_{DD}	Match
0	0	0	1	1	1	GND	Mismatch
	0	0	2	0	1	V_{DD}	Match
	1	1	0	0	0	GND	Mismatch
1	1	1	1	1	1	V_{DD}	Match
	1	1	2	0	1	V_{DD}	Match
	0	1	0	0	0	V_{DD}	Match
2	0	1	1	1	1	V_{DD}	Match
	0	1	2	0	1	V_{DD}	Match

Table 1 shows the operation of the proposed TCAM comparator circuit. An ambipolar transistor is ON only when the voltages at its gate and polarity gate are different. When two ambipolar transistors are connected in series (Figure 3b), the match line voltage discharges only when a '0' (as data) is stored in the cell and searching for a '1' (or vice versa). This matches with the search operation of a TCAM. The circuit in Figure 3b is used as comparator circuit of the proposed TCAM cell. Consider a CMOS-based comparator circuit for TCAM (Figure 3c); similar to the ambipolar-based comparator, the match or mismatch outcome of a TCAM cell is accomplished by precharging the match line voltage (V_{ML}) to V_{DD}, while delivering the search (stored) data as voltages at lines S1 (O1) and S2 (O2).

5. SIMULATION RESULTS

The simulation results of the proposed TCAM cell are presented in this section. HSPICE is used as simulation tool and the model of [4] is employed for the PCM; its resistance range is initially given by 7kΩ – 200kΩ. The macroscopic model of Figure 1a is utilized for the ambipolar transistor; its transistor sizes are adjusted to generate the symmetric conduction between the PMOS and NMOS behaviors. Simulation is initially performed at a CMOS feature

size of 32nm and a supply voltage (V_{DD}) of 0.9V. The performance of the memory cells is obtained by combining the performance of the different circuits.

5.1 1T1P Memory Core

The two basic operations (read and write) of the 1T1P core are considered first. For the write operation, the bitline voltage (V_{BL}) must be controlled when the word line voltage (V_{WL}) is set to V_{DD}, V_{BL} is passed through M1 and is dropped across the PCM. The PCM resistance is switched to the ON-state value, and its crystalline fraction (C_x) is changed. The write time (i.e. from the amorphous to a crystalline phase) linearly increases when increasing the range of the PCM resistance. For the read operation, the bitline voltage (V_{BL}) must be precharged to V_{read}; when V_{WL} is at V_{DD}, the data in the memory core is read and detected from the bitline voltage. The relationship between the read time and V_{BL} is plotted in Figure 4.

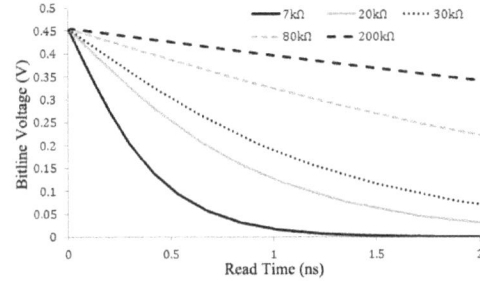

Figure 4. Bitline voltage of 1T1P memory core for a read operation (bitline capacitance is 0.03pF)

As shown in Figure 4, the bitline voltage is higher at a larger PCM resistance. As the PCM resistance of state '0' is larger than the resistance for either state '2' or '1', the bitline voltage during the read operation for state '0' is larger than the bitline voltage for either state '2' or state '1'. Since ternary data are stored in a TCAM, the value of the intermediate PCM resistance of 1T1P core for the "don't care" state ('2') is considered. The value of intermediate PCM resistance for state '2' is chosen as the resistance such that its bitline voltage is in the middle of the voltages for state '0' (200kΩ) and state '1' (7kΩ). Such a value should be not biased toward none of these two states; therefore for the read operation, voltage difference between state '0' and intermediate state must be nearly equal to the voltage difference between state '1' and intermediate state.

Table 2. Read time and bitline voltage difference (between state '0' and intermediate state and between state '1' and intermediate state) at intermediate PCM resistance values

Intermediate PCM Resistance	Read Time (ns)	Bitline Voltage Difference (V)
20kΩ	0.378	0.135
30kΩ	0.83	0.19
50kΩ	1.64	0.178
70kΩ	2.514	0.15
80kΩ	3.015	0.14

Table 2 shows the read time of a 1T1P memory core at different values of possible intermediate PCM resistance. At 30kΩ, the bitline voltage difference between state '0' and the intermediate state (equal to the difference between state '1' and the intermediate state) has the highest value at the least read time. Therefore based also on the simulation results of Table 2, 30kΩ is the appropriate intermediate PCM resistance to represent state '2' of a 1T1P memory core. So the read time is then selected such that the values of the voltage differences between the states are high and nearly the same; this occurs at 0.83ns.

5.2 Differential Sense Amplifier

After reading the 1T1P core, bitline voltage takes the value of the stored data through two differential sense amplifiers.

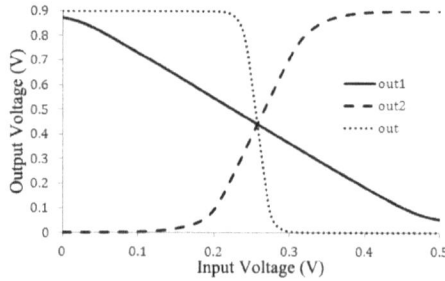

Figure 5. Output voltage of differential sense amplifier when $V_{ths} = 0.15V$

Figure 5 shows the output voltage of differential sense amplifier when changing the input voltage; the threshold voltage of the differential amplifier (V_{ths}) is given by 0.15V. The output voltage of the differential sense amplifier switches at 0.25V (Figure 5). So when the input voltage of the differential sense amplifier (V_{BL}) is less than 0.25V, the voltage at out is V_{DD}; however if V_{BL} is higher than 0.25V, the voltage at out is at GND (0V). Table 3 presents the voltages at O1 and O2 when the 1T1P core is connected to the differential sense amplifiers in a TCAM (Figure 3a).

Table 3. Bitline voltage of 1T1P core and output voltages of differential sense amplifiers for TCAM operation at read times

State	PCM (kΩ)	V_{BL} (0.83ns)	V_{O1} (V)	V_{O2} (V)
0	200	0.407	0	0
2	30	0.230611	0	0.9
1	7	0.0386	0.9	0.9

The switching voltage of the differential sense amplifier is different from the threshold voltage of the differential amplifier (V_{ths}). Figure 6 shows that the switching voltage changes linearly with the threshold voltage of the differential sense amplifier.

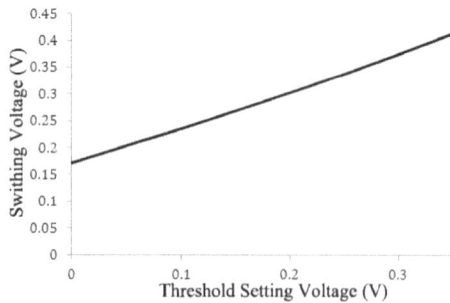

Figure 6. Threshold voltage of differential sense amplifier (V_{ths}) and its switching voltage

Consider the delay of the differential sense amplifier; when the input voltage of the differential sense amplifier is changed from GND to the holding voltage (V_h), the voltage at node out does not suddenly change, i.e. there is a delay in the switching process. The delay of the differential sense amplifier at a 32nm CMOS feature size is given by 0.067ns.

5.3 Comparator Circuit

The data stored in the 1T1P core must be changed to a two-valued voltage by the differential sense amplifiers; so for the search operation of a TCAM cell, a circuit is required for comparing the stored data with the search data. In this paper, the ambipolar-based (Figure 3b) and CMOS-based (Figure 3c) comparator circuits are assessed. The model in Figure 1a is employed to simulate ambipolar-based comparison circuit of TCAM. The initial values for the voltages at nodes A1 and B1 in the model for the ambipolar transistor are given by V_{DD} and GND respectively; the characteristics of the ambipolar transistor are then generated and the delay of the comparison circuit is established.

Table 4. Search time of the CMOS and ambipolar-based TCAM comparator circuits at a supply voltage (V_{DD}) of 0.9V

Search	V_{S1}	V_{S2}	Stored	V_{O1}	V_{O2}	Search Time (ns)	
						CMOS	Ambipolar
0	0	0	1	1	1	4.814	0.347
1	1	1	0	0	0	4.814	1.55

The match line voltage (V_{ML}) is discharged only when the stored and search data are mismatched, so only the mismatch delay is considered. As shown in Table 4, the comparison circuit based on ambipolar transistors is faster than the CMOS-based circuit. Also it should be noted that the ambipolar-based comparison circuits requires a significantly lower number of transistors (at most two, if the ambipolar transistors are implemented by CNTFETs for TCAM operation [3]).

5.4 Delay

By adding the delay of each circuit in the cell, the total delay for the search operation is reported in Table 5.

Table 5. Delay of proposed TCAM cell for a search operation

Circuit	Delay (ns)
1T1P Memory Core	0.83
Differential Sense Amplifier [11]	0.067
Comparison Circuit	1.55
Total Delay	2.447

So, the total delay of the ambipolar-based TCAM cell is 2.447ns (Table 5). However, if an ambipolar transistor is implemented by utilizing a SB-CNTFET [3] (as equivalent to the macromodel of the ambipolar transistor of Figure 1a), the delay of the comparison circuit can be significantly reduced because [3] has shown that the inverter delay of a SB-CNTFET at a diameter of 1nm, is nearly 1ps [3].

5.5 Power Dissipation

Only the power dissipation during a search operation is considered. Table 6 shows the average power dissipation, average miss delay and power delay product (PDP) of each circuit in the proposed ambipolar-based TCAM cell. State '1' of the 1T1P cell consumes the highest power, while state '0' consumes the least due to the high resistance value (200kΩ). Moreover, in state '1' (7kΩ), the bitline voltage can be passed easier to GND, thus dissipating more power than for the other two states with larger PCM resistance values. For the average power dissipation of the comparison circuit, the macromodel of the ambipolar transistor is used; this is a very pessimistic value, because the power dissipation in Table 6 accounts for the 10 transistors used in this macromodel (Figure 1a) rather than the power dissipation of a fabricated device (using for example a single CNTFET [3]). The average power dissipation and the PDP of comparator circuit made of a single CNTFET should be even lower than the values obtained for the macromodel of the ambipolar transistor (Figure 1a).

Table 6. Average power dissipation, average miss delay and power delay product of each circuit in the proposed TCAM cell

Circuit	State /outcome	Average Power (μW)	Average Miss Delay (ns)	PDP (fJ)
1T1P	0	1.3542	0.83	1.1240
	1	4.4175	0.83	3.6726
	2	3.4963	0.83	2.9019
Differential Sense Amplifier	N/A	22.3939	0.067	1.5004
Comparator	mismatch	24.696	1.55	38.2788

5.6 PCM Resistance Range

In this section, the influence of increasing the PCM resistance range (i.e. by varying the resistance of the highest value) is assessed for the read/write times as well as the PDP. The resistance for state '0' is changed to 100kΩ and 300kΩ.

Table 7. 1T1P core performance under different PCM resistance ranges; at 32nm feature size and 0.9V supply voltage

PCM Resistance Range	Write time (ns)	Read time (ns)	PDP (fJ)
7kΩ-100kΩ	94.81	1.046	3.693
7kΩ-200kΩ	199.34	0.83	3.6726
7kΩ-300kΩ	301.78	0.795	3.6666

Table 7 shows the write time of the 1T1P core (when the data in the memory core is changed from '0' to '1'), the read time and the power delay product (PDP) of the 1T1P core (for the read '1' operation). As shown in Table 7, the write time of the 1T1P core changes depending on the PCM resistance range. As for the read time of the TCAM, the read time of a smaller PCM resistance range results in a larger value. The same effect is observed for the PDP.

5.7 1T1P Cores/Bitlines

In this section, the number of 1T1P cores connected to a single bitline is initially considered at a read time of 0.83ns for TCAM operation as described previously. Figure 7 shows that the bitline voltage of states '1' (7kΩ) and '2' (30kΩ) increases when the number of 1T1P cores connected to it is increased. However for state '0' (i.e. the PCM resistance is high at 200kΩ), the bitline voltage is almost constant, because its value is close to V_h (as precharged during the read operation). The difference between the bitline voltages of each state are still large, hence the read operation can be still executed correctly.

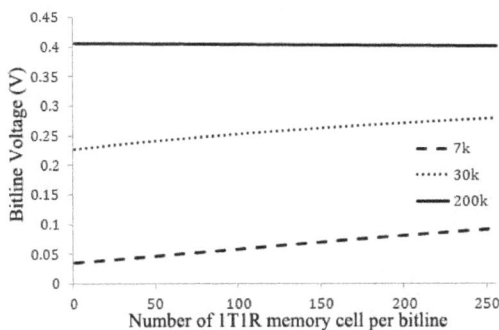

Figure 7. Bitline voltage vs number of 1T1P cores per bitline, (read time of 0.83ns and TCAM operation)

5.8 CMOS Feature Size

Previously, the CMOS feature size of the proposed TCAM design has been fixed to 32nm. Next, the design is also assessed when different HP (high performance). PTMs are utilized at the lower feature sizes of 22 and 16nm. Table 8 shows the delay of the proposed TCAM cell for the search operation when the supply voltage is either kept constant or varied as per PTM specifications. Smaller features sizes show a significant reduction in total delay at the constant supply voltage (i.e. 0.9V). As the values in the PCM resistance are still the same, a reduction in power supply is not as beneficial to the search time as the feature size.

Table 8. Delay of proposed TCAM cell for the search operation when varying CMOS feature size and supply voltage

Circuit	CMOS Feature Size (nm)					
	16	22	32	16	22	32
1T1P Memory Cell	0.738	0.78	0.83	1.023	0.93	0.83
Differential Sense Amplifier	0.024	0.045	0.067	0.039	0.053	0.067
Comparator	0.334	0.53	1.55	0.698	0.87	1.55
Total Delay	1.096	1.355	2.447	1.76	1.853	2.447
Voltage Supply(V)	0.9			0.7	0.8	0.9

6. COMPARISON

In this section, the proposed TCAM cell is compared with different schemes found in the technical literature employing PCM, memristor and CMOS.

6.1 PCM-Based TCAM Cell [9]

As presents in Figure 1b, the cell of [9] employs 2 PCMs and 2 CMOS transistors to store data in a TCAM. The PCMs are used as storage elements. The search operation of a TCAM [9] starts by setting the match voltage (V_{ML}) at 0.4V, while the voltage at the search lines (SL and $\overline{SL}$) is based on the search data. The output of the search operation is presented in the form of a match line current (I_{ML}). The *match* or *mismatch* outcome of the TCAM requires the adjustment of the search voltage V_{SL} as function of I_{ML}. Hence, a *current differential amplifier* [9] is required.

Table 9. Comparison between proposed 1T1P TCAM and TCAM [9] at 32nm CMOS feature size and 0.9 supply voltage

Circuit	TCAM	
	[9]	Proposed
Write Time (ns)	209.53	199.34
Search Time (ns)	1.346	2.447
Number of Transistors/Core	2	1
Number of PCM s/Core	2	1
Power Dissipation (μW)	35.9658	17.757
PDP of Search Operation (fJ)	48.41	43.4518

Table 9 shows the comparison results; the write time of the proposed TCAM cell is faster than the TCAM of [9] due to the higher number of resistive elements per core. As for the search time, the search time of the proposed TCAM cell is slower than the TCAM of [9]; this occurs, because in the proposed TCAM cell, the search time is based on the selection of the time at which the values of the bitline voltage differences between state pairs of the TCAM are closest. Moreover, the comparison circuit of the proposed TCAM consists of two ambipolar transistors, so the discharging rate of the match line is slower. The proposed TCAM cell employs less transistors and PCM devices than the TCAM of [9], so the area of the proposed TCAM cell is lower. Furthermore, as for power dissipation and PDP, the proposed cell is better than

[9]. Hence, the proposed TCAM is better suited in low power applications.

6.2 CMOS Based TCAM Cell

In this section, a comparison between the proposed TCAM cell with a CMOS-based TCAM [9] and a NAND Flash-Based TCAM [12] is pursued at 32nm feature size. The non-volatile circuit of [12] is utilized for the NAND flash-based memory to store data; a comparison circuit is then employed for the TCAM operation.

Table 10. Comparison of the proposed and CMOS-based TCAM cell (in which a 6T SRAM is used as storage core)

Circuit	TCAM		
	PCM	CMOS	NAND-Flash
Write time/Erase time	199.34ns	0.033ns	300μs/2ms
Search Time	2.447ns	0.562ns	25μs
Write Operating Voltage (V)	0.9	0.9	3
Read Operating Voltage (V)			3
Number of Transistors/Core	1	16	4

Table 10 shows the simulation results; as expected, the deterioration in write and search times of the proposed cell with respect to a CMOS cell is compensated by the lower number of transistors required for implementation and the non-volatile nature of the proposed memory cells. The proposed cell is however significantly better than the other non-volatile scheme, i.e. the NAND flash-based TCAM cell of [12].

6.3 1T1M Memristor-Based Cell

The proposed memory cell using a PCM is compared with the 1T1M (memristor-based) memory cell. Simulation has been performed by using the same resistance range (7kΩ - 200kΩ) and supply voltage (0.9V) for both cores. The (programming) temperatures of the PCM during the write operation from state '0' to state '1' and state '1' to state '0' are fixed to 705K and 1200K degrees respectively [4], while the threshold resistance of the memristor for a refresh operation is given by 96.5kΩ.

Table 11. Write time, read time and number of read operations prior to refresh for 1T1P and 1T1M cores

	Core	CMOS Feature Size (nm)		
		16	22	32
Write time ('0' to '1')	PCM	198.66ns	198.93ns	199.34ns
	Memristor	1.837μs	2.023μs	2.202μs
Write time ('1' to '0')	PCM	6.49ns	6.50ns	6.51ns
	Memristor	1.263μs	1.385μs	1.435μs
Read time (ns)	PCM	0.738	0.78	0.83
	Memristor	0.738	0.78	0.83
Number of Reads prior to refresh (*10^3)	PCM	N/A	N/A	N/A
	Memristor	3.08	3.17	3.24

Table 11 shows that the 1T1P core has a faster write time than the 1T1M core, because the changing rate of the PCM resistance is faster than the changing rate of the memristance. The read times of the 1T1P and 1T1M cores are the same, because in both cases data is stored in terms of resistance (of equal value and range). When the CMOS feature size is reduced, the write and read times for both the 1T1P and 1T1M cores decrease. Moreover the number of (successive) read operations that the 1T1M core can undertake prior to a refresh operation is also considered. A memristor based core requires a refresh operation to be performed following a number of consecutive read '0' operations; this is required to prevent the stored value of the memristance to reach the threshold value. When reducing its CMOS feature size, the number of consecutive read operations prior to the refresh operation of a

1T1M core is also reduced, i.e. at a lower CMOS feature size, the bitline voltage is transferred easier to the memristor, so the read time is faster. Note that for the proposed 1T1P core, no refresh operation is required because the read voltage is limited to the holding voltage (V_h) and the PCM resistance retains its value.

7. CONCLUSION

In this paper, the PCM-based TCAM cell is proposed. This design utilize a single phase change memory (PCM) as storage element and ambipolarity for comparison. The proposed comparator circuits have been shown to be superior to their CMOS-based counterparts. Also it should be noted that the ambipolar-based comparison circuit requires a significantly lower number of transistors. Compared with other non-volatile memory cells using emerging technologies (such as PCM-based, and memristor-based), simulation results show that the proposed non-volatile TCAM cell offer significant advantages in terms of power dissipation, PDP for the search operation, write time and reduced circuit complexity (in terms of lower counts in transistors and storage elements).

8. REFERENCES

[1] K. Pagiamtzis, A.Sheikholeslami "Content-Addressable Memory (CAM) Circuits and Architectures: A Tutorial and Survey" *IEEE Journal of Solid-State Circuits*, Vol. 41 No.3 March 2006

[2] P. Junsangsri, F. Lombardi "A Memristor-based TCAM (Ternary Content Addressable Memory) Cell: Design and Evaluation" *GLSVLSI* 22nd, pp. 311-314, Salt Lake City, Utah, USA, May 2012

[3] H.S.P. Wong, Jie Deng, A. Hazeghi, T. Krishnamohan, G. C. Wan "Carbon Nanotube Transistor Circuits – Models and Tools for Design and Performance Optimization" ICCAD'06 Nov 2006 pp. 651- 654

[4] P. Junsangsri, J. Han, F. Lombardi "Macromodeling a Phase Change Memory (PCM) Cell by HSPICE" *Proc. Nanoarch'12* pp. 77-84, Amsterdam Netherland July 2012

[5] Y.-M. Lin, J. Appenzeller, J. Knoch, P. Avouris "High-performance Carbon Nanotube field-effect Transistor with Tunable Polarities," *IEEE Trans. Nanotechnology*, vol. 4, pp. 481–489, 2005

[6] K. S. Novoselov, A. K. Geim, S. V. Morozov, D. Jiang, Y. Zhang, S. V. Dubonos, I.V.Grigorieva, A.A.Firsov "Electric field effect in atomically thin carbon films" *Science*, Vol. 306, No. 5696, pp. 666– 669, 2004

[7] A. Dodabalapur, H. E. Katz, L. Torsi, R. C. Haddon "Organic Heterostructure Field-effect Transistors," *Science*, vol. 269, no. 5230, pp. 1560–1562, 1995.

[8] M. H. B. Jamaa, K. Mohanram, G. D. Michel"Novel Library of Logic Gates with Ambipolar CNTFETs: Opportunities for Multi-Level Logic Synthesis," in *DATE2009.*, 2009, pp. 622–627

[9] B. Rajendran, R. W. Cheek, L. A. Lastra, M. M. Franeschini, M. J. Breitwisch, A. G. Schrott, Jing Li, R. K. Montoye, L. Chang, C. Lam "Demonstration of CAM and TCAM using Phase Change Devices" Memory Workshop (IMW), 2011 3rd IEEE, pp.1-4, May 2011

[10] K. Eshraghian, K.R. Cho, O. Kavehei, S.K. Kang, D. Abbott, S.M. Steve Kang, "Memristor MOS Content Addressable Memory (MCAM): Hybrid Architecture for Future High Performance Search Engines" *IEEE Transactions on VLSI Systems*, vol. 19, no. 8, pp. 1407-1417, 2011

[11] R. J. Baker "CMOS, Circuit Design, Layout, and Simulation" IEEE Press Series on Microelectronic Systems 2nd Edition 2011

[12] Micron Corporation, Product Specifications, found at http://download.micron.com/pdf/datasheets/flash/nand/2gb_nand_salesbrief_m29a.pdf

Characterization of SWCNT Bundle Based VLSI Interconnect with Self-heating Induced Scatterings

K. M. Mohsin and Ashok Srivastava[*]

Division of Electrical and Computer Engineering
Louisiana State University, Baton Rouge
LA 70803, U. S. A.
*Author to whom correspondence should be addressed; E-Mail: ashok@ece.lsu.edu

ABSTRACT

Performance of single walled carbon nanotube (SWCNT) bundle- based VLSI interconnects has been studied under the strong influence of scatterings induced by self-heating. Landauer Büttiker formalism along with Fourier heat transfer equation have been used to compute interconnect scattering parameters at various cross sectional areas of the interconnection. Cross sectional temperature calculation was performed using finite difference method considering temperature dependent thermal conductivity for primitive defect-less SWCNT bundles. Using the relaxation time approximation, we have studied scattering dynamics in calculating equivalent resistance. Electronic and thermal transport equations have been coupled and solved iteratively to get accurate estimation of temperatures and resistances. Study of scattering parameters shows low backscattering however significant transmission loss. Below 100GHz, for a 1μm long interconnect with 10 nm by10 nm cross sectional area shows S_{21} as high as 80dB. In terahertz regime transmission parameter S_{21} is in the range of few hundreds dB.

Categories and Subject Descriptors: B.7.1 [Types and Design Styles]: VLSI (very large scale integration)

Keywords: SWCNT bundle; VLSI; Interconnect; Joule heating; Self- heating; Scattering.

1. INTRODUCTION

Carbon nanotube (CNT) has received immense attraction as future interconnects material for very large scale integration (VLSI) nano electronic circuits. Due to high electro-thermal conductivities of different variants of carbon nanotube (CNT) and graphene, research has advanced further to explore potential of these nano-materials as future VLSI interconnect [1-6] and sensors [7, 8]. Because of high thermal conductivity, CNT interconnects can quickly drain out heat energy to make interconnect more thermally stable [4, 9]. Considering all these benefits metallic single-wall carbon nanotube (SWCNT) and multiwall carbon nanotube (MWCNT) have been studied intensely as a future VLSI interconnects material [10-15]. It is now a common trend to study the performances of interconnects made of all the variants of CNT and their bundles [3, 13-15]. Most of these previous works focused on electronic transport rather than giving focus to thermal transport, thermal instability induced performance degradation and ultimately thermal breakdown of interconnect. After Chiang et al.'s study on impact of Joule heating and performance degradation of Cu/low-k interconnects [16] researchers started evaluating the performance of CNT interconnects in light of thermal transport. Pop [17], Yamada et al. [18] and Kitsuki et al. [19] studied the thermal breakdown and tried to model the breakdown with one-dimensional Fourier heat equation in cylindrical coordinate system. In our recent works, we have reported theoretical study of electro-thermal transport in SWCNT and MWCNT interconnects considering Joule heating induced scatterings [20, 21]. Since geometry of bundle is unlike the SWCNT and MWCNT it is essential to study the SWCNT bundle to compare the performance of all these CNT variants in regards to thermal stability. In this work, we have studied high frequency performance of SWCNT bundle-based VLSI interconnects at various bias currents. Thermal performance greatly depends on dimensions of interconnect hence we also studied effects of various scaling factors of interconnect. We have coupled electronic transport with heat equation and solved coupled electro-thermal equation in two-dimensional Cartesian coordinate system for temperature distribution in a cross section of interconnects. Geometry of interconnect along with electrical properties of SWCNT bundle has been discussed in Section 2. Thermal properties and heat equation formalism have been discussed in Section 3. Results and discussion have been presented in Section 4. At the end, we have drawn conclusive remarks based on the limitations of this work and future scope in Section 5.

2. ELECTRICAL TRANSPORT AND GEOMETRY

2.1 SWCNT Bundle as Interconnect

An isolated SWCNT can be used as a VLSI interconnect which can be approximated as one-dimensional conductor [20]. Although the physics of SWCNT is well understood and SWCNT based interconnect is easy to model, it is very challenging to implement in VLSI because of technology limitation toward alignment and growth of single chirality SWCNT. However, it is a lot easier to pile SWCNTs of natural mix to implement as VLSI interconnects. Although SWCNT bundle can be obtained by piling SWCNTs in different geometrical shapes; in this work, we only considered rectangular shape as shown in Figure 1(C) and this is the most common interconnect geometry for VLSI technology. Each of this SWCNT is just rolled up single layer graphene sheet consisting sp^2 hybridized carbon atoms with 0.142 nm bond length as

GLSVLSI '15, May 20 - 22, 2015, Pittsburgh, PA, USA
Copyright 2015 ACM 978-1-4503-3474-7/15/05$15.00
http://dx.doi.org/10.1145/2742060.2742074

shown in Figure 1(A). In a bundle, different SWCNT wires are bounded by Van der Walls attraction forces with spacing 0.34 nm [22].

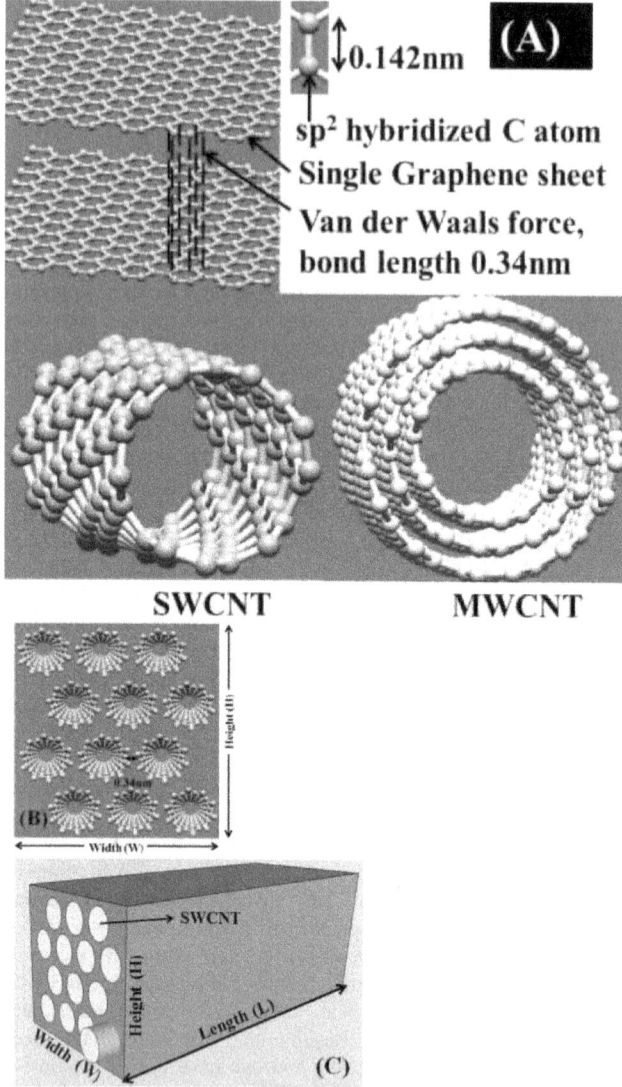

Figure 1. (A) sp^2- sp^2 hybridized sheet of carbon atoms, SWCNT, MWCNT, (B) SWCNT bundle and (C) Geometry for interconnects.

Here we have considered bundle of SWCNT instead of traditional Cu/low-k dielectric as interconnect material surrounded by inter layer dielectrics in present CMOS process technology. Figure 1(B) shows the bundle of SWCNT and Figure 1(C) is the geometry of interconnect. In this study, we have taken the length (L) of interconnect as 1μm, width (W) 5nm, height (H) 5nm and diameter (D) of each of SWCNT shell as 1nm. At different bias currents, we have studied the cross sectional temperature distribution and temperature dependent resistance. Electrically SWCNT bundle is actually parallel SWCNT wires running side-by-side maintaining Van der Walls distance from each other. Electrical parameters can be modeled as done for SWCNT in our previous work [20] and then the combined effect of all parallel running wires can be obtained. Naturally in SWCNT bundle, one third of these shells are metallic and rest of these is semiconducting. Here, we are assuming that only metallic shells will be contributing in

electron transport. Hence, considering the spin degeneracy, number of conducting channels (M) in each of SWCNT shell is 2/3 as long as temperature is well below the melting point of SWCNT [23]. Since we have statistically averaged the number of conducting channels we can assume that each of the SWCNT shell is contributing with 2/3 channels. Total number of shells can be calculated using following equations:

$$N_W = Int\left\{\frac{W-D}{D+d}\right\}+1 \qquad (1)$$

$$N_H = Int\left\{\frac{2(H-D)}{\sqrt{3}(D+d)}\right\}+1 \qquad (2)$$

$$N_{shell} = N_W N_H - Int\left\{\frac{N_H}{2}\right\} \qquad (3)$$

Here N_w and N_H are number of CNT shell in the direction of width and height of interconnect, respectively. Function Int is to take the integer value for everything enclosed by curly brackets. In equation (3), N_{shell} is total number of SWCNT shells which could be fit for a given geometry of interconnect. Here, d=0.34 nm which is the inter distance between of shells.

2.2 Equivalent Resistance (R_{eqv})

From Landauer-Büttiker formalism, dc resistance (R_k) of each shell can be calculated from equation (4),

$$R_k = \frac{h}{2q^2}\frac{1}{M}\left(1+\frac{l}{\lambda_{eff}(L,D,T_k,V)}\right). \qquad (4)$$

In equation (4), q is electronic charge, h is Plank constant, λ_{eff} is effective mean free path of an electron that takes into account electrons scattering with acoustic and optical phonons which is discussed in Section 2.4. T_k is temperature of a particular shell. Not all the shells will be at the same temperature because cross sectional temperature is not same everywhere. Length of interconnect is L and V is voltage across interconnect due to constant bias current (I). Considering contribution from all parallel shells; total resistance can be calculated from equation (5). M is the equivalent number of conducting channels, which is 2/3 here.

$$R_{eqv} = \left(\frac{1}{R_1}+\frac{1}{R_2}+...+\frac{1}{R_k}..+\frac{1}{R_{N_{shell}}}\right)^{-1}$$

$$= \frac{h}{2q^2}\left(\sum_{k=1}^{N_{shell}}\frac{M\lambda_{eff}(L,D,T_k,V)}{\lambda_{eff}(L,D,T_k,V)+L}\right)^{-1} \qquad (5)$$

2.3 Equivalent Inductance (L_{eqv}) and Capacitance (C_{eqv})

Equivalent quantum inductance can be calculated from equation (6) where v_F is Fermi velocity (8.854×10^5 ms^{-1}) [14] and ℏ is reduced Plank constant.

$$L_{eqv} = \frac{\pi\hbar}{2q^2 v_F \sum_{k=1}^{N_{shell}} M_k} = \frac{3\pi\hbar}{4q^2 v_F N_{shell}} \qquad (6)$$

While taking all parallel shells into consideration magnetic inductance can be neglected for more number of shells. Quantum capacitance can be obtained from following equation (7). Electrostatic capacitance is dominant over quantum capacitance only for few numbers of shells. Our focus here is to show how Joule heating affects electron transport in interconnects. Mostly the Joule heating affects the resistance of interconnects. Hence, we neglected negligible amount of magnetic inductance and electrostatic capacitance in this study. Of course electrostatic capacitance are always present in a wire and there is magnetic inductance along with mutual inductance in between the wires is always there and dominant for a single wire. One can always include those inductances and capacitances to obtain more accurate results at the cost of far complex calculations and these complex ladder inductance and capacitance networks are well reported in literatures [13, 14].

$$C_{eqv} = \frac{2q^2}{hv_F} \sum_k^{N_{shell}} M_k = \frac{4q^2 N_{shell}}{3hv_F} \qquad (7)$$

2.4 Effective Mean Free Path

In equation (8), Matthiessen's rule has been used to estimate effective mean free path (λ_{eff}) of an electron. In this equation, first term is due to spontaneous acoustic phonon. Second term is the contribution of optical emission and third term is related to scattering length due to optical emission induced by the field across interconnect. The right most term in equation (8) is due to optical absorption. Using equation (8) we can calculate the overall effective mean free path of an electron considering all scatterings. A detail calculation method of effective mean free path has been presented in an earlier work [21].

$$\frac{1}{\lambda_{eff}} = \frac{1}{\lambda_{ac}} + \frac{1}{\lambda_{op,ems}^{abs}} + \frac{1}{\lambda_{op,ems}^{fld}} + \frac{1}{\lambda_{op,abs}} \qquad (8)$$

2.5 Transmission Line Model

For interconnect characterization we have adopted the single conductor transmission line model developed by Sarto et al. [14] as shown in Figure 2. For scattering parameter calculations, this equivalent single conductor model has been used along with per unit length circuit parameters. Per unit length circuit parameters have been listed in Table II of Section 4.

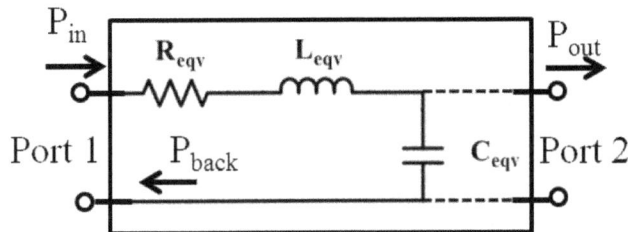

Figure 2: Single conductor transmission line model for SWCNT bundle based interconnect.

3. THERMAL TRANSPORT MODELING

After calculating electrical parameters of SWCNT bundle interconnect, it is essential to model heat transport for temperature distribution calculation and to study thermal stability of interconnect. Unlike a single wire, SWCNT bundle has a finite cross section and it is expected to have different temperature in each point of rectangular cross section. A distribution of temperature in a cross section means different SWCNT wire will be at different temperatures causing different temperature dependent resistance (R_k). For temperature profile, we have solved Fourier heat equation in two-dimensional rectangular cross section,

$$\kappa(T)\frac{\partial^2 T}{\partial x^2} + \kappa(T)\frac{\partial^2 T}{\partial y^2} + p = 0 . \qquad (9)$$

In equation (9), κ is temperature dependent thermal conductivity of SWCNT and modeled as $(3600 \times 300)/T$ Wm^{-1}K^{-1} [24] and p is the heat generation term, which is I^2R per unit volume. Right hand side of equation is zero because steady state solution was expected. Geometry of SWCNT bundle based interconnect is a three dimensional rectangular bar and it has steady state solution for diffusion equations. Being a three dimensional wire, SWCNT bundle-based interconnects are inherently thermally stable unlike single SWCNT wire. Because of nonlinear inter-dependence of resistance and temperature in between, we have to solve coupled electro-thermal transport equations iteratively until consistency achieved for total equivalent resistance (R_{eqv}). We assumed $T_0 = 300$K as initial temperature for each points of rectangular cross section as our starting temperature for nonlinear iterative calculation. Tolerance in this calculation was taken as 0.01K and does not have any effect in any physical parameters other than slow convergence. Temperatures on all the boundaries were taken as 300K. No heat sink was considered in this model for the sake of simplicity. However, heat sink can be incorporated in this model by knowing interfacial thermal resistance in between SWCNT bundles and substrate. Knowing interfacial thermal resistance a more detailed study can be performed using the same scheme presented in this work. Using equation (5), R_{eqv} can be obtained and then Joule heating per unit volume can be obtained from p= $(I^2R_{eqv})/(W \times L \times H)$. Here W, L, and H are width, length and height of interconnect. Using the value of p in equation (9) we have solved for T(x,y). Again T(x,y) can be used in equation (4), (5) and (7) to obtain the updated temperature dependent R_{eqv}. Iteratively consistent solution can be obtained for a particular bias current (I). Summary of this iterative scheme has been shown in Figure 3.

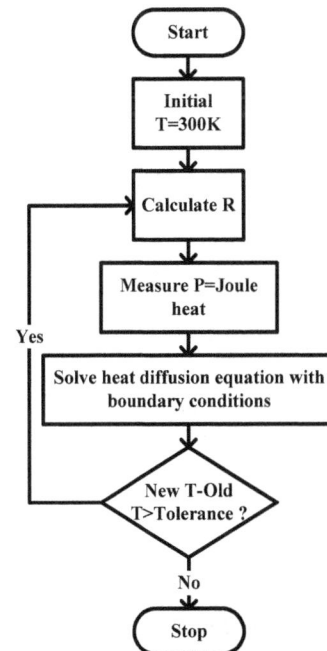

Figure 3: Iterative scheme for electro-thermal coupled equations.

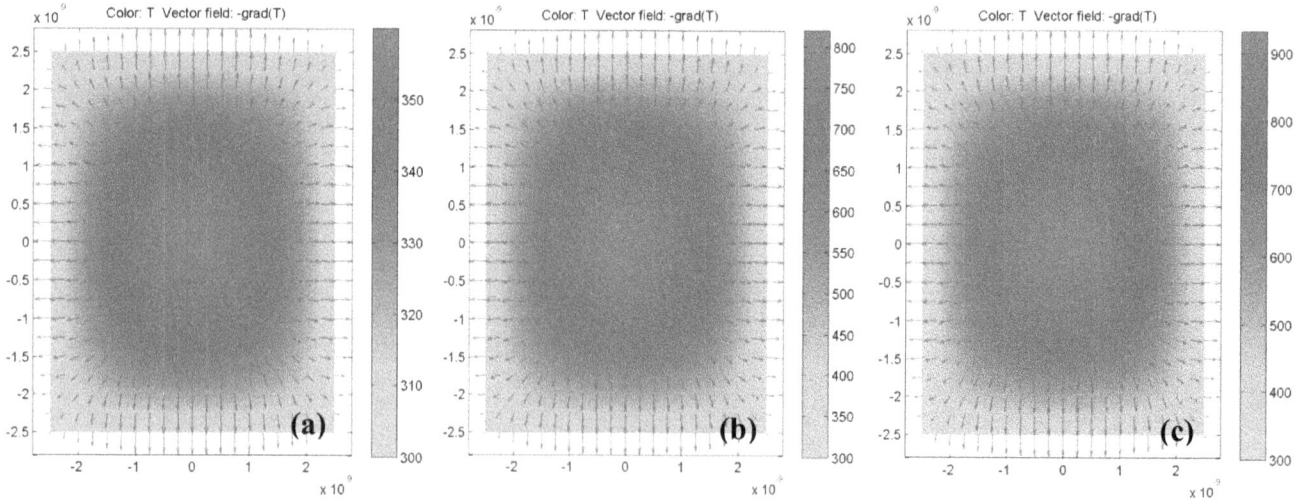

Figure 4: Cross sectional temperature distributions (color) and heat flow vector (arrow) for (a) 10mA, D=1nm, L=1μm, (b) 23mA, D=1nm, L=1μm and (c) 10mA, D=4nm, L=1μm.

Table I: Temperatures and equivalent resistances of SWCNT bundle interconnect at various bias currents

Bias current (mA)	Width=Height (nm)	Number of SWCNTs	Heat Dissipated (J/m^3)	Current Density (A/cm^2)	Highest Temperature (K)	Equivalent Resistance $(K\Omega)$	Comments on Break down
10	5	14	1.0729×10^{23}	4.0×10^{10}	360	26.8	No
	10	52	7.0643×10^{21}	1.0×10^{10}	303	7	No
23	5	14	5.7013×10^{23}	9.2×10^{10}	820	27	Critical
10	5, D=4nm	3	7.6945×10^{23}	9.2×10^{10}	>800	N/A	Yes

Table II: Two port network parameters

Bias current (mA)	Width=Height (nm), D=1nm, L=1um (unless mentioned)	Number of SWCNTs	Highest Temperature (K)	Equivalent Resistance (Ω/m)	Equivalent Inductance (H/m)	Equivalent Capacitance (F/m)
10	5	14	360	2.6800×10^{10}	0.0017	9.0394×10^{-10}
	10	52	303	7.0000×10^{9}	4.6538×10^{-4}	3.3575×10^{-09}
5	5 (D=4nm)	3	320	3.6320×10^{10}	0.0081	1.9370×10^{-10}
5	5 (L=2um)	14	316	3.3071×10^{10}	0.0017	9.0394×10^{-10}

4. RESULTS AND DISCUSSION

Temperature distributions in cross sections of SWCNT bundle-based interconnect considering Joule heating has been calculated with finite difference method. Figure 4 shows various temperature distributions at different bias currents and geometries. All these temperatures have been calculated in steady state condition. It is assumed that the temperature is concentrated in central shells even though heat is generating uniformly everywhere inside all SWCNTs. This is because heat can easily diffuse from the outer surface of interconnect towards the dielectric materials. However, it is very difficult for center to diffuse heat radially with low thermal conductivity $(5 Wm^{-1}K^{-1})$ in radial direction [25]. On the other hand, temperature profile is almost uniform in the direction of length because of high thermal conductivity towards the length of SWCNT. This is the prime reason for reducing the heat equation from an actual three-dimensional problem to a two-dimensional one. Figure

4(a) is for the bundle of SWCNT with 1nm diameter and 1μm long, 5nm by 5nm cross section under the bias current of 10 mA. In this case, steady state temperature goes up to 360K. For the same geometry, if we increase the current up to 23mA temperature reaches above 800K as shown in Figure 4(b). Beyond this temperature C-C bonds in SWCNT will be breaking. Hence, for this geometry breaking current is 23mA. In Figure 4(c), we have varied the diameter to 4 nm instead of 1nm to see how it affects the temperature profile. For a fixed cross sectional area, increasing diameter is decreasing number of total shells and hence increasing the current per shell causes temperature to rise above the melting point. For example, an interconnection of 5 nm by 5 nm cross section, 1μm long consisting of SWCNT each of them having 4nm diameter will not withstand at 10mA bias current. In Table I, we have summarized the thermal stability parameters study at different geometries and bias currents. In general, with more shells, total

268

number of parallel conducting channels increases causing equivalent resistance to decreases. In Table II, two port network parameters (R, L, and C) have been shown in per unit length along with the current density and peak temperature. Two ports network parameters S_{11} and S_{21} calculations have been carried out with distributed elements and normalized by 50 Ω. S_{11} is the ratio of power reflected from the transmission line to the incident power while S_{21} is the ratio of power transmitted through the transmission line to the incident power (Figure 2). S-parameters calculations have been carried out by the method described in [26] with per unit values of resistances, inductances, and capacitances from Table II for various interconnect dimensions and at different bias currents. Magnitudes of S_{11} and S_{21} at various scaling factors of cross section and currents are shown in Figures 5 and 6. Figure 5 shows that S_{11} is low enough for the whole band of 1GHz to 100THz and is more than -6dB. At high frequencies, reactive components dominate over resistive component causing significant back scatterings and increase in transmission losses. In VLSI applications, we expect low back scattering and high transmission. Hence, low values for S_{11} parameter is desirable. However, S_{21} parameter, which is a measure of forward signal transmission, is very low for VLSI applications. It is found to be always below -80dB in all frequencies shown in Figure 6. Interconnect with 10 nm by 10 nm cross section (Green line in Figure 6) shows better than any other combinations at 10mA current bias below 100GHz. It is an indicative that increase in cross sectional area will increase thermal stability and at the same time decrease high frequency signal transmission loss. After all, Figures 5 and 6 confirm how Joule heating affects the scattering parameters, which is a major concern in designing future CNT based VLSI interconnects

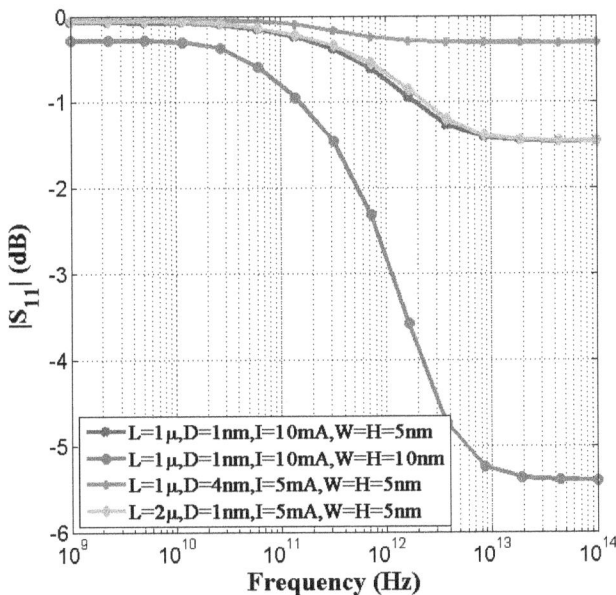

Figure 6: $|S_{21}|$ at various SWCNT bundle-based interconnects.

5. CONCLUSION

Cross sectional area scaling dependence in electro-thermal characterization of SWCNT bundle has been theoretically studied with Joule heating induced scattering. We have used heat equation coupled with electronic transport to get accurate temperature distribution in the cross section of interconnect. Coupled electro-thermal nonlinear equations have been iteratively solved to obtain equivalent circuit parameters for SWCNT bundle-based interconnect. Using these circuit parameters we have studied two-port network based scattering parameters to evaluate the performance of different scaling factor of cross section and effect of bias currents. Optimum interconnect dimension and critical breaking current can be estimated using this presented work. We neglected the non-uniformity of diameter induced from void or from any other form of defect originated during growth or deposition process. . Experimental validation of theoretical study is beyond the scope of this present work since integration of CNT bundles with CMOS is still in primitive stage and such theoretical studies would assist in better understanding of integration process.

6. ACKNOWLEDGMENT

Part of this work is supported by the United States Air Force Research Laboratory under agreement number FA9453-10-1-0002. The U.S. Government is authorized to reproduce and distribute reprints for Government purposes notwithstanding any copyright notation thereon.

7. REFERENCES

[1] N. Srivastava and K. Banerjee, "Performance analysis of carbon nanotube interconnects for VLSI applications," *Proc. IEEE/ACM International Conference on Computer-Aided Design (ICCAD)*, pp. 383-390, 2005.

[2] L. Hong, X. Chuan and K. Banerjee, "Carbon nanomaterials: the ideal interconnect technology for next-generation ICs," *IEEE Design & Test of Computers*, vol. 27, no. 4, pp. 20-31, 2010.

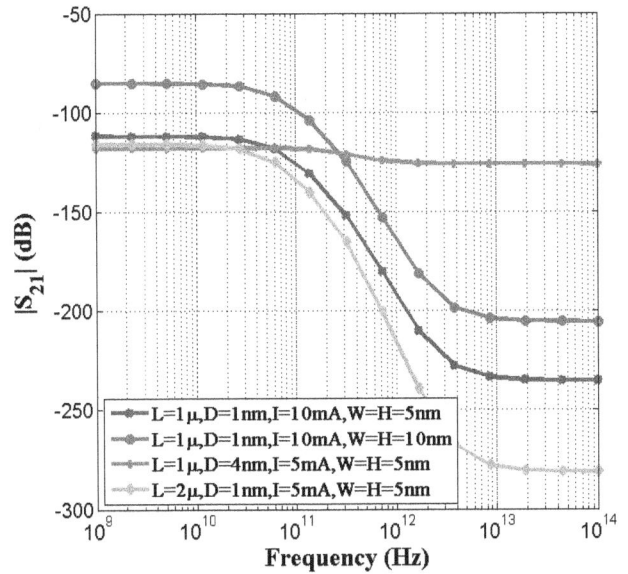

Figure 5: $|S_{11}|$ at various SWCNT bundle-based interconnects.

[3] A. Srivastava, Y. Xu and A. K. Sharma, "Carbon nanotubes for next generation very large scale integration interconnects," *Journal of Nanophotonics,* vol. 4, no. 1, pp. 041690, 1-26, 2010.

[4] S. Berber, Y.-K. Kwon and D. Tománek, "Unusually high thermal conductivity of carbon nanotubes," *Physical Review Letters,* vol. 84, no. 20, pp. 4613-4616, May 15, 2000.

[5] A. Naeemi and J. D. Meindl, "Carbon nanotube interconnects," *Annual Review of Materials Research,* vol. 39, no. 1, pp. 255-275, 2009.

[6] M. Nihei, A. Kawabata, D. Kondo, M. Horibe, S. Sato and Y. Awano, "Electrical properties of carbon nanotube bundles for future via interconnects," *Japanese Journal of Applied Physics,* vol. 44, no. 4A, pp. 1626, 2005.

[7] K. M. Mohsin, Y. M. Banadaki and A. Srivastava, "Metallic single-walled, carbon nanotube temperature sensor with self heating," *Proc. SPIE Smart Structures and Materials,* vol. 9060, pp. 906003-906003-7, 2014.

[8] Y. M. Banadaki, K. M. Mohsin and A. Srivastava, "A graphene field effect transistor for high temperature sensing applications," *Proc. SPIE Smart Structures and Materials,* vol. 9060, pp. 90600F-90600F-7, 2014.

[9] K. Sun, M. A. Stroscio and M. Dutta, "Thermal conductivity of carbon nanotubes," *Journal of Applied Physics,* vol. 105, no. 7, pp. 074316, 2009.

[10] P. L. McEuen, M. S. Fuhrer and H. Park, "Single-walled carbon nanotube electronics," *IEEE Transactions on Nanotechnology,* vol. 1, no. 1, pp. 78-85, 2002.

[11] A. Naeemi and J. D. Meindl, "Performance modeling for single- and multiwall carbon nanotubes as signal and power interconnects in gigascale systems," *IEEE Transactions on Electron Devices,* vol. 55, no. 10, pp. 2574-2582, 2008.

[12] P. Lamberti, M. S. Sarto, V. Tucci and A. Tamburrano, "Robust design of high-speed interconnects based on an MWCNT," *IEEE Transactions on Nanotechnology,* vol. 11, no. 4, pp. 799-807, 2012.

[13] X. Yao, A. Srivastava and A. K. Sharma, "A model of multi-walled carbon nanotube interconnects," *Proc. 52nd IEEE International Midwest Symposium on Circuits and Systems,* pp. 987-990, 2009.

[14] M. S. Sarto and A. Tamburrano, "Single-conductor transmission-line model of multiwall carbon nanotubes," *IEEE Transactions on Nanotechnology,* vol. 9, no. 1, pp. 82-92, 2010.

[15] M. D'Amore, M. S. Sarto and A. Tamburrano, "SPICE-model of multiwall carbon nanotube through-hole vias," *Proc. Asia-Pacific Symposium on Electromagnetic Compatibility (APEMC),* pp. 1104-1107, 2010.

[16] C. Ting-Yen, B. Shieh and K. C. Saraswat, "Impact of Joule heating on scaling of deep sub-micron Cu/low-k interconnects," *Proc. Digest of Technical Papers in Symposium on VLSI Technology,* pp. 38-39, 2002.

[17] E. Pop, D. A. Mann, K. E. Goodson and H. Dai, "Electrical and thermal transport in metallic single-wall carbon nanotubes on insulating substrates," *Journal of Applied Physics,* vol. 101, no. 9, pp. 093710, 2007.

[18] T. Yamada, T. Saito, D. Fabris and C. Y. Yang, "Electrothermal analysis of breakdown in carbon nanofiber interconnects," *IEEE Electron Device Letters,* vol. 30, no. 5, pp. 469-471, May, 2009.

[19] H. Kitsuki, T. Yamada, D. Fabris, J. R. Jameson, P. Wilhite, M. Suzuki and C. Y. Yang, "Length dependence of current-induced breakdown in carbon nanofiber interconnects," *Applied Physics Letters,* vol. 92, no. 17, pp. 173110, 2008.

[20] K. M. Mohsin, A. Srivastava, A. K. Sharma and C. Mayberry, "A thermal model for carbon nanotube interconnects," *Nanomaterials,* vol. 3, no. 2, pp. 229-241, April 26, 2013.

[21] K. M. Mohsin, A. Srivastava, A. K. Sharma and C. Mayberry, "Characterization of MWCNT VLSI interconnect with self-heating induced scatterings," *Proc. IEEE Computer Society Annual Symposium on VLSI,* pp. 368-373, 2014.

[22] L. Forró and C. Schönenberger, *"Physical Properties of Multi-wall Nanotubes,"* in *Carbon Nanotubes: Synthesis, Structure, Properties and Applications,* M. S.Dresselhaus, G. Dresselhaus and P. Avouris, eds., Berlin: Springer, 2000.

[23] C. Forestiere, A. Maffucci and G. Miano, "On the evaluation of the number of conducting channels in multiwall carbon nanotubes," *IEEE Transactions on Nanotechnology,* vol. 10, no. 6, pp. 1221-1223, 2011.

[24] E. Pop, D. Mann, J. Cao, Q. Wang, K. Goodson and H. Dai, "Negative differential conductance and hot phonons in suspended nanotube molecular wires," *Physical Review Letters,* vol. 95, no. 15, pp. 155505, 10/07/, 2005.

[25] H. Hayashi, T. Ikuta, T. Nishiyama and K. Takahashi, "Enhanced anisotropic heat conduction in multi-walled carbon nanotubes," *Journal of Applied Physics,* vol. 113, no. 1, Jan, 2013.

[26] A. A. Bhatti, "A computer based method for computing the n-dimensional generalized abcd parameter matrices of n-dimensional systems with distributed parameters," Proc. *22nd Southeastern Symposium on System Theory (SSST) Conference,* pp. 590–593, 1990.

A Novel True Random Number Generator Design Leveraging Emerging Memristor Technology

Yandan Wang[1], Wei Wen[1], Miao Hu[2], Hai Li[1]

[1]Dept. of Electrical & Computer Engineering, University of Pittsburgh, Pittsburgh, PA, 15261, USA
[2]Hewlett-Packard Laboratories, Palo Alto, CA, 94304, USA

wangyandan418@gmail.com,   wew57@pitt.edu,   miaozxc@gmail.com,   HAL66@pitt.edu

ABSTRACT

Memristor, the fourth basic circuit element, demonstrates obvious stochastic behaviors in both the static resistance states and the dynamic switching. In this work, a novel *memristor-based true random number generator* (MTRNG) is presented which leverages the stochastic property when switching a device between its binary states. Compared to conventional random number generators that require amplifiers or comparators with high complexity, the use of memristors significantly reduces the design cost: a basic MTRNG consists of only one memristor, six transistors, and one D Flip-flop. To maximize the entropy of the random bit generation, we further enhanced the design to a 2-branch scheme which can provide a uniform bit distribution. Our simulation results show that the proposed MTRNGs offer high operating speed and low power consumption: the reading clocks of the basic 1-branch and the enhanced 2-branch schemes can reach at 1.05GHz and 0.96GHz with power assumptions of 31.1μW and 80.3μW, respectively. Moreover, the zero-versus-one distributions and sampling rates of MTRNGs can be flexibly reconfigured by modulating the width and amplitude of the programming pulse applied on a memristor and therefore adjusting its switching probability between ON and OFF states.

Categories and Subject Descriptors

B.7.1 [**Integrated Circuits**]: Types and Design Styles–*VLSI (very large scale integration)*.

Keywords

Memristor; random number generator; stochastic switching.

1. INTRODUCTION

Random number generators (RNGs) are broadly used in various systems and applications where unpredictable data are required, such as communication systems, statistical sampling, computer simulation, and cryptography systems [1]. There are two types of typical RNG designs, *pseudo random number generator* (PRNG) and *true random number generator* (TRNG). PRNG generates a sequence of numbers by injecting an initial seed to a given computing algorithm. Because the initial seed is deterministic, the properties (correlation, probability distribution, *etc.*) of these numbers can only be an approximation of true randomness, that is, the number sequence is *pseudo* random. TRNG, instead, usually leverages unpredictable physical phenomenon, such as thermal noise, *random*

GLSVLSI'15, May 20–22, 2015, Pittsburgh, PA, USA.
Copyright 2015 ACM 978-1-4503-3474-7/15/05 …$15.00.
http://dx.doi.org/10.1145/2742060.2742088

telegraph noise (RTN), atmospheric noise, electromagnetic and quantum [2]. Random data plays a crucial role in system protection of many applications where the true stochastic characteristic is highly appreciated.

Thermal noise is an intrinsic noise induced by thermal agitation of charge carriers (usually the electrons) inside an electrical conductor at equilibrium, which occurs regardless of applied voltage. RTN refers to a kind of electronic noise in semiconductors: when applying discrete voltage or current levels on semiconductors, sudden step-like RTN signals can be generated. Traditional thermal-noise-based TRNG usually is composed of a stochastic signal source, multi-level amplifiers, A/D converter and post-processing circuits [3]. Recently, a TRNG based on RTN in *contact resistive random access memory* (CRRAM) was proposed in which the *high- and low-resistance states* (HRS and LRS) of CRRAM are subject to RTN and therefore the resistance fluctuations can be converted to a stream of random bits [4]. Some TRNG designs leveraging the nanotechnologies have also been investigated. For example, Vivoli *et al.* presented a device-independent quantum TRNGs using a photon pair source based on *spontaneous parametric down conversion* (SPDC) which can gain both high entropy and high rate of random bit generation [5]. *Spin dice* is a spintronic-based TRNG that utilizes the stochastic nature of spin-torque switching in a *magnetic tunnel junction* (MTJ) to generate random numbers [6].

Memristors, as emerging two-terminal nonlinear dynamic electronic devices [7], have been extensively studied in recent years. Because of the advantages of good scalability, high endurance and ultra-low power consumption [8], memristors have been applied in non-volatile memory storage, logic implementation and neuromorphic computing systems [9][10][11]. Moreover, the memristive behaviors in various memristive devices have been thoroughly investigated, in which the stochastic processes have been clearly demonstrated [12][13]. For instance, the distribution of static memristances at HRS/LRS can be approximated with a lognormal probability density function, and the cumulative probability of dynamic switching from one static state to the other is also a lognormal function of the applied voltage. The standard deviation of the static stochastic behavior is negligible compared to the large gap between HRS and LRS, making memristor as an ideal component for binary data storage. Due to the big variance of physical materials and the flexible configuration in programming operation, the dynamic switching of memristive devices demonstrates a very large scalability. The state-of-the-art switching performance in real tantalum-oxide based memristors showed the cycling endurances of over 10^{12} cycles and fast switching speed below 10ns [14]. Moreover, the sub-nanosecond switching time has been demonstrated through tantalum-oxide based memristors with durations of 10^5 and 120ps for low- and high-memristance switching, respectively [15].

In this work, we propose a novel *memristor-based true random number generator* (MTRNG) design by leveraging the stochastic behaviors of memristor. By modulating the width and amplitude of programming pulses applied on memristor devices, the zero-ver-sus-one distribution and the sampling rate of bit streams can be flexibly adjusted. More importantly, the adoption of memristor technology effectively simplifies the structure of TRNG, offering a compact, fast and energy-efficient design. To further improve the entropy of random bit streams, we propose to enhance the design by integrating two basic (1-branch) MTRNGs through an XOR gate. The circuit simulations show that the clock of 1-branch and 2-branch designs based on TiO₂ memristors [20][21] can reach at 1.05GHz and 0.96GHz with the power assumptions of 31.1μW and 80.3μW, respectively.

2. PRELIMINARY

2.1 Memristor

As the fourth fundamental component besides resistor, capacitor and inductor, memristor describes the dynamic relationship between charge (q) and flux (φ) [16]. Particularly, it can "remember" the total electric flux flowing through the device and represent it as the memristance (M).

Figure 1 illustrates the structure of a TiO₂ memristor sandwiched between two metal wires. The device consists of two titanium dioxide layers: the doped layer TiO$_{2-x}$ is filled with oxygen vacancies and therefore has a high conductivity; the pure TiO₂ (undoped layer), in contrast, has the character of insulator. While there is a positive bias voltage ($V+$) applying to the device, the oxygen vacancies will be forced into the undoped area and therefore the total resistance (or *memristance*) continuously reduces. On the contrary, a reversed bias voltage ($V-$) will force the vacancies back to its original position and raise the memristance. Without enough external voltage, the oxygen vacancies within the structure remain so as that the memristance maintains [17].

For ease of explanation, we define the following terminologies and variables that will be referred in this paper:

- **Static states** – the state in which the equivalent resistance is high (R_{off}) or low (R_{on}). *OFF state* and *ON state* denote the states of R_{off} and R_{on}, respectively.

- **Dynamic switching** – the process of switching from one static state to the other. *OFF switching* refers to the process switching from *ON* to *OFF*, while *ON switching* corresponds to the opposite operation.

- **Programming pulse** – the voltage pulse applied on the memristor to trigger the dynamic switching process.

2.2 Stochastic Behaviors of Memristors

Stochastic behaviors have been widely observed in metal oxide based memristor devices, including the variations in static states and dynamic switching processes.

- **Static stochastic behavior**: The final resistance value of a memristor during a programming operation is not deterministic but a stochastic variable related to the voltage amplitude and duration of the programming pulse. The randomness of R_{on} and R_{off} is denoted as the static stochastic behavior of memristors. The distributions of R_{on} and R_{off} usually follow the lognormal probability density functions [18][19].

- **Dynamic stochastic behavior** is resulted by means of the complicated stochastic oxide electroforming process during ON/OFF switching [18], in which the successful switching probability monotonically increases along with the increase of the amplitude and/or duration of programming pulse. More specific, the cumulative probability function of a successful switching between R_{on} and R_{off} follows a lognormal distribution [20].

3. METHODOLOGY

In this work, we propose a new *memristor-based true random number generator* (MTRNG) design. The reconfigurable dynamic stochastic behavior of memristors provides a flexible design space for various applications with different sampling rate requirements. Though the memristance value of each programming is not deterministic due to the static stochastic behavior, the stability of the design can still be promised by the large gap between the high and low memristance states. Moreover, we design and customize a 2-branch MTRNG which integrates two pieces of basic 1-branch MTRNGs. Markov chain analysis shows that the 2-branch scheme further maximizes the entropy of the random number sequence. Our work not only presents a novel circuit to generate random number streams but also can be generalized to a statistical methodology for memristor-based design.

3.1 Stochastic Model of TiO₂ Memristor

Because of the static stochastic behavior, the memristor resistance in ON or OFF state is not deterministic but random, even for a single identical device. In a TiO₂ memristor, the distributions of static state resistance R_{on} and R_{off} both can be approximated to the lognormal probability density function (pdf) such as [20]:

$$f_x(x;\mu,\sigma) = \frac{1}{x\sigma\sqrt{2\pi}} \cdot \exp\left(-\frac{(\ln x/\mu)^2}{2\sigma^2}\right), \quad x > 0, \qquad (1)$$

where, μ is the normal mean and σ is the standard deviation of the normal distribution of the initial barrier width of the memristor device. Certainly, the parameters of μ and σ for R_{on} and R_{off} are different. Figure 2 presents the real measurement data of a TiO₂ memristor [21].

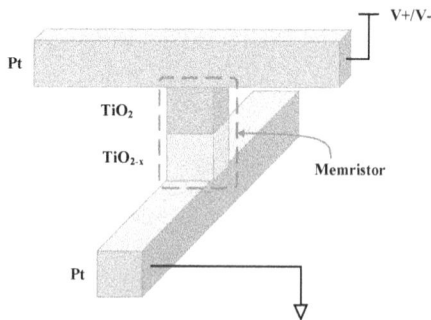

Figure 1. The structure of a TiO₂ memristor

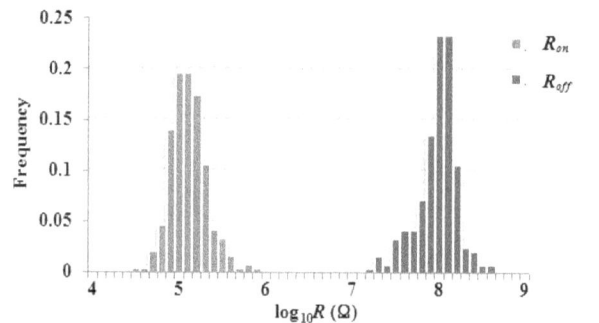

Figure 2. Static stochastic behavior

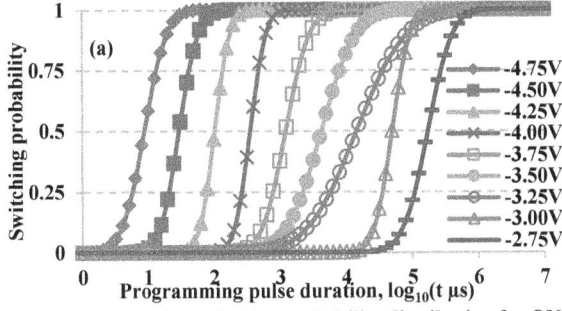

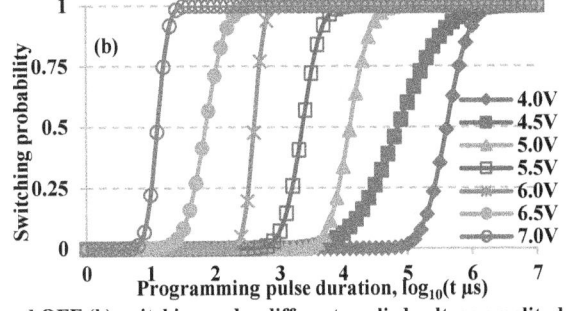

Figure 3. Cumulative switching probability distribution for ON (a) and OFF (b) switching under different applied voltage amplitude

Giving $E[R_{on}]$ and $E[R_{off}]$ as the means of R_{on} and R_{off}, respectively; and their standard deviations are $D[R_{on}]$ and $D[R_{off}]$, respectively. The device demonstrated in Figure 2 has $E[R_{on}] \approx 10^5\Omega$ and $E[R_{off}] \approx 10^8\Omega$. Both $D[R_{on}]$ and $D[R_{off}]$ are more than 2 orders smaller than the gap between the means ($E[R_{off}] - E[R_{on}]$). Such a highly isolated binary characteristic in memristors guarantees an ideal physical mechanism for MTRNG design. Details shall be presented and discussed in Section 4.

The dynamic stochastic behavior refers to the successful switching probability between ON and OFF state. Under an external programming pulse, the switching probability is determined by the voltage amplitude and the pulse width (duration) t. The cumulative distribution can be approximated by lognormal distribution [20]:

$$F(t;\tau,\sigma_t) = \int_0^t \frac{1}{\sqrt{2\pi}\sigma_t T} e^{-\left(\frac{\ln T}{\sqrt{2}\sigma_t}\right)^2} dT = \frac{1}{2} erfc\left(-\frac{\ln t}{\sqrt{2}\tau\sigma_t}\right). \quad (2)$$

Where, τ is the mean of the switching time, which has an exponential dependency on the applied voltage amplitude, while its deviation σ_t only has a weak dependence on the voltage [20]. Figure 3 shows the cumulative switching probability distributions of ON and OFF switching. Both results reveal that increasing the programming duration of a constant-amplitude pulse can increase the switching probability. Moreover, a larger voltage amplitude decreases the required programming duration to reach a given switch probability.

3.2 The MTRNG Design

Our proposed MTRNG design switches between the programming mode and the reading mode to generate the random bit stream. In the programming mode, a programming pulse is applied on the

memristor to trigger a dynamic switching between the ON and OFF states. In the reading mode, the programmed binary resistance is converted to a binary bit. In the design, the selection of the programming pulse amplitude determines the maximal allowable sampling rate of the bit stream. We can control the ratio of the probability of 0's and 1's by modulating the programming duration. Ideally, a uniform distribution of 0/1 bit stream can be obtained by aligning the pulse width to the switching probability of 0.5 under a given pulse voltage (refer Figure 3).

Figure 4 depicts the proposed MTRNG circuit with the following key control and internal signals:

- V_{dc_r}, V_{dc_on} and V_{dc_off} are the DC voltage sources used in reading mode, the ON switching and the OFF switching programming, respectively.

- V_{read} is the control signal to enable the reading mode to detect the state of the memristor.

- V_{p_on} and V_{p_off} are used for program the memristor to ON and OFF states, respectively.

- V_d is the bias voltage representing the state of memristor. It determines the generated output bit of the MTRNG.

- V_g is used to modulate V_d for bit generation.

- *Clk* is the clock signal to control the data capture at D flip-flop.

The sequence of control signals is also illustrated in Figure 4. V_{p_on} and V_{p_off} are turned on alternatively to enable the ON and OFF switching. Under the ideal condition with the sufficient programming voltage and pulse duration, the memristor can always be programmed, that is, the device switches between ON and OFF states. By properly controlling the programming voltage amplitude together with the pulse duration corresponding to the required bit distribution, the switching of the memristor becomes more random. In our design, following every programming period is a read operation enabled by V_{read}. The ON and OFF states of the memristor will be transferred to 1 or 0, respectively, under appropriate V_g setup. Here, a D flip-flop is used to recover distorted binary signal resulted by stochastic memristance values. More details of design configuration and the simulation results shall be conveyed in Section 4.

The simple MTRNG in Figure 4 can be used to generate a stream of random bits. However, the scheme cannot obtain the maximal entropy because the memristor will keep at the ON or OFF state if the previous switching fails. Take the signal sequence in Figure 4 as an example and assume the previous state of the memristor is OFF: if an ON switching triggered by V_{p_on} fails so that the memristor remains as OFF, the following OFF switching initialized by V_{p_off} does not affect the state of the memristor. In such a case, this OFF switching is not a stochastic process.

To improve the entropy of the random bit stream, we further enhance the design. As illustrated in Figure 5, it integrates two basic

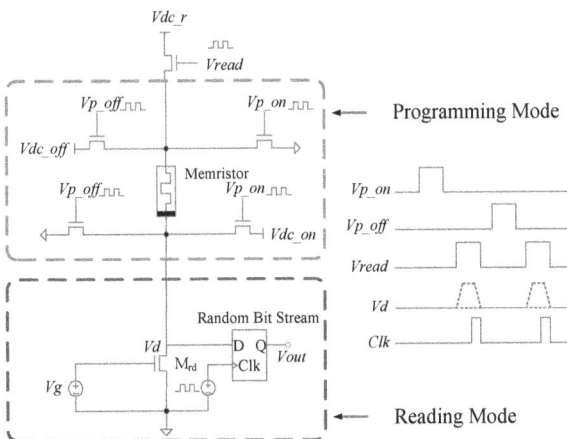

Figure 4. The scheme of the basic 1-branch MTRNG design

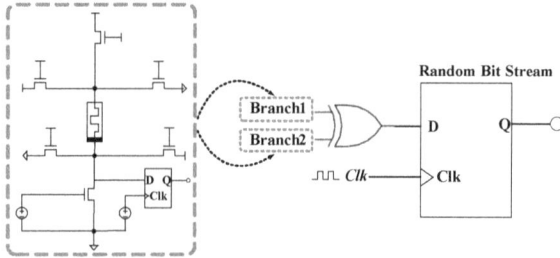

Figure 5. The scheme of the enhanced 2-branch MTRNG design

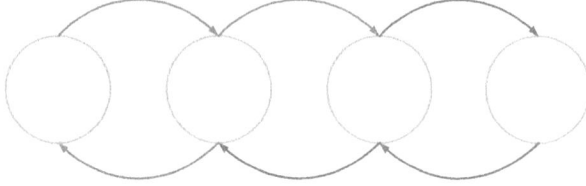

Figure 6. The state transition diagram

(1-branch) MTRNGs through an XOR gate. Because the stochastic switching of one memristor is independent to the other, the entropy of the random bit stream through the XOR function can be maximized under appropriate dynamic switching probability. We name this scheme as 2-branch MTRNG design.

3.3 MTRNG Markov Chain Analysis

Here, we will give a detailed probability analysis for both the basic 1-branch and the enhanced 2-branch MTRNG designs based on the Markov chain analysis. The variables used include:

- $P_{even}(i)$ – the probability of an even bit in the random bit stream as logic state $i \in (0,1)$ after ON switching operation.

- $P_{odd}(i)$ – the probability of an odd bit in the random bit stream as logic state $i \in (0,1)$ after OFF switching operation.

- P_{on} – the ON switching probability to which the V_{p_on} cumulates, which is also the successful switching probability from OFF to ON state shown in Figure 3(a).

- P_{off} – the OFF switching probability to which the V_{p_off} cumulates. It is equivalent to the successful switching probability from ON to OFF state shown in Figure 3(b).

- S – the state space of a bit in the random stream, $S = \{S_{mn} \mid m=0,1$ and $n=0,1\}$. m and n denote the position and value of the bit, respectively. The bit is the even-th (odd-th) one in the stream if $m=0$ ($m=1$) and its value is n. $n=0$ ($n=1$) corresponds to R_{off} (R_{on}).

- $\mathbf{P}_{even}^{(2)}$ – the two-step transition matrix between two sequential even bits.

- $\mathbf{P}_{odd}^{(2)}$ – the two-step transition matrix between two sequential odd bits.

- $P_{2\text{-}branch}(i)$ – the probability distribution of the output of 2-branch MTRNG ($i=0,1$).

Figure 6 summarizes the state transition diagram. As aforementioned in Section 3.2, the transition probability of 1 exists because of the invalid ON (OFF) switching operation on ON (OFF) state.

The stochastic process of generating the random bit stream is a first-order Markov chain. To simplify the Markov chain analysis, we separately calculate the 0/1 probability distributions of the even and the odd bits, such as:

$$\mathbf{P}_{even}^{(2)} = \begin{vmatrix} 1 & 0 \\ P_{off} & 1-P_{off} \end{vmatrix} \cdot \begin{vmatrix} 1-P_{on} & P_{on} \\ 0 & 1 \end{vmatrix}, \text{ and} \qquad (3)$$

$$\mathbf{P}_{odd}^{(2)} = \begin{vmatrix} 1-P_{on} & P_{on} \\ 0 & 1 \end{vmatrix} \cdot \begin{vmatrix} 1 & 0 \\ P_{off} & 1-P_{off} \end{vmatrix}. \qquad (4)$$

Given $0 < P_{off} < 1$ and $0 < P_{on} < 1$, every element in $\mathbf{P}_{even}^{(2)}$ and $\mathbf{P}_{odd}^{(2)}$ is larger than 0. As such, the Markov chains with the transition matrixes of Eqs. (3) and (4) have stationary distributions $\boldsymbol{\pi}_{even}$ and $\boldsymbol{\pi}_{odd}$, denoting the stationary 0/1 distributions of even and odd bits, respectively. They satisfy

$$\begin{cases} \boldsymbol{\pi}_{even} \cdot \mathbf{P}_{even}^{(2)} = \boldsymbol{\pi}_{even} = \left[P_{even}(0), P_{even}(1) \right] \\ \boldsymbol{\pi}_{odd} \cdot \mathbf{P}_{odd}^{(2)} = \boldsymbol{\pi}_{odd} = \left[P_{odd}(0), P_{odd}(1) \right] \end{cases}. \qquad (5)$$

Given P_{on} and P_{off}, the solution of the equation set is

$$\begin{cases} P_{even}(0) = 1 - P_{even}(1) = \dfrac{P_{off} - P_{on} \cdot P_{off}}{P_{on} + P_{off} - P_{on} \cdot P_{off}} \\ P_{odd}(0) = 1 - P_{odd}(1) = \dfrac{P_{off}}{P_{on} + P_{off} - P_{on} \cdot P_{off}} \end{cases}. \qquad (6)$$

To maximize the Shannon entropy of random bit stream generated by MTRNG, the probability should be uniformly distributed:

$$P_{odd}(0) = P_{odd}(1) = P_{even}(0) = P_{even}(1) = 0.5. \qquad (7)$$

Note that Eq. (7) cannot be a solution of Eq. (6), indicating that the basic 1-branch MTRNG design cannot generate an entropy-maximized random number sequence. Only skewed probability distribution can be produced where $P_{even}(i) \neq 0.5$ or $P_{odd}(i) \neq 0.5$.

The enhanced 2-branch MTRNG design, in contrast, can obtain the maximized entropy by appropriately setting P_{on} and P_{off}, e.g., aligning V_{p_off} of a branch to V_{p_on} of the other branch and setting $P_{even}(0) = P_{even}(1) = 0.5$, uniformly distributed $P_{2\text{-}branch}(i)$ can be satisfied because

$$\begin{cases} P_{2\text{-}branch}(0) = P_{even}(0) \cdot P_{odd}(0) + P_{even}(1) \cdot P_{odd}(1) = 0.5 \\ P_{2\text{-}branch}(1) = P_{even}(0) \cdot P_{odd}(1) + P_{even}(1) \cdot P_{odd}(0) = 0.5 \end{cases}. \qquad (8)$$

In this case,

$$P_{on} = \frac{P_{off}}{1 + P_{off}}. \qquad (9)$$

P_{off} and P_{on} shall be carefully selected for the enhanced 2-branch design. From the one hand, smaller P_{off} and P_{on} are more preferable because the circuit can operate under a faster sampling rate. From the other hand, we tend to avoid the steep slope of switching probability curve because a tiny fluctuation of programming duration can result in a large drift of the switch probability.

4. EXPERIMENT

We evaluate the proposed MTRNG designs through circuit simulations in Cadence Virtuoso environment. The 180nm CMOS technology and the memristor device parameters in [20] were adopted. Here, we first discuss the design configuration followed by the simulation of MTRNGs and the probability distribution of random bits. At the end, the speed and power consumptions of the proposed designs are evaluated and analyzed.

4.1 The Selection of Gate Voltage V_g

The gate voltage of transistor M_{rd} (V_g) in Figure 4 is a crucial parameter to modulate the bias voltage V_d and the finally output V_{out}. As aforementioned in Section 3.1, the distributions of R_{on} and R_{off} are approximated to the lognormal probability density function. Based on the real measured resistance distribution of a TiO$_2$

memristor in Figure 2, the means of the high and low resistance states, $E[R_{on}]$ and $E[R_{off}]$, are about $10^5\Omega$ and $10^8\Omega$, respectively. Even considering the worst situation where R_{on} is $10^6\Omega$ and R_{off} is $10^7\Omega$, R_{off} is still one order higher than R_{on}. Comparing the difference between $E[R_{on}]$ and $E[R_{off}]$ and the noise margin of CMOS transistors, we are able to map the static memristor resistances to binary code by constraining V_g within a critical range.

We start the evaluation with the typical condition when $R_{on}=10^5\Omega$ and $R_{off}=10^8\Omega$. To find the critical range for V_g, the memristor resistance is fixed and V_g is scanned from 0V to $V_{dc}=1.8$V. The simulation results in Figure 7(a) show that V_{out} falls from high to low when V_g is higher than a critical voltage and therefore the equivalent resistance of M_{rd} is smaller than a threshold. More specific, under the typical situation when $R_{off}=10^8\Omega$, V_{out} drops to low as V_g approaches to 0.34V. For $R_{on}=10^5\Omega$, the critical falling point is around 0.66V. Thus, the ON and OFF states of memristor can be respectively mapped to HIGH and LOW of V_{out} if setting V_g within the range from 0.34V to 0.66V.

We also verify the circuit stability under the worst scenario condition when $R_{on}=10^6\Omega$ and $R_{off}=10^7\Omega$. Figure 7(b) presents the simulation results. A similar trend as Figure 7(a) can be observed except that the allowable range of V_g reduces to 0.43V ~ 0.53V. The narrower critical range indicates the degraded circuit stability. Even though, the inclusion relationship of the critical ranges in Figure 7(a) and (b) shows that V_g in the intersection set can guarantee our MTRNG functions properly even under the worst scenario condition. Based on the analysis, we set the gate voltage V_g to 0.5V in the following simulations.

4.2 MTRNG Simulation

Figure 8 and Figure 9 show the simulation results of the basic 1-branch MTRNG at the typical ($R_{on}=10^5\Omega$ and $R_{off}=10^8\Omega$) and the worst-case ($R_{on}=10^6\Omega$ and $R_{off}=10^7\Omega$) conditions, respectively. The simulations show that stochastic binary states of memristor can be successfully converted to random bit stream. Even in the extreme situation when R_{off} is very close to R_{on}, the basic 1-branch MTRNG design still functions properly. Figure 10 shows the simulation result of the enhanced 2-branch MTRNG, the output random bit

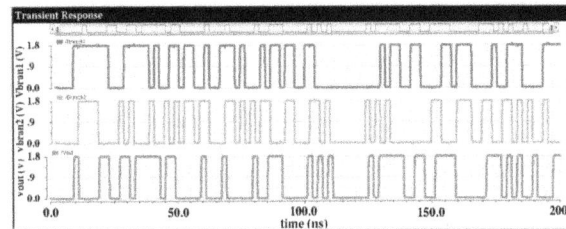

Figure 8. Simulation of 1-branch MTRNG ($R_{on}=10^5\Omega$ and $R_{off}=10^8\Omega$)

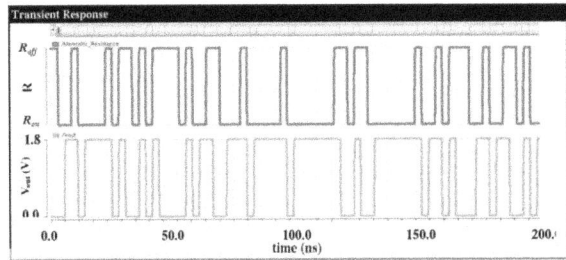

Figure 9. Simulation of 1-branch MTRNG ($R_{on}=10^6\Omega$ and $R_{off}=10^7\Omega$)

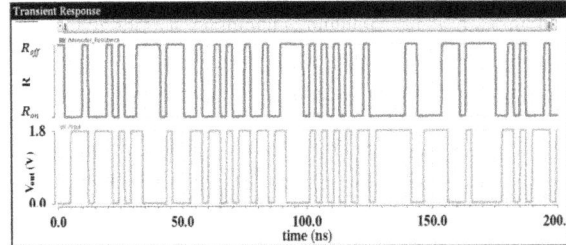

Figure 10. Simulation of 2-branch MTRNG

stream of which is dependent on the signals of two bit sequences generated by the two 1-branch MTRNGs.

To analyze the probability distribution of the 1-branch and 2-branch MTRNG designs, the memristor ON switching and OFF switching probabilities are set to $P_{on}=1/4$ and $P_{off}=1/3$, respectively. To ease the explanation, we show the probability distributions of the first 100 bits generated by 1-branch and 2-branch MTRNG in Figure 11. Here, each point represents the probability of logic 1 at the bit. Simulation shows that both MTRNG schemes rapidly converge towards their stationary distributions after only a few steps because of the ergodicity of the Markov chain. The fast convergence of the Markov chain guarantees that the bit probability approaches to the desired distributions quickly.

For the 1-branch MTRNG design, the probability distribution of the odd-*th* bits is non-uniform. The situation can be solved by passing two bit streams of the 1-branch design through an XOR gate. Consistent to the theoretical analysis in Section 3.3, a uniformly distributed random bit stream can be generated via the 2-branch MTRNG design.

4.3 The Design Evaluation

Traditional thermal noise based TRNGs usually require multi-stage voltage amplifiers to magnify the weak signals, resulting in high design complexity and cost [21]. The latest random telegraph noise (RTN) based TRNG requires an analogy comparator to convert RTN to binary code [4]. For the reason, its sampling rate is relatively low at only 11.4Hz. Thus, its applications are limited to low-speed systems such as encryption system [4].

Amplifier is not necessary in our MTRNGs for the large bias voltage V_d. The design is realized in a much simpler form: the basic

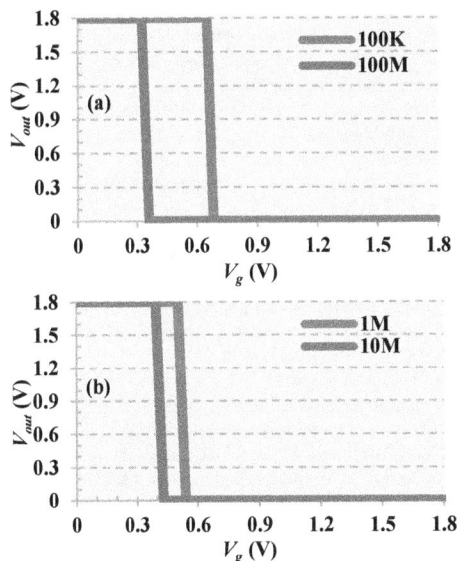

Figure 7. V_g vs. V_{out}: (a) under the means of the high and low resistance states, as $R_{on}=10^5\Omega$ and $R_{off}=10^8\Omega$; (b) at the worst condition when $R_{on}=10^6\Omega$ and $R_{off}=10^7\Omega$.

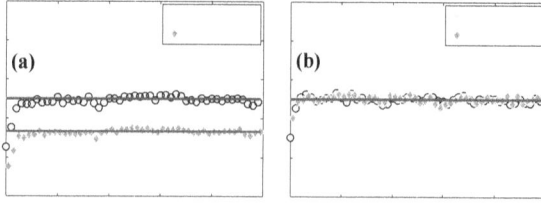

Figure 11. The probability distribution of random bit in the stream generated by 1-branch (a) and 2-branch (b) MTRNG

Table I. Power Consumption of MTRNGs.

	HRS (μW)	LRS (μW)	Average (μW)
1-branch	16.5	45.6	31.1
2-branch	44.6	115.9	80.3

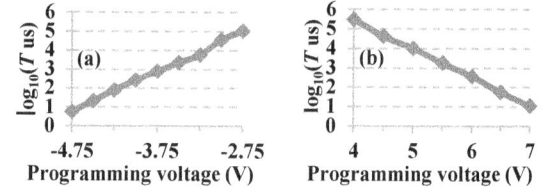

Figure 12. Dependence of programming voltage for random bit stream sampling period in ON switching (a) and OFF switching (b)

1-branch MTRNG consists of only one memristor, six access control transistors, and one D flip-flop. Determined by the memristor programming voltage and duration, the proposed MTRNGs can operate under a large frequency range varying from Hz to GHz. Our simulations show that the minimal reading periods of the 1-branch and 2-branch designs are only 0.95ns (1.05GHz) and 1.04ns (0.96GHz), respectively. Moreover, Figure 12 shows the relationship between the random bit stream sampling period T and the voltage of programming pulse for the 2-branch MTRNG when setting P_{off}=1/3 and P_{on}=1/4. The log function of sampling period approximately linearly decreases with the voltage amplitude.

The detailed power consumption results of the 1-branch and 2-branch MTRNGs are summarized in Table I. Benefiting from the simple structure and the ultra-low energy characteristic of memristors, MTRNGs obtain low power consumption of tens of μW regardless of 1-branch or 2-branch design styles.

5. CONCLUSION

A *memristor-based true random number generator* (MTRNG), which leverages the stochastic behavior of memristors and converts the programmed resistances to random binary bit stream, has been proposed in this work. Besides the basic 1-branch MTRNG, we also enhance the design to 2-branch scheme which can obtain the identical generating probability of bit 1 and bit 0, promising the maximum entropy of random number generation. Sampling rate of our designs can reach at GHz with minimum power consumption of 31.1μW. The proposed MTRNG designs exhibit characteristics of simple structure, compact area, high frequency, low power and flexible configurability.

ACKNOWLEDGEMENT

This work was supported in part by DARPA D13AP00042, NSF EECS-1311747 and NSF CNS-1342566. Any opinions, findings and conclusions or recommendations expressed in this material are those of the authors and do not necessarily reflect the views of DARPA, NSF, or their contractors.

REFERENCES

[1] T. L. Blackwell, "Applications of randomness in system performance measurement," Citeseer, 1998.

[2] R. S. DeBellis, R. M. Smith Sr, and P. C.-C. Yeh, "Pseudo random number generator," US Patents US6061703, 2000.

[3] S. Fujita, K. Uchida, S. Yasuda, R. Ohba, H. Nozaki, and T. Tanamoto, "Si nanodevices for random number generating circuits for cryptographic security," in *2004 IEEE International Solid-State Circuits Conference (ISSCC)*, 2004, pp. 294-295.

[4] C.-Y. Huang, W. C. Shen, Y.-H. Tseng, Y.-C. King, and C.-J. Lin, "A contact-resistive random-access-memory-based true random number generator," *IEEE Electron Device Letters*, vol. 33, pp. 1108-1110, 2012.

[5] V. C. Vivoli, P. Sekatski, J. D. Bancal, C. C. W. Lim, A. Martin, R. T. Thew, *et al.*, "Device-independent quantum random number generator with a photon pair source," *arXiv preprint arXiv:1409.8051*, 2014.

[6] A. Fukushima, T. Seki, K. Yakushiji, H. Kubota, H. Imamura, S. Yuasa, *et al.*, "Spin dice: A scalable truly random number generator based on spintronics," *Applied Physics Express*, vol. 7, p. 083001, 2014.

[7] Y. Yang and W. Lu, "Nanoscale resistive switching devices: mechanisms and modeling," *Nanoscale*, vol. 5, pp. 10076-10092, 2013.

[8] S. Gaba, P. Knag, Z. Zhang, and W. Lu, "Memristive devices for stochastic computing," in *2014 IEEE International Symposium on Circuits and Systems (ISCAS)*, 2014, pp. 2592-2595.

[9] S. Kim, S. Choi, and W. Lu, "Comprehensive Physical Model of Dynamic Resistive Switching in an Oxide Memristor," *ACS nano*, vol. 8, pp. 2369-2376, 2014.

[10] L. Chua, "Resistance switching memories are memristors," *Applied Physics A*, vol. 102, pp. 765-783, 2011.

[11] M. Hu, H. Li, Y. Chen, Q. Wu, G. Rose, and W. Linderman, "Memristor Crossbar Based Neuromorphic Computing System: A Case Study," *IEEE Transactions on Neural Network and Learning System (TNNLS)*, vol. 25, no 10, pp. 1864-1878, Oct. 2014.

[12] A. F. Vincent, J. Larroque, W. S. Zhao, N. B. Romdhane, O. Bichler, C. Gamrat, *et al.*, "Spin-transfer torque magnetic memory as a stochastic memristive synapse," in *Circuits and Systems (ISCAS), 2014 IEEE International Symposium on*, 2014, pp. 1074-1077.

[13] S. Gaba, P. Sheridan, J. Zhou, S. Choi, and W. Lu, "Stochastic memristive devices for computing and neuromorphic applications," *Nanoscale*, vol. 5, pp. 5872-5878, 2013.

[14] M.-J. Lee, C. B. Lee, D. Lee, S. R. Lee, M. Chang, J. H. Hur, *et al.*, "A fast, high-endurance and scalable non-volatile memory device made from asymmetric Ta_2O_{5-x}/TaO_{2-x} bilayer structures," *Nature materials*, vol. 10, pp. 625-630, 2011.

[15] A. C. Torrezan, J. P. Strachan, G. Medeiros-Ribeiro, and R. S. Williams, "Sub-nanosecond switching of a tantalum oxide memristor," *Nanotechnology*, vol. 22, p. 485203, 2011.

[16] L. O. Chua, "Memristor-the missing circuit element," *IEEE Transactions on Circuit Theory*, vol. 18, pp. 507-519, 1971.

[17] R. Williams, "How we found the missing memristor," *IEEE Spectrum*, vol. 45, no. 12, pp. 28-35, 2008.

[18] M. Hu, Y. Wang, Q. Qiu, Y. Chen, and H. Li, "The stochastic modeling of TiO2 memristor and its usage in neuromorphic system design," in *Asia and South Pacific Design Automation Conference (ASP-DAC)*, 2014, pp. 831-836.

[19] S. Yu, B. Gao, Z. Fang, H. Yu, J. Kang, and H.-S. P. Wong, "Stochastic learning in oxide binary synaptic device for neuromorphic computing," *Frontiers in neuroscience*, vol. 7, 2013.

[20] G. Medeiros-Ribeiro, F. Perner, R. Carter, H. Abdalla, M. D. Pickett, and R. S. Williams, "Lognormal switching times for titanium dioxide bipolar memristors: origin and resolution," *Nanotechnology*, vol. 22, p. 095702, 2011.

[21] W. Yi, et al., "Feedback write scheme for memristive switching devices," *Appl. Phys. A*, vol.102, pp.973-982, 2011.

TFET-based Operational Transconductance Amplifier Design for CNN Systems

Qiuwen Lou*, Indranil Palit*, Andras Horvath**, X. Sharon Hu*, Michael Niemier*, Joseph Nahas*

*Department of Computer Science and Engineering University of Notre Dame Notre Dame, IN 46556, USA
**Faculty of Information Technology, Pazmany Peter Catholic University, Budapest, Hungary
*{qlou,ipalit,shu,mniemier,jnahas}@nd.edu, horvath.andras@itk.ppke.hu

ABSTRACT

A Cellular Neural Network (CNN) is a powerful processor that can significantly improve the performance of spatio-temporal applications such as pattern recognition, image processing, motion detection, when compared to the more traditional von Neumann architecture. In this paper, we show how tunneling field effect transistors (TFETs) can be utilized to enhance the performance of CNNs. Specifically, power consumption of TFET-based CNNs can be significantly lower when compared to MOSFET-based CNNs due to improved voltage controlled current sources (VCCSs) - an important component in CNN systems. We demonstrate that CNNs can benefit from low power conventional linear VCCSs implemented via TFETs. We also show that T-FETs can be useful to realize non-linear VCCSs, which are either not possible or exhibit degraded performance when implemented via CMOS. Such non-linear VCCSs help to improve the performance of certain CNN operations (e.g., global maximum/minimum). We provide two case studies – image contrast enhancement and maximum row selection – that illustrate the benefits of non-linear VCCSs (e.g., reduced computation time, energy dissipation, etc.) when compared to CMOS-based approaches.

Categories and Subject Descriptors

B.7.1 [**Hardware**]: Integrated Circuits—*VLSI*

Keywords

tunnel-FET; operational transconductance amplifier; cellular neural/nonlinear network

1. INTRODUCTION

It is generally accepted that CMOS scaling and its performance gains have either slowed down or stopped. Further scalibility of von Neumann architectures based on MOSFET technology are power constrained and do not offer significant performance improvements[1]. Moreover, data centric computation, e.g., the need to process and analyze large amounts of imagery, demands alternative computational models. As such, many new architectures are being investigated - that often exploits new emerging device technologies - to meet the information processing needs [2, 3, 5, 4].

A Cellular Nonlinear/Neural Network (CNN) is an analog computing architecture [6] that could be well suited for emerging information processing tasks. In a CNN, identical processing units (called cells) process analog information in concurrent manner. Interconnection between cells is typically local (i.e., nearest neighbor) and space-invariant [7]. For spatio-temporal applications, CNNs can offer vastly superior performance and power efficiency when compared to conventional von Neumann architectures. However, there are many ways in which both the performance and implementation complexity of a CNN system could be improved. For example, in a CNN, the task to be performed is typically specified by tuning the feedforward or feedback weights from cell-to-cell. This is typically accomplished via a linear voltage controlled current source (VCCS) when the feedback and feedforward relationships are linear. That said, theory suggests that by employing non-linear relationships between cells, it is possible to perform certain computational tasks much more efficiently [8]. Furthermore, some applications simply require nonlinear relationship [8]. Unfortunately, the circuitry required to realize non-linear template operations can become quite complex - ultimately overwhelming any benefit of a nonlinear approach. Moreover, VCCSs regardless of linear or nonlinear types, can dominate both the area and power of a CNN system. As such, any way to mitigate VCCS should have a more significant impact on system-level power and performance.

Previous research [9, 10, 11, 12] have shown positive results by utilizing emerging devices in multiple CNN contexts. Specifically, [9] shows TFETs can be utilized as non-linear resistive element in CNNs to improve power efficiency without sacrificing performance. [10] further uses TFETs to construct circuits to realize ternary outputs.

In this paper, we investigate the use of TFETs: (a) to realize nonlinear template operation in an efficient manner, and (b) to reduce VCCS overhead in general. We show that TFETs can improve both power efficiency and performance of CNNs. More specifically, we first present a TFET-based VCCS designs, compare its performance, power, area, efficiency to a CMOS equivalent. Notably, the TFET-based VCCS exhibits 1.5X power improvement. We next discuss how TFET-based VCCSs can enable non-linear template operations. As an initial case study, we show how we can use said hardware to perform several image pre-processing functions - specifically "globalmax" and "globalmin" operations (i.e., finding the pixel with the highest or lowest intensities).

GLSVLSI'15 May 20–22, 2015, Pittsburgh, PA, USA.
Copyright © 2015 ACM 978-1-4503-3474-7/15/05 ...$15.00.
http://dx.doi.org/10.1145/2742060.2742089

We also use CMOS to build circuits with similar functions, and compare with TFET-based designs. Lastly, we show how specific non-linear operators can be employed to solve large scale problems. As initial examples, we consider an image contrast enhancement problem and a maximum row selection problem (i.e., determining which row of an input image has the highest number of black pixels). Notably, for both the globalmax/globalmin and maximum row selection problems, improvements of up to 2.5X and 6X in energy dissipation, respectively, are observed for TFET-based non-linear solution when compared to a CMOS-based equivalent or TFET-based linear solution.

2. BACKGROUND
2.1 Conventional CNN

The single-layer, spatially invariant CNN architecture [6] is an $M \times N$ array (Fig. 1(a)) of identical cells, where each cell, C_{ij}, $(i,j) \in \{1, ..., M\} \times \{1, ..., N\}$, has identical connections with all the adjacent cells in a predefined neighborhood, $N_r(i,j)$ of radius r. The size of the neighborhood is $m = (2r + 1)^2$, where r is a positive integer. A conventional CNN cell (Fig. 1(b)) consists of one resistor, one capacitor, $2m$ linear VCCSs, one fixed current source, and one specific type of non-linear voltage controlled voltage source. The nodal voltages, u_{ij}, x_{ij}, and y_{ij}, correspond to the input, state, and output of a given cell C_{ij}, respectively. The input and output voltages of the each neighbor contribute a feedback, and a feedforward current to a given cell via the VCCSs. The dynamics of the CNN can be expressed by a system of $M \times N$ ordinary differential equations (ODEs), each of which is simply the Kirchhoffâ㥎Žs Current Law (KCL) at the state nodes of the corresponding cells per Eq. 1. To ensure fixed binary output levels, a conventional CNN cell typically employs a non-linear sigmoid-like transfer function [6] at the output.

$$C\frac{dx_{ij}(t)}{dt} = -\frac{x_{ij}(t)}{R} + \sum_{C_{kl} \in N_r(i,j)} a_{ij,kl} y_{kl}(t)$$
$$+ \sum_{C_{kl} \in N_r(i,j)} b_{ij,kl} u_{kl} + Z \qquad (1)$$

The parameters $a_{ij,kl}$, and $b_{ij,kl}$ act as weights for the feedback and feedforward currents from cell C_{kl} to cell C_{ij}. Due to their space invariant nature, these parameters are denoted by two $(2r + 1) \times (2r + 1)$ matrices (i.e., 3×3 when $r = 1$), namely the feedback template A and the feedforward template B. The fixed bias current, Z, provides a mechanism to adjust the total current flowing into the cell, and thus enhances design flexibility. By carefully selecting the values of the A and B templates (as well as Z). A CNN can solve a wide range of image processing problems or more general "binary classification" problems. (Here we call a series of successfully applied template operations as a "program.")

The VCCSs can be realized via various analog circuits such as an inverter, a Gilbert multiplier, an operational transconductance amplifier (OTA), etc[13, 14, 15]. OTAs are particularly interesting as they provide a large linear range for voltage to current conversion. OTAs can also implement a wide range of transconductances allowing for different CNN templates (i.e., applications) to be executed on a given CNN hardware via reprogramming. However, OTA's power consumption is a bottleneck in CNN.

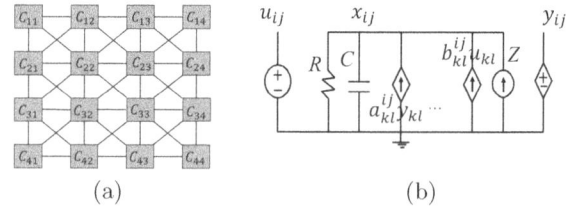

Figure 1: (a) CNN architecture, (b) circuitry in CNN cell.

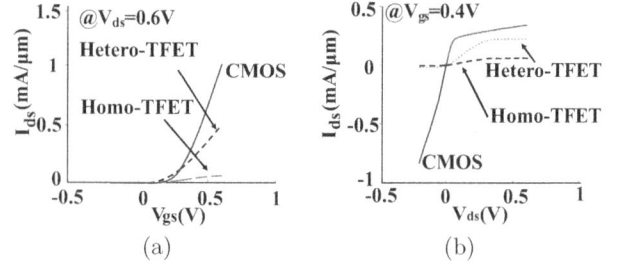

Figure 2: (a) I_d versus V_{gs}, (b) I_d versus V_{gs}.

2.2 TFET characteristics

TFET is a beyond-CMOS device that exhibits sub-threshold swing below 60mV/dec and can operate at very low voltages [17, 16]. TFET shows strong promises for ultra-low power applications. Previous research has demonstrated the use of TFETs to efficiently design logic circuit [18] and analog circuits such as DRAM, amplifier, ADC, [19, 20]. Furthermore, TFETs conduct current through band-to-band tunneling which has very weak sensitivity to temperature variation [17]. As a result, their operations are robust in the presence of thermal noise – an important design consideration for analog circuits. TFETs also demonstrate small drain currents when $V_{ds} < 0$, which is helpful for realizing non-linear functionality (see Sec. 4).

In this work, we consider two III-V TFET devices: InAs homojunction TFET (HomTFET) and GaSb-InAs heterojunction TFET (HetTFET) [21, 22]. Characteristics of the two TFET devices are shown in Fig. 2. More detailed device characteristics are discussed in [19]. In summary, the model for HomTFET has a larger effective I-V characteristic range, while the data from HetTFET demonstrates a better steep slope characteristic with smaller parasitic capacitance.

2.3 Global maximum and Global minimum Problems

Here we briefly introduce globalmax and globalmin functions, and its realization by nonlinear CNN templates. These two functions aim to find the pixels with maximum and minimum intensities in the image, respectively. In image processing, globalmax and globalmin help to expand dynamic range expansion, which is crucial in some applications. For example, histogram stretching at the sensor level is essential in many modern cameras. Low power and small size are required for this module. Other applications include that in newspaper printing where, any image should map to a gray scale image, or in image watermarking where, the dynamic range should be found before making watermark [23].

In the CNN context, these problems can be defined as propagating types. The pixel with maximum or minimum density propagates to all the pixels. Then, by arbitrarily selecting an image pixel, we can find the global maximum or minimum value. With linear CNN templates, the prob-

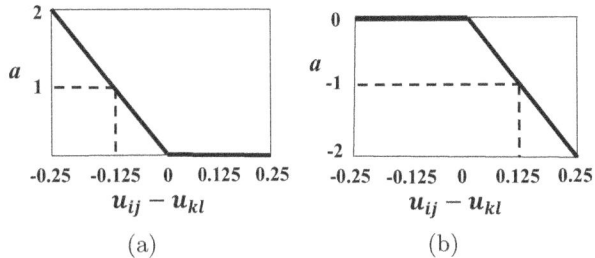

Figure 3: Nonlinear templates for (a) global maximum, (b) global minimum problem.

lems can be solved in multiple steps. Each pixel needs to be compared with all its neighboring pixels, then an AND operation is required to identify the local maximum/minimum pixel. In total, the whole computation requires 15 steps. To reduce the computation steps for these problems, [8] investigates nonlinear templates. Their solution requires a single step to find the local maximum/minimum pixel. The corresponding non-linear templates for global maximum and global minimum are as follows:

$$A = \begin{pmatrix} a & a & a \\ a & 1 & a \\ a & a & a \end{pmatrix}, B = \begin{pmatrix} 0 & 0 & 0 \\ 0 & 0 & 0 \\ 0 & 0 & 0 \end{pmatrix}, Z = 0 \quad (2)$$

The non-linear function, a is shown in Fig. 3. u_{ij} and u_{kl} represents the state voltage of current cell ij, and its neighbor cell kl, respectively. Note that a is not a fixed template value unlike in traditional CNN. For a given cell, the value of a changes non-linearly as a function of how different its state voltage is from that of a neighbor. Thus, when the intensity of any neighboring cell's state is larger than that of a given cell, the corresponding VCCS begins to charge the capacitor of the given cell to raise its state voltage.

3. LINEAR OTA IMPLEMENTATION

In this section, we propose a TFET-based linear OTA, and demonstrate its performance and power benefits compared to CMOS-based OTA. The schematics of the TFET-based and CMOS-based OTAs are shown in Fig. 4 (a) and (b), respectively. Previous research has proposed a different TFET-based OTA design with TFET working in subthreshold region [15]. That circuit demonstrates linearity for a narrow input range. In the proposed OTA, TFETs are in saturation region. Thus the circuit is more suitable for CNN implementation due to its larger linear range and changeable G_m.

The circuit schematics for OTAs based on both HomTFET and HetTFET are the same (Fig. 4(a)). In the differential pair, one input, V_{in}, connects to signals from neighboring cells, reflecting the coupling. And the other input, V_{ref}, of the differential pair connects to a fixed bias voltage. There is a resistor acting as source degeneration to widen the input linear range and stabilize transconductance.

To evaluate performance and power fairly, we use the technology with the same minimum gate length for both the CMOS and TFET devices. The key parameters of the three circuits are summarized in Table 1. A scale parameter, M, is introduced here. By tuning M, the transconductance, G_m of the circuit can be scaled to meet different requirements. HetTFET has a steeper slope than other two devices, making the W/L smaller compared with the other two. To

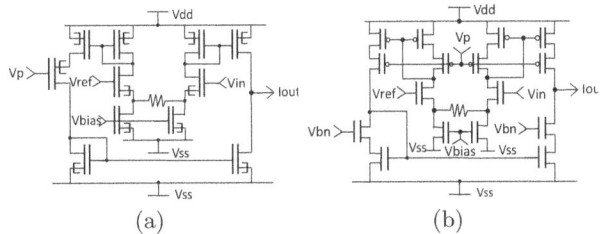

Figure 4: (a) TFET-based linear OTA, (b) CMOS-based linear OTA.

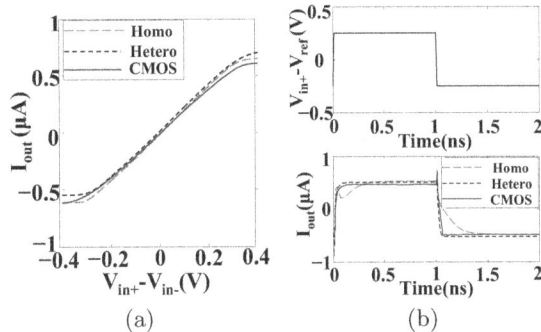

Figure 5: (a) DC characteristic of OTA, (b) Transient waveform of OTA.

benchmark the OTA, a target $G_m = 200\mu A/V$ is set (i.e., M=100). The DC characteristics and transient waveforms for the OTAs are shown in Fig. 5 (a) and (b), respectively. All three circuits demonstrate similar DC characteristics (Fig. 5(a)) because of their same target G_m value. As shown in Fig. 5(b), the HomTFET based OTA is slower than the other two.

We further study the power and performance of the three types of OTAs. The corresponding power and performance results obtained from HSPICE simulation are given in Table 2. As seen from Row 4 in Table 2, both TFET OTAs dissipate less power than the CMOS one. The difference in power is largely due to lower supply voltage, which attributes to TFET's steep slope characteristic. The performances of the CMOS and Hetero-TFET OTA, measured by delay and rise time (Row 5 and Row 6 in Table 2), are almost the same. They are much smaller than HomTFET OTA. In summary, HomTFET OTA has the benefit in both power and performance, while Hetero-TFET and CMOS OTAs have advantage in power and performance, respectively.

4. NONLINEAR OTA IMPLEMENTATION

We now introduce the circuits based on both TFET and CMOS nonlinear OTA in the CNN context to realize the globalmax and globalmin function. The TFET model used here is the HomTFET since it has a larger efficient range. We first show how to implement circuit with nonlinear coupling between cells (i.e., nonlinear OTA). We then compare the circuit performance for both TFET and CMOS in terms of computation time, image quality and energy.

Table 1: Configurations in three circuits

	CMOS	HomTFET	HetTFET
W/L for input pair	$3.2 \times M$	$3.2 \times M$	$2 \times M$
Tail current (μA)	$0.8 \times M$	$0.8 \times M$	$0.75 \times M$
Reference voltage (V)	0.6	0.45	0.45
Resistor (Ω)	$800k/M$	$800k/M$	$1200k/M$

Table 2: Power and performance of three circuits

	CMOS	HomTFET	HetTFET
Linear range (mV)	250	250	250
$V_{DD}(V)$	1	0.85	0.8
Power (μW)	1.5	1.1	1
Delay (ps)	23.4	92.3	20.1
Rise time (ps)	99	320	95

For TFET-based non-linear OTA, the circuit schematics for globalmax and globalmin are shown in Fig. 6(a) and Fig. 6(b), respectively. The circuit is similar to the linear OTA. However, the resistor in Fig. 4 are replaced with a single TFET, T_{r1}. A gate voltage for T_{r1} is added to make it biased properly. For globalmax, T_{r1} is on when $V_{in+} < V_{in-}$, providing a much larger output current compared to $V_{in+} > V_{in-}$ (i.e., T_{r1} is off). For globalmin, T_{r1} operates in $V_{ds} < 0$ when $V_{in+} < V_{in-}$. T_{r1} is on when $V_{in+} > V_{in-}$. The DC characteristic of the circuit is shown in Fig. 7. As seen from the figure, the characteristics mimic the non-linear templates for the globalmax and globalmin functions (shown in Fig. 3).

One could also design a CMOS non-linear OTA based on the same idea (see Fig. 6(c) and (d)). Here, instead of applying an external gate voltage, the T_{r1} in Fig. 4(b) is diode-connected. Other part of the CMOS-based circuit is unchanged compared with its linear equivalent. In this design, T_{r1} is on when $V_{in+} < V_{in-}$ for globalmax, $V_{in+} > V_{in-}$ for globalmin. T_{r1} is off in all other cases. Our simulation result shows that the CMOS design can indeed realize the globalmax and globalmin function (Fig. 7).

Although the characteristics demonstrated by our TFET and CMOS-based non-linear OTA circuits mimic the ideal characteristics of globalmax and globalmin, they are not exactly the same. We use CNNs with CMOS/TFET nonlinear OTA implementation, as well as ideal nonlinear characteristic, to show their comparison. First we define the output error. The output error is measured by the difference between the global maximum/minimum value produced by the TFET/CMOS CNN, and the actual maximum/minimum value. The error can be reduced by decreasing computation time. The decrease of computation time requires larger output current of OTA. That causes the increase of OTA's power.

To study the figures of merit of our non-linear OTA designs, we consider a worst-case input setup with 16×16 pixel image. It is defined as the input image that requires longest computation time in a given size. The pixel propagation follows diagonal route from top to the bottom. A black pixel (maximum intensity) in the top left of the image with other pixels all white for globalmax. We use a CNN to propagate the black pixel value to the image, so that when we arbitrarily select a pixel in the image, we can find the global maximum in the image. For globalmin, we use all-black image with a white pixel in the top left. Three nonlinear characteristics: ideal characteristic, TFET-based characteristic, and CMOS-based characteristic are shown in Fig. 7 for the comparison. The output current I_{out} of VCCS can be scaled by scaling the bias current and the width of T_{r1} in both circuits, resulting in the change of both power, performance and error. We study three cases to compare CMOS design and TFET design: i) iso-power, ii) iso-time, and iii) iso-error. In iso-time comparison, the result for ideal charac-

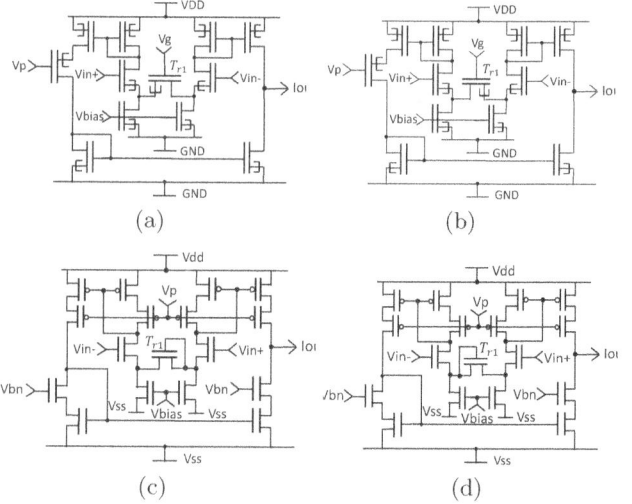

Figure 6: (a) TFET-based nonlinear OTA for globalmax, (b) TFET-based nonlinear OTA for globalmin, (c) CMOS-based nonlinear OTA for globalmax, (d) CMOS-based nonlinear OTA for globalmin.

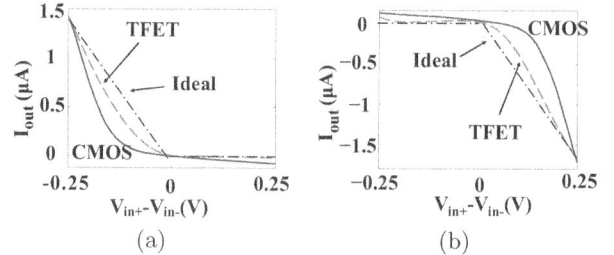

Figure 7: (a) TFET and CMOS-based nonlinear characteristic for globalmax, (b) TFET and CMOS-based nonlinear characteristic for globalmin.

teristic is also given as a contrast. In iso-error comparison, we set the target error - 7% for these cases. Actual errors must be below this error. In each case, we scale the I_{out} of CMOS design so that the power, speed and error changes. The results are shown in Fig. 8.

First we study the error (Fig. 8(a)). In $V_{in+} > V_{in-}$ for globalmax, and $V_{in+} < V_{in-}$ for globalmin, I_{out} for both TFET and CMOS designs are not exactly 0. This current discharges the capacitor in CNN cell, resulting in the decrease of state voltage. Therefore, there is some error in the final globalmax and globalmin value of the image. Moreover, CMOS design has a larger absolute value of I_{out} compared with TFET design in this region, which indicates larger error in iso-time and iso-power case. In the iso-error case, the decrease of error is due to the decrease of computation time, leading to the increase of power. Then we study the computation time (Fig. 8(b)). Computation time mainly depends on the output current, I_{out} of OTA, in $V_{in+} < V_{in-}$ for globalmax, and $V_{in+} > V_{in-}$ for globalmin. The computation time for TFET design is close to ideal one. The ideal characteristic has the similar curve with TFET nonlinear OTA in this region. However, CMOS design gives larger computation time in the iso-power case. In CMOS design T_{r1} works in sub-threshold region when V_{in+} and V_{in-} are close. It makes the output current smaller than TFET equivalent. TFET design also has a larger peak output current com-

280

pared to CMOS equivalent in iso-power case due to its steep slope characteristic. In the iso-time and iso-error cases, the I_{out} grows, making power of CMOS nonlinear OTA grows, and the computation time decrease. We last exam energy (Fig. 8(c)) in all three cases, energy dissipation for CMOS is larger than TFET. However, the ratio is similar as the decrease of computation time is proportional to the increase of power.

Overall, the TFET-based CNN is better than the CMOS-based one in all aspects of interests.

5. CASE STUDY ON GLOBALMAX AND GLOBALMIN

In this section we present two case studies that make use of globalmax and globalmin to reduce computation steps. They demonstrate the benefits of implementing non-linearity by utilizing TFETs.

5.1 Image contrast enhancement

Image contrast enhancement is a normalization problem[24]. It first finds the maximum/minimum intensity of the image, then applies a linear mapping between global maximum and the maximum value to a specific range to increase the image contrast. In this section we focus on the first step. Here we use an actual case to compare designs based on the T-FET, CMOS, and ideal characteristics. As the study for the worst case, we investigate the same three cases here: iso-power, iso-performance and iso-error designs. We also compare globalmax and globalmin functions by TFET, CMOS with ideal nonlinear characteristics.

Compared with the worst case, computation time here is about 1/16 shorter in each case because the intensity levels in this image are closer to one another. Furthermore, it is observed that not only the computation time, but also the image quality as well as energy all decrease proportionally compared with each case in the worst case set up. Our simulation results also validate that the TFET design outperforms the CMOS design in this case study. Due to the page limit, we omit the actual data.

5.2 Maximum row selection

The maximum row selection problem (MRS) selects the row with the maximum number of black pixels in an image. The input image is a binary image. In this section, we present solutions to MRS by both linear CNN and nonlinear CNN. Our results show that nonlinear CNN has advantage in both performance, energy dissipation and hardware complexity.

The processing steps based on linear templates and nonlinear templates are shown in Fig. 9(a) and (b), respectively. Output images for some steps are also shown. For the flow with linear templates, all the black pixels are first shifted to the left of the image by the PROJECTION operations. Then, the rightmost black pixel is selected by the AND operation. The HORIZONTAL SHADOW operation follows to fill the row having the rightmost black pixel. The nonlinear case achieves the goal in a more efficient way. First all the pixels diffuse horizontally by the DIFFUSION operation, making the intensities of the pixels in the row all at the same value - the average intensity of this row. Then the GLOBALMAX operation is utilized to propagate the maximum intensity to the entire image, and use that value as current max. It follows by the THRESHOLD operation with the current max as threshold value. Then in the image after the

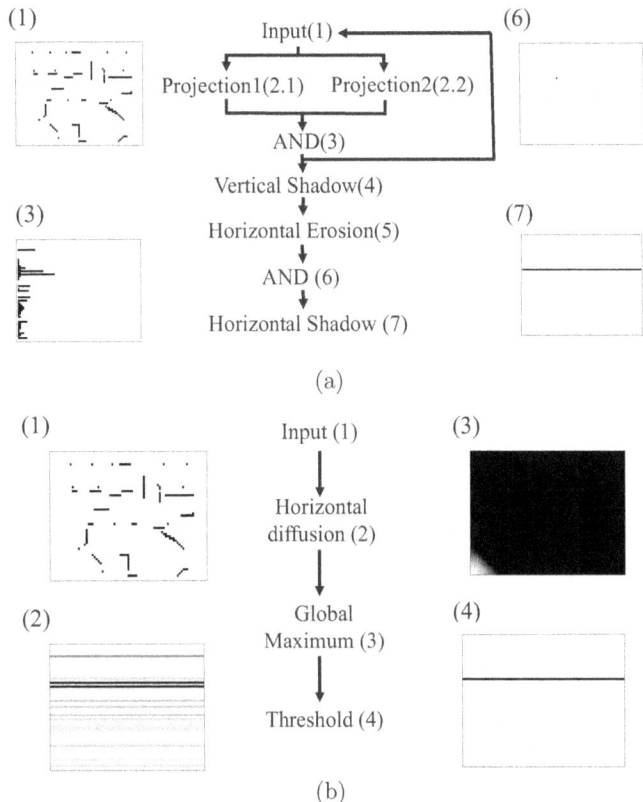

(a)

(b)

Figure 9: (a) Linear templates based MRS, (b) Nonlinear templates based MRS[25].

Table 3: Time and power for MRS

Linear case			Nonlinear case		
Operator	Time (μs)	Power (μW)	Operator	Time (μs)	Power (μW)
Project/And	640	5	Diffusion	500	2.5
Shadow	300	15	Global Max	300	2.5
ERO/And	30	10	Threshold	10	5
Shadow	300	15			
Total	1270		Total	810	

DIFFUSION operation, the row (or rows) with an intensity equal to the threshold value is/are the row (or rows) with the maximum number of black pixels. The THRESHOLD operation makes these rows all black. It is straightforward to see that the nonlinear solution for this problem greatly reduces the computation steps. This directly leads to reduced hardware complexity.

We investigate how the non-linear template based design impacts the time and energy. For each step, we consider the time required in the worst case to guarantee that each image can reach its stable state. We define this time as the computation time for that step. The HSPICE simulation results for the computation time and the power consumption of each step are shown in the Table 3.

For the linear case, the proposed TFET-based OTA is utilized. G_m of the OTA is tuned to meet the templates. Then the power is measured correspondingly. For the nonlinear case, the proposed nonlinear TFET-based OTA is utilized. The results show that nonlinear solution is 1.5X better in computation time compared with linear case (810μs vs. 1270μs). By multiplying the power and time in each step,

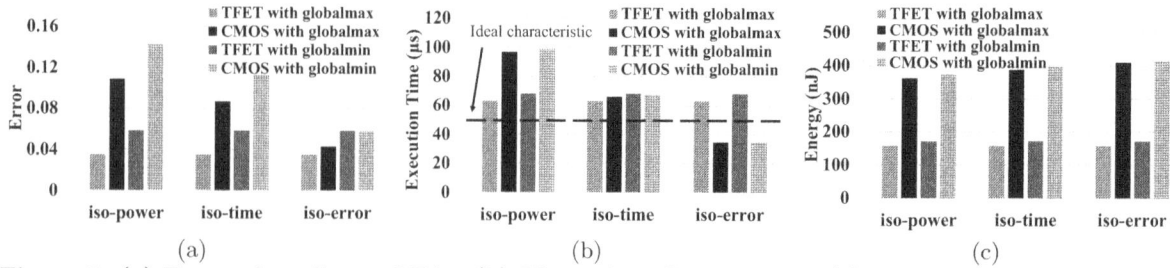

Figure 8: (a) Error of nonlinear OTAs, (b) Time of nonlinear OTAs, (c) Energy of nonlinear OTAs.

we obtain the total energy. For the linear case the energy dissipation $E_{linear} = 12.5nJ$, while $E_{nonlinear} = 2.05nJ$ for nonlinear case. Therefore, 6X improvement in terms of energy is observed. Moreover, as mentioned above, the linear case require 6 steps to finish its computation, while nonlinear case only requires 3 steps, resulting in the reduction of hardware complexity.

6. CONCLUSIONS

We introduce a TFET-based linear OTA design for the CNN architecture. It shows 1.5X power efficiency compared with CMOS-based VCCS due to the steep slope characteristic of TFET. Moreover, we demonstrate using TFET and CMOS to realize nonlinear templates in CNN, and compare the two designs. Two case studies, image contrast enhancement and maximum row selection, are conducted. They show that TFET-based CNN systems with non-linear templates not only reduce computation steps but also improves computation time and power when compared with TFET CNNs with only linear templates.

7. ACKNOWLEDGMENTS

This work was supported in part by the Center for Low Energy Systems Technology (LEAST), one of six centers of STARnet, a Semiconductor Research Corporation program sponsored by MARCO and DARPA.

8. REFERENCES

[1] Paul A. Merolla *et al.*, "A million spiking-neuron integrated circuit with a scalable communication network and interface," in *Science* 345, no. 6197, pp. 668-673, 2014.

[2] R. Dominguez-Castro *et al.*, "A 0.8-μm CMOS Two-Dimensional Programmable Mixed-Signal Focal-Plane Array Processor with On-Chip Binary Imaging and Instructions Storage," in *IEEE Journal of Solid-State Circuits*, vol. 32, no. 7, pp. 1013-1026, 1997.

[3] T. Chen *et al.*, "Benchnn: On the broad potential application scope of hardware neural network accelerators," in *IEEE International Symposium on Workload Characterization*, 2012, pp. 36-45.

[4] P. Zhao *et al.*, "SymFET: A Proposed Symmetric Graphene Tunneling Field Effect Transistor," in *IEEE Transaction on Electron Devices*, vol. 60, no. 2, pp. 951-957, 2013.

[5] M. Niemier *et al.*, "Shape Engineering for Controlled Switching With Nanomagnet Logic," in *IEEE Transaction on Nanotechnology*, vol. 11, no. 2, pp. 220-230, 2012.

[6] L. O. Chua *et al.*, "Cellular Neural Network: Theory," *IEEE Transaction on Circuits and Systems*,vol. 35, no. 10, pp. 1257-1272, 1988.

[7] G. Linan, *et al.*, "ACE4k: An analog I/O 64 × 64 visual microprocessor chip with 7–bit analog accuracy," *International Journal of Circuit Theory and Applications*, vol.30, no. 2-3, pp. 89-116, 2002.

[8] K. Karacs *et al.*, "Software library for cellular wave computing engines," version 3.1, 2010.

[9] I. Palit *et al.*, "TFET-based cellular neural network architectures," in *International Symposium on Low Power Electronics and Design (ISLPED)*, 2013, pp. 236-241.

[10] I. Palit *et al.*, "Impact of steep-slope transistors on non-von neumann architectures: CNN case study," in *Design, Automation & Test in Europe (DATE)*, 2014, pp. 1-6.

[11] A. Horvath *et al.*, "Architectural impacts of emerging transistors," in *IEEE International NEW Circuits And Systems*, 2014, pp. 69-72.

[12] I. Palit*et al.*, "Cellular neural networks for image analysis using steep slope devices," in *Proceedings of the 2014 IEEE/ACM ICCAD*, 2014, pp. 92-95.

[13] J. Molinar-Solis *et al.*, "Programmable CMOS CNN cell based on floating-gate inverter unit," in *Journal of VLSI Signal Processing systems for Signal, Image, and Video Technology*, vol. 49, no. 1, pp. 207-216, 2007.

[14] L. Wang *et al.*, "Time multiplexed color image processing based on a CNN with cell-state outputs," in *IEEE Transaction on VLSI*, vol. 6, no. 2, pp. 314-322, 2002.

[15] A. Trivedi *et al.*, "Exploring Tunnel-FET for ultra low power analog applications: a case study on operational transconductance amplifier," in *Design Automation Conference (DAC)*, 2013, pp. 1-6.

[16] H. Kam *et al.*, "Design requirements for steeply switching logic devices," in *IEEE Transaction on Device*, vol. 59, no. 2, pp. 326-334, 2012.

[17] A. C. Seabaugh *et al.*, "Low-Voltage Tunnel Transistors for Beyond CMOS Logic," *Proceedings of the IEEE*, vol.98, no.12, pp. 2095-2110, 2010.

[18] Y. Khatami *et al.*, "Steep Subthreshold Slope n- and p-Type Tunnel-FET Devices for Low-Power and Energy-Efficient Digital Circuits," *IEEE Transaction on Electron Devices*, vol. 56, no. 11, pp. 2752-2761, 2009.

[19] B. Sedighi *et al.*, "Analog Circuit Design using Tunnel-FETs," *IEEE Transaction on Circuits and Systems*, vol.99, no.0, 2014.

[20] H. Liu *et al.*, "Tunnel FET-Based Ultra-Low Power, Low-Noise Amplifier Design for Bio-signal Acquisition," *International Symposium on Low Power Electronics and Design (ISLPED)*, 2014, pp. 57-62.

[21] U.E. Avci *et al.*, "Comparison of performance, switching energy and process variations for the TFET and MOSFET in logic," *IEEE VLSI Technology Symposium on*, 2011, pp. 124-125.

[22] G. Zhou *et al.*, "Novel gate-recessed vertical InAs/GaSb TFETs with record high I_{on} of 180 uA/um at $V_{DS} = 0.5V$," *IEEE International Electron Devices Meeting*, 2012, pp. 32.6.1-4.

[23] C. Tang *et al.*, "A Feature-Based Robust Digital Image Watermarking Scheme," *IEEE Transaction on Signal Processing*, vol. 51, no. 4, pp. 950-959, 2003.

[24] J. Stark, "Adaptive image contrast enhancement using generalizations of histogram equalization," *IEEE Transaction on Image Processing*, vol. 9, no. 5, pp.889-896, 2000.

[25] D. Balya, "CNN universal machine as classification platform" an art-like clustering algorithm," *International Journal of Neuron System*, vol.13, no. 6, pp.415-425, 2003.

Clock Skew Scheduling in the Presence of Heavily Gated Clock Networks

Weicheng Liu, Emre Salman
Department of Electrical and Computer
Engineering
Stony Brook University
Stony Brook, NY 11794
[weicheng.liu,
emre.salman]@stonybrook.edu

Can Sitik, Baris Taskin
Department of Electrical and Computer
Engineering
Drexel University
Philadelphia, PA 19104
as3577@drexel.edu,
taskin@coe.drexel.edu

ABSTRACT

Clock skew scheduling is a common and well known technique to improve the performance of sequential circuits by exploiting the mismatches in the data path delays. Existing clock skew scheduling techniques, however, cannot effectively consider heavily gated clock networks where a local clock tree exists between clock gating cells and registers. A methodology is proposed in this paper to efficiently achieve clock skew scheduling in circuits with gated clock networks. The methodology is implemented via both linear programming and constraint graph based approaches, and evaluated using the largest ISCAS'89 benchmark circuits with clock gating. The results demonstrate up to approximately 21% reduction in clock period while maintaining the power savings achieved by clock gating. A conventional design flow is used for the experiments, demonstrating the applicability of the proposed algorithms to automation.

Categories and Subject Descriptors

B.7 [**Integrated Circuits**]: VLSI (very large scale integration)

General Terms

Design

Keywords

Clock Skew Scheduling, Clock Gating, Low Power

1. INTRODUCTION

In IC design process, clock distribution networks are vital to synchronize all of the sequential elements in a circuit [1]. Due to the process-voltage-temperature (PVT) variations and design margins, the arrival time of the clock signal to each sequential element (latch or flip-flop) is not

GLSVLSI'15, May 20–22, 2015, Pittsburgh, PA, USA
Copyright 2015 ACM 978-1-4503-3474-7/15/05 ...$15.00
http://dx.doi.org/10.1145/2742060.2742092.

identical, resulting in non-zero clock skew [2–4]. Historically, the clock skew is managed in three ways: i) zero skew, ii) bounded skew and iii) useful skew approaches, *i.e.*, clock skew scheduling.

The zero skew and bounded skew approaches ensure that the clock arrival time of all of the sequential elements is either identical (for zero skew) or within a margin (for bounded skew). Alternatively, the useful skew approach considers clock skew scheduling where the skew of each sequential element that belongs to the same timing path is individually considered for timing optimization. In clock skew scheduling, the available timing slack at each sequential element is utilized to improve clock period of the IC. Specifically, slower data paths "borrow" time from faster data paths. Thus, skew scheduling exploits the mismatches in the timing characteristics of the data paths to decrease clock period.

Conventional clock skew scheduling techniques rely on linear programming (LP) with a minimum clock period objective [2,5,6] or a graph-based solution to utilize existing graph algorithms [7,8]. In [9], delay insertion methodology in clock skew scheduling is proposed. In [10], a linear programming approach is proposed to minimize the overall delay insertion while maintaining the minimum clock period. In order to mitigate the effect process variations on skew, multi-domain clock skew scheduling [11] is proposed. In [12,13], two optimal algorithms are developed to implement a multi-domain clock skew scheduling.

The global clock signal has the highest switching activity in an IC, making clock gating a popular technique to reduce dynamic power. Although clock gating is shown to be effective [14], it may introduce timing related challenges. One such challenge is to utilize useful skew since conventional clock gating structures consider zero skew. Furthermore, the timing constraints (setup and hold) and the insertion delay of the local clock tree (between clock gating cells and registers) produce other challenges that need to be addressed during clock skew scheduling, as discussed in this paper.

Existing clock skew scheduling methods (including those mentioned above) consider only *non-gated* clock distribution networks, which is impractical since industrial clock trees are heavily clock gated. A recent methodology proposed in [15] performs clock skew scheduling in a clock gated design where a linear programming framework is used with a minimum insertion delay objective. However, it is assumed that each sequential element has an individual clock gate, which is not practical in modern industrial designs. Furthermore, the clock arrival time at the clock gate and its corresponding sequential element are assumed to be identical, which is typically not the case when there is a local clock tree after the clock gating cell. Thus, a practical clock skew scheduling approach for gated clock trees is required, as proposed in this paper. Specifically, the challenges of skew scheduling in the presence of gated clock networks are addressed to improve timing performance (clock period) while maintaining the power savings achieved by clock gating.

The rest of the paper is organized as follows. Traditional clock skew scheduling methods that utilize linear programming and constraint based approaches are summarized in Section 2. The challenges introduced by clock gating are also discussed. The proposed method is described in Section 3. Experimental results on largest ISCAS'89 benchmark circuits are presented in Section 4. Finally, paper is concluded in Section 5.

2. BACKGROUND AND PROBLEM FORMULATION

Traditional clock skew scheduling is briefly summarized in Section 2.1. Unique challenges introduced due to clock gating are discussed in Section 2.2.

2.1 Traditional Clock Skew Scheduling

In a sequential timing path P, assume R_i and R_j represent two registers, t_i and t_j are clock arrival times for registers R_i and R_j, respectively. For each data path P in the circuit, two types of timing constraints exist: setup time (max delay) and hold time (min delay) constraints, which are represented, respectively, by (1) and (2),

$$t_i - t_j \leq T - DP_{max}, \qquad (1)$$

$$t_i - t_j \geq -DP_{min}, \qquad (2)$$

where T is the clock period, DP_{max} and DP_{min} are the maximum and minimum data path delays that include setup and hold time, respectively [16].

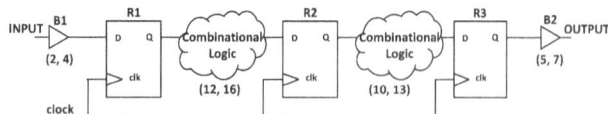

Figure 1: Simple sequential circuit consisting of three registers without clock gating.

A simple sequential circuit with three registers $R1$, $R2$ and $R3$ and without clock gating is shown in Fig. 1. Two buffers $B1$ and $B2$ are inserted at the primary input and the output load, respectively. A pair of delay values (D_{min}, D_{max}) is denoted with each buffer, where $D_{min,buf}$ and $D_{max,buf}$ are the minimum and maximum propagation delay of the buffer, respectively. There are two data paths in this circuit, $R1 \rightarrow R2$ and $R2 \rightarrow R3$, which are also associated with a pair of delay values $(DP_{min,path}, DP_{max,path})$ representing minimum and maximum data path delays.

Conventional clock skew scheduling approaches find a set of clock arrival times corresponding to each register, which should satisfy each data path's timing constraints represented by (1) and (2). In [5], the proposed clock skew scheduling methodology is formulated as a simple linear programming (LP) problem where the objective function is to

Table 1: LP based formulation of skew scheduling for the simple circuit shown in Fig. 1.

LP based formulation
Objective: min T
1    $-12 \leq t_1 - t_2 \leq T - 16$
2    $-10 \leq t_2 - t_3 \leq T - 13$
3    $-2 \leq t_{host} - t_1 \leq T - 4$
4    $-5 \leq t_3 - t_{host} \leq T - 7$
5    $0 \leq t_1, t_2, t_3, t_{host} \leq T$

minimize the clock period. The linear programming model of the motivational example shown in Fig. 1 is listed in Table 1. Lines 1 to 4 represent the timing constraints of the two data paths and the primary input and the primary output paths. Line 5 is included to limit the maximum global skew within one clock period. The linear programming determines the minimum clock period as 10 units with the following set of skew schedule: $t_1 = 0$, $t_2 = 6$, $t_3 = 9$ and $t_{host} = 6$.

In addition to utilizing linear programming to perform clock skew scheduling, a sequential circuit can also be modeled as a constraint graph $G(V, E)$, in which each vertex represents a register and two edges (with opposite directions) connecting two vertices represent setup and hold time constraints, respectively. In [8], a constraint graph based approach is proposed to optimize clock skew. In this graph-based approach, each data path from R_i to R_j in a sequential path has two edges: 1) an edge (R_j, R_i) with weight $T - DP_{max}$ models the setup time constraint in (1) and 2) an edge (R_i, R_j) with weight DP_{min} models the hold time constraint in (2). In order to synchronize the primary input and the primary output, a special vertex $Host$ is added. This constraint graph provides skew schedule only if no negative weight cycle exists in the constraint graph. The well-known Bellman-Ford algorithm [17] is utilized to detect a negative weight cycle and increase the clock period T until all of the negative weight cycles are eliminated.

Using the circuit of the motivational example in Fig. 1, the constructed constraint graph is shown in Fig. 2(a). The solid lines represent setup time constraints, and the dashed lines represent hold time constraints. After applying the graph-based method, a minimum clock period of 10 units (similar to LP result) is computed with the set of clock arrival times as: $t_1 = 1$, $t_2 = 7$, $t_3 = 10$ and $t_{host} = 7$. As depicted in Fig. 2(b), there is no negative weight cycle after substituting clock period with 10 units.

2.2 Clock Skew Scheduling with Clock Gating

Clock gating is a popular technique to save dynamic power by deactivating the clock signal of the idle registers [14, 18]. Typically, an integrated clock gating (ICG) cell, as shown in Fig. 3, is utilized to prevent the clock signal from switching. The enable pin within an ICG cell creates a clock enable (or control) path in addition to the data paths. Thus, a clock enable (or control) path refers to the combinational logic from the output pin of a register to the enable pin of an ICG cell.

In practice, one ICG cell gates multiple registers since an ICG cell placed at higher levels of a clock tree can save more dynamic power. Thus, in industrial designs, it is common to have *a local clock tree* between an ICG cell and the reg-

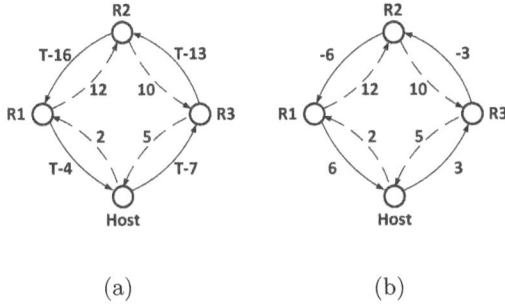

Figure 2: Constraint graph based formulation of skew scheduling for the circuit shown in Fig. 1: (a) constraint graph, (b) after applying a clock period of 10 units eliminating all of the negative weight cycles.

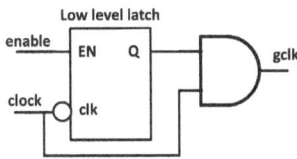

Figure 3: Integrated clock gating (ICG) cell.

isters that are gated by this ICG cell. A *clock propagation path* on the local clock tree is therefore defined as the path from the output pin of an ICG cell to the clock pin of a register that is gated by this ICG cell. Since an ICG cell typically gates multiple registers, there are more than one clock propagation paths for an ICG cell. The delay of the clock propagation path (the delay between the clock arrival time to the ICG cell and the clock arrival time to the register gated by this ICG cell) is at least the ICG cell delay and is bounded by the longest path within the local tree. Thus, each ICG cell is associated with a lower and upper bound of clock propagation path delay.

A simplified motivational example with clock gating is shown in Fig. 4 to better illustrate the aforementioned definitions. For simplicity, the circuit in this example has one ICG cell $ICG1$, gating two registers $R1$ and $R2$. A local sub-tree including two buffers $B5$ and $B6$ is synthesized to drive the two registers. Each buffer is denoted with a pair of delay values, which indicates the minimum and the maximum clock propagation path delays. The clock enable (or control) path is from $R1$ to $ICG1$ and consists of a single combinational gate, $C1$. Note that for simplicity, data paths are omitted in this example so that the issues related with clock gating can be emphasized.

Conventional clock skew scheduling methodologies cannot consider the unique challenges introduced by clock gating. In [15], the authors have recently proposed a linear programming approach to investigate the clock gated designs. In this work, useful skew is utilized in a gated design via considering both the data paths and clock enable paths with the objective function of minimum insertion delay [15]. However, it is assumed that the clock arrival time to an ICG cell is the same as the clock arrival time to the registers gated by this ICG. This assumption is impractical since in practice, the clock signal is distributed with a local clock tree that has larger and non-identical clock propagation delays (as depicted in Fig. 4). A method to perform clock skew

Table 2: LP based approach to clock skew scheduling in a clock gated design.

LP based approach for ICs with clock gating
Objective: min T
1   $t_i - t_j \geq -DP_{min}(data\ path)$
2   $t_i - t_j \leq T - DP_{max}(data\ path)$
3   $\boldsymbol{t_{icg,j} - t_i \geq -CP_{max}}(propagation\ path)$
4   $\boldsymbol{t_{icg,j} - t_i \leq -CP_{min}}(propagation\ path)$
5   $\boldsymbol{t_i - t_{icg,j} \geq -EP_{min}}(enable\ path)$
6   $\boldsymbol{t_i - t_{icg,j} \leq T - EP_{max}}(enable\ path)$
7   $0 \leq t_i, t_{icg,j} \leq T$

scheduling in clock gated design with a local sub-tree is proposed in this paper, as described in the following section.

3. PROPOSED APPROACH

Since ICG cell has a clock pin, in the proposed approach, each ICG cell is treated as a register with an associated clock arrival time. Since there is a local clock tree between an ICG cell and registers gated by this ICG, the associated clock propagation delays can be treated as clock skew. However, note that the clock signal should arrive to the ICG cell earlier than it arrives to the registers gated by this ICG cell due to positive clock propagation path delay. This constraint is different than conventional data paths where skew can be both positive and negative. The linear programming based solution to skew scheduling in gated clock trees is described in Section 3.1 whereas the constrained graph based approach is discussed in Section 3.2.

3.1 Linear Programming Based Solution

The arrival time of a clock signal to a register gated by an ICG cell is larger than the arrival time of the clock signal to the ICG cell (see Fig. 4). The lower bound for each clock propagation path delay is determined by the AND gate delay and a local clock tree. This inequality is given by,

$$t_{icg,j} - t_i \leq -CP_{min}, \qquad (3)$$

where $t_{icg,j}$ and t_i are the clock arrival times to ICG cell ICG_j and register R_i, respectively. CP_{min} is the minimum clock propagation path delay.

An upper bound on clock propagation path delay is also required to represent the maximum delay of the local clock tree,

$$t_i - t_{icg,j} \leq CP_{max}, \qquad (4)$$

where CP_{max} is the maximum delay of the corresponding clock propagation path. Combining the constraints in (3) and (4) with the traditional, data path related constraints, an improved linear programming solution for skew scheduling in ICs with gated clock trees is obtained, as listed in Table 2. The bold lines represent the *new* constraints required for gated clock networks.

The first two lines are the data path related constraints whereas lines 3 and 4 are the constraints related with clock propagation paths. Lines 5 and 6 represent the timing constraints of the enable (control) path. Line 7 is added to limit the global skew within one clock period. The linear programming based solution for the motivational example in Fig. 4 is listed in Table 3. The program determines the minimum clock period as 22 units and a set of clock arrival times as $t_1 = 0$, $t_2 = 1$, $t_3 = 2$, $t_{icg,1} = 0$, and $t_{host} = 0$.

285

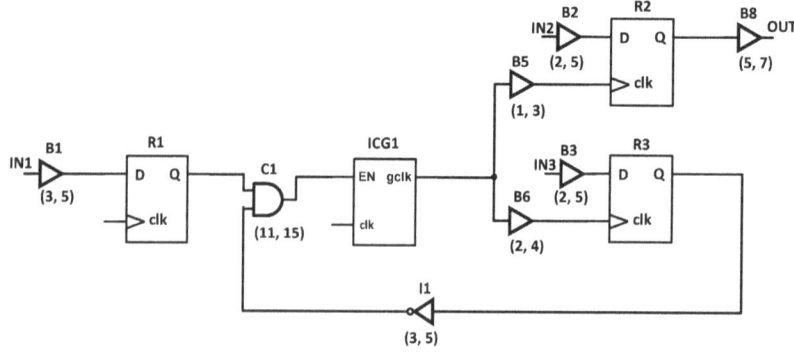

Figure 4: Simple sequential circuit consisting of an ICG cell, two registers gated by this ICG cell, a local clock sub-tree, and a timing loop formed by clock propagation path and clock enable path.

Table 3: Application of the LP based approach to circuit shown in Fig. 4.

LP based approach for ICs with clock gating
Objective: min T
s.t. $-3 \leq t_{host} - t_1 \leq T - 5$
$-2 \leq t_{host} - t_2 \leq T - 5$
$-2 \leq t_{host} - t_3 \leq T - 5$
$-5 \leq t_2 - t_{host} \leq T - 7$
$-3 \leq t_{icg,1} - t_2 \leq -1$
$-4 \leq t_{icg,1} - t_3 \leq -2$
$-11 \leq t_1 - t_{icg,1} \leq T - 15$
$-14 \leq t_3 - t_{icg,1} \leq T - 20$
$0 \leq t_1, t_2, t_3, t_{icg,1}, t_{host} \leq T$

3.2 Constraint Graph Based Solution

In addition to linear programming, constraint graph based solution is also proposed to compare the efficacy and confirm the accuracy of the proposed methods. Each ICG cell is treated as a register and added to the directed graph as a vertex. The maximum and minimum clock propagation path delays are treated, respectively, as setup and hold time constraints of a traditional data path. Specifically, (3) is treated as a setup time constraint and modeled by a directed edge (R_i, ICG_j) with weight $-CP_{min}$. Similarly, (4) is treated as a hold time constraint and modeled by a directed edge (ICG_j, R_i) with weight CP_{max}.

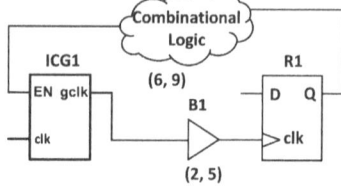

Figure 5: Simple example to illustrate the timing loop formed by an ICG cell and a register gated by this ICG cell.

An important issue in graph based solution of skew scheduling in gated clock networks is a possible timing loop that can form between an ICG cell and one of the registers gated by this ICG cell. Assume that the enable signal of the ICG cell is provided from the output pin of one of the registers that is gated by the same ICG cell (such as $ICG1$ and $R3$ in Fig. 4), then the ICG cell and the register form a loop. Unlike conventional data paths, the clock signal should arrive to the register *later* than it arrives to the ICG. Thus, this

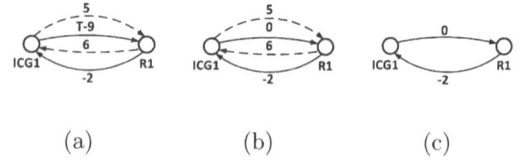

Figure 6: Constraint graph of the circuit shown in Fig. 5: (a) original graph, (b) after one iteration with clock period as 11 units, (c) after breaking the timing loop.

timing loop should be broken from the directed graph while still maintaining accurate results. As observed from experimental results on ISCAS'89 benchmark circuits, breaking the loop is necessary to obtain a feasible skew schedule.

Table 4: Graph based solution for ICs with clock gating, including the proposed mechanism to break the timing loop.

Graph based approach (timing data)
1:    start with a clock period T
2:    for each edge(u,v) with weight w
3:      if (u,v) ∃ in G(V,E)
4:        if weight(u,v)>w
5:          weight(u,v)=w
6:      else
7:        add edge(u,v)
8:    end for
9:    add a source node
10:    for each V ∈ G(V,E) except source node
11:      add edge(source,V) with weight T
12:    end for
13:    apply Bellman-Ford algorithm on G(V,E)
14:    if ∃ negative weight cycle
15:      increase clock period
16:      repeat Line 1-13
17:    else
18:      return clock period T and skew schedule

To better describe this issue, consider the example shown in Fig. 5 where the enable signal of $ICG1$ is generated by the output signal of $R1$, forming a timing loop. The constraint graph of this circuit is depicted in Fig. 6. Due to the loop, there are two sets of max and min delay constraints: 1) $t_{icg,1} - t_1 \leq -2$, $t_{icg,1} - t_1 \geq -5$ and 2) $t_1 - t_{icg,1} \leq T - 9$, $t_1 -$

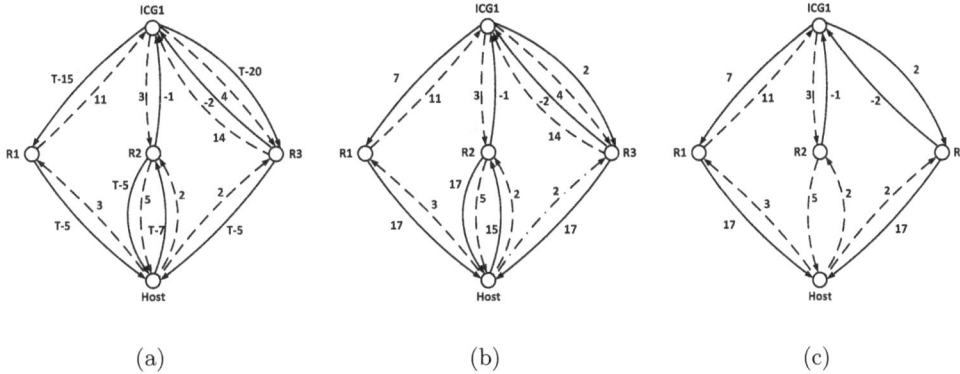

Figure 7: Constraint graph of the circuit shown in Fig. 4: (a) original graph, (b) after one iteration with clock period as 22 units, (c) after breaking the timing loop.

$t_{icg,1} \geq -6$, as shown in Fig. 6(a). To break the loop, only the tighter constraints of the same directed edge (*i.e.* smaller weight) should be preserved. For example, assume that in one of the iterations, clock period T is determined as 9 units, producing the following inequalities: $-5 \leq t_{icg,1} - t_1 \leq -2$ and $0 \leq t_{icg,1} - t_1 \leq 6$, as shown in Fig. 6(b). Since only the tighter constraint of the same edge should be preserved, the edges with weights 5 and 6 are dropped, breaking the loop, as shown in Fig. 6(c). According to Fig. 6(c), a negative weight cycle exists, indicating that the chosen clock period should be increased. If the process is repeated with a clock period of 11 units, the cycle weight becomes zero, indicating that the minimum clock period has been determined while satisfying the timing constraints.

The pseudo-code of the proposed constraint graph based solution is provided in Table 4. The algorithm takes the timing data as the input and generates a constraint graph in lines 2 to 12. In lines 3 to 5, the timing loops formed by ICG cells and registers gated by the same ICG cells are detected and broken by the proposed method (*i.e.*, preserving only the smaller weight of the same directed edges). In line 13, Bellman-Ford algorithm [17] is utilized to detect negative weight cycles. If found, clock period is increased until all of the negative weight cycles are removed. In line 18, the algorithm returns the minimum clock period and the skew schedule, *i.e.*, clock arrival time to each register and ICG cell.

As an example, the proposed algorithm is applied to the circuit shown in Fig. 4. The original constraint graph that corresponds to this circuit is depicted in Fig. 7(a). T is replaced with the minimum clock period 22 units, producing the graph shown in Fig. 7(b). The timing loop formed by $ICG1$ and $D3$ are broken using the proposed method, producing the final graph shown in Fig. 7(c). The algorithm returns the clock arrival times as $t_1 = 22$, $t_2 = 22$, $t_3 = 22$, $t_{icg} = 20$, and $t_{host} = 22$.

4. EXPERIMENTAL RESULTS

The proposed LP based and constraint graph based approaches for skew scheduling in gated clock networks are evaluated using the largest ISCAS'89 benchmark circuits consisting of up to approximately 2000 registers. Each benchmark is synthesized with Synopsys Design Compiler [19] using the 45 nm NanGate open cell library [20]. ICG cells are inserted by the tool during the synthesis stage. An open source GLPK (GNU Linear Programming Kit) [21] is used as the linear programming solver, running on a Linux system with Intel Xeon processor.

The experimental results are listed in Table 5 for both linear programming and graph based solutions. It is important to note that both solutions provide the same minimum clock period in each circuit, verifying the accuracy of the algorithms. The maximum reduction in clock period after skew scheduling is approximately 21%, which highly depends upon the timing data. In some benchmarks, higher gating percentage corresponds to less reduction in clock period, such as S1423 and S38417. However, this behavior does not hold in other benchmarks such as S38584 where 16% reduction in clock period is achieved with approximately 72% gating. It is also shown in Table 5 that the graph based solution produces smaller global skew than LP based solution.

The run time of both solutions is compared in Fig. 8 for some of the benchmark circuits. LP based solution runs faster than or equal to graph based solution. Note that the graph based approach utilizes Bellman-Ford algorithm with a computational complexity of $O(V \cdot E)$ [17], where V is the overall number of registers and ICG cells in the circuit, and E is the overall number of data paths, enable paths and clock propagation paths. Lines 2 to 8 in Table 4 have a complexity of $O(E)$ and lines 9 to 11 have a complexity of $O(V)$. Therefore, the computational complexity of the graph based method is maintained at $O(V \cdot E)$. The LP based solution utilizes the simplex algorithm and in practice, runs faster. However, note that with certain inputs, simplex algorithm may require exponential time to reach a solution [17].

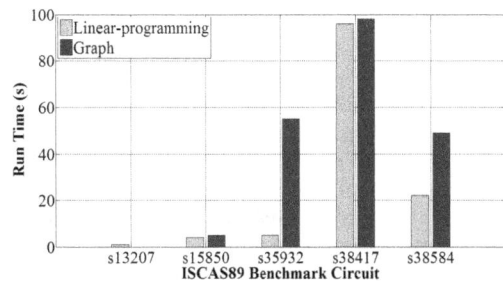

Figure 8: The run time comparison of linear programming and graph based approaches.

Table 5: Experimental results demonstrating the reduction in clock period of gated ISCAS'89 benchmark circuits after clock skew scheduling (CCS).

Circuit	No. of DFFs	No. of ICGs	Gating%	Clock Period (ns)			Max Global Skew (ns)	
				Zero Skew	After CSS	Reduction	LP	Graph
S1423	74	30	90.54%	4.9212	4.6618	5.27%	0.2594	0.2374
S9234	125	15	51.20%	2.9278	2.7369	6.52%	0.7171	0.1909
S13207	240	37	44.17%	2.4436	2.0678	15.38%	0.3897	0.3896
S15850	434	57	66.36%	4.9466	4.1436	16.23%	0.8030	0.1342
S35932	1728	4	0.23%	3.8314	3.0419	20.61%	0.7895	0.0773
S38417	1459	236	49.62%	4.8895	4.6490	4.92%	0.2926	0.2487
S38584	1240	251	71.61%	4.5806	3.8425	16.11%	0.7381	0.0570

5. CONCLUSIONS

Existing clock skew scheduling methods cannot effectively consider clock gating where an ICG cell gates multiple registers. In such cases, a local clock tree typcially exists between the ICG cell and registers gated by this ICG cell, introducing additional and unbalanced *clock propagation paths*. A methodology is proposed in this paper to efficiently implement skew scheduling for gated clock networks. Each ICG cell is treated as a register and additional constraints are included to accurately consider clock propagation paths. A mechanism is also proposed to break the register-to-ICG timing loops in the graph based solution to ensure accuracy. The proposed algorithms are evaluated using the largest IS-CAS'89 benchmark circuits with gated clock networks. A conventional design flow is utilized, demonstrating that the proposed algorithms are feasible for automation. Up to 21% reduction in clock period is demonstrated.

6. ACKNOWLEDGMENTS

This research is supported by Semiconductor Research Corporation (SRC) under contract No. 2013-TJ-2449 and 2013-TJ-2450.

7. REFERENCES

[1] E. Salman and E. G. Friedman, *High Performance Integrated Circuit Design*. McGraw-Hill, 2012.

[2] E. G. Friedman, "Clock Distribution Networks in Synchronous Digital Integrated Circuits," *Proceedings of the IEEE*, Vol. 89, No. 5, pp. 665-692, May 2001.

[3] I. S. Kourtev, B. Taskin, and E. G. Friedman, *Timing Optimization Through Clock Skew Scheduling*. Springer, 2009.

[4] J. Neves and E. G. Friedman, "Optimal clock skew scheduling tolerant to process variations," *Design Automation Conference*, pp. 623-628, June 1996.

[5] J. P. Fishburn, "Clock Skew Optimization," *IEEE Transactions on Computers*, Vol. 39, No. 7, pp. 945-951, July 1990.

[6] T.G.Szymanski, "Computing Optimal Clock Schedules," *ACM/IEEE Design Automation Conference*, pp. 399-404, June 1992.

[7] N.Shenoy, R.K.Brayton, and A.L.Sangiovanni-Vincentelli, "Graph Algorithms for Clock Skew Optimization," *International Conference on Computer-Aided Design*, pp. 132-136, November 1992.

[8] R. Deokar and S. Sapatnekar, "A Graph-theoretic Approach to Clock Skew Optimization," *Int. Symp. on Circuits and Systems*, pp. 407-410, May 1994.

[9] B. Taskin and I. S. Kourtev, "Delay Insertion Method in Clock Skew Scheduling," *IEEE Transactions on Computer-Aided Design of Integrated Circuits and Systems*, Vol. 25, No. 4, pp. 651-663, April 2006.

[10] S.-H. Huang, C.-H. Cheng, C.-M. Chang, and Y.-T. Nieh, "Clock Period Minimization with Minimum Delay Insertion," *Design Automation Conference*, pp. 970-975, June 2007.

[11] K. Ravindran, A. Kuehlmann, and E. Sentovich, "Multi-domain Clock Skew Scheduling," *International Conference on Computer-Aided Design*, pp. 801-808, November 2003.

[12] M. Ni and S. O. Memik, "A Fast Heuristic Algorithm for Multidomain Clock Skew Scheduling," *IEEE Transactions on Very Large Scale Integration (VLSI) Systems*, Vol. 18, No. 4, pp. 630-637, April 2010.

[13] L. Li, Y. Lu, and H. Zhou, "Optimal and Efficient Algorithms for Multidomain Clock Skew Scheduling," *IEEE Trans. on Very Large Scale Integration (VLSI) Systems*, Vol. 22, No. 9, pp. 1888-1897, Sept. 2014.

[14] Q. Wu, M. Pedram, and X. Wu, "Clock-gating and Its Application to Low Power Design of Sequential Circuits," *IEEE Transactions on Circuits and Systems-I: Fundamental Theory and Applications*, Vol. 47, No. 103, pp. 415-420, March 2000.

[15] W.-P. Tu, S.-H. Huang, and C.-H. Cheng, "Co-synthesis of Data Paths and Clock Control Paths for Minimum-Period Clock Gating," *Design, Automation And Test in Europe Conference And Exhibition (DATE)*, pp. 1831-1836, March 2013.

[16] E. Salman, A. Dasdan, F.Taraporevala, K. Kucukcakar and E. G. Friedman, "Exploiting Setup-Hold Time Interdependence in Static Timing Analysis," *IEEE Transactions on Computer-Aided Design of Integrated Circuits and Systems*, Vol. 26, No. 6, pp. 1114-1125, June 2007.

[17] T. H. Cormen, C. E. Leiserson, R. L. Rivest, and C. Stein, *Introduction to Algorithms*. The MIT Press, 2001.

[18] M. Donno, A. Ivaldi, L. Benini, and E. Macii, "Clock-tree Power Optimization based on RTL Clock-gating," *Design Automation Conference*, pp. 622-627, June 2003.

[19] Synopsys. Design Compiler. http://www.synopsys.com/home.aspx.

[20] NanGate. 45nm Open Cell Library. http://www.nangate.com.

[21] GNU. GNU Linear Programming Kit. https://www.gnu.org/software/glpk/.

Standard Cell Layout Regularity and Pin Access Optimization Considering Middle-of-Line

Wei Ye[†♭],   Bei Yu[†],   Yong-Chan Ban[‡],   Lars Liebmann[♯],   David Z. Pan[†]

[†] ECE Department, University of Texas at Austin, Austin, TX, USA
[♭] College of Electrical Engineering, Zhejiang University, Hangzhou, China
[‡] System IC R&D Lab, LG Electronics, Seoul, South Korea
[♯] IBM Corporation, Hopewell Junction, NY, USA

wei_ye@zju.edu.cn, {bei,dpan}@cerc.utexas.edu, yc.ban@lge.com, lliebman@us.ibm.com

ABSTRACT

As minimum feature size and pitch spacing further decrease in advanced technology nodes, many new design constraints and challenges are introduced, such as regularity, middle of line (MOL) structures, and pin-access challenges. In this work, we propose a comprehensive study on standard cell layout regularity and pin access optimization. Given irregular cell layout from old technology nodes, our cell optimization tool can search unidirectional migrated result where the self-aligned double patterning (SADP) and MOL based design constraints are satisfied, and the pin-accessibility is optimized. This problem is formulated as a general integer linear programming (ILP), which may suffer from long runtime for some large standard cell cases. Therefore, we also develop a set of hybrid techniques to quickly search for high-quality solutions. The experimental results demonstrate the effectiveness of our approaches.

Categories and Subject Descriptors

B.7.2 [**Hardware, Integrated Circuit**]: Design Aids

Keywords

Standard Cell Design, Layout Regularity, Middle of Line, Self-Aligned Double Patterning, Pin Access

1. INTRODUCTION

As VLSI technology continues scaling down into advanced technology nodes, the semiconductor industry is greatly challenged by the printability and the design complexity issues. On the one hand, under the constraint of $193nm$ wavelength lithography, circuit designs are vulnerable to open/shorts, performance degradation, or even parametric yield loss. Although various resolution enhancement techniques are utilized, random geometrical configurations are still hard to implement due to lithography limitation [1]. Therefore, unidirectional layout styles have been proposed to improve the manufacturability and achieve manageable post-layout pro-

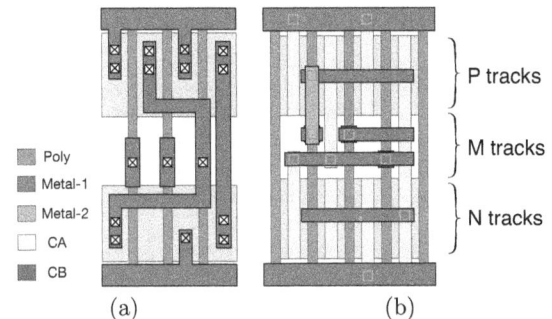

Figure 1: Example of cell regularity and pin access optimization. (a) The input layout with ten tracks. (b) The optimized layout with nine tracks.

cessing complexity [2, 3, 4]. On the other hand, the technology scaling also translates denser I/O pins to the standard cells, which may cause severe local congestion problem. That means if a standard cell is not properly designed, it cannot be easily accessed by physical design routing tool [5].

To improve the regularity of standard cell, a Tungsten-based middle of line (MOL) structure is introduced to connect intra-cell transistors [6]. MOL structure is made up of two different local interconnection layers, CA and CB (sometimes called IM1 and IM2, respectively) [7]. In addition, MOL is able to achieve better manufacturability while paying little performance penalty [8]. Due to the regularity, both Metal-1 and MOL layers can be manufactured through self-aligned double patterning (SADP) technique [9], which has better overlap and line edge roughness control than multiple litho-etch based techniques [10, 11, 12]. Therefore, SADP with extreme unidirectional layout is a viable candidate for lower layer metallization at the $10nm$ technology node.

To overcome the local congestion problem, physical design tools should be aware of the congestion derived from the dense I/O pin cells. For instance, in placement stage local congestion mitigation can be applied to prevent placing hard-to-routed cells too close together [5]. Due to limited local routing resources and dense I/O pins, pin access is becoming a serious problem for detailed routing. More importantly, the standard cell library should be carefully designed to enhance the pin accessibility. That is, I/O pins need to be balanced distributed within a cell, as the alignment or the densely packing of pins make the cell more difficult to be accessed.

Based on these motivations, there has been growing interest in standard cell design toward regularity and pin access optimization. Tang and Yuan [13] studied the cell migration problem where the conventional shape-based layouts are transformed to simplified layouts with restrictive design rule constraints. There are some cell synthesis works for conventional 2D cells [14, 15], or 1D cells [16, 17, 18, 19]. Recently, an I/O pin extension approach was proposed to alleviate the pin access problem [20]. However, these existing studies suffer from one or more of the following issues. (1) Conventional layout migration or pin extension is with the assumption that the topologies of all pins and intra-cell wires are fixed, which limits the ability to resolve some very challenging cell designs. (2) When considering MOL structure, so far most of the cells are manually designed and there is no automatic flow to transform conventional 2D cell layout into unidirectional layout patterns. (3) Existing approaches may be ad hoc, thus there is very limited work providing a robust and generic flow to automatically optimize cell layout toward all the design metrics and requirements.

In this paper we study the problem of cell layout regularity and pin access optimization under MOL structure. Fig. 1 gives an example of our proposed cell optimization, where the input 2D cell in older technology node is shown in Fig. 1 (a), while the optimized unidirectional cell is in Fig. 1 (b). The MOL structure is utilized that CA connecting drain or source is parallel to gates, while CB is enabling connections between via0 to polys. Due to the unidirectional shapes of MOL and Metal-1 layers, the patterns are SADP friendly. That is, the line-space array decomposition can be applied to SADP with trim masks, with tight control on overlay and wafer-print artifacts. To the best of our knowledge, this is the first systematic work toward cell regularity and pin access optimization under MOL structure. Our contributions are highlighted as follows.

- We propose a general integer linear programming (ILP) formulation to solve the unidirectional cell optimization under MOL structure.

- We propose a set of hybrid techniques to search for high quality cell optimization solution.

- We have successfully migrated a set of library cells from the conventional 2D layout to the legal unidirectional layout while satisfying a set of gridded based design rules.

- Our framework is very generic that it can not only provide SADP friendly, but also be extended to consider other lithography techniques, e.g., LELE type double patterning.

The rest of this paper will be organized as follows. Section 2 gives the problem formulation. Section 3 proposes the details of unidirectional cell routing and pin access optimization algorithms. Section 4 presents the experimental results, followed by conclusion in Section 5.

2. PROBLEM FORMULATION

In this paper we utilize a regular cell layout that both polys and metal layers have fixed directions, i.e., Metal-1 has horizontal direction while poly and Metal-2 have vertical direction. Metal-1 connects to active areas of transistors through Via-0 and CA, while it connects to polys through Via-0 and CB. MOL is a contactless structure that makes routing denser. That is, CA-to-diffusion and CB-to-poly are directly

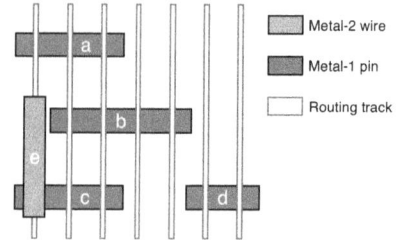

Figure 2: An example of pin access value calculation.

connected by shape overlap. CA strips can be extended in vertical direction to make power and ground connections to the transistors or to connect P transistors and N transistors together. All the Metal-1 and MOL wires must be compliant with a set of design rules [19, 20]. Since CA and Metal-1 are different layers, intersection of two perpendicular wire segments is allowed.

Metric 1 (Metal Wirelength). Wirelength is a good metric to evaluate the quality of standard cells. Performance and pin capacitance may be degraded due to longer wirelength. Therefore, a cell with shorter wirelength on metal layers is preferred.

Metric 2 (Pin Access Value). Optimized cell layout is required to provide flexible I/O pin access. Since most modern standard cell designs primarily use Metal-1 for local connections and I/O pins, Metal-1 wires present a new set of problems to standard cell I/O pin access. To evaluate pin accessibility of each pair of I/O pins, we define its corresponding pin access value as follows:

$$p(i,j) = h_i + h_j - \alpha \cdot o(i,j) \qquad (1)$$

where h_i is the available routing track number on pin i, h_j is the available routing track number on pin j, $o(i,j)$ is the number of vertical routing tracks overlapping pin i and pin j simultaneously, and α is a parameter to evaluate the effect of the overlapping part to pin accessibility. Note that if one vertical track is occupied by a Metal-2 intra-cell wire, the available routing track number would be reduced by 1.

Pin access value in Eq. (1) is decided by two factors: the available length of the two pins and the overlapping track numbers. Longer pins have more routing tracks, which allows better flexibility for Via-1 position. However, if there are vertical routing tracks overlapping two pins, Metal-2 access to the overlap part is restricted. Thus we consider the overlapping issue in the pin access value calculation. A simple example is demonstrated in Fig. 2, where a, b, c and d are pins, and e is intra-cell Metal-2 wire. Due to the wire e, the available routing track number of c is 2. If α is set to 0.6, due to Eq. (1), $p(a,c) = 3.8, p(a,d) = 5, p(c,d) = 4, p(a,b) = 5.8$, and $p(b,d) = 6$. Note that Metal-2 pitch is not necessarily equal to the grid width.

For a standard cell, the total pin access value is calculated as follows:

$$PA = \sum_{i=1}^{m} \sum_{j>i}^{m} p(i,j) \qquad (2)$$

where PA represents the total pin access value of all pin pairs in a standard cell, and m is the total pin number.

Based on above metrics, the **Unidirectional Routing with Pin Access Optimization (URPAO)** problem is defined as follows.

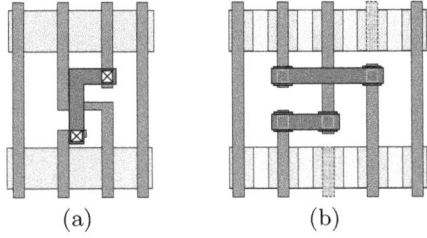

Figure 3: Dummy columns to resolve the native interconnect conflict.

Problem 1 (URPAO). *Given an original standard cell, a required total track number T and a maximum M track number T_m, URPAO problem seeks a unidirectional cell layout considering the MOL and SADP friendly. The objective is to minimize the cell wirelength, and maximize the pin access value PA.*

3. ALGORITHMS

In this section we detail our algorithms to solve the URPAO problem. Given an input cell layout, all the geometric information is parsed into a grid graph. Then ILP based approach and fast hybrid approach are proposed, respectively.

3.1 Dummy Column Insertion

In some complex standard cells such as DFF, there may be some cross-couple gate connection structures. As shown in Fig. 3 (a), one pair of polys is joined by bending Metal-1 wire, and another pair is merged into a single bent poly. Without modification, there will be no legal unidirectional routing solutions as their polys always overlap mutually. As illustrated in Fig. 3 (b), to resolve the cross-couple poly conflict, we insert a dummy poly column. The useless polys (shadow rectangles in Fig. 3 (b)) can be removed in final layout, or kept with floating for better lithography variation.

3.2 Grid Graph Construction

The geometric information of an input cell layout is parsed and stored in a grid graph. We use a coarse grain grid graph to indicate all the intra-cell interconnections. As illustrated in Fig. 4, polys are placed at regular intervals, and CA strips lie between these intervals. We use columns to represent them. Besides, as mentioned in Fig. 1, we divide routing area into three parts: P tracks, M tracks and N tracks. Utilizing grid graph effectively can simplify design rules. Since the SADP-specific parameters in [20] are much smaller than the grid width, the layout derived from the grid graph is SADP friendly intrinsically.

For a typical net, there are three types of terminals: poly gates, diffusion terminals on P transistors, and diffusion terminals on N transistors, which are denoted as M-terminals, P-terminals, and N-terminals, respectively. Besides, we distinguish power/ground nets from local interconnect nets. Since all power/ground nets only connect to power/ground rails located in the top or the bottom of the standard cell, we do not take them into consideration during cell routing stage.

3.3 M/P/N Track Number Negotiation

The input of URPAO problem specifies a total track number T and a maximum allowed M track number T_m. Under these specific track number constraints, our framework will auto-

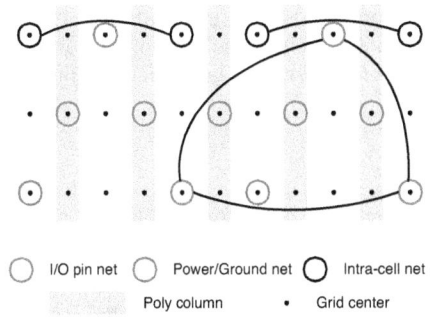

Figure 4: A grid graph example for AOI221_X1 Gate.

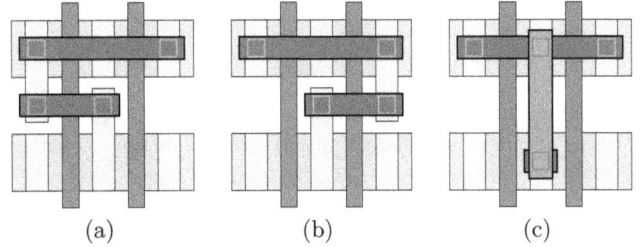

Figure 5: An example of P/N terminals connection for a net.(a), (b), and (c) are the three possible routes for the net with two P-terminals and one N-terminal.

matically decide track numbers among M tracks, P tracks, and N tracks. The basic idea is that the M track number will be determined first, followed by the track numbers for P/N tracks. The segment length in M tracks of each intra-cell net will be estimated, then we can further estimate the required minimum M track number. The M track number for the cell is set to this number if it is smaller than T_m, otherwise is set to T_m. Once the middle track number is fixed, the P/N track numbers would be decided evenly.

3.4 ILP Based URPAO

In this subsection the URPAO problem is formulated as an integer linear programming (ILP). For each net we enumerate all its possible routing geometries, all of which will be considered in the ILP formulation.

3.4.1 Intra-Cell Net Topology Enumeration

We are given a standard cell with a set of intra-cell nets $N = \{n_1, n_2, \ldots, n_m\}$. If a net has P-terminals or N-terminals, its P-terminals are connected by a wire segment running on one of P tracks and its N-terminals are connected by a wire segment running on one of N tracks. Then we choose one P-terminal and one N-terminal respectively, and join them through a middle wire segment. Taking combination of P-terminals and N-terminals into consideration, there are many possible routes for a net. For instance, as shown in Fig. 5, three possible routes exist for the net. In addition, deciding which tracks to assign these horizontal wire segments adds some more possible routes. Note that sometimes the middle wire segment needs to extend to guarantee the connection between P-terminals and N-terminals. Improvement of I/O pin accessibility is another purpose to extend wire segments.

3.4.2 ILP Formulation

After intra-cell net topology enumeration, each net n_i constructs a set of routes R_i. For each $r_i^p \in R_i$, we introduce a binary decision variable x_i^p such that x_i^p is 1 if the route r_i^p is selected for net n_i, otherwise route r_i^p is not selected.

In the ILP formulation, the objective function is to maximize

$$\beta \cdot PA - WL \tag{3}$$

where PA represents the total pin access value, WL represents the total wirelength of all the nets in the cell, and β is user specified parameter to assign the importance of pin access value. PA and WL are calculated as follows.

$$PA = \sum_{p_i, p_j \in N} \sum_{r_i^p \in R_i} \sum_{r_j^q \in R_j} p_{i,j}^{p,q} \cdot x_i^p \cdot x_j^q \tag{4}$$

$$WL = \sum_{n_i \in N} \sum_{r_i^p \in R_i} w_i^p \cdot x_i^p \tag{5}$$

Next, we describe the constraints for the ILP formulation. Since each net is assigned only to a route, we have constraint below

$$\sum_{r_i^p \in R_i} x_i^p = 1 \quad \forall n_i \in N \tag{6}$$

$$x_i^p \in \{0, 1\} \quad \forall r_i^p \in R_i , \forall n_i \in N \tag{7}$$

Violation of design rules is modeled as conflicts between pair of routes as follows.

$$x_i^p + x_j^q \leq 1, \quad \text{if } r_i^p, r_j^q \text{ conflict} \tag{8}$$

which indicates that, to ensure the final layout satisfies correct electrical connection and specific design rules, two routes conflict with each other cannot be chosen at the same time. The rules to check whether there is any conflict between route r_i^p and route r_j^q are adapted from the 1-D gridded design rules in [19] and the SADP-specific design rules in [20].

Note that Eq. (4) is not linear equation, thus we introduce a new variable $x_{i,j}^{p,q}$ to replace $x_i^p \cdot x_j^q$ with the additional constraints:

$$\begin{cases} x_{i,j}^{p,q} \geq x_i^p + x_j^q - 1 \\ x_{i,j}^{p,q} \leq x_i^p, \quad x_{i,j}^{p,q} \leq x_j^q \\ x_{i,j}^{p,q} \in \{0, 1\} \end{cases} \tag{9}$$

Similarly, we can rewrite Eq. (4) as

$$PA = \sum_{p_i, p_j \in N} \sum_{r_i^p \in R_i} \sum_{r_j^q \in R_j} w_{i,j}^{p,q} \cdot x_{i,j}^{p,q} \tag{10}$$

3.5 Fast URPAO with Hybrid Techniques

Although the 0-1 ILP formulation in the preceding section provides high-quality results, it may suffer from runtime overhead problem, especially for some cell cases with a large number of variables. In this section we propose a fast URPAO approach with hybrid techniques. The basic idea is that instead of search for optimal total metal wirelength and pin access value simultaneously, we divide the whole problem into two sub-problems. Firstly, each net is selected one basic topology through track assignment. Secondly, I/O pin extension is carried out to optimize the pin accessibility.

The details of the fast URPAO approach is summarized in Algorithm 1. Given the grid graph, we construct all horizontal wire segments of each net (line 1). We choose the middle wire segments with the shortest length. Therefore,

---

Algorithm 1 Fast URPAO
Input: Grid graph;
1: Generate all wire segments from nets N;
2: M track assignment using LP;
3: P/N track assignment using 2-SAT;
4: I/O pin extension using LP;
5: Transfer the wire segments to layout;

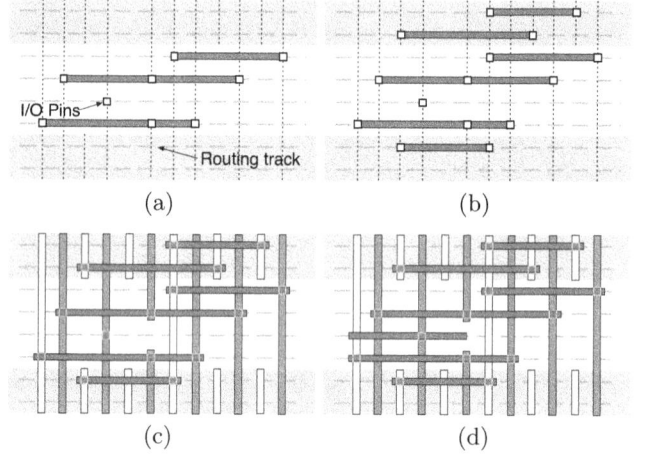

Figure 6: Example of fast URPAO approach, (a) M track assignment, (b) P/N track assignment, (c) Before pin extension, and (d) After pin extension.

sometimes P-terminal and N-terminal are directly connected through CA. After processing each net $n_i \in N$, we get a set of horizontal wire segments. The second step is M track assignment using linear programming (LP) (line 2), followed by track assignment for P/N tracks (line 3). After all wire segments are assigned to tracks, the I/O pin wire segments are extended to achieve better pin accessibility (lines 4). In the last step (line 5), we transfer the wire segments information into layout and dump out the final layout. Fig. 6 illustrates the corresponding steps of our URPAO approach.

3.5.1 LP Formulation for M Track Assignment

In MOL structure, some horizontal wire segments prefer to be assigned to M tracks, if they are connected to poly terminals (Fig. 7 (a)). In fast URPAO approach, given a set of horizontal segments, we identify those ones preferring on M tracks. However, since the M track number is limited, sometimes not all of them can be successfully assigned. If a segment connecting to poly terminal cannot be assigned to M tracks, additional Metal-2 wires are introduced to shift it to P/N tracks (Fig. 7 (b)). Besides, some poly grids are blocked due to connection to these Metal-2 wires, which are called block points. Since the M track assignment directly impact the intra-cell routability and the Metal-2 wirelength, we rely on an LP formulation to search for a reasonable assignment solution.

Let a variable x_i indicates whether the wire segment w_i is assigned to a M track. For each column c_i in the grid graph, there exist two sets $BLK(i)$ and $NET(i)$. If net n_j produces no block points when assigned to a P/N track, n_j is added to $NET(i)$ of the columns c_i which n_j overlaps when it is assigned to a M track. Otherwise, net n_j is added to set $BLK(i)$ of the columns c_i which n_j blocks when not assigned to a M

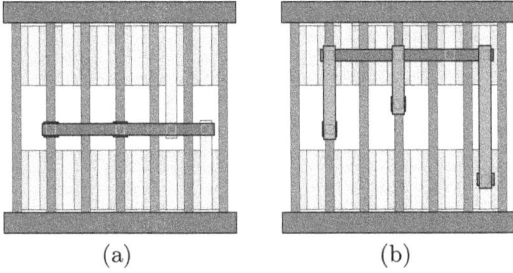

Figure 7: (a) Assign the horizontal wire segment to a M track. (b) Additional Metal-2 wires when assign wire segment to a P/N track.

track. Based on the above definitions, the LP formulation is as follows.

$$\max \sum_i b_i \cdot x_i \tag{11}$$

$$\text{s.t.} \sum_{i \in NET(j)} x_i \leq T_m - |BLK(j)|, \quad \forall \text{ column } j \tag{12}$$

where b_i is the benefit of w_i when it is assigned to one of M tracks. $|BLK(j)|$ is the cardinality of set $BLK(j)$. After solving LP, selected wire segments are assigned to M tracks one-by-one according to the order. The sequence of wire segments is determined based on the LP solutions in descending order. That is, the wire segment with the biggest x_i is assigned first. After a segment is assigned, the capacity of the corresponding track is dynamically updated, and the next segment would be assigned to an available track which can accommodate this segment and has highest capacity.

3.5.2 2-SAT Formulation for P/N Track Assignment

Several wire segments may not be assigned during the M track assignment. Besides, there are some horizontal segments that only connects P-terminals or N-terminals. All these segments are assigned to P/N tracks. It is observed that certain pairs of wire segments have vertical constraints. For example, one segment w_i cannot be placed below another segment w_j. To consider these constraints during P/N track assignment, we define a binary variable x_i for each wire segment w_i. $x_i = 1$ if and only if the i-th segment is assigned to a P track, otherwise it is assigned into an N track. Then all vertical constraints are considered by a 2-SAT formulation.

$$\text{FALSE} = \bar{x}_i \cdot x_j \Leftrightarrow \text{TRUE} = (x_i + \bar{x}_j) \tag{13}$$

That is, the clause $(x_i + \bar{x}_j)$ is introduced into the 2-conjunctive normal form (CNF) formula. 2-SAT problem can be optimally solved in linear time [21] based on strongly connected component. The track type for each segment is set according to the topological order of each component. Then the similar algorithm in Section 3.5.1 is adopted to determine the detailed track for each wire segment.

3.5.3 LP Formulation for I/O Pin Extension

After all wire segments are assigned to the tracks, the next step is line end extension for pin wire segments. Here we denote PW as all the pin wire segments. Because we want to maximize the total amount of line end extensions, the objective function is defined in (14). Constraints (15) - (16) define the line end extension limits, while constraint (17) indicates the minimum wire length of each pin wire segment.

For each pair of pin wire segments, the initial relative order in x-coordinate is determined. Suppose that pin wire segment w_i is on the left of pin wire segment w_j, constraint (18) is developed to prevent overlap of pairs of extended pins.

$$\max \sum_{i=1}^m (l_i^0 - l_i) + (r_i - r_i^0) \tag{14}$$

$$\text{s.t.} \quad c_L \leq l_i \leq l_i^0 \qquad \forall w_i \in PW \tag{15}$$

$$r_i^0 \leq r_i \leq c_R \qquad \forall w_i \in PW \tag{16}$$

$$r_i - l_i \geq l_0 \qquad \forall w_i \in PW \tag{17}$$

$$l_j - r_i \geq l_1 \qquad \forall w_i, w_j \in \text{same track} \tag{18}$$

We can simplify the objective function by omitting item l_i^0 and r_i^0, which are constants for the pin extension problem. It shall be noted that the dual problem of the line end extension is a min-cost flow problem [22]. But in our implementation the line end extension is formulated and solved through LP, as for standard cell level design problem the LP solver is fast enough.

4. EXPERIMENTAL RESULTS

The proposed standard cell routing algorithms are implemented in C++, and tested on a Linux machine with 3.3GHz CPU. The GUROBI solver [23] is used to generate the ILP/LP solutions. The experiments are carried out on Nangate $45nm$ standard cell library [24]. In our implementation the α value in (1) is set to 0.6, the β value in (3) is set to 0.02. Our cell routing framework is targeting at $10nm$ technology node with SADP process. The regular gridded based design rules [19] and SADP-specific design rules [20] are adapted in our work.

In Table 1 we compare two proposed algorithms for URPAO problem, where ILP based URPAO (Section 3.4) and fast URPAO with hybrid techniques (Section 3.5) are applied, respectively. Since the Nangate $45nm$ library consists of more than 130 standard cells, it is hard to list all the results. Therefore, ten typical standard cells are listed here. Columns "WL(nm)", "PA" and "CPU(s)" are the total metal wirelength, pin accessibility, and the cell routing runtime in seconds. We can see that although ILP based cell routing can achieve optimal solutions in theory, for some cells it suffers from long runtime overhead. Compared with expensive ILP based cell routing, our fast cell routing can achive more than $10000\times$ speed-up. Besides, the fast method can get very comparable results, in terms of both wire-length and pin access values. That is, through fast cell routing the pin access value is 2% less, the wirelength is increased 0.7%.

5. CONCLUSION

In this paper, we propose a comprehensive study for the MOL based unidirectional cell layout regularity and pin access optimization. To the best of our knowledge, this work is so far the only one to automatically perform cell synthesis toward regularity, pin access optimization, and SADP friendly design. In addition, our framework is generic and flexible that it can be easily extended to consider other lithography techniques, e.g., LELE type patterning. As MOL structure ensures better regularity and better routability, we hope this paper will stimulate more future research into the automatic cell design for emerging technology nodes.

Table 1: Comparison of Two Cell Routing Approaches

Cell Name	Net#	T	ILP Based URPAO			Fast URPAO		
			WL(nm)	PA	CPU(s)	WL(nm)	PA	CPU(s)
XOR2_X2	5	9	3072	101.6	1.99	3072	101.6	0.14
		10	3072	101.6	8.05	3072	99.2	0.13
HA_X1	7	9	2448	91.2	0.55	2448	91.2	0.13
		10	2448	91.2	0.95	2448	91.2	0.14
MUX2_X1	6	9	1920	66.6	33.51	1920	66.6	0.11
		10	1920	66.6	242.99	1920	66.0	0.12
AND2_X1	4	9	864	21.0	1.57	864	21.0	0.13
		10	864	21.0	16.17	1008	23.4	0.12
AOI21_X1	5	9	960	38.4	22.30	960	38.4	0.13
		10	1104	42.0	57.51	1104	42.0	0.12
CLKGATE_X1	8	9	3552	30.0	3.60	3600	30.0	0.14
		10	3312	30.0	4.80	3312	30.0	0.11
DLL_X2	7	9	3120	29.4	76.09	3120	28.8	0.11
		10	2928	29.4	297.47	2928	28.8	0.11
DFFS_X1	12	9	8496	145.6	185.48	8880	149.0	0.13
		10	8064	145.6	520.69	8352	149.0	0.13
AOI221_X1	8	9	2208	181.2	>7202	2160	175.4	0.13
		10	2256	184.8	>7201	2160	177.2	0.12
NAND4_X1	5	9	1440	118.2	2087.63	1296	108.4	0.13
		10	1488	120.8	>7202	1296	109.6	0.12
avg.			2776.8	82.8	>1260	2796.0	81.3	0.12
ratio			**1.0**	**1.0**	**1.0**	**1.007**	**0.982**	**0.0001**

Acknowledgment

This work is supported in part by NSF and SRC.

6. REFERENCES

[1] D. Z. Pan, B. Yu, and J.-R. Gao, "Design for manufacturing with emerging nanolithography," *IEEE Transactions on CAD*, vol. 32, no. 10, pp. 1453–1472, 2013.

[2] T. Jhaveri, V. Rovner, L. Liebmann, L. Pileggi, A. J. Strojwas *et al.*, "Co-optimization of circuits, layout and lithography for predictive technology scaling beyond gratings," *IEEE Transactions on CAD*, vol. 29, no. 4, pp. 509–527, 2010.

[3] Y. Du, H. Zhang, M. D. F. Wong, and K.-Y. Chao, "Hybrid lithography optimization with e-beam and immersion processes for 16nm 1D gridded design," in *ASPDAC*, 2012, pp. 707–712.

[4] L. Liebmann, A. Chu, and P. Gutwin, "The daunting complexity of scaling to 7nm without EUV: Pushing DTCO to the extreme," in *Proc. of SPIE*, vol. 9427, 2015.

[5] T. Taghavi, C. Alpert, A. Huber, Z. Li, G.-J. Nam *et al.*, "New placement prediction and mitigation techniques for local routing congestion," in *ICCAD*, 2010, pp. 621–624.

[6] T. Kauerauf, A. Branka, G. Sorrentino, P. Roussel, S. Demuynck *et al.*, "Reliability of MOL local interconnects," in *IRPS*, 2013, pp. 2F–5.

[7] A. Mallik, P. Zuber, T.-T. Liu, B. Chava, B. Ballal *et al.*, "TEASE: a systematic analysis framework for early evaluation of FinFET-based advanced technology nodes," in *DAC*, 2013, pp. 24:1–24:6.

[8] M. Rashed, N. Jain, J. Kim, M. Tarabbia, I. Rahim *et al.*, "Innovations in special constructs for standard cell libraries in sub 28nm technologies," in *IEDM*, 2013, pp. 9.7.1–9.7.4.

[9] G. Luk-Pat, B. Painter, A. Miloslavsky, P. De Bisschop, A. Beacham *et al.*, "Avoiding wafer-print artifacts in spacer is dielectric (SID) patterning," in *Proc. of SPIE*, vol. 8683, 2013.

[10] B. Yu, Y.-H. Lin, G. Luk-Pat, D. Ding, K. Lucas *et al.*, "A high-performance triple patterning layout decomposer with balanced density," in *ICCAD*, 2013, pp. 163–169.

[11] B. Yu and D. Z. Pan, "Layout decomposition for quadruple patterning lithography and beyond," in *DAC*, 2014, pp. 53:1–53:6.

[12] B. Yu, S. Roy, J.-R. Gao, and D. Z. Pan, "Triple patterning lithography layout decomposition using end-cutting," *Journal of Micro/Nanolithography, MEMS, and MOEMS (JM3)*, vol. 14, no. 1, pp. 011 002–011 002, 2015.

[13] X. Tang and X. Yuan, "Technology migration techniques for simplified layouts with restrictive design rules," in *ICCAD*, 2006, pp. 655–660.

[14] N. Ryzhenko and S. Burns, "Standard cell routing via boolean satisfiability," in *DAC*, 2012, pp. 603–612.

[15] S. Hougardy, T. Nieberg, and J. Schneider, "BonnCell: Automatic layout of leaf cells," in *ASPDAC*, 2013, pp. 453–460.

[16] B. Taylor and L. Pileggi, "Exact combinatorial optimization methods for physical design of regular logic bricks," in *DAC*, 2007, pp. 344–349.

[17] H. Zhang, M. D. F. Wong, and K.-Y. Chao, "On process-aware 1-D standard cell design," in *ASPDAC*, 2010, pp. 838–842.

[18] P.-H. Wu, M. Lin, T.-C. Chen, T.-Y. Ho, Y.-C. Chen *et al.*, "1-D cell generation with printability enhancement," *IEEE Transactions on CAD*, vol. 32, no. 3, pp. 419–432, 2013.

[19] J. Cortadella, J. Petit, S. Gómez, and F. Moll, "A boolean rule-based approach for manufacturability-aware cell routing." *IEEE Transactions on CAD*, vol. 33, no. 3, pp. 409–422, 2014.

[20] X. Xu, B. Cline, G. Yeric, B. Yu, and D. Z. Pan, "Self-aligned double patterning aware pin access and standard cell layout co-optimization," in *ISPD*, 2014, pp. 101–108.

[21] B. Aspvall, M. F. Plass, and R. E. Tarjan, "A linear-time algorithm for testing the truth of certain quantified boolean formulas," *Information Processing Letters*, vol. 8, no. 3, pp. 121–123, 1979.

[22] R. K. Ahuja, T. L. Magnanti, and J. B. Orlin, *Network Flows: Theory, Algorithms, and Applications.* Prentice Hall/Pearson, 2005.

[23] Gurobi Optimization Inc., "Gurobi optimizer reference manual," http://www.gurobi.com, 2014.

[24] "NanGate FreePDK45 Generic Open Cell Library," http://www.si2.org/openeda.si2.org/projects/nangatelib.

Inevitability of Phase-locking in a Charge Pump Phase Lock Loop using Deductive Verification

Hafiz ul Asad
City University London
EC1 0HB London,UK
hafiz.ul-asad.1@city.ac.uk

Kevin D. Jones
Plymouth University
PL4 8AA Plymouth,UK
kevin.jones@plymouth.ac.uk

ABSTRACT

Phase-locking in a charge pump (CP) phase lock loop (PLL) is said to be inevitable if all possible states of the CP PLL eventually converge to the equilibrium, where the input and output phases are in lock and the node voltages vanish. We verify this property for a CP PLL using deductive verification. We split this complex property into two sub-properties defined in two disjoint subsets of the state space. We deductively verify the first property using multiple Lyapunov certificates for hybrid systems, and use the Escape certificate for the verification of the second property. Construction of deductive certificates involves positivity check of polynomial inequalities (which is an NP-Hard problem), so we use the sound but incomplete Sum of Squares (SOS) relaxation algorithm to provide a numerical solution.

Categories and Subject Descriptors

B.7.2 [**INTEGRATED CIRCUITS**]: Design Aids—*Verification and Simulation*

General Terms

Verification

Keywords

Deductive Verification; AMS Circuits; Lyapunov Certificate; Escape Certificate; SOS Programming

1. INTRODUCTION

Formal methods are in their infancy in Analog and Mixed Signal (AMS) circuits verification. Start up problems (Inevitability) have been very common in PLL circuits, i.e., for certain initial states of voltages on the nodes, the circuits do not converge to the desired behaviour. Furthermore, when perturbed by an external disturbance, designers need to know if the system will return to the desired behaviour.

Hybrid systems are well known modelling paradigm for a CP PLL [16], [2], [6]. Techniques for the verification of hybrid

systems can be classified as, reach-set methods, abstraction based methods, and certificate based methods. Reach-set method has been used to prove the inevitability property. Hundreds of discrete transitions are required by the hybrid model of the CP PLL before it reaches the locking state. This results in a large number of continuous set computations followed by the guard conditions describing the switching laws, making the reachability computations prohibitively expensive.

In this paper, we use certificate based deductive verification of the inevitability of phase-locking in higher order CP PLL circuits. Due to its complexity, we adopt a two-pronged verification approach and divide the inevitability property in to the conjunction of two sub-properties. Verification of these two properties determine the truth value of the inevitability property in two disjoint subsets of the state space. The first property specifies, that in a compact set, all system trajectories eventually converge to the equilibrium locking state. The second property is specified, such that trajectories in the second subset, will eventually escape the set and reaches the set where the first property holds. The first property is verified by computing an attractive invariant region (ROA), utilizing the deductive Lyapunov stability theory for hybrid systems [5]. We construct multiple Lyapunov certificates for different modes of the CP PLL hybrid system. The maximized level curves of these Lyapunov certificates characterize the level sets whose union is the ROA. Similarly, we use Escape certificates to verify the second property, and establish that trajectories in the second set will eventually leave and reach the ROA. Our certificate (Lyapunov-Escape) based deductive approach involves checking positivity of polynomial inequalities, which is an NP-hard problem. Therefore, we utilize the sound but incomplete SOS relaxation to construct these certificates.

1.1 Related Work

A survey of the formal verification of AMS circuits can be found in [17]. In [6], the author verified the 'time to locking' property for a digitally extensive PLL. [16] verified 'global convergence' property for an all digital PLL. They divided the state space into linear and non-linear regions, and applied linear Lyapunov stability theory (using Quadratic Lyapunov Certificate) for linear and reachability analysis for non-linear regions respectively. Time-outs of the reachability tool has been reported by the author due to the large number of discrete transitions needed by the PLL hybrid automata. To avoid discrete jumps, [2] presented a continuization technique and verified the 'time to locking' property of a CP PLL.

Inevitability of an equilibrium state is closely related to the global asymptotic stability of a dynamical system . Lyapunov theory is a well known approach for the verification of such properties [5]. Hybrid system models have different flavours that can be found in [8],[1]. Here we consider the framework outlined in [4]. In the last decade, SOS programming has been the major tool used in the algorithmic construction of Lyapunov certificates for continuous as well as hybrid systems [9], [11]. Barrier certificates has been used for safety verification of the hybrid systems in [11]. Deductive verification of continuous and hybrid systems have been demonstrated in [14], [13].

This paper is organized as follows: In Sec.II, we introduce the preliminaries of this paper. Sec.III illustrates verification of the inevitability of phase-locking in CP PLL. Experimental results are shown in Sec.IV. Sec.V concludes the paper.

2. PRELIMINARIES

2.1 Hybrid Systems Model

We use the hybrid system formalism described in [4]. We consider a hybrid system described by the tuple $(\mathcal{C}, \mathcal{F}, \mathcal{D}, \mathcal{G})$. Here, $\{\mathcal{C} = \bigcup_{i \in I_C} C_i\} \subset \mathbb{R}^n$, and $\{\mathcal{D} = \bigcup_{i \in I_D} D_i\} \subset \mathbb{R}^n$ are the flow set and jump set for $i \in \mathbb{N}$, respectively. I_C and I_D are finite disjoint index sets and it is possible that $C_i \cap D_i \neq \emptyset$. The flow and jump maps are, respectively, $\mathcal{F} = \bigcup_{i \in I_C} F_i$, and $\mathcal{G} = \bigcup_{i \in I_C} G_i$, where each $F_i : \mathbb{R}^n \times \mathbb{R}^m \to \mathbb{R}^{m+n}$, and, $G_i = \mathbb{R}^n \to \mathbb{R}^n$. These two mappings characterize the continuous and discrete evolution of the system, whereas C_i and D_i describe subsets of $\mathbb{R}^n$ where such evolution may occur. We represent a hybrid system $\mathcal{H}$ as

$$\mathcal{H} = \begin{cases} \dot{x} = F_i(x, u) \in \mathcal{F} & x \in \mathcal{C}, \ u \in \mathcal{U} \\ x^+ = G_i(x) \in \mathcal{G} & x \in \mathcal{D} \end{cases} \quad (1)$$

Here $u \in \mathcal{U} \subset \mathbb{R}^m$ is a vector of uncertain parameters. The state of the hybrid system consists of alternate flows in jumps through $\mathcal{C}$ and $\mathcal{D}$ according to F_i and G_i, respectively. This hybrid phenomena can be described by a notion of time called hybrid time.

Definition 1 (Hybrid Time Domain).
A set $\mathcal{T} \subset \mathbb{R}_{\geq 0} \times \mathbb{N}$ is a hybrid time domain if

$$\mathcal{T} = \bigcup_{j=0}^{j-1} ([t_j, t_{j+1}], j)$$

where $0 = t_0 \leq t_1 \leq t_2 \leq, ...,$ with the last interval possibly of the form $[t_j, t_{j+1}] \times \{j\}$, $[t_j, t_{j+1}) \times \{j\}$, or $[t_j, \infty) \times \{j\}$.

Definition 2 (Hybrid Arc).
A mapping $x : \mathcal{T} \to \mathbb{R}^n$ is a hybrid arc if $\mathcal{T}$ is a hybrid time domain and for each $j \in \mathbb{N}$, the function $t \mapsto x(t, j)$ is locally absolutely continuous on the interval $I_j = \{t : (t, j) \in \mathcal{T}\}$.

We denote by dom x, the domain of the hybrid arc which is the hybrid time domain. A hybrid arc x is a solution to the hybrid system $\mathcal{H}$, if $x(0, j) \in \mathcal{C} \cup \mathcal{D}$ and (i) for each $j \in \mathbb{N}$ such that I_j has a non-empty interior,

$$\dot{x}(t, j) = F_i(x(t, j)), \ \forall t \in I_j,$$
$$x(t, j) \in C_i, \ \forall i \in I_C, \ \forall t \in [min \ I_j, sup \ I_j) \quad (2)$$

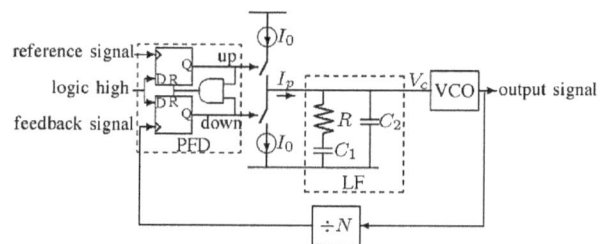

Figure 1: *Charge Pump (CP) Phase Lock Loop (PLL)*

Assumption 1.
The flow maps $F_i(x, u)$ and the jump maps $G_i(x)$ are polynomials.

Definition 3 (Equilibrium point).
A point $x(t, j) \in \mathcal{C} \cup \mathcal{D}$ is called an equilibrium, if $\exists t, \ \exists j$, $F_j(x(t, j), u) = 0$.

Definition 4 (Inevitability of Equilibrium).
The equilibrium point x_e is said to be inevitable, if $\forall x(0, j) \in \mathcal{C} \cup \mathcal{D}$ and bounded t, $x(t, j) \to x_e$.

2.2 CP PLL Model

A CP PLL circuit consists of a reference signal, a phase frequency detector (PFD), a charge pump (CP), a loop filter (LF), and a voltage controlled oscillator (VCO). In this paper we consider a single path higher order (Third and fourth) CP PLL shown in Fig. 1[1]. We use a behavioural model of the PLL, where we consider a linear model for VCO, a linear model for the third order LF, and a non-linear model for the PFD. We denote by ϕ_{ref}, and ϕ_{VCO}, the phases of the reference and VCO output feedback signals respectively. We model the CP PLL as a hybrid system such that the non-linearities of the PFD is modelled as a piecewise continuous signal. Ignoring the cycle slip phenomena, the PFD output in the form of the charge pump current I_p, is given by the following piecewise linear inclusion:

$$I_p = \begin{cases} \in [I_p^U \ I_P^U] & \text{UP=1, Down=0, } 0 \leq \phi_{VCO} < 2\pi \leq \phi_{ref} \\ \in [I_p^D \ I_P^D] & \text{UP=0, Down=1, } 0 \leq \phi_{ref} < 2\pi \leq \phi_{VCO} \\ \in [0^R \ 0^R] & \text{UP=0, Down=0, } 0 \leq \phi_{VCO}, \phi_{ref} < 2\pi \end{cases} \quad (3)$$

We denote the three modes as mode1 (UP=0, Down=0), mode2 (UP=1, Down=0) and mode3 (UP=0, Down=1). The transition from one mode to another is based on the reference and feedback signals hitting the 2π threshold. Due to the cyclic behaviour of the PLL and to keep the analysis modulo 2π, we need to ensure the phases remain in the range $0 \leq \phi_{VCO}, \phi_{VCO} < 2\pi$ (Similarly ϕ_{ref}) after resetting the PFD. This is achieved by resetting the two phases such that $(\phi_{ref} := 0, \ \phi_{VCO} := \phi_{VCO} - 2\pi)$, and $(\phi_{ref} := \phi_{ref} - 2\pi, \ \phi_{VCO} := 0)$, while taking transitions from mode1 to mode2 and mode1 to mode3, respectively. Identity resets are used for transitions from mode2 to mode1 and mode3 to mode1.

Our model consists of the state variables, ϕ_{VCO}, ϕ_{ref}, voltage v_1 across the capacitor C_1, and the voltage v_2 across the capacitor C_2 (Fourth order has an additional voltage variable across the third capacitor). Let f_{VCO}, and f_{ref}, represent the frequencies of the VCO output and the refer-

---

[1]Third order shown here,fourth order has an additional resistor-capacitor in its LF

ence signal respectively. If K_p is the gain of the LF, then $f_{VCO} = K_p v_2/2\pi + f_O$, where f_O is the free running frequency of the VCO. Therefore, $\dot{\phi}_{VCO} = 2\pi f_{VCO}/N$, $\dot{\phi}_{ref} = 2\pi f_{ref}$. By Kirchhoff's current law and using the three modes of the PFD, we get the following hybrid system of the third order CP PLL

$$\mathcal{H} = \begin{cases} \begin{pmatrix} \dot{v_1} \\ v_2 \\ \phi_{ref} \\ \phi_{VCO} \end{pmatrix} = A \begin{pmatrix} v_1 \\ v_2 \\ \phi_{ref} \\ \phi_{VCO} \end{pmatrix} + BI_p + c \quad x \in \mathcal{C}, \\ x^+ = G_i(x) \qquad\qquad\qquad\quad x \in \mathcal{D} \end{cases} \quad (4)$$

where, $A = \begin{pmatrix} -1/RC_1 & 1/RC_1 & 0 & 0 \\ 1/RC_2 & -1/RC_2 & 0 & 0 \\ 0 & 0 & 0 & 0 \\ 0 & K_p/N & 0 & 0 \end{pmatrix}$,

$B = \begin{pmatrix} 0 \\ I_p/C_2 \\ 0 \\ 0 \end{pmatrix}$, $c = \begin{pmatrix} 0 \\ 0 \\ 2\pi f_{ref} \\ 2\pi f_o/N \end{pmatrix}$, I_p as given by Eq. 3.

From the three modes and their invariants, we can easily find the sets $\mathcal{C}$, $\mathcal{D}$, and the jump maps $G_i(x)$. We notice, that the state variables ϕ_{ref} and ϕ_{VCO} do not settle to zero in their steady state. Instead the system has a limit cycle like behaviour in the (ϕ_{ref}, ϕ_{VCO}) plane. Here, we are interested in the stability of the equilibrium point (locking condition) where the difference of these two phases becomes zero. We therefore, use the difference $\phi_{ref} - \phi_{VCO}$ as a state variable instead of ϕ_{ref}, and ϕ_{VCO}.

Remark 1.
This change of state variables transforms all jump maps G_i in to identity maps ($G_i(x) = x$), as the same constant 2π is subtracted from ϕ_{VCO} and ϕ_{ref}, leaving their difference $\phi_{ref} - \phi_{VCO}$ before and after the jumps unchanged.

2.3 Attractive Invariants in Hybrid Systems using Lyapunov Certificates

Contrary to the safety, where existence of an invariant set is sufficient for proving/dis-proving the property, we use the concept of "attractive invariants" to verify inevitability property. These are compact semi-algebraic sets inheriting the properties of invariance and attractivity; trajectories stay there indefinitely and eventually converge to the equilibrium state. Stability and attractivity concepts for an equilibrium state of the continuous dynamical systems are discussed in [5], and have been extended to hybrid systems in [4]. The equilibrium point, $x_e = 0$, is called asymptotically stable if it is both stable and attractive. There are several versions of the stability theorems for hybrid systems based on the global Lyapunov certificate, and multiple Lyapunov certificates [12]. We use the following theorem of asymptotic stability of the equilibrium and define the attractive invariant.

Theorem 1.
Let, $\mathcal{I}_0 \subseteq I_C$ be the set of indices that contain the equilibrium. For a hybrid system $\mathcal{H}$ having an equilibrium point $x_e = 0$, if there exist Lyapunov certificates V_i such that,

1. $V_i(x) > 0$, $\forall i \in I_C$, $\forall x \in \mathcal{C} \setminus x_e$,

2. $V_i(0) = 0$, $\forall i \in \mathcal{I}_0$,

3. $\frac{\partial V_i}{\partial x}(x)F_i(x,u) < 0$, $\forall i \in I_C$, $\forall x \in \mathcal{C} \setminus x_e$, $F_i \in \mathcal{F}$, $u \in \mathcal{U}$,

4. $V_j(G_i(x)) - V_{j'}(x) < 0$, $\forall j \; \forall j' \in I_C$, $j \neq j'$, $\forall i \in I_D$, $\forall x \in \mathcal{D} \setminus x_e$, $G_i \in \mathcal{G}$,

then x_e is asymptotically stable. Furthermore, the set $\mathcal{AI} = \bigcup_i (V_i \leq c_{max}^i) \subset \mathcal{C} \cup \mathcal{D}$ is an "attractive invariant" set.

Proof. Similarly to [12]. □

2.4 Escape of Trajectories from a Set using Escape Certificates

In this paper, we also use an another important characteristic of the trajectories in a semi-algebraic set and term it as the "Escape" property. This property ensures that trajectories in a compact set can not converge to an invariant set (Equilibrium,Limit Cycle), and will eventually leave that set.

Proposition 1.
For a compact set $\mathcal{X} \subset C_i$, if there is a differentiable Escape certificate, $E : \mathbb{R}^n \to \mathbb{R}$, and $\epsilon > 0$, such that

$$\frac{\partial E}{\partial x}(x)F_i(x,u) \leq -\varepsilon, \; \forall x \in \mathcal{X}, \; u \in \mathcal{U} \qquad (5)$$

then $\forall x(t, i) \in \mathcal{X}$, $x(t+T, i) \notin \mathcal{X}$, $T > t$.

Proof. Assume that there exists $x_0 \in \mathcal{X}$ such that $x(t, i)$ starting at x_0 remain in $\mathcal{X}$ as $t \to \infty$. From Eq. 5, $E(x) = \int_0^\infty \frac{\partial E}{\partial x}(x)F_i(x,u) \leq -\varepsilon$. As $t \to \infty$, $E(x) \to -\infty$. This contradicts the assumption as $E(x)$ should be bounded if $x(t, j)$ has to remain in the bounded set $\mathcal{X}$. Therefore, $x(t, j)$ has to eventually "Escape" the set $\mathcal{X}$ in finite time. □

Lemma 1.
If the hybrid arc $x(t, j)$ is bounded and belong to a set $\mathcal{X}$ for the hybrid time $(t, j) \geq 0$, then $x(t, j)$ approaches a compact invariant set as $(t, j) \to \infty$.

Proof. See [5]. □

2.5 SOS Programming

Our deductive verification approach involves checking the positivity of polynomials in semi-algebraic sets. To solve this NP-Hard problem, a sound relaxation method based on SOS programming has been presented in [10], [12]. A sufficient condition for a multivariate polynomial $p(x)$ to be non-negative everywhere, is that it can be decomposed as a sum of squares of polynomials. A polynomial $p(x)$ is a sum of squares, if there exist polynomials $p_1(x), ..., p_m(x)$ such that $p(x) = \sum_{i=1}^m p_i^2(x)$. We denote the set of polynomials in n variables with real coefficients by $\mathcal{P}_n$. A subset of this set is the set of SOS polynomials in n variables denoted by $\mathcal{S}_n$. For a differentiable scalar polynomial $q : \mathbb{R}^n \to \mathbb{R}$, we define the 0-sub-level-set of q as $\mathcal{Z}(q) = \{x \in \mathbb{R}^n \mid q(x) \leq 0\}$. We present an important lemma to be used for polynomial level sets operations such as intersection, union, and set inclusion [15].

Lemma 2.
For polynomials $p1, p2 \in \mathcal{P}_n$, if there exist SOS polynomials $s0$, $s1 \in \mathcal{S}_n$ such that

$$s0 - s1p1 + p2 = 0 \; \forall x \in \mathbb{R}^n \qquad (6)$$

Then $\mathcal{Z}(p1) \subset \mathcal{Z}(p2)$

Proof. See for example [15] and the references there in. □

3. VERIFICATION OF INEVITABILITY OF PHASE-LOCKING IN CP PLL

To verify inevitability of the CP PLL equilibrium, we introduce two compact sets $S1$, and $S2$, such that $S1 \cap S2 = \emptyset$, and $S1 \cup S2 = C \cup D$. We define two properties whose verification implies verification of the inevitability of the equilibrium.

Property 1.
$\forall x(0,j) \in S1, \; x(t,j) \to x_e$ for $t \to \infty$.

Property 2.
$\forall x(0,j) \in S2 = (C \cup D) \setminus S1, \; x(t,j) \in S1$ for $t \to b \in \mathbb{R}_{>0}$.

If we denote the inevitability property by φ, Property.1 by $\varphi1$ and Property.2 by $\varphi2$, then $\varphi = \varphi1 \wedge \varphi2$. A hybrid arc x satisfies φ iff it satisfies $\varphi1$ in $S1$ and $\varphi2$ in $S2$, i.e., $\forall x \in C \cup D, \; x \models \varphi \iff (x \models \varphi1 \; \forall x \in S1) \wedge (x \models \varphi2 \; \forall x \in S2)$. We verify property $\varphi1$ using Lyapunov certificates, and property $\varphi2$ using Escape certificates.

Theorem 2.
If there are feasible Lyapunov certificates (fulfilling Th. 1), $\{V_1, V_2, V_3\}$, then, $x \models \varphi1, \; \forall x(0,j) \in S1 = \{(V_1 \leq \gamma1_{max}) \cup (V_2 \leq \gamma2_{max}) \cup (V_3 \leq \gamma3_{max})\}$, and $AI = S1$ is the attractive invariant set.

Proof. Follows directly from Th. 1, since the level sets defined by the level curves of the Lyapunov certificates represent attractive invariant sets with the negative Lie-derivative along the system trajectories. Therefore, eventually all system trajectories starting in these level sets converge to the equilibrium phase-locking state. $\square$

Theorem 3.
If in a compact set $S2$, such that $S1 \cup S2 = C \cup D$, where $S1$ is an attractive invariant set, we have an Escape certificate $E = \cup_{i \in \{1,2,3\}} E_i(x) \; \forall x \in S2$, then, $\forall x(t,j) \in S2, \; x(t,j) \in S1$ as $t + j \to \infty$.

Proof. Follows directly from Lemma. 1. The boundedness of $x(t,j)$ is guaranteed by the supply voltage and ground of the CP PLL circuit. Existence of an Escape certificate for $x(t,j) \in S2$ (Prop. 1), guarantees that trajectories will eventually leave $S2$, and being the only invariant set, they will eventually reach $S1$. $\square$

Following Th. 2, we verify $\varphi1$ using Alg. 1. The truth value of $\varphi1$ depends on the existence of the attractive invariant set $S1$. The set $S1$ is computed from the maximized level sets defined by the three candidate Lyapunov certificates V_1, V_2, V_3, Line (1-6). We compute these certificates using SOS programming and a mathematical technique called the S-procedure (to incorporate domain constraints [3]). We encode the verification of $\varphi1$ as two SOS programs. The first SOS program is given below:

(a) $V_i(x) - \sum_{k=1}^{n_{C_i}} s_1^{(ik)}(x) g_{ik}(x) \in S_n, \; \forall x \neq 0,$
$i \in \{1,2,3\}, \forall k \in \{1,..,n_{C_i}\}, s_1^{(ik)} \in S_n,$

(b) $\left[-\frac{\partial V_i}{\partial x}(x) F_i(x,u) - \sum_{k=1}^{n_{C_i}} s_2^{(ik)}(x) g_{ik}(x) - \right.$

$\left. \sum_{j=1}^{m} s_3^{(j)}(x) a_j(u) \right] \in S_n,$

$\forall i \in \{1,2,3\}, \forall k \in \{1,..,n_{C_i}\}, \; \forall j \in \{1,..,m\}, s_2^{(ik)}, s_3^{(j)} \in S_n,$

(c) $\left[V_j(x) - V_{j'}(G_i(x)) - s_4^{(i0)}(x) h_{i0}(x) - \right.$

$\left. \sum_{k=1}^{m_{D_i}} s_5^{(ik)}(x) h_{ik}(x) \right] \in S_n, \; \forall j \forall j' \in \{1,2,3\},$

$j \neq j', \; \forall i \in \{1,2,3,4\}, \forall k \in \{1,..,n_{D_i}\},$
$s_4^{(i0)} \geq 0, s_5^{(ik)} \in S_n$

Here $V_i(x), V_j(x), V_{j'}(x), s_1^{(ik)}, s_2^{(ik)}, s_3^{(j)}, s_4^{(i0)}, s_5^{(ik)}$, are polynomials of degree d.

SOS constraints (a) and (b) enforce positive definiteness on the Lyapunov certificates, and negative semi-definiteness on their Lie-derivatives respectively. Furthermore, these constraints have to be satisfied in their respective domains C_i's, where, $C_i = \{x \in \mathbb{R}^n : g_{ik} \geq 0, \text{ for } k \in \{1,..,n_{C_i}\}, i \in \{1,2,3\}\}$. Constraint (b) also ensures parameters u to belong to the set, $\{a(u) \geq 0, \text{ for } j \in \{1,..,m\}\}$. Constraint in (c) ensures that Lyapunov certificates $V_j(x)$ decrease along the discrete jumps in the sets, $D_i = \{x \in \mathbb{R}^n : h_{ik} \geq 0, h_{i0} = 0, \text{ for } k \in \{1,..,n_{D_i}\}, i \in \{1,2,3,4\}\}$, through the mappings $G_i(x)$'s. SOS polynomials $s_1^{(ik)}, s_2^{(ik)}, s_3^{(j)}, s_4^{(i0)}, s_5^{(ik)}$ are used to enforce domain constraints through the S-procedure. A feasible solution of the above SOS program results in Lyapunov certificates V_i. If this SOS program is infeasible, then either the program is repeated for an increased degree d of the polynomials, or we conclude that the truth value of the property $\varphi1$ can not be established Line (11-16).

The second SOS program for maximizing the level curves for every $V_i \leq (\gamma_i \in \mathbb{R}_{>0})$ is (Line-7),

maximize $\quad \gamma_i$

subject to $\quad s5 + \sum_{k=1}^{n_{C_i}} s6^{ik}(-g_{ik}) - (V_i - \gamma_i) + \epsilon = 0,$

$\quad s5, s6^{ik} \in S_n, \; i \in \{1,2,3\}, \; k \in \{1,...,n_{C_i}\}.$

This algorithm maximizes the level curves of the Lyapunov certificates V_i such that $\mathcal{Z}(V_i - \gamma_i) \subset \mathcal{Z}(-g_{ik})$, for $k \in \{1,..,n_{C_i}\}$ (Lemma. 2). The set $S1 = \bigcup_{i=1}^{3}(V_i \leq (\gamma_i)_{max})$. The non-emptiness of the set $S1$ shows that $x \models \varphi1, \; \forall x \in S1$.

Algorithm 2 Verification of Property $\varphi 2$

INPUT: : Hybrid System Model of CP PLL, Set $\mathcal{S}2 = \cup_{i \in 1,2,3} \mathcal{S}2_i$

OUTPUT: : $\varphi 2$ Verified/No-answer

1: **for** $i \leftarrow 1$ **to** $i \leftarrow 3$ **do**
2:     $E_i \leftarrow Parametrize(E_i)$; _{Setting degree of E_i Polynomials}
3: **end for**
4: **if** $E_i, \forall i \in \{1,2,3\}$, are feasible (fulfilling Prop. 1) **then**
5:     $E_{multiple} \leftarrow \{E_{multiple}, E_i\}, \forall i \in \{1,2,3\}$
6:     $x \models \varphi 2, \forall x \in \mathcal{S}2 = \cup_{i \in 1,2,3} \mathcal{S}2_i$
7: **else**
8:     $E_i \leftarrow Infeasible$
9:     Increase degree of Escape Certificates
10: **end if**
11: **if** degree = maximum possible value & E_i are Infeasible **then**
12:     No Answer about $\varphi 2$
13: **end if**
14: **return** Truth value of $\varphi 2$

Similarly, following Th. 3, we verify property $\varphi 2$ utilizing Alg. 2. We search for three Escape certificates (Prop. 1) in three disjoint sets $\mathcal{S}2_i$, $i \in \{1,2,3\}$, such that $\mathcal{S}2 = \cup_{i \in 1,2,3} \mathcal{S}2_i$. After parametrizing the three Escape certificates, we establish the feasibility of these Escape certificates by the following SOS program,

$$-\frac{\partial E_i}{\partial x}(x) F_i(x,u) - \sum_{k=1}^{n_{C_i}} s_1^{(ik)}(x) g2_{ik}(x) - ..$$

$$\sum_{j=1}^{m} s_2^{(j)}(x) a_j(u) + \varepsilon \in \mathcal{S}_n$$

$$s_1^{(ik)}, s_2^{(j)} \in \mathcal{S}_n, \ \varepsilon > 0$$

This SOS program ensures that the Lie-derivative of E_i is strictly negative in the set, $\mathcal{S}2_i = \{x \in \mathbb{R}^n : g2_{ik} \geq 0, \text{ for } k \in \{1,..,n_{C_i}\}, i \in \{1,2,3\}\}$. The second constraint in this SOS program is such that the parameters u belong to the set, $\{a(u) \geq 0, \text{ for } j \in \{1,..,m\}\}$. Here ε is a small positive real number. Feasibility of this SOS program indicates existence of the Escape certificates for each mode of the CP PLL hybrid system, and consequently the property $\varphi 2$ is verified Line(4-6). Alternatively, in case of infeasible solution of the SOS program, we increase the degree of the Escape certificates and repeat the process Line(8-10). If the property $\varphi 2$ is still not verified, we conclude inconclusiveness about the truth value of $\varphi 2$ (respectively φ) Line 12.

4. EXPERIMENTAL EVALUATION

We used YALMIP [7] solver within MATLAB for the verification of the inevitability property (respectively subproperties) on a 2.6 GHZ Intel Core i5 machine with 4 GB of memory. The CP PLL parameters are listed in Table. 1, with all phases normalized by 2π. We computed degree-6 multiple Lyapunov certificates for the third order, and degree-4 multiple Lyapunov certificates for the fourth order CP PLL. Their attractive invariant sets as projected onto different planes are shown in Fig. 2, and Fig. 3 respectively. We constructed three Escape certificates for each mode of the the third order and fourth order CP PLL hybrid models. For both benchmarks, we computed degree 2 Escape certificates for mode2 and mode3. For mode1, we computed degree 12

Parameters	Third Order	Fourth Order
C_1	$[1.98\ 2.2]e-12F$	$[31\ 29]e-12F$
C_2	$[6.1\ 6.4]e-12F$	$[3.2\ 3.4]e-12F$
C_3		$[1.8\ 2.2]e-12F$
R	$[7.8\ 8.2]e3\Omega$	$[48\ 52]e3\Omega$
$R2$		$[7\ 9]e3\Omega$
f_{ref}	27MHZ	5MHZ
f_O	27e3MHZ	5MHZ
I_p	$[495\ 505]e-6A$	$[395\ 405]e-6A$
K_p	$[198\ 202]$	$[495\ 502]$

Table 1: *PLL Parameters used in the Experimentation*

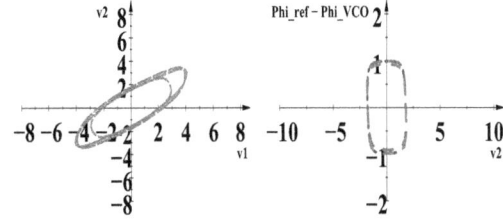

Figure 2: *3-Order $\mathcal{AI}$ Projected onto $(v1, v2)$, and $(v2, (\phi_{ref} - \phi_{VCO})$*

and degree 10 Escape certificates for third and fourth order CP PLL respectively. We chose, $\varepsilon = 1e-4$, for all Escape certificates. We noticed that decreasing the value of ε resulted in a higher degree Escape certificate for both benchmarks. However, this is at the cost of higher computation time. We therefore opted for the value $1e-4$. A simulation trace along with the derivative of the Escape certificate patched up from the three Escape certificates of each benchmark are depicted in Fig. 4 and Fig. 5 respectively. Note that due to space constraints, we have shown projections on only two planes for each benchmark. Simulation traces show that the derivative of the Escape certificate is negative along the trajectories. Computation time of different steps of our verification methodology is given in Table. 2. Though the maximum degree of certificates (Lyapunov,Escape) for the fourth order is less than that of the third order, however, the dimensionality factor is dominant as far as the computation time is concerned.

Results show the effectiveness of our approach to the verification of the inevitability property of a complex real circuit. We have proved the inevitability property avoiding hundred of discrete transitions as well as the complex continuization as in [2]. Computation time is comparable to [2], and infact is less by an order of atleast three considering their approach using gridding of the state space for a third order PLL only. Our Lyapunov and Escape certificate based deductive methods, though needs user input in the formalization of the problem, are applicable to infinite domain (oppose to bounded) and avoid approximating (under or over) solutions of the differential equations. Furthermore, SOS based relaxation, in addition to solve the NP-hard problem of positivity check, offers an easy way of incorporating parameter variations as well.

5. CONCLUSION

We have presented a scalable deductive verification methodology for the inevitability verification of phase-locking in higher order CP PLL. We benefited from the Lyapunov sta-

Verification Step	3-Order Time(Sec)	4-Order Time(Sec)
Attractive Invariants	1381.7(Degree 6)	10021(Degree 4)
Max.Level Curves	15.5	12
Escape Certificates	100	900

Table 2: *Computation Time of the Inevitability Verification*

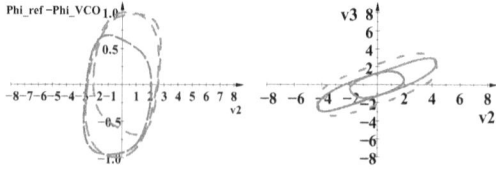

Figure 3: *4-Order $\mathcal{AI}$ Projected onto $(v2, v3)$, and $(v2, (\phi_{ref} - \phi_{VCO})$*

bility of hybrid systems and Non-linear continuous systems theory, and came up with some interesting local properties. Successful verification of these local properties resulted in the global inevitability property verification of a CP PLL. Involving an NP-Hard problem of checking the positivity of polynomials inequalities, we used the sound SOS relaxation algorithm for the verification of these properties. Experimental results show the effectiveness of our approach avoiding expensive discretization and reach set computations.

6. REFERENCES

[1] T. A.Henzinger, P.-H. Ho, and H. Wong-Toi. Algorithmic analysis of nonlinear hybrid systems. *IEEE Transactions on Automatic Control*, 43(4):540–554, Apr 1998.

[2] M. Althoff, A. Rajhans, B. H. Krogh, S. Yaldiz, X. Li, and L. Pileggi. Formal verification of phase-locked loops using reachability analysis and continuization. In *Proceedings of the International Conference on Computer-Aided Design ICCAD*, pages 659–666, 2011.

[3] S. P. Boyd, L. El Ghaoui, E. Feron, and V. Balakrishnan. *Linear matrix inequalities in system and control theory*, volume 15. SIAM, 1994.

[4] R. Goebel, R. G. Sanfelice, and A. R. Teel. *Hybrid dynamical systems: modeling, stability, and robustness*. Princeton University Press, 2012.

[5] H. K.Khalil. *Nonlinear Systems*. Prentice Hall, third edition, 2002.

[6] H. Lin, P. Li, and C. J. Myers. Verification of digitally-intensive analog circuits via kernel ridge regression and hybrid reachability analysis. In *Proceedings of the 50th Annual Design Automation Conference*, page 66. ACM, 2013.

[7] J. Lofberg. Yalmip: A toolbox for modeling and optimization in matlab. In *Computer Aided Control Systems Design, 2004 IEEE International Symposium on*, pages 284–289. IEEE, 2004.

[8] J. Lygeros, K. H. Johansson, S. N. Simić, J. Zhang, and S. S. Sastry. Dynamical properties of hybrid automata. *IEEE TRANSACTIONS ON AUTOMATIC CONTROL*, 48(1):2–17, January 2003.

[9] A. Papachristodoulou and S. Prajna. On the construction of lyapunov functions using the sum of squares decomposition. In *41st IEEE Conference on Decision and Control*, volume 3, pages 348–3487, 2002.

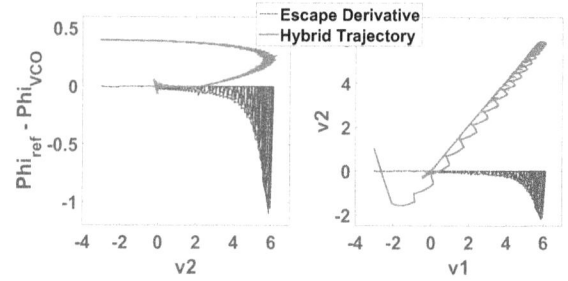

Figure 4: *3-Order Derivative of Escape Certificates, Trajectory Trace Projected onto $(v1, v2)$, and $(v2, (\phi_{ref} - \phi_{VCO}))$*

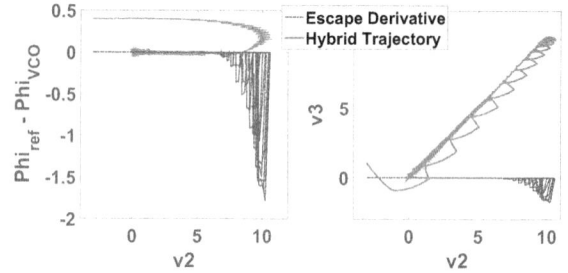

Figure 5: *4-Order Derivative of Escape Certificates, Trajectory Trace Projected onto $(v2, v3)$, and $(v2, (\phi_{ref} - \phi_{VCO}))$*

[10] P. A. Parrilo. *Structured semidefinite programs and semialgebraic geometry methods in robustness and optimization*. PhD thesis, Citeseer, 2000.

[11] S. Prajna and A. Jadbabaie. Safety verification of hybrid systems using barrier certificates. In *Hybrid Systems: Computation and Control*, pages 477–492. Springer, 2004.

[12] S. Prajna and A. Papachristodoulou. Analysis of switched and hybrid systems-beyond piecewise quadratic methods. In *American Control Conference, 2003. Proceedings of the 2003*, volume 4, pages 2779–2784. IEEE, 2003.

[13] T. Sturm and A. Tiwari. Verification and synthesis using real quantifier elimination. In *Proceedings of the 36th international symposium on Symbolic and algebraic computation*, pages 329–336. ACM, 2011.

[14] A. Taly and A. Tiwari. Deductive verification of continuous dynamical systems. In *LIPIcs-Leibniz International Proceedings in Informatics*, volume 4. Schloss Dagstuhl-Leibniz-Zentrum für Informatik, 2009.

[15] T. Wang, S. Lall, and M. West. Polynomial level-set method for polynomial system reachable set estimation. 2013.

[16] J. Wei, Y. Peng, G. Yu, and M. Greenstreet. Verifying global convergence for a digital phase-locked loop. In *Formal Methods in Computer-Aided Design (FMCAD), 2013*, pages 113–120. IEEE, 2013.

[17] M. H. Zaki, S. Tahar, and G. Bois. Formal verification of analog and mixed signal designs: A survey. *Microelectronics Journal*, 39(12):1395–1404, 2008.

A Novel Static D-Flip-Flop Topology
for Low Swing Clocking

Mallika Rathore
Marvell Semiconductor
Printer and Custom Solutions
Business Unit
Boise, ID 83713
mrathore@marvell.com

Weicheng Liu
Emre Salman
Department of ECE
Stony Brook University
Stony Brook, NY 11794
weicheng.liu
@stonybrook.edu

Can Sitik
Baris Taskin
Department of ECE
Drexel University
Philadelphia, PA 19104
as3577@drexel.edu,
taskin@coe.drexel.edu

ABSTRACT

Low swing clocking is a well known technique to reduce dynamic power consumption of a clock network. A novel static D flip-flop topology is proposed that can reliably operate with a low swing clock signal (down to 50% of the V_{DD}) despite the full swing data and output signals. The proposed topology enables low swing signals within the entire clock network, thereby maximizing the power saved by low swing operation. The proposed flip-flop is compared with existing low swing flip-flops using a 45 nm technology node at a clock frequency of 1.5 GHz. The results demonstrate an average reduction of 38.1% and 44.4% in, respectively, power consumption and power-delay product. The sensitivity of each circuit to clock swing is investigated. The robustness of the proposed topology is also demonstrated by ensuring reliable operation at various process, voltage, and temperature corners.

Categories and Subject Descriptors

B.7 [**Integrated Circuits**]: VLSI (very large scale integration)

General Terms

Design

Keywords

Flip-flop, low power, low swing, clock

1. INTRODUCTION

Reducing power consumption is a major objective for almost any application [1]. Voltage scaling is a common method to achieve quadratic savings in power consumption with considerable penalty in performance [2, 3]. Near-threshold computing has recently received attention to widen the application scope of sub-threshold circuits due to relatively more acceptable delay penalty [4]. Reducing the power supply voltage to the levels of threshold voltage, however, is not suitable for a majority of the applications where

GLSVLSI'15, May 20–22, 2015, Pittsburgh, PA, USA
Copyright 2015 ACM 978-1-4503-3474-7/15/05 ...$15.00
http://dx.doi.org/10.1145/2742060.2742095.

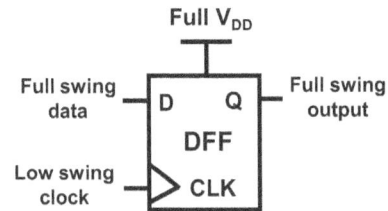

Figure 1: Flip-flop that operates with a low swing clock signal whereas the data and output signals have full swing voltage.

performance is also a critical concern. Furthermore, the effect of process and environmental variations is exacerbated at the near-threshold voltage levels [5].

Another approach to reduce power consumption with negligible impact on performance is low swing clocking [6–8]. Low swing clock distribution networks have been investigated in existing literature since clock networks typically consume a significant portion of the overall power [9, 10]. Thus, low swing clock networks implemented either with a dedicated low voltage power grid or single voltage level-shifters can achieve considerable reduction in dynamic power while maintaining the performance.

Existing works on low swing clock networks, however, rely on full swing operation at the sinks (flip-flops) to maintain performance and the timing characteristics of the data paths [9, 10]. This approach significantly limits the power savings since the last stage of a clock network typically has large switching capacitance. Thus, it is desirable to maintain low swing clock signals even at the sink stages (*i.e.,* at the clock pins of the flip-flops). However, a typical flip-flop designed for full swing operation cannot reliably operate with a low swing clock signal. Furthermore, the data (D) and output (Q) signals of the flip-flop have full swing operation since the transistors along the D-to-Q path are connected to full power supply voltage, as illustrated in Fig. 1. A novel D flip-flop topology is therefore required to reliably operate with a low swing clock signal despite the full swing data and output signals.

The most commonly used static D flip-flop topology is redesigned in a novel fashion to accommodate low swing clock signals while ensuring reliable operation without any contention current. The proposed topology enables utilizing low swing clock signals at the clock pins of the flip-flops, thereby increasing the overall power savings that can be achieved via low swing clocking.

The rest of the paper is organized as follows. Background information is provided in Section 2. Previous work on low swing flip-flops is summarized in Section 3. The proposed topology is described in Section 4. Simulation results including a comparative

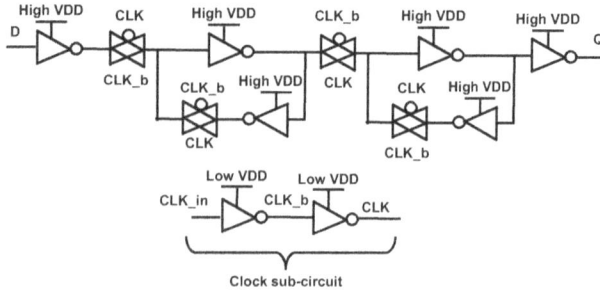

Figure 2: Conventional, transmission gate based D flip-flop driven by a low swing clock signal.

analysis with existing works are presented in Section 5, demonstrating an average reduction of 38.1% and 44.4% in, respectively, power consumption and power-delay product. The effect of process and environmental variations is also investigated. Finally, the paper is concluded in Section 6.

2. BACKGROUND

In a typical flip-flop, clock signals drive both NMOS and PMOS transistors (as in transmission gated based and tri-state inverter based flip-flops). If the same flip-flop is used with a low swing clock signal, the PMOS transistors driven by the clock signal fail to completely turn off when the clock signal is high. For example, consider a 45 nm technology with a nominal V_{DD} of 1 V. If the clock swing is reduced to $0.7 \times V_{DD}$, the gate-to-source voltage of the PMOS transistors -0.3 V since the data signal is at full swing and the inverters within the flip-flop are connected to full V_{DD}. -0.3 V is sufficiently close to the threshold voltage of PMOS transistors in this technology. This behavior significantly affects the operation reliability of a traditional flip-flop driven by a low swing clock signal. As an example, consider a rising-edge triggered master-slave flip-flop. When the clock signal is high, the master latch should be turned off. However, due to low swing clock signal, the transmission gate (or tri-state inverter) within the master latch cannot completely turn off. If the data signal is in a different state than the stored data within the master latch, a race condition occurs which can possibly generate a metastable state.

To better illustrate the unreliability of conventional flip-flops operating with a low swing clock signal, a traditional transmission gate based D flip-flop, as shown in Fig. 2, is simulated with a 45 nm technology node when the clock swing is 0.7 V. Note that the clock signal and inverted clock signal are internally generated by using two inverters. This circuit is referred to as the clock sub-circuit in this paper, as also depicted in Fig. 2. Note that the inverters within the clock sub-circuit are connected to a low supply voltage to provide low swing clock signals. Since the PMOS transistors driven by the clock signals are not completely turned off, internal nodes experience a glitch as high as 400 mV and clock-to-Q delay increases by more than 15%. Furthermore, in the slow corner, the flip-flop fails to correctly latch the data signal. Thus, a new flip-flop topology is required that can reliably operate with a low swing clock signal.

3. PREVIOUS WORK

Existing flip-flop topologies developed for a low swing clock signal are summarized in this section. The strengths and weaknesses of each topology are discussed.

A flip-flop topology for a low swing clock signal based on clocked CMOS method (C^2MOS) and sense amplifier (SA) has been pro-

posed in [11], as illustrated in Fig. 3(a). This circuit, referred to as L-C^2MOS-SA, reduces the charge-discharge capacitance and implements the conditional pre-charge and discharge technique to achieve low power consumption. The circuit is area efficient and a considerable reduction in leakage current is also obtained. The original version of this topology utilizes diode-connected PMOS transistors within the clock sub-circuit to reduce voltage swing, as depicted in Fig. 3(a). Diode-connected PMOS transistors, however, significantly degrade clock slew due to reduced supply voltage in stacked PMOS transistors, making this topology impractical for industrial circuits. Thus, to achieve a fair comparison, this topology is modified in this work where the clock sub-circuit has a second power supply voltage for low swing operation rather than having diode-connected PMOS transistors. This modified version is referred to as L-C^2MOS-SA-2. Also note that this topology requires a full swing clock signal at the slave stage (transistor N5), which defies our primary objective of having only a low swing clock signal throughout the entire clock network.

Another flip-flop topology has been proposed in [12] for low swing operation. This topology, referred to as reduced clock swing flip-flop (RCSFF), is depicted in Fig. 3(b). As shown in this figure, this design utilizes an additional low supply voltage within the clock sub-circuit to provide low swing clock signal, similar to the proposed topology in this paper. However, in [12], the low swing clock signal is used to drive PMOS transistors (P2 and P4) that are connected to a higher (full) supply voltage. As mentioned earlier, these transistors cannot completely turn off, producing functionality and reliability issues in addition to significantly increasing both short-circuit and leakage current. To alleviate this issue, in [12], authors have utilized the well known bulk biasing technique. Specifically, the bulk nodes of P2 and P4 are connected to a separate well biased at a greater voltage, thereby increasing the threshold voltage of these PMOS transistors. An additional well, however, not only increases the physical area and complexity of the design, but also requires a triple-well process that is not common in standard digital CMOS technologies. Furthermore, in the slowest corner, this issue is exacerbated despite the use of well biasing.

The NAND-type keeper flip-flop topology proposed in [13], referred to as NDKFF, is illustrated in Fig. 3(c). As opposed to the previous topology, this circuit does not require a separate well at the expense of excessive leakage current that flows through transistors P2, N1-N3 when node X is at logic low. Furthermore, a contention occurs at node X since the level-keeping transistors, *i.e.*, P2, N4, N5 and I1-I2 have a race condition when node X transitions from logic low to logic high, thereby increasing the transition time and clock-to-Q delay of the output. This issue is exacerbated during the worst-case delay analysis of the circuit, which can be partially controlled by carefully sizing the transistors.

In [14], authors have proposed a contention reduced flip-flop referred to as CRFF and is depicted in Fig. 3(d). This circuit utilizes a pulsed clock signal to provide a short transparency window during which the output is discharged through the NMOS transistors N1-N4. During this transparency window, the clocked transistors P5 and P6 disconnect the latch (I1-I2), thereby reducing contention current. Transistors P1 and P2 are controlled by input D through P3 and P4 which further reduces the contention current. However, low swing clock signal is used to drive PMOS transistors P5 and P6, thereby suffering from the aforementioned issues of functionality and reliability.

4. PROPOSED D FLIP-FLOP TOPOLOGY

As observed in some of the previously proposed topologies, if a low swing clock signal drives PMOS transistors, functionality and

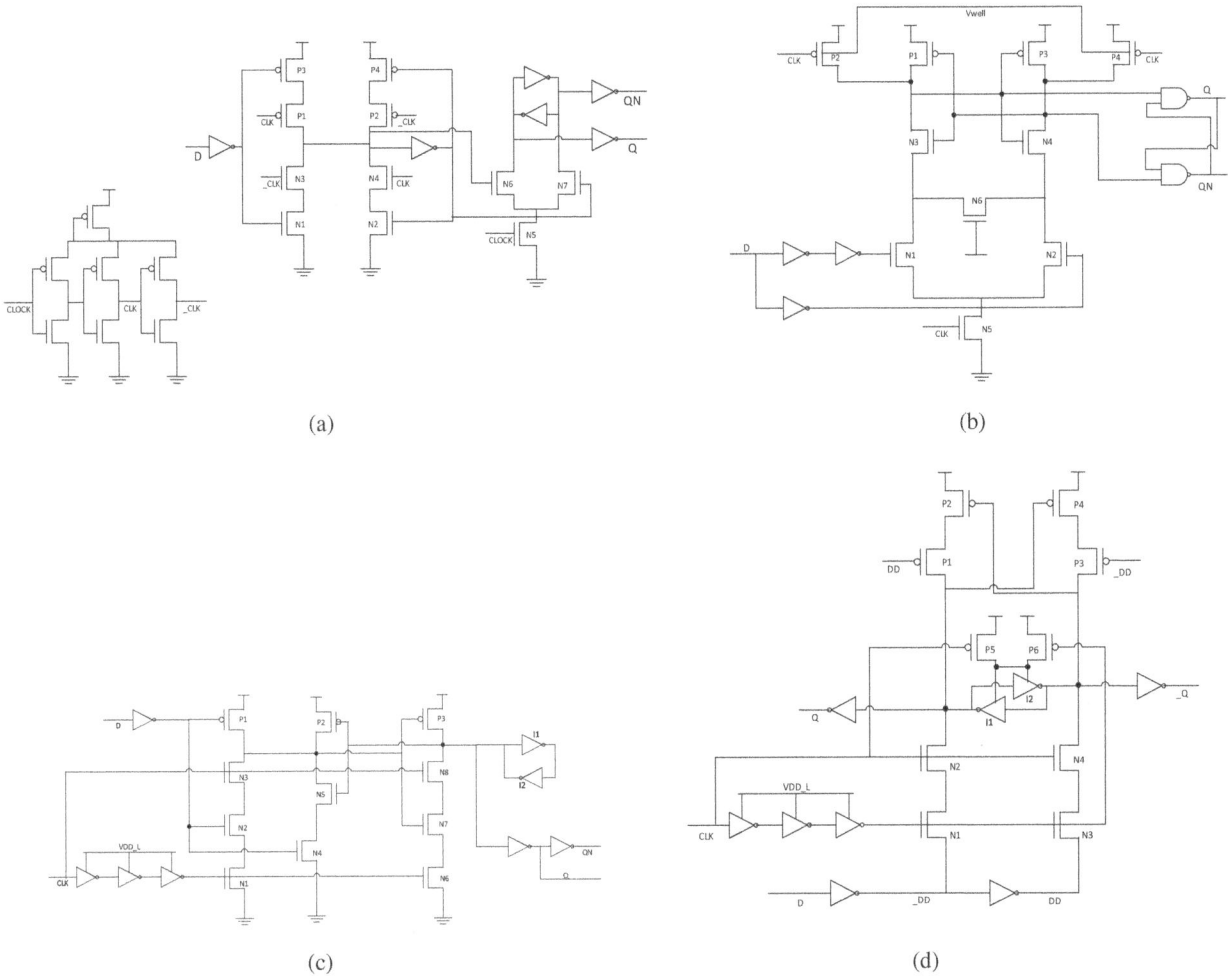

(a)

(b)

(c)

(d)

Figure 3: Existing low swing flip-flop topologies that are compared with the proposed topology in this work: (a) C^2MOS and sense amplifier based low swing flip-flop, L-C^2MOS-SA [11], (b) reduced clock swing flip-flop, RCSFF [12], (c) NAND-type keeper flip-flop, NDKFF [13], and (d) contention reduced flip-flop, CRFF [14].

reliability are compromised, particularly in nanoscale technologies where the supply voltage is in the range of 0.8 to 1.1 V and threshold voltage is in the range of 0.3 to 0.5 V. Thus, in the proposed topology, as depicted in Fig. 4, low swing clock signal drives only NMOS transistors.

The proposed topology is based on the most commonly used, static D flip-flop shown in Fig. 2. However, rather than using transmission gates, pass gates with NMOS transistors (N2, N4, N13, and N14) are utilized as the switches in both master and slave latches. Thus, when the low swing clock signal is at logic high, N2 and N13 can completely turn off. Replacing the transmission gates with pass gates, however, introduces another issue since the pass gates cannot transfer a full voltage to the output. This issue is critical since the incoming data signal operates at full swing. Thus, node Y cannot reach a full V_{DD} which increases the short-circuit and leakage current in the following stages in addition to increasing clock-to-Q delay. Furthermore, pass transistors are known to be less robust to process variations. To alleviate these issues, a pull-up network consisting of two PMOS transistors is added to both master and slave latches (P4 to P7). When the master node (input of N4) transitions to logic low, P4 turns on. If the data signal D is also at logic low, then node Y is pulled to full V_{DD} through P4 and P6. Note that P6 (and P7 in the slave latch) are added to prevent contention current

(and therefore reduce power consumption) when the data signal D is at logic high and clock signal is at logic low. In this situation, N2 is on and node Y is discharged through N2 and N1. If P6 does not exist, a race condition occurs at node Y since N2 and N1 should be stronger than P4, which pulls node Y to full V_{DD}. Finally, a pull-down logic is added to both master and slave latches to enhance clock-to-Q delay and setup time (N6 to N9). Specifically, when data and clock signals are at logic low, the pull-down logic is active and pulls the master node (input of N4) to ground, triggering P4. Thus, node Y quickly reaches full V_{DD}. Note that the master node does not need to wait for node Y to rise through a weak pass transistor and turn on N3. Instead, the pull-down logic completes this transition relatively faster. Also note that the clock sub-circuit is not shown in Fig. 4, but is identical to the sub-circuit shown in Fig. 2.

The operation of the proposed flip-flop is depicted in Fig. 5 in a 45 nm technology node where the nominal V_{DD} is 1 V. The clock voltage swing is 0.7 V. The flip-flop successfully latches the full swing data and produces a full swing output while operating with a low swing clock signal.

The proposed topology is relatively less complex than the previously proposed flip-flops described in Section 3 since the proposed topology is static and does not require a separate well (bulk biasing)

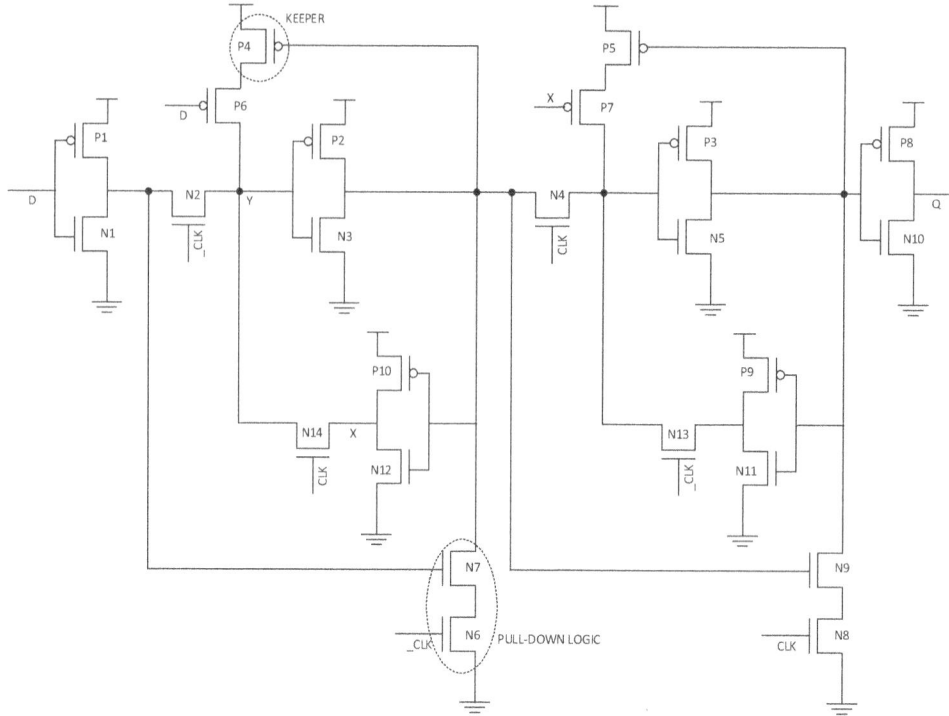

Figure 4: Proposed flip-flop topology where the low swing clock signal drives only NMOS transistors.

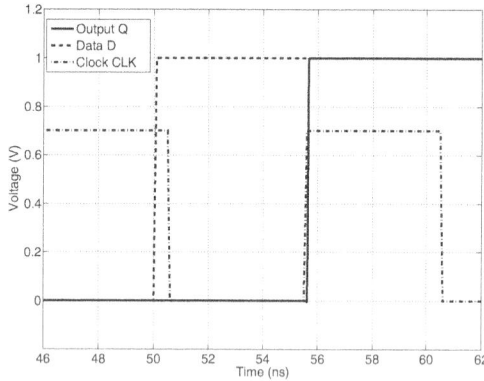

Figure 5: Operation of the proposed flip-flop in a 45 nm technology node where the nominal V_{DD} is 1 V. Clock swing is set to 0.7 V.

or sense amplifier. Furthermore, the performance characteristics of the proposed topology outperform existing flip-flops, as discussed in the following section.

5. SIMULATION RESULTS

The simulation setup is described in Section 5.1 and the simulation results including a comparative analysis with existing work are presented in Section 5.2. Robustness of each topology to process, voltage, and temperature variations is investigated in Section 5.3.

5.1 Simulation Setup

The proposed flip-flop topology and the previous circuits in existing work (L-C^{2}MOS-SA [11], L-C^{2}MOS-SA-2 [11], RCSFF [12], NDKFF [13], and CRFF [14]) are designed using a 45 nm technology with a nominal supply voltage of 1 V and all of the simulations are performed using Spectre [15]. The clock signal has a reduced swing of 0.7 V. The clock and data frequencies are, respectively,

1.5 GHz and 150 MHz. Each flip-flop drives an output load capacitance of 5 fF. To achieve a fair comparison, all of the flip-flops are sized to produce approximately equal clock-to-Q delay.

5.2 Comparative Analysis

The simulation results are listed in Table 1, comparing clock-to-Q delay, power consumption, power-delay product (PDP), leakage power, overall transistor size, and setup and hold times of all of the flip-flops. Note that the leakage power listed in this table is obtained by averaging the leakage power obtained from four possible static combinations of the data and clock signals.

As listed in Table 1, the proposed topology achieves, on average, 38.1% and 44.4% reduction in, respectively, dynamic power and power-delay product while exhibiting similar clock-to-Q delay. L-C^{2}MOS-SA [11] achieves the least leakage power that is approximately 45% less than the proposed topology. L-C^{2}MOS-SA [11], however, exhibits degraded behavior at the worst-case corners, as described in Section 5.3. The proposed topology exhibits the second lowest leakage power, achieving significant reduction, particularly as compared to NDKFF [13] and CRFF [14]. Overall transistor width of the proposed topology is less than the other topologies except L-C^{2}MOS-SA [11]. The setup-hold time characterization of each topology is also performed, as listed in the last two columns [16]. Similar to some other topologies, the proposed flip-flop exhibits a negative setup time.

The effect of clock swing voltage level on clock-to-Q delay and power consumption is also investigated for each flip-flop, as depicted in Fig. 6. According to Fig. 6(a), clock-to-Q delay increases as the clock swing is reduced in each topology. For L-C^{2}MOS-SA [11], NDKFF [13], and CRFF [14], clock swing cannot be reduced below 0.6 V since these circuits fail to latch the input data at clock swings lower than 0.6 V. Note that the clock-to-Q delay is highly sensitive to voltage swing for NDKFF [13]. The proposed topology can reliably latch the input data for a clock swing

Table 1: Comparison of the proposed topology with existing work under nominal operating conditions with a clock voltage swing of $0.7 \times V_{DD}$. Each topology is sized to achieve approximately equal clock-to-Q delay.

Flip-flop topology	CLK-to-Q delay (ps)	Overall power (μW)	PDP (fW.s)	Leakage power (nW)	Overall transistor width		Setup time (ps)	Hold time (ps)
					NMOS (nm)	PMOS (nm)		
L-C^{2}MOS-SA [11]	69.7	8.0	0.56	37.2	2395	2950	27.9	0.9
L-C^{2}MOS-SA-2 [11]	71.3	9.3	0.67	34.5	4195	3550	17.5	-9.2
RCSFF [12]	70.6	17.2	1.22	82.0	6840	5500	-26.9	42.6
NDKFF [13]	69.4	12.0	0.83	196.6	5050	3900	-6.0	-62.7
CRFF [14]	70.3	10.5	0.74	201.5	4650	5300	-20.2	92.9
This work	**64.1**	**6.6**	**0.42**	**68.1**	**2650**	**3450**	**-1.7**	**17.8**

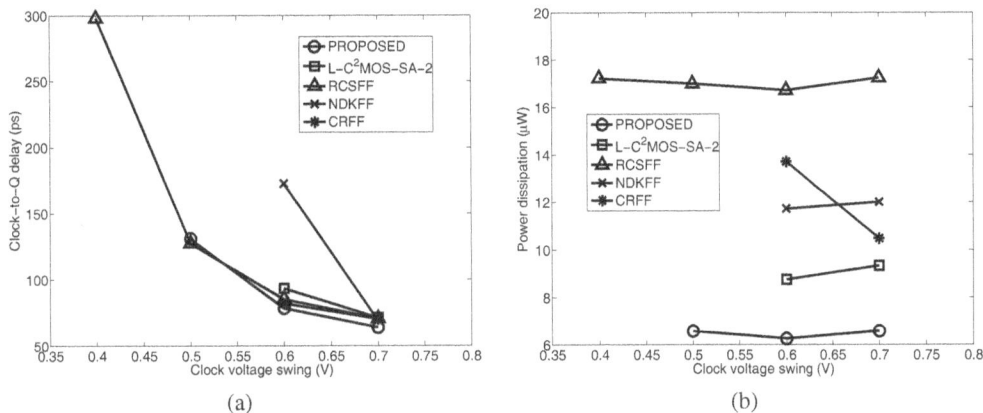

Figure 6: Effect of clock swing voltage level on clock-to-Q delay and power consumption for each flip-flop topology: (a) Clock-to-Q delay vs. clock voltage swing, (b) power consumption vs. clock voltage swing.

as low as 0.5 V (half V_{DD}). Furthermore, the proposed topology exhibits relatively low sensitivity to voltage swing. RCSFF [12] is the only topology that can work with a clock swing as low as 0.4 V. However, the clock-to-Q delay significantly increases below 0.5 V, making this operating point impractical. Furthermore, RCSFF [12] consumes significantly more power than the proposed topology, as listed in Table 1.

The dependence of power dissipation on clock voltage swing is shown in Fig. 6(b). According to this figure, the proposed topology exhibits the lowest power consumption at each clock swing voltage. Note that from 0.7 V to 0.6 V, the overall power is slightly reduced whereas from 0.6 V to 0.5 V, there is a slight increase. The overall effect of clock swing on power depends upon two factors: 1) partial reduction in power since the clock sub-circuit consumes less power with a lower swing, 2) partial increase in power due to a greater contention current with a lower clock swing. If the first factor outweighs the second factor, overall power is reduced as the clock swing is reduced. Note that CRFF [14] is the only topology where power consumption significantly increases with a lower clock swing, indicating the dominance of the second factor.

5.3 Robustness to Variations

A critical challenge in nanoscale ICs is the variations incurred during fabrication and fluctuations in operating voltage and temperature. The behavior of a circuit to these variations is important to evaluate the overall robustness. To investigate this issue, each flip-flop topology is simulated in the worst-case corner for delay, transient power, and leakage power. The results are listed in Table 2. Note that L-C^{2}MOS-SA [11] and RCSFF [12] fail to latch

the input data at the worst-case corner for delay, determined by the slow process models for both NMOS and PMOS transistors, 0.9 V V_{DD} (90% of the nominal V_{DD}) and 165°C temperature.

The proposed topology exhibits the lowest clock-to-Q delay (approximately 20% lower, on average) in the worst-case corner even though each topology exhibits similar delays in the nominal case (see Table 1). This trend demonstrates that the clock-to-Q delay of the proposed topology exhibits the least sensitivity to process and environmental variations.

Similar to the nominal case, the proposed topology consumes the least transient power in the worst-case, as determined by the fast process models for both NMOS and PMOS transistors and 1.1 V V_{DD} (110% of the nominal V_{DD}). Note that the temperature that corresponds to the worst-case corner for overall power depends upon the topology due to inverted temperature dependence [17]. Specifically, in RCSFF [12] and the proposed topologies, the worst-case transient power occurs at the lowest temperature whereas the other topologies consume the largest power at the highest temperature. Note that inverted temperature dependence also applies to the worst-case delay analysis and therefore each topology is simulated with both the lowest and highest temperatures. However, largest clock-to-Q delay occurs at the highest temperature in each topology, as shown by the second column in Table 1. Finally, the worst-case leakage power, determined by the fast process models, 1.1 V V_{DD}, and highest temperature, is provided in the last column. The trend is similar to the nominal results where the proposed topology consumes the second least leakage power, after L-C^{2}MOS-SA [11].

The variation analysis provided in this section demonstrates that the proposed topology can reliably operate at the worst-case delay

Table 2: Comparison of the proposed topology with existing work under worst-case operating conditions for clock-to-Q delay, overall transient power, and leakage power. FF and SS correspond, respectively, to fast and slow models for both NMOS and PMOS transistors.

Flip-flop topology	CLK-to-Q delay (ps) at SS-0.9V-165°C	Overall transient power (μW) at FF-1.1V	Leakage power (μW) at FF-1.1V-165°C
L-C²MOS-SA [11]	Failure	10.8 (T=165°C)	0.6
L-C²MOS-SA-2 [11]	178.8	11.3 (T=165°C)	0.6
RCSFF [12]	Failure	21.5 (T=-40°C)	1.5
NDKFF [13]	210.0	17.2 (T=165°C)	2.5
CRFF [14]	175.7	17.7 (T=165°C)	3.8
This work	**150.8**	**8.9 (T=-40°C)**	**1.1**

and power corners, unlike some of the existing topologies that fail at the worst-case delay corner. Furthermore, the proposed topology consumes the least worst-case power consumption and exhibits the least sensitivity to worst-case delay corner.

6. CONCLUSIONS

In existing low swing clocking approaches, clock signal is restored to full swing before arriving to the clock pins of the flip-flops since traditional flip-flops cannot reliably operate with a low swing clock signal. This approach, however, significantly limits the power savings since the last stage of a clock network typically has the largest capacitance and therefore benefits the most from low swing clocking. A novel static D flip-flop topology is proposed in this paper that can reliably operate with a low swing clock signal, thereby enabling a *true* low swing clocking methodology. The proposed topology is compared with existing low swing flip-flops, demonstrating an average reduction of 38.1% and 44.4% in, respectively, power consumption and power-delay product. It is shown that the proposed topology is less sensitive to clock voltage swing than existing circuits. Furthermore, worst-case corner analysis for clock-to-Q delay and power consumption demonstrates that the proposed flip-flop exhibits a robust operation.

7. ACKNOWLEDGMENTS

This research is supported by Semiconductor Research Corporation (SRC) under contract No. 2013-TJ-2449 and 2013-TJ-2450.

8. REFERENCES

[1] E. Salman and E. G. Friedman, *High Performance Integrated Circuit Design*. McGraw-Hill, 2012.

[2] R. Gonzalez, B. M. Gordon, and M. A. Horowitz, "Supply and Threshold Voltage Scaling for Low Power CMOS," *IEEE Journal of Solid-State Circuits*, Vol. 32, No. 8, pp. 1210-1216, August 1997.

[3] J.-M. Chang and M. Pedram, "Energy Minimization Using Multiple Supply Voltages," *IEEE Transactions on Very Large Scale Integration (VLSI) Systems*, Vol. 5, No. 4, pp. 436-443, December 1997.

[4] R. Dreslinski, *et al.*, "Near-Threshold Computing: Reclaiming Moore's Law Through Energy Efficient Integrated Circuits," *Proceedings of the IEEE*, Vol. 98, No. 2, pp. 253-266, 2010.

[5] F. Chang *et al.*, "Practical Strategies for Power-Efficient Computing Technologies," *Proceedings of the IEEE*, Vol. 98, No. 2, pp. 215-236, 2010.

[6] H. Zhang, G. Varghese, and J. M. Rabaey, "Low-Swing On-Chip Signaling Techniques: Effectiveness and Robustness," *IEEE Transactions on Very Large Scale Integration (VLSI) Systems*, Vol. 8, No. 3, pp. 264-272, June 2000.

[7] C. Sitik, E. Salman, L. Filippini, S. J. Yoon, and B. Taskin, "FinFET-Based Low Swing Clocking," *ACM Journal on Emerging Technologies in Computing Systems*, in press.

[8] C. Sitik, L. Filippini, E. Salman, and B. Taskin, "High Performance Low Swing Clock Tree Synthesis with Custom D Flip-Flop Design," *Proceedings of the IEEE Computer Society Annual Symposium on VLSI*, pp. 498–503, July 2014.

[9] J. Pangjun and S. Sapatnekar, "Low-Power Clock Distribution Using Multiple Voltages and Reduced Swings," *IEEE Transactions on Very Large Scale Integration (VLSI) Systems*, Vol. 10, No. 3, pp. 309-318, June 2002.

[10] F. H. A. Asgari and M. Sachdev, "A Low-Power Reduced Swing Global Clocking Methodology," *IEEE Transactions on Very Large Scale Integration (VLSI) Systems*, Vol. 12, No. 5, pp. 538-545, May 2004.

[11] Z. Jianjun and S. Yihe, "A low clock swing, power saving and generic technology based D flip-flop with single power supply," *IEEE International Conference on ASIC*, pp. 142-144, October 2007.

[12] H. Kawaguchi and T. Sakurai, "A reduced clock-swing flip-flop (RCSFF) for 63% power reduction," *IEEE Journal of Solid-State Circuits*, Vol. 33, No. 5, pp. 807-811, 1998.

[13] M. Tokumasu, *et al.*, "A new reduced clock-swing flip-flop: NAND-type keeper flip-flop (NDKFF)," *Proceedings of the IEEE Custom Integrated Circuits Conference*, pp. 129-132, 2002.

[14] D. Levacq, *et al.*, "Half V_{DD} Clock-Swing Flip-Flop with Reduced Contention for up to 60% Power Saving in Clock Distribution," *Proceedings of the IEEE European Solid State Circuits Conference*, pp. 190-193, 2007.

[15] Cadence. Spectre. http://www.cadence.com.

[16] E. Salman, A. Dasdan, F. Taraporevala, K. Kucukcakar, and E. G. Friedman,, "Exploiting Setup-Hold Time Interdependence In Static Timing Analysis," *IEEE Transactions on Computer-Aided Design of Integrated Circuits and Systems*, Vol. 26, No. 6, pp. 1114–1125, June 2007.

[17] A. Dasdan and I. Hom, "Handling Inverted Temperature Dependence in Static Timing Analysis," *ACM Transactions on Design Automation of Electronic Systems*, Vol. 11, No. 2, pp. 306-324, April 2006.

Voltage-Boosted Synchronizers

Yaoqiang Li, Pierce I-Jen Chuang, Andrew Kennings, Manoj Sachdev
Department of Electrical and Computer Engineering, University of Waterloo
Waterloo, Ontario, Canada
{lyaoqian,pichuang,akenning,msachdev}@uwaterloo.ca

ABSTRACT

With a specified Mean Timing Between Failure (MTBF), the metastability resolution time of synchronizers possibly constrains the system performance. To enhance metastability resolution time under single low-voltage supply environments, Voltage-Boosted Synchronizers (VBSs) consisting of a basic minimum-sized Jamb latch and a switched-capacitor-based charge pump are proposed. The capacitor of the charge pump is sized 13 times the area of the Jamb latch. Two powering strategies of the charge pump, namely Metastability-driven VBS (MVBS) and Clock-driven VBS (CVBS), are proposed. For a 1-year MTBF specification, MVBS and CVBS show 2.0-2.7 and 5.1-9.8 times the performance improvement over the basic Jamb latch, respectively, without incurring large power consumption.

Categories and Subject Descriptors

B.6.1 [**LOGIC DESIGN**]: Design Styles—*Sequential circuits*; B.7.1 [**INTEGRATED CIRCUITS**]: Types and Design Styles—*VLSI (very large scale integration)*

General Terms

Design

Keywords

Synchronizers; metastability; MTBF; charge pump

1. INTRODUCTION

Flip-flops and latches are used as synchronizers in digital systems to synchronize the incoming asynchronous signals. Synchronizers are not only imperative for asynchronous communication systems but also key components for building energy-efficient resilient systems [1]. However, in these systems with specific reliability requirements, the clock frequencies are constrained not only by the traditional data-path delays but also by the synchronizer delays that are mainly de-

termined by the metastability resolution time. As technologies scale, the metastability problem becomes more severe [2]. Even though there may be only a few synchronizers in a digital system, their performance can become the bottleneck in the overall system performance. Therefore, the metastability performance of a synchronizer is often weighted more heavily than its energy and/or area.

Several techniques have been developed to improve the metastability resolution time of a synchronizer. However, some of these techniques do not work effectively at lower supply voltages. In this paper, we propose Voltage-Boosted Synchronizers (VBSs) that integrate a basic Jamb latch and a charge pump implemented by switched capacitors [3] [4] capable of working at low-voltage supply environments. The proposed synchronizers provide a temporary voltage boost to the latching element which improves its metastability resolution time.

The remaining paper is organized as follows. Section 2.1 provides a background on synchronizers. It also discusses existing circuit techniques to improve the metastability resolution time of a synchronizer. Section 3, introduce the proposed synchronizers. A new methodology of metastability parameter extraction is described. Section 4 presents and compares the simulation results for the baseline and proposed synchronizers. Finally, in Section 5 conclusions are drawn.

2. BACKGROUND KNOWLEDGE AND EXISTING SYNCHRONIZER TECHNIQUES

2.1 Background Knowledge

The delay, t_d, of a synchronizer such as a Jamb latch [5] in Fig. 1a is approximated as [6]

$$t_d \simeq t_{norm} + t_r \tag{1}$$

where t_{norm} and t_r are the normal delay and the metastability resolution time, respectively. The metastability failure probability per operation, i.e., the probability that the metastability resolution time reaches t_r is [7]

$$P_{meta} = f_c T_w e^{-\frac{t_r}{\tau}} \tag{2}$$

and the MTBF due to metastability is [7]

$$MTBF = \frac{1}{P_{meta} f_d} = \frac{e^{\frac{t_r}{\tau}}}{T_w f_c f_d} \tag{3}$$

where T_w is the asymptotic width of the metastability window, τ is the resolution time constant and f_d, f_c are data and clock frequencies, respectively. T_w is usually a small portion of the clock period and $T_w f_c$ is calculated as 0.05 for a 90nm technology at $0.3V$ in [6]. For synchronizers with constant τ, t_r can be expressed as

$$t_r = N_r \cdot \tau \tag{4}$$

where N_r is the *normalized* value of the metastability resolution time. Both analytical and empirical studies show that N_r is a dominant term for the MTBF (Eq. 3). For a given N_r, i.e., for a given MTBF specification, it is desirable to design a synchronizer with a smaller τ so as to minimize t_d in Eq. 1.

The overall system MTBF is upper-bounded by the smallest MTBF among various kinds of failure mechanisms. Thus it is necessary to set a proper overall requirement for the metastability-induced MTBF. Researchers in [1] report this MTBF 10^{10} times greater than the targeted Single Event Upset (SEU) induced MTBF. Similarly, authors in [8] calculates $P_{meta} = 2E - 30$ in its system, which is roughly converted into $N_r = 65$. Conventional synchronizer design suggests a N_r around 29-40 for single stage synchronizing. This work applies a $N_r = 35$ specification for one synchronizing latch, indicating a 1-year MTBF for the latch assuming $T_w f_c = 0.05$ [6] and $f_d = 10^9$. For the same overall metastability-induced MTBF requirement, the N_r specification of each stage can be reduced by using multiple synchronizing stages. However, this cascading technique causes increased t_{norm}. More importantly, it significantly increases the timing latency and data-path complexity [9]. Thus, we focus on circuit-level techniques to improving the circuit parameters of metastability resolution in synchronizers, especially the τ which is determined by

$$\tau = \frac{C}{g_{m,sum}} \tag{5}$$

where $g_{m,sum}$ is the sum of the transconductances g_m of an inverter in the Jamb latch and C is lumped capacitance at nodes A and B of the Jamb latch. Furthermore, $g_{m,sum}$ is expressed as

$$g_{m,sum} = g_{mP} \parallel g_{mN} = g_{mP} + g_{mN} \tag{6}$$

where g_{mP} and g_{mN} are the transconductances for PMOS and NMOS, respectively. The transconductance of a single MOS is calculated as

$$g_{m,MOS} = k' \frac{W}{L}(V_{GS} - V_t) = \sqrt{2 I_D k' \frac{W}{L}} \tag{7}$$

where k' is a process parameter, W and L are width and length respectively, V_{GS} is the gate-source voltage, V_t is the threshold voltage, I_D the drain current of the transistor.

2.2 Existing Synchronizer Technique

According to Eq. 5, τ can be improved by a few different ways [10], however, they either increase the transconductance of the latch or reduce its parasitic capacitance. New circuit topologies and/or transistor sizing are usually at an expense of t_{norm} [11] and need trade-off between τ and t_{norm} to optimize t_d. Transistor sizing is also an inefficient way since g_m and C are both increased. The bias current can be increased by enlarging the overdrive voltage [12]. Fig. 1b illustrates grounded PMOS load transistors to provide increased bias current [13], [6]. Thus the inverter amplifiers are transformed into common-source amplifiers with a larger

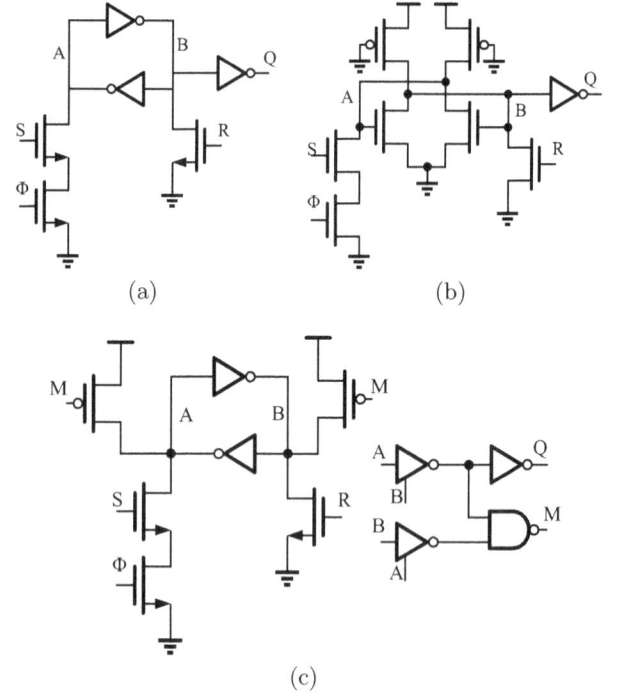

Figure 1: The Jamb Latch: (a) 'ORI'; (b) 'GNDed'; (c) 'GATEd'.

bias current. However, the common-source amplifiers have two significant drawbacks: (i) the transconductance of the amplifier is reduced as expressed in Eq. 6; and (ii) the large direct-path or leakage current. A metastability detector can be used to control the switch on-off of the biasing transistors [6] as illustrated in Fig. 1c. However, the performance improvement is significantly degraded due to the additional capacitance at the latching nodes and the long feedback response time of the metastability detector. Similarly, forward body bias technique can also be exploited to reduce the V_t of transisitors [6]; however, its implementation is not trivial and requires expensive process option.

3. PROPOSED VOLTAGE-BOOSTED SYNCHRONIZERS

To address the mentioned problems and further improve t_r without incurring large energy consumption, we propose Voltage-Boosted Synchronizers (VBSs) that integrate the basic Jamb latch (Fig. 2a) with a charge pump (Fig. 2b). Since the Cross-Coupled Inverters (CCIs) of Jamb latch remains, thus the characteristics of *double transconductors* and *self switch-off* persist. The Jamb latch uses minimum-sized transistors to minimize the power consumption. The charge pump is sized to provide a large current and sufficient electrical charge for powering the CCIs without direct impacts on the lumped capacitance of the CCIs. The charge pump works in two phases, *Precharging* and *Powering*. This characteristic is naturally matched with the transparent and latching modes of the Jamb latch, which is further easily controlled by the clock high and low phases. During the precharging (transparent) phase, the Jamb latch receives new data and the charge pump is precharged by PMOS $P1$.

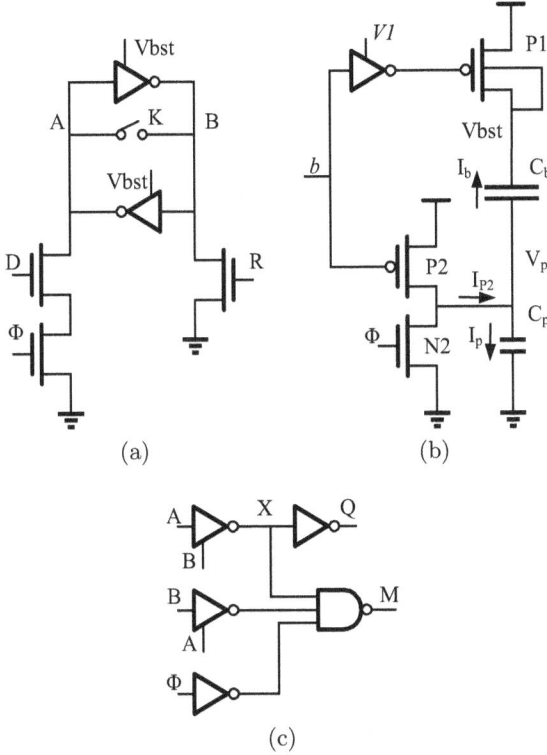

Figure 2: VBS. (a) the basic Jamb latch, (b) the charge pump, (c) the metastability detector. PMOSs in the CCIs are source-body connected. For MVBS, b and M, $V1$ and V_{dd} are connected, respectively; for CVBS, b and Φ (the clock), $V1$ and V_{bst} are connected, respectively.

During the powering (latching) phase, the control signal b turns on PMOS $P2$ and turns off $P1$. The voltage at the $P2$ side of the capacitor C_b is boosted up and the voltage V_{bst} at the $P1$ side of C_b rises beyond V_{dd}, thus speeding up the metastability resolution of the CCIs. $P1$ is drain-body connected to force the current unidirectionally flowing from the supply rail to the charge pump.

3.1 The Powering Strategies of Charge Pump

Two Powering strategies of the charge pump on the powering phase have been developed, including Metastability-driven VBS (MVBS) and Clock-driven VBS (CVBS). MVBS powers the CCIs only when the CCIs is metastable. MVBS utilizes the metastability detector (Fig. 2c) to detect the metastable status and generate the control signal M for the input b of the charge pump. CVBS powers the CCIs every powering phase. The supply voltage $V1$ for the inverter in the charge pump is connected with V_{bst} to perform the same function as the $P1$ drain-body connection does. During the powering phase, the synchronizer is targeting a specified N_r for the metastable resolution and possibly enters the following situations:

Situation 1: There is no metastability. This occupies the majority of all the possible situations. The charge pump of MVBS will not be triggered, thus no extra energy is wasted. However, CVBS will raise the V_{bst} and the transistors including $P1$, $P2$ and the CCIs will dissipate dynamic energy due to the raised V_{bst}. Nevertheless, the energy loss in

these small inverters is much smaller than that of the fully switched-on 'GNDed' synchronizer.

Situation 2: Metastability is unresolved before N_r is reached. To guarantee the overall metastability resolution performance, τ should be maintained smaller than those of the baseline synchronizers.

Situation 3: Metastability is resolved before N_r is reached. The Jamb latch switches off, however, still consumes the leakage current. This current is provided by both the charge pump and the small current of $P1$ when $V_{bst} < V_{dd}$ in CVBS, or, by the switched-on $P1$ in MVBS. The stability for this situation is determined by other failure factors such as SEU [14]. In this sense, MVBS is more flexible to frequency scaling than CVBS.

Situation 4: Metastability is unresolved after N_r is reached. Though electrical charge on C_b may be consumed further and possible run out due to the *switched-on* CCIs, the N_r specification for this stage is already met. The subsequent synchronizing stages (if exist) will provide more metastability resolution time.

In summary, MVBS targets low power and high flexibility for frequency scaling while CVBS targets the high performance.

3.2 The Transistor-Sizing Strategy of Charge Pump

As mentioned, the charge pump shall be properly sized. $P2$ and C_b should be sized large to provide a large current and sufficient electrical charges, respectively; $P1$ should be sized larger than $P2$ so as to precharge C_b in time; $N2$ can be minimum-sized for discharging the electrical charge stored in C_p.

According to KCL, the current flowing through $P2$ is

$$I_{P2}(t_r) = I_b(t_r) + I_p(t_r) \tag{8}$$

where $I_b(t_r)$ and $I_p(t_r)$ are the currents flowing through C_b and C_p, respectively. The voltage $V_b(t_r)$ across C_b is determined by

$$V_b(t_r) = V_{b0} - \frac{1}{C_b} \int_0^{t_r} I_b(t) \, dt \tag{9}$$

where V_{b0} is the initial voltage across C_b (in our case V_{b0} is V_{dd}). The voltage $V_p(t_r)$ across C_p is determined by

$$V_p(t_r) = V_{p0} + \frac{1}{C_p} \int_0^{t_r} I_p(t) \, dt \tag{10}$$

where V_{p0} is the initial value of $V_p(t_r)$ (in our case V_{p0} is near $0V$). Normally, during the powering phase, the condition holds

$$V_p(t_r) \leq V_{dd}. \tag{11}$$

The output voltage $V_{bst}(t_r)$ of the charge pump is given by

$$V_{bst}(t_r) = V_b(t_r) + V_p(t_r) \tag{12}$$

Situation 2 requires

$$V_{bst}(t_r) > V_{dd}. \tag{13}$$

This requirement is combined together with condition (11) to produce

$$V_b(t_r) > 0. \tag{14}$$

That is

$$\int_0^{t_r} I_b(t)\, \mathrm{d}t \leq C_b V_{b0} \tag{15}$$

where $Q_{b0} = C_b V_{b0}$ is the total electrical charge stored during the precharging phase. In other words, Q_b provides the entire electrical charge needed for the metastability resolution and C_b should be sized according to the designed τ and N_r.

Eq. 12 can be differentiated to obtain the $V_{bst}(t_r)$ derivative over t_r

$$\frac{dV_{bst}}{dt_r} = \frac{I_p(t_r)}{C_p} - \frac{I_b(t_r)}{C_b} \tag{16}$$

$$= \frac{I_{P2}(t_r)}{C_p} - I_b(t_r)(\frac{1}{C_b} + \frac{1}{C_p}) \tag{17}$$

$$\simeq \frac{1}{C_p}[I_{P2}(t_r) - I_b(t_r)] \tag{18}$$

assuming $C_b \gg C_p$. This indicates that when $I_{P2}(t_r)$ is greater than $I_b(t_r)$, $V_{bst}(t_r)$ is raised to increase the load current or else $V_{bst}(t_r)$ is reduced to reduce the load current. In other words, *The charge pump maintains the $I_{P2}(t_r) \simeq I_b(t_r)$ relationship by adapting V_{bst} to adjust the load current $I_b(t_r)$.* Giving that $C_b \gg C_p$, P2 negatively charges C_b, forcing $V_b(t_r)$ to drop from V_{dd} towards 0 during the powering phase.

3.3 Metastability Parameters Calculation

It is difficult to extract τ using Eq. 5. A τ extraction methodology is developed in [5] and performed as follows: in Fig. 2a, an ideal switch K is placed in between nodes A and B; K is first closed to force A and B to enter the true metastability status and then released to let them resolve; The slope of the time t_r versus the log-scaled the voltage difference between A and B during the metastability resolution is calculated as τ; t_r is further obtained by Eq. 4. This methodology assumes a constant bias current and a constant τ during the metastability resolution for the 'ORI' and the 'GNDed', however, the assumption is not the case for 'GATEd' and VBSs with temporally changing V_{bst} and τ. Thus here we have developed a new methodology for calculating t_r and the average $\bar{\tau}$ for a given N_r.

(1) **Metastability Simulations**. τ is extracted using the mentioned methodology parametrically over V_{bst}. In each simulation, the charge pump is replaced with an extra voltage source that provides a constant V_{bst} while the metastability detector remains in MVBS. The extracted simulation data build a mapping function between V_{bst} and τ in

$$\tau = \tau(V_{bst}) \tag{19}$$

Similarly, for the baseline 'GATEd', the control signal of two PMOS current sources is disconnected from the metastability detector and connected to ground or V_{dd} to extract τ_{on} and τ_{off}, respectively.

(2) **Voltage-Boosting Simulation** . The temporally changing V_{bst} is extracted. Opposite from the metastability simulations, the switch K is first open to initialize the VBSs and then closed to force the CCIs in the persisting metastable status to evaluate the V_{bst} response (including the feedback response of metastability detector in MVBS).

$$V_{bst} = V(t_s) \tag{20}$$

Similarly, the feedback response time t_{FB} of the 'GATEd' is extracted.

(3) N_r **Integration**. The total N_r is obtained by integrating over t_r as a function of t_r

$$N_r = \int_0^{t_r} \frac{1}{\tau(V_{bst}(t))}\, \mathrm{d}t = N(t_r) \tag{21}$$

For constant V_{bst} and τ, Eq. 21 is degenerated as Eq. 4.

(4) t_r **and** $\bar{\tau}$ **Calculation**. t_r for a given N_r is calculated using the inverse function of Eq. 21

$$t_r = N^{-1}(N_r) \tag{22}$$

The t_r of the 'GATEd' is calculated as

$$t_r = t_{FB} + (N_r - \frac{t_{FB}}{\tau_{off}})\tau_{on}. \tag{23}$$

$\bar{\tau}$ is calculated using Eq. 4.

3.4 Energy Consumption Estimation

The overall average energy consumption E_{total} can be estimated as

$$E_{total} = (1 - a\%)E_{idle} + a\%[(1 - b\%)E_{norm} + b\%E_{meta})] \tag{24}$$

where E_{idle}, E_{norm} and E_{meta} are the energy consumption during the idle status, a normal data activity and metastability, respectively. $a\% = \frac{f_d}{f_c}$ is the data activity and $b\% = T_w f_c$ is the metastability probability with data activities. For asynchronous communication systems or the final synchronizers in resilient digital system, $a\%$ is usually very small due to the hand-shake protocol or the small timing-error rate setting. For synchronizers used as data samplers such as the shadow flip-flop in the Razor-style designs, $a\%$ is the same as data-path activities. $b\%$ is very small as calculated. Thus E_{total} is mainly determined by E_{idle} and E_{norm}.

4. SIMULATION RESULTS

In Cadence 5.1 using the TSMC 65nm technology, The ideal capacitor C_b is $20fF$ and C_p is the parasitic capacitance in the transistors; the widths of $P1$ and $P2$ are $0.8um$ and $1.2um$, respectively, for both CVBS and MVBS; all other transistors are minimum-sized.

Simulations are first carried out at $V_{dd} = 0.7V$. In Fig. 3, the trend of the curves indicates that as V_{bst} becomes larger, τ becomes smaller due to a larger overdrive voltage. The gap between the CVBS and MVBS curves shows that the metastability detector deteriorates τ. Fig. 4 shows that in the powering phase the charge pump raises V_{bst} to power the CCIs and is precharged in the precharging phase. Fig. 5 demonstrates the bias currents flowing through the CCIs of the five synchronizers. MVBS and CVBS need smaller bias currents than 'GATEd' and 'GNDed' do. The feedback response time of MVBS is larger than that of 'GATEd' due to the charge pump. However, due to the PMOS transconductors, MVBS and CVBS have better τ than 'GATEd' and 'GNDed', as shown in Fig. 6. In Fig. 7, CVBS and MVBS reach the specified N_r (such as 35) earlier than 'GNDed' and 'GATED' do, respectively.

Simulations are carried out parametrically for $V_{dd} = 0.4$V, 0.5V, 0.6V, 0.7V. The energy of each synchronizer is calculated by integrating the power (including that of the charge pump) with respect to the corresponding clock period $2t_d$.

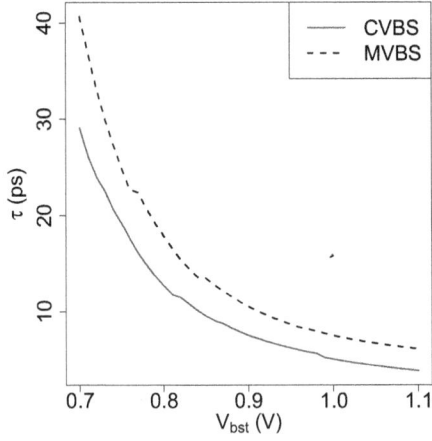

Figure 3: Metastability simulations for VBSs at $V_{dd} = 0.7V$.

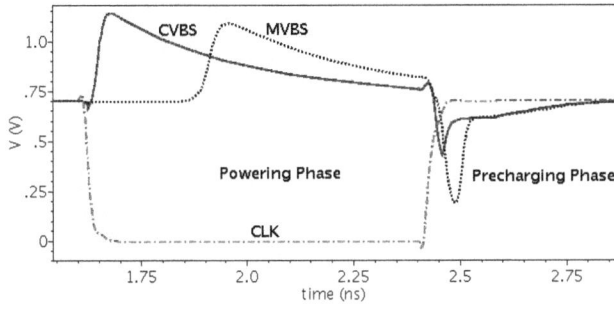

Figure 5: The bias current flowing through the CCIs at $V_{dd} = 0.7V$.

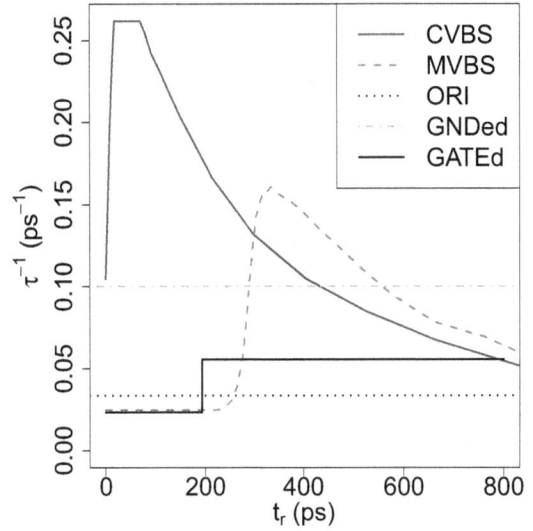

Figure 4: Voltage-boosting simulations at $V_{dd} = 0.7V$.

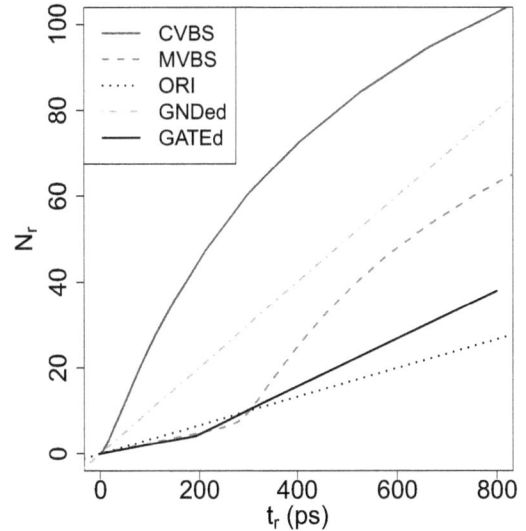

Figure 6: τ^{-1} vs t_r at $V_{dd} = 0.7V$.

The results are shown in Tab. 1 and Tab. 2. Some conclusions can be drawn as follows.

(1) Performance. The r_0 column represents the performance (frequency) ratio of the corresponding synchronizer over the basic Jamb latch. The r_0 for the 'GATEd' and MVBS are 1.3-2.2 and 2.0-2.7, respectively. The r_0 for the 'GNDed' and CVBS shows 3.0-7.9 and 5.1-9.8, respectively. The r_1 column represents the performance (frequency) ratio of MVBS over the 'GATEd' or CVBS over the 'GNDed'. The r_1 values show that MVBS and CVBS are 1.12-1.49 and 1.19-1.73 faster than the 'GATEd' and 'GNDed', respectively.

(2) Energy. E_{idle} of the 'ORI' and 'GATED' are the least primarily because of low clock energy. However, $71\% - 95\%$ of E_{idle} of MVBS comes from the clock inverter (in Fig. 2c) that is usually also required by practical master-slave flip-flop designs. Thus we believe that 'ORI', 'GATED' and MVBS consume the same level of idle energy. E_{idle} of CVBS and 'GNDed' are 5-8 and 30-50 times of that of MVBS, respectively. The other synchronizers consumes similar amount of E_{norm} except the 'GNDed' consumes 4-5 times more.

(3) Area. C_b is approximately equivalent to 120 minimum PMOSs, roughly 13 times large as the minimum-sized 9-MOS Jamb latch, comparable to the additional flip-flops used in [15]. However, it do not introduce a large overall area expense since synchronizers are usually much less than the storage flip-flops.

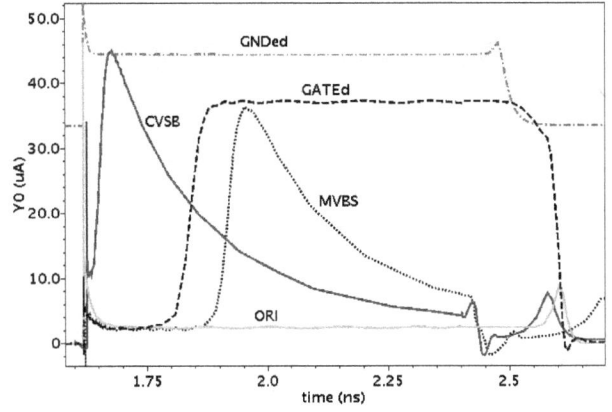

Figure 7: N_r vs. t_r at $V_{dd} = 0.7V$.

Table 1: The Performance of the 'GATEd' synchronizer

Vdd (V)	0.7	0.6	0.5	0.4
τ_{off} (ps)	46	125	448	1086
τ_{on} (ps)	18	24	42	143
t_{FB} (ps)	193	477	1430	4360

Table 2: The Energy Consumption and Performance of the Baseline and Proposed Synchronizers with a given $N_r = 35$

Vdd (V)	Energy (fJ)		Delay(ps)					
ORI								
Vdd	E_{idle}	E_{norm}	τ	t_r	t_{norm}	t_d	r_0	r_1
0.7	0.02	3.90	31	1085	98	1183	1.00	
0.6	0.03	3.19	86	3010	180	3190	1.00	
0.5	0.05	2.56	206	7210	445	7655	1.00	
0.4	0.07	1.65	566	19810	1578	21388	1.00	
GNDed								
Vdd	E_{idle}	E_{norm}	τ	t_r	t_{norm}	t_d	r_0	r_1
0.7	19.49	20.82	10	350	50	400	2.96	
0.6	13.19	14.04	13	455	78	533	5.99	
0.5	8.94	9.42	23	805	161	966	7.93	
0.4	6.51	6.76	80	2800	560	3360	6.37	
GATEd								
Vdd	E_{idle}	E_{norm}	$\bar{\tau}$	t_r	t_{norm}	t_d	r_0	r_1
0.7	0.02	3.89	21	747	154	901	1.31	
0.6	0.02	3.18	35	1225	287	1512	2.11	
0.5	0.03	2.54	79	2766	719	3485	2.20	
0.4	0.06	1.64	251	8791	2522	11313	1.89	
MVBS								
Vdd	E_{idle}	E_{norm}	$\bar{\tau}$	t_r	t_{norm}	t_d	r_0	r_1
0.7	0.42	3.30	14	477	126	603	1.96	1.49
0.6	0.32	2.64	27	961	225	1186	2.69	1.27
0.5	0.24	2.02	71	2498	534	3032	2.52	1.15
0.4	0.19	1.33	235	8229	1882	10111	2.12	1.12
CVBS								
Vdd	E_{idle}	E_{norm}	$\bar{\tau}$	t_r	t_{norm}	t_d	r_0	r_1
0.7	2.93	4.12	4	147	85	232	5.11	1.73
0.6	2.15	3.41	6	218	151	369	8.65	1.44
0.5	1.49	2.44	12	423	357	780	9.81	1.24
0.4	0.96	1.65	48	1667	1163	2830	7.56	1.19

5. CONCLUSIONS

To solve the performance bottleneck due to synchronizers at low supply voltages, we proposed two VBSs consisting of a basic Jamb latch and a charge pump, MVBS and CVBS. The capacitor of the charge pump is sized as large as 13 basic Jamb latches, trading the area with a high powering capability to speed up the metastability resolution in the Jamb latch. For a equivalent 1-year MTBF specification, MVBS and CVBS show 2.0-2.7 and 5.1-9.8 times performance improvements over the basic Jamb latch, respectively, without incurring large power consumption.

6. REFERENCES

[1] K. Bowman, J. Tschanz, N. S. Kim, J. Lee, C. Wilkerson, S.-L. Lu, T. Karnik, and V. De, "Energy-Efficient and Metastability-Immune Resilient Circuits for Dynamic Variation Tolerance," *IEEE Journal of Solid-State Circuits*, vol. 44, no. 1, pp. 49–63, jan. 2009.

[2] S. Beer, R. Ginosar, M. Priel, R. Dobkin, and A. Kolodny, "The Devolution of Synchronizers," in *IEEE Symp. on Asynchronous Circuits and Systems (ASYNC), 2010*, May 2010, pp. 94–103.

[3] P. Favrat, P. Deval, and M. Declercq, "A high-efficiency CMOS voltage doubler," *Solid-State Circuits, IEEE Journal of*, vol. 33, no. 3, pp. 410–416, Mar 1998.

[4] B. Razavi, *Design of Analog CMOS Integrated Circuits*, 1st ed. New York, NY, USA: McGraw-Hill, Inc., 2001.

[5] C. Dike and E. Burton, "Miller and noise effects in a synchronizing flip-flop," *IEEE Journal of Solid-State Circuits*, vol. 34, no. 6, pp. 849–855, jun 1999.

[6] J. Zhou, M. Ashouei, D. Kinniment, J. Huisken, and G. Russell, "Extending Synchronization from Super-Threshold to Sub-threshold Region," in *2010 IEEE Symp. on Asynchronous Circuits and Systems (ASYNC)*, May 2010, pp. 85–93.

[7] C. Portmann and H. Meng, "Metastability in CMOS library elements in reduced supply and technology scaled applications," *IEEE Journal of Solid-State Circuits*, vol. 30, no. 1, pp. 39–46, jan 1995.

[8] S. Das, D. Roberts, S. Lee, S. Pant, D. Blaauw, T. Austin, K. Flautner, and T. Mudge, "A self-tuning DVS processor using delay-error detection and correction," *IEEE Journal of Solid-State Circuits*, vol. 41, no. 4, pp. 792–804, April 2006.

[9] M. Fojtik, D. Fick, Y. Kim, N. Pinckney, D. Harris, D. Blaauw, and D. Sylvester, "Bubble Razor: Eliminating Timing Margins in an ARM Cortex-M3 Processor in 45 nm CMOS Using Architecturally Independent Error Detection and Correction," *Solid-State Circuits, IEEE Journal of*, vol. 48, no. 1, pp. 66–81, jan. 2013.

[10] S. Beer and R. Ginosar, "Eleven Ways to Boost Your Synchronizer," *IEEE Trans. on Very Large Scale Integration Systems*, vol. PP, no. 99, pp. 1–1, 2014.

[11] D. Li, D. Rennie, P. Chuang, D. Nairn, and M. Sachdev, "Design and analysis of metastable-hardened and soft-error tolerant high-performance, low-power flip-flops," in *Int. Symp. on Quality Electronic Design (ISQED)*, 2011, pp. 1–8.

[12] D. J. Kinniment, *Synchronization and Arbitration in Digital Systems*. Wiley Publishing, 2008.

[13] J. Zhou, D. Kinniment, G. Russell, and A. Yakovlev, "A robust synchronizer," in *IEEE Computer Society Annual Symposium on Emerging VLSI Technologies and Architectures, 2006.*, March 2006, p. 2.

[14] J. M. Rabaey, A. P. Chandrakasan, and B. Nikolic, *Digital integrated circuits: a design perspective*, 2nd ed., ser. Prentice Hall electronics and VLSI series. Pearson Education, Jan. 2003.

[15] J. Zhou, D. Kinniment, G. Russell, and A. Yakovlev, "Adapting Synchronizers to the Effects of on Chip Variability," in *IEEE Int. Symp. on Asynchronous Circuits and Systems, 2008.*, April 2008, pp. 39–47.

Recent Advances in Brain-controlled Prosthetics for Paralysis

[Friday Keynote]

Andrew Schwartz
Neurobiology
University of Pittsburgh
E1440 BSTWR, 200 Lothrop Street
Pittsburgh, PA 15213-2536
abs21@pitt.edu

ABSTRACT

Neurons encode many parameters simultaneously, but the encoding fidelity at the level of individual neurons is weak. In contrast, with a better understanding of neural population function we can now decode complex arm and hand movement. We have developed a simple extraction algorithm to capture arm movement data and shown that a paralyzed patient who cannot move any part of her body below her neck can control a high-performance "modular prosthetic limb" using 10 degrees-of-freedom simultaneously. The control of this artificial limb is intuitive, with coordinated, graceful motion, closely resembling natural arm and hand movement.

Categories and Subject Descriptors

A.0 [**General Literature**]: GENERAL—*Conference proceedings*

General Terms

Keynote

BIOGRAPHY

Dr. Schwartz received his Ph.D. in Physiology from the University of Minnesota in 1984. He then went on to a postdoctoral fellowship with Dr. Apostolos Georgopoulos, who was developing the concept of directional tuning and population-based movement representation in the motor cortex. After building research programs in Phoenix and San Diego, he moved to the University of Pittsburgh in 2002. Schwartz' research is centered on the exploration of cortical signals generated during volitional arm movements. This effort showed that a high-fidelity representation of movement intention could be decoded from the motor cortex and enabled technology now being used by paralyzed subjects to operate a high-performance prosthetic arm and hand.

GLSVLSI'15, May 20–22, 2015, Pittsburgh, PA, USA.
ACM 978-1-4503-3474-7/15/05.
http://dx.doi.org/10.1145/2742060.2742124.

Formal Analysis Provides Parameters for Guiding Hyperoxidation in Bacteria using Phototoxic Proteins

Qinsi Wang
Computer Science
Department
Carnegie Mellon University
qinsiw@cs.cmu.edu

Natasa Miskov-Zivanov
Electrical and Computer
Engineering Department
Carnegie Mellon University
nmiskov@andrew.cmu.edu

Cheryl Telmer
Biological Sciences
Department
Carnegie Mellon University
ctelmer@cmu.edu

Edmund M. Clarke
Computer Science
Department
Carnegie Mellon University
emc@cs.cmu.edu

ABSTRACT

In this work, we developed a methodology to analyze a bacteria model that mimics the stages through which bacteria change when phage therapy is applied. Due to the widespread misuse and overuse of antibiotics, drug resistant bacteria now pose significant risks to health, agriculture and the environment. Therefore, we were interested in an alternative to conventional antibiotics, a phage therapy. Our model was designed according to an experimental procedure to engineer a temperate phage, Lambda (λ), and then kill bacteria via light-activated production of superoxide. We applied formal analysis to our model and the results show that such an approach can speed up evaluation of the system, which would be impractical or possibly not even feasible to study in a wet lab.

1. INTRODUCTION

The discovery of antibiotics has been quickly followed by the development of antibiotic resistance. New medicines are becoming increasingly scarce in tackling this issue. The document released by CDC (Centers for Disease Control and Prevention), "Antibiotic Resistance Threats in the United States, 2013" [1], intends to raise public awareness of the problems associated with overuse and misuse of antibiotics and to outline the threats to society caused by these organisms. The organisms have been categorized by hazard level as urgent, serious and concerning. Over 2 million illnesses and $23,000$ deaths per year are a direct result of antibiotic resistance.

There are multiple mechanisms of antibiotic resistance. First, altered permeability of the antimicrobial agent is suggested to be due to the inability of the agent to enter the

bacterial cell, or alternatively, due to the active export of the agent from the cell. Second, resistance is often the result of the production of an enzyme that is capable of inactivating the antimicrobial agent. Next, resistance can arise due to alteration of the target site for the antimicrobial agent. Finally, resistance can result from the acquisition of a new enzyme to replace the sensitive one, thus replacing the pathway that was originally sensitive to antibiotic to another pathway.

The CDC outlines four core actions that will help fight deadly infections [1]: (a) preventing infections and the spread of resistance; (b) tracking resistant bacteria; (c) improving the use of today's antibiotics; and (d) promoting the development of new antibiotics and developing new diagnostic tests for resistant bacteria. Recently, we have addressed this problem by designing a new system that relies on phage-based therapy. Phages, or bacteriophages, are viruses that infect bacteria and have evolved to manipulate the bacterial cells and genome, making resistance to bacteriophages difficult to achieve. Bacteriophages are complex and utilize many host pathways such that they cannot be inactivated or bypassed. Bacteriophages infect only specific hosts and can kill the host by cytolysis. However, many phages are temperate, meaning that they can enter a lysogenic phase and therefore not lyse and kill the host bacteria. The addition of a phototoxic protein to the system offers a second method of killing those bacteria targeted by a lysogenic phage. Thus, our system, shown in Figure 1, explores the possibility that temperate phages can also be used for phage therapy and bacteria killing applications. We incorporated several proteins (KillerRed [8], SuperNova [10]), that have been shown to be phototoxic and that provide another level of controlled bacteria killing.

In this paper, we describe our computational model of the phage-bacteria system in section 2, which has been developed as an extension of an initial model described in [2]. Then, a formal analysis technique used to deal with the parameter estimation and parameter sensitivity evaluation of our hybrid model is introduced in section 3. Section 4 presents the analysis results, and demonstrates that our model and methodology allow for studying the behavior and final state of the system at a number of points in the pa-

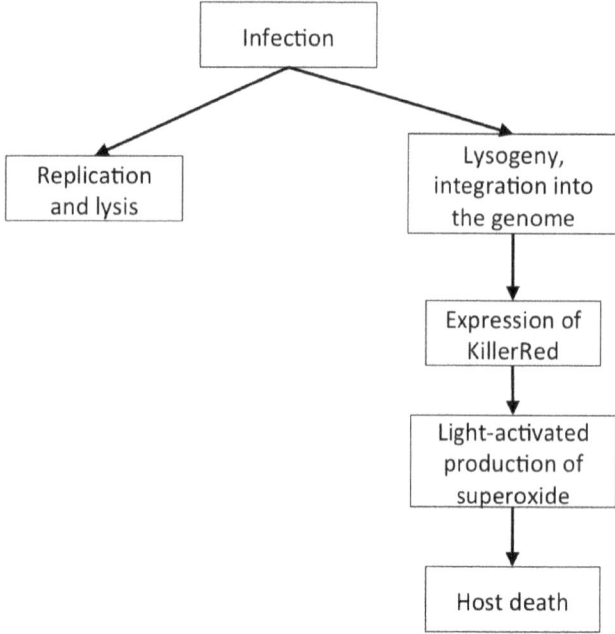

Figure 1: Interactions between phage and bacteria used in our model

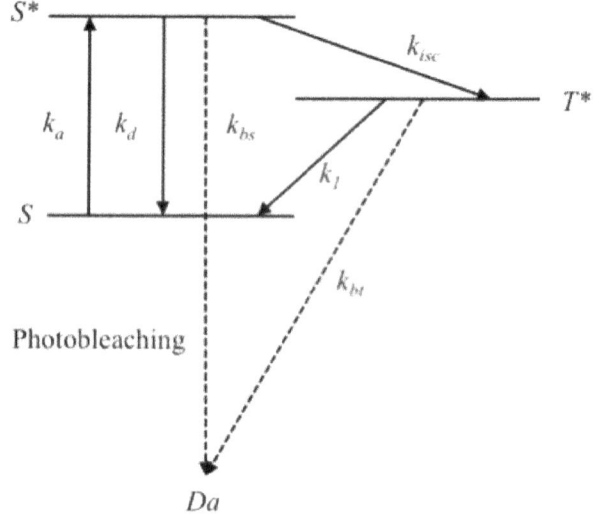

Figure 2: Energy diagram for a generic fluorochrome [9]

rameter space, and for checking properties that are often impractical to characterize using wet lab procedures only. Section 5 concludes the paper.

2. THE KILLERRED MODEL

We have modeled synthesis and action of KillerRed that occurs over three main phases of a typical photobleaching experiment: induction at $37°C$, storage at $4°C$ to allow for protein maturation, and photobleaching at room temperature. Within these phases, we identify several stages of interest in KillerRed synthesis and activity as follows.
- mRNA synthesis and degradation
- KillerRed synthesis, maturation, and degradation
- KillerRed states: singlet (S), singlet excited (S^*), triplet excited (T^*), and deac-tivated (Da)
- Superoxide production (by KillerRed)
- Superoxide elimination (by superoxide dismutase)

We implemented these system stages with distinct model states, and outlined them in Figure 3, together with state variables (values are included if variables are fixed within a state), transitions between states, and events that trigger state transitions. In Table 1 we list the model states that are used to describe the stages of the system. In the following, we detail our implementation of system stages within the model. We also list equations that we derived for each stage.

Cell exposure to light
In [11], the authors describe a method for determining the rate coefficient of activation from the ground state k_a: $k_a = \sigma I$. In detail, σ is the optical cross-section per molecule and I is the excitation intensity in photons per unit area. The lamp used for photobleaching gave $I = 11027\ photons/cm^2 s$ (about $1W$). σ is given by $\sigma = \varepsilon(1000cm^3/L)(ln10)NA$, where ε is the extinction coefficient and NA is Avogadro's number. We calculated $k_a = 1.721011s^{-1}$ for KillerRed for our photobleaching experiments. The rate constant for returning to the ground state is $k_f = ln2/\tau$, where τ is the

half-life for KillerRed in the excited state. τ for KillerRed is assumed to be similar to τ for dsRed (about $3.0ns$ [3]), since their chromophores are identical. Thus, by assuming that KillerRed is always in the excited state (if it has not been deactivated) during photobleaching, we have that $k_f = 2.3108s^1$ and $F = k_a/(k_a + k_f) = 0.9987$.

Production of superoxide
Production of the superoxide radical is governed by several reactions. Fluorescein is used as a model chromophore. S, S, T, and Da are the singlet, excited singlet, excited triplet, and deactivated states, respectively, of the chromophore. Figure 2 outlines transitions between different forms of the chromophore. In detail, fluorochrome molecules absorb photon energy at a rate k_a and go from the ground singlet state S up to the excited singlet state S^*. Then they may return to the ground state by radiative (fluorescence) or non-radiative (internal conversion) pathway at a combined rate k_d. They may also undergo non-radiative intersystem crossing, at a rate k_{isc}, to T^*, where they may return to the ground state at a rate k_1. Photobleaching may take place from both S^* and T^* at rates k_{bs} and k_{bt}, respectively. Those photobleached molecules can no longer participate in the excitation-emission cycle.

Superoxide dismutase
Superoxide dismutase is $E.\ coli's$ main defense against superoxide. Its action was incorporated using Michaelis-Menten kinetics:
$$-\frac{d[O_2^{\cdot-}]}{dt} = \frac{V_{max}[O_2^{\cdot-}]}{K_m + [O_2^{\cdot-}]},$$
where V_{max} estimated using $k_c at$ from [7], and K_m was estimated using k_m and k_{cat}/k_m from [4, 7].

Cell without λ-phage genome
The first system stage that we model is a bacteria cell that does not have phage genome injected, and gene transcription is not induced. Thus, all of the model elements are at their initial level, assumed to be 0. In the model, we assume that λ-phage genome is injected into bacteria cell with rate k_1, or t_1 time units after the start of time counting. When analyzing individual cells this does not have an effect, but

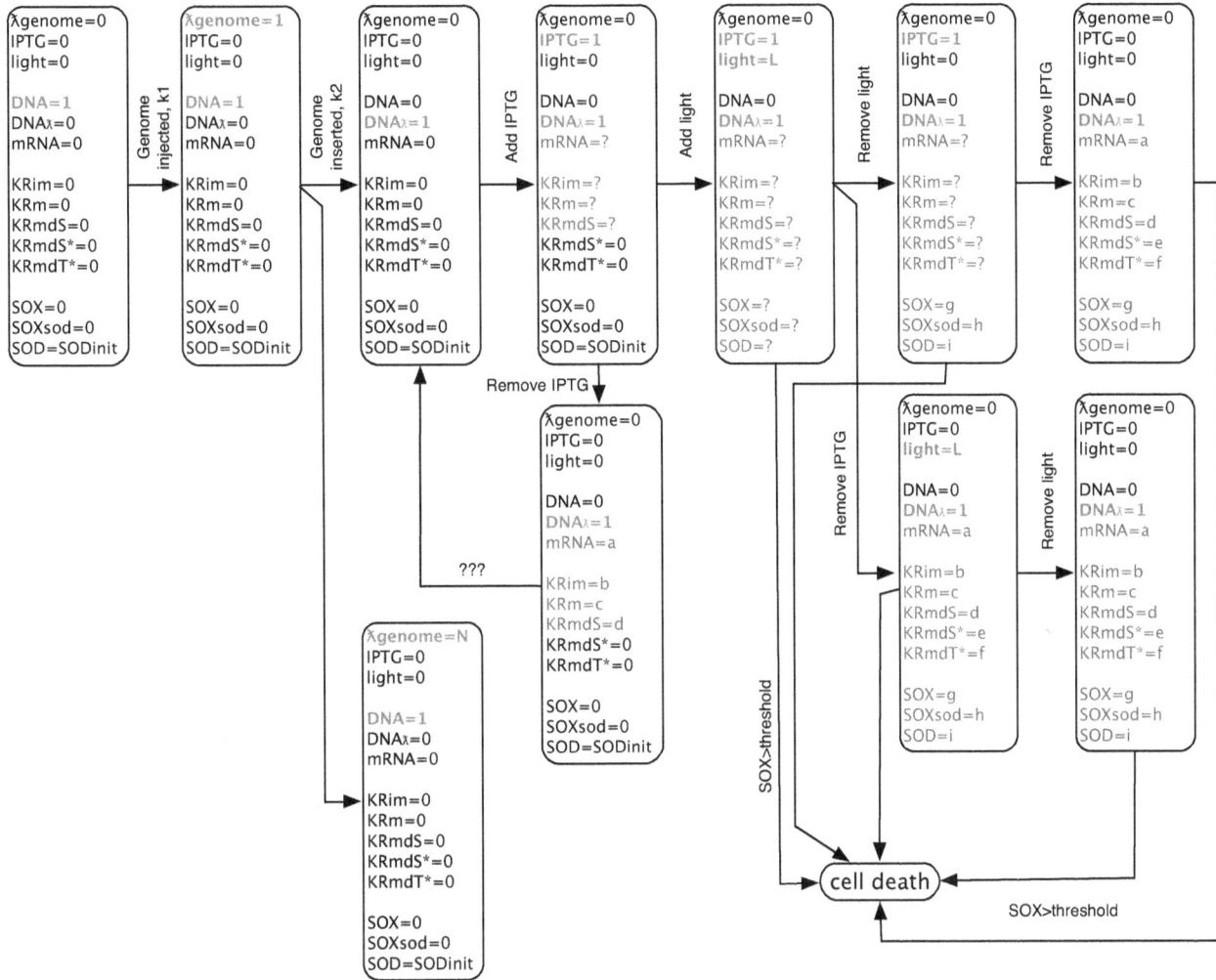

Figure 3: Hybrid automaton for our KillerRed model

is important to take into account when analyzing cell population.

Cell with injected λ-phage genome

After the injection of phage genome into the cell, the genome will be inserted into the bacterial DNA with rate k_2. Or, in terms of counting time units, it will take t_2 time units to integrate the phage genome into bacterial plasmid once it is inside the cell. However, since IPTG is still not added to the cell, we assume that gene transcription is not induced yet. Therefore, similar to previous two states, initial state and the state of phage genome injected, this state is assumed to be static.

Addition of IPTG

When IPTG is added to the system, the transcription starts. Measure of transcriptional efficiency is the rate of mRNA synthesis, k_{RNAsyn}. Our construct uses a wild-type lac promoter, so we assume that its transcription rates are similar to the lac operon. Next, mRNA transforms into immature KillerRed molecules with translational efficiency, k_{KRsyn}. The maximum translation rate in the model is three orders of magnitude lower to reflect the presents of several rare codons. This adjustment is suggested by comparisons of

our fluorescence data for KillerRed and mRFP, which have nearly identical brightness.

Immature synthesized KillerRed (KR_{im}) requires additional time to become mature KillerRed form (KR_m), and to fold and create a dimer (KR_{md}). These two events together occur with the overall rate of k_{KR_m}. This folded and dimerized form of KillerRed that can be activated by light is called singlet form (KR_{mdS}). Degradations of synthesized mRNA and KillerRed in both modeled forms are included in equations with rates $k_{mRNAdeg}$ (characteristic half-life), $k_{KR_{im}deg}$, and k_{mdSdeg}, respectively. In this model state, resulting from addition of IPTG and ending with either removal of IPTG or addition of light, we use the following ordinary differential equations (ODEs) to describe the continuous dynamics.

$$\frac{\mathrm{d}[mRNA]}{\mathrm{d}t} = k_{RNAsyn} \cdot [DNA] - k_{RNAdeg} \cdot [mRNA]$$

$$\frac{\mathrm{d}[KR_{im}]}{\mathrm{d}t} = k_{KR_{im}syn} \cdot [mRNA] - (k_{KR_m} + k_{KR_{im}deg}) \cdot [KR_{im}]$$

$$\frac{\mathrm{d}[KR_{mdS}]}{\mathrm{d}t} = k_{KR_m} \cdot [KR_{im}] - k_{KR_{mdS}deg} \cdot [KR_{mdS}]$$

State	State description	Input	Next state(s)
S_0	Initial system state, bacteria cell, without phage	n/a	S_1 (ex.)
S_1	Phage genome injected	λ-phage genome	S_2 (in.), S_3 (in.)
S_2	Phage genome replication (lytic cycle)	Genome replication	n/a
S_3	Phage genome within bacterial DNA (lysogenic cycle)	Genome insertion	S_4 (ex.)
S_4	Gene transcription, translation	Addition of IPTG	S_5 (ex.), S_6 (ex.)
S_5	Gene transcription decrease	Removal of IPTG	S_3 (in.) [1]
S_6	Activation of KillerRed	Light turned ON	S_7 (ex.), S_8 (ex.), S_{11} (in.)
S_7	Mixture of KillerRed forms, no activation	Light turned OFF	S_9 (ex.), S_{11} (in.)
S_8	Mixture of KillerRed forms, transcription decrease	Removal of IPTG	S_{10} (ex.), S_{11} (in.)
S_9	Mixture of KillerRed forms, no activation, transcription decrease	Removal of IPTG	S_{11} (in.)
S_{10}	Mixture of KillerRed forms, transcription decrease, no activation	Light turned OFF	S_{11} (in.)
S_{11}	Cell death	SOX>threshold	n/a

Table 1: List of modeled system states, their description, inputs and next state(s) with indication whether transition was triggered by external input (ex.) or by internal variable (in.) reaching some specified value.

Addition of light

Addition of light results in moving from the state with Killer-Red synthesis into the state of activating KillerRed, S. In the state that assumes systemâĂŹs exposure to light, other forms of KillerRed are present, including excited singlet state S^*, (KR_{mdS^*}) and triplet state T^*, (KR_{mdT^*}). Transitions between different forms of KillerRed can occur and therefore, in this state, we include the above model equations and modified equation, and add equations for other forms of KillerRed (KR_{mdS^*}, KR_{mdT^*}), as well as equations for produced superoxide (SOX) and for the effect of superoxide dismutase (SOX_{sod}).

$$\frac{d[KR_{mdS}]}{dt} = k_{KR_m} \cdot [KR_{im}] + k_{KR_f} \cdot [KR_{mdS^*}]$$
$$+ k_{KR_{ic}} \cdot [KR_{mdS^*}] + k_{KR_{nrd}} \cdot [KR_{mdT^*}]$$
$$+ k_{KR_{SOXd1}} \cdot [KR_{mdT^*}] - k_{KR_{ex}} \cdot [KR_{mdS}]$$
$$- k_{KR_{mdS}deg} \cdot [KR_{mdS}]$$

$$\frac{d[KR_{mdS^*}]}{dt} = k_{KR_{ex}} \cdot [KR_{mdS}] - k_{KR_f} \cdot [KR_{mdS^*}]$$
$$- k_{KR_{ic}} \cdot [KR_{mdS^*}] - k_{KR_{isc}} \cdot [KR_{mdS^*}]$$
$$- k_{KR_{mdS^*}deg} \cdot [KR_{mdS^*}]$$

$$\frac{d[KR_{mdT^*}]}{dt} = k_{KR_{isc}} \cdot [KR_{mdS^*}] - k_{KR_{nrd}} \cdot [KR_{mdT^*}]$$
$$- k_{KR_{SOXd1}} \cdot [KR_{mdT^*}]$$
$$- k_{KR_{SOXd2}} \cdot [KR_{mdT^*}]$$
$$- k_{KR_{mdT^*}deg} \cdot [KR_{mdT^*}]$$

$$\frac{d[SOX]}{dt} = k_{KR_{SOXd1}} \cdot [KR_{mdT^*}] + k_{KR_{SOXd2}}$$
$$\cdot [KR_{mdT^*}] - \frac{d[SOX_{sod}]}{dt}$$

$$\frac{d[SOX_{sod}]}{dt} = k_{SOD} \cdot V_{maxSOD} \cdot \frac{[SOX]}{K_m + [SOX]}$$

Rates of KillerRed transitioning from state S^* to state S, through fluorescence or internal conversion are denoted with k_{KR_f} and $k_{KR_{ic}}$, respectively. Rates of KillerRed transitioning from state T^* to state S, through non-radiative deactivation or by production of SOX with deactivation are denoted with $k_{KR_{nrd}}$ and $k_{KR_{SOXd1}}$, respectively. The excited form of KillerRed, S^*, is formed at rate $k_{KR_{ex}}$, and is reduced in several ways: (a) by fluorescence with rate k_{KR_f}, (b) by internal conversion with rate $k_{KR_{ic}}$, (c) by inter-system crossing $k_{KR_{isc}}$, and (d) by degradation with rate

$k_{KR_{mdS^*}deg}$. The triplet form, T^*, is formed through inter-system crossing with rate $k_{KR_{isc}}$, and is reduced in several ways, by non-radiative deactivation with rate $k_{KR_{nrd}}$, by superoxide (ROS) production with deactivation to state S with rate $k_{KR_{SOXd1}}$, by superoxide (ROS) production with photobleaching with rate $k_{KR_{SOXd2}}$, and by degradation with rate $k_{KR_{mdS^*}deg}$. In addition, $k_{KR_{SOXd1}}$ and $k_{KR_{SOXd2}}$ can be computed taking into account relative propensity for KillerRed to generate superoxide without becoming deactivated (c), photo-bleaching rate obtained from experiments $(k_{KR_{pb}})$, and quantum yield (Φ) as follows.

$$k_{KR_{SOXd1}} = c \cdot \frac{k_{KR_{pb}}}{\Phi} \qquad k_{KR_{SOXd2}} = \frac{k_{KR_{pb}}}{\Phi}$$

3. δ-DECISIONS FOR HYBRID MODELS

In order to overcome the undecidability of reasoning about hybrid systems, Gao *et al.* recently defined the concept of δ-satisfiability over the reals, and presented a corresponding δ-complete decision procedure [5, 6]. The main idea is to decide correctly whether slightly *relaxed* sentences over the reals are satisfiable or not. The following definitions are from [6].

Definition 1 A bounded quantifier is one of the following:

$$\exists^{[a,b]} x = \exists x : (a \leq x \wedge x \leq b)$$
$$\forall^{[a,b]} x = \forall x : (a \leq x \wedge x \leq b)$$

Definition 2 A bounded Σ_1 sentence is an expression of the form:

$$\exists^{I_1} x_1, ..., \exists^{I_1} x_n : \psi(x_1, ..., x_n)$$

where $I_i = [a_i, b_i]$ are intervals, $\psi(x_1, ..., x_n)$ is a Boolean combination of atomic formulas of the form $g(x_1, ..., x_n)$ op 0, where g is a composition of Type 2-computable functions and op $\in \{<, \leq, >, \geq, =, \neq\}$.

Note that any bounded Σ_1 sentence is equivalent to a Σ_1 sentence in which all the atoms are of the form $f(x_1, ..., x_n) = 0$ (*i.e.*, the only op needed is '='). Essentially, Type 2-computable functions can be approximated arbitrarily well by finite computations of a special kind of Turing machines (Type 2 machines); most 'useful' functions over the reals are Type 2-computable. The notion of δ-weakening of a bounded sentence is central to δ-satisfiability.

Definition 3 Let $\delta \in \mathbb{Q}^+ \cup \{0\}$ be a constant and ϕ a bounded Σ_1-sentence in the standard form

$$\phi = \exists^{I_1} x_1, ..., \exists^{I_n} x_n : \bigwedge_{i=1}^{m} (\bigvee_{j=1}^{k_i} f_{ij}(x_1, ..., x_n) = 0) \quad (1)$$

where $f_{ij}(x_1, ..., x_n) = 0$ are atomic formulas. The δ-*weakening* of ϕ is the formula:

$$\phi^\delta = \exists^{I_1} x_1, ..., \exists^{I_n} x_n : \bigwedge_{i=1}^{m} (\bigvee_{j=1}^{k_i} |f_{ij}(x_1, ..., x_n)| \leq \delta) \quad (2)$$

Note that ϕ implies ϕ^δ, while the converse is obviously not true. The bounded δ-satisfiability problem asks for the following: given a sentence of the form (1) and $\delta \in \mathbb{Q}^+$, correctly decide whether **unsat** (ϕ is false), or **δ-sat** (ϕ^δ is true). If the two cases overlap either decision can be returned: such a scenario reveals that the formula is *fragile* — a small perturbation (*i.e.*, a small δ) can change the formula's truth value.

A qualitative property of hybrid systems that can be checked is bounded δ-reachability. It asks whether the system reaches the unsafe region after $k \in \mathbb{N}$ discrete transitions.

Definition 4 Bounded k step δ-reachability in hybrid systems can be encoded as a bounded Σ_1-sentence

$$\exists \mathbf{x}_{0,q_0}^0, \exists \mathbf{x}_{0,q_0}^t, ..., \exists \mathbf{x}_{0,q_m}^0, \exists \mathbf{x}_{0,q_m}^t, ..., \exists \mathbf{x}_{k,q_m}^0, \exists \mathbf{x}_{k,q_m}^t :$$
$$(\bigvee_{q \in Q} (\text{init}_q(\mathbf{x}_{0,q}^0) \wedge \text{flow}_q(\mathbf{x}_{0,q}^0, \mathbf{x}_{0,q}^t)))$$
$$\wedge (\bigwedge_{i=0}^{k-1} (\bigvee_{q,q' \in Q} (\text{jump}_{q \to q'}(\mathbf{x}_{i,q}^t, \mathbf{x}_{i+1,q'}^0) \quad (3)$$
$$\wedge (\text{flow}_{q'}(\mathbf{x}_{i+1,q'}^0, \mathbf{x}_{i+1,q'}^t))) \wedge (\bigvee_{q \in Q} \text{unsafe}_q(\mathbf{x}_{k,q}^t))))$$

where $\mathbf{x}_{i,q}^0$ and $\mathbf{x}_{i,q}$ represent the continuous state in the mode q at the depth i, and q' is a successor mode.

Intuitively, the formula above can be understood as follows: the first conjunction is asking for a set of continuous variables which satisfy the initial condition in one of the modes and the flow in that mode; the second conjunction is looking for a set of vectors which satisfy any k discrete jumps and flows in each successor mode defined by the jumps; the third conjunction is verifying whether the state of the system (the mode and the set of continuous variables in the mode after k jumps) belongs to the unsafe region. Note that the previous definition asks for reachability in *exactly* k steps. One can build a disjunction of formula (3) for all values from 1 to k, thereby obtaining reachability *within* k steps.

The δ-reachability problem can be solved using the described δ-complete decision procedure, which will correctly return one of the following answers:
- **unsat**: the system never reaches the bad region U,
- **δ-sat**: the δ-perturbation of (3) is true, and a witness, *i.e.*, an assignment for all the variables, is returned.

We now show that this δ-decisions technique for hybrid models can be used to handle problems such as model falsification, parameter estimation, and parametric sensitivity analysis.

Model Falsification. The model falsification problem with existing experimental observations is basically a bounded reachability question: Expressing each experimental observation as a goal region, is there any number of steps k in which the model reaches the goal region? If none exists, the model is incorrect regarding the given observation. If, for each observation, a witness is returned, we can conclude that the model is correct with regard to a given set of experimental results. This is a bounded Model Checking problem, where all experimental observations can be expressed as reachability properties.

Parameter Estimation. The parameter estimation problem can also be encoded as a k-step reachability problem: Does it exist a parameter combination for which the model reaches the given goal region in k steps? Considering an assignment of a certain set of system parameters, if a witness is returned, this assignment is potentially a good estimation for those parameters. The goal here is to find an assignment with which all the given goal regions can be reached in bounded steps.

Parametric Sensitivity Analysis. The sensitivity analysis can be conducted by a set of bounded reachability queries as well. For different possible values of a certain system parameter, are the results of reachability analysis the same? If so, the model is insensitive to this parameter with regard to the given experi-mental observations.

4. FORMAL ANALYSIS RESULTS

4.1 Effect of delay in turning light ON

First, we have studied the relation between the time to turn ON the light after adding IPTG ($t_{lightON}$), and the total time needed until the bacteria cells being killed (t_{total}). We fixed the values of several other parameters as follows.
- SOX_{thres} = 5e-4m - threshold for the concentration level of SOX which is sufficient to kill the bacteria cells
- $t_{lightOFF_1}$ = 2 time units (t.u.) - time to turn the light OFF after turning it ON
- $t_{lightOFF_2}$ = 2 t.u. - time to turn the light OFF after removing IPTG
- t_1 = 1 t.u. - time to inject genome
- t_2 = 1 t.u. - time to insert genome into DNA after injecting it into bacteria cell
- $t_{addIPTG_3}$ = 1 t.u. - time to add IPTG after inserting phage genome into bacteria DNA

As shown in the first two rows of Table 2, the earlier we turn on the light after adding IPTG, the quicker the bacteria cells will be killed.

4.2 Lower bound for the duration of exposure to light

The δ-decisions technique has also been adopted to analyze the impact of the time duration that the cells are exposed to light ($t_{lightOFF_1}$) on the system, and estimate an appropriate range for $t_{lightOFF_1}$ which leads to the successful killing of bacteria cells by KillerRed. By setting SOX_{thres}, $t_{lightOFF_2}$, t_1, t_2, and $t_{addIPTG_3}$ with the same values in Section 4.1, and assigning 2 t.u. to $t_{lightON}$ (time to turn the light OFF after turning it ON), we have found that, in order to kill bacteria cells, the system has to keep the light ON for at least 4 time units (see row 3-4 of Table 2).In addition, we have also found that the bacteria cells can be killed within 100 time units when light is ON for 4 time units.

$t_{lightON}$ (t.u.)	1	2	3	4	5	6	7	8	9	10
t_{total} (t.u.)	16	17.2	18.5	20	21.3	22.7	23.5	24.1	25	30
$t_{lightOFF_1}$ (t.u.)	1	2	3	4	5	6	7	8	9	10
killed bacteria cells	failed	failed	failed	succ	succ	succ	succ	succ	succ	succ
t_{rmIPTG_3} (t.u.)	1	2	3	4	5	6	7	8	9	10
killed bacteria cells	succ	succ	succ	succ	succ	succ	succ	succ	succ	succ
SOX_{thres} (M)	1e-4	2e-4	3e-4	4e-4	5e-4	6e-4	7e-4	8e-4	9e-4	1e-3
t_{total} (t.u.)	5.1	5.2	5.4	17	19	48	61	71	36	42

Table 2: Formal analysis results for our KillerRed hybrid model

4.3 Time to remove IPTG as an insensitive role

The sensitivity of the time difference between removing the light and removing IPTG (t_{rmIPTG_3}) with regard to the successful killing of bacteria cells has also been studied. We have noticed that t_{rmIPTG_3} has insignificant impacts on the cell killing outcome (see row 5-6 of Table 2). This is in accordance with our understanding of this system, since any additional KillerRed that will be synthesized will not be activated in the absence of light. Note that, for other involved system parameters, we used the same values for SOX_{thres}, $t_{lightON}$, $t_{lightOFF_2}$, t_1, t_2, and $t_{addIPTG_3}$ as in Section 4.2, and set $t_{lightOFF_1}$ as 4 t.u..

4.4 Necessary level of superoxide

Finally, we have used the δ-decisions to discuss the correctness of our hybrid model by considering various values of SOX_{thres} within the suggested range - [100uM, 1mM]. We have used the same values for variables SOX_{thres}, $t_{lightON}$, $t_{lightOFF_1}$, $t_{lightOFF_2}$, t_1, t_2, and $t_{addIPTG_3}$ as in Section 4.3. As we can see from row 7-8 of Table 2, the bacteria cells can be killed in reasonable time for all 10 point values of SOX_{thres}, which was uniformly chosen from [100uM, 1mM]. Furthermore, we have also found a broader range for SOX_{thres} - (0M, 0.6667M], with which bacteria cells can be killed by KillerRed.

5. CONCLUSIONS

In this work, we have studied a novel method of killing bacteria using bacteriophage instead of antibiotics. A bacteriophage can be engineered to include code for proteins, which when inside bacteria can get activated and result in bacteria killing. Specifically, in this work we studied photosensitizing proteins, those that produce reactive oxygen species (ROS) when exposed to light. Excess amounts of ROS result in cell death. We created a hybrid model expressing both continuous and discrete dynamics. We defined this model within each of the stages that bacteria can go through, and used our tool (implemented the δ-decisions technique) for hybrid system reachability analysis to define parameters of the model that are otherwise hard or not possible to be found in experiments. We were especially interested in the timing effects, when the cells should be exposed to light, how long the light exposure should be, and how long it takes photosensitized proteins to kill bacteria cells after exposure to light.

Our analysis shows that the timing will be critical if this treatment, using bacteriophage and photosensitized proteins, is used for killing bacteria: the delay in exposure to light can significantly delay bacteria killing and could potentially lead to complications such as sepsis; and the duration of exposure to light is critical - turning light off too early may also

not result in killing. Interestingly, we found that a broader range of SOX could kill bacteria, although the time to reach this effect may again be too long for practical purposes. We noticed that very low levels of SOX are efficient in bacteria killing, while medium levels result in the longest time to killing, and we are further investigating these results, as they point to potential improvements in our model. Our next step is to validate the results that we obtained with wet lab experiments, and to use guidance from the experiments to improve accuracy of the model.

6. REFERENCES

[1] Antibiotic resistance threats in the united states. The Center for Disease Control, 2013.

[2] Carnegie mellon university, igem. http://2013.igem.org/Team:Carnegie_Mellon, 2013.

[3] B. Bowen and N. Woodbury. Single-molecule fluorescence lifetime and anisotropy measurements of the red fluorescent protein, dsred, in solution. *Photochemistry and photobiology*, 77(4):362–369, 2003.

[4] M. Falconi, P. O'Neill, M. E. Stroppolo, and A. Desideri. Superoxide dismutase kinetics. *Methods in enzymology*, 349:38–49, 2002.

[5] S. Gao, S. Kong, and E. M. Clarke. dReal: An SMT solver for nonlinear theories over the reals. In *CADE*, pages 208–214. Springer, 2013.

[6] S. Gao, S. Kong, and E. M. Clarke. Satisfiability modulo ODEs. In *FMCAD*, pages 105–112, Oct. 2013.

[7] H. Karadag and R. Bilgin. Purification of copper-zinc superoxide dismutase from human erythrocytes and partial characterization. *Biotechnology & Biotechnological Equipment*, 24(1):1653–1656, 2010.

[8] S. Pletnev, N. G. Gurskaya, N. V. Pletneva, K. A. Lukyanov, D. M. Chudakov, V. I. Martynov, et al. Structural basis for phototoxicity of the genetically encoded photosensitizer killerred. *Journal of Biological Chemistry*, 284(46):32028–32039, 2009.

[9] L. Song, E. Hennink, I. T. Young, and H. J. Tanke. Photobleaching kinetics of fluorescein in quantitative fluorescence microscopy. *Biophysical journal*, 68(6):2588, 1995.

[10] K. Takemoto, T. Matsuda, N. Sakai, D. Fu, M. Noda, S. Uchiyama, I. Kotera, Y. Arai, M. Horiuchi, K. Fukui, et al. Supernova, a monomeric photosensitizing fluorescent protein for chromophore-assisted light inactivation. *Scientific reports*, 3, 2013.

[11] R. Y. Tsien and A. Waggoner. Fluorophores for confocal microscopy: Photophysics and photochemistry. In *Handbook of biological confocal microscopy, 3rd edition*. Springer, 2006.

Design Automation for Biological Models: A Pipeline that Incorporates Spatial and Molecular Complexity

[Extended Abstract]

Devin P. Sullivan[*][†]
Computational Biology
Department
Carnegie Mellon University
Pittsburgh,PA 15213
devins@cmu.edu

Jose-Juan Tapia[†]
Department of Computational
and Systems Biology
University of Pittsburgh
Pittsburgh,PA 15260
jjtapia@pitt.edu

Rohan Arepally
Computational Biology
Department
Carnegie Mellon University
Pittsburgh,PA 15213
rarepall@andrew.cmu.edu

Robert F. Murphy
Computational Biology
Department
Carnegie Mellon University
Pittsburgh,PA 15213
murphy@cmu.edu

Markus Dittrich
Biomedical Applications Group
Pittsburgh Supercomputing
Center
Pittsburgh,PA 15213
dittrich@psc.edu

James R. Faeder
Department of Computational
and Systems Biology
University of Pittsburgh
Pittsburgh,PA 15260
faeder@pitt.edu

ABSTRACT

Understanding the dynamics of biochemical networks is a major goal of systems biology. Due to the heterogeneity of cells and the low copy numbers of key molecules, spatially resolved approaches are required to fully understand and model these systems. Until recently, most spatial modeling was performed using geometries obtained either through manual segmentation or manual fabrication both of which are time-consuming and tedious. Similarly, the system of reactions associated with the model had to be manually defined, a process that is both tedious and error-prone for large networks. As a result, spatially resolved simulations have typically only been performed in a limited number of geometries, which are often highly simplified, and with small reaction networks.

CCS Concepts

•**Applied computing** → **Systems biology**; *Imaging; Biological networks;*

---

[*]Current address: Science for Life Laboratory. KTH-Royal Institute of Technology. Stockholm, Sweden. devin.sullivan@scilifelab.se

[†]These authors contributed equally to this work.

Keywords

Spatial Modeling, Cellular Modeling, Rule-based modeling, Protein Subcellular Localization, High Throughput, Automation of Research

1. BACKGROUND

Reaction network complexity arises from the fact that a typical signaling protein may possess multiple interaction sites with activities and rates that may be modified by the state of neighboring sites [3]. This multivalency can result in a combinatorial explosion of the number of possible chemical species and reactions [6]. Rule-based modeling (RBM) provides an explicit mechanism to specify in a precise and compact way reaction networks involving multi-component and multivalent objects, such as proteins in a cell regulatory network [1, 3]. RBM also provides efficient methods for simulating such networks even when the combinatorial complexity is prohibitive for standard network simulation tools [12].

The spatial complexity of cells is also a major bottleneck for the development of realistic cellular models. Manual segmentation of images is often used to obtain realistic spatial geometries [10], but this imposes a significant limitation on the number of geometries available. Recently, statistical generative models have been developed that can address this limitation [2, 9, 11]. These methods use imaging data to learn statistical models of cellular organization that capture the underlying variances within cell populations.

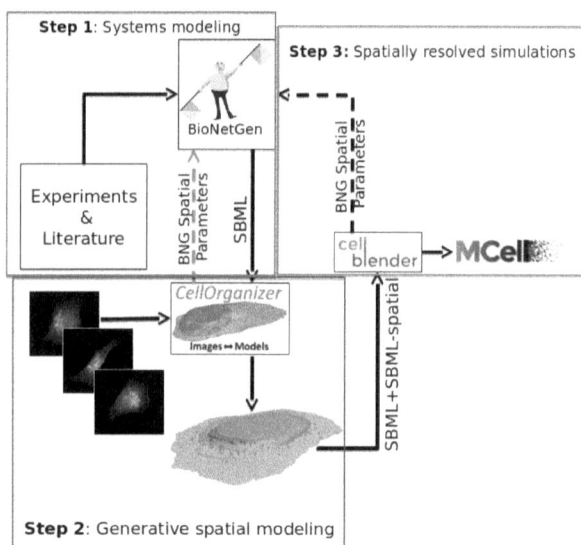

Figure 1: Modeling pipeline.

2. METHODS

We developed a high-throughput pipeline for combining synthetic cells that harnesses the power of both rule-based modeling and generative modeling to create high-throughput spatially resolved biochemical systems (in Fig. 1). This system allows the user to sample in a targeted manner from the distribution of possible cell shapes and organizations to probe the effects of spatial variation directly while controlling other variables. Combining these *in-silico* instances with complex biochemical models of cellular behavior we analyze what direct impact shape and spatial variance have on system behavior.

The pipeline begins with the definition of a rule-based model using literature or experimental data. In our implementation we used the BioNetGen software [4]. BioNetGen also possesses functionality to define compartmental models [5], such that the chemical space is divided into well-mixed sub-volumes that can communicate through transport reactions. In our modeling pipeline, these compartments are later mapped to specific organelle geometries. Once we have defined our model BioNetGen is instructed to export a reaction network definition which is then passed to our statistical generative modeling platform, the CellOrganizer software [9]. CellOrganizer recognizes the set of compartments that the model employs and maps them to existing geometries in its library of geometries previously created from imaging data. After finding an adequate geometry configuration, it exports a unified reaction-network/geometry definition which is then passed to MCell, a spatial modeling framework [8] through the CellBlender interface. Once imported the modeler can use the geometry analysis tools found in CellBlender to pass precise spatial parameters back to the BioNetGen model definition, or continue to simulate the system. All necessary simulation and optimization settings are managed by the pipeline scripts to minimize user involvement.

By leveraging generative models trained with CellOrganizer using fluorescent imaging data we are able to easily create a nearly unlimited number of realistic synthetic cells *in-silico* [9]. By combining these geometries with biochemi-

cal models we can perform high-throughput simulations in a spatially resolved manner at the sub-cellular level. Another important advantage to using generative models in CellOrganizer is that we can sample from specific areas in the set of all possible cells and subcellular organizations describable by our models and investigate specific shape and organization changes that may be associated with a diseased state of interest, or perform a general parameter sweep for a specific part of cellular organization [2].

Biochemical models were moved between the different pieces of software in the pipeline using the Systems Biology Markup Language (SBML) [7]. The SBML standard is widely used in systems biology, however it currently lacks the ability to describe spatial instances (geometries). We addressed this issue by contributing to the development of the new spatial extension to the SBML package (SBML-spatial). We also improved the SBML export capabilities for BioNetGen to include more detailed compartment information and implemented SBML and SBML-spatial import functionality in CellBlender.

3. PRELIMINARY RESULTS

To demonstrate the utility of the pipeline we used a prototype signal transduction model presented in [5] (Fig. 2a). This system contains several geometric compartments including plasma membrane, cytoplasm, nucleus, and endosomes encompassing a simplified but still rather large network of 354 reactions. A CellOrganizer model was trained using 2D microscopy images of HeLa cells and used to generate the specific instance shown in 2b. Figure 2c shows the effect of varying cytoplasmic volume, nuclear volume, and the number of endosomes on a specific model observable, the concentration of phosphorylated transcription factor dimers in the nucleus. There appear to be statistically significant differences in the time-course of this observable between cell morphologies. Future work will investigate these effects in greater detail.

This example and the overall pipeline was presented during a hands-on lab session at the MMBioS Workshop on Computational Methods for Spatially Realistic Microphysiological Simulations held in April, 2014. An online tutorial can be found at [13].

4. CONCLUSION

The modeling pipeline we have developed automates the process of creating simulation models of cellular processes that are realistic both spatially and biochemically. This system greatly reduces the required effort to systematically investigate the effect of spatial and reaction network complexity on cell signaling processes.

5. ACKNOWLEDGMENTS

We gratefully acknowledge funding from NIH grants GM103712, GM090033 and EB009403. We thank Rory Donovan, Tom Bartol and Bob Kuczewski for helpful discussions related to this work.

6. ADDITIONAL AUTHORS

Additional authors: Jacob Czech (Pittsburgh Supercomputing Center), email: jczech@pscuxa.psc.edu.

(a)

(b)

(c)

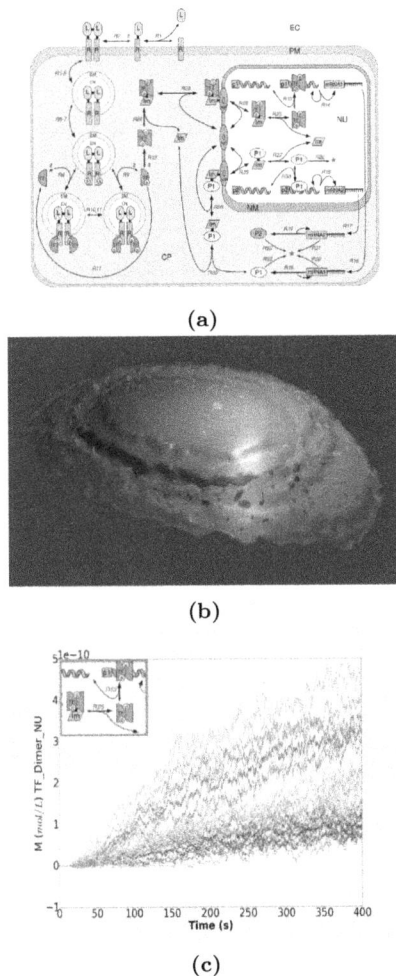

Figure 2: a: Reaction network diagram taken from [5] of the model signal transduction network used to demonstrate high throughput spatial modeling. b: Example geometry generated by CellOrganizer that was used for the MCell simulation. The nucleus is shown in blue, endosomes based on GFP tagged TfR are shown in green and the cytoplasm is shown in yellow. c: Impact of cell morphologies on the mean expression levels of dimerized nuclear transcription factor. Colors correspond to different geometries. Dashed lines indicate +/- 1 standard deviation around the mean molecule counts for 6 MCell simulations.

7. REFERENCES

[1] M. L. Blinov, J. R. Faeder, B. Goldstein, and W. S. Hlavacek. Bionetgen: software for rule-based modeling of signal transduction based on the interactions of molecular domains. *Bioinformatics*, 20(17):3289–3291, 2004.

[2] T. E. Buck, J. Li, G. K. Rohde, and R. F. Murphy. Toward the virtual cell: Automated approaches to building models of subcellular organization "learned" from microscopy images. *Bioessays*, 34(9):791–799, 2012.

[3] L. A. Chylek, L. A. Harris, C.-S. Tung, J. R. Faeder, C. F. Lopez, and W. S. Hlavacek. Rule-based modeling: a computational approach for studying biomolecular site dynamics in cell signaling systems. *Wiley Interdisciplinary Reviews: Systems Biology and Medicine*, 6(1):13–36, 2014.

[4] J. R. Faeder, M. L. Blinov, and W. S. Hlavacek. Rule-based modeling of biochemical systems with bionetgen. In *Systems Biology*, pages 113–167. Springer, 2009.

[5] L. A. Harris, J. S. Hogg, and J. R. Faeder. Compartmental rule-based modeling of biochemical systems. In *Winter Simulation Conference*, pages 908–919. Winter Simulation Conference, 2009.

[6] W. S. Hlavacek, J. R. Faeder, M. L. Blinov, A. S. Perelson, and B. Goldstein. The complexity of complexes in signal transduction. *Biotechnology and Bioengineering*, 84(7):783–794, 2003.

[7] M. Hucka, A. Finney, H. M. Sauro, H. Bolouri, J. C. Doyle, H. Kitano, A. P. Arkin, B. J. Bornstein, D. Bray, A. Cornish-Bowden, et al. The systems biology markup language (SBML): a medium for representation and exchange of biochemical network models. *Bioinformatics*, 19(4):524–531, 2003.

[8] R. A. Kerr, T. M. Bartol, B. Kaminsky, M. Dittrich, J.-C. J. Chang, S. B. Baden, T. J. Sejnowski, and J. R. Stiles. Fast monte carlo simulation methods for biological reaction-diffusion systems in solution and on surfaces. *SIAM Journal on Scientific Computing*, 30(6):3126–3149, 2008.

[9] R. F. Murphy. Cellorganizer: Image-derived models of subcellular organization and protein distribution. *Methods in Cell Biology*, 110:179, 2012.

[10] S. R. Neves, P. Tsokas, A. Sarkar, E. A. Grace, P. Rangamani, S. M. Taubenfeld, C. M. Alberini, J. C. Schaff, R. D. Blitzer, I. I. Moraru, et al. Cell shape and negative links in regulatory motifs together control spatial information flow in signaling networks. *Cell*, 133(4):666–680, 2008.

[11] G. K. Rohde, A. J. Ribeiro, K. N. Dahl, and R. F. Murphy. Deformation-based nuclear morphometry: Capturing nuclear shape variation in hela cells. *Cytometry Part A*, 73(4):341–350, 2008.

[12] M. W. Sneddon, J. R. Faeder, and T. Emonet. Efficient modeling, simulation and coarse-graining of biological complexity with nfsim. *Nature Methods*, 8(2):177–183, 2011.

[13] J.-J. Tapia and D. Sullivan. A spatially realistic model of cell regulatory processes. Website, 2014. `http://www.mcell.org/tutorials/cell_regulatory_processes.html`.

Mammalian Synthetic Gene Circuits

Jason J. Lohmueller
University of Pittsburgh
200 Lothrop St. 1017 EBST
Pittsburgh, PA 15213
+1 603-819-9492
jasonloh@pitt.edu

ABSTRACT

Synthetic gene networks enable the programming of living cells to perform novel behaviors. Mammalian synthetic gene networks have largely been used as research tools to probe cellular function and more recently to engineer therapeutic capabilities. To create these networks researchers have developed a vast array of DNA - encoded parts that can serve as sensors, computational regulators, and actuators. Many of these gene circuit components have varying temporal characteristics and sensitivities making them well - suited for engineering systems that can act on different time scales and at different molecular concentrations. These components have been combined to create increasingly complex gene circuits. Major challenges for engineering mammalian synthetic gene networks include further improving scalability and predictability. Recent technological advancements in site - directed genome engineering and programmable DNA binding domains will likely aid in addressing these issues. Other important future directions will include incorporating new regulators that act at the levels of chromatin remodeling and DNA methylation and the division of computational loads among different cell types with population - based computing.

Categories and Subject Descriptors

J.3 [**Computer applications**]: Life and Medical Sciences – *Biology and genetics.*

General Terms

Measurement, Performance, Design.

Keywords

Synthetic biology, gene circuit, cell therapy, chimeric antigen receptor.

1. SYNTHETIC GENE CIRCUITS

1.1 Circuit Architectures and Examples

Several types of synthetic gene circuits have been engineered in mammalian cells to date. These circuits include gene switches that control the induction of a gene in response to small molecule drugs [1], gene oscillators that express a gene in regulated pulses [2], genetic logic gates and classifiers that express a gene in response to combinations of input molecules [3,4], and memory circuits that can remember whether or not a cell has experienced a particular stimulus [5]. While early versions of these networks were proof - of - principle designs using ideal circuit components and inputs, many circuits have now been generated for medically - relevant applications. For instance a cell memory device has been created to remember whether a cell has undergone DNA damage or experienced a hypoxic environment, and a gene classifier circuit was created that could identify and kill cancer cells based on combinations of microRNAs expressed in cancer vs. healthy cells [5,4]. Finally, one type of gene circuit currently having success in the clinic is chimeric antigen receptor (CAR) T cell cancer therapy. For these systems engineered T cell receptors containing antibody fragments re - direct T cell killing to cancer cells displaying specific antigens on their surface. These systems have had unprecedented success in treating some previously untreatable leukemias [6,7]. In addition to directly saving lives the success of these therapies will likely move forward the use of synthetic gene networks as a whole and pave the way for treating other diseases.

1.2 Circuit Components

There are many gene regulatory components available for creating mammalian synthetic gene networks. These components have recently been reviewed in detail in Lienert et al. [8]. The most commonly used regulators to date have been transcription factor proteins that bind to a specific DNA sequence and lead to increase or decrease in RNA transcription. Recently programmable transcription factors such as zinc finger and TALE proteins have been designed that allow the user to define their DNA binding sequence. Using these factors allows for the creation of a common computational framework of similar molecules that will not interfere with one another [3]. RNA - based molecules comprise a second class of sensors and regulators. RNAs have the advantage of being easily selected to bind to specific targets, and in mammalian cells, RNA components are particularly well - suited to sensing microRNAs. However, in general for signal computation RNA - based systems can show lower fold changes compared to those constructed using transcription factors. As RNA only undergoes transcription and not translation, these systems generally act on faster time scales than transcription factor - based networks. Post - translational protein systems represent yet another class of circuit regulator. These are of interest because they operate on very rapid time scales, and much of a cell's natural signal transduction works in this manner such as with signaling from cell surface receptors and phosphorylation cascades. Other systems using protease cleavage as a signal transduction method have also been demonstrated [9].

2. CHALLENGES AND FUTURE DIRECTIONS

The major existing challenges in the field are improving gene circuit predictability and scalability. Recent advancements in site - directed genome engineering techniques using programmable DNA nucleases should help by improving the number of system variants that can be rapidly tested in the same context. Another underlying cause of issues with scale is that by creating a gene network consisting of highly - expressed molecules the cell's natural transcription and translation machinery are likely to be exhausted leading to a failure in system behavior. One approach to avoid this resource drain is to use regulators of different classes in single circuits [10]. In the future systems could also incorporate new regulators acting at the levels of chromatin remodeling and DNA methylation [11], important components of mammalian cell's natural gene regulatory circuits, as well as dividing computational activities among different cell types for cell population based computing.

3. ACKNOWLEDGMENTS

I would like to offer special thanks to Natasa Miskov-Zivanov for the opportunity to speak at the GLSVLSI 2015 conference.

4. REFERENCES

[1] Brown M., Figge J., Hansen U., Wright C., Jeang K.T., Khoury G., Livingston D.M., Roberts T.M. 1987. lac repressor can regulate expression from a hybrid SV40 early promoter containing a lac operator in animal cells. *Cell.* 49(5): 603-612.

[2] Tigges M., Marquez-Lago T.T., Stelling J., Fussenegger M. 2009. A tunable synthetic mammalian oscillator. *Nature.* 457(7227): 309-12.

[3] Lohmueller J. J., Armel T.Z., Silver P.A. (2012). A tunable zinc finger-based framework for Boolean logic computation in mammalian cells. *Nucleic Acids Res.* 40(11): 5180-5187.

[4] Xie Z., Wroblewska L., Prochazka L., Weiss R., Benenson Y. (2011). Multi-input RNAi-based logic circuit for identification of specific cancer cells. *Science.* 333(6047): 1307-1311.

[5] Burrill, D. R., M. C. Inniss, Boyle P.M., Silver P.A. (2012). Synthetic memory circuits for tracking human cell fate. *Genes & Dev.* 26(13): 1486-1497.

[6] Porter D.L., Levine B.L., Kalos M., Bagg A., June C.H. 2011. Chimeric antigen receptor-modified T cells in chronic lymphoid leukemia. *N. Engl. J. Med.* 365(8):725-33.

[7] Grupp S.A., Kalos M., Barrett D., Aplenc R., Porter D.L., Rheingold S.R., Teachey D.T., Chew A., Hauck B., Wright J.F., Milone M.C., Levine B.L., June C.H. Chimeric antigen receptor-modified T cells for acute lymphoid leukemia. *N. Engl. J. Med.* 368(16):1509-18.

[8] Lienert F., Lohmueller J.J., Garg A., Silver P.A. 2014 Synthetic biology in mammalian cells: next generation research tools and therapeutics. Nat. Rev. Mol. Cell Biol. 15(2):95-107.

[9] Daringer N.M., Dudek R.M., Schwarz K.A., Leonard J.N. Modular extracellular sensor architecture for engineering mammalian cell-based devices. ACS Synth. Biol. 3(12):892-902.

[10] Ausländer S., Ausländer D., Müller M., Wieland M., Fussenegger M. 2012. Programmable single-cell mammalian biocomputers. *Nature.* 487(7405):123-7.

[11] Maeder M.L., Angstman J.F., Richardson M.E., Linder S.J., Cascio V.M., Tsai S.Q., Ho Q.H., Sander J.D., Reyon D., Bernstein B.E., Costello J.F., Wilkinson M.F., Joung J.K. Targeted DNA demethylation and activation of endogenous genes using programmable TALE-TET1 fusion proteins. *Nat. Biotechnol.* 31(12):1137-42.

Automation of Biological Model Learning, Design and Analysis

Natasa Miskov-Zivanov
Electrical and Computer Engineering,
Carnegie Mellon University
5000 Forbes Avenue, Pittsburgh PA 15213
nmiskov@andrew.cmu.edu

ABSTRACT

Although there have been several recent attempts to automate steps of the process of model development and analysis in cell signaling networks, closing the overall cycle between information extraction, model assembly and analysis, and design of questions to guide new information search and experiments still requires a significant amount of human intervention. In this paper, we give an overview of challenges in this process, and outline our approaches to tackle these challenges.

Categories and Subject Descriptors

I. Computing Methodologies: I.6 SIMULATION AND MODELING: I.6.3 Applications.

General Terms

Algorithms, Measurement, Documentation, Design, Reliability, Experimentation, Standardization, Languages, Theory.

Keywords: Model design. Information extraction. Automation. Model analysis. Cell signaling. Pathways and networks.

1. INTRODUCTION

When building complex models, systems biologists usually start by searching for relevant models in existing databases, and published literature, and continue by checking how models differ, overlap and complement one another. The common next step is comparison of models with experimental observations or data to identify missing mechanisms and inconsistencies between models and data. Although there have been attempts to automate different parts of this process, most often modelers conduct these steps manually, with multiple iterations between model design, model analysis, and comparison with ever-increasing experimental data.

The reason that the developed automation techniques or databases are not very much utilized by modelers often lays in the fact that modelers are not aware of these resources since they are published in different areas, spreading from medicine, biology and chemistry to mathematics, physics, computer science and engineering. Moreover, it is not uncommon that, during model development, new experimental results are published, which seemingly contradict previously known results, and these inconsistencies, often very

subtle, call for human expert interpretation. Finally, model development of the same system is often repeated by different researchers, due to the fact that the results are not shared in a consistent fashion.

To allow for efficient handling of the complexity of the disease, and of the ever-increasing amount of information existing in published work, enabled by large-scale acquisition of data during experiments, it is critical to employ the computational power we have at hand, and even more, existing techniques in computer science and engineering, such as data mining, machine learning, or circuit design automation.

In order to automate this process, one needs to tackle challenges in all components of modeling shown in Figure 1: information extraction from different sources (*e.g.*, experimental data, literature, *etc.*), model assembly, model analysis, and explanation of results. Here, we describe several components of this automation flow that we recently implemented. First, an approach to selection of model types and level of details in models is described. Next, we describe (using cancer as an example) types of information that need to be taken into account as model context when drawing conclusions from models. Finally, we outline model design and analysis techniques that we have been developing.

2. MODEL TYPES

Biochemical pathways are interlinked and interdependent within the cell. However, they are often divided into signaling pathways, metabolic networks, gene regulatory networks, etc., and studied only within those groups. There exist a number of public databases that catalog biochemical pathways and allow access to their computational models, necessary for reasoning about pathways. Still, complex and paradoxical relationships that are more nuanced and context dependent can be lost in these databases. At the same

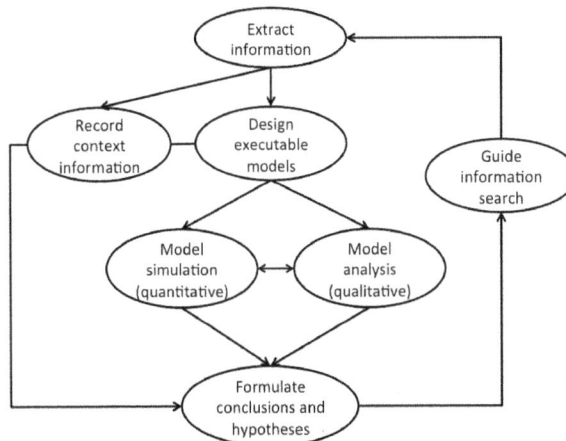

Figure 1. Components of the modeling flow.

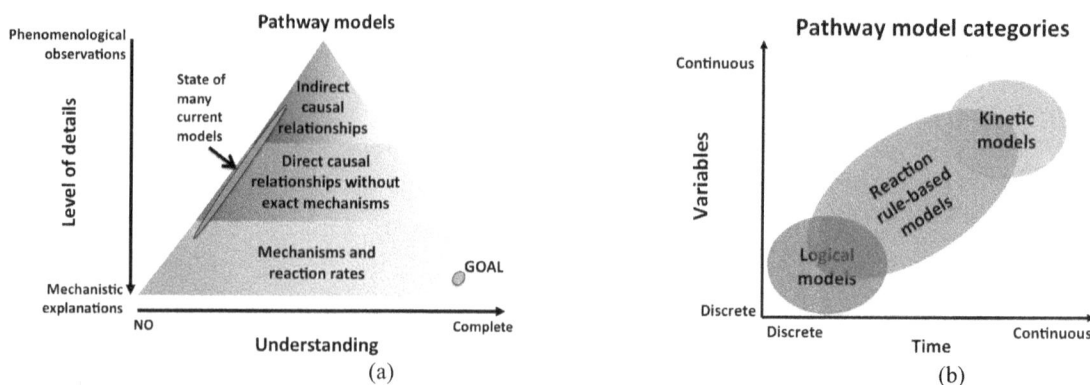

Figure 2. Granularity of (a) knowledge and (b) models of cell signaling pathways.

time, model building is usually done according to specific project goals, for specific cell types, or specific cell processes. In addition, modeling largely depends on the experimental data available and thus, pathway models have different levels of granularity for modeled elements and different degrees of precision for element update functions. To this end, different types of models exist, for example, kinetic models, reaction rule-based models, discrete logical models, multi-agent models.

Having a knowledge base (KB) that is organized in a hierarchical manner seems to be critical in modeling cell signaling, where the granularity of our current understanding of component relationships varies both across different cell signaling pathways and along a single pathway: some pathways or fragments of pathways are explored to the finest mechanistic details, while in many other cases only indirect causal relationships between elements or, even less, only element correlations are known. Still, even models derived on the basis of such knowledge have been shown to be invaluable for reasoning about cellular networks, given that pathways often contain many intertwined feedback loops, and thus reasoning only intuitively about them becomes impractical. Therefore, existing models of cell signaling pathways span from purely phenomenological to fully mechanistic in terms of biology they describe (Figure 2(a)), from discrete to continuous in terms of variable and time implementation (Figure 2(b)), or from deterministic to stochastic in terms of modeled event occurrences.

The goal of our work is to allow for the KB to expand in two directions, top→down and left→right, as shown in Figure 2(a). As in the design of computer systems, where different levels of abstraction, from system level through architecture and logic to transistor level, are all important in the design process, pathway modeling can follow similar approach. Pathway integration can be done hierarchically, and as we learn we can add new information at the appropriate level. In situations where mechanisms are not well understood, but observations about cause and effect are available, this information should be integrated into pathway models at the higher level of abstraction. Often, such information can be sufficient to guide new experiments, which in turn will explain additional mechanisms.

3. MODEL CONTEXT

Models need to be put in the right context in order to draw useful conclusions or create new hypotheses from them. In cancer, we identify many dimensions that are critical for our understanding of the disease and for treatment development. When designing models of cancer pathways, relationships between pathway components and

their roles can vary depending on the specifics of the disease being explored.

We approach *intracellular* events by taking into account relationships between the three commonly studied cell network types: metabolic, signal transduction and gene regulatory networks. The interconnections between these network types are often important in cell responses to stimuli or treatments, and need to be modeled accordingly. For example, signaling events can lead to activation of transcription factors that initiate gene transcription and expression of proteins, which are then involved in other signaling processes. However, these different networks can also comprise of mechanisms that occur at different time scales (*e.g.*, less than a second in signaling vs. hours in gene regulation). Moreover, proteins can belong to different types of networks and have different roles, depending on the environment. For example, moonlighting proteins regulate both metabolism and cell growth but play different roles in these two processes. In addition, research in recent years has shown that epigenetic modifications (e.g., DNA methylation or histone modifications) can play critical role in gene regulation.

At the level of *intercellular* communication, there is an increasing interest in cancer microenvironment and the response of immune system cells to cancer. It is also important to account for the fact that immune response differs at different stages of cancer progression, as different cell processes prevail during different phases. There is also growing evidence that understanding not only data, but even more importantly, metadata, is critical in defining treatments. Differences between individuals such as family history, drug history, or carcinogen exposure (*e.g.*, ultraviolet light exposure) can affect cancer pathways, and thus may lead to different responses to drug or treatment. Finally, cancer-related data sources include not only clinical data, but also experiments in cell lines or in mice, and thus, pathway description should take into account this context information as well.

Current ontologies, include some of the above information, but not all of it, while existing databases and model representation formalisms often do not include such information, since models are developed for very specific scenarios (*e.g.*, cancer type, cell type, stimuli type, subset of pathways, *etc.*) without any intent to later merge them with other models.

4. MODEL DESIGN AND ANALYSIS

Here, we briefly describe our previous and recent efforts towards model design and analysis. As outlined in Figure 1, these steps follow the information extraction step and provide inputs for the step where new hypotheses are formulated.

328

4.1 Model design

Previously, we automated several steps of model design, namely those steps that use the information extracted from literature or data, and result in executable model rules. The automation steps are described in [1].

4.2 Model analysis

In our modeling framework, we have thus far used simulation and formal methods in studying models, and both software and hardware approaches to speed up model analysis.

4.2.1 Model simulation methods

The approaches to simulating cell network models can be divided into two main groups: deterministic and stochastic. A deterministic approach usually provides information about steady-states, while stochastic simulation also gives insights into transient behavior. We have developed a tool that uses both simulation methods [1-2], as well as a combination of the two. The simulation algorithms we implemented allow for capturing different levels of detail that are available in literature or are extracted from data.

4.2.2 Perturbation and sensitivity analysis

Perturbation analysis usually includes scenarios such as (*i*) changes in causal relationships between elements (*e.g.*, re-wiring pathways, changing logic rule operations from "and" to "or"), (*ii*) turning elements permanently "on" or "off" to mimic constitutive presence, gene knock-outs or addition of inhibitors, or (*iii*) adding temporary "faults" to the model to mimic transient changes in environment. Previous work analyzed the difference between robustness to perturbations in state vs. function in synchronous, deterministic models, and only considered steady-state results [3]. Recently, we studied (semi-automatically) the effect of perturbations on both transient behavior and steady-state values in the biological models that we have developed [4], assuming stochastic simulation approach.

There also exist many methods to study sensitivity, often grouped into "local" and "global" sensitivity analysis. We created a tool to analyze two types of sensitivity of model outputs or internal variables to inputs or other model variables: using information dynamic sensitivity using information obtained from simulation trajectories, and static sensitivity derived from element update rules.

4.2.3 Model checking

In addition to the simulation-based methods, we have also applied formal methods, probabilistic and statistical model checking, in the analysis of models, which allowed for efficient and systematic testing of a large number of system properties in different scenarios, while assuming both types of simulations (deterministic and stochastic) [5].

4.2.4 Model emulation methods

We have also created an emulation tool that can directly compile discrete logical models on programmable logic devices (*e.g.*, Field Programmable Gate Arrays – FPGAs). Hardware emulation can provide significant speed-up of up to four or five orders of magnitude over software simulation tools [6-7]. The use of hardware allows for parallelization of model analysis in many ways. For example, one can compare alternative models to identify those

that best match experimental observations, or compare results from the same model but starting from different initial states. As the size of models increases, parallelization within a single model will be important as well, and therefore hardware emulation will provide means for further speed up.

5. CONCLUSION

The focus of our work is on automation of the overall modeling process, first for models of cell signaling networks, and next for cell-cell interaction models. We have already implemented several steps of the automation framework, including model design, different model simulation methods, and some steps of model analysis. Our next steps will focus on automation of the front and back ends of the framework, and the implementation of their seamless connections to already developed parts of the framework.

6. ACKNOWLEDGMENTS

This work is supported in part by DARPA award W911NF-14-1-0422. The author gratefully acknowledges the team of collaborators that work on different aspects of model learning, assembly and explanation: Peter Spirtes, William Cohen, Diana Marculescu, and Michael Lotze.

7. REFERENCES

[1] N. Miskov-Zivanov, D. Marculescu, and J. R. Faeder, "Dynamic behavior of cell signaling networks: model design and analysis automation." in *Proc. of Design Automation Conference (DAC)*, Article 8, 6 p., June 2013.

[2] N. Miskov-Zivanov, P. Wei, C.S.C. Loh, "THiMED: Time in Hierarchical Model Extraction and Design," in *Proc. of Computational Methods in Systems Biology (CMSB)*, pp. 260-263, November 2014.

[3] A. Garg, K. Mohanram, A. Di Cara, G. De Micheli, and I. Xenarios, "Modeling stochasticity and robustness in gene regulatory networks," *Bioinformatics*, vol. 25, pp. i101-i109, 2009.

[4] N. Miskov-Zivanov, M. S. Turner, L. P. Kane, P. A. Morel, and J. R. Faeder, "The duration of T cell stimulation is a critical determinant of cell fate and plasticity," in *Science Signaling*, 6, ra97, November 2013.

[5] N. Miskov-Zivanov, P. Zuliani, E. M. Clarke, and J. R. Faeder, "Studies of biological networks with statistical model checking: application to immune system cells," in *Proc. of ACM Conference on Bioinformatics, Computational Biology and Biomedicine (ACM-BCB)*, September 2013, pp. 728.

[6] N. Miskov-Zivanov, A. Bresticker, S. Venkatakrishnan, P. Kashinkunti, D. Krishnaswamy, D. Marculescu and J. R. Faeder, "Regulatory Network Analysis Acceleration with Reconfigurable Hardware," in *Proc. of International Conference of the IEEE Engineering in Medicine and Biology Society (EMBC)*, pp. 149-152, September 2011.

[7] N. Miskov-Zivanov, A. Bresticker, D. Krishnaswamy, S. Venkatakrishnan, D. Marculescu and J. R. Faeder, "Emulation of Biological Networks in Reconfigurable Hardware," in *Proc. of ACM Conference on Bioinformatics, Computational Biology and Biomedicine (ACM-BCB)*, pp. 536-540, August 2011.

On the Functions Realized by Stochastic Computing Circuits

Armin Alaghi and John P. Hayes
Advanced Computer Architecture Laboratory
Department of Electrical Engineering and Computer Science
University of Michigan, Ann Arbor, MI, 48109, USA
{alaghi, jhayes}@eecs.umich.edu

ABSTRACT

Stochastic computing (SC) employs conventional logic circuits to implement analog-style arithmetic functions acting on digital bit-streams. It exploits the advantages of analog computation —powerful basic operations, high operating speed, and error tolerance—in important applications such as sensory image processing and neuromorphic systems. At the same time, SC exhibits the analog drawbacks of low precision and complex underlying behavior. Although studied since the 1960s, many of SC's fundamental properties are not well known or well understood. This paper presents, in a uniform manner and notation, what is known about the relations between the logical and stochastic behavior of stochastic circuits. It also considers how correlation among input bit-streams and the presence of memory elements influences stochastic behavior. Some related research challenges posed by SC are also discussed.

Categories and Subject Descriptors

B.2.1 [**Arithmetic and Logic Structures**]: Design styles.

General Terms

Algorithms, design, theory.

Keywords

Stochastic computing, Boolean functions, logic design.

1. INTRODUCTION

Computing hardware has traditionally been partitioned into two broad classes: *analog* acting on continuous data and *digital* acting on discrete data, with real and integer arithmetic being the corresponding mathematical methods. In the digital case where the fundamental data units are the bits 0 and 1, Boolean algebra plays a key role. Analog computing was eclipsed by digital in the mid-twentieth century due to the latter's greater generality, higher precision, and ease of use [19]. Nevertheless, analog computing continues to be found in applications that can exploit its performance advantages (high speed, complex basic operations, and error insensitivity) while tolerating its disadvantages. Of interest here are *hybrid* systems that combine analog and digital features. These include biological systems, in which digital neural signals control analog functions like motion, and a class of artificial computing systems called stochastic [1][12], which are the topic of this paper. Stochastic computing (SC) is so called because it computes with analog probabilities, but represents them by digital bit-streams and processes them with conventional logic circuits.

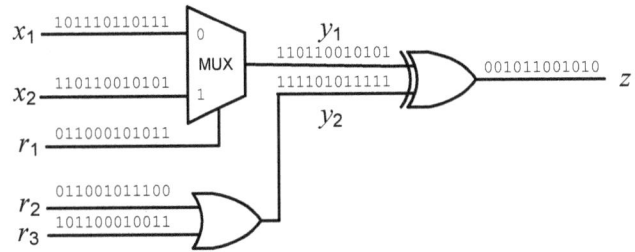

Figure 1. Stochastic circuit implementing the arithmetic function $Z = -0.25(X_1 + X_2)$ using bipolar format.

Figure 1 shows a typical stochastic circuit with bit-streams of length $N = 12$. It comprises an OR gate, an XOR gate, and a multiplexer (MUX). On one level, this is just a simple logic circuit realizing the Boolean function

$$z(x_1, x_2, r_1, r_2, r_3) = (x_1 \wedge \bar{r}_1 \vee x_2 \wedge r_1) \oplus (r_2 \vee r_3) \quad (1)$$

On another level, it is a relatively powerful stochastic circuit realizing the arithmetic function

$$Z(X_1, X_2) = -0.25(X_1 + X_2) \quad (2)$$

Here, X_1, X_2 and Z denote *stochastic numbers* (SNs) implemented by (pseudo) random bit-streams applied to lines x_1, x_2 and z, respectively.

An N-bit SN X containing N_1 1s and $N - N_1$ 0s has the (*unipolar*) *value* $p_X = N_1/N$. For example, the SN on output line z of Figure 1 has the value $p_Z = 5/12$. Since p_X always lies in the real-number interval $[0,1]$, it can be seen as the probability of observing 1 in any randomly selected position of X. The value p_X is also referred to as signal intensity, pulse rate, or frequency in different contexts. In neurobiology, for instance, a neural spike train can be modeled by a bit-stream X and its intensity can be represented by p_X [8].

The foregoing probabilistic interpretation along with the randomness of SNs are at the heart of SC, and effectively convert logic gates into analog-style arithmetic components operating on probabilities. For example, a MUX serves as a scaled adder computing the function $0.5(p_{X_1} + p_{X_2})$. With suitable off-line scaling and value approximation, stochastic circuits can be applied to numbers over various ranges. For example, to handle signed numbers, we map p_X to $2p_X - 1$, which changes the SN range from $[0,1]$ to $[-1,1]$. This is the *bipolar* format and is the interpretation needed for Figure 1 to implement Eq. (2). The output bit-stream Z of Figure 1 then represents $2(5/12) - 1 = -2/12$. Figure 1's XOR gate computes $-(2 p_{Y_1} - 1)(2 p_{Y_2} - 1)$ and so contributes both multiplication and negation to Eq. (2). This circuit implements a fairly complex arithmetic operation using just a handful of logic gates. A conventional implementation operating on ordinary binary numbers requires many more gates to implement Eq. (2). The hardware simplicity illustrated by Figure 1 is SC's chief attraction.

The three SNs R_1, R_2 and R_3 appearing on inputs r_1, r_2 and r_3, respectively, of Figure 1 are examples of *stochastic constants*. They are typically seen as auxiliary inputs and have the unipolar value 0.5. This value requires an SN with equal numbers of 0s and 1s, which is easily generated by (pseudo) random sources. It can be transformed

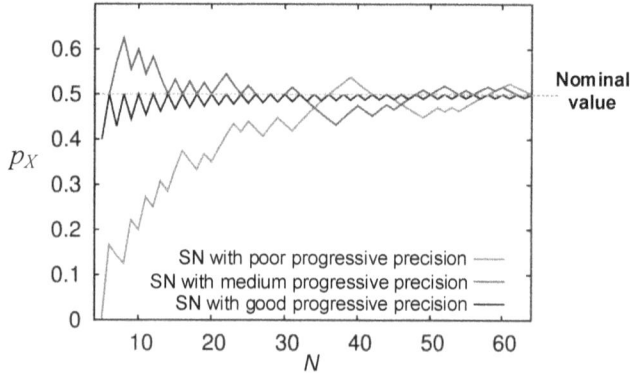

Figure 2. Fluctuations in p_X for 3 bit-streams as their length N increases.

to other constant values via suitable logic circuits [24]. For instance, the OR gate of Figure 1 generates the constant $p_{R_2} + p_{R_3} - p_{R_2}p_{R_3} = 0.75$ (unipolar) = 0.5 (bipolar), which combined with R_1, gives the 0.25 coefficient required by Eq. (2).

Two other key factors affecting stochastic circuit behavior are the length N and the randomness of the bit-streams. SN formats are highly redundant since $p_X = N_1/N$ is represented by $\binom{N}{N_1}$ different bit patterns. This skewed distribution implies low arithmetic precision. To represent p_X with a precision of n bits, requires X to have length $N \geq 2^n$. Consequently, stochastic circuits tend to have low precision and/or very large N. This can offset the speed advantage of SC's relatively simple arithmetic components. Moreover, such basic questions as— What should N be to guarantee that results are correct to k bits?—are surprisingly hard to answer. Figure 2 shows how p_X fluctuates as N increases for SNs of nominal value $p = 1/2$ generated by a typical stochastic number generator (SNG). SNs that rapidly converge to p are said to have (good) *progressive precision*.

Yet another basic problem in SC is that interacting bit-streams are usually required to be independent or *uncorrelated*, otherwise the results can be unacceptably inaccurate. For example, if two identical (maximally correlated) copies of a bipolar SN X are applied to an XOR gate, the result will be the all-0 bit-stream instead of the expected bipolar product $-X^2$. Ensuring that SNs are sufficiently long and uncorrelated can require an excessive number of SNGs and become the major cost factor in SC [25].

Compensating somewhat for these drawbacks is the fact that long SNs are inherently far less sensitive than ordinary binary numbers to errors caused by environmental noise or hardware faults. Not only do bit-flips occurring in SN X have a small effect on p_X, but two bit-flips in opposite directions cancel one another. Progressive precision can be exploited to speed-up applications where variable degrees of precision are acceptable [2]. Correlation may also be less of a problem than it seems at first sight. While the XOR multiplier is sensitive to correlation among its inputs, the MUX adder is insensitive to input correlations. Moreover, correlation can sometimes be deliberately used to increase the functional range of stochastic circuits and reduce their complexity [4], as will be discussed in Sec. 3. Figure 3 summarizes the advantages and disadvantages of stochastic computing.

Stochastic computing can be traced back to the pioneering ideas of Gaines and Poppelbaum in the 1960s [12][23]. Since then, it has found its major applications in control systems [29] and artificial neural networks [7][26]. More recently, new applications have appeared that involve probabilistic or error-tolerance issues for which SC is well suited, such as image processing [2][17], simulation of probabilistic systems [9][21], data recognition and mining [11], and decoders for channel codes ranging from LDPC to polar codes [13][28]. Furthermore, novel physical technologies are emerging such as memristors that have native stochastic features [16]. Despite these successes, many gaps exist in our understanding of SC and its potential applications.

Feature	Advantages	Disadvantages
Circuit size and power	Tiny arithmetic components	Many random number sources and stochastic-binary conversion circuits
Operating speed	Short clock periods Massive parallelism	Very long bit-streams
Result quality	High error tolerance Progressive precision	Low precision Random number fluctuations Correlation-induced inaccuracies
Design issues	Rich set of arithmetic components	Theory not fully understood Little CAD tool support at present

Figure 3. Advantages and disadvantages of stochastic computing.

The goal of this paper is review and unify recent results on the behavioral or functional properties of stochastic circuits. Section 2 defines stochastic behavior formally, and examines the links between a circuit's logical and stochastic properties, as exemplified by Eqs. (1) and (2). Correlation is examined in Sec. 3, while Sec. 4 addresses sequential design issues. Section 5 draws some conclusions and discusses challenges for future SC research.

2. STOCHASTIC FUNCTIONS

In this section, we discuss the links between combinational logic circuits and their stochastic functions (SFs). We show that that the SFs are functions over the real numbers, which can be expressed in many forms. Later, we will see how factors like correlation and the presence of memory elements can change the SFs.

Suppose some n-input single-output combinational circuit C realizes the Boolean function (BF) $z(x_1, x_2, ..., x_n)$. This function has the canonical sum-of-minterms form

$$z(x_1, x_2 ..., x_n) = \bigvee_{i=0}^{2^n-1} c_i \wedge m_i \qquad (3)$$

where the c_i's are 0-1 constants. The m_i's are *minterms* of the form $\tilde{x}_{i,1} \wedge \tilde{x}_{i,2} \wedge \cdots \wedge \tilde{x}_{i,n}$ where $\tilde{x}_{i,j}$ is either $x_{i,j}$ or $\bar{x}_{i,j}$. For example, the sum-of-minterms representation of the XOR function $z_{XOR}(x_1, x_2)$ is $m_2 \vee m_3 = (x_1 \wedge \bar{x}_2) \vee (\bar{x}_1 \wedge x_2)$.

Now suppose n SNs are applied to the inputs of C. If X_i is the (unipolar) probability value of the SN on x_i, i.e., $X_i = p_{X_i}$, then $\bar{x}_i$ has the probability value $1 - X_i$. The following theorem gives C's output probability Z, and so defines its stochastic function (SF).

Theorem 1: Let $z(x_1, x_2 ..., x_n)$ be a Boolean function defined by Eq. (3). The stochastic function $Z(X_1, X_2 ..., X_n)$ implemented by z, assuming all input SNs are independent, is

$$Z(X_1, X_2 ..., X_n) = \sum_{i=0}^{2^n-1} c_i M_i \qquad (4)$$

where $M_i = \widetilde{M}_{i,1}\widetilde{M}_{i,2} \cdots \widetilde{M}_{i,n}$ with $\widetilde{M}_{i,j} = p_{X_{i,j}} = X_{i,j}$ if the corresponding minterm m_i of Eq. (3) has $\tilde{x}_{i,j} = x_{i,j}$; $\widetilde{M}_{i,j}$ is $1 - p_{X_{i,j}} = 1 - X_{i,j}$ if $\tilde{x}_{i,j} = \bar{x}_{i,j}$.

This key result was first shown by Parker and McCluskey [22] using rather ad hoc notation. Note that each M_i corresponds to a minterm and is the probability of the corresponding input combination. These probabilities have the form stated in Thm. 1 when the input SNs are independent. As will be shown in Sec. 3, if the input SNs are correlated, the M_i's may take a different form. For the XOR gate with independent inputs, Thm. 1 implies

$$Z_{XOR}(X_1, X_2) = X_1(1 - X_2) + (1 - X_1)X_2$$

which, when multiplied out, becomes

$$Z_{XOR}(X_1, X_2) = X_1 + X_2 - 2X_1X_2 \qquad (5)$$

The sum-of-minterms-style probability expression (4) can be seen as a *canonical representation* of the stochastic function Z realized by the Boolean function z. It thus captures z's stochastic behavior with respect to the basic unipolar format. When the X_i's are restricted to 0 and 1, and sum is interpreted as OR, Eq. (4) reduces to Eq. (3), so Z is effectively an interpolation of z in the real-number domain. Equation (4) is also easily converted to other SN formats. To convert from

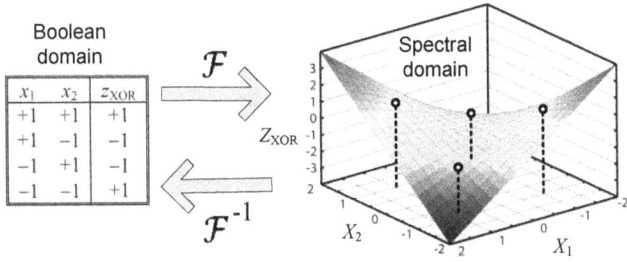

Figure 4. Spectral transformation of the XOR function.

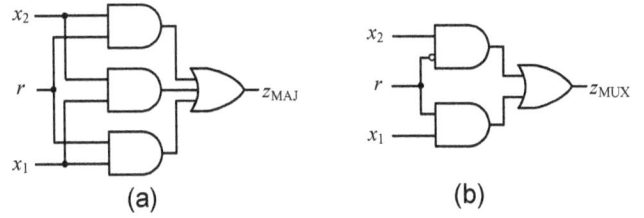

Figure 5. Two circuits implementing scaled addition when $R = 0.5$.

unipolar to bipolar, for instance, replace $p_{X_{i,j}}$ by $2p_{X_{i,j}} - 1$, and re-define the SN value $X_{i,j}$ to be $2p_{X_{i,j}} - 1$.

The canonical representation of Eq. (4) can also be expressed as the inner product of two vectors. The first is the truth-table vector $C_z = [c_0 \ c_1 \ \cdots \ c_{2^n-1}]$ defining z in terms of the constant coefficients in Eq. (3). The second is the input vector $M = [M_0 \ M_1 \ \cdots \ M_{2^n-1}]$ specifying the probability distribution of the input combinations, or equivalently, the stochastic minterm functions. We can now rewrite Eq. (4) as follows, where "·" denotes the inner-product operation:

$$Z(X_1, X_2 \ldots, X_n) = C_z \cdot M$$
$$= [c_0 \ c_1 \ \cdots \ c_{2^n-1}] \cdot [M_0 \ M_1 \ \cdots \ M_{2^n-1}] \quad (6)$$

The c_i elements in Eqs. (3), (4) and (6) are the same and belong to the binary set $\{0,1\}$. Since SFs deal with real numbers, we can further generalize Thm. 1 by allowing the c_i's to be any numbers in the real interval $[0,1]$. Such generalized c_i coefficients can be interpreted as constant SNs applied to the circuit when the corresponding minterm m_i is activated or set to 1. For example, if $c_0 = 0$, $c_1 = 0.5$, $c_2 = 0.5$, and $c_3 = 1$ (or in vector form $[0 \ 0.5 \ 0.5 \ 1]$), then Eq. (4) becomes

$$Z(X_1, X_2) = 0.5X_1(1 - X_2) + 0.5(1 - X_1)X_2 + X_1X_2 \quad (7)$$

which is the scaled add function $0.5(X_1 + X_2)$. The coefficients $c_1 = c_2 = 0.5$ in (7) imply that when minterms m_1 and m_2 are activated, a constant SN of value 0.5 should propagate to the output. Such constant probabilities can be obtained from (pseudo) random number sources. These sources often appear as auxiliary inputs in the corresponding circuit. For example, the r_i inputs of Figure 1 are auxiliary inputs that are fed with SNs of value 0.5.

Like BFs, SFs can be expressed and interpreted in different forms, which are associated with different, and sometimes useful, circuit design styles. When Eq. (4) is expanded in the manner illustrated by Eq, (5), Z takes the form of a *multi-linear polynomial*, i.e., one which can contain products of X_i variables, but no variable appears with a power of two or higher. If bipolar instead of unipolar format is used then, as we saw in the case of Figure 1, Eq. (5) changes to $Z_{XOR} = -X_1X_2$, a different multi-linear polynomial. Qian et al. observed that these expressions can be replaced by another interesting class of polynomials called Bernstein polynomials [25].

Alaghi and Hayes showed that the spectrum of a BF z obtained via the Fourier transform reveals z's stochastic behavior in useful ways [3]. First, to facilitate the use of spectral transforms, we map the usual 0 and 1 values of C_z into the real numbers $+1$ and -1, respectively; see Figure 4. Then we multiply C_z by an appropriate matrix, such as the Walsh-Hadamard matrix H_n. This produces a 2^n-dimensional vector (z's spectrum) which defines yet another polynomial form of Z. In the case of z_{XOR}, we get $Z_{XOR} = X_1X_2$.

Spectral transformation can be expressed symbolically as $Z = \mathcal{F}(z)$. An advantage of the spectral viewpoint is that the design problem of finding a z to implement a given SF Z reduces to computing the inverse spectral transform

$$z = \mathcal{F}^{-1}(Z) \quad (8)$$

A difficulty here is that there may be no BF z satisfying Eq. (8). This problem can be resolved by approximating Z by another function Z^* for which Eq. (8) has a solution in the Boolean domain. This entails expressing Z^* in a suitable (polynomial) form and introducing new

stochastic variables and constants, a complex process for which only heuristic methods are known [3][10][25]. For example, the function $Z = X^{0.45}$, commonly used in image processing, has no suitable polynomial form. However, it is approximated by $Z^* = -0.75X^2 + 1.5X + 0.25$ [3]. Applying the inverse spectral transform to Z^* yields

$$z(x_1, x_2, r_1, r_2) = x_1 \lor x_2 \lor r_1 \land r_2$$

which includes several new inputs. Variables x_1 and x_2 are supplied with two independent SNs representing X, while r_1 and r_2 are auxiliary inputs supplied with constant SNs of value 0.5.

Although every BF has a unique sum-of-minterms form (3), it turns out, surprisingly, that several different BFs can lead to the same SF [3][10]. This happens when generalized minterm coefficients, i.e., real-valued constant inputs, are allowed in stochastic functions. Consider, for instance, the majority function $z_{MAJ} = (x_1 \land x_2) \lor (x_1 \land r) \lor (x_2 \land r)$ and the multiplexer function $z_{MUX} = (x_1 \land r) \lor (x_2 \land \bar{r})$. They map to two different SFs $Z_{MAJ}(X_1, X_2, R)$ and $Z_{MUX}(X_1, X_2, R)$, as is easily shown using Eq. (4). However, if R is set to 0.5, both SFs become the same, i.e.

$$Z_{MAJ}(X_1, X_2, 0.5) = Z_{MUX}(X_1, X_2, 0.5) = 0.5(X_1 + X_2) \quad (9)$$

This, again, is the scaled addition operation of SC. Figure 5 shows two-level realizations of z_{MAJ} and z_{MUX}. Although each is optimal in the usual circuit-cost sense, the multiplexer has somewhat lower cost. However, in some emerging nanotechnologies, majority gates are the fundamental building block [15] so a majority-based scaled adder might be preferred.

The preceding discussion shows that SC adds an interesting new twist to logic optimization, namely: Find the "best" Boolean function z that implements a target SF Z (or an approximation thereto) in the form $z(X_V; X_C)$, where X_V denotes inputs to which variable SNs are applied, and X_C denotes auxiliary inputs to which constant SNs are applied. (For notational simplicity. X_V may refer either to Boolean variables or SNs.) With slight loss of generality, we assume all members of X_C are 0.5, i.e., 0s and 1s are applied with equal probability to constant inputs. This reflects the nature of the random sources normally used in SC.

With these assumptions, we can now define various types of stochastic equivalence among Boolean functions. For example, two BFs $z_1(X_V; X_C)$ and $z_2(X_V; X_C)$ are *stochastically equivalent*, denoted $z_1 \equiv z_1$, if $Z_1(X_V; X_C) = Z_2(X_V; X_C)$ [10]. Equation (9) shows that $z_{MAJ} \equiv z_{MUX}$. For any given size parameters $|X_V| = s$ and $|X_C| = t$, the $\equiv$ relation partitions the set of SFs $Z(X_V; X_C)$ into stochastic equivalence classes (SECs). With $s = 2$ and $t = 1$, the $2^{2^3} = 256$ distinct BFs form 81 SECs, including a 4-member class E containing z_{MAJ} and z_{MUX}. (The other two members of E result from replacing r by $\bar{r}$, whose value is also 0.5.) Each SEC represents a potentially useful arithmetic component or circuit for designing stochastic circuits. Note that although X_C is usually seen as a set of secondary inputs, they form an intrinsic part of an SF and consume significant circuit resources. This is clear from Figure 1 where the two-input SF of Eq. (2) requires a five-input logic circuit in which X_C with $t = 3$ has a non-trivial role comparable in complexity to that of X_V.

The foregoing SEC concept can also play a useful role in optimizing stochastic circuits [10]. For small s and t, an SEC representing some SF $Z(X_V; X_C)$ can be searched systematically either to find an optimal BF $z(X_V; X_C)$ implementing Z, or else to

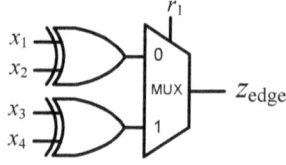

Figure 6. Stochastic edge detector [2].

evaluate the optimality of a known z. To illustrate, consider the stochastic function

$$Z_{\text{edge}} = 0.5 \times (|X_1 - X_2| + |X_3 - X_4|) \qquad (10)$$

which defines the Roberts Cross function for edge detection in black-and-white images. It employs a four-pixel window which outputs four Boolean variables x_1, x_2, x_3, x_4 on which random bit-streams appear that measure light intensity. Figure 6 shows a stochastic logic circuit implementing Eq. (10) which was derived by ad hoc means [2]. (Its input SNs must meet certain correlation requirements, which we consider in Sec. 3, but they do not affect SEC membership.) This circuit's area cost is about 100x less than that of a non-stochastic implementation of Eq. (10), and was thought to be optimal. Its BF is

$$z_{\text{edge}} = \bar{x}_1 \wedge x_2 \wedge \bar{r}_1 \vee x_1 \wedge \bar{x}_2 \wedge \bar{r}_1 \vee \bar{x}_3 \wedge x_4 \wedge r_1 \vee x_3 \wedge \bar{x}_4 \wedge r_1 \qquad (11)$$

whose inputs x_1, x_2, x_3 and x_4 define X_V, while r_1 defines X_C. The SEC for z_{edge} contains 256 functions. The implementation cost of these functions was computed in terms of literal count [14] for an optimal two-level design using a conventional CAD tool, and found to range from 16 to 45. Since z_{edge}'s literal cost is 16, as can be seen from Eq. (11), the optimality of the edge-detector design in Figure 6 is confirmed.

3. IMPACT OF CORRELATION

In stochastic computations, it is often necessary to convert inputs from a number style such as analog or weighted-binary to stochastic form. This requires *stochastic number generators* (SNGs) which tend to cost far more than other SC components. The large numbers of them found in traditional designs—Figure 1 needs up to five SNGs for its five inputs—render many such designs impractical.

As shown in Figure 7, a typical SNG comprises a comparator and a random number source (RNS). In each clock cycle, a new random number is compared with the input number X^* and a bit of the corresponding SN X appears at the output. Over the years, many variants of this design have been proposed. Most implement the RNS by a deterministic sequential circuit such as a linear feedback shift register (LFSR) that produces pseudo-random outputs. Alternative SNG designs can be found in [1][5]. It is also possible to combine non-random and pseudo-random bit-streams, but the results have been unpromising. "True" random sources, made possible by nanotechnologies like memristors [16] and magnetic-tunnel junction devices [20] have also been proposed recently for SC.

As noted earlier, the inputs of a stochastic circuit must usually be independent or uncorrelated in order to achieve the desired functionality. Correlation is caused by insufficient randomness among SNs and is a key source of inaccuracy. Reducing correlation requires many costly SNGs with independent RNSs. Alaghi and Hayes [4][6] however, show that some circuits are inherently *correlation insensitive* (CI), meaning that correlation among their input SNs does not alter their stochastic function. A formal definition of CI is given in [6], where it is shown that exploiting correlation insensitivity can reduce stochastic circuit area substantially.

Correlation insensitivity is most readily seen in the scaled adder realized by the multiplexer of Figure 5b. The output z_{MUX} is x_1 if $r = 1$ and x_2 if $r = 0$. Hence, the inputs x_1 and x_2 never affect z_{MUX} simultaneously, so any correlation between the SNs X_1 and X_2 is masked by the circuit. Knowledge of this kind can be used to reduce the SNG costs. For instance, it implies that a scaled adder's inputs x_1 and x_2 can share an RNS, as shown in Figure 8.

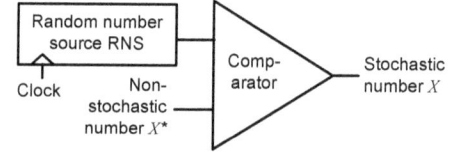

Figure 7. Generic stochastic number generator (SNG).

The stochastic function of a circuit with correlated inputs can be expressed using modified versions of Eqs. (4) or (6). The M_i's of these equations are the probabilities of the circuit's various input combinations. For example, when $n = 2$, $\boldsymbol{M} = [M_0 \quad M_1 \quad M_2 \quad M_3]$ denotes the probability of $x_1 x_2$ being 00, 01, 10, and 11, respectively. Suppose X_1 and X_2 are constant SNs with values 0.3 and 0.2, respectively. By Thm. 1, $\boldsymbol{M}$ is $\boldsymbol{M}_1 = [0.56 \quad 0.14 \quad 0.24 \quad 0.06]$ when X_1 and X_2 are independent. But if X_1 and X_2 are correlated, the M_i's generally take different values. Suppose that, in the current example, whenever X_2 applies 1 to x_2, X_1 always applies a 1 is to x_1, implying that X_1 and X_2 have a high degree of correlation. Then $\boldsymbol{M}_1$ changes to $\boldsymbol{M}_2 = [0.7 \quad 0 \quad 0.1 \quad 0.2]$.

Earlier we observed that a MUX-based scaled adder is CI with respect to X_1 and X_2 using the intuitive argument that the output function z_{MUX} does not depend on both inputs and at the same time. This argument does not apply to a MAJ-based scaled adder. To determine whether it too is CI, consider the majority circuit of Figure 5a. On assigning a constant SN of value 0.5 to its r input (assuming it is independent of the other input SNs), its truth-table vector becomes $\boldsymbol{C}_{\text{MAJ}} = [0 \quad 0.5 \quad 0.5 \quad 1]$, which implements stochastic scaled addition if the inputs are independent. Now assume a generic input vector $\boldsymbol{M} = [M_0 \quad M_1 \quad M_2 \quad M_3]$ with no specific assumptions about correlation between X_1 and X_2. From Eq. (6), we can write

$$\begin{aligned} Z_{\text{MAJ}}(X_1, X_2) &= [M_0 \quad M_1 \quad M_2 \quad M_3] \cdot [0 \quad 0.5 \quad 0.5 \quad 1] \\ &= 0.5M_1 + 0.5M_2 + M_3 \\ &= 0.5(M_1 + M_3) + 0.5(M_2 + M_3) \end{aligned}$$

Noting that $M_1 + M_3 = X_1$ and $M_2 + M_3 = X_2$ for any possible level of correlation between X_1 and X_2, we get $Z_{\text{MAJ}}(X_1, X_2) = 0.5(X_1 + X_2)$. This implies that the majority gate is CI with respect to X_1 and X_2 when the SN constant 0.5 is assigned to r.

Systematic correlation among input SNs of a circuit is not necessarily a source of inaccuracy. In fact, it can change a circuit's underlying stochastic function to a more desirable one [4]. For example, consider the upper XOR gate of Figure 6. As shown by Eq. (5), it has the stochastic function $Z_{\text{XOR}}(X_1, X_2) = X_1 + X_2 - 2X_1 X_2$ when its inputs are independent SNs. However, with maximally correlated input SNs, the XOR gate implements the stochastic function $Z_{XOR}(X_1, X_2) = |X_1 - X_2|$, which turns out to be a key part of the Z_{edge} function implemented by the circuit of Figure 6.

To quantify systematic correlation among SNs, a measure called SCC (*stochastic computing correlation*) is proposed in [4]. Zero *SCC* between two SNs implies their independence. If $SCC = +1$, then the SNs have maximum overlap of 1s and 0s; if SCC = -1, then the SNs have a minimum overlap of 1s and 0s. It is important to note that these conditions hold for SNs of arbitrary value. For example, if $X_1 = 11110000$ and $X_2 = 1100000$, then $SCC(X_1, X_2) = +1$, while if $X_1 = 11110000$ and $X_2 = 0000011$, we get $SCC(X_1, X_2) = -1$. In contrast, the standard Pearson correlation measure imposes constraints on the

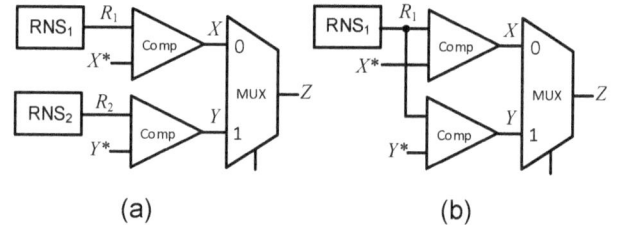

Figure 8. Stochastic number generation for a scaled adder with (a) two independent RNSs, and (b) one shared RNS.

SN values. For instance, a correlation of +1 implies that the SNs are identical, and hence must have the same value. Thus SCC is a more suitable correlation measure for SC. More importantly, we can incorporate SCC into Thm. 1 and extend it as follows.

Theorem 2: The correlation-dependent stochastic function $Z(X_1, X_2)$ implemented by the Boolean function $z(x_1, x_2)$ defined by Eq. (3) with $n = 2$ is

$$Z(X_1, X_2) = \sum_{i=0}^{3} c_i M_i'$$

where representative M_i''s are given by Figure 9.

	$SCC(X_1, X_2) = 0$	$SCC(X_1, X_2) = -1$	$SCC(X_1, X_2) = +1$
M_0'	$(1 - X_1)(1 - X_2)$	$\max(1 - X_1 - X_2, 0)$	$\min(1 - X_1, 1 - X_2)$
M_1'	$(1 - X_1)X_2$	$\min(1 - X_1, X_2)$	$\max(X_2 - X_1, 0)$
M_2'	$(1 - X_2)X_1$	$\min(1 - X_2, X_1)$	$\max(X_1 - X_2, 0)$
M_3'	$X_1 X_2$	$\max(X_1 + X_2 - 1, 0)$	$\min(X_1, X_2)$

Figure 9. Correlation-dependent probabilities for Thm. 2.

To illustrate this theorem, consider the upper XOR gate of Figure 6 which has the two minterms m_1 and m_2. When supplied by SNs with $SCC = +1$, it implements the stochastic function

$$Z_{XOR} = \max(X_2 - X_1, 0) + \max(X_1 - X_2, 0) = |X_1 - X_2|$$

In contrast, the SF implemented by the multiplexer of Figure 5b remains the same for all possible SCC values among its inputs.

4. SEQUENTIAL STOCHASTIC CIRCUITS

Stochastic circuits are highly sequential in that their behavior is determined by long sequences of binary data involving synchronous sequential components like SNGs and I/O registers. So far in this paper (and throughout the SC literature) it has been assumed that the data-processing functions are fully defined by combinational circuits. Introducing memory into these circuits changes the picture.

Consider the circuit of Figure 10a which combines an AND gate with a D-flip-flop. The AND acts as a stochastic multiplier implementing the function $Z = X(1 - Y)$. The D-flip-flop simply shifts its input bit-stream by 1 bit, and implements the stochastic function $Y = Z$. Eliminating Y from the preceding equations, gives $Z = X/(1 + X)$, which is the SF implemented by the circuit of Figure 10a. This function does not have an appropriate polynomial form, and so cannot be directly implemented by combinational stochastic circuits. A similar example is the JK-flip-flop shown in Figure 10b, which has the SF $Z = X_1/(X_1 + X_2)$, and is used to approximate stochastic division.

Figure 11 shows the general structure of an n-input sequential circuit with k flip-flops. The combinational block generates the output z and the next state variables $y_1^+, \ldots, y_k^+$ based on the inputs and the current state variables $y_1, \ldots, y_k$. The memory block merely copies the y_i^+'s values to y_i at the active clock edge. The stochastic functions implemented by a sequential circuit C are defined by the stationary distribution Y of its states and the primary output Z, which can be derived by solving the Markov chain equations for C [12].

As an example, let $n = k = 1$ in the circuit of Figure 11, and assume that the Boolean functions $y^+(x, y)$ and $z(x, y)$ realized by the combinational block, have the following truth-table vectors.

$$\boldsymbol{C}_{y^+} = \begin{bmatrix} c_0^y & c_1^y & c_2^y & c_3^y \end{bmatrix} \text{ and } \boldsymbol{C}_z = \begin{bmatrix} c_0^z & c_1^z & c_2^z & c_3^z \end{bmatrix}$$

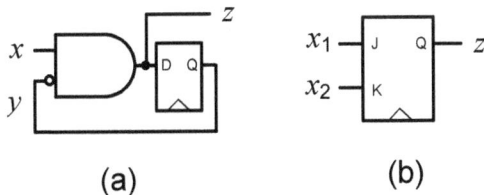

Figure 11. An n-input sequential circuit with k flip-flops.

Then the stationary state distribution at Y is obtained by assigning $Y^+ = Y$ in the following equation

$$Y^+(X, Y) = \boldsymbol{C}_{y^+} \cdot [(1 - X)(1 - Y) \quad (1 - X)Y \quad X(1 - Y) \quad XY]$$

Solving this equation gives Y's SF.

$$Y(X) = \frac{c_0^y + X(c_2^y - c_0^y)}{1 + c_0^y - c_1^y - X(c_0^y - c_1^y - c_2^y + c_3^y)}$$

The SF at Z can be derived similarly.

By assigning different values to the M_i^y's and M_j^z's, one can obtain all the possible stochastic sequential circuits with one input and one flip-flop. Interestingly, many of these circuits implement similar stochastic functions, showing that there are many equivalence classes of sequential stochastic circuits analogous to the combinational SECs mentioned in Sec. 2. For instance, the two circuits shown in Figure 12 implement exactly the same SF $Z(X) = (2X - 2)/(X - 2)$, so they are stochastically equivalent. Within the 256 single-input single-flip-flop sequential circuits, there are only 55 distinguished equivalent classes of SFs.

These small examples show that sequential circuits implement a larger class of SFs than combinational circuits, namely, rational functions of the form

$$Z(X_1, \ldots, X_n) = \frac{P(X_1, \ldots, X_n)}{Q(X_1, \ldots, X_n)}$$

in which P and Q are polynomials.

As noted, the stochastic function of sequential circuits can be obtained by solving the corresponding equations for Y and Z, but this can be very difficult when many state variables are involved. To sidestep this problem, Gaines proposed restricting attention to finite-state machines (FSMs) with a chain structure in which the states are ordered and transitions only occur between adjacent states; jumping over states is not allowed [12]. This restriction allows easy Markov chain analysis. Figure 13 shows the state behavior of one such chain-structured FSM, the ADDIE (*ADaptive Digital Element*). Gaines also argued that state transitions should be local to avoid excessive fluctuations in SF values. ADDIEs have been used in various analog-style stochastic circuits such as filters [12]. Similar chain structured sequential circuits can implement non-polynomial functions such as *tanh* and *exp* efficiently [7][18].

Variations and extensions of Gaines's ADDIE model have been proposed over the years. A 2-dimensional extension of the chain-structured FSM was proposed by Li et al. [18]. A more general form of ADDIE was used by Saraf et al. [27] to implement SFs such as trigonometric functions. Evidently, sequential implementations can be more efficient than combinational for certain classes of SFs.

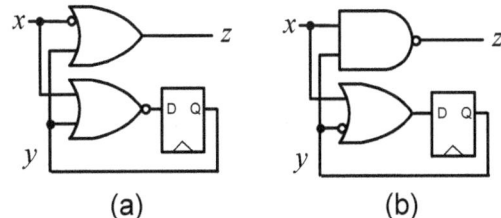

(a)

(b)

Figure 10. Sequential stochastic circuits implementing (a) $Z = X/(1 + X)$ and (b) $Z = X_1/(X_1 + X_2)$.

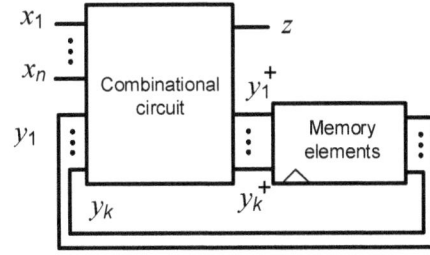

(a)

(b)

Figure 12. Two sequential circuits implementing $Z(X) = (2X - 2)/(X - 2)$.

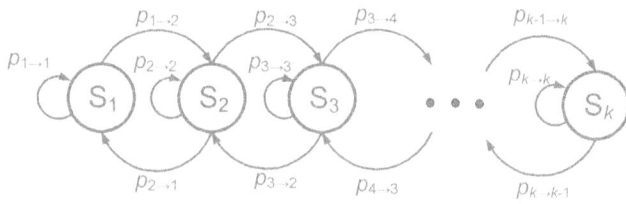

Figure 13. State diagram of a generalized ADDIE [12].

However, many optimal combinational stochastic circuits exist. For example, the sequential edge-detection circuit in [17] is more than 20 times larger than the combinational edge detector of Figure 6.

A drawback of sequential circuits is that they require a transition (warm-up) period before settling to the desired stationary distribution. During this period, which can be quite long, the circuit may produce inaccurate results. Another disadvantage of sequential circuits is that their behavior is affected by *auto-correlation* among the SNs. This refers to the correlation between a SN and its shifted or delayed versions. Auto-correlation imposes new requirements for the SNGs used for sequential circuits. Combinational circuits, being memory-less, are not affected by auto-correlation.

Finally, we note that unlike combinational circuits, a general design methodology for sequential stochastic circuits is not known. Most existing methods are limited to chain-structured designs.

5. DISCUSSION

Stochastic computing is a fascinating blend of analog and digital concepts. By associating data values with signal probabilities, SC enables analog computation to be performed using digital bit-streams and circuits. This hybrid approach tends to merge the advantages and disadvantages of analog and digital. Unsurprisingly, SC is best suited to applications that benefit most from the advantages (powerful low-cost primitives and error tolerance) and are least affected by the disadvantages (low precision, scaling issues, and complex behavior).

We have examined the dual nature of SC from a functional perspective, starting from the fact that a stochastic circuit implements both a Boolean function z and a stochastic function Z. Theorem 1 states the basic connection between z and Z. This connection can be expressed in many different, but equivalent, ways (multi-linear polynomials, spectral transforms, etc.), some of which have interesting and potentially useful design implications. By introducing auxiliary variables and constants, and accounting for phenomena like correlation and sequential behavior, the range of stochastic functions and their implementations can be greatly expanded.

Many questions, old and new, about SC remain unanswered. We have only begun to investigate the full range of stochastic functions that are realizable, even by relatively small logic circuits. Sequential stochastic circuits still present many challenges. Most of what we know about correlation, precision, scalability and the like derives from studies of circuits involving just a few gates and flip-flops. It seems likely that many of the problems of building large stochastic systems have not yet been fully recognized, let alone solved.

ACKNOWLEDGEMENT

This work was supported by Grant CCF-1318091 from the National Science Foundation.

REFERENCES

[1] Alaghi, A. and Hayes, J.P. 2013. Survey of stochastic computing. *ACM Trans. Embed.Comp. Syst.*12, 92:1-92:12.

[2] Alaghi, A. et al. 2013. Stochastic circuits for real-time image-processing applications. In *Proc. DAC,* 136:1-136-6.

[3] Alaghi, A. and Hayes, J.P. 2012. A spectral transform approach to stochastic circuits. In *Proc. ICCD,* 315-312.

[4] Alaghi, A. and Hayes, J.P. 2013. Exploiting correlation in stochastic circuit design. In *Proc. ICCD*, 39-46.

[5] Alaghi, A. and Hayes, J.P. 2014. Fast and accurate computation using stochastic circuits. In *Proc. DATE.* 1-4.

[6] Alaghi, A. and Hayes, J.P. 2015. Dimension reduction in statistical simulation of digital circuits. In *Proc. Symp. Theory of Modeling and Simulation* (TMS). To appear.

[7] Brown, B.D. and Card, H.C. 2001. Stochastic neural computation I: computational elements. *IEEE Trans. Computers.* 50, 891-905.

[8] Brown, E.N. 2004. Multiple neural spike train data analysis: state-of-the-art and future challenges. *Nature Neuroscience.*7, 456-461.

[9] Chen, H. and Han, J. 2010. Stochastic computational models for accurate reliability evaluation of logic circuits. In *Proc. GLSVLSI*, 61-66.

[10] Chen, T.H. and Hayes, J.P. 2015. Equivalence among stochastic logic circuits and its application. In *Proc DAC.* To appear.

[11] Chippa V.K. et al. 2014. StoRM: a stochastic recognition and mining processor. In *Proc. ISLPED*, 39-44.

[12] Gaines, B.R. 1969. Stochastic computing systems. In *Advances in Information Systems Science*, Springer. 2, 37-172.

[13] Gross, W.J. et al. 2005. Stochastic implementation of LDPC decoders. In *Proc. Asilomar Conf.* 713-717.

[14] Hachtel, G.D. and Somenzi, F. 1996. *Logic Synthesis and Verification Algorithms.* Kluwer.

[15] Zhang, R. et al. 2007. Majority and minority network synthesis with application to QCA-, SET-, and TPL-based nanotechnologies. *IEEE Trans. CAD.* 26, 1233-1245.

[16] Knag, P. et al. 2014. A native stochastic computing architecture enabled by memristors. *IEEE Trans. Nanotech.* 13, 283-293.

[17] Li, P. et al. 2013. Computation on stochastic bit streams: digital image processing case studies. *IEEE Trans. VLSI.* 22, 449-462.

[18] Li, P. et al. 2014. Logical computation on stochastic bit streams with linear finite-state machines. *IEEE Trans. Computers.* 63, 1473-1485.

[19] MacLennan, B.J. 2009. Analog computation. In *Encyclopedia of Complexity and System Science*, Springer, 271-294.

[20] Onizawa, N. et al. 2014. Analog-to-stochastic converter using magnetic-tunnel junction devices. In *Proc. NANOARCH*, 59-64.

[21] Paler, A. et al. 2013. Approximate simulation of circuits with probabilistic behavior. In *Proc. DFT Symp.* 95-100.

[22] Parker, K.P. and McCluskey, E.J. 1975. Probabilistic treatment of general combinational networks. *IEEE Trans. Computers.* C-24, 668-670.

[23] Poppelbaum, W.J. 1976. Statistical processors. In *Advances in Computers*, Academic Press, 187-230, 1976.

[24] Qian, W. et al. 2011. Transforming probabilities with combinational logic. *IEEE Trans. CAD.* 30, 1279-1292.

[25] Qian, W. et al. 2011. An architecture for fault-tolerant computation with stochastic logic. *IEEE Trans. Computers.* 60, 93-105.

[26] Rossello, J.L. et al. 2010. Hardware implementation of stochastic-based neural networks. In *Proc. IJCNN.* 1-4.

[27] Saraf, N. et al. 2013. Stochastic functions using sequential logic. In *Proc. ICCD*, 507-510.

[28] Yuan, B and Parhi, K.K. 2015. Successive cancellation decoding of polar codes using stochastic computing. In *Proc. ISCAS.* To appear.

[29] Zhang D. and Li, H. 2008. A stochastic-based FPGA controller for an induction motor drive with integrated neural network algorithms. *IEEE Trans. Industrial Electronics*, 55, 551-561.

ApproxMA: Approximate Memory Access for Dynamic Precision Scaling

Ye Tian, Qian Zhang, Ting Wang, Feng Yuan, and Qiang Xu
CUhk REliable computing laboratory (CURE)
Department of Computer Science, The Chinese University of Hong Kong
Shatin, N.T., Hong Kong
tianye,qzhang,twang,fyuan,qxu@cse.cuhk.edu.hk

ABSTRACT

Motivated by the inherent error-resilience of emerging recognition, mining, and synthesis (RMS) applications, approximate computing techniques such as precision scaling has been advocated for achieving energy-efficiency gains at the cost of small accuracy loss. Most existing solutions, however, focus on the approximation of on-chip computations without considering that of off-chip data accesses, whose energy consumption may contribute to a significant portion of the total energy. In this work, we propose a novel approximate memory access technique for dynamic precision scaling, namely ApproxMA. To be specific, by taking both runtime data precision constraints and error-resilient capabilities of the application into consideration, ApproxMA determines the precision of data accesses and loads scaled data from off-chip memory for computation. Experimental results with mixture model-based clustering algorithms demonstrate the efficacy of the proposed methodology.

Categories and Subject Descriptors

C.4 [**Computer Systems Organization**]: Performance of Systems—*Design studies*

Keywords

Approximate Computing, Precision Scaling, Memory Access

1. INTRODUCTION

By trading off computation quality with computational effort, approximate computing [1–5] is a promising energy-efficient technique for emerging Recognition, Mining and Synthesis (RMS) applications due to their inherent error-resilience characteristics. Firstly, they are usually used to process large amounts of data that are often noisy and redundant; Secondly, there is usually no specific "golden" output value but rather many "acceptable" outputs; Finally, the algorithms used in many of these applications are stochastic in nature and often resort to error-resilient methods for solution-finding.

Precision scaling, which decreases the operand bit-width in computations according to application quality requirements,

GLSVLSI'15, May 20–22, 2015, Pittsburgh, PA, USA.
Copyright © 2015 ACM 978-1-4503-3474-7/15/05$15.00.
http://dx.doi.org/10.1145/2742060.2743759.

is one of the most effective approximate computing techniques [6–8]. Considering the fact that the computation quality requirement may vary significantly at runtime, various dynamic precision scaling [9, 10] techniques have been presented in the literature, which adaptively adjust operand bit-width to improve energy efficiency under quality constraints.

For RMS applications that are used to process a large volume of data, there are inevitably frequent interactions between off-chip memory and on-chip computational units, and the energy needed for such communication can be much higher than that of computations. Intuitively, if we could selectively load certain most significant bits (instead of all the bits) of data from off-chip under quality constraints, significant energy-efficiency gains can be achieved. Most existing precision scaling techniques, however, only target at energy-efficient on-chip computations without much consideration of off-chip memory accesses.

Motivated by the above, in this work, we propose an approximate memory access framework, namely *ApproxMA*, for dynamic precision scaling with emphasis on off-chip memory accesses, and we validate its effectiveness on mixture model-based clustering problem. Mixture model-based clustering [11] assumes that data were generated by a mixture of models and tries to recover the original model from the data, which provides great flexibility for fitting any data set according to a particular distribution. It has a wide range of applications [12]. For instance, it is the essential part in grouping products and customers in massive retail datasets, gene sequence analysis to find genes that work together, and image segmentation and denoising in image/video processing. Mixture model-based clustering problem is inherently error-resilient and needs large amount of data accesses from off-chip memory. The computation demand for this task is usually quite high and hence how to improve its energy-efficiency is of great interest.

The remainder of this paper is organized as follows. Section 2 provides related works and motivates this paper. Section 3 demonstrates mechanism of approximate memory access for dynamic precision scaling. Case study of mixture model-based clustering with ApproxMA is then presented in Section 4. Finally, Section 5 concludes this paper.

2. RELATED WORKS AND MOTIVATION

Precision scaling is a commonly used approximate design technique, in which the bit-width (precision) of the input operands is modulated for energy efficiency. Many research efforts have been dedicated to precision scaling for tradeoff energy and quality in the literature [6, 8, 9, 13–15]. For example, QUORA [6] applies dynamic precision scaling into processing elements (PEs) with error monitoring and compensation to facilitate quality-programmable execution. A

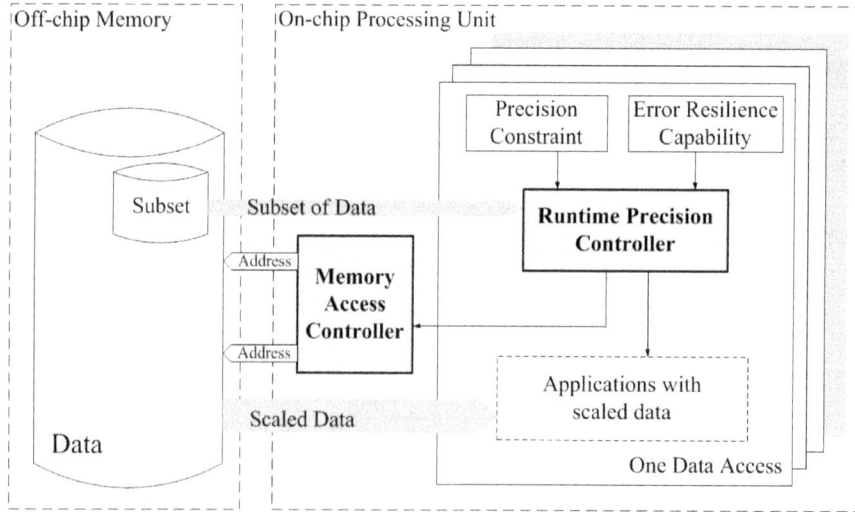

Figure 1: The Framework of Approximate Memory Access.

significant amount of energy is saved by adjusting the precision based on application quality constraints. Analysis of the intermediate variables has been proposed to set the bit-width of the input data under a given error bound of the computation [7]. In [8], word-length tunable architecture for OFDM (Orthogonal Frequency Division Multiplexing) Demodulator determines data word-length at runtime based on the observed error of the system output. [9, 13] optimize the word-length used in the operation according to the time-varying environment of wireless communication systems. There were also other works that apply precision scaling for FPGAs [14] and GPUs [15]. All the above works only apply precision scaling on the processing units.

In big-data era, RMS applications require to deal with extremely large size of dataset, thereby requiring frequent data communications between off-chip memory and on-chip computational units. On the other hand, due to much longer bus length and larger on-board parasitic capacitance, the energy consumption of loading data from off-chip memory is up to 19x comparing with that from on-chip memory [16]. Therefore, off-chip memory accesses could be the dominant factor of the total energy consumption for these communication-intensive RMS applications.

Motivated by the above, we propose an approximate memory access framework for dynamic precision scaling, namely *ApproxMA*. One related work is presented in [17], wherein the authors apply lossy compression for data transferred between the GPU and its off-chip memory, but it requires microarchitectural changes to the system.

3. THE PROPOSED FRAMEWORK

The proposed ApproxMA framework is presented in Fig. 1, which is comprised of *runtime precision controller* and *memory access controller*. For data accesses, runtime precision controller firstly generates the customized bit-width according to runtime quality requirements, and then memory access controller loads the scaled data from off-chip for computations. Although consequent computations also bring energy savings, our work mainly focuses on the communications with scaled data.

3.1 Runtime Precision Controller

Our runtime precision controller works based on the principle that it is not necessary to perform fully-accurate com-

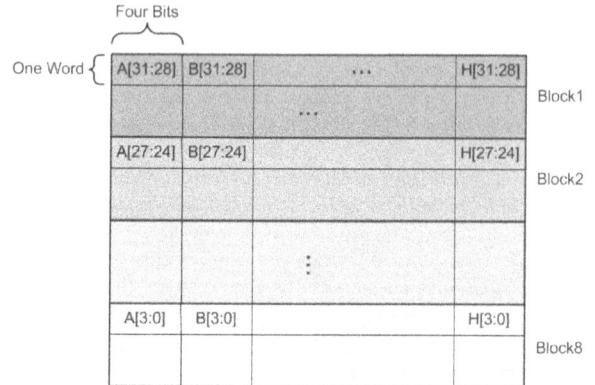

Figure 2: Data Format in Off-chip Memory

putation with approximate computing. On the one hand, lower precision data does not always lead to functional error. On the other hand, as many RMS applications are inherently error-resilient, certain amount of functional errors are acceptable, which can sometimes be recovered and have no influence on the final output quality. We denote this property as *error resilience capability* of the algorithm.

By analyzing subset of data and/or intermediate computational results, runtime precision controller calculates precision constraints (when there will be a functional error) and error resilience capability (how many functional errors are tolerable), and then decides the required bit-width for the current data access.

3.2 Memory Access Controller

To realize loading certain most significant bits of data from off-chip memory, we need to reorganize the data. Bits of the same significance in different words are combined to form new words and stored in off-chip memory. For example, assuming each word has 32 bits and we divide it into 8 parts, each of which then has 4 bits. We will store them in the format shown in Fig. 2, where $A, B, \ldots, H$ respectively represent the eight original words. The first block in off-chip memory stores the first 4 bits of all data, the second block stores the second 4 bits, and so on.

Knowing the starting address of dataset, the number of blocks and the bit-width of data to load, memory access

338

```
Input:
        startAdd (starting address of dataset),
        sizeOfData (original total size of dataset
    in off-chip memory),
        nOfBlock (number of blocks data are
    divided to),
        bitwidth (bit-width of data to load for
    current data access)
 1  offset = sizeOfData/nOfBlock;
 2  calculate nOfBlockToLoad (number of blocks to
    load) with bitwidth;
 3  while (nOfBlockToLoad > 0) do
 4  |   Load data from the address startAdd to the
    |   address startAdd + offset − 1;
 5  |   startAdd = startAdd + offset;
 6  |   nOfBlockToLoad = nOfBlockToLoad − 1;
 7  end
```

Algorithm 1: Load Precision Scaled Data from Off-chip Memory

controller loads the corresponding scaled data from off-chip memory as shown in Algo. 1. For example, assuming we are able to read m 32-bit original data words from off-chip memory once, if the current required precision is 16 bits, we can instead read $32 \times m \div 16 = 2m$ samples once. The access sequence is, bits [31:28] of the first $2m$ samples, then bits [27:24], [23:20] and [19:16] of these $2m$ samples. Having processed the first $2m$ samples, the processor then read the former 16 bits of the second $2m$ samples, and so on.

ApproxMA can be applied to general processor/accelerator architecture without necessarily changing the hardware, in which case, the access control of off-chip memory is conducted at the processor side with a software-based memory management unit MMU). Data reorganization needs to be performed before computation. Runtime precision controllers and memory access controllers can be realized by many kinds of algorithms in our framework depending on the specific applications and datasets. We will detail how ApproxMA can be applied for mixture model-based clustering problem in Sec. 4.

4. CASE STUDY FOR MIXTURE MODEL-BASED CLUSTERING PROBLEM

4.1 Preliminaries

Data clustering is commonly used to find the structure of a given dataset. To be specific, clustering algorithm groups a-like samples based on certain distance metric (e.g., euclidean distance, probability-based distance) and finally outputs k clusters to represent the whole samples. As no pre-knowledge on the different clusters or labels provided, clustering is a typical unsupervised learning procedure. Mixture model-based clusterings use certain models (e.g., distributions, centroids) for clusters and attempt to optimize the fitness between the samples and the models based on an objective function (e.g., maximize the likelihood or minimize the distances). In practice, each model can be mathematically represented by a parametric distribution, such as Gaussian (continuous) or Poisson (discrete). The entire dataset is therefore modeled by a *mixture* of these distributions.

Without loss of generality, let us consider Gaussian mixture model-based clustering (GMM). First, with given data $X = \{x_1, x_2, ...x_n\}$, we assume these samples are from

k Gaussians (i.e., specific *model*), and each of them can be uniquely identified by $G_i(\mu_i, \Sigma_i)$. Then, samples will be assigned with different labels based on the probability (i.e., specific *distance metric*) that they belong to each Gaussian. Next, all the parameters consisting such mixture models will be determined by optimizing the likelihood function (i.e., specific *objective function*) in an Expectation-Maximization (EM) manner. The algorithm is as follows:

Repeat until convergence : {
    $E - Step(Calculate\ current\ measurement)$:
        For each data t and cluster j
            calculate the probability that t belongs to j
    $M - Step(Optimize\ objective\ function)$:
        For each cluster j
            update μ_j and Σ_j by Maximum Likelihood
}

In the E-step, it "guesses" the values of the probabilities (i.e., calculating the similarities for current model), and in the M-step, it updates the model parameters by Maximum Likelihood (i.e., optimizing objective function) based on the E-step's guesses. Although the distance metrics of various models are different, the above iterative EM-based learning procedure is the main-stream technique used for clustering.

4.2 Runtime Precision Controller

A functional error of clustering algorithm happens only if one sample is assigned to an incorrect cluster, and thus the computation with lower precision data does not always lead to functional errors if the relative distances hold. Precision constraints can be decided according to the lowest precision with no functional errors. From the point view of error resilience capability, an appropriate amount of functional errors (i.e., error rate[1]) are acceptable. The iterative nature of clustering algorithm is to continuously correct the mixture models and re-label all the samples. Therefore, the correctness of clustering results can be guaranteed in the later iteration with higher data precision. Such capability is oscillating until the convergence of clustering procedure.

4.2.1 Overview of Runtime Precision Controller

In our proposed runtime precision controller, we represent the relationship between error rates and data precision levels with precision constraint table, and then precision is scaled according to the application's error resilience capability. In each iteration, both precision constraint table and error resilience capability are updated based on runtime information. However, it is a challenging problem, because (i) constraints and error resilience capabilities are all highly dependent on datasets and mixture models; (ii) modern datasets usually feature large amounts of high-dimensional data and there will be significant overhead to analyze all of them.

Fig. 3 depicts the overall flow of our runtime precision controller. It can be observed that *precision constraint table* is constructed from a subset of all the samples, and *error resilience capability* is obtained from intermediate computation results (i.e., classification membership changes between two iterations). The precision of data is determined based on the outputs of the above two blocks (i.e., constraint and relaxations). In addition, a *precision prediction calibration* module is applied to avoid the bit-width prediction error due

---

[1]The percentage of functional errors among all the samples

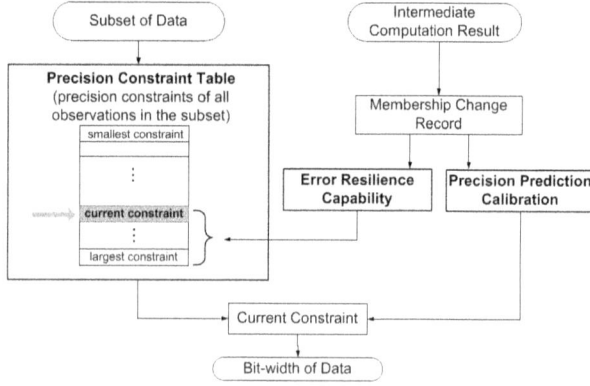

Figure 3: Runtime Precision Controller

to the incomplete or inexact information extraction (i.e., subset of samples). In the following parts, we will detail these functional blocks.

4.2.2 Precision Constraint Table

The precision constraint table lists the data precision constraints and the corresponding predicted error rates.

Suppose the subset we used to construct this table is denoted as

$$x = \{x_1, x_2, ...x_m\}.$$

For each sample, we would estimate the minimal precision requirement (i.e., bit-width bound) to avoid functional error, and then, construct the corresponding precision constraint table with precision requirements of all samples in the subset.

Let us take Fig. 4 as an example to illustrate how to estimate the minimal precision constraint for a single sample.

Given the number of clusters k, the clustering algorithm first computes the distances between the current sample and these k clusters based on the specific distance metric used in the clustering algorithm, and then assigns it to the cluster with the smallest distance. That is, we get

$$d = \{d_1, d_2, ...d_k\},$$

where each d_i indicates the distance between the current sample and the i_{th} cluster, and if d_s is the smallest value in d, the current sample will be assigned to s_{th} cluster.

Based on the above, as long as the relative relationship between any other d_i and d_s is correct (i.e., $\forall d_i > d_s, i \neq s$), the functional error for this sample is avoided.

Specifically, for $d_j > d_s$ ($j \neq s$), the tolerable relative error for keeping this relative relationship can be represented as

$$min(\frac{d_j - d_s}{d_j}, \frac{d_j - d_s}{d_s}) = \frac{d_j - d_s}{d_j} = 1 - \frac{d_s}{d_j}, j \neq s.$$

As there are totally $k - 1$ relative relationships needed to be maintained, we get $k - 1$ tolerable relative errors. Given d_s must be smaller than any other d_i, the final relative error bound for labeling the current sample correctly must be the smallest one of these $k - 1$ values.

For specific distance metric

$$d = f(x),$$

by conducting the above procedure, we get the final relative error bound on distance computation (i.e., bounds on d). Then, the bit-width constraint c for the current data can be determined accordingly. That is, as long as we load c-bit of this sample, it will be classified correctly.

Then, for the entire selected subset, we get

$$C = \{c_1, c_2, ...c_m\},$$

wherein each c_i indicates the bit-width constraint for the i_{th} sample in the subset. After sorting these values in ascending order, we can predict the error rate with any c_i as follows:

$$rate = \frac{No.(entries\ in\ C\ that\ is\ smaller\ than\ c_i)}{m}$$

Finally, we obtain the precision constraint table.

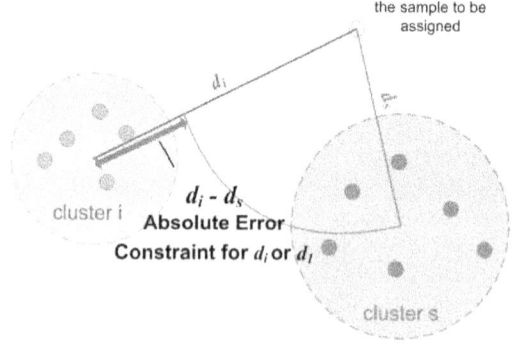

Figure 4: Absolute Error Constraint for One Comparison

4.2.3 Error Resilience Capability

Membership of a sample depicts which cluster the sample belongs to. We define the change of memberships in one iteration as the percentage of samples whose membership changes comparing with that of last iteration. The change of membership tends to decrease along with the algorithm approaching convergence and will finally reach zero. This value reflects the converging rate of the clustering algorithm, and thus we leverage it as the indicator of error resilience capability. For example, if 30% samples change their memberships, the error resilience capability is set as $\alpha \times 30\%$, which means we can tolerate at most $\alpha \times 30\%$ functional errors, where α is a user-defined parameter.

Error resilience capability works cooperatively with precision constraint table to select data precision. First of all, error resilience capability determines the worst case error rate. Then, based on the precision constraint table, the most inaccurate data precision among all acceptable configurations is selected.

4.2.4 Precision Prediction Calibration

Sometimes the predicted precision is not good enough due to the incompleteness of data subset and the inaccuracy of error resilience capability estimation model, leading to endless membership vibrations for some of the samples and significant energy consumption, which appears at the final stage of clustering algorithm.

To avoid the above situation, we keep track of the membership changes within the most recent two iterations. Whenever similar membership changes are detected, we would upgrade the data precision to be the next more accurate one.

4.3 Experimental Results

4.3.1 Experimental Setup

Experiments are conducted on two widely used clustering algorithms: Gaussian mixture model-based clustering (GMM) and k-means clustering (which is the hard assign version

Table 1: Applications and Datasets

Application	Dataset	Source	Dimension	Distance Metric
k-means	svmguide	[19]	4	Least square distance with ℓ_2 norm
	codrna	[19]	8	
	shuttle	[19]	9	
GMM	image noise	[20]	3	Mahalanobis distance with ℓ_2 norm
	irisflowers	[19]	2	
	fourclasses	[21]	2	

Table 2: Mixture Model-based Clustering with ApproxMA

Application	Datasets	Model Deviation	Testing Data Error Rate	Energy Savings
k-means	svmguide	0.3	0	58.08%
	codrna	1.22e-04	0	41.92%
	shuttle	9.39e-05	0	56.17%
GMM	image noise	4.34e-05	0.07%	51.41%
	irisflowers	1.01e-06	0	42.08%
	fourclasses	4.51e-03	0.60%	59.64%

of mixture model-based clustering [11]) with various datasets. Detailed information is listed in Table 1, wherein column "Source" gives the download source of our used datasets, and column "Dimension" indicate the dimension of features. column "Distance Metric" shows the distance metrics for each applications, which will be used in our runtime precision controller.

We apply two metrics to illustrate approximation quality loss on the final results. The first one is named as *model deviation*, which reflects distance between the approximated model and the accurate one. Here the distance is a model-specific metric, and we define it as follows: for k-means, Deviation of Models is calculated with the average Euclidean squared distance between the approximate and the accurate centroids (denoted as c_{app} and c_{acc}, respectively), which is calculated as:

$$D = \frac{1}{k} \sum_{i=1}^{k} d(c_{app,i}, c_{acc,i}),$$

wherein k is the number of clusters; For clustering with Gaussian mixtures, "Deviation of Models" is calculated with the weighted sum of Bhattacharyya distances between approximate and accurate Gaussian mixture models, which is calculated as,

$$D = \sum_{i=1}^{k} weight_i \times d(model_{app,i}, model_{acc,i}).$$

$d(model_{app,i}, model_{acc,i})$ denotes the Bhattacharyya distance between $model_{app,i}$ and $model_{acc,i}$. And $weight_i$ is the weight of accurate model.

The second metric is named as *Testing Data Error Rate*, which means the percentage of testing data that are assigned to a wrong cluster with our calculated approximate model. It should be noted that testing data is different from the training data that is used to calculated the model.

4.3.2 Energy Benefits

In this work, we mainly consider the energy savings of the proposed ApproxMA solution for memory accesses and the values are obtained with CACTI [18]. Note that, there is slight increase of energy consumption due to data reorganiza-

tion before computation, but it is ignored in our experiments due to its relatively small contribution.

Table 2 demonstrates the quality loss and energy benefit for k-means clustering and Gaussian mixture clustering, separately. We can observe from the results that our proposed technique is able to achieve significant energy savings (from 40% to 60%) when comparing with fully accurate off-chip memory accesses. At the same time, the resultant quality loss is almost negligible. One interesting phenomenon illustrated by dataset *svmguide* is that the model deviation is as much as 0.3 while there is no testing data error detected. This is because the clusters are well separated in this dataset so that labeling the testing samples become easy and error-tolerant. Therefore, we are able to gain the best energy savings in this case, which illustrates that our proposed technique is very powerful to capture error resilience capability featured by specific dataset.

4.3.3 Comparison with Static Precision Scaling

We also conduct comparison with static precision scaling that uses a pre-determined fixed bit-width for approximation.

Experimental results for k-means clustering are shown in Table 3. For all the datasets, ApproxMA obtains the most accurate result. "Model Deviation" of dynamic precision scaling is the smallest (9.39e-05 vs 6.13 and 49.18 in Table 3(c)). Correspondingly, "Testing Data Error Rate" is zero indicating that models built with dynamic precision assign all testing data correctly. At the same time, the energy savings are significant, and sometimes better than the case when the bit-width is set as 16. This is because, static precision scaling with small bit-width may cause increase of iterations or even no convergence of the algorithm and therefore consumes more energy.

Generally speaking, the output quality decreases along with the reduction of bit-widths with static precision scaling, and the quality itself is not guaranteed, as shown in the unacceptable results in Table 3(b) and Table 3(c), where nearly half of the testing data are clustered incorrectly when the bit-width is set to be 12. This is a serious problem for static precision scaling because it has no knowledge on the actual data set used in practice.

Table 3: Comparison of Static and Dynamic Precision Scaling

Bitwidth	(a) svmguide			(b) shuttle			(c) cod-rna		
	Model Deviation	Testing Data Error Rate	Energy Savings	Model Deviation	Testing Data Error Rate	Energy Savings	Model Deviation	Testing Data Error Rate	Energy Savings
16	0.45	0.13%	54.55%	1.81e-03	0.03%	50.00%	6.13	4.11%	74.44%
12	6.73	1.49%	69.32%	0.086	44.04%	53.84%	49.18	39.95%	94.17%
dynamic	0.3	0	58.08%	1.22e-04	0	41.92%	9.39e-05	0	56.17%

5. CONCLUSION

Precision scaling is an effective approximate computing technique to improve energy-efficiency. However, most existing works focus on approximation of on-chip computations without considering the energy consumption of off-chip memory accesses. Since emerging Recognition, Mining, and Synthesis applications typically involve huge amounts of data accesses, in this work, we design an approximate memory access framework for dynamic precision scaling, namely ApproxMA. We apply this framework to mixture model-based clustering as a case study. As the precision requirements can vary significantly during runtime, we also propose a lightweight runtime bit-width calculator by jointly considering runtime data precision constraints and application's error resilience capabilities. Experimental results with two widely-used mixture model-based clustering algorithms (k-means and clustering with Gaussian mixtures) demonstrate the efficacy of the proposed methodology.

6. ACKNOWLEDGEMENT

This work was supported in part by National Natural Science Foundation of China (NSFC)/Hong Kong Research Grants Council (RGC) Joint Research Scheme N_CUHK444/12, and in part by NSFC Key Project 61432017.

7. REFERENCES

[1] V. Gupta, D. Mohapatra, S. P. Park, A. Raghunathan, and K. Roy, "Impact: imprecise adders for low-power approximate computing," in *Proceedings of the 17th IEEE/ACM international symposium on Low-power electronics and design*, pp. 409–414, 2011.

[2] J. Han and M. Orshansky, "Approximate computing: An emerging paradigm for energy-efficient design," in *Proceedings of the 18th IEEE European Test Symposium (ETS)*, pp. 1–6, 2013.

[3] V. K. Chippa, S. T. Chakradhar, K. Roy, and A. Raghunathan, "Analysis and characterization of inherent application resilience for approximate computing," in *Proceedings of the 50th Annual Design Automation Conference*, p. 113, 2013.

[4] Q. Zhang, F. Yuan, R. Ye, and Q. Xu, "Approxit: An approximate computing framework for iterative methods," in *Proceedings of the 51st Annual Design Automation Conference*, pp. 97:1–97:6, 2014.

[5] Q. Zhang, T. Wang, Y. Tian, F. Yuan and Q. Xu, "ApproxANN: An Approximate Computing Framework for Artificial Neural Network," *Proceedings IEEE/ACM Design, Automation, and Test in Europe (DATE)*, to appear, 2015.

[6] S. Venkataramani, V. K. Chippa, S. T. Chakradhar, K. Roy, and A. Raghunathan, "Quality programmable vector processors for approximate computing," in *Proceedings of the 46th Annual IEEE/ACM International Symposium on Microarchitecture*, pp. 1–12, 2013.

[7] O. Sarbishei and K. Radecka, "Analysis of precision for scaling the intermediate variables in fixed-point arithmetic circuits," in *Proceedings of the International Conference on Computer-Aided Design*, pp. 739–745, 2010.

[8] S. Yoshizawa and Y. Miyanaga, "Tunable wordlength architecture for a low power wireless OFDM demodulator," *IEICE Transactions on fundamentals of electronics, communications and computer sciences*, vol. 89, no. 10, pp. 2866–2873, 2006.

[9] S. Lee and A. Gerstlauer, "Fine grain word length optimization for dynamic precision scaling in dsp systems," in *2013 IFIP/IEEE 21st International Conference on Very Large Scale Integration (VLSI-SoC)*, pp. 266–271, 2013.

[10] R. Ye, T. Wang, F. Yuan, R. Kumar, and Q. Xu, "On reconfiguration-oriented approximate adder design and its application," in *Proceedings of the IEEE/ACM International Conference on Computer-Aided Design*, pp. 48–54, 2013.

[11] V. Melnykov, R. Maitra, "Finite mixture models and model-based clustering," *Statistics Surveys*, vol. 4, pp. 80–116, 2010.

[12] C.M. Bishop *et al.*, *Pattern recognition and machine learning*, vol. 1. springer New York, 2006.

[13] H.-N. Nguyen, D. Menard, and O. Sentieys, "Dynamic precision scaling for low power WCDMA receiver," in *IEEE International Symposium on Circuits and Systems*, pp. 205–208, 2009.

[14] Y. Lee, Y. Choi, S.-B. Ko, and M. H. Lee, "Performance analysis of bit-width reduced floating-point arithmetic units in FPGAs: a case study of neural network-based face detector," *EURASIP Journal on Embedded Systems*, vol. 2009, p. 4, 2009.

[15] N. Luehr, I. S. Ufimtsev, and T. J. Martínez, "Dynamic precision for electron repulsion integral evaluation on graphical processing units (GPUs)," *Journal of Chemical Theory and Computation*, vol. 7, no. 4, pp. 949–954, 2011.

[16] H. Sangki, "3D super-via for memory applications," in *Micro-Systems Packaging Initiative Packaging Workshop (WSPI)*, 2007.

[17] V. Sathish, M. J. Schulte, and N. S. Kim, "Lossless and lossy memory I/O link compression for improving performance of GPGPU workloads," in *Proceedings of ACM International Conference on Parallel Architectures and Compilation Techniques*, 2012.

[18] "CACTI," http://www.hpl.hp.com/research/cacti/.

[19] http://www.csie.ntu.edu.tw/ cjlin/libsvm/

[20] http://scikit-learn.org/stable/modules/classes.html#module-sklearn.datasets

[21] T. K. Ho and E. M. Kleinberg, "Building projectable classifiers of arbitrary complexity," in *Proceedings of the 13th IEEE International Conference on Pattern Recognition*, vol. 2, pp. 880–885, 1996.

A Comparative Review and Evaluation of Approximate Adders

Honglan Jiang
Department of Electrical and
Computer Engineering
University of Alberta
Edmonton, Alberta, Canada
T6G 2V4
honglan@ualberta.ca

Jie Han
Department of Electrical and
Computer Engineering
University of Alberta
Edmonton, Alberta, Canada
T6G 2V4
jhan8@ualberta.ca

Fabrizio Lombardi
Department of Electrical and
Computer Engineering
Northeastern University
Boston, MA 02115, USA
lombardi@ece.neu.edu

ABSTRACT

As an important arithmetic module, the adder plays a key role in determining the speed and power consumption of a digital signal processing (DSP) system. The demands of high speed and power efficiency as well as the fault tolerance nature of some applications have promoted the development of approximate adders. This paper reviews current approximate adder designs and provides a comparative evaluation in terms of both error and circuit characteristics. Simulation results show that the equal segmentation adder (ESA) is the most hardware-efficient design, but it has the lowest accuracy in terms of error rate (ER) and mean relative error distance (MRED). The error-tolerant adder type II (ETAII), the speculative carry select adder (SCSA) and the accuracy-configurable approximate adder (ACAA) are equally accurate (provided that the same parameters are used), however ETATII incurs the lowest power-delay-product (PDP) among them. The almost correct adder (ACA) is the most power consuming scheme with a moderate accuracy. The lower-part-OR adder (LOA) is the slowest, but it is highly efficient in power dissipation.

Categories and Subject Descriptors

B.2.0 [**Arithmetic and Logic Structures**]: General; B.6.1 [**Logic Design**]: Design Styles *combinational logic*; B.7.1 [**Integrated Circuits**]: Types and Design Styles *VLSI*; B.8.0 [**Performance and Reliability**]: General

Keywords

Approximate Computing; Adder; Power; Accuracy.

1. INTRODUCTION

As the physical dimensions of CMOS scale down to a few tens of nanometers, it has been increasingly difficult to improve circuit performance and/or to enhance power

efficiency. Approximate computing has been advocated as a new approach to saving area and power dissipation, as well as increasing performance at a limited loss in accuracy [3]. While computation errors are in general not desirable, applications such as multimedia (image, audio and video) processing, wireless communications, recognition, and data mining are tolerant to some errors. Due to the statistical/probabilistic nature of these applications, small errors in computation would not impose noticeable degradation in performance [22].

Generally, there are two types of methodologies for improving speed and power efficiency by approximation. The first methodology uses a voltage-over-scaling (VOS) technique for CMOS circuits to save power [4,15,19]. The second methodology is based on redesigning a logic circuit into an approximate version. While the VOS technique is applicable to most circuits for error-tolerant applications, an approximate redesign pertains to the functionalities of different logic circuits. Approximately redesigned adders (simply referred to as approximate adders) are reviewed and a comparative evaluation is performed in this paper.

2. REVIEW

Adders are utilized for calculating the addition (or sum) of two binary numbers. Two common types of adders are the ripple-carry adder (RCA) and the carry lookahead adder (CLA) [9, 21]. In an n-bit RCA, n 1-bit full adders (FAs) are cascaded; the carry of each FA is propagated to the next FA, thus the delay of RCA grows in proportion to n (or $O(n)$). An n-bit CLA consists of n SPGs, which operate in parallel to produce the sum, generate ($g_i = a_i b_i$) and propagate ($p_i = a_i + b_i$) signals, and connected to a carry lookahead generator. For CLA, all carries are generated directly by the carry lookahead generator using only the generate and propagate signals, so the delay of CLA is logarithmic in n (or $O(log(n))$), thus significantly shorter than that of RCA. However, CLA requires larger circuit area and higher power dissipation. The carry lookahead generator becomes very complex for large n. The area complexity of CLA is $O(nlog(n))$ when the fan-in and fan-out of the constituent gates are fixed [16].

Many approximation schemes have been proposed by reducing the critical path and hardware complexity of the accurate adder. An early methodology is based on a speculative operation [16, 23]. In an n-bit speculative adder, each sum bit is predicted by its previous k less significant bits

(LSBs) ($k < n$). A speculative design makes an adder significantly faster than the conventional design. Segmented adders are proposed in [7,19,27]. An n-bit segmented adder is implemented by several smaller adders operating in parallel. Hence, the carry propagation chain is truncated into shorter segments. Segmentation is also utilized in [1,5,8,10, 12,25], but their carry inputs for each sub-adder are selected differently. This type of adder is referred to as a carry select adder. Another method for reducing the critical path delay and power dissipation of a conventional adder is by approximating the full adder [2,17,20,24]; the approximate adder is usually applied to the LSBs of an accurate adder. In the sequel, the approximate adders are divided into four categories.

2.1 Speculative Adders

As the carry chain is significantly shorter than n in most practical cases, [23] has proposed an almost correct adder (ACA) based on the speculative adder design of [16]. In an n-bit ACA, k LSBs are used to predict the carry for each sum bit ($n > k$), as shown in Fig. 1. Therefore, the critical path delay is reduced to $O(log(k))$ (for a parallel implementation such as CLA, the same below). As an example, four LSBs are used to calculate each carry bit in Fig. 1. As each carry bit needs a k-bit sub-carry generator in the design of [16], ($n - k$) k-bit sub-carry generators are required in an n-bit adder and thus, the hardware overhead is rather high. This issue is solved in [23] by sharing some components among the sub-carry generators. Moreover, a variable latency speculative adder (VLSA) is then proposed with an error detection and recovery scheme [23]. VLSA achieves a speedup of 1.5× on average compared to CLA.

2.2 Segmented adders

2.2.1 The Equal Segmentation Adder (ESA)

A dynamic segmentation with error compensation (DSEC) is proposed in [19] to approximate an adder. This scheme divides an n-bit adder into a number of smaller sub-adders; these sub-adders operate in parallel with fixed carry inputs. In this paper, the error compensation technique is ignored because the focus is on the approximate design, so the equal segmentation adder (ESA) (Fig. 2) is considered as a simple structure of the DSEC adder. In Fig. 2, $\lceil \frac{n}{k} \rceil$ sub-adders are used, l is the size of the first sub-adder ($l \le k$), and k is the size of the other sub-adders. Hence, the delay of ESA is $O(log(k))$ and the hardware overhead is significantly less than ACA.

2.2.2 The Error-Tolerant Adder Type II (ETAII)

Another segmentation based approximate adder (ETAII) is proposed in [27]. Different from ESA, ETAII consists of carry generators and sum generators, as shown in Fig. 3 (n is the adder size; k is the size of the carry and sum generators). The carry signal from the previous carry generator propagates to the next sum generator. Therefore, ETAII utilizes more information to predict the carry bit and thus, it is more accurate compared with ESA for the same k. Because the sub-adders in ESA produce both sum and carry, the circuit complexity of ETAII is similar to ESA, however its delay is larger ($O(log(2k))$). In addition to ETAII, several other error tolerant adders (ETAs) have been proposed by the same authors in [26,28,29].

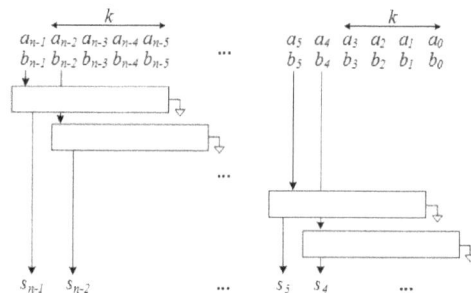

Figure 1: The almost correct adder (ACA). ☐ : the carry propagation path of the sum bit.

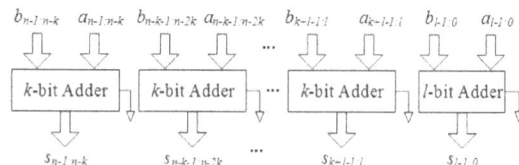

Figure 2: The equal segmentation adder (ESA). k: the maximum carry chain length; l: the size of the first sub-adder ($l \le k$).

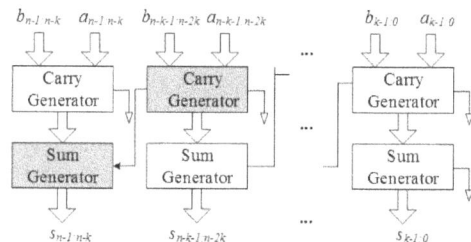

Figure 3: The error-tolerant adder type II (ETAII) [27]: the carry propagates through the two shaded blocks.

2.2.3 Accuracy-Configurable Approximate Adder

An accuracy-configurable approximate adder (ACAA) is proposed in [7]. As accuracy can be configured at runtime by changing the circuit structure, a tradeoff of accuracy versus performance and power can be achieved. In an n-bit adder, $\lceil \frac{n}{k} - 1 \rceil$ $2k$-bit sub-adders are required. Each sub-adder adds $2k$ consecutive bits with an overlap of k bits, and all $2k$-bit sub-adders operate in parallel to reduce the delay to $O(log(2k))$. In each sub-adder, the half most significant sum bits are selected as the partial sum. An error detection and correction (EDC) circuit is used to correct the errors generated by each sub-adder. The accuracy configuration is implemented by the approximate adder and its EDC with a pipelined architecture. For the same k, the carry propagation path is the same for each sum bit as in ACAA and ETAII; hence they have the same error characteristics.

2.2.4 The Dithering Adder

The dithering adder [18] starts by dividing a multiple-bit adder into two sub-adders. The higher sub-adder is an accurate adder and the lower sub-adder consists of a conditional upper bounding module and a conditional lower bounding module. An additional "Dither Control" signal

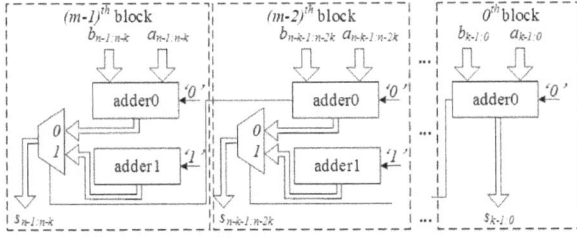

Figure 4: The speculative carry selection adder (SCSA).

is used to configure an upper or lower bound of the lower sum and carry into the higher accurate sub-adder, resulting in a smaller overall error variance.

2.3 Carry Select Adders

In the carry select adders, several signals are commonly used: generate $g_j = a_j b_j$, propagate $p_j = a_j \oplus b_j$, and $P^i = \prod_{j=0}^{k-1} p_j^i$. $P^i = 1$ means that all k propagate signals in the ith block are true.

2.3.1 The Speculative Carry Select Adder (SCSA)

The SCSA is proposed in [1]. An n-bit SCSA consists of $m = \lceil \frac{n}{k} \rceil$ sub-adders (window adders). Each sub-adder is made of two k-bit adders: adder0 and adder1, as shown in Fig. 4. Adder0 has carry-in "0" while the carry-in of adder1 is "1"; then the carry-out of adder0 is connected to a multiplexer to select the addition result as a part of the final result. Thus, the critical path delay of SCSA is $t_{adder} + t_{mux}$, where t_{adder} is the delay of the sub-adder ($O(log(k))$), and t_{mux} is the delay of the multiplexer. SCSA and ETAII achieve the same accuracy for the same parameter k, because the same function is used to predict the carry for every sum bit. Compared with ETAII, SCSA uses an additional adder and multiplexer in each block and thus, the circuit of SCSA is more complex than ETAII.

2.3.2 The Carry Skip Adder (CSA)

Similar to SCSA, an n-bit carry skip adder (CSA) [8] is divided into $\lceil \frac{n}{k} \rceil$ blocks, but each block consists of a sub-carry generator and a sub-adder. The carry-in of the $(i+1)^{th}$ sub-adder is determined by the propagate signals of the ith block: the carry-in is the carry-out of the $(i-1)^{th}$ sub-carry generator when all the propagate signals are true ($P^i = 1$), otherwise it is the carry-out of the ith sub-carry generator. Therefore, the critical path delay of CSA is $O(log(2k))$. This carry select scheme enhances the carry prediction accuracy.

2.3.3 The Gracefully-Degrading Accuracy-Configurable Adder (GDA)

An accuracy-configurable adder, referred to as the gracefully-degrading accuracy-configurable adder (GDA), is presented in [25]. Control signals are used to configure the accuracy of GDA by selecting the accurate or approximate carry-in using a multiplexer for each sub-adder. The delay of GDA is determined by the carry propagation and thus by the control signals to multiplexers.

2.3.4 The Carry Speculative Adder

Different from SCSA, the carry speculative adder (CSPA) in [12] contains one sum generator, two internal carry gener-

ators (one with carry-0 and one with carry-1) and one carry predictor in each block. The output of the ith carry predictor is used to select carry signals for the $(i + 1)^{th}$ sum generator. l input bits (rather than k, $l < k$) in a block are used in a carry predictor. Therefore, the hardware overhead is reduced compared to SCSA.

2.3.5 The Consistent Carry Approximate Adder

The consistent carry approximate adder (CCA) [10] is also based on SCSA. Likewise, each block of CCA comprises adder0 with carry-0 and adder1 with carry-1. The select signal of a multiplexer is determined by the propagate signals, i.e., $S_i = (P^i + P^{i-1})SC + \overline{(P^i + P^{i-1})}C_{out}^{i-1}$, where C_{out}^{i-1} is the carry out of the $(i - 1)^{th}$ adder0, and SC is a global speculative carry (referred to as a consistent carry). In CCA, the carry prediction depends not only on its LSBs, but also on the higher bits. The critical path delay and area complexity of CCA are similar to SCSA.

2.3.6 The Generate Signals Exploited Carry Speculation Adder (GCSA)

In [5], the generate signals are used for carry speculation. GSCA has a similar structure as CSA. The only difference between them is the carry selection; the carry-in for the $(i + 1)^{th}$ sub-adder is selected by its own propagate signals rather than its previous block. The carry-in is the most significant generate signal g_{k-1}^i of the ith block if $P^i = 1$, or else it is the carry-out of the ith sub-carry generator. The critical path delay of GCSA is $O(log(2k))$ due to the carry propagation. This carry selection scheme effectively controls the maximal relative error.

2.4 Approximate Full Adders

2.4.1 The Lower-Part-OR Adder (LOA)

LOA [17] divides an n-bit adder into an $(n - l)$-bit more significant sub-adder and an l-bit less significant sub-adder. For the less significant sub-adder, its inputs are simply processed by using OR gates (as a simple approximate full adder). The more significant $(n - l)$-bit sub-adder is an accurate adder. An extra AND gate is used to generate the carry-in signal for the more significant sub-adder by AND-ing the most significant input bits of the less significant sub-adder. The critical path of LOA is from the AND gate to the most significant sum bit of the accurate adder, i.e., approximately $O(log(n - l))$. LOA has been utilized in a recently-proposed approximate floating-point adder [14].

2.4.2 Approximate Mirror Adders (AMAs)

In [2], five AMAs are proposed by reducing the number of transistors and the internal node capacitance of the mirror adder (MA). The AMA adder cells are then used in the LSBs of a multiple-bit adder. However, the critical paths of AMA1-4 are longer than LOA because the carry propagates through every bit. As for AMA5, the carry-out is one of the inputs; thus, no carry propagation exists in the LSBs of an approximate multiple-bit adder.

2.4.3 Approximate Full Adders using Pass Transistors

Three approximate adders (AXAs) based on XOR/XNOR gates and multiplexers (implemented by pass transistors) have been presented in [24]. Several approximate complementary pass transistor logic (CPL) adders have been proposed by reducing the number of transistors in the accurate CPL adder [20]. Significant area and power savings have been obtained for both types of approximate designs.

3. COMPARATIVE EVALUATION

In the evaluation, SCSA is selected as a typical carry select adder and LOA is considered as a representative design using approximate full adders. All adders and sub-adders are implemented as CLA in this paper.

3.1 Error Characteristics

To evaluate the accuracy of approximate adders, analytical and simulation-based approaches have been proposed [6, 11, 13, 18, 22]. In this paper, Monte Carlo simulation is performed. The error rate (ER, the probability of producing an incorrect result), the normalized mean error distance (NMED, the normalization of mean error distance (MED) by the maximum output of the accurate adder) and the mean relative error distance (MRED, the average value of all possible relative error distances (REDs)) are used to assess the error characteristics of the approximate designs. Error distance (ED) and RED are calculated as: $ED = |M' - M|$ and $RED = \frac{ED}{M}$, where M' is the approximate result and M is the accurate result [11]. MED is the mean of all possible EDs.

The functions of the approximate adders ($16-$bit) are implemented in MATLAB and simulated with 10^8 random input combinations. The error measures in ER, NMED and MRED are obtained. Fig. 5 shows the simulation results where each adder's name is followed by the value of its parameter k. For ACA, ETAII and ESA, k is the size of the sub-adder, while k is the size of the less significant adder for LOA (as implemented by OR gates).

The NMED and MRED values of the approximate adders with data sorted by the MRED are shown in Fig. 5(a). The logarithms (base 10) of the NMED and MRED are plotted, and the vertical axis is labeled by negative numbers. In this figure, ETAII-k represents ETAII-k, SCSA-k and ACAA-k because they have the same carry propagation chain for each sum bit and hence, the same error characteristics (ER, NMED and MRED). The NMED and MRED show the same trend, so we only consider MRED in the comparison. Fig. 5(b) shows the comparison of ER and MRED of the approximate adders with data sorted by ER.

Among these approximate adders, ETAII-6 has the smallest MRED, while ESA-3 has the largest. LOA (shown in different patterns in Fig. 5(b)) has a structure different from the other approximate adders. Its higher part is totally accurate, while the approximate part is less significant. Therefore, the MRED of LOA is rather small but its ER is very large. The information used to predict each carry in ESA is rather limited, so its MRED and ER are the largest (excluding LOA). Specifically, a lower ER usually indicates a smaller MRED; a larger k normally means a lower ER and MRED for all the approximate adders (except for LOA). Compared with ETAII, SCSA and ACAA (represented by ETAII in Fig. 5), ACA gives slightly higher ER and MRED for the same k due to the shorter carry propagation chain (thus, less information is used for predicting the carry bits).

In summary, ETAII-6, SCSA-6 and ACAA-6 are the most accurate adders among the compared designs since they have the smallest ER and MRED. ESA-3 is the least accurate design in terms of ER and MRED.

3.2 Circuit Characteristics

To assess circuit characteristics, the considered 16-bit approximate adders and the accurate CLA are implemented in VHDL and synthesized using the Synopsys Design Compiler based on an STM 65-nm process; delay, area and power are then obtained. Among ETAII, SCSA and ACAA (with the same error characteristics when the same parameter k is selected), SCSA incurs the largest power dissipation because two sub-adders and one multiplexer are utilized in each block, and ACAA is the slowest because of its critical path ($2k$) is twice that of the other two adders. The block of ETAII (a carry generator and a sum generator) is significantly simpler than those of SCSA and ACAA. Therefore, ETAII has a shorter delay and consumes less power and area than SCSA and ACAA, thus ETAII is selected for circuit comparisons.

A circuit with larger area is likely to consume more power, so only power and delay are considered in the comparison. Fig. 6 shows the delay and power of the approximate adders with ascending delay (Fig. 6(a)) and power (Fig. 6(b)) from left to right. Obviously, the accurate CLA has the longest delay among all adders, but not the highest power dissipation. LOA (shown in different patterns) is the slowest, but it is very power efficient compared with the other approximate adders. With the same k, ESA is the fastest (when k is 3 or 4) and most power efficient due to its simple segment structure. ETAII is the slowest (except for $k = 3$) excluding LOA, and ACA incurs the largest power consumption due to its complex speculation circuit. Among all the approximate adders shown in Fig. 6, ESA-3 is the fastest, while LOA-8 is the slowest. The delays of all ACAs are very close (less than 400 ps), and all the LOAs have a delay larger than 600 ps. For ESA and ETAII, a smaller k leads to a smaller delay and power dissipation, a larger k also shows significantly larger values of these metrics.

Since a smaller delay does not always imply lower power dissipation, the power-delay-product (PDP) is used as a joint metric to evaluate the circuit characteristics of the approximate adders. Fig. 7 shows in ascending order the PDPs of the approximate adders from left to right. ESA-3 has the smallest PDP, while the accurate CLA has the largest value. LOA-10 and LOA-9 have moderate PDPs (due to large delay and low power dissipation). In terms of PDP, the approximate adders can be classified into three classes: ESA-3, ESA-4 and ETAII-3 have the smallest PDP with less than 10 fJ, then ESA-5, LOA-10, ETAII-4 and ACA-3 with around 20 fJ, and the PDPs of the other approximate adders are larger than 20 fJ and less than 45 fJ.

4. DISCUSSION AND CONCLUSION

In this paper, current approximate adders are reviewed; their error and circuit characteristics are evaluated. Fig. 8 shows the MRED and PDP of the approximate adders in a two-dimension (2-D) plot. ESA-3 and ESA-4 have rather small PDP but a considerably large MRED; LOA-8, LOA-7 and ETAII-6 are the opposite, i.e., they have a small MRED but a large PDP. These approximate adders do not show the best tradeoff, but they can be used for special applications where either hardware efficiency or high accuracy is required. The best tradeoff is met by ETAII-3 with a small PDP and

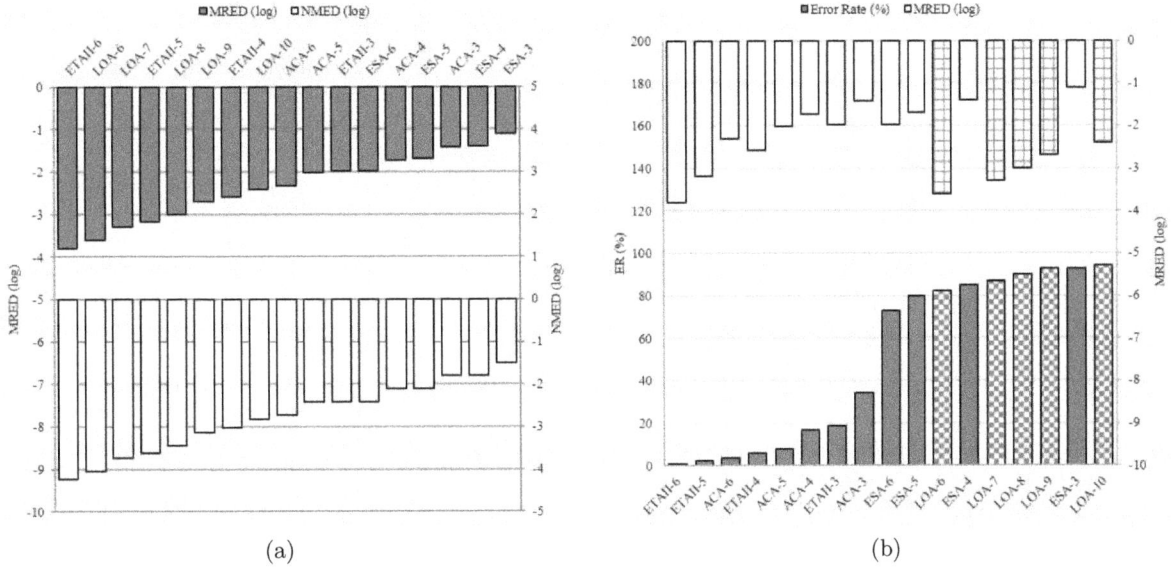

(a)   (b)

Figure 5: A comparison of error characteristics of approximate adders with data sorted on (a) MRED and (b) ER.

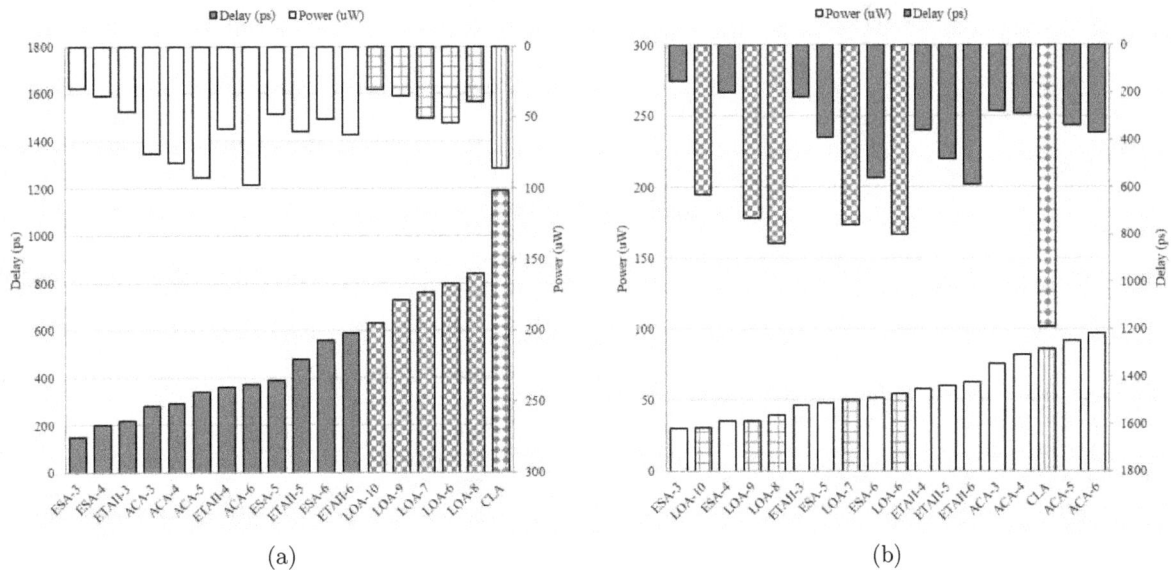

(a)   (b)

Figure 6: A comparison of delay and power of approximate adders with data sorted on (a) delay and (b) power.

MRED. ESA-5, ACA-3 and ACA-4 show moderate MRED and PDP.

Overall, ESA is the most hardware-efficient design but it is also the least accurate. ETAII, SCSA and ACAA have the same accuracy when their parameters are the same, whereas ETATII shows the smallest PDP among them. ACA is the most power consuming design with a moderate accuracy, while LOA is the slowest but it is highly power efficient among all approximate adders.

5. REFERENCES

[1] K. Du, P. Varman, and K. Mohanram. High performance reliable variable latency carry select addition. In *DATE*, pages 1257 1262, 2012.

[2] V. Gupta, D. Mohapatra, A. Raghunathan, and K. Roy. Low-power digital signal processing using approximate adders. *IEEE Trans. CAD*, 32(1):124 137, 2013.

[3] J. Han and M. Orshansky. Approximate Computing: An Emerging Paradigm For Energy-Efficient Design. In *ETS*, pages 1 6, Avignon, France, 2013.

[4] R. Hegde and N. Shanbhag. Soft digital signal processing. *IEEE Trans. VLSI Syst.*, 9(6):813 823, 2001.

[5] J. Hu and W. ian. A new approximate adder with low relative error and correct sign calculation. In *DATE*, in press, 2015.

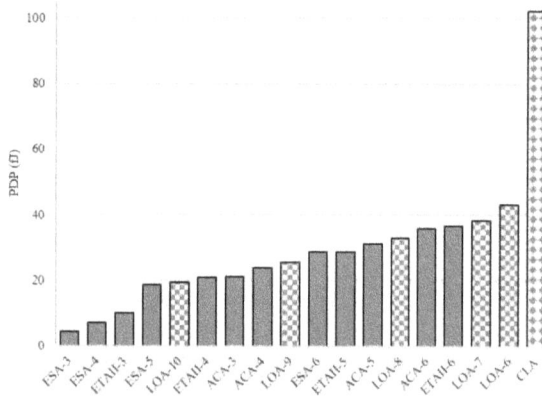

Figure 7: Sorted PDP of the approximate adders.

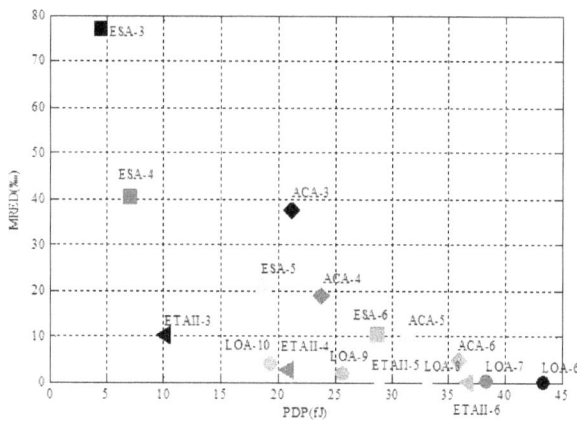

Figure 8: MRED and PDP of the approximate adders.

[6] J. Huang, J. Lach, and G. Robins. A methodology for energy-quality tradeoff using imprecise hardware. In *DAC*, pages 504 509, 2012.

[7] A. B. Kahng and S. Kang. Accuracy-configurable adder for approximate arithmetic designs. In *DAC*, pages 820 825, 2012.

[8] Y. Kim, Y. Zhang, and P. Li. An energy efficient approximate adder with carry skip for error resilient neuromorphic vlsi systems. In *ICCAD*, pages 130 137, 2013.

[9] I. Koren. *Computer Arithmetic Algorithms, 2nd edition*. A K Peters/CRC Press, Natick, 2001.

[10] L. Li and H. Zhou. On error modeling and analysis of approximate adders. In *ICCAD*, pages 511 518, 2014.

[11] J. Liang, J. Han, and F. Lombardi. New metrics for the reliability of approximate and probabilistic adders. *IEEE Trans. Comput.*, 62(9):1760 1771, 2013.

[12] I. Lin, Y. Yang, and C. Lin. High-performance low-power carry speculative addition with varible latency. *IEEE Trans. VLSI Syst.*, in press, 2014.

[13] C. Liu, J. Han, and F. Lombardi. An analytical framework for evaluating the error characteristics of approximate adders. *IEEE Trans. Comput.*, 2014.

[14] W. Liu, L. Chen, C. Wang, M. ONeill, and F. Lombardi. Inexact floating-point adder for dynamic

image processing. In *IEEE-NANO*, pages 239 243, 2014.

[15] Y. Liu, T. Zhang, and K. Parhi. Computation error analysis in digital signal processing systems with overscaled supply voltage. *IEEE Trans. VLSI Syst.*, 18(4):517 526, 2010.

[16] S.-L. Lu. Speeding up processing with approximation circuits. *Computer*, 37(3):67 73, 2004.

[17] H. R. Mahdiani, A. Ahmadi, S. M. Fakhraie, and C. Lucas. Bio-Inspired Imprecise Computational Blocks for Efficient VLSI Implementation of Soft-Computing Applications. *IEEE Trans. Circuits Syst.*, 57(4):850 862, 2010.

[18] J. Miao, K. He, A. Gerstlauer, and M. Orshansky. Modeling and synthesis of quality-energy optimal approximate adders. In *ICCAD*, pages 728 735, 2012.

[19] D. Mohapatra, V. Chippa, A. Raghunathan, and K. Roy. Design of voltage-scalable meta-functions for approximate computing. In *DATE*, pages 1 6, 2011.

[20] D. Nanu, R. P. K., D. Sowkarthiga, and K. S. A. Ameen. Approximate adder design using cpl logic for image compression. *International Journal of Innovative Research and Development*, 3(4):362 370, 2014.

[21] B. Parhami. *Computer Arithmetic: Algorithms and Hardware Designs, 2nd edition*. Oxford University Press, New York, 2010.

[22] R. Venkatesan, A. Agarwal, K. Roy, and A. Raghunathan. Macaco: Modeling and analysis of circuits for approximate computing. In *ICCAD*, pages 667 673, 2010.

[23] A. K. Verma, P. Brisk, and P. Ienne. Variable latency speculative addition: A new paradigm for arithmetic circuit design. In *DATE*, pages 1250 1255, 2008.

[24] Z. Yang, A. Jain, J. Liang, J. Han, and F. Lombardi. Approximate XOR/XNOR-based adders for inexact computing. In *IEEE-NANO*, pages 690 693, 2013.

[25] R. Ye, T. Wang, F. Yuan, R. Kumar, and . Xu. On reconfiguration-oriented approximate adder design and its application. In *ICCAD*, pages 48 54, 2013.

[26] N. Zhu, W. L. Goh, G. Wang, and K. S. Yeo. Enhanced low-power high-speed adder for error-tolerant application. In *SOCC*, pages 323 327, 2010.

[27] N. Zhu, W. L. Goh, and K. S. Yeo. An enhanced low-power high-speed adder for error-tolerant application. In *ISIC 2009*, pages 69 72, 2009.

[28] N. Zhu, W. L. Goh, and K. S. Yeo. Ultra low-power high-speed flexible Probabilistic Adder for Error-Tolerant Applications. In *SOCC*, pages 393 396, 2011.

[29] N. Zhu, W. L. Goh, W. Zhang, K. S. Yeo, and Z. H. Kong. Design of Low-Power High-Speed Truncation-Error-Tolerant Adder and Its Application in Digital Signal Processing. *IEEE Trans. VLSI Syst.*, 18(8):1225 1229, 2010.

Minimizing Error of Stochastic Computation through Linear Transformation

Yi Wu, Chen Wang, and Weikang Qian
University of Michigan-Shanghai Jiao Tong University Joint Institute
Shanghai Jiao Tong University, Shanghai, China
Email: {eejessie, wangchen_2011, qianwk}@sjtu.edu.cn

ABSTRACT

Stochastic computation is an unconventional computational paradigm that uses ordinary digital circuits to operate on stochastic bit streams, where signal value is encoded as the probability of ones in a stream. It is highly tolerant of soft errors and enables complex arithmetic operations to be implemented with simple circuitry. Prior research has proposed a method to synthesize stochastic computing circuits to implement arbitrary arithmetic functions by approximating them via Bernstein polynomials. However, for some functions, the method cannot find Bernstein polynomials that approximate them closely enough, thus causing a large computation error. In this work, we explore linear transformation on a target function to reduce the approximation error. We propose a method to find the optimal linear transformation parameters to minimize the overall error of the stochastic implementation. Experimental results demonstrated the effectiveness of our method in reducing the computation error and the circuit area.

Categories and Subject Descriptors

B.6.1 [**Logic Design**]: Design Styles

General Terms

Design, Performance

Keywords

stochastic computing; stochastic circuit; approximation error; stochastic variation

1. INTRODUCTION

Stochastic computation is a method to explicitly use randomness to perform computation [1]. Like conventional digital computation, stochastic computation uses digital circuits to process information encoded by zeros and ones. However, stochastic circuits take random bit streams as their inputs and outputs. Each bit stream encodes a value equal to the ratio of ones in that stream. For example, a stream of 8 random bits 1, 0, 1, 0, 0, 1, 0, 0 encodes the value 3/8.

GLSVLSI'15, May 20–22, 2015, Pittsburgh, PA, USA.
Copyright © 2015 ACM 978-1-4503-3474-7/15/05 ...$15.00.
http://dx.doi.org/10.1145/2742060.2743761.

One advantage of stochastic computation is that many complex arithmetic operations can be realized using very simple circuitry. As shown in Fig. 1, an AND gate can implement multiplication: given that the two input stochastic bit streams are independent, the probability of ones in the output bit stream equals the product of the probabilities of ones in the input streams. Previous works have also introduced various simple circuits to implement other functions such as addition, division, and square root [2,3].

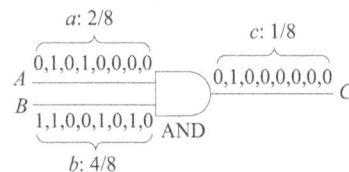

Figure 1: Multiplication on stochastic bit streams with an AND gate. Here the inputs are 2/8 and 4/8. The output is 2/8 × 4/8 = 1/8, as expected.

Besides area efficiency, stochastic computation is also highly tolerant of soft errors, because a single bit flip occurring anywhere in the stream changes the value only slightly. The strong fault tolerance of stochastic computation was visually demonstrated by several image processing applications [4,5].

To apply stochastic computation to a wide variety of applications, an automatic way to synthesize stochastic computing circuits is required. Recently, several synthesis approaches have been proposed [4,6,7]. One method proposed by Qian et al. is to first approximate an arbitrary function via a Bernstein polynomial [8] and then implement that Bernstein polynomial through a specific stochastic computing circuit [4].

However, we observe that for some functions, we cannot find Bernstein polynomials of a low degree that approximate them closely enough, hence causing a large approximation error. In this case, Bernstein polynomial of a higher degree is needed to reach a close approximation, which increases area cost.

In this work, we propose a linear transformation technique to reduce the approximation error. We perform a proper linear transformation on the original function to obtain a function that can be approximated very closely by a Bernstein polynomial of a low degree. We then synthesize a circuit to compute the transformed function. The value of the original function can be easily obtained through an inverse linear transformation, which is achieved by a simple modification to the original design.

Although the linear transformation technique could reduce the approximation error, it will amplify the error due to random fluctuation, which is another major error component of stochastic computation. In order to minimize the overall error of stochastic computation, we further propose a method to find the optimal linear transformation parameters. The proposed technique dramatically reduces the overall error.

The remainder of the paper is organized as follows. Section 2 introduces the background on the Bernstein polynomial based approach to synthesize stochastic computing circuit. Section 3 describes the linear transformation technique that decreases the approximation error. Section 4 proposes a method to determine the optimal linear transformation parameters to minimize the overall error of stochastic computation. Section 5 shows the experimental results. Conclusions are drawn in Section 6.

2. BACKGROUND

2.1 Bernstein Polynomial Based Synthesis Method

The method proposed in [4] first approximates the target function by a Bernstein polynomial [8] and then implements the Bernstein polynomial through a specific stochastic computing circuit. A *Bernstein polynomial* of degree n is of the form

$$B_n(x) = \sum_{i=0}^{n} b_i B_{i,n}(x),$$

where each real number b_i is a constant, called *Bernstein coefficient*, and each $B_{i,n}(x)$ $(i = 0, 1, 2, \cdots, n)$ is a *Bernstein basis polynomial* of the form

$$B_{i,n}(x) = \binom{n}{i} x^i (1 - x)^{n-i}.$$

A Bernstein polynomial *with all the coefficients in the unit interval* can be implemented by a stochastic computing circuit shown in Fig. 2. Since it is the core of the stochastic computing system, to be discussed later, we call the circuit *stochastic computing core*. The core consists of an adder and a multiplexer. An analysis in [4] showed that the probability of the output Y to be one is in the form of a Bernstein polynomial of degree n. As shown in the figure, the Bernstein coefficients b_i's are probability values. Therefore, the Bernstein polynomial that can be realized by the stochastic computing core must have all the coefficients in the unit interval, i.e., $0 \le b_i \le 1$ for all $i = 0, \ldots, n$.

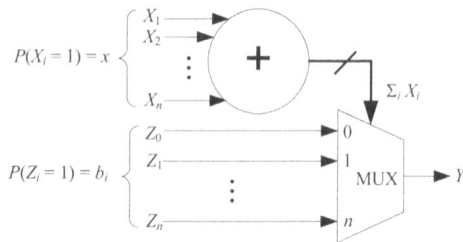

Figure 2: The stochastic computing core that implements a Bernstein polynomial $B_n(x) = \sum_{i=0}^{n} b_i B_{i,n}(x)$ with all the coefficients in the unit interval.

Given an arbitrary target function f, a Bernstein polynomial closest to f with all the coefficients in the unit interval is obtained by solving the following optimization problem on $b_0, \ldots, b_n$:

$$\text{minimize} \int_0^1 (f(x) - \sum_{i=0}^{n} b_i B_{i,n}(x))^2 \, \mathrm{d}x \qquad (1)$$

$$\text{subject to } 0 \le b_0, \ldots, b_n \le 1.$$

The computation of the target function f is realized by implementing the approximate Bernstein polynomial using the stochastic computing core.

2.2 Error Components of Stochastic Computation

The result of stochastic computation based on the Bernstein approximation is affected by two major error components — the approximation error and the error due to random fluctuation [4]. Since the stochastic computing core implements a Bernstein polynomial $B_n(x)$ which approximates the target function $f(x)$, we have the approximation error as $e_1 = |B_n(x) - f(x)|$.

The output of the stochastic computing core is a stochastic bit stream $(Y_1, \ldots, Y_N)$ of length N, where each Y_i is a random bit having probability $B_n(x)$ of being one. For this encoding mechanism, the final output of the stochastic computing core is

$$S = \frac{1}{N} \sum_{i=1}^{N} Y_i, \qquad (2)$$

which is a binomial random variable taking values from the set $\{0, \frac{1}{N}, \ldots, \frac{N-1}{N}, 1\}$. Therefore, although the output probability of the stochastic computing core is $B_n(x)$, the actual value encoded by the output bit stream is random and may not be equal to $B_n(x)$. The difference is $e_2 = |S - B_n(x)|$, which is an error due to random fluctuation.

The expectation of S, denoted as $E[S]$, and the variance of S, denoted as $Var(S)$, can be calculated as

$$E[S] = B_n(x), \quad Var[S] = \frac{B_n(x)(1 - B_n(x))}{N}. \qquad (3)$$

Since $Var[S] = E[(S - E[S])^2] = E[(S - B_n(x))^2]$, we have

$$E[e_2^2] = \frac{B_n(x)(1 - B_n(x))}{N}.$$

The overall error of stochastic computation is $e = |S - f(x)|$. It is bounded by the sum of the approximation error and the error due to random fluctuation:

$$e \le |S - B_n(x)| + |B_n(x) - f(x)| = e_1 + e_2.$$

2.3 Stochastic Computing System

Fig. 3 shows a stochastic computing system [4], which consists of the stochastic computing core and the input/output interface circuits. The circuit shown in the figure implements a Bernstein polynomial of degree 3. The input interface consists of uniform random number generators (URNGs) and comparators. The URNGs produce independent random numbers, which are fed into different comparators. As shown in the figure, the inputs to the adder are independent stochastic bit streams with the same probability to have a one. The multiplexer selects one of the numbers $b_0, \ldots, b_n$ represented in binary radix form. The output of the multiplexer is then compared with a random number to generate the output stochastic bit stream Y. Finally, a counter converts a stochastic bit stream into a binary radix number.

3. REDUCING THE APPROXIMATION ERROR THROUGH LINEAR TRANSFORMATION

The approach proposed in [4] requires the Bernstein polynomial to have all of its coefficients in the unit interval. Given this constraint, it is impossible to find a low degree Bernstein polynomial to approximate some target functions closely. For example, consider a target function $f(x) = 0.5\sin(8x) + 0.5$. If we set the degree to 6, by solving the

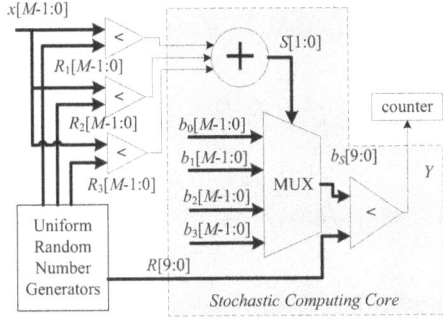

Figure 3: The stochastic computing system.

optimization problem in (1), we obtain a Bernstein polynomial with coefficients as $[b_0, b_1, b_2, b_3, b_4, b_5, b_6] = [0.735, 1, 0.832, 0, 0, 0.455, 1]$.

Fig. 4 shows the approximation effect, from which we can see that the approximation error is quite large. In the previous approach, in order to reduce the approximation error, a Bernstein polynomial with a higher degree is required. This causes a larger area for the stochastic computing system, since the area of the system increases with the degree.

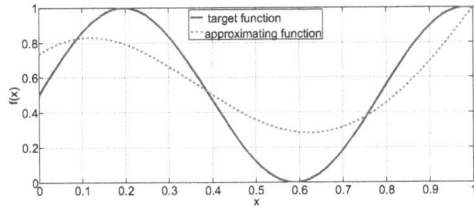

Figure 4: Approximating the target function $f(x) = 0.5\sin(8x) + 0.5$ **by the optimal Bernstein polynomial with all the coefficients in the unit interval.**

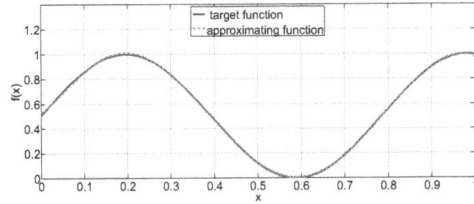

Figure 5: Approximating the target function $f(x) = 0.5\sin(8x) + 0.5$ **by the optimal unconstrained Bernstein polynomial.**

For the same target function $f(x) = 0.5\sin(8x) + 0.5$, if we remove the constraint on the Bernstein coefficients, we can obtain the coefficients of the optimal Bernstein polynomial approximation as $[b'_0, b'_1, b'_2, b'_3, b'_4, b'_5, b'_6] = [0.530, 0.905, 2.898, -2.415, -0.088, 1.193, 0.979]$. Its approximation effect is illustrated in Fig. 5. We can see that without the constraint on the Bernstein coefficients, we are able to find a very close Bernstein polynomial approximation to the target function. However, such a Bernstein polynomial cannot be implemented by the stochastic computing core. To reduce the approximation error while making the Bernstein polynomial suitable for stochastic implementation, we propose to change the target function through a linear transformation.

In our method, we use a linear transformation of the original function $g(x) = cf(x) + d$ as the target. The transforma-

tion parameters c and d are determined as follows: Suppose that the optimal *unconstrained* Bernstein polynomial that approximates $f(x)$ is $B_o(x) = \sum_{i=0}^{n} b_i B_{i,n}(x)$. We then select c and d so that for all $i = 0, \ldots, n$, $0 \le cb_i + d \le 1$.

Given $B_o(x)$ and the transformation parameters c and d, we use $B_g(x) = cB_o(x) + d$ to approximate the new target function $g(x)$. Based on the property that $\sum_{i=0}^{n} B_{i,n}(x) = 1$ [9], we have

$$B_g(x) = cB_o(x) + d = c\sum_{i=0}^{n} b_i B_{i,n}(x) + d\sum_{i=0}^{n} B_{i,n}(x)$$

$$= \sum_{i=0}^{n} (cb_i + d)B_{i,n}(x).$$

Thus, $B_g(x)$ is a Bernstein polynomial with coefficients $(cb_0 + d), \ldots, (cb_n + d)$. Based on our choice of c and d, all the coefficients of $B_g(x)$ are in the unit interval. Thus, we can implement $B_g(x)$ using the stochastic computing core. In the ideal situation where there is no error due to random fluctuation, the output S of the core is

$$S = B_g(x) \approx g(x) = cf(x) + d.$$

Thus, we can approximate the original function $f(x)$ from the output S using an inverse linear transformation $(S-d)/c$.

The above inverse linear transformation can be realized by replacing the final counter used in the stochastic computing system with an accumulator shown in Fig. 6. The signal Y shown in Fig. 3 is connected to the EN input of the accumulator.

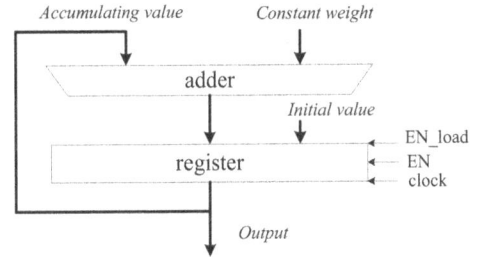

Figure 6: An accumulator for implementing the inverse linear transformation.

Assume that the length of the stochastic bit streams is N. Before the stochastic computing system starts, the signal EN_load is set to one and an initial value $-Nd/c$ is loaded into the register. For each clock cycle, if the signal Y shown in Fig. 3 is a one, then the signal EN is also a one. Then, the register will be updated with the sum of a constant weight $1/c$ and the previous value in the register. After N clock cycles, the final value in the register is

$$\frac{1}{c}\sum_{i=1}^{N} Y_i - N\frac{d}{c} \tag{4}$$

where Y_i is the i-th bit in the output bit stream Y. From Eq. (2) and (4), the final value is $N(S-d)/c$. If we choose length N to be a power of 2, then we can obtain the stochastic computing result $(S - d)/c$ by shifting the value in the register.

Using the linear transformation method, the *approximation error* is reduced. The approximation error is defined as the difference between $f(x)$ and the ideal output of the system (i.e., output result without considering the error due to random fluctuation), which is $(B_g(x) - d)/c$. Thus, the approximation error is

$$|f(x) - (B_g(x) - d)/c| = |f(x) - B_o(x)|.$$

Since $B_o(x)$ is the optimal unconstrained Bernstein polynomial to approximate $f(x)$, it gives the smallest approximation error $|f(x) - B_n(x)|$ among all Bernstein polynomials, including the one with all the coefficients in the unit interval that best approximates $f(x)$. Thus, using the proposed linear transformation technique, we can reduce the approximation error compared to the previous approach.

4. DETERMINING THE LINEAR TRANSFORMATION PARAMETERS TO MINIMIZE THE ERROR OF STOCHASTIC COMPUTATION

As we stated in Section 2.2, the result of the stochastic computation is also subject to error due to random fluctuation, which makes the output value of the stochastic computing core, S, different from the Bernstein polynomial after linear transformation, $B_g(x)$. As a result, the actual output of the system $(S - d)/c$ is different from its ideal output $(B_g(x) - d)/c$. The error caused by random fluctuation is $|S - B_g(x)|/c$. To make this error small, c should be large. However, a large c will not help reduce the approximation error. Thus, to minimize the overall error, we need to choose a proper c. In this section, we propose a mathematical formulation to find the optimal choice of the linear transformation parameters c and d to minimize the overall error of stochastic computation.

4.1 Formulation of the Optimization Problem

To indicate that the actual output S of the stochastic computing core is related to the input x, we will rewrite S as $S(x)$. The final output of the system is $(S(x) - d)/c$. For a given x, the overall computation error is

$$e(x) = \left| \frac{S(x) - d}{c} - f(x) \right|. \tag{5}$$

To measure the average error of stochastic computation for all $x \in [0,1]$, we use the square of the L^2-norm of the function $e(x)$:

$$T = \int_0^1 e(x)^2 \, dx. \tag{6}$$

Since T is a random variable, we use the expectation on T, represented as $E[T]$, as a measure of the error of the stochastic computation. Our target is to find c and d to minimize $E[T]$. From Eq. (5) and (6), we have

$$E[T] = E\left[\int_0^1 \left(\frac{S(x) - d}{c} - f(x) \right)^2 dx \right].$$

Define

$$U = \frac{S(x) - B_g(x)}{c}, \quad V = \frac{B_g(x) - d}{c} - f(x),$$

where $B_g(x)$ is the Bernstein polynomial implemented by the stochastic computing core. Note that U is a random variable and V is a deterministic value. Thus, we have

$$E[T] = E\left[\int_0^1 (U + V)^2 \, dx \right]$$
$$= \int_0^1 \left(E[U^2] + 2VE[U] + V^2 \right) dx. \tag{7}$$

From Eq. (3), we have

$$E[S(x)] = B_g(x), \ E[(S(x) - B_g(x))^2] = \frac{B_g(x)(1 - B_g(x))}{N}.$$

Given the above two equations, we could further simplify Eq. (7) as

$$E[T] = \int_0^1 \frac{B_g(x)(1 - B_g(x))}{c^2 N} \, dx$$
$$+ \int_0^1 \frac{(B_g(x) - cf(x) - d)^2}{c^2} \, dx. \tag{8}$$

Eq. (8) shows how the parameters c and d affect our error measurement $E[T]$. From that equation, we can see that the value of $E[T]$ also depends on the Bernstein polynomial $B_g(x)$, or more specifically, its Bernstein coefficients. However, with c and d not known yet, we do not know $B_g(x)$ neither. Thus, we will also treat the coefficients of $B_g(x)$ as unknowns. Suppose that the Bernstein polynomial $B_g(x)$ of degree n is

$$B_g(x) = \sum_{i=0}^n b_i B_{i,n}(x).$$

Our target is to find a set of values $b_0, b_1, \ldots, b_n, d, c$ to minimize the objective function (8). Note that $b_0, \ldots, b_n$ should satisfy the constraint that $0 \le b_i \le 1$ for all $i = 0, \ldots, n$.

4.2 Solution of the Optimization Problem

In this section, we will show how to transform the optimization problem into a standard quadratic programming problem. For this purpose, we first define the following new variables

$$b_i^* = \frac{1}{c} b_i, \text{ for } i = 0, \ldots, n \tag{9}$$

$$c^* = \frac{1}{c}, d^* = \frac{d}{c}. \tag{10}$$

Define

$$B_g^*(x) = \sum_{i=0}^n b_i^* B_{i,n}(x). \tag{11}$$

Then, $B_g^*(x) = \frac{1}{c} B_g(x)$. We can rewrite objective function (8) as

$$E[T] = \int_0^1 \frac{B_g^*(x)(c^* - B_g^*(x))}{N} \, dx$$
$$+ \int_0^1 (B_g^*(x) - f(x) - d^*)^2 \, dx. \tag{12}$$

Now our target is to find a set of values $b_0^*, \ldots, b_n^*, d^*, c^*$ to minimize the objective function (12).

By substituting (11) into (12) and expanding (12), we can rewrite the objective function as

$$f_{obj}(\mathbf{z}) = \frac{1}{2} \mathbf{z}^T \mathbf{H} \mathbf{z} + \mathbf{c}^T \mathbf{z} + \int_0^1 f^2(x) \, dx, \tag{13}$$

where

$$\mathbf{z} = [b_0^*, \ldots, b_n^*, d^*, c^*]^T, \mathbf{c} = [c_1, c_2]^T, \mathbf{H} = \begin{bmatrix} H_1 & H_2 \\ H_2^T & H_3 \end{bmatrix}$$

with

$$c_1 = \left[-2 \int_0^1 f(x) B_{0,n}(x)\, dx, \ldots, -2 \int_0^1 f(x) B_{n,n}(x)\, dx\right],$$

$$c_2 = \left[2 \int_0^1 f(x)\, dx, 0\right]$$

$$H_1 = \frac{2(N-1)}{N} H_1',$$

$$H_1' =$$

$$\begin{bmatrix} \int_0^1 B_{0,n}(x) B_{0,n}(x) dx & \cdots & \int_0^1 B_{0,n}(x) B_{n,n}(x) dx \\ \int_0^1 B_{1,n}(x) B_{0,n}(x) dx & \cdots & \int_0^1 B_{1,n}(x) B_{n,n}(x) dx \\ \vdots & \ddots & \vdots \\ \int_0^1 B_{n,n}(x) B_{0,n}(x) dx & \cdots & \int_0^1 B_{n,n}(x) B_{n,n}(x) dx \end{bmatrix},$$

$$H_2 = \begin{bmatrix} -2 \int_0^1 B_{0,n}(x) dx & \frac{1}{N} \int_0^1 B_{0,n}(x) dx \\ \vdots & \vdots \\ -2 \int_0^1 B_{n,n}(x) dx & \frac{1}{N} \int_0^1 B_{n,n}(x) dx \end{bmatrix},$$

$$H_3 = \begin{bmatrix} 2 & 0 \\ 0 & 0 \end{bmatrix}.$$

Note that $\mathbf{c}$ and $\mathbf{H}$ in Eq. (13) are all known matrices. The original set of constraints that $0 \le b_i \le 1$, for $i = 0, \ldots, n$, is now transformed into a new set of constraints on b_i^* and c^* as

$$0 \le b_i^* \le \frac{1}{c} = c^*, \text{ for } i = 0, \ldots, n. \qquad (14)$$

By now, we have transformed the problem of minimizing the error of stochastic computation to finding a set of values $b_0^*, \ldots, b_n^*, c^*, d^*$ to minimize the objective function (13) subject to the constraint (14). This is a standard quadratic programming problem and can be solved using standard techniques. Once we obtain the optimal solution, we can get the optimal Bernstein coefficients $b_0, \ldots, b_n$ and the optimal linear transformation parameters c and d based on Eq. (9) and (10).

5. EXPERIMENTAL RESULTS

We performed experiments on five test functions shown in Table 1 to study the effect of the proposed linear transformation technique. For each test function, we can find an unconstrained Bernstein polynomial of degree 6 to approximate it very closely. However, for the first four functions, if we approximate them by Bernstein polynomials with coefficients in the unit interval, we need polynomials of degree at least 12 to get a close approximation. For Test5, we can still find a degree 6 Bernstein polynomial with all the coefficients in the unit interval to approximate it closely. Test5 was used here to show that our method takes the previous method as a special case. For all the experiments, we fixed the length of the stochastic bit streams N as 1024.

Table 1: Five test functions used in our experiments.

Test1	$0.5 \sin(8x) + 0.5$
Test2	$1 - 4(x - 0.5)^2$
Test3	$4x^2 \log(x + 0.1) + 0.53$
Test4	$59.2x^4 - 118.7x^3 + 74.9x^2 - 15.4x + 1$
Test5	e^{-3x}

5.1 Error of Stochastic Computation

In this section, we studied the computation error of the system designed using our method. We used the first four

test functions as the targets. Since an unconstrained Bernstein polynomial of degree 6 can approximate each test function very closely, we chose the degree of $B_g(x)$ as 6. For each test function, we solved the quadratic programming problem proposed in Section 4.2 and obtained the optimal choice of $B_g(x)$ and the linear transformation parameters c and d. The parameters c and d for the four test functions are listed in Table 2.

Table 2: Linear transformation parameters c and d for the first four test functions.

	Test1	Test2	Test3	Test4
c	0.405	0.893	0.961	0.308
d	0.379	0	0.039	0.538

With these design parameters, we simulated our stochastic computing system to obtain the computation error. For each function, we obtained computation errors for 101 inputs $x = 0, 0.01, \ldots, 1$. For each function and each input x, we simulated the stochastic computing system 100 times. We then averaged the errors for these 100 simulations. Finally, for each function, we averaged the errors over all input points.

For comparison purpose, we also simulated the system designed using the previous method [4]. The system was designed based on a Bernstein polynomial of degree 6, but with all the coefficients in the unit interval. We obtained its computation error in the same way as above.

The errors of the two methods for each test function are listed in Table 3. We can see that when the degrees of the Bernstein polynomials implemented by the two systems are the same, the proposed method reduces the computation error significantly in comparison with the previous method.

Table 3: Average error of the proposed method and the previous method [4].

	Test1	Test2	Test3	Test4
proposed method	0.0396	0.0128	0.0103	0.0422
method in [4]	0.1539	0.0354	0.0251	0.1959

5.2 Hardware Cost

In this section, we studied the hardware cost of the proposed stochastic computing system. Still, we used the first four test functions as the targets.

The previous stochastic computing system is shown in Fig. 3. The proposed system is similar, but with the final counter replaced by the accumulator shown in Fig. 6. We used linear feedback shift registers (LFSR) as URNGs. The precision M of the binary radix numbers was chosen as 10. In order to count the number of ones in a stream of 1024 bits, the counter in the previous system has 10 bits. The accumulator in our system works on binary numbers with 10 and 6 bits before and after the binary point, respectively.

We fixed the degree of the Bernstein polynomial used in the proposed system as 6. For the previous system, we manually adjusted the degree n of the Bernstein polynomial until the system produces an average error close to that of the proposed system. The degrees n we obtained are listed in the second row of Table 4.

With the above design parameters, we used the Synopsys Design Compiler [10] to synthesize the two systems and evaluate their areas. The designs were mapped to the Nangate FreePDK45 library [11]. The area of each system for each test function is listed in Table 4. We also showed the percentage of area saving of the proposed system over the previous system. We can see that for these four test functions, when the amount of computation errors are close, the proposed method produces a system with smaller area than the previous system.

Table 4: The degree of the Bernstein polynomial required by the method [4] in order to achieve close error to our proposed method, the areas for the two systems, and the percentage of area saving of the proposed system.

		Test1	Test2	Test3	Test4
degree of Bernstein polynomial in [4]		17	14	12	17
area (μm^2)	method in [4]	1497	1266	1136	1497
	proposed method	775			
area saving (%)		48.2	38.8	31.8	48.2

The proposed system replaces the counter in the previous system with an accumulator, which has a larger area than the counter. Therefore, when the degrees of the Bernstein polynomials implemented by the two systems are the same, the proposed system has a larger hardware cost. In order to determine when our proposed design will have advantage in area over the previous design, we further used Design Compiler to synthesize the two stochastic computing systems for different degrees of the Bernstein polynomials. Fig. 7 plots the areas of the two systems versus degrees. We performed linear regression on each set of points and obtain a linear relation between the circuit area a and the degree d. The relations for the proposed method and the previous method are shown by Eq. (15) and (16), respectively.

$$a_1 = 75.9d_1 + 319.2. \quad (15)$$
$$a_2 = 75.9d_2 + 204.1. \quad (16)$$

When the area of the proposed system is smaller than that of the previous system, i.e., $a_1 \leq a_2$, we have $d_2 - d_1 \geq 1.52$. Therefore, if the degree of the Bernstein polynomial required by the previous method is larger than the degree required by the proposed method by 2, the proposed method is more area efficient.

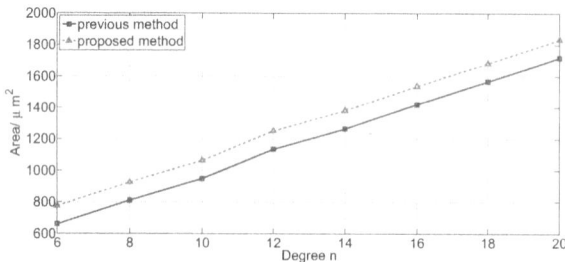

Figure 7: The areas of the proposed system and the previous system for implementing Bernstein polynomials with different degrees.

5.3 The Relation between the Proposed Method and the Previous Method [4]

In this section, we took Test5 as the target function and implement it using the proposed technique. Note that Test5 can be approximated closely by a degree 6 Bernstein polynomial with all the coefficients in the unit interval. In the proposed technique, we chose the degree of $B_g(x)$ as 6. After solving the quadratic programming problem shown in Section 4.2, we obtained the optimal linear transformation parameters as $c = 1$ and $d = 0$. This means that there is no

linear transformation needed in order to implement Test5. Therefore, the system synthesized by the proposed method essentially degenerates to the system synthesized by the previous method [4]. This indicates that our method takes the previous method as a special case.

6. CONCLUSION AND DISCUSSION

In this paper, we proposed a technique using linear transformation to synthesize stochastic computing systems. We formulated an optimization problem to find the best linear transformation parameters to reduce the overall computation error. The design technique is effective to those functions which cannot be approximated closely by a Bernstein polynomial with all the coefficients in the unit interval. Compared with the previous method without linear transformation, our method could reduce the computation error as well as the circuit area.

The proposed technique performs the final inverse linear transformation through an accumulator, which converts the output stochastic bit stream into a binary radix number. Thus, the proposed system is applicable when the final result of the stochastic computation should be encoded in binary radix form.

The proposed linear transformation technique is applied in the context of the Bernstein polynomial-based synthesis approach. However, we believe that the technique can also be applied to the finite state machine (FSM)-based approach introduced in [6]. The details will be studied in our future work.

Acknowledgement

This work is supported by National Natural Science Foundation of China (NSFC) under Grant No. 61204042.

7. REFERENCES

[1] B. Gaines, "Stochastic computing systems," in *Advances in Information Systems Science*. Plenum, 1969, vol. 2, ch. 2, pp. 37–172.

[2] B. Brown and H. Card, "Stochastic neural computation I: Computational elements," *IEEE Transactions on Computers*, vol. 50, no. 9, pp. 891–905, 2001.

[3] S. Toral, J. Quero, and L. Franquelo, "Stochastic pulse coded arithmetic," in *International Symposium on Circuits and Systems*, vol. 1, 2000, pp. 599–602.

[4] W. Qian, X. Li, M. Riedel, K. Bazargan, and D. Lilja, "An architecture for fault-tolerant computation with stochastic logic," *IEEE Transactions on Computers*, vol. 60, no. 1, pp. 93–105, 2011.

[5] P. Li and D. Lilja, "Using stochastic computing to implement digital image processing algorithms," in *International Conference on Computer Design*, 2011, pp. 154–161.

[6] P. Li, D. Lilja, W. Qian, K. Bazargan, and M. Riedel, "The synthesis of complex arithmetic computation on stochastic bit streams using sequential logic," in *International Conference on Computer-Aided Design*, 2012, pp. 480–487.

[7] A. Alaghi and J. Hayes, "A spectral transform approach to stochastic circuits," in *International Conference on Computer Design*, 2012, pp. 315–321.

[8] G. Lorentz, *Bernstein Polynomials*. University of Toronto Press, 1953.

[9] R. Farouki and V. Rajan, "On the numerical condition of polynomials in Bernstein form," *Computer Aided Geometric Design*, vol. 4, no. 3, pp. 191–216, 1987.

[10] *Design Compiler*, Synopsys Inc.

[11] *Nangate FreePDK45 library*, Silicon Integration Initiative, Inc.

Experimental Validation of a Faithful Binary Circuit Model

Robert Najvirt
ECS group, TU Wien
rnajvirt@ecs.tuwien.ac.at

Matthias Függer
MPI-INF
mfuegger@mpi-inf.mpg.de

Thomas Nowak
ENS Paris
thomas.nowak@ens.fr

Ulrich Schmid
ECS group, TU Wien
s@ecs.tuwien.ac.at

Michael Hofbauer
Inst. EMCE, TU Wien
michael.hofbauer@tuwien.ac.at

Kurt Schweiger
Avago Technologies
kurt.schweiger@avagotech.com

ABSTRACT

Fast digital timing simulations based on continuous-time, digital-value circuit models are an attractive and heavily used alternative to analog simulations. Models based on analytic delay formulas are particularly interesting here, as they also facilitate formal verification and delay bound synthesis of complex circuits.

Recently, Függer et al. (arXiv:1406.2544 [cs.OH]) proposed a circuit model based on so-called involution channels. It is the first binary circuit model that *realistically* captures solvability of short-pulse filtration, a non-trivial glitch propagation problem related to building one-shot inertial delays.

In this work, we address the question of whether involution channels also *accurately* model the delay of real circuits. Using both Spice simulations and physical measurements, we confirm that modeling an inverter chain by involution channels accurately describes reality. We also demonstrate that transitions in vanishing pulse trains are accurately predicted by the involution model. For our Spice simulations, we used both UMC-90 and UMC-65 technology, with varying supply voltages from nominal down to near sub-threshold range. The measurements were performed on a special-purpose UMC-90 ASIC that combines an inverter chain with low-intrusive high-speed on-chip analog amplifiers.

1. INTRODUCTION

Modern digital circuit design relies heavily on fast timing analysis techniques. In contrast to fully-fledged analog simulations, using Spice [1], for example, which are based on detailed analog models of all elements of a digital standard-cell library, several state-of-the-art tools use less detailed component models to speed-up simulation times. For example, the Synopsis CCS Timing model [2] characterizes the delay of a cell via input/output current waveforms given in tabular form, depending on parameters such as input slew rate and output capacitive load.

This research was partially funded by the Austrian Science Fund (FWF) projects SIC (P26436) and Rise (S11405).

GLSVLSI'15, May 20–22, 2015, Pittsburgh, PA, USA.
ACM 978-1-4503-3474-7/15/05.
http://dx.doi.org/10.1145/2742060.2742081.

Whereas such models facilitate a very *accurate* and reasonably fast timing simulation and functional correctness verification of a given circuit design, they are not suited for gaining a deeper understanding of the timing behavior of a complex circuit, its dependence on various parameters, and general performance and correctness characterizations of classes of circuits. To be more specific, consider some input-to-output delay characteristics Δ of a complex circuit, which typically depends on the input-to-output delay characteristics $\delta_1, \ldots, \delta_k$ of the constituent cells.

Determining Δ with empiric tabular-based delay models like the CCS Timing model inevitably introduces interpolation errors, discontinuities, cutoffs of unbounded function values, etc., which may not only lead to quantitatively wrong results, but may also predict qualitatively wrong circuit behaviors. Moreover, this approach admits only numerical solution methods for computing, e.g., fixed points in case of feedback-loops (see below).

A designer who tries to meet constraints on Δ thus would greatly benefit from having an accurate *analytic* expression $\Delta = f(\delta_1, \ldots, \delta_k)$ in terms of the constituent delays, which is sufficiently simple to highlight dependencies and may even facilitate a formal characterization of the solution space for Δ. This is particularly true at early design stages, where such knowledge may guide the search for alternative architectural designs.

As a long-term goal of our research, we hence target an *analytic framework* for the timing and correctness analysis of complex digital circuits. Such a framework, supported by tools, would not only allow for accurate performance and even power estimation [3, 4] at early design stages, but also pave the way to a thorough formal verification of a complex circuit's correctness. After all, a key concern for the latter is the detection of potential race conditions and hazardous glitches, which rests upon a rigorous timing analysis.

It is important to note, though, that statements about the correctness of a circuit *in a model* are meaningful only if they also imply correctness of the corresponding *real* circuit implementation. We hence call a model *realistic*, if a given problem can be solved in the model if and only if it can be solved by a real circuit, and *faithful* if it is both realistic and provides accurate timing predictions. Obviously, our ultimate target is a faithful analytic circuit model.

Unfortunately, determining analytic expressions for Δ, not to speak of characterizing its solution space, is complicated by the fact that the delay δ_i of a circuit's component i may depend on its input history and, hence, on the way it is used

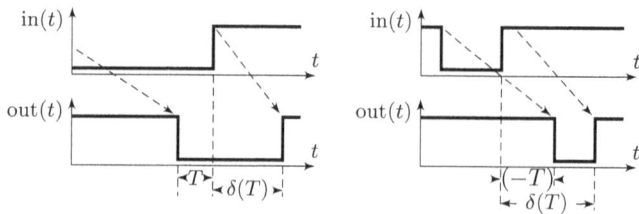

Figure 1: Left: Input/output signal of a single-history channel, involving the input-to-previous-output delay T and the resulting output-to-input delay $\delta(T)$. Right: Input transition with $T < 0$.

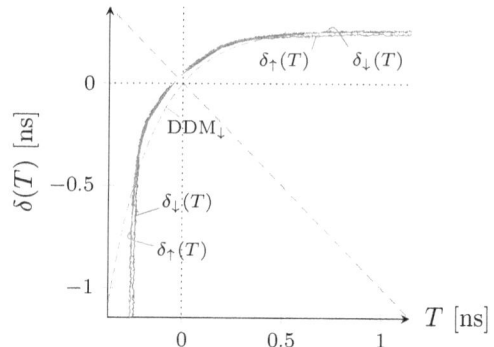

Figure 2: Measured $\delta_\downarrow$ (blue) and $\delta_\uparrow$ (red) for UMC-90 inverter chain for $V_{DD} = 0.6$ V, which support the involution hypothesis. By contrast, there is no perfect fit for the exponential DDM delay function (dashed green).

within the circuit. Even worse, in case of circuits involving feedback loops, computing Δ may involve solving a fixed-point problem, as δ_i may in fact depend on (the history of) Δ. Developing an analytic timing framework for complex circuits is hence a major challenge.

Particularly interesting for complex circuits are models that involve only discrete-valued, typically binary, continuous-time signals, as they facilitate a purely digital analysis framework. For example, the circuit model introduced in [5] combines zero-time Boolean gates with *single-history channels* that model circuit delays. Such channels are primarily characterized by a delay function δ that maps a transition occurring at the channel input at time t to its corresponding output transition at time $t + \delta(T)$, where T is the input-to-previous-output delay. Fig. 1 shows two examples. Note that single-history channels do not only allow to model decaying pulse propagation, but also vanishing pulses: If two succeeding input transitions would, according to $\delta(T)$, occur at the output in reversed order, they cancel each other. Further, single-history channels allow for different rising and falling transition delays, specified by two delay functions $\delta_\uparrow$ and $\delta_\downarrow$, respectively. Well-known instances of single-history channels are *pure* or *inertial delay* channels [6]; a more advanced example is the *Delay Degradation Model* (DDM) [7, 8] by Bellido-Díaz et al.

In [5], it was formally proved that no *bounded* single-history channel (i.e., where δ is also bounded from below) can be realistic, and hence faithful: For the simple *Short-Pulse Filtration* (SPF) problem, which is related to a circuit's ability to suppress a single glitch, the authors showed that every bounded single-history channel either contradicts the unsolvability of SPF in bounded time or the solvability of SPF in unbounded time in physical circuits.

In [9], however, Függer et al. provided what seems to be the first candidate for a realistic circuit model: It is based on *involution channels*, which are single-history channels with delay functions that are not bounded from below. Due to a continuity property of an involution channel output with respect to the presence of glitches at the input, which is due to the involution property, they proved that SPF can be solved precisely when this is possible with physical circuits.

Major contributions: The purpose of this paper is to experimentally explore the applicability of the involution model with respect to modern VLSI circuits. Our primary target is a chain of inverters, which allows to track the reshaping of pulse trains along the inverter stages. In order to extend the generality of our experimental results, we consider both two different VLSI technologies (UMC-65 nm and UMC-90 nm) as well as different supply voltages (from nom-

inal down to close to the sub-threshold regime, which causes the delays to increase). Moreover, as we operate our inverter chains at their speed limits, we also employed dedicated experiments to validate the accuracy of (part of) our Spice simulations. For our validation measurements, we used a custom UMC-90 ASIC [10] containing an inverter chain monitored by low-intrusive high-speed on-chip analog amplifiers attached to a high-speed real-time oscilloscope. Comparing the measurement results with corresponding simulations (using the post-layout netlists extracted from the ASIC design) indeed showed a very good match.

Our experiments have been used to validate the following two features of the involution model:

(*Involution property*) By using input pulses of decreasing width, we empirically determine $\delta_\uparrow$ and $\delta_\downarrow$ for a single inverter. The resulting graphs for a supply voltage of $V_{DD} = 0.6$ V are depicted in Fig. 2. The involution property $-\delta_\downarrow(-\delta_\uparrow(T)) = T$ [9] has been used to extrapolate the functions' values for small T that do not allow direct delay measurements. The graphs support our claim that real delay functions are well approximated by involutions. By contrast, the exponential delay function of the DDM [8] is not an involution and cannot be fit to the experimental data over the whole range of T.

(*Good accuracy*) Using representative examples of pulse trains, we show that the involution model with the empirically determined $\delta_\uparrow$ and $\delta_\downarrow$ provides very good accuracy. We provide an explicit simulation algorithm for this purpose, which has also been implemented in ModelSim and thus allows timing simulations in our model. Fig. 3 shows an example pulse train (analog) together with the digital predictions from both the involution model and the DDM. We can see that the DDM both overly decays some short pulses (cp. the pulse at $t = 4$ ns in the middle waveform) and produces spurious pulses (bottom waveform at $t = 12$ ns).

2. RELATED WORK

Whereas there is a wealth of research devoted to the analog modeling of digital circuits (see [1, 11, 12, 13, 14] for a few references), none addressed the issue of characterizing delay functions with respect to solvability of problems. To the best of our knowledge, Függer et al. [9] have been the first to do so. As an underpinning of their involution model, they showed that, for any pair of involution delay functions

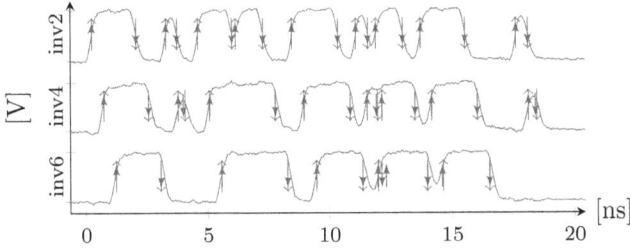

Figure 3: Measured waveform (solid) for the UMC-90 inverter chain, along with the corresponding predictions according to the involution model (red long up/down-arrows) ($\uparrow\downarrow$) and the DDM (blue short up/down arrows) ($\uparrow\downarrow$).

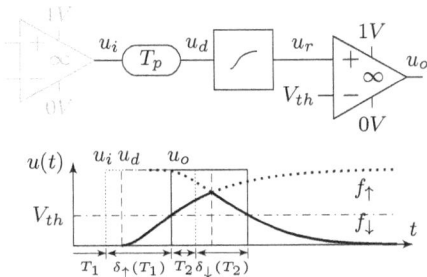

Figure 4: Simple analog channel model.

$\delta_\uparrow$, $\delta_\downarrow$, there are matching analog channel models consisting of a pure delay component with delay T_p, a slew-rate limiter with generalized switching waveforms $f_\uparrow$ and $f_\downarrow$, and a comparator with threshold V_{th}, as shown in Fig. 4.

On the other hand, digital circuit models have been proposed as a general approach for modeling asynchronous sequential switching circuits long time ago: Unger [6] introduced the well-known pure and inertial delay channels, which have been heavily used both in research and in industrial timing simulators. Bellido-Díaz et al. [8] proposed the PID model, and justified its appropriateness both analytically and by comparing model predictions against Spice simulations. In [15], the PID model (now called *Delay Degradation Model* DDM) was generalized from inverters to (N)AND and (N)OR gates. In the meantime, thanks to considerable efforts like [16, 15] spent on the question of how to extract the DDM model parameters from technology parameters, the DDM model has already made its way into digital timing analysis tools [7].

3. MODEL DESCRIPTION AND SIMULATION ALGORITHM

In this section, we briefly survey the cornerstones of the involution model and provide an explicit simulation algorithm, which iteratively constructs the execution, i.e., the traces of all signals, of a given circuit and trace of its inputs.

3.1 General model and simulation algorithm

The involution model rests on a binary-value continuous-time signal model. The state transitions of a signal are identified by *events* (t, x), where t is the event's time and x is the signal's new value. All state transition times are non-negative, but every signal has an initial value that is set at time $t = -\infty$. A signal can hence be represented by a (fi-

Algorithm 1 Initialization of the simulation algorithm

1: **for all** input ports I **do**
2: $\quad$ Pending(I) $\leftarrow$ Events(I); Events(I) $\leftarrow \emptyset$
3: **end for**
4: **for all** gates B **do**
5: $\quad (C_1, \ldots, C_d) \leftarrow$ Incoming(B)
6: $\quad i \leftarrow B\big(\text{Init}(C_1), \ldots, \text{Init}(C_d)\big)$
7: $\quad$ add $(-\infty, i)$ to Events(B)
8: **end for**
9: **for all** channels (B_1, B_2) **do**
10: $\quad$ Last(B_1, B_2) $\leftarrow (-\infty, \text{Init}((B_1, B_2)))$
11: $\quad$ add Last(B_1, B_2) to Events((B_1, B_2))
12: $\quad$ **if** Init(B_1) $\neq$ Init((B_1, B_2)) **then**
13: $\quad\quad$ add $(0, \text{Init}(B_1))$ to Pending((B_1, B_2))
14: $\quad$ **end if**
15: **end for**

nite or infinite) sequence of events with increasing times and alternating values, whose first event is at time $-\infty$.

A circuit is a directed graph consisting of vertices that are either *input ports* or zero-time Boolean *gates*, and edges that are *channels*. Input ports have no incoming channels, every gate is assigned a Boolean function whose arity is equal to the number of its incoming edges. A gate can be declared to also form an *output port*, although they do not receive special treatment. Every channel is assigned a pair $(\delta_\uparrow, \delta_\downarrow)$ of delay functions; one for rising and one for falling transitions. Both gates and channels have a Boolean initial value.

The simulation algorithm takes as input a time T up to which the circuit should be simulated, and a sequence of events Events(I) up to time T for every input port I. Its output are sequences of events Events(C) for every component C (gate or channel) output of the circuit.

During the execution of the algorithm, it distinguishes *pending* and *fixed* events. Pending events are stored in the variable Pending(C), while fixed ones are transferred to Events(C). We write Incoming(B) for the ordered tuple of incoming edges of gate B and Delay(B_1, B_2) for the pair of delay functions of channel (B_1, B_2). Further, each channel (B_1, B_2) stores its last generated output event, whether it is canceled or not, in Last(B_1, B_2). We write Init(C) for the initial value of component C and we use the symbol f_B for the Boolean function of gate B.

Algorithm 1 performs the initializations needed for the following iterations of the simulation algorithm. Note that lines 12–14 produce a channel input event at time $t = 0$ if the initial values of a gate and an outgoing channel mismatch.

The main simulation algorithm is given in Algorithm 2. It uses function Latest(C, t) for a vertex (component) C and a time t, which is equal to the Boolean value of the most recent event for vertex C before or at time t. Note that both fixed and pending events are considered for Latest(C, t) and in line 14. When the loop terminates, the variables Events(C) contain the event sequences up to time T for all vertices C.

The algorithm proceeds by looking at the earliest pending events, declaring them as fixed, and propagating their effect to the other vertices via the channels. We highlight two noteworthy properties of the algorithm: (a) The delay $\delta(T)$ is a function of the input-to-previous output delay $T = t - t'$ (see line 15). (b) A pending output event of a channel is removed if a later input event causes an output event that occurs earlier (code line 17). In this case, the two events cancel at the channel output (pulse cancellation).

We implemented a custom VHDL involution channel module based on this simulation algorithm in Mentor Graphics

Algorithm 2 Timing prediction algorithm until time T

1: **while** there is a pending event at a time $\leq T$ **do**
2:   $t \leftarrow$ earliest time of a pending event
3:   **for all** comp. C with a pending event (t, x) at time t **do**
4:     move (t, x) from Pending(C) to Events(C)
5:   **end for**
6:   **for all** gates B **do**
7:     $(C_1, \ldots, C_d) \leftarrow$ Incoming(B)
8:     $v \leftarrow f_B\big(\text{Latest}(C_1, t), \ldots, \text{Latest}(C_d, t)\big)$
9:     add (t, v) to Events(B) if $v \neq \text{Latest}(B, t)$
10:   **end for**
11:   **for all** channels (B_1, B_2) **do**
12:     $(\delta_\uparrow, \delta_\downarrow) \leftarrow$ Delay(B_1, B_2)
13:     **if** $\exists$ an event (t, x) in Events(B_1) at time t **then**
14:       $(t', x') \leftarrow$ Last(B_1, B_2)
15:       $\delta \leftarrow \delta_\uparrow(t - t')$ if $x = 1$ and $\delta \leftarrow \delta_\downarrow(t - t')$ otherwise
16:       Last(B_1, B_2) $\leftarrow (t + \delta, x)$
17:       **if** $t + \delta \leq t'$ **then**
18:         remove (t', x') from Pending((B_1, B_2))
19:       **else**
20:         add $(t + \delta, x)$ to Pending((B_1, B_2))
21:       **end if**
22:     **end if**
23:   **end for**
24: **end while**

ModelSim, which thereby supports digital timing simulations in the involution model.

3.2 Involution Channels

An involution channel is a channel whose pair of delay functions $(\delta_\downarrow, \delta_\uparrow)$ satisfies the following properties: Each delay function is defined on an open unbounded interval of the form $(z, +\infty)$ with $z \in \mathbb{R}$. The delay functions $\delta_\downarrow(T)$ and $\delta_\uparrow(T)$ are strictly increasing, concave, differentiable, and bounded as $T \to \infty$. Both $-\delta_\uparrow\big(-\delta_\downarrow(T)\big) = T$ and $-\delta_\downarrow\big(-\delta_\uparrow(T)\big) = T$ for all T in the respective domains. The domains are maximal in the sense that neither $\delta_\uparrow$ nor $\delta_\downarrow$ is bounded from below.

An involution channel is called *strictly causal* if $\delta_\downarrow(0) > 0$. By the above properties, this is equivalent to $\delta_\uparrow(0) > 0$.

Geometrically speaking, the properties for an involution channel say that $\delta_\uparrow$ is equal to $\delta_\downarrow$ reflected over the line $y = -x$. The defining property for strict causality means that the two curves meet in the second quadrant ($x \leq 0$, $y \geq 0$), at some point $(-\delta_{\min}, \delta_{\min})$ that gives the minimal delay $\delta_{\min}$ by which a non-canceled transition is propagated; Fig. 2 shows an example.

Függer et al. [9] proved that the simulation algorithm terminates with a unique, consistent collection of event sequences if all channels are strictly causal involution channels.

4. EXPERIMENTAL SETUP

The target of all our experiments is an inverter chain, which is a natural choice for validating involution channels. We consider two different bulk CMOS implementation technologies, namely, UMC-90 nm and UMC-65 nm. For UMC-65, we resorted to Spice simulations of a 7-stage inverter chain from a standard cell library. In case of UMC-90, we relied on a custom ASIC described in [10], which has been developed for on-chip measurements of single-event transient pulse shapes in VLSI circuits. It provides a 7-stage inverter chain built from 700 nm x 80 nm (W x L) pMOS and 360 nm x 80 nm nMOS transistors, with threshold voltages 0.29 V and 0.26 V, respectively, and a nominal supply voltage of

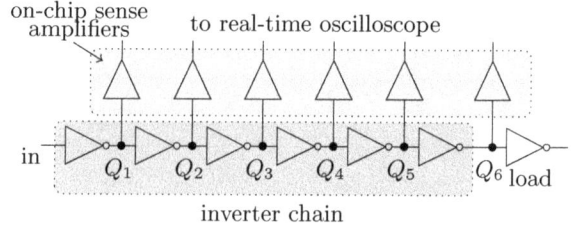

Figure 5: Schematics of the ASIC used for validation measurements. It combines an inverter chain with analog high-speed sense amplifiers.

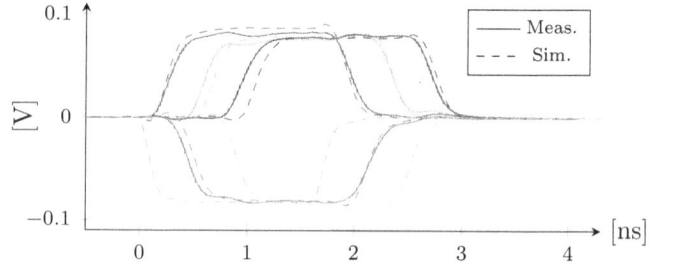

Figure 6: Measured (solid) vs. simulated (dashed) waveforms at Q_1, Q_3, Q_5 (bottom, shifted by $-V_{DD}$) and Q_2, Q_4, Q_6 (top), for $V_{DD} = 0.6$ V. Note the amplifier gain of 0.15.

$V_{DD} = 1$ V. Detailed post-layout simulation models for the entire circuit are also available.

What makes this ASIC an ideal target for our experiments is the fact that all inverter outputs are connected to on-chip low-intrusive high-speed analog sense amplifiers, as shown in Fig. 5. As the amplifiers can drive the 50 Ω input of a high-speed real-time oscilloscope, they allow faithful analog recording of the output signal waveforms. The amplifiers have a measured gain of 0.15 with an overall -3 dB cutoff frequency of approximately 8.5 GHz, and constitute an additional (low) load approximately equivalent to 3 inverter inputs. Independent power supplies and grounds for inverters and amplifiers facilitate measurements with different digital supply voltages V_{DD}. According to [10], extensive simulations and measurements have revealed excellent measurement accuracy (within the linear bandwidth of the amplifiers).

The availability of both the ASIC and the corresponding post-layout simulation model allowed us to validate our simulation results: Given that we operate the inverters at their bandwidth limits, it is important to make sure that they indeed match reality.

For our measurements, we bonded the ASIC directly to an RF-substrate PCB (Rogers RO 4350), which routes the pins to dedicated SMP connectors. The PCB with the ASIC itself is mounted on a Peltier-cooled copper heat sink, which guarantees a stable operating temperature. In our final measurement setup, four high-performance RF cables of identical length connect the SMP outputs of the amplifiers attached to inverters 2,3,4, and 6 to the inputs of a 4-channel 12 GHz Tektronix TDS 6154B real-time oscilloscope, which records the waveforms with a sampling rate of 20 GS/s. The input of the first inverter is directly driven by a 3.35 GHz Agilent 81134A pulse/pattern generator. The entire setup was optimized to minimize distortions of the pulse shapes.

Validation measurements have been conducted for digital supply voltages in the range $V_{DD} \in \{0.3 \ldots 1\}$ V, which result in inverter output waveforms within the linear operation range of the sense amplifiers. In order to "hide" the much better driving capabilities of the pulse generator, we only considered inverters 3–6 in our measurements, that is, the output of inverter 2 was considered as the actual input of the chain. Note that the output bias due to AC coupling and the gain of the sense amplifiers had to be compensated when evaluating our results; the (identical) amplifier and cable delays automatically cancel out for stage to stage delay measurements.

The comparison of the measured waveforms with the ones obtained in corresponding analog simulations showed a very good match, see Fig. 6 for an example. As a consequence, we can reasonably infer that Spice simulations faithfully represent reality also in situations where no measurement results are available: For UMC-90 in settings near $V_{DD} = 1$ V, where the measurement results are inaccurate due to amplifier bandwidth limitations, and for UMC-65 in general, as there was no measurement ASIC available.

All post-processing, including averaging, curve fitting and extraction of the delay functions based on threshold crossing times, was done in Matlab.

5. INVOLUTION VALIDATION

For determining $\delta_{\downarrow}(T)$ of a single inverter output channel, we used a sweep of 1-0-1 pulses with different widths at the inverter input. Analogously, $\delta_{\uparrow}(T)$ was determined using 1-0-1 input pulses. In order to mitigate noise and measurement errors, we computed the average of 1000 single pulse experiments for every measured pulse width.

For values $T \geq \delta_{\min}$, where no output cancellation takes place, both T and $\delta(T)$ can be directly observed from the input/output waveforms by determining the points in time where the threshold voltage V_{th} was crossed. The delay $\delta_{\downarrow}(T)$, e.g., was computed as the difference between the threshold crossing of the falling output and that of the rising input. T as the time from the latter to the threshold crossing of the rising output, i.e., the previous output transition (cp. Fig. 4). Note that we assume the same logical threshold voltage V_{th} for both rising and falling transitions, as in Fig. 4.

Measuring $\delta_{\downarrow}(T)$ and $\delta_{\uparrow}(T)$ for $T < \delta_{\min}$ is impossible, however, as such transitions are not propagated to the output: Expressed in terms of the analog waveforms, this corresponds to the situation where the output never reaches the threshold voltage V_{th}. We hence used the involution property $\delta_{\downarrow}(T) = -\delta_{\uparrow}(-T)$ established in [9] to extrapolate these values for $\delta_{\downarrow}$ from $\delta_{\uparrow}$ and vice versa.

Fig. 2 already provided in Sec. 1 shows the delays $\delta_{\downarrow}$ and $\delta_{\uparrow}$ drawn from the measurements of inverter 3 (which has Q_2 as its input and Q_3 as its output) in the chain depicted in Fig. 5, with $V_{DD} = 0.6$ V. For this supply voltage, we are sure that the sense amplifiers are within their linear operating range. Similar results have been obtained for all reasonable values of V_{DD}, both for UMC-90 and UMC-65: Fig. 7 shows $\delta_{\downarrow}$ drawn from the measurements and one drawn from simulations of inverter 3 in the UMC-90 inverter chain, Fig. 8 shows some simulated $\delta_{\downarrow}$ for UMC-65.

Our results clearly support our claim that real delay functions are well-approximated by means of involutions. By contrast, it is impossible to fit the exponential delay of the DDM [8] over the whole range of T: Fig. 2 and Fig. 8 also

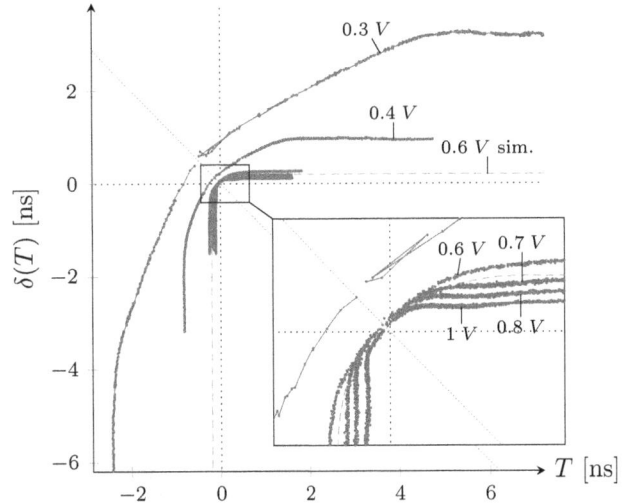

Figure 7: Measured $\delta_{\downarrow}$ for UMC-90 inverter chain for $V_{DD} \in \{0.3, 0.4, 0.6, 0.7, 0.8, 1\}$ V and simulated (dashed brown) $\delta_{\downarrow}$ for $V_{DD} = 0.6$ V.

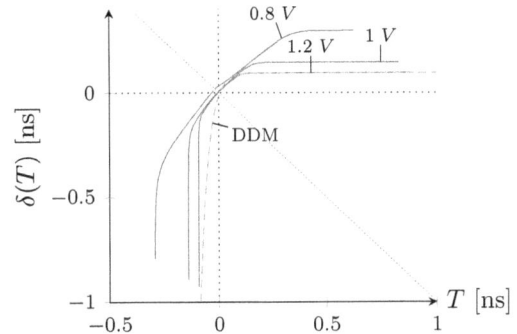

Figure 8: Simulated $\delta_{\downarrow}$ for UMC-65 inverter chain for $V_{DD} \in \{0.8, 1, 1.2\}$ V. DDM fitting for $V_{DD} = 1.2$ V.

show the exponential delay function of the DDM for parameters T_0 and $\tau = (T_{95} - T_0)/3$ chosen according to Eq. (5) in [8], where T_{95} is such that $\delta(T_{95}) = 0.95\delta_{\infty}$. The parameter T_0 has been determined empirically to fit the measured delays best: For $V_{DD} = 0.6\,V$, we obtained $T_0 = 0$ ps and $T_{95} = 684$ ps (falling transitions) resp. $T_{95} = 527$ ps (rising) for UMC-90 and $T_0 = 5$ ps and $T_{95} = 115$ ps (falling) resp. $T_{95} = 151$ ps (rising) for UMC-65. It is apparent that there is a substantial mismatch for small values of the input-to-previous-output delay T for both UMC-90 and UMC-65.

6. MODELING ACCURACY

We next complement the results obtained in Sec. 5, which focused on the validation of the involution property, by experiments devoted to the accuracy of the involution model. More specifically, using the empirically determined functions $\delta_{\uparrow}$ and $\delta_{\downarrow}$ as well as the fitted exponential delay function of the DDM in the simulation algorithm Alg. 2, we compare the simulated/measured analog output waveforms obtained for certain input pulse trains with the corresponding model predictions. Our results reveal that the modeling accuracy is very good in general, and that the involution model outperforms the DDM in scenarios with short pulses.

Fig. 3 already provided in Sec. 1 shows the measured waveforms for the UMC-90 inverter chain (outputs Q_2, Q_4 and

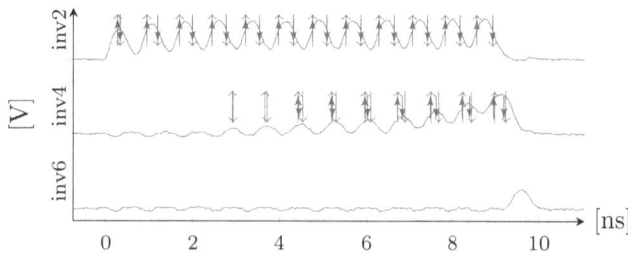

Figure 9: Measured fixed-frequency 1:1.31 duty cycle pulse train (solid) for the UMC-90 inverter chain, along with the corresponding predictions according to the involution model (red long up/down-arrows) (↑↓) and the DDM (blue short up/down arrows) (↑↓).

Q_6 in Fig. 5) when stimulated with a pulse train that incorporates pulses of various lengths. The crossings of the waveforms with the imaginary horizontal line at $V_{th} = 0.5V_{DD}$ give the times when the real circuit would change state. The long (red) up/down-arrows represent the signal transitions predicted by the involution model, the short (blue) up/down arrows give the DDM predictions. Whereas both models provide accurate predictions in most cases, the DDM tends to overly decay short pulses like the one at $t = 4$ ns in the middle waveform. In addition, the DDM produces spurious pulses (that do not exist in the real waveform), as can be seen e.g. in the bottom waveform at $t = 12$ ns. Similar results have been obtained for UMC-65.

We also investigated the model predictions in the case of a high frequency pulse train with a 0:1 duty cycle of 1:1.31, which captures the accumulation of energy even from non-propagated pulses. They are presented in Fig. 9, which again shows the measured waveforms for our UMC-90 inverter chain. Whereas both the DDM and the involution model accurately predict the output Q_2 (top waveform), both generate spurious pulses (before $t = 8$ ns) in the case of Q_4 (middle waveform), but not for Q_6 (bottom waveform). We conjecture that this inaccuracy is the price for the simplicity of any single-history model, which can only rely on the input-to-previous-output delay T in its predictions.

7. CONCLUSIONS

We experimentally evaluated the accuracy of the involution channel model, which is the first candidate for a realistic circuit model proposed so far. Using simulations of an inverter chain in both UMC-90 nm and UMC-65 nm technology, as well as measurements using a special-purpose ASIC, we could strengthen the hypothesis that real circuit delays are indeed well-approximated by involutions. Moreover, the model predictions obtained by using the empirically determined involution delay functions in the timing simulation algorithm match the analog waveforms quite accurately.

Whereas these findings further support the hypothesis that involution channels are indeed a promising candidate for the first faithful circuit model known so far, important issues are left for further research. Among these is the question of how to efficiently determine the actual involutions for a given circuit technology.

8. REFERENCES

[1] L. W. Nagel and D. Pederson, "SPICE (Simulation Program with Integrated Circuit Emphasis)," Tech. Rep. UCB/ERL M382, EECS Department, University of California, Berkeley, 1973.

[2] Synopsis, "CCS timing." Technical white paper v2.0, 2006.

[3] F. Najm, "A survey of power estimation techniques in vlsi circuits," *Very Large Scale Integration (VLSI) Systems, IEEE Transactions on*, vol. 2, no. 4, pp. 446–455, 1994.

[4] M. Favalli and L. Benini, "Analysis of glitch power dissipation in cmos ics," in *Proceedings of the 1995 international symposium on Low power desig n*, ISLPED '95, (New York, NY, USA), pp. 123–128, ACM, 1995.

[5] M. Függer, T. Nowak, and U. Schmid, "Unfaithful glitch propagation in existing binary circuit models," in *Proceedings 19th IEEE International Symposium on Asynchronous Cir cuits and Systems (ASYNC'13)*, pp. 191–199, IEEE Computer Society, 2013.

[6] S. H. Unger, "Asynchronous sequential switching circuits with unrestricted input changes," *IEEE ToC*, vol. 20, no. 12, pp. 1437–1444, 1971.

[7] M. J. Bellido-Díaz, J. Juan-Chico, and M. Valencia, *Logic-Timing Simulation and the Degradation Delay Model*. London: Imperial College Press, 2006.

[8] M. J. Bellido-Diaz, J. Juan-Chico, A. Acosta, M. Valencia, and J. L. Huertas, "Logical modelling of delay degradation effect in static cmos gates," *Circuits, Devices and Systems, IEE Proceedings -*, vol. 147, no. 2, pp. 107–117, 2000.

[9] M. Függer, R. Najvirt, T. Nowak, and U. Schmid, "Faithful glitch propagation in binary circuit models," *arXiv:1406.2544*, 2014. (appears in Proc. DATE'15).

[10] M. Hofbauer, K. Schweiger, H. Dietrich, H. Zimmermann, K.-O. Voss, B. Merk, U. Schmid, and A. Steininger, "Pulse shape measurements by on-chip sense amplifiers of single event transients propagating through a 90 nm bulk CMOS inverter chain," *IEEE Transactions on Nuclear Science*, vol. 59, pp. 2778–2784, Dec. 2012.

[11] M. A. Horowitz, *Timing Models for MOS Circuits*. PhD thesis, Stanford University, 1984.

[12] T.-M. Lin and C. Mead, "Signal delay in general RC networks," *IEEE TCAD*, vol. 3, no. 4, pp. 331–349, 1984.

[13] L. Pillage and R. Rohrer, "Asymptotic waveform evaluation for timing analysis," *IEEE TCAD*, vol. 9, no. 4, pp. 352–366, 1990.

[14] A.-C. Deng and Y.-C. Shiau, "Generic linear RC delay modeling for digital CMOS circuits," *IEEE TCAD*, vol. 9, no. 4, pp. 367–376, 1990.

[15] J. Juan-Chico, M. J. Bellido, P. Ruiz-de Clavijo, A. J. Acosta, and M. Valencia, "Degradation delay model extension to CMOS gates," in *Integrated Circuit Design*, LNCS 1918, pp. 149–158, Springer, 2000.

[16] A. Millan, J. Juan, M. J. Bellido, P. Ruiz-de Clavijo, and D. Guerrero, "Characterization of normal propagation delay for delay degradation model (DDM)," in *Integrated Circuit Design*, LNCS 2451, pp. 477–486, Springer, 2002.

Lookup Table Based Discrete Gate Sizing for Delay Minimization with Modified Elmore Delay Model

Jiani Xie
Syracuse University
Syracuse, New York, 13244
jixie@syr.edu

C.Y. Roger Chen
Syracuse University
Syracuse, New York, 13244
crchen@syr.edu

ABSTRACT

Gate sizing is one of the most important techniques for circuit optimization. Over the years, Elmore delay model (EDM) has been the predominant timing model used in gate sizing due to its simplicity. However, EDM is no longer effective in meeting the increasing demand of timing accuracy. In this paper, we propose a new gate delay model, which characterizes the timing information of lookup tables and creates a model which is mathematically similar to EDM, and can be easily incorporated into well-known EDM based gate sizing techniques using Lagrangian Relaxation (LR) with minor modifications. Experimental data show that it can produce even better results than those directly based on lookup tables, while keeping the benefit of the simplicity of EDM.

Keywords

Delay minimization, discrete gate sizing, Elmore delay model, gate model, lookup table

1. INTRODUCTION

Gate sizing is a critical technique for optimizing circuit delay and power consumption. Existing works primarily use Elmore Delay Model (EDM), which is known to be unsatisfactory in meeting the increasing demand of timing accuracy due mainly to its inability to model input waveform and transition times. Instead, most recent works have all proposed to directly obtain timing information from lookup tables that come with standard cell library. Two challenges arise. First, timing information is no longer expressed in simple, EDM like, mathematical formula and the development of gate sizing techniques becomes tedious and difficult. Second, all previous EDM based research works are no longer considered useful. In this work, we are focusing on the problem of discrete gate sizing for delay minimization. Note that most existing gate sizing techniques are addressing the issue of optimizing area or power, while treating delay as a given constraint. Only few works have directly addressed the issue of optimizing circuit delay.

Prior researchers were mainly focusing on solving continuous sizing problems. Fishburn et al. [1] used convex optimization technique TILOS to size transistors. Chen et al. [2] solved constrained continuous gate and wire sizing problems using Lagrangian relaxation, which was later refined by Wang et al. in [3]. Tennakoon et al. [4] utilized a gradient based approach. More recently, researchers have started working on the discrete sizing problems. Coudert [5] proposed a randomization-based greedy search algorithm. Hu et al. [6] applied a dynamic programming approach guided by continuous solutions.

EDM [7] has played an important role in the history of gate sizing research. Elmore delay is a simple approximation in calculating circuit delay through an RC network. The delay of each gate is calculated as its resistance times its direct down-stream capacitance. Because of its simplicity, EDM has been widely used in gate sizing problems. Chen et al. [2] built gate and wire delay models based on EDM. In [4], EDM is adopted to formulate the problems.

With modern complex timing models, classic Elmore delay cannot fully characterize the timing information of current standard cell libraries, especially input and output transition time. Thus nowadays, researchers tend to directly use lookup tables for describing gate delays, transition times, etc. However, it is hard to incorporate the lookup table information into optimization techniques. Ozdal et al. [8] proposed a graph model to capture library cell information.

Circuit performance is evaluated by delay, area, power, etc. Among them, circuit delay is of vital importance, since smaller circuit delay will lead to faster circuit speed. However, previous researchers were primarily focusing on optimizing power or area rather than delay. Nguyen et al. [9] used linear programming to minimize dynamic and static power. Livramento et al. [10] introduced a Lagrangian relaxation-based method to minimize leakage power with delay constraint. Liu et al. [11] proposed a systematic combinatorial approach with threshold voltage assignment. Constraint free delay minimization, which is addressed in this paper, is very important but rarely studied in literature. Only few researchers [2, 6, 12] have performed work on this, and they were limited to continuous sizing [2] or outdated EDM [6], or required much more complicated approach than our proposed one [12].

In this work, we show how to modify the classic EDM to characterize the timing information of the discrete lookup tables, thus retaining its mathematical simplicity and flexibility. We present an algorithm to solve the gate sizing problems using Lagrangian relaxation with the proposed modified EDM.

The rest of this paper is organized as follows. In Section 2, we first define the notations and terminology in this work. And in Section 3, we show how to modify the classic EDM to characterize the lookup tables from ISPD 2012 standard cell library [13]. In Section 4, we present our algorithm to solve the delay minimization problem using Lagrangian relaxation with the proposed modified EDM. In Section 5, we project the continuous solution to discrete domain using nearest rounding with delay cost refinement. Experimental results and summary are presented in Sections 6 and 7, respectively.

2. PRELIMINARIES

We first define the notations and terminology in this work. For simplicity. Following that described in [2], for a circuit with n sizable gates, we model it as a directed acyclic graph (DAG). The DAG is denoted as $G(V, E)$, where V is the set of individual gates and E is the set of wires connecting the gates. We use $v_i \in V$ to represent an individual gate in the DAG, where i, $1 \leq i \leq n$, is the index of the gate. We use PI and PO to represent the set of primary inputs and primary outputs, respectively. We add a pseudo output P_0 to connect all the primary outputs. Reverse topological sorting is used to label all the gates from output to input such that if gate i is closer to the pseudo output than gate j, then $i < j$. Thus, in the circuit with n resizable gates and s primary inputs, P_0 is labeled as gate 0, all the resizable gates are labeled from 1 to n, and the primary inputs are labeled from $n + 1$ to $n + s$. We add a pseudo input P_m to connect to all the primary inputs, where $m = n + s + 1$.

Then we use $X = (x_1, x_2, \ldots, x_n)$ to represent the discrete sizes of all sizable gates in the circuit. Each x_i, where $i = 1, \ldots, n$, represents a discrete size for gate i. x_i is referred to as the ith component of X, and X is simply referred to as a solution point in the following discussions. For each of gate i, it comes with a lower bound and an upper bound of its size, denoted as L_i and U_i, i.e., $L_i \leq x_i \leq U_i$.

For each gate i, where $1 \leq i \leq n$, we use $input(i)$ to represent the set of indexes of components that are directly connected to the inputs of component i. We use $output(i)$ to represent the set of indexes of components that are directly connected to the outputs of component i. In addition, for each component i, where $1 \leq i \leq n + s$, a_i, D_i and TT_i are used to refer to as its arrival time, gate delay and transition time, respectively. OC_i represents its output load capacitance, and $Input\_TT_i$ represents the input transition time of gate i. We use the proposed modified EDM to calculate the component delay, which will be discussed in the next section.

3. PROPOSED ELMORE-DELAY-LIKE MODEL

In this section, we propose to modify the classic EDM to model the characteristics of the lookup tables from ISPD 2012 standard cell library [13].

First we would like to review the timing model from ISPD 2012 standard cell library. The cell timing delay and output transition time are organized as lookup tables, and these lookup tables take the input transition time and output load capacitance as inputs and generate gate delay and output transition time. Mathematically, we use function $d_i = f_{d_i}(x_i, Input\_TT_i, OC_i)$ and $TT_i = f_{TT_i}(x_i, Input\_TT_i, OC_i)$ to represent the delay and output transition time of gate i. We can use a simple 2-dimensional linear interpolation model for specific values from the table.

3.1 Delay and Transition Time

Each cell from ISPD 2012 standard cell library comes with fall/rise delay and fall/rise transition time, which are delays and transition times for fall or rise transitions, respectively. Even though it comes with four types of lookup tables, their values at each parameter are so close that we can use only one of the four to represent all of them. On the other hand, since EDM only deals with delay, we suggest to use the delay of a gate to approximate its output transition time. This is the case in the ISPD 2012 library. For libraries with

considerable discrepancy between the two, we can introduce some additional form of approximation.

We have the following equations for defining the output transition time TT_i and input transition time $Input\_TT_i$ using delay only:

$$TT_i = D_i \tag{1}$$

$$Input\_TT_i = max\left(\begin{array}{c} TT_j \\ j \in input(i) \end{array}\right) = max\left(\begin{array}{c} D_j \\ j \in input(i) \end{array}\right) \tag{2}$$

3.2 Gate Model

As in EDM, we model the gates using resistors and capacitors only. However, we make some changes on the gate capacitance c_i and gate resistance r_i as follows:

$$c_i = \hat{c}_i \times x_i \tag{3}$$

$$r_i = \hat{r}_i / x_i + r_{i0} \tag{4}$$

In the above two equations, $\hat{c}_i$ is the unit size gate capacitance, $\hat{r}_i$ is the unit output resistance, and r_{i0} is the intrinsic resistance. We can obtain the variable values from the lookup tables of library cells.

3.3 Maximum Output Load Capacitance Limit

Each cell from the standard library comes with a maximum output load capacitance, which defines the maximum output load capacitance that the output pin can drive. In general, the maximum output load capacitance is a linear function of the cell size from ISPD 2012 library. As specified in the library, the maximum output capacitance for gate i is as follows:

$$Max\_cap\_load_i = Unit\_cap_i \times x_i \tag{5}$$

where $Unit\_cap_i$ is the maximum capacitance that can be driven by a unit size cell.

3.4 Modified Elmore Delay Model

The traditional Elmore delay equation $D_i = r_i \cdot OC_i$ is no longer satisfactory for modern standard cell library as it cannot fully characterize the effect of input transition time and output load capacitance. Thus, we introduce two correction factors, $\alpha_i(Input\_TT_i)$ and $\beta_i(OC_i)$, to refine it. From the lookup tables of ISPD 2012 standard cell library, under the same output load, the rate for gate delay to increase with respect to input transition time is faster than linear. We thus use $\alpha_i(Input\_TT_i)$ as a function of the input transition time of gate i to reflect this feature. $\alpha_i(Input\_TT_i)$ can be described either as a linear function of $Input\_TT_i$ or as a piecewise linear function for more precision. Similarly, we have observed that, with the same input transition time, the rate for gate delay to increase with respect to output load capacitance is slower than linear. We thus use $\beta_i(OC_i)$ to reflect this. We propose a new model for gate delay D_i, where $1 \leq i \leq n$, by modifying EDM as follows:

$$D_i = \alpha_i(Input\_TT_i) \times \beta_i(OC_i) \times (r_i \cdot OC_i + D_{i0})$$
$$= \alpha_i \cdot \beta_i \cdot \left((\hat{r}_i / x_i + r_{i0}) \cdot OC_i + D_{i0}\right) \tag{6}$$

In the above equation, D_{i0}, the intrinsic delay of gate i, is the delay of gate i when its output load capacitance is 0. We use α_i and β_i, respectively, to represent the two parameters $\alpha_i(Input\_TT_i)$ and $\beta_i(OC_i)$ for short. The specific values for those variables can be obtained from the standard cell library. The proposed model is summarized in Table 1.

3.5 Gate Model Example

We use the inverter cell in01m01 in Table 2 as an example to compare our new delay model with the original lookup table. We list all the new delay model parameters in Table 3. Since the transition time constraint sets the slew between $5ps - 300ps$ and the maximum output load capacitance of cell in01m01 is $14.4fF$, we only consider the input transition time between $5ps - 300ps$ and output load capacitance less than $14.4fF$. The delay obtained from the proposed model for inverter cell in01m01 is shown in Table 4.

Table 5 shows the delay comparison between modified Elmore delay model and lookup table. They are very close when the input transition time and output load capacitance are far less than the maximum value, and still only differ slightly when reaching the

Table 1. Modified Elmore Delay Model Parameters.

Gate capacitance	$c_i = \hat{c}_i \times x_i$
Gate resistance	$r_i = \hat{r}_i/x_i + r_{i0}$
Gate delay	$D_i = \alpha_i(Input\_TT_i) \times \beta_i(OC_i) \times (r_i \cdot OC_i + D_{i0})$ $= \alpha_i \cdot \beta_i \cdot \left((\hat{r}_i/x_i + r_{i0}) \cdot OC_i + D_{i0} \right)$
Transition time	$TT_i = D_i$
Input transition time	$Input\_TT_i = max\left(\begin{matrix} TT_j \\ j \in input(i) \end{matrix} \right)$ $= max\left(\begin{matrix} D_i \\ j \in input(i) \end{matrix} \right)$
Maximum output capacitance	$Max\_cap\_load_i = Unit\_cap_i \times x_i$

Table 2. Lookup Table of Cell in01m01 from ISPD 2012 [13].

Output Load Cap. (fF)	Input Transition Time (ps)						
	5	30	50	80	140	200	300
0.0	10.2	16.3	20.2	24.8	32.4	38.7	47.4
1.0	14.6	20.9	25.6	31.2	39.9	47.4	58.1
2.0	19.1	25.3	30.3	36.8	46.8	55.0	67.1
4.0	28.0	34.2	39.2	46.7	58.9	68.7	82.5
8.0	45.9	52.1	57.1	64.5	79.4	92.0	109.3

Table 3. Modified Elmore Delay Parameters for Cell in01m01.

$\hat{c}_i$	$1fF$
$\hat{r}_i$	$4.465\ k\Omega$
r_{i0}	$0\ k\Omega$
D_{i0}	$10.17\ ps$
$\alpha_i(Input\_TT_i)$	$\begin{cases} 0.8 & Input\_TT_i \in [5ps, 30ps) \\ 0.97 & Input\_TT_i \in [30ps, 50ps) \\ 1.14 & Input\_TT_i \in [50ps, 80ps) \\ 1.35 & Input\_TT_i \in [80ps, 140ps) \\ 1.7 & Input\_TT_i \in [140ps, 200ps) \\ 2.05 & Input\_TT_i \in [200ps, 300ps) \\ 2.5 & Input\_TT_i = 300ps \end{cases}$
$\beta_i(OC_i)$	$\begin{cases} 1.75 & OC_i \in [0fF, 1fF) \\ 1.55 & OC_i \in [1fF, 2fF) \\ 1.4 & OC_i \in [2fF, 4fF) \\ 1.23 & OC_i \in [4fF, 8fF) \\ 1.1 & OC_i \in [8fF, 16fF) \\ 1 & OC_i = 16fF \end{cases}$
$Unit\_cap_i$	$14.4\ fF$

maximum limit. Since in most cases, the input transition time and output load capacitance are far below the maximum value, the accuracy of the proposed model is quite high. Similar accuracy has been be observed for other library cells, and the errors are on average within 5% for most of the cells.

Table 4. Modified Elmore Delay for Cell in01m01.

Output Load Cap. (fF)	Input Transition Time (ps)						
	5	30	50	80	140	200	300
0.0	10.2	17.3	20.3	24.0	30.3	36.5	44.5
1.0	14.6	22.0	25.9	30.6	38.6	46.5	56.7
2.0	19.1	25.9	30.5	36.1	45.5	54.8	66.9
4.0	28.0	33.4	39.3	46.5	58.6	70.7	86.2
8.0	45.9	49.0	57.5	68.1	85.8	103.5	126.2

Table 5. Delay Comparison between Modified Elmore Delay Model and Lookup Table (%).

Output Load Cap. (fF)	Input Transition Time (ps)						
	5	30	50	80	140	200	300
0.0	0.0	5.7	0.3	-3.2	-6.6	-5.8	-6.2
1.0	0.0	5.6	1.1	-1.7	-3.4	-1.9	-2.3
2.0	0.0	2.5	0.6	-1.9	-2.8	-0.3	-0.3
4.0	0.0	-2.3	0.2	-0.2	-0.5	3.0	4.5
8.0	0.0	-6.0	0.8	5.6	8.1	12.4	15.5

4. GATE SIZING WITH DELAY MINIMIZATION USING LAGRANGIAN RELAXATION

In this section, we solve the problem of minimizing the maximum delay in continuous domain with Lagrangian relaxation.

4.1 Problem Formulation

The delay of the circuit can be defined as the maximal delay of all the paths in the circuit. Minimizing the circuit delay is the same as minimizing the arrival time of the pseudo output. Thus, similar to [2], the primal problem of minimizing maximum delay can be formulated as following:

Primal Problem: Find $X^* = (x_1^*, \ldots, x_n^*)$ that Minimizes a_0

Subject to: $a_j \leq a_0,$ $j \in input(0)$ /* outputs */

$a_j + D_i \leq a_i,$ $i = 1, \ldots, n$ and $\forall j \in input(i)$

$D_i \leq a_i,$ $i = n + 1, \ldots, n + s$ /* inputs */

$L_i \leq x_i \leq U_i,$ $i = 1, \ldots, n$

$Min\_TT_i \leq D_i \leq Max\_TT_i,$ $i = 1, \ldots, n$

/* transition time constraints */

$OC_i \leq Unit\_cap \times x_i,$ $i = 1, \ldots, n$

/* output load capacitance constraints */   (7)

4.2 Lagrangian Relaxation

We use Lagrangian relaxation to solve the primal problem. For each constraint on arrival time, we introduce a nonnegative Lagrange multiplier λ to formulate a new subproblem L_λ as follows:

$L_\lambda = a_0 + \sum_{j \in input(0)} \lambda_{j0}(a_j - a_0) + \sum_{i=1}^{n} \sum_{j \in input(i)} \lambda_{ji}(a_j + D_i - a_i) + \sum_{i=n+1}^{n+s} \lambda_{mi}(D_i - a_i)$ (8)

Then the Lagrangian relaxation subproblem associated with the Lagrange multipliers λ is:

LRS/λ: Minimize $L_\lambda(x, a)$

Subject to: $L_i \leq x_i \leq U_i$,

$$Min\_TT_i \leq D_i \leq Max\_TT_i,$$

$$OC_i \leq Unit\_cap \times x_i,$$

$$i = 1, ..., n \quad (9)$$

From the Kuhn-Tucker conditions [14], which imply $\partial L/\partial a_j = 0$, $1 \leq j \leq n + s$, for optimal solutions of the primal problem, we have the following optimality conditions on λ:

$$1 = \sum_{j \in input(0)} \lambda_{j0} \quad (10)$$

$$\sum_{i \in output(k)} \lambda_{ki} = \sum_{j \in input(k)} \lambda_{jk}, \text{where } 1 \leq k \leq n + s \quad (11)$$

Then for λ satisfying the conditions, we can simplify LRS/λ to form the following problem:

LRS/μ: Minimize $L_\mu(x, a)$

Subject to: $L_i \leq x_i \leq U_i$,

$$Min\_TT_i \leq D_i \leq Max\_TT_i,$$

$$OC_i \leq Unit\_cap \times x_i,$$

$$i = 1, ..., n$$

where $\mu = (\mu_0, ..., \mu_{n+s}), \mu_i = \sum_{j \in input(i)} \lambda_{ji}$ for $0 \leq i \leq n + s$, and $L_\mu(x) = \sum_{i=1}^{n+s} \mu_i D_i$.

4.3 Solving LRS/μ

With the modified Elmore delay model discussed in Section 3, we will show how to solve LRS/μ with any fixed $\mu \geq 0$.

$$L_\mu(x) = \sum_{i=1}^{n+s} \mu_i D_i = \sum_{i=n+1}^{n+s} \mu_i D_i + \sum_{i=1}^{n} \mu_i D_i$$

For primary inputs $n + 1 \leq i \leq n + 1$, we set $\alpha_i = \beta_i = 1$, and for gate $1 \leq i \leq n$, with Eq (3),(4) and (6), we have:

$$L_\mu(x) = \sum_{i=n+1}^{n+s} \mu_i \alpha_i \beta_i r_i \cdot OC_i + \sum_{i=1}^{n} \mu_i \alpha_i \beta_i \cdot \left(\frac{\widehat{r}_i}{x_i}\right) \cdot OC_i$$

$$+ \sum_{i=1}^{n} \mu_i \alpha_i \beta_i \cdot r_{i0} \cdot OC_i + \sum_{i=1}^{n} \mu_i \alpha_i \beta_i \cdot D_{i0} \quad (12)$$

For any $1 \leq i \leq n$, if $j \notin input(i)$, $\mu_j \alpha_i \beta_i r_j \cdot OC_j$ is independent of x_i. If $j \in input(i)$, $\mu_j \alpha_i \beta_i r_j \cdot OC_j = \mu_j \alpha_j \beta_j r_j \cdot \widehat{c}_i x_i +$ terms independent of x_i. Thus, we have:

$$L_\mu(x) = \left(\sum_{j \in input(i)} \mu_j \alpha_j \beta_j r_j \widehat{c}_i\right) \cdot x_i + \frac{\mu_i \alpha_i \beta_i \widehat{r}_i \cdot OC_i}{x_i}$$
$$+ \text{ terms independent of } x_i \quad (13)$$

Then the optimal value of x_i is:

$$x_i^* = \sqrt{\frac{\mu_i \alpha_i \beta_i \widehat{r}_i \cdot OC_i}{\sum_{j \in input(i)} \mu_j \alpha_j \beta_j r_j \widehat{c}_i}} \quad (14)$$

Taking into consideration of the transition time constraints and output capacitance constraints, we have the following constraints:

$$L_i \leq x_i \leq U_i$$

$$Min\_TT_i \leq D_i \leq Max\_TT_i$$

$$OC_i \leq Unit\_cap \times x_i$$

Considering the modified EDM of Eq. (6), we have

$$\frac{\widehat{r}_i}{(Max\_TT_i/\alpha_i\beta_i - D_{i0})/OC_i - r_{i0}} \leq x_i$$

$$\leq \frac{\widehat{r}_i}{(Min\_TT_i/\alpha_i\beta_i - D_{i0})/OC_i - r_{i0}}$$

and $x_i \geq OC_i/Unit\_cap_i$

Thus, combining all the constraints, we set new lower bound L_i^* and upper bound U_i^* as:

$$L_i^* = max\left\{L_i, OC_i/Unit\_cap_i, \frac{\widehat{r}_i}{(Max\_TT_i/\alpha_i\beta_i - D_{i0})/OC_i - r_{i0}}\right\} \quad (15)$$

$$U_i^* = min\left\{U_i, \frac{\widehat{r}_i}{(Min\_TT_i/\alpha_i\beta_i - D_{i0})/OC_i - r_{i0}}\right\} \quad (16)$$

Combining the Eq. (14), (15) and (16), the optimal local resizing of component i is then given by the following equation:

$$x_i^* = min\left\{U_i^*, max\left(L_i^*, \sqrt{\frac{\mu_i \alpha_i \beta_i \widehat{r}_i \cdot OC_i}{\sum_{j \in input(i)} \mu_j \alpha_j \beta_j r_j \widehat{c}_i}}\right)\right\} \quad (17)$$

As shown by Chen et al. in [2], the algorithm to solve LRS/μ always converges and the solution is optimal for LRS/μ.

Hence, with a fixed $\mu \geq 0$, we can solve LRS/μ by an iterative and greedy algorithm which resizes the gate components. Figure 1 outlines the algorithm, denoted as $SOLVE\_LRS/\mu$. Initially, we set all the gates with minimum sizes. For each iteration, we adjust the gates one at a time. Then each time, we only adjust one gate based on Eq. (17), and keep all other gates fixed. Thus, we examine all the gates until they converge to the optimal sizes. Obviously, each iteration takes $O(n)$ time. Chen et al. [2] showed the complexity of $SOLVE\_LRS/\mu$ is $O(rn)$, where r is the number of iterations.

4.4 Adjust λ

Chen et al. [2] introduced the method called subgradient-based direction, which calculates the subgradient direction by adding the

---

Algorithm $SOLVE\_LRS/\mu$

Input: $\mu = (\mu_0, ..., \mu_{n+s})$ and all gate information

Output: $X = (X_1, ..., X_n)$, which minimizes $L_\mu(x)$

---

1. **Repeat**

2.   Update timing information

3.   For each gate i, where $1 \leq i \leq n$

4. $L_i^* = max\left\{L_i, OC_i/Unit\_cap_i, \frac{\widehat{r}_i}{(Max\_TT_i/\alpha_i\beta_i - D_{i0})/OC_i - r_{i0}}\right\}$

5. $U_i^* = min\left\{U_i, \frac{\widehat{r}_i}{(Min\_TT_i/\alpha_i\beta_i - D_{i0})/OC_i - r_{i0}}\right\}$

6. $x_i^* = min\left\{U_i^*, max\left(L_i^*, \sqrt{\frac{\mu_i \alpha_i \beta_i \widehat{r}_i OC_i}{\sum_{j \in input(i)} \mu_j \alpha_j \beta_j r_j \widehat{c}_i}}\right)\right\}$

7. **Until** no further improvement

Figure 1. Pseudo code for $SOLVE\_LRS/\mu$ algorithm

product of step size ρ_k and the difference between the current arrival time and the expected arrival time. However, this method sometimes is not effective and may easily lead to negative λ in some cases. Zhou et al. [12] introduced a subgradient method to update the multipliers according to the percentage of the current arrival time to the expected arrival time. We further refine it such that it has different updates depending on its locations in the circuit. We define the following equations to update multipliers λ_{ji}, where $j \in input(i)$:

$$\lambda_{ji} = \begin{cases} \lambda_{ji} \times (\frac{a_j}{a_0})^{\rho_k} & if\ i = 0 \\ \lambda_{ji} \times (\frac{a_j + D_i}{a_i})^{\rho_k} & if\ 1 \leq i \leq n \\ \lambda_{ji} \times (\frac{D_i}{a_i})^{\rho_k} & if\ n + 1 \leq i \leq n + s \end{cases} \quad (18)$$

We have outlined the pseudo code for delay minimization by Lagrangian relaxation (DMLR) in Figure 2.

Algorithm DMLR

Input: Circuit and library information

Output: Solution X with minimum circuit delay

---

1. Set initial sizes as minimum cell sizes
2. **Repeat**
3.   Update timing information
4.   Adjust λ with Eq. (18)
5.   Project λ to satisfy Kuhn-Tucker conditions:

$$1 = \sum_{j \in input(0)} \lambda_{j0}$$

$$\sum_{l \in output(k)} \lambda_{ki} = \sum_{j \in input(k)} \lambda_{jk}$$

6.   Call $SOLVE\_LRS/\mu$ to find the X
7. **Until** no further improvement

Figure 2. Pseudo code for DMLR algorithm

5. MODIFIED NEAREST ROUNDING AND POST POWER OPTIMIZATION

In this section, we present our algorithm to project continuous solutions to discrete solutions and keep reducing extra delay cost during nearest rounding. We apply a post power optimization afterwards to further reduce the power consumption. Our algorithm presented in Section 4 gives us an optimal continuous solution. After getting the continuous solution, we usually use nearest rounding to project to discrete solution. However, during the nearest rounding, it is hard to tell whether we should round up or round down the continuous size, since it may introduce extra cost when the continuous solution is either rounded up or rounded down. Then we propose a quick procedure to reduce the extra delay cost by considering resizing the gates with either one size up or one size down. And we use the local delay difference to calculate delay cost of gate i as $\Delta D(i)$, which is much more time efficient. Figure 3 shows the pseudo code of Modified Nearest Rounding (MNR). We have observed that projecting a continuous gate size beyond its two direct neighboring discrete sizes will not further improve the results and is unnecessary. We further reduce the power consumption by replacing certain gates with those with less power consumption and keeping the same circuit delay. Our entire algorithm of discrete gate sizing with Lagrangian relaxation (DSLR) is outlined in Figure 4.

6. EXPERIMENTAL RESULTS

We implemented the algorithm in C++ and the experiments were performed on a 3.4 GHz Intel Core i7 computer. We use the test cases from ISCAS 87' benchmark, and the standard cell library provided by the ISPD 2012 Discrete Gate Sizing Contest [13]. To validate the effectiveness of our algorithm, we compare our algorithm with the previous work from Liu et al. [11], who proposed a method that employs bi-directional solution search. However, the method [11] cannot predict the effect of cell change on its input side, which causes imprecision in searching and pruning solution space. We implemented the JRR from [11] to obtain the minimum delay solution first. As the data in Table 6 show, we can see the delay of our algorithm is on average 5.03% less than that of [11]. Note that there is no noticeable difference in runtime. Moreover, it is interesting to notice an important implication of our work. Over the past decades, numerous papers have been published for optimization problems in gate sizing, buffer insertion, placement, routing, timing analysis, etc. using EDM. Because nowadays EDM is generally considered inaccurate, the EDA industry has started to abandon EDM, and moved into lookup tables from standard cell library. Although the lookup tables provide much more accuracy, it completely loses the conciseness of EDM, making analysis very difficult. Thus, the numerous EDM based existing works are considered invalid. This paper shows that it is possible to modify the EDM to properly include information in lookup tables such that earlier EDM based techniques in many EDA problems can still be re-utilized. This might be a most significant contribution of this paper.

Figure 5 shows the delay sequence of circuit c1355, c1908 and c2670. As we can see, the delay decreases as the iterations go on, and finally converges to the optimal solution. And it usually takes more iterations to converge for circuits with more gates.

Figure 6 shows the runtime versus the number of gates. Polynomial-like curve is plotted for comparison.

Algorithm MNR

Input: Continuous solution X with minimum circuit delay

Output: Discrete solution X'

---

1. Project continuous solution X to discrete solution X' using classic nearest rounding
2. Foreach gate i
3. $v_i.resizable = true$
4. **Repeat**
5.   Update timing information
6.   Foreach gate i
7.   If $v_i.resizable == true$
8.   Find i with max $\Delta D(i)$
9. $x_i = x_i'$ and $v_i.resizable = false$
10. **Until** no further improvement

Figure 3. Pseudo code for modified nearest rounding (MNR)

Algorithm DSLR

Input: Circuit and library information

Output: Solution $X^{*\prime}$ with minimum circuit delay and optimized leakage power consumption

---

1. Find continuous solution X with minimum delay by DMLR

2. Project continuous solution X to discrete solution X' by MNR

3. Apply post power optimization to further reduce power

Figure 4. Pseudo code for discrete gate sizing with Lagrangian relaxation (DSLR)

7. CONCLUSIONS

We modified the classic EDM to model the characteristics of the lookup tables from ISPD 2012 standard cell library and presented a new algorithm to solve the discrete gate sizing problems by re-using the Lagrangian relaxation method, which was previously used to solve the continuous gate sizing problem. We showed how to use the modified EDM to minimize circuit delay using the revised Lagrangian relaxation approach. We also take into consideration the input transition time constraints and output load capacitance constraints. With the Kuhn-Tucker conditions, we can solve the Lagrangian subproblem with an iterative algorithm,

Table 6. Delay and Power Comparison between Our Algorithm (NEW) and Liu's Algorithm [11]. *Delays* are in *ps. Powers* are in *µW*.

Circuit	New		Liu [11]		New vs Liu [11]	
	Delay	Power	Delay	Power	Delay	Power
c432	752.6	2152	870.4	2684	-13.54%	-19.82%
c499	564.8	4864	627.2	3664	-9.95%	32.75%
c880	884.0	3340	1052.7	4574	-16.02%	-26.98%
c1355	868.4	5072	960.5	5176	-9.59%	-2.01%
c1908	1054.5	7104	1074.4	6246	-1.86%	13.74%
c2670	1020.0	9154	1068.3	9388	-4.52%	-2.49%
c3540	1517.5	13230	1687.9	17618	-10.09%	-24.91%
c5315	1446.4	20474	1338.9	23904	8.03%	-14.35%
c6288	4150.6	26216	3837.4	30484	8.16%	-14.00%
c7552	1216.7	26608	1227.9	27450	-0.91%	-3.07%
Avg.	1347.5	11821.4	1374.6	13118.8	-5.03%	-6.11%

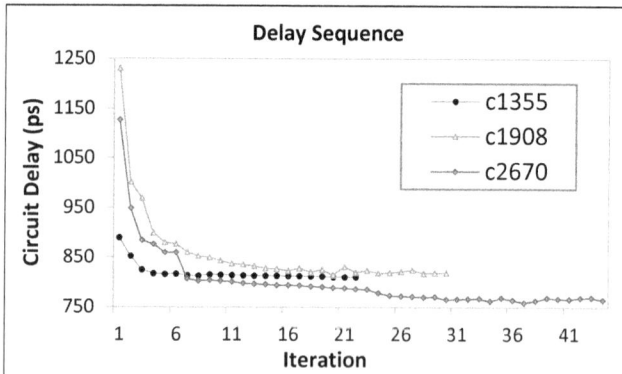

Figure 5. Delay sequence of circuit c1355, c1908 and c2670.
Delays are in *ps*.

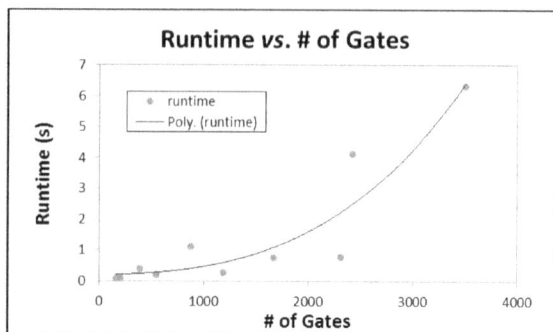

Figure 6. Runtime comparison vs. # of gates.
Runtimes are in *seconds(s)*.

which is shown to converge to the global optimal solutions. The proposed subgradient optimization method is used to update the Lagrangian multipliers. We presented an algorithm to transform the continuous solutions to discrete solutions, and a post-processing algorithm to minimize power consumption.

8. REFERENCES

[1] J. Fishburn and A. Dunlop. Tilos: A polynomial programming approach to transistor sizing. In *Proc. Int. Conf. Comput – Aided Des.*, 1985, pp. 326-328.

[2] C.-P Chen, C. Chu, and D. Wong. Fast and exact simultaneous gate and wire sizing by Lagrangian relaxation. *IEEE Trans. Comput.-Aided Design Intergr. Circuits Syst.*, vol. 18, no. 7, pp. 1014-1025, Jul. 1999.

[3] J. Wang, D. Das and H. Zhou. Gate sizing by Lagrangian relaxation revisited. In *2007 IEEE/ACM International Conference on Computer-Aided Design*, pp. 111-118.

[4] H. Tennakoon and C. Sechen. Gate sizing using lagrangian relaxation combined with a fast gradient-based pre-processing step. In *Proc. ICCAD*, 2002, pp. 395-402.

[5] O. Coudert. Gate sizing for constrained delay/power/area optimization. *IEEE Trans. VLSI Syst.*, vol. 5, no. 4, pp. 465-472, Dec. 1997.

[6] S. Hu, M. Ketkar, and J. Hu. Gate sizing for cell-library-based designs. *IEEE Trans. Comput.-Aided Des.*, vol. 28, no. 6, pp. 818-825, Jun. 2009.

[7] W. C. Elmore. The Transient Response of Damped Linear Networks with Particular Regard to Wideband Amplifiers. *Journal of Applied Physics*, January 1948, Volume 19, Issue 1, pp. 55-63.

[8] M. M. Ozdal, S. Burns, and J. Hu. Algorithms for gate sizing and device parameter selection for high-performance designs. *IEEE Trans. On CAD*, vol. 31, no. 10, pp. 1558-1571, Oct 2012.

[9] D. Nguyen, A. Davare, M. Orshansky, D. Chinnery, B. Thompson, and K. Keutzer. Minimization of dynamic and static power throught joint assignment of threshold voltages and sizing optimization. In *Proc, ISLPED*, 2003, pp. 158-163.

[10] V. S. Livramento, C. Guth, J. L. Guntzel and M. O. Johann. Fast and efficient Lagrangian relaxation-based discrete gate sizing. *Proceedings of the conference on Design, Automation and Test in Europe. EDA Consortium*, 2013.

[11] Y. Liu and J. Hu. A new algorithm for simultaneous gate sizing and threshold voltage assignment. *IEEE Trans. Computer-Aided Design*, Vol. 29, No. 2, pp. 223-234, Feb 2010.

[12] S. Zhou, H. Yao, Q. Zhou, and Y. Cai. Minimization of circuit delay and power through gate sizing and threshold voltage assignment. In *Proc. ISVLSI*, 2011, pp. 212-217.

[13] M. M. Ozdal, C. Amin, A. Ayupov, S. Burns, G. Wilke, C. Zhuo. The ISPD -2012 Discrete Cell Sizing Contest and Benchmark Suite. *Proc. ACM International Symposium on Physical Design*, pp. 161-164, 2012.

[14] M. S. Bazaraa, H. D. Sherali, and C. M. Shetty. *Nonlinear Programming: Theory and Algorithms*. John Wiley & Sons, Inc., second edition, 1993.

A Novel Framework for Temperature Dependence Aware Clock Skew Scheduling

Mineo Kaneko
Japan Advanced Institute of Science and Technology
1-1 Asahidai, Nomi-shi, Ishikawa, Japan
mkaneko@jaist.ac.jp

ABSTRACT

Temperature is one of the major sources of delay variations which may cause timing violations. In this paper, an approach to temperature aware clock skew scheduling for a general class of sequential circuits is proposed. At first, an alternative interpretation of the affine type (linear model) of temperature dependency is shown, which is not merely a "linearized" model applicable to a limited temperature range, but it can cover a class of nonlinear temperature dependency, and hence its applicability is not limited in temperature range. After that, a graph-theoretic skew scheduling considering the lower and the upper temperature bounds, which can work in a polynomial time complexity with respect to the circuit size, is derived. This framework can be applicable to the variants of temperature aware optimizations, such as maximizing upper temperature bound, maximizing clock frequency under a given temperature range, etc. Experiments using ISCAS'89 benchmark circuits show us that our approach achieves maximum 70% improvement in the upper temperature range (in a linear temperature scale) compared with a conventional skew scheduling which maximizes the minimum timing slack.

Categories and Subject Descriptors

B.8.2 [**PERFORMANCE AND RELIABILITY**]: Performance Analysis and Design Aids

Keywords

Delay variation, timing skew, delay test, setup timing constraint, hold timing constraint

1. INTRODUCTION

Temperature is one of the major sources of delay variations which may cause timing violations. Since the timing issues are closely related to a clock distribution, thermal aware clock tree construction has been intensively studied in many literatures[1][2] [3]. Most of those works target a zero-skew (or bounded skew) implementation, and their objectives are set on the minimization of variation-induced skew considering temperature distribution (temperature profile) on a chip. Chakraborty, et al., proposed clock skew compensation using tunable delay[4], which aims to bound skew from zero skew dynamically in compensation for hardware overhead. Compared with those approaches, SACTA[5][6] proposed by Long, et al., is a unique approach to mitigate the risk of thermal-induced timing violation by the use of intentional thermal-dependent clock skew. This approach is attractive, but is applied to a simple pipeline architecture without feedback and feedforward paths.

In this paper, a novel approach to temperature aware clock skew scheduling for sequential circuits is proposed. Being different from SACTA, we target a general sequential circuit which may have feedback paths, but on the other hand, we consider uniform temperature variation. In this sense, current version of our approach may be applicable only to a small size controller circuit, but it provides us alternative insights into temperature dependence aware skew scheduling than SACTA provides.

Similar to several papers treating temperature aware design, a linear temperature dependence model[5][7] will be employed. In order to extend the applicability of this mode, an alternative interpretation of the affine type (linear model) of temperature dependency is demonstrated, which is not merely a "linearized" model applicable to a limited temperature range, but it can cover a class of nonlinear temperature dependency. The major contribution of this paper is a graph-theoretic skew scheduling considering the lower and the upper temperature bounds, that is, the skew scheduling which guarantees a correct operation in clock timing at any temperature between lower and upper temperature bounds.

The algorithm can work in a polynomial time complexity with respect to the circuit size, and is applicable to the variants of temperature aware optimizations, such as maximizing upper temperature bound, maximizing clock frequency under a given temperature range, etc. Exploration of the best suitable temperature dependency for delays of intentional skew is another application of this framework.

The rest of this paper is organized as follows. In Section 2, one possible applicability of linear temperature dependence model to a class of nonlinear temperature dependence model. After that, temperature aware skew scheduling problem is formulated and is solved using a graph-theoretic approach in Sections 3 and 4. Several experimental results

GLSVLSI '15, May 20–22, 2015, Pittsburgh, PA, USA
Copyright © 2015 ACM 978-1-4503-3474-7/15/05 ...$15.00.
http://dx.doi.org/10.1145/2742060.2742073.

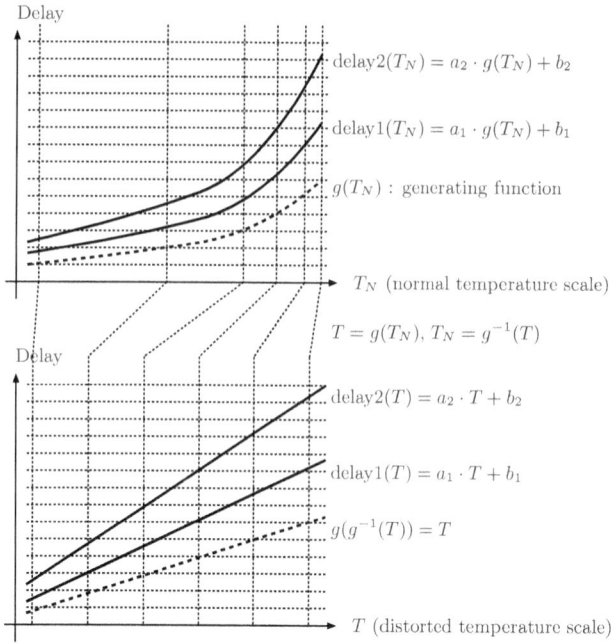

Figure 1: Delay in normal temperature scale and one in distorted temperature scale.

are shown in Section 5, and concluding remarks are given in Section 6.

2. MEANING OF LINEAR TEMPERATURE-DEPENDENCE MODEL

In this paper, we will use a linear temperature dependence model for circuit delay $\text{delay}(T)$,

$$\text{delay}(T) = \text{delay}(T_0)\left(1 + \beta \cdot (T - T_0)\right)$$

where T is a temperature at run time, T_0 is a reference temperature, and β is a relative coefficient in this first order temperature dependence model.

The temperature dependence of LSI performances has been intentionally studied in many literatures[8][9][10]. Since the temperature affects multiple parameters such as carrier mobility, threshold voltage, etc., the temperature dependency model of circuit delay has a degree of nonlinearity and several empirical constants. In spite of such spontaneous nonlinearity of temperature dependence, the validity of linear function model, when we limit the target technology, target temperature range, etc., has been pointed out in several literatures[5][7].

Here, we will introduce an alternative interpretation of linear temperature dependence model.

Now we do not specify any particular delay model as a function of the temperature (in the normal scale) T_N, instead we simply assume the following.
(1) Delay is monotonic with respect to the temperature T_N.
(2) When we consider a digital circuit, all delays in a circuit have a common generating function $g(T_N)$ as their temperature dependency, and they are represented with

$$\text{delay}(T_N) = a \cdot g(T_N) + b,$$

where a and b are two constants inherent to each delay. Note that, from (1), $g(T_N)$ is monotonic with respect to T_N.

Now we will introduce another temperature scale T (a distorted temperature scale) as,

$$T = g(T_N),$$

and, from the monotonicity of $f(T_N)$, we have

$$T_N = g^{-1}(T).$$

If we discuss the temperature-dependency of delays with using the distorted temperature scale T instead of the normal temperature scale T_N, delay can be represented as,

$$
\begin{aligned}
\text{delay}(T) &= a \cdot g(g^{-1}(T)) + b \\
&= a \cdot T + b \\
&= (a \cdot T_0 + b)\left(1 + \frac{a}{a \cdot T_0 + b}(T - T_0)\right) \\
&= \text{delay}(T_0)\left(1 + \tilde{a}(T - T_0)\right)
\end{aligned}
$$

where $T_0 = g(T_{N0})$ and T_{N0} is a reference temperature in the normal scale.

In the following of this paper, temperature and constants relevant to temperature are all represented in the distorted temperature scale specified by a generating function which might be inherent to a target technology.

3. TIMING CONSTRAINT WITH TEMPERATURE DEPENDENT CLOCK SKEW

In this paper, any specific application is not considered, and a standard sequential circuit together with intentional clock skew[11]-[14] is our target for the discussion.

3.1 Setup and Hold Constraints

Let $\boldsymbol{y}_{ij}$ be a set of combinatorial paths starting from ith flip-flop (FF_i) and terminating at jth flip-flop (FF_j), and let $d_{ij}^{max}(T)$ and $d_{ij}^{min}(T)$ be the maximum path delay and the minimum path delay over $\boldsymbol{y}_{ij}$ at the temperature (distorted temperature) T. On the other hand, let $x_i(T)$ be the clock skew for FF_i at the temperature T. All those delays are assumed to obey the linear temperature dependency model such as,

$$
\begin{aligned}
d_{ij}^{max}(T) &= d_{ij}^{max}(T_0)\left(1 + \beta_{i,j} \cdot (T - T_0)\right) \\
d_{ij}^{min}(T) &= d_{ij}^{min}(T_0)\left(1 + \beta_{i,j} \cdot (T - T_0)\right) \\
x_i(T) &= x_i(T_0)\left(1 + \gamma_i \cdot (T - T_0)\right)
\end{aligned}
$$

where T_0 is a reference temperature specified occasionally. Of course, we always consider the domain of the temperature T in the distorted scale such that

$$
\begin{aligned}
1 + \beta_{i,j} \cdot (T - T_0) &> 0 \\
1 + \gamma_i \cdot (T - T_0) &> 0
\end{aligned}
$$

holds. In the following discussions, we further assume that all $\beta_{i,j}$ and all γ_i are the same values as β and γ, respectively. We assume also $\beta > 0$ and $\gamma > 0$.

The correct operation of a sequential circuit relies on the setup timing constraint and the hold timing constraint. In order to apply those constraints to design problem, timing margins as design parameters specified by a designer are included in the following formulations.

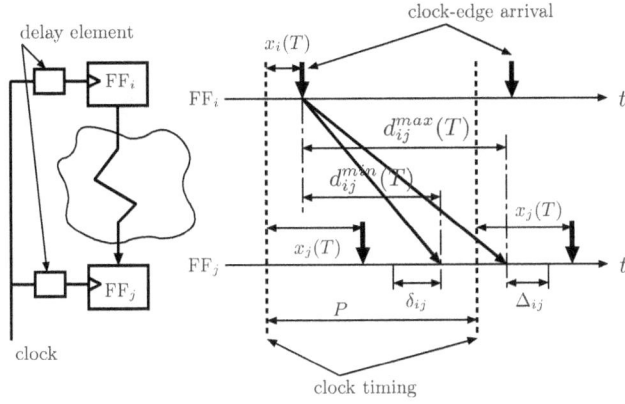

Figure 2: Setup timing constraint and hold timing constraint under intentional skew environment.

Setup timing constraint:

$$P + x_j(T) \geq x_i(T) + d_{ij}^{max}(T) + \Delta_{ij}$$

where P is a clock period, and Δ_{ij} is a specified timing margin (design parameter) for setup timing condition.

Hold timing constraint:

$$x_j(T) \leq x_i(T) + d_{ij}^{min}(T) - \delta_{ij}$$

where δ_{ij} is a specified timing margin (design parameter) for hold timing condition.

3.2 Temperature Dependency on Timing Constraints

Here we consider a constant T_0 as a reference temperature, and let $\Sigma_{ij} \geq 0$ be a timing slack of the setup timing constraint evaluated at temperature $T = T_0$, i.e.,

$$\Sigma_{ij} = \{P + x_j(T_0)\} - \{x_i(T_0) + d_{ij}^{max}(T_0) + \Delta_{ij}\} \quad (1)$$

Similarly, let $\sigma_{ij} \geq 0$ be a timing slack of the hold timing constraint evaluated at $T = T_0$.

$$\sigma_{ij} = \left\{x_i(T_0) + d_{ij}^{min}(T_0) - \delta_{ij}\right\} - x_j(T_0) \quad (2)$$

In order to check the effect of the temperature, we will substitute the temperature dependency models into the original setup and hold timing constraints.

$$P + x_j(T_0)\left(1 + \gamma \cdot (T - T_0)\right)$$
$$\geq x_i(T_0)\left(1 + \gamma \cdot (T - T_0)\right)$$
$$+ d_{ij}^{max}(T_0)\left(1 + \beta \cdot (T - T_0)\right) + \Delta_{ij}$$

$$x_j(T_0)\left(1 + \gamma \cdot (T - T_0)\right)$$
$$\leq x_i(T_0)\left(1 + \gamma \cdot (T - T_0)\right)$$
$$+ d_{ij}^{min}(T_0)\left(1 + \beta \cdot (T - T_0)\right) - \delta_{ij}$$

Finally we substitute Eq.(1) and Eq.(2) into the above formulations, and have final form of temperature dependent setup and hold constraints.

$$x_j(T_0) \cdot \gamma \cdot (T - T_0)$$
$$\geq x_i(T_0) \cdot \gamma \cdot (T - T_0)$$
$$+ d_{ij}^{max}(T_0) \cdot \beta \cdot (T - T_0) - \Sigma_{ij} \quad (3)$$

$$x_j(T_0) \cdot \gamma \cdot (T - T_0)$$
$$\leq x_i(T_0) \cdot \gamma \cdot (T - T_0)$$
$$+ d_{ij}^{min}(T_0) \cdot \beta \cdot (T - T_0) + \sigma_{ij} \quad (4)$$

3.3 Available Temperature Range

From Eq.s (3) and (4), we can compute an available temperature range for a designed circuit to operate correctly.

Eq.(3) can be rewritten as,

$$\left\{d_{ij}^{max}(T_0) \cdot \beta - (x_j(T_0) - x_i(T_0)) \cdot \gamma\right\}(T - T_0) \leq \Sigma_{ij}$$

Here we assume(see Section 3.4)

$$d_{ij}^{max}(T_0) \cdot \beta - (x_j(T_0) - x_i(T_0)) \cdot \gamma > 0, \quad (5)$$

and we have,

$$T \leq T_0 + \frac{\Sigma_{ij}}{d_{ij}^{max}(T_0) \cdot \beta - (x_j(T_0) - x_i(T_0)) \cdot \gamma} \quad (6)$$

Similarly, from Eq.(4) with assuming(see Section 3.4)

$$d_{ij}^{min}(T_0) \cdot \beta - (x_j(T_0) - x_i(T_0)) \cdot \gamma > 0, \quad (7)$$

we have,

$$T \geq T_0 - \frac{\sigma_{ij}}{d_{ij}^{min}(T_0) \cdot \beta - (x_j(T_0) - x_i(T_0)) \cdot \gamma} \quad (8)$$

Note that Eq.s (6) and (8) are obtained from each pair of source and destination flip-flops, and the maximum available temperature T_{max} and the minimum one T_{min} (both in distorted temperature) for a whole circuit to operate correctly are given as follows.

$$T_{max} = T_0$$
$$+ \min\left\{\frac{\Sigma_{ij}}{d_{ij}^{max}(T_0) \cdot \beta - (x_j(T_0) - x_i(T_0)) \cdot \gamma}\right\} \quad (9)$$

$$T_{min} = T_0$$
$$- \min\left\{\frac{\sigma_{ij}}{d_{ij}^{min}(T_0) \cdot \beta - (x_j(T_0) - x_i(T_0)) \cdot \gamma}\right\} \quad (10)$$

where "min" is the minimum over all pairs of i and j such that $y_{ij} \neq \emptyset$.

THEOREM 1. *If there is a temperature T_0 for which the set of setup and hold timing constraints has a feasible solution of skew values $x_i(T_0)$, i for all flip-flops, and if*

$$d_{ij}^{min}(T_0) \cdot \beta - (x_j(T_0) - x_i(T_0)) \cdot \gamma > 0$$

is satisfied for all pairs of i and j such that $y_{ij} \neq \emptyset$, then the setup timing constraint dominates only the maximum available temperature T_{max}, and the hold timing constraint dominates only the minimum available temperature T_{min}, where T_{max} and T_{min} are given in Eq.s (9) and (10), respectively.

COROLLARY 1. *For the case that the condition in Theorem 1 is satisfied, the setup timing constraint is always fulfilled for every temperature below T_{max}, and the hold timing constraint is always fulfilled for every temperature above T_{min}.*

3.4 Positiveness of the Denominators

During the derivation process of Theorem 1, we have introduced two assumptions on the sign of the weighted summation of delays, Eq.s (5) and (7). In general, those assumptions are not always true depending on the values of $d_{i,j}^{max/min}(T_0)$, $x_{i/j}(T_0)$, β and γ. Hence, as for more general discussions, we need to discuss not only the case that those assumptions are true, but also the case that those assumptions are not always true. However, in this paper, as the first attempt to establish the framework of temperature dependency aware skew design, we will focus our attention on the former case. In fact, the former seems more basic than the latter since all setup timing constraints (and all hold timing constraints, respectively) of all signal paths in a circuit can be treated in the same way for the former, while for the latter we need to check one path to another whether the assumption is satisfied or not, and apply different treatment depending on the check-result. In addition, those two assumptions are not so special, but rather likely to happen as it is shown below.

Because of $\beta > 0$ and $\gamma > 0$, if $x_j(T_0) \leq x_i(T_0)$, the assumptions Eq.s (5) and (7) are always true without depending on parameter values. For the case of $x_j(T_0) > x_i(T_0)$, $\beta \geq \gamma$ is one possible sufficient condition for the truth of those assumptions since

$$
\begin{aligned}
& d_{ij}^{max}(T_0) \cdot \beta - (x_j(T_0) - x_i(T_0)) \cdot \gamma \\
& \geq \ d_{ij}^{min}(T_0) \cdot \beta - (x_j(T_0) - x_i(T_0)) \cdot \gamma \\
& \geq \ \beta \left\{ d_{ij}^{min}(T_0) - (x_j(T_0) - x_i(T_0)) \right\} \\
& \geq \ \beta \cdot \delta_{ij} \geq 0.
\end{aligned}
$$

4. TEMPERATURE AWARE SKEW SCHEDULING

Several basic temperature aware skew scheduling problems can be considered. For example,

1. Find a set of skews satisfying correct operation with a given clock period P and a given temperature range $[T_L, T_H]$.

2. Find a set of skews which achieves $T_{max} \to$ max with a given clock period P subject to and $T_{min} \leq T_L$ (or $T_{min} \to$ min subject to $T_{max} \geq T_H$).

3. Find a set of skews which achieves $P \to$ min subject to the correct operation in a given temperature range $[T_L, T_H]$.

Note that the second one (and the third one as well) can be solved, for example, by using bisection search of the maximum T_{max} (clock period P for the third one) in which the solution of the first problem is used repeatedly during the search process. Hence, we will focus on the first problem in this section.

Temperature-Aware Skew Scheduling (TASS) Problem:

Given circuit information ($d_{ij}^{max}(T_0)$, $d_{ij}^{min}(T_0)$, β, γ) as well as a clock period P, required setup timing margin Δ, hold timing margin δ, and two real numbers T_L and T_H, $T_L \leq T_0 \leq T_H$, find the set of skew values $x_i(T_0)$, i for all flip-flops, such that the given circuit operates without violating setup and hold timing constraints in the temperature range $[T_L, T_H]$.

A method to solve this problem is derived in the rest of this section.

4.1 Enumeration of Design Constraints

Treatment of Upper Temperature Bound

From Eq. (6), for each pair of i and j such that $\boldsymbol{y}_{ij} \neq \emptyset$,

$$
T_H \leq T_0 + \frac{\Sigma_{ij}}{d_{ij}^{max}(T_0) \cdot \beta - (x_j(T_0) - x_i(T_0)) \cdot \gamma}
$$

is requested, where Σ_{ij} is a setup timing slack at temperature T_0, which is given as,

$$
\Sigma_{ij} = \{ P + x_j(T_0) \} - \{ x_i(T_0) + d_{ij}^{max}(T_0) + \Delta \}
$$

and Σ_{ij} should be non-negative (equivalent to the setup timing constraint at temperature T_0).

Combining these two formulas and assuming the positiveness of the denominator of the last term in the former (Eq.(5), Section 3.4), we have,

$$
\begin{aligned}
& (T_H - T_0) \left(d_{ij}^{max}(T_0) \cdot \beta - (x_j(T_0) - x_i(T_0)) \cdot \gamma \right) \\
& \leq \ P + x_j(T_0) - x_i(T_0) - d_{ij}^{max}(T_0) - \Delta,
\end{aligned}
$$

and finally we have,

$$
\begin{aligned}
& x_j(T_0) - x_i(T_0) \\
& \geq \frac{\{1 + (T_H - T_0)\beta\} \, d_{ij}^{max}(T_0) - P + \Delta}{1 + (T_H - T_0)\gamma}
\end{aligned} \tag{11}
$$

This one can be interpreted as the setup timing constraint at temperature T_H, which is represented using the skew at temperature T_0. Remark that, under the situation $\beta \geq \gamma$, when Eq. (11) holds, $\Sigma_{ij} \geq 0$ holds as well.

Treatment of Lower Temperature Bound

Similar to the case of upper temperature bound, from Eq.(8) and Eq.(2),

$$
T_L \geq T_0 - \frac{x_i(T_0) + d_{ij}^{min}(T_0) - \delta - x_j(T_0)}{d_{ij}^{min}(T_0) \cdot \beta - (x_j(T_0) - x_i(T_0)) \cdot \gamma}
$$

is requested. By applying modifications, finally we have,

$$
\begin{aligned}
& x_i(T_0) - x_j(T_0) \\
& \geq \frac{- \{1 + (T_L - T_0)\beta\} \, d_{ij}^{min}(T_0) + \delta}{1 + (T_L - T_0)\gamma}
\end{aligned} \tag{12}
$$

From the above discussions, we can conclude that TASS Problem can be solved by enumerating all setup constraints given by Eq. (11) and all hold constraints given by Eq. (12), and finding $x_i(T_0)$ satisfying all those constraints.

4.2 Graph Theoretic Approach

Graph theoretic approach to the conventional skew scheduling is well known[12]. Fortunately, a similar approach can be applied to our TASS Problem.

In our proposed framework, timing constraints for solving TASS Problem have a uniform style like

$$
x_t(T_0) \geq x_s(T_0) + w_{st}
$$

where $x_t(T_0)$ and $x_s(T_0)$ are two skew variables (unknown variables), and w_{st} is a fixed constant. When a problem is formulated as the set of inequalities in this form, we can find a feasible solution by computing the longest path lengths on a weighted graph (constraint graph) generated by given inequalities.

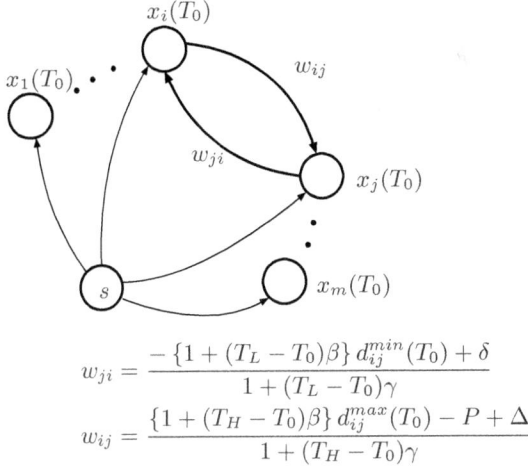

$$w_{ji} = \frac{-\{1 + (T_L - T_0)\beta\} d_{ij}^{min}(T_0) + \delta}{1 + (T_L - T_0)\gamma}$$

$$w_{ij} = \frac{\{1 + (T_H - T_0)\beta\} d_{ij}^{max}(T_0) - P + \Delta}{1 + (T_H - T_0)\gamma}$$

Figure 3: Constraint graph for computing feasible skew. Edges between $x_i(T_0)$ and $x_j(T_0)$ with their weights w_{ij} and w_{ji} are placed for representing hold and setup timing constraints for y_{ij}.

In order to solve our TASS Problem, the constraint graph is constructed by (1) placing vertices corresponding to skew variables, (2) for each setup timing constraint given by Eq.(11), placing a direct edge $(x_i(T_L), x_j(T_L))$ with its weight

$$\frac{\{1 + (T_H - T_0)\beta\} d_{ij}^{max}(T_0) - P + \Delta}{1 + (T_H - T_0)\gamma},$$

(3) for each hold timing constraint given by Eq.(12), placing a direct edge $(x_j(T_0), x_i(T_0))$ with its weight

$$\frac{-\{1 + (T_L - T_0)\beta\} d_{ij}^{min}(T_0) + \delta}{1 + (T_L - T_0)\gamma},$$

and (4) placing an auxiliary vertex s and directed edge from s to all other vertices with their weights 0s.

If (and only if) the constraint graph has no positive cycle, the given set of inequalities has a feasible solution, and the longest path lengths from s provide feasible solution $x_i(T_0)$, i for all flip-flops.

5. EXPERIMENTS

In this section, several experimental results are shown. Unfortunately, we do not have practical information on temperature dependency of logic circuits, delay components, etc., and hence we cannot demonstrate practical gain of performance in real application fields. Instead of them, using computer simulation together with several artificial parameter setting, we will demonstrate somewhat idealized features of our method. The major purposes of these experiments include (1) verifying the performance gain achieved by our temperature- dependency aware skew scheduling, and (2) providing materials to discuss better situations in temperature-dependent behavior.

Recall that our approach relies on the linear temperature-dependency model based on the concept of distorted temperature scale. Temperature-relevant values are all presented in the distorted temperature scale in this section also.

Table 1: Comparison of maximum available temperature. "maxM" denotes a conventional skew scheduling which maximizes timing slack, and "maxTH" denotes the proposed skew scheduling which maximizes maximum available temperature.

| Circuit | Maximum temperature (maxTH/maxM in %) | | | |
| | $\gamma = 0.0$ | | $\gamma = 0.25$ | |
	maxM	maxTH	maxM	maxTH
s208	1.85	2.16 (117%)	2.09	2.66 (127%)
s298	1.46	1.63 (112%)	1.52	1.85 (122%)
s344	1.23	1.79 (146%)	1.24	2.12 (171%)
s386	1.20	1.20 (100%)	1.20	1.20 (100%)
s400	1.85	2.28 (123%)	2.07	2.53 (122%)
s444	1.89	2.19 (116%)	2.14	2.78 (130%)
s510	1.18	1.19 (101%)	1.19	1.19 (100%)
s526	1.47	1.63 (111%)	1.53	1.85 (121%)
s641	1.24	1.33 (107%)	1.26	1.40 (111%)
s713	1.24	1.32 (106%)	1.25	1.39 (111%)
s838	1.69	1.83 (108%)	1.83	1.83 (100%)
s953	1.28	1.41 (110%)	1.31	1.47 (112%)
s1196	1.25	1.30 (104%)	1.26	1.30 (103%)
s1423	1.18	1.25 (106%)	1.19	1.30 (109%)

5.1 Improvement of Maximum Available Temperature

First we will evaluate the effectiveness of skew scheduling considering temperature dependency. Sequential circuits from ISCAS'89 benchmark are used for this experiment.

In the first experiment, we have set the clock period P at the maximum of maximum path delays between flipflops in each circuit, and compare the maximum available temperature achieved by our proposed temperature aware skew scheduling (given T_L as a constraint and maximize T_H) with the one achieved by a conventional skew scheduling which maximizes the minimum timing slack evaluated at the reference temperature T_0. We have set the setup timing margin $\Delta = 0.0$ and the hold timing margin $\delta = 0.0$ since we are not considering any practical technique nor any practical application, and hence there is no reasonable way to fix those values. In addition, the effect of those values is not essential in the comparison of our thermal-aware skew scheduling with a conventional one. As for temperature-dependency parameters, we set $\beta = 0.25$ and $\gamma = 0.0$ or $\gamma = 0.25$. The value 0.25 has no practical meaning here. $(\beta, \gamma) = (0.25, 0.25)$ is a model in which delay elements for intentional skew has the same temperature characteristics with combinatorial signal paths between flipflops, while $(\beta, \gamma) = (0.25, 0.0)$ is a kind of virtual model in which the intentional skew has zero temperature dependency.

Table 1 shows the result. Similar to the fact that the effect (typically, the improvement of the clock frequency) of intentional skew depends on circuit configuration, the maximum available temperature optimized by skew scheduling varies circuit by circuit. The maximum available temperature is improved maximally 71% for s344, while it is not improved for s386 and s510. Detailed study of circuit-dependency of the maximum available temperature is left as one of future works.

One other issue observed from those results is the effect of γ, the temperature-dependency of the delay for intentional skew, i.e., the case $\gamma = 0.25$ is better in the maximum avail-

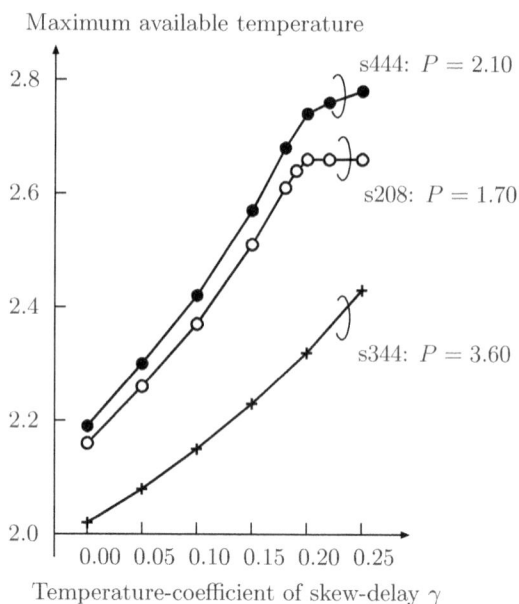

Maximum available temperature

Figure 4: γ-dependency of the maximum available temperature for s208.1, s344 and s444.

able temperature than the case $\gamma = 0.0$ for most circuits. This issue will be verified again later.

5.2 Choice of Temperature Coefficient

Fig.4 shows γ-dependency of the maximum available temperature for benchmark circuits s208.1, s344 and s444. Individual dependency-curve changes circuit by circuit, but it is common for those three circuits that as γ approaches to β, the maximum available temperature is improved. It indicates that the concept of self-compensation of temperature variation by a temperature-dependent delay for skew is valid not only for simple pipeline circuits but also a certain class of sequential circuits having feedback paths. Detailed discussions on this issue are beyond the scope of this paper.

6. CONCLUSION

This paper proposed an approach to temperature-aware skew scheduling for a general class of sequential circuits. Our approach improves the available temperature range of a circuit compared with a conventional skew scheduling which maximizes the minimum timing slack. On the other hand, during the formulation process, we have encountered several conditional branches, and have chosen one of alternatives for each branch. One of serious choices arises from the sign of $d_{ij}^{min}(T_0) \cdot \beta - (x_j(T_0) - x_i(T_0)) \cdot \gamma$, and we have discussed only the case of positive sign by assuming $\beta \geq \gamma$. A complete formulation including all possible choices is an important future work. Optimization of a combinatorial circuit part and delay components for generating skew considering the temperature aware timing behavior is also an interesting future work.

7. ACKNOWLEDGEMENTS

The author would like to thank Dr. Renyuan Zhang, JAIST, for useful discussions. This work is partly supported by JSPS KAKENHI Grant Number 26420303.

8. REFERENCES

[1] M. Cho, S. Ahmed, D. Z. Pan, "TACO: Temperature Aware Clock-tree Optimization", Proc. ICCAD'05, pp.581-586, 2005.

[2] A. Chakraborty, P. Sithambaram, K.Duraisami, A. Macii, E. Macii, M. Poncino, "Thermal Resilient Bounded-Skew Clock Tree Optimization Methodology", Proc. DATE'06, pp.832-837, 2006.

[3] C.-C. Liu, J. Su, Y. Shi, "Temperature-Aware Clock Tree Synthesis Considering Spatiotemporal Hot Spot Correlations", Proc. ICCAD'08, pp.107-113, 2008.

[4] A. Chakraborty, K. Duraisami, A. Sathanur, P. Sithambaram, L. Benini, A. Macii, E. Macii, M. Poncino, "Dynamic Thermal Clock Skew Compensation Using Tunable Delay Buffers", IEEE Trans. VLSI Systems, Vol. 16, No. 6, pp.639-649, 2008.

[5] J. Long, J. C. Ku, S. O. Memik, Y. Ismail, "A Self Adjusting Clock Tree Architectgure to Cope with Temperature Variations", Proc. ICCAD'07, pp.75-82, 2007.

[6] J. Long, J. C. Ku, S. O. Memik, Y. Ismail, "SACTA: A Self-Adjusting Clock Tree Architecure for Adapting to Thermal-Induced Delay Variation", IEEE Trans. VLSI Systems, Vol.18, No.9, pp.1323-1336, 2010.

[7] J. Ku, Y. Ismail, "Thermal-Aware Methogology for Repeater Insertion in Low-Power VLSI Circuits", IEEE Trans. VLSI Systems, Vol. 15, No. 8, pp.963-970, August 2007.

[8] R. Cobbold, "Temperature Effects on MOS Transistors", Electron Letter, Vol.2, pp.190-192, 1966.

[9] Y.Cao et al., "New Paradigm of Predictive MOSFET and Interconnect Modeling for Early Circuit Design", Proc. IEEE Custom Integrated Circuits Conference, pp.201-204, 2000.

[10] W. Liao, L. He, K. Lepak, "Temperature and Supply Voltage Aware Performance and Power Modeling at Microarchitecture Level", IEEE Trans. Computer-Aided Design of Integrated Circuits and Systems, Vol.24, No.7, pp.1042-1053, 2005.

[11] J. P. Fishburn, "Clock Skew Optimization", IEEE Trans. Computers, vol. 39, no. 7, pp.945-951, 1990.

[12] R. B. Deokar, and S. S. Sapatnekar, "A Graph Theoretic Approach to Clock skew Optimization", Proc. ISCAS, vol.1, pp.407-410, 1994.

[13] E. Takahashi, M. Murakawa, K. Toda, T. Higuchi, "An Evolvable-hardware-based Clock Timing Architecuture towards GigaHz Digital Systems", Proc. of AAAI Genetic Algorithm and Evolutionary Computation Conference, pp.1204-1210, 1999.

[14] J.-L. Tsai, D.-H. Baik, C. C.-P. Chen, K. Saluja, "A Yield Improvement Methodology Using Pre- and Post-Silicon Statistical Clock Scheduling", ICCAD, 2004.

Dynamic Task Priority Scaling for Thermal Management of Multi-core Processors with Heavy Workload

Ali Akbari §, Hamid Noori †, Saadat Pour Mozafari §, Farhad Mehdipour ‡

§ Amirkabir University of
Technology
424 Hafez Ave, Tehran, IRAN
ali-akbari@aut.ac.ir

saadat@aut.ac.ir

† Ferdowsi University of Mashhad
Azadi Sq., Mashhad, IRAN
hnoori@um.ac.ir

‡ E-JUST Center, Graduate
School of ISEE, Kyushu
University
Fukuoka, JAPAN
farhad@ejust.kyushu-u.ac.jp

ABSTRACT

This paper presents a task priority scaling algorithm for dynamic thermal management of multi-core processors. The unique features of this algorithm include: 1) enabling task-level Dynamic Frequency Scaling (DFS) capability through software, 2) reducing task migration and provide load balancing using dynamic task priority scaling, 3) targeting DTM for systems with high workload. This algorithm is evaluated on a commercial quad-core processor. The experimental results indicate that the proposed approach can decrease the average and peak temperature by 9.73% and 7.1%, respectively, compared to Linux standard scheduler.

Categories and Subject Descriptors

C.4 [**Performance of Systems**]: *Design studies, Measurement techniques, Performance attributes*; B.8.2 [**Performance and Reliability**]: Performance Analysis and Design Aids

General Terms

Management, Performance, Reliability, Experimentation

Keywords

Dynamic Thermal Management; Dynamic Task Priority Scaling; DVFS; Task Migration

1. INTRODUCTION

The size of transistors is decreasing due to advances in technology which allows further integration in a specified area and hence, designing faster and more complex processors. More integration density is associated with more power consumption and thus, higher temperature. Higher temperature results in problems such as less reliability, more propagation delay, shorter aging and higher costs required for cooling [1]. Therefore, thermal management is essential to address the aforementioned issues.

Different strategies have been proposed for thermal management including static and dynamic techniques. Both hardware and

software approaches exist for dynamic thermal management. stop-go [1], dynamic voltage and frequency scaling (DVFS) can be categorized as hardware-based DTM techniques and task scheduling and task migration are software-based DTM techniques.

Dynamic voltage and frequency scaling (DVFS) is the most effective hardware technique for thermal management [2]. This technique can be implemented locally or globally. In the global approach, the frequency/voltage of all cores is adjusted in group while in the local method, the frequency/voltage of each core is tuned individually.

Both methods have their advantages and disadvantages. The implementation of global method is easier, but it reduces the performance of all cores. Although the temperature of only one core may be higher than a certain threshold, the speed of all cores degrades. The local method is a more efficient strategy [3]. Disadvantages of local DVFS include lack of scalability and high implementation costs.

Most of the DTM software solutions have been proposed for the light workloads, i.e. the cases where the number of tasks is less than of number of cores [4-7]. They are not typically applicable for the heavy workloads, i.e. the cases where the number of tasks is higher than the number of cores. In light workloads, the task migration technique is more effective for DTM. However, when the workload is heavy, task migration is not very effective, because all the cores are busy running the tasks.

There are several techniques to measuring the temperature of the cores including the use of physical sensors, performance counters and thermal models. For effective DTM predicting the future temperature is very important. Accordingly, critical conditions can be predicted to prevent the violation of temperature threshold in a processor. By tracking the thermal behavior of a core, the future temperature can be predicted and the proper actions can be taken based on the predicted temperature.

In this paper, we propose a new technique for dynamic thermal management of multicore processors with high workload (when the number of tasks is higher than the number of cores) based on *dynamic task priority scaling* (DTPS). The proposed software technique provides dynamic frequency scaling at task level through task priority scaling on the cores. Thus, local dynamic frequency scaling can be achieved at no cost in the systems lacking this hardware feature. Moreover, due to less number of task migrations due to task priority scaling, the proposed technique enhances performance degradation imposed due to applying DTM.

The proposed approach is evaluated on Intel's Core i7-3770 processor. The results for running various number of applications from SPEC CPU2006 Suite show that the proposed scheduling technique reduces the average and peak temperature by 9.73% and 7.1%, respectively compared to standard Linux scheduler. It results in a performance overhead of 1.25% compared to standard Linux scheduler.

Our concrete contributions in this work are as follows:

- The software technique presented in this paper provides dynamic frequency scaling at task level in multi-core processors.
- Due to less number of task migration using the task priority scaling, runtime overhead is significantly reduced.
- The target of the proposed approach is DTM for processors with high workloads.

The paper is organized as follows: Section 2 reviews the literature on DTM of multicore processors. Section 3 explains the prerequisites. The proposed algorithm is described in Section 4. The results are presented in Section 5, and concluding remarks are given in Section 6.

2. Related Works

Various techniques have been proposed for DTM of modern processors. These techniques can be classified into three groups: 1) hardware based, 2) software based, and 3) hybrid hardware/software techniques. The major disadvantage of hardware methods is their high performance overhead. The software techniques have lower performance overhead than hardware methods, but their effectiveness to manage and reduce the temperature is lower. Dynamic software thermal management techniques such as task scheduling [8, 9, 10] and task migration [2, 4, 5, 6, 9] are able to reduce the temperature with low performance overhead without additional hardware. The third method involves a combination of software and hardware techniques for dynamic thermal management [5, 9].

In paper [8] first, the tasks are assigned to the cores to establish thermal equilibrium. If the core is overheated, the hot applications are deferred and a cooling loop is run. Authors in [9] proposed a DTM approach to reduce the on-chip temperature variance and the occurrence of hot spots by considering transient thermal effects. This method performs the task migrations to reduce the temperature variations across the chip. Authors in [10] proposed a thermal-aware round-robin scheduling algorithm in the Linux kernel for multiple threads (more than the number of cores). Authors in [5] use a combination of hardware and software techniques for thermal management. The work of [11] introduces a simulation-based technique for parallel applications, called thread shuffling. This technique dynamically maps threads with similar criticality degrees into the same core and then applies DVFS to non-critical cores which execute fast threads. Their use of local DVFS restricts the proposed algorithm to only a few specific processors.

An effective approach in thermal management is to estimate the future core temperature. Using the predicted temperatures, the core temperature can be reduced before reaching the threshold temperature. Authors in [6] introduce one of the first attempts to predict the core temperature. In this technique, the temperature is predicted using the thermal model of applications and the cores. In critical conditions, the applications migrate from the overheated core to the coldest future core in favor of reducing the processor's temperature.

The work in [7] uses the idle cycle injection into the core rather than DVFS. Using the least square method, a model has been proposed to estimate the temperature and the required idle cycle injection. DTM techniques have been developed mostly for the cases light workloads (where the number of tasks is less than the number of cores) [2, 4, 5, 6, 7]. Thus, it is essential to find solutions for the cases of high workloads.

3. Algorithm Prerequisites

In this section, the preliminary issues used in different sections are explained.

3.1 Problem Definition

The system studied in this paper is a multicore processor with N cores, denoted as (core$_1$, core$_2$, ..., core$_N$). Each of N cores has a physical thermal sensor. Since in this paper we focus on high workload, it is also assumed that there are at least $2N$ tasks for executing on each core. The problem considered in this paper is how to schedule this tasks among cores dynamically such that the average and peak temperature of the processor is minimized under minimum performance loss and also temperature does not violate (T_{max}). We propose a heuristic method to solve the problem using task priority scaling and DVFS. It has been assumed that the processor supports global DVFS and performance counters. First, the proposed algorithm predicts the future temperature of the each core considering their workload of the cores. According to the predicted temperature and the temperature of the tasks, the time slice which should be devoted to each task in the core is calculated and determined so that the threshold temperature (T_{Max}) is not violated.

3.2 Physical Features of Cores

The cores of a processor do not have the same thermal behavior due to various reasons such as packaging technology [6] and process variation [12]. This makes a thermal difference of 10~15 °C between the cores while running the same applications. This phenomenon is known as physical features of cores [4]. According to [4], we conducted different experiments on Intel's Core i7 3770 processor to identify the cold and hot cores. The results are shown in Table 1.

Table 1. The thermal difference between the cores.

Benchmark	gcc	hmmer	bzip2
	Intel Core i7-3770		
Core 0	56∘C	60∘C	59∘C
Core 1	56∘C	60∘C	59∘C
Core 2	57∘C	62∘C	60∘C
Core 3	55∘C	58∘C	58∘C

CPU2006 SPEC benchmark programs were used for this purpose. The results were obtained for the cases when a core runs an application and other cores are idle. All the experiments are done while the CPU fan speed is constant and fixed. The reported temperature is the peak temperature among the cores. The selected benchmark programs includes *hmmer*, *gcc* and *bzip2*. When the core 2 is running *hmmer* and other cores are idle, the highest temperature among the four cores of Core i7 3770 processor is 62 °C.

According to Table 1, despite the fact that all four cores have the same settings, the cores 3 and 2 are always the coldest and hottest cores, respectively.

3.3 Prediction Model

Performance counters are used to identify hot and cold tasks for task priority scaling. In this study, Instructions Per Cycle (IPC) performance counter is used for determining hot and cold tasks. When the IPC of a task is higher, the task is hotter and thus produces a higher temperature. Given the IPC of each task, the priority of tasks is set such that the temperature would not exceed the threshold. For this purpose, we need an IPC-based temperature predictor. Hence, a predictor is proposed to estimate the future temperature using the IPC. The predictor makes use of current temperature $T(t)$, current IPC $(IPC(t))$ and next IPC $(IPC(t+1))$ to estimate the temperature of the cores for the next time slot (t+1). The predicted temperature is calculated using the equation (1):

$$T(t + 1) = a.T(t) + b.IPC(t) + c.IPC(t + 1) + d \qquad (1)$$

where $IPC(t)$ is the IPC of core N at time t, $T(t)$ is the temperature of core N at time t. The offline coefficients a, b and c are obtained using regression and d is a constant.

Replacing the threshold temperature with the estimated temperature, the next IPC $(IPC(t+1))$ is obtained to apply in the proposed algorithm. According to equation (2):

$$IPC(t + 1) = \frac{T(t + 1) - a.T(t) - b.IPC(t) - d}{c} \qquad (2)$$

4. Proposed Algorithm

We plan to manage the temperature for a system where the number of tasks is more than the number of cores. Accordingly, we need to schedule tasks on each core. The thermal properties of each task differs with other tasks, thus the tasks are divided into cold and hot tasks. The IPC of a core is defined as the summation (IPC times core utilization percentage) of all the tasks running on that core. By adjusting the contribution of execution time of each task (core utilization percentage), the temperature of each task can be managed without reducing the working frequency, doing task migration or injecting idle cycle in high workload. For this purpose, the operating system time slices are adapted using the command, "*niceness*" [13]. In this case, the priority of tasks are set in the range of -20 (highest priority) to 19 (lowest priority). The Linux Completely Fair Scheduler (CFS) calculates a weight based on the niceness. The weight of τ_i is roughly equivalent to equation (3):

$$W\tau_i = \frac{1024}{1.25^{\wedge}nice\ value} \qquad (3)$$

As the nice value decreases the weight increases exponentially. The time slice allocated for the τ_i is proportional to the weight of the task divided by the total weight of all runnable tasks. According to equation (4):

$$T_i = \frac{W\tau_i}{\sum_0^i W\tau_i} \times T_{Total} \qquad (4)$$

where (T_i) is the time slice allocated for the τ_i and T_{Total} is the time slice of core.

Figure 1 shows the flowchart of the proposed algorithm. In this algorithm, first, the tasks are sorted in terms of their temperature according to their IPC and then they are assigned to the cores. The hottest task is assigned to the coldest core (considering the physical features) and the second hottest task is assigned to the second coldest core. This process is repeated to fill up all the cores with all the tasks.

There are two temperature thresholds in our proposed algorithm. The first is T_{Max}, which is the temperature that is supposed not to be violated. The second is $T_{Critical}$, the threshold that is less than T_{Max}. The frequency of processor is not increased until the temperature is above $T_{Critical}$.

The required IPC is predicted by replacing (T_{Max}) with the next temperature $T(t+1)$ using equation (2). If the predicted IPC of core N $(IPC_{Predict})$ is higher than the IPC of the hottest task in core N (IPC_{HotN}), the total CPU time is assigned to the hottest task (I). If the predicted IPC of core N is lower than the IPC of the coldest task in core N (IPC_{ColdN}), the total CPU time is assigned to the coldest task (II). If the IPC of core N is between the IPC of the hottest task of core N and the coldest task of core N, the core utilization percentage of these two hottest and coldest tasks are determined so that the estimated IPC can be achieved (III).

The CPU time percentage (core utilization percentage) is assigned to the tasks in the operating system scheduler in a competitive manner. In other words, if we have only one task in the core even with the lowest priority, the 100% core utilization percentage is assigned to that task, because this task has no competitor in the core and thus will be the winner of the competition. Due to the competitive nature of the tasks, equation (5) is obtained:

$$IPC_N = \alpha.IPC_{\tau_{HotN}} + \beta.IPC_{\tau_{ColdN}} \qquad (5)$$

$$\alpha + \beta = 1$$

where IPC_N is IPC of the core N and $IPC_{\tau_{HotN}}$ and $IPC_{\tau_{ColdN}}$ are IPCs of the hottest and coldest tasks. According to equation (3), α and β, the core utilization percentage the tasks. The estimated IPC is achieved by task priority scaling. After priority scaling of the tasks, if the core temperature is still greater than threshold, the frequency is scaled down by one step. Conversely, if the temperature is lower the critical temperature $(T_{Critical})$, the frequency is scaled up by one step. Whenever a task is completed, the tasks are re-scheduled according to the new IPC and are re-assigned to the cores.

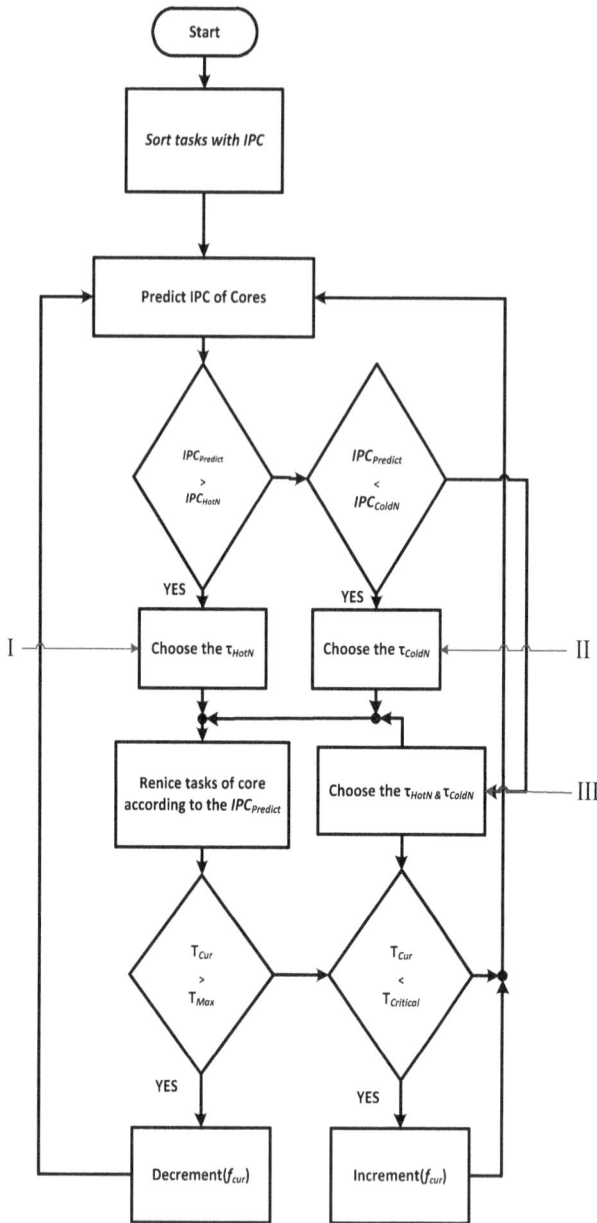

Figure 1. The flowchart of the proposed DTPS algorithm.

5. Experimental Results

This section provides experimental results for evaluating the proposed approach for different number of applications from SPEC CPU2006 benchmarks and an analysis on the obtained results.

5.1 Experimental Setup

The results obtained under high workloads (more than 8 applications) using SPEC CPU2006 applications are presented in this section. Table 2 shows the selected applications from SPEC CPU2006 suite. These applications have been simultaneously run and scheduled on Intel's Core i7 3770 when Simultaneous Multi-Threading (SMT) feature is disabled. The features of the target

system is 8GB RAM, Linux 3.2.0 as the operating system and Lm-sensor tool is used to get the cores temperature [14].

Cpufreq and *libpfm* tools are used to control the processor frequency and get the performance counters, respectively. The speed of the CPU fan is kept constant, hence, all the experiments are performed under the same conditions. The processor has 16 frequency steps from 1.6 GHz to 3.9 GHz. The temperature threshold (T_{max}) and critical temperatures $(T_{Critical})$ are set to be 62°C and 58 °C, respectively.

Table 2. SPEC CPU2006 applications used in experimental results (each benchmark is run separately in processor).

Benchmarks	bzip2	cactusADM	gcc	gromacs
Average Temperature	53.1∘C	53.5∘C	49.7∘C	54.3∘C
Benchmarks	hmmer	lbm	libquantum	mcf
Average Temperature	56.1∘C	55.2∘C	51.9∘C	50.1∘C
Benchmarks	namd	perlbench	sjeng	soplex
Average Temperature	52.2∘C	51.1∘C	52.8∘C	50.5∘C

5.2 Thermal Management Results

During running various number of applications under the proposed scheduling technique and Linux scheduler on Intel's Core i7 3770 processor, the cores temperature are recorded. The average and peak core temperatures and runtime obtained from the proposed algorithm and Linux scheduler are compared in Figure 2.

The results obtained from our algorithm and Linux standard scheduler are summarized in Table 3. The results show that the proposed technique reduces the average and peak temperatures by 9.73% and 7.1%, respectively. It shows a performance overhead (increase in runtime) of 1.25% compared with the standard Linux. It is worth mentioning that the average temperature means the average temperatures of 4 cores when applications are run simultaneously from beginning to end. Figure 3 shows the peak temperature at any moment.

Table 3. Comparison of DTPS and Linux scheduler running 8 to 12 applications simultaneously.

	Average Temperature	Peak Temperature	Runtime (sec)
DTPS	55.42∘C	62∘C	2557
Linux	60.81∘C	66.4∘C	2589
Improvement	9.73%	7.1%	-1.25%

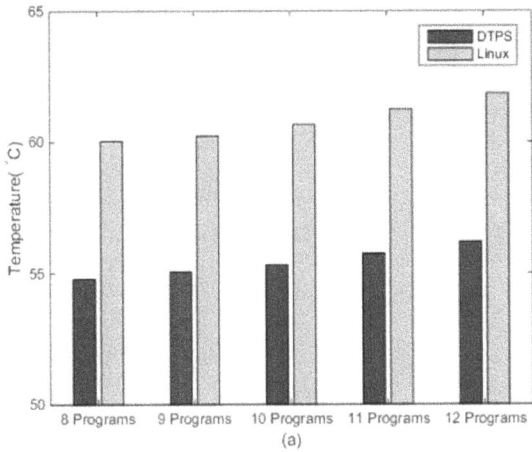

(a)

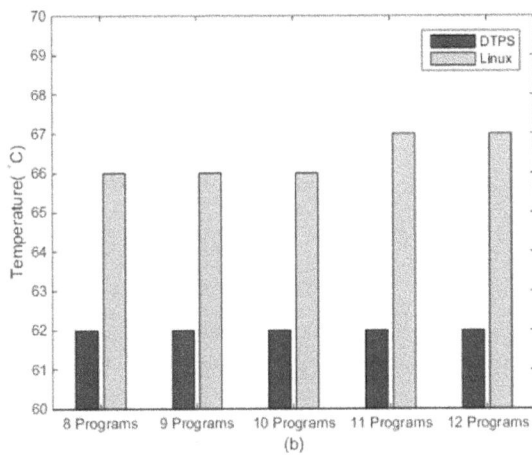

Figure 3. Peak temperature obtained from Linux scheduler and the proposed algorithm (DTPS) when 12 applications are run simultaneously.

5.3 Physical Features Analysis

To evaluate the effectiveness of physical features, we disable that part of the algorithm. By considering the physical features, 1.4% (0.8°C) and 2.1% (65 seconds) improvement is obtained on average temperature and performance compared to the case when the cores are selected randomly and their physical features are not considered (Figure 4).The temperature difference between the coldest and hottest core is 2.4°C in the case physical features are not considered and 1.4°C in the case physical features are considered.

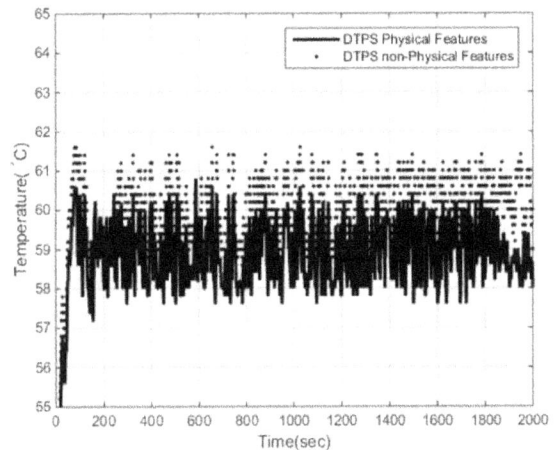

(b)

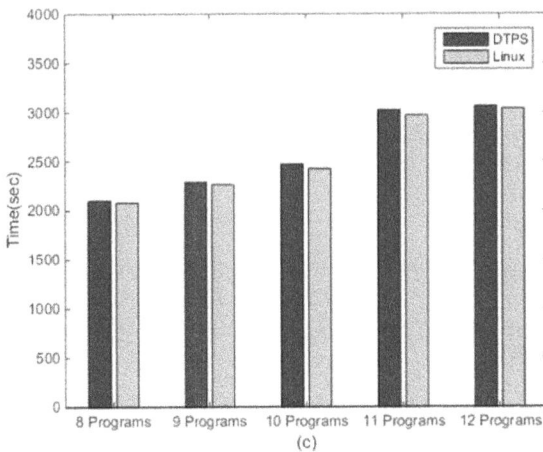

(c)

Figure 2. Comparison of DTPS and Linux with various number of programs in terms of (a) average temperature (b) peak temperature, and (c) runtime.

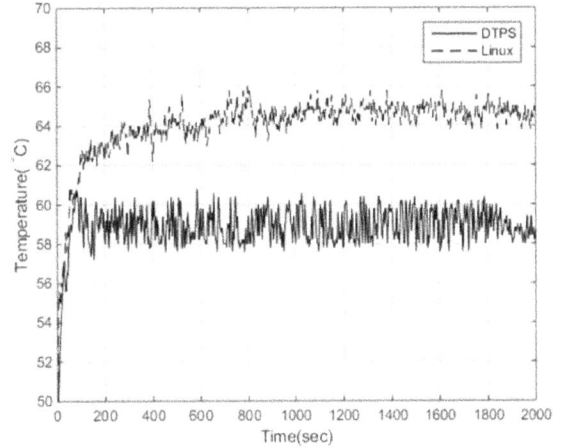

Figure 4. Peak temperature obtained from the proposed algorithm (DTPS) at two state of considering and do not consider physical features.

5.4 Performance Counter Analysis

Our algorithm uses performance counters to predict the temperature of tasks and to enable to sort the applications according to their temperature. We need to evaluate the correlation between the performance counter that we've chosen and temperature. To do so, we first run different programs and profile the IPC counter of these programs, then the correlation between IPC and temperature of programs is calculated using Pearson Product-Moment Correlation Coefficient (PPMCC) [15]. It is used as a criterion to measure the correlation between two variables X and Y. The r coefficient is calculated using equation (6):

$$r = \frac{\sum_{i=1}^{N}(X_i - \overline{X})(Y_i - \overline{Y})}{\sqrt{\sum_{i=1}^{N}(X_i - \overline{X})^2}\sqrt{\sum_{i=1}^{N}(Y_i - \overline{Y})^2}}, \qquad (6)$$

where N is number of sampled data, $\overline{X}$, $\overline{Y}$ are the averages for X and Y variables, respectively. The relationship between X and Y is perfect when r is 1 or -1. The average correlations between IPC and applications temperature of twelve programs (Table 2) is 0.42.

6. Conclusion

We proposed an algorithm for dynamic thermal management using a temperature predictor and task priority scaling for a multi-core processor with a temperature sensor for each core. The proposed algorithm manages the processor temperature by considering the physical characteristics of the cores. For dynamic thermal management, it is essential to set the priority of tasks (task priority scaling) without the need for task migration using physical characteristics of cores, thermal behavior of applications and appropriate performance counters. These factors have a significant impact on the efficiency of thermal management. Experimental results obtained from SPEC CPU2006 benchmark applications on a desktop platform (Intel's Core i7-3770) indicates that the proposed algorithm outperforms the standard Linux scheduler in terms of thermal management with minimal performance overhead.

7. REFERENCES

[1] Sheikh, H. F., Ahmad, I., Wang, Z., & Ranka, S. (2012). An overview and classification of thermal-aware scheduling techniques for multi-core processing systems. *Sustainable Computing: Informatics and Systems*, *2*(3), 151-169.

[2] Kong, J., Chung, S. W., & Skadron, K. (2012). Recent thermal management techniques for microprocessors. *ACM Computing Surveys (CSUR)*, *44*(3), 13.

[3] Donald, J., & Martonosi, M. (2006, June). Techniques for multicore thermal management: Classification and new exploration. In *ACM SIGARCH Computer Architecture News* (Vol. 34, No. 2, pp. 78-88). IEEE Computer Society.

[4] Salami, B., Baharani, M., Noori, H., & Mehdipour, F. (2014). Physical-aware task migration algorithm for dynamic thermal management of SMT multi-core processors. In *ASP-DAC* (pp. 292-297).

[5] Kumar, A., Shang, L., Peh, L. S., & Jha, N. K. (2006, July). HybDTM: a coordinated hardware-software approach for dynamic thermal management. In *Proceedings of the 43rd annual Design Automation Conference* (pp. 548-553). ACM.

[6] Yeo, I., Liu, C. C., & Kim, E. J. (2008, June). Predictive dynamic thermal management for multicore systems. In *Proceedings of the 45th annual Design Automation Conference* (pp. 734-739). ACM.

[7] Sironi, F., Maggio, M., Cattaneo, R., Del Nero, G. F., Sciuto, D., & Santambrogio, M. D. (2013, September). ThermOS: System support for dynamic thermal management of chip multi-processors. In *Parallel Architectures and Compilation Techniques (PACT), 2013 22nd International Conference on* (pp. 41-50). IEEE.

[8] Choi, J., Cher, C. Y., Franke, H., Hamann, H., Weger, A., & Bose, P. (2007, August). Thermal-aware task scheduling at the system software level. In *Proceedings of the 2007 international symposium on Low power electronics and design* (pp. 213-218). ACM.

[9] Liu, Z., Xu, T., Tan, S. D., & Wang, H. (2013, January). Dynamic thermal management for multi-core microprocessors considering transient thermal effects. In *Design Automation Conference (ASP-DAC), 2013 18th Asia and South Pacific* (pp. 473-478). IEEE.

[10] Xia, L., Zhu, Y., Yang, J., Ye, J., & Gu, Z. (2010). Implementing a thermal-aware scheduler in linux kernel on a multi-core processor. *The Computer Journal*, *53*(7), 895-903.

[11] Qiong, C., González, J., Magklis, G., Chaparro, P., & González, A. (2011, August). Thread shuffling: Combining DVFS and thread migration to reduce energy consumptions for multi-core systems. In *Low Power Electronics and Design (ISLPED) 2011 International Symposium on* (pp. 379-384). IEEE.

[12] Kursun, E., & Cher, C. Y. (2008, October). Variation-aware thermal characterization and management of multi-core architectures. In *Computer Design, 2008. ICCD 2008. IEEE International Conference on* (pp. 280-285). IEEE.

[13] Mauerer, W. (2010). *Professional Linux kernel architecture*. John Wiley & Sons.

[14] Lm sensors linux hardware monitoring [Online]. Available: http://www.lm-sensors.org.

[15] Lee Rodgers, J., & Nicewander, W. A. (1988). Thirteen ways to look at the correlation coefficient. *The American Statistician*, *42*(1), 59-66.

Reinforcement Learning For Thermal-Aware Many-Core Task Allocation

Shiting (Justin) Lu, Russell Tessier, and Wayne Burleson
University of Massachusetts
Department of Electrical and Computer Engineering
Amherst, MA, USA
{jlu, tessier, burleson}@ecs.umass.edu

ABSTRACT

To maintain reliable operation, task allocation for many-core processors must consider the heat interaction of processor cores and network-on-chip routers in performing task assignment. Our approach employs *reinforcement learning*, a machine learning algorithm that performs task allocation based on current core and router temperatures and a prediction of which assignment will minimize maximum temperature in the future. The algorithm updates prediction models after each allocation based on feedback regarding the accuracy of previous predictions. Our new algorithm is verified via detailed many-core simulation which includes on-chip routing. Our results show that the proposed technique is fast (scheduling performed in < 1 ms) and can efficiently reduce peak temperature by up to $8°C$ in a 49-core processor ($4.3°C$ on average) versus a competing task allocation approach for a series of SPLASH-2 benchmarks.

Categories and Subject Descriptors

B.8 [**Performance and Reliability**]: Miscellaneous

General Terms

Performance, Design, Reliability

Keywords

Thermal aware, task allocation, reinforcement learning

1. INTRODUCTION

The thermal behavior of many-cores has grown to become a major performance and fault tolerance concern. High power density impacts circuit reliability and chip lifetime and can lead to the frequent initiation of remediation techniques such as DVFS. Although chip cooling technologies are frequently deployed, system-level thermal management techniques are necessary to prevent thermal emergencies and maintain high processor performance.

Data intensive applications implemented on many-cores benefit from low latency and high bandwidth on-chip communication. The heat dissipated by the routers not only affects router temperature, but also the temperature of neighboring cores. Effective task scheduling for thermal management considers power dissipated in all many-core components, including NoC routers. In this paper, a new task allocation scheme based on machine learning is described which considers both processor core and NoC router temperatures. The allocation scheme aims to reduce the peak temperature of the chip, a leading cause of device failure. In performing task assignment, the allocator uses *current* chip temperature information and stochastic *predictions* about how each possible task assignment is likely to affect maximum many-core temperature in the future. During the next allocation interval, the accuracy of the previous prediction is checked and the model used to make the prediction is updated. As allocation proceeds, the accuracy of the model converges. This *reinforcement learning* is adaptive and scalable and it results in rapid convergence within about 200 task allocations.

Our work is supported by careful thermal analysis of typical many-cores and their reaction to task allocation. It is observed that many-cores running the same workloads but with different allocations can have a hot spot temperature difference of up to $8°C$ due to heat interactions with neighboring cores. Experiments show that our approach can reduce peak temperature by $4.3°C$ on average for a many-core which is moderately loaded versus a previous approach [1].

2. BACKGROUND

Approaches to reduce many-core overheating have been developed using a variety of techniques including remediation (e.g. DVFS), thermal-aware floorplans, and run-time task allocation. Issues impacting thermal-aware task allocation for core- and network-level management are summarized below.

Thermal Constraint Optimization: For multi-core systems, thermal-aware task allocation assigns tasks to cores to optimize thermal conditions. Different task distributions can result in substantially varied thermal chip profiles [2], so task allocation must consider the spatial thermal correlation of cores, caches, NoC routers and other processor components. A number of popular many-core allocation techniques [2] [3] use objective functions to minimize maximum temperature subject to constraints to meet physical design limits. Since it is computationally expensive in such systems to model the thermal behavior of all system components, in general, existing allocators do not consider many-core router temperatures or the thermal impact of earlier allocation decisions while performing task assignment.

In Yu *et al.* [2], a thermal-aware allocation technique was developed that focused on maximizing computation throughput and meeting the peak temperature requirement for 3D architectures. Similarly, K-means clustering was used to perform multi-core task scheduling in Yeo *et al.* [4] with a goal of temperature reduction. In Coskun *et al.* [3], the authors formulated multi-core task scheduling statically as an integer linear programing problem by taking temperature into account. Hanumaiah *et al.* [5] provided an online thread migration technique focused on thermal balancing. Our approach differs from these previous approaches by learning from and adapting to thermal dynamics rather than relying on static thermal models. Our technique implicitly includes the thermal impact of circuit components and also considers the impact of thermal interface materials and cooling conditions, among other factors.

Adaptive Random: To evaluate the effectiveness of our new approach in Section 5, we compare against a widely-used thermal-aware allocation algorithm. The heuristic *adaptive random* algorithm selects the coolest core for task allocation [1] under a set of calculated probabilities. Potential allocations to cores are assigned weights based not only on the current temperatures, but also on their thermal history. These weights measuring thermal history are adjusted in real time as the cores execute a dynamic workload. Stochastic assignment is employed to allocate a new task to a core based on its current temperature, thermal history, and the thermal conditions of neighboring cores. The storage of thermal histories incurs memory cost. The temperatures for each core are stored for a period of time (1∼10K samples per core) to capture the thermal characteristics for specific workloads.

Thermal Impact of Network-on-Chip: Hot spots can occur in routers when heavy data traffic is present. If the system is dedicated to a specific application, static task mapping on NoC systems can achieve thermal balance over the on-chip network [6]. In a general-purpose system, tasks are dynamically mapped to cores, so heat generated by the NoC should be carefully managed by routing packets in a thermally-aware fashion [7]. However, these approaches do have limitations: (a) the thermal impact of processor cores is underestimated or ignored and (b) application-specific designs are employed, so they have limited generality.

Machine learning for thermal and power management: Ge and Qiu [8] proposed a temperature reduction technique based on reinforcement learning for media applications. The agent learns the workload and dynamically adjusts frequency to control thermal violations. Similar techniques were applied in a power management context [9] [10]. Chen *et al.* [11] proposed workload allocation based on reinforcement learning to reduce the peak temperature in a data center. The approach avoids local heating by assigning workloads in a spatially dispersed fashion.

3. THERMAL AWARE TASK ALLOCATION USING REINFORCEMENT LEARNING

This section introduces a task allocation approach based on reinforcement learning (RL). After performing an allocation, the approach "learns" how well its core selection was during the previous allocation, and updates decision-making models accordingly. This technique effectively *rewards* good allocation choices. Thus, the two main contributions are (1) the use of rewards in determining task allocation and (2) the inclusion of localized NoC router temperatures in making allocation decisions for neighboring cores.

3.1 Thermal-Aware Task Allocation Overview

At a high level, the steps taking place during each task allocation can be described as follows: (1) Temperature readings are collected from temperature sensors located in each processor core; (2) The maximum temperature T_{max} among all sensors is recorded; (3) The temperature values are used to determine the best assignment of a task to an idle processor core based on a temperature-based *utility function*; (4) The model used to formulate the utility function is updated.

The *utility function* effectively determines which assignment is likely to affect the maximum temperature of the chip the least. This effect is determined by considering the processor core's instantaneous temperature and the temperature of the attached router and surrounding cores. The formulation of the utility function and its model is based on RL.

3.2 Reinforcement Learning

In RL [12], an agent (the task allocator in our case) explores an environment by taking actions and observing the resultant reward. The reward of a particular action (assigning a task to a specific core) reflects the metric to be optimized (maximum temperature). For our system, as task allocations are performed, the model used to make assignments is refined in a learning process. The task allocator gradually refines the model based on temperatures measured a time period after an allocation is performed. Effectively, the allocator *learns* how to respond to a specific environmental condition (e.g. temperatures measured from temperature sensors) based on the results of previous assignments when cores and routers had a similar temperature profile. Formally, reinforcement learning consists of the following

- A set of environment states: $\mathcal{S}$, in this case temperature readings from sensors;
- A set of available actions on the current state : $\mathcal{A}$, task assignments to specific cores;
- A rule to evaluate the reward for taking the action at a specific state: $\mathcal{R}$;
- The goal is to find a policy $\pi : \mathcal{S} \rightarrow \mathcal{A}$, i.e. what action (assignment) should be taken at the current environmental (temperature) state.

A *utility function* can be developed to allow for the desired mapping. Our *Q learning* approach provides a reinforcement learning formulation for task allocation. A utility value is defined to find a policy π for Q learning as follows.

$$Q(s, a) = E\left[\sum_{i=0}^{\infty} (\gamma^i r_{t+i} | s_t = s, a_t = a)\right] \quad (1)$$

The utility $Q(s, a)$ indicates the expected temperature *rewards*, r, (both present, $i = 0$, and future) which can be obtained by performing task assignment action a for temperature vector state s at time step t. Predicted future rewards are discounted via a discount factor γ. The optimal policy takes action which maximizes the utility Q. During each task assignment at time $t + 1$, utility Q for temperature vector s and assignment a in (1) can be approximated

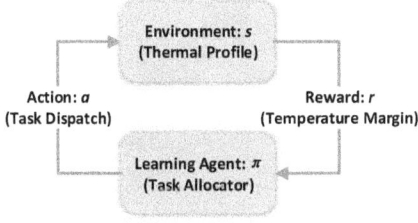

Figure 1: RL cycle for thermal-aware task allocation

as follows [12]:

$$Q_{t+1}(s_{t+1},a) = Q_t(s_t,a) + \alpha \big(\underbrace{r_t(s,a)}_{\substack{current \\ reward}} + \underbrace{\gamma \max_{a'} Q_t(s_{t+1},a')}_{future\ reward} - Q_t(s_t,a) \big)$$

(2)

In (2), α is the *learning rate*, which helps control the convergence of the algorithm. The new utility includes a combination of the previous utility, the current reward, and a discounted version of the future reward (Q_t values for other processors a'). This iterative equation is known to converge to an optimal point [12]. Fig. 1 shows the iterative reinforcement learning process. Each cycle represents one task allocation. In our implementation, the task allocator serves as the learning agent and the environmental state is the chip thermal profile which is read from on-chip temperature sensors. Task allocation decisions impact the thermal condition of the whole chip. After each task allocation, the allocator collects system thermal information to assess the reward of the *last* allocation action and to select a core for the next task. The details on how to apply Q and update the model used to determine it are discussed subsequently.

3.3 Definitions

On-chip thermal sensors are often deployed in processors to assist thermal management [13]. In our approach, a set of thermal sensor readings from m temperature sensors are used to represent the thermal state of the silicon. To apply RL in thermal-aware task allocation, the environment state is a temperature vector,

$$s = \big[s^1, s^2, s^3, ..., s^m \big].$$

(3)

Each temperature value in the vector is a temperature reading from one of m different on-chip thermal sensors deployed in different locations on the chip. In a many-core, the task allocator is implemented in a dedicated core which typically performs other system-level management functions. This core dispatches new tasks to other available, working cores. So a task allocation selects a specific, idle core for a task execution. If processor cores are indexed from 1 to n, the possible actions are defined as:

$$\mathcal{A} = \{1, 2, 3, ..., n-1, n\}$$

(4)

where $\mathcal{A}$ represents all possible assignments to processors. An assignment to a specific processor is an action a.

The construction of the reward function is a key step in effectively performing RL-based allocation. Since the *maximum* temperature adversely impacts the performance and reliability of a many-core, reduction of this value is the goal. Generally, a many-core will have a pre-set *emergency* threshold temperature T_{em} which serves as a temperature bound-

ary. System remediation (e.g. voltage scaling, task migration) is needed if a maximum temperature passes this point. We define the reward of an action as the difference between the emergency temperature and the current peak temperature T_{max}:

$$r = T_{em} - T_{max}$$

(5)

The higher the reward, the bigger the temperature margin.

3.4 Utility Function Approximation

In our approach, a processor which has a high utility Q value is more likely to receive a task assignment. If the number of possible temperatures for a core and associated router is relatively small, the utility function $Q(s,a)$ in (2) can be represented as a lookup table using temperature vector s and target processor core a as inputs. In other words, for every input temperature vector s, a Q value which has been previously determined and refined for a core a can be identified and used to make the current allocation decision. This approach leads to two issues: (1) Q values must be learned over time and stored in the lookup table and (2) temperature readings can span a large range of continuous values that would have to be discretized. As the state space of temperatures becomes large, using a lookup table for Q learning becomes intractable due to memory limitations and the difficulty of updating it in a timely fashion. Therefore, a continuous function is needed to map state-action (temperature-target processor) pairs to Q values.

Due to the high complexity of (2), it is not realistic to find a closed form representation for the Q function. However, the function can be approximated by the linear combination of a series of basis functions, $\phi_i(s)$.

$$Q(s,a) = \sum_{i=0}^{k} \theta_i^a \times \phi_i(s)$$

(6a)

$$a = 1, 2, ..., n$$

(6b)

Here, θ_i^a are k weight parameters for core a that are refined after each allocation to the core (k is defined in the next section). Each task assignment to a core (e.g. an action) corresponds to a set of weight parameters θ_i^a for core a. Following the updating of Q values at time $t+1$, weight parameters (θ_i^a) for the processor selected during the previous allocation t are updated according to the gradient descent technique [14]. Here a' includes all cores except a.

$$\theta_i^a(t+1) = \theta_i^a(t) + \alpha(r_t + \gamma \max_{a'} Q(s_{t+1}, a') - Q(s_t, a))\phi_i(s_t)$$

(7)

3.5 Basis Function

The basis function for Q value function approximation is a radial basis function (RBF), defined as follows:

$$\phi_i(s) = \frac{1}{\sqrt{2\pi\sigma^2}} e^{-||c-s||^2/2\sigma^2}$$

(8)

$$c = \big[c^1, c^2, c^3, ..., c^m \big]$$

(9)

The formulation includes constant parameters σ^2, a scalar, and m-element vector c. The elements of $c - s$ provide context regarding the temperature difference between sensor readings s and typical temperature measurements c. We assume that the usual working temperature range of a chip is $[330, 360]$ Kelvin. Temperature *centers* are specified in

Algorithm 1 RL-based Task Allocation Algorithm

1: Initialize weight parameters $\theta_i^a \leftarrow 0$;
2: Read temperature values s from temperature sensors;
3: Apply a random task allocation;
4: **for** each task allocation episode **do**
5:    Get current temperature values s_{t+1};
6:    Calculate reward function for the last action based on (5);
7:    For state s_{t+1}, calculate utility value, $Q(s_{t+1}, a)$, for all processors a;
8:    Find maximum Q value from the above step and update the selected processor for the task: $a \leftarrow \max_{a'} Q(s_t, a')$;
9:    Update weight parameters for θ_i^a according to (7);
10:   Apply action a with probability p or an alternative action with probability $1 - p$;
11: **end for**

Table 1: Core Config.

L1-I	16KB
L1-D	16KB
L2	256KB
ITLB	16 entries
DTLB	16 entries

Table 2: Router Config.

port number	5
frequency	2.0 Ghz
VC per port	8
flit size	144 bits
buffer length	24 flits

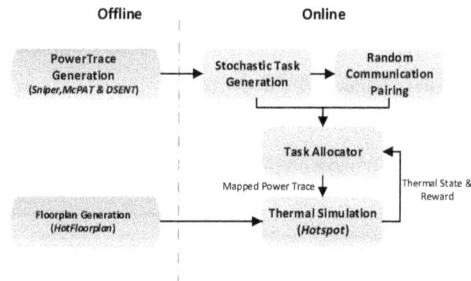

Figure 2: Simulation flow for thermal-aware task allocation experimentation

this range. The value of each of the elements in c is defined as one of v temperature centers within this range:

$$c^1, c^2, ..., c^m \in \{340, 350\} \tag{10}$$

The above example shows $v = 2$ centers. Since each of the values in the c vector can take on any of the v values, there are $k = v^m$ combinations for the c vector. Thus, v^m basis functions are available to approximate one Q function for each processor a. Since there are n total processors (possible allocation actions), the total number of parameters is $n * v^m$. Note that v is generally quite small (2 or 3).

3.6 RL-based Task Allocation Algorithm

In a many-core system, the task dispatcher is responsible for monitoring thermal state and assigning tasks to cores. Algorithm 1 describes the task allocation procedure performed by the dispatcher. Initially, the θ_i^a weight parameters of the Q function (6a) are initialized to zero. Steps 5-10 are performed for each task allocation. An allocation can be invoked when a new task arrives or an overheating situation is detected and a task must be migrated. The reward is calculated for the last allocation action at Step 6 and current thermal states are obtained by collecting temperatures from thermal sensors at Step 5. Steps 7 and 8 determine the task assignment to an idle core (action a) which leads to the maximum Q. Information is updated once the appropriate allocation action is determined. Our technique is stochastic, i.e. the determined action is taken with probability $p = 0.9$, a value determined empirically. Other assignments for a specific allocation are applied with equal probability of $\frac{1-p}{n-1}$. Using this approach, potentially good actions are not excluded and the environment is extensively explored.

4. EXPERIMENTAL APPROACH

Power, temperature and performance simulation was used to verify the effectiveness of our new task allocation scheme and to perform comparisons to *adaptive random* task allocation. In this section, detailed descriptions of the simulation platform, task models and the simulator flow are presented.

Many-core Floorplan: A mesh topology was used to build many-core systems for verification. Both routers and processor cores in 45 nm technology were evaluated. McPAT

[15] was used to estimate the area and power consumption for the ten architectural component in the processor based on the parameters in Table 1. DSENT [16] was used to estimate the area and power for the router based on the configuration in Table 2 and estimated router usage based on traffic flow in the floorplan. HotFloorPlan was used to generate the floorplan. It was fed with core and router area information to generate the floorplan for a single core. The many-core floorplan was obtained by replicating single-core building blocks.

Benchmark Workload: Twelve benchmarks from the SPLASH-2[1] suite were used to test our platform. Each allocated task consists of an instantiation of one of the benchmarks. Communication between tasks was randomly assigned. To determine dynamic temperature values during many-core execution, power values for all processor core components and associated routers were determined. The power traces of the SPLASH-2 benchmarks were captured using the McPAT-integrated Sniper simulator [17]. HotSpot[2] was used to convert power values into temperature values. We use an $M/M/c$ queuing model to mimic the task arrival and task execution duration in the many-core system. In this model, task arrival is modeled as a Poisson process whose inter-arrival time is exponentially distributed; the execution time of tasks is also exponentially distributed. The number of cores in the system is n. The task arrival rate is defined as λ and the service rate is defined as μ. The system utilization, ρ, is given by $\rho = \frac{\lambda}{n\mu}$. Effectively, $n\rho$ defines the steady-state number of processor cores which is used to service tasks.

Simulation Flow: The simulation flow is shown in Fig. 2. As a first step, the power traces for each benchmark for a single-core floorplan are generated. Router power consumption under different loads is also calculated. The task allocator is implemented in conjunction with HotSpot which reports simulated chip temperatures. The task allocator retrieves temperature points which represent the s vector in

---

[1]http://liuyix.org/splash2-benchmark
[2]http://lava.cs.virginia.edu/HotSpot

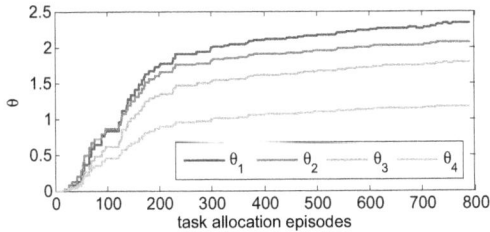

Figure 3: Convergence of θ_i values for a 25-core processor

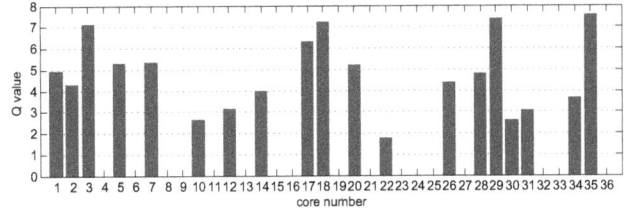

Figure 5: Q values for different actions at the thermal state given in Fig. 4.

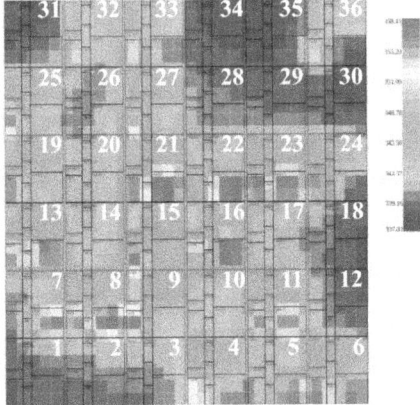

Figure 4: A thermal map snapshot for a 36-core system

(3). When a new task is generated for allocation, its communication is paired with other tasks. The appropriate power trace for the task is identified and mapped onto the floorplan. The HotSpot simulator reads the mapped power trace and performs thermal simulation. The maximum temperature is then reported to the allocator for reward calculation.

5. RESULTS

Our approach has been validated via simulation using 16-core, 25-core, 36-core and 49-core systems. To implement the reinforcement learning technique, the learning rate is set to $\alpha = 0.8$ and the discount rate is set to $\gamma = 0.8$ (Section 3.2). These parameters were determined empirically.

5.1 Effectiveness Validation

The convergence of our reinforcement learning model was evaluated over a series of task allocations. In the experiment, task allocations of randomly-selected SPLASH-2 benchmarks were performed to all 25 processor cores. A selection of θ_i values is shown in Fig. 3. Initially, θ_i values are all zeros and they begin to converge after $200 \sim 300$ allocation episodes. Other θ_i values showed similar behavior.

Fig. 4 shows a thermal snapshot of a 36-core processor at the seven minute time point. Q values are calculated for all possible allocation choices at this time point. Fig. 5 shows the magnitude of Q values for corresponding cores indexed in Fig. 4. As seen in the figure, the non-zero Q value for action 22 is lowest among all actions because the heat stress for core 22 is significant. An allocation to core 22 will negatively impact the chip peak temperature. Actions 3, 18, 29 and 35 have relatively high Q values. From the chip thermal map, it is seen that cores 3, 18, 29 and 35 are relatively cool and their neighboring cores are also in

a favorable thermal condition. We also notice that cores 1 and 31 are cool, but their Q values are not as high as the previous four cores. These two cores are in the corner of the chip and the thermal conductivity of air is much lower than silicon. The allocator effectively learns this information over time via reinforcement.

5.2 Peak Temperature Reduction

The peak temperature can be effectively reduced versus previous approaches through the use of the proposed allocation technique. A series of experiments are conducted to observe the peak temperature of the chip in comparison with the *adaptive random* approach [1] over five minute execution runs. This allocator assigns tasks to one of the coolest available cores based on probabilities determined from core temperature histories. In our implementation of the adaptive random approach, we also included the impact of router temperatures on allocation to allow for a fair comparison versus reinforcement learning. Table 3 shows the average peak temperature over time for different core counts and system utilization ratios for the two approaches. For a low system utilization (ρ), adaptive random and reinforcement learning have almost the same performance in terms of peak temperature. In this case, chip temperature is impacted more by the workload intensity inside specific cores and less by the distribution of tasks. Our technique performs better when the system is moderately loaded (about half used). For example, compared to adaptive random, our approach reduces peak temperature by $8.1^{\circ}C$ in a 49-core system ($4.3^{\circ}C$ across all many-core configurations for $\rho = 0.4$ and 0.6). Fig. 6 shows the differences in the peak temperatures over time between the two approaches for 16-, 25-, and 36-core systems. Comparisons between reinforcement learning and adaptive random indicate that the former approach is more effective.

The time cost of the reinforcement learning allocator was evaluated for different numbers of sensors, m, and two sets of temperature centers, v. Table 4 shows the average computational time for one task allocation. The temperature centers used in (8) are selected from two sets, $\{340, 350\}$ and $\{335, 345, 355\}$, respectively. For most cases, the computational time of task allocation is $< 1\ ms$. Since the task allocation is only invoked when there is an incoming task or a thermal emergency, the frequency of allocation is typically on the order of seconds. Therefore, the percentage time cost of allocation with respect to the allocation interval is negligible. Although the adaptive random technique also has very low overhead time cost ($<< 1\ ms$) for each task allocation, it must track temperature sensor readings over time (one sample per 100 ms) regardless of task allocation rate. As a result, the technique becomes less favorable in a system which has a low task arrival rate.

Table 3: Peak temperature comparison between reinforcement learning (ours) and adaptive random [1]. The value ρ indicates the average number of cores used during execution. A random sampling of SPLASH-2 benchmarks were used as tasks.

core number	System Utilization											
	$\rho = 0.1$			$\rho = 0.4$			$\rho = 0.6$			$\rho = 0.8$		
	ours ($^{\circ}C$)	[1] ($^{\circ}C$)	$\Delta^{\circ}C$	ours ($^{\circ}C$)	[1] ($^{\circ}C$)	$\Delta^{\circ}C$	ours ($^{\circ}C$)	[1] ($^{\circ}C$)	$\Delta^{\circ}C$	ours ($^{\circ}C$)	[1] ($^{\circ}C$)	$\Delta^{\circ}C$
16	73.2	74.1	0.9	81.5	86.4	4.9	86.8	88.5	1.7	93.8	93.5	-0.3
25	74.6	74.3	-0.3	83.1	86.7	3.6	87.5	90.8	3.3	95.1	96.0	0.9
36	72.8	73.2	0.4	83.8	88.3	4.5	87.3	91.1	3.8	96.4	96.1	-0.3
49	70.5	71.4	0.9	78.0	86.1	8.1	86.2	90.8	4.6	93.1	93.8	0.7

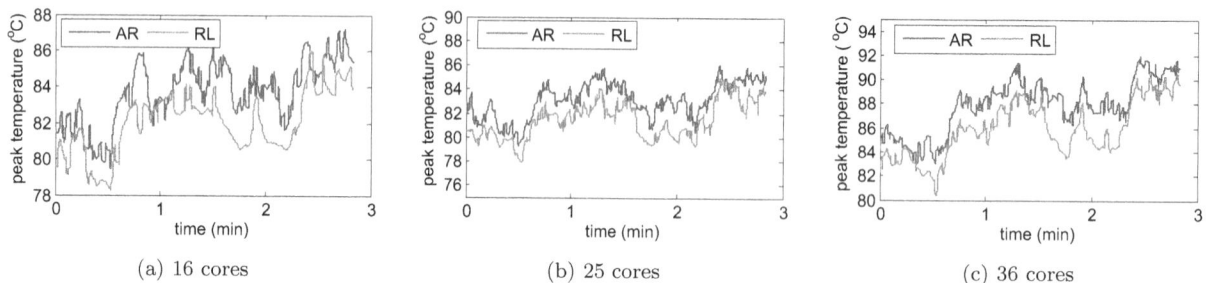

(a) 16 cores

(b) 25 cores

(c) 36 cores

Figure 6: Peak temperature comparison over time for $\rho = 0.4$ for reinforcement learning (RL) and adaptive random (AR)

Table 4: Time cost For RL task allocation (ms)

Temperature Center Set	Sensor Numbers				
	5	6	7	8	9
{340, 350}	0.014	0.024	0.043	0.081	0.150
{335, 345, 355}	0.074	0.216	0.635	1.927	6.210

6. CONCLUSIONS

A reinforcement learning based task allocation strategy is presented to address localized overheating in many-core systems. RL quality metrics are used to make optimized allocation decisions based on the accuracy of previous allocation choices. The experiments show that the proposed technique is capable of capturing the complex on-chip thermal environment induced by dynamic workload distribution. Our results show that the proposed technique is fast (scheduling performed in <1 ms) and can efficiently reduce peak temperature by $4.3^{\circ}C$ on average in moderately-loaded many-core processors for a collection of SPLASH-2 benchmarks.

7. REFERENCES

[1] A. K. Coskun, T. S. Rosing, and K. Whisnant, "Temperature aware task scheduling in MPSoCs," in *Proc. DATE*, Mar. 2007, pp. 1659–1664.

[2] C. H. Yu, C.-L. Lung, Y.-L. Ho, R.-S. Hsu, D.-M. Kwai, and S.-C. Chang, "Thermal-aware on-line scheduler for 3-D many-core processor throughput optimization," *IEEE TCAD*, vol. 33, no. 5, May 2014.

[3] A. Coskun, T. Rosing, K. Whisnant, and K. Gross, "Static and dynamic temperature-aware scheduling for multiprocessor SoCs," *IEEE TVLSI*, vol. 16, no. 9, pp. 1127–1140, Sep. 2008.

[4] I. Yeo and E. J. Kim, "Temperature-aware scheduler based on thermal behavior grouping in multicore systems," in *Proc. DATE*, May 2009, pp. 946–951.

[5] V. Hanumaiah, S. Vrudhula, and K. Chatha, "Performance optimal online DVFS and task migration techniques for thermally constrained multi-core processors," *IEEE TCAD*, vol. 30, no. 11, pp. 1677–1690, Nov. 2011.

[6] W. Hung et al., "Thermal-aware IP virtualization and placement for networks-on-chip architecture," in *Proc ICCD*, Oct. 2004, pp. 430–437.

[7] Z. Qian and C.-Y. Tsui, "A thermal-aware application specific routing algorithm for network-on-chip design," in *Proc. ASP-DAC*, 2011.

[8] Y. Ge and Q. Qiu, "Dynamic thermal management for multimedia applications using machine learning," in *Proc. DAC*, June 2011, pp. 95–100.

[9] T. Ebi, D. Kramer, W. Karl, and J. Henkel, "Economic learning for thermal-aware power budgeting in many-core architectures," in *Proc. CODES+ISSS*, Oct 2011.

[10] G.-Y. Pan, J.-Y. Jou, and B.-C. Lai, "Scalable power management using multilevel reinforcement learning for multiprocessors," *ACM Trans. Des. Autom. Electron. Syst.*, vol. 19, no. 4, pp. 33:1–33:23, Aug. 2014.

[11] H. Chen and etc, "Spatially-aware optimization of energy consumption in consolidated data center systems," in *ASME 2011 Pac. Rim Tech. Conf. and Exhibition on Packaging and Integration of Elec. and Phot. Sys.*

[12] A. G. Barto, *Reinforcement learning: An introduction*. MIT press, 1998.

[13] E. Rotem et al., "Power management architecture of the 2nd generation Intel core microarchitecture, formerly codenamed Sandy Bridge," in *Hot Chips*, August 2011.

[14] L. Baird and A. W. Moore, "Gradient descent for general reinforcement learning," *Adv. in Neural Information Proc. Sys.*, pp. 968–974, 1999.

[15] L. Sheng et al., "McPAT: An integrated power, area, and timing modeling framework for multicore and manycore architectures," in *Proc. IEEE/ACM Micro*, 2009.

[16] C. Sun et al., "DSENT - a tool connecting emerging photonics with electronics for opto-electronic networks-on-chip modeling," in *Proc. IEEE/ACM Int'l Symp. on NoC*, 2012, pp. 201–210.

[17] T. E. Carlson, W. Heirman, and L. Eeckhout, "Sniper: Exploring the level of abstraction for scalable and accurate parallel multi-core simulations," in *Int'l Conf. for High Perf. Comput., Network., Stor. and Analysis*, 2011.

Revisiting Dynamic Thermal Management Exploiting Inverse Thermal Dependence

Katayoun Neshatpour
George Mason University
kneshatp@gmu.edu

Amin Khajeh
Broadcom Corporation
amink@broadcom.com

Wayne Burleson
AMD
University of Massachusetts,
Amherst
burleson@ecs.umass.edu

Houman Homayoun
George Mason University
hhomayou@gmu.edu

ABSTRACT

As CMOS technology scales down towards nanometer regime and the supply voltage approaches the threshold voltage, increase in operating temperature results in increased circuit current, which in turn reduces circuit propagation delay. This paper exploits this new phenomenon, known as inverse thermal dependence (ITD) for power, performance, and temperature optimization in processor architecture. ITD changes the maximum achievable operating frequency of the processor at high temperatures. Dynamic thermal management techniques such as activity migration, dynamic voltage frequency scaling, and throttling are revisited in this paper, with a focus on the effect of ITD. Results are obtained using the predictive technology models of 7nm, 10nm 14nm and 20nm technology nodes and with extensive architectural and circuit simulations. The results show that based on the design goals, various design corners should be re-investigated for power, performance and energy-efficiency optimization. Architectural simulations for a multi-core processor and across standard benchmarks show that utilizing ITD-aware schemes for thermal management improves the performance of the processor in terms of speed and energy-delay-product by 8.55% and 4.4%, respectively.

Keywords

ITD, memory-intensive, compute-intensive, IPS, energy-delay-product

1. INTRODUCTION

Reducing the feature sizes has been an ongoing trend in the processor design technology. If the dimensions are scaled without scaling of the supply and the threshold voltage, the power density of the processor will increase dramatically, which will cause overheating and reliability issues. Thus, while heat sinks are used to extract the heat out of the processor, supply and threshold voltage scaling is done to

control the increase in the power density. It should be noted that various design concerns do not allow the supply and threshold voltages to be scaled at the same rate as the processor dimensions are scaling. Thus, finding techniques for low-power and low-temperature designs has been a hot topic in the processor design.

As the integrated circuits enter into the deep-sub-micron CMOS technologies, their thermal behavior changes significantly. Traditionally, as temperature increases, propagation delay of the circuit also increases due to the lower mobility, which slows down the circuit. In the sub-micron technologies however, at low operating voltage an opposite behavior is observed - the circuit propagation delay reduces. This phenomenon is called the inverse temperature dependence (ITD).

ITD introduces many new aspects in the design and optimization of the circuit. Design corners will have to be re-investigated and power reduction and thermal management techniques will have to be adapted, accordingly. With ITD, at high temperatures the circuit will be able to benefit from the frequency headroom offered due to reduction in propagation delay. For applications in which the performance is heavily impacted by the operating frequency (frequency-sensitive applications), this headroom can be exploited to enhance the performance.

This paper investigates ITD in future CMOS technologies to understand whether further scaling will increase the significance of the ITD. In this work, several design optimal points are explored for the 7nm, 10nm, 14nm and 20nm predictive technology models (PTM). At the circuit level, we use fully synthesizable LEON3 core to understand the impact of ITD on processor maximum achievable operating frequency. For circuit simulations the complete critical paths were explored rather than just a few basic cells (NAND, XOR, etc.) or an invert-based ring oscillator. The results of circuit characterizations are used at the architectural level to simulate the impact of ITD on dynamic thermal management (DTM) techniques to explore opportunities for improvements. For architecture simulation, a multi-core architecture is studied. Different temperature-aware techniques including throttling, activity migration (AM), and dynamic voltage frequency scaling (DVFS) are explored to find the best solution in terms of performance, power, thermal behavior, and energy-delay product. To the best of our knowledge, this is the first paper that analyzes the impact of ITD on a fully synthesizable processor core at the circuit level and in deep nanometer technologies, and exploits this new phenomenon to manage power, performance and temperature at the architectural level.

This paper in brief makes the following contributions: (1) ITD characterization by performing spice-level analysis on LEON3 processor at various voltage and temperature corners for PTM technologies to understand ITD trends with technology scaling. (2) Proposing ITD-aware dynamic thermal management including throttling, AM and DVFS. (3) Analyzing simulation results for the comparison of different thermal management techniques in the presence of ITD at various operating points.

The paper is organized as follows: Section 2 provides background on ITD and reports its impact on maximum achievable operating clock frequency in LEON3 processor for four predictive models. In section 3, a number of SPEC and media applications are characterized in terms of frequency-sensitivity and thermal behavior. In section 4, we introduce ITD-aware thermal management techniques. Section 5 introduces the simulation framework. Section 6 presents the results of the simulations and evaluates them. Section 8 presents our conclusion remarks.

2. INVERSE THERMAL DEPENDENCE

2.1 Background

In order to understand the effect of temperature on the behavior of CMOS transistors, a proper model should be utilized. Numerous models have been used to model the behavior of the CMOS transistors. The square law model in (1) estimates the drain current of CMOS transistor operating in the saturation mode [1].

$$I_D = \mu \times C_{ox} \frac{W}{L} (V_{gs} - V_t)^2. \qquad (1)$$

In (1), I_D is the drain current, μ is the mobility, C_{ox} is the oxide capacitance, W and L are the channel width and length, V_{gs} is the gate-source voltage and V_t is the threshold voltage. Mobility and the threshold voltage are two parameters that are dependent on the temperature; however, they work on opposite directions. While an increase in the temperature reduces the mobility, and thus slows down the device, it reduces the threshold voltage, which will enhance the device speed according to (1). At high operating voltages, the threshold voltage change will have little effect on $(V_{gs} - V_t)$ and thus, the mobility will determine the effect of the temperature on the device speed. However, at low operating voltages, the threshold voltage will determine the effect of temperature. As the technology scales down, the operating voltage approaches the threshold voltage. Thus, when working at slightly lower than the nominal voltage, the device is switching faster at higher temperature. This phenomenon is called the inverse thermal dependence.

2.2 ITD in predictive technologies

Latest work have explored the effect of ITD in current technology nodes [2], [3] and [4]; however, it is important to explore ITD impact in the future nodes, as well. This paper first investigates ITD in future CMOS technologies to understand whether further scaling will increase the significance of the ITD. We use PTM for this purpose [5]. PTM provides accurate, customizable, and predictive models for future transistor and interconnect technologies.

We synthesize LEON3, a fully synthesizable VHDL model for open SPARC V8 32-bit architecture [6] using Design Compiler and extract the critical path for further explorations. Based on the PTM transistor models, we run Spice

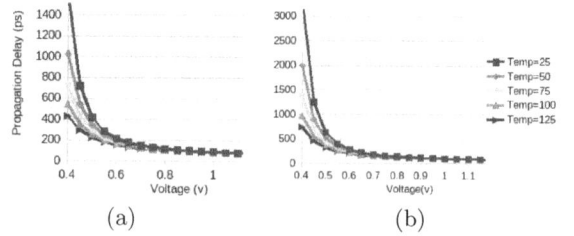

(a)   (b)

Figure 1: Propagation delay of a critical path in LEON3 for (a) 7nm (b) 14nm.

simulations at different temperatures with variable supply voltages to find the effect of temperature on the the critical path delays. To provide more accurate analysis of ITD characteristics in processor design, in these simulations the complete critical paths were explored rather than just a few basic cells. (NAND, XOR, etc.) or an invert-based ring oscillator.

Additionally, since gate-level netlist from Design Compiler does not include RC delay, we simulated dominated paths using π-Models for Metal4-Metal7 layers (that are usually used for signal routing) for 20nm. For our simulations, we assumed different wire lengths (1μm, 50μm and 100μm). Moreover, we selected appropriate drivers for each case, that resulted in maximum acceptable slew rate as physical design tools do. Our simulation results show that the worst-case delay degradation occurs for the lower metal layer (Metal4) and longer wire length. Assuming 20% of our post-layout top critical path will be RC-delay and 80% cell-delay, the difference between pre-layout and post-layout speedup for 25°C to 125°C, will be 7% lower in 20nm at nominal voltage. In other words, post-layout speedup as a result of increase in temperature is lower than that of pre-layout. This is mostly due to the fact that resistance (R) increases with temperature, which in turn increases the RC delay at higher temperatures. Since we don't have access to a full library of cells at 14nm, 10nm, and 7nm, for the remainder of the paper we will use the pre-layout results.

It should be noted that, several factors such as device aging may change the critical paths of a design. The intent here, is to show the trend of temperature effect as we scale down the technology and build a model for selected case-study in this paper using PTM device models. To apply the proposed technique to other designs, an accurate temperature-delay at different process-voltage-temperature (PVT) should be devised and utilized.

Fig. 1 shows LEON3 critical path delays, for the 7nm and 14nm PTM technologies. The nominal voltages are 0.7v and 0.8v for 7nm and 14nm technologies, respectively.

Fig. 1(b) shows that for 14nm technology, with an operating voltage that is 85% of the nominal voltage, the critical path delay at 75°C, 100°C and 125 °C is 7%, 14% and 17% lower than the critical path delay at 50°C, respectively. For 7nm technology, with the same operating voltage of 85% of the nominal voltage, the critical path delay at 75°C, 100°C and 125 °C is 8%, 18% and 28% lower than the critical path delay at 50°C. This indicates that the impact of ITD on critical path delay increases further as the technology scales down. Thus, for these technologies, there will be a headroom at high temperatures for increasing the frequency as long as overheating of the device does not introduce reliability issues.

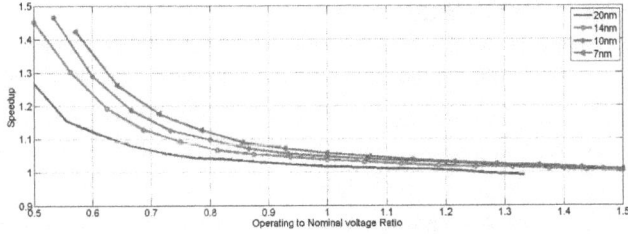

Figure 2: The reduction in propagation delay (speedup) when the temperature rises from 50°C to 75°C.

A comparison of Fig. 1(a) and 1(b) shows that, as the technology scales down, the ITD effect is observed more significantly. Moreover, for each technology the reduction in the critical path due to the elevated temperature is more significant at low operating voltages.

Fig. 2 shows the ratio of the critical path delay at 75°C to the delay at 50°C for the 7nm, 10nm, 14nm and 20nm PTM technologies at different operating voltages, which defines the speedup of the circuit when the temperature rises from 50°C to 75°C. The X-axis shows the ratio of the operating voltage to the nominal voltage. According to the figure, as we move away from the nominal voltage towards threshold voltage, the effect of temperature on the critical path delay increases. Moreover, Fig. 2 shows that the speedup at elevated temperatures is less significant for larger technologies.

As discussed earlier, the frequency headroom available at elevated temperatures due to the ITD effect can be used to speed up the processor. However, it should be noted that the circuit will have to operate at low voltages (lower than the nominal) in order to observe the ITD effect. Table 1 shows the range of speedup at elevated temperatures for various operating points for the 7nm, 10nm, 14nm and 20nm technologies. Arguably, when the circuit is operating at voltages lower than the nominal voltage, the maximum frequency is typically lower. Thus, in order to make a better comparison with the speed of the circuit working at the nominal voltage, Table 1 also shows the speedup of the circuit, if we run it at the nominal voltage. On the other hand, running the circuit at the nominal voltage will result in higher power dissipation and increased temperature. Thus, thermal management techniques will have to be used, which will in turn slow down the circuit. An overview of Table 1 shows that, the operating condition that yields the best performance cannot be easily determined, as it heavily depends on power and thermal profile of the processor, which is decided at run-time, is application dependent and requires architecture-level control.

3. CHARACTERIZATION OF APPLICATIONS UNDER ITD

3.1 Performance analysis under ITD

Traditionally, with large feature sizes (45nm and above), the increase in the temperature results in an increase in the propagation delay in all high-temperature paths in the processor. Thus, the operating frequency needs to be reduced to ensure that there is no failing path in the processor. Therefore, processor throughput is affected by its operating temperature. In order to take frequency into consideration for performance estimation, instructions committed per second (IPS) is calculated. (IPS = frequency× IPC)

Table 1: Speedup of the circuit at elevated temperatures

Tech.	$\frac{Op.\ Voltage}{Nom.\ Voltage}$	Speedup $50°C \rightarrow 75°C$	Speedup $50°C \rightarrow 100°C$	Speedup Nom. Voltage
7nm	0.65	1.261	1.542	3.680
	0.75	1.15	1.297	2.101
	0.85	1.089	1.81	1.426
10nm	0.65	1.186	1.377	3.636
	0.75	1.118	1.236	1.990
	0.85	1.07	1.137	1.405
14nm	0.65	1.166	1.334	3.263
	0.75	1.091	1.19	1.903
	0.86	1.052	1.121	1.384
20nm	0.65	1.089	1.178	2.406
	0.75	1.043	1.07	1.653
	0.85	1.035	1.069	1.292

With ITD, the increase in the temperature reduces the delay and allows a headroom for increasing the frequency. As long as the critical paths, which generally conclude the operating frequency, lie in the core, an increase in the temperature, will allow running the processor at higher frequencies. However, it should be noted, that colder regions including the L2 and last level cache (LLC), which are normally operating at low temperature [7], will still maintain their path delays. For example, for a cache delay of 100ns, increasing the frequency from 1GHz to 2GHz, will increase the access time from 100 cycles to 200 cycles, which will negatively affect the instruction per cycle (IPC). Thus the IPS does not increase linearly with the frequency, since the IPC might be dropping at higher frequencies.

In order to evaluate the effect of IPC drop on the performance for various applications, we use SMTSIM simulator [8] with Spec2000, Spec2006 [9], and Media benchmarks. Table 2 shows the micro-architecture parameters of our studied multicore architecture. The access time for individual SRAM units was captured using McPAT [10].

Based on the operating frequency, the number of cycles to access the memory and cache subsystem is varied, and the new IPC at each frequency level is calculated, accordingly. The performance results (i.e., IPS) for a selected group of Spec2000, Spec2006, and Media benchmarks are shown in Fig. 3. The results show that for memory-intensive applications, e.g. lbm_06, the high number of accesses to the cache subsystem, reduces the IPC at high frequencies (achieved at high core temperature) and therefore, limits the potential performance gain of elevated frequency. Thus, for these applications, the increased frequency at elevated core temperatures is not useful, as it only increases the power and temperature, and negatively affect the reliability without enhancing the performance. For compute-intensive applications however, due to the lower number of accesses to the memory, the higher cache access cycles at higher frequencies can be tolerated as it does not affect the IPC significantly. Therefore, for this group of applications the performance increases with the increased frequencies.

In Fig. 3, the IPS drops for a number of applications at specific frequency points. For the frequency-sensitive applications, a small increase in the frequency may cause the cache access latency to increase by one cycle which reduces the IPC consequently. This reduction in the IPC can nullify the effect of frequency increase on the IPS and could even result in a reduction in the IPS.

3.2 Thermal behavior analysis

For thermal characterization of studied applications we used HotSpot [7]. The numbers next to each application

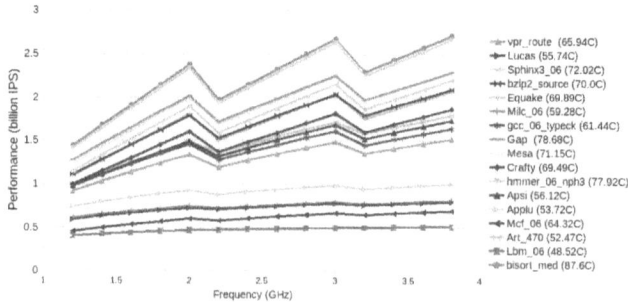

Figure 3: performance of Spec benchmarks as a function of frequency

Table 2: Architectural specification

	Specification
Core	8
Issue, Commit width	4
INT instruction queue	24 entries
FP instruction queue	24 entries
Reorder Buffer entries	48 entries
INT registers	128
FP registers	128
L1 cache	64KB, 8-way, 1ns
L2 cache	512KB, 8-way, 7.5ns

name in Fig. 3 show the steady state temperature of the hottest unit in processor derived from Hotspot for selected applications. As shown, the steady state temperature of hottest unit (register file in most applications) varies from 48.52°C to 78.6°C for these applications, which is about 30°C variation.

By comparing the performance and temperature results in Fig. 3, we observe that the applications with higher IPC, which are mostly the compute-sensitive applications, are generally the ones that have higher temperature.

It is also important to gather information about the transient temperatures, as some applications reach critical temperatures during their execution time. In such applications, dynamic thermal control techniques are of high importance. If the compute-intensive application (hot application) is running on a single core without any feedback from the transient temperature, the core might reach critical temperatures which may damage the device or cause reliability issues.

Based on the results in Fig. 3, the applications are divided into two groups, the memory-intensive applications and the memory-non-intensive applications. For the memory-non-intensive applications, which could also be referred to as compute-intensive applications, using higher frequencies is more desirable, as the increased frequency will contribute significantly to the performance. Thus, these applications are categorized as frequency-sensitive. For the memory-intensive application, higher frequencies are not desirable as they will increase the power consumption with little contribution to the performance.

4. DYNAMIC THERMAL MANAGEMENT

DVFS [11], AM [12] and throttling [7,13] are among the most well studied techniques to manage performance, power, and temperature in multi-core architectures. These techniques have been developed with the assumption that the device is slower at elevated temperatures. In this section, we will study how these techniques are effective in managing power, temperature and performance in the presence of ITD.

4.1 Throttling

The simplest way to prevent an application from reaching critical temperatures is throttling. In throttling when an application reaches a threshold temperature, the pipeline is halted until the core cools down [7]. During the throttling time the core remains idle. This results in an under-utilization and therefore loss of performance.

4.2 Activity Migration

AM is another effective technique to reduce temperature. In AM, the application that reaches critical temperature faster, is migrated to the colder core in order to avoid high temperatures.

4.3 Dynamic Voltage and Frequency Scaling

Another effective technique for managing temperature is DVFS, in which the processor supply voltage and frequency are adapted dynamically to respond to thermal emergencies [11]. The number of voltage and frequency pair varies from two in Intels SpeedStep technology to 40 or even more in Intel XScale [14].

4.4 ITD-aware throttling, AM and DVFS

After running a frequency-sensitive application on a single core, the temperature will increase. With ITD, this elevated temperature will increase the maximum allowable frequency on the core. Thus, dynamic frequency changing will allow the application to run at higher frequencies when it reaches higher temperature.

Before reaching the critical temperature, the core will reach a mid-point threshold (In our simulations we set this mid-point temperature to 75°C). In the ITD-aware schemes, when the temperature of the core is higher than this mid-point threshold, we increase the frequency of the core to benefit from the frequency headroom offered by the ITD. Afterwards, we keep monitoring the temperature until it reaches the critical temperature (i.e., 90°C in this paper), at which point, throttling, AM or DVFS is done to reduce the temperature. If the temperature drops below the mid-point temperature at any time, the operating frequency is set back to its lower value. This technique allows us to run the core at higher frequency for the time interval when the temperature is between the mid-point threshold and the critical value, to increase the overall IPS.

Note, that in addition to two different frequencies for 2 temperature thresholds, more level of temperature-frequency pair may be explored. Fig. 4 shows the ITD-aware AM algorithm for an n-core system with m levels of temperature-frequency pairs. Array T contains core temperatures, t_h is a hash table with temperature as its key and task numbers as its value. FL and TL arrays contain frequency and temperature levels, with the first term being the starting/lowest frequency and temperature point.

5. SIMULATION PLATFORM

In order to study the thermal characteristic of various applications, we study the behavior of SPEC2000, SPEC2006, and Media applications. Due to space limitation we only report the results for a representative subset of these benchmarks. We use an integrated version of SMTSIM, McPAT [10], and HotSpot-5.02 [7] for performance, power and temperature simulations. Each benchmark was simulated for 1 billion instructions after fast forwarding for 1 billion instructions.

The DTM techniques introduced in Section 4 including throttling, AM and DVFS are implemented in the integrated

```
Inputs:  CoreTemp: T[1..n];  CoreFreq: F[1:n];  FreqLevel: FL[1:m];
TempLevel: TL[1:m]
Core Hash: t_h{Temp}→{1,....n}
Sort_descending(T)
For i = 1 to n/2:
    If T[i]>Critical_temp:
        Task[t_h(T[i])]→Core[t_h(T[n-i])]  -- <perform task migration>
    Else:
        For j=1:m:
            If T[i]>TL[j]:
                F[i]=FL[j]      -- <ITD-aware frequency changing>
Run(benchmark)
T←new Temperature
```

Figure 4: ITD-aware acitivty migration algorithm

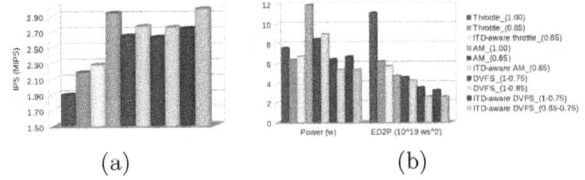

(a)   (b)

Figure 5: (a) Performance(b) Power and ED2P of thermal control techniques for various operating voltages for the 7nm PTM technology

simulation framework. The ITD-aware modified versions of these techniques are also studied to evaluate the performance enhancement from the frequency headroom offered at elevated temperatures in the presence of the ITD.

For this purpose, we study various processor operating voltage points for the 7nm PTM technology. In order to make a fair comparison, the power and frequencies for different operating voltages are derived based on the values form Table 1. E.g., for the 7nm technology, if the maximum frequency is 3.565 GHz at the nominal voltage at temp=50°C, the maximum frequency at 85% of nominal voltage is 2.5GHz and 2.722GHz at temperatures of 50°C and 75°C, respectively. Moreover, at 75% of the nominal voltage the maximum frequency is 1.696GHz and 1.951GHz at temperatures of 50°C and 75°C, respectively.

For temperature study, we simulate 400ms of transient thermal behavior. Every time-interval, (for this study, 1m and 0.1ms) the transient temperature is checked and if it reaches to 90°C, a DTM mechanism is activated. This include throttling, AM, or DVFS. For the AM, the cost of each migration is set one thousand cycles according to [15], which is the cost to bring up a completely power-gated core. For the DVFS, two levels of voltage frequency pairs are used for each operating point, the higher being the operating point (either nominal or 85% of the nominal voltage) and the lower being 75% of the nominal voltage, which is used when the core reaches critical temperatures.

As described in Section 2.2, in order to see the ITD phenomenon, we have to operate the core at lower than nominal voltages. Thus, for the ITD-aware schemes the operating point of 85% and 75% of the nominal voltage are investigated. For $v = 0.85v_{nom}$, the frequency is increased from 2.50GHz to 2.722GHz and for $v = 0.75v_{nom}$, the frequency is increased from 1.696GHz to 1.951GHz for the frequency-sensitive application when it reaches a temperature of 75°C.

The simulations are done for workloads combining hot and cold applications (e.g., bisort_med and lbm_06). Based on the simulation results in Section 3, these two applications showed high contrast in their thermal profile. Moreover, one of them is frequency-sensitive and the other is frequency-insensitive. While other cold-hot applications can be paired with the same simulation framework, pairing hot-hot application and cold-cold applications will yield no performance gain, as there is no thermal difference to exploit ITD.

6. SIMULATION RESULTS

Fig. 5(a) shows the overall performance of the frequency-sensitive application (i.e. bisort_med) for different thermal control techniques and various operating voltages for the 7nm PTM technology. The values in the parenthesis show the ratio of the operating voltage to the nominal voltage.

Table 3: Simulation Results

Scheme	$\frac{op.voltage}{nom.voltage}$	IPS (MIPS)	power (w)	EDP ($10^{13}ws^2$)	ED2P ($10^{19}ws^3$)	max. temp. (°C)
Throttle	1	1.898	7.59	21.10	11.11	90.6
Throttle	0.85	2.182	6.40	13.5	6.17	91.16
ITD throttle	0.85	2.277	6.73	13.00	5.71	92.32
AM	1	2.934	11.93	13.86	4.72	90.59
AM	0.85	2.644	8.50	12.16	4.60	91.10
ITD AM	0.85	2.765	8.98	11.75	4.25	92.86
DVFS	(1,0.75)	2.627	6.43	9.32	3.55	90.07
DVFS	(0.85,0.75)	2.749	5.37	7.10	2.58	90.13
ITD DVFS	(1,0.75)	2.735	6.68	8.93	3.27	90.07
ITD DVFS	(0.85,0.75)	2.984	6.11	6.86	2.30	90.41

As mentioned earlier, with the operating point of $v = v_{nom}$, the change in the operating frequency at different temperatures is negligible, thus for this operating point, dynamic frequency changing is not useful and only the results for throttling and activity migration are reported. For $v = 0.85v_{nom}$, the results for all techniques in Section 4 are reported. For $v = 0.75v_{noml}$, the cores will never reach critical temperatures, thus no thermal control technique is used. Fig. 5(a) shows that the ITD-aware techniques yield better performance compared to their corresponding DTM technique.

Table 3 shows the summary of the results for various DTM techniques at different operating points. In Table 3, EDP stands for the energy delay product. The cost of migration has been included in the results reported in the table. The number of task migrations during a 400ms simulation in the AM technique was 126 and 550 at $v = 0.85v_{nom}$ and $v = v_{nom}$, respectively, while it was 126 for the ITD-aware technique at $v = 0.85v_{nom}$.

Fig. 5 illustrates the power and EDP comparison between the DTM techniques. According to Table 3 and Fig. 5, using the ITD-aware scheme will enhance the performance of all DTM techniques. For throttling, AM and DVFS, the ITD-aware scheme increases the IPS by 4.39%, 4.59% and 8.55%, respectively at $v = 0.85v_{nom}$. At the operating voltage of $v = v_{nom}$ the ITD-aware scheme is used when DVFS technique in working at a lower voltage level (i.e. $v = 0.75v_{nom}$) and it enhances the performance of DVFS technique by 3.9%. Among the DTM techniques studied in this paper, AM and DVFS show better performance in comparison to the throttling.

While the AM at the nominal voltage yields the best performance, its behavior in other design metrics including power and EDP is not desirable. Moving to a lower operating voltage point would result in better power profile at the cost of decreased performance. The ITD-aware algorithms allow us to compensate for this reduced performance by exploiting the frequency headroom at high temperatures. The DVFS algorithm shows a behavior close to the AM algorithm in terms of IPS when equipped with ITD-aware scheme; however, its lower power and EDP makes it a better candidate for low-power designs.

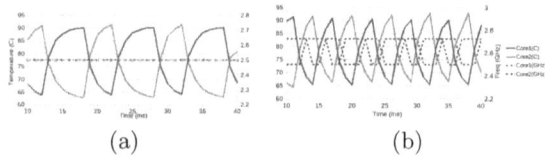

(a)   (b)

Figure 6: Transient temperature for (a) AM (b) ITD-aware AM at $v = 0.85 v_{nom}$

Fig. 6 shows the thermal behavior of the AM and ITD-aware AM techniques for $v = 0.85 v_{nom}$. The dashed lines show the changes in the operating frequency. In the conventional AM algorithm in Fig. 6(a), the frequency is kept unchanged; however, in the ITD-aware algorithm, the frequency increases whenever the temperature of the core increases above 75 °C. Moreover, these figures show that increasing the frequency of the core at the mid-point temperature threshold, will result in the core temperature reaching the critical temperature faster. Thus, in case of the ITD-aware scheme, the number and thus the cost of migration increases.

7. RELATED WORK

Prior works have focused on the implication of the ITD on circuit design and how it changes the device behavior and design corners. In [2], the effect of ITD is investigated for the behavior of the clock tree mapped on an industrial 65nm CMOS technology, and ITD is shown to occur at low operating voltages. In [3], a dual-v_t circuit is proposed for a commercial low-power 65 nm CMOS technologies under ITD to ensure the temperature-insensitive behavior of the circuit. In [4], the authors use the available power headroom at low temperatures to increase the voltage when the temperature is bellow a certain level to enhance the performance. Latest work have explored the effect of ITD in current technology nodes [2], [3] and [4]; however, it is important to explore ITD impact in the future nodes, as well. This work investigates ITD in future CMOS technologies to understand whether further scaling will increase the significance of the ITD.

On dynamic thermal management, processor thermal characteristics at the architectural level have been studied extensively in recent years [7]. Several techniques have been proposed to reduce the chip temperature in single core [7] as well as multicore architectures [13]. These techniques either migrate the processor activity [12] or adapt processor resources to reduce temperature [7]. In the latter, the utilization across processor units are balanced to control the power density. DVFS has also shown to be effective in balancing the temperature of processor [13,16].

These techniques have been widely studied at the architectural and operating system levels without considering the ITD phenomenon. This work shows how ITD can be exploited to enhance the benefits of DTM techniques for power, performance and energy-efficiency improvement.

8. CONCLUSION

This paper exploited ITD for power, performance, and temperature optimization in processor architecture. It investigated ITD in future CMOS technologies showing further scaling would increase the significance of the ITD. In Future CMOS technologies, while working at the nominal voltage yields the best performance, due to high power densities the power profile and thermal behavior of a chip is not

desirable. On the other hand, moving to a lower operating voltage results in better power profile at the cost of lowering the performance. The ITD-aware algorithm proposed in this paper, allows us to compensate for this reduced performance by exploiting the frequency headroom at high temperatures, while maintaining a low power profile. Simulation results were provided for a workload consisting of a hot-cold combination of applications for the proposed ITD-aware schemes.

9. REFERENCES

[1] B. Razavi, *Design of Analog CMOS Integrated Circuits*, 1st ed. New York, NY, USA: McGraw-Hill, Inc., 2001.

[2] A. Sassone et. al, "Investigating the effects of inverted temperature dependence (ITD) on clock distribution networks," *DATE*, 2012.

[3] A. Calimera et. al, "Temperature-insensitive dual- vth synthesis for nanometer cmos technologies under inverse temperature dependence," *TVLSI*, 2010.

[4] M. Latif and et. al., "Design for cold test elimination - facing the inverse temperature dependence (ITD) challenge," *ISCAS*, 2012.

[5] Y. K. Cao, "Predictive techonology models," Nanoscale Integration and Modeling (NIMO) Group, 2012. [Online]. Available: http://www.ptm.asu.edu

[6] A. Gaisler, "Leon3 processor," Nanoscale Integration and Modeling (NIMO) Group, 2010. [Online]. Available: http://www.gaisler.com/index.php/ products/processors/leon3

[7] K. Skadron et. al, "Temperature-aware microarchitecture," *ISCA*, 2003.

[8] D. M. Tullsen, "Simulation and modeling of a simultaneous multithreading processor," *In Proc. of CMG Conference*, 1996.

[9] "Standard performance evaluation corporation," Open Systems Group (OSG), 2013. [Online]. Available: http://www.spec.org

[10] L. Sheng et. al, "McPAT: An integrated power, area, and timing modeling framework for multicore and manycore architectures," *MICRO-42*, 2009.

[11] Liu Yongpan et. al, "Thermal vs energy optimization for DVFS-enabled processors in embedded systems," *ISQED*, 2007.

[12] V. Hanumaiah et. al, "Performance optimal online DVFS and task migration techniques for thermally constrained multi-core processors," *TCAD*, 2011.

[13] J. Donald and M. Martonosi, "Techniques for multicore thermal management: Classification and new exploration," in *Computer Architecture News*, 2006.

[14] Coskun et. al, "Evaluating the impact of job scheduling and power management on processor lifetime for chip multiprocessors," in *ACM SIGMETRICS Performance Evaluation Review*, 2009.

[15] R. Kumar et. al, "Processor power reduction via single-isa heterogeneous multi-core architectures," *Computer Architecture Letters*, 2003.

[16] C. Zhu and et. al., "Three-dimensional chip-multiprocessor run-time thermal management," *TCAD*, 2008.

Adaptive Bandwidth Management for Performance-Temperature Trade-offs in Heterogeneous HMC+DDRx Memory

Mohammad Hossein Hajkazemi, Michael Chorney, Reyhaneh Jabbarvand Behrouz,
Mohammad Khavari Tavana, Houman Homayoun
George Mason University, Fairfax, VA, USA
Email: {mhajkaze, mchorney, rjabbarv, mkhavari, hhomayou}@gmu.edu

ABSTRACT

High fabrication cost per bit and thermal issues are the main reasons that prevent architects from using 3D-DRAM alone as the main memory. In this paper, we address this issue by proposing a heterogeneous memory system that combines a DDRx DRAM with an emerging 3D hybrid memory cube (HMC) technology. Bandwidth and temperature management are the challenging issues for such a memory architecture. To address these challenges, first we introduce a memory page allocation policy for the heterogeneous memory system to maximize performance. Then, using the proposed policy, we introduce a temperature-aware algorithm that adaptively distributes the requested bandwidth between HMC and DDRx DRAM to reduce the thermal hotspot while maintaining high performance. The results show that the proposed memory page allocation policy can utilize the memory bandwidth close to 99% of the ideal bandwidth utilization. Moreover our temperate-aware bandwidth adaptation reduces the average steady-state temperature of the HMC hotspot across various workloads by $4.5^{\circ}K$ while incurring 2.5% performance overhead.

Categories and Subject Descriptors

B.3.1 [**Memory Structures**]: Semiconductor Memories–*Dynamic memory (DRAM)*.

Keywords

Heterogeneous Memories, Bandwidth, HMC, Temperature

1. INTRODUCTION

3D-integration is a recent technology that addresses the memory wall problem [13][14]. With 3D-integration, different layers of dies are stacked using fast through-silicon TSV interconnects (TSV) with a latency as low as few picoseconds. Therefore, by exploiting 3D-integration, we are able to stack multiple layers of DRAM resulting in shorter memory access latency to potentially address the memory wall problem. Moreover, stacking DRAM gives us the opportunity to have parallel accesses to DRAM banks, which results in higher maximum achievable bandwidth.

Compared to the conventional DRAM architecture (2D), 3D-DRAM results in better performance. Hybrid memory cube (HMC) is an emerging 3D memory interface and design introduced by Micron to address the inefficiency of DDRx DRAMs [14]. HMC

stacks up to eight layers of standard DRAM building blocks on a memory controller. However, 3D-integration used in HMC imposes a drastic power density as highlighted in 2013 report by Rambus [20]. Higher power density causes many temperature-related problems including extra cooling costs, reliability, wear-out, and leakage power issues [7]. For example, more stacked layers increases the heat resistivity of the entire chip package that results in higher peak and steady-state temperature. It also complicates the chip packaging process which makes the design more vulnerable to various failure mechanisms [21].

Beside the thermal issues, fabrication cost is another challenge, which could limit the application of HMC. As the capacity of each HMC cube is limited to 2~4GB [9], several cubes need to be chained together to build a larger capacity required. In terms of cost and design feasibility this may not be a practical option. Therefore, conventional 2D, DDRx DRAM, is indispensable in order to maintain high capacity requirement of DRAM to achieve high performance and avoid the thermal and cost challenges associated with the new 3D technology.

A heterogeneous memory system that combines 2D- and 3D-DRAM can exploit the high capacity, low cost and low thermal footprint of 2D, and high bandwidth and low access latency of 3D, simultaneously. However the challenge is how to manage the two substantially different designs effectively to exploit their benefits. [10] attempts to address this issue, however it does not model HMC, and instead, it studies a generic 3D-stacked DRAM. Moreover, despite proposing a policy to achieve higher QoS, the thermal challenge of 3D memory is not addressed in [10].

In this paper we introduce a heterogeneous HMC+DDRx memory system. The focus of this paper is to address both performance and temperature challenges associated with the proposed memory architecture, simultaneously, by introducing performance-temperature aware memory management mechanisms. Over-utilization of either HMC or DDRx DRAM results in bandwidth congestion and incurs a large performance loss. Furthermore, utilizing the HMC to maximize the performance benefits can lead to thermal hotspots, which in turn can severely affects performance, due to thermal emergency response such as throttling. In order to utilize both HMC and DDRx DRAM efficiently, our memory management mechanism allocates the memory pages in an interleaving manner considering the system temperature and performance. To the best of our knowledge this is the first paper to simultaneously address the performance and temperature challenges in a heterogeneous HMC+DDRx DRAM memory subsystem. The main contributions of this work are as follows:

- We show that a heterogeneous HMC+DDRx, is an alternative for conventional DDRx and plain HMC memory system, which addresses the performance challenge and thermal issues of 3D-integartion, while maintaining high performance.

- We show that in heterogeneous DDRx+HMC, the average memory access latency changes substantially across various bandwidth allocation, therefore suggests the need for a bandwidth allocation policy to minimize the latency. We propose a run-time memory page allocation policy to efficiently utilize the bandwidth.
- We introduce a dynamic temperature-aware policy that utilizes our proposed heterogeneous DRAM based on the operating temperature of the HMC and the current phase of the workload. As a result, by allocating bandwidth to HMC and DDRx DRAM dynamically, we reduce the steady-state temperature.

The rest of this paper is organized as follows. Section 2 describes our heterogeneous memory system. Section 3 introduces our heterogeneous memory management. Section 4 presents the framework and Section 5 shows the results. Section 6 introduces some related works. Finally, Section 7 concludes the paper.

2. HETEROGENEOUS HMC+DDRx

Prior research [15][16] has shown that 3D-DRAM provides significant advantages in terms of performance while enabling energy-efficient computing. 3D-DRAMs including HMC offer much higher bandwidth compared to DDRx technologies. They are also more power efficient [22][14][12]. This is achieved by having more parallel accesses to the DRAM enabled by short and fast interconnect. However, in terms of cost per pit and relative power density (and temperature footprint) DDRx is a better technology [22][14]. While the HMC cost might even go further down in future, as DRAM is a very cost-sensitive market DDRx will not going away any time soon [12]. Therefore, a memory system consisting of both HMC and DDRx interfaces can address power, performance, temperature, and cost challenges.

Our studied architecture in this work is shown in Fig.1. In our heterogeneous memory system, HMC is combined with a conventional DDRx DRAM to exploit the high memory bandwidth and the low memory latency of the HMC as well as the high capacity and the low cost of the DDRx DRAM. The memory management we employ for the proposed heterogeneous DRAM integrates the OS virtual to physical address translation so that the heterogeneous memory is transparent to the CMP (chip multiprocessor) and the cores see a unified address space.

As Fig. 1 illustrates, the cores' memory requests are pushed to the memory request distributer (MRD). Decoding the coming request, MRD transfers the request to the corresponding memory controller (i.e., either HMC or DDRx memory controller). Each controller has its own queue for memory requests. By generating appropriate DRAM commands, the memory controller services the requests in the queue and accesses the DRAM cells. Then, depending on the request type (i.e., read/write) the data is either written to or read

from the memory and sent back to the core through the memory controller's read queue. As shown in Fig. 1, our proposed heterogeneous DRAM has two distinct memory channels: one connecting to HMC using two high-speed links, and the other connecting to DDRx DRAM. Without loss of generality, similar to [1][10], we assume in this paper that The HMC and DDRx DRAM employ two and one memory controllers, respectively.

The main question for our proposed heterogeneous memory system is how to manage each memory component including the HMC and the DDRx DRAM to gain the best performance while addressing the bandwidth, capacity, and temperature challenges. The key to answer this question is to understand the application's behavior in terms of memory access pattern and utilization. For instance, the more requests the HMC receives in burst, the more its bandwidth is utilized. However, utilizing the HMC aggressively, results in longer memory latency if the application has a large number of memory requests that are coming in burst. On the other hand, applications with a large number of memory requests cause more dynamic power dissipation and thus, higher average temperature. Therefore, a dynamic bandwidth and temperature adaptation is required.

3. HMC+DDRX MANAGEMENT

In this section, we explain how to allocate the application requested memory bandwidth between the HMC and the DDRx DRAM.

3.1 Bandwidth Allocation Policy

Memory access latency is a function of memory bandwidth utilization [1] [10]. As the bandwidth utilization increases, the memory access latency becomes longer, mainly due to congestion in the memory controller and links. While there are several solutions to mitigate this problem [17], above certain bandwidth utilization, due to queuing effect the memory access latency increases significantly [1][10]. In Fig. 2 we investigate this phenomenon for both the DDRx DRAM and the HMC independently. As shown in Fig. 2 we increase the bandwidth utilization of HMC and DDRx DRAM by allocating more number of memory requests for each type of workloads. The x-axis illustrates the memory request portion that each DRAM receives form the entire accesses. For example, in Fig. 2(a) 10/90 means that while 10% of requests are serviced by HMC, 90% of requests are serviced by DDRx DRAM. It is important to note that in Fig. 2(a) and 2(b), we show the average memory latency from HMC and DDRx DRAM perspective, respectively. We categorize application into three groups; the memory-intensive applications, the memory-non-intensive applications and a mixture of them. The workloads are classified based on their LLC misses per 1K instructions (MPKI) which varies from 0.0005 to 24 for our studied benchmarks. We refer to a benchmark as memory-intensive if its MPKI is greater than twelve and non-intensive if MPKI is less than

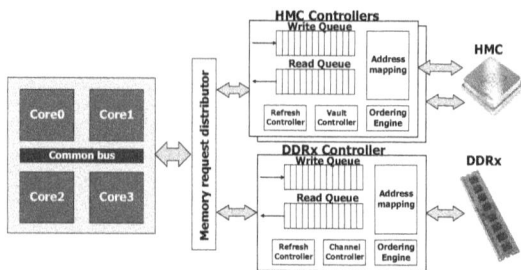

Figure 1. Studied architecture employing heterogeneous DRAM.

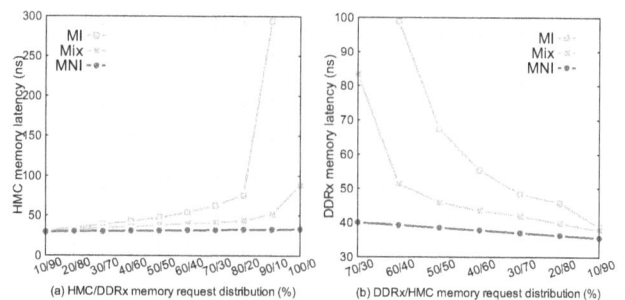

(a) HMC/DDRx memory request distribution (%) (b) DDRx/HMC memory request distribution (%)

Figure 2. Memory access latency of (a) HMC and (b) DDRx DRAM as a function of memory request allocation.

Table 1. Inaccuracy of proposed bandwidth allocation policy.

Workload	(+/-) inaccuracy %	Workload	(+/-) inaccuracy %
MI1	1.53	Mix3	5.53
MI2	0.33	Mix4	0.74
MI3	0.33	MNI1	2.23
MI4	0.23	MNI2	0.51
Mix1	1.99	MNI3	1.02
Mix2	0.99	MNI4	0.38
Average		**1.32**	

one. For simplicity, we refer to memory-intensive, memory-non-intensive and mixture applications throughout the paper as MI, MNI and Mix applications. Workloads used in Fig. 2 are representatives of their categories.

As Fig. 2(b) shows, for the DDRx DRAM, the MI workload has the highest rise in memory access latency when request allocation increases from 10% to 60% for DDRx DRAM. For bandwidth above 70%, due to queuing effect the memory access latency for MI workload becomes so large that we could not show it in the figure (for instance with 90% utilization this is 8891ns). In Mix and MNI workloads the memory latency is affected much less as the bandwidth utilization increases. The results show that for MNI workloads, the memory access latency is somewhat linear while for Mix applications it grows exponentially, but at much slower rate compared to MI workloads. We show the results for HMC in Fig. 2(a). As shown, when the memory request allocation is between 10% and 80%, the latency is almost linear across all groups of workloads. For larger bandwidth utilizations, except for MNI, in Mix and MI workloads, HMC latency increases exponentially, however at much slower rate compared to DDRx DRAM (Fig. 2(b)). It is notable that, generally, the memory latency increases in DDRx DRAM more quickly compared to HMC, since HMC has a higher memory bandwidth and faster interconnects, TSVs.

Motivated by the observation from Fig. 2, we introduce a bandwidth allocation policy to effectively utilize both HMC and DDRx DRAM, so that we gain the minimum average memory

access latency for any given workload. In this technique, we allocate new memory pages in an interleaving scheme between HMC and the DDRx DRAM, to achieve the minimum average access latency for the entire system. The minimum access latency is achieved at a specific bandwidth utilization of each DRAM which is different across various workloads. We refer to this point as **O**ptimum **B**andwidth **U**tilization or OBU in brief. For instance, for a given workload OBU of 70% means that to achieve the minimum access latency we need to allocate the requests to HMC and DDRx DRAM by 70% and 30% respectively. To satisfy this goal, out of each ten new consecutive writes (page faults), we assign the first seven access (pages) to the first seven free blocks of HMC and the remaining to the three free blocks of the DDRx DRAM. This necessitate a mechanism (using a simple counter) to determine the DRAMs' turn. This helps meeting the OBU for the new incoming write accesses. Nonetheless, since not all the accesses are new writes (i.e., the requested data already resides in the DRAM), and the access pattern to the previously allocated memory blocks may not be uniform, the target bandwidth allocation might not be satisfied. However, our experimental results show that our memory allocation policy can satisfy the target bandwidth, indicating that the access pattern is somewhat uniform. Table 1 reports the average inaccuracy of our allocation technique from the OBU for all other target bandwidths (0 to 100 in step of 10), which indicates how accurate it meets the target bandwidth. As reported in Table 1, the average inaccuracy of the proposed allocation policy is 1.32%, i.e., close to 99% of the ideal bandwidth utilization.

The proposed interleaving memory page allocation policy is shown in Fig. 3. As it shows, upon generating a new request by the CMP, the corresponding core accesses its own TLB and then page table to check whether the address is available in the main memory or not. If so, using MRD, the correspondent DRAM is accessed to read/write the data. Otherwise a page fault occurs, and *bandwidth manager* transfers the page which contains the data from the hard disk to the proper DRAM (i.e., HMC or DDRx). In order to do so, with the help of OS, the bandwidth manager checks whether any of the DRAMs (i.e., HMC and DDRx) has a free page. If any of the DRAMs is full, bandwidth manager accesses the other one that is not full, otherwise it employs page replacement policies to bring the new page to the heterogeneous DRAM. Moreover, bandwidth manager needs to know about DRAM's turn to accommodate the new page in the proper DRAM. This is done with the help of the distribution factor variable that stores the OBU. We will discuss *Temperature-aware distribution factor regulator* in section 3.2.

As discussed, every workload type have different OBU and the interleaving policy results in the minimum memory latency only if the proper bandwidth utilization is set. Therefore, it is important to detect the type of workload, whether it is an intensive, mix or non-intensive, to set the proper OBU. Our studies on workload memory access pattern show that, although the memory access pattern may change through different phases of a program, consistent with prior

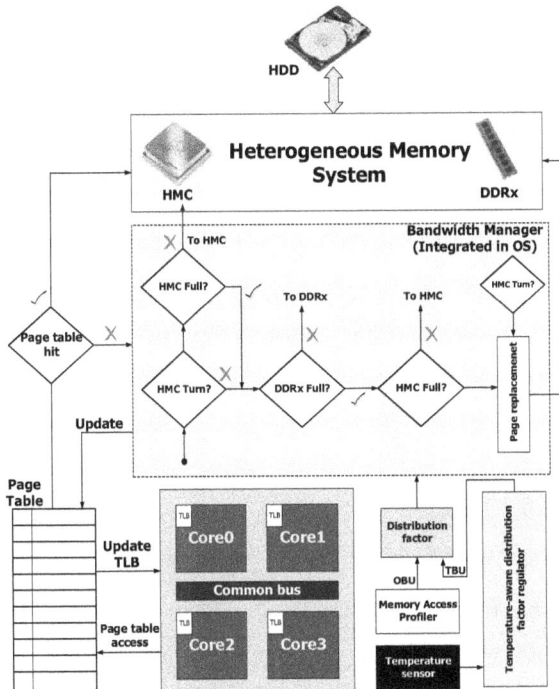

Figure 3. Bandwidth- and temperature-aware memory management.

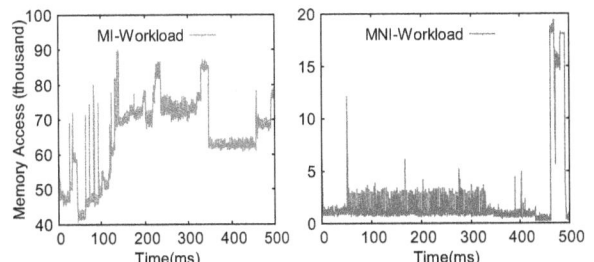

Figure 4. Memory access pattern for different workloads.

work [17], the average intensity of memory requests in a given phase is deterministic and highly predictable. Fig. 4 illustrates the memory access pattern for two representatives of MI and MNI workloads. The samples are collected every 1 million cycles.

As shown in Fig. 4, MNI applications can be clearly distinct from MI workloads, as the number of memory requests in this class of workload remains almost consistently small throughout the 500M cycles studied intervals. Therefore by profiling memory access pattern we can decide the workload type and the relevant OBU accordingly. As Fig. 3 depicts, the *memory access profiler* provides the proper OBU for the bandwidth manager. This can be done every 10 milliseconds, as most operating systems performs context switching at this rate and therefore the memory access pattern will change. After all, as soon as the new page resides in the memory, the corresponding TLB and the page table need to be updated.

Since bandwidth allocation policy brings the memory blocks in page granularity, and given that we use the same page size as homogeneous memory system does, our memory management does not affect the data locality. Applying our memory allocation policy, we estimate the average memory access latency of the proposed heterogeneous memory system when running different workloads using equation 1:

$$L_T = (P * L_{HMC}) + ((1 - P) * L_{DDRx}) \qquad (1)$$

where L_T is the total latency, P is the HMC desired allocated bandwidth, L_{HMC} is the HMC latency and L_{DDRx} is the DDRx DRAM latency.

Fig. 5 presents the total memory access latency for two groups of workloads and for various target bandwidths. It is noteworthy that memory access latency (Y axis) for MI and MNI is in the range of microseconds and nanoseconds, respectively. We observe such a high difference in memory latency (us vs. ns) only when the queuing effect occurs in MI workloads. Moreover, as Mix workload behavior is somewhat close to MI workload behavior, due to space limitation, in Fig. 5 we only report the results for the first two studied workloads in MI and MNI categories.

As Fig. 5 shows, different types of workloads have different OBU to achieve minimum average memory access latency. In MI workloads the average memory latency is more sensitive to the bandwidth allocation than the other workload. In Fig. 5(a), for MI workloads, miss utilization of the heterogeneous memory system results in a large performance loss. For example, for the first workload, if the HMC bandwidth allocation is less than 50% or more than 80%, the memory access latency is becoming large in a microsecond range (note that 50% and 80% of HMC allocation means 50% and 20% of DDRx bandwidth allocation). This occurs for the second workload as well, if the HMC bandwidth allocation

is less than 30% or equal to 100%. This large penalty is due to the queuing effect. It is important to note that as the simulations for both workloads took so long, we were not able to report the memory access latency for 10% and 20% of HMC bandwidth allocation, in Fig. 5 (a). This shows that the performance loss is even more, compared to 30% of HMC bandwidth allocation. Our observation shows that allocating 60% of the entire bandwidth to HMC gives the best performance for all MI workloads. Therefore, the OBU is set to 60% for this class of workloads. Since Mix workloads show the same behavior as MI workloads do, we set OBU to 60% as well for this class of workloads.

As Fig. 5 (b) presents, in MNI workload, the performance penalty due to DRAMs miss utilization is very small compared to MI workload. Unlike MI and Mix workloads in which we observed the queuing effect, in memory-non-intensive workloads, as we allocate higher bandwidth to HMC we gain a better performance up to the point where we reach to 90% of the entire bandwidth. If we allocate the entire bandwidth to HMC we lose a small performance. Therefore, we can set the OBU at 90% for this class of workloads. Our observation shows that the average memory access latency of our heterogeneous memory system at the OBU for MI, Mix and MNI applications are 64ns, 44ns and 33ns respectively. It is worth mentioning that the workloads that are not presented in these figures have somewhat similar behavior and the illustrated workloads can be representative of its corresponding workload category.

3.2 Temperature-aware Policy

In this section, we propose our algorithm that reduces the steady sate temperature while maintaining the high-performance benefit of bandwidth allocation policy presented earlier. Fig. 6 shows the steady state temperature in HMC as a function of bandwidth allocation, for different types of workloads. As Fig. 6 shows, for the MI and the Mix workloads allocating higher bandwidth to HMC from 10% to 100% results in 25°K and 43°K steady state temperature increase. For workloads with high memory requests (MI) a sharp rise in temperature is observed when higher bandwidth is allocated. As shown, for MNI workload higher bandwidth allocation does not affect the temperature, mainly due to the fact that these workloads do not generate significant memory accesses and therefore they have small power dissipation.

While higher DRAM bandwidth allocation is desired, it comes with a large temperature rise. Such a large thermal rise is not tolerable as it can affect the performance, reliability and the cooling cost of the design [7][21]. Therefore, we need a smart mechanism to dynamically adapt DRAM bandwidth allocation to manage the temperature.

3.2.1 Temperature-aware Bandwidth Allocation
Bandwidth allocation of the heterogeneous DRAM affects DRAM

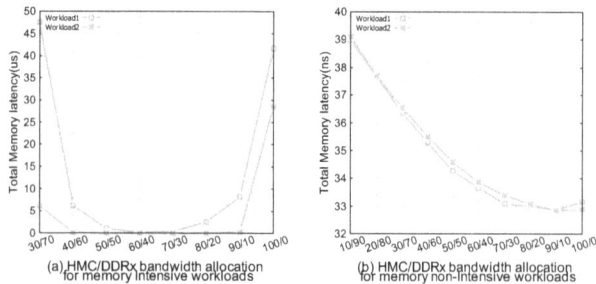

Figure 5. Total memory access latency in the heterogeneous memory system, as a function of HMC/DDRx bandwidth allocation for (a) MI and (b) MNI workloads.

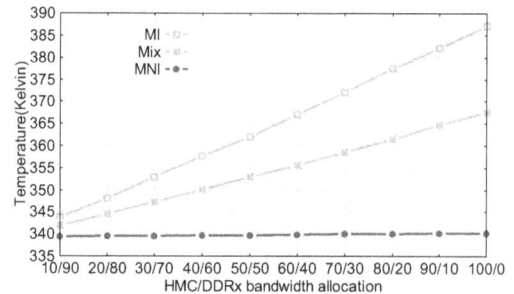

Figure 6. HMC steady state temperature of hot spot for various bandwidth allocations across different workloads.

power dissipation. The power and therefore the temperature of HMC are highly decided by its bandwidth allocation. As indicated in Fig. 6, for MI and Mix workloads there is a large gap in steady state temperature. Motivated by this observation, we propose our dynamic temperature-aware bandwidth allocation technique (DTBA in brief) to reduce the steady-state temperature of HMC while maintaining high performance benefit.

In DTBA, first we define two operating temperature regions, namely normal and hot. As long as the HMC operates in the normal region it can be utilized to gain the highest performance using the bandwidth allocation policy. However, whenever HMC enters the hot region we allocate lower bandwidth to it while dedicating higher bandwidth to the DDRx DRAM at the same time to compensate for possible performance loss. This results in lowering HMC power consumption and therefore reduces steady state temperature. We implement DTBA using the proposed memory allocation technique explained in Section 3.1 (see Fig. 3).

As presented in Fig. 6, MNI workloads' temperatures are almost bandwidth insensitive. Therefore these workloads do not require a thermal-aware adaptation and we can simply use the bandwidth allocation technique to manage their bandwidth utilization.

As Fig. 3 shows, our temperature-aware algorithm works as follows. We profile the memory accesses to detect the running workload type. Then, based on the workload type, we set the OBU using bandwidth allocation policy. The temperature sensor on HMC monitors the temperature periodically. If the HMC temperature rises into the hot region, the distribution factor variable is over-written with the new bandwidth referred to as Temperature-aware Bandwidth Utilization (TBU). This is done by temperature-aware distributer factor regulator. Otherwise, we continue with the previous bandwidth allocation based on the OBU provided by the memory access profiler. Our temperature-sampling interval is set at 1 millisecond [5][8].

Note that bandwidth allocation policy and DTBA work cooperatively to find the target bandwidth that delivers the highest performance while maintaining the HMC operation below the hot region. As shown in Fig. 5, although allocating 90% of the entire bandwidth to HMC gives the highest performance for MNI workloads, it hurts performance significantly for MI and Mix workloads. Therefore, starting with 60% of bandwidth allocation is an optimal choice as it provides a good performance across all workloads.

4. METHODOLOGY

We use a quad-core CMP architecture with a total of 3GBs of DRAM including 1 GB HMC and 2 GB of DDRx as our target system. For the DDRx DRAM we model a Micron DDR3 SDRAM [3]. Table 2 summarizes the detailed parameters of CMP

Table 2. CMP and heterogeneous memory system parameters.

Core	
Core Clock	3GHz
Issue, Commit width	4
INT & FP Instruction queue	32 entries
ROB size, INT Reg, FP Reg	128
L1 cache	64KB, 8-way, 2 cycle
L2 cache	512KB, 20 cycle
HMC and DDRx DRAM	
DRAM Clock	800MHz
Column Access Strobe (t_{CAS})	10 (DDRx), 6 (HMC)
Row Access Strobe (t_{RAS})	24 (DDRx), 24 (HMC)
Row Buffer Policy	Close page
Page Size	4 KB

architecture and heterogeneous memory system modeled in this work.

We integrate SMTSIM simulator [2] and DRAMsim2 [3] for architecture simulation. We use SPEC2000, SPEC2006, NAS [18] and Olden [19] benchmarks to create the 12 studied workloads. We modify DRAMSim2 memory simulator extensively to model the proposed heterogeneous memory. Moreover, DRAMsim2 is extended with a profiler that periodically monitors workload to predict whether it is memory-intensive in the current program phase. It is also equipped with a power profiler to generate the memory system power trace.

To calculate the memory controller power consumption, we use the results reported in [14]. As [14] presents, in an HMC the average power dissipation of the memory controller is 1.8 of the DRAM layers. We employ HotSpot [5] to measure the HMC temperature. DRAMSim2 receives the transient temperature (running temperature) from HotSpot [5] periodically, i.e., every 1 millisecond. We assume that the power dissipation is distributed evenly across all eight DRAM layers, as well as within each layers. We assume the area of the HMC layers including DRAM and controller layers to be 68 mm^2 which is adopted from [6]. We consider the thickness of HMC dies and heat-sink to be 0.05 mm and 0.01 mm, respectively. Other thermal specifications are borrowed from [5]. Similar to [6], since the HMC and CMP are integrated using a PCB, we consider an inexpensive heat-sink for the HMC.

5. DTBA RESULTS

This section evaluates DTBA when applied in the proposed heterogeneous DRAM. To find how effective DTBA can optimize temperature and performance simultaneously, we compare it with a performance-optimized (bandwidth allocation) baseline where the bandwidth adaptation is performed to minimize average DRAM access latency and therefore maximize performance. Hence, the OBU is set to 60%, based on the results discussed in Section 3.1. In order to have a better understating of DTBA impact on temperature, we consider different TBU for the hot region

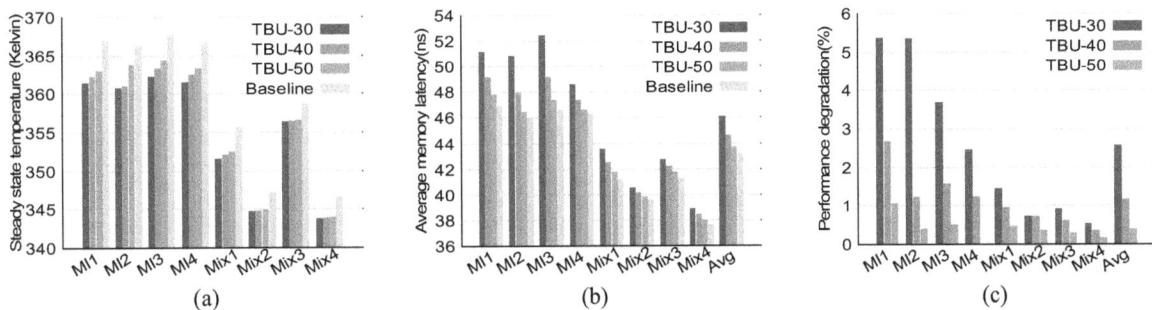

Figure 7. (a) Steady-state temperature of HMC, (b) Average latency of the entire DRAM and (c) Performance degradation for different workloads when different TBU is applied.

discussed in Section 3.2. Fig. 7(a) shows the steady state temperature of DTBA. Note that since MNI workloads are not temperature sensitive as discussed earlier, only results for MI and Mix workload are presented.

As shown in Fig. 7(a), TBU=30% configuration achieves the highest temperature reduction. The largest thermal reduction is 5.5°K which is observed in MI4 workload. TBU=40% and TBU=50% results have slightly lower thermal reduction. Moreover, it is important to note that as memory-intensive workloads are more temperature sensitive, temperature results are more sensitive to the TBU compared to Mix workloads. Since DTBA trade-offs temperature with performance, it comes with a small performance penalty compared to the bandwidth allocation policy, which is only optimized for performance. This performance loss is due to the longer memory latency. Fig. 7(b) and 7(c) show the DTBA performance loss for different workloads in terms of memory latency and IPC.

As shown in Fig. 7(b), the average memory access latency increases when DTBA is applied, compared to bandwidth allocation policy. Similar to Fig. 7(a), since there is a negligible performance loss for memory-non-intensive workloads, we do not report the results. As Fig. 7(b) depicts, for all workloads, configurations with more temperature reduction, result in larger memory latency. The largest increase in average memory latency is observed in MI3 workload. Note that, this is the same workload with highest temperature reduction benefit.

As Fig. 7(c) reports, the average performance loss is around 2.5% in the worst case (TBU=30%). The loss in performance is more noticeable in MI workloads. This is consistent with the thermal improvement we show in Fig. 7(a) in which we achieve higher temperature reduction for MI workloads.

6. RELATED WORK

3D stacking can be used in many ways including logic on logic stacking [4], memory on logic stacking [13] and memory on memory stacking [14] to address some of the major challenges microprocessor industry is facing. 3D-DRAM stacking can potentially resolves the memory wall problem and delivers lower power consumption for the memory subsystem.

Although thermal management in 2D deigns for both core and DRAM has been a challenge for architects, introducing 3D stacking even exacerbates the problem. Therefore, many studies have focused to address this issue, especially for stacked memory. These studies either propose static methods at design level [11] or dynamic techniques at runtime [7][13] to reduce the transient or steady state temperature. For instance, [7] proposes a dynamic power and temperature management for a 3D design with stacked cache. Monitoring the runtime application behavior, [13] attempts to choose the best voltage-frequency setting to achieve the maximum throughput while maintaining the power and temperature constraints in 3D multicore system with a stacked DRAM. In a recent work Zhao [8] proposes a migration technique to reduce temperature in a multicore architecture with stacked DRAM. Migrating threads between cores according to their temperature, is the key of their work to reduce the steady state temperature of the system.

[10] proposes a heterogeneous memory management which exploits a stacked DRAM alongside a 2D DRAM. However, unlike to our work, their research does not investigate the thermal characteristics of the design and onl focuses on the quality of service of applications, which also needs the programmer intervention. Another recent work has been on thermal mitigation

in hybrid memory cubes (HMC) [6] that tries to reduce the number of read/write burst by compressing data in the logic layer (memory controller). This scheme is orthogonal to ours when used in HMC.

7. CONCLUSION

This paper proposes an adaptive bandwidth allocation and a temperature-aware memory management to exploit the high bandwidth and low latency of 3D hybrid memory cube (HMC) and high capacity and low temperature of the DDRx DRAM. The bandwidth allocation memory management policy profiles workload at run-time and based on memory access pattern allocates DRAM and HMC bandwidth accordingly, to reduce memory bandwidth congestion. While this ensures high performance, it causes significant thermal rise in HMC. To address this challenge, the temperature-aware policy monitors run-time temperature of HMC to adapt the bandwidth. Temperature-aware policy reduces the temperature while maintaining the high-performance benefit of bandwidth allocation technique. This is all done based on application memory access patterns and at run-time. Simulation results show that the bandwidth allocation memory management can utilize the memory bandwidth close to 99% of the ideal bandwidth utilization. Combined with the thermal-aware policy, our proposed memory management reduces steady-state temperature by 4.5°K, on average, across different workloads while maintaining the performance benefits of bandwidth-adaptive technique.

8. REFERENCES

[1] Dong, X., et al. "Simple but effective heterogeneous main memory with on-chip memory controller support" IEEE/ACM SC'2010.

[2] Tullsen, D. M. "Simulation and Modeling of a Simultaneous Multithreading Processor" CMG, Part 2(of 2), pp. 819-828, 1996.

[3] Rosenfeld, P., et al. "DRAMSim2: A Cycle Accurate Memory System Simulator" Computer Architecture Letters, 2011.

[4] Vasileios K., et al. "Enabling Dynamic Heterogeneity Through Core-on-Core Stacking" Proceedings of the 51st Annual Design Automation Conference on Design Automation Conference. ACM, 2014.

[5] Skadron, K., et al. "Temperature-aware microarchitecture," ISCA 2003.

[6] Khurshid, et al. "Data compression for thermal mitigation in the Hybrid Memory Cube," ICCD 2013.

[7] Kang, K., et al. "Temperature-Aware Runtime Power Management for Chip-Multiprocessors with 3-D Stacked Cache" ISQED 2014.

[8] Zhao, D., et al. "Temperature aware thread migration in 3D architecture with stacked DRAM" ISQED 2013.

[9] Hybrid Memory Cube Specification 1.1. 2014.http://hybridmemorycube.org/files/SiteDownloads/HMC%20Rev%201_%20Specification.pdf

[10] Tran L., et al. "Heterogeneous memory management for 3D-DRAM and external DRAM with QoS" ASP-DAC, 2013.

[11] Puttaswamy, K., et al. "Thermal Herding: Microarchitecture Techniques for Controlling Hotspots in 3D-Integrated Processors" HPCA 2007.

[12] Elsasser, W., 5 Emerging DRAM Interfaces You Should Know for Your Next Design, Cadence white paper, 2013.

[13] Meng, J., et al. "Optimizing energy efficiency of 3-D multicore systems with stacked DRAM under power and thermal constraints", DAC 2012.

[14] Jeddeloh, J., et al. "Hybrid Memory Cube – New DRAM Architecture Increases Density and Performance", VLSIT 2012.

[15] Wu, Q., et al., "Impacts of though-DRAM vias in 3D processor-DRAM integrated systems" IEEE 3DIC 2009.

[16] Kang, U., et al. "8 Gb 3-D DDR3 DRAM using through-silicon-via technology" Solid-State Circuits, IEEE Journal of 45, 2010.

[17] Kim, Y., et al. "ATLAS: A scalable and high-performance scheduling algorithm for multiple memory controllers" HPCA 2010.

[18] Bailey, D. H., et al. "The NAS parallel benchmarks" International Journal of High Performance Computing Applications 5.3 (1991): 63-73.

[19] Rogers, A., et al. "Supporting dynamic data structures on distributed-memory machines" ACM TOPLAS 17.2 (1995): 233-263.

[20] Li M., 3D Packaging for Memory Application, Rambus, 2013. http://www.avsusergroups.org/joint_pdfs/2013_6Li.pdf

[21] Srinivasan, J., et al. "Lifetime reliability: Toward an architectural solution" Micro, IEEE 25.3 (2005): 70-80.

[22] Pawlowski, J. T. "Hybrid Memory Cube: Breakthrough DRAM Performance with a Fundamentally Re-Architected DRAM Subsystem" In Proceedings of the 23rd Hot Chips Symposium, 2011.

Optimizing VMIN of ROM Arrays without Loss of Noise Margin

Avijit Chakraborty
Texas A&M University
Dept. Electrical and Computer Eng.
College Station TX 77843-3128
+1 (979) 676-0674
avijit.chakraborty@tamu.edu

D. M. H. Walker
Texas A&M University
Dept. Electrical and Computer Eng.
College Station TX 77843-3128
+1 (979) 862-4387
walker@cse.tamu.edu

ABSTRACT

The minimum voltage of operation (Vmin) for memory arrays often limits the lowest system operating voltage. This paper introduces a novel read assist topology for a domino-based evaluation architecture in a read only memory (ROM). The implementation incorporates an assist pull-down (PD) device, which activates during the evaluation phase in order to increase the effective pull-down strength of the bit cells. This implementation maintains Vmin without increasing the size of pull down devices inside the bit cells. The assist topology improves read delay by 11-30% and increases noise margin. Area overhead can be limited to 27% in a typical ROM.

Categories and Subject Descriptors

B.7.1 [**Integrated Circuits**]: Types and Design Styles – Memory Technologies.

General Terms: Performance, Design

Keywords

Vmin; Dynamic evaluation; DC Droop; Area optimization

1. INTRODUCTION

Minimum operating voltage (Vmin) is a key design parameter in low-power circuits, as lower Vmin results in lower power. The Vmin of embedded memories often limits system Vmin. In addition, embedded memories can take up to 94% of the area of a system-on-chip [1]. Therefore, Vmin and area optimization are the key design goals for embedded memories.

In this paper, we will focus on Vmin and area optimization for read only memory (ROM) circuits. The general approach to Vmin reduction is the addition of a read assist circuit on the bit line (BL). Various assist topologies appear in the literature. The drawback of these schemes is that they add devices to the bit cell or add power supply rails [2]-[7]. These schemes have significant area and routing overhead.

The proposed read assist topology in this paper does not require any voltage level modification on the power line or the BL node. BL lowering has been used previously [2], which partially reduces the BL node level from its precharged state of VDD. The lowered BL level reduces the margin between the BL node and the reference threshold of the sensing logic to improve performance. However, this requires additional control circuit and complex logic operation in order to carry out such BL lowering operation. The proposed topology in this paper increases the

GLSVLSI '15, May 20 -22, 2015, Pittsburgh, PA, USA.
Copyright 2015 ACM 978-1-4503-3474-7/15/05...$15.00.
http://dx.doi.org/10.1145/2742060.2742100

effective strength of the pull down device and does not require any changes to the BL node's precharged state in order to gain performance.

BL lowering schemes also reduce the noise margin of the design. For a domino evaluated ROM, a lowered BL voltage level in the logic-0 read phase will lower the amount of noise the BL node can withstand before flipping to cause an erroneous logic-1 state.

There is always a tradeoff between achieving lower Vmin and saving area. In this paper, we propose a domino based dynamic evaluation scheme that minimizes the area overhead. The read assist topology uses an assist pull-down (APD) device that is selectively activated during the evaluation phase of the read operation. The effective strength of the PD device in the bit cell is thus increased during the evaluation phase. Since the bit cell PD device remains unchanged, the bit cell area and its leakage remains unchanged. The APD device however requires an enable signal derived from word line (WL) signals. This introduces an area overhead. By exploiting the low percentage of '1' values in a typical ROM, the area overhead can be limited.

The remainder of the paper is organized as follows. In section 2, we discuss the read assist circuit and operation in detail. Section 3 discusses the design of the assist enable circuit. Section 4 describes the experimental results and Section 5 concludes with directions for future work.

2. READ ASSIST SCHEME

The generic architecture of a ROM array is depicted in Figure 1. The address decoders generate WL signals. The WLs drive the gate of the PD device inside each bit cell. In a ROM, the bit cell consists of a single NMOS PD device that pulls down the BL during the evaluation phase of the read operation. Two sets of bit cells are used to form the array, corresponding to logic values '0' and '1'. The values are programmed using via or diffusion layers. Essentially the presence of a connection from the PD drain to the BL represents a logic '1' and the absence a logic '0'.

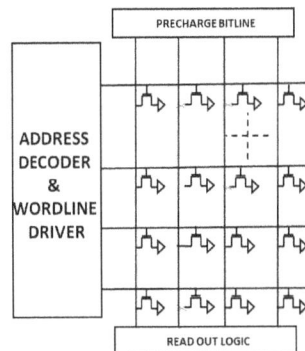

Figure 1. Architecture of ROM Array

The precharge logic block shown in Figure 1 pulls the BLs to VDD during the precharge phase. The readout logic can vary depending on the architecture. For the purpose of this paper, only domino evaluation is considered. Domino based dynamic evaluation is useful for embedded memories such as register files and ROMs [8][9]. Figure 2 shows the basic structure of a single bit line of a domino ROM. This structure is then used in a flat or hierarchical fashion to form the ROM array. It consists of a precharge device MP0 that is clocked with the precharge clock PCLK. The keeper device MP1 is driven by the feed-forward (FFWD) inverter which turns the keeper off during the evaluation phase. MN_0 to MN_n constitute the PD devices within the bit cells on the bit line. The PD devices are driven by the word line signals WL_0 to WL_n generated by the address decoder. The additional assist PD (APD) device that is driven by the ASSIST_ENABLE signal is the read assist device.

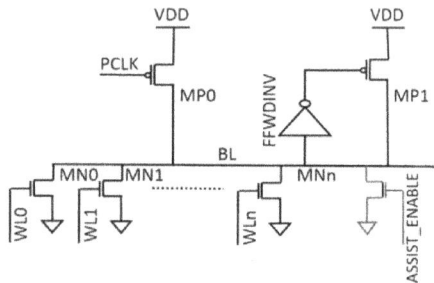

Figure 2. Assisted ROM domino evaluation architecture

2.1 Read Operation in Domino ROM

Domino based evaluation has two phases of operation. In the precharge phase, the BL is pulled up to VDD. We will consider this voltage to be a logic '0'.

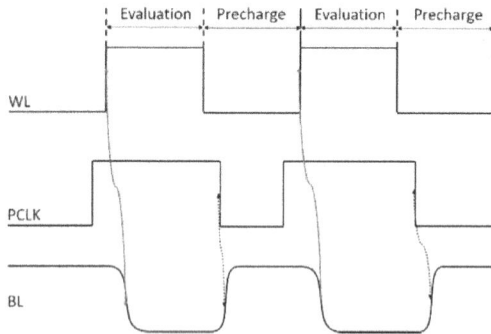

Figure 3. Read cycle operation for ROM

The read cycle of a ROM using the domino approach is shown in Figure 3. In the precharge phase, the WL signals are kept low, so there is no pull down path from the BL. The precharge clock PCLK goes low, which turns on the precharge device (MP0 in Figure 1), charging the BL to VDD. In the evaluation phase, the PCLK signal goes high, turning off the pull up device (MP0). Then the appropriate WL signal is driven high, which creates a pull down path on the BL node, if the corresponding bit cell PD has its drain connected to the BL. This causes the BL node to be pulled low. This represents logic '1' according to the convention used in this paper. If there is no PD path, then the high BL level will drive the FFWD inverter output low, turning on the keeper device (MP1), which will hold the BL high, a logic '0'. The keeper device is small enough that the PD devices will overpower

it. Once the BL voltage starts to fall, the inverter is driven high, turning off the keeper.

As can be seen in Figure 3, the duty cycle of PCLK is maintained such that the high phase of the signal covers the high phase of the WL signal. This avoids contention between MP0 and any PD devices.

The slew rate of the BL during evaluation determines the evaluation delay, which largely determines the maximum operating frequency of the ROM. The evaluation delay, defined as the delay between the WL rise and BL fall, is determined mainly by the size of the PD devices, the strength of the keeper and the slew rate of the WL signal. The delay can be reduced by increasing the size of the PD devices, reducing the size of the keeper, or doing both. A balance needs to be maintained between the strength of the PD devices and the keeper device. If the PD devices are too strong, the off-state leakage from these devices will overpower the keeper, causing the BL to droop so much during a read '0' condition that a logic '1' may be read instead. On the other hand, if the keeper is too strong, the contention during evaluation will increase the time for the BL to fall low.

Considering the above scenario, for a given keeper strength, the only way to reduce evaluation delay is to increase PD device size. For FinFET technology, this would mean doubling the number of fins if the PD originally had a single fin. This will increase the area and leakage and reduce the noise margin.

The read assist topology effectively increases the PD device strength without a corresponding increase in leakage or bit cell area or reduction in noise margin. For a given number of PD devices (bit cells) on the BL, the addition of one extra PD device in the form of the APD results in only a slight increase in leakage.

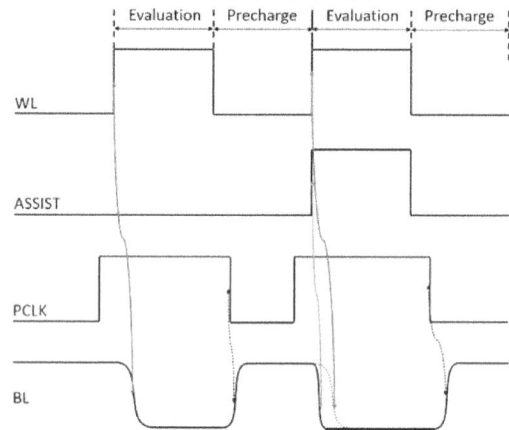

Figure 4. Assisted read cycle operation for ROM

Figure 4 shows a read cycle without assist, and then one with assist. During the first cycle, the assist signal is kept low. During the second cycle, the assist signal is enabled in the same phase as the WL signal. As a result, the slew rate of the BL increases. This can be understood from the red dashed line that shows the BL value during the first read cycle. The faster slew rate in the assisted cycle reduces the read evaluation delay.

3. ASSIST ENABLE LOGIC DESIGN

The assist enable signal to drive the APD device is derived from the WL values and bit cell content in such a way that the APD device is only activated for a logic '1' evaluation. That is, the selected bit cell is pulling down the BL. If the APD device is activated during logic '0' evaluation, it will pull down the BL, resulting in an incorrect logic '1'. This section describes the design of the assist enable logic. In addition to activating the APD only for a logic '1' evaluation, the delay between the WL and assist enable signal must be as small as possible, in order to maximize the improvement in the BL slew rate.

The assist enable logic can be implemented using either static or dynamic gates. The common requirement is that the assist enable signal is only asserted when a WL selects a bit cell encoding a logic '1' (a connected PD device). Essentially the assist enable signal is the logical OR of the WLs selecting logic '1' bit cells. We use the following example of eight bit cells connected on the same BL to understand derivation of the assist enable signal.

If the bits 11000010 are stored in eight bit cells on the same BL, with the bit cells selected by word lines WL0 to WL7, then the logic to derive the assist enable is WL0+WL1+WL6. Similarly, given bits 01110110, the assist enable signal will be WL1+WL2+WL3+WL5+WL6. Both of these examples are shown in Figure 5.

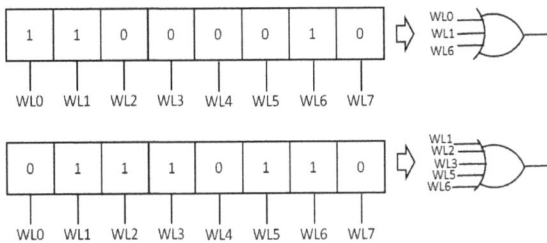

Figure 5. Assist Enable Logic derivation from the WLs

In a static gate design approach, the assist enable logic is formulated using static NAND and NOR gates to realize the desired OR function. This approach has two major drawbacks. First, the gate delay will be large if it has a high fan-in (large number of WL signals). Second, the area required for this logic could be quite large. For example, the first bit pattern above would require eight transistors (six transistors for a 3-input NOR gate and two transistors for an inverter). The second pattern above would require 12 transistors, assuming a 5-input NOR gate and inverter. These transistor counts are already as high as the bit cells themselves. Decoding larger numbers of WLs will require decomposing the logic into multiple logic levels, increasing area and delay. Area can be optimized by sharing common min terms across multiple BL assist signals or by inverting the logic implementation (decoding on logic '0') if the number of logic '1' bit cells is too high on a BL. Both approaches increase complexity and introduce routing overhead for the WL and assist enable signals.

An alternative is to implement the assist enable logic using a dynamic gate to optimize the delay between the WL and the assist enable signal. The dynamic gate is also area efficient. Compared to static gate implementation, it requires six and eight transistors for the bit streams in Figure 5. The design of the assist enable gate is shown in Figure 6.

The number of PD devices in this gate will depend on the number of bit cells on the BL containing a logic '1' bit. Inputs i_0 to i_n are connected to those WLs connected to the logic '1' bit cells. The pull up device MP0 is controlled by the signal EN, which can be the precharge clock. This forces the assist enable signal low during BL precharge. Folding the ROM (multiple short BLs sharing each output) increases the number of BLs with the same bit pattern, reducing the amount of logic required to control the ASSIST_ENABLE.

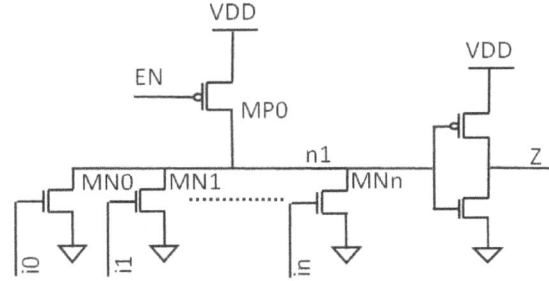

Figure 6. Dynamic gate design for assist enable

4. EXPERIMENTAL RESULTS

A series of circuit simulation experiments were performed on variations of the baseline ROM design and versions with read assist, to evaluate the designs for performance, noise margin, area, and Vmin improvement.

4.1 Performance Improvement

The BL evaluation delay was analyzed using circuit simulation with nominal 22 nm HP PTM models. Evaluation delay is defined as the delay between 50% rise on the WL and 90% rise on the FFWD inverter that drives the keeper. The different configurations considered are:

- *PD1X_NA*: 1-fin bit cell PD device and no APD
- *PD1X_WA1X*: 1-fin bit cell PD device with 1-fin APD
- *PD1X_WA2X*: 1-fin bit cell PD device with 2-fin APD
- *PD2X_NA*: 2-fin bit cell PD device and no APD

Figure 7 shows the evaluation delay for a 32-bit BL with VDD ranging from 0.4V to 0.6V, with the different configurations.

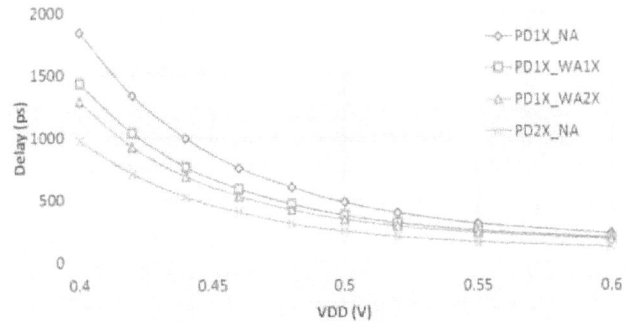

Figure 7. Assist circuit performance analysis

Figure 7 shows that the assist circuit reduces the evaluation delay throughout the VDD range and the percentage improvement increases at lower voltage. The *PD2X* configuration has the lowest evaluation delay. However, the *PD2X* bit cell will be considerably larger than the *PD1X* bit cell and have twice the leakage power.

The performance improvement provided by the assist circuit was evaluated as the number of bit cells (NWL) on the BL ranged from eight to 48. Table 1 shows the percentage improvement in the evaluation delay relative to the *PD1X_NA* configuration for different NWL numbers at a clock frequency of 250MHz. BL evaluation fails for *PD1X_NA* with NWL=48 at 0.4V. Hence, the corresponding entry in Table 1 is empty. As NWL increases, the load on the BL node increases as well, which causes the evaluation delay to increase. If the FFWD inverter output does not cross 90% of VDD by the end of the evaluation phase, the evaluation is considered incomplete. As can be seen in Table 1, at lower VDD, the percentage improvement in evaluation time is lower for more bit cells (word lines). However, at higher VDD, the opposite is true. In the middle VDD range, performance improvement is lower for an intermediate number of bit cells.

Table 1. Percentage improvement in evaluation delay

VDD	0.40	0.42	0.44	0.46	0.48	0.50	0.52	0.55	0.60
NWL8	29.84	29.79	29.46	29.26	27.06	25.88	23.60	17.62	10.72
NWL16	25.05	25.88	25.97	24.78	24.05	21.42	21.26	17.89	11.90
NWL24	22.76	23.13	23.11	21.93	22.36	20.49	19.26	15.49	12.11
NWL32	22.20	22.40	23.09	22.46	22.52	21.51	20.53	18.23	15.17
NWL48	-	22.24	22.41	22.99	23.24	22.47	22.37	22.50	17.84

This behavior can be understood with the help of Figure 8. Figure 8 shows the BL voltage level (as a percentage of VDD) when the APD turns on. The voltage level at which the APD turns on is higher for increasing NWL. For smaller NWL, the kick-in voltage falls with rising VDD. However, the kick-in voltage stays relatively constant for higher NWL. This translates into the trends seen in Table 1.

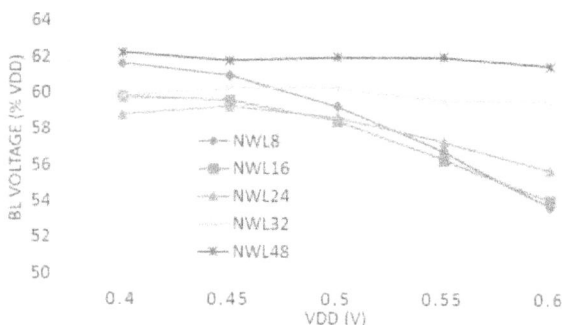

Figure 8. BL voltage at assist circuit turn-on

The key take away from Table 1 is that higher speed up is achieved at lower VDD for configurations with smaller NWL. For larger NWL, the speed up is similar across the VDD range.

4.2 Noise Margin

We evaluate the noise margin by considering the voltage droop on the BL during the read '0' evaluation phase. The droop should be small in order to avoid incorrectly reading a '1' value. The droop comes from two sources. The first source is the leakage of the bit cell PD and APD devices working against the keeper. A 1-fin PD device will have half the leakage of a 2-fin PD device. The second source is the noise on the WLs that are being held low. The WLs run perpendicular to the BLs, and capacitively couple to them [10][11]. The more BLs that a WL runs across, the greater the potential noise.

Figure 9 depicts the noise coupling model for a victim net *VICT,* which is routed alongside two attacker nets *ATK1* and *ATK2* on either side, with GND (or stable) nets above and below. The cross coupling capacitance has two components. The capacitance between adjacent net is denoted as C_{couple} and the capacitance to the GND net is denoted as C_{GND}.

The coupling capacitance on the WL signal is calculated using Synopsys® Raphael 3D parasitic extraction tool. The WL signal is routed perpendicular to multiple BL nodes. The green net in the

upper layer in Figure 9 represents the WL signal and the adjacent blue nets represent attackers. The yellow nets in the lower layer represent bit lines. The extracted capacitances are incorporated into the circuit simulation.

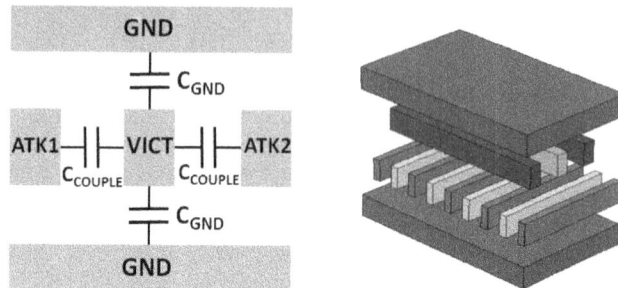

Figure 9. Word line noise modeling

The circuit model for measuring the noise on the WL from capacitive coupling is shown in Figure 10. The WL is driven with a steady low voltage. The adjacent nets are driven with rising signal transitions. The voltage on the WL is measured at the far end of the net. The values of C_x are obtained from the model shown in Figure 9. The value of R is obtained from the resistivity of the nets. The length of each wire segment in the distributed RC network is kept equal to the height of a bit cell since the WL signal is routed perpendicular to the BL signal. Parametric simulation is run with different number of bit cells (number of BL nets routed beneath the WL signal, denoted by NBL) that are driven by the WL signal. The simulations capture the noise coupled on the WL signal at the far end as a function of NBL.

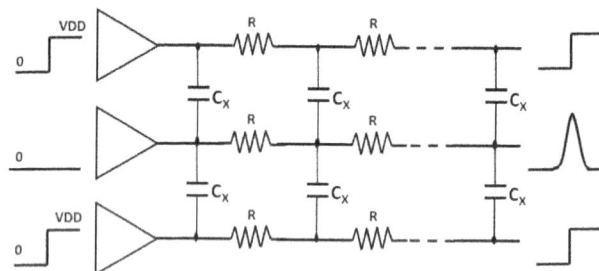

Figure 10. Noise modelling in SPICE simulation

The calculated noise is applied to the gates of all of the deselected bit cell PD devices in a separate simulation that models reading '0' on the BL. The droop on the BL is measured by calculating the minimum voltage on the BL in the evaluation phase. This model is conservative since it assumes only rising transitions on the nets coupled to the WLs, when some will be stable or have falling transitions.

Table 2 lists the DC voltage droop for different circuit configurations, as a percentage of the nominal '0' BL voltage level. The top two rows list the noise (mV) that can appear at the far end of a WL (away from the WL driver) due to the corresponding number of BLs (NBL), based on the models in Figures 9 and 10. The left column lists the BL configurations. A configuration of *8PD1X* means eight bit cells on the bit line, each with 1-fin PD devices, *8PD2X* means eight bit cells on the bit line, each with 2-fin PD devices, and so on, up to 64 bit cells.

The table shows that the droop is significantly higher for higher NBL and NWL, and higher for the *PD2X* configurations. A droop of 99.99% means that the noise droop was greater than the '0' BL voltage level (i.e. the BL voltage dropped to 0V). The noise droop for *PD1X* with assist is not shown, but is nearly the same as *PD1X* without assist. Hence, the assist topology has a higher noise margin than a design with a 2-fin PD device in the bit cell. This permits word lines to cross more bit lines for a given noise margin.

Table 2. DC Droop on BL node as a function of noise on WL

noise(mV)	24	44	60	74	96	118	176
NBL	8	16	24	32	48	64	128
8PD1X	1.88	2.49	3.14	3.78	5.06	6.63	12.39
8PD2X	3.59	4.73	5.86	7.02	9.14	11.63	20.06
16PD1X	3.36	4.48	5.56	6.66	8.70	11.14	19.36
16PD2X	6.31	8.16	9.90	11.59	14.60	18.03	29.40
24PD1X	4.68	6.15	7.55	8.95	11.49	14.43	24.18
24PD2X	8.48	10.78	12.88	14.90	18.43	22.42	36.84
32PD1X	5.84	7.59	9.23	10.85	13.74	17.06	27.99
32PD2X	10.28	12.91	15.26	17.51	21.42	25.85	99.99
48PD1X	7.83	10.00	12.00	13.94	17.34	21.18	34.36
48PD2X	13.22	16.28	19.01	21.59	26.09	31.31	99.99
64PD1X	9.51	11.99	14.25	16.41	20.18	24.42	99.99
64PD2X	15.57	18.95	21.94	24.78	29.80	36.28	99.99

4.3 Area Overhead

The area overhead of different assist configurations is shown in Table 3. The structure for which area is calculated consists of all the bit cell devices connected to the BL and the domino circuit involving the precharge, keeper and FFWD inverter. For the case of an assisted array, all the devices associated with the assist circuit - the dynamic gate and the APD device are also included in the area calculation.

The following notations are used in the table:

- *% One*: percentage of bit cells with '1' values
- *NWL*: number of word lines (bit cells) on the bit line
- *NA1X:* area without assist topology for bit cells with 1-fin PD devices
- *NA2X:* area without assist topology for bit cells with 2-fin PD devices, relative to *NA1X*
- *WA1X/WA2X:* area with assist topology with a 1 or 2-fin assist device and bit cells with 1-fin PD devices, relative to *NA1X*

The bit cell has a single polysilicon line for the 1-fin structure. The content of the bit cell defines the diffusion sharing with the adjacent bit cell. Figure 11 illustrates the layout of two rows, each with four bit cells. The polysilicon and the diffusion layers are at minimum spacing. It can be seen from Figure 11 that the area of a single bit cell can be expressed in the form of $A=dxl \cdot (dyl+D1)$ where dxl is the sum of the width of the polysilicon gate and the diffusion area under source and drain, dyl is the minimum diffusion width, and $D1$ is the minimum distance between two adjacent diffusion edges in the direction parallel to the polysilicon grid.

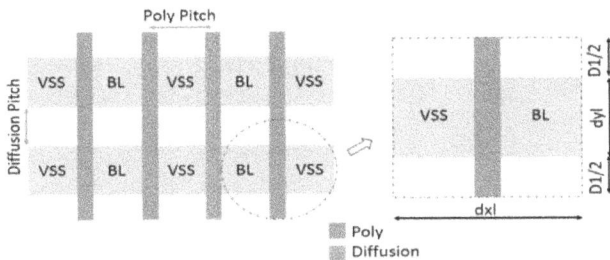

Figure 11. Bit cell array layout

The bit cell area A is used to normalize the *NA1X* area in Table 3. The other area values are relative to the *NA1X* area. The area of the *NA2X* configuration is simply double the area of *NA1X*. The *NA2X* bit cell is drawn using two polysilicon grids, both of which are connected to the same WL signal.

The BL runs in M1 or M2 layer perpendicular to the polysilicon line. The choice of metal layer is determined by the architecture and the array metal usage methodology, which does not affect the area calculation. The WL signal runs in M1 or M3 in parallel to the polysilicon grid, contacting it periodically.

As noted above, the area calculation for Table 3 assumes minimum design rules. The area overhead of the assist enable logic and the APD device is independent of the physical location of the devices used in the assist enable logic. We consider two approaches to placing the dynamic gate and the APD device. The bit cell could be drawn in two polysilicon grids to incorporate the PD device for the dynamic assist enable gate inside the corresponding bit cell. Since a PD is only required only for logic '1' bit cells, the bit cells encoding logic '0' would remain unchanged in the layout. The APD device and the precharge device inside the dynamic gate can be placed outside the bit cell array structure, adjacent to the BL precharge and keeper devices. Alternatively, the dynamic gate PD devices can be placed outside the bit cell array structure along with the precharge device and the APD device. The second approach achieves better layout efficiency since all the devices in the dynamic gate are placed together, which ensures most efficient device sharing, minimizes routing complexity, and optimizes the delay.

Table 3. Area comparison of assisted and unassisted array

% One	NWL	NA1X	NA2X	WA1X	WA2X
25	8	32	2	1.38	1.41
25	16	64	2	1.31	1.33
25	24	96	2	1.29	1.30
25	32	128	2	1.28	1.29
25	48	192	2	1.27	1.28
50	8	32	2	1.63	1.66
50	16	64	2	1.56	1.58
50	24	96	2	1.54	1.55
50	32	128	2	1.53	1.54
50	48	192	2	1.52	1.53
75	8	32	2	1.88	1.91
75	16	64	2	1.81	1.83
75	24	96	2	1.79	1.80
75	32	128	2	1.78	1.79
75	48	192	2	1.77	1.78

The number of bit cells containing logic value '1' determines the size of the dynamic gate generating the ASSIST_ENABLE signal. So the higher the *% One* value, the higher the area overhead. For a given *% One*, the area overhead is always lower than using the *NA2X* configuration. The overhead of using the *NA2X* configuration is always 2X irrespective of *% One* or *NWL*. Hence, the key observation is that for lower *% One*, it is more beneficial to use the assist topology to improve performance when the design is area sensitive. Note that for *% One* above 50%, it is possible to invert the dynamic gate logic. The 2-fin APD has nearly the same area overhead as that of a 1-fin APD, while providing lower evaluation delay, so is the preferred choice.

4.4 Vmin Improvement

Table 4 summarizes Vmin for different operating frequency and circuit configurations. The notation follows the previous tables. For example, *PD1XWA1X* is a configuration with bit cells with 1-fin PD devices and a 1-fin APD. We assume that the precharge and evaluation phases have equal delay, so the clock period is twice the evaluation period.

Table 4. Vmin comparison of multiple configurations

NWL	Frequency	500MHz	1GHz	1.5GHz	2GHz	2.5GHz	3GHz
8	PD1XNA	0.42	0.47	0.5	0.53	0.56	0.58
	PD1XWA1X	0.4	0.44	0.47	0.5	0.53	0.56
	PD1XWA2X	0.4	0.42	0.46	0.49	0.52	0.55
	PD2XNA	0.4	0.42	0.44	0.46	0.48	0.5
16	PD1XNA	0.43	0.48	0.51	0.54	0.58	-
	PD1XWA1X	0.41	0.45	0.49	0.52	0.55	0.58
	PD1XWA2X	0.4	0.44	0.48	0.51	0.54	0.57
	PD2XNA	0.4	0.43	0.45	0.48	0.5	0.51
24	PD1XNA	0.43	0.49	0.53	0.56	0.6	-
	PD1XWA1X	0.42	0.47	0.5	0.54	0.57	-
	PD1XWA2X	0.41	0.46	0.49	0.53	0.56	0.6
	PD2XNA	0.4	0.44	0.47	0.49	0.51	0.53
32	PD1XNA	0.44	0.5	0.54	0.59	-	-
	PD1XWA1X	0.43	0.48	0.52	0.56	0.6	-
	PD1XWA2X	0.42	0.47	0.51	0.54	0.58	-
	PD2XNA	0.4	0.45	0.48	0.5	0.53	0.55
48	PD1XNA	0.46	0.53	0.58	-	-	-
	PD1XWA1X	0.44	0.5	0.55	0.59	-	-
	PD1XWA2X	0.44	0.49	0.53	0.58	-	-
	PD1XNA	0.42	0.47	0.5	0.53	0.56	0.59

The table shows that all assisted configurations have lower Vmin across all operating frequencies than an unassisted *PD1X* configuration. Although the *PD2X* configuration provides slightly lower Vmin than any *PD1X* assisted topologies, it has much higher area overhead and leakage power, and lower noise margin. An assisted topology provides a better design option for constructing an array with less area overhead and similar Vmin at a given clock frequency. The entries that do not list a Vmin fail to meet the operating frequency for any VDD in the 0.4V to 0.6V range. The assisted topologies reach higher operating frequency than the corresponding bit cell configuration without assist. The 2-fin APD assist configurations achieve slightly lower Vmin than the 1-fin APD configurations, with minimal area overhead.

5. CONCLUSIONS AND FUTURE WORK

The assist circuit topology introduced in this paper improves the performance of the domino read evaluation in a ROM array across various configurations. For a given operating frequency, the assisted configuration can be run at a lower VDD. It also provides better noise margin. If area is of higher priority, the assisted configuration provides better area for arrays with a lower percentage of logic '1' bits, than an area with 2-fin bit cells. In essence, the assist circuit provides area and performance benefits without modifying the bit cell. The proposed assist approach does not add any additional complexity in terms of power grid design or other power control circuits present in other read assist topologies. As a result, it can be seamlessly integrated into existing unassisted designs.

In the future, we will consider process variation in our circuit analysis. Since the assist enable gate sits outside the bit cell, lower threshold or larger devices can be used to speed up the assist circuit, while limiting area overhead and maintaining noise margin. Different layouts need to be evaluated to better understand the area overhead for routing the WL signals to the dynamic gate.

6. ACKNOWLEDGMENTS

This research was funded in part by the National Science Foundation under grant CCF-1117982.

7. REFERENCES

[1] Zorian, Y. 2002. Embedded memory test and repair: infrastructure IP for SOC yield In *IEEE Int'l Test Conf.* 340-349. doi: 10.1109/TEST.2002.1041777.

[2] Khellah, M.M., Keshavarzi, A., Somasekhar, D., Karnik, T., De, V. 2008. Read and write circuit assist techniques for improving Vccmin of dense 6T SRAM cell. In *IEEE Int'l Conf. Integrated Circuit Design and Technology*, 185-188. doi: 10.1109/ICICDT.2008.4567275.

[3] Valaee, A., Al-Khalili, A.J. 2011. SRAM read-assist scheme for high performance low power applications. In *Int'l SoC Design Conf.* 179-182. doi: 10.1109/ISOCC.2011.6138676.

[4] Pilo, H., Barwin, C., Braceras, G., Browning, C., Lamphier, S., Towler, F. 2007. An SRAM Design in 65-nm Technology Node Featuring Read and Write-Assist Circuits to Expand Operating Voltage. In *IEEE J. Solid-State Circ.* 813-819. doi: 10.1109/JSSC.2007.892153.

[5] Abouzeid, F., Clerc, S., Pelloux-Prayer, B., Roche, P. 2013. 0.42-to-1.20V read assist circuit for SRAMs in CMOS 65nm. In *IEEE SOI-3D-Subthreshold Microelectronics Technology Unified Conf.* 1-2. doi: 10.1109/S3S.2013.6716578.

[6] Zhang, K., Bhattacharya, U., Chen, Z.; Hamzaoglu, F., Murray, D., Vallepalli, N., Wang, Y., Zheng, B., Bohr, M. 2005. A 3-GHz 70MB SRAM in 65nm CMOS technology with integrated column-based dynamic power supply. In *IEEE Int'l Solid-State Circuits Conf.* 474,611. doi: 10.1109/ISSCC.2005.1494075.

[7] Eustis, S. 2004. An embedded read only memory architecture with a complementary and two interchangeable power/performance design points. In *IEEE Int'l SOC Conf.* 187-190. doi: 10.1109/SOCC.2004.1362403.

[8] Lin Hu, Zhibiao Shao. 2003. High-performance ROM design for embedded applications. In *5th Int'l Conf. on ASIC*. 494-497. doi: 10.1109/ICASIC.2003.1277594.

[9] Ching-Rong Chang., Jinn-Shyan Wang., Cheng-Hui Yang, . 2001. Low-power and high-speed ROM modules for ASIC applications. In *IEEE J. Solid-State Circ.* 1516-1523. doi: 10.1109/4.953480.

[10] Meng-Fan Chang, Kuei-Ann Wen, Ding-Ming Kwai. 2005. Via-programmable read-only memory design for full code coverage using a dynamic bit-line shielding technique. In *IEEE Int'l Workshop on Memory Technology, Design, and Testing.* 16-21. doi: 10.1109/MTDT.2005.36.

[11] Chang, M.-F., Wen, K-A; Chiou, L.Y. 2005. Code-pattern insensitive embedded ROMs using dynamic bitline shielding technique. In *ElectronicsLetters*. 834-835. doi: 10.1049/el:2005173.

Author Index